October 1–4, 2017
Amsterdam, The Netherlands

I0027570

**Association for
Computing Machinery**

Advancing Computing as a Science & Profession

ICTIR'17

Proceedings of the 2017 ACM SIGIR

International Conference Theory
of Information Retrieval

Sponsored by:

ACM SIGIR

Supported by:

**Bloomberg, Booking.com, ESF Elias, Facebook, Google, Microsoft,
NWO, SIKS, University of Amsterdam, WGI, & the City of Amsterdam**

Association for Computing Machinery

Advancing Computing as a Science & Profession

The Association for Computing Machinery
2 Penn Plaza, Suite 701
New York, New York 10121-0701

ISBN: 978-1-4503-4490-6 (Digital)

ISBN: 978-1-4503-5612-1 (Print)

Additional copies may be ordered prepaid from:

ACM Order Department
PO Box 30777
New York, NY 10087-0777, USA

Phone: 1-800-342-6626 (USA and Canada)
+1-212-626-0500 (Global)
Fax: +1-212-944-1318
E-mail: acmhelp@acm.org
Hours of Operation: 8:30 am – 4:30 pm ET

Chairs' Welcome

Welcome to ICTIR 2017, the 7th International Conference on the Theory of Information Retrieval and the 3rd conference with that name to be fully sponsored by the ACM Special Interest Group on Information Retrieval (SIGIR). This year's conference continues its tradition of being the premier forum for presentation of research on theoretical aspects of Information Retrieval (IR) including (a) conceptual papers that explore key concepts, (b) theoretical papers that model concepts and/or relations between concepts, and (c) papers that study theory in experimental or industrial settings. To highlight the increasingly strong connections between Information Retrieval and neighboring disciplines this year's conference explicitly welcomed papers in IR areas that overlap with Human Information Access, Machine Learning, Natural Language Processing and Perception.

We are also happy to welcome you to Amsterdam, The Netherlands. The Netherlands has a number of strong and vibrant IR groups, e.g. at the University of Amsterdam, Twente University, Radboud University Nijmegen, Centrum Wiskunde en Informatica, Delft University of Technology, and University of Leiden and counts about 150 IR researchers, the largest number per capita in worldwide. These groups are successfully engaged in both theoretical and practical work. They are young groups consisting of enthusiastic people, with a track record in high quality publications.

The call for papers attracted submissions from all over the world. The program committee reviewed 97 contributions – 54 long and papers 43 short papers – and accepted 27 long papers and 25 short papers, all of which will be presented during the conference. We received three excellent tutorial proposals and two workshop proposals, and we hope those will aid in laying down foundational ideas in information retrieval research.

We thank everyone who helped us organize the conference: short paper chairs Katja Hofmann and Christina Lioma, workshop chair Grace Hui Yang, tutorial chair Josiane Mothe, core IR track program chairs Peter Bruza and Lynda Tamine-Lechani, IR & Human Information Access track chair Diane Kelly, IR & Machine Learning track chairs Qiaozhu Mei and Alessandro Sordoni, IR & Natural Language Processing track chair Alessandro Moschetti, IR & Perception track chairs Maria Eskevich and Stefan Rueger, and the members of the program committee who worked hard to review papers and provide feedback for authors. We also thank our sponsors and supporters: ACM SIGIR, Bloomberg, Booking.com, Facebook, Gemeente Amsterdam, Google, Microsoft, NWO, SIKS, University of Amsterdam, Werkgemeenschap Informatiewetenschap. Finally, we thank the authors for providing superb technical content, the workshop organizers, the tutorial lecturers and our keynote speakers Oren Kurland, Jennifer Neville and Suju Rajan.

We hope that you will find the conference program interesting and thought-provoking and that the conference will provide you with a valuable opportunity to share ideas with other researchers and practitioners from institutions around the world.

Enjoy the conference!

Jaap Kamps, Evangelos Kanoulas & Maarten de Rijke
ICTIR'17 General Chairs
University of Amsterdam, Netherlands

Hui Fang & Emine Yilmaz
ICTIR'17 Program Chairs
University of Delaware & University College London

Table of Contents

Paper Session 4: Retrieval Models

Paper Session 5: Social Media

Keynote 3

Paper Session 6: Interactive and Session Search

Paper Session 7: User Modelling

Short Papers

Tutorials

Workshop Summaries

Author Index

ICTIR 2017 Conference Organization

General Chairs: Jaap Kamps *(University of Amsterdam, The Netherlands)*
Evangelos Kanoulas *(University of Amsterdam, The Netherlands)*
Maarten de Rijke *(University of Amsterdam, The Netherlands)*

Program Chair: Hui Fang *(University of Delaware, USA)*
Emine Yilmaz *(University College London, UK)*

Short Papers Chair: Katja Hofmann *(Microsoft Research, UK)*
Christina Lioma *(University of Copenhagen)*

Tutorials Chair: Josiane Mothe *(IRIT, France)*

Workshops Chair: Grace Hui Yang *(Georgetown University, USA)*

IR Track Chair: Peter Bruza *(Queensland University of Technology, Australia)*
Lynda Tamine-Lechani *(IRIT, France)*

**IR & Human Information
Access Track Chair:** Diane Kelly *(University of Tennessee, USA)*

IR & Machine Learning Track Chair: Qiaozhu Mei *(University of Michigan, USA)*
Alessandro Sordoni *(University of Montreal, Canada)*

**IR & Natural Language
Processing Chair:** Alessandro Moschitti *(Hamad bin Khalifa University, Qatar)*

IR & Perception Track Chair: Maria Eskevich *(Radboud University, The Netherlands)*
Stefan Rueger *(The Open University, UK)*

Publicity Chair: Julia Kiseleva *(University of Amsterdam, The Netherlands)*

Proceedings Chair: Hosein Azarbonyad *(University of Amsterdam, The Netherlands)*

Booklet Chair: Dan Li *(University of Amsterdam, The Netherlands)*
Chang Li *(University of Amsterdam, The Netherlands)*
Christophe Van Gysel *(University of Amsterdam, The Netherlands)*

Program Committee: Enrique Amigó *(UNED, Spain)*
Jaime Arguello *(University of North Carolina at Chapel Hill, USA)*
Leif Azzopardi *(University of Strathclyde, UK)*
Phil Bachman *(Microsoft, Canada)*
Alberto Barrón-Cedeño *(Qatar Computing Research Institute, Qatar)*
Gaurav Baruah *(University of Waterloo, Canada)*
Pavel Braslavski *(Ural Federal University, Russia)*
Jamie Callan *(Carnegie Mellon University, USA)*
Pablo Castells *(Universidad Autónoma de Madrid, Spain)*
Chang Chia-Hui *(National Central University, Taiwan)*
Kevyn Collins-Thompson *(University of Michigan, USA)*
Ingemar Cox *(University College London, UK)*

Program Committee (continued): Matt Crane *(University of Waterloo, Canada)*
Fabio Crestani *(University of Lugano, Switzerland)*
Danilo Croce *(University of Roma Tor Vergata, Italy)*
Bruce Croft *(University of Massachusetts Amherst, USA)*
Ronan Cummins *(University of Cambridge, UK)*
Jeff Dalton *(University of Massachusetts Amherst, USA)*
Kareem Darwish *(Qatar Computing Research Institute, Qatar)*
Arjen de Vries *(Radboud University, The Netherlands)*
Gianluca Demartini *(University of Sheffield, UK)*
Tamer Elsayed *(Qatar University, Qatar)*
Ralph Ewerth *(Leibniz Universität Hannover, Germany)*
James Fan *(HelloVera.ai, USA)*
Nicola Ferro *(University of Padua, Italy)*
Simone Filice *(University of Roma Tor Vergata, Italy)*
Ingo Frommholz *(University of Bedfordshire, UK)*
Norbert Fuhr *(University of Duisburg-Essen, Germany)*
Shlomo Geva *(Queensland University of Technology, Australia)*
Julio Gonzalo *(UNED, Spain)*
Martin Halvey *(University of Strathclyde, UK)*
Morgan Harvey *(Northumbria University, UK)*
Ben He *(University of Chinese Academy of Sciences, China)*
Jiyin He *(CWI, The Netherlands)*
Djoerd Hiemstra *(University of Twente, The Netherlands)*
Jimmy Huang *(York University, Canada)*
Mohit Iyyer *(University of Maryland, USA)*
Jing Jiang *(Singapore Management University, Singapore)*
Jussi Karlgren *(Gavagai & KTH, Sweden)*
Bevan Koopman *(CSIRO, Australia)*
Wai Lam *(The Chinese University of Hong Kong, Hong Kong)*
Birger Larsen *(Aalborg University Copenhagen, Denmark)*
Cheng Li *(University of Michigan, USA)*
Hang Li *(Huawei Technologies, Hong Kong)*
Joo-Hwee Lim *(Nanyang Technological University, Singapore)*
Chang Liu *(Peking University, China)*
Haiming Liu *(University of Bedfordshire, UK)*
Yiqun Liu *(Tsinghua University, China)*
Joao Magalhaes *(Universidade Nova de Lisboa, Portugal)*
Ilya Markov *(University of Amsterdam, The Netherlands)*
Massimo Melucci *(University of Padua, Italy)*
Bhaskar Mitra *(Microsoft, UK)*
Alistair Moffat *(The University of Melbourne, Australia)*
Boughanem Mohand *(IRIT University Paul Sabatier Toulouse, France)*
Yashar Moshfeghi *(University of Strathclyde, UK)*
Jayanta Mukherjee *(IIT Kharagpur, India)*

ICTIR 2017 Sponsor & Supporters

Sponsor:

SIGIR
Special Interest Group
on Information Retrieval

Gold Supporters:

Elias
evaluating information access systems

Booking.com

Silver Supporter:

NWO
Netherlands Organisation
for Scientific Research

Bronze Supporters:

Google

Bloomberg

Contributing Supporters:

SIKS

Werkgemeenschap
Informatiewetenschap

facebook

Gemeente Amsterdam

Microsoft

Institutional Supporters:

UNIVERSITY OF AMSTERDAM

Information Retrieval Meets Game Theory

Oren Kurland

Technion — Israel Institute of Technology

kurland@ie.technion.ac.il

ABSTRACT

In competitive search settings such as the Web, authors of documents may have an incentive to have their documents highly ranked for certain queries. This can drive corpus dynamics as documents may be manipulated in response to induced rankings (e.g., by applying search engine optimization). Such post-ranking corpus effects are not directly modeled in ad hoc retrieval models and, more generally, are not accounted for by the formal foundations of retrieval paradigms.

In this talk I will discuss how (algorithmic) game theory can be used to analyze some aspects of the competitive search setting. I will first discuss the probability ranking principle (PRP) [3] which is the theoretical underpinning of most ad hoc retrieval methods. As it turns out, the PRP is sub-optimal in competitive settings [1]. In addition, I will discuss some initial theoretical and empirical results regarding the strategic behavior of document authors in competitive retrieval settings, specifically with respect to the foundations of classical ad hoc retrieval models [2]. I will then discuss future directions.

CCS CONCEPTS

• **Information systems → Retrieval models and ranking;**

KEYWORDS

ad hoc retrieval; game theory; probability ranking principle

BIOGRAPHY

Oren Kurland is an Associate Professor at the Technion — Israel Institute of Technology. He holds a Ph.D. in Computer Science from Cornell University. Oren's main research focus is information retrieval. He serves on the editorial board of the Information Retrieval Journal, and has also served on the editorial boards of the Journal of Artificial Intelligence Research and Information Processing and Management Journal. Oren served as the first chair of the ACM SIGIR ICTIR steering committee. He has also served as program committee co-chair of the ICTIR and SPIRE conferences. Oren was awarded best-paper honorable mention awards in the SIGIR 2013 and ECIR 2016 conferences. He has received faculty research awards from IBM, Google and Yahoo.

REFERENCES

[1] Ran Ben-Basat, Moshe Tennenholtz, and Oren Kurland. 2015. The Probability Ranking Principle is Not Optimal in Adversarial Retrieval Settings. In *Proceedings of ICTIR*. 51–60.
[2] Nimrod Raifer, Fiana Raiber, Moshe Tennenholtz, and Oren Kurland. 2017. Information Retrieval Meets Game Theory: The Ranking Competition Between Documents' Authors. In *Proceedings of SIGIR*. 465–474.
[3] Stephen E. Robertson. 1977. The Probability Ranking Principle in IR. *Journal of Documentation* (1977), 294–304. Reprinted in K. Sparck Jones and P. Willett (eds), *Readings in Information Retrieval*, pp. 281–286, 1997.

ICTIR '17, October 1–4, 2017, Amsterdam, Netherlands
© 2017 Copyright held by the owner/author(s).
ACM ISBN 978-1-4503-4490-6/17/10.
DOI: https://doi.org/10.1145/3121050.3121079

Structural Regularities in Text-based Entity Vector Spaces

Christophe Van Gysel
University of Amsterdam
Amsterdam, The Netherlands
cvangysel@uva.nl

Maarten de Rijke
University of Amsterdam
Amsterdam, The Netherlands
derijke@uva.nl

Evangelos Kanoulas
University of Amsterdam
Amsterdam, The Netherlands
e.kanoulas@uva.nl

ABSTRACT

Entity retrieval is the task of finding entities such as people or products in response to a query, based solely on the textual documents they are associated with. Recent semantic entity retrieval algorithms represent queries and experts in finite-dimensional vector spaces, where both are constructed from text sequences.

We investigate entity vector spaces and the degree to which they capture structural regularities. Such vector spaces are constructed in an unsupervised manner without explicit information about structural aspects. For concreteness, we address these questions for a specific type of entity: experts in the context of expert finding. We discover how clusterings of experts correspond to committees in organizations, the ability of expert representations to encode the co-author graph, and the degree to which they encode academic rank. We compare latent, continuous representations created using methods based on distributional semantics (LSI), topic models (LDA) and neural networks (word2vec, doc2vec, SERT). Vector spaces created using neural methods, such as doc2vec and SERT, systematically perform better at clustering than LSI, LDA and word2vec. When it comes to encoding entity relations, SERT performs best.

CCS CONCEPTS

•**Information systems → Content analysis and feature selection;**

ACM Reference format:
Christophe Van Gysel, Maarten de Rijke, and Evangelos Kanoulas. 2017. Structural Regularities in Text-based Entity Vector Spaces. In *Proceedings of ICTIR '17, October 1–4, 2017, Amsterdam, Netherlands.*, , 8 pages.
DOI: https://doi.org/10.1145/3121050.3121066

1 INTRODUCTION

The construction of latent entity representations is a recurring problem [11, 14, 19, 24, 60] in natural language processing and information retrieval. So far, entity representations are mostly learned from relations between entities [11, 60] for a particular task in a supervised setting [24]. How can we learn latent entity representations if (i) entities only have relations to documents in contrast to other entities (e.g., scholars are represented by the papers they authored), and (ii) there is a lack of labeled data?

As entities are characterized by documents that consist of words, can we use word embeddings to construct a latent entity representation? Distributed representations of words [25], i.e., word embeddings, are learned as part of a neural language model and have been shown to capture semantic [15] and syntactic regularities [39, 43]. In addition, word embeddings have proven to be useful as feature vectors for natural language processing tasks [51], where they have been shown to outperform representations based on frequentist distributional semantics [7]. A downside of word embeddings [8] is that they do not take into account the document a word sequence occurred in or the entity that generated it.

Le and Mikolov [29] address this problem by extending word2vec models to doc2vec by additionally modeling the document a phrase occurred in. That is, besides word embeddings they learn embeddings for documents as well. We can apply doc2vec to the entity representation problem by representing an entity as a pseudo-document consisting of all documents the entity is associated with. Recent advances in entity retrieval incorporate real-world structural relations between represented entities even though the representations are learned from text only. Van Gysel et al. [56] introduce a neural retrieval model (SERT) for an entity retrieval task. In addition to word embeddings, they learn representations for entities.

In this paper, we study the regularities contained within entity representations that are estimated, in an unsupervised manner, from texts and associations alone. Do they correspond to structural real-world relations between the represented entities? E.g., if the entities we represent are people, do these regularities correspond to collaborative and hierarchical structures in their domain (industrial, governmental or academic organizations in the case of experts)? Answers to these questions are valuable because if they allow us to better understand the inner workings of entity retrieval models and give important insights into the entity-oriented tasks they are used for [29]. In addition, future work can build upon these insights to extract structure within entity domains given only a document collection and entity-document relations so to complement or support structured information.

Our working hypothesis is that text-based entity representations encode regularities within their domain. To test this hypothesis we compare latent text-based entity representations learned by neural networks (word2vec, doc2vec, SERT), count-based entity vector representations constructed using Latent Semantic Indexing (LSI) and Latent Dirichlet Allocation (LDA), dimensionality-reduced adjacency representations (Graph PCA) and random representations sampled from a standard multivariate normal distribution. For evaluation purposes we focus on expert finding, a particular case of entity ranking. Expert finding is the task of finding the right person with the appropriate skills or knowledge [5], based on a document collection and associations between people and documents. These associations can be extracted using entity linking methods or from document meta-data (e.g., authorship). Typical queries are descriptions of expertise areas, such as *distributed computing*, and expert search engines answer the question "Who are experts on *distributed computing*?" asked by people unfamiliar with the field.

Our main finding is that, indeed, semantic entity representations encode domain regularities. Entity representations can be used as feature vectors for clustering and that partitions correspond to structural groups within the entity domain. We also find that similarity between entity representations correlates with relations between entities. In particular, we show how representations of experts in the academic domain encode the co-author graph. Lastly, we show that one of the semantic representation learning methods, SERT, additionally encodes importance amongst entities and, more specifically, the hierarchy of scholars in academic institutions.

2 RELATED WORK

2.1 Representations and regularities

The idea that representations may capture linguistic and semantic regularities or even stereotyped biases that reflect everyday human culture has received considerable attention [13]. The idea of learning a representation of the elements of a discrete set of objects (e.g., words) is not new [25, 46]. However, it has only been since the turn of the last century that Neural Probabilistic Language Models (NPLM), which learn word embeddings as a side-effect of dealing with high-dimensionality, were shown to be more effective than Markovian models [8].

Even more recently, Collobert and Weston explain how the ideas behind NPLMs can be applied to arbitrary Natural Language Processing (NLP) tasks, by learning one set of word representations in a multi-task and semi-supervised setting. Turian et al. [51] compare word representations learned by neural networks, distributional semantics and cluster-based methods as features in Named Entity Recognition (NER) and chunking. They find that both cluster-based methods and distributed word representations learned by NPLMs improve performance, although cluster-based methods yield better representations for infrequent words. Baroni et al. [7] confirm the superiority of context-predicting (word embeddings) over context-counting (distributional semantics) representations.

Later algorithms are specifically designed for learning word embeddings [39, 43], such that, somewhat ironically, NPLMs became a side-product. These embeddings contain linguistic regularities [31, 40], as evidenced in syntactic analogy and semantic similarity tasks. Multiple *word* representations can be combined to form *phrase* representations [38]. Clusterings of word embeddings can be used to discover word classes [38]. And insights gathered from word embedding algorithms can be used to improve distributional semantics [30].

2.2 Entity retrieval

Around 40% of web queries [44] and over 90% of academic search queries [33] concern entities. Entity-oriented queries express an information need that is better answered by returning specific entities as opposed to documents [6]. The entity retrieval task is characterized by a combination of (noisy) textual data and semi-structured knowledge graphs that encode relations between entities [21].

As a particular instance of entity retrieval, expert finding became popular with the TREC Enterprise Track [50]. The task encompasses the retrieval of experts instead of documents. This is useful in enterprise settings, where employers seek to facilitate information exchange and stimulate collaboration [17]. Expert finding diverges from the generic entity retrieval task due to the lack of explicit relations between experts. Balog et al. [2] introduce language models for expert finding. In the maximum-likelihood language modeling paradigm, experts are represented as a normalized bag-of-words vector with additional smoothing. These vectors are high-dimensional and sparse due to the large vocabularies used in expert domains. Therefore, bag-of-words vectors are unsuited for use as representations as lower-dimensional and continuous vector spaces are preferred in machine learning algorithms [59]. Demartini et al. [19] introduce a framework for using document vector spaces in expert finding. Fang et al. [22] explore the viability of learning-to-rank methods in expert retrieval. van Dijk et al. [52] propose methods for detecting potential experts in community question-answering.

Van Gysel et al. [54, 56] propose a neural language modeling approach to expert finding; they also release the Semantic Entity Retrieval Toolkit (SERT) that we use in this paper. Closely related to expert finding is the task of expert profiling, of which the goal is to describe an expert by her areas of expertise [3], and similar expert finding [4]; see [5] for an overview.

2.3 Latent semantic information retrieval

The mismatch between queries and documents is a critical challenge in search [32]. Latent Semantic Models (LSMs) retrieve objects based on conceptual, or semantic, rather than exact word matches. The introduction of Latent Semantic Indexing (LSI) [18], followed by probabilistic LSI (pLSI) [26], led to an increase in the popularity of LSMs. Salakhutdinov and Hinton [47] perform unsupervised learning of latent semantic document bit patterns using a deep auto-encoder. Huang et al. introduced Deep Structured Semantic Models [27, 49] that predict a document's relevance to a query using click data. Neural network models have also been used for learning to rank [12, 20, 34].

3 TEXT-BASED ENTITY VECTOR SPACES

For text-based entity retrieval tasks we are given a document collection D and a set of entities X. Documents $d \in D$ consist of a sequence of words $w_1, \ldots, w_{|d|}$ originating from a vocabulary V, where $|\cdot|$ denotes the document length in number of words. For every document d we have a set $X_d \subset X$ of associated entities (X_d can be empty for some documents) and conversely $D_x \subset D$ consists of all documents associated with entity x. The associations between documents and experts can be obtained in multiple ways. E.g., named-entity recognition can be applied to the documents and mentions can subsequently be linked to entities. Or associations can be extracted from document meta-data (e.g., authorship).

Once determined, the associations between entities X and documents D encode a bipartite graph. If two entities $x_i, x_j \in X$ are associated with the same document, we say that x_i and x_j are co-associated. However, the semantics of a co-association are equivocal as the semantics of an association are ambiguous by itself (e.g., author vs. editor). Therefore, instead of relying solely on document associations, we use the textual data of associated documents to construct an entity representation.

Vector space models for document retrieval, such as LSI [18] or LDA [10], can be adapted to entity retrieval. We substantiate this for a specific entity retrieval task: expert finding. As there are many more documents than experts, it is not ideal to estimate a vector space directly on the expert-level using bag-of-word vectors (e.g., by representing every expert as a concatenation of its documents) due to data sparsity. Therefore, it is preferable to first estimate a vector space on the document collection and then use the obtained document representations to construct an entity vector. Demartini et al. [19] take an entity's representation to be the sum of its documents:

$$e_i = \sum_{d_j \in D_{x_i}} g(d_j),$$ (1)

where e_i is the k-dimensional vector representation of entity $x_i \in X$ and g is the function mapping a document to its vector space representation (e.g., LSI). The dimensionality k depends on the underlying vector space. For simple bag-of-words representations, k is equal to the number of words in the vocabulary. For latent vector spaces (e.g., LSI), the k-dimensional space encodes latent concepts and the choice of k is left to the user.

Vector space models for document retrieval are often constructed heuristically. E.g., Eq. 1 does not make optimal use of document-entity associations as document representations are added without taking into consideration the significance of words contained within them [35]. And if many diverse documents are associated with an expert, then Eq. 1 is likely to succumb to the noise in these vectors and yield meaningless representations.

To address this problem, Le and Mikolov [29] introduced doc2vec by adapting the word2vec models to incorporate the document a phrase occurs in. They optimize word and document embeddings jointly to predict a word given its context and the document the word occurs in. The key difference between word2vec and doc2vec is that the latter considers an additional meta-token in the context that represents the document. Instead of performing dimensionality reduction on bag-of-words representations, doc2vec learns representations from word phrases. Therefore, we use the doc2vec model to learn expert embeddings by representing every expert $x_j \in X$ as a pseudo-document consisting of the concatenation of their associated documents D_{x_j}.

A different neural language model architecture than doc2vec was proposed by Van Gysel et al. [56], specifically for the expert finding task. For a given word w_i and expert x_j:

$$\text{score}(w_i, x_j) = \exp\left(v_i^\intercal \cdot e_j + b_j\right),$$ (2)

where v_i (e_j, resp.) are the latent k-dimensional representations of word w_i (and expert x_j, respectively) and b_j is the bias scalar associated with expert x_j. Eq. 2 can be interpreted as the unnormalized factor product of likelihood $P(w_i \mid x_j)$ and prior $P(x_j)$ in log-space. The score is then transformed to the conditional probability

$$P(X = x_j \mid w_i) = \frac{\text{score}(w_i, x_j)}{\sum_{x_l \in X} \text{score}(w_i, x_l)}.$$

Unlike Eq. 1, the conditional probability distribution $P(X = x_j \mid w_i)$ will be skewed towards relevant experts if the word w_i is significant as described by Luhn [35]. The parameters v_i, e_j and b_j are learned from the corpus using gradient descent. See [56] for details.

Our focus lies on representations of entities e_j and how these correspond to structures within their domains (i.e., organizations for experts). These representations are estimated using a corpus only and can be interpreted as vectors in word embedding space that correspond to entities (i.e., people) instead of words.

4 EXPERIMENTAL SET-UP

4.1 Research questions

We investigate regularities within text-based entity vector spaces, using expert finding as our concrete test case, and ask how these representations correspond to structure in their respective domains. We seek to answer the following research questions:

RQ1 Do clusterings of text-based entity representations reflect the structure of their domains?

Many organizations consist of smaller groups, committees or teams of experts who are appointed with a specific role. When we cluster expert representations, do the clusters correspond to these groups?

RQ2 To what extent do different text-based entity representation methods encode relations between entities?

The associations within expert domains encode a co-association graph structure. To what extent do the different expertise models encode this co-association between experts? In particular, if we rank experts according to their nearest neighbors, how does this ranking correspond to the academic co-author graph?

4.2 Expert finding collections

We use publicly-available expert finding collections provided by the World Wide Web Consortium (W3C) and Tilburg University (TU); see Table 1.

W3C. The W3C collection was released as part of the 2005–2006 editions of the TREC Enterprise Track [16]. It contains a heterogeneous crawl of W3C's website (June 2004) and consists of mailing lists and discussion boards among others. In the 2005 edition, TREC released a list of working groups and their members. Each working group is appointed to study and report on a particular aspect of the World Wide Web to enable the W3C to pursue its mission. We use the associations provided by Van Gysel et al. [56], which they gathered by applying named entity recognition and linking these mentions to a list of organization members, as proposed by Balog et al. [2].

TU. The TU collection consists of a crawl of a university's internal website and contains bi-lingual documents, such as academic publications, course descriptions and personal websites [9]. The document-candidate associations are part of the collection. For every member of the academic staff, their academic title is included as part of the collection.

Table 1: An overview of the two expert finding collections (W3C and TU).

	W3C	TU
Documents in collection	331,037	31,209
Average tokens per document	1,237.23	2,454.93
Number of candidate experts	715	977
Number of document-candidate associations	200,939	36,566
Number of documents (with $|X_d| > 0$)	93,826	27,834
Number of associations per document	2.14 ± 3.29	1.13 ± 0.39
Number of associations per candidate	281.03 ± 666.63	37.43 ± 61.00

4.3 Implementations and parameters

We follow a similar experimental set-up as previous work [2, 19, 38, 56]. For LSI, LDA, word2vec and doc2vec we use the Gensim[1] implementation, while for the log-linear model we use the Semantic Entity Retrieval Toolkit[2] (SERT) [55].

The corpora are normalized by lowercasing and removing punctuation and numbers. The vocabulary is pruned by removing stop words and retaining the 60k most frequent words. We sweep exponentially over the vector space dimensionality ($k = 32, 64, 128$ and 256) of the methods under comparison. This allows us to evaluate the effect of differently-sized vector spaces and their modeling capabilities.

For word2vec, a query/document is represented by its average word vector, which is effective for computing short text similarity [28]. We report both Continuous Bag-of-Words (CBOW) and Skip-gram (SG) variants of word2vec. For LDA, we set $\alpha = \beta = 0.1$ and train the model for 100 iterations or until topic convergence is achieved. Unlike Van Gysel et al. [56], for SERT, we do not initialize with pre-trained word2vec embeddings. Default parameters are used in all other cases.

For LSI, LDA and word2vec, expert representations are created from document representations according to Eq. 1.

In addition to text-based representations, we also include two baselines that do not consider textual data. For the first method (Graph PCA), we construct a weighted, undirected co-association graph where the weight between two entities is given by the number of times they are co-associated. We then apply Principal Component Analysis to create a latent representation for every entity. Secondly, we include a baseline where experts are represented as a random vector sampled from a standard multivariate normal distribution.

5 REGULARITIES IN ENTITY VECTOR SPACES

We investigate regularities within latent text-based entity vector spaces. In particular, we first build latent representations for experts and ground these in the structure of the organizations where these experts are active. First, we cluster latent expert representations using different clustering techniques and compare the resulting clusters to committees in a standards organization of the World

Wide Web (RQ1). We continue by investigating to what extent these representations encode entity relations (RQ2). We complement the answers to our research questions with an analysis of the prior (the scalar bias in Eq. 2) associated with every expert in one of the models we consider, SERT, and compare this to their academic rank.

5.1 Answers to research questions

RQ1 Do clusterings of text-based entity representations reflect the structure of their domains?

The World Wide Web Consortium (W3C) consists of various working groups.[3] Each working group is responsible for a particular aspect of the WWW and consists of two or more experts. We use these working groups as ground truth for evaluating the ability of expert representations to encode similarity. The W3C working groups are special committees that are established to produce a particular deliverable [45, p. 492] and are a way to gather experts from around the organization who share areas of expertise and who would otherwise not directly communicate. Working groups are non-hierarchical in nature and represent clusters of experts. Therefore, they can be used to evaluate to what extent entity representations can be used as feature vectors for clustering.

We cluster expert representations using K-means [36]. While K-means imposes strong assumptions on cluster shapes (convexity and isotropism), it is still very popular today due to its linear time complexity, geometric interpretation and absence of hard to choose hyper-parameters (unlike spectral variants or DBSCAN). We cluster expert representations of increasing dimensionality k ($k = 2^i$ for $5 \leq i < 9$) using a linear sweep over the number of clusters K ($10^0 \leq K < 10^2$).

During evaluation we transform working group memberships to a hard clustering of experts by assigning every expert to the smallest working group to which they belong as we wish to find specialized clusters contrary to general clusters that contain many experts. We then use Adjusted Mutual Information, an adjusted-for-chance variant of Normalized Information Distance [58], to compare both clusterings. Adjusting for chance is important as non-adjusted measures (such as BCubed precision/recall[4] as presented

---

[1]https://radimrehurek.com/gensim
[2]https://github.com/cvangysel/SERT

[3]http://www.w3.org/Consortium/activities
[4]This can be verified empirically by computing BCubed measures for an increasing number of random partitions.

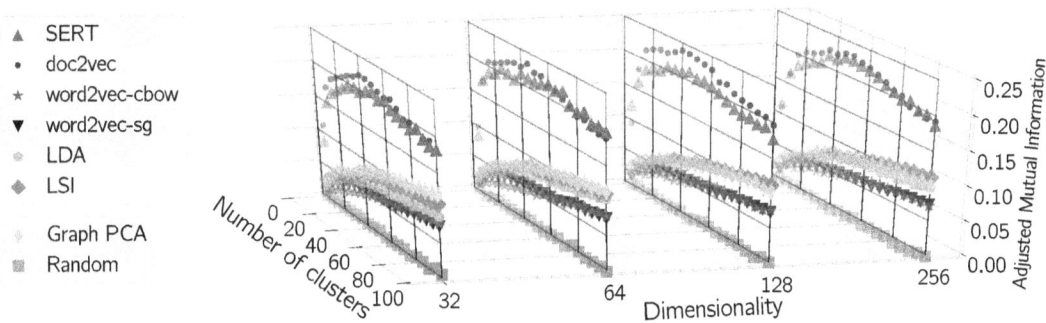

Figure 1: Comparison of clustering capabilities of expert representations (random, Graph PCA, LSI, LDA, word2vec, doc2vec and SERT) using K-means for $10^0 \leq K < 10^2$ (y-axis). The x-axis shows the dimensionality of the representations and the z-axis denotes the Adjusted Mutual Information.

by Amigó et al. [1]) have the tendency to take on a higher value for a larger value of K. Performing the adjustment allows us to compare clusterings for different values of K. We repeat the K-means clustering 10 times with different centroids initializations and report the average.

Figure 1 shows the clustering capabilities of the different representations for different values of K and vector space dimensionality. Ignoring the random baseline, representations built using word2vec perform worst. This is most likely due to the fact that document representations for word2vec are constructed by averaging individual word vectors. Next up, we observe a tie between LSI and LDA. Interestingly enough, the baseline that only considers entity-document associations and does not take into account textual content, Graph PCA, outperforms all representations constructed from document-level vector space models (Eq. 1). Furthermore, doc2vec and SERT perform best, regardless of vector space dimensionality, and consistently outperform the other representations. If we look at the vector space dimensionality, we see that the best clustering is created using 128-dimensional vector spaces. Considering the number of clusters, we see that doc2vec and SERT peak at about 40 to 60 clusters. This corresponds closely to the number of ground-truth clusters. The remaining representations (word2vec, LSI, LDA, Graph PCA) only seem to plateau in terms of clustering performance at $K = 100$, far below the clustering performance of the doc2vec and SERT representation methods.

To answer our first research question, we conclude that expert representations can be used to discover structure within organizations. However, the quality of the clustering varies greatly and use of more advanced methods (i.e., doc2vec or SERT) is recommended.

RQ2 To what extent do different text-based entity representation methods encode relations between entities?

The text-based entity representation problem is characterized by a bipartite graph of entities and documents where an edge denotes an entity-document association. This differs from entity finding settings where explicit entity-entity relations are available and fits into the scenario where representations have to be constructed

from unstructured text only. If latent text-based entity representations encode co-associations, then we can use this insight for (1) a better understanding of text-based entity representation models, and (2) the usability of latent text-based entity representations as feature vectors in scenarios where relations between entities are important.

We evaluate the capacity of text-based expert representations to encode co-associations by casting the problem as a ranking task. Contrary to typical expert finding, where we rank experts according to their relevance to a textual query, for the purpose of answering RQ2, we rank experts according to their cosine similarity w.r.t. a query expert [4]. This task shares similarity with content-based recommendation based on unstructured data [42].

In expert finding collections, document-expert associations can indicate many things. For example, in the W3C collection, entity-document associations are mined from expert mentions [2]. However, for the TU collection, we know that a subset of associations corresponds to academic paper authorship. Therefore, we construct ranking ground-truth from paper co-authorship and take the relevance label of an expert to be the number of times the expert was a co-author with the query expert (excluding the query expert themselves). Our intention is to determine to what extent latent entity representations estimated from text can reconstruct the original co-author graph. Given that we estimate the latent entity representations using the complete TU document collection, by design, our evaluation is contained within our training set for the purpose of this analysis.

Table 2 shows NDCG and R-Precision [37, p. 158] for various representation models and dimensionality. SERT performs significantly better than the other representations methods (except for the 256-dimensional representations where significance was not achieved w.r.t. LDA). SERT is closely followed by word2vec (of which both variants score only slightly worse than SERT), LDA and LSI. The count-based distributional methods (LSI, LDA) perform better as the dimensionality of the representations increases. This is contrary to SERT, where retrieval performance is very stable across dimensionalities. Interestingly, doc2vec performs very poorly at reconstructing the co-author graph and is even surpassed

Table 2: Retrieval performance (NDCG and R-Precision) when ranking experts for a query expert by the cosine similarity of expert representations (random, Graph PCA, LSI, LDA, word2vec, doc2vec and SERT) for the TU expert collection (§4.2) for an increasing representation dimensionality. The relevance labels are given by the number of times two experts were co-authors of academic papers. Significance of results is determined using a two-tailed paired Student t-test (* $p < 0.10$, ** $p < 0.05$, *** $p < 0.01$) between the best performing model and second best performing method.

Dimensionality $k =$	32		64		128		256	
	NDCG	R-Precision	NDCG	R-Precision	NDCG	R-Precision	NDCG	R-Precision
Random	0.18	0.01	0.18	0.01	0.18	0.01	0.18	0.01
Graph PCA	0.38	0.18	0.39	0.20	0.41	0.23	0.39	0.23
LSI	0.39	0.17	0.43	0.21	0.46	0.23	0.47	0.23
LDA	0.44	0.19	0.45	0.20	0.46	0.22	0.52	0.28
word2vec-sg	0.46	0.22	0.49	0.24	0.49	0.24	0.50	0.25
word2vec-cbow	0.46	0.23	0.47	0.24	0.48	0.25	0.48	0.25
doc2vec	0.35	0.14	0.36	0.15	0.36	0.16	0.35	0.15
SERT	**0.53*****	**0.29*****	**0.54*****	**0.31*****	**0.53*****	**0.30*****	**0.53**	**0.31***

by the Graph PCA baseline. This is likely due to the fact that doc2vec is trained on expert profiles and is not explicitly presented with document-expert associations. The difference in performance between doc2vec and SERT for RQ2 reflects a difference in architecture: while SERT is directly optimized to discriminate between entities, doc2vec models entities as context in addition to language. Hence, similarities and dissimilarities between entities are preserved much better by SERT.

We answer our second research question as follows. Latent text-based entity representations do encode information about entity relations. However, there is a large difference in the performance of different methods. SERT seems to encode the entity co-associations better than other methods, by achieving the highest performance independent of the vector space dimensionality.

5.2 Analysis of the expert prior in SERT

One of the semantic models that we consider, SERT, learns a prior $P(X)$ over entities. The remaining representation learning methods do not encode an explicit entity prior. It might be possible to extract a prior from generic entity vector spaces, e.g., by examining the deviation from the mean representation for every entity. However, developing such prior extraction methods is a topic of study by itself and is out of scope for this paper.

In the case of expert finding, this prior probability encodes a belief over experts without observing any evidence (i.e., query terms in SERT). Which structural information does this prior capture? We now investigate the regularities encoded within this prior and link it back to the hierarchy among scholars in the Tilburg University collection. We estimate a SERT model on the whole TU collection and extract the prior probabilities:

$$P(X = x_i) = \frac{\exp{(b_i)}}{\sum_l \exp{(b_l)}}, \quad (3)$$

where b is the bias vector of the SERT model in Eq. 2.

For 666 out of 977 experts in the TU collection we have ground truth information regarding their academic rank [9].[5] Figure 2 shows box plots of the prior probabilities, learned automatically by the SERT model from only text and associations, grouped by academic rank. Interestingly, the prior seems to encode the hierarchy amongst scholars at Tilburg University, e.g., Post-docs are ranked higher than PhD students. This is not surprising as it is quite likely that higher-ranked scholars have more associated documents.

The prior over experts in SERT encodes rank within organizations. As mentioned earlier, this is not surprising, as experts (i.e., academics in this experiment) of higher rank tend to occur more frequently in the expert collection. This observation unveils interesting insights about the expert finding task and consequently models targeted at solving it. Unlike unsupervised ad-hoc document retrieval where we assume a uniform prior and normalized document lengths, the prior over experts in the expert finding task is of much greater importance. In addition, we can use this insight to gain a better understanding of the formal language models for expertise retrieval [2]. Balog et al. [2] find that, for the expert finding task, the document-oriented language model performs better than a entity-oriented language model. However, the document-oriented model [2] will rank experts with more associated documents higher than experts with few associated documents. On the contrary, the entity-oriented model of Balog et al. [2], imposes a uniform prior over experts. SERT is an entity-oriented model and performs better than the formal document-oriented language model [56]. This is likely due to the fact that SERT learns an empirical prior over entities instead of making an assumption of uniformity, in addition to its entity-oriented perspective.

In the case of general entity finding, the importance of the number of associated documents might be of lesser importance. Other sources of prior information, such as link analysis [41], recency [23] and user interactions [48], can be a better way of modeling entity importance than the length of entity descriptions.

---

[5]126 PhD Students, 49 Postdoctoral Researchers, 210 Assistant Professors, 89 Associate Professors and 190 Full Professors; we filtered out academic ranks that only occur once in the ground-truth, namely Scientific Programmer and Research Coordinator.

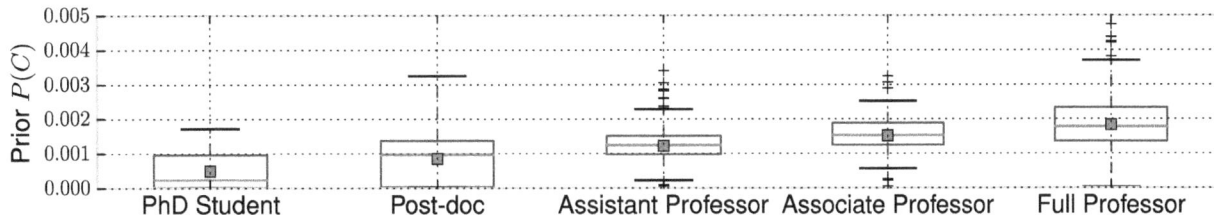

Figure 2: Box plots of prior probabilities learned by SERT, grouped by the experts' academic rank, for the TU collection. We only show the prior learned for a SERT model with $k = 32$, as the distributions of models with a different representation dimensionality are qualitatively similar.

6 CONCLUSIONS

In this work we have investigated the structural regularities contained within latent text-based entity representations. Entity representations were constructed from expert finding collections using methods from distributional semantics (LSI), topic models (LDA) and neural networks (word2vec, doc2vec and SERT). For LSI, LDA and word2vec, document-level representations were transformed to the entity scope according to the framework of Demartini et al. [19]. In the case of doc2vec and SERT, entity representations were learned directly. In addition to representations estimated only from text, we considered non-textual baselines, such as: (1) random representations sampled from a Normal distribution, and (2) the rows of the dimensionality-reduced adjacency matrix of the co-association graph.

We have found that text-based entity representations can be used to discover groups inherent to an organization. We have clustered entity representations using K-means and compared the obtained clusters with a ground-truth partitioning. No information about the organization is presented to the algorithms. Instead, these regularities are extracted by the documents associated with entities and published within the organization. Furthermore, we have evaluated the capacity of text-based expert representations to encode co-associations by casting the problem as a ranking task. We discover that text-based representations retain co-associations up to different extents. In particular, we find that SERT entity representations encode the co-association graph better than the other representation learning methods. We conclude that this is due to the fact that SERT representations are directly optimized to discriminate between entities. Lastly, we have shown that the prior probabilities learned by semantic models encode further structural information. That is, we find that the prior probability over experts (i.e., members of an academic institution), learned as part of a SERT model, encodes academic rank. In addition, we discuss the similarities between SERT and the document-oriented language model [2] and find that the document association prior plays an important role in expert finding.

Our findings have shown insight into how different text-based entity representation methods behave in various applications. In particular, we find that the manner in which entity-document associations are encoded plays an important role. That is, representation learning methods that directly optimize the representation of the entity seem to perform best. When considering different neural representation learning models (doc2vec and SERT), we find that their difference in architecture allows them to encode different regularities: doc2vec models an entity as context in addition to language, whereas SERT learns to discriminate between entities given their language. Thus, doc2vec can more adequately model the topical nature of entities, while SERT more closely captures the similarities and dissimilarities between entities. In the case of expert finding, we find that the amount of textual data associated with an expert is a principal measure of expert importance.

Future work includes the use of text-based entity representations in end-to-end applications. For example, in social networks these methods can be applied to cluster users in addition to network features [53, 57], or to induce graphs based on thread participation or hashtag usage. In addition, text-based entity representations can be used as item feature vectors in recommendation systems. Beyond text-only entity collections, there is also a plenitude of applications where entity relations are available. While there has been some work on learning latent representations from entity relations [11, 60], there has not been much attention given to combining textual evidence and entity relations. Therefore, we identify two additional directions for future work. First, an analysis showing in what capacity entity representations estimated from text alone encode entity-entity relations (beyond the co-associations considered in this work). Secondly, the incorporation of entity-entity similarity in the construction of latent entity representations.

ACKNOWLEDGMENTS

We would like to thank the anonymous reviewers for their valuable comments and suggestions. This research was supported by Ahold Delhaize, Amsterdam Data Science, the Bloomberg Research Grant program, the Criteo Faculty Research Award program, the Dutch national program COMMIT, Elsevier, the European Community's Seventh Framework Programme (FP7/2007-2013) under grant agreement nr 312827 (VOX-Pol), the Google Faculty Research Award scheme, the Microsoft Research Ph.D. program, the Netherlands Institute for Sound and Vision, the Netherlands Organisation for Scientific Research (NWO) under project nrs 612.001.116, HOR-11-10, CI-14-25, 652.002.001, 612.001.551, 652.001.003, and Yandex. All content represents the opinion of the authors, which is not necessarily shared or endorsed by their respective employers and/or sponsors.

REFERENCES

[1] Enrique Amigó, Julio Gonzalo, Javier Artiles, and Felisa Verdejo. 2009. A comparison of extrinsic clustering evaluation metrics based on formal constraints. *Information Retrieval* 12, 4 (2009), 461–486.

[2] Krisztian Balog, Leif Azzopardi, and Maarten de Rijke. 2006. Formal models for expert finding in enterprise corpora. In *SIGIR*. 43–50.

[3] Krisztian Balog and Maarten de Rijke. 2007. Determining Expert Profiles (With an Application to Expert Finding). In *IJCAI*. 2657–2662.

[4] Krisztian Balog and Maarten de Rijke. 2007. Finding similar experts. In *SIGIR*. ACM, 821–822.

[5] Krisztian Balog, Yi Fang, Maarten de Rijke, Pavel Serdyukov, and Luo Si. 2012. Expertise Retrieval. *Found. & Tr. in Information Retrieval* 6, 2-3 (2012), 127–256.

[6] Krisztian Balog, Pavel Serdyukov, and Arjen P. de Vries. 2010. Overview of the TREC 2010 entity track. In *TREC*. NIST.

[7] Marco Baroni, Georgiana Dinu, and Germán Kruszewski. 2014. Don't count, predict! A systematic comparison of context-counting vs. context-predicting semantic vectors.. In *ACL*. 238–247.

[8] Yoshua Bengio, Réjean Ducharme, Pascal Vincent, and Christian Janvin. 2003. A Neural Probabilistic Language Model. *JMLR* 3 (2003), 1137–1155.

[9] Richard Berendsen, Maarten de Rijke, Krisztian Balog, Toine Bogers, and Antal van den Bosch. 2013. On the Assessment of Expertise Profiles. *JASIST* 64, 10 (2013), 2024–2044.

[10] David M. Blei, Andrew Y. Ng, and Michael I. Jordan. 2003. Latent Dirichlet allocation. *JMLR* 3 (2003), 993–1022.

[11] Antoine Bordes, Jason Weston, Ronan Collobert, and Yoshua Bengio. 2011. Learning structured embeddings of knowledge bases. In *AAAI*.

[12] Chris Burges, Tal Shaked, Erin Renshaw, Ari Lazier, Matt Deeds, Nicole Hamilton, and Greg Hullender. 2005. Learning to rank using gradient descent. In *ICML*. 89–96.

[13] Aylin Caliskan, Joanna J. Bryson, and Arvind Narayanan. 2017. Semantics derived automatically from language corpora contain human-like biases. *Science* 356, 6334 (2017), 183–186.

[14] Kevin Clark and Christopher D Manning. 2016. Improving Coreference Resolution by Learning Entity-Level Distributed Representations. arXiv 1606.01323. (2016).

[15] Ronan Collobert and Jason Weston. 2008. A unified architecture for natural language processing: Deep neural networks with multitask learning. In *ICML*. 160–167.

[16] Nick Craswell, Arjen P. de Vries, and Ian Soboroff. 2005. Overview of the TREC 2005 Enterprise Track. In *TREC*.

[17] Thomas H. Davenport and Laurence Prusak. 1998. *Working knowledge: How organizations manage what they know.* Harvard Business Press.

[18] Scott C. Deerwester, Susan T. Dumais, and Richard A. Harshman. 1990. Indexing by latent semantic analysis. *Journal of the American Society for Information Science* 41, 6 (1990), 391–407.

[19] Gianluca Demartini, Julien Gaugaz, and Wolfgang Nejdl. 2009. A vector space model for ranking entities and its application to expert search. In *ECIR*. Springer, 189–201.

[20] Li Deng, Xiaodong He, and Jianfeng Gao. 2013. Deep stacking networks for information retrieval. In *ICASSP*. 3153–3157.

[21] Laura Dietz, Alexander Kotov, and Edgar Meij. 2016. Utilizing Knowledge Bases in Text-centric Information Retrieval. In *ICTIR*. ACM, 5–5.

[22] Yi Fang, Luo Si, and Aditya P. Mathur. 2010. Discriminative models of integrating document evidence and document-candidate associations for expert search. In *SIGIR*. ACM, 683–690.

[23] David Graus, Manos Tsagkias, Wouter Weerkamp, Edgar Meij, and Maarten de Rijke. 2016. Dynamic collective entity representations for entity ranking. In *WSDM*. ACM, 595–604.

[24] Zhengyan He, Shujie Liu, Mu Li, Ming Zhou, Longkai Zhang, and Houfeng Wang. 2013. Learning Entity Representation for Entity Disambiguation.. In *ACL*. 30–34.

[25] Geoffrey E. Hinton. 1986. Learning distributed representations of concepts. In *8th Annual Conference of the Cognitive Science Society*, Vol. 1. Amherst, MA, 12.

[26] Thomas Hofmann. 1999. Probabilistic latent semantic indexing. In *SIGIR*. ACM, 50–57.

[27] Po-sen Huang, N Mathews Ave Urbana, Xiaodong He, Jianfeng Gao, Li Deng, Alex Acero, and Larry Heck. 2013. Learning Deep Structured Semantic Models for Web Search using Clickthrough Data. In *CIKM*. 2333–2338.

[28] Tom Kenter and Maarten de Rijke. 2015. Short text similarity with word embeddings. In *CIKM*. ACM, 1411–1420.

[29] Quoc V Le and Tomas Mikolov. 2014. Distributed Representations of Sentences and Documents. In *ICML*. 1188–1196.

[30] Omer Levy, Yoav Goldberg, and Ido Dagan. 2015. Improving distributional similarity with lessons learned from word embeddings. *TACL* 3 (2015), 211–225.

[31] Omer Levy, Yoav Goldberg, and Israel Ramat-Gan. 2014. Linguistic Regularities in Sparse and Explicit Word Representations. In *CoNLL*. 171–180.

[32] Hang Li and Jun Xu. 2014. Semantic Matching in Search. *Found. & Tr. in Information Retrieval* 7, 5 (June 2014), 343–469.

[33] Xinyi Li, Bob Schijvenaars, and Maarten de Rijke. 2017. Investigating queries and search failures in academic search. *Information Processing & Management* 53, 3 (May 2017), 666–683.

[34] Tie-Yan Liu. 2011. *Learning to Rank for Information Retrieval.* Springer.

[35] Hans Peter Luhn. 1958. The automatic creation of literature abstracts. *IBM Journal of research and development* 2, 2 (1958), 159–165.

[36] James B. MacQueen. 1967. Some methods for classification and analysis of multivariate observations. In *Proceedings of the Fifth Berkeley Symposium on Mathematical Statistics and Probability, Volume 1: Statistics.* 281–297.

[37] Christopher D. Manning, Prabhakar Raghavan, and Hinrich Schütze. 2008. *Introduction to Information Retrieval.* Cambridge University Press, New York, NY, USA.

[38] Tomas Mikolov, Kai Chen, Greg Corrado, and Jeffrey Dean. 2013. Distributed Representations of Words and Phrases and their Compositionality. In *NIPS*. 3111–3119.

[39] Tomas Mikolov, Greg Corrado, Kai Chen, and Jeffrey Dean. 2013. Efficient Estimation of Word Representations in Vector Space. arXiv 1301.3781. (2013).

[40] Tomas Mikolov, Wen-tau Yih, and Geoffrey Zweig. 2013. Linguistic Regularities in Continuous Space Word Representations. In *HLT-NAACL*. 746–751.

[41] Lawrence Page, Sergey Brin, Rajeev Motwani, and Terry Winograd. 1999. *The PageRank citation ranking: bringing order to the web.* Technical Report. Stanford InfoLab.

[42] Michael J Pazzani and Daniel Billsus. 2007. Content-based recommendation systems. In *The adaptive web*. Springer, 325–341.

[43] Jeffrey Pennington, Richard Socher, and Christopher D. Manning. 2014. GloVe: Global Vectors for Word Representation. In *EMNLP*. 1532–1543.

[44] Jeffrey Pound, Peter Mika, and Hugo Zaragoza. 2010. Ad-hoc Object Retrieval in the Web of Data. In *WWW*. ACM, 771–780.

[45] Henry Martyn Robert, Sarah Corbin Robert, and Daniel H Honemann. 2011. *Robert's rules of order newly revised.* Da Capo Press.

[46] David E. Rumelhart, Geoffrey E. Hinton, and Ronald J. Williams. 1985. *Learning internal representations by error propagation.* Technical Report. DTIC Document.

[47] Ruslan Salakhutdinov and Geoffrey Hinton. 2009. Semantic hashing. *Int. J. Approximate Reasoning* 50, 7 (2009), 969–978.

[48] Anne Schuth. 2016. Search Engines That Learn from Their Users. *SIGIR Forum* 50, 1 (June 2016), 95–96.

[49] Yelong Shen, Xiaodong He, Jianfeng Gao, Li Deng, and Grégoire Mesnil. 2014. A Latent Semantic Model with Convolutional-Pooling Structure for Information Retrieval. In *CIKM*. 101–110.

[50] TREC. 2005–2008. Enterprise Track. (2005–2008).

[51] Joseph Turian, Lev Ratinov, and Yoshua Bengio. 2010. Word representations: a simple and general method for semi-supervised learning. In *ACL*. 384–394.

[52] David van Dijk, Manos Tsagkias, and Maarten de Rijke. 2015. Early Detection of Topical Expertise in Community Question Answering. In *SIGIR*. ACM, 995–998.

[53] Christophe Van Gysel. 2014. Listening to the Flock - Towards opinion mining through data-parallel, semi-supervised learning on social graphs. (2014).

[54] Christophe Van Gysel, Maarten de Rijke, and Evangelos Kanoulas. 2016. Learning Latent Vector Spaces for Product Search. In *CIKM*. ACM, 165–174.

[55] Christophe Van Gysel, Maarten de Rijke, and Evangelos Kanoulas. 2017. Semantic Entity Retrieval Toolkit. In *Neu-IR SIGIR Workshop*.

[56] Christophe Van Gysel, Maarten de Rijke, and Marcel Worring. 2016. Unsupervised, Efficient and Semantic Expertise Retrieval. In *WWW*. ACM, 1069–1079.

[57] Christophe Van Gysel, Bart Goethals, and Maarten de Rijke. 2015. Determining the Presence of Political Parties in Social Circles. In *ICWSM*, Vol. 2015. 690–693.

[58] Nguyen Xuan Vinh, Julien Epps, and James Bailey. 2010. Information theoretic measures for clusterings comparison: Variants, properties, normalization and correction for chance. *JMLR* 11 (2010), 2837–2854.

[59] Roger Weber, Hans-Jörg Schek, and Stephen Blott. 1998. A quantitative analysis and performance study for similarity-search methods in high-dimensional spaces. In *VLDB*. 194–205.

[60] Yu Zhao, Liu Zhiyuan, and Maosong Sun. 2015. Representation learning for measuring entity relatedness with rich information. In *IJCAI*. 1412–1418.

Knowledge Questions from Knowledge Graphs

Dominic Seyler
University of Illinois at
Urbana-Champaign
dseyler2@illinois.edu

Mohamed Yahya
Bloomberg LP, London
myahya6@bloomberg.net

Klaus Berberich
Max Planck Institute for Informatics
HTW Saar
kberberi@mpi-inf.mpg.de

ABSTRACT

We address the problem of automatically generating quiz-style knowledge questions from a knowledge graph such as DBpedia. Questions of this kind have ample applications, for instance, to educate users about or to evaluate their knowledge in a specific domain. To solve the problem, we propose a novel end-to-end approach. The approach first selects a named entity from the knowledge graph as an answer. It then generates a structured triple-pattern query, which yields the answer as its sole result. If a multiple-choice question is desired, the approach selects alternative answer options as distractors. Finally, our approach uses a template-based method to verbalize the structured query and yield a natural language question. A key challenge is estimating how difficult the generated question is to human users. To do this, we make use of historical data from the Jeopardy! quiz show and a semantically annotated Web-scale document collection, engineer suitable features, and train a logistic regression classifier to predict question difficulty. Experiments demonstrate the viability of our overall approach.

1 INTRODUCTION

In this work, we address the problem of generating quiz-style knowledge questions from knowledge graphs (KGs). As shown in Figure 1, starting from a KG and a topic such as *US Presidents*, we generate a quiz question whose unique answer is an entity from that topic. The question starts its life as an automatically generated triple-pattern query, which our system verbalizes. Each generated question is adorned with a difficulty level, providing an estimate for how hard it is to answer, and optionally a set of distractors, which can be listed alongside the correct answer to obtain a multiple-choice question. Our system is able to judge the impact of distractors on the difficulty of the resulting multiple-choice question.

Applications of automatically generated knowledge questions include education and evaluation. One way to educate users about a specific domain (e.g., Politics) is to prompt them with questions, so that they pick up facts as they try to answer – reminiscent of flash cards used by pupils. When qualification for a task needs to be ensured, such as knowledge about a specific domain, automatically generated knowledge questions can serve as a qualification test. Crowdsourcing is one concrete use case as outlined in [35].

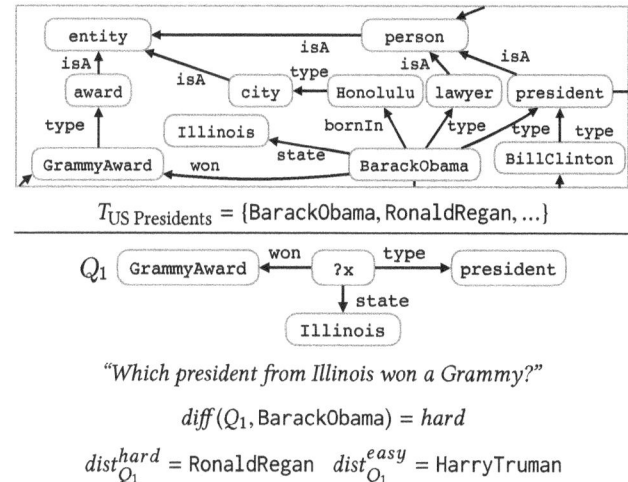

$T_{\text{US Presidents}} = \{\text{BarackObama}, \text{RonaldRegan}, \ldots\}$

"Which president from Illinois won a Grammy?"

$$\textit{diff}(Q_1, \text{BarackObama}) = \textit{hard}$$

$$\textit{dist}_{Q_1}^{\textit{hard}} = \text{RonaldRegan} \quad \textit{dist}_{Q_1}^{\textit{easy}} = \text{HarryTruman}$$

Figure 1: A KG fragment, a topic, a hard question, and two distractors (one easy and one hard).

Likewise, knowledge questions can serve as a form of CAPTCHA to exclude likely bots.

Challenges. To discriminate how much people know about a domain it is typical to ask progressively more difficult questions. In our setting, this means that we need to automatically quantify the difficulty of a question. This is not trivial as it requires us to consider multiple signals and their interaction. One might consider all questions whose answer is BarackObama to be easy, as he is a prominent entity. However, few people would know that he won a GrammyAward. Therefore, signals that predict question difficulty need to be identified and combined in a meaningful manner.

An answer should be easy to verify automatically and disputes about the correctness of an answer should be minimal. We envision a setting with minimal human involvement, which we achieve by ensuring that each question has exactly one correct answer. We deal with possible variation in user input (e.g., *'Barack Obama'* vs *'Barack H. Obama'*) by turning fill-in-the-blank questions into multiple-choice questions. Here, we carefully consider the impact distractors have on question difficulty.

A final challenge is the production of well-formed questions that look natural. Such questions provide a better experience to users and make them hard to identify as having been automatically generated. Two important factors here are question coherence and linguistic variety. For example, while a *KG* may classify BarackObama as an entity and a formerSenator, we use the latter in asking about him, as the first is unnatural. Similarly, while a relation of an actor to a movie is called actedIn, we want to vary it's expression (e.g., *'acted in'* or *'starred in'*).

ICTIR '17, October 1–4, 2017, Amsterdam, The Netherlands
© 2017 ACM. ISBN 978-1-4503-4490-6/17/10…$15.00
DOI: http://dx.doi.org/10.1145/3121050.3121073

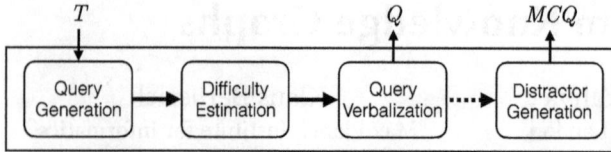

Figure 2: Question generation pipeline.

Contributions. We propose a novel end-to-end approach for generating quiz-style knowledge questions from knowledge graphs. Our approach has three major components: query generation, difficulty estimation, and query verbalization. In a setting where multiple-choice questions are desired, a fourth component can generate distractors and quantify their impact on question difficulty. Figure 2 depicts our pipeline.

The query generation component generates a structured query that will serve as the basis of the final question shown to a human. By starting from a structured query, we are able to generate questions that are certain to have one unique, correct answer in our KG. We discuss challenges that need to be addressed so that the resulting cues are meaningful.

To estimate the difficulty of a question we leverage different signals about named entities, which we derive from a Web-scale document collection annotated with named entities from the KG. We use these signals as features to train a difficulty classifier with supervision obtained from more than thirty years of data from the Jeopardy! quiz show.

Since our questions start their life as structured queries over the KG, we verbalize them to generate a corresponding natural language question. Following earlier work, we adopt a template-based approach. However, we extend this approach with automatically mined paraphrases for relations and classes in the KG, ensuring diversity in the resulting natural language questions.

Outline. The rest of this paper unfolds as follows. Section 2 introduces preliminaries and provides a formal problem statement. Section 3 describes how a SPARQL query can be generated that has a unique answer in the KG. Our approach for estimating the difficulty of the generated query is presented in Section 4. Section 5 describes how the query can be verbalized into natural language. Extensions for multiple-choice questions are described in Section 6. Section 7 lays out the setup and results of our experiments. We put our work in the context of prior research in Section 8, before concluding in Section 9.

2 PRELIMINARIES & PROBLEM STATEMENT

Knowledge Graphs (KGs) such as as Freebase [9] and Yago [38] describe *entities* E (e.g., BarackObama) by connecting them to other entities, *types* T — also called classes (e.g., president, leader), and *literals* L (e.g., '1985-02-05') using *predicates* P (e.g., bornIn, birthdate, type). A KG is thus a set of facts (or triples), $\{f \mid f \in E \cup T \times P \times E \cup T \cup L\}$. A triple can also be seen as an instance of a binary predicate, with the first argument called *subject* and the second called *object*, hence the model is referred to as subject-predicate-object (SPO) model. Figure 1 shows a KG fragment.

Pattern matching is used to query a KG. Given a set of variables V that are always prefixed with a question mark (e.g., ?x), a *triple-pattern-query* is a set of triple patterns $Q = \{q \mid q \in V \cup E \cup T \times V \cup$

$P \times V \cup E \cup T \cup L\}$. An answer a to a query is a total mapping of variables to items in the KG such that the application of a to each q results in a fact in the KG. In our setting, inspired by Jeopardy!, we restrict ourselves to queries having a single variable for which a unique answer exists in the KG.

We use Yago2s [39] as our reference KG, which contains 2.6M entities, 300K types organized into a type hierarchy, and more than 100 predicates that form over 48M facts. Yago entities are associated with Wikipedia entries, whereas Yago types correspond to WordNet synsets [13] or Wikipedia categories. For estimating question difficulty, we utilize the ClueWeb09/12 document collections and the FACC annotations provided by Google [16]. The latter provide semantic annotations of disambiguated named entities from Freebase, which we map to Yago2s via their Wikipedia article.

Jeopardy! is a popular U.S. TV quiz show that features questions referred to as clues. Each clue comes with a monetary value, corresponding to the amount added to a contestant's balance when answering correctly. We reckon that monetary values correlate with human performance and thus question difficulty – a hypothesis which we investigate in Section 4.

Problem Statement. Put formally, our objective is to automatically generate a question Q whose unique answer is an entity $e \in \mathfrak{T}$ which can be supported by facts in the KG. $\mathfrak{T}$ is a thematic set of entities called a *topic*, which allows us to control the domain from which knowledge questions are generated (e.g., *American Politics*). Moreover, we assume a predefined set of *difficulty levels* $D = \{d_1, ..., d_n\}$ with a strict total order $<$ defined over its elements, and we want to estimate the difficulty of providing the answer a to Q, denoted $diff(Q, a)$. An extension of the above problem which we also deal with in this work is the generation of *multiple choice questions* (MCQs), where the task is to extend a question Q into an MCQ by generating a set of incorrect answers, called *distractors*, and quantifying their difficulty.

In our concrete instantiation of the above problem, we use Wikipedia categories as topics and Yago2s as our KG. As a first attempt to address the above problem, we consider a setting with two difficulty levels, $D = \{easy, hard\}$, where $easy < hard$. For our purposes, a *question* is any natural language sentence that requires an answer. It can be an interrogative sentence, or a declarative one in the style of Jeopardy! clues.

Generality. All methods and tools proposed in this work are general enough to apply to a setting other than ours of Jeopardy! and Yago. Our approach can be applied to any KG that is represented as triples and abides by the standards described earlier in this section. In addition, lexical knowledge is required in the form of surface forms for entities (e.g., BarackObama → "Barack Obama") and relations (e.g., actedIn → "starred in"). For difficulty estimation, our approach requires a question-answer corpus with annotated difficulties. Statistics are required about salience of entities and coherence of entity pairs, which can be estimated using external corpora like Wikipedia.

3 QUERY GENERATION

The first stage is the generation of a query that has a unique answer in the KG. This query serves as the basis for generating a question that will be shown to human contestants. The unique answer needs to be provided by the user in order to correctly answer the question. Ensuring that a question has a single answer simplifies verification.

The input to the query generation step is a topic $\mathfrak{T}$ (e.g., US Presidents). The unique answer to the generated query will be an entity $e \in \mathfrak{T}$ randomly drawn from the KG (e.g., BarackObama). After drawing e, a subset of triple patterns is selected from the KG where e is either subject or object in the pattern. These triples form the question's content.

The selection of triple patterns is guided by the following desiderata: i) the query should contain at least one type triple pattern, which is crucial when verbalizing the query to generate a question, and ii) entities mentioned in the query should not give any obvious clues about the answer entity. In what follows we present the challenges in achieving each of these desiderata, and our solutions to these challenges.

3.1 Answer Type Selection

Questions asking for entities always require a type that is either specified implicitly (e.g., 'who' for person) or explicitly (e.g., "Which president ... "). KGs tend to contain a large number of types and typically associate an entity with multiple types. Some of these types usually appear in text talking about an entity (e.g., president, lawyer). Other types, however, are artifacts of attempts to have an ontologically complete and formally sound type system. Such types are meaningful only in the context of a type system, but not on their own (e.g., the type entity).

To address the problem of selecting a type for an answer entity, we use our entity-annotated corpus to capture the salience of a semantic type t for an entity e, denoted $s(t, e)$. We start by collecting occurrences of an entity e along with *textual types* to which it belongs t_{text} in our entity-annotated corpus. We use the following patterns, inspired by Hearst [19], to collect (t_{text}, e) pairs:

P1: ENTITY ('is a'| 'is an'|', a'| 'and other'| 'or other') TYPE
"BarackObama *and other* presidents attended the ceremony."
P2: TYPE ('like'| 'such as'| 'including'| 'especially'|) ENTITY
"...several *attorneys* including BarackObama"

The next step is to disambiguate (t_{text}, e) pairs to (t, e) pairs — note that entities are already disambiguated in the corpus, so we only need to disambiguate t_{text} to a semantic type t in the KG. Relying on the fact that our semantic types are WordNet synsets, we use the WordNet lexicon (e.g., {lawyer, attorney} → lawyer) for generating a set of semantic type candidates for a given textual type. We then use a heuristic where a textual type t_{text} paired with an entity e is disambiguated to a semantic type t if i) t is in the set of candidates for t_{text} and ii) $e \in t$. We compute salience $s(t, e)$ as the relative frequency with which the disambiguated (t, e) pair was observed in our corpus. To select a type for the answer entity e, we draw one of its types randomly based on $s(t, e)$.

3.2 Triple Pattern Generation

We now have an answer entity e and one of its semantic types t that will be used to refer to e in the question. We now need to create a query whose unique answer over the KG is e. Creating a query means selecting facts where e is either the subject or object

and turning these into triple patterns by replacing e with a variable (?x). Not all facts can be used here, as some reveal too much about the answer and render the question too trivial. Other facts will be redundant given the facts already used.

Elimination of Textual Overlap with the Answer. The first restriction we impose on a fact is that the surface forms of entities that appear in it cannot have any textual overlap with surface forms of the answer entity. The question *"Which president is married to Michelle Obama?"* reveals too much about the answer entity. For overlap, we look at the set of words in the surface forms, excluding common stop words.

Elimination of Redundant Facts. Given a set of facts that has been chosen, a new fact does not always add new information. Keeping this redundant fact in a query will allow humans to clearly identify a question as being automatically generated. To eliminate this issue, we check each new type fact against all existing ones. If the new type is a supertype (e.g., person) of an existing one (e.g., president), we discard it.

4 DIFFICULTY ESTIMATION

We now describe our approach to estimating the difficulty of answering the knowledge query generated in Section 3. There are several, seemingly contradictory, signals that affect the difficulty of a question. As discussed earlier, one might expect any question asking for a popular entity such as BarackObama to be an easy one. However, if we were to ask *"Which president from Illinois won a Grammy Award?"*, few people are likely to think of BarackObama. We use a classification model trained on a corpus of questions paired with their difficulties to predict question difficulty. Note that the difficulty is computed based on the query and not its verbalization. Our goal here is to create questions that measure factual knowledge rather than linguistic ability.

Since we rely on supervised training for difficulty estimation, we make the natural assumption that difficulty labels in the 'training' and 'testing' questions are drawn from the same underlying distribution for some target audience. We also assume that for this population, it is possible to capture the difficulty of a question. As evidence for this, in the Jeopardy! dataset [1] we find a positive correlation between the attempted questions for a certain difficulty-level and the number of times a question of this difficulty-level could not be answered. For the five difficulty-levels ($200, $400, $600, $800, $1000), 4.46%, 8.35%, 12.69%, 17.82% and 25.69% of the questions could not be answered, respectively.

4.1 Preparing Training Data

We use the Jeopardy! quiz-game show data described in Section 2 for training and testing our difficulty-estimation classifier. The larger goal is to estimate the difficulty of answering queries generated from a knowledge graph, so we restrict ourselves to a subset of the Jeopardy! questions answerable from Yago [38], which we collected as described below.

We say a question is answerable from Yago if i) all entities mentioned in the question and its answer are in Yago, and ii) all relations connecting these entities are captured by Yago. To find these questions, we automatically annotate Jeopardy! questions with Yago entities using the AIDA tool for named entity disambiguation [21]. An example of a disambiguated question is:

ShahJahan *built this complex in* Agra *to immortalize* MumtazMahal, *his favorite wife.* TajMahal

We retain an entity-annotated question if i) its answer can be mapped to a Yago entity, ii) its body has at least one entity (the one that will be given in the question, not the answer), and iii) considering all entities in the question and the answer entity, each entity can be paired with another entity to which it has a direct relation in Yago. The last condition ensures that we have questions that can be captured by the relationships in Yago. However, it does not identify this relation, and such a match may be spurious. Since this is hard to establish automatically, we invoke humans at this point.

We run a crowdsourcing task on the questions that survive the above automated annotation and filtering procedure. The task is to label a question/answer pair as *Good* if i) all entities in the question have been captured and disambiguated correctly, ii) the question can be captured by relations in Yago, and iii) the answer is a unique one. The crowdsourcing task ran until we obtained a total of 500 questions that we use in our experiments.

4.2 Difficulty Classifier

After obtaining the training/testing data, we turn our attention to building the difficulty classifier and its features. Formally, our goal is to learn a function $diff(Q, e) \in \{easy, hard\}$ that estimates the difficulty of providing the answer e to the query Q. We use logistic regression due to the ease with which it can be trained and because it allows easy inspection of feature weights, which proved helpful during development. As we are dealing with a binary classification case ($easy, hard$), we train our model to learn the probability of the question being an *easy* one, $P(diff(Q, e) = easy)$, and set a decision boundary at 0.5. We judge a question to be *easy* if $P(diff(Q, e) = easy) > 0.5$ and *hard* otherwise.

The model, however, only works if provided with the right features. Table 1 provides a summary of our features. The key ingredients in our feature repertoire are:

Entity Salience (ϕ) is a normalized score that is used as a proxy for an entity's popularity. As our entities come from Wikipedia, we use the Wikipedia link structure to compute entity salience as the relative frequency with which the Wikipedia entry for an entity is linked to from all other entries. We also consider salience on a per-coarse-semantic-type basis. The second group of Table 1 defines a set of templates. We consider the coarse semantic types person, location, and organization and define a fourth coarse semantic type other that collects entities not in any of the three aforementioned coarse types (e.g., movies, inventions). Having specialized features for individual coarse-grained types allows us to take into account some particularities of these coarse types. For example, locations tend to have disproportionately high salience. By having a feature that accounts for this specific semantic type, we can mitigate this. Without this feature, a location in a question would always result in our classifier labeling the question as *easy*.

Coherence of entity pairs (φ) captures the relative tendency of two entities to appear in the same context. This feature essentially informs us about how much the presence of one entity indicates the

Table 1: Difficulty estimator features and their description. $\mathcal{T}$ is one of person, organization, location, or other.

Feature	Description
Entity Salience	
ϕ_{target}	answer entity salience
ϕ_{min}	min. salience of question entities
ϕ_{max}	max. salience of question entities
ϕ_{Σ}	sum over salience of entities
ϕ_{μ}	mean salience of question and answer entities
ϕ_{μ}^{q}	mean salience of entities in question
Per-coarse-semantic-type Salience	
$\phi_{min}^{\mathcal{T}}$	min. salience of entities of type $\mathcal{T}$
$\phi_{max}^{\mathcal{T}}$	max salience of entities of type $\mathcal{T}$
$\phi_{\Sigma}^{\mathcal{T}}$	sum over salience of entities of type $\mathcal{T}$
$\phi_{\mu}^{\mathcal{T}}$	mean salience of entities of type $\mathcal{T}$
Coherence	
φ_{min}	maximum pairwise coherence of all entity pairs
φ_{Σ}	sum over coherence of all entity pairs
φ_{μ}	average coherence of all entity pairs
φ_{μ}^{QTA}	average coherence of entity pairs that involve answer
Answer Type	
$I_{\mathcal{T}}$	binary indicator: answer entity is of type $\mathcal{T}$

presence of the other entity. For example, we would expect a question asking for BarackObama using the WhiteHouse in the question to be easier than one asking for him using GrammyAward. Intuitively, coherence counteracts the effect of salience. Since BarackObama is a salient entity, we would expect questions asking for him to be relatively easy. However, asking for him using GrammyAward is likely to make the question difficult, as people are unlikely to make a connection between the two entities.

We capture coherence using Wikipedia's link structure. Given two entities e_1 and e_2, we define their coherence as the Jaccard coefficient of the sets of Wikipedia entries that link to their respective entries in Wikipedia. The intuition here is that any overlap corresponds to a mention of the relation between these two entities. For the above measures, we take their maximum, minimum, average, and sum over the question as features as detailed in Table 1.

5 QUERY VERBALIZATION

We now turn to the problem of query verbalization, whereby we transform a query constructed in Section 3 into a natural language question. A human can digest this question without the technical expertise required to understand a query. Our questions test factual knowledge as opposed to linguistic ability. The way a question is formulated is not a factor in predicting its difficulty. This guides our approach to query verbalization, which ensures uniformity in how questions are phrased. Our final goal is to construct well-formed questions that are easy to understand.

We rely on a hand crafted *verbalization template* and automatically generated *lexicons* for transforming a query into a question. The verbalization template specifies where the different components of the query appear in the question. The lexicon serves as a bridge between knowledge graph entries and natural language.

Input: Query, $Q = \{q_1, ..., q_n\}$

$Q_{type} := \{q_i \in Q \mid \text{has the predicate type}\} = \{q_{t_1}, ..., q_{t_m}\}$
$Q_{instance} := Q \setminus Q_{type} = \{q_{i_1}, ..., q_{i_l}\}$

$\textit{Which}\ \texttt{verbalize}(q_{t_1}), ...,\ \textit{and}\ \texttt{verbalize}(q_{t_m})$
$\texttt{verbalize}(q_{i_1}), ...,\ \textit{and}\ \texttt{verbalize}(q_{i_l})$?

Figure 3: Verbalization Template

5.1 Verbalization Template

Our approach to verbalizing queries is based on templates. Such approaches are standard in the natural language generation literature [22, 30]. We adopt a template suitable for a quiz game show given in Figure 3. Most of the work is done in the function `verbalize`.

The function `verbalize` takes a triple pattern and produces its verbalization. How this verbalization is performed depends on the nature of the triple pattern. More concretely, there are three distinct patterns possible in our setting (see Section 3):

- **Type**: if the predicate is `type`, then this results in verbalizing the object, which is a semantic type.
- **PO**: where the triple pattern is of form (`?var p o`) and `p` is not `type`.
- **SP**: where the triple pattern is of form (`s p ?var`) and `p` is not `type`.

By considering these cases individually we ensure that linguistically well-formed verbalizations are created.

5.2 Verbalization Lexicons

Semantic items in the knowledge graph are simply identifiers that are not meant for direct human consumption. It is therefore important that we map each semantic item to phrases that can be used to represent it in a natural language string such as a question.

Entities. To verbalize entities we follow the approach of Hoffart et al. [21] and rely on the fact that our entities come from Wikipedia. We resort to Wikipedia for extracting surface forms of our entities. For each entity e, we collect the surface forms of all links to e's Wikipedia entry. We consider this text to be a possible verbalization of e. The above process extracts many spurious verbalizations of an entity e. To overcome this issue, we associate with each candidate verbalization the number of times it was used to link to e's Wikipedia entry and restrict ourselves to the five most frequent ones, which we add to the lexicon for the entry corresponding to e.

Predicates. Predicate verbalization depends on the pattern in which it is observed (SP or PO). We rely on our large entity-annotated corpus described in Section 2 for mining predicate verbalizations sensitive to the SP and PO patterns. For each triple $(e_1\ p\ e_2) \in KG$, we collect all sentences in our corpus that match the patterns $Pat_{SP} = $ "$e_1\ w_1...w_n\ e_2$" (e.g., "`BarackObama` *was born in* `Hawaii`") and $Pat_{PO} = $ "$e_2\ w_1...w_n\ e_1$" (e.g., "`Hawaii` *is the birthplace of* `BarackOmaba`"). Following the distant supervision assumption [27], we hypothesize that '$w_1...w_n$' is expressing p. The above hypothesis does not always hold. To filter out possible noise we resort to a combination of heuristic filtering and scoring. We remove from the above verbalization candidate set any phrases that are longer than 50 characters or contain a third entity e_3. We subsequently score how good of a fit a phrase '$w_1...w_n$' is for a

predicate p using normalized pointwise mutual information (npmi). For each predicate p, we retain the 5 highest scoring verbalizations for each of the two patterns, Pat_{SP} and Pat_{PO}, which are used for verbalizing SP and PO triple patterns, respectively.

Types. As explained in Section 2, our types are WordNet synsets. We therefore rely on the lexicon distributed as part of WordNet for type paraphrasing. Each of the three lexicons provides several ways to verbalize a semantic item. We verbalize a semantic item by choosing a verbalization uniformly at random from the corresponding lexicon to ensure variety.

6 MULTIPLE-CHOICE QUESTIONS

The final component in our question generation framework turns a question into a multiple-choice question (MCQ). This has several advantages: in general, it is easier to administer a MCQ as the problem of answer verification can be completely mechanized. In general, where knowledge questions are involved (as opposed to free response questions that might involve opinion), the use of MCQs is widespread as observed in such tests as the GRE.

To turn a question into an MCQ we need *distractors*: entities presented to the user as candidate answers, but are in fact incorrect answers. Of course, not all entities constitute reasonable distractors. Distractors should ideally be related to the correct answer entity and it should generally be possible to confuse a distractor with the correct answer. We call this the *confusability* of a distractor. The more confusable a distractor is with the correct answer, the more likely a test taker is to choose it as an answer, making the MCQ more challenging.

6.1 Distractor Generation

Our starting point for generating distractors is the query $Q = \{q_1, ..., q_n\}$ generated in Section 3, which formed the basis of the question verbalized in Section 5. By starting with a query, we have a fairly simple but powerful scheme for generating distractors. By removing one or more triple patterns from Q we obtain a query $Q' \subset Q$ that has more than one answer entity. All but one of these entities are an incorrect answer to Q.

The relaxation scheme described above can generate a large number of candidate distractors. However, not all relaxations stay close to the original query. If a relaxation deviates too much from Q, the obtained distractors become meaningless. We address this by imposing two restrictions on relaxed queries: (i) a semantic type restriction, and (ii) a relaxation distance restriction.

Semantic type restriction ensures that the answer and distractor are type-compatible. For example, an MCQ asking for a location should not have a person as one of its distractors. The semantic type restriction requires that a semantic type triple pattern is relaxed to the corresponding coarse type.

The relaxation distance restriction refers to relaxations involving instance triple patterns (as opposed to triple patterns specifying type constraints). We define the distance between a query Q and a query $Q' \subseteq Q$ as follows:

$$dist(Q, Q') = |answers(Q')| - |answers(Q)|,$$

where $answers(Q')$ is the set of answers of Q' ($|answers(Q)|$ is always 1). We restrict relaxed queries to have a distance of no more than α, which we set to 10. By pooling the results of all relaxed queries, we form a set of candidate distractors. The choice of distractor is based on how much difficulty we want the distractors to introduce using our notion of distractor confusability.

6.2 Distractor Confusability

An MCQ can be made more or less difficult by the choice of distractors. If one of the distractors is highly confusable with the answer entity, the MCQ is difficult. If none of the distractors is easy to confuse with the answer entity, the MCQ is easy.

Based on this observation we regard a distractor as confusable if it is likely to be the answer to the original question based on our difficulty model. This implies that if an entity is very likely to be the answer to a question asking about a different entity, this entity pair must be similar. We can therefore define confusability between the question's answer e_a and a distractor entity e_{dist} as follows:

$$conf(Q, e_a, e_{dist}) =$$
$$1 - |P(diff(Q, e_a) = easy) - P(diff(Q, e_{dist}) = easy)|.$$

Since we can have more than one distractor in an MCQ, we capture the above intuition regarding how multiple distractors affect the overall difficulty of the question. We observe that an MCQ is as confusing as its most confusing distractor and define the confusability of a distractor set $Dist = \{e_{dist1}, e_{dist2}, ...\}$ as:

$$conf(Q, e_a, Dist) = \max_{e_{dist} \in Dist} conf(Q, e_a, e_{dist}).$$

Looking at the big picture, we relate the notion of confusability in an MCQ with our earlier notion of difficulty by combining $diff(Q, e_a) \in \{easy, hard\}$ and $conf(Q, e_a, Dist) \in [0, 1]$. An easy question can be turned into a hard one when a very confusable distractor is added, since the user has to distinguish between two very similar entities. However, adding an easy distractor to a hard question will not change its difficulty because even when both entities are not similar to each other, the user still has to know which entitiy is the correct answer.

7 EXPERIMENTAL EVALUATION

In the following section we evaluate our approach to knowledge question generation from knowledge graphs. We perform two user studies which focus on evaluating the difficulty model and our distractor generation framework.

7.1 Human Assessment of Difficulty

An important motivation for automating difficulty assessment of questions is the fact that it is difficult to judge for the average human what constitutes an easy or hard question. Beinborn et al. [6] has already shown this result for language proficiency tests, where language teachers were shown to be bad at predicting the difficulty of questions when considering the actual performance of students. We would like to observe if the same applies to our setting. To create fair and informative tests, it is crucial that we are able to correctly assess the difficulty of a question.

We start with the assumption that the creators of Jeopardy! are good at automatically assessing question difficulty. Evidence for this was discussed in Section 4, where we showed that there exists a correlation between the monetary value of a question and the likelihood of an incorrect answer by Jeopardy! contestants.

Table 2: Agreement between human evaluators (all measurements are Fleiss' Kappa)

	$eval_2$	$eval_3$	majority
$eval_1$	0.192	0.325	0.500
$eval_2$		0.443	0.661
$eval_3$			0.810

In our experiment we want to show how well the average human can predict the difficulty of a question. To do so, we randomly sampled 100 easy ($200) and 100 hard ($1000) questions from the 500 questions generated in Section 4 to maximize the discrepancy in question difficulty. We then asked three human evaluators ($eval_1$, $eval_2$, $eval_3$) to annotate each of the 200 questions as easy or hard. We then compared their answers with each other and with the ground truth according to Jeopardy!.

Table 2 shows the agreement between each pair of human evaluators and the majority vote difficulty assessment using Fleiss' Kappa [15]. When looking at pairwise agreement between evaluators, it ranges from fair to moderate [24]. This leads us to conclude that it is hard for non-experts to properly judge question difficulty.

We also compared the majority vote of the evaluators on the difficulty of the questions with the ground truth provided by Jeopardy!. The result was agreement on 62.5% of questions. This suggests that there is a need to automate the task.

7.2 Question Difficulty Classification

We start by looking at the quality of our scheme for assigning difficulty levels to questions. The scheme is described in Section 4, where the possible difficulty levels are $D = \{easy, hard\}$. We train our logistic regression classifier on 500 Jeopardy! questions annotated as described in Section 4. Using ten-fold cross validation, our classifier was able to correctly identify the difficulty levels of questions with an accuracy of 66.4%.

To gain insight into how informative our features are, we performed a feature ablation study where we look at the results for all combinations of our features. For this part, we grouped our features into three classes:

- **SAL:** "Salience" features as in Table 1, with additional log-transformation of salience values to deal with long-tail entities.
- **COH:** "Coherence" features in Table 1.
- **TYPE:** "Per-coarse-semantic-type Salience" and "Answer Type" features in Table 1.

Table 3 shows the results of this experiment. Each row corresponds to a certain combination of features enabled or disabled. Rows are shown in descending order of ten-fold cross validation accuracy. It can be seen that best performance is achieved when all of our features are integrated. From this observation it can be reasoned that all features are necessary and give complementary signals. The bottom row corresponds to a random classifier.

7.3 User Study on Difficulty Estimation

In the following we perform an experiment on how well our classifier agrees with relative difficulty assessments of humans for questions generated by our system. It is important to note that we

Table 3: Ablation study results for features introduced in Section 4. Accuracy is based on ten-fold cross-validation.

SAL	COH	TYPE	Accuracy
yes	yes	yes	**66.4%**
yes	no	yes	65.8%
yes	yes	no	62.6%
yes	no	no	62.2%
no	no	yes	60.0%
no	yes	yes	57.8%
no	yes	no	52.4%
no	no	no	50.0%

ask humans for relative difficulty assessments as opposed to absolute difficulties, since we have shown in Section 7.1 that humans are not very proficient in judging absolute difficulties.

For the user study we sampled a set of 50 entities with at least 5 non-type facts in Yago. For each entity, we generated a set of three questions and presented them with the answer entity to human annotators. The annotators were asked to order these questions by their relative difficulty and were allowed to skip a set of questions about an entity if they were not familiar with the entity.

We then compared the correlation between the ranking given by each of the human annotators and the output of our logistic regression classifier. For this we used Kendall's τ, which ranges from -1, for perfect disagreement, to 1, for perfect agreement.

A total of 13 evaluators took part in the study and evaluated 92.5 questions on average. Rankings produced by the difficulty classifier moderately agree with the human annotators with $\tau = 0.563$. When the τ-values for users are weighted by study participation, the average rises to $\bar{\tau} = 0.593$. Here, each user's contribution to the final average depends on how many questions she evaluated to avoid overly representing users that evaluated only few questions.

7.4 Distractor Confusability

When generating distractors for MCQs, our goal is to accurately predict the confusability of a distractor given a question's correct answer. In Section 6.2 we presented our scheme for quantifying distractor confusability, which we evaluate here.

For this experiment we automatically generate 10,000 MCQs. Each question has three answer choices, which are the correct answer and two distractors. We then restricted ourselves to 400 MCQs whose distractor pair has the largest difference in confusability. This was done to maximize the probability that study participants can discriminate more confusable from less confusable distractors.

We ran each MCQ through a crowdsourcing platform and asked workers to judge which distractor is more confusing. Each MCQ was judged by 5 workers so we could take the majority vote if judgments where not unanimous. We compare this majority vote with the result of our confusability estimator. Our estimator agreed with the human annotations on 76% of the 400 MCQs. This translates to a Cohen's κ of 0.521, indicating moderate agreement [11].

7.5 Examples

To demonstrate the viability of our approach we provide a few selected examples in Table 4. The table contains generated questions

as described in the paper for five topics. For each question Q the verbalization is given, as well as the answer entity e_a and the difficulty of the question being easy $[P(diff(Q, e_a) = easy)]$. Furthermore, we provide two distractors (e_{dist1}, e_{dist2}) with their corresponding confusabilities $[conf(Q, e_a, e_{dist1}), conf(Q, e_a, e_{dist2})]$, where the confusability of $dist1$ is smaller than the confusability of $dist2$. Further examples can be downloaded from http://bit.ly/kg-questions.

The dataset was created by choosing for each topic the ten most salient entities according to our salience measure presented in Section 4. Questions were randomly generated with the constraint that each question should contain at least three triple patterns.

8 RELATED WORK

There has been work on knowledge question generation for testing linguistic knowledge and reading comprehension. The generation of language proficiency tests has been tackled in several works [17, 28, 31]. Here, the focus is on generating cloze (fill-in-the-blank) tests. Beinborn et al. [6] presents an approach for predicting the difficulty of answering such questions with multiple blanks using SVMs trained on four classes of features that look at individual blanks, their candidate answers, their dependence on other blanks, and the overall question difficulty.

Question generation for reading comprehension is aimed at evaluating knowledge from text corpora. This includes general Wikipedia knowledge [7, 20] and specialized domain knowledge, such as medical texts [2, 42]. While the above works focus on generating a question from a single document, Questimator [18] generates multiple choice questions from the textual Wikipedia corpus by considering multiple documents related to a single topic to produce a question. Work in this area has mostly taken the approach of overgeneration and ranking [20, 42]. Multiple questions are generated for a given passage using rules. A learned model ranks the questions in terms of "acceptability", where acceptable answers should be sensical, grammatical, and not obvious.

Recent work has started to look at the problem of generating questions, including multiple choice ones, from KGs and ontologies [3, 33, 34, 37]. Strong motivations for studying this problem, compared to question generation from text, are scenarios where structured data is available at hand, and the ability to generate deeper, structurally more complex questions. Our system is an end-to-end solution for this problem over a large KG.

In Section 5 we presented a simple approach for query verbalization that fits our needs. The query verbalization problem has been tackled by Ngomo et al. for SPARQL [29], and Koutrika et al. for SQL [23], with a focus on usability. Similar to our approach, these earlier works take a template-based approach to verbalization, which are widely used for natural language generation from logical forms, such as SPARQL queries [22, 30].

Much recent work has focused on keyword search [8] and question answering, rather than generation, from knowledge graphs [5, 12, 26, 36, 40, 43], possibly in combination with textual data [4, 32, 44]. The value of knowledge graphs is that they return crisp answers and allow for complex constraints to answer structurally complex questions. Of course, question answering has a long history, with one of the major highlights being IBM's Watson [14],

Table 4: Examples of generated questions for different topics.

$verbalize(Q)$	$e_a[P(diff(Q, e_a) = easy)]$	$e_{dist1}[conf(Q, e_a, e_{dist1})]$	$e_{dist2}[conf((Q, e_a, e_{dist2})]$
Topic: Theoretical Physicists			
Which scientist is a citizen of Weimar Republic and died in Princeton, New Jersey?	Albert Einstein[0.870]	Aaron Lemonick[0.154]	Grover Cleveland[0.963]
Which physicist was awarded the Nobel Prize in Physics and Goethe Prize?	Max Planck[0.745]	Richard Kuhn[0.683]	Albert Schweitzer[1.000]
Topic: Internet Companies of the United States			
Which company created Android (operating system) and Network Security Services?	Google[0.576]	Open Handset Alliance[0.504]	AOL[0.914]
Which company is located in Washington (state) and was created by the person Jeff Bezos?	Amazon.com[0.243]	Cdigix[0.760]	Starbucks[0.991]

which won the Jeopardy! game show combining both structured and unstructured sources for answering.

One important contribution of our work is an approach to compute the difficulty of questions generated. This topic has received attention lately in community question answering [25, 41], by using a competition-based approach that tries to capture how much skill a question requires for answering. There has also been work on estimating query difficulty in the context of information retrieval [10, 45] to learn an estimator that predicts the expected precision of the query by analyzing the overlap between the results of the full query and the results of its sub-queries.

9 CONCLUSION

We proposed a novel end-to-end approach to the problem of generating quiz-style knowledge questions from knowledge graphs. Our approach addresses the challenges inherent to this problem, most importantly estimating the difficulty of generated questions. To this end, we engineer suitable features and train a model of question difficulty on historical data from the Jeopardy! quiz show, which is shown to outperform humans on this difficult task.

REFERENCES

[1] J! Archive. http://j-archive.com.
[2] M. Agarwal and P. Mannem. Automatic gap-fill question generation from text books. In *BEA*, 2011.
[3] T. Alsubait et al. Generating multiple choice questions from ontologies: Lessons learnt. In *OWLED*, 2014.
[4] H. Bast et al. Semantic Search on Text and Knowledge Bases. *Foundations and Trends in IR*, 10(2-3), 2016.
[5] H. Bast and E. Haussmann. More Accurate Question Answering on Freebase. In *CIKM*, 2015.
[6] L. Beinborn et al. Predicting the Difficulty of Language Proficiency Tests. *TACL*, 2, 2014.
[7] A. S. Bhatia et al. Automatic generation of multiple choice questions using wikipedia. In *PReMI*, 2013.
[8] R. Blanco et al. Effective and efficient entity search in RDF data. In *ISWC*, 2011.
[9] K. D. Bollacker et al. Freebase: a Collaboratively Created Graph Database for Structuring Human Knowledge. In *SIGMOD*, 2008.
[10] D. Carmel and E. Yom-Tov. *Estimating the Query Difficulty for Information Retrieval*. Morgan & Claypool Publishers, 2010.
[11] J. Cohen. A Coefficient of Agreement for Nominal Scales. *Educational and Psychological Measurement*, 20(1):37, 1960.
[12] W. Cui et al. KBQA: an Online Template Based Question Answering System over Freebase. In *IJCAI*, 2016.
[13] C. Fellbaum, editor. *WordNet: an Electronic Lexical Database*. MIT Press, 1998.
[14] D. A. Ferrucci. Introduction to "this is watson". *IBM Journal of Research and Development*, 2012.
[15] J. L. Fleiss. Measuring Nominal Scale Agreement among Many Raters. *Psychological Bulletin*, 1971.
[16] E. Gabrilovich et al. FACC1: Freebase annotation of ClueWeb corpora, Version 1, 2013.
[17] D. M. Gates. How to Generate Cloze Questions from Definitions: A Syntactic Approach. In *AAAI*, 2011.
[18] Q. Guo et al. Questimator: Generating Knowledge Assessments for Arbitrary Topics. In *IJCAI*, 2016.
[19] M. A. Hearst. Automatic Acquisition of Hyponyms from Large Text Corpora. In *COLING*, 1992.
[20] M. Heilman and N. A. Smith. Question Generation via Overgenerating Transformations and Ranking. Technical report, 2009.
[21] J. Hoffart et al. Robust Disambiguation of Named Entities in Text. In *EMNLP*, 2011.
[22] N. Indurkhya et al., editors. *Handbook of Natural Language Processing*. Chapman and Hall/CRC, 2010.
[23] G. Koutrika et al. Explaining Structured Queries in Natural Language. In *ICDE*, 2010.
[24] J. R. Landis and G. G. Koch. The Measurement of Observer Agreement for Categorical Data. *Biometrics, Vol. 33*, 1977.
[25] J. Liu et al. Question difficulty estimation in community question answering services. In *EMNLP*, 2013.
[26] V. López et al. Scaling up question-answering to linked data. In *EKAW*, 2010.
[27] M. Mintz et al. Distant supervision for relation extraction without labeled data. In *ACL*, 2009.
[28] A. Narendra et al. Automatic Cloze-Questions Generation. In *RANLP*, 2013.
[29] A.-C. Ngonga Ngomo et al. Sorry, I Don'T Speak SPARQL: Translating SPARQL Queries into Natural Language. In *WWW*, 2013.
[30] E. Reiter et al. *Building Natural Language Generation Systems*. Cambridge University Press, 2000.
[31] K. Sakaguchi et al. Discriminative Approach to Fill-in-the-Blank Quiz Generation for Language Learners. In *ACL*, 2013.
[32] D. Savenkov and E. Agichtein. When a knowledge base is not enough: Question answering over knowledge bases with external text data. In *SIGIR*, 2016.
[33] I. V. Serban et al. Generating factoid questions with recurrent neural networks: The 30m factoid question-answer corpus. In *ACL*, 2016.
[34] D. Seyler et al. Generating quiz questions from knowledge graphs. In *WWW*, 2015.
[35] D. Seyler et al. Automated question generation for quality control in human computation tasks. In *WebSci*, 2016.
[36] S. Shekarpour et al. Question answering on interlinked data. In *WWW*, 2013.
[37] L. Song and L. Zhao. Domain-specific question generation from a knowledge base. *arXiv*, 2016.
[38] F. M. Suchanek et al. Yago: A Core of Semantic Knowledge. In *WWW*, 2007.
[39] F. M. Suchanek et al. Yago2s: Modular high-quality information extraction with an application to flight planning. In *BTW*, volume 214, 2013.
[40] C. Unger et al. Template-based question answering over RDF data. In *WWW*, 2012.
[41] Q. Wang et al. A regularized competition model for question difficulty estimation in community question answering services. In *EMNLP*, 2014.
[42] W. Wang et al. Automatic question generation for learning evaluation in medicine. In *ICWL*, 2007.
[43] K. Xu et al. What Is the Longest River in the USA? Semantic Parsing for Aggregation Questions. In *AAAI*, 2015.
[44] P. Yin et al. Answering Questions with Complex Semantic Constraints on Open Knowledge Bases. In *CIKM*, 2015.
[45] E. Yom-Tov et al. Learning to estimate query difficulty: including applications to missing content detection and distributed information retrieval. In *SIGIR*, 2005.

DSRIM: A Deep Neural Information Retrieval Model Enhanced by a Knowledge Resource Driven Representation of Documents

Gia-Hung Nguyen
IRIT, Université de Toulouse, CNRS
Toulouse, France
gia-hung.nguyen@irit.fr

Laure Soulier
Sorbonne Universités, UPMC Univ Paris 06 CNRS, LIP6
UMR 7606, 4 place Jussieu 75005 Paris, France
laure.soulier@lip6.fr

Lynda Tamine
IRIT, Université de Toulouse, CNRS
Toulouse, France
tamine@irit.fr

Nathalie Bricon-Souf
IRIT, Université de Toulouse, CNRS
Toulouse, France
nathalie.souf@irit.fr

ABSTRACT

The state-of-the-art solutions to the vocabulary mismatch in information retrieval (IR) mainly aim at leveraging either the relational semantics provided by external resources or the distributional semantics, recently investigated by deep neural approaches. Guided by the intuition that the relational semantics might improve the effectiveness of deep neural approaches, we propose the Deep Semantic Resource Inference Model (DSRIM) that relies on: 1) a representation of raw-data that models the relational semantics of text by jointly considering objects and relations expressed in a knowledge resource, and 2) an end-to-end neural architecture that learns the query-document relevance by leveraging the distributional and relational semantics of documents and queries. The experimental evaluation carried out on two TREC datasets from TREC Terabyte and TREC CDS tracks relying respectively on WordNet and MeSH resources, indicates that our model outperforms state-of-the-art semantic and deep neural IR models.

CCS CONCEPTS

•**Information systems** → **Retrieval models and ranking;**
•**Computing methodologies** → **Semantic networks;** *Neural networks;*

KEYWORDS

Ad-hoc IR; knowledge resource; semantic document representation; deep neural architecture

1 INTRODUCTION

Tackling the vocabulary mismatch has been a long-standing and major goal in information retrieval (IR). To infer and match discrete word senses within the context of documents and queries being matched, one line of work makes use of hand-labeled external knowledge resources such as linguistic resources and knowledge graphs. In IR, such resources allow exploiting the objects and their relations (e.g., synonymy, hyperonymy) within, e.g., query or document expansion [1, 33] to lower the vocabulary mismatch between queries and documents; this is referred to as the *relational semantics.*

Another line of work attempts to automatically infer hidden word senses from corpora using word collocations by performing dimensionality reduction techniques, such as latent semantic indexing [7] or, more recently, representation learning [19, 26] leading to *distributional semantics.* The latter was successfully exploited within deep neural networks for supporting search tasks [10, 12, 27]. One of the first contributions in the field relies on siamese architectures, opposing queries and documents in a two-branch network [12, 27]. However, these architectures are not yet mature since the learning of a relevance function suffers from several limitations: 1) tackling traditional IR models (e.g., BM25 or language models) remains a difficult task [10–12] and 2) learning the relevance function on full text does not allow the network convergence, even though evaluated on search logs of commercial search engines, leading to focus on a query-document title matching [10, 12, 27].

Guided by the intuition that the relational semantics could complement distributional semantics and the motivation that siamese networks are under-explored in IR [21], we investigate how to leverage both knowledge resources and siamese architecture to perform ad-hoc IR. Specifically, we first model in a low-dimensional vector the relational semantics of text by jointly considering objects and relations expressed in knowledge resources. Then, we investigate the hypothesis that combining the distributional and the relational representations of text would enhance its representation for a ranking task. To the best of our knowledge, this is one of the first approach combining distributional and relational semantics in a neural architecture with the goal to enhance document-query ranking. More particularly, our contributions are twofold:

• A *Deep Semantic Resource Inference Model (DSRIM)* leveraging:

- An input raw level representation of queries and documents relying on a *knowledge resource-driven representation.* More particularly, the premise of the latter representation relies on assumptions that a text is a bag of identified objects from a knowledge resource, and that semantically similar texts are deemed to entail similar/related objects. To deal with a large number of object-to-object relations, we propose the *relation mapping* method that aims at projecting pairs in a low-dimensional space of object clusters.

ICTIR'17, October 1–4, 2017, Amsterdam, Netherlands.
© 2017 ACM. ISBN 978-1-4503-4490-6/17/10...$15.00
DOI: https://doi.org/10.1145/3121050.3121063

Our method is flexible since it can be used with any resource providing objects and relations between objects.

- An end-to-end siamese neural network which learns an enhanced document-ranking function using input vectors combining both the distributional and the knowledge resource-driven representations of document/query.

• A thorough experimental evaluation aiming at assessing the quality of the knowledge resource-driven representation and the effectiveness of DSRIM. We use two TREC datasets, namely TREC PubMed CDS and TREC GOV2 Terabyte, and two knowledge resources, respectively MeSH[1] and WordNet[2]. It is worth mentioning that, unlike previous work [12, 27] experimentally evaluated on document titles, our experiments are performed using full-texts.

The rest of this paper is organized as follows: Section 2 reviews the related work. We motivate and then describe the DSRIM model in Section 3. Section 4 details the experimental protocol. Section 5 discusses the experimental results. Section 6 concludes the paper.

2 RELATED WORK

2.1 On the Semantic Representation of Words, Documents, Objects, and Relations.

The potential of word semantic representations learned through neural approaches has been introduced in [19, 26], opening several perspectives in NLP and IR tasks. Indeed, several work focuses on the representation of sentences [20], documents [15, 29], and also objects and relations expressed in knowledge resources [4, 13, 30]. Within the latter, the main principle consists in learning the representation of objects and relations on the basis of object-relation-object triplets, relying on the assumption that the embedding of object o_i should be close to the embedding translation of object o_j by relation r, namely $o_i \simeq o_j + r$ (TransE model) [4]. Extensions have been proposed considering, e.g., different object representations according to the semantic relation type (TransH) [30]. Moreover, knowledge resources have been used to enhance the distributed representation of words for representing their underlying concepts [9, 17, 34, 35]. Faruqui et al. [9] propose a "retrofitting" technique consisting in a leveraging of lexicon-derived relational information, namely adjacent words of concepts, to refine word embeddings. Other work [34, 35] introduces an end-to-end approach that rather adjusts the objective function of the neural language model by either leveraging the relational and categorical knowledge to learn a higher quality word embeddings (RC-NET model) [34] or extending the CBOW model using prior relational knowledge [35].

2.2 On using Knowledge Resources in IR.

Both general/specific linguistic bases (e.g., WordNet or UMLS respectively) and large-scale knowledge graphs (e.g., Freebase) represent external resources that offer valuable information about word semantics through objects (e.g., words, entities, or concepts) and their associated relations (e.g., "is-a", "part-of"). Based on the use of such resources, the first line of work in IR aims at increasing the likelihood of term overlap between queries and documents through query expansion [22, 33] or document expansion [1]. Among models expanding queries, Xiong et al. [33] propose two algorithms

relying on the category of terms in FreeBase. While the unsupervised approach estimates the similarity between the category distribution of terms in documents and queries, the supervised approach exploits the ground truth to estimate the influence of terms. Authors in [22] propose a query expansion technique using terms extracted from multiple sources of information. For each query term, candidate expansion terms in top retrieved documents are ranked by combining their importance in pseudo-relevant documents and their semantic similarity based on their definition in WordNet. Unlikely, Agirre et al. [1] propose a document expansion technique based on the use of a random walk algorithm identifying from WordNet the most related concepts. The second line of work leverages relations modeled in knowledge resources at the document ranking level [32]. For instance, the authors propose a learning-to-rank algorithm based on objects of knowledge resources that are related to a given pair of query-document.

2.3 On using Deep Neural Networks in IR.

A large amount of work has shown that deep learning approaches are highly efficient in several IR tasks. The first category of work uses neural models for IR tasks [2, 29, 36] to integrate embeddings in IR relevance functions. The second category of work, closer to our contribution, consists in end-to-end models that learn the relevance of document-query pairs via latent semantic features [11, 12]. For instance, the Deep Semantic Structured Model (DSSM) [12] applies a siamese deep feed-forward network on document and query representations obtained by a word hashing method. The network aims at learning their latent representations and then measuring their relevance score using a cosine similarity. As an extension, Shen et al. [28] use a convolutional-pooling structure, called Convolutional Latent Semantic Model (CLSM). In the same mind, Severyn and Moschitti [27] apply a convolution to learn the optimal representation of short text pairs as well as the similarity function. However, these model parameters are hard to learn, which leads authors to only consider the matching between query-title pairs. Guo et al. [10] also argue that tackling traditional IR models (e.g., BM25 or language models) remains a difficult task. To bypass this limitation, another line of work [10, 18, 23] rather aims at building a local interaction map between inputs, then uses deep neural networks to learn hierarchical interaction patterns. The DeepMatch model [18] integrates a topic model into a fully connected deep network based on the word interaction matrix while the Match-Pyramid model [23] applies a convolution to an interaction matrix estimated using word representation. Guided by the intuition that interaction matrix is more appropriate for the global matching and lacks of the term importance consideration, authors in [10] model local interactions of query-document terms through occurrence histograms.

3 DSRIM: DEEP SEMANTIC RESOURCE INFERENCE MODEL

3.1 Motivation

The literature review highlights that: 1) plain text and knowledge resources are complementary for both learning distributional representations and enhancing IR effectiveness [1, 22, 33], and that

---

[1]https://www.nlm.nih.gov/mesh/
[2]http://wordnet.princeton.edu

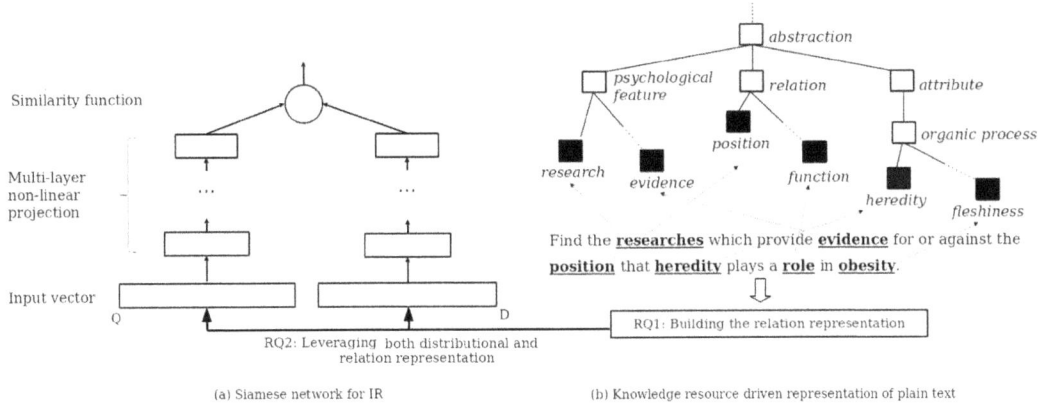

Figure 1: General issue of our contribution and research questions

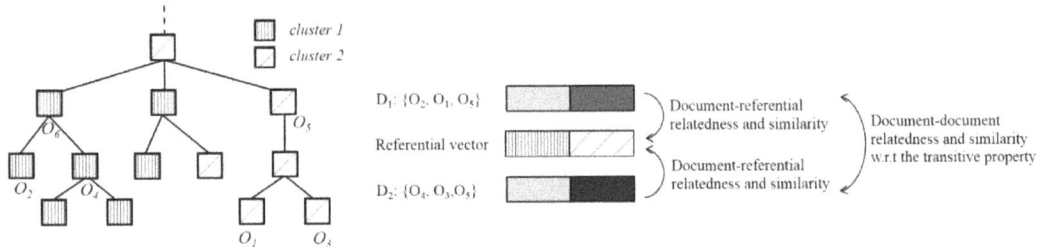

Figure 2: Intuition of the transitive property in knowledge resource-driven representation of documents

2) neural approaches in IR, and more particularly siamese architectures, have a great potential for ad-hoc search but could still be improved to compete with traditional IR models [10]. In this contribution, we address the problem of bridging the semantic gap in IR by leveraging both deep learning approaches [12, 27] and valid knowledge expressed in knowledge resources [22, 33]. In contrast to previous work in deep IR models [11, 12, 23, 27] relying only on the distributional semantics of texts and work on the semantic representation of objects and relations only leveraging knowledge resources [4, 9, 30, 34], our main concern is to estimate a relevance function leveraging a semantic representation of documents that simultaneously takes into consideration objects and their pairwise relations expressed in a knowledge resource. With this in mind, we investigate the potential of siamese neural architectures, such as DSSM [12], on full-text retrieval. In this paper, we specifically address the two following research questions, illustrated in Figure 1:

• **RQ1**: How to model the relational semantics of texts at the raw data level by jointly leveraging objects and their relations expressed in knowledge resources?

• **RQ2**: How to learn the query-document relevance function by combining the relational and distributional semantics of text in a siamese neural architecture?

Below, we detail our contributions w.r.t. each research question.

3.2 Knowledge Resource driven Representation

Our aim is to model a text representation that conveys their semantics with respect to a knowledge resource. The premise of this representation relies on two assumptions: (A1) a text is a bag of identified objects from a knowledge resource, and (A2) semantically similar texts are deemed to entail similar and related objects.

Formally, a knowledge resource is built upon a relational graph $G = (V, E)$ where V is a node set and E is an edge set. Each node $v_i = <o_i, desc_i, >$ includes an object o_i (e.g., word, entity) and its textual label $desc_i$ (e.g., preferred entry). Each object o_i is associated to a distributional representation x_i^d (e.g., its *ParagraphVector* [2] obtained on the basis of its textual labels $desc_i$). Each edge $e_{i,i'}$ expresses a semantic relation between objects o_i and $o_{i'}$. We suppose that given the set O of objects in the knowledge resource G, we can identify, for each text T, a set $O(T) \subset O$ of objects o.

While assumption A1 is easy to formalize through a binary vector modeling objects $o_i \in V$ or a vector combining their distributional representation x_i^d, it does not allow to fulfill assumption A2. To cope with this issue, the perspective of a vector representing object-object pairs could be a good option to simultaneously capture: 1) the objects belonging to a text and 2) their similarity as well as their relatedness. However, a large number of potential pairwise objects, or more precisely object-to-object relations, in a knowledge resource would lead to a high dimensional and sparse vector. To face this issue, we propose the *relation mapping method*, that: 1) similarly to the word hashing method [12], aims at reducing the dimensionality and the sparsity of the vector representation to make it scalable, and 2) allows building representations of both objects belonging to text T and their relations according to assumption A2. We describe below our approach for achieving these two sub-goals.

• Sub-goal 1) *Text representation vector space:* A naive approach consists in considering objects from the knowledge resource as unit vectors of a $|V|$-dimensional space. Even if the number of objects in the resource is significantly lower than the number of object-to-object relations, the scalability of the underlying framework remains questionable. To fit with sub-goal 1) and lower the dimensionality of the vectorial representation space, we rather consider clusters of objects as representative of each dimension of the vectorial space. Assuming that object-to-object relations might express topical relatedness between objects, we propose to build k topical clusters c_j of objects $o_i \in O$ assumed to be mutually independent. The latter refers to the referential $\mathcal{R} = \{c_1, \ldots, c_k\}$ of the knowledge resource. In practice, we use the k-means clustering algorithm on the topical representation of objects, where the number of topical clusters k would be experimentally tuned (see Section 5.1). Thus, we consider a k-dimensional space, in which k is the number of topical clusters of objects.

• Sub-goal 2) *Knowledge resource-driven text representation:* The representation x^{KR} of text T is a k-dimensional vector $x^{KR} = (x_1^{KR}, \ldots, x_k^{KR})$. To fulfill sub-goal 2, our intuition is that two documents are likely to be similar if they mention objects that are gathered around the same topical clusters. Naturally, the degree of similarity between those documents would depend on the average relatedness and similarity of their objects with each object in the topical clusters c_j of the referential $\mathcal{R}$. This refers to as a transitive property, illustrated in Figure 2. Each document D_1 and D_2 is modeled through a 2-dimensional vector in which each element represents a topical cluster. The gray levels in the document representation express the relatedness and similarity degree of document objects with respect to the topical clusters. Although documents D_1 and D_2 are not characterized by the same objects, they are as close to the referential and have similar representations. We compute each element x_j^{KR} as a combination of the importance w_j^T of topical cluster c_j given text T and the relatedness $S_{relat}(c_j, O(T))$ of objects $O(T)$ belonging to text T w.r.t. topical cluster c_j:

$$x_j^{KR} = w_j^T * S_{relat}(c_j, O(T)) \tag{1}$$

3.2.1 Topical cluster importance score. The importance score w_j^T of the topical cluster c_j expresses to what extent the set $O(T)$ of objects belonging to text T are topically similar to objects belonging to topical cluster c_j. Intuitively, the more topically similar the objects mentioned in the representations of texts T and T' with respect to the topical clusters, the more similar texts T and T'. Assuming that objects belonging to a text represent a topical cluster, we rely on previous work dealing with clustering similarity [14] suggesting to estimate the similarity between two sets of objects by aggregating similarities between objects of these two different sets. More formally, the topical cluster importance score between topical cluster c_j and object set $O(T)$ is estimated as:

$$w_j^T = Agg\_Function_{(o_m, o_n) \in O(T) \times c_j} sim_t(o_m, o_n) \tag{2}$$

where *Agg_Function* expresses an aggregation function (we consider here the maximum to capture the best topical similarity between objects); sim_t estimates the topical similarity between vector representations of objects (here, the cosine similarity between the vectorial representations of object textual descriptions).

3.2.2 Topical cluster-text relatedness score. The topical cluster-text relatedness score $S_{relat}(c_j, O(T))$ measures to what extent objects $o_i \in O(T)$ belonging to text T are related to those of topical cluster c_j. Our intuition is that if the objects mentioned in texts T and T' are related to the representative of the same topical clusters, texts T and T' are more likely to be similar. Having in mind that state-of-the-art relatedness measures [25] rely on the computation

of paths between objects, a scalable way allowing to measure this score is to consider the relatedness of objects $O(T)$ with respect to a representative object $R(c_j)$ of topical cluster c_j (e.g., the most frequent object in the collection among objects belonging to topical cluster c_j). The impact of the method used for identifying the representative is experimentally investigated (see Section 6.1). More formally, given a representative object $R(c_j)$ of topical cluster c_j, the topical cluster-text relatedness $S_{relat}(c_j, O(T))$ estimates the path length between object $R(c_j)$ and the object set $O(T)$:

$$S_{relat}(c_j, O(T)) = \sum_{o_m \in O(T)} \log\left(1 + sim_r(R(c_j), o_m)\right) \cdot \frac{avg\_no}{|O(T)|} \tag{3}$$

where o_m is an object of the object set $O(T)$ characterizing text T. sim_r is a relatedness measure between objects (here the Leacock measure [16]); avg_no is the average number of objects per document in the collection. The normalization factor $\frac{avg\_no}{|O(T)|}$ avoids bias due to differences in text lengths in terms of the number of objects.

3.3 Model Architecture

3.3.1 Input. We propose to characterize each text T (whether extracted from a document or a query) by an input vector $x_{input} = (x^t, x^{KR})$ modeled as a vector composed of two parts:

• *Plain text representation x^t.* This feature represents words of full text T. Based on previous findings highlighting the effectiveness of distributed semantic representations to tackle the issue of large vocabulary in IR, we use the *ParagraphVector* model [2].

• *Knowledge resource-driven representation x^{KR}.* This feature expresses the objects belonging to text T and their semantic relations expressed in the knowledge resource. This representation is built upon the *relation mapping* method (see Section 3.2).

3.3.2 Learning the latent representation. For each sub-network branch, the input vector x_{input} of text T is projected into a latent space by means of L hidden layers l_i ($i = 1, \cdots, L$) so as to obtain a latent semantic vector y combining the distributional and relational semantics of text T. Each hidden layer l_i and the latent semantic vector y are respectively obtained by non-linear transformations:

$$l_0 = x_{input}$$
$$l_i = f(W_{i-1} \cdot l_{i-1} + b_{i-1}) \ i = 1, \ldots, L \tag{4}$$
$$y = f(W_L \cdot l_L + b_L)$$

where W_i and b_i are respectively the weight matrix and bias term of the ith layer. The activation function $f(x)$ performs a non-linear transformation, namely the ReLU: $f(x) = max(0, x)$, also used in [8]. The use of the ReLU function is motivated by the fact that it does not saturate to 1 when x is high in contrast to the hyperbolic tangent [12], avoiding to face to the gradient vanishing problem.

The latent semantic vectors y_D and y_Q of document D and query Q obtained through the non-linear transformations are used to estimate the document-query cosine similarity score $R(D|Q)$.

3.3.3 Loss function. Since retrieval tasks refer to a ranking problem, we optimize the parameters of the neural network using a pairwise ranking loss based on the distance Δ of similarity between relevant document-query pairs, noted (Q, D^+), and irrelevant document-query pairs, noted (Q, D_p^-). Unlike [12], it worth mentioning that we use the hinge loss function, more adapted for

Table 1: Statistics of the GOV2 and the PMC datasets

	GOV2	PMC
# Documents	25,000,000	733,138
Average length of documents (#words)	1132.8	477.1
# Queries	150	60
# Relevant pairs	25,100	8,346

learning-to-rank tasks [5, 8]. As suggested in [12], we build a sample of document-query pairs in which we oppose, for the same query Q, one relevant document D^+ for n irrelevant documents D_p^-, $p = [1..n]$. The difference Δ between the similarity of the relevant pair (Q, D^+) and the irrelevant ones (Q, D_p^-) is defined as:

$$\Delta = \left[sim(Q, D^+) - \sum_{p=1}^{n} sim(Q, D_p^-) \right] \quad (5)$$

where $sim(\bullet, \bullet)$ is the output of the neural network. Then, the DSRIM network is trained to maximize the similarity distance Δ using the hinge loss function L: $L = max(0, \alpha - \Delta)$ where α is the margin of L, depending on the Δ range.

4 EVALUATION PROTOCOL

4.1 Datasets

We consider two datasets (statistics are presented in Table 1):
• The GOV2 dataset gathering .gov sites used in the TREC Terabyte campaign. We use topics from the 2004, 2005, and 2006 campaigns and the narrative part of each topic as a query.
• The PMC OpenAccess dataset with biomedical full-texts from PubMed used in the TREC-CDS campaign. The summaries of topics of the 2014 and 2015 evaluation campaigns are used as queries.

4.2 Implementation Details and Evaluation Methodology

To build the input layer, we pre-train a *ParagraphVector* model on the plain text corpus for learning vector x^t. The vectors are sized to 100, as suggested in [2]. The concepts used for building our knowledge resource-driven representation are extracted using appropriate tools, namely *SenseRelate* on WordNet resource [24] for the GOV2 dataset and Cxtractor relying on *MaxMatcher* [38] applied on the 2015-MeSH version the PMC dataset. We used for both the 'IS-A' relation. For modeling the representation x^{KR}, we tune two parameters: 1) the number of topical clusters: we set the number k of topical clusters to $k \in \{100, 200\}$; 2) the choice of the representative object $\mathcal{R}(c_j)$ within each topical cluster: we use three strategies: idf_{min}, namely the most frequent object; idf_{max}, the less frequent one; and *centroid*, the closest object to the centroid. Concerning our model architecture, we set the number of hidden layers to 2 with a hidden vector size equals to 64 leading to an output layer of 32 nodes. Similarly to [12], the number n of irrelevant document-query pairs opposed to a relevant one is 4 (Equation 5). Relevant/irrelevant document-query sets are randomly extracted from each dataset ground truth, supplying graded relevance judgments from 0 to 2 (relevance criteria: 1 and 2).

To train our model parameters, we apply the 5-fold cross-validation method. The topics in each dataset are divided into

5 folds. For each fold retained as the test set for model evaluation, the other 4 folds are used to train and validate the model. The final retrieval results are averaged over the test results on 5 folds. The model is optimized using a 5-sample mini-batch stochastic gradient descent (SGD) regularized with a dropout equals to 0.3. Our model generally converges after 50 epochs over the training dataset.

For evaluating the ranking performance of our model and the different baselines, we perform a re-ranking [10] which is carried out over the top 2,000 documents retrieved by the BM25 model on Lucene. Final results are estimated using the top 1000 documents of each re-ranking model according to the MAP metric.

4.3 Baselines

To evaluate the quality of our knowledge resource-driven representation, we use two models building representations of documents:
• **Top_concepts**: A naive version of our knowledge resource-driven representation selecting the top k frequent objects in the document collection as the representative objects ($k \in \{100, 200\}$).
• **LDA**: The well-known LDA topic model representing topic clusters from plain text [3] (vs. topical cluster relying on concepts and relations in DSRIM).

To evaluate the model effectiveness, we use three types of baselines:
1) Exact term matching models to highlight the impact of both leveraging relational semantics and deep learning approaches:
• **BM25**: The well-known probabilistic model (*BM25*).
• **LM-DI**: The language model based on Dirichlet smoothing [37].
2) Enhanced semantic matching models to outline the impact of a deep neural model guided by knowledge resources for capturing text semantics:
• **LM-QE**: A language model applying a concept-based query expansion technique [22] in which candidate terms are ranked based on their similarity with descriptions in the knowledge resource. Default parameters mentioned in the paper are used.
• **LM-LDA**: The LM-LDA is a latent topical model using the language modeling framework [31].
3) Deep neural semantic matching models, also based on a siamese architecture, to highlight the impact of combining relational and distributional semantics in neural approaches:
• **DSSM**: The state-of-the-art DSSM model [12]. We adopt the publicly released code[3] with default parameter values. We evaluate the DSSM on full-text documents.
• **CLSM**: The DSSM extension in which the feed-forward network is replaced by a convolution. We also apply the publicly released CLSM code[8] on full-texts and use the default parameter values.

To measure the impact of the different evidence sources taken into consideration for representing texts, we use three scenarios:
• $DSRIM^{p2v}$: Our proposed neural model based on an input representation of texts restricted to the plain text, namely x^t.
• $DSRIM^{kr}$: Our proposed neural model based on our knowledge resource-driven representation of text, namely x^{KR}.
• $DSRIM^{kr+p2v}$: Our proposed neural model based on an enhanced representation of texts combining plain text representation x^t and our knowledge resource-driven representation x^{KR}.

---

[3]https://www.microsoft.com/en-us/research/project/dssm/

Table 2: Cosine similarities of the knowledge resource-driven representation on most similar (Top_10) and less similar (Less_10) documents, averaged on 100 random pivotal documents. diff: difference between Top_10 and Less_10

	#Clusters k	Repres. obj. $R(c_i)$	GOV2			PMC		
			Top_10	Less_10	diff	Top_10	Less_10	diff
Clustering	#Cluster 100	idf_max	0.7490	0.5776	0.1714	0.5455	0.3035	0.2420
		centroid	0.7411	0.5693	0.1719	0.4807	0.2862	0.1945
		idf_min	0.7018	0.5501	0.1518	0.4975	0.2717	0.2259
	#Cluster 200	idf_max	0.7595	0.5814	0.1781	0.6359	0.3885	0.2475
		centroid	0.7344	0.5536	0.1808	0.6464	0.3842	0.2621
		idf_min	0.7645	0.5660	0.1985	0.6485	0.4234	0.2251
Baselines	Top_concept, $k = 200$		0.9034	0.9013	0.0021	0.9861	0.9616	0.0245
	Top_concept, $k = 100$		0.9123	0.9049	0.0074	0.9817	0.9572	0.0245
	LDA		0.4377	0.3189	0.1188	0.2884	0.0518	0.2639

Table 3: Effectiveness comparison of baselines and DSRIM on GOV2 and PMC collections. % Chg: Significant improvement/degradation of $DSRIM^{kr+p2v}$ (+/-). p-value: Significance t-test: * : $0.01 < \alpha \leq 0.05$, ** : $0.001 < \alpha \leq 0.01$, *** : $\alpha \leq 0.001$

Model Type	Model	GOV2			PMC		
		MAP	%change	p-value	MAP	%change	p-value
Exact	BM25	0.1777	+4.84	0.6691	0.0348	-1.15	0.9628
Matching	LM-DI	0.1584	+17.61	0.1644	0.0379	-9.23	0.7109
Semantic	LM-QE	0.0738	+152.44	0.0001 ***	0.0106	+224.53	0.0008 ***
Matching	LM-LDA	0.0966	+92.86	0.0001 ***	0.0185	+85.95	0.0323 *
Deep	DSSM	0.0418	+345.69	0.0001 ***	0.0095	+262.11	0.0008 ***
Matching	CLSM	0.0365	+410.41	0.0001 ***	0.0069	+398.55	0.0001 ***
Our approach	$DSRIM^{p2v}$	0.1115	+67.09	0.0001 ***	0.0183	+87.98	0.0460 *
	$DSRIM^{kr}$	0.1801	+3.44	0.7461	0.0307	+12.05	0.6829
	$DSRIM^{kr+p2v}$	0.1863			0.0344		

5 RESULTS

5.1 Analyzing the Semantic Representation of Documents

In this section, we propose to analyze our knowledge resource-driven representation through a twofold objective: 1) identifying the optimal parameter setting of the vectorial representation and 2) assessing the validity of the built document vectors x^{KR}.

We assess the vectorial representation quality based on the intuition that semantically similar texts, modeled as bags of concepts, should have similar vectorial representations built following our approach; such representations should also discard non-similar documents [15, 19]. In practice, given a randomly selected document (called a "pivotal document"), a good vectorial representation should 1) ensure that the distance between the pivotal document and each other document of the collection is non-uniform, and 2) maximize the distance between its most similar documents and its less similar ones. To this end: 1) we first identify for each given pivotal document, the set $\mathcal{D}_+^p$ of its 10 most semantically similar documents and the set $\mathcal{D}_-^p$ of the 10 less semantically similar documents over the whole dataset using a concept-oriented metric proposed in [6], called in the remaining the *Corley* measure; and 2) then we compute the average cosine similarity of the representations of the pivotal documents with the sets $\mathcal{D}_+^p$ and $\mathcal{D}_-^p$. Table 2 presents the comparative results for 100 randomly selected pivotal documents and suggests the following statements:

• The difference in terms of cosine value range between both datasets (higher for GOV2) conjectures that representing texts using objects and relations expressed in a knowledge resource seems to be more difficult for the PMC dataset. This could be explained by the fact that this dataset focuses on a particular application domain (namely, the medical vs. general for GOV2) that might imply a more technical vocabulary.

• Regarding the method used for defining the vectorial representation space (sub-goal 1; Section 4.1), we can see that our proposed approach for identifying the referential based on the object clustering is more effective than both baselines, respectively Top_concept and LDA. Indeed, the similarity differences of both document sets $\mathcal{D}_+^p$ and $\mathcal{D}_-^p$ obtained by the baselines are very small (< 0.11 for both datasets, except LDA for PMC, vs. higher than 0.15 for our clustering approach). It is worth to mention that the Top_concept baseline particularly fails to discriminate between the most/less similar documents for both datasets given the high values of cosine values (> 0.90). Also, the small cosine values obtained using the LDA baseline for the most similar documents (< 0.5) show that the LDA representation is not able to build close document representations. In contrast, we outline that cosine values for our clustering approach seem to be more intuitive, with an average cosine for the GOV2 dataset higher than 0.6 for the most similar documents and lower than 0.6 for the less similar ones (respectively 0.5 for the PMC dataset). These statements suggest that our referential building approach based on topical clustering seems reasonable.

• Focusing on the methods used for the knowledge resource-driven representation (sub-goal2; Section 4.1) and the one used for choosing the topical cluster representative, we can notice that the average similarities between pivotal documents and the set of top similar ones are more important for a higher number of clusters (e.g., up to 0.6485 for $k = 200$ vs. 0.5455 for $k = 100$ for PMC). Also, this setting allows obtaining higher differences between the most vs. less similar documents (with at least 0.2251 vs. 0.1945 for respectively $k = 200$ and $k = 100$ for PMC , and 0.1781 vs. 0.1518 for GOV2). These results highlight the importance of achieving a reasonable ratio between the knowledge resource size (w.r.t. the number of object-object-relations) and the number of representative clusters of objects to better capture the semantic representation of documents. With this in mind, the best scenario for $k = 200$ allowing to distinguish the most vs. the less similar documents consists in selecting the closest object to the cluster *centroid* as the representative object for PMC while these are no significant differences between the three methods for GOV2. Given that the *centroid* method is more intuitive with the assumptions used for building the referential, we retain the setting with 200 topical clusters and the *centroid* method for encoding the representative object.

5.2 Measuring the Model Effectiveness

We present here the performance of our model on both GOV2 and PMC datasets. Table 3 shows a summary of effectiveness values in terms of MAP for our model and the different baselines.

Comparing different configurations of our approach, namely $DSRIM^{p2v}$, $DSRIM^{kr}$, and $DSRIM^{kr+p2v}$, we can see that the DSRIM model applied only on our knowledge resource-driven representation $x^{\overline{KR}}$ provides significant better performance (p-value<0.001) according to the MAP metric than the one with only the plain text-based representation x^t (e.g., respectively 0.0307 and 0.0183 for the PMC dataset). This result reinforces the intuition claimed in recent work dealing with the use of text representations based on local interactions of terms and/or non-learned features [10]. Moreover, when combining the distributional and the relational semantics through the $DSRIM^{kr+p2v}$ model, we could see that the MAP value slightly increases, with for instance a significant improvement of +67.09% and +87.98% for the GOV2 and PMC datasets respectively with respect to $DSRIM^{p2v}$. This opens interesting perspectives in the combination of those word-sense approaches as we claim in this paper.

With this in mind, we comment the baseline results with respect to the $DSRIM^{kr+p2v}$ model. From a general point of view, we can see, on the one hand, that exact matching models are non-significantly different from our proposed model, with a particular attention to the GOV2 dataset with small improvements with respect to BM25 (+4.84%) and LM-DI (+17.61%). On the other hand, our approach overpasses semantic and deep matching models with significant improvements. For instance, our model reports significant better results for the GOV2 dataset according to the MAP compared with the LM-QE, LM-LDA, DSSM, and CLSM models for which our model obtains a MAP value up to +410.41% of improvement rate. Those observations are similar for both datasets, highlighting the fact that our model is effective for leveraging general (WordNet) as well as domain-oriented (MeSH) knowledge resources. More particularly, we can formulate the following statements:

Table 4: Statistics on queries w.r.t their difficulty level

	Difficulty level	#Words	#Objects	%Change
GOV2	Easy	22.95	12.11	-16.60%
	Medium	20.79	11.79	-5.15%*
	Difficult	22.15	12.14	+87.15%***
PMC	Easy	13	5.4	-0.22%
	Medium	16.68	5.36	-25.78%
	Difficult	18.5	6.3	+63.60%*

• The BM25 and the language models are well-known as strong IR baselines which are difficult to outperform with deep matching models learned with small training datasets that do not allow to generalize the task. The results presented in Table 3 lead us to confirm this statement. However, it is worth noting that, in contrast to most previous neural approaches based on siamese architecture [12, 27, 28] that rank short documents (titles) and use large-scale real collection for training their model, we rather experiment our model on long full-text document collections (average length is 1132.8 words for GOV2 and 477.1 for PMC). To get a better understanding of these results, we investigate to what extent the effectiveness of our model depends on the level of difficulty of queries. More particularly, we classify queries according to three levels of difficulty ("easy", "medium", "difficult") using the k-means algorithm applied on the BM25 MAP values. Statistics of each class are presented in Table 4. We can outline that, for the PMC dataset, difficult queries significantly include more terms and more objects than easy and medium ones. However, there is no significant differences between the different query types with respect to the number of terms and objects for the GOV2 dataset. Focusing on the retrieval effectiveness, it can be seen that $DSRIM^{kr+p2v}$ improvements according to BM25 are both positive and significant for difficult queries for both GOV2 and PMC. Moreover, it is worth mentioning that the improvement rates for difficult queries (+63.60% for the PMC dataset) are significantly different from the ones for medium and easy queries (respectively −25.78% and −0.22% for the PMC dataset, with no significant improvement difference between easy and medium queries, $p > 0.5$). Interestingly, combining the improvement rates and the number of objects for medium queries of the GOV2 dataset, we can see that the significant effectiveness decrease of our model (−5.15%) could be explained by the lowest number of objects associated with this query set. These results highlight that leveraging the relational semantics through our knowledge resource-driven representation is more effective for solving difficult queries. This is coherent since those queries are generally characterized by a high number of words and extracted objects. Accordingly, we can reasonably argue that our model is particularly devoted to lowering the semantic gap between word-based and concept-based representations of documents and queries which probably favors the discrimination between relevant and irrelevant documents.

• The LM-QE baseline performs a knowledge resource-based query expansion. Since the DSRIM outperforms the LM-QE model, we can suggest that the semantic based representations of documents and queries which are learned from the input built upon the relation mapping method, is more effective than the expanded queries with relevant object descriptors.

• The LDA-LM model is based on a probabilistic generative model able to identify relevant topics. Our model generally outperforms this baseline with a significant improvement of 89.95% for the MAP metric on the PMC dataset. This is consistent with previous work [12], highlighting the effectiveness of deep latent representations of texts in comparison to those obtained by generative models.

• In the category of neural IR models, our model outperforms the DSSM and the CLSM models (with a MAP reaching 0.0418 and 0.0095 for both datasets respectively). These results suggest that the integration of relational as well as the distributional semantics at the document level (rather than the word level) into the input representation allows enhancing the learning of the deep neural matching model while considering small collections (instead of real search logs) and full texts (instead of titles). Interestingly, the convolutional CLSM model initially overpassing the DSSM in [28] through experiments carried out on a large-scale real-world data, is less effective than the DSSM. One explanation might be that it is trained using TREC collections characterized by a limited number of queries (as also shown in [10]). A further analysis based on the cosine similarity between document-query vectors of input and output relevant pairs obtained using both DSSM and DSRIM highlights that the use of evidence from relational semantics underlying queries and documents allows a better discrimination between relevant and irrelevant documents. Indeed, the similarity improvement between input/output representations is more important for our model than for the DSSM model for both datasets: 166.88% for DSSM vs. 271.51% for DSRIM for the GOV2 dataset, 5.91% for DSSM vs. 71.71% for the PMC dataset.

6 CONCLUSION

We propose the DSRIM model, a deep neural IR model that leverages both distributional semantics through the *ParagraphVector* algorithm, and relational semantics, through a knowledge resource-driven representation of texts aiming at jointly modeling embedded objects and structured relations between objects. Experimental evaluation on two TREC datasets is performed to evaluate the quality of the input representations as well as their impact on document ranking effectiveness. Results show that 1) our knowledge resource-driven representation allows to discriminate semantically similar from non-semantically similar texts, and that 2) our model overpasses semantic-driven approaches as well as state-of-the-art neural IR models. In the near future, we plan to further the knowledge resource-driven representation by taking into account both the heterogeneity of objects and relations between objects.

ACKNOWLEDGEMENT

This work was supported by the French FUI research program SparkInData.

REFERENCES

[1] Eneko Agirre, Xabier Arregi, and Arantxa Otegi. 2010. Document expansion based on WordNet for robust IR. In *ICCL*. 9–17.
[2] Qingyao Ai, Liu Yang, Jiafeng Guo, and W. Bruce Croft. 2016. Analysis of the Paragraph Vector Model for Information Retrieval. In *ICTIR*. ACM, 133–142.
[3] David M. Blei, Andrew Y. Ng, and Michael I. Jordan. 2003. Latent Dirichlet Allocation. *J. Mach. Learn. Res.* 3 (2003), 993–1022.
[4] Antoine Bordes, Nicolas Usunier, Alberto García-Durán, Jason Weston, and Oksana Yakhnenko. 2013. Translating Embeddings for Modeling Multi-relational Data. In *NIPS*. 2787–2795.
[5] Wei Chen, Tie yan Liu, Yanyan Lan, Zhi ming Ma, and Hang Li. 2009. Ranking Measures and Loss Functions in Learning to Rank. In *NIPS*. 315–323.
[6] Courtney Corley and Rada Mihalcea. 2005. Measuring the semantic similarity of texts. In *Workshop on empirical modeling of semantic equivalence and entailment*.

[7] Scott Deerwester, Susan T. Dumais, George W. Furnas, Thomas K. Landauer, and Richard Harshman. 1990. Indexing by latent semantic analysis. *Journal of the American Society for Information Science* 41, 6 (1990), 391–407.
[8] Mostafa Dehghani, Hamed Zamani, Aliaksei Severyn, Jaap Kamps, and W Bruce Croft. 2017. Neural Ranking Models with Weak Supervision. *arXiv:1704.08803* (2017).
[9] Manaal Faruqui, Jesse Dodge, Sujay K. Jauhar, Chris Dyer, Eduard Hovy, and Noah A. Smith. 2015. Retrofitting Word Vectors to Semantic Lexicons. In *NAACL*.
[10] Jiafeng Guo, Yixing Fan, Qingyao Ai, and W Bruce Croft. 2016. A Deep Relevance Matching Model for Ad-hoc Retrieval. In *CIKM*. 55–64.
[11] Baotian Hu, Zhengdong Lu, Hang Li, and Qingcai Chen. 2014. Convolutional neural network architectures for matching natural language sentences. In *NIPS*. 2042–2050.
[12] Po-Sen Huang, Xiaodong He, Jianfeng Gao, Li Deng, Alex Acero, and Larry Heck. 2013. Learning deep structured semantic models for web search using clickthrough data. In *CIKM*. 2333–2338.
[13] Guoliang Ji, Shizhu He, Liheng Xu, Kang Liu, and Jun Zhao. 2015. Knowledge Graph Embedding via Dynamic Mapping Matrix. In *ACL*. 687–696.
[14] Benjamin King. 1967. Step-Wise Clustering Procedures. *J. Amer. Statist. Assoc.* 62, 317 (1967), 86–101.
[15] Quoc V Le and Tomas Mikolov. 2014. Distributed Representations of Sentences and Documents.. In *ICML*. 1188–1196.
[16] Claudia Leacock and Martin Chodorow. 1998. Combining local context and WordNet similarity for word sense identification. *WordNet: An electronic lexical database* 49, 2 (1998), 265–283.
[17] Xiaojie Liu, Jian-Yun Nie, and Alessandro Sordoni. 2016. Constraining Word Embeddings by Prior Knowledge – Application to Medical Information Retrieval. In *AIRS*.
[18] Zhengdong Lu and Hang Li. 2013. A deep architecture for matching short texts. In *NIPS*. 1367–1375.
[19] Tomas Mikolov, Kai Chen, Greg Corrado, and Jeffrey Dean. 2013. Efficient estimation of word representations in vector space. *arXiv:1301.3781* (2013).
[20] Tomas Mikolov, Ilya Sutskever, Kai Chen, Gregory S. Corrado, and Jeffrey Dean. 2013. Distributed Representations of Words and Phrases and their Compositionality. In *NIPS*. 3111–3119.
[21] Gia-Hung Nguyen, Lynda Tamine, Laure Soulier, and Nathalie Bricon-Souf. 2016. Toward a deep neural approach for knowledge-based IR. *arXiv:1606.07211* (2016).
[22] Dipasree Pal, Mandar Mitra, and Kalyankumar Datta. 2014. Improving query expansion using WordNet. *JASIST* 65, 12 (2014), 2469–2478.
[23] Liang Pang, Yanyan Lan, Jiafeng Guo, Jun Xu, Shengxian Wan, and Xueqi Cheng. 2016. Text Matching As Image Recognition. In *AAAI*. 2793–2799.
[24] Ted Pedersen and Varada Kolhatkar. 2009. WordNet::SenseRelate::AllWords: A Broad Coverage Word Sense Tagger That Maximizes Semantic Relatedness. In *NAACL-Demonstrations*. 17–20.
[25] Ted Pedersen, Serguei V.S. Pakhomov, Siddharth Patwardhan, and Christopher G. Chute. 2007. Measures of semantic similarity and relatedness in the biomedical domain. *Journal of Biomedical Informatics* 40, 3 (2007), 288 – 299.
[26] Jeffrey Pennington, Richard Socher, and Christopher Manning. 2014. Glove: Global Vectors for Word Representation. In *EMNLP*. 1532–1543.
[27] Aliaksei Severyn and Alessandro Moschitti. 2015. Learning to rank short text pairs with convolutional deep neural networks. In *SIGIR*. 373–382.
[28] Yelong Shen, Xiaodong He, Jianfeng Gao, Li Deng, and Grégoire Mesnil. 2014. A latent semantic model with convolutional-pooling structure for information retrieval. In *CIKM*. 101–110.
[29] Ivan Vulić and Marie-Francine Moens. 2015. Monolingual and Cross-Lingual Information Retrieval Models Based on (Bilingual) Word Embeddings. In *SIGIR*. ACM, 363–372.
[30] Zhen Wang, Jianwen Zhang, Jianlin Feng, and Zheng Chen. 2014. Knowledge Graph Embedding by Translating on Hyperplanes. In *AAAI*. 1112–1119.
[31] Xing Wei and W Bruce Croft. 2006. LDA-based document models for ad-hoc retrieval. In *SIGIR*. ACM, 178–185.
[32] Chenyan Xiong and Jamie Callan. 2015. EsdRank: Connecting Query and Documents Through External Semi-Structured Data. In *CIKM*. 951–960.
[33] Chenyan Xiong and Jamie Callan. 2015. Query expansion with Freebase. In *ICTIR*. ACM, 111–120.
[34] Chang Xu, Yalong Bai, Jiang Bian, Bin Gao, Gang Wang, Xiaoguang Liu, and Tie-Yan Liu. 2014. Rc-net: A general framework for incorporating knowledge into word representations. In *CIKM*. 1219–1228.
[35] Mo Yu and Mark Dredze. 2014. Improving Lexical Embeddings with Semantic Knowledge.. In *ACL*. 545–550.
[36] Hamed Zamani and W. Bruce Croft. 2016. Estimating Embedding Vectors for Queries. In *ICTIR*. ACM, 123–132.
[37] Chengxiang Zhai and John Lafferty. 2001. A Study of Smoothing Methods for Language Models Applied to Ad Hoc Information Retrieval. In *SIGIR*. 334–342.
[38] Xiaohua Zhou, Xiaodan Zhang, and Xiaohua Hu. 2006. MaxMatcher: Biological Concept Extraction Using Approximate Dictionary Lookup. In *PRICAI*. Springer.

On Type-Aware Entity Retrieval

Darío Gargliotti
University of Stavanger
dario.gargliotti@uis.no

Krisztian Balog
University of Stavanger
krisztian.balog@uis.no

ABSTRACT

Today, the practice of returning entities from a knowledge base in response to search queries has become widespread. One of the distinctive characteristics of entities is that they are typed, i.e., assigned to some hierarchically organized type system (type taxonomy). The primary objective of this paper is to gain a better understanding of how entity type information can be utilized in entity retrieval. We perform this investigation in an idealized "oracle" setting, assuming that we know the distribution of target types of the relevant entities for a given query. We perform a thorough analysis of three main aspects: (i) the choice of type taxonomy, (ii) the representation of hierarchical type information, and (iii) the combination of type-based and term-based similarity in the retrieval model. Using a standard entity search test collection based on DBpedia, we find that type information proves most useful when using large type taxonomies that provide very specific types. We provide further insights on the extensional coverage of entities and on the utility of target types.

CCS CONCEPTS

•Information systems →Retrieval Models and Ranking;

KEYWORDS

Entity retrieval, entity types, semantic search

ACM Reference format:
Darío Gargliotti and Krisztian Balog. 2017. On Type-Aware Entity Retrieval. In *Proceedings of ICTIR'17, October 1–4, 2017, Amsterdam, Netherlands.*, , 8 pages.
DOI: https://doi.org/10.1145/3121050.3121054

1 INTRODUCTION

Entities, such as people, organizations, or locations are natural units for organizing information; they can provide not only more focused responses, but often immediate answers, to many search queries [30]. Indeed, entities play a key role in transforming search engines into "answer engines" [24]. The pivotal component that sparked this evolution is the increased availability of structured data published in knowledge bases, such as Wikipedia, DBpedia, or the Google Knowledge Graph, now primary sources of information for entity-oriented search. Major web search engines also shaped users' expectations about search applications; the single-search-box

paradigm has become widespread, and ordinary users have little incentive (or knowledge) to formulate structured queries. The task we consider in this paper, referred to as *ad-hoc entity retrieval* [30], corresponds to this setting: returning a ranked list of entities from a knowledge base in response to a keyword user query.

One of the unique characteristics of entity retrieval is that entities are typed, this is, grouped into more general classes, i.e., *types*, of entities. Types are typically organized in a hierarchy, which we will refer to as *type taxonomy* hereinafter. Each entity in the knowledge base can be associated with (i.e., is an *instance of*) one or more types. For example, in DBpedia, the type of the entity Albert Einstein is Scientist; according to Wikipedia, that entity belongs to the types Theoretical physicists and People with acquired Swiss citizenship, among others. It is assumed that by identifying the types of entities sought by the query (*target types*, from now on), one can use this information to improve entity retrieval performance; see Figure 1 for an illustration. The main high-level research question we are concerned with in this study is: *How to use entity type information in ad-hoc entity retrieval?*

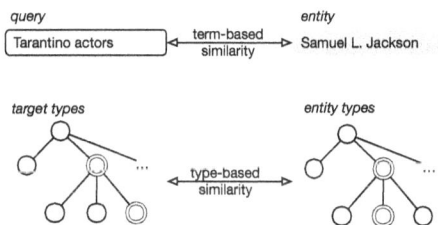

Figure 1: Entity retrieval using entity type information.

The concept of entity types, while seemingly straightforward, turns out to be a multifaceted research problem that has not yet been thoroughly investigated in the literature. Most of the research related with the usage of type information has been conducted in the context of the INEX Entity Ranking track [9]. There, it is assumed that the user complements the keyword query with one or more target types, using Wikipedia's category system as the type taxonomy. The focus has been on expanding the set of target types based on hierarchical relationships and dealing with the imperfections of the type system [1, 8, 18, 29]. Importantly, these developments have been motivated and driven by the peculiarities of Wikipedia's category system. It is not known whether the same methods prove effective, and even if these issues persist at all, in case of other type taxonomies. One important contribution of this paper is that we consider and systematically compare multiple type taxonomies (DBpedia, Freebase, Wikipedia, and YAGO). Additionally, there is the matter of representing type information, i.e., to what extent the hierarchy of the taxonomy should be preserved. Yet another piece of the puzzle is how to combine type-based and text-based similarity in the retrieval model. Therefore, the research questions we address are as follows:

RQ1 What is the impact of the particular choice of type taxonomy on entity retrieval performance?

RQ2 How to represent hierarchical entity type information for entity retrieval?

RQ3 How to combine term-based and type-based information?

To answer the above questions, we conduct a series of experiments for all possible combinations of three dimensions:

i) The way term-based and type-based information is combined in the retrieval model; see Section 3.

ii) The representation of hierarchical entity type information; see Section 4.

iii) The choice of the type taxonomy; see Section 5.

In summary, our work is the first comprehensive study on the usage of entity type information for entity retrieval. Our main contributions are twofold. First, we present methods for representing types in a hierarchy, establishing type-based similarity, and combining term-based and type-based similarities. Second, we perform a thorough experimental comparison and analysis of all possible configurations across the above identified three dimensions. Our overall finding is that type information has the most benefits in case of large, deep type taxonomies that provide very specific types.

2 RELATED WORK

The task of entity ranking has been studied in different flavors, including ad-hoc entity retrieval [26, 30], list search [5, 10], related entity finding [2], and question answering [23]. Our interest in this work lies in the usage of type information for general-purpose entity retrieval against a knowledge base (KB), where queries may belong to either of the above categories.

Retrieval models. Early works represented type information as a separate field in a fielded entity model [40]. In later works, types are typically incorporated into the retrieval method by combining term-based similarity with a separate type-based similarity component. This combination may be done using (i) a linear interpolation [1, 18, 29] or (ii) in a multiplicative manner, where the type-based component essentially serves as a filter [6]. Raviv et al. [32] introduce a particular version of interpolation using Markov Random Fields, linearly aggregating each of the scores for the joint distribution of the query with entity document, type, and name. All the mentioned works have consistently reported significant performance improvements when a type-based component is incorporated into the (term-based) retrieval model. However, type-aware approaches have not been systematically compared to date. We formalize these two general combination strategies, interpolation and filtering, in Section 3, and then compare them in Section 7.

Type taxonomies. The choice of a particular type taxonomy is mainly motivated by the problem setting, depending on whether a wide-coverage type system (like Wikipedia categories) or a curated, well-designed ontology (e.g., the DBpedia Ontology) is desired. The most common type system used in prior work is Wikipedia categories [1, 6, 8, 18, 32]. This is in part for historical reasons, as this was the underlying type system used at the INEX Entity Ranking track, where type information was first exploited. Further choices

include the DBpedia Ontology [3, 35], YAGO types [8, 25, 33, 35], Freebase [21], and schema.org [35]. We are not aware of any work that compared different type taxonomies for entity retrieval.

Representations of type information. Target types are commonly considered either as a set [8, 18, 29, 32] or as a bag (weighted set) [1, 33, 36]. Various ways of measuring type-based similarity have been proposed [7, 17, 37, 38, 40]. In this work we employ a state-of-the-art probabilistic approach by Balog et al. [1] (cf. Section 3.3). Within a taxonomy, types are arranged in a hierarchy. Several approaches have attempted to expand the set of target types based on the hierarchical structure of the type system [1, 6, 8, 29]. Importantly, the investigation of type hierarchies has been limited to Wikipedia, and, even there, mixed results are reported [7, 16, 37, 40]. It remains an open question whether considering the hierarchical nature of types benefits retrieval performance. We aim to fill that gap.

Target Type Identification. The INEX Entity Ranking track [10] and the TREC Entity track [5] both featured scenarios where target types are provided by the user. In the lack of explicit target type information, one might attempt to infer types from the keyword query. This subtask is introduced by Vallet and Zaragoza [36] as the *entity type ranking* problem. They extract entity mentions from the set of top relevant passages, then consider the types associated with the top-ranked entities using various weighting functions. Kaptein et al. [19] similarly use a simple entity-centric model. Manually assigned target types tend to be more general than automatically identified ones [18]. Having a hierarchical structure, therefore, makes it convenient to assign more general types. In [3], a hierarchical version of the *target type identification* task is addressed using the DBpedia Ontology and language modeling techniques. Sawant and Chakrabarti [33] focus on telegraphic queries and assume that each query term is either a type hint or a "word matcher." They consider multiple interpretations of the query and tightly integrate type detection within the ranking of entities. Their approach further relies on the presence of a large-scale web corpus. In our case, an oracle process generates the query target type distribution from its set of known relevant entities (cf. Section 6).

Entity Types. A further complicating issue is that the type information associated with entities in the knowledge base is incomplete, imperfect, or missing altogether for some entities. Automatic typing of entities is a possible solution for alleviating some of these problems. For example, approaches to extend entity type assignments in DBpedia include mining associated Wikipedia articles for wikilink relations [28], patterns over logical interpretations of the deeply parsed natural language definitions [13], or linguistic hypotheses about category classes [12]. Several works have addressed entity typing over progressively larger taxonomies with finer-grained types [11, 15, 22, 31, 39]. Regarding the task of detecting and typing *emerging entities*, having fine-grained types for new entities is of particular importance for informative knowledge [21, 25].

3 TYPE-AWARE ENTITY RETRIEVAL

In this section we formally describe the type-aware entity retrieval models we will be using for investigating the research questions stated in Section 1. Our contributions do not lie in this part; the techniques we present were shown to be effective in prior research.

We formulate our retrieval task in a generative probabilistic framework. Given an input query q, we rank entities e according to

$$P(e|q) \propto P(q|e)P(e) . \tag{1}$$

When uniform entity priors are assumed, the final ranking of entities boils down to the estimation of $P(q|e)$. We consider the query in the term space as well as in the type space. Hence, we write $q = (q_w, q_t)$, where q_w holds the query terms (words) and q_t holds the *target types*. Two ways of factoring the probability $P(q|e)$ are presented in Section 3.1. All models share two components: term-based similarity, $P(q_w|e)$, and type-based similarity, $P(q_t|e)$. These are discussed in Sections 3.2 and 3.3, respectively.

3.1 Retrieval Models

We present two alternative approaches for combining term-based and type-based similarity.

3.1.1 Filtering. Assuming conditional independence between the term-based and type-based components, the final score becomes a multiplication of the components:

$$P(q|e) = P(q_w|e)P(q_t|e) . \tag{2}$$

This approach is a generalization, among others, of the one used in [6] (where the term-based information itself is unfolded into multiple components, considering not only language models from textual context but also estimations of entity co-occurrences). We consider two specific instantiations of this model:

Strict filtering where $P(q_t|e)$ is 1 if the target types and entity types have a non-empty intersection, and is 0 otherwise.

Soft filtering where $P(q_t|e) \in [0..1]$ and is estimated using the approach detailed below in Section 3.3.

3.1.2 Interpolation. Alternatively, a mixture model may be used, which allows for controlling the importance of each component. Nevertheless, the conditional independence between q_w and q_t is still imposed by this model:

$$P(q|e) = (1 - \lambda_t)P(q_w|e) + \lambda_t P(q_t|e) . \tag{3}$$

Examples of this approach include [1, 18, 29, 32].

3.2 Term-based Similarity

We base the estimation of the term-based component, $P(q_w|e)$, on statistical language modeling techniques since they have shown to be an effective approach in prior work, see, e.g., [1, 4, 6, 18]. Specifically, we employ the Mixture of Language Models method from [4] with two fields, title and content. Following [27], the weights are set to 0.2 and 0.8, respectively. This is a simple, yet solid baseline approach. We note that the term-based component is not the focus of this work; any other approach could also be plugged in (provided that the retrieval scores are mapped to probabilities).

3.3 Type-based Similarity

Rather than considering types simply as a set, we assume a distributional representation of types, also referred to as *bag-of-types*. Namely, a type in the bag may occur with repetitions, naturally

rendering it more important. Following [1], we represent type information as a multinomial probability distribution over types, both for queries and for entities. Specifically, let θ_q denote the target type distribution for the query q (such that $\sum_t P(t|\theta_q) = 1$). We assume that there is some mechanism in place that estimates this distribution; in our experiments, we will rely on an "oracle" that provides us exactly with this information (cf. Section 6). Further, let θ_e denote the target type distribution for entity e. We assume that a function $n(t, e)$ is provided, which returns 1 if e is assigned to type t, otherwise 0. We present various ways of setting $n(t, e)$ based on the hierarchy of the type taxonomy in Section 4. We note that $n(t, e)$ is not limited to having a binary value; this quantity could, for example, be used to reflect how important type t is for the given entity e. We use a multinomial distribution to allow for such future extensions. Based on these raw counts, the type-based representation of an entity e is estimated using Dirichlet smoothing:

$$P(t|\theta_e) = \frac{n(t, e) + \mu P(t)}{\sum_{t'} n(t', e) + \mu} , \tag{4}$$

where $P(t)$ is the background type model obtained by a maximum-likelihood estimate, and μ is the smoothing parameter, which we set to the average number of types assigned to an entity.

With both θ_q and θ_e in place, we estimate type-based similarity using the Kullback-Leibler (KL) divergence of the two distributions:

$$P(q_t|e) = z(\max_{e'} KL(\theta_q \| \theta_{e'}) - KL(\theta_q \| \theta_e)) , \tag{5}$$

where z is a normalization factor. Note that the smaller the divergence the more similar the distributions are, therefore in Eq. (5) we subtract it from the maximum KL-divergence, in order to obtain a probability distribution. For further details we refer to [1].

4 REPRESENTING HIERARCHICAL ENTITY TYPE INFORMATION

This section presents various ways of representing hierarchical entity type information. That is, how to set the quantity $n(t, e)$, which is needed for estimating type-based similarity between target types of the query and types assigned to the entity in the knowledge base. Before proceeding further, let us introduce some terminology and notation.

- T is a type taxonomy that consists of a set of hierarchically organized entity types, and $t \in T$ is a specific entity type.
- E is the set of all entities in the knowledge base, and $e \in E$ is a specific entity.
- $T(e)$ is the set of types that are assigned to entity e in the knowledge base. We refer to this as a set of *assigned types*. Note that $T(e)$ might be an empty set.

We impose the following constraints on the type taxonomy.

i) There is a single root node t_0 that is the ancestor of all types (e.g., <owl:Thing>). Since all entities belong to this type, it is excluded from the set of assigned types by definition.

ii) We restrict the type taxonomy to subtype-supertype relations; each type t has a single parent type denoted as $\pi(t)$.

iii) Type assignments are transitive, i.e., an entity that belongs to a given type also belongs to all ancestors of that type: $t \in T(e) \wedge \pi(t) \neq t_0 \implies \pi(t) \in T(e)$.

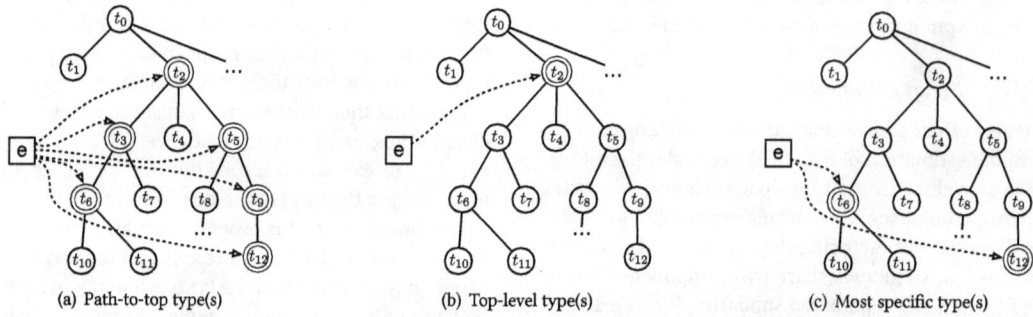

(a) Path-to-top type(s)   (b) Top-level type(s)   (c) Most specific type(s)

Figure 2: Alternative ways of representing entity-type assignments with respect to the type taxonomy. The dashed arrows point to the types that are assigned to entity e. The root node of the taxonomy is labeled with t_0.

We further note that an entity might belong to multiple types under different branches of the taxonomy. Assume that t_i and t_j are both types of e. It might be then that their nearest common ancestor in the type hierarchy is t_0.

While $T(e)$ holds the types assigned to entity e, there are multiple ways of turning it into a numerical value, $n(t, e)$, which reflects the type's importance or weight with respect to the given entity. This weight is taken into account when building the type-based entity representation in Eq. (4). In this work, we treat all types equally important for an entity, i.e., use binary values for $n(t, e)$.

We consider the following three options for representing hierarchical type information; see Figure 2 for an illustration. In our definitions, we use $\mathbb{1}(x)$ as an indicator function, which returns the value 1 if condition x is true and returns 0 otherwise.

Path-to-top It counts all types that are assigned to the entity in the knowledge base, excluding the root (from constraint (iii) it follows that $T(e)$ contains all the types to the top-level node):

$$n(t, e) = \mathbb{1}\big(t \in T(e)\big).$$

Top-level type(s) Only top-level types are considered for an entity, that is, types that have the root node as their parent:

$$n(t, e) = \mathbb{1}\big(t \in T(e) \wedge \pi(t) = t_0\big).$$

Most specific type(s) From each path, only the most specific type is considered for the entity:

$$n(t, e) = \mathbb{1}\big(t \in T(e) \wedge \nexists t' \in T(e) : \pi(t') = t\big).$$

Even though there may be alternative representations, these three are natural ways of encoding hierarchical information.

5 ENTITY TYPE TAXONOMIES

In this paper we study multiple type taxonomies from various knowledge bases: DBpedia, Freebase, Wikipedia, and YAGO. These vary a lot in terms of hierarchical structure and in how entity-type assignments are recorded. We normalize these type taxonomies to a uniform structure, adhering to the constraints specified in Section 4. Table 1 presents an overview of the type systems (after normalization). The number of type assignments are counted according to the path-to-top representation. Properties of the four type systems and details of the normalization process are discussed below.

Table 1: Overview of normalized type taxonomies and their statistics. The top block is about the taxonomy itself; the bottom block is about type assignments of entities.

Type system	DBpedia	Freebase	Wikipedia categories	YAGO
#types	713	1,719	423,636	568,672
#top-level types	22	92	27	61
#leaf-level types	561	1,626	303,956	549,754
height	7	2	35	19
#types used	408	1,626	359,159	314,632
#entities w/ type	4.87M	3.27M	3.52M	2.88M
avg #types/entity	2.8	4.4	20.8	13.4
mode depth	2	2	11	4

5.1 Type Taxonomies

Wikipedia categories. The Wikipedia category system, developed and extended by Wikipedia editors, consists of textual labels known as categories. This categorization is not a well-defined "is-a" hierarchy, but a graph; a category may have multiple parent categories and there might be cycles along the path to ancestors [19]. Also, categories often represent only loose relatedness between articles; category assignments are neither consistent nor complete [9].

We transformed the Wikipedia category graph, consisting of over 1.16M categories, into a type taxonomy as follows. First, we selected a set of 27 top-level categories covering most of the knowledge domains.[1] These became the top-level nodes of the taxonomy, all with a single common root type <owl:Thing>. All super-categories that these selected top-level categories might have in the graph were discarded. Second, we removed multiple inheritances by selecting a single parent per category. For this, we considered the population of a category to be the set of its assigned articles. Each category was linked in the taxonomy with a single parent in the graph whose intersection between their populations is the maximal among all possible parents; in case of a tie, the most populated parent was

---

[1] The selected top-level categories are the main categories for each section of the portal https://en.wikipedia.org/wiki/Portal:Contents/Categories. (As an alternative, we also considered the categories from https://en.wikipedia.org/wiki/Category:Main_topic_classifications, and found that it comprises a similar category selection).

chosen. Under this criterion, and for the purpose of understanding hierarchical relations, any category without a parent was discarded. Lastly, from this partial hierarchy (which is still a graph, not a tree), we obtained the final taxonomy by performing a depth-first exploration from each top-level category, and avoiding to add those arcs that would introduce cycles. The resulting taxonomy contains over 423K categories and reaches a maximum depth of 35 levels.[2]

DBpedia ontology. The DBpedia Ontology is a well-designed hierarchy since its inception; it was created manually by considering the most frequently used infoboxes in Wikipedia. It continues to be properly curated to address some weaknesses of the Wikipedia infobox space. While the DBpedia Ontology is clean and consistent, its coverage is limited to entities that have an associated infobox. It consists of 712 classes organized in a hierarchy of 7 levels.

YAGO taxonomy. YAGO is a huge semantic knowledge base, derived from Wikipedia, WordNet, and GeoNames [34]. Its classification schema is constructed by taking leaf categories from the category system of Wikipedia and then using WordNet synsets to establish the hierarchy of classes. The result is a deep subsumption hierarchy, consisting of over 568K classes. We work with the YAGO taxonomy from the current version of the ontology (3.0.2). We normalized it by adding a root node, <owl:Thing>, as a parent to every top-level type.

Freebase types. Freebase has a two-layer categorization system, where types on the bottom level are grouped under high-level domains. We used the latest public Freebase dump (2015-03-31), discarding domains meant for administering the Freebase service itself (e.g.; base, common). Additionally, we made <owl:Thing> the common root of all the domains, and finally obtained a taxonomy of 1,719 types.

5.2 Entity-Type Assignments

Now that we have presented the four type taxonomies, we also need to discuss how type assignments of entities are obtained. We use DBpedia 2015-10 as our knowledge base, which makes DBpedia types, Wikipedia categories, and YAGO type assignments readily available. For the fourth type taxonomy, Freebase, we followed same-as links from DBpedia to Freebase (which exist for 95% of the entities in DBpedia) and extracted type assignments from Freebase. It should be noted that entity-type assignments are provided differently for each of these taxonomies; DBpedia and Freebase supply a single (most specific) instance type for an entity, Wikipedia assignments include multiple categories for a given entity (without any restriction), while YAGO adheres to the path-to-top representation. We treat all entity-type assignments transitively, adhering to constraint (iii) in Section 4.

6 EXPERIMENTAL SETUP

We base our experiments on the DBpedia knowledge base (version 2015-10). DBpedia [20], as a central hub in the Linked Open Data cloud, provides a large repository of entities, which are mapped—directly or indirectly—to each of the type taxonomies of interest.

Test Collection. Our experimental platform is based on the test collection developed in [4]. The dataset contains 485 queries, synthesized from various entity-related benchmarking evaluation campaigns. These range from short keyword queries to natural language questions.

Target Types Oracle. Throughout all our experiments, we make use of a so-called *target type oracle.* We assume that there is an "oracle" process in place that provides us with the (distribution of) correct target types for a given query. This corresponds to the setting that was employed at previous benchmarking campaigns (such as the INEX Entity Ranking track [9] and the TREC Entity track [5]), where target types are provided explicitly as part of the topic definition. We need this idealized setting to ensure that our results reflect the full potential of using type information, without being hindered by the imperfections of an automated type detector.

For a given query q, we take the union of all types of all entities that are judged relevant for that query. Each of these types t becomes a target type, and its probability $P(t|\theta_q)$ is set proportional to the number of relevant entities that have that type.

Retrieval Models. As our baseline, we use a term-based approach, specifically the Mixture of Language Models [4], which we described in Section 3.2. We compare three type-aware retrieval models (cf. Section 3.1): strict filtering, soft filtering, and interpolation. For the latter, we perform a sweep over the possible type weights $\lambda_t \in [0, 1]$ in steps of 0.05, and use the best performing setting when comparing against other approaches. (Automatically estimating the λ_t parameter is outside the scope of this work.)

Type Assignments. To ensure that the differences we observe are not a result of missing type assignments, we distinguish between two settings in our experiments.

4TT We restrict our set of entities to those that have types assigned to them from all four type systems (1.51M entities in total). This ensures that the results we obtain are comparable across the different type systems. We also restrict the set of queries to those that have target types in all four type systems; queries without any relevant results (as a consequence of these restrictions) are filtered out. This leaves us with a total of 419 queries.

ALL We include all entities from the knowledge base and use the original set of relevance assessments without any modifications. Hence, some entities and queries do not have types assigned from one or more taxonomies.

7 RESULTS

In this section we present evaluation results for all combinations of the three proposed dimensions: type taxonomies, type representation modes, and retrieval models. When discussing the results, we use the term *configuration* to refer to a particular combination of type taxonomy, type representation, and retrieval model.

Figure 3 shows the results, corresponding to the two settings we distinguished in Section 6: in the top histograms, we consider only entities that have types assigned to them in all four type taxonomies (4TT); in the bottom histograms, we rank all entities in the knowledge base (ALL). The red line corresponds to the term-based baseline. Our evaluation metric is Mean Average Precision (MAP).

---

[2]We have confirmed experimentally that enforcing the Wikipedia category graph to satisfy the taxonomical constraints does not hurt retrieval performance. In fact, it is the opposite: it results in small, but statistically significant improvements.

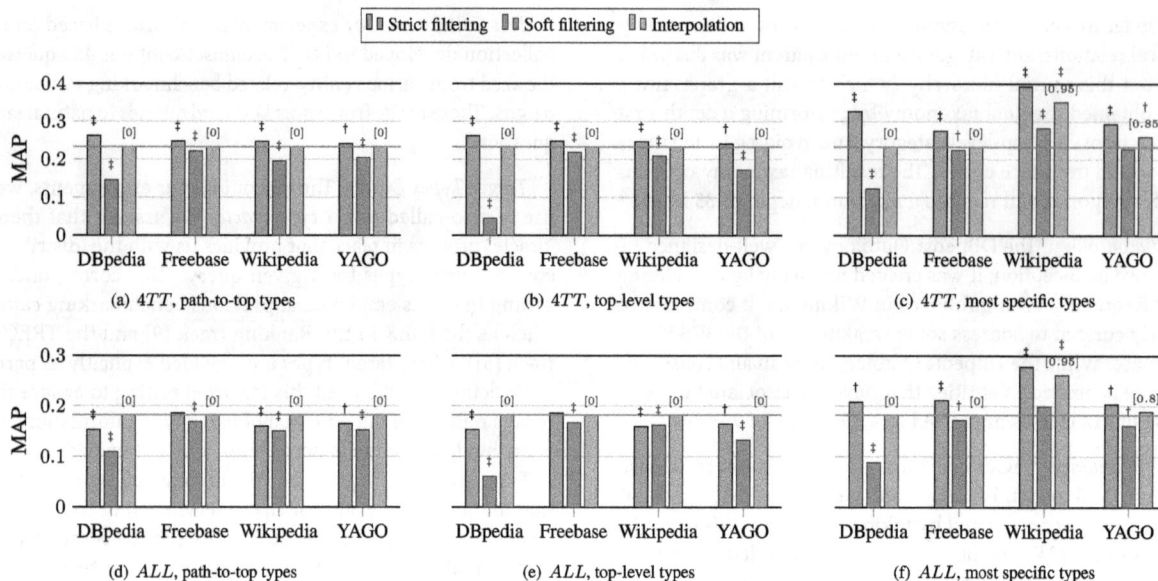

Figure 3: Entity retrieval performance for all combinations of type taxonomies, type representation modes, and retrieval models. (Top): only entities with types from all four type taxonomies; (Bottom): all entities in the knowledge base. The red line corresponds to the term-based baseline. Above each bar, the symbols † and ‡ indicate statistical significance against the baseline; the numbers in brackets show the type weight (empirically found best λ_t) used by the interpolation model.

We report on statistical significance using a two-tailed paired t-test at $p < 0.05$ and $p < 0.001$, denoted by † and ‡, respectively.

RQ1. Let us turn to our first research question, which concerns the impact of the particular choice of type taxonomy. It is clear that Wikipedia, in combination with the most specific type representation, performs best (for both 4TT and ALL). In particular, for the 4TT setting (top right plot in Figure 3), the improvements for Wikipedia are highly significant for all three retrieval models. As for the rest, there is no easy way to compare taxonomies, as the performance varies depending on the other dimensions. E.g., for 4TT using strict filtering and more general types (i.e., the purple bars in the top left and top middle histograms in Figure 3), the smaller, shallower type taxonomies (DBpedia and Freebase) tend to outperform the larger, deeper ones (Wikipedia and YAGO).

RQ2. The second research question, which is about type representation, has a clear answer: keeping only the most specific types in the hierarchy provides the best performance (right vs. left and middle histograms in Figure 3). This is also in line with findings in past work (cf. Section 2). As for the other two representations, i.e., types along path to top vs. top-level types, two things are worth pointing out. Firstly, the results are the same for both type representations when using strict filtering, which is explained by how the representations are defined in Section 4; if an entity is retained (given that the intersection between the entity's types and the target types is non-empty), this filtering does not change by adding more specific types. Secondly, for the interpolation model, we can observe that the λ_t weights are always 0 for these representations. This means that type information is not used at all. Overall, we

could not find any evidence that hierarchical relationships from ancestor types would benefit retrieval effectiveness.

RQ3. Answering our final research question, concerning the type-aware retrieval model, requires a more elaborate treatment. In the 4TT setting, strict filtering is the best retrieval model for every configuration, outperforming the baseline with high significance in almost all cases. This no longer holds in the ALL setting; in fact, all MAP scores drop with respect to the corresponding 4TT configuration. This is expected, as in the more realistic setting, many relevant entities may have incomplete type assignments. Only the interpolation model can deal with this in a robust manner.

Figure 4 shows the performance of the interpolation model when varying the weight of the type-based component (value of λ_t). Due to space constraints, we present the plots only for the 4TT setting; the figures look very similar for the ALL setting. We find that for the smaller, shallower type taxonomies, DBpedia and Freebase, assigning more weight to type-based information is increasingly more harmful, independently of the type representation or type assignment setting. The same occurs for Wikipedia and YAGO using the more general type representations. On the other hand, when using only the most specific types (right plot in Figure 4), for Wikipedia and YAGO, performance increases with higher λ_t values. Yet, MAP scores peak at $\lambda_t < 1$, meaning that term-based similarity is still needed for optimal performance.

The only configurations performing worse than the baseline, even in the 4TT setting, are the ones using the soft filtering model. In particular, the MAP scores for DBpedia with soft filtering are noticeably low. We plan to perform a deeper investigation of this phenomenon in future work.

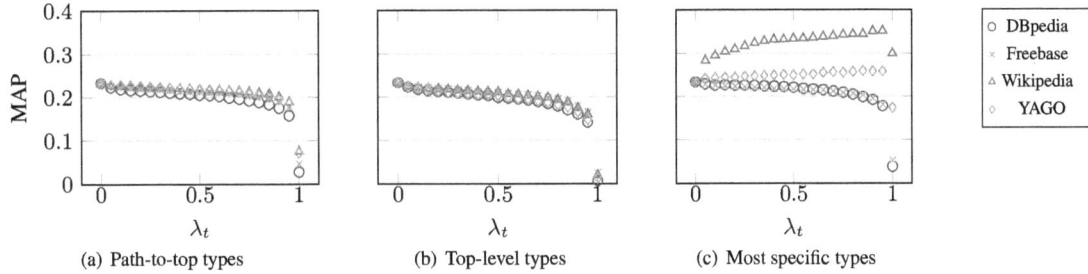

Figure 4: Retrieval performance (4TT setting) using the interpolation model with different type weights, λ_t.

Table 2: Number of entities with missing type information.

Entities	DBpedia	Freebase	Wikipedia	YAGO
All entities	35,390	1,369,636	1,113,299	1,755,480
Relevant entities	3,341	1,594	2,567	2,532

8 ANALYSIS AND DISCUSSION

Now that we have presented our results, we proceed with further analysis of some of the issues we identified in the previous section.

8.1 Missing Type Information

In order to make a fair comparison between different type taxonomies, we had to account for the fact that the entity type assignments in the knowledge bases may be incomplete (cf. the 4TT setting in Section 6). Indeed, results in Section 7 have shown that the benefits of using type information are more obvious when entities are not missing type assignments. Table 2 shows, for each of the type taxonomies, the number of entities that have no types assigned to them in the KB (i.e., "non-typed" entities). Interestingly, while DBpedia has the least number of non-typed entities (only 35K out of 4.6M), it lacks types for over 25% of the relevant entities (3.3K out of 12.9K). Even for Freebase, which has the best coverage of relevant entities, over 12% of the relevant entities have no type assignments in the KB. Clearly, the problem of missing type information, frequently referred to as partial *extensional* coverage of type systems [13], is an important area of research (cf. Section 2).

8.2 Revisiting the Target Types Oracle

Another aspect of type-based information we are concerned about is the quality of target types. Previously, we have included all types associated with known relevant entities, proportional to their frequency, in the target type distribution (θ_q); we shall refer to it as the *default oracle*. Here, we consider another variant, referred to as *filtered oracle*, where a frequency threshold is applied. Specifically, we include type t as a target type iff at least 3 relevant entities have t assigned to them. As a consequence of this filtering, many queries have an empty set of types; for this experiment, we discard those from the ground truth set, leaving us with 182 queries in total.

A comparison of the two oracles is presented in Figure 5. For the more general type representations, the filtered oracle turns out to be slightly less effective for most of the configurations. Yet, the differences are barely noticeable. When using the most specific

Table 3: Coverage of relevant entities by top-K types, in terms of precision, recall, and F1, averaged over all queries.

Top-K types	Type Taxonomy	P	R	F1
$K = 1$	DBpedia	0.0027	0.5863	0.0046
	Freebase	0.0060	**0.7254**	0.0076
	Wikipedia	**0.1147**	0.4798	**0.1287**
	YAGO	0.0418	0.6303	0.0488
$K = 3$	DBpedia	0.0006	0.7199	0.0012
	Freebase	0.0004	**0.7805**	0.0008
	Wikipedia	**0.0402**	0.5847	**0.0614**
	YAGO	0.0036	0.7025	0.0062

types, we find that MAP scores drop, especially for larger, deeper taxonomies (Wikipedia and YAGO); some configurations no longer outperform the term-based baseline. Hence, it is important to consider all possible target types, even those with a low probability.

8.3 What is in a Target Type?

Our ultimate interest in this work is in understanding the usefulness of type information for ad-hoc entity retrieval. What portion of relevant entities can target types help to capture? To shed some light on this, we measure the coverage of relevant entities by (i) the top ranked type and (ii) the set of top 3 types.[3] Table 3 reports the results. We find that Wikipedia has, by far, the highest precision and F1-score among all type taxonomies; YAGO comes second. Notice that these are the two taxonomies that performed best, when using the most specific type representations, in Figure 3.

In summary, we have found that specific types from large, fine-grained taxonomies provide the best performance. Yet, it appears that it is not the hierarchical nature of the taxonomy that brings benefits, but rather the fact that these fine-grained types provide semantic sets or classes that can capture (some subset of) the relevant entities with high precision.

9 CONCLUSIONS

In this paper we have furthered our understanding on the usage of target type information for entity retrieval over structured data sources. A main contribution of this work is the systematic comparison of four well-known type taxonomies (DBpedia, Freebase,

---

[3]For this experiment, we take the type assignments "as-recorded" in Wikipedia, without enforcing the taxonomical constraints.

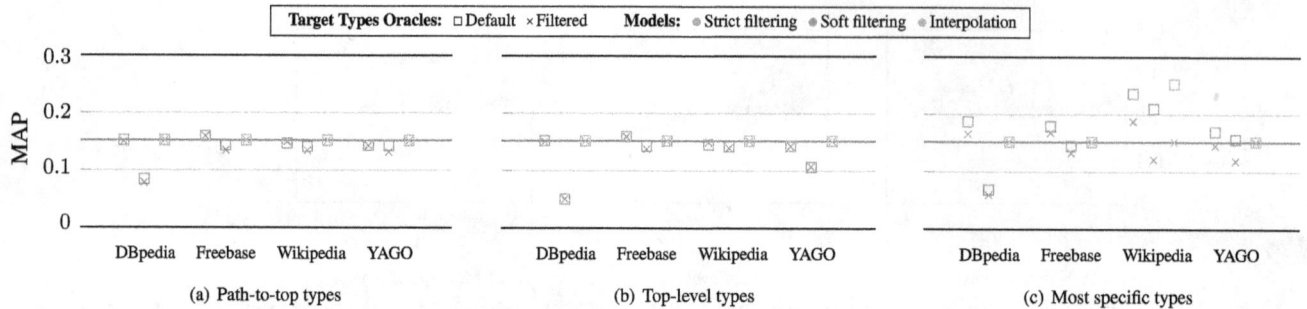

Figure 5: Retrieval performance using the default vs. filtered target types oracle. The red line is the term-based baseline.

Wikipedia, and YAGO) across three dimensions of interest: the representation of hierarchical entity type information, the way to combine term-based and type-based information, and the impact of choosing a particular type taxonomy. We have found that using the most specific types in a fine-grained taxonomy, like Wikipedia, leads to the best retrieval effectiveness.

We identify two directions for future work. First, we plan to report on an even deeper query-level analysis, which was not possible here due to space limitations. Second, our investigations so far have taken place in an idealized environment, assuming that an "oracle" process can provide us with the target types for each query. We wish to perform a similar analysis using automatically identified target types [14].

REFERENCES

[1] Krisztian Balog, Marc Bron, and Maarten De Rijke. 2011. Query modeling for entity search based on terms, categories, and examples. *ACM Trans. Inf. Syst.* 29, 4 (2011), 22:1–22:31.
[2] K. Balog, A. P. de Vries, P. Serdyukov, P. Thomas, and T. Westerveld. 2010. Overview of the TREC 2009 Entity Track. In *Proc. of TREC*.
[3] Krisztian Balog and Robert Neumayer. 2012. Hierarchical target type identification for entity-oriented queries. In *Proc. of CIKM*. 2391–2394.
[4] Krisztian Balog and Robert Neumayer. 2013. A Test Collection for Entity Search in DBpedia. In *Proc. of SIGIR*. 737–740.
[5] Krisztian Balog, Pavel Serdyukov, and Arjen P. De Vries. 2012. Overview of the TREC 2011 Entity Track. In *Proc. of TREC*.
[6] Marc Bron, Krisztian Balog, and Maarten de Rijke. 2010. Ranking Related Entities: Components and Analyses. In *Proc. of CIKM*. 1079–1088.
[7] Gianluca Demartini, Claudiu S. Firan, and Tereza Iofciu. 2008. Focused Access to XML Documents. Springer, Chapter L3S at INEX 2007, 252–263.
[8] Gianluca Demartini, Claudiu S. Firan, Tereza Iofciu, Ralf Krestel, and Wolfgang Nejdl. 2010. Why finding entities in Wikipedia is difficult, sometimes. *Information Retrieval* 13, 5 (may 2010), 534–567.
[9] Gianluca Demartini, Tereza Iofciu, and Arjen P. De Vries. 2010. Overview of the INEX 2009 Entity Ranking Track. In *Focused Retrieval and Evaluation, and INEX*. 254–264.
[10] Gianluca Demartini, Tereza Iofciu, and Arjen P. De Vries. 2010. Overview of the INEX 2009 Entity Ranking Track. In *Focused Retrieval and Evaluation*. 254–264.
[11] Michael Fleischman and Eduard Hovy. 2002. Fine Grained Classification of Named Entities. In *Proc. of COLING*. 1–7.
[12] Marco Fossati, Dimitris Kontokostas, and Jens Lehmann. 2015. Unsupervised Learning of an Extensive and Usable Taxonomy for DBpedia. In *Proc. of SEMANTICS*. 177–184.
[13] Aldo Gangemi, Andrea Giovanni Nuzzolese, Valentina Presutti, Francesco Draicchio, Alberto Musetti, and Paolo Ciancarini. 2012. Automatic Typing of DBpedia Entities. In *Proc. of ISWC*. 65–81.
[14] Darío Garigliotti, Faegheh Hasibi, and Krisztian Balog. 2017. Target Type Identification for Entity-Bearing Queries. In *Proc. of SIGIR*. 845–848.
[15] Claudio Giuliano. 2009. Fine-grained Classification of Named Entities Exploiting Latent Semantic Kernels. In *Proc. of CoNLL*. 201–209.
[16] Janne Jämsen, Turkka Näppilä, and Paavo Arvola. 2008. Focused Access to XML Documents. Springer, Chapter Entity Ranking Based on Category Expansion, 264–278.

[17] Rianne Kaptein and Jaap Kamps. 2009. Finding Entities in Wikipedia using Links and Categories. In *Advances in Focused Retrieval, INEX*. 273–279.
[18] Rianne Kaptein and Jaap Kamps. 2013. Exploiting the category structure of Wikipedia for entity ranking. *Artificial Intelligence* 194 (jan 2013), 111–129.
[19] Rianne Kaptein, Pavel Serdyukov, Arjen P. De Vries, and Jaap Kamps. 2010. Entity ranking using Wikipedia as a pivot. In *Proc. of CIKM*. 69–78.
[20] Jens Lehmann, Robert Isele, Max Jakob, Anja Jentzsch, Dimitris Kontokostas, Pablo N. Mendes, Sebastian Hellmann, Mohamed Morsey, Patrick van Kleef, Sören Auer, and Christian Bizer. 2015. DBpedia - A large-scale, multilingual knowledge base extracted from Wikipedia. *Semantic Web* 6, 2 (2015), 167–195.
[21] Thomas Lin, Mausam, and Oren Etzioni. 2012. No Noun Phrase Left Behind: Detecting and Typing Unlinkable Entities. In *Proc. of EMNLP-CoNLL*. 893–903.
[22] Xiao Ling and Daniel S. Weld. 2012. Fine-grained Entity Recognition. In *Proc. of AAAI*. 94–100.
[23] Vanessa Lopez, Christina Unger, Philipp Cimiano, and Enrico Motta. 2013. Evaluating Question Answering over Linked Data. *Web Semantics: Science, Services and Agents on the World Wide Web* 21 (aug 2013), 3–13.
[24] Peter Mika. 2013. Entity Search on the Web. In *Proc. of WWW*. 1231–1232.
[25] Ndapandula Nakashole, Tomasz Tylenda, and Gerhard Weikum. 2013. Fine-grained Semantic Typing of Emerging Entities. In *Proc. of ACL*. 1488–1497.
[26] Robert Neumayer, Krisztian Balog, and Kjetil Nørvåg. 2012. On the modeling of entities for ad-hoc entity search in the web of data. In *Proc. of ECIR*. 133–145.
[27] Robert Neumayer, Krisztian Balog, and Kjetil Nørvåg. 2012. When simple is (more than) good enough: effective semantic search with (almost) no semantics. In *Proc. of ECIR*. 540–543.
[28] Andrea Giovanni Nuzzolese, Aldo Gangemi, Valentina Presutti, and Paolo Ciancarini. 2012. Type inference through the analysis of Wikipedia links. In *Proc. of LDOW*.
[29] Jovan Pehcevski, James A Thom, Anne-Marie Vercoustre, and Vladimir Naumovski. 2010. Entity ranking in Wikipedia: utilising categories, links and topic difficulty prediction. *Information Retrieval* 13, 5 (2010), 568–600.
[30] Jeffrey Pound, Peter Mika, and Hugo Zaragoza. 2010. Ad-hoc object retrieval in the web of data. In *Proc. of WWW*. 771–780.
[31] Altaf Rahman and Vincent Ng. 2010. Inducing Fine-grained Semantic Classes via Hierarchical and Collective Classification. In *Proc. of COLING*. 931–939.
[32] Hadas Raviv, David Carmel, and Oren Kurland. 2012. A Ranking Framework for Entity Oriented Search Using Markov Random Fields. In *Proc. of JIWES*. 1:1–1:6.
[33] Uma Sawant and S Chakrabarti. 2013. Learning Joint Query Interpretation and Response Ranking. In *Proc. of WWW*. 1099–1109.
[34] Fabian M Suchanek, Gjergji Kasneci, and Gerhard Weikum. 2007. Yago: A Core of Semantic Knowledge. In *Proc. of WWW*. 697–706.
[35] Alberto Tonon, Michele Catasta, Gianluca Demartini, Philippe Cudré-Mauroux, and Karl Aberer. 2013. TRank: Ranking Entity Types Using the Web of Data. In *Proc. of ISWC*. 640–656.
[36] David Vallet and Hugo Zaragoza. 2008. Inferring the most important types of a query: a semantic approach. In *Proc. of SIGIR*. 857–858.
[37] Anne-Marie Vercoustre, Jovan Pehcevski, and James A. Thom. 2008. Focused Access to XML Documents. Springer, Chapter Using Wikipedia Categories and Links in Entity Ranking, 321–335.
[38] W. Weerkamp, K. Balog, and E. J. Meij. 2009. A Generative Language Modeling Approach for Ranking Entities. In *Advances in Focused Retrieval, INEX*. 292–299.
[39] Mohamed Amir Yosef, Sandro Bauer, Johannes Hoffart Marc Spaniol, and Gerhard Weikum. 2012. HYENA: Hierarchical Type Classification for Entity Names. In *Proc. of COLING*. 1361–1370.
[40] Jianhan Zhu, Dawei Song, and Stefan Rüger. 2008. Focused Access to XML Documents. Springer, Chapter Integrating Document Features for Entity Ranking, 336–347.

Enhanced Mean Retrieval Score Estimation for Query Performance Prediction

Haggai Roitman, Shai Erera, Oren Sar-Shalom, Bar Weiner
IBM Research - Haifa
Haifa, Israel 31905
haggai,shaie,orensr,barw@il.ibm.com

ABSTRACT

We study the problem of mean retrieval score estimation for query performance prediction (QPP). We propose an enhanced estimator which estimates the mean based on calibrated retrieval scores. Each document score is adjusted based on features that model potential tradeoffs that may exist in the retrieval process of that specific document. Using the proposed estimator, we derive several previously suggested QPP methods, from which we gather an initial set of calibration features. Based on these features and few additional ones, we propose two estimator instantiations. Using an evaluation over several TREC benchmarks, we demonstrate the effectiveness of our estimation approach.

1 INTRODUCTION

In the absence of relevance judgements, query performance prediction (QPP) methods may be used for estimating search quality [4]. Similar to many previous post-retrieval QPP works [7–9, 12, 27, 30–32], we estimate query performance by analyzing retrieval scores. Specifically, we focus on the mean retrieval score as the search effectiveness indicator. The mean score captures the *central tendency* of the retrieval scores' distribution. The higher this tendency is, the more we shall assume that the observed retrieval scores represent actual effectiveness.

Our goal is to estimate the mean retrieval score as accurate as possible so as to improve prediction. We build on top of Kurland et al.'s [14] probabilistic QPP framework and derive a general "calibrated" mean score estimator. To this end, each document's retrieval score is calibrated based on several generative terms; each such term models a different aspect of the document's retrieval process that may affect its relevance. We further derive two variants of this estimator. While the first variant emphasizes more on query-related retrieval issues, the second one emphasizes more on corpus-related issues.

Evidently, there are tradeoffs in the design of such estimators. To address these tradeoffs, we treat the score calibration problem as a *multi-criteria decision problem*; and suggest an alternative estimator based on a discriminative calibration approach. For that, we represent the retrieval process of each document by a set of calibration features; each feature captures a different retrieval quality criterion that may govern the actual document's relevance. We then combine the various features using their weighted product.

Using our proposed approach, we derive several previously suggested QPP methods, including Clarity [7], where we show that they share the same basic grounds of mean estimation. Using this connection allows us to gather and study an initial set of calibration features that can be utilized, in addition to several other features that we study.

Using an evaluation over several TREC benchmarks, we demonstrate that, overall, our calibrated mean score estimator results in an enhanced QPP. Moreover, we demonstrate that, those previously suggested QPP methods can be further improved by redesigning them as private instances of our proposed estimator.

The rest of this paper is organized as follows. We discuss related works in Section 2, followed by the description of our mean estimation framework in Section 3. Using this framework, we study several previously suggested methods in Section 4 and suggest two new instantiations in Section 5. We then evaluate the proposed approach in Section 6 and shortly conclude in Section 7.

2 RELATED WORK

Retrieval scores in IR have been extensively studied [6–10, 13, 20, 27, 30–32]. Among previous works, those related to QPP can be further classified based on two main types of descriptive statistics that are being utilized for prediction, either the mean score [7, 31, 32] or score dispersion [9, 20, 27, 30, 31]. Similar to [7, 31, 32], we utilize the mean retrieval score as the main indicator for QPP and aim at estimating it as accurately as possible. We show that, such previous works can be viewed as private instances of our proposed approach. Compared to [6, 8, 10, 13], we do not try to fit a generative (mixed) model of score distributions. Rather, we calibrate the scores provided by the underlying retrieval model in a discriminative way by adjusting them according to **multiple retrieval quality criteria**.

Our proposed mean estimation approach is built on top of Kurland et al.'s [14] probabilistic QPP framework. Using this framework, the authors explained several of previously suggested QPP methods [14]. Yet, our work differs from [14]. First, we describe a general mean score estimation framework for QPP, a venue of research, that, to the best of our knowledge, was not previously explored. Similar to [14], we show how to derive some of previously suggested QPP methods such as Clairty and WIG. Yet, our work has a different motivation, where we propose **new interpretations** to these methods. In addition, compared to [14], we are further able to improve such baseline methods and derive a general predictor that outperforms them all.

Raiber and Kurland [22] have studied several document level features for identifying representative "relevant" documents for retrieval. While we share some motivation with [22], our goal is completely different. The main goal in [22] is to improve document and cluster retrieval using a learning-to-rank method, trained over several document and cluster features; while our goal is to predict the effectiveness of a given retrieval, **without modifying it**.

Finally, some other previous works have combined the prediction of several QPP methods [3, 5, 23, 24, 26, 29]. Yet, within these works, such combination was performed **on whole lists basis**. This is in comparison to our approach that combines predictions based on the retrieval effectiveness of individual documents. Moreover, while we acknowledge that [3, 24] did utilize additional document-level retrieval features, their actual prediction is based on the **aggregations of each document-level feature** (e.g., the mean retrieval score itself, standard deviation, maximum/minimum scores, etc). Hence, similar to [5, 23, 26, 29], the actual combined predictor derived in [3, 24] is based on **list-level** properties.

3 FRAMEWORK

For a given query q, let D be a subset of documents, retrieved from a given corpus C by some underlying retrieval method $\mathcal{M}$. Let $s(d)$ further denote the corresponding retrieval score assigned by method $\mathcal{M}$ to document $d \in C$. Unless stated otherwise, we assume that D includes the top-k documents $d \in C$ with the highest scores.

In this work, we focus on post-retrieval QPP [4]. Let r denote the relevance event, our goal is, therefore, to estimate $p(D|q, r)$ – *the likelihood of finding relevant information for q in D* [14]. Similar to many previous works [7–9, 12, 30–32], we estimate $p(D|q, r)$ by analyzing the retrieval scores $s(d)$ of the documents in D. Specifically, we focus on the mean retrieval score $\mathbb{E}(s|D)$ as an indicator of QPP, whose value we wish to estimate as accurately as possible. The mean score "encodes" the *central tendency* of the retrieval scores's distribution. The higher this tendency is, the more confidence we assign to the ability of the underlying method $\mathcal{M}$ to retrieve relevant documents in D [4].

3.1 Towards a general mean estimator for QPP

Our main goal is to estimate the mean retrieval score $\mathbb{E}(s|D)$ as accurately as possible. To accomplish that, we wish to derive a general mean estimator that would adjust retrieval scores based on various retrieval quality criteria.

We start by setting the theoretical grounds (and motivation) behind our approach. As a first step, we now build on top of Kurland et al.'s [14] probabilistic QPP framework. Using their framework, $p(D|q, r)$ can be derived as follows[1]:

$$p(D|q, r) \overset{def}{=} p(r|D) \sum_{d \in D} p(d|q, r)p(d|D, r). \qquad (1)$$

$p(r|D)$ denotes the probability that D is relevant regardless of a specific query [14]. $p(r|D)$ may be estimated, for example, by analyzing properties of D that may indicate the existence of relevant information in D. Such properties may include, among others,

---
[1]See Eq. 4 in [14].

D's cohesion (e.g., by measuring list diameter), its clustering tendency, diversity, etc [14]. $p(d|q, r)$ denotes the probability that document $d \in D$ provides a relevant answer to query q [14]. $p(d|q, r)$ may be estimated, for example, using d's (normalized) query likelihood [15]. Finally, $p(d|D, r)$ is the probability that document d is generated by the relevant document set D, representing the strength of d's association with D [14]. This probability may be estimated according to the likelihood of generating d from D's induced relevance model compared to the likelihood of generating it from the background model induced from C [14].

Next, noting that $p(d|q, r) \overset{def}{=} \frac{p(q|d, r)p(r|d)p(d)}{p(r|q)p(q)}$ and assuming that $p(q)$ is uniform, we now obtain:

$$p(D|q, r) \propto \frac{p(r|D)}{p(r|q)} \sum_{d \in D} p(q|d, r)p(r|d)p(d)p(d|D, r) \qquad (2)$$

Here, $p(q|d, r)$ represents the query likelihood of document d [21], which is commonly estimated according to the observed score $s(d)$ determined by the underlying retrieval method $\mathcal{M}$. In many retrieval model implementations, such a score is usually determined according to the similarity between the query q and the document d. $p(r|q)$ denotes the probability that query q is a relevant representation of the (hidden) information need I_q. Estimating this probability is the primary goal of many pre-retrieval QPP methods [11].

Further assuming that documents $d \in D$ are uniformly distributed over D, i.e., $p(d) \overset{def}{=} \frac{1}{|D|}$; and noting that $s(d) \overset{def}{=} p(q|d) \approx p(q|d, r)$, we now obtain our first proposed general mean estimator:

$$p(D|q, r) \overset{def}{=} \frac{1}{|D|} \sum_{d \in D} s(d) \cdot \left[\frac{p(r|d)p(d|D, r)p(r|D)}{p(r|q)} \right] \qquad (3)$$

3.2 Deriving alternative estimators

We next derive two variants of the general mean estimator in Eq. 3. The first, is a *query-sensitive* estimator, which emphasizes more on query-related properties that may govern document d's retrieval quality. On the other hand, the second is a *corpus-sensitive* estimator, which emphasizes more on corpus-related properties. These two variants are further derived from the prior document relevance probability $p(r|d)$. On the theoretical side, we wish to show that, putting more emphasis on query-related properties would mean that less attention can be given to corpus-related ones, and vice versa. This in turn, suggests the existence of **tradeoffs** in the design of such "general" mean estimators.

3.2.1 Query-sensitive estimator. To derive a query-sensitive variant of the proposed general mean estimator in Eq. 3, we first note that $p(r|d) \overset{def}{=} \frac{p(r|d, q)p(q|d)}{p(q|d, r)}$. Using again the assumption that $p(q|d) \approx p(q|d, r)$ we get that $p(r|d) \approx p(r|d, q)$. Putting this back into Eq. 3, we now obtain a query-sensitive mean estimator:

$$p(D|q, r) \overset{def}{=} \frac{1}{|D|} \sum_{d \in D} s(d) \cdot \left[\frac{p(r|d, q)p(d|D, r)p(r|D)}{p(r|q)} \right] \qquad (4)$$

$p(r|d, q)$ serves as the basis of all *probabilistic relevance models*, commonly estimated in proportion to $\log \frac{p(d|r)}{p(d|\bar{r})}$, e.g., using the Okapi-BM25 document score [25].

Finally, please note that, since $p(r|D) \overset{def}{=} \frac{p(r|D,q)p(q|D)}{p(q|D,r)}$, we could potentially make this estimator variant even more sensitive to query-related issues.

3.2.2 *Corpus-sensitive estimator.*
To derive a corpus-sensitive variant of the proposed general mean estimator in Eq. 3, we first note that $p(r|d) \overset{def}{=} \frac{p(r|d,C)p(C|d)}{p(C|d,r)}$. Putting this back into Eq. 3, we now obtain a corpus-sensitive mean estimator:

$$p(D|q,r) \overset{def}{=} \frac{1}{|D|} \sum_{d \in D} s(d) \cdot \left[\frac{p(r|d,C)p(C|d)p(d|D,r)p(r|D)}{p(r|q)p(C|d,r)} \right] \quad (5)$$

Here $p(r|d, C)$ denotes the probability that document d is the most relevant document in C (i.e., "most focused"), regardless of a specific query. In Section 5 we suggest one new option of how to estimate this probability. $p(C|d)$ models the relative importance of document d in C, which can be estimated, for example, by measuring the document's centrality in C (e.g., PageRank [19]). Finally, $p(C|d, r)$ further denotes the probability that a relevant document d belongs to corpus C. Since $p(C|d, r) \propto p(d|C, r)$, this term can be potentially estimated in a similar manner to $p(d|D, r)$. In this case, $p(d|C, r)$ will capture the association strength of document d with the (presumably) relevant corpus. Yet, compared to $p(d|D, r)$, in this case, the weaker such association is, the more we shall assume that document d is relevant.

Finally, similar to the query-sensitive case, noting that $p(r|D) \overset{def}{=} \frac{p(r|D,C)p(C|D)}{p(C|D,r)}$, we could potentially make this variant even more sensitive to corpus-related issues.

3.3 Calibrated mean retrieval score estimation

Estimating $p(D|q, r)$ according to either of the three proposed alternatives (i.e., Eq. 3, Eq. 4 or Eq. 5) dictates a generic estimation scheme that adjusts the original retrieval scores $s(d)$ according to several retrieval quality criteria. To better reflect this fact, we now further define the following (generic) calibrated version of the proposed estimators:

$$p(D|q,r) \overset{def}{=} \frac{1}{|D|} \sum_{d \in D} s(d) \cdot \phi_r(d), \quad (6)$$

where $\phi_r(d) \equiv \phi(r|q, C, D, d)$ is a (generic) score **calibration factor** that denotes the overall calibration that is applied on a given document score $s(d)$. The score calibrator $\phi_r(d)$ should basically consider all quality aspects that may affect document d's relevance during its retrieval process. Apart from considering document d's own properties, the properties of the query q, the corpus C and document d's associated result list D should be also considered. Therefore, the original document score $s(d)$ should be adjusted based on the likelihood that, at the end of this process, the "emitted" document d will be relevant. If the observed score $s(d)$ over- or underestimates this likelihood, then $\phi_r(d)$ should rescale $s(d)$ accordingly.

3.3.1 *Score calibration as tradeoff analysis.*
We now make the observation that, the retrieval process of document d evaluated by the calibrator $\phi_r(d)$ is potentially a *multi-criteria decision making process*. Closer examination of the relationship between the three alternative mean estimators we previously derived, demonstrates that, capturing every possible retrieval quality aspect within $\phi_r(d)$ may be very hard, sometimes even impossible. This becomes more evident, for example, by examining the two query-sensitive (Eq. 4) and corpus-sensitive (Eq. 5) estimators, side by side. For example, putting more emphasis on corpus-related aspects would mean that we can put less emphasis on query-related aspects.

In an idle case, the retrieval process (implemented by the underlying retrieval method $\mathcal{M}$) provides the best possible response $D^* \subseteq C$ by considering all possible quality criteria that may govern an effective retrieval. Yet in practice, an effective retrieval process may be governed by several, possibly contradicting, quality aspects that need to be considered in parallel, e.g., relevance, retrievability, diversity, personalization, etc. Hence, not all retrieval quality criteria can be fully satisfied by the underlying method, and therefore, in many cases a **tradeoff** may exist among many of such criteria.

3.3.2 *Discriminative score calibration.*
It becomes more evident that, it is eminently impossible to derive a (single) general generative mean estimator that can consider all possible retrieval quality criteria at once. Using different generative factors for the various retrieval components, will commonly instantiate a mean estimator that may prioritize the retrieval quality criteria in a different way. Every such instantiation further dictates the specific calibration $\phi_r(d)$ scheme that needs to be applied on D's document scores $s(d)$. Trying to overcome this "hurdle", we next describe an alternative way in which $\phi_r(d)$ can be effectively derived.

To this end, instead of calculating $\phi_r(d)$ directly in a generative form, we propose to calculate it in a discriminative fashion. Accordingly, we now associate with each retrieved document $d \in D$ a set of features $F(d) = \{f_1(d), \ldots, f_h(d)\}$. Each feature $f_j(d) \in F(d)$ is assumed to encode some unique aspect of the document's retrieval that might affect its actual relevance. Let $\phi_{r,F}(d)$ further denote this discriminative version of the calibrator. $\phi_{r,F}(d)$ now gets $F(d)$ as an input and outputs the calibration value for $s(d)$. Whenever $|F(d)| = \emptyset$, we get the null calibrator which is simply defined as $\phi_{r,\emptyset}(d) \overset{def}{=} 1$ (meaning we estimate the mean score using only the original document scores $s(d)$).

3.3.3 *$\phi_{r,F}(d)$ implementation.*
Since the calibration problem by itself is a multi-criteria decision problem, we now propose to derive $\phi_{r,F}(d)$ using the *Weighted Product Model* [17] (WPM for short). WPM is a general multi-criteria decision analysis (MCDA) approach that can be used to combine different decision criteria. In our case, each calibration feature $f_j(d) \in F(d)$ defines a single decision criterion. Our goal is, therefore, to find the best criteria combination policy. Based on WPM, such a policy is defined by a set of (nonnegative) real weights, having weight $\alpha_j \geq 0$ ($1 \leq j \leq h$) model the relative importance of feature $f_j(d) \in F(d)$. We note that, the weights do not depend on a specific document, but rather on the feature type.

Overall, the calibrator $\phi_{r,F}(d)$ is implemented by calculating the weighted product of the feature values: $\phi_{r,F}(d) \stackrel{def}{=} \prod_{j=1}^{h} \left(f_j(d)\right)^{\alpha_j}$. Note that, zeroing all weights also results in null (no) calibration.

Finally, "plugging" the defined $\phi_{r,F}(d)$ calibrator back into Eq. 6, we obtain our proposed (general) mean score estimator, hereinafter, termed **WPM** estimator. Later on, in Section 5 we shall propose two instantiations of WPM.

4 DERIVING PREVIOUS PREDICTORS

We next demonstrate that, several previously suggested QPP methods, namely Clarity [7], WIG [32] and SMV [31], can be directly derived as private instantiations of our calibrated-mean score estimation approach. Using this connection in mind, therefore, allows us to obtain and study a preliminary set of calibration features $F(d)$ that can be utilized within our approach.

4.1 Deriving Clarity

The Clarity [7] method estimates query performance proportionally to the divergence between a relevance language model [15] induced from D and that induced from C. Higher divergence is assumed to imply that D is more "focused" [7].

Given D, Clarity's prediction is calculated as follows:

$$p_{Clarity}(D|q,r) \stackrel{def}{=} \sum_w p(w|R) \log \frac{p(w|R)}{p(w|C)}, \qquad (7)$$

where $p(w|R) \stackrel{def}{=} \sum_{d \in D} p(d)p(w|d)p(q|d)$ denotes the likelihood that term w is generated by the relevance model R induced from D [15]. Using again $s(d) \stackrel{def}{=} p(q|d)$ and $p(d) = \frac{1}{|D|}$, we get that:

$$p_{Clarity}(D|q,r) = \frac{1}{|D|} \sum_{d \in D} s(d) \cdot \left[\sum_w p(w|d) \log \frac{p(w|R)}{p(w|C)} \right] \qquad (8)$$

Next, let $p(w|d) \stackrel{def}{=} \frac{c(w,d)}{|d|}$, where $c(w,x)$ denotes term w's occurrence count in text x and $|d| \stackrel{def}{=} \sum_{w \in d} c(w,d)$ is document d's length. We now further obtain:

$$p_{Clarity}(D|q,r) = \frac{1}{|D|} \sum_{d \in D} s(d) \cdot \left[\sum_w \frac{c(w,d)}{|d|} \log \frac{p(w|R)}{p(w|C)} \right] \qquad (9)$$

$$= \frac{1}{|D|} \sum_{d \in D} s(d) \cdot \left[\frac{1}{|d|} \log \frac{\prod_w p(w|R)^{c(w,d)}}{\prod_w p(w|C)^{c(w,d)}} \right]$$

$$\stackrel{def}{=} \frac{1}{|D|} \sum_{d \in D} s(d) \cdot \left[\frac{1}{|d|} \cdot \log \frac{p(d|R)}{p(d|C)} \right].$$

Hence, using the following equal feature weights $\alpha_1 = \alpha_2 = 1$ yields that, Clarity is basically a private case of our calibrated mean score estimator. In Clarity's case, two calibration features are utilized as follows. The first feature, $f_1(d) = \frac{1}{|d|}$ (denoted **invDocLen**), calibrates the document score $s(d)$ by scaling it reversely to

its document length $|d|$. Therefore, such calibration prefers shorter documents to longer ones. The shorter the document is, the higher its chance for being retrieved, regardless of a specific query in mind [2]; whereas, longer documents have a higher chance of being relevant. Therefore, in this case: $f_1(d) \propto \frac{1}{p(r|d)}$.

The second feature, $f_2(d) = \log \frac{p(d|R)}{p(d|C)}$ (denoted **dLogRel**), calibrates $s(d)$ according to the log-likelihood ratio between d's generation from the relevance model induced from D to its generation from the background model induced from C. Therefore, $f_2(d) \propto p(d|D,r)$, and $s(d)$ is calibrated based on d's association strength with D [14], where the later is assumed by Clarity to be relevant [7].

All in all, it becomes apparent that, Clarity's calibration scheme aims at capturing the tradeoff between relevance and retrievability [2]. In Clarity, such tradeoff is implemented by a simple product of a couple of calibration features. As will be shown in our evaluation, a simple extension of Clarity with a weighted calibration scheme for its two identified basic features, leads to a significantly better query performance prediction.

4.2 Deriving WIG

The WIG method [32] estimates query performance according to the difference between the average retrieval score in D and that of C. The larger the difference is, the better query performance is assumed to be [32]. WIG prediction is given as follows:

$$p_{WIG}(D|q,r) = \frac{1}{\sqrt{|q|}} \cdot \frac{1}{|D|} \sum_{d \in D} (s(d) - s(C)), \qquad (10)$$

where $s(C) \approx p(q|C)$ denotes the corpus query likelihood [32]. $s(C)$ can be calculated, for example, by treating the corpus as a single document [32].

Noting that $s(d) - s(C) = s(d) \cdot \left(1 - \frac{s(C)}{s(d)}\right)$, we can rewrite:

$$p_{WIG}(D|q,r) = \frac{1}{|D|} \sum_{d \in D} s(d) \cdot \left[\frac{1}{\sqrt{|q|}} \cdot \left(1 - \frac{s(C)}{s(d)}\right) \right] \qquad (11)$$

Therefore, fixing again $\alpha_1 = \alpha_2 = 1$, we observe that, WIG is also a private case of our proposed estimator. Moreover, similar to Clarity, WIG utilizes two (yet different) calibration features. The first feature $f_1(d) = \frac{1}{\sqrt{|q|}}$ (denoted **invQLen**) is document-independent, which calibrates $s(d)$ reversely to query q's (scaled) length $|q| \stackrel{def}{=} \sum_{w \in q} c(w,q)$. In this case $f_1(d) \propto p(r|q)$, where the longer the query is, the more difficult it may be to answer such a query [11]. In accordance, $f_1(d)$ down-scales $s(d)$ more for longer queries; regardless of the document's identity.

The second feature, $f_2(d) = 1 - \frac{s(C)}{s(d)}$ (denoted **invCd**), is document-dependent and shares resemblance with the second calibration feature of Clarity. In this case $f_2(d) \propto \frac{1}{p(C|d,r)} \propto \frac{1}{p(d|C,r)}$ (see $p(C|d,r)$ derivation in Eq. 5). As we already noted, the probability $p(d|C,r)$ shares the same motivation with the definition of the $p(d|D,r)$ term. Therefore, $f_2(d)$ estimates document d's association strength with the corpus, when the later is assumed to be relevant. The higher such association is, the more difficult it would be to separate it from the corpus, and hence, the document score will be down-scaled. When $s(C) \to 0$, then $f_2(d) \to 1$, which implies that no association is evident between the document and the corpus. Therefore, in this case, $s(d)$ shall remain unaffected.

Similar to Clarity, WIG's performance can be further boosted by tuning the weights of its two calibration features.

4.3 Deriving SMV

Another QPP method that is based on assessing score magnitudes is the SMV method [31], whose prediction can be directly expressed using our approach as follows:

$$p_{SMV}(D|q,r) = \frac{1}{|D|} \sum_{d \in D} s(d) \cdot \left[\frac{1}{|s(C)|} \cdot \left| \ln \frac{s(d)}{\hat{\mu}_D} \right| \right], \quad (12)$$

where $\hat{\mu}_D = \frac{1}{|D|} \sum_{d \in D} s(d)$ denotes D's mean document score.

Similar to the two previous methods, SMV also utilizes two (yet again, different) calibration features (with $\alpha_1 = \alpha_2 = 1$). The first feature is $f_1(d) = \frac{1}{|s(C)|}$ (denoted **invCS**), which is document-independent. Here, $f_1(d)$ inversely rescales the document score according to the corpus's similarity to the query. Hence, in this case $f_1(d) \propto \frac{1}{p(r|q,C)}$. The higher the similarity $s(C)$ is, the more documents in C may be similar to q, and hence, the more difficult it would be to point out that document d is the one relevant to q. Therefore, higher corpus-query similarity will down-scale $s(d)$.

The second feature $f_2(d) = \left| \ln \frac{s(d)}{\hat{\mu}} \right|$ (denoted **invSD**), is document-dependent, which adjusts the document's score $s(d)$ relatively to its absolute "divergence" from the mean score $\hat{\mu}_D$. In this case, the mean score $\hat{\mu}_D$ which represents the score of D's centroid [30] is assumed to capture the uncertainty in whether documents in D are either relevant or not. Hence, $f_2(d) \propto \frac{1}{p(d|D,q)}$, the more $s(d)$ is different from $\hat{\mu}_D$, the less uncertainty is associated with $s(d)$ [30].

Finally, similar to the two previous methods, tuning SMV's two feature weights can further boost its performance.

5 WPM ESTIMATOR INSTANTIATIONS

We now propose two calibration feature sets, used for instantiating the WPM estimator that we derived in Section 3. As the first feature set, we reutilize the six features that we identified and studied in Section 4, namely: **invDocLen**, **dLogRel**, **invQLen**, **invCd**, **invCS** and **invSD**. We now denote the resulting estimator instance as **WPM1**. By learning WPM1's feature weights, we expect to obtain a more accurate estimator.

As a second instantiation, denoted **WPM2**, we utilize an additional set of calibration features to that of WPM1. Our purpose here is not to design or explore many such features, but rather to demonstrate, as a proof of concept, that, with more features, a further improvement may be achieved. We only choose additional features that are **document-level dependent**, which we believe are more interesting to explore in the context of our work. We note again that, various combinations of other feature types (i.e., ones that aim to capture $p(r|D)$, $p(r|C)$ or additional $p(r|q)$ features), were already studied by several previous works [3, 5, 23, 29].

Overall, we use the following four additional features in WPM2. The first feature **dEnt**, borrowed from [22], captures $p(r|d)$ and estimates the document's content diversity according to its induced entropy: $- \sum_{w \in d} p(w|d) \log p(w|d)$. The second feature **dClarity**,

also borrowed from [22], captures $p(d|C,r)$ which estimates the focus of d according to the KL divergence: $\sum_{w \in d} p(w|d) \log \frac{p(w|d)}{p(w|C)}$. The third feature **BM25**, captures $p(r|q,d)$ and is simply calculated as the Okapi-BM25 [25] score of document d given q.

Finally, the last feature **dCFocus**, aims at capturing $p(r|d,C)$, i.e., the probability that document d is the **most focused document in** C. Document d's relative focus is estimated by measuring to what extent d's term saliency "agrees" with C's global term importance. To this end, we now define the normalized inverse document frequency $nidf(w) = \frac{idf(w)}{\sum_{w'} idf(w')}$. **dCFocus** is then calculated as the KL-divergence based similarity: $\exp\left(- \sum_{w \in d} p(w|d) \log \frac{p(w|d)}{nidf(w)} \right)$.

6 EVALUATION

6.1 Datasets

Corpus	#documents	Queries	Disks
AP	242,918	51-150	1-3
TREC4	567,529	201-250	2-3
TREC5	524,929	251-300	2&4
ROBUST	528,155	301-450, 601-700	4&5-{CR}
WT10g	1,692,096	451-550	WT10g
GOV2	25,205,179	701-850	GOV2

Table 1: TREC benchmarks used for experiments.

The TREC corpora and queries used for the evaluation are specified in Table 1. These benchmarks were used by many previous QPP works [4]. Titles of TREC topics were used as queries, except for the TREC4 benchmark, where no titles are available and topic descriptions were used instead. The Apache Lucene[2] open source search library was used for indexing and searching documents. Documents and queries were processed using Lucene's English text analysis (i.e., tokenization, Porter stemming, stopwords, etc.). As the underlying retrieval method $\mathcal{M}$ we used Lucene's Dirichlet-smoothed query-likelihood implementation. Following previous works [14, 23, 28, 30], we fixed the Dirichlet parameter to $\mu = 1000$.

6.2 Baselines

We compared the two instantiations of the WPM estimator, **WPM1** and **WPM2**, with several different baseline methods. As a trivial baseline, we considered D's original mean score (denoted **Mean**(org)). It was simply implemented using the null calibrator $\phi_{r,\emptyset}(d)$.

As a first line of baselines we considered **Clarity** [7], **WIG** [32] and **SMV** [31], whose details were already discussed in Section 4. As we have shown, each of these baselines can be directly derived as a private instance of the WPM estimator employed with two different calibration features whose weights equal to 1. For each method, we further implemented its calibrated (weighted) version which utilized the same pair of features, except for the weights which were treated as free parameters. This resulted in three more corresponding calibrated baselines, which we further refer to as **C-Clarity**, **C-WIG** and **C-SMV**.

---
[2]http://lucene.apache.org

Next, we implemented several competitive baseline methods as follows. The first is the **ImpClarity** [12] method, a variant of Clarity, which given a parameter t, induces a relevance model from D using only those terms w that appear in less than $t\%$ of the documents in C. We also implement **NQC** [30], a method that shares resemblance to **SMV** and is commonly used as a strong baseline that also utilizes retrieval scores. **NQC** predicts query performance according to the standard deviation of (D's documents) retrieval scores $s(d)$. Higher deviation is assumed to testify for lower chance of query drift, hence better performance [30]. Similar to **SMV**, **NQC** further normalizes the standard deviation by the corpus query likelihood $s(C)$. As another common strong baseline, we also implemented the **QF** method [32], which was proposed as an alternative to **WIG** by the same authors of [32]. **QF** predicts query performance according to the overlap between D and another list $D' \subseteq C$, obtained by evaluating a new (weighted) query q' over C. q' is formulated from the top-n terms with the highest contribution to the KL-divergence between the relevance model induced from D and the background (corpus) model. The higher the overlap is (which is simply measured as $|D \cap D'|$), the better the performance is predicted to be [32].

As another (strong) alternative, we also implemented the **UEF** method [28]. **UEF** predicts the query performance of a given result list D based on the combination of two features. The first, is the similarity of D with its re-ranked version π_D (measured using Pearson's-ρ correlation between scores [28]). π_D is obtained by scoring documents in D according to a relevance model (RM1) induced from $D^{[m]} \subseteq D$ - the top-m scored documents in D. Higher similarity is assumed to result in a better performance [28]. The second feature is the estimated performance of $D^{[m]}$ itself. For this estimation, any baseline QPP method can be applied on $D^{[m]}$ [28]. The final prediction is obtained by multiplying both feature values [28]. We employed **UEF** with Clarity, WIG and SMV as its baseline methods and obtained three corresponding UEF variants: **UEF[Clarity]**, **UEF[WIG]** and **UEF[SMV]**.

Finally, we further implemented the **LTRoq** method [23], a predictor inspired by the Markov Random Field (MRF) model. **LTRoq** combines several list-level post-retrieval QPP features (e.g., Clarity, WIG, NQC, UEF, etc) with several pre-retrieval features [23] (e.g., various variants of SCQ, VAR, and IDF [11]). **LTRoq** learns to combine the various QPP features using SVM^{rank} [23]. Therefore, we consider **LTRoq** as a very strong baseline.

6.3 Setup

We predicted the performance of each query based on its top-1000 retrieved documents [4]. Following the common practice [4], we assessed prediction over queries quality according to the correlation between the predictor's values and the actual average precision (AP@1000) values calculated using TREC's relevance judgments. To this end, we report the Pearson's-ρ (P-ρ) and Kendall's-τ (K-τ) correlations which are the most common measures [4].

Most of the methods that we evaluated (including WPM variants) required to tune some free parameters. Common to all methods is the free parameter $k \stackrel{def}{=} |D|$, which is the number of top scored documents (out of a total of 1000 retrieved documents) **to**

be used for the prediction. To this end, for each method we selected $k \in \{5, 10, 20, 50, 100, 150, 200, 500, 1000\}$.

Next, some of the methods we evaluated required additional parameters to tune. For example, **Clarity**, **ImpClarity**, **QF** and **UEF** variants all utilize a relevance model (RM1) that is induced from D. For the first two, we used all documents in D [7, 12], while for **QF** and **UEF** variants we only used the top-m scored docs in D [28, 32] (i.e., $D^{[m]}$), with $m \in \{1, 3, 5, \dots, |D|\}$. Following the common practice [7, 12, 28, 32], in all these methods, we further clipped the induced relevance model at the top-n terms cutoff, with $n \in \{5, 10, 20, 50, 100, 150, 200\}$. For **ImpClarity**, its term selection parameter t was further selected as follows: $t \in \{1, 2, 3, 5, 10\}$.

To implement **LTRoq**, we used the same set of post-retrieval and pre-retrieval features[3] that was used in [23]. For training **LTRoq**, we further closely followed [23]'s two-phase learning approach[4].

To have a direct way of measuring the impact of feature calibration (weighing) in our WPM variants (i.e., **C-Clarity**, **C-WIG**, **C-SMV**, **WPM1** and **WPM2**), we fixed the $\langle k, n \rangle$ parameters to the same configuration that was initially learned for the non-calibrated baselines (i.e., **Clarity**, **WIG** and **SMV**). For the **dEnt**, **dClarity** and **dCFocus** features utilized by WPM2, we further tuned the number of top-l terms in d (i.e., term cutoff according to $p(w|d)$) that should be considered for each feature calculation, with $l \in \{5, 10, 20, 50, 100\}$. For the **BM25** feature we used its common parameters $k1 = 1.2, b = 0.75$ [25]. We further smoothed each feature used by the WPM variants as follows $f_j(d; \epsilon) \stackrel{def}{=} \max(f_j(d), \epsilon)$, where $\epsilon = 10^{-10}$ is a hyperparameter.

To learn the calibration feature weights of the WPM variants, we used a Coordinate Ascent approach [16]. To this end, we selected the feature weights $\{\alpha_j\}_{j=1}^{h}$ in the grid $[0, 5]^h$, assuming there are $h \in \{2, 6, 10\}$ such different features, depending on the WPM variant (with a step size of 0.1 within each dimension).

Training and testing of all methods was performed similarly to previous works [23, 29, 30] using an holdout (2-fold cross validation) approach. Accordingly, on each benchmark, we generated 30 random splits of the query set; each split had two folds. The first fold was used as the (query) train set, where parameters were tuned to maximize P-ρ. The second fold was kept untouched for testing. We recorded the average prediction quality (i.e., P-ρ and K-τ) over the 30 splits. Finally, we measured statistical significant differences of prediction quality using a two-tailed paired t-test with $p < 0.05$ computed over all 30 splits (with a Bonferroni correction whenever more than two methods were compared).

6.4 Results

6.4.1 Impact of score calibration. Table 2 depicts the results of the comparison of each non-calibrated version of **Clarity**, **WIG** and **SMV** (i.e., all weights α_j are set to the value of 1) with its corresponding calibrated (weighted) version, i.e., **C-Clarity**, **C-WIG** and **C-SMV**. For each calibrated version we also report the relative improvement in prediction quality over its corresponding non-calibrated version.

---

[3]The full set of features is described in Section 3.5.1 in [23].

[4]Due to space considerations, we cannot describe in details this learning approach. The reader is kindly encouraged to refer to Section 4.1.1 in [23] for more details.

	AP		TREC4		TREC5		Robust		WT10g		GOV2	
Method	$P-\rho$	$K-\tau$	$P-\rho$	$K-\tau$	$P-\rho$	$K-\tau$	$P-\rho$	$K-\tau$	$P-\rho$	$K-\tau$	$P-\rho$	$K-\tau$
Mean(org)	.383	.326	.356	.340	.215	.152	.314	.290	.375	.290	.411	.297
Clarity	.596	.428	.456	.380	.490	.258	.477	.328	.380	.240	.407	.305
C-Clarity	.626* (+5.0%)	.447* (+4.4%)	.537* (+17.8%)	.392 (+3.3%)	.492 (+0.4%)	.271 (+5.0%)	.532* (+11.5%)	.370* (+12.8%)	.456* (+20%)	.313* (+30.4%)	.435* (+6.9%)	.323* (+5.9%)
WIG	.526	.380	.533	.502	.347	.252	.411	.358	.434	.364	.535	.387
C-WIG	.672* (+27.8%)	.400* (+5.3%)	.561* (+5.2%)	.535* (+6.5%)	.375* (+8.1%)	.278* (+10.3%)	.551* (+34.1%)	.383* (+7.0%)	.454* (+4.6%)	.374* (+2.74%)	.550* (+2.8%)	.391* (+1.0%)
SMV	.631	.398	.524	.499	.459	.268	.586	.432	.292	.206	.418	.304
C-SMV	.668* (+5.9%)	.450* (+13.1%)	.572* (+9.2%)	.541* (+8.4%)	.483* (+5.3%)	.283* (+4.4%)	.601* (+2.6%)	.433 (+0.2%)	.432* (+47.9%)	.330* (+60.2%)	.589* (+40.9%)	.423* (+39.1%)

Table 2: Comparison between each non-calibrated baseline method and its corresponding calibrated version. Percentages reported in parentheses "()" represent the relative change in quality of each calibrated version over its corresponding non-calibrated version. The superscript * further denotes a statistically significant difference between the two ($p < 0.05$).

	AP		TREC4		TREC5		Robust		WT10g		GOV2	
Method	$P-\rho$	$K-\tau$	$P-\rho$	$K-\tau$	$P-\rho$	$K-\tau$	$P-\rho$	$K-\tau$	$P-\rho$	$K-\tau$	$P-\rho$	$K-\tau$
ImpClarity	.582	.418	.502	.389	.501	.291	.514	.354	.422	.272	.520	.359
NQC	.554	.361	.624	.562	.483	.318	.575	.406	.486	.354	.432	.304
QF	.575	.385	.632	.570	.413	.378	.483	.371	.436	.343	.515	.383
UEF[Clarity]	.620	.435	.618	.532	.554	.327	.560	.387	.483	.360	.427	.307
UEF[WIG]	.574	.389	.625	.542	.507	.308	.542	.384	.450	.371	.527	.361
UEF[SMV]	.652	.427	.568	.527	.537	.317	.594	.430	.358	.229	.571	.389
LTRoq	.684	.506	.653	.588	.566	.345	.570	.391	.367	.312	.582	.410
WPM1	$.730^c_b$ (+8.6%) [+6.7%]	$.539^c_b$ (+19.8%) [+6.5%]	$.682^c_b$ (+19.2%) [+4.4%]	$.600^c$ (+10.9%) [+2.0%]	$.702^c_b$ (+42.7%) [+24.0%]	$.386^c$ (+37.0%) [+2.1%]	$.628^c_b$ (+4.5%) [+5.7%]	$.464^c$ (+7.2%) [+7.9%]	$.497^c$ (+9.0%) [+2.3%]	$.378$ (+1.1%) [+1.9%]	$.634^c_b$ (+7.6%) [+8.9%]	$.462^c_b$ (+9.2%) [+12.7%]
WPM2	$.738^c_b$ (+9.8%) [+7.9%]	$.553^c_b$ (+22.9%) [+9.3%]	$.702^c_b$ (+22.7%) [+7.5%]	$.613^c_b$ (+13.3%) [+4.2%]	$.738^c_b$ (+50.0%) [+30.4%]	$.412^c$ (+45.6%) [+3.0%]	$.640^c_b$ (+6.5%) [+7.7%]	$.495^c_b$ (+14.3%) [+15.1%]	$.540^c_b$ (+18.4%) [+11.1%]	$.433^c_b$ (+15.8%) [+16.7%]	$.655^c_b$ (+11.2%) [+12.5%]	$.478^c_b$ (+13.0%) [+16.6%]

Table 3: Comparison between WPM1 and WPM2 and the alternative baseline methods. Percentages reported in parentheses "()" represent the relative change in quality of each WPM instance over the best calibrated baseline (i.e., either C-Clarity, C-WIG or C-SMV). Percentages reported in brackets "[]" further represent the relative change in quality of each WPM instance over the best alternative baseline. The superscript c and subscript b further denote a statistically significant difference of WPM1/WPM2 with the calibrated and alternative baselines, respectively (Bonferroni corrected for $p < 0.05$).

Overall, calibrating all three methods by tuning the two calibration feature weights of each method resulted in an enhanced prediction quality. The average improvement, regardless of specific correlation measure, was 10.3(±2.5)%, 9.5(±3.0)% and 19.7(±6.0)% for C-Clarity, C-WIG and C-SMV, respectively. This attests the merits of using calibration within these methods. By better tuning their identified calibration features, tradeoffs that exist within the core design of these methods could be better handled.

Table 3 further reports the prediction quality of all other baselines we implemented (including WPM1 and WPM2). A comparison of C-Clarity, C-WIG, and C-SMV with ImpClarity, NQC, QF and the UEF variants, reveals that, each one of the three calibrated versions, in at least 50% of the usecases, resulted in a better prediction quality than that of its potential alternative (i.e., C-Clarity vs. ImpClarity and UEF[Clarity]; C-WIG vs. QF and UEF[WIG]; C-SMV vs. NQC and UEF[SMV]). This is yet another empirical testimony to the potential of calibration. We next investigate this potential more closely.

6.4.2 WPM vs. alternative baselines. We now compare WPM1 and WPM2 (whose details were described in Section 5) with all the other baselines. To recall, WPM1 uses the super-set of calibration features (six in total) of the calibrated baseline methods C-Clarity, C-WIG and C-SMV. WPM2 further uses 4 additional features. For WPM1 and WPM2 we also report the relative improvement over the best calibrated baseline (i.e., out of C-Clarity, C-WIG and C-SMV) and the relative improvement over the best alternative baseline in Table 3 (excluding WPM1 and WPM2).

First, comparing WPM1 side-by-side with the three calibrated baselines, shows a significant boost in prediction quality over these methods (an average improvement of 15.0(±4.0)% regardless of the correlation measure). This is yet another empirical proof that, considering more tradeoffs that govern an effective retrieval of a given document, results in an enhanced prediction quality. This is further supported by examining WPM2 side-by-side with WPM1. WPM2's additional calibration features provide further improvement (an average additional improvement of 3.8(±1.1)% regardless

AP	TREC4	TREC5	Robust	WT10g	GOV2
dLogRel	invSD	invCd	invCS	dEnt	dEnt
invCS	invCS	invSD	invSD	dLogRel	invCd
invSD	dCFocus	invDLen	invDLen	BM25	invCS
BM25	invDLen	dLogRel	dLogRel	dCFocus	invQLen
invCd	invCd	invCS	BM25	invCd	dClarity

Table 4: The top-5 calibration features with the highest contribution to WPM2's prediction quality.

of the correlation measure). This actually comes with no surprise, as **WPM2** considers even more retrieval effectiveness tradeoffs that may govern an effective document retrieval.

We next compare **WPM1** and **WPM2** with the other baselines in Table 3. As can be observed, both WPM instances **completely outperformed all other baselines** (significantly in most cases). The average improvement over the **best alternative baseline** was 7.8(±1.9)% for **WPM1** and 13.0(±1.9)% for **WPM2**, regardless of the correlation measure. Quite notable is the significant difference with the **LTRoq** method, one of the strongest baselines in the QPP literature to date that also utilizes supervised learning. We attribute this difference to the fact that WPM learns to combine document-level features for QPP; this in comparison to **LTRoq**, which similarly to previous supervised approaches [3, 5], uses only list-level post-retrieval and pre-retrieval features [23].

6.4.3 Calibration feature analysis. Table 4 reports the top-5 calibration features with the highest contribution to **WPM2**'s prediction quality[5]. Among these features, both **invCS** and **invCd** are the most notable (appearing in 5 out of the 6 top-5 lists). This suggests that, corpus-sensitivity should play a major role in the design of retrieval score calibrators.

The next significant features are **invSD** and **dLogRel** (appearing in 4 out of the 6 top-5 lists). This suggests that, the next line of calibration features that should get closer attention are those that consider the association of a given document d with its containing result list D. A score of a document that is associated with an effective list (captured by **dLogRel**) should be trusted more than one that is associated with an ineffective list (captured by **invSD**). Another feature that "stands out" in Table 4 is **BM25**. Such feature importance implies that, rather than using only document scores that were obtained from a single retrieval method, it would be better to use also document scores that were obtained from another (preferably indepedent) retrieval method. Indeed, some of previously suggested QPP methods share a similar motivation [1].

Finally, another notable feature is **dEnt**, which appears to be (very) important in Web corpora. This strongly supports the merits of considering content diversification aspects in the design of QPP methods for Web corpora [18].

7 CONCLUSIONS

Our empirical evaluation has served as a solid evidence on the effectiveness of our proposed discriminative calibrated mean estimator. By re-designing several of previously suggested QPP methods according to our approach, we were able to significantly improve

their prediction quality. We also demonstrated the merits of using additional and diverse calibration features within our approach, which resulted in a prediction quality which outperformed that of several strong alternative baselines.

REFERENCES

[1] Javed A. Aslam and Virgil Pavlu. Query hardness estimation using jensen-shannon divergence among multiple scoring functions. In *Proceedings of ECIR'07*.
[2] Leif Azzopardi and Vishwa Vinay. Retrievability: An evaluation measure for higher order information access tasks. In *Proceedings of CIKM '08*.
[3] Niranjan Balasubramanian, Giridhar Kumaran, and Vitor R. Carvalho. Predicting query performance on the web. In *Proceedings of SIGIR '10*.
[4] David Carmel and Oren Kurland. Query performance prediction for ir. In *Proceedings of SIGIR '12*.
[5] Kevyn Collins-Thompson and Paul N. Bennett. Predicting query performance via classification. In *Proceedings of ECIR'2010*.
[6] William S. Cooper, Fredric C. Gey, and Daniel P. Dabney. Probabilistic retrieval based on staged logistic regression. In *Proceedings of SIGIR '92*.
[7] Steve Cronen-Townsend, Yun Zhou, and W. Bruce Croft. Predicting query performance. In *Proceedings of SIGIR '02*.
[8] Ronan Cummins. Document score distribution models for query performance inference and prediction. *ACM Trans. Inf. Syst.*, 32(1):2:1–2:28, January 2014.
[9] Ronan Cummins, Joemon Jose, and Colm O'Riordan. Improved query performance prediction using standard deviation. In *Proceedings of SIGIR '11*.
[10] Keshi Dai. *Modeling Score Distributions for Information Retrieval.* PhD thesis, Boston, MA, USA, 2012. AAI3542649.
[11] Claudia Hauff, Djoerd Hiemstra, and Franciska de Jong. A survey of pre-retrieval query performance predictors. In *Proceedings of CIKM '08*.
[12] Claudia Hauff, Vanessa Murdock, and Ricardo Baeza-Yates. Improved query difficulty prediction for the web. In *Proceedings of CIKM '08*.
[13] Evangelos Kanoulas, Virgil Pavlu, Keshi Dai, and Javed A Aslam. Modeling the score distributions of relevant and non-relevant documents. In *Conference on the Theory of Information Retrieval*, pages 152–163. Springer, 2009.
[14] Oren Kurland, Anna Shtok, Shay Hummel, Fiana Raiber, David Carmel, and Ofri Rom. Back to the roots: A probabilistic framework for query-performance prediction. In *Proceedings of CIKM '12*.
[15] Victor Lavrenko and W. Bruce Croft. Relevance based language models. In *Proceedings of SIGIR '01*.
[16] Donald Metzler and W. Bruce Croft. Linear feature-based models for information retrieval. *Inf. Retr.*, 10(3):257–274, June 2007.
[17] David William Miller et al. Executive decisions and operations research. 1963.
[18] A. M. Ozdemiray and Ismail S. Altingovde. Query performance prediction for aspect weighting in search result diversification. In *Proceedings of CIKM '14*.
[19] Lawrence Page, Sergey Brin, Rajeev Motwani, and Terry Winograd. The pagerank citation ranking: Bringing order to the web, 1999.
[20] Joaquín Pérez-Iglesias and Lourdes Araujo. Standard deviation as a query hardness estimator. In *Proceedings of SPIRE'10*.
[21] Jay M. Ponte and W. Bruce Croft. A language modeling approach to information retrieval. In *Proceedings of SIGIR '98*.
[22] Fiana Raiber and Oren Kurland. On identifying representative relevant documents. In *Proceedings of CIKM '10*.
[23] Fiana Raiber and Oren Kurland. Query-performance prediction: Setting the expectations straight. In *Proceedings of SIGIR '14*.
[24] Fiana Raiber and Oren Kurland. Using document-quality measures to predict web-search effectiveness. In *Proceedings of ECIR'13*.
[25] Stephen Robertson and Hugo Zaragoza. The probabilistic relevance framework: Bm25 and beyond. *Found. Trends Inf. Retr.*, 3(4):333–389, April 2009.
[26] Haggai Roitman. An enhanced approach to query performance prediction using reference lists. In *Proceedings of SIGIR '17*.
[27] Haggai Roitman, Shai Erera, and Bar Weiner. Robust standard deviation estimation for query performance prediction. In *Proceedings of ICTIR '17*.
[28] Anna Shtok, Oren Kurland, and David Carmel. Using statistical decision theory and relevance models for query-performance prediction. In *Proceedings of SIGIR '10*.
[29] Anna Shtok, Oren Kurland, and David Carmel. Query performance prediction using reference lists. *ACM Trans. Inf. Syst.*, 34(4):19:1–19:34, June 2016.
[30] Anna Shtok, Oren Kurland, David Carmel, Fiana Raiber, and Gad Markovits. Predicting query performance by query-drift estimation. *ACM Trans. Inf. Syst.*, 30(2):11:1–11:35, May 2012.
[31] Yongquan Tao and Shengli Wu. Query performance prediction by considering score magnitude and variance together. In *Proceedings of CIKM '14*.
[32] Yun Zhou and W. Bruce Croft. Query performance prediction in web search environments. In *Proceedings of SIGIR '07*.

---

[5]Features are ordered according to their relative contribution and were selected using a sequential forward selection approach.

Can Short Queries Be Even Shorter?

Peilin Yang, Hui Fang
{franklyn,hfang}@udel.edu
Department of Electrical and Computer Engineering
University of Delaware

ABSTRACT

It is well known that query formulation could affect retrieval performance. Empirical observations suggested that a query may contain extraneous terms that could harm the retrieval effectiveness. This is true for both verbose and title queries. Given a query, it is possible that using its subqueries can generate more satisfying search results than using the original query. Although previous studies proposed method to reduce verbose queries, it remains unclear how we could reduce title queries given the short length of the title queries. In this paper, we focus on identifying the best performed subqueries for a given query. In particular, we formulate this problem as a ranking problem, where the goal is to rank subqueries of the query based on its predicted retrieval performance. To tackle this problem, we propose a set of novel post-retrieval features that can better capture relationships among query terms, and apply a learning-to-rank algorithm based on these features. Empirical results over TREC collections show that these new features are indeed useful in identifying the best subqueries.

CCS CONCEPTS

•**Information systems** →**Query representation; Query reformulation;**

ACM Reference format:
Peilin Yang, Hui Fang. 2017. Can Short Queries Be Even Shorter?. In *Proceedings of ICTIR'17, October 1–4, 2017, Amsterdam, The Netherlands, ,* 8 pages.
DOI: https://doi.org/10.1145/3121050.3121056

1 INTRODUCTION

The retrieval performance is closely related to the quality of a query. Not all terms in a query are equally important. Given a query, it is possible that its *subqueries*, i.e., the ones generated by removing terms from the query, can lead to better search results.

The problem of query reduction has been studied intensively for *verbose queries* (usually long, more than 6 terms, e.g., queries that are formulated based on the description of TREC topics) [1, 8, 13]. Previous studies showed that although a subquery does not always perform as well as the original query, the best subquery could be much better – 23% improvement in terms of MAP for verbose

queries [1, 13]. However, reducing *keyword queries* (usually short, 2-6 terms in total, e.g. queries that are formulated based on the title of TREC topics) has drawn less attention than its counterpart. Previous study [8] showed that *title queries can also be reduced to obtain better performances* on ClueWeb collection. We made similar observations based on the results on other TREC collections too. Table 1 compares the performance when using the original keyword queries with those using the best performed subqueries. Although the table only contains the queries with length 3, it can be seen that the performance of using the best subqueries has more than 10% of gain in terms of the effectiveness. It is clear that *reducing keyword queries could lead to better performance*, but the problem is how to identify the best-performed subquery for a given query when we do not have any information about the relevance judgments.

Reducing keyword queries is a challenging task. Given a keyword query is already very short, how can we ever remove terms from that? One simplest solution would be to remove the terms based on their IDF values. Unfortunately, it does not work well. Let us consider query "pheromone scents work" (from WT10G). Among all the query terms, "work" has the lowest IDF. However, removing "work" from the query would not achieve our goal since the best-performed subquery for this query is "pheromone work". Similarly, other features, such as mutual information and clarity score [13] are not as useful as what they are supposed to be (more details in Section 3).

In this paper, we focus on the problem of identifying best-performed subquery for a given keyword query. In particular, we formulate the problem as ranking all the subqueries of a keyword query based on their predicted performance. To tackle this problem, we propose a set of novel features that can better capture the relations among query terms, and then apply a learning-to-rank algorithm to rank the subqueries based on these new features as well as some existing ones.

All the proposed new features are post-retrieval ones, meaning that they are computed based on the retrieval results. These features are designed to capture different relationships among query terms from different aspects: query term proximity, the aggregated ranking scores of query terms, and the compactness and position of term tensors. Specifically, *term proximity based features* are designed to capture the intuition that some query terms should be viewed as phrases as opposed to individual terms. Let us consider query "family leave law". Its best subquery is "family leave", which is a law code. And only when the two terms occur next to each other and in the right order in a document, we are sure that the document is relevant. To capture this intuition, we propose to compute the statistics of the ranking scores that are computed based on term dependency model [14] for each subquery. We also leverage the correlations between these ranking scores with the ranking scores of the original query for this category of features. Furthermore, we

Table 1: Comparison of the MAP between using original queries and optimal subqueries. Only queries of length 3 are shown and the ranking function is BM25

Collection	Original	Upper Bound	Diff.
Disk12	0.2597	0.2880	+10.9%
Disk45	0.2399	0.2772	+15.5%
AQUAINT	0.2107	0.2426	+15.1%
WT2G	0.3285	0.3580	+9.0%
WT10G	0.1720	0.2051	+19.2%
GOV2	0.3060	0.3221	+5.3%

proposed another set of *term score based* features that are designed to measure the balance between TF and IDF weighting [7]. These features are computed based on different ways of aggregating the term scores of individual query terms. The assumption is that these statistics could capture the key properties of the best subquery at the term score level and thus are useful. Finally, we proposed a set of features based on the *compactness and positions of the term score tensors*. For this set of features, we investigate the spatial properties of the term scores. We view the term scores from top ranked documents as tensors in the multi-dimensional space and then compute the compactness and the position of the tensors cluster.

Empirical results show that the proposed new features are effective in identifying the best-performed subquery. Moreover, we intensively analyze the important features by comparing the performance difference between the subset of features and all features. The results validate the utility of the proposed new features.

2 IDENTIFYING BEST SUBQUERY

We now discuss how to identify the best-performed subquery for a given keyword query.

2.1 Problem Formulation

Given a query, it is possible that some of the terms in the query are not informative and including them in the query could harm the performance. Thus, the goal of best-performed subquery identification is to identify the best query representation by using the terms in the original query. The solution could be the original query or part of the original query.

The best-performed subquery identification problem can be formally defined as follows. Given an arbitrary query $Q = \{t_1, t_2, ..., t_{|QL|}\}$ where t_i is the ith term in Q and $|QL|$ is the length (number of terms) of the query, let P^Q denote the power set of Q, which includes all possible subqueries of Q. Let f be a retrieval function used for ranking the documents in the collection for any query in P. Let $m(P, f)$ denote a metric for the ranking effectiveness of retrieval function f using query P. The best-performed subquery identification problem aims at finding a subquery $P^* = \arg\max_{P \in PQ} m(P, f)$.

We formulate the best-performed subquery identification problem as a subqueries ranking problem. The ranking is based on the *predicted* performance of the subqueries without prior knowledge of relevance. More specifically, given a query, we will generate all the subqueries and rank the subqueries based on their predicted retrieval performance. We leverage existing learning-to-rank algorithm such as LambdaMART [3] and focus on feature identification in our study.

Table 2: Notations and Explanations

Notations	Explanations
$Q = \{t_1, t_2, ..., t_{|QL|}\}$	The original query and its terms
$|QL|$	Query length
$P^Q = \{q_1, q_2, ..., q_i, ...\}$	The power set of Q which contains all subqueries
q	The general notation for any subquery including the original query.
c	Ranking list cutoff position
d_i	Document i in the ranking list
$ds_{q,i}$	Ranking score of document i for query q
$L_{q,c}(f) = \{d_1, ..., d_c\}$	Ranking list of q using model f cutoff at c.
$SL_{q,c}(f) = \{ds_{q,1}, ..., ds_{q,c}\}$	Ranking scores in $L_{q,c}(f)$.
$\vec{t_{q,d_i}}(f) = \{f_{t_1,d_i}, ..., f_{t_n,d_i}\}$	Terms scores of d_i for query q computed by model f. $n = |QL|$.
$TL_{t_i,c}(f) = \{f_{t_i,d_1}, ..., f_{t_i,d_c}\}^T$	Column term scores for t_i.
$ML_{q,c}(f) = \{\vec{t_{q,d_1}}(f), ..., \vec{t_{q,d_c}}(f)\}$	Terms scores matrix of $L_{q,c}(f)$.
$g(\vec{x}), h(\vec{x}) \in \Re$	Feature function. One of **MIN**, **MAX**, **MAX-MIN** (difference), **MAX/MIN** (division), **SUM**, **MEAN**, **STD** (standard deviation), **GMEAN** (geometric mean)

2.2 Subquery Ranking Features

2.2.1 Terms Relationship Features. We introduce the newly proposed features that can better capture the relations among query terms – the motivation behind them as well as the detailed steps to compute them. These features are designed to capture different relationships among query terms from different aspects: query term proximity, the aggregated ranking scores of query terms, and the compactness and position of term tensors. The above mentioned features are *post-retrieval features* where we explore the scores in the ranking list of the subquery and generate the features from that. The variables and the notations that will be used in the following sections are summarized in Table 2.

Term Proximity Based Features (PXM) When identifying useful subqueries, it is important to consider the relations among terms in the subqueries. One of the important term relations is phrases. Intuitively, a subquery containing a phrase makes more sense than the combination of a few random terms. Let us consider an example query "family leave law". It is clear that its subquery "family leave" and "family law" are better choices than "leave law".

To distinguish subqueries with phrases from those without, we proposed to utilize the statistics of the ranking results when using the term dependency model [14]. When ranking documents using dependency model, the documents that have exact or close matching with the subquery will be favored. Thus, when a subquery is a phrase, the scores of the top-ranked results could have larger variance since some documents have the exact matching while others do not. On the contrary, when a subquery is not a phrase, the score variance is often small since few documents would have the exact matching. Clearly, we should use the statistics of ranking results based on the term dependency model as features for the

subquery ranking. More specifically, we first rank the documents in the collection using one of the following term proximity models: unordered window model (UW), ordered window model (OW) and the combination of the two models (UWOW). The window parameter (i.e. terms must appear with at most how many terms between each) wd is set to $4 \cdot (|QL| - 1)$. For example, a sample query of UWOW using Indri query language is
#combine(#uw4(family leave) #ow4(family leave)).
After getting the results, we extract high level statistics from the document scores at cutoff c as the features by applying the feature functions $h(\vec{x})$ to the scores. The feature function h is defined in Table 2 and it consists of a set of statistical functions that can be applied to a vector of values such as summation and standard deviation. The use of feature function was shown to be beneficial in order of aggregating the raw values in the previous studies [2, 5]. Formally, the features can be computed as follows:

$$PXM(w)_h = h(\vec{SL_{q,c}}(w)) \qquad (1)$$

where $w \in UW, OW, UWOW$ and $\vec{SL_{q,c}}(w)$ is the documents scores vector of the term proximity model.

Another way to identify the phrase-based subquery is to examine how similar the search results are when using the term dependency model and when using the basic retrieval models. By comparing the the scores in the two ranking lists we might have more insights about the subqueries. Presumably, if a specific subquery performs much better than the original query because of the subquery is the key phrase in the original query, the scores of the two ranking lists should be different from each other. Take our previous subquery "family leave" for example, our method assumes that this subquery (actually the term proximity model) should have different ranking scores from the original query "family leave law" ranking scores and we are expected to capture such feature. Based on the above reasoning we measure the correlation between the documents scores of the term proximity model of the subquery and the regular ranking scores of the original query Q using Kendall's Tau (τ_B) and Pearson's r as two additional features. Formally, the correlation-based PXM features can be computed as:

$$PXM(w)_{corr} = Corr(\vec{SL_{Q,c}}(w), \vec{SL_{q_i,c}}(w)) \qquad (2)$$

where $Corr \in \{\tau_B, \rho\}$.

Term Score Based Features (TS)

For this set of features, we continue to explore the ranking list of the subqueries – the scores of individual query terms instead of the score of the document. The intuition of TS is originated from the term frequency constraint and the term discrimination constraint from previous work [7]. The constraint essentially introduces the balance between document term frequency (TF) and inverted document frequency (IDF). This really inspires us that there should be some interesting properties in the term score of top ranked documents. Instead of separately considering the TF and IDF, we choose to directly look at the individual term score computed by any ranking function that has reasonable TF and IDF components (e.g. BM25) for two reasons: (1) the ranking list is determined by the scores computed by the ranking function, and (2) the ranking function has the TF and IDF components and thus it already naturally adopts the TF-IDF constraint [7]. We wonder, for

Figure 1: Individual term scores. Term scores are computed using BM25 model. Colors of the dots are the probability of relevant document at that point. Axis labels show the IDF values computed by $\log \frac{N}{df}$.

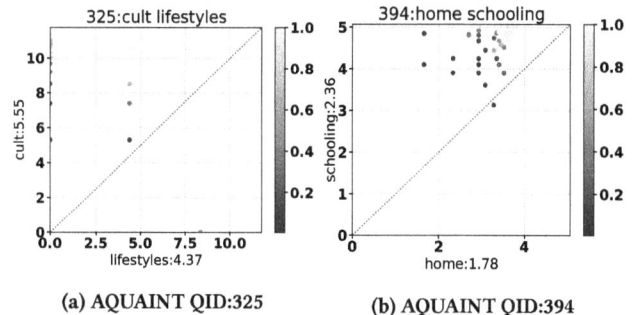

(a) AQUAINT QID:325 **(b) AQUAINT QID:394**

instance, do the top ranked documents have more balanced term scores or do they have highly skewed term scores? Or is the performance of subquery related to the minimum of the term scores in the top ranked documents? Figure 1 illustrates the intuition: the two subfigures are the term scores computed by BM25 model for the two queries for TREC keyword topics. From the figures we find two distinct patterns: for query "cult lifestyle" its relevant documents have higher probability along the y-axis indicating that "cult" is more important than "lifestyle" for this query. But for query "home schooling" the term scores are more balanced.

The TS features are then computed as follows: we first generate the ranking list $\vec{L_{q,c}}(f)$ for subquery q using any ranking function that has reasonable TF and TD components. For each document d_i in $\vec{L_{q,c}}(f)$, we compute the score for each individual term. This would generate the term scores vector $\vec{t_{q,d_i}}(f)$ for d_i. We then apply the feature function h to $\vec{t_{q,d_i}}(f)$ to get the aggregated statistics for d_i as $h(\vec{t_{q,d_i}}(f))$. The result of this step is a list of statistics with each element corresponding to one document. We then apply the feature function g again to each column of the previously generated list $h(\vec{t_{q,d_i}}(f))$ to generate the final TS features. Formally, TS is computed as:

$$TS(f, h, g) = g(h(\vec{t_{q,d_i}}(f))) \qquad (3)$$

For example, $TS(BM25, MEAN, STD)$ for query "home schooling" first rank the documents in the collection using BM25 function and then we compute the terms scores for "home" and "schooling" for each document in the ranking list again using BM25 function. The average value of terms scores for each document in the ranking list is then calculated and this results in a list of average values. Finally the standard deviation of the average values is computed and the value is served as the feature.

Compactness and Positions of Term Score Tensors (TCP)

Using document scores in the ranking list as query prediction features has been proposed in the previous studies [17]. In their work, the feature Normalized Query Commitment (NQC), which is essentially defined as the standard deviation of document scores in the ranking list, was used as a post-retrieval feature to predict the query performance. Larger deviation values were correlated with potentially lower query drift, and thus indicating the better

45

Figure 3: Terms scores (computed by BM25) of the top 50 ranked documents in the list. The numbers in the titles are the Average Precision of the corresponding subquery. Green dots are relevant documents and red dots are non-relevant documents. For each query only the optimal subquery and the original query are shown.

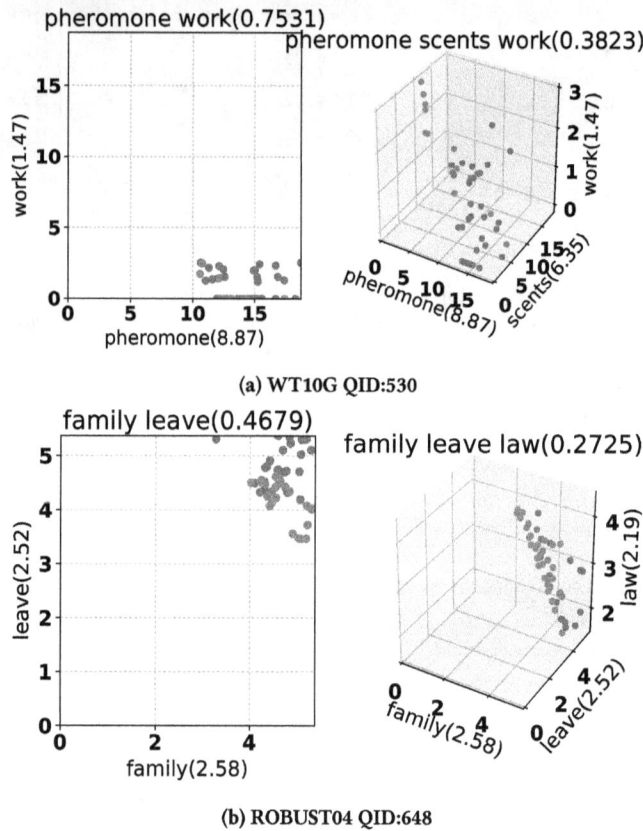

(a) WT10G QID:530

(b) ROBUST04 QID:648

effectiveness [17]. We also find the deviation and other statistics of ranking scores are indeed useful. However, we focus on the term level scores instead of document level scores.

Figure 3 shows two example queries from WT10G and RO-BUST04 respectively. The x-axis and y-axis are the term scores computed by BM25 model and only the top 50 ranked documents are included in the figures. For both queries, the best subqueries are the queries with fewer query terms, i.e. not the original query. We find the similarity and difference for the chosen queries. First, it can be seen that for both best subqueries the term scores from top ranked documents are more compactly clustered. Second, the two queries are different in the sense that the term scores clusters are located at the different position in the two dimensional space. Such difference indicates that for the best subquery the ranking model has its own preference among query terms. For WT10G-530 "pheromone" receives much higher score. But for ROBUST04-648 both query terms receive similar scores. We name this category of features as compactness and positions of term score tensors since we intensively compute the all kinds of distances in the multi-dimensional term space and the term scores from the documents

are essentially N dimensional vectors. We formally define three types of features in this category as follows:

- Tensor Compactness (**TCP(TC)**): The average and the standard deviation of the distances for the tensors to their centroid. This feature captures the compactness of the tensors cluster.

$$TCP(TC)_\mu = \frac{\sum_{d \in L_{q,c}(f)} \|t_{q,\vec{d_i}}(f), t_{q,\vec{d_\mu}}(f)\|}{c} \quad (4)$$

$$TCP(TC)_\sigma = \sqrt{\frac{1}{c} \sum_{d \in L_{q,c}(f)} \|t_{q,\vec{d_i}}(f), TCP(TC)_\mu\|^2} \quad (5)$$

where f is BM25 ranking model, $\|T_A, T_B\|$ is the distance between tensor A and tensor B, $t_{q,\vec{d_\mu}}$ is centroid of all the tensors in the list which is essentially

$$t_{q,\vec{d_\mu}}(f) = \left(\frac{\sum TL_{t_1,c}(f)}{c}, \frac{\sum TL_{t_2,c}(f)}{c}, ... \right) \quad (6)$$

- Tensor Closeness to Diagonal (**TCP(CDG)**): The distance from the tensors centroid to the diagonal line in multi-dimensional space, the average and the standard deviation of the distances from the tensors to the diagonal line in multi-dimensional space. These features capture part of the position information of the tensors.

$$TCP(CDG)_c = \|t_{q,\vec{d_\mu}}(f), l_{dg}\| \quad (7)$$

$$TCP(CDG)_\mu = \frac{\sum_{d \in L_{q,c}(f)} \|t_{q,\vec{d_i}}(f), l_{dg}\|}{c} \quad (8)$$

$$TCP(CDG)_\sigma = \sqrt{\frac{1}{c} \sum_{d \in L_{q,c}(f)} \|t_{q,\vec{d_i}}(f), TCP(CDG)_\mu\|^2} \quad (9)$$

where l_{dg} is the diagonal line in the multi-dimensional space and $\|T, l\|$ is the distance from tensor T to line l.

- Tensor Closeness to Nearest Axis (**TCP(CNA)**): We compute the distance from the tensors centroid to its nearest axis, the average/standard deviation distance from the tensors to the nearest axis in multi-dimensional space. TCNA and TCD together define the position property of the tensors.

$$TCP(CNA)_c = \|t_{q,\vec{d_\mu}}(f), l_{na}\| \quad (10)$$

$TCP(CNA)_\mu$ and $TCP(CNA)_\sigma$ can be computed similarly with Equation 8 and 9 with replacement of l_{dg} to l_{na} where l_{na} is the nearest axis to the centroid of all tensors and is computed as:

$$l_{na} = \min_{1 \le i \le N} \|t_{q,\vec{d_\mu}}, l_i\| \quad (11)$$

where l_i is ith-axis and N is the number of the dimensions.

We first computed the tensor closeness related features for the terms in the subquery q_i. Later on we found that it is beneficial to compute the tensor closeness related features for all the terms in the original query Q. We apply this in all our experiments.

2.2.2 Basic Features. Besides the aforementioned features (PXM, TS, TCP) we also applied other features proposed by others which we will further refer as "basic features".

Mutual Information We compute the mutual information by first counting the co-occurrence of pairwise terms within N terms window in the matching documents. The value is then normalized by the product of the document frequencies of the two terms. Finally we apply all possible feature functions h to the the pairwise terms list. The formula [13] is shown as follows:

$$MI = h(I(x, y)) = h\left(\frac{\frac{\sum O(x,y)}{T}}{\frac{O(x)}{T} \cdot \frac{O(y)}{T}}\right) \quad (12)$$

where $O(x, y)$ is the number of times term x and term y co-occur within a window of 50 terms in each matched documents, $O(t)$ is the total occurrence of term t in the collection and T is the total number of terms in the collection.

Collection Term Frequency (CTF)

The collection level term frequency of term t. Then we apply feature function h to the list of CTFs as $h(CTF_q)$.

Document Frequency (DF)

This is simply the document frequency for each term in the subquery $q_{i,j}$. Then we apply feature function h to the terms DFs as $h(DF_q)$.

Inversed Document Frequency (IDF)

The IDF here is the modified $log(IDF)$ component used in the modified BM25 model [6]:

$$IDF_t = log\frac{N+1}{DF_t}$$

where N is the number of documents in the collection. We then apply the feature function h to the list of IDF_t as $h(IDF_q)$.

Min Document Term Frequency (MINTF) and Max Document Term Frequency (MAXTF)

MINTF is the minimum term frequency in the collection and is computed as:

$$MINTF_t = \min_{1 \le i \le DF_t} TF_{t, d_i}$$

Similarly

$$MAXTF_t = \max_{1 \le i \le DF_t} TF_{t, d_i}$$

Final features are masked using feature function as $h(MINTF_q)$ and $h(MAXTF_q)$.

Average Document Term Frequency (AVGTF) and Standard Deviation Document Term Frequency (STDTF)

This AVGTF applies to each individual term as:

$$AVGTF_t = \frac{\sum_{i=1}^{DF_t} TF_{t, d_i}}{DF_t}$$

The STDTF is the standard deviation of $AVGTF_t$. We apply feature function masks to both features as $h(AVGTF_q)$ and $h(STDTF_q)$.

Average Document Term Frequency with IDF (AVGTFIDF)

We also incorporate the average document term frequency with IDF to capture the term salience in the collection. Formally we have:

$$AVGTFIDF_t = AVGTF_t \cdot IDF_t.$$

Table 3: Collections and Queries

Collection	#qry	$|QL| = 2$	$|QL| = 3$	$|QL| = 4$
Disk12	150	30(20%)	37(25%)	41(27%)
Disk45	250	75(33%)	147(59%)	17(7%)
AQUAINT	50	21(42%)	27(54%)	1(2%)
WT2G	50	24(48%)	23(46%)	0(0%)
WT10G	100	30(30%)	25(25%)	20(20%)
GOV2	150	44(29%)	65(43%)	35(23%)

Average Document Term Frequency with Collection Occurrence Probability (AVGTFCOP)

Similar to AVGTFIDF, we can also leverage the average collection occurrence probability to capture the term salience in the collection. Formally we have:

$$AVGTFCOP_t = AVGTF_t + \mu \cdot p(t|C)$$

where $p(t|C)$ is the probability of term t occurred in the whole collection and is computed as $p(t|C) = \frac{CTF_t}{|C|}$. $|C|$ is the total number of terms in the collection. We choose $\mu = 1000$ based on the preliminary results.

Simplified Clarity Score (SCS)

This feature was firstly proposed by He and Ounis [9] to reduce the computational cost of original query clarity and it was used as a pre-retrieval query performance predicator. It is computed as:

$$SCS_q = \sum_{t \in q} p(t|q) \cdot log_2 \frac{p(t|q)}{p(t|C)}$$

where $p(t|q)$ is the probability of term occurred in the query q.

3 EXPERIMENTS AND RESULTS

In this section we test our subquery ranking method using TREC collections and topics. We will describe the details of the experiment setup as well as the analysis of the results.

3.1 Experiment Setup

We use six TREC Ad-hoc/Web collections in our experiments: Disk12, Disk45 with ROBUST04 query set, AQUAINT News Collection with ROBUST05 query set (ROBUST04 hard queries), WT2G, WT10G and GOV2. The title part of the query topics is used to test the proposed subquery ranking method. Stopwords are removed from both the collections and the queries and porter stemmer is applied to the indexes. Table 3 lists the details of the collections and the corresponding queries. As we can see that for most title topics their lengths are within 2 to 4.

Since we are targeting the subquery ranking, single term queries will not be included [1]. Lots of features can not be directly applied to the queries of length 2 such as MI since the subqueries are single term query (other than the original query) and thus we separate the queries by their lengths. In our experiments we focus on queries of length 2 and 3 since even for queries of length 4 AQUAINT and WT2G do not have enough queries for both training and testing. When tested on one collection, queries from other 5 collections are used together as training examples. All the features are normalized to the range [0, 1] before being fed to the learning algorithm.

---

[1][20] provided the performance upper bound for single term queries

LambdaMART is leveraged to rank the subqueries based on their features and the average precision of the subquery is used as the labels. Since LambdaMART favors the scalar labels we convert the AP values to integers based on the relative AP values distribution. The relative AP values are the differences between the AP of a subquery and the AP of the best subquery. The mapping from AP to integer should reflect the relative importance of a query whose best subquery performs much better than the rest of its subqueries. We do not show the actual distribution due to space limit and the rule of the mapping is:

$$Label(q) = \begin{cases} 4, & \text{if } AP_q = MaxAP_{OQ(q)} \\ 3, & \text{if } MaxAP_{OQ(q)} - AP_q \leq 0.1 \\ 2, & \text{if } MaxAP_{OQ(q)} - AP_q > 0.1 \cap MaxAP_{OQ(q)} - AP_q \leq 0.3 \\ 1, & \text{if } MaxAP_{OQ(q)} - AP_q > 0.3 \cap MaxAP_{OQ(q)} - AP_q \leq 0.5 \\ 0, & \text{otherwise} \end{cases}$$

where q is a subquery, $OQ(q)$ denotes the original query of q, AP_q denotes the average precision of the subquery q, and $MaxAP_Q$ denotes the best AP of all the subqueries of Q. Basically we only care about which subquery should be labeled as the best-performed subquery thus the metric for LambdaMART is set to nDCG@1. The number of leaves for each tree is chosen from [2, 10] and the best performance averaged among all collections is reported. When generating the ranking list or compute the features like TS and TCP where ranking function is needed we always apply BM25 [2] with optimal parameter b ($k_1 = 1.2$ always) set based on the results reported in [21]. For performance metrics we report the accuracy and MAP. We also compare the MAP of best-performed subqueries identified by our method with the theoretical upper bound.

3.2 Results of Subquery Ranking

The results of subquery ranking (SR) using all features (mentioned in Section 2.2 and normalized) for queries of length 2 and 3 are listed in Table 4. The accuracy is computed as the number of queries whose best-performed subqueries are correctly identified divided by the total number of queries. MAP is computed by first picking the best subqueries identified by our model and then taking the average precision for these best subqueries. It can be seen that our SR method is better than using original query for most of the collections. The only exception is the GOV2 with queries of length 2 where the upper bound of the optimal performance is almost the same with the performance of using original queries. We also find that in general the our model performs better with queries of length 3 than the queries of length 2 in terms of percentage improvement. This is mainly because some features such as MI and PXM simply can not be applied to the queries of length 2.

Figure 5 shows the length distribution of the best subqueries for the queries of length 3. Basically it shows how many queries of which its best subquery of length N. For example, for Disk12 there are 6 queries whose best subquery are of length 1 and 23 of the queries have their optimal subquery length of 2. From the figure we can see that in general our model has balanced number of best subqueries in different length and the numbers are very close to the upper bound. We also find that our model slightly favors the

---

[2] We also tried using Dirichlet language model and found using BM25 leads to slightly better performance.

Table 4: Results of using all features. *OG* represents the original query. *SR* represents our subquery ranking model. *UB* represents the upper bound where the optimal subquery for each original query is picked.

$|QL|$	Collection	Accuracy	MAP		
			OG	SR	UB
2	Disk12	90%	0.3216	0.3309 +2.89%	0.3372 +4.85%
	Disk45	82%	0.2506	0.2566 +2.39%	0.2662 +6.23%
	AQUAINT	76%	0.2063	0.2091 +1.36%	0.2184 +5.87%
	WT2G	83%	0.2983	0.2983 +0.00%	0.3083 +3.35%
	WT10G	83%	0.2544	0.2663 +4.68%	0.2738 +7.63%
	GOV2	96%	0.2912	0.2911 -0.03%	0.2913 +0.03%
3	Disk12	92%	0.2597	0.2833 +9.09%	0.2880 +10.90%
	Disk45	89%	0.2399	0.2643 +10.17%	0.2772 +15.55%
	AQUAINT	88%	0.2107	0.2323 +10.25%	0.2426 +15.14%
	WT2G	90%	0.3285	0.3380 +2.89%	0.3580 +8.98%
	WT10G	94%	0.1720	0.1949 +13.31%	0.2051 +19.24%
	GOV2	95%	0.3060	0.3113 +1.73%	0.3221 +5.26%

Figure 5: Optimal Subqueries Lengths of queries with 3 terms. *UB-1* denotes the number of ground truth best subqueries that has 1 term. *SR-1* denotes the number of subquery ranking model ranked best subqueries that has 1 term. *UB-2, UB-3, SR-2, SR-3* follow the same notation.

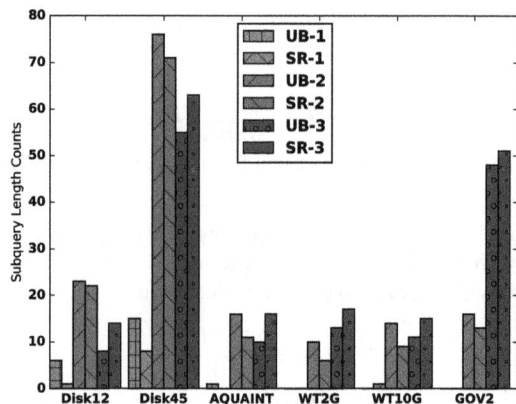

original queries as the number of best queries that have three terms in our model is always larger than the values of the upper bound.

3.3 Feature Importance Analysis

In order to quantify the feature importance we set up another experiment in which a subset of features are taken off from the

the feature space and the performance difference between using all features and using the subset of features is compared. The results are in Table 5 and we only show the results of queries of length 3 due to space limit.

In Table 5 there are two main sections: the top important features from basic features are on the left and the detailed feature importance of terms relationship features on the right. For basic features the features with the largest performance drops if they were removed from the feature space are listed. For terms relationship features we present the details of PXM, TS and TCP by showing the importance of the sub-features. Sub-features are the features like $PXM(w)_h$ and $TCP(CDG)$ which essentially reflect specific intuitions of the newly proposed features. First, we notice that in general the terms relationship features have the performance drop larger than -13%. Comparing to the top basic features where two of them have the performance drop below than -13% it validates the utility of these features. Second, Detailed collection-wise performance drop indicates different features contribute differently for the collections. For example, AVGTFCOP is important to AQUAINT while TS(SUM,SUM) is specifically useful for WT2G. Third, detailed analysis on terms relationship features reveal that: for PXM $PXM(w)_h$ is better than $PXM(w)_c orr$. For TS features TS(SUM,SUM) which is actually the sum of the top ranked documents scores (the first sum of all query terms equals to the document score) is more vital. For TCP features the TCP(CNA) which captures the position of the terms scores tensors and the TCP(TC) which captures the tensors compactness are all important with performances drops larger than -14% and this validates the utility of such features.

4 RELATED WORK

Reducing verbose queries to shorter queries has been intensively studied in recent years [1, 13].

Most previous work involves in generating the features for either the original query Q, the subquery q or groups of terms. Basically there are several features categories:

Statistical Features TF-IDF based features are the most widely used set of statistical features [2, 5, 10, 13, 16, 18] which include various statistics such as collection TF, IDF, residual IDF, TF in matching Wikipedia titles, count of passages containing the subquery etc. Other popular features include simplified clarity score [5, 13] and mutual information (MI) between query terms [11, 12, 19], domain specific dictionaries based features such as whether the term indicating a brand [19].

Query Features Query features are only based on the query itself and no collection context is involved. Similarity Original Query measures the cosine similarity between TF-IDF vectors of each subquery and the original query [13]. Presence of Stop Words [1, 16] computes the ratio of stop words in subquery. IsRightMost and IsLeftMost [19] are the features that capture the position of the subquery in the original query.

Term Dependency Features These features capture the dependencies between query words. Park et al. [16] proposed four types of dependencies among query terms: parent-child, ancestor-descendant, siblings and c-commanding. The final features include the number of dependent clauses in the query; the ratio of the dependent term pairs which have parent-child; ancestor-dependent, siblings, and c-commanding in the query.

Post Retrieval Features These features are based on the ranking results of subqueries. Typically, these features are expensive to compute but they have been proven to be effective. Query-document Relevance Scores [1, 4] are the LambdaRank and BM25 scores of top K documents, the click through counts of top K documents and the page-rank scores of top K documents. Query scope [13] of a subquery is the size of the retrieved document set relative to the size of the collection. Weighted Information Gain [2] is the difference of the retrieval quality by comparing the state where only the average document is retrieved to the state where the actual results are observed. Query drift among results [5] is a set of features which include the standard deviation of the ranking scores at 100 documents, the maximum standard deviation in the ranking list, etc.

Our proposed features are all *post-retrieval features* and some of them share the similar ideas with previous studies, e.g. term proximity based features are inspired by the term dependency features mentioned above. Different from the previous work, we are interested in the document score of the proposed term proximity models and various properties of the term scores.

A large number of research efforts have been made towards combining the features using a classification or a regression model. The classification problem is equivalent to pick the best subquery and it typically decides whether a term in the original query should be included in the best subquery. The regression problem is to learn a weight for each term denoting its importance score or to learn a weight for a sub-query; the top terms or the subquery with highest weight is then chosen. RankSVM [1, 13, 15], decision trees, AdaBoost, logistic regression [19] are popular classification models while random forests [1] is the most popular regression model. We adopt the classification model in our work where we apply the LambdaMART to the features from all subqueries and the model learns which subquery should be the best subquery.

5 CONCLUSIONS AND FUTURE WORK

This paper focuses on the problem of identifying the best-performed subquery for a given keyword query. Our main contribution lies in the identification of new features that can be used to predict the performance of a subquery. These new features are designed to capture different types of term relations based on the retrieval results, i.e., the proximity among query terms, the aggregated relevance score of query terms, and the compactness and positions of the term score tensors. The newly proposed features together with other basic features are used to train a LambdaMART model to identify the best subqueries. Experiment results show that by using the terms relationship features together with other popular basic features could lead to promising performance in terms of both accuracy and MAP. Detailed analysis on feature importance validates the usefulness of our proposed features.

One of the limitations of the proposed features is related to the computational cost. Since these features are post-retrieval, it would inevitably increase the processing time and make it less practical to apply this method to reduce the keyword queries online.

Table 5: Feature importance analysis for queries of length 3, the lower the better. The lowest value of each collection is bolded.

Collection	Top Basic Features			Terms Relationship Features							
	AVGTFCOP	SCS	CTF	$PXM(w)_h$	$PXM(w)_{corr}$	TS1	TS2	TS3	TCP(TC)	TCP(CDG)	TCP(CNA)
Disk12	0.2399	0.2497	0.2445	0.2535	0.2497	0.2532	0.2536	0.2536	**0.2374**	0.2492	0.2498
0.2833	-15.3%	-11.9%	-13.7%	-10.5%	-11.9%	-10.6%	-10.5%	-10.5%	**-16.2%**	-12.0%	-11.8%
Disk45	0.2292	0.2293	**0.2224**	0.2306	0.2354	0.2294	0.2313	0.2313	0.2330	0.2337	0.2267
0.2643	-13.3%	-13.2%	**-15.9%**	-12.8%	-10.9%	-13.2%	-12.5%	-12.5%	-11.8%	-11.6%	-14.2%
AQUAINT	**0.1882**	0.1999	0.2003	0.1974	0.1970	0.2029	0.1949	0.1949	0.1884	0.2005	0.1999
0.2323	**-19.0%**	-13.9%	-13.8%	-15.0%	-15.2%	-12.7%	-16.1%	-16.1%	-18.9%	-13.7%	-13.9%
WT2G	0.2561	0.2756	0.2853	0.2785	0.2760	0.2641	**0.2191**	0.2191	0.2828	0.2826	0.2795
0.3380	-24.2%	-18.5%	-15.6%	-17.6%	-16.3%	-21.9%	**-35.2%**	-35.2%	-16.4%	-17.3%	-18.3%
WT10G	0.1587	0.1643	0.1663	0.1454	0.1510	0.1671	0.1617	0.1617	0.1589	**0.1435**	0.1441
0.1949	-18.6%	-15.7%	-14.7%	-25.4%	-22.5%	-14.3%	-17.0%	-17.0%	-18.5%	**-26.4%**	-26.1%
GOV2	0.3040	0.2990	0.3029	0.2989	0.3025	**0.2857**	0.2927	0.2947	0.3046	0.3087	0.2990
0.3113	-2.3%	-4.0%	-2.7%	-4.0%	-2.8%	**-8.2%**	-6.0%	-5.3%	-2.2%	-0.8%	-4.0%
AVG	0.2294	0.2363	0.2370	0.2341	0.2364	0.2337	**0.2256**	0.2259	0.2342	0.2359	0.2329
0.2707	-15.5%	-12.9%	-12.7%	-14.2%	-13.3%	-13.5%	**-16.2%**	-16.1%	-14.0%	-13.6%	-14.7%

TS1: TS(MAX/MIN,SUM); TS2: TS(SUM,SUM); TS3: TS(GMEAN,MEAN)

We acknowledge this limitation and plan to study more efficient ways of computing features in our future work. However, we also want to emphasize that one benefit of the proposed new features is to help us better understand the impact of term relations on the retrieval performance. And these features might shed some lights on developing more effective retrieval functions.

As for future work, there are two interesting directions. The first one is to continue on the features so that the identification of the best subquery can be further improved. For example, the semantic features would be the promising perspective. Incorporating the outside resources as the potential feature source would be another choice. The second direction is to leverage the terms relationship features and the experimental results presented in this paper to do more theoretical studies. For example, we could get inspiration from the features and try to prove the performance upper bound of multiple-terms queries.

Acknowledgments. This research was supported by the U.S. National Science Foundation under IIS-1423002.

REFERENCES
[1] N. Balasubramanian, G. Kumaran, and V. R. Carvalho. Exploring reductions for long web queries. In *Proceedings of the 33rd International ACM SIGIR Conference on Research and Development in Information Retrieval*, SIGIR '10, pages 571–578, New York, NY, USA, 2010. ACM.

[2] M. Bendersky and W. B. Croft. Discovering key concepts in verbose queries. In *Proceedings of the 31st Annual International ACM SIGIR Conference on Research and Development in Information Retrieval*, SIGIR '08, pages 491–498, New York, NY, USA, 2008. ACM.

[3] C. J. Burges. From ranknet to lambdarank to lambdamart: An overview. Technical Report MSR-TR-2010-82, June 2010.

[4] Y. Chen and Y.-Q. Zhang. A query substitution-search result refinement approach for long query web searches. In *Proceedings of the 2009 IEEE/WIC/ACM International Joint Conference on Web Intelligence and Intelligent Agent Technology - Volume 01*, WI-IAT '09, pages 245–251, Washington, DC, USA, 2009. IEEE Computer Society.

[5] R. Cummins, M. Lalmas, C. O'Riordan, and J. M. Jose. Navigating the user query space. In *Proceedings of the 18th International Conference on String Processing and Information Retrieval*, SPIRE'11, pages 380–385, Berlin, Heidelberg, 2011. Springer-Verlag.

[6] H. Fang, T. Tao, and C. Zhai. A formal study of information retrieval heuristics. In *Proceedings of the 27th Annual International ACM SIGIR Conference on Research and Development in Information Retrieval*, SIGIR '04, pages 49–56, New York, NY, USA, 2004. ACM.

[7] H. Fang, T. Tao, and C. Zhai. Diagnostic evaluation of information retrieval models. *ACM Trans. Inf. Syst.*, 29(2):7:1–7:42, Apr. 2011.

[8] H. Fang and H. Wu. An exploration of query term deletion. 2011.

[9] B. He and I. Ounis. Inferring query performance using pre-retrieval predictors. In *In Proc. Symposium on String Processing and Information Retrieval*, pages 43–54. Springer Verlag, 2004.

[10] S. Huston and W. B. Croft. Evaluating verbose query processing techniques. In *Proceedings of the 33rd International ACM SIGIR Conference on Research and Development in Information Retrieval*, SIGIR '10, pages 291–298, New York, NY, USA, 2010. ACM.

[11] G. Kumaran and J. Allan. A case for shorter queries, and helping users create them. In *HLT-NAACL*, pages 220–227, 2007.

[12] G. Kumaran and J. Allan. Effective and efficient user interaction for long queries. In *Proceedings of the 31st Annual International ACM SIGIR Conference on Research and Development in Information Retrieval*, SIGIR '08, pages 11–18, New York, NY, USA, 2008. ACM.

[13] G. Kumaran and V. R. Carvalho. Reducing long queries using query quality predictors. In *Proceedings of the 32Nd International ACM SIGIR Conference on Research and Development in Information Retrieval*, SIGIR '09, pages 564–571, New York, NY, USA, 2009. ACM.

[14] D. Metzler and W. B. Croft. A markov random field model for term dependencies. In *Proceedings of the 28th annual international ACM SIGIR conference on Research and development in information retrieval*, pages 472–479. ACM, 2005.

[15] J. H. Park and W. B. Croft. Query term ranking based on dependency parsing of verbose queries. In *Proceedings of the 33rd International ACM SIGIR Conference on Research and Development in Information Retrieval*, SIGIR '10, pages 829–830, New York, NY, USA, 2010. ACM.

[16] J. H. Park, W. B. Croft, and D. A. Smith. A quasi-synchronous dependence model for information retrieval. In *Proceedings of the 20th ACM International Conference on Information and Knowledge Management*, CIKM '11, pages 17–26, New York, NY, USA, 2011. ACM.

[17] A. Shtok, O. Kurland, D. Carmel, F. Raiber, and G. Markovits. Predicting query performance by query-drift estimation. *ACM Trans. Inf. Syst.*, 30(2):11:1–11:35, May 2012.

[18] X. Xue, S. Huston, and W. B. Croft. Improving verbose queries using subset distribution. In *Proceedings of the 19th ACM International Conference on Information and Knowledge Management*, CIKM '10, pages 1059–1068, New York, NY, USA, 2010. ACM.

[19] B. Yang, N. Parikh, G. Singh, and N. Sundaresan. A study of query term deletion using large-scale e-commerce search logs. In *Proceedings of the 36th European Conference on IR Research on Advances in Information Retrieval - Volume 8416*, ECIR 2014, pages 235–246, New York, NY, USA, 2014. Springer-Verlag New York, Inc.

[20] P. Yang and H. Fang. Estimating retrieval performance bound for single term queries. In *Proceedings of the 2016 ACM International Conference on the Theory of Information Retrieval*, ICTIR '16, pages 237–240, New York, NY, USA, 2016. ACM.

[21] P. Yang and H. Fang. A reproducibility study of information retrieval models. In *Proceedings of the 2016 ACM International Conference on the Theory of Information Retrieval*, ICTIR '16, pages 77–86, New York, NY, USA, 2016. ACM.

Deriving Differentially Private Session Logs
for Query Suggestion

Sicong Zhang
Department of Computer Science
Washington, D.C., USA
sz303@georgetown.edu

Grace Hui Yang
Department of Computer Science
Washington, D.C., USA
huiyang@cs.georgetown.edu

ABSTRACT

Query logs are valuable resources for Information Retrieval (IR) research. However, the huge concern about user privacy has become an obstacle preventing data from being released and interfering with the advance of IR. It is understandable but still quite disappointing. Recent privacy research has begun to address the problem by anonymizing queries in query logs. In that, each query and its associated user actions are treated as one block for anonymization; each block is independent from each other. It might be sufficient to support ad-hoc retrieval that handles queries independently but will be not adequate for more complex IR tasks that require the knowledge of query sequences. In this paper, we tackle this challenge by keeping session information in differentially privately anonymized logs so that an anonymized log is able to support IR tasks, such as query suggestion and session search, that need query sequence information as well. We also provide analysis on how to achieve a proper balance between privacy and search utility.

KEYWORDS

Differential Privacy; Query Log Anonymization; Query Suggestion

1 INTRODUCTION

Query logs are essential research materials for understanding how users interact with the search engine. However, the large and 'real' query logs are not readily accessible by the general research community due to privacy concerns. The dominance of these research materials by only a few commercial companies might have been negatively impacting the research field as a whole. We suspect an increasing split in the Information Retrieval (IR) community – academic researchers who have no access to query logs and could not conduct related research vs. industrial researchers who have the data but miss the opportunities to learn more diversified ideas from their academic colleagues. The authors of this paper believe that this split could be one of the reasons that premium IR conferences such as SIGIR are experiencing a decline.[1] We probably won't be able to make changes to the situation in one day, but we do hope the

issue of privacy in IR could be alleviated at least from a technical point of view. The authors of this paper are highly motivated to propose query log anonymization methods to enable data release for research in IR.

The principle challenge of privacy protection is to safeguard the data from being identifiable at the individual level – which is *data anonymization*. Anonymization is a lossy process. Unavoidably, an anonymized dataset would become less useful than the original one. Therefore, another challenge of privacy protection is to preserve the utility of the anonymized data as much as we can.

In the early years, most query log anonymization techniques were quite straightforward [1, 11, 19]. Those approaches had no proved privacy guarantee and the anonymized information could be easily re-identified. Unfortunately, however, those poorly-proved methods are still in use during recent data releases. For instance, in 2014, Yandex released a detailed query log containing over 167 million search records from 5 million users using only hash coding and data deletion.[2] The resulting query log contains no meaningful natural language words but can still be easily deciphered if one has knowledge of popular website frequencies. A theoretically and practically sound way to anonymize query logs is very much needed to remove us from such high risks.

More recently, a technique called *k-anonymity* has been applied to query log anonymization [9, 18]. The basic idea is to hide sensitive information among many (say k) similar copies of data. It is like *concealing a drop in the sea*. However, a serious shortcoming exists in k-anonymity, which is that it assumes knowing what knowledge an adversary has access to. In the real world, however, such assumption could never hold because an adversary could always gather extra knowledge from unknown sources and use that to decipher the k-anonymized data. Therefore, it is really not safe to use k-anonymity for data protection.

Until lately, researchers have explored stronger privacy protection mechanisms. The state-of-the-art method is Differential Privacy (DP) [12]. DP is effective in anonymizing statistics about a dataset as well as is able to provide mathematically proved privacy guarantee. By adding noise to sample statistics in a dataset, DP creates disturbed (anonymized) statistics that no one could tell whether one exists in the dataset or not. In this way, DP hides the information of each individual. The idea is that if no one could tell a user's existence, it would be even more impossible for them to find the user out. It is like what is described in the *Platform Sutra – if fundamentally there is not a single thing, where could any dust be attracted?* DP is perhaps the strictest way to protect data privacy since the data 'seems' to no longer exist. Due to its strong privacy protection, there is usually no need for DP to make assumptions

---

[1]http://sigir.org/files/forum/2016J/p001.pdf

ICTIR '17, October 01-04, 2017, Amsterdam, Netherlands
© 2017 Association for Computing Machinery
ACM ISBN 978-1-4503-4490-6/17/10...$15.00
https://doi.org/.1145/3121050.3121076

---

[2]https://www.kaggle.com/c/yandex-personalized-web-search-challenge/data

Table 1: Toy example for Differential Privacy (DP): After anonymization, from an anonymized sum, it is difficult to tell whether Carol is in Dataset 1 and/or Dataset 2.

	Dataset 1	Dataset 2
Raw Data	Alice has 5 apples	Alice has 5 apples
	Bob has 4 apples	Bob has 4 apples
	Carol has 2 apples	
Sum of apples	5+4+2=11	5+4=9
Anonymized Sum	11+Noise=10	9+Noise =10

on what knowledge or what method an adversary would use to attack a dataset. The no requirement of assumptions makes DP very plausible to be used in practice.

Table 1 shows a toy example and explains how DP works. Suppose we would like to release a database about users' possession of apples. We are not going to release the raw data. Instead, we would like to release a summary statistic to the public. Would there be any privacy concern when we release sum as the statistic? The answer is 'yes'. Suppose we will release either Dataset 1 or Dataset 2, which are two databases differ by exactly one user, Carol. The summary statistic, the sum of apples, for the two datasets will be different by 2, that is what is contributed by Carol (11-9=2). If an adversary happens to know that (a) Carol has 2 apples and (b) everybody else has either 4 or 5 apples, then it is easy to identify that Carol is in Dataset 1 and not in Dataset 2. The re-identification can be done by exausitively calculating a few possible decompositions for the released statistic. In this case, the only possible decomposition for 11 is 5+4+2 and for 9 is 5+4. The adversary can thus identify which dataset Carol is in since Carol must be included in Dataset 1 and excluded from Dataset 2. Once knowing where Carol is, it would become fairly easy to figure out other information about Carol by the adversary. To obscure an individual's identity, DP adds randomized noise to the summary statistic. The anonymized data then follows a distribution, whose mean equals to the original mean, but the end results would not be distinguishable between datasets with or without Carol. In other words, after applying DP, the adversary would not be able to figure out whether or not Carol is in a given dataset based on the released statistics.

Researchers have made progresses in applying DP in query log anonymization [14, 22, 29]. There are two main limitations of the current approaches. First, most approaches simply measure the utility of anonymized logs by the percentage of what is remaining, instead of evaluating through actual IR tasks and IR effectiveness measures [22]. In this study, we find that percentage of the kept data and real IR utility could contradict each other. We argue that we should use the latter. Second, existing work only takes care of single record privacy protection [29]. This simplification is not sufficient for complex IR tasks that require the use of sessions, a particular form of sequential data, from a query log.

A major challenge of session log anonymization is the sparsity of re-occurring sessions. The sparsity comes from the large number of possible query sequences. From the perspective of privacy research, the sparsity of sessions would require a greater scale of noises to be added and would make the privacy protection harder to stay under control. From the perspective of IR utility, the sparsity of sessions also makes it more complicated to distinguish higher frequency

sessions, which may be more valuable to support IR applications, from the other sessions.

In this paper, we tackle the challenge and propose a releasing mechanism to produce a DP-protected query log with both click-through data and session data. We show that our anonymized query log can be used to support complex IR application such as query suggestion and report the remaining IR utility of the anonymized log. We wish this work can contribute to our research community by better enabling data release for IR studies.

2 RELATED WORK

Naive Privacy Techniques: In 2006, an outbreak of tremendous privacy concerns was triggered by that many users were re-identified from a query log released by America Online (AOL) [3]. The AOL log was "anonymized" by hash coding the ID of each user, which was soon proved a poor mechanism. Since then, privacy-enhancing techniques [1, 11, 14, 20] have been tried on query logs. Early attempts include *log deletion, hashing queries, identifier deletion, hashing identifiers, scrubbing query content, deleting infrequent queries* and *shortening sessions* [11]. Those methods all tried to directly modify or remove individual data entries. However, there would always be some other traits left to re-identify an individual. It is like you may still recognize a friend who stands in front of you, even if he covers his name tag (hashing identifier) or wears a mask (scrubbing query content). Researchers have reached a consensus that those early techniques do not work [1, 14, 20]. Jones et al. [20] showed that after removing unique terms from a query log, personal information could still be re-identified with a simple classifier at an accuracy as high as 97.5%. We urge our research community or anyone who intends to release a query log to stop using those naive techniques.

K-Anonymity: K-Anonymity [9, 25] has been a popular privacy protection technique since 2002. The main idea is that any released record for an individual can not be distinguished from at least k-1 other individuals whose information are released too [25]. In the query log anonymization scenario, to satisfy k-anonymity, an anonymization algorithm would only release query click records appearing at least k times in the original query log [9]. Here k is usually the cut-off threshold of some frequency. However, the privacy of k-anonymity is not strong because it depends on assumptions made about an adversary [25]. To develop data protection mechanisms with proved privacy guarantee, privacy research has moved on to differential privacy.

Differential Privacy: Differential privacy [13, 14, 22, 23, 26, 28, 29] is the state-of-art privacy protection mechanism especially for statistical data release. The key idea of differential privacy is to make the released statistics affected very limited by adding or removing a single record or a single user. Whether achieving record level DP or user-level DP depends on the neighboring dataset's definition. In this paper, we implement user-level DP. Recent work [14, 22, 28] has been proposed to use histogram based DP algorithms for query log anonymization. Gotz et al. [14] and Korolova et al. [22] proposed to release queries and clicks based on their frequencies. They were among the first to release queries as natural language words instead of as hash codes. Their work achieved (ϵ, δ)-differential privacy. However, the utility of the released query log was evaluated by the quantity of queries that can be released and how similar the released statistics are to the original statistics. They showed that more than 10% of the search volume and 0.75% distinct queries from the original log could be privately released. Zhang et al. [28] proposed another algorithm that could achieve ϵ-differential privacy with greater ϵ and zero δ. The work used web document retrieval to evaluate the utility of the released log. However, their use of an external query pool may raise other privacy concerns. The existing DP work focuses on protecting single queries. In this paper, we propose an (ϵ, δ)-differential privacy method for anonymizing a session of multiple queries in sequences.

Data Sequence Release: Frequent sequence mining [4, 7, 10, 24, 27] is relevant to our work because it studies how to anonymize sequences of data. Their techniques can be grouped by types of sequences being released – consecutive subsequence mining [7, 10], unconstrained subsequence mining [27], and frequent itemset mining [24]. It is worthy noting that these techniques cannot be directly applied to query log anonymization. The reason lies deep in the difference between IR and data mining (DM)/database (DB). IR handles free text in natural languages, which can be considered as an infinite domain of data. On the contrary, DM and DB handle structured data, which is generated from a limited domain, also called a limited or controlled vocabulary. Most frequent sequence mining approaches would function at a very high cost for even a small controlled vocabulary, which makes it inapplicable on free text tasks. To the best of our knowledge, this paper is the first to study how session data can be released anonymously and can be useful to support IR tasks.

Query Suggestion: Query Suggestion [16] is an important task in IR. Although under specific settings, query suggestion can be done in the absence of query logs [5], most query suggestion approaches utilize query logs to suggest queries [2, 6, 8, 17, 21]. There are two main types of log-based query suggestion approaches. The first type cluster queries based on a query-click bipartite graph. For instance, Baeza-Yates et al. [2] proposed a method based on query clustering which groups semantically similar queries together. The click-through data in the log is used to represent and cluster the queries. The other approaches employ query sequences to predict the follow-up queries. For instance, Boldi et al. [6] utilized a query-flow graph to generate query suggestion results. Here, the most valuable pieces of information for query suggestion are click-through data and query sequences. In this paper, we anonymize both pieces of information in order to support query suggestion.

3 ANONYMIZATION ALGORITHM

In this section, we first introduce the related definitions of DP. Then we present our DP query log anonymization algorithm, followed by a brief proof of privacy.

3.1 Differential Privacy and Other Definitions

Neighboring is an important concept upon which differential privacy is defined. We therefore start from defining what neighboring datasets are.

Definition 1: Neighboring. Two query logs, or more generally two datasets, Q_1 and Q_2, are said to be neighboring to each other if they differ by at most one user.

The toy example we presented in Table 1 shows two neighboring datasets. The only difference between them is the information from one person, Carol. When we define differential privacy later, any possible pairs of neighboring datasets could be under consideration. It means that the datasets could also differ by Alice or by Bob.

Definition 2: Differential Privacy. A randomized query log anonymization algorithm A satisfies differential privacy, or more specifically (ϵ, δ)-differential privacy, iff for all neighboring query logs Q_1 and Q_2 and for all possible output logs Q', the following inequality holds:

$$Pr[A(Q_1) = Q'] \leq e^{\epsilon} \times Pr[A(Q_2) = Q'] + \delta \qquad (1)$$

where A is the randomized anonymization algorithm that inputs an original query log and outputs an anonymized query log Q'. ϵ and δ indicate privacy levels of A and control the probabilities of getting certain outputs from the neighboring inputs.

Based on Eq. 1, the smaller the values of ϵ and δ, the stronger the privacy guarantee. The ranges of ϵ and δ can be $0 \leq \epsilon \leq \infty$ and $0 \leq \delta \leq 1$. However, we usually expect ϵ and δ to be much smaller than their upper bounds. In general there is no hard rule for selecting their values and proper settings vary quite a lot depending on the actual applications. However, usually we consider an ϵ no more than 10 and a δ less or around 1/#of released users.

According to Eq. 1, the values of ϵ and δ directly affect how different two neighboring query logs are after applying the anonymization algorithm A. Therefore it is necessary to quantitively define the difference between two neighboring input query logs Q_1 and Q_2. The following defines *sensitivity*:

Definition 3: Sensitivity. Given a function f that takes a query log Q as the inputs and produces a numerical vector as the output. The sensitivity of f is denoted as Δf:

$$\Delta f = \max_{\forall \text{ neighboring } Q_1, Q_2} ||f(Q_1) - f(Q_2)||_1 \qquad (2)$$

where $||.||_1$ is the l_1 norm. The maximum is taken over all pairs of neighboring query logs Q_1 and Q_2. In the scenario of query log anonymization, the numerical vector output, $f(Q)$, is a vector of the raw count statistics generated from query log Q. The sensitivity value Δf indicates the maximum overall statistical difference between the two neighboring inputs Q_1 and Q_2, which would largely influence the privacy levels, i.e. the values of ϵ and δ.

3.2 Query Log Anonymization Algorithm

Our query log anonymization algorithm releases two types of data: query sequences in a session and click-throughs. The nonymization algorithm also consists of two parts, $A_{Session}$ and A_{Click}, to produce the two types of data. Both parts take the original query log Q as the input and satisfy the (ϵ, δ)-differential privacy. $A_{Session}$ releases frequent search sessions as the output, while A_{Click} releases frequent query click-through data as the output. We merge their outputs and release both.

3.2.1 Releasing Session Data. Because of the property of nature of natural language, the total number of unique search queries could be infinite. Exact match of the two search sessions is thus rare because sessions are ordered sequences of natural language queries. As we know that it is difficult to protect low frequency data from being re-identified. To address this challenge, we propose to increase the session and query counts by adding all non-trivial subsequences in sessions.

We propose the $A_{Session}$ algorithm to release search sessions with (ϵ, δ)-differential privacy. Each non-trivial subsequences of the original sessions would contribute a count to reduce the sparsity of sessions. We add noise to the session frequency by applying the Laplace mechanism [14, 22].

Algorithm $A_{Session}$ takes in the following inputs. The original query log Q, the session timeout threshold T_{Gap}, the max number of sessions per user l_s, the max number of queries per session l_q, Laplace noise scale b, and the session frequency cut-off threshold K. The algorithm is described as the following:

1) Session segmentation. We define each session S as an ordered sequence of search queries:

$$S = [q_1, q_2, ..., q_{|S|}] \qquad (3)$$

where $|S|$ is the number of queries in S.

We segment the sessions in Q based on either i) if they are from two different users, or ii) if the timestamp difference between these two queries are greater than the session timeout threshold T_{Gap}. Practically, we take 30 minutes as the timeout threshold according to previous work in session search [15]. Then we transfer Q into Q_{seg}, which is a set of sessions:

$$Q_{seg} = \{S_1, S_2, ..., S_{|Q_{seg}|}\} \qquad (4)$$

Without loss of generality, we only keep non-trivial sessions that consist of at least two queries. "Sessions" with only a single query are excluded from Q_{seg}.

2) Subsequence mining. To increase the number of repeated sessions, we take into consideration all non-trivial subsequences within a session and treat them as sessions too. The relative orders from the original session are reserved. with the permission to have some original queries missing in the new subsequences. That is to say, each subsequence of a session $S = [q_1, q_2, ..., q_{|S|}]$ is a sequence $S' = [q'_1, ...q'_{|S'|}]$ defined by $q'_t = q_{n_t}$, where the indices $n_1 < n_2 < ... < n_{|S'|}$ is monotonically increasing and $|S'| >= 2$. For example, if the original session is (q_1, q_2, q_3, q_4), our algorithm adds one count to each of the following 11 sessions:

$$(q_1, q_2, q_3, q_4), (q_1, q_2, q_3), (q_1, q_2, q_4), (q_1, q_3, q_4), (q_2, q_3, q_4)$$
$$(q_1, q_2), (q_1, q_3), (q_1, q_4), (q_2, q_3), (q_2, q_4), (q_3, q_4)$$
$$(5)$$

Hence, the search sessions, or query sequences, may get greater frequency of occurrence from the same raw dataset.

3) Sensitivity control. In order to make sure the presence or absence of each individual user would not make impact too much on the statistics that we release, the sensitivity Δf of $A_{session}$ is controlled by adjusting the max number of sessions per user l_s and the max number of queries per session l_q. Sessions longer than l_q queries are trimmed down to only the first l_q queries. As a result, the sensitivity is kept as $\Delta f = l_s \times (2^{l_q} - 1 - l_q)$. The proof can be found in Section 3.3.

4) Session release decision. We denote the session counts for a session S after subsequence mining as $C(S)$. Then we apply the Laplace mechanism on the session counts by adding i.i.d. noise to each count. We release session S iff. $C(S) + noise > K$, where $noise \sim Lap(0, b)$, and K is the session frequency cut-off threshold. The

decision of whether to release session S is made based on:

$$\begin{cases} \text{if } C(S) + Lap(0, b) > K, & \text{Release session } S \\ \text{otherwise,} & \text{Do not release } S \end{cases}$$

5) Session count release. For all session S that we have decided to release, their counts generated from the previous step form a biased sample since they are all selected because their values are greater than K. However, we need to make sure the actual released counts still follow an unbiased Laplace distribution $Lap(C(S), b)$. We therefore need to do the sampling again and release the sessions together with their perturbed count $C(S) + Lap(0, b)$. The released perturbed frequency count $C(S) + Lap(0, b)$ follows the distribution of $Lap(C(S), b)$, which becomes the Laplace Mechanism [13] for Differential Privacy.

6) Output: A set of frequent sessions along with their corresponding counts, $\{(S, C(S))\}$, while each session S is in the form of an ordered sequence of free text queries. Table 2 shows an example outputted by $A_{Session}$.

3.2.2 Releasing click-through data. We also release click-through data, i.e. a query and the urls that a user clicked for the query. Algorithm A_{Click} releases the click-through data as a tuple of query, clicked document and the count for the pair, $[q, d, c(q, d)]$. The released data satisfies the (ϵ, δ)-differential privacy. The count $c(q, d)$ is the frequency after adding Laplacian noise for a query-URL pair (q, d).

The A_{Click} algorithm takes in the following inputs: the query log Q, query click records limit per user l, the Laplace noise scale b (the same as in $A_{Session}$), and the frequency threshold K (the same as in $A_{Session}$). Note that both $A_{session}$ and A_{Click} need to share the same privacy parameter settings b and K. It is because the overall privacy guarantee is bottlenecked by the algorithm that has the weaker differential privacy guarantee.

The A_{Click} algorithm releases the click-through data to assist session data release using the following steps:

1) Sensitivity control for clicks. For each user in Q, we only keep the first l click records for each user and ignore the rest from the same user to make sure that data from any user won't contribute too much to the overall frequency statistics.

2) Query-clickthrough release decision. This is similar to step 4 in $A_{Session}$. We first count the total number of occurrences for each query-clickthrough pair as $C(q, d)$. We then decide to release a pair (q, d) iff. $C(q, d) + noise > K$, where $noise \sim Lap(0, b)$ and K is the frequency cut-off threshold.

3) Release query-clickthrough tuples. This is similar to step 5 in $A_{Session}$. If a (q,d) pair has been decided to be released at the previous step, we perform a sampling again from the Laplacian distribution for added noise and release a 3-tuple $[q, d, C(q, d) + noise]$ where the new i.i.d. $noise \sim Lap(0, b)$; otherwise, we won't release anything for the (q, d) pair.

4) Output: A set of query-clickthrough tuples in the form of (Query q, Document d, Fuzzed Count $C(q, d) + noise$). Table 3 shows an example outputted by A_{Click}.

3.3 Proof of Privacy

According to the definition of (ϵ, δ)-differential privacy, a query log anonymization algorithm A should satisfy the following two

Table 2: Session output example.

Session 1	Session 2
q_1=daily record morristown nj	q_1=ny lottery
q_2=star ledger newark nj	q_2=pa lottery
q_3=google	q_3=nj lottery
	q_4=ny lottery
Counts: 11	Counts: 16

Table 3: Click-through output example.

Query	Clicked URL	Counts
weather	http://www.weather.com	4190
weather	http://weather.yahoo.com	1035
aol weather	http://weather.aol.com	30
aol weather	http://aolsvc.weather.aol.com	16

inequalities for all neighboring query logs Q_1 and Q_2 in order to achieve DP.

$$P[A(Q_1) \in \hat{Q}] \leq \alpha P[A(Q_2) \in \hat{Q}] + \delta \tag{6}$$

$$P[A(Q_2) \in \hat{Q}] \leq \alpha P[A(Q_1) \in \hat{Q}] + \delta \tag{7}$$

A major difference between our algorithm $A_{Session}$ and previous DP algorithms [14, 22, 29] is that we consider the query sequence of search sessions, rather than individual queries or click-throughs as the unit to be counted and to be protected. However, a common mechanism is shared by all the work, which is achieving the requirements of (ϵ, δ)-differential privacy (Equa. 6 and 7) by adding i.i.d noise from the Laplace distribution on the data. A proof of the mechanism can be found in the *Lemma 1.* of Section 5.1 of Korolova et al. [22]. It shows that adding Laplacian noise would be able to achieve $(d \cdot ln(\alpha), \delta_{alg})$-differential privacy, where $\alpha = Max\{e^{1/b}, 1 + \frac{1}{2e^{(K-1)/b}-1}\}$, $\delta_{alg} = 0.5d \cdot exp(\frac{d-K}{b})$.

Now let's evaluate the ϵ and δ values in our algorithm. In [22], d is the max number of queries per user and equals the sensitivity in their algorithm. That is to say, $d = \Delta f$ [22]. In our algorithm, the sensitivity Δf can be greater than the maximum of sessions per user l_s because the subsequences of original sessions also contribute to the sensitivity value. If we consider each of the Δf counts caused by a user as an individual record, the privacy guarantee of the Step 4 in $A_{Session}$ would be equivalent to $d = \Delta f$ as in Lemma 1. Hence the Step 1 to Step 4 (to decide which session may be released) of $A_{Session}$ satisfies $(\Delta f \cdot ln(\alpha), \delta_{alg})$-differential privacy, where $\alpha = Max\{e^{1/b}, 1 + \frac{1}{2e^{(K-1)/b}-1}\}$, $\delta_{alg} = 0.5\Delta f \cdot exp(\frac{\Delta f - K}{b})$. Step 5 of $A_{Session}$ is a standard procedure in differential privacy [13]. Such released session counts could be used to weigh query transitions in a session, which is helpful for the IR algorithms. This step itself achieves $(\Delta f/b, 0)$ differential privacy. Therefore, the overall $A_{Session}$ algorithm achieves $(\Delta f \cdot (ln(\alpha) + 1/b), \delta_{alg})$-differential privacy, while α and δ_{alg} are defined as earlier.

Next, we need to calculate the exact value of Δf in order to finalize the privacy level ϵ and δ. Sensitivity Δf is defined as the maximum difference of the statistics could be made by the data generated from one user. In the worst case, the particular user differing between two neighboring datasets may issue l_s sessions,

and each session may contain at most l_q queries. Given a session containing l_q queries, the amount of subsequences containing at least two queries is 2^{l_q} (total subsequences) -1 (the empty sequence) - l_q (subsequences containing only 1 query). Hence each input session with l_q queries contributes a count by at most $2^{l_q} - 1 - l_q$ sessions. Therefore, the overall sensitivity of our algorithm is:

$$\Delta f = l_s \times (2^{l_q} - 1 - l_q) \tag{8}$$

By plugging in the sensitivity value Δf into $\epsilon = \Delta f \cdot (ln(\alpha) + 1/b)$ and $\delta = 0.5\Delta f \cdot exp(\frac{\Delta f - K}{b})$, our session release approach can achieve (ϵ, δ)-differential privacy while ϵ and δ are:

$$\epsilon = l_s(2^{l_q} - 1 - l_q) \cdot (ln(Max\{e^{1/b}, 1 + \frac{1}{2e^{(K-1)/b} - 1}\}) + 1/b)$$

$$\delta = 0.5l_s(2^{l_q} - 1 - l_q) \cdot exp(\frac{l_s(2^{l_q} - 1 - l_q) - K}{b})$$

$$\tag{9}$$

4 UTILITY MEASUREMENT

Data utility should be evaluated task-dependently. However, most prior work simply measures the utility by how much data is kept. In our experiments (Section 5), we reveal that amount of kept data and the actual task-dependent utility do not agree. In this research, we a real IR task – query suggestio – and classic IR evaluation metrics to measures the utility of a query log after anonymization.

4.1 The Task of Query Suggestion

Query suggestion is a popular IR task. The goal of the task is to predict the next search query that a user is going to write. Given a session S with $n + t$ queries, $S = [q_1, q_2, ..., q_{n-1}, q_n, q_{n+1}, ..., q_{n+t}]$ the task of query suggestion is to generate a ranked list of suggested queries $\{q'_1, ..., q'_m\}$ as the candidates of the next query after q_n. For evaluation purpose, we use the queries that are after q_n in the same session and are generated by the same user as the ground truth. That is, $Truth(q_n) = \{q_{n+1}, ..., q_{n+t}\}$. The results can then be evaluated by comparing between the generated ranked list $\{q'_1, ..., q'_m\}$ and the ground truth set $Truth(q_n)$.

4.2 Query Suggestion Using Anonymized logs

We build two graphs G_s and G from the anonymized log Q' to support query suggestion. We use the first graph, a query-flow graph $G_s = (V_s, E_s)$, to organize queries in sessions. We use the second graph, a query-URL bipartite graph $G = (V_q, V_d, E)$, to organize relations between queries and URLs in anonymized click-through data.

With the help of the anonymized session information, we are able to create a query-flow graph as in Boldi et al. [6]. The query-flow graph G_s organizes the ordered query transitions from the query sequences in Q'. In particular, $G_s = (V_s, E_s)$. V_s contains the set of query vertex in the graph and E_s is the set of edges connecting queries that have occurred adjacently. In G_s, we denote $e(q_i, q_j)$ as the edge weight between the transition from q_i to q_j, which is number of co-occurrences of q_i and q_j in the anonymized session log. Note that q_j is any query that appears after q_i and is not restricted to be the query immediately after q_i in the session. We also denote $d(q_i)$ as the out-degree of q_i. Then the probability of q_j

following q_i in the same session can be calculated as $e(q_i, q_j)/d(q_i)$, if only based on the session data.

We also use the query click-through data. We organize queries and their corresponding click-through URLs into a query-URL bipartite graph $G = (V_q, V_d, E)$. V_q is the set of query nodes, V_d is the set of document (URL) nodes, and E is the set of weighted edges in G. According to this bipartite graph, we represent each query $q \in V_q$ as a vector of weighted documents $\vec{q}$. Then we calculate the similarities between any two queries q_i and q_j by their normalized dot product $\vec{q_i} \cdot \vec{q_j}/(|\vec{q_i}| \cdot |\vec{q_j}|)$. We use a variation of a state-of-the-art query suggestion approach [8] to quantify the similarities between the queries. The difference is that we generate a ranked list of relevant queries for each query q, rather than allocating queries into clusters [8]. The ranked lists of the relevant queries is equivalent to the results generated based on the Euclidean distance between the normalized feature vectors as in [8] according to the geometric properties of the vector space.

Finally, we combine the two scores from both G_s and G. The overall probability of having the candidate query q_j follow q_i is calculated as:

$$P(q_i, q_j) = \lambda \frac{\vec{q_i} \cdot \vec{q_j}}{|\vec{q_i}| \cdot |\vec{q_j}|} + (1 - \lambda) \frac{e(q_i, q_j)}{d(q_i)} \qquad (10)$$

where λ is a parameter to control the value contributed between G and G_s.

4.3 Using Classic IR Metrics

In this paper, we use classic IR metrics Precision and Recall to evaluate the utility for query suggestion. In particular, we report Precision@5 and Recall@5:

$$Precision@5 = \frac{1}{5} \sum_{i=1}^{5} Hit(i); \; Recall@5 = \frac{1}{t} \sum_{i=1}^{5} Hit(i) \qquad (11)$$

$$Hit(i) = \begin{cases} 1, & \text{if } q_i' \in Truth(q_n). \\ 0, & \text{otherwise.} \end{cases}$$

where $t = |Truth(q_n)|$, $Hit(i)$ shows whether the ith predicted query q_i' hits the ground truth, $1 \le i \le 5$.

5 EXPERIMENTS

We evaluate our algorithms on the 2006 AOL dataset. The entire query log contains 36,389,567 search records. In total, there are 10,154,742 unique queries and 19,442,629 clickthrough records from 657,426 unique users over three months. We use nine-tenths of the query log as the original log Q to be anonymized, and reserve one-tenth of the data as the test set Q_{Test} for evaluating the IR applications. In the experiments, we compare a few query log anonymization schemes and use the anonymized logs Q' generated from each of them to test on the query suggestion task.

5.1 Anonymized Methods to Compare

The logs used in our experiments include the Original, KA (logs anonymized by k-anonymity), DP_C (logs anonymized by differential privacy, clickthrough data only), and DP_S (logs anonymized by differential privacy, containing both session and clickthrough data). The details of them are described as follows:

Table 4: Privacy levels ϵ and δ for typical $A_{Session}$ runs.

Detail Parameters in DP_S	ϵ	δ
b=1, K=10, T_{Gap}=30, l_s=1, l_q=3	ϵ=8.00	$\delta = 4.95 * 10^{-3}$
b=1, K=20, T_{Gap}=30, l_s=1, l_q=3	ϵ=8.00	$\delta = 2.25 * 10^{-7}$
b=1, K=30, T_{Gap}=30, l_s=1, l_q=3	ϵ=8.00	$\delta = 1.02 * 10^{-11}$
b=3, K=20, T_{Gap}=30, l_s=1, l_q=3	ϵ=2.67	$\delta = 9.66 * 10^{-3}$
b=3, K=30, T_{Gap}=30, l_s=1, l_q=3	ϵ=2.67	$\delta = 3.44 * 10^{-4}$
b=1, K=20, T_{Gap}=30, l_s=1, l_q=4	ϵ=22.00	$\delta = 6.79 * 10^{-4}$
b=2, K=30, T_{Gap}=30, l_s=1, l_q=4	ϵ=11.00	$\delta = 4.12 * 10^{-4}$
b=1, K=20, T_{Gap}=30, l_s=2, l_q=3	ϵ=16.00	$\delta = 2.46 * 10^{-5}$
b=2, K=30, T_{Gap}=30, l_s=2, l_q=3	ϵ=8.00	$\delta = 6.68 * 10^{-5}$

Table 5: Query Suggestion results using different query logs

Run	Precision@5	Recall@5	# of Evaluated Sessions
Original	0.0421	0.1402	**18,475**
KA	0.0693	0.2312	9,494
DP_C	0.1133	0.3891	4,144
DP_S	**0.1139**	**0.3911**	4,119

- Original: The original query log Q without anonymization.
- KA(K): The query log anonymized by the k-anonymity [25]. This log contains frequent clickthrough data from the original log while preserving certain privacy with k-anonymity. Major steps of the k-anonymity query log anonymization algorithm are as follow:
  (1) Input: a query log Q, query clickthrough frequency threshold K.
  (2) Count the number of users who formulates query q and clicks document d as $c(q, d)$.
  (3) Release all tuples $[q, d, c(q, d)]$ iff. $c(q, d) > K$, where K is the frequency cut-off threshold.
  (4) Output: A set of tuples in the form of [Query q, Document d, User Count c(q,d)].
- $DP_C(\epsilon, \delta;l,b,K)$: The query log anonymized by (ϵ, δ)-differentially private algorithm A_{Click} as presented in section 3.2.2, where l is the query click limits per user, b is the Laplacian noise scale, K is the frequency threshold. The output format of the log is the same as KA(K).
- $DP_S(\epsilon, \delta;T_{Gap},l_s,l_q,b,K)$: This anonymized query log consists of the session-based differentially private output and a copy of $DP_C(\epsilon, \delta;l,b,K)$. The session-based output query log is anonymized via $A_{Session}$ and A_{Click} as in section 3.2. T_{Gap} is the session timeout threshold in minutes, l_s is the session limits per user, l_q is the query limits per session, b is the Laplacian noise scale, K is the frequency threshold. The anonymized log contains both session and query clickthrough data.

5.2 Query Suggestion

The query suggestion approach we proposed earlier is based on the calculation of similarities between query pairs which can be generated from Q'. In this section, we use four different types of query logs as presented in section 5.1 to support query suggestion.

The effectiveness of a query suggestion approach is evaluated by comparing between the predicted ranked list of candidate queries and the ground truth. For each session in the test set, we perform query suggestion for each of the prefix query sequence and use the remaining queries of the session as the ground truth.

Table 5 presents Precision and Recall at the ranking position 5 for query suggestion, and the number of sessions in the test set that can still be used by query suggestion, the number of the evaluated or remaining sessions. The major parameters for the anonymized query logs we used are:

- KA(K=20)
- $DP_C(\epsilon=8, \delta=2.25 * 10^{-7}; l=4, b=1, K=20)$
- $DP_S(\epsilon=8, \delta=2.25 * 10^{-7}; T_{Gap}=30, l_s=1, l_q=3, b=1, K=20)$.

where all three anonymized runs share the same frequency threshold value $k = 20$ for a fair comparison.

As we can see, the number of test sessions that our algorithm successfully evaluated in DP_C and DP_S (4,144 and 4,119) are much fewer than in KA (9,494) and Original (18,475). Such information loss is inevitable for getting strong privacy protection. The two runs based on differential privacy successfully suggest queries for a similar amount of sessions. The KA run based on k-anonymity suggests queries for sessions as twice many as the runs based on differential privacy would do. It is because k-anonymity doesn't limit the number of records from each individual while differential privacy does. Therefore, in terms of the quantity of the test sessions that could be evaluated, k-anonymity wins differential privacy, if both constrained by the same cut-off threshold k.

Table 5 also presents the IR utility measures: Precision and Recall. DP_C and DP_S outperform the other runs. Especially, DP_S achieves the best utility results in both Precision and Recall. The KA run works less effective in terms of IR utilities than DP_C and DP_S.

An interesting finding is that the number of evaluated sessions contradicts with task-specific IR utility measures. That is, the runs releasing less sessions yield better IR utility scores. We think the underlying reason roots from the nature of IR. It is because (a) the records with the higher frequency (the more common ones) have a greater chance to be released by differential privacy; (b) they are also records that are positively correlated to producing relevant results for an IR task because they reflect similar behaviors from many different users and are better and more effective data records. That is to say, although DP_C and DP_S release fewer data and suggest less sessions/queries, their released content happen to be more useful to IR. This result is very encouraging for us to advocate the use of actual IR utility metrics over data percentage.

5.3 Parameter Settings

In Table 4, we compare the privacy level in DP_S with different parameter settings. By showing the typical runs and their parameter settings, we observe that ϵ is very sensitive to the max number of sessions per user l_s and the max number of queries per session l_q. Moreover, δ is also very sensitive to the noise scale b and the frequency threshold K.

There are no hard rules for setting the parameters. Generally, smaller ϵ and δ values lead to stronger privacy guarantees but δ can

not be too large. This gives the query log owner, usually the commercial search companies, more flexibility to pick proper privacy parameter values in order to achieve a good balance between privacy and utility. In Table 4, many listed runs are acceptable to use, for instance $DP_S(\epsilon = 8, \delta = 2.25 \times 10^{-7}; T_{Gap}=30, l_s=1, l_q=3, b=1, k=20)$ is one of the good runs that we use in the experiments.

5.4 Privacy Utility Tradeoff

In this section, we run further experiments to analyze the privacy-utility tradeoff during query log anonymization. It is important to show the consequences of using varying anonymization algorithms and using different parameter settings. The comparisons and suggestions we provide in this section should be able to help data owners to make decisions when they need to anonymize a query log.

Figure 1 shows the scale of the anonymized data with varying frequency threshold K. Each data point in the figure corresponds to an anonymized query log. While changing the K values, we fix the other parameters in Figure 1 as $T_{Gap}=30, l_s=1, l_q=3, l = 4$, b=1. Figure 1 (a) presents the change of distinct clickthrough tuples in query logs anonymized by KA; Figure 1 (b) presents the change of distinct clickthrough tuples in query logs anonymized by DP_C, while Figure 1 (c) presents the variation of different released sessions by DP_S. According to Figure 1, the scale of the anonymized query log is very sensitive to the frequency threshold parameter K. The anonymized log suffers a significant amount of data loss as K increases. Based on Eq. 9, the differential privacy parameters ϵ and δ (especially δ) decrease as K increases, which leads to even stronger privacy. Hence, the stronger privacy we require for differential privacy, the more data would lose in the anonymized query logs.

Figure 2 shows the relations between the number of sessions being evaluated and (a) the frequency threshold K, (b) Precision@5 and (c) Recall@5 for the query suggestion task. Figure 2(a) reveals that if we want to evaluate a certain amount of sessions, the K used in differential privacy could be much less than the K used in k-anonymity. Figures 2(b) and (c) present the relationship between the application-based utility score and the amount of evaluated sessions. We observe that the differential privacy runs have better utility than the k-anonymity runs when the sessions being evaluated is no more than a certain value, around 5,500 in our case, while the k-anonymity runs may achieve even better utility than the differential privacy runs if there are more sessions evaluated.

Moreover, we observe from the analysis and experimental results that fewer input records from each user lead to stronger privacy. According to the mathematical characteristics of (ϵ, δ)-differential privacy, the δ value is linearly related to the sensitivity value in our scenario. In other words, the fewer records we take from each user, the smaller δ value we can guarantee and thus achieves stronger privacy, and vice versa. For instance, if we double the number of input records per user l (or l_s), the anonymization mechanism will be with a doubled δ value. We, therefore, suggest to include raw data from more users while limiting fewer sessions and clickthroughs accepted from each user. The experiments based on different anonymization algorithms reveal an privacy-utility tradeoff. It seems that the balance between privacy and utility should be considered at the very beginning when we are selecting the parameters for the anonymization methods.

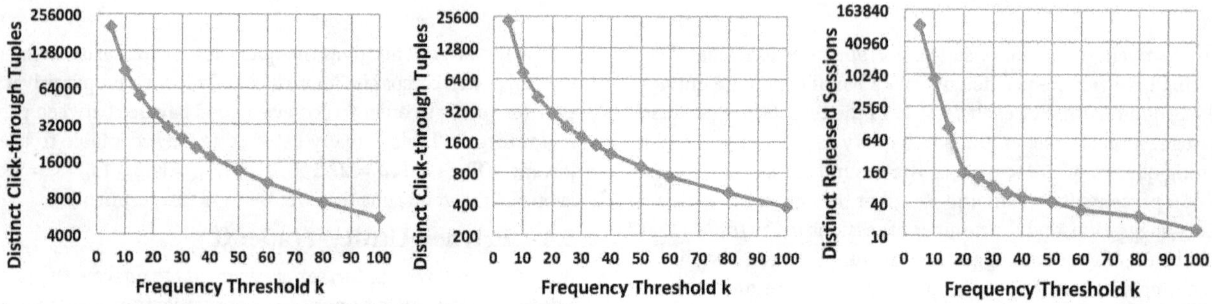

(a) KA Runs

(b) DP_C Runs

(c) DP_S Runs

Figure 1: Data lost: distinct clickthrough tuples and sessions after anonymization with varying frequency threshold k values.

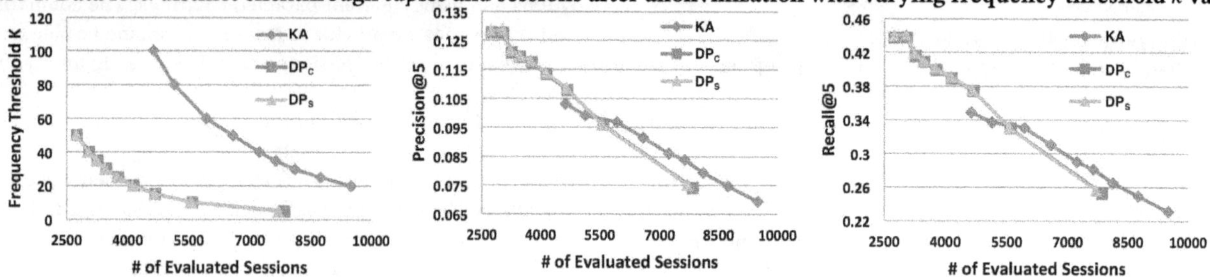

(a) Frequency Threshold K

(b) Precision@5

(c) Recall@5

Figure 2: Query Suggestion: Utility versus # of Evaluated Sessions

6 CONCLUSIONS

Query log anonymization is challenging. When a session of multiple queries are involved, it has becomes even more challenging. In this paper, we research on how to release session data from query logs with differential privacy. We propose methods to evaluate the utility of the anonymized session data and support query suggestion with those anonymized query logs. The results show that our session-based query log anonymization algorithm not only satisfies differential privacy but also is sufficiently capable of supporting complex IR applications. We wish this work can contribute to our research community to better enable data release for IR research.

7 ACKNOWLEDGMENTS

This research was supported by NSF grant IIS-145374 and DARPA grant FA8750-14-2-0226. Any opinions, findings, conclusions, or recommendations expressed in this paper are of the authors, and do not necessarily reflect those of the sponsor.

REFERENCES

[1] Eytan Adar. User 4XXXXX9: Anonymizing query logs. In *Query Logs Workshop at the WWW'07*.
[2] Ricardo Baeza-Yates, Carlos Hurtado, and Marcelo Mendoza. 2004. Query recommendation using query logs in search engines. In *International Conference on Extending Database Technology*. Springer, 588–596.
[3] Michael Barbaro and Tom Zeller. Aug 2006. A Face Is Exposed for AOL Searcher No. 4417749. In *New York Times*.
[4] Raghav Bhaskar, Srivatsan Laxman, Adam Smith, and Abhradeep Thakurta. 2010. Discovering Frequent Patterns in Sensitive Data. In *KDD '10*.
[5] Sumit Bhatia, Debapriyo Majumdar, and Prasenjit Mitra. 2011. Query Suggestions in the Absence of Query Logs. In *SIGIR '11*.
[6] Paolo Boldi, Francesco Bonchi, Carlos Castillo, Debora Donato, and Sebastiano Vigna. 2009. Query Suggestions Using Query-flow Graphs. In *WSCD '09*.
[7] Luca Bonomi and Li Xiong. 2013. A Two-phase Algorithm for Mining Sequential Patterns with Differential Privacy. In *CIKM '13*. ACM, New York, NY, USA.
[8] Huanhuan Cao, Daxin Jiang, Jian Pei, Qi He, Zhen Liao, Enhong Chen, and Hang Li. 2008. Context-aware Query Suggestion by Mining Click-through and Session Data. In *KDD '08*.
[9] Claudio Carpineto and Giovanni Romano. Semantic Search Log K-anonymization with Generalized K-cores of Query Concept Graph. In *ECIR'13*.
[10] Rui Chen, Gergely Acs, and Claude Castelluccia. 2012. Differentially Private Sequential Data Publication via Variable-length N-grams. In *CCS '12*.
[11] Alissa Cooper. 2008. A Survey of Query Log Privacy-enhancing Techniques from a Policy Perspective. *ACM Trans. Web* 2, 4, Article 19 (Oct. 2008), 27 pages.
[12] Cynthia Dwork. 2008. Differential privacy: A survey of results. In *Theory and Applications of Models of Computation*. Springer, 1–19.
[13] Cynthia Dwork. 2011. *Differential Privacy*. Springer US, Boston, MA, 338–340.
[14] Michaela Gotz, Ashwin Machanavajjhala, Guozhang Wang, Xiaokui Xiao, and Johannes Gehrke. 2012. Publishing search logs:a comparative study of privacy guarantees. *IEEE Transactions on Knowledge and Data Engineering* 24, 3 (2012).
[15] Dongyi Guan, Sicong Zhang, and Hui Yang. Utilizing Query Change for Session Search. In *SIGIR '13*.
[16] Morgan Harvey, Claudia Hauff, and David Elsweiler. 2015. Learning by Example: Training Users with High-quality Query Suggestions. In *SIGIR '15*.
[17] Q. He, D. Jiang, Z. Liao, S. C. H. Hoi, K. Chang, E. P. Lim, and H. Li. 2009. Web Query Recommendation via Sequential Query Prediction. In *ICDE'09*.
[18] Yuan Hong, Xiaoyun He, Jaideep Vaidya, Nabil Adam, and Vijayalakshmi Atluri. Effective Anonymization of Query Logs. In *CIKM '09*.
[19] Rosie Jones, Ravi Kumar, Bo Pang, and Andrew Tomkins. "I Know What You Did Last Summer": Query Logs and User Privacy. In *CIKM '07*.
[20] Rosie Jones, Ravi Kumar, Bo Pang, and Andrew Tomkins. Vanity Fair: Privacy in Querylog Bundles. In *CIKM '08*.
[21] Makoto P. Kato, Tetsuya Sakai, and Katsumi Tanaka. 2012. Structured Query Suggestion for Specialization and Parallel Movement: Effect on Search Behaviors. In *WWW '12*.
[22] Aleksandra Korolova, Krishnaram Kenthapadi, Nina Mishra, and Alexandros Ntoulas. Releasing Search Queries and Clicks Privately. In *WWW '09*.
[23] Haoran Li, Li Xiong, Xiaoqian Jiang, and Jinfei Liu. 2015. Differentially Private Histogram Publication for Dynamic Datasets: an Adaptive Sampling Approach. In *CIKM '15*.
[24] S. Su, S. Xu, X. Cheng, Z. Li, and F. Yang. 2015. Differentially Private Frequent Itemset Mining via Transaction Splitting. *IEEE TKDE* 27, 7 (July 2015).
[25] Latanya Sweeney. 2002. k-anonymity: A model for protecting privacy. *International Journal of Uncertainty, Fuzziness and Knowledge-Based Systems* 10, 05 (2002), 557–570.
[26] Jia Xu, Zhenjie Zhang, Xiaokui Xiao, Yin Yang, Ge Yu, and Marianne Winslett. 2013. Differentially private histogram publication. *The VLDB Journal* 22, 6 (2013).
[27] S. Xu, S. Su, X. Cheng, Z. Li, and L. Xiong. 2015. Differentially private frequent sequence mining via sampling-based candidate pruning. In *ICDE'15*.
[28] Sicong Zhang, Grace Hui Yang, Lisa Singh, and Li Xiong. 2016. Safelog: Supporting Web Search and Mining by Differentially-Private Query Logs. In *2016 AAAI Fall Symposium Series*.
[29] Sicong Zhang, Hui Yang, and Lisa Singh. 2016. Anonymizing Query Logs by Differential Privacy. In *SIGIR '16*.

Graph-based Semi-supervised Learning for Text Classification

Natalie Widmann
Artificial Intelligence, Radboud University
Nijmegen, The Netherlands
NatalieWidmann@gmx.de

Suzan Verberne
LIACS/Leiden Centre of Data Science
Leiden, The Netherlands
s.verberne@liacs.leidenuniv.nl

ABSTRACT

In this paper, we propose a graph-based representation of document collections in which both documents and features are represented by nodes. The nodes are connected with weights based on word order, context similarity and word frequency. Graph-based representations can overcome the limitations of bag-of-words based representations that suffer from sparseness for collections with short documents. In a series of experiments, we evaluate multiple types of graph-based text features in the context of semi-supervised text classification, and investigate the effect of the number of labeled documents in the collection. We find that graph-based semi-supervised learning outperforms bag-of-words semi-supervised learning but not bag-of-words supervised learning in 20-class text categorization. A large asset of graph-based representations is that they are flexible in the types of nodes and relations that are included.

CCS CONCEPTS

• **Information systems** → **Clustering and classification**; **Content analysis and feature selection**; • **Mathematics of computing** → *Graph algorithms*; • **Theory of computation** → *Semi-supervised learning*;

KEYWORDS

text representation, graph models, text classification, semi-supervised learning

ACM Reference format:
Natalie Widmann and Suzan Verberne. 2017. Graph-based Semi-supervised Learning for Text Classification. In *Proceedings of ICTIR'17, Amsterdam, The Netherlands., October 1–4, 2017,* 8 pages.
DOI: http://dx.doi.org/10.1145/10.1145/3121050.3121055

1 INTRODUCTION

Semi-supervised learning offers the possibility to reduce the burden of data labeling. This is important in many text classification tasks where limited labeled data is available, such as the classification of short and sparse web texts [15], email categorization [19] and Twitter sentiment classification [23]. Most text classification methods are based on the vector space model [27], where the dimensions represent word frequencies without information about word order or semantic relations between words [1, 9]. When applied to short

texts, these methods suffer from sparseness – the use of different words among documents belonging to the same class [22].

In this paper we investigate whether a graph-based text representation can overcome this limitation and is able to improve text categorization quality in semi-supervised learning. Graph-based representations are flexible in the types of nodes and relations that are included and provide a much richer representation in terms of sentence structure and semantics of the underlying data [1]. We propose a graph-based text representation that includes documents and features connected with weights based on word order, context similarity and word frequency. We evaluate multiple types of graph-based text features in semi-supervised learning with label propagation [33]. We compare our methods to a standard supervised learning method, and to a semi-supervised method that uses a bag-of-words (BOW) representation in the vector space model.

As evaluation set, we use the 20-Newsgroup benchmark dataset.[1] On this dataset, [34] demonstrate that semi-supervised learning is able to efficiently exploit the structure of unlabeled data. We address the following research questions:

(1) Which graph-based features are the most successful in semi-supervised text categorization?

(2) How does graph-based semi-supervised learning compare to supervised classification and semi-supervised learning with BOW-features when varying the number of labeled documents?

Since scalability is a key issue in graph-based semi-supervised learning [17], we also address the computational complexity of our method.

Our contributions are: (1) we propose a graph-based representation of document collections that can be flexibly adapted to the specific task; (2) we show that adding word relations to the standard (frequency-based) representation improves classification quality and thereby (3) we lay foundations for further research into the potential of graph representations for text retrieval and classification.

2 BACKGROUND

In previous research, many approaches have been proposed to take into account word order and semantics in text representation. Here (Section 2.1), we limit ourselves to graph representations. In Sections 2.2 and 2.3 we provide a background on semi-supervised learning and label propagation respectively.

2.1 Graph representations of text

There is a large body of previous work on graph models in Information Retrieval and Natural Language Processing [13], partly brought together in the TextGraphs workshops since 2006.[1] Many graph

[1] http://qwone.com/~jason/20Newsgroups/
[1] http://textgraphs.org/

models represent relations between documents such as hyperlinks on the web [2], or ontological relations in a knowledge graph. Here, we focus on graph representations of document collections that include vocabulary items as nodes. The connecting edges then indicate consecutive syntactic relations, semantic similarities or word co-occurrences [1, 13, 21].

Graph representations of text have proven to be particularly successful for short texts, such as reviews [7, 16] and Tweets [4, 26], because the graph representation overcomes the sparseness of information by enriching the word nodes with (syntactic and/or semantic) relations. A recent application is semantic clustering of suggested short response messages in email clients [10].

As many machine learning algorithms rely on similarity or distance measures, as well as the computation of centroids and other numerical values [20], graph-based text representations require further processing (e.g. conversion to a matrix) or specially adapted graph-based machine learning methods [9, 13]. The required operations are often computationally expensive as graph-based text representations add an additional level of complexity by including different types of relevant structural and semantic information [9]. Recent advances in graph methods and computational power have resulted in a growing interest in graph-based text representations [1].

2.2 Semi-Supervised Learning

The idea of semi-supervised learning is that the distribution of unlabeled data can add relevant information to a supervised learning algorithm and hence, positively influence the ability to classify unseen data [6].

Graph-based methods for semi-supervised learning have been applied to sentiment classification of reviews [8] and tweets [30], and genre classification of web pages [2]. In the paper by [2], the graph represents the structure of the web, with nodes representing documents documents and edges representing hyperlinks. In [30], nodes represent hashtag and edges the cooccurrence of hashtags in a tweet.

A number of works describe semi-supervised learning methods evaluated on (subsets of) the here used 20-Newsgroup dataset [14, 24, 32, 34]. Zhou et al. [32] show that smoothing the classification function with respect to the intrinsic structure revealed by the labeled and unlabeled data points decreases the error rates of 4-class text categorization. Zhu et al. [34] demonstrate that semi-supervised learning approach based on Gaussian random fields is able to efficiently exploit the structure of unlabeled data to improve accuracy on a binary text classification task selected from the 20-Newsgroup dataset. Nigam et al. [14] illustrate the use of Expectation-Maximization (EM) techniques with Naive Bayes classification. They report an 66% accuracy with 300 labeled documents (15 documents per class). More recently, Su et al. [24] proposed a semi-supervised extension of multinomial Naive Bayes, called Semi-supervised Frequency Estimate. They report accuracy scores ranging from 41.92% for 64 labeled documents to 66.29% for 512 labeled documents.

2.3 Label Propagation

In this section we have a detailed look at label propagation which is a commonly used graph-based semi-supervised learning approach. Labeled and unlabeled data points are represented as nodes in a graph and connected with weighted edges representing their similarity [11]. The known labels are then propagated through the graph until all nodes are labeled [33].

For the understanding of label propagation it is necessary to introduce a standardized mathematical notation of graph structure and the representation of the labels [35]: A data set $\mathcal{X}$ consists of labeled samples $\{(\mathbf{x}_1, y_1), (\mathbf{x}_2, y_2), ...(\mathbf{x}_l, y_l)\}$ with $y \in \{1...C\}$, and unlabeled samples $\{\mathbf{x}_{l+1}, ...\mathbf{x}_u\}$. All n data points are either labeled or unlabeled, hence, $n = l + u$, where normally $l << u$. A weighted graph $\mathcal{G} = (\mathcal{X}, \mathbf{W})$ is constructed such that every data point $\mathbf{x}_i$ is represented as a node, connected with node of point $\mathbf{x}_j$ with weight w_{ij}. All the edge weights together form the weight matrix $\mathbf{W}$.

To estimate $\hat{Y} = (\hat{Y}_l, \hat{Y}_u)$ the weight matrix $\mathbf{W}$ is normalized with it degree matrix $\mathbf{D}$ with $\mathbf{D}_{ii} = \sum_j \mathbf{W}_{ij}$ corresponding to the total number of out going edges of node x_i. Therefore, the matrix product $\mathbf{D}^{-1}\mathbf{W}$ corresponds to the normalized transition matrix which indicates how probable the transition from one node to another node is. Labels are then propagated through the graph by multiplying the transition probability with the actual labels: $\hat{Y} = \mathbf{D}^{-1}\mathbf{W}Y$. With $\hat{Y}_l = Y_l$ we ensure that the original labels are fixed and repeat the process with $Y = \hat{Y}$ until convergence is reached.

The original label propagation algorithm was introduced in 2002 by Zhu and Ghahramani [33] and was since then modified and extended many times. The original label propagation algorithm ensures that the initially known labels do not change over time. This minimizes the following function [3]:

$$\sum_{i \in V_l} (\hat{y}_i - y_i)^2 = ||\hat{Y}_l - \hat{Y}_l||^2 \qquad (1)$$

To include the smoothness assumption (points that are similar or closely related are likely to have the same label), rapid changes in the predicted labels $\hat{Y}$ between similar data points are penalized by minimizing the following function:

$$\frac{1}{2} \sum_{i,j \in V} A_{ij}(\hat{y}_i - \hat{y}_j)^2 = \hat{Y}^T (D - A)\hat{Y} = \hat{Y}^T L\hat{Y} \qquad (2)$$

The combination of (1) and (2) results in a cost function that covers the tradeoff between the smoothness of the predicted labels over the entire graph and the accuracy of the predicted labels in fitting the given hard labels on the labeled nodes $\mathcal{X}_l$ [11]:

$$C(\hat{Y}) = ||\hat{Y}_l - \hat{Y}_l||^2 + \mu \, \hat{Y}^T L\hat{Y} \qquad (3)$$

with μ regulating the corresponding relevance.

Based on this simple idea, more and more algorithms are developed that try to improve the quality of semi-supervised learning such that noisy labeled data can be used, more explicit consistency assumptions can be modeled and the results are more stable. As mentioned in the introduction, the main disadvantage of graph-based methods is their computational complexity. But with advancing technology, new approaches to tackle this issue are developed, for example [17] who present the EXPANDER algorithm for approximated graph-base semi-supervised learning that scales up to large data scenarios. Its effectiveness for semantic clustering on short response messages has been demonstrated by [10].

In this paper we combine different ideas from graph-based text representation and label propagation. Similarly to [10], we present documents as well as features in one graph. However, while their feature space is limited to very frequent responses which are clustered manually, we extend their approach such that entire texts documents can be represented and the graph construction, including the computation of similarity is fully automized.

3 METHODS AND EXPERIMENTS

We conduct two experiments: one to investigate the graph-based features that improve text classification quality in semi-supervised learning, and another one to compare its success in dealing with a low number of labeled documents with standard approaches for graph and vector based text categorization.

Figure 1 gives an overview of the steps involved in graph-based semi-supervised learning. In the following subsections each of the steps are explained in detail. The general script for processing, label propagation and analysis was implemented in python 2.7 under usage of the natural language toolkit (nltk)[2] and scikit-learn.[3] Furthermore, the graph database management system Neo4j is used for storing the graph representations.[4] We will publish our source code for re-use by other researchers.

3.1 Data and preprocessing

We use the 20-Newsgroup corpus, a popular benchmark dataset for text classification, to evaluate and compare our methods. The collection[5] consists of about 11,300 newsgroup texts divided into 20 different topics in which some are closely related [18]. The average document length is 185 words and the categories are quite balanced as most of the topics contain between 550 and 600 documents.

Headers, footers and references were removed from the Newsgroup documents. As we use documents as well as all unique words as nodes in the graph, a first step to reduce the dimensionality of the problem, was to reduce the amount of unique words. Therefore, every document was tokenized[6], all words were lowercased and lemmatized using the nltk WordNetLemmatizer and stopwords were removed.[6] Furthermore words that appear fewer than 10 times in the entire document collection, as well as words that appear in more than 50% of the documents were removed. The remaining words were grouped together in a vocabulary and documents that did not include any word from the vocabulary were excluded from the analysis. Every remaining document was separated into lists of sentences containing the unique words.

3.2 Graph Construction

Based on the preprocessed documents a graph of the entire newsgroup collection is constructed in Neo4j. We distinguish between

two different node types: Document Nodes represent a document, in this case a newsgroup post, and contain a unique name as well as a property indicating their label. Feature Nodes represent a feature of a document, for example a word. To create the graph we iterate through each document of the collection and add all sentences word by word to the graph if it is not yet present. For every word appearing in a document their corresponding feature and document nodes get connected via the *is_in* relation.

The word order in a document is grasped by relating successive words in a sentence with the directed edge *followed_by*. Furthermore, the start and end of every sentence is indicated by the special feature nodes *$Start$* and *End* which are as any other feature node connected to the succeeding and preceding features, and as well as the corresponding document nodes. Both edge types, *followed_by* and *is_in*, have a count that is increased as soon as for example a word appears a second or third time in the same document or a sequence of words is repeated within the same document or within another one.

After constructing the entire collection graph, the edge weights are normalized by dividing them by the total number of out-going edges from the corresponding node. The normalized relation between feature nodes now indicates the transition probability from a certain word to another. Similarly, the document–feature relation now indicates the relative frequency of a word in a document.

3.3 Graph-based features

In this section, we explore what kind of information is contained in the graph and how further features can be constructed. Conventional semi-supervised learning approaches, like label propagation, require a matrix representation of the graph. Therefore, we analyze the graph-based features with respect to the corresponding matrix representation. A matrix representation contains each node with its corresponding relations to all other nodes. We distinguish between document and feature nodes. Assuming we have n documents and m features the corresponding matrix representation $\mathbf{W}$ has the shape $n + m \times n + m$. Splitting the matrix up into a document matrix $\mathbf{DD}$, a feature matrix $\mathbf{FF}$ and a document feature matrix $\mathbf{DF}$ matrix helps to avoid confusions and facilitates having a closer look at each of them and the text features they represent:

$$W = \begin{pmatrix} \mathbf{DD} & \mathbf{DF} \\ \mathbf{DF}^T & \mathbf{FF} \end{pmatrix}$$

The document-matrix, $\mathbf{DD}$, describes the relations or similarity between documents which for example can be based on the author, publication time, topic or any other measure that directly or indirectly relates two documents. As we do not include any information of this kind, the document matrix corresponds to a $n \times n$ dimensional identity matrix. $\mathbf{DD} = \mathbf{I}_n$ reflects that each document is identical to itself while different to all others. The document–feature matrix, $\mathbf{DF}$, captures information that relates document with feature nodes, for example based on their frequency. In the complete matrix representation the document–feature matrix appears twice, once in its original form and once transposed. In the following we list the different document–feature relations that we consider in our experiments:

---

[2]http://www.nltk.org/
[3]http://scikit-learn.org
[4]https://neo4j.com/
[5]Different versions of the 20-Newsgroup dataset exist. We obtained the corpus from scikit-learn for which more information can be found on http://scikit-learn.org/stable/datasets/twenty_newsgroups.html
[6]The code for tokenization and the list of stopwords are taken from [28]. The full list of stopwords can be found here: https://github.com/suzanv/termprofiling/blob/master/stoplist.txt

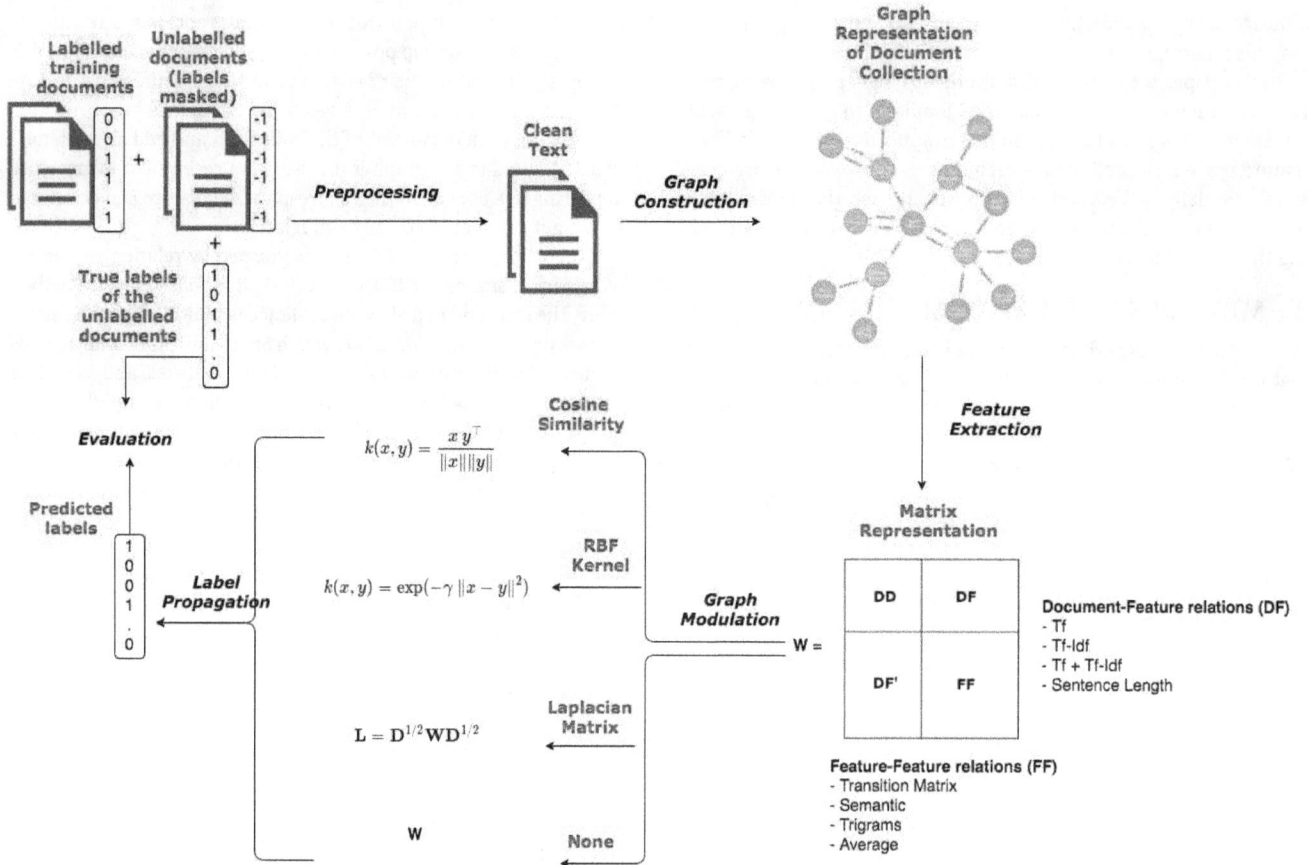

Figure 1: Visualization of the step-by-step process for graph-based semi-supervised learning. The raw documents and the corresponding label vector (unlabeled data indicated with -1) are the starting point of the approach. By preprocessing the documents, clean text that is split in sentences represented as lists of words is obtained. In graph construction, we iterate through the sentences and add respective words and relations to the graph until the full collection of documents is represented. In order to use the graph properties for label propagation, relevant features have to be extracted and converted into a square matrix consisting of document–document, document–feature and feature–feature relations.

- Term frequency (tf), normalized by the total number of terms in a document.
- Term frequency – Inverse document frequency (tf-idf). We use the implementation in `scikit-learn`.
- Tf+Tf-Idf As the weight matrix W includes twice the document–feature relations, once as DF and once as DF^T the previously two features can be combined.
- Sentence Count, implemented as edges between the \$Start\$ and \$End\$ features and the document.

The feature matrix **FF** describes how features relate to each other. With m features **FF** is a $m \times m$ matrix. Dependent on the chosen weight metric the matrix is either symmetric or asymmetric. The following text properties expressible with **FF** are evaluated in our experiments:

- *Transition Probability (word order).* We constructed the graph such that successive words in a sentence are linked with an edge; the feature–feature relation indicates how often a certain feature f_j follows feature f_i. The transition probability matrix follows from normalizing the count weights.
- *Trigrams.* The weights in the transition probability matrix indicate how likely it is that a feature is followed by any other feature, or in other words that a path between those two features exists. By multiplying the transition matrix n times with it self, paths of length n are detected [25]. Therefore, the square matrix of **W** gives information about 3-gram feature sequences in the sentence structures of the document collection.
- *Context Similarity* indicates whether two words appear in a similar context and hence, can be substituted for each other [12]. For example *Monday* and *Thursday* have a common context as they are both weekdays. The same is true for words from other semantic classes and subclasses such as animals, birds, objects, body parts, etc. Including this information to the label propagation algorithm can link documents that talk about the same semantic class but use

different words. The context of feature is defined as all the words to which it is directly linked, where we distinguish between preceding and succeeding words. The context similarity between two features is computed by averaging over the similarity of the preceding and the similarity of the succeeding context of each of the features. The Jaccard index is used to measure the similarity between two context sets C_1 and C_2:

$$J(C_1, C_2) = \frac{\|C_1 \cap C_2\|}{\|C_1 \cup C_2\|}$$

To ensure the computational feasibility of this method, only connected features with a normalized edge weight higher than 0.1 are considered as context features.

- *Average of the above three FF properties.*

3.4 Graph Modulation

To successfully use the modeled matrix **W** in label propagation for text classification, it has to include relevant features of the text documents, but also fulfill the smoothness and cluster assumptions which we discussed in Section 2.3. Kernel methods compute the pairwise similarity of all elements in the matrix and are often used to implement the smoothness assumptions in semi-supervised learning. We evaluate three different kernels and their combinations and investigate how they effect the quality of text classification: (1) *Cosine Similarity*, which is commonly used for measuring the similarity between two documents in the vector space model; (2) an *RBF Kernel*, which is commonly used in support vector machines and defined as:

$$k(x, y) = \exp(-\gamma \|x - y\|^2) = \exp(-\frac{1}{\sigma^{-2}} \|x - y\|^2)$$

where σ^{-2} describes the variance of a Gaussian distribution. In other words, γ indicates the reach or the influence of a single data point. The higher the gamma, the more local the reach, the lower the more global. The gamma value has a significant influence on the model [29]. The values of the RBF kernel range between 0 and 1. (3) a *Laplacian Matrix*, used on top of the RBF kernel, as [11] argues that while the RBF kernel is effective to establish local consistency, by additionally smoothing it with the Laplacian also global consistency is achieved as unreliable edges between points that are relatively far apart are removed. The normalized Laplacian matrix is defined as: $L = D^{1/2}WD^{1/2}$, with **W** being the weight or similarity matrix and **D** its corresponding degree matrix, defined as $D = diag([D_{11}, ... D_{nn}])$ with $D_{ii} = \sum_{j=1}^{n} W_{ij}$.

3.5 Experimental setup

For semi-supervised learning, slightly modified versions of the label propagation and label spreading algorithm in the module sklearn.semi_supervised are used. The modification ensures that implemented graph modulations such as the RBF kernel can be circumvented or replaced by different modulations.

Graph-based Feature Analysis. First, we compare the different combinations of document–feature relations. For the feature–feature relations the transition matrix is used as a default. These different matrix settings are then compared to label propagation with Tf-Idf weighting which is a standard approach for bag-of-words based

semi-supervised learning. In the result section this latter condition is indicated as *baseline*. Furthermore, for each setting different combinations of graph-modulations (cosine similarity, RBF kernel and Laplacian matrix) are applied. A 3-fold cross-validated parameter search in the interval of [0.15, 10] for the γ value in the RBF kernel yielded $\gamma = 5$ which is used for all experiments that include an RBF kernel.

As Tf+Tf-Idf emerges to have the highest performance with different graph modulations, this will be used as default for the **DF** matrix when different feature–feature relations are investigated. For each of the different settings, 100 documents from each class (around one fifth of all documents) are randomly selected as labeled data points. To ensure that the quality is not dependent on the selected labeled documents, the experiment is repeated three times and the resulting mean F-scores and standard deviations are reported.

Percentage of labeled documents. From the first experiment the best performing **DF** and **FF** matrix with their corresponding graph modulation is chosen. The best performing **DF** matrix was found to be *Tf+Tf-idf* and the best performing **FF** matrix was context similarity. In addition to the RBF kernel with $\gamma = 5$, the Laplacian matrix is used for graph modulation. This setting will be referred to as *graph-based SSL*.

To evaluate the influence of the *graph-based text representation*, this setting is compared to semi-supervised learning with the same graph modulations based on the *tf-idf* vector representation (*bag-of-words SSL*). Furthermore, to assess the quality of semi-supervised learning compared to a standard supervised learning approach, linear support vector classification as implemented in sklearn.svm.LinearSVC is also evaluated. It is trained on the *tf-idf* vector representation. The C parameter was optimized in grid search on 2000 held-out documents with a grid ranging from 2^{-5} to $2^{1}5$ with steps of 2. The optimal parameter setting found is $C = 1$. We will refer to this setting to as *bag-of-words SL*.

The different approaches are compared by using different amounts of labeled documents that vary from 1 to 350 documents per class. The labeled documents are selected randomly. To marginalize the effect of the random selection the full experiment is conducted ten times and the average F-scores with their corresponding standard deviations are reported. Note that since the unlabeled documents (labels masked) from the semi-supervised training are used as test documents (see Figure 1), the number of test documents varies from from $n = 11280$ with 1 labeled document per class to $n = 4300$ with 350 labeled documents per class.

Evaluation. The 20-Newsgroup dataset provides the true labels for all documents. We evaluate our methods on the documents for which the true labels were masked during the training phase. These documents are used to evaluate the predicted labels in the different learning approaches, in terms of precision and recall. We will report the macro averaged F1 as main evaluation metric as the different classes in the 20-Newsgroup dataset are relatively balanced.

4 RESULTS

The result section is separated into the two different experiments about graph-based feature analysis and the text categorization quality with varying amount of labeled documents.

During preprocessing stopwords and low-frequent words were removed, which causes 335 documents to be empty. These were removed from the dataset and 10979 documents remain. Also, the number of unique words is important, as they are used as nodes in the graph representation. There are 7002 features consisting of the the 7000 most frequent unique words and the special features $Start$ and End that indicate the beginning and end of a sentence.

4.1 Graph-based Feature Analysis

For both categorization tasks the results in terms of F-scores are summarized in Tables 1 and 2. In Table 1 different document–feature relations and graph modulations are compared. Note that the label propagation algorithm is based on matrix multiplication requiring a square matrix as input. Therefore, the *Tf-Idf* vector representation ('Baseline') does not yield any results without being modulated by a kernel ('None'). Table 2 shows the effect of different **FF** relations, while using *Tf+Tf-Idf* as **DF** matrix. Statistical significance is assessed with a t-test at significance level 0.05.

Table 1 shows that without the use of an RBF kernel the semi-supervised learning performances are almost zero (around 0.5%). However, if an RBF kernel is applied the *Tf-Idf* and *Tf+Tf-Idf* condition are always significantly better than the *baseline* or the *Tf* condition.

Table 2 shows that context similarity gives the highest F-scores when no cosine similarity is applied. However, these scores of about 62% are only significantly different from the F-scores obtained in the transition matrix with added sentence length information. The other **FF** settings (transition matrix, T trigram and context similarity) do not significantly differ from each other. When cosine similarity is added, the best mean F-score drops about 6% points, and this effect is even larger in the context similarity setting, where the drop from *RBF* to *RBF+cos* is almost 10% points. Information about sentence length leads to a significant deviation form the best results when cosine similarity is not used. A more detailed discussion of the results is in Section 5.

4.2 Percentage of labeled documents

Figure 2 displays how the number of labeled documents per class influences the quality of 20-class text categorization. The plot shows the F-score averaged over 10 runs in which the labeled documents used for training are randomly selected. The corresponding standard deviations are plotted as error bars. The best graph-based SSL setting (with *Tf+Tf-Idf* and the context similarity as **FF** matrix), is compared to *tf-idf* based bag-of-words semi-supervised (bag-of-words SSL) and supervised learning (bag-of-words SL). For both semi-supervised learning approaches the graph is modulated by an RBF kernel with $\gamma = 5$ and the Laplace matrix. The number of labeled documents per class ranges from 1 to 350. The best performing method, surprisingly, is bag-of-words SL. Graph-based SSL reaches an F-score of 0.62 with 100 labeled documents, and up to 0.68 with 350 labeled documents. Interestingly, the difference with

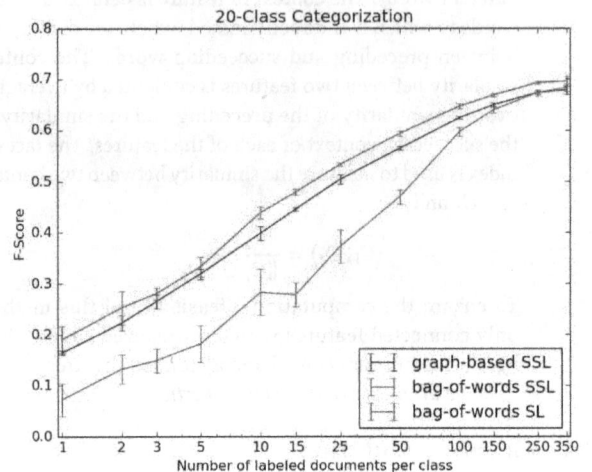

Figure 2: Comparison of the performance in 20-class text categorization with an increasing number of labeled documents per class. From ten independent runs the mean F-scores with their corresponding standard deviation are plotted.

bag-of-words SSL is the largest with a small number of labeled documents.

For significance testing, we apply a Welch two-sample t-test to the mean F-scores obtained by the different methods for each number of labeled documents (each point on the X-axis). This test indicates that the differences between the methods are significant with $p < 0.0001$ for each number of labeled documents, despite the seemingly small difference between graph-based SSL (the blue line) and bag-of-words SL (red line). This is a result of the large sample size (ranging from $n = 11280$ with 1 labeled document per class to $n = 4300$ with 350 labeled documents per class), which makes a the smallest difference statistically significant.

All in all, graph-based SSL outperforms bag-of-words SSL, but not bag-of-words SL in 20-class text categorization. With respect to the standard deviations, graph-based SSL and bag-of-words SL seem to be more stable than bag-of-words SSL. Thus, in our semi-supervised learning setting, the graph representations do clearly outperform the bag-of-words representations for this dataset, but our semi-supervised learning method was not able to outperform supervised learning with SVM.

5 DISCUSSION

In this section we discuss in detail the obtained results, describe the potential application of our methods, and discuss computational complexity.

5.1 Discussion of the results

One of our findings was that graph-based semi-supervised learning performs poorly without an RBF kernel. This implies that the required connection between nodes that indicates smoothness and clustering in the graph is not sufficiently present in the obtained

Table 1: Average F-scores with corresponding standard deviations for the 20-class text categorization task with 100 labeled documents per class. The baseline is semi-supervised learning with the *Tf-Idf* vector representation. The best results are printed in bold and the ones that differ significantly from them are marked with an asterisk.

	Baseline	Tf	Tf-Idf	Tf - Tf-Idf
None	-	0.50 ±0.01	0.52 ±0.00	0.49 ±0.00
cos	0.52 ±0.00	0.52 ±0.00	0.52 ±0.00	0.52 ±0.00
RBF	52.88* ±1.91	0.52* ±0.02	60.82 ±1.70	**61.97** ±0.36
RBF + cos	46.67* ±0.37	9.55* ±6.51	54.91±0.68	**55.48** ±0.61
RBF + Laplace	59.69* ±0.81	0.68* ±0.28	61.00 ±1.44	**62.01** ±0.28
RBF + Laplace + cos	48.05 *±0.25	7.01* ±2.69	**57.37** ±0.21	56.76 ±0.82

Table 2: Average F-scores with corresponding standard deviations for the 20-class text categorization task with 100 labeled documents per class, with different feature–feature relations, all using the *Tf+Tf-Idf* as DF matrix. The best results are printed in bold and the ones that differ significantly from them are marked with an asterisk.

	Transition Matrix	Trigram	Context Similarity	Average	Transition Matrix Sentence Length
RBF	61.97 ±0.36	62.00 ±0.35	**62.07** ±0.37	62.03 ±0.34	46.73* ±2.87
RBF + cos	**55.48** ±0.61	55.36 ±0.51	52.70* ±0.41	52.88* ±0.35	54.27 ±0.55
RBF + Laplace	62.01 ±0.28	62.04 ±0.28	**62.09** ±0.28	62.05 ±0.31	52.08* ±1.33
RBF + Laplace + cos	**56.76** ±0.82	56.05 ±0.79	55.30 ±0.63	55.05 ±0.82	56.53 ±0.64

weight matrix. Applying an RBF kernel on the weight matrix helps to convey this information.

Our graph based semi-supervised learning approach improves text categorization quality compared to bag-of-words based semi-supervised learning. As both approaches use *tf-idf* feature weights, the improvement comes from the word relations that are only present in the graph representation. However, it seems that the performance is not significantly influenced by the choice of different word relations: the results for the feature–feature relations (transition matrix, trigram and context similarity) do not significantly differ from each other. Several explanations are possible: besides the fact that the DF matrix appears twice in the weight matrix, it might be that the tf-idf weights of the DF matrix are in general higher and therefore the FF does contribute but the actual values are very small such that tiny changes do not lead to significant improvement of the overall classification quality.

We looked into the big influence of the sentence length and how it can be explained. We found that as we remove stopwords from the newsgroup posts, the sentences become very short which in turn increases the probability of a word to connect to the start or end of a sentence than to connect to another word. Therefore, the weights that resemble the transition probability from and to a special feature indication sentence start and length are in general higher than other transition probabilities. Also in the document–feature relation that they a fairly big role due to the shortness of sentences and the special features appearing twice.

In the second experiment, graph-based semi-supervised learning was compared to bag-of-words (semi-)supervised learning with a varying number of labeled documents. All three classifiers differed significantly from each other. Graph-based semi-supervised learning did outperform the bag-of-words semi-supervised learning, but not the supervised learning baseline. Given the previous success with semi-supervised learning on the same dataset [14, 24], we

conclude that semi-supervised learning with label propagation is sub-optimal for 20-class document categorization.

5.2 Potential of graph-based text representation

Graph-based learning offers the possibility to get insights into the document collection. Firstly, transition probabilities indicate frequent word sequences, which helps to identify key phrases. Secondly, words with a high context similarity indicate synonyms in the collection's topic domain (following the distributional hypothesis). Thirdly, by including words or other features into the representation of a document collection, labels are not only assigned to the documents but also its features. This helps to understand based on what criteria a classifier assigns labels to documents. This aspect can also be used for direct application: For example, if a collection of documents is already labeled with topics, the graph representation can identify keywords that relevant for a specific topic, which in turn can be used for a different completely unlabeled dataset [10].

The main advantage of graph-based semi-supervised learning is its flexibility to adapt and weight graph properties dependent on the specific task at hand. In our experiments we focused on document–feature and feature–feature relations, but the graph representation could be extended with document–document relations representing the similarity of documents (based on author, journal, year of publication, etc.) Many other feature–feature relations are also thinkable, e.g. the word co-occurrence in a larger windows of n-words, similarity based on the length of words or word2vec based similarity.

5.3 Computational Complexity

The proposed graph representation of a document collection requires iterating through all documents and their corresponding words. Every word and relation is checked for existence and if necessary modified or created. This leads to a time complexity linear to the number of documents n plus the number of words m $O(n + m)$. For the purpose of label propagation a matrix containing the corresponding relation of each node to all other nodes has to be constructed, leading to a squared complexity $O(f^2)$ in the number of features.

Similarly, kernel operations like the cosine similarity or the RBF kernel, correspond to the dot-product of the feature vectors [31], that computes the similarity of each object to all other. For a m dimensional feature space a kernel function results requires the computation of a $m \times m$ feature matrix and its storage [5].

In conclusion, scalability of graph-based semi-supervised learning is limited, especially when documents as well as features are represented in the graph. Therefore, graph-based semi-supervised learning is especially interesting for collections of short documents in which the addition of document–document and feature–feature relations overcome the sparseness of short documents in a standard bag-of-words representation.

6 CONCLUSION

We showed that graph-based semi-supervised learning has a number of advantages compared to bag-of-words based semi-supervised learning. However, we were not able to prove the advantage of graph-based semi-supervised learning over the supervised learning baseline.

A large asset of graph-based representations is that they are flexible in the types of nodes and relations that are included. We propose a graph-based text representation that includes documents and features connected with weights based on word order, context similarity and word frequency, but more node types and relation types could be included as well, depending on the task at hand. One particular direction that we would like to explore in the future is the inclusion of user interaction data (queries, clicks on documents, document reading and writing) in the document collection graph.

REFERENCES

[1] Charu C Aggarwal and Peixiang Zhao. 2013. Towards graphical models for text processing. *Knowledge and information systems* 36, 1 (2013), 1–21.
[2] Noushin Rezapour Asheghi, Katja Markert, and Serge Sharoff. 2014. Semi-supervised Graph-based Genre Classification for Web Pages. *TextGraphs-9* (2014), 39.
[3] Yoshua Bengio, Olivier Delalleau, and Nicolas Le Roux. 2006. 11 Label Propagation and Quadratic Criterion. In *Semi-Supervised Learning*, O. et al. Chapelle (Ed.). MIT Press.
[4] Esteban Castillo, Ofelia Cervantes, Darnes Vilarino, David Báez, and Alfredo Sánchez. 2015. Udlap: sentiment analysis using a graph based representation. In *Proceedings of the 9th International Workshop on Semantic Evaluation (SemEval 2015)*,. Association for Computational Linguistics, 556–560.
[5] Nicolo Cesa-Bianchi, Yishay Mansour, and Ohad Shamir. 2015. On the Complexity of Learning with Kernels. In *Journal of Machine Learning Research: Workshop and Conference Proceedings*. PMLR Press, 1–29.
[6] Olivier Chapelle, Bernhard Scholkopf, and Alexander Zien. 2009. Semi-supervised learning. *IEEE Transactions on Neural Networks* 20, 3 (2009), 542–542.
[7] Kavita Ganesan, ChengXiang Zhai, and Jiawei Han. 2010. Opinosis: a graph-based approach to abstractive summarization of highly redundant opinions. In *Proceedings of the 23rd international conference on computational linguistics*. Association for Computational Linguistics, 340–348.
[8] Andrew B Goldberg and Xiaojin Zhu. 2006. Seeing stars when there aren't many stars: graph-based semi-supervised learning for sentiment categorization. In *Proceedings of the First Workshop on Graph Based Methods for Natural Language Processing*. Association for Computational Linguistics, 45–52.
[9] Chuntao Jiang, Frans Coenen, Robert Sanderson, and Michele Zito. 2010. Text classification using graph mining-based feature extraction. *Knowledge-Based Systems* 23, 4 (2010), 302–308.

[10] Anjuli Kannan, Karol Kurach, Sujith Ravi, Tobias Kaufmann, Andrew Tomkins, Balint Miklos, Greg Corrado, László Lukács, Marina Ganea, Peter Young, and others. 2016. Smart Reply: Automated Response Suggestion for Email. In *Proceedings of the ACM SIGKDD Conference on Knowledge Discovery and Data Mining (KDD)*, Vol. 36. 495–503.
[11] Wei Liu, Jun Wang, and Shih-Fu Chang. 2012. Robust and scalable graph-based semisupervised learning. *Proc. IEEE* 100, 9 (2012), 2624–2638.
[12] William Lyon. 2015. Natural Language Processing with Neo4j – Mining Paradigmatic Word Associations. (2015). http://www.lyonwj.com/2015/06/16/nlp-with-neo4j/
[13] Rada Mihalcea and Dragomir Radev. 2011. *Graph-based natural language processing and information retrieval.* Cambridge University Press.
[14] Kamal Nigam, Andrew McCallum, and Tom Mitchell. 2006. Semi-supervised text classification using EM. In *Semi-Supervised Learning*. The MIT Press, Cambridge, MA, 33–56.
[15] Xuan-Hieu Phan, Le-Minh Nguyen, and Susumu Horiguchi. 2008. Learning to classify short and sparse text & web with hidden topics from large-scale data collections. In *Proceedings of the 17th international conference on World Wide Web*. ACM, 91–100.
[16] Lakshmi Ramachandran and Edward Gehringer. 2013. Graph-structures matching for review relevance identification. *Proceedings of TextGraphs-8 Graph-based Methods for Natural Language Processing* (2013), 53–60.
[17] Sujith Ravi and Qiming Diao. 2015. Large Scale Distributed Semi-Supervised Learning Using Streaming Approximation. In *Proceedings of the 19th International Conference on Artificial Intelligence and Statistics (AISTATS)*. JMLR, 519–528.
[18] Jason Rennie. 2008. 20 Newsgroup. (2008). http://qwone.com/~jason/20Newsgroups/
[19] Maya Sappelli, Suzan Verberne, and Wessel Kraaij. 2014. E-mail categorization using partially related training examples. In *Proceedings of the 5th Information Interaction in Context Symposium*. ACM, 86–95.
[20] Adam Schenker. 2003. Graph-theoretic techniques for web content mining. (2003).
[21] SS Sonawane and PA Kulkarni. 2014. Graph based Representation and Analysis of Text Document: A Survey of Techniques. *International Journal of Computer Applications* 96, 19 (2014).
[22] Ge Song, Yunming Ye, Xiaolin Du, Xiaohui Huang, and Shifu Bie. 2014. Short Text Classification: A Survey. *Journal of Multimedia* 9, 5 (2014), 635–643.
[23] Michael Speriosu, Nikita Sudan, Sid Upadhyay, and Jason Baldridge. 2011. Twitter polarity classification with label propagation over lexical links and the follower graph. In *Proceedings of the First workshop on Unsupervised Learning in NLP*. Association for Computational Linguistics, 53–63.
[24] Jiang Su, Jelber S Shirab, and Stan Matwin. 2011. Large scale text classification using semi-supervised multinomial naive bayes. In *Proceedings of the 28th International Conference on Machine Learning (ICML-11)*. 97–104.
[25] Raluca Tanase and Remus Radu. 2017. The Mathematics of Web Search - Lecture 2: Directed Graphs - Transition. (2017). http://www.math.cornell.edu/~mec/Winter2009/RalucaRemus/Lecture2/lecture2.html
[26] Erik Tromp and Mykola Pechenizkiy. 2011. Graph-based n-gram language identification on short texts. In *Proc. 20th Machine Learning conference of Belgium and The Netherlands*. 27–34.
[27] Peter D Turney and Patrick Pantel. 2010. From frequency to meaning: Vector space models of semantics. *Journal of artificial intelligence research* 37 (2010), 141–188.
[28] Suzan Verberne, Maya Sappelli, Djoerd Hiemstra, and Wessel Kraaij. 2016. Evaluation and analysis of term scoring methods for term extraction. *Information Retrieval Journal* 19, 5 (2016), 510–545.
[29] Fei Wang and Changshui Zhang. 2008. Label propagation through linear neighborhoods. *IEEE Transactions on Knowledge and Data Engineering* 20, 1 (2008), 55–67.
[30] Xiaolong Wang, Furu Wei, Xiaohua Liu, Ming Zhou, and Ming Zhang. 2011. Topic sentiment analysis in twitter: a graph-based hashtag sentiment classification approach. In *Proceedings of the 20th ACM international conference on Information and knowledge management*. ACM, 1031–1040.
[31] Dmitry Zelenko, Chinatsu Aone, and Anthony Richardella. 2003. Kernel methods for relation extraction. *Journal of machine learning research* 3, Feb (2003), 1083–1106.
[32] Dengyong Zhou, Olivier Bousquet, Thomas Navin Lal, Jason Weston, and Bernhard Schölkopf. 2003. Learning with local and global consistency.. In *NIPS*, Vol. 16. 321–328.
[33] Xiaojin Zhu and Zoubin Ghahramani. 2002. Learning from labeled and unlabeled data with label propagation. (2002).
[34] Xiaojin Zhu, Zoubin Ghahramani, John Lafferty, and others. 2003. Semi-supervised learning using gaussian fields and harmonic functions. In *ICML*, Vol. 3. 912–919.
[35] Xiaojin Zhu, John Lafferty, and Ronald Rosenfeld. 2005. *Semi-supervised learning with graphs.* Carnegie Mellon University, language technologies institute, school of computer science.

Are IR Evaluation Measures on an Interval Scale?

Marco Ferrante
Dept. Mathematics
University of Padua, Italy
ferrante@math.unipd.it

Nicola Ferro
Dept. Information Engineering
University of Padua, Italy
ferro@dei.unipd.it

Silvia Pontarollo
Dept. Mathematics
University of Padua, Italy
spontaro@math.unipd.it

ABSTRACT

In this paper, we formally investigate whether, or not, IR evaluation measures are on an interval scale, which is needed to safely compute the basic statistics, such as mean and variance, we daily use to compare IR systems. We face this issue in the framework of the representational theory of measurement and we rely on the notion of difference structure, i.e. a total equi-spaced ordering on the system runs.

We found that the most popular set-based measures, i.e. precision, recall, and F-measure are interval-based. In the case of rank-based measures, using a strongly top-heavy ordering, we found that only RBP with $p = \frac{1}{2}$ is on an interval scale while RBP for other p values, AP, DCG, and ERR are not. Moreover, using a weakly top-heavy ordering, we found that none of RBP, AP, DCG, and ERR is on an interval scale.

CCS CONCEPTS

• **Information systems → Retrieval effectiveness**;

KEYWORDS

evaluation measures; representational theory of measurement; interval scale

1 INTRODUCTION

Information Retrieval (IR) is deeply rooted in experimentation but there is a growing need for stronger theoretical foundations [10]. Even if experimental evaluation is a main driver of progress and IR measures are a core part of it, our theoretical understanding of what IR measures are is still quite limited, despite the several studies both in the past [4, 5, 22] and more recently [2, 6, 8, 19].

When measuring something, the notion of *measurement scale* plays a central role [13, 21], since it determines the operations that can be performed and, as a consequence, the statistical analyses that can be applied. Stevens [21] identifies four major types of scales with increasing properties: (i) the *nominal scale* consists of discrete unordered values, i.e. categories; (ii) the *ordinal scale* introduces a natural order among the values; (iii) the *interval scale* preserves the equality of intervals or differences; and (iv) the *ratio scale* preserves the equality of ratios.

ICTIR '17, October 01-04, 2017, Amsterdam, Netherlands
© 2017 Association for Computing Machinery.
ACM ISBN 978-1-4503-4490-6/17/10...$15.00
https://doi.org/10.1145/3121050.3121058

Many of the operations we perform daily in IR, such as computing averages and variances, are possible only from interval scales onwards but, due to our limited knowledge of IR measures, we do not actually know which scales they rely on. Robertson [17] points out that the assumption of *Average Precision (AP)* being on an interval scale is somehow arbitrary while Ferrante et al. [8] shows that, only under some strong restrictions on the system runs being compared, we can ensure that IR measures use at least an ordinal scale.

We investigate whether IR measures are on an interval scale or not. We rely on the *representational theory of measurement* [13], which is the measurement theory adopted in both physical and social sciences. According to this framework, the key point is to understand how real world objects are related to each other since measure properties are then derived from these relations. Moreover, it is important that these relations among real world objects are intuitive and sensible to "everybody" and that they can be commonly agreed on.

In our context, this means that being on an interval scale is not just a numeric property of an IR measure but we need first to understand how system runs are ordered and what *intervals* of system runs are. Then, once we come to commonly agreed notions of order and interval among system runs, we can verify whether an IR measure complies with these notions and determine whether it is on an interval scale or not.

Therefore, we introduce a notion of interval among system runs by relying on *posets* and *lattices* [20] and we exploit *Hasse diagrams* to provide a graphical representation of such intervals. Then, we define a *difference* which quantifies the "length" of such intervals.

In the case of set-based measures and system runs of fixed length, we show that our notions of interval and difference induce a *difference structure* [13, 18] on the set of system runs and this guarantees the existence of an interval scale measure M while a uniqueness theorem ensures that any other interval scale measure is just a positive linear transformation of such M. We then show how to construct such interval scale measure M and we prove that Precision, Recall, and F-measure are all on an interval scale by finding a positive linear transformation with such measure M.

In the case of rank-based measures and system runs of fixed length, we explore two different notions of interval and difference based on the *top-heaviness* property, i.e. the preference towards highly ranked relevant documents. Using a *strong top-heaviness* notion, we find how it induces a difference structure and we prove that only *Rank-Biased Precision (RBP)* [16] with $p = \frac{1}{2}$ is on an interval scale while RBP for other values of p and other popular measures – namely AP, *Discounted Cumulated Gain (DCG)* [11], and *Expected Reciprocal Rank (ERR)* [7] – are not. Using a *weak top-heaviness* notion, we find that it induces another difference structure and we prove that the previously mentioned IR measures are not on an interval scale.

The paper is organized as follows: Section 2 introduces some basic concepts about the representational theory of measurement and how to determine if a measure is on an interval scale; Section 3 recalls some definition and properties of posets and Hasse diagrams; Section 4 analyses set-based IR measures while Section 5 deals with rank-based IR measures; finally, Section 6 wraps up the discussion and outlooks some future work.

2 MEASUREMENT THEORY

2.1 Representational Theory of Measurement

The *representational theory of measurement* [13] sees measurement as the process of assigning numbers to the entities in the real world according to some property under examination. Therefore, the relations among the entities in the real world determine the relations among the numbers we assign.

More precisely, a **relational structure** [13, 18] is an ordered pair $X = \langle X, R_X \rangle$ of a domain set X and a set of relations R_X on X, where the relations in R_X may have different arities, i.e. they can be unary, binary, ternary relations and so on. Given two relational structures X and Y, a *homomorphism* $M : X \to Y$ from X to Y is a mapping $M = \langle M, M_R \rangle$ where: (i) M is a function that maps X into $M(X) \subseteq Y$, i.e. for each element of the domain set there exists one corresponding image element; (ii) M_R is a function that maps R_X into $M_R(R_X) \subseteq R_Y$ such that $\forall r \in R_X$, r and $M_R(r)$ have the same arity, i.e. for each relation on the domain set there exists one (and it is usually, and often implicitly, assumed: and only one) corresponding image relation; (iii) $\forall r \in R_X, \forall x_i \in X$, if $r(x_1, \ldots, x_n)$ then $M_R(r)\big(M(x_1), \ldots, M(x_n)\big)$, i.e. if a relation holds for some elements of the domain set then the image relation must hold for the image elements.

A relational structure E is called *empirical* if its domain set E spans over the entities under consideration in the real world, i.e. the system runs in our case; a relational structure S is called *symbolic* if its domain set S spans over a given set of numbers. A **measurement (scale)** is the homomorphism $M = \langle M, M_R \rangle$ from the real world to the symbolic world and a **measure** is the number assigned to an entity by this mapping.

2.2 Measurement Scales

As discussed in Section 1, there are four major types of measurement scales [21] which can be ordered by their increasing properties and allows for different computations: *nominal scales* allow us to compute the number of cases and the mode; in addition, *ordinal scales* allow us to compute median and percentiles; *interval scales* add the possibility to compute mean, variance, product-moment correlation and rank correlation; finally, *ratio scales* add the capability to compute the coefficient of variation. Over the years, there has been debate [23] on whether these rules are too strict or not but they are applied widely.

If we already know that on an empirical structure there is an interval scale M, the uniqueness theorem – see e.g. Theorem 3.18 in [18] – ensures that any other measurement M' on that structure is a linear positive transformation of M, that is $M' = \alpha M + \beta$, $\alpha, \beta \in \mathbb{R}$.

However, in the case of IR measures, we lack a known interval scale M which we can use to compare all the other IR measures against. Actually, the core issue is even more severe and it is the lack of any notion of interval on the empirical set E of the system runs and, consequently, we cannot define an interval scale M.

Therefore, following [13, 18], we will rely on the notion of *difference structure* to introduce a definition of interval among system runs in such a way that it ensures the existence of an interval scale. Given E, a weakly ordered empirical structure is a pair $(E, \preceq)$ where, for every $a, b, c \in E$,

- $a \preceq b$ or $b \preceq a$;
- $a \preceq b$ and $b \preceq c \Rightarrow a \preceq c$.

Given $(E, \preceq)$, we have to define a **difference** Δ_{ab} between two elements $a, b \in E$, which is a kind of signed distance we exploit to compare intervals. Then, we have to define a weak order $\preceq_d$ between these Δ_{ab} differences. We can proceed as follows: if two elements $a, b \in E$ are such that $a \sim b$, i.e. $a \preceq b$ and $b \preceq a$, then the interval $[a, b]$ is null and, consequently, we set $\Delta_{ab} \sim_d \Delta_{ba}$; if $a < b$ we agree upon choosing $\Delta_{aa} <_d \Delta_{ab}$ which, in turn implies that $\Delta_{aa} >_d \Delta_{ba}$.

DEFINITION 1. *Let E be a finite (not empty) set of objects. Let $\preceq_d$ be a binary relation on $E \times E$ that satisfies, for each $a, b, c, d, a', b', c' \in E$, the following axioms:*

i. $\preceq_d$ *is weak order;*
ii. *if $\Delta_{ab} \preceq_d \Delta_{cd}$, then $\Delta_{dc} \preceq_d \Delta_{ba}$;*
iii. *if $\Delta_{ab} \preceq_d \Delta_{a'b'}$ and $\Delta_{bc} \preceq_d \Delta_{b'c'}$ then $\Delta_{ac} \preceq_d \Delta_{a'c'}$;*
iv. *Solvability Condition: if $\Delta_{aa} \preceq_d \Delta_{cd} \preceq_d \Delta_{ab}$, then there exists $d', d'' \in R$ such that $\Delta_{ad'} \sim_d \Delta_{cd} \sim_d \Delta_{d''b}$.*

*Then $(E, \preceq_d)$ is a **difference structure**.*

Particular attention has to be paid to the *Solvability Condition* which ensures the existence of an equally spaced gradation between the elements of E, indispensable to construct an interval scale measurement.

The *representation theorem* for difference structures states:

THEOREM 1. *Let E be a finite (not empty) set of objects and let $(R, \preceq_d)$ be a difference structure. Then there exist a measurement scale $M : E \to \mathbb{R}$ such that for every $a, b, c, d \in E$*

$$\Delta_{ab} \preceq_d \Delta_{cd} \Leftrightarrow M(b) - M(a) \leq M(d) - M(c).$$

This theorem ensures us that, if there is a difference structure on the empirical set E, then there exists an interval scale M. We can then resort to the uniqueness theorem mentioned above and look for a linear positive transformation between this M and any another measurement M' to determine if the latter one is on an interval scale as well.

3 POSET, LATTICE, AND HASSE DIAGRAM

As anticipated in Section 1, we will rely on the notion of *poset* and other constructs to introduce a definition of interval on the empirical set E of the system runs. In this section, following [20], we recall some definitions and results that will be useful afterwards.

A partially ordered set P, **poset** for short, is a set with a partial order $\leq$ defined on it. A **partial order** $\leq$ is a binary relation over P which is reflexive, antisymmetric and transitive. Given $s, t \in P$, we say that s and t are *comparable* if $s \preceq t$ or $t \preceq s$, otherwise they are *incomparable*.

EXAMPLE. Given a set A, let us consider the set $B = \{E : E \subseteq A\}$ and then define the following ordering: given $E, F \in B$, we say that $E \preceq F$ if $E \subseteq F$. B is the set of all subsets of A *ordered by inclusion* and it is a poset.

Note that a **total order** over a set P is a partial order where every pair of elements are comparable, whereas a **weak order** is a total order without the antisymmetric relation.

A closed **interval** is a subset of P defined as $[s, t] := \{u \in P : s \preceq u \preceq t\}$, where $s, t \in P$ and $s \preceq t$. Moreover we say that t **covers** s if $s \prec t$ and $[s, t] = \{s, t\}$, that is there does not exist $u \in P$ such that $s \prec u \prec t$.

We can represent a finite poset P by using the **Hasse diagram** which is a graph where vertices are the elements of P, edges represent the *covers* relations, and if $s \prec t$ then s is below t in the diagram. Note that if $s, t \in P$ lie on the same horizontal level of the diagram, then they are incomparable by construction. Furthermore, elements on different levels may be incomparable as well.

EXAMPLE. Let $N = 30$ and P the set of all divisors of N, that is $P = \{1, 2, 3, 5, 6, 10, 15, 30\}$. Let us define the following ordering on P: given $a, b \in P$ we say that $a \preceq b$ if a divide b. P is a poset with respect to the ordering $\preceq$, and its Hasse diagram is:

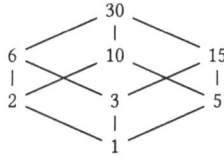

2, 3 and 5 are on the same horizontal level and they are incomparable since, for example, neither 2 divides 3 nor 3 divides 2. Moreover 3 and 10 lie on different levels and they are incomparable.

A subset C of a poset P is a **chain** if any two elements of C are comparable: a chain is a totally ordered subset of a poset. If C is a finite chain, the **length** of C, $\ell(C)$, is defined by $\ell(C) = |C| - 1$. A **maximal chain** of P is a chain that is not a proper subset of any other chain of P. Referring to the previous example, a chain is the subset $\{1, 10, 30\}$, while an example of maximal chain is the subset $\{1, 2, 10, 30\}$.

If every maximal chain of P has the same length n, we say that P is **graded of rank** n; in particular there exists a unique function $\rho : P \to \{0, 1, \ldots, n\}$, called the **rank function**, such that $\rho(s) = 0$, if s is a minimal element of P, and $\rho(t) = \rho(s) + 1$, if t covers s. The poset $P = \{1, 2, 3, 5, 6, 10, 15, 30\}$ defined above is graded of rank 3 since any maximal chain of P has length equal to 3.

Finally, since any interval on a graded poset is graded, the **length of an interval** $[s, t]$ is given by $\ell(s, t) := \ell([s, t]) = \rho(t) - \rho(s)$.

Given $s, t \in P$, an upper bound is $u \in P$ such that $s \preceq u$ and $t \preceq u$. A *least upper bound* (or supremum) of s and t, denoted by $s \vee t$, is an upper bound u such that every other upper bound $v \in P$ of s and t satisfies $v \succeq u$. Dually it is defined the *greatest lower bound* (or infimum) $s \wedge t$. Note that not every pair of elements in a poset has necessarily the infimum or the supremum. A poset L for which every pair of elements has a least upper bound and a greatest lower bound is called **lattice**. The poset P from the previous example is a

lattice: for example the elements $2, 15 \in P$ are such that $2 \vee 15 = 30$ and $2 \wedge 15 = 1$, and for any other pair of elements $s, t \in P$ one has $s \vee t = $ *least common multiple* and $s \wedge t = $ *greatest common divisor*.

PROPOSITION 1. *Let L be a finite lattice. The following two conditions are equivalent:*

   i. *L is graded, and the rank function ρ of L satisfies*

$$\rho(s) + \rho(t) \geq \rho(s \wedge t) + \rho(s \vee t),$$

  for all $s, t \in L$.

  ii. *If s and t both covers $s \wedge t$, then $s \vee t$ covers both s and t.*

Moreover, Foldes [9] proves that in a graded poset P the length $\ell(\cdot, \cdot)$ of any interval, also called the **natural distance**, equals the length of the shortest path connecting the two endpoints of the interval in its Hasse diagram.

4 SET-BASED MEASURES

We recall some basic definitions from [8]. Let $(REL, \preceq)$ be a totally ordered set of **relevance degrees** with minimum called the non-relevant relevance degree nr $= \min(REL)$ and a maximum rr $= \max(REL)$. In this work, we assume binary relevance, that is we set $REL = \{0, 1\}$ without any loss of generality.

Let us consider a set of **documents** D and a set of **topics** T. For each pair $(t, d) \in T \times D$, the **ground-truth** GT is a map which assigns a relevance degree $rel \in REL$ to a document d with respect to a topic t.

Given a positive natural number N called the *length of the run*, we define the **set of retrieved documents** as $D(N) = \{\{d_1, \ldots, d_N\} : d_i \in D\}$ and the **universe set of retrieved documents** as $\mathcal{D} := \bigcup_{N=1}^{|D|} D(N)$.

A **run** r_t, retrieving a set of documents $D(N)$ in response to a topic $t \in T$, is a function from T into $\mathcal{D}$

$$t \mapsto r_t = \{d_1, \ldots, d_N\}.$$

A *multiset* (or bag) is a set which may contain the same element several times and its multiplicity of occurrences is relevant [12]. A **set of judged documents** is a multiset $(REL, m) = \{0, 1, 0, \ldots, 0, 0, 1, \ldots\}$, where $m = (m_0, m_1)$ and m_0, m_1 are two functions from REL into $\mathbb{N}_0$ representing the multiplicity of the 0 and 1 relevance degrees, respectively [14]; if the multiplicity is 0, a given relevance degree is not present in the multiset. Let $\mathcal{M}(N)$ be the set of all the possible multiplicity functions m, such that $m_0 + m_1 = N$; then, $\mathcal{R} := \bigcup_{N=1}^{|D|} \bigcup_{m \in \mathcal{M}(N)} (REL, m)$ is the **universe set of judged documents**, i.e. the set of all the possible sets of judged documents (REL, m). We denote by RB_t the **recall base**, i.e. the total number of relevant documents for a topic.

We call **judged run** the function $\hat{r}_t$ from $T \times \mathcal{D}$ into $\mathcal{R}$, which assigns a relevance degree to each retrieved document

$$(t, r_t) \mapsto \hat{r}_t = \{GT(t, d_1), \ldots, GT(t, d_N)\} = \{\hat{r}_{t,1}, \ldots, \hat{r}_{t,N}\}.$$

In the following, we omit the dependence on the topic and we simplify the notation into $\hat{r} := \{\hat{r}_1, \ldots, \hat{r}_N\}$, RB, and so on.

As discussed in Section 2.2, we have to start from introducing an order relation $\preceq$ on the set of judged runs. Therefore, we order judged runs with same length by how many relevant documents they retrieve, i.e. by their total mass of relevance:

$$\hat{r} \preceq \hat{s} \Leftrightarrow \sum_{i=1}^{N} \hat{r}_i \le \sum_{i=1}^{N} \hat{s}_i . \tag{1}$$

Note that this order is quite intuitive and just corresponds to common sense; therefore it respects the requirement of defining intuitive, sensible and commonly agreeable relations discussed in Section 1.

The order $\preceq$ is a partial order on $\mathcal{R}$, since runs with different length are incomparable. However, to define a difference structure on $\mathcal{R}$ and apply Theorem 1, we need a weak order, that is a totally ordered subset of $\mathcal{R}$ since the antisymmetric relation is satisfied on $\mathcal{R}$.

Let us define $\mathcal{R}(N) := \bigcup_{m \in \mathcal{M}(N)} (REL, m)$ as the set of the judged runs with length fixed to N. $\mathcal{R}(N) \subseteq \mathcal{R}$ and it is a totally ordered set with respect to the ordering $\preceq$ defined in (1) since every pair of runs on this set is comparable. Moreover, $\mathcal{R}(N)$ is a maximal chain of $\mathcal{R}$ since runs with same length are all and only the comparable runs.

Since $\mathcal{R}(N)$ is a totally ordered set and $|\mathcal{R}(N)| = N + 1$, it is *graded of rank* N. Therefore, as discussed in Section 3, there is a unique *rank function* $\rho : \mathcal{R}(N) \rightarrow \{0, 1, \dots, N\}$ which is given by $\rho(\hat{r}) = \sum_{i=1}^{N} \hat{r}_i$. Indeed, $\rho(\{0, \dots, 0\}) = 0$; if $\hat{s}$ cover $\hat{r}$, that is $\hat{s}$ has one more relevant document than $\hat{r}$, then $\rho(\hat{s}) = \rho(\hat{r}) + 1$ by definition of rank function. This leads for any $r \preceq s$ to the following *natural distance* on $\mathcal{R}(N)$: $\ell(\hat{r}, \hat{s}) = \rho(\hat{s}) - \rho(\hat{r}) = \sum_{i=1}^{N} (\hat{s}_i - \hat{r}_i)$.

We can finally rely on this natural distance to introduce the definition of difference Δ, which is the core building block for an interval scale as explained in Section 2.2.

DEFINITION 2. *Given two runs $\hat{r}, \hat{s} \in \mathcal{R}(N)$, the* **difference** *between $\hat{r}$ and $\hat{s}$ is defined as $\Delta_{\hat{r}\hat{s}} = \sum_{i=1}^{N} (\hat{s}_i - \hat{r}_i)$, that is $\Delta_{\hat{r}\hat{s}} = \ell(\hat{r}, \hat{s})$ if $\hat{r} \preceq \hat{s}$, otherwise $\Delta_{\hat{r}\hat{s}} = -\ell(\hat{s}, \hat{r})$.*

Let $\le_d$ be the *less than or equal to* relation on $\mathcal{R}(N) \times \mathcal{R}(N)$, where the subscript d is to highlight its connection with intervals as described in Section 2.2; note that $\le_d$ is exactly the order relation $\le$ among real numbers. We show that $(\mathcal{R}(N), \le_d)$ is a *difference structure*. Indeed the first three axioms of Theorem 1 follow immediately from the fact that the ordering $\le_d$ between intervals is given by the well known order $\le$, thanks to the definition of difference. Whereas the *Solvability Condition*, i.e. having an equally-spaced gradation on $\mathcal{R}(N)$, is satisfied by construction: if $\hat{s}$ covers $\hat{r}$, the difference $\Delta_{\hat{r}\hat{s}}$ is constant and equal to 1 $(\Delta_{\hat{r}\hat{s}} = \ell(\hat{r}, \hat{s}) = \rho(\hat{s}) - \rho(\hat{r}) = \rho(\hat{r}) + 1 - \rho(\hat{r}) = 1)$.

Let us show how we can construct an interval scale measure M on $\mathcal{R}(N)$. The rank function ρ counts the number of relevant retrieved documents and, if $\hat{s}$ covers $\hat{r}$, the difference $\Delta_{\hat{r}\hat{s}} = \rho(\hat{s}) - \rho(\hat{r})$ is always equal to 1, by construction. Thus an interval scale measure M on $(\mathcal{R}(N), \le_d)$ is given by the rank function itself:

$$M(\hat{r}) = \rho(\hat{r}) = \sum_{i=1}^{N} \hat{r}_i ,$$

which satisfies the condition imposed by Theorem 1: let $\hat{r}, \hat{s}, \hat{u}, \hat{v} \in \mathcal{R}(N)$ such that $\Delta_{\hat{r}\hat{s}} \le \Delta_{\hat{u}\hat{v}}$, then $\Delta_{\hat{r}\hat{s}} \le \Delta_{\hat{u}\hat{v}} \Leftrightarrow \sum_{i=1}^{N} (\hat{s}_i - \hat{r}_i) \le \sum_{i=1}^{N} (\hat{v}_i - \hat{u}_i) \Leftrightarrow M(\hat{s}) - M(\hat{r}) \le M(\hat{v}) - M(\hat{u})$; thus M is an interval scale on $(\mathcal{R}(N), \le_d)$.

We can finally proceed with the last step of Section 2.2 and check whether an IR measure uses an interval scale on $(\mathcal{R}(N), \le_d)$ by looking for a linear positive transformation with M.

Let us consider *Precision*

$$\text{Prec@}[N](\hat{r}) = \frac{1}{N} \sum_{i=1}^{N} \hat{r}_i = \frac{M(\hat{r})}{N} ;$$

thus Precision is an interval scale.

Similarly, *Recall*

$$\text{Recall}(\hat{r}) = \frac{1}{RB} \sum_{i=1}^{N} \hat{r}_i = \frac{M(\hat{r})}{RB}$$

is an interval scale.

The *F-measure*, that is the harmonic mean of Precision and Recall,

$$\text{F}(\hat{r}) = 2 \frac{\text{Prec}(\hat{r}) \cdot \text{Recall}(\hat{r})}{\text{Prec}(\hat{r}) + \text{Recall}(\hat{r})} = \frac{2}{N + RB} \sum_{i=1}^{N} \hat{r}_i = \frac{2M(\hat{r})}{N + RB}$$

is an interval scale as well.

4.1 Related Work

van Rijsbergen [22] exploited conjoint structures to study Precision and Recall by considering all the possible Precision and Recall pairs, i.e. $R \times P$, as the empirical set E and then creating a kind of "second order" measure on this set E whose properties are examined, e.g. if this "second order" measure is interval based. We take a different approach since we consider system runs as the empirical set E and not the set of all the possible Precision and Recall pairs; moreover, we directly determine if an IR measure is on an interval scale by exploiting the ordering and difference among system runs.

Bollmann and Cherniavsky [5] introduced the *MZ-metric* and, following the example of van Rijsbergen [22], they defined a conjoint structure on the contingency table relevant/not relevant and retrieved/not retrieved in order to determine under which transformations the MZ-metric was on an interval scale. Instead of a conjoint structure on the contingency table, we directly created a difference structure on the set of system runs that can be used to determine if any set-based IR measure is on an interval scale.

Moreover, the MZ-metric is not on a interval scale if we use the structure we defined above. Indeed, if MZ is the *MZ-metric*, let us consider the measure $\overline{MZ} := 1 - MZ$, since we are working with effectiveness measures, defined as $\overline{MZ}(\hat{r}) = \dfrac{\sum_{i=1}^{N} \hat{r}_i}{RB + N - \sum_{i=1}^{N} \hat{r}_i}$ for $\hat{r} \in \mathcal{R}(N)$. This measure is not interval scale on $(\mathcal{R}(N), \le_d)$, since replacing a non relevant document with a relevant one yields to a not constant increment of the measure which depends on the run at hand. This further stresses that the core issue in determining what are the properties of a measure is to agree on what are the appropriate relations among the entities in the empirical set E, from which the properties of a measure are then derived.

Finally, Bollmann [4] studied set-based measures by showing that measures complying with a monotonicity and an Archimedean axiom are a linear combination of the number of relevant retrieved documents and the number of not relevant not retrieved documents. We address a completely different issue, that is determining which scales are used by IR measures.

5 RANK-BASED MEASURES

Given N, the length of the run, we define the **set of retrieved documents** as $D(N) = \{(d_1, \ldots, d_N) : d_i \in D, d_i \neq d_j$ for any $i \neq j\}$, i.e. the ranked list of retrieved documents without duplicates, and the **universe set of retrieved documents** as $\mathcal{D} := \bigcup_{N=1}^{|D|} D(N)$. A **run** r_t, retrieving a ranked list of documents $D(N)$ in response to a topic $t \in T$, is a function from T into $\mathcal{D}$

$$t \mapsto r_t = (d_1, \ldots, d_N)$$

We denote by $r_t[j]$ the j-th element of the vector r_t, i.e. $r_t[j] = d_j$.

We define the **universe set of judged documents** as $\mathcal{R} := \bigcup_{N=1}^{|D|} REL^N$, where REL^N is the set of the ranked lists of judged retrieved documents with length fixed to N. Since in our case $REL = \{0, 1\}$, $REL^N = \{0, 1\}^N$ refers to the space of all N−length vectors consisting of 0 and 1. As for the set-based case, we denote by RB_t the **recall base**, i.e. the total number of relevant documents for a topic.

We call **judged run** the function $\hat{r}_t$ from $T \times \mathcal{D}$ into $\mathcal{R}$, which assigns a relevance degree to each retrieved document in the ranked list

$$(t, r_t) \mapsto \hat{r}_t = \big(GT(t, d_1), \ldots, GT(t, d_N)\big)$$

We denote by $\hat{r}_t[j]$ the j-th element of the vector $\hat{r}_t$, i.e. $\hat{r}_t[j] = GT(t, d_j)$.

As for the set-based case, we can simplify the notation omitting the dependence on topics, $\hat{r} := \big(\hat{r}[1], \ldots, \hat{r}[N]\big)$, RB, and so on.

5.1 Strong Top-Heaviness

Top-heaviness is a central property in IR, stating that the higher a system ranks relevant documents the better it is. If we apply this property at each rank position (not only at the first ones) and we take to extremes the importance of having a relevant document ranked higher, we can define a **strong top-heaviness** property which, in turn, will induce total ordering among runs with fixed length N.

We start from the definition of an order among system runs. Let $\hat{r}, \hat{s} \in REL^N$ such that $\hat{r} \neq \hat{s}$, then there exists $k = \min\{j \leq N : \hat{r}[j] \neq \hat{s}[j]\}$ and we order system runs as follows

$$\hat{r} < \hat{s} \iff \hat{r}[k] < \hat{s}[k] . \tag{2}$$

This ordering prefers a single relevant document ranked higher to any number of relevant documents ranked just below it; more formally, $(\hat{u}[1], \ldots, \hat{u}[m], 1, 0, \ldots, 0)$ is greater than $(\hat{u}[1], \ldots, \hat{u}[m], 0, 1, \ldots, 1)$, for any length $N \in \mathbb{N}$ and for any $m \in \{0, 1, \ldots, N-1\}$. This is why we call it *strong top-heaviness*. This ordering makes sense and it is quite intuitive but it might be considered too radical; therefore, it is a matter of future discussion to determine if it can also be commonly agreed on.

REL^N is totally ordered with respect to $\leq$, since for every pair of runs $\hat{r}, \hat{s} \in REL^N$, if k is the smallest depth at witch the two runs differ, we establish which one is the biggest by just looking at the values of $\hat{r}[k]$ and $\hat{s}[k]$.

Moreover, REL^N is *graded of rank* $2^N - 1$ since $|\{0, 1\}^N| = 2^N$ and $REL^N = \{0, 1\}^N$ is a maximal chain. Therefore, there is a unique rank function $\rho : REL^N \longrightarrow \{0, 1, \ldots, 2^N - 1\}$ which is

given by:

$$\rho(\hat{r}) = \sum_{i=1}^{N} 2^{N-i} \hat{r}[i] .$$

If we look at the runs as binary strings, the rank function is exactly the representation in base 10 of the number identified by a run and the ordering among runs $\leq$ corresponds to the ordering $\leq$ among binary numbers.

EXAMPLE. Let $\hat{r}, \hat{s} \in REL^5$ be such that $\hat{r} = (0, 0, 1, 1, 1)$ and $\hat{s} = (0, 1, 0, 0, 0)$. Since $\hat{r}[1] = \hat{s}[1]$, while $\hat{r}[2] = 0 < 1 = \hat{s}[2]$, we have $\hat{r} < \hat{s}$. Moreover $\rho(\hat{r}) = 2^2 + 2^1 + 2^0 = 7 < 8 = 2^3 = \rho(\hat{s})$ and, in particular, $\hat{s}$ covers $\hat{r}$ (indeed $\rho(\hat{s}) = \rho(\hat{r}) + 1$).

The *natural distance* is then given by $\ell(\hat{r}, \hat{s}) = \rho(\hat{s}) - \rho(\hat{r})$, for $\hat{r}, \hat{s} \in REL^N$ such that $\hat{r} \leq \hat{s}$, and we can define the difference as $\Delta_{\hat{r}\hat{s}} = \ell(\hat{r}, \hat{s})$ if $\hat{r} \leq \hat{s}$, otherwise $\Delta_{\hat{r}\hat{s}} = -\ell(\hat{s}, \hat{r})$.

DEFINITION 3. Given two runs $\hat{r}, \hat{s} \in REL^N$, the **difference** between $\hat{r}$ and $\hat{s}$ is defined as $\Delta_{\hat{r}\hat{s}} = \sum_{i=1}^{N} 2^{N-i}\big(\hat{s}[i] - \hat{r}[i]\big) .$

Let $\leq_d$ be the *less than or equal to* relation on $REL^N \times REL^N$, which as in the set-based case is exactly the order relation $\leq$ among real numbers, then $(REL^N, \leq_d)$ is a difference structure. Indeed, as shown for the set-based case, the first three axioms of Theorem 1 follow immediately from the fact that the ordering $\leq_d$ between intervals is given by the well known order $\leq$, thanks to the definition of difference. Finally, the *Solvability Condition*, that is needed to have an equally-spaced gradation on REL^N, is satisfied by construction of the rank function, since $\Delta_{\hat{r}\hat{s}} = \rho(\hat{s}) - \rho(\hat{r}) = 1$ for every $\hat{r}, \hat{s} \in REL^N$ such that $\hat{s}$ covers $\hat{r}$.

Similarly to the set-based case, an interval scale measure M on $(REL^N, \leq_d)$ is given by the rank function itself

$$M(\hat{r}) = \rho(\hat{r}) = \sum_{i=1}^{N} 2^{N-i} \hat{r}[i]$$

which is an interval scale since it satisfies the condition imposed by Theorem 1. To prove it, let $\hat{r}, \hat{s}, \hat{u}, \hat{v} \in REL^N$ such that $\Delta_{\hat{r}\hat{s}} \leq_d \Delta_{\hat{u}\hat{v}}$; then, $\Delta_{\hat{r}\hat{s}} \leq_d \Delta_{\hat{u}\hat{v}} \iff \sum_{i=1}^{N} 2^{N-i}(\hat{s}[i] - \hat{r}[i]) \leq \sum_{i=1}^{N} 2^{N-i}(\hat{v}[i] - \hat{u}[i]) \iff M(\hat{s}) - M(\hat{r}) \leq M(\hat{v}) - M(\hat{u})$, as we have to show.

Remember that a measure M′ is an ordinal scale on REL^N if, for every $\hat{r}, \hat{s} \in REL^N$, the following statement is true:

$$\hat{r} \leq \hat{s} \iff M'(\hat{r}) \leq M'(\hat{s}) .$$

Let us show that RBP_p is ordinal scale on REL^N, with respect to the total ordering defined above, if and only if $p \leq 1/2$. Even though we work with N fixed, note that we want RBP_p ordinal for some $p \geq 0$ to hold regardless of the chosen value for N.

Let us consider $\hat{r}, \hat{s} \in REL^N$ such that $\hat{r} < \hat{s}$. Then there exist $k \in \{1, \ldots, N\}$ such that $\hat{r} = (\hat{r}[1], \ldots, \hat{r}[k-1], 0, \hat{r}[k+1], \ldots, \hat{r}[N])$ and $\hat{s} = (\hat{r}[1], \ldots, \hat{r}[k-1], 1, \hat{s}[k+1], \ldots, \hat{s}[N])$. Let moreover $\hat{\bar{r}}, \hat{\bar{s}} \in REL^N$ be such that $\hat{\bar{r}} = (\hat{r}[1], \ldots, \hat{r}[k-1], 0, 1, \ldots, 1)$ and $\hat{\bar{s}} = (\hat{r}[1], \ldots, \hat{r}[k-1], 1, 0, \ldots, 0)$. Clearly $\hat{r} \leq \hat{\bar{r}} < \hat{\bar{s}} \leq \hat{s}$, let us prove that $RBP_p(\hat{\bar{r}}) < RBP_p(\hat{\bar{s}})$ iff $p \leq 1/2$.

$$RBP_p(\hat{\bar{r}}) - RBP_p(\hat{\bar{s}}) = (1-p)\left(\sum_{i=1}^{k-1} \hat{r}[i]p^{i-1} + \sum_{i=k+1}^{N} p^{i-1}\right) - (1-p)\left(\sum_{i=1}^{k-1} \hat{r}[i]p^{i-1} + p^{k-1}\right) = (1-p)\left(\sum_{i=k+1}^{N} p^{i-1} - p^{k-1}\right) = (1-p)\left(\frac{p^k - p^N}{1-p} - p^{k-1}\right) = -p^{k-1}(1 - 2p + p^{N-k+1}).$$

Note that $\text{RBP}_p(\hat{\bar{r}}) < \text{RBP}_p(\hat{\bar{s}}) \Leftrightarrow \text{RBP}_p(\hat{\bar{r}}) - \text{RBP}_p(\hat{\bar{s}}) < 0 \Leftrightarrow 1 - 2p + p^{N-k+1} > 0$. If $p > 1/2$ then there exists $N \in \mathbb{N}$ big enough such that $1 - 2p + p^{N-k+1} < 0$ since $1 - 2p < 0$, while if $p \leq 1/2$ then $1 - 2p \geq 0$ and it is true that $1 - 2p + p^{N-k+1} > 0$. Then we have shown that $\text{RBP}_p(\hat{\bar{r}}) < \text{RBP}_p(\hat{\bar{s}}) \Leftrightarrow p \leq 1/2$.

Moreover $\text{RBP}_p(\hat{r}) \leq \text{RBP}_p(\hat{\bar{r}})$ since $\hat{r}[i] \leq 1$, and $\text{RBP}_p(\hat{\bar{s}}) \leq \text{RBP}_p(\hat{s})$ since $\hat{s}[i] \geq 0$, for all $i \in \{k+1, \ldots, N\}$. Thus we can conclude that, for $p \leq 1/2$, $\hat{r} < \hat{s} \Rightarrow \text{RBP}_p(\hat{r}) < \text{RBP}_p(\hat{s})$. Moreover, if $\hat{r} = \hat{s}$, then simply $\text{RBP}_p(\hat{r}) = \text{RBP}_p(\hat{s})$. Therefore, for $p \leq 1/2$, $\hat{r} \leq \hat{s} \Rightarrow \text{RBP}_p(\hat{r}) \leq \text{RBP}_p(\hat{s})$.

To show the other implication of the *iff*, that is $\text{RBP}_p(\hat{r}) \leq \text{RBP}_p(\hat{s}) \Rightarrow \hat{r} \leq \hat{s}$, we just prove that not$\{\hat{r} \leq \hat{s}\} \Rightarrow$ not$\{\text{RBP}_p(\hat{r}) \leq \text{RBP}_p(\hat{s})\}$, i.e. we need to prove that $\hat{r} > \hat{s} \Rightarrow \text{RBP}_p(\hat{r}) > \text{RBP}_p(\hat{s})$. But this last relation is exactly what we have already proven above, exchanging $\hat{r}$ and $\hat{s}$, hence the proof is complete.

RBP_p with $p > 1/2$ and other IR measures – namely DCG, AP and ERR – are not even ordinal scale on REL^N. Indeed, let us for example consider the runs $\hat{r} = (0, 0, 1, 1, 1)$ and $\hat{s} = (0, 1, 0, 0, 0)$ on REL^5: clearly $\hat{r} \leq \hat{s}$. Note instead that $\text{DCG}_2(\hat{r}) = 1/\log_2 3 + 1/\log_2 4 + 1/\log_2 5 > 1 = \text{DCG}_2(\hat{s})$; $RB \cdot \text{AP}(\hat{r}) = 1/3 + 2/4 + 3/5 > 1/2 = RB \cdot \text{AP}(\hat{s})$, where RB is the recall base; $\text{ERR}(\hat{r}) = 1/6 + 1/16 + 1/40 > 1/4 = \text{ERR}(\hat{s})$; finally, $\text{RBP}_p(\hat{r}) = (1-p)(p^2 + p^3 + p^4) > (1-p)p = \text{RBP}(\hat{s})$ for $p > 0.544$, and such an example can be found for any other values of $p > 1/2$. Hence, these measures cannot be on interval scale, since an interval scale measure is also ordinal scale.

Therefore, only RBP_p with $p \leq 1/2$ may be on interval scale. Note that only $\text{RBP}_{1/2}$ is a linear positive transformation of the M defined above:

$$\text{RBP}_{1/2}(\hat{r}) = \frac{1}{2} \sum_{i=1}^{N} \frac{1}{2^{i-1}} \hat{r}[i] = \frac{1}{2^N} \sum_{i=1}^{N} 2^{N-i} \hat{r}[i] = \frac{1}{2^N} \text{M}(\hat{r}),$$

for every $\hat{r} \in REL^N$. While RBP_p with $p < 1/2$ is not a linear positive transformation of M, since it does not preserve the equivalence between differences. Indeed, let us consider $\hat{r} = (0, 0, 0, 0, 1)$, $\hat{s} = (0, 0, 0, 1, 0)$, $\hat{u} = (0, 0, 0, 1, 1)$ and $\hat{v} = (0, 0, 1, 0, 0)$, four runs on REL^5. Note that $\hat{s}$ covers $\hat{r}$ and $\hat{v}$ covers $\hat{u}$, but $\text{RBP}_p(\hat{s}) - \text{RBP}_p(\hat{r}) = \text{RBP}_p(\hat{v}) - \text{RBP}_p(\hat{u}) \Leftrightarrow (1-p)(p^3 - p^4) = (1-p)(p^2 - p^3 - p^4)$, that is *iff* $p = 1/2$, as we expect.

Therefore we have shown that, given the total order (2) induced by the strong top-heaviness, $\text{RBP}_{1/2}$ is the only one among the considered IR measures that is on an interval scale with respect to the difference structure defined above.

5.2 Weak Top-Heaviness

In this section, we abandon the total ordering induced by the strong top-heaviness and we explore another ordering, induced by a weaker form of top-heaviness. This ordering is based on these two *monotonicity-like* properties proposed by Ferrante et al. [8]:

- **Replacement** A measure of retrieval effectiveness should not decrease when replacing a document with another one in the same rank position with higher degree of relevance.
- **Swap** If we swap a less relevant document with a more relevant one in a lower rank position, the measure should not decrease.

These two properties lead to the following partial ordering among system runs

$$\hat{r} \leq \hat{s} \Leftrightarrow \sum_{j=1}^{k} \hat{r}[j] \leq \sum_{j=1}^{k} \hat{s}[j] \;\; \forall k \in \{1, \ldots, N\} . \tag{3}$$

This ordering considers a run bigger than another one when, for each rank position, it has more relevant documents than the other one up to that rank. With respect to the strong top-heaviness of eq. (2), this ordering is less extreme because it is sensitive to the total mass of relevance accumulated at the different rank positions instead of "cutting" everything just because of a single relevant document ranked higher. This is why we call it *weak top-heaviness*. Moreover, this ordering is based on two monotonicity-like properties which are common-sense and have been somehow pointed out also in other previous works [2, 15]. Therefore, being also intuitive and sensitive, this ordering might be commonly agreed on in an easier way than the strong top-heaviness ordering.

The ordering $\leq$ is a partial ordering on REL^N: for example, when $N = 5$ the runs $\hat{r} = (0, 1, 1, 0, 1)$ and $\hat{s} = (1, 0, 0, 0, 1)$ are incomparable, since $\hat{s}[1] > \hat{r}[1]$ while $\sum_{i=1}^{3} \hat{s}[i] = 1 < 2 = \sum_{i=1}^{3} \hat{r}[i]$. Thus REL^N is a poset.

Since REL^N is a poset, that is it does not have a weak order, we have no chance to find a difference structure defined on the whole set, as we did in Section 5.1. Thus we first have to highlight some properties associated to REL^N as a poset, and then we will make use of totally ordered subsets of REL^N, i.e. chains, where it is possible to define a difference structure.

PROPOSITION 2. *Let $N \in \mathbb{N}$ be fixed and $REL = \{0, 1\}$. The poset REL^N is graded, i.e. every maximal chain of REL^N has the same length.*

PROOF. Thanks to Lemma 2.1 of [3] it can be proved that REL^N is a lattice. Then, using Proposition 1 it is sufficient to show that for each $\hat{r}, \hat{s} \in REL^N$ that both cover $\hat{r} \wedge \hat{s}$, $\hat{r} \vee \hat{s}$ covers both $\hat{r}$ and $\hat{s}$.

Let $\hat{r}, \hat{s} \in REL^N$ be such that $\hat{r} < \hat{s}$, define $c = \left| \{ k \leq N : \sum_{i=1}^{N} \hat{r}[i] < \sum_{i=1}^{N} \hat{s}[i] \} \right|$ and denote with $k_1 < \cdots < k_c$ the depths where the strict inequality on (3) hold. Firstly note that if $\hat{r} < \hat{s}$ then $c \geq 1$.

If $c = 1$ and $k_1 < N$, then $\hat{s}$ and $\hat{r}$ differ in a **swap** of length one $\hat{s} = (\ldots, \hat{s}[k_1 - 1], 1, 0, \hat{s}[k_1 + 2], \ldots)$, $\hat{r} = (\ldots, \hat{s}[k_1 - 1], 0, 1, \hat{s}[k_1 + 2], \ldots)$. If $c = 1$ and $k_1 = N$, then $\hat{s}$ and $\hat{r}$ differ in a **replacement** in the last position: $\hat{s} = (\ldots, \hat{s}[k_1 - 1], 1)$, $\hat{r} = (\ldots, \hat{s}[k_1 - 1], 0)$.

In both cases, for every $\hat{u} \in REL^N$ such that $\hat{r} \leq \hat{u} \leq \hat{s}$, then $\hat{u} = \hat{r}$ or $\hat{u} = \hat{s}$, and this follows immediately from the partial order recalled above.

On the contrary, if $c > 1$, there are two cases to study: $k_2 > k_1 + 1$ or $k_2 = k_1 + 1$. In the first case we have the following situation: $\hat{s} = (\ldots, \hat{s}[k_1 - 1], 1, 0, \hat{s}[k_1 + 2], \ldots, \hat{s}[k_2 - 1], 1, \hat{s}[k_2 + 1], \ldots)$, $\hat{r} = (\ldots, \hat{s}[k_1 - 1], 0, 1, \hat{s}[k_1 + 2], \ldots, \hat{s}[k_2 - 1], 0, \hat{r}[k_2 + 1], \ldots)$. Note that $\hat{r}[k_1 + 1] = 1$ while $\hat{s}[k_1 + 1] = 0$ since $\sum_{i=1}^{k_1 + 1} \hat{r}[i]$ has to be equal to $\sum_{i=1}^{k_1 + 1} \hat{s}[i]$ as $k_2 > k_1 + 1$. Then the following run $\hat{u} = (\ldots, \hat{s}[k_1 - 1], 0, 1, \hat{s}[k_1 + 2], \ldots, \hat{s}[k_2 - 1], 1, \hat{s}[k_2 + 1], \ldots)$ is such that $\hat{r} < \hat{u} < \hat{s}$.

Similarly, when $k_2 = k_1 + 1$ a run $\hat{u} \in REL^N$ such that $\hat{r} < \hat{u} < \hat{s}$ can be found.

Thus we have shown that the "cover" relations, that is the operation for which from a run we can obtain a new run that covers the first one, are swap of length one and replacements in the last position.

Now let $\hat{r}, \hat{s} \in \{0, 1\}^N$ such that both cover $\hat{r} \wedge \hat{s}$, which implies that $\hat{r}$ and $\hat{s}$ are incomparable. This means that does not exists $\hat{z} \in REL^N$ such that $\hat{r} \wedge \hat{s} \prec \hat{z} \prec \hat{r}$ nor $\hat{r} \wedge \hat{s} \prec \hat{z} \prec \hat{s}$. Thus, if $\hat{u} := \hat{r} \wedge \hat{s} := (\hat{u}[1], \dots, \hat{u}[N])$, there exist an index $i \in \{1, \dots, N-1\}$ such that $u[i] = 0$ and $u[i + 1] = 1$. Since $\hat{r}$ and $\hat{s}$ both cover $\hat{u}$, we have two possibilities (up to symmetries):

i. $\hat{r} = (\hat{u}[1], \dots, \hat{u}[i - 1], 1, 0, \hat{u}[i + 2], \dots, \hat{u}[N])$ and $\hat{s} = (\hat{u}[1], \dots, \hat{u}[j - 1], 1, 0, \hat{u}[j + 2], \dots, \hat{u}[N])$, if $\hat{u}[j] = 0$, $\hat{u}[j + 1] = 1$, where $1 \le j \le i - 1$ or $i + 1 \le j \le N - 1$;

ii. $\hat{r} = (\hat{u}[1], \dots, \hat{u}[i - 1], 1, 0, \hat{u}[i + 2], \dots, \hat{u}[N])$ and $\hat{s} = (\hat{u}[1], \dots, \hat{u}[N - 1], 1)$, if $\hat{u}[N] = 0$.

Respectively, let us define $\hat{t} \in REL^N$ as

i. $\hat{t} = (\hat{u}[1], \dots, \hat{u}[i - 1], 1, 0, \hat{u}[i + 2], \dots, \hat{u}[j - 1], 1, 0, \hat{u}[j + 2], \dots, \hat{u}[N])$ if $j > i + 1$, exchanging i and j if $j < i - 1$;

ii. $\hat{t} = (\hat{u}[1], \dots, \hat{u}[i - 1], 1, 0, \hat{u}[i + 2], \dots, \hat{u}[N - 1], 1)$.

The notes made above entail that $\hat{t}$ covers both $\hat{r}$ and $\hat{s}$, since $\hat{t}$ differs from each of them only for one swap or a replacement in the last position. Then $\hat{t} = \hat{r} \vee \hat{s}$ and the proof is complete. □

As discussed in Section 3, REL^N graded implies that the natural distance $\ell(\cdot, \cdot)$ is well defined for every two comparable elements $\hat{r}, \hat{s} \in REL^N$ as the length of a maximal chain in $[\hat{r}, \hat{s}]$ minus 1. Equivalently, given the *rank function* $\rho : REL^N \longrightarrow \mathbb{N}$, the natural distance is defined as $\ell(\hat{r}, \hat{s}) = \rho(\hat{s}) - \rho(\hat{r})$ and, if $\hat{s}$ covers $\hat{r}$, then $\rho(\hat{s}) = \rho(\hat{r}) + 1$.

Remember that the natural length of any interval of a graded poset equals the numbers of edges in every shortest path connecting the endpoints of the interval in its Hasse diagram. The next example highlights this fact.

EXAMPLE. Let us fix $N = 4$. The Hasse Diagram of REL^N is

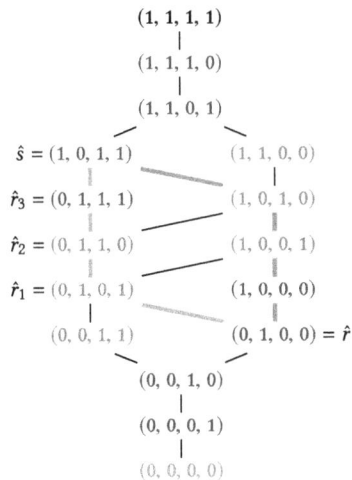

where different colours of the runs correspond to different total numbers of relevant retrieved documents.

Given $\hat{r} = (0, 1, 0, 0)$, $\hat{s} = (1, 0, 1, 1)$, let us consider one of the shortest paths between the two runs, for example the one with orange edges: it starts from $\hat{r}$, goes through $\hat{r}_1, \hat{r}_2, \hat{r}_3$, and ends in $\hat{s}$.

Note that $\{\hat{r}_0 := \hat{r}, \hat{r}_1, \hat{r}_2, \hat{r}_3, \hat{r}_4 := \hat{s}\}$ is also a maximal chain, since there does not exist $\hat{u} \in REL^4$ such that $\hat{r}_i \prec \hat{u} \prec \hat{r}_{i+1}$ for some $i \in \{0, 1, 2, 3\}$. Moreover this shortest path has length 4, and every other shortest path between $\hat{r}$ and $\hat{s}$ has the same length, e.g. the one with dark green edges. Thus the natural length of $[\hat{r}, \hat{s}]$ is 4.

The explicit expression for the rank function is

$$\rho(\hat{r}) = \sum_{i=1}^{N} (N - i + 1)\hat{r}[i] \, .$$

Indeed, recalling that given two runs one covers the other if they differ only for a swap of length one or a replacement in the last position, in order to compute $\rho(\hat{r})$ we need to count the number of replacements and swaps needed to go from the smallest run possible, i.e. $(0, \dots, 0)$ to $\hat{r}$ along a path in the Hasse diagram, where the edges are the "cover" relations.

EXAMPLE. Let us consider $\hat{s} = (1, 0, 1, 1)$ from the previous example. Since $\hat{s}[1] = 1$, from $\hat{0} = (0, 0, 0, 0)$ we need a replacement in $\hat{0}[4]$ plus three swaps to reach $\hat{s}[1]$, that is we have to do four "cover" operation to go from $\hat{0}$ to $(1, 0, 0, 0)$ and, equivalently, the path in the Hasse diagram has length equal to 4. Since $\hat{s}[3] = 1$, from $(1, 0, 0, 0)$ to $(1, 0, 1, 0)$ we need a replacement in the last position plus a swap, that is 2 more "cover" operations. Eventually, with another replacement, we reach $\hat{s}$. Hence $\rho(\hat{s}) = 4 + 2 + 1 = 7 = \sum_{i=1}^{4}(4 - i + 1)\hat{s}[i]$, as stated.

Therefore, from the natural distance and the rank function, we can define the difference as $\Delta_{\hat{r}\hat{s}} = \ell(\hat{r}, \hat{s})$ if $\hat{r} \le \hat{s}$, otherwise $\Delta_{\hat{r}\hat{s}} = -\ell(\hat{s}, \hat{r})$.

DEFINITION 4. Given two comparable runs $\hat{r}, \hat{s} \in REL^N$, the **difference** between $\hat{r}$ and $\hat{s}$ is $\Delta_{\hat{r}\hat{s}} = \sum_{i=1}^{N}(N - i + 1)(\hat{s}[i] - \hat{r}[i])$.

Note that, contrary to the previous cases, since the ordering given by (3) is only partial, in order to compare differences between intervals we need to restrict our study to a maximal chain, i.e. a totally ordered subset of REL^N. Thus, denoted with $C(REL^N)$ a maximal chain of REL^N, and given the *less than or equal to* $\preceq_d$ relation, which as in the previous cases coincides with the order relation $\le$ among real numbers, the relational structure $(C(REL^N), \preceq_d)$ is a difference structure. This follows from the same discussion we have done for the difference structure in the strong top-heaviness case in the previous section.

Therefore, an interval scale measure M on $(C(REL^N), \preceq_d)$ is given by the rank function, that is

$$M(\hat{r}) = \rho(\hat{r}) = \sum_{i=1}^{N}(N - i + 1)\hat{r}[i] \, ,$$

for $\hat{r} \in C(REL^N)$.

AP, RBP, DCG, and ERR are on a ordinal scale with respect the partial ordering (3) induced by the weak top-heaviness, as demonstrated by [8]. However, none of them is on an interval scale since there does not exist any positive linear transformation between M and any of them. In particular, the next example shows how each of them fails on intervals with same length.

EXAMPLE. Consider the following runs on $REL^4 : \hat{r} = (0, 1, 0, 0)$, $\hat{s} = (1, 0, 0, 0)$, $\hat{u} = (0, 0, 0, 1)$ and $\hat{v} = (0, 0, 1, 0)$. These runs are comparable, that is they belong to the same maximal chain on REL^4.

Moreover, $\hat{s}$ covers $\hat{r}$ and $\hat{v}$ covers $\hat{u}$, that is the differences $\Delta_{\hat{r}\hat{s}}$ and $\Delta_{\hat{u}\hat{v}}$ are equal.

Hence an interval scale measure M should satisfy M($\hat{s}$) − M($\hat{r}$) = M($\hat{v}$)−M($\hat{u}$), as a consequence of Theorem 1. However, in the case of AP we have that $RB\cdot(\text{AP}(\hat{s})-\text{AP}(\hat{r})) = 1-1/2 > 1/3-1/4 = (\text{AP}(\hat{v})-\text{AP}(\hat{u})) \cdot RB$, where RB is the recall base. In the case of RBP we have that $\text{RBP}_p(\hat{s})-\text{RBP}_p(\hat{r}) = (1-p)^2 > (1-p)^2p^2 = \text{RBP}_p(\hat{v})-\text{RBP}_p(\hat{u})$ since $p < 1$. In the case of DCG we have that $\text{DCG}_2(\hat{s}) - \text{DCG}_2(\hat{r}) = 1 - 1 < 1/\log_2 3 - 1/\log_2 4 = \text{DCG}_2(\hat{v}) - \text{DCG}_2(\hat{u})$. Finally, in the case of ERR we have that $\text{ERR}(\hat{s}) - \text{ERR}(\hat{r}) = 1/2 - 1/4 > 1/6 - 1/8 = \text{ERR}(\hat{v}) - \text{ERR}(\hat{u})$. This proves that none of these measures is an interval scale on $(C(REL^N), \leq_d)$, where $C(REL^N)$ is such that $\hat{r}, \hat{s}, \hat{u}, \hat{v} \in C(REL^N)$.

5.3 Related Work

Both Amigó et al. [2] and Moffat [15] studied the properties of IR measures, in a formal and a numeric way respectively, defining, e.g., how an IR measure should behave when a relevant document is added or removed from a system run. All the identified properties could be exploited to introduce some sort of structure among the system runs but these authors did not do that explicitly. Moreover, they did not study what scales are adopted by IR measures, which is the core topic of this paper instead.

Busin and Mizzaro [6] used the notion of scale and mapping among scale to model different kinds of similarity and to introduce constraints and axioms over them. However, they did not address the problem of determining the scales used by an IR measure.

6 CONCLUSIONS AND FUTURE WORK

In this paper we have explored the question whether IR evaluation measures are based on an interval scale or not. This is a core issue since the validity of the statistics, such as mean and variance, and the statistical tests we use to compare IR systems depends on the scale adopted by IR measures.

We have relied on the representational theory of measurement and highlighted that the key point to understand the properties of IR measures is to have a clear understanding of the relations among system runs. In particular, to determine if an IR measure is on a interval scale, we need first to have a commonly agreed notion of ordering and a notion of interval among system runs. We have shown how to define such notions of ordering and interval and how to exploit them to determine whether an IR measure is on an interval scale.

In the case of set-based measures and system runs of fixed length, we found that the most popular ones – namely Precision, Recall, and F-measure – are on an interval scale. In the case of rank-based measures and system runs of fixed length, adopting a strongly top-heavy ordering, we found that: RBP with $p = \frac{1}{2}$ is on an interval scale; RBP with $p < \frac{1}{2}$ is on an ordinal scale but not on an interval one; RBP with $p > \frac{1}{2}$, AP, DCG, and ERR are not on an interval scale and not even on an ordinal one. Using a weakly top-heavy ordering, we found that RBP, AP, DCG, ERR are not on an interval scale even if they are on an ordinal one.

Future work will concern further investigation of rank-based measures and we will explore two alternatives. Firstly, instead of

defining a notion of ordering among the system runs, we will use the ordering of systems induced by an IR measure itself and we will check if, at least in this case, IR measures are on an interval scale. Secondly, we will relax the properties of Definition 1 by removing the Solvability Condition. This will cause the intervals of system runs to not be anymore equi-spaced but could allow us to introduce a notion of partially interval scale which IR measures might (or not) comply to.

REFERENCES

[1] J. Allan, W. B. Croft, A. P. de Vries, C. Zhai, N. Fuhr, and Y. Zhang (Eds.). 2015. *Proc. 1st ACM SIGIR International Conference on the Theory of Information Retrieval (ICTIR 2015)*. ACM Press, New York, USA.

[2] E. Amigó, J. Gonzalo, and M. F. Verdejo. 2013. A General Evaluation Measure for Document Organization Tasks. In *Proc. 36th Annual International ACM SIGIR Conference on Research and Development in Information Retrieval (SIGIR 2013)*, G. J. F. Jones, P. Sheridan, D. Kelly, M. de Rijke, and T. Sakai (Eds.). ACM Press, New York, USA, 643–652.

[3] A. Bjorner, P. H. Edelman, and G. M. Ziegler. 1990. Hyperplane Arrangements with a Lattice of Regions. *Discrete & Computational Geometry* 5, (1990), 263–288.

[4] P. Bollmann. 1984. Two Axioms for Evaluation Measures in Information Retrieval. In *Proc. of the Third Joint BCS and ACM Symposium on Research and Development in Information Retrieval*, C. J. van Rijsbergen (Ed.). Cambridge University Press, UK, 233–245.

[5] P. Bollmann and V. S. Cherniavsky. 1980. Measurement-theoretical investigation of the MZ-metric. In *Proc. 3rd Annual International ACM SIGIR Conference on Research and Development in Information Retrieval (SIGIR 1980)*, C. J. van Rijsbergen (Ed.). ACM Press, New York, USA, 256–267.

[6] L. Busin and S. Mizzaro. 2013. Axiometrics: An Axiomatic Approach to Information Retrieval Effectiveness Metrics. In *Proc. 4th International Conference on the Theory of Information Retrieval (ICTIR 2013)*, O. Kurland, D. Metzler, C. Lioma, B. Larsen, and P. Ingwersen (Eds.). ACM Press, New York, USA, 22–29.

[7] O. Chapelle, D. Metzler, Y. Zhang, and P. Grinspan. 2009. Expected Reciprocal Rank for Graded Relevance. In *Proc. 18th International Conference on Information and Knowledge Management (CIKM 2009)*, D. W.-L. Cheung, I.-Y. Song, W. W. Chu, X. Hu, and J. J. Lin (Eds.). ACM Press, New York, USA, 621–630.

[8] M. Ferrante, N. Ferro, and M. Maistro. 2015. Towards a Formal Framework for Utility-oriented Measurements of Retrieval Effectiveness, See [1], 21–30.

[9] S. Foldes. 2013. On distances and metrics in discrete ordered sets. *arXiv.org, Combinatorics (math.CO)* arXiv:1307.0244 (June 2013).

[10] N. Fuhr. 2012. Salton Award Lecture: Information Retrieval As Engineering Science. *SIGIR Forum* 46, 2 (December 2012), 19–28.

[11] K. Järvelin and J. Kekäläinen. 2002. Cumulated Gain-Based Evaluation of IR Techniques. *ACM TOIS* 20, 4 (October 2002), 422–446.

[12] D. E. Knuth. 1981. *The Art of Computer Programming – Volume 2: Seminumerical Algorithms* (2nd ed.). Addison-Wesley, USA.

[13] D. H. Krantz, R. D. Luce, P. Suppes, and A. Tversky. 1971. *Foundations of Measurement. Additive and Polynomial Representations*. Vol. 1. Academic Press, USA.

[14] S. Miyamoto. 2004. Generalizations of Multisets and Rough Approximations. *International Journal of Intelligent Systems* 19, 7 (July 2004), 639–652.

[15] A. Moffat. 2013. Seven Numeric Properties of Effectiveness Metrics. In *Proc. 9th Asia Information Retrieval Societies Conference (AIRS 2013)*, R. E. Banchs, F. Silvestri, T.-Y. Liu, M. Zhang, S. Gao, and J. Lang (Eds.), Vol. 8281. LNCS 8281, Springer, Heidelberg, Germany, 1–12.

[16] A. Moffat and J. Zobel. 2008. Rank-biased Precision for Measurement of Retrieval Effectiveness. *ACM TOIS* 27, 1 (2008), 2:1–2:27.

[17] S. Robertson. 2006. On GMAP: and Other Transformations. In *Proc. 15th International Conference on Information and Knowledge Management (CIKM 2006)*, P. S. Yu, V. Tsotras, E. A. Fox, and C.-B. Liu (Eds.). ACM Press, New York, USA, 78–83.

[18] G. B. Rossi. 2014. *Measurement and Probability. A Probabilistic Theory of Measurement with Applications*. Springer-Verlag, New York, USA.

[19] F. Sebastiani. 2015. An Axiomatically Derived Measure for the Evaluation of Classification Algorithms, See [1], 11–20.

[20] R. P. Stanley. 2012. *Enumerative Combinatorics – Volume 1* (2nd ed.). Cambridge Studies in Advanced Mathematics, Vol. 49. Cambridge University Press, Cambridge, UK.

[21] S. S. Stevens. 1946. On the Theory of Scales of Measurement. *Science, New Series* 103, 2684 (June 1946), 677–680.

[22] C. J. van Rijsbergen. 1974. Foundations of Evaluation. *Journal of Documentation* 30, 4 (1974), 365–373.

[23] P. F. Velleman and L. Wilkinson. 1993. Nominal, Ordinal, Interval, and Ratio Typologies Are Misleading. *The American Statistician* 47, 1 (February 1993), 65–72.

Considering Assessor Agreement in IR Evaluation

Eddy Maddalena
University of Southampton
Southampton, UK
e.maddalena@soton.ac.uk

Kevin Roitero
University of Udine
Udine, Italy
roitero.kevin@spes.uniud.it

Gianluca Demartini
University of Queensland
Brisbane, Australia
g.demartini@uq.edu.au

Stefano Mizzaro
University of Udine
Udine, Italy
mizzaro@uniud.it

ABSTRACT

The agreement between relevance assessors is an important but understudied topic in the Information Retrieval literature because of the limited data available about documents assessed by multiple judges. This issue has gained even more importance recently in light of crowdsourced relevance judgments, where it is customary to gather many relevance labels for each topic-document pair. In a crowdsourcing setting, agreement is often even used as a proxy for quality, although without any systematic verification of the conjecture that higher agreement corresponds to higher quality.

In this paper we address this issue and we study in particular: the effect of topic on assessor agreement; the relationship between assessor agreement and judgment quality; the effect of agreement on ranking systems according to their effectiveness; and the definition of an agreement-aware effectiveness metric that does not discard information about multiple judgments for the same document as it typically happens in a crowdsourcing setting.

CCS CONCEPTS

• **Information systems → Relevance assessment**;

KEYWORDS

TREC, evaluation, test collections, agreement, disagreement

ACM Reference format:
Eddy Maddalena, Kevin Roitero, Gianluca Demartini, and Stefano Mizzaro. 2017. Considering Assessor Agreement in IR Evaluation. In *Proceedings of ICTIR '17, Amsterdam, Netherlands, October 1–4, 2017,* 8 pages.
https://doi.org/10.1145/3121050.3121060

1 INTRODUCTION

Gathering relevance assessments is a crucial activity in Information Retrieval (IR) effectiveness evaluation. However, as it is well known, relevance is often uncertain: a query can be ambiguous, a term can have multiple meanings, a document can be considered from different viewpoints, an information need might be unclear, the "need behind a query" might be unknown, relevance assessors might work in non-ideal conditions, or be inadequate or even malicious, and so on. This is even more prominent when crowdsourcing is used to gather document relevance labels, as it has often been done in the last few years [1]. When crowdsourcing relevance assessments, usually each document is redundantly assessed by several crowd workers, who judge the relevance of the document to a specific topic. Generally speaking, all the relevance judgments received for a document by different workers are aggregated to compute the final relevance score: by doing so, only the final aggregated scores are subsequently considered to compute IR evaluation metrics, and all the information about the distributions of the judgments scores before the aggregation, and assessors's agreement, are lost. This could be valuable information, though: high disagreement between workers could suggest the presence of unreliable judgments, or a high intrinsic document or topic ambiguity.

Previous work has shown that while assessor agreement is typically low, the effect on the final IR system ranking generated using IR test collections is limited [7, 19]. While some work on measuring assessor disagreement and its effects on IR evaluation has been performed, it is somehow surprising that a comprehensive understanding of agreement in relevance assessment is still missing also given the recent rise in popularity of crowdsourcing.

In this paper we address this issue and propose novel evaluation metrics that preserve agreement information rather than just aggregating relevance labels collected from different human assessors for the same topic-document pair. More specifically, we focus on the following research questions, each one divided into sub-questions.

RQ1. Agreement, topic, and relevance. Is there a relationship between assessor agreement, topic and relevance level?

RQ1a. Is agreement level different on different topics?

RQ1b. Is agreement related to topic ease/difficulty?

RQ1c. Is agreement different on different relevance levels?

RQ2. Agreement and system evaluation. Is there a relation between assessor agreement and effectiveness evaluation?

RQ2a. What is the effect of agreement on measures of retrieval effectiveness?

RQ2b. What is the effect of agreement on systems ranking? Are system ranks more affected when removing high agreement or low agreement topics?

RQ3. Agreement-Aware metric. Is it possible to take agreement into account and define an agreement-aware IR evaluation metric? What is the effect on evaluation and system rankings of such a metric?

RQ3a. How to define an agreement-aware metric?

RQ3b. What is the effect of an agreement-aware metric on effectiveness evaluation and system rankings?

This paper is structured as follows. Section 2 surveys the related work in the area of assessor agreement. Section 3 presents the datasets used in our experiments, the agreement measures that we rely on, and highlights some issues. Each of Sections 4, 5, and 6 addresses one of the three research question RQ1, RQ2, and RQ3. Section 7 concludes the paper.

2 RELATED WORK

Inter-annotator agreement (IAA) is a measure of labeling quality used across several fields. For example, when creating linguistics collections IAA measures are used to validate the quality of the collection [10]. In IR evaluation the classic approach to create test collections is to rely on one human assessor to judge the relevance of a retrieved result with respect to the search topic. To preserve judgment consistency, in traditional IR evaluation one topic is entirely judged by one single assessor. Despite this common approach, previous work has looked at the expected level of agreement among assessors judging the same set of topic-document pairs.

Agreement in TREC Collections. Early research work has looked at agreement levels among different groups of human assessors (e.g., experts and non-experts) for TREC collections. For example, in [2, 15] authors looked at how the same evaluation collection created by different groups of assessors can lead to different evaluation results due to low IAA. An early measure used to look at disagreement was the overlap of relevant documents identified by different assessors [19]. In this and earlier work by Cleverdon [7], authors showed that, while IAA can be low, it has a limited impact on the evaluation results measured by the final IR system ranking correlation.

Causes of Disagreement. An analysis of what are the main causes for low IAA in relevance judgment tasks showed that document readability and length have a significant impact [6]. Another study which looked at the causes of judgment errors and disagreement [17] observed an existing 'assessor inertia' where a certain judgment is unconsciously affected by the previous ones done by the human assessor. Another cause of disagreement is the more or less detailed assessment guidelines [20]. Related to this is a recent study on how the order of documents presented to assessors impacts IAA levels, which showed that ordering documents by decreasing levels of relevance leads to higher levels of disagreement [8].

Crowdsourced Relevance Judgments. With the rising of the use of crowdsourcing as a means to collect relevance judgments for search results, a new approach to create IR evaluation collections is to collect *multiple* relevance labels for the same topic-document pair and to then aggregate such labels into a final relevance judgment [1]. This is typically done to improve the quality of the judgments by removing possible noise introduced by randomly assigned labels or adversaries. Previous work on crowdsourced relevance judgments has shown how collections built with such an approach lead to reliable results, and are repeatable if created again [3].

Several ways to aggregate labels collected from the crowd have been proposed, starting with the simple majority vote [12] up to complex weighted aggregation models that combine labels together by looking at common patterns at the crowd level [18]. However, performing such operation of label aggregation leads to a loss of information about the level of agreement among the different human assessors who looked at the same topic-document pair. On the other hand, we claim it is important to preserve such information in the IR evaluation process and to incorporate assessor agreement levels into the evaluation by, for example, giving less importance to judgments where lower agreement was observed.

Agreement-aware IR evaluation. Related to our work is the model presented in [9] where the hypothesis used is that non-relevant results judged with high disagreement should be retrieved higher than those with high agreement. Authors proposed an evaluation framework that integrates information about disagreement. Based on such previous work, in our paper we present a comprehensive study of assessor agreement and of the effects that high/low agreement rates have on IR system evaluation: We first perform an extensive analysis of assessor disagreement across different test collections and measure the effects on IR system evaluation. We then propose IR evaluation measures that integrate assessor agreement levels by looking at the distribution of relevance labels and compare such novel agreement-aware metrics with traditional ones in terms of the generated IR system ranking.

3 EXPERIMENTAL METHODOLOGY

3.1 Datasets

To study agreement, we need datasets featuring several relevance assessments for the same ⟨topic, document⟩ pair. We use two such datasets in our experiments, as detailed below.

3.1.1 RF: Relevance Feedback. The first dataset, denoted in the following by *RF* for Relevance Feedback, is described by Demeester et al. [9]. For the Relevance Feedback track 2010 [4] some of the ClueWeb documents used in TREC 2009 Million Query Track [5] have been re-assessed by up to 11 assessors each. Since we are interested in assessor agreement, we select the documents that were judged by at least 5 assessors; when more than 5 assessments are available, we select the first five only. We thus obtain around 15,000 usable re-assessments.

We also transform the original scale (that included −2 for "broken link" and −1 for "unknown (no gold label)") into 0, 1, 2 (by collapsing −1 and −2 into 0). For all these documents the original NIST assessments are available; we refer to them as *Gold* assessments.

The RF dataset contains re-assessments on 100 topics, however in some cases we cannot use all of them. Of the 100 topics, 11 do not have re-judged documents for all the three Gold relevance levels. In other terms, it is only for 89 topic that we can find re-assessed documents for all Gold relevance levels of 0, 1, and 2. Since in some cases we are interested to measure, and compare, the agreement of the documents at a given relevance level, sometimes we use those 89 topics only. Furthermore, some of the original summary files in the TREC 2009 Million Query Track data do not contain the NDCG values. This is not a problem when measuring agreement; however, when comparing agreement and effectiveness or ease (as we will sometimes do in the following) we need to filter some data. This leaves us with 81 topics. Finally, when combining all the above filters, we are left with 71 topics to work with.

3.1.2 ME: Magnitude Estimation. The second dataset, denoted *ME* for Magnitude Estimation, is the datasets used for the experiments by Maddalena et al. [14]. They re-assessed 18 TREC-8 topics by crowdsourcing. For each topic, the top ten retrieved documents by the systems that participated in TREC-8 were pooled and re-assessed, each one by 10 Crowdflower workers. Several quality checks were used to ensure that the collected data were reliable. One particularity of this dataset is that relevance scores were not on a graded, or category, scale as it is usually done; instead, magnitude estimation was used. With this psychophysical technique workers could express the relevance of a document to a topic using any number in the $]0, +\infty[$ range (note that 0 was not admissible).

For those documents Gold from NIST assessors (the original TREC-8 assessors) are available.

3.2 Measures: Effectiveness, Ease, Agreement

In this paper we use mainly NDCG as a measure of system effectiveness. For each topic we define *topic ease* as the average effectiveness on that topic of the systems participating in the evaluation exercise (for RF we use the Million Query 2009 runs; for ME we use the TREC-8 runs). On terminology, we notice that we prefer to use "topic ease" instead of the probably most common "topic difficulty" for symmetry with system effectiveness: higher e would mean both higher topic ease and higher average system effectiveness.

Several agreement measures have been defined in the past: variance, standard deviation, entropy, ICC, Cohen's kappa, Fleiss's kappa, etc. Throughout this paper we use Krippendorff's α [13], a standardized measure of agreement that adapts to items having different numbers of evaluators, different scales, missing values. α assumes values ranging from -1 (complete disagreement) through 0 random (agreement obtained by random evaluations) to 1 (complete agreement). We use two versions of α:

1 α interval/ordinal for RF data. The scale is the usual graded scale $0, 1, 2$ and using the interval version means that we weight more the difference between 0 and 2 than the difference between 0 and 1. Results are equivalent to using α ordinal.

2 α interval for ME data. Normalized ME scores are log-normally distributed [14]. We take the logarithm the scores, to obtain a normal distribution and avoid precision issues. Since ME scores are on a ratio scale [14], by taking the logarithm we obtain an interval scale; therefore we adopt the interval version of α.

α (and other agreement measures) works on a set of assessments and computes the overall agreement for that set. Using it to compute the agreement on a single ⟨topic, document⟩ pair would be absolutely not standard and open to criticisms. Therefore our experiments are topic-based. As we will see shortly, it is indeed the case that there is a topic-related notion of agreement, and it makes sense to speak of *agreement for a topic*: agreement is somehow intrinsic in a topic, and there are high- and low-agreement topics.

Table 1 summarizes the measures for the two datasets. For each topic we have its ease e, its agreement computed using all the assessed documents (α^A, A stands for "All"), and its agreement computed using a subset of the documents having a specific relevance value in the Gold. For RF we have Gold on a three level scale $(0, 1, 2)$, so we can compute α^0, α^1, and α^2; for ME we have Gold on a binary scale $(0, 1)$ and therefore only α^0 and α^1 can be computed. We will also refer to α^{01}, α^{02}, and α^{12} as the α values computed on the basis of documents having two Gold relevance values.

Table 1: Datasets. The α superscripts indicate the set of documents used to compute α, i.e., A=All, or having Gold = 0, Gold = 1, or Gold = 2 (the latter only for the RF dataset).

Topic	Ease (e)	Agreement (α^A)	(α^0)	(α^1)	(α^2)
t_1	e_1	α_1^A	α_1^0	α_1^1	α_1^2
t_2	e_2	α_2^A	α_2^0	α_2^1	α_2^2
...					
t_n	e_n	α_n^A	α_n^0	α_n^1	α_n^2

3.3 Justifications and Issues

We provide a justification for the choice of those two datasets, and highlight some issues for each of them. Of course we need datasets featuring several relevance assessments for the same ⟨topic, document⟩ pair. In this respect, both datasets are adequate.

For some of our experiments on RF data we had to "interpolate" some effectiveness values by filling NDCG values for specific ⟨topic, system⟩ pairs. 26% of such values we missing. We created those values by taking the mean of all the other available NDCG values for that topic and that system. Intuitively this interpolation makes sense. In practice it does not affect the results significantly: when evaluating system effectiveness or topic ease with the "interpolated" values or with the original values, the results is in practice unchanged (we obtain correlations around 0.98).

RF has three levels relevance judgments. When the relevance scale used is bounded, as it is in this case, some subtle issues arise with agreement metrics. When focusing on one end of the scale (maximum relevance or complete irrelevance), a decrease in agreement implies a decrease in judgment quality (since agreement can be decreased only by "going away in one direction" from the true value). This is not true for the central part of the scale, where, however, another phenomenon arises: for the central value of the scale, maximum disagreement means also maximum quality of the aggregated judgment (since the maximum disagreement is obtained "going away in two symmetrical directions" from the true value). In an attempt to overcome these problems, we also use ME data. ME does not have the same limitations, since it is based on an unbounded scale $]0, +\infty[$; however a somehow non-standard scale is used, and therefore another dataset is needed to find confirmations and avoid results depending on effects of the used scale only.

We additionally report results obtained by grouping together topics with similar agreement levels to smooth noise in the data: after ordering topics by their α score, we create groups of topics of the same size (referred to as topic binning).

4 RQ1: AGREEMENT, TOPIC, RELEVANCE

RQ1 is aimed at understanding if there is a relationship between assessor agreement, topic, and relevance level. Each sub-question is addressed in the following subsections.

4.1 RQ1a: Agreement Over Topics

To answer RQ1a, we analyze the variation of Krippendorff's α over topics. Figure 1 shows that there is quite some variation of α values over the 100 topics of the RF dataset: the range is approximately $[-0.1, 0.3]$. On the ME dataset the variation is more limited, approximately in the $[0.25, 0.45]$ range (this can be seen from the red top series in Figure 3, bottom chart—the figure will be described in

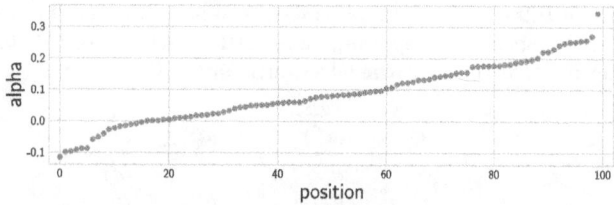

Figure 1: Agreement over topics

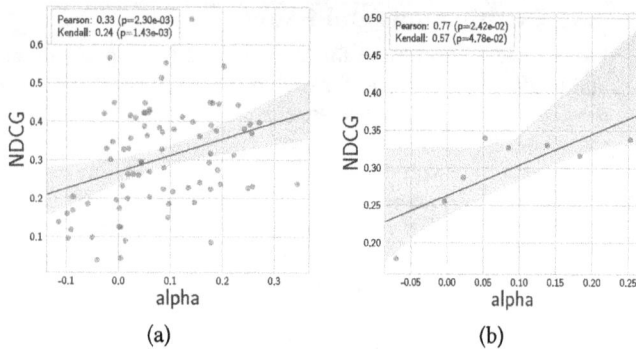

(a)

(b)

Figure 2: Agreement and topic ease: individual topics (a) and topics binned according to their agreement (b)

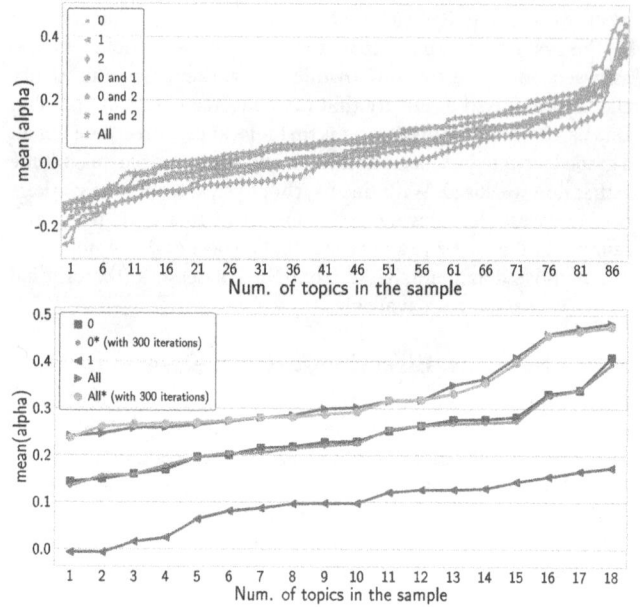

Figure 3: Agreement over topics: breakdown on relevance levels and combinations, RF above and ME below.

Section 4.3), but the topics are only 18. After this first analysis, there seems to be a significant effect of topic on agreement, so the answer to RQ1a is positive. Also note that this result should be quite stable since it is obtained using topics with dozens of documents each.

4.2 RQ1b: Agreement and Topic Ease/Difficulty

As anticipated in Section 3.2 we speak of topic ease. To understand if agreement is related to topic ease (RQ1b) we plot for each topic its agreement value (α) against its ease value (e, NDCG in our case). Figure 2(a) shows the scatter plot for RF data (using 81 topics, as detailed in Section 3.1.1): there is a mild, though significant, correlation between agreement and topic ease on the RF dataset. In other terms, topics with a higher agreement among the five assessors also tend to also be easier topics, i.e., systems tend to obtain a higher NDCG on them. The correlation is mild but it becomes stronger (and still statistically significant) when binning the topics, as shown in Figure 2(b). In this figure each dot is a bin of topics of similar agreement; the values on the axes are the averages of α and NDCG for the topics in that bin.

However, when turning to the ME datasets, we do not find any significant correlation between α and NDCG. We do not report the data for space limits, but correlations are around zero and not significant. We can formulate a conjecture for understanding this difference. One important difference on the two datasets is that the topics in ME are TREC-8 topics, with the usual Title plus Description plus Narrative rich structure; whereas RF topics are Million Query 2009 queries, selected from a query log and consisting of simply a few terms. When the latter contain ambiguous terms, those are ambiguous for both human assessors (thus probably leading to low agreement) and systems (thus probably leading to lower

effectiveness as well). TREC-8 topics, instead, are probably less ambiguous for human assessors, that can exploit topic Description and Narrative to build a context and disambiguate meaning; of course, systems can rely on the query terms only, and therefore "human" and "system" ambiguity become more independent.

As an answer to RQ1b we can state that there seems to be some relation between topic ease and agreement, although a positive and significant correlation has been observed in the RF dataset only.

4.3 RQ1c: Agreement Over Relevance Levels

As discussed in Section 3.1, the individual documents of each topic have a Gold relevance assessment. Then, we can repeat the previous analyses to understand if the same results hold when a breakdown of the documents on the different relevance levels is done. Also, we can study what are the relations among the different relevance levels. Therefore, to answer RQ1c we proceed with a breakdown on relevance levels according to the Gold, keeping in mind that RF has three levels (0, 1, 2), whereas ME has two (0, 1). Since there seems to be an effect of the topics on agreement, we still work on the individual topics (instead of putting all the topics together).

Figure 3 shows, for the two datasets, the agreement values considering the documents at a given relevance level, across the various topics: α^A, α^0, α^1, and (for RF only) α^2, as well as α^{01}, α^{02}, and α^{12} values for each topic. On the x axis, topics are ranked by increasing agreement (within each series). As anticipated in Section 3.1.1, to be able to compare agreement over different relevance levels, we use 89 topics for RF. The figure shows that the relevance level causes some variation, on both datasets. The curves do not overlap (as they would do if there were no effect of the relevance level).

The charts show another result: agreement is lower for relevant documents: when focusing on documents having Gold = 2 in RF or Gold = 1 in ME, the α values are lower. However, in RF the

Table 2: Pearson's ρ correlations of agreement computed over different topic subsets on the basis of relevance levels for the RF dataset (* means $p < .005$).

	α^0	α^1	α^2	α^{01}	α^{02}	α^{12}	α^A
α^0		.13	.06	.78*	.80*	.19	.71*
α^1			.06	.51*	.16	.74*	.47*
α^2				.07	.29*	.53*	.31*
α^{01}					.7*	.46*	.87*
α^{02}						.45*	.88*
α^{12}							.68*

Table 3: α - NDCG Pearson's ρ correlation over relevance levels combinations, for RF data (* means $p < .005$).

num. of bins	α^0	α^1	α^2	α^{01}	α^{02}	α^{12}	α^A
8	.76	.78	.84*	.71	.80	.66	.77
16	.67*	.51	.65*	.69*	.67*	.62	.64*
32	.48*	.29	.58*	.58*	.61*	.46*	.62*
89 = no bins	.42*	.24	.40*	.43*	.41*	.39*	.48*

intermediate relevance (Gold = 1) does not have lower α values than irrelevant (Gold = 0). We verified that in our data lower α values do not depend on the number of documents involved in each α calculation. For the ME dataset we recomputed α on a subset of all the documents, and on a subset of the irrelevant documents, having a cardinality equal to the set of relevant documents for that topic. We also repeated the process 300 times and took the average α. The resulting α values are plotted on the bottom chart of Figure 3 as the two more pale curves. Those are in practice overlapping with the curves obtained using the full data. If the amount of data used had an effect, those two curves would be much more similar to the red curve. It has to be noted however that, the metric α decreases when judgments are distributed across more values (which makes sense because intuitively "it is easier to disagree when there is more space / possibility to disagree").

4.4 RQ1 Again: Agreement Over Topics and Relevance, Revisited

To answer RQ1 in a more complete way, we report on some further analysis. Since there seems to be an effect of *both* topics and relevance levels, we study the two combined.

From the results presented in Table 2 it is clear that there is no correlation between α^i, α^j, and α^k, neither between α^{ij} and α^k for $i, j, k \in \{0, 1, 2\}$. Note that the higher correlation of α^i and α^{ij} with α^A (last column) is to be expected since for the latter a superset of the same data is used. The same results hold for the ME dataset (although of course in that case we can speak only of α^0, α^1, and α^A). In other terms, even when focusing on a topic, the agreement level on documents having a certain relevance value according to the gold is not a good predictor of the agreement level on documents with a different relevance value.

As a general conclusion about RQ1, we can state that agreement does not seem related to topic only. One needs to take into account the relevance levels too.

5 RQ2: EFFECT OF AGREEMENT ON RETRIEVAL EVALUATION

With RQ2 we are interested not only in the agreement per se, but more specifically in its effect on effectiveness evaluation.

5.1 RQ2a: Effect on Effectiveness Measures

We begin by analyzing how NDCG values vary when varying the topic subset on the basis of agreement, and also taking into account the relevance level in the Gold (RQ2a).

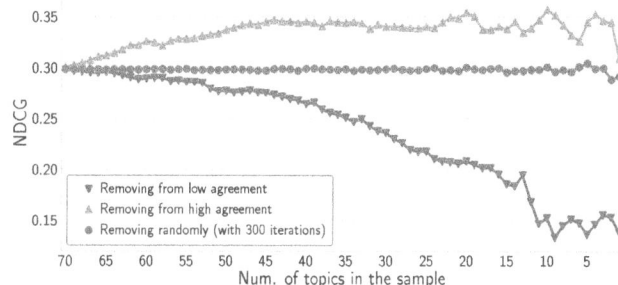

Figure 4: NDCG variation when removing topics (with high agreement, low agreement and randomly).

Table 3 shows correlation values between α and NDCG values, on RF data. This is a similar table to Figure 2, with only fewer data items used because we selected the 71 RF topics having at least one document for each relevance level and for which we found an NDCG value from the summary files (see Section 3.1.1). The results show that, although no correlation is found between α^i, α^j, and α^k, neither between α^{ij} and α^k for $i, j, k \in \{0, 1, 2\}$ (as we have seen in Table 2), the correlation between agreement (α^A) and ease shown by Figure 2 does persist when agreement is computed on a subset of the topics only.

To better understand how NDCG is affected by agreement levels we observe how NDCG changes by computing it only on high/low agreement topics and removing the others. Figure 4 provides some further insight. In the chart, the x axis represents the number of topics used to compute NDCG: at the extreme left all 71 topics are used, and topics are removed while going to the right of the chart. We use three strategies to remove the topics: randomly (with 300 random repetitions), removing the high agreement topics first, and removing the low agreement topic first. The figure (consistently with the previous results) shows that when computing NDCG after removing high agreement topics NDCG decreases, as expected since those are the easier topics. Conversely, when removing low agreement topics, NDCG increases. As a baseline, when removing topics randomly, NDCG remains constant (with some normal fluctuations). Similar patterns are observed when binning topics.

5.2 RQ2b: Effect on System Ranks

Having understood that high and low agreement topics impact differently on NDCG values, it is natural to ask how system ranks are likewise affected (RQ2b). We address this issue by trying to estimate system ranks by using a subset of topics. In other terms, we compute the Kendall's τ correlation between (i) NDCG computed on the whole topic set and (ii) NDCG computed on a subset formed by selecting the high agreement topics, or the low agreement ones, or random ones (with the usual 300 sampling repetitions). This is

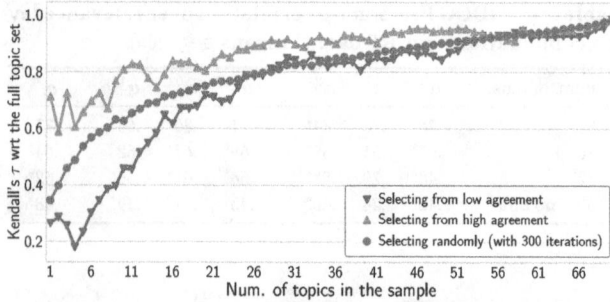

Figure 5: Effect of removing topics on system ranks. The Y axis shows the Kendall's τ correlation between the rankings obtained computing NDCG using the full 80 topics or a subset of the size shown on the x axis. Subsets are formed by low agreement, high agreement, and random topics.

a similar methodology to that used by Guiver et al. [11]. Figure 5 shows the result. The x axis represents the number of topics in the topic subset (differently from previous figures here cardinality increases while moving right; we can use 71 topics from RF). The three series show the τ values for the three topic subset selection strategies. The figure shows that when using the topics with high agreement one can predict better the system ranks than when using low agreement topics. In other terms, system ranks are more affected by high agreement topics.

6 RQ3: AN AGREEMENT AWARE METRIC

Having shown that agreement has an effect on evaluation, we now turn to RQ3. Whereas in the previous section we have been focusing on RF data only, in this section we use the ME dataset as it provides relevance judgments on a continuous scale thus displaying a score distributions that can be considered in the proposed metrics. We first define an agreement aware IR evaluation metrics and provide some intuition. We then re-evaluate systems with the new effectiveness and topic ease metrics on ME data, comparing the outcome with the official evaluation results.

6.1 RQ3a: Definition of the Agreement-Aware NDCG Metric

To answer RQ3a we provide a generalization of NDCG@k.

6.1.1 Generalizing DCG. Classic[1] DCG@k is defined as:

$$DCG@k = g_1 + \sum_{i=2}^{k} \frac{g_i}{\log(i)}.$$

This assumes that it is possible to define a gain value g_i, which in turn assumes that it can be determined with certainty. A first generalization incorporating the notion of assessor agreement could be to consider gain intervals in place of individual gains g_i. Interval DCG@k (IDCG@k) could be defined as:

$$IDCG@k = (g_1 \pm \delta) + \sum_{i=2}^{k} \frac{(g_i \pm \delta)}{\log(i)}.$$

---

[1]We follow the well known original formulation where the first retrieved document is considered individually. We use $\log_2$ in this paper without loss of generality.

IDCG@k is an interval, not a number. We might use generic, i.e., non symmetric, intervals, but we can generalize it even more by considering in place of individual gains g_i not simply intervals, but *gain distributions* G_i. The individual gain g_i is the expected value of G_i. We therefore define Uncertain DCG at k (UDCG@k) as:

$$UDCG@k = G_1 + \sum_{i=2}^{k} \frac{G_i}{\log(i)}.$$

Thus UDCG@k is neither a number, nor an interval but a (discounted) gain distribution. In other terms, we are not cumulating the gain values g_i but we are cumulating (discounted) gain distributions G_i. This is a generalization of IDCG@k, that can be obtained from UDCG@k by using uniform distributions over an interval.

6.1.2 Generalizing NDCG. However, DCG@k needs to be normalized to take into account different "quantities of relevance" for different topics. Classic normalized DCG@k ($NDCG@k$) is obtained by dividing the obtained DCG@k by the ideal DCG@k, i.e., the DCG@k that would be obtained with the ideal ranking of documents. Ideal DCG@k is defined as:

$$iDCG@k = ig_1 + \sum_{i=2}^{k} \frac{ig_1}{\log(i)},$$

where i stand for ideal and ig for the gain of the ideal document. Then NDCG@k is defined as: $NDCG@k = \frac{DCG@k}{iDCG@k}$. We can do almost the same to normalize UDCG@k, using mixture distributions [16], that are weighted sums of probability distributions. They are almost what we need; mixture distributions have the requirement that the sum of the weights is 1, which is not true in our case (our weights are the inverse of the logarithms of the ranks). But we can divide our sums in UDCG@k by the sum of the weights. We can define the constant value:

$$C@k = 1 + \sum_{i=2}^{k} \frac{1}{\log(i)}.$$

We can therefore build a mixture distribution for both the actual rank of documents retrieved by a system and the ideal rank, provided that we divide the results by $C@k$

$$DCG'@k = \frac{DCG@k}{C@k} \text{ and } iDCG'@k = \frac{iDCG@k}{C@k}.$$

We now normalize $DCG'@k$ by subtracting the expected value of $iDCG'@k$ (we use the mean μ): $NDCG@k = DCG'@k - \mu$. This has the effect of translating the distribution "towards zero". Note that μ of the ideal case will alway be greater than or equal to the actual case. The alternative of dividing by μ is also sensible and perhaps more similar to what is done in original NDCG@k; however we feel that the effect of subtracting μ is more intuitive and therefore we leave the alternative as future work.

With this process we can associate a gain distribution to each ⟨system, topic⟩ pair. The gain distributions can provide insight on both effectiveness / ease and agreement. Furthermore, from each gain distribution we can derive its mean (that can be used as single value of effectiveness, or ease) and its standard deviation (that can be used to measure assessor agreement). The mean over all topics is an effectiveness / ease measure, that we call AANDCG@k (Agreement Aware NDCG@k).

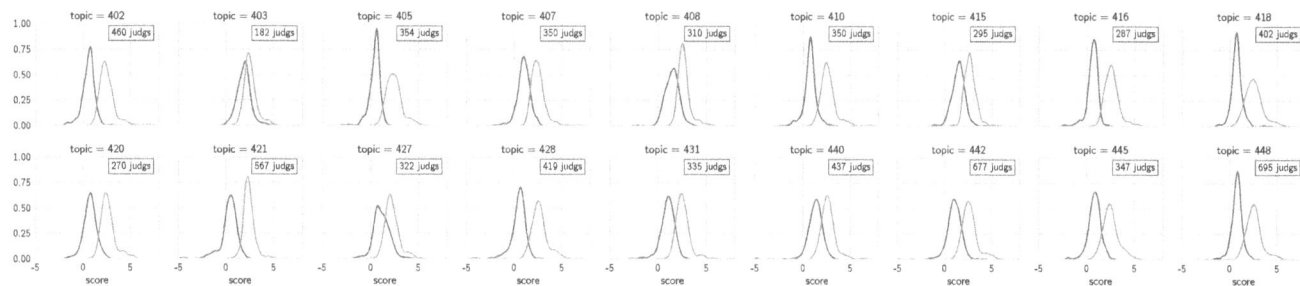

Figure 6: Distribution of the relevance scores for the 18 ME topics. Relevant documents are represented by the green distributions, not relevant documents by the blue distributions.

6.1.3 Relevance / Gain Distributions. We attempt to make more concrete the idea that each document can have its own relevance / gain distribution, in place of the standard single value. In the ME dataset, for each of the 18 topics, there are two documents, named H_K and N_K in the original paper [14], that received many relevance assessment. The number of relevance assessment varied across topic, from 182 to 695. Those documents, one highly relevant (H_K) and one very irrelevant (N_K) were used in the original work as quality checks and to normalize the scales, but by using those assessment we can have an idea of what relevance distribution to expect, at least for those relevance levels. Figure 6 shows the distributions of the (logarithm of) the relevance scores. The figure shows that, as expected, relevant documents (green distributions) have higher values than irrelevant (blue ones), but it overall confirms the idea of associating to each document its own relevance distribution rather than a single relevance value as a measure of assessor agreement. Then, in place of associating a gain value g_i to each relevance value as it is done in DCG, it is natural to think of gain distributions G_i as done in Section 6.1.2.

6.2 RQ3b: AANDCG at Work

To analyze the effect of agreement on system rankings (RQ3b) we provide two kinds of results. The first is in graphic form. Figure 7 represents the gain distributions for a given ⟨system, topic⟩ pair, and shows the subset of 100 intervals having positive values. The figure shows that there is indeed some variation across both systems and topics. Some of the gain distributions are unimodal, some are bimodal; some have a lower standard deviation; the means are in general different. Both system effectiveness and topic ease are affected by agreement.

The second result is numeric. When computing AANDCG@k (i.e., the means as described at the end of Section 6.1.2) over systems and topics, and comparing them to the original evaluation of system effectiveness and topic ease we obtain the two scatter plots, with their correlation values, in Figure 8. It is clear that the two measurements are related, but different: assessor agreement has an effect on system ranks as well as on topic ease.

7 CONCLUSIONS AND FUTURE WORK

IR evaluation results are heavily influenced by relevance judgments done by human assessors. The use of crowdsourcing to scale the collection of relevance judgments has introduced the novel aspect of judgments for the same topic-document pair being collected

from multiple assessors and their labels being then aggregated. Such approach has the advantage of increasing judgment quality, but, at the same time, it disregards the information about agreement levels among assessors judging the same document.

In this paper we performed an in-depth study of the effects of assessor agreement on IR evaluation results across different datasets looking at how topics with different agreement levels affect the evaluation. We additionally proposed agreement-aware IR evaluation metrics (AANDCG) that preserve and leverage information about assessor agreement. We have observed how using topics with high-agreement judgments lead to more robust evaluation results. Our experimental results also show the benefits of defining relevance as a distribution (and thus incorporating agreement information) rather than as an absolute value attached to a retrieved document with respect to the search topic.

This paper leaves many indications for future work. We worked on a topic-wise definition of agreement; this allowed to use the standard agreement measure by Krippendorff but of course it leaves room to different approaches. Also, variants of AANDCG@k (like dividing by the mean in place of subtracting) need to be studied. We took particular care to verify our results on two independent datasets, but of course further confirmation on other data is needed.

Acknowledgments

This project has received funding from the European Union's Horizon 2020 research and innovation programme under grant agreement No 732328 and was partially supported by the UK EPSRC grant number EP/N011589/1. We want to thank the Erasmus+ traineeships program for facilitating collaborations, and the European Science Foundation for funding the Science Meeting SM 5917 under the ELIAS Research Networking Programme. We thank the crowd workers who participated in our experiments.

REFERENCES

[1] Omar Alonso and Stefano Mizzaro. 2012. Using Crowdsourcing for TREC Relevance Assessment. *Inf. Process. Manage.* 48, 6 (Nov. 2012), 1053–1066.
[2] Peter Bailey, Nick Craswell, Ian Soboroff, Paul Thomas, Arjen P. de Vries, and Emine Yilmaz. 2008. Relevance Assessment: Are Judges Exchangeable and Does It Matter. In *Proceedings of the 31st ACM SIGIR.* 667–674.
[3] Roi Blanco, Harry Halpin, Daniel M. Herzig, Peter Mika, Jeffrey Pound, Henry S. Thompson, and Thanh Tran Duc. 2011. Repeatable and Reliable Search System Evaluation Using Crowdsourcing. In *Proceedings of the 34th ACM SIGIR.* 923–932.
[4] Chris Buckley, Matthew Lease, and Mark D Smucker. 2010. Overview of the TREC 2010 Relevance Feedback Track. In *19th Text Retrieval Conference.*
[5] Ben Carterette, Virgiliu Pavlu, Hui Fang, and Evangelos Kanoulas. 2009. Million Query Track 2009 Overview. In *TREC.*

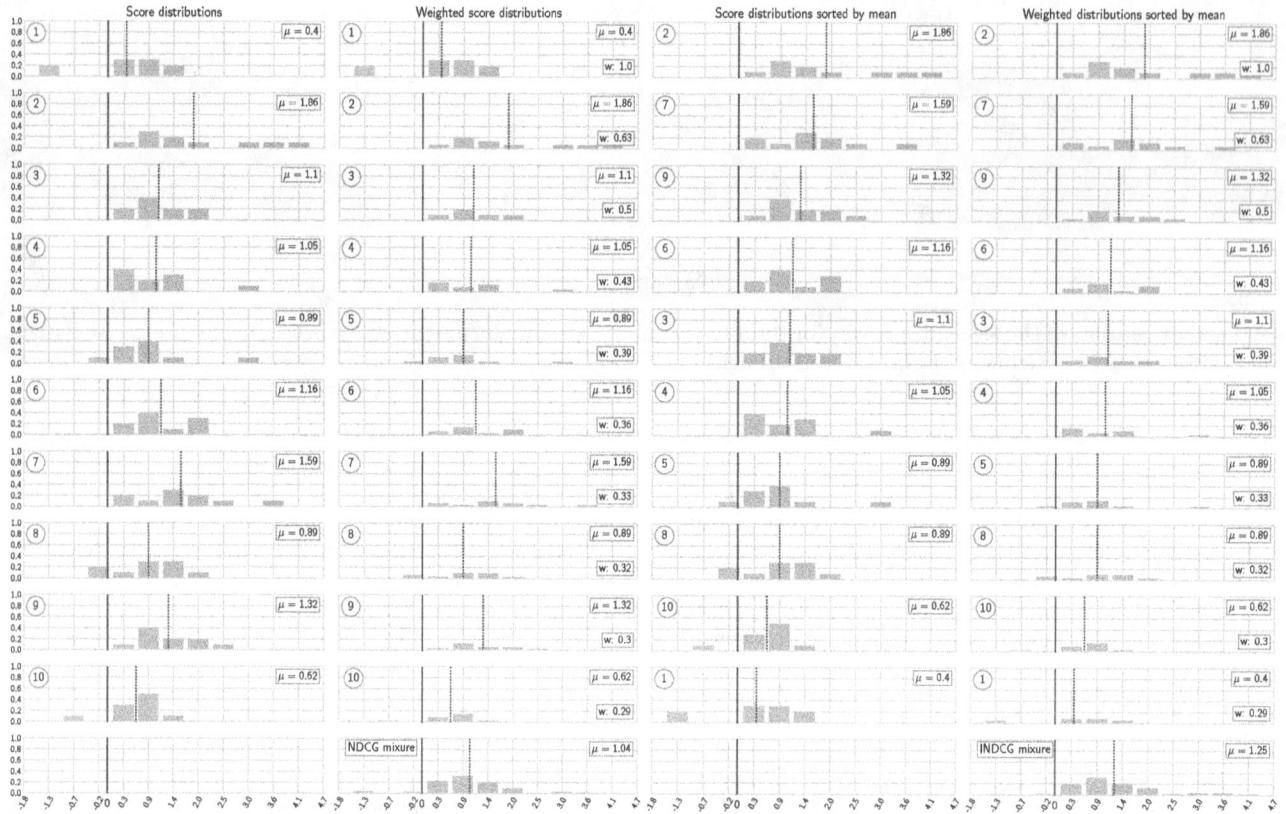

Figure 7: Gain distributions for the ME datasets. Each plot shows the binned distribution of the document relevance scores, obtained considering crowd judgments. The first column shows the first 10 documents as retrieved by an IRS; the second column shows the same distribution discounted by the log of the rank; the third column shows the top 10 documents in the ideal rank (i.e., the most relevant first; the mean value is shown, and graphically represented as a dotted vertical line); the fourth column shows the ideal rank discounted by the log of the rank (i.e., as col.2). In the bottom row we see 2 mixture distributions: on the left, the mixture distribution obtained cumulating the distributions produced by the IRS; on the right, the distribution obtained cumulating the distributions according to the ideal order.

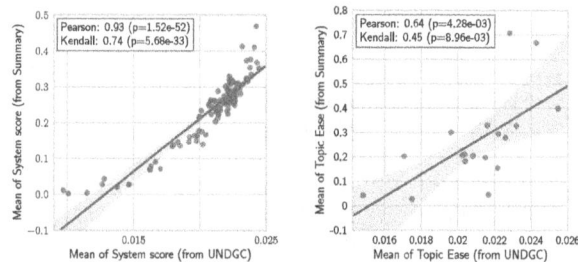

Figure 8: AANDCG vs MAP, for systems (left) and topics (right) on the ME dataset.

[6] Praveen Chandar, William Webber, and Ben Carterette. 2013. Document Features Predicting Assessor Disagreement. In *36th ACM SIGIR*. 745–748.

[7] Cyril W Cleverdon. 1970. *The effect of variations in relevance assessments in comparative experimental tests of index languages*. Technical Report. Cranfield University; Aslib.

[8] Tadele T. Damessie, Falk Scholer, Kalvero Järvelin, and J. Shane Culpepper. 2016. The Effect of Document Order and Topic Difficulty on Assessor Agreement. In *Proceedings of the 2016 ACM International Conference on the Theory of Information Retrieval (ICTIR '16)*. 73–76.

[9] Thomas Demeester, Robin Aly, Djoerd Hiemstra, Dong Nguyen, Dolf Trieschnigg, and Chris Develder. 2014. Exploiting User Disagreement for Web Search Evaluation: An Experimental Approach. In *Proceedings of the 7th ACM International Conference on Web Search and Data Mining (WSDM '14)*. 33–42.

[10] Leon Derczynski, Kalina Bontcheva, and Ian Roberts. 2016. Broad Twitter Corpus: A Diverse Named Entity Recognition Resource. In *COLING 2016, 26th International Conference on Computational Linguistics*. 1169–1179.

[11] J. Guiver, S. Mizzaro, and S. Robertson. 2009. A few good topics: Experiments in topic set reduction for retrieval evaluation. *ACM TOIS* 27, 4 (2009).

[12] Gabriella Kazai. 2011. In Search of Quality in Crowdsourcing for Search Engine Evaluation. In *33rd ECIR Conference*. 165–176.

[13] Klaus Krippendorff. 2007. *Computing Krippendorff's alpha reliability*. Technical Report. University of Pennsylvania. 43 pages.

[14] Eddy Maddalena, Stefano Mizzaro, Falk Scholer, and Andrew Turpin. 2017. On Crowdsourcing Relevance Magnitudes for Information Retrieval Evaluation. *ACM Trans. Inf. Syst.* 35, 3, Article 19 (Jan. 2017), 32 pages.

[15] Joao Palotti, Guido Zuccon, Johannes Bernhardt, Allan Hanbury, and Lorraine Goeuriot. 2016. *Assessors Agreement: A Case Study Across Assessor Type, Payment Levels, Query Variations and Relevance Dimensions*. 40–53.

[16] Surajit Ray and Bruce G Lindsay. 2005. The topography of multivariate normal mixtures. *Annals of Statistics* (2005), 2042–2065.

[17] Falk Scholer, Andrew Turpin, and Mark Sanderson. 2011. Quantifying Test Collection Quality Based on the Consistency of Relevance Judgements. In *Proceedings of the 34th ACM SIGIR*. 1063–1072.

[18] Matteo Venanzi, John Guiver, Gabriella Kazai, Pushmeet Kohli, and Milad Shokouhi. 2014. Community-based Bayesian Aggregation Models for Crowdsourcing. In *23rd International Conference on World Wide Web (WWW '14)*. 155–164.

[19] Ellen M. Voorhees. 1998. Variations in Relevance Judgments and the Measurement of Retrieval Effectiveness. In *Proceedings of the 21st ACM SIGIR*. 315–323.

[20] William Webber, Bryan Toth, and Marjorie Desamito. 2012. Effect of Written Instructions on Assessor Agreement. In *35th ACM SIGIR*. 1053–1054.

Dealing with Incomplete Judgments in Cascade Measures

Kai Hui
Max Planck Institute for Informatics
Saarbrücken Graduate School of
Computer Science
Saarbrücken, Germany
khui@mpi-inf.mpg.de

Klaus Berberich
htw saar
Max Planck Institute for Informatics
Saarbrücken, Germany
kberberi@mpi-inf.mpg.de

Ida Mele
Faculty of Informatics
Università della Svizzera italiana
Lugano, Switzerland
ida.mele@usi.ch

ABSTRACT

Cascade measures like α-nDCG, ERR-IA, and NRBP take into account novelty and diversity of query results and are computed using judgments provided by humans, which are costly to collect. These measures expect that all documents in the result list of a query are judged and cannot make use of judgments beyond the assigned labels. Existing work has demonstrated that condensing the query results by taking out documents without judgment can address this problem to some extent. However, how highly incomplete judgments can affect cascade measures and how to cope with such incompleteness have not been addressed yet. In this paper, we propose an approach which mitigates incomplete judgments by leveraging the content of documents relevant to the query's subtopics. These language models are estimated at each rank taking into account the document and the upper ranked ones. Then, our method determines gain values based on the Kullback-Leibler divergence between the language models. Experiments on the diversity tasks of the TREC Web Track 2009–2012 show that with only 15% of the judgments our method accurately reconstructs the original rankings determined by the established cascade measures.

CCS CONCEPTS

•**Information systems →Retrieval models and ranking;** *Web searching and information discovery;*

ACM Reference format:
Kai Hui, Klaus Berberich, and Ida Mele. 2017. Dealing with Incomplete Judgments in Cascade Measures. In *Proceedings of ICTIR '17, October 1–4, 2017, Amsterdam, The Netherlands, , 8 pages.*
DOI: http://dx.doi.org/10.1145/3121050.3121064

1 INTRODUCTION

Information retrieval systems are evaluated based on their ability to return documents that are relevant to the query as well as on the novelty and diversity of the results. This is of valuable importance especially for faceted/ambiguous queries (e.g., java, jaguar, python) which have more than one possible interpretation. To avoid redundant information, the information retrieval system is supposed to show results that cover all possible different subtopics of the query

(also known as *aspects* or *facets*). Recent years have seen an increasing interest in novelty and diversity as features complementary to relevance [13–15]. Cascade measures, such as α-nDCG, ERR-IA, and NRBP, have been proposed and adopted widely to evaluate novelty and diversity of a ranked list of query results. They reward the documents that diversify the result list in order to cover all possible information needs behind a faceted/ambiguous query. To quantify the novelty and diversity of the ranked list of query results, the cascade measures usually sum up the gain value of each result which is evaluated based on the relevance to the query and the novelty to the ranking. Such measures require manual judgments done by humans, which is costly to collect in terms of time and of money. An alternative is to partially evaluate the results which could lead to inaccurate computations. Hence, it is desirable to have a more effective use of the available judgments to better trade off the cost for evaluating results and the inaccurateness of the measure computations.

Several authors have investigated the reusability of test collections for diversification, comparing the influence of pooling depths and system bias [6, 20, 22]. Specifically, in Sakai et al. [22], the reusability is examined in terms of employing judgments collected for different pooling depths and of system bias in a leave-one-out experiment [6]. Moreover, a condensed-list method [20] was employed to improve the reusability by removing unjudged documents from the query results before the evaluation. It has been demonstrated that a condensed list can address the issue of incomplete judgments, but still a significant amount of judgments is needed (e.g., more than 50% of judgments [22]). A natural question that arises is how cascade measures and the condensed-list approach behave when substantially fewer judgments (e.g., less than 30%) are available. Subsequently, a second question worth exploring is how the very few judgments can be fully leveraged, namely, beyond a single label, to assess the effectiveness of the retrieval task.

To address these questions, we first investigate the behavior of cascade measures when judgments are highly incomplete and are only available for less than 30% of documents. In addition, inspired by the work on dealing with incomplete judgments in ad-hoc retrieval [6, 16, 18], we devise novel measures that use documents' contents to approximate the established cascade measures for novelty and diversity. The proposed measures are especially useful when very few judgments are available, by adequately employing the content of the judged documents in place of the labels.

Instead of directly using relevance judgments, our measures compare the language models estimated based on the contents of the returned documents against the language models estimated based on the contents of those documents that are judged as relevant to the different subtopics of the query. We estimate the gain values of the documents from the language models' divergences which are then plugged into the established cascade measures. Intuitively, a system is rewarded, if it returns documents that are content-wise similar to documents considered relevant to the different subtopics of a query. If the system returns a non-relevant document, though, the language model estimated based on its result will diverge more from the subtopic language models.

We first examine the effectiveness of the established cascade measures over the raw list and a condensed list based on few judgments. Beyond that, we propose methods based on the observations that relevant documents for a subtopic tend to be homogeneous, i.e., relatively similar to each other. Irrelevant documents, in contrast, tend to exhibit widely different contents. To model the features that make the documents relevant to the possible subtopics of a query, our approach estimates a language model from the documents' contents. Likewise, our method estimates a language model at each rank of the returned results to characterize what the users can see when they go through the ranked list of the results of a query. Gain values are then determined based on the Kullback-Leibler divergence between the estimated language models. Exploring the design space, we consider different approaches with different ways to determine the gain values and aggregate them into a single measure. In total, we end up with four novel cascade measures, coined as ABSNB, ABSRB, DELTANB, and DELTARB. Differently from existing measures which explicitly penalize redundancy in the form of repetitions of the same label (on the same subtopic), our measures implicitly capture redundancy via the estimated language models.

The contribution of this paper is threefold:

- We study the robustness of the established cascade measures, i.e., α-nDCG, ERR-IA, and NRBP, as well as their condensed-list versions in presence of highly incomplete judgments;
- We propose four novel cascade measures that can robustly approximate α-nDCG, ERR-IA, and NRBP with very few judgments. Such novel measures allow reusing relevance judgments collected on one document collection to evaluate systems on another document collection;
- We performed a comprehensive experimental evaluation of our novel cascade measures based on CLUEWEB09 datasets, using queries and runs from the TREC Web Track 2009–12.

Organization. The rest of this paper is organized as follows. We discuss related work in Section 2. Section 3 gives some background on effectiveness measures for novelty and diversity. Section 4 introduces our novel cascade measures. Our experimental evaluation is described in Section 5, before concluding in Section 6.

2 RELATED WORK

Measures for Novelty and Diversity. Standard effectiveness measures evaluate IR systems only in terms of the relevance of returned results, while other measures attempt to capture also their diversity and novelty. Zhai et al. [28] proposed the *subtopic recall* to measure the percentage of subtopics covered by a list of query results. Agrawal et al. [1] focused on ambiguous queries and presented intent-aware variants of established effectiveness measures. Differently from nDCG [17], which assumes independence of documents' relevance, Chapelle et al. [10] proposed the Expected

Reciprocal Rank (ERR) measure, capturing the dependency among the documents by assuming a cascade-style user model. Extending ERR, Chapelle et al. [9] proposed ERR-IA to further measure the diversification of the ranking, following the general approach by Agrawal et al. [1]. Clarke et al. [11] considered underspecified queries, namely, queries with faceted interpretations. They presented α-nDCG which decomposes the information needs behind a query into so-called *information nuggets* and defines the utility of a document as the number of novel nuggets covered by it. In a follow-up work they proposed NRBP [12] which considers both ambiguous and underspecified (faceted) queries by combining α-nDCG and *Rank-Biased Precision* (RBP) proposed by Moffat and Zobel [19]. More recently, Want et al. [25] presented several hierarchical measures that consider the relationships among different subtopics. Our measures follow the cascade models, but differ from them since we implicitly capture the dependency between the returned results in the estimated query-result language model.

Dealing with Incomplete Judgments. To deal with the incompleteness of judgments, researchers have developed novel measures for robust evaluation when judgments are incomplete. Buckley and Voorhees [5] proposed *bpref* which uses binary relevance and completely ignores search results for which no relevance information is available. Yilmaz and Aslam [26] as well as Aslam et al. [3] presented approaches for random sampling to estimate the actual values of the average precision when relevance judgments are incomplete. Similarly, Sakai and Kando [23] applied traditional effectiveness measures to "condensed" lists which are ranked lists of documents obtained by removing all unjudged documents. Carterette et al. [8] analyzed the distribution of average precision over all possible assignments of relevance to all unjudged documents and proposed a method to construct a test collection with minimal relevance judgments. All of these works focused on traditional effectiveness measures (e.g., average precision), whereas we focus on more recent cascade measures for novelty and diversity. Moreover, differently from these works, we use the contents of documents judged as relevant when determining our measures. Beyond that, Amitay et al. [2] used the relevant and irrelevant term sets to evaluate IR systems, enabling evaluation on a dataset without judgments. Carterette and Allan [7] as well as Büttcher et al. [6] tried to make up for missing relevance judgments by predicting them using machine learning. Similarly to our work, they also make use of relevant documents' contents in their prediction models. Making use of machine learning and plugging predicted relevance judgments into cascade measures for novelty and diversity is an interesting direction for future research but orthogonal to our approach.

Finally, the works [21, 22] are the closest to ours in the sense that the incomplete judgments are considered in the context of diversification. In both papers, the situation of incomplete judgments from leave-one-out experiments and from expansion of judgment pooling are examined, but more than 50% of judgments are assumed to be available. Differently, in our work, we consider the situation when judgments are highly incomplete, that is, only between 1% and 50% are available, as shown in Section 5.2. Moreover, we also take into account the situation when no judgment is available at all by evaluating on disjoint document collections as shown in

Section 5.3. Hence, our work can be regarded as complementary to [21, 22] when established cascade measures fail to work.

3 BACKGROUND

In this section, we briefly describe existing evaluation measures for novelty and diversity, namely α-nDCG, ERR-IA, and NRBP.

α-**nDCG.** Clarke et al. [11] extended the traditional nDCG [17] to α-nDCG to capture novelty and diversity in query results. α-nDCG scores a query-result list by rewarding results relevant to new subtopics and penalizing the ones relevant to already covered subtopics. It balances relevance and diversity through the tuning of the α parameter. We used $\alpha = 0.5$ for our experiments to give equal importance to relevance and diversity, following the default setting in TREC[1]. α-nDCG includes a *novelty-biased gain* as indicated in Equation 1, where m is the number of query subtopics, k the number of results. $J_i(r)$ indicates the relevance of the document at rank r relative to the intent i, $C_i(r-1)$ is the number of times the subtopic i has been covered by documents appearing before rank r, and $IDCG$ serves to normalize the measure.

$$\alpha\text{-}nDCG = \frac{\sum\limits_{r=1}^{k} \frac{\sum\limits_{i=1}^{m} J_i(r)(1-\alpha)^{C_i(r-1)}}{\log_2(1+r)}}{IDCG} \ . \tag{1}$$

ERR-IA. The intent-aware version of the *Expected Reciprocal Rank* (ERR) has been proposed by Chapelle et al. [10], which is defined as the weighted average of ERR computed separately for each query subtopic [9] as summarized in Equation 2. $R_i(j)$ is a function of the relevance grade for subtopic i of the document at position j in the ranking. It is commonly defined as $(2^g - 1)/2^{g_{max}}$, where g is the grade given by the judges to the document. The scores are weighted by p_i which is the probability of the intent i.

$$ERR - IA = \sum_{i=1}^{m} p_i \sum_{r=1}^{k} \frac{1}{r} R_i(r) \prod_{j=1}^{r-1} (1 - R_i(j)) \ , \tag{2}$$

NRBP. The *Novelty- and Rank-Biased Precision* was proposed by Clarke et al. [12] to combine α-nDCG and *Rank-Bias Precision* (RBP) as originally proposed by Moffat and Zobel [19]. It is defined as in Equation 3. This measure uses two discount mechanisms. Redundancy is penalized based on the parameter α, whereas the persistence by the parameter β. For our experiments we set α and β as 0.5, following the default configuration in TREC.

$$NRBP = \frac{1 - (1 - \alpha)\beta}{m} \sum_{r=1}^{\infty} \beta^{r-1} \sum_{i=1}^{m} J_i(r)(1 - \alpha)^{C_i(r)} \ . \tag{3}$$

4 DIVERGENCE-BASED MEASURES

In this section we introduce a family of novel measures. In contrast to existing ones, which only digest relevance judgments provided by humans, our measures operate on the content of the judged documents. Our approach indirectly provides robust measures which are able to deal with substantially incomplete relevance judgments, as we demonstrate in our experimental results.

---

[1]http://trec.nist.gov/data/web2012.html

4.1 Model

The document collection is denoted as $\mathcal{D}$. Each document is represented as a bag of words drawn from a vocabulary $\mathcal{V}$ consisting of indexed terms. For a term $v \in \mathcal{V}$ we use $tf(v,d)$ to denote its term frequency in document $d \in \mathcal{D}$ and let $|d| = \sum_{v \in \mathcal{V}} tf(v,d)$ be the document length. We refer to the subtopics of a query q as $\{q_1, \ldots, q_m\}$ with m subtopics, and let $r(q_i, d)$ be a predicate indicating the (binary) relevance of document d to subtopic q_i. Finally, we refer to a query result list as $R = \langle d_1, \ldots, d_{|R|} \rangle$ and as $R_k = \langle d_1, \ldots, d_k \rangle$ to its corresponding top-k results.

4.2 Statistical Language Models

Within the last two decades, statistical language models have also been successfully applied to Information Retrieval tasks [27]. In this work, language models serve two purposes. First, they can be used to model the characteristics that make a document relevant to a specific subtopic. Second, they capture what the users can see while sifting through the query's result list. While more advanced language models have been proposed (e.g., based on n-grams or allowing for term translations), for simplicity, we will focus on unigram language models with Dirichlet smoothing.

Top-k Query Result Language Model. From the top-k query result R_k we estimate a language model Θ_{R_k} as in Equation 5, where μ is a tunable parameter (set as $\mu = 2,500$ [27]) which controls the influence of Dirichlet smoothing with the language model $\Theta_{\mathcal{D}}$ estimated from the document collection as in Equation 4.

$$P[v|\Theta_{\mathcal{D}}] = \frac{\sum_{d \in \mathcal{D}} tf(v,d)}{\sum_{d \in \mathcal{D}} |d|} \ . \tag{4}$$

$$P[v|\Theta_{R_k}] = \frac{\sum_{d \in R_k} tf(v,d) + \mu}{\sum_{d \in R_k} |d| + \mu \, P[v|\Theta_{\mathcal{D}}]} \ . \tag{5}$$

The language model Θ_{R_k} thus captures what users see when they inspect all the documents up to rank k in the query's result list. The smoothing with the document collection language model $\Theta_{\mathcal{D}}$ can be interpreted as their prior knowledge about general documents from the collection. By its definition, Θ_{R_k} captures the degree of diversity in the top-k query results. Intuitively, when homogeneous documents related to a single subtopic are returned, the estimated language model Θ_{R_k} will have lower entropy than in the case when heterogeneous documents related to various subtopics are returned. Moreover, Θ_{R_k} comes with an inherent bias against documents returned at lower ranks. When comparing Θ_{R_k} and $\Theta_{R_{k+1}}$ it is clear from the definition that the influence of the additional result on the estimate decreases as k increases.

Subtopic Language Models. Given a query q and its subtopics $\{q_1, \ldots, q_{|q|}\}$, we estimate a language model

$$P[v|\Theta_{q_i}] = \frac{\sum_{d \in \mathcal{D} \, : \, r(q_i,d)} tf(v,d) + \mu}{\sum_{d \in \mathcal{D} \, : \, r(q_i,d)} |d| + \mu \, P[v|\Theta_{\mathcal{D}}]} \tag{6}$$

for each subtopic based on its relevant documents, again smoothed with the document collection language model $\Theta_{\mathcal{D}}$. The purpose of smoothing is twofold, namely, to avoid zero probabilities and to achieve a relative weighting of terms for the following divergence computation.

4.3 Divergence-Based Gain

We obtain the document gain values by comparing the language models estimated for subtopics and top-k results. In more details, let Θ_{q_i} be a subtopic language model and Θ_{R_k} be a top-k query result language model estimated as described above. For comparing the language models we can apply the Kullback-Leibler divergence

$$KLD(\Theta_{q_i} \| \Theta_{R_k}) = \sum_{v \in \mathcal{V}} P[v|\Theta_{q_i}] \log\left(\frac{P[v|\Theta_{q_i}]}{P[v|\Theta_{R_k}]}\right) , \quad (7)$$

which ranges in $[0, \infty]$. We thus obtain high values of $KLD(\Theta_{q_i} \| \Theta_{R_k})$ when the top-k results in R_k are different from the documents relevant to the subtopic q_i, for instance, they use different terminology or key terms. Hence, we compute the per-subtopic gain value as

$$g(i, k) = max\left(0, 1 - \frac{KLD(\Theta_{q_i} \| \Theta_{R_k})}{KLD(\Theta_{q_i} \| \Theta_{\mathcal{D}})}\right) , \quad (8)$$

which is normalized with the Kullback-Leibler divergence observed for the document collection language model $\Theta_{\mathcal{D}}$. According to our preliminary experiments, there always exist $KLD(\Theta_{q_i} \| \Theta_{R_k}) \le KLD(\Theta_{q_i} \| \Theta_{\mathcal{D}})$ in our data, leading to $g(i, k) \in [0, 1]$. To turn these per-subtopic gain values $g(i, k)$ into per-rank gain values, which can then be aggregated, we consider two alternative formulations, coined as ABS and DELTA.

ABS determines a per-rank gain value as

$$g(j) = \max_{1 \le i \le |q|} g(i, j) , \quad (9)$$

thus rewarding query results whose top-j covers at least one of the subtopics well.

DELTA derives per-rank gain values from the observed differences in per-subtopic gain values as

$$g(j) = \max\left(0, \max_{1 \le i \le |q|} \left(g(i, j) - g(i, j - 1)\right)\right) . \quad (10)$$

Note that the outer maximum function in Equation 10 guarantees that $g(j) \ge 0$. Given a query result, to obtain a high per-rank gain value under this formulation, its document at rank j must be closely related to a subtopic that has not been covered yet.

4.4 Position Bias

As a final step, we describe how the per-rank gain values $g(j)$ can be aggregated into a single measure reflecting the quality of a top-k result list. We propose NB and RB formulations.

NB. By definition, as described above, in our approach the influence of documents at lower ranks is diminishing. Thus, we can simply sum up the per-rank gain values observed at ranks up to k as

$$\sum_{1 \le j \le k} g(j) . \quad (11)$$

This formulation is referred to as NB which stays for *no bias*.

RB. We borrow the position-bias model from Rank-Biased Precision [19] and aggregate the per-rank gain values as

$$(1 - \theta) \cdot \sum_{1 \le j \le k} g(j) \cdot \theta^{j-1} . \quad (12)$$

The parameter θ (set as $\theta = 0.8$ based on our pilot experiments to force a dramatic decay) models the user's persistence in sifting

through the query result, or put differently, at each rank the user decides to stop inspecting query results with probability $(1 - \theta)$.

5 EXPERIMENTAL EVALUATION

In this section, we design experiments to investigate the reliability of established cascade measures and to examine our proposed measures under three different aspects: (i) the robustness when only few judgments available, (ii) how well they can reuse relevance judgments to evaluate systems on a previously unseen document collection, and (iii) their correlation with existing cascade measures.

5.1 Setup

Document Collection. We use CLUEWEB09 [2] as a document collection. In our experiments, we focus on the subset of more than 500 million English web pages, which are known as CLUEWEB09 Category A (CwA). For our robustness and reusability experiments, we also make use of CLUEWEB09 Category B (CwB), as a well-defined subset of about 50 million English web pages. As a third subset of English web pages, called CwC, we consider all 450 million web pages that are part of CwA but not of CwB.

Queries & Relevance Judgments. We use data from the diversity track of the TREC Web Track 2009–2012. This leaves us with a total of 200 queries (50 per year) and their corresponding relevance judgments. For our methods we convert graded labels into binary ones by treating labels -2 (spam) and 0 (non-relevant) as irrelevant and all other labels as relevant. To compare our measures against existing cascade measures, we also obtained the runs submitted by participants of the TREC Web Track. There are 48 runs for 2009, 32 runs for 2010, 62 runs for 2011, and 48 runs for 2012. Some of the runs were produced considering only CwB; others considered the whole document collection CwA. As standard in TREC Web Track, we consider top-20 query results when comparing different systems.

Cascade Measures. As established cascade measures we consider α-nDCG, ERR-IA, and NRBP which are described in Section 3. Regarding our novel cascade measures, we combine the different design choices of per-rank gain and position bias and obtain four novel measures:

- ABSNB combining the absolute gain ABS from Eq. 9 with no position bias NB as in Eq. 11;
- ABSRB combining the absolute gain ABS from Eq. 9 with the ranking bias RB as in Eq. 12;
- DELTANB combining the delta gain DELTA from Eq. 10, with no position bias NB as in Eq. 11;
- DELTARB combining the delta gain DELTA from Eq. 10 with the ranking bias RB as in Eq. 12.

Rank Correlation. We use Kendall's τ as a correlation measure between system rankings determined by different cascade measures. Kendall's τ is the difference between concordant and discordant pairs divided by the total number of pairs. It ranges in $[-1, 1]$ with 1 (-1) indicating perfect agreement (disagreement). Vorhees [24] suggests 0.9 as a threshold to consider two rankings as equivalent, whereas a correlation below 0.8 reflects a significant difference. In this work, however, given the difficulty of our task, exploiting test

---

[2]http://www.lemurproject.org/clueweb09.php/

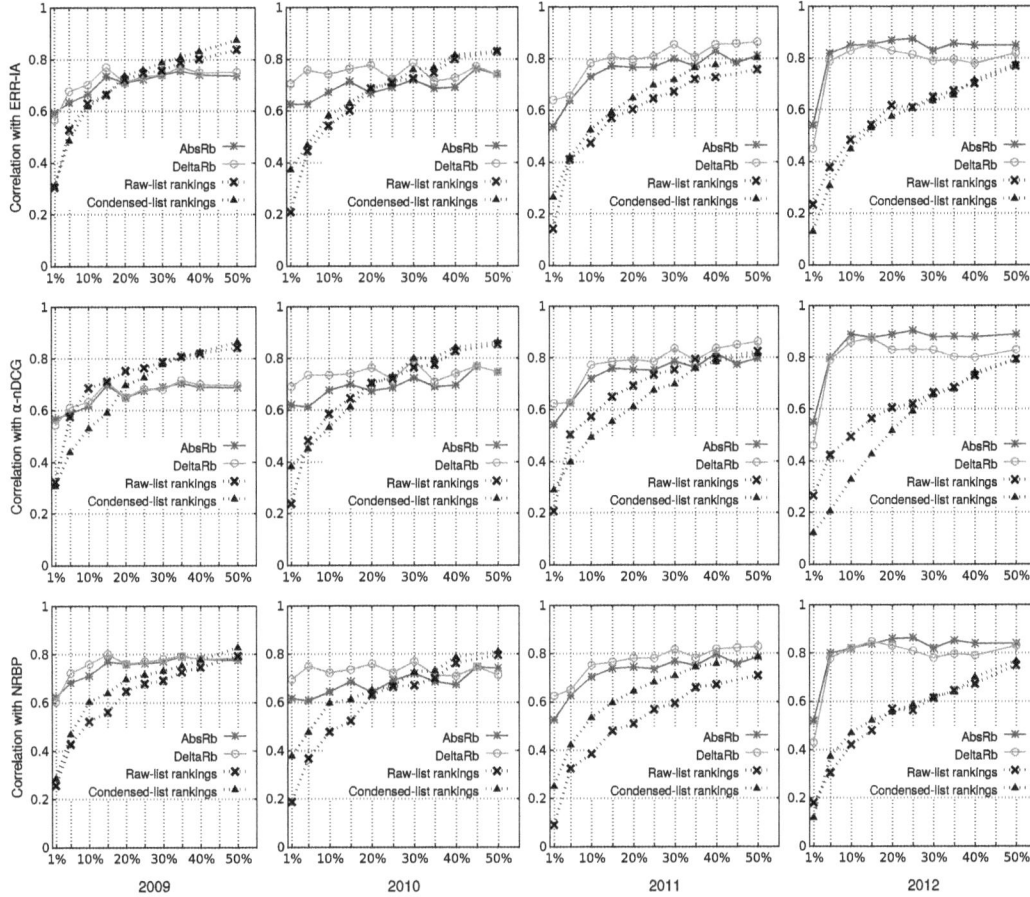

Figure 1: Effectiveness of cascade measures over the raw list and the condensed list. Rows correspond to ERR-IA, α-nDCG, and NRBP (top to bottom). Columns correspond to TREC Web Track 2009–2012 (left to right). In each figure, the x-axis indicates the sampling percentage $p\%$ and the y-axis indicates the Kendall's τ correlation.

collections with very few available judgments, namely, below 50%, we choose 0.8 as a threshold.

5.2 Robustness over Highly Incomplete Judgments

Firstly, we analytically investigate the effectiveness of different cascade measures when evaluating the raw list and the condensed list [20] of search results. Beyond that, we evaluate the proposed measures under the same set of judgments and make comparisons. In particular, we inspect the correlation between system rankings determined by different measures on incomplete judgments and the ones determined by established cascade measures over complete judgments. To do so, we follow Bompada et al. [4] and Buckley et al. [5] and denote the full relevance judgment document set as $qrel$. Given a query, we randomly shuffle the relevant documents in $qrel$ and pick up the first $max(1, \lceil p\%|qrel|\rceil)$ relevant documents from $qrel$ to build Θ_q. For each query we require at least one relevant document to construct our measures, and the relevance judgments are all that is required by our proposed measures. To compare with results based on established measures over condensed lists,

we further sample $p\%$ non-relevant documents to construct an incomplete judgment set including only $p\%$ of the judgments. To remove the randomness of this sampling procedure, we report the average results based on 30 repetitions. Although this stratified random sampling is analytical, it can cover different situations through dozens of samplings.

The Kendall's τ correlations between our rankings and the ones under complete judgments with established measures are summarized in Figure 1. Each column corresponds to a query set (i.e., one year of TREC topics); each row represents one of the established cascade measures. The two dashed curves represent the system rankings determined by established measures, namely, ERR-IA, α-nDCG and NRBP, when measuring on raw lists and condensed lists, respectively. We only display results for ABSRB and DELTARB, denoted as two solid curves, which look similar to ABSNB and DELTANB, respectively. The x-axis indicates the sample percentage $p\%$, and the y-axis is the Kendall's τ correlation.

From Figure 1, it can be seen that the established measures require more than 40%-50% judgments to achieve 0.8 Kendall's τ correlation. Sakai et. al [22] demonstrated that the condensed-list

Table 1: Reusability of our measures. Relevance judgments collected on CwC (i.e., CwA-CwB) are used to evaluate systems on the disjoint document collection CwB. Kendall's τ above 0.8 are shown in bold.

		AbsNb	AbsRb	DeltaNb	DeltaRb
2009	α-nDCG	.72	.70	.73	.69
	ERR-IA	.78	.78	.76	.76
	NRBP	.74	.74	.70	.74
2010	α-nDCG	.72	.66	.74	.76
	ERR-IA	.70	.66	.72	.75
	NRBP	.68	.65	.71	.73
2011	α-nDCG	.71	.76	.79	**.81**
	ERR-IA	.67	.75	.73	**.81**
	NRBP	.64	.74	.69	.79
2012	α-nDCG	.23	.40	.31	.51
	ERR-IA	.26	.44	.31	.54
	NRBP	.26	.45	.31	.54

methods can address the incomplete-judgment issues in leave-one-out experiment [6]. However, it is clear from Figure 1 that with highly incomplete judgments (i.e., when less than 30% judgments are available), the correlation for condensed lists can be very low, e.g., lower than 0.4 when less than 1% judgments are available. This is not surprising since the highly incomplete judgments make the computation of the established measures highly depend on the very few documents that have been judged. Put differently, an unjudged document directly corresponds to a missing component in the formula of these measures. Our proposed measures behave much more smoothly, because they make use of all the judged documents instead of few documents labeled for a single query. Actually, even with only a single judged relevant documents, one can still estimate a reasonable language model Θ_q based on it, given that documents relevant to a query tend to have similar content. As a concrete example, the correlation numbers for the established measures vary a lot among different years, while the DeltaRb still has a Kendall's τ correlation above 0.8 for the year 2011 with as little as 15% of relevance judgments. Likewise, for the year 2012 we can observe a Kendall's τ correlation above 0.8 with as little as 5% relevance judgments. For the years 2009 and 2010, the proposed measures fail to get beyond 0.8 Kendall's τ, yet they achieve significantly higher correlation compared to the established measures when less than 15% judgments are available. Note that, differently from the established measures, both DeltaRb and AbsRb behave rather robustly when different amounts of judgments are available, and the correlation values do not increase monotonically. This is due to the fact that more judgments can only adjust Θ_q by including more observations of the distribution, which is fundamentally different from the way when computing established measures by taking individual relevant judgments into computation.

5.3 Reusability on Disjoint Document Collection

As a second aspect, we examine whether our measures are able to reuse relevance judgments collected on one document collection to evaluate systems on another (disjoint) document collection. Note that this setting is different from the one described in Section 5.2 with $p = 0\%$, which corresponds to having no relevance judgments available at all and is beyond hope for any measure. Instead, we estimate subtopic language models based on documents from CwC. Our objective is then to approximate the system rankings determined by ERR-IA and α-nDCG on CwB, which by construction is disjoint from CwC (we recall that CwC is the set of documents that appear in CwA but not in CwB). In this context, it is worth mentioning that CwB, despite of its smaller size, comes with 1.5× more relevance judgments than CwC, which is due to the facts that a lot of systems in TREC opted to work on CwB.

Table 1 reports the obtained Kendall's τ correlations. It can be seen that DeltaRb performs better among the proposed measures. Although only in 2011 over 0.8 correlation can be achieved, in other years the correlation is beyond 0.5, and in 2009-10 it is around 0.75. Note that the established cascade measures, in contrast, can not be employed in this setting due to the complete mismatch between relevance judgments and result documents. This actually highlights the advantages of our proposed measures in fully utilizing judged documents that do not appear in the evaluated query results.

In Table 1, we can observe relatively low values for the year 2012. Digging deeper we wanted to investigate the question to what extent the reusability depends on the document collection on which the relevance judgments were collected. Therefore, for the year 2012, we further employ all our document collections CwA, CwB, and CwC as a source of relevance judgments and study correlation with α-nDCG, ERR-IA, and NRBP on all these three document collections. Recall that CwC is disjoint from CwB, while both CwB and CwC are subsets of CwA. Table 2 shows Kendall's τ correlations for all combinations of document collections. From the table we can see that the choice of document collection on which relevance judgments are collected can have a significant impact. Thus, Kendall's τ correlations are generally higher for relevance judgments collected on CwA and CwB than on CwC. This is not completely surprising, given that many participants of TREC Web Track 2009-2012 initially focused on CwB, and CwC was constructed artificially. What is promising is that using relevance judgments from CwB to evaluate systems on the much larger CwA works fine when using our measures. It is confirmed by fact that the observed values of Kendall's τ decrease only slightly if at all. It is also worth mentioning that we performed analogous experiments for the years 2009–2011 with similar results which are omitted here for the space limitation.

5.4 Correlation

We now examine the correlation between our proposed measures and the established cascade measures. While our measures aim at addressing the cases when only highly incomplete judgments are available, one may desire to know the relationship between them and the established ones. To this end, we compute Kendall's τ between the system rankings determined by our measures and the

Table 2: Impact of the document collections used for collecting relevance judgments. The first row indicates the document collection on which relevance judgments were collected; the second row indicates the document collection on which query results were determined. Kendall's τ correlations above 0.8 are shown in bold.

Pair of measures	Test collections	CwA			CwB			CwC		
		CwA	CwB	CwC	CwA	CwB	CwC	CwA	CwB	CwC
α–nDCG	AbsNb	**.87**	**.89**	.71	.79	**.90**	.73	.30	.23	.71
	AbsRb	**.89**	**.89**	.71	**.84**	**.89**	.73	.43	.40	.71
	DeltaNb	.71	.79	.67	.61	**.81**	.67	.23	.31	.69
	DeltaRb	**.82**	**.88**	.69	.79	**.88**	.67	.41	.51	.70
ERR-IA	AbsNb	**.85**	**.87**	.65	**.81**	**.88**	.69	.29	.26	.67
	AbsRb	**.86**	**.88**	.69	**.85**	**.89**	.71	.43	.44	.68
	DeltaNb	.69	.75	.63	.60	.78	.60	.20	.31	.65
	DeltaRb	**.80**	**.86**	.65	**.80**	**.87**	.64	.41	.54	.66
NRBP	AbsNb	**.84**	**.83**	.60	**.82**	**.83**	.64	.26	.26	.63
	AbsRb	**.85**	**.84**	.64	**.86**	**.85**	.66	.40	.45	.63
	DeltaNb	.68	.70	.59	.61	.72	.55	.19	.31	.60
	DeltaRb	**.80**	**.82**	.60	**.82**	**.84**	.59	.39	.54	.61

ones determined by the established cascade measures with complete judgments. For comparison, Table 3 lists pairwise correlations between α-nDCG, ERR-IA, and NRBP in terms of their average Kendall's τ on TREC Web Track 2009–2012. As we can see, the established cascade measures are highly correlated.

Table 3: Average Kendall's τ between α-nDCG, ERR-IA, NRBP on TREC Web Track 2009–2012.

	α-nDCG	ERR-IA	NRBP
α-nDCG			
ERR-IA	.93		
NRBP	.88	.87	

Table 4 reports Kendall's τ between our four measures AbsNb, AbsRb, DeltaNb and DeltaRb, and the cascade measures α-nDCG, ERR-IA, and NRBP. For a different perspective, Figure 2 plots the system ranks assigned by our four methods against those assigned by ERR-IA on TREC Web Track 2009–2012. For a measure having perfect correlation with ERR-IA, the points in this plot would lie on the main diagonal $y = x$. Due to the space limitation, we only show plots against ERR-IA. From Table 4, we can see that the correlation between our measures and α-nDCG, ERR-IA, and NRBP varies across different query sets. The correlation is lowest for queries from the year 2010 and highest for queries from the year 2012. Comparing our methods, we observe a positive effect of the position bias with AbsRb and DeltaRb, consistently showing higher correlation than their non-biased counterparts. While our measures do not consistently achieve a Kendall's τ correlation above 0.8, we argue that the proposed measures are still useful since they can better deal with incomplete judgments and more effectively reuse relevance judgments, as we have discussed in Section 5.2

Table 4: Correlations between our measures and the established cascade measures. Kendall's τ correlations above 0.8 are shown in bold.

		AbsNb	AbsRb	DeltaNb	DeltaRb
2009	α-nDCG	.78	.70	.78	.73
	ERR-IA	**.81**	.75	.79	.78
	NRBP	**.80**	.79	.73	.78
2010	α-nDCG	.70	.73	**.81**	.76
	ERR-IA	.68	.73	.77	.76
	NRBP	.65	.71	.75	.72
2011	α-nDCG	.74	**.81**	.76	**.85**
	ERR-IA	.74	**.81**	.75	**.85**
	NRBP	.71	.78	.70	**.81**
2012	α-nDCG	**.87**	**.89**	.71	**.82**
	ERR-IA	**.85**	**.86**	.69	**.80**
	NRBP	**.84**	**.85**	.68	**.80**

and 5.3. From Figure 2, it can be seen that all points distribute along the $y = x$, indicating that the system rankings determined by the proposed measures are close to the ones from ERR-IA.

6 CONCLUSION

Our work investigates the performance of the established cascade measures (i.e., α-nDCG, ERR-IA, and NRBP) when less than 50% judgments are available. We found out that their ability to rank systems deteriorates quickly as we remove more and more relevance judgments. To mitigate this, we proposed novel cascade measures

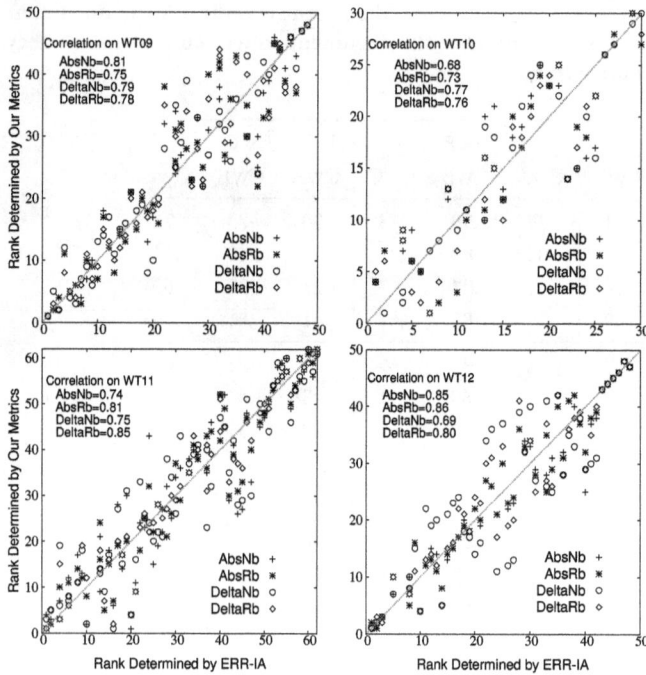

Figure 2: System rank assigned by ERR-IA vs. system rank assigned by our measures on TREC Web Track 2009–2012.

that are based on the Kullback-Leibler divergence between language models estimated for queries' subtopics and returned results. Our experiments showed that our novel measures correlate well with the established ones and, more importantly, are robust in the presence of highly incomplete judgments. Even with as little as 15% of relevance judgments, our cascade measures still get close to the established ones on complete judgments. Moreover, our measures can assess the retrieval performance of a system on unlabelled collections leveraging the relevance judgments gathered for a completely disjoint document collection.

REFERENCES

[1] R. Agrawal, S. Gollapudi, A. Halverson, and S. Ieong. Diversifying search results. In *Proceedings of the Second ACM International Conference on Web Search and Data Mining*, WSDM '09, pages 5–14, New York, NY, USA, 2009. ACM.
[2] E. Amitay, D. Carmel, R. Lempel, and A. Soffer. Scaling IR-system Evaluation Using Term Relevance Sets. In *Proceedings of the 27th Annual International ACM SIGIR Conference on Research and Development in Information Retrieval*, SIGIR '04, pages 10–17, New York, NY, USA, 2004. ACM.
[3] J. A. Aslam, V. Pavlu, and E. Yilmaz. A statistical method for system evaluation using incomplete judgments. In *Proceedings of the 29th Annual International ACM SIGIR Conference on Research and Development in Information Retrieval*, SIGIR '06, pages 541–548, New York, NY, USA, 2006. ACM.
[4] T. Bompada, C.-C. Chang, J. Chen, R. Kumar, and R. Shenoy. On the robustness of relevance measures with incomplete judgments. In *Proceedings of the 30th Annual International ACM SIGIR Conference on Research and Development in Information Retrieval*, SIGIR '07, pages 359–366, New York, NY, USA, 2007. ACM.
[5] C. Buckley and E. M. Voorhees. Retrieval evaluation with incomplete information. In *Proceedings of the 27th Annual International ACM SIGIR Conference on Research and Development in Information Retrieval*, SIGIR '04, pages 25–32, New York, NY, USA, 2004. ACM.
[6] S. Büttcher, C. L. A. Clarke, P. C. K. Yeung, and I. Soboroff. Reliable information retrieval evaluation with incomplete and biased judgements. In *Proceedings of the*

[7] 30th Annual International ACM SIGIR Conference on Research and Development in Information Retrieval, SIGIR '07, pages 63–70, New York, NY, USA, 2007. ACM.
[7] B. Carterette and J. Allan. Semiautomatic evaluation of retrieval systems using document similarities. In *Proceedings of the 16th ACM Conference on Conference on Information and Knowledge Management*, CIKM '07, pages 873–876, New York, NY, USA, 2007. ACM.
[8] B. Carterette, J. Allan, and R. Sitaraman. Minimal test collections for retrieval evaluation. In *Proceedings of the 29th Annual International ACM SIGIR Conference on Research and Development in Information Retrieval*, SIGIR '06, pages 268–275, New York, NY, USA, 2006. ACM.
[9] O. Chapelle, S. Ji, C. Liao, E. Velipasaoglu, L. Lai, and S.-L. Wu. Intent-based diversification of web search results: metrics and algorithms. *Information Retrieval*, 14(6):572–592, 2011.
[10] O. Chapelle, D. Metlzer, Y. Zhang, and P. Grinspan. Expected reciprocal rank for graded relevance. In *Proceedings of the 18th ACM conference on Information and knowledge management*, CIKM '09, pages 621–630, New York, NY, USA, 2009. ACM.
[11] C. L. Clarke, M. Kolla, G. V. Cormack, O. Vechtomova, A. Ashkan, S. Büttcher, and I. MacKinnon. Novelty and diversity in information retrieval evaluation. In *Proceedings of the 31st annual international ACM SIGIR conference on Research and development in information retrieval*, SIGIR '08, pages 659–666, New York, NY, USA, 2008. ACM.
[12] C. L. Clarke, M. Kolla, and O. Vechtomova. An effectiveness measure for ambiguous and underspecified queries. In *Proceedings of the 2nd International Conference on Theory of Information Retrieval: Advances in Information Retrieval Theory*, ICTIR '09, pages 188–199, Berlin, Heidelberg, 2009. Springer-Verlag.
[13] V. Dang and W. B. Croft. Diversity by proportionality: an election-based approach to search result diversification. In *Proceedings of the 35th international ACM SIGIR conference on Research and development in information retrieval*, pages 65–74. ACM, 2012.
[14] V. Dang and W. B. Croft. Term level search result diversification. In *Proceedings of the 36th international ACM SIGIR conference on Research and development in information retrieval*, pages 603–612. ACM, 2013.
[15] S. Hu, Z. Dou, X. Wang, T. Sakai, and J.-R. Wen. Search result diversification based on hierarchical intents. In *Proceedings of the 24th ACM International on Conference on Information and Knowledge Management*, pages 63–72. ACM, 2015.
[16] K. Hui and K. Berberich. Selective labeling and incomplete label mitigation for low-cost evaluation. In *International Symposium on String Processing and Information Retrieval*, pages 137–148. Springer International Publishing, 2015.
[17] K. Järvelin and J. Kekäläinen. Cumulated gain-based evaluation of IR techniques. *ACM Transactions on Information Systems*, 20:422–446, October 2002.
[18] G. K. Jayasinghe, W. Webber, M. Sanderson, and J. S. Culpepper. Improving test collection pools with machine learning. In *Proceedings of the 2014 Australasian Document Computing Symposium*, ADCS '14, pages 2:2–2:9, New York, NY, USA, 2014. ACM.
[19] A. Moffat and J. Zobel. Rank-biased precision for measurement of retrieval effectiveness. *ACM Trans. Inf. Syst.*, 27(1):2:1–2:27, Dec. 2008.
[20] T. Sakai. Alternatives to bpref. In *Proceedings of the 30th annual international ACM SIGIR conference on Research and development in information retrieval*, pages 71–78. ACM, 2007.
[21] T. Sakai. The unreusability of diversified search test collections. In *EVIA@ NTCIR*, 2013.
[22] T. Sakai, Z. Dou, R. Song, and N. Kando. The reusability of a diversified search test collection. In *Asia Information Retrieval Symposium*, pages 26–38. Springer, 2012.
[23] T. Sakai and N. Kando. On information retrieval metrics designed for evaluation with incomplete relevance assessments. *Inf. Retr.*, 11(5):447–470, 2008.
[24] E. M. Voorhees. Evaluation by highly relevant documents. In *Proceedings of the 24th Annual International ACM SIGIR Conference on Research and Development in Information Retrieval*, SIGIR '01, pages 74–82, New York, NY, USA, 2001. ACM.
[25] X. Wang, Z. Dou, T. Sakai, and J.-R. Wen. Evaluating search result diversity using intent hierarchies. In *Proceedings of the 39th International ACM SIGIR conference on Research and Development in Information Retrieval*, pages 415–424. ACM, 2016.
[26] E. Yilmaz and J. A. Aslam. Estimating average precision with incomplete and imperfect judgments. In *Proceedings of the 15th ACM International Conference on Information and Knowledge Management*, CIKM '06, pages 102–111, New York, NY, USA, 2006. ACM.
[27] C. Zhai. Statistical language models for information retrieval a critical review. *Found. Trends Inf. Retr.*, 2:137–213, March 2008.
[28] C. X. Zhai, W. W. Cohen, and J. Lafferty. Beyond independent relevance: methods and evaluation metrics for subtopic retrieval. In *Proceedings of the 26th annual international ACM SIGIR conference on Research and development in information retrieval*, SIGIR '03, pages 10–17, New York, NY, USA, 2003. ACM.

Evaluation Measures for Relevance and Credibility in Ranked Lists

Christina Lioma, Jakob Grue Simonsen
Department of Computer Science
University of Copenhagen
Copenhagen, Denmark
{c.lioma,simonsen}@di.ku.dk

Birger Larsen
Department of Communication
University of Aalborg in Copenhagen
Copenhagen, Denmark
birger@hum.aau.dk

ABSTRACT

Recent discussions on *alternative facts*, *fake news*, and *post truth* politics have motivated research on creating technologies that allow people not only to *access* information, but also to *assess* the credibility of the information presented to them by information retrieval systems. Whereas technology is in place for filtering information according to relevance and/or credibility [15], no single measure currently exists for evaluating the accuracy or precision (and more generally *effectiveness*) of *both* the relevance *and* the credibility of retrieved results. One obvious way of doing so is to measure relevance and credibility effectiveness separately, and then consolidate the two measures into one. There at least two problems with such an approach: (I) it is not certain that the same criteria are applied to the evaluation of both relevance and credibility (and applying different criteria introduces bias to the evaluation); (II) many more and richer measures exist for assessing relevance effectiveness than for assessing credibility effectiveness (hence risking further bias).

Motivated by the above, we present two novel types of evaluation measures that are designed to measure the effectiveness of both relevance and credibility in ranked lists of retrieval results. Experimental evaluation on a small human-annotated dataset (that we make freely available to the research community) shows that our measures are expressive and intuitive in their interpretation.

KEYWORDS

relevance; credibility; evaluation measures

ACM Reference format:
Christina Lioma, Jakob Grue Simonsen and Birger Larsen. 2017. Evaluation Measures for Relevance and Credibility in Ranked Lists. In *Proceedings of ICTIR '17, Amsterdam, Netherlands, October 1–4, 2017,* 8 pages.
DOI: http://dx.doi.org/10.1145/3121050.3121072

1 INTRODUCTION

Recent discussions on *alternative facts*, *fake news*, and *post truth* politics have motivated research on creating technologies that allow people, not only to *access* information, but also to *assess* the credibility of the information presented to them [8, 14]. In the broader area of information retrieval (IR), various methods for approximating [10, 23] or visualising [11, 17, 18, 21] information credibility have been presented, both stand-alone and in relation to relevance [15]. Collectively, these approaches can be seen as steps in the direction of building IR systems that retrieve information that is both relevant and credible. Given such a list of IR results, which are ranked decreasingly by both relevance and credibility, the question arises: how can we evaluate the quality of this ranked list?

One could measure retrieval effectiveness first, using any suitable existing relevance measure, such as NDCG or AP, and then measure separately credibility accuracy similarly, e.g. using the F-1 or the G-measure. This approach would output scores by two separate metrics[1], which would need to somehow be consolidated or considered together when optimising system performance. In such a case, and depending on the choice of relevance and credibility measures, it would not be always certain that the same criteria are applied to the evaluation of both relevance and credibility. For instance, whereas the state of the art metrics in relevance evaluation treat relevance as graded and consider it in relation to the rank position of the retrieved documents (we discuss these in Section 2), no metrics exist that consider graded credibility accuracy in relation to rank position. Hence, using two separate metrics for relevance and credibility may, in practice, bias the overall evaluation process in favour of relevance, for which more thorough evaluation metrics exist.

To provide a more principled approach that obviates this bias, we present two new types of evaluation measures that are designed to measure the effectiveness of both relevance and credibility in ranked lists of retrieval results *simultaneously* and *without bias* in favour of either relevance or credibility. Our measures take as input a ranked list of documents, and assume that assessments (or their approximations) exist both for the relevance and for the credibility of each document. Given this information, our Type I measures define different ways of measuring the effectiveness of both relevance and credibility based on differences in the *rank position* of the retrieved documents with respect to their ideal rank position (when ranked only by relevance or credibility). Unlike Type I, our Type II measures operate directly on *document scores* of relevance and credibility, instead of rank positions. We evaluate our measures both axiomatically (in terms of their properties) and empirically on a small human-annotated dataset that we build specifically for the purposes of this work. We find that our measures are expressive and intuitive in their interpretation.

---

[1]In this paper, we use *metric* and *measure* interchangeably, as is common in the IR community, even though the terms are not synonymous. Strictly speaking, *measure* should be used for more concrete or objective attributes, and *metric* should be used for more abstract, higher-level, or somewhat subjective attributes [2]. When discussing effectiveness, which is generally hard to define objectively, but for which we have some consistent feel, Black et al. argue that the term *metric* should be used [2].

2 RELATED WORK

The aim of evaluation is to measure how well some method achieves its intended purpose. This allows to discover weaknesses in the given method, potentially leading to the development of improved approaches and generally more informed deployment decisions. For this reason, evaluation has been a strong driving force in IR, where, for instance, the literature of IR evaluation measures is rich and voluminous, spanning several decades. Generally speaking, relevance metrics for IR can be split into three high-level categories:

  (i) earlier metrics, assuming binary relevance assessments;
  (ii) later metrics, considering graded relevance assessments, and
  (iii) more recent metrics, approximating relevance assessments from user clicks.

We overview some among the main developments in each of these categories next.

2.1 Binary relevance measures

Binary relevance metrics are numerous and widely used. Examples include:

Precision @ k (P@k): the proportion of retrieved documents that are relevant, up to and including position k in the ranking;

Average Precision (AP): the average of (un-interpolated) precision values (proportion of retrieved documents that are relevant) at all ranks where relevant documents are found;

Binary Preference (bPref): this is identical to AP except that bPref ignores non-assessed documents (whereas AP treats non-assessed documents as non-relevant). Because of this, bPref does not violate the *completeness assumption*, according to which "all relevant documents within a test collection have been identified and are present in the collection") [5];

Mean Reciprocal Rank (MRR): the reciprocal of the position in the ranking of the first relevant document only;

Recall: the proportion of relevant documents that are retrieved;

F-score: the equally weighted harmonic mean of precision and recall.

2.2 Graded relevance measures

There exist noticeably fewer graded relevance metrics than binary ones. The two main graded relevance metrics are NDCG and ERR:

Normalised Discounted Cumulative Gain (NDCG): the cumulative gain a user obtains by examining the retrieval result up to a rank position, where the relevance scores of the retrieved documents are:

  • *accumulated* over all the rank positions that are considered,
  • *discounted* in order to devaluate late-retrieved documents, and
  • *normalised* in relation to the maximum score that this metric can possibly yield on an ideal reranking of the same documents.

Two useful properties of NDCG are that it rewards retrieved documents according to both (i) their degree (or grade) of relevance, and (ii) their rank position. Put simply, this means that the more relevant a document is *and* the closer to the top it is ranked, the higher the NDCG score will be [12].

Expected Reciprocal Rank (ERR): ERR operates on the same high-level idea as NDCG but differs from it in that it penalises documents that are shown below very relevant documents. That is, whereas NDCG makes the *independence assumption* that "a document in a given position has always the same gain and discount independently of the documents shown above it", ERR does not make this assumption, and, instead, considers (implicitly) the immediate context of each document in the ranking. In addition, instead of the discounting of NDCG, ERR approximates the expected reciprocal length of time that a user will take to find a relevant document. Thus, ERR can be seen as an extension of (the binary) MRR for graded relevance assessments [6].

2.3 User click measures

The most recent type of evaluation measures are designed to operate, not on traditionally-constructed relevance assessments (defined by human assessors), but on approximations of relevance assessments from user clicks (actual or simulated). Most of these metrics have underlying user models, which capture how users interact with retrieval results. In this case, the quality of the evaluation measure is a direct function of the quality of its underlying user model [24].

The main advances in this area include the following:

Expected Browsing Utility (EBU): an evaluation measure whose underlying user click model has been tuned by observations over many thousands of real search sessions [24];

Converting click models to evaluation measures: a general method for converting any click model into an evaluation metric [7]; and

Online evaluation: various different algorithms for interleaving [19] or multileaving [3, 4, 20] multiple initial ranked lists into a single combined ranking, and by approximating clicks (through user click models) on the resulting combined ranking, assigning credit (hence evaluating) the methods that produced each initial ranked list [9].

In addition to the above three types of IR evaluation measures, there also exists further literature on IR measures that consider additional dimensions on top of relevance, such as query difficulty for instance [16]. To the best of our knowledge, none of these measures consider credibility. The closest to a credibility measure we could find is the work by Balakrishnan et al. [1] on source selection for deep web databases: their method considers the agreement between different sources in answering a query as an indication of the credibility of the sources. An adjusted version of this agreement is modeled as a graph with vertices representing sources. Given such a graph, the credibility (or quality) of each source is calculated as the stationary visit probability of a random walk on this graph.

The evaluation measures we present in Sections 4 - 5 are the only ones, to our knowledge, that are designed to operate both on relevance and credibility. Beyond these two particular dimensions, reasoning more generally about different dimensions of effectiveness, the F-score, and its predecessor, van Rijsbergen's E-score [22], are early examples of a single evaluation measure combining two different aspects, namely precision and recall. We return to this discussion in Section 5, where we present a variant of the F-score for aggregating relevance and credibility.

3 EVALUATION DESIDERATA

Given a ranked list of documents, the aim is to produce a measure that reflects how effective this ranking is with respect to *both* the relevance of these documents to some query *and* also the credibility of these documents (irrespective of a query).

There are at least two basic ways to produce such a metric: Either

(I) gauge the difference in rank position(s) between an input ranking and "ideal" relevance and credibility rankings,

or

(II) employ relevance and credibility *scores* to gauge how well the input ranking reflects high versus low scores.

Note that while (II) is reminiscent of existing measures for relevance ranking, the fact that two distinct kinds of scores (relevance and credibility) – perhaps having different ranges and behaviour – must be combined may lead to further complications.

Accordingly, in the remainder of the paper, we call measures *Type I* if they are based primarily on differences in rank position, and *Type II* if they are based primarily on relevance and credibility scores.

Regardless of whether it is Type I or Type II, we reason that any measure must be easily interpretable. Hence, its scores should be normalised between 0 and 1, where low scores should indicate poor rankings, and high scores should indicate good rankings. The extreme points (0 and 1) of the scale should preferably be attainable by particularly bad or particularly good rankings; as a minimum, if the ranking can be measured against an "ideal" ranking (as in, e.g. NDCG), the value 1 should be attainable by the ideal ranking.

In addition to the above, there also exist desiderata for evaluation measures that are more debatable (e.g., how the measure should act in case of identical ranking scores for distinct documents). Below, we list what we believe to be the most pertinent desiderata. The list encompasses desiderata tailored to evaluate measures that gauge ranking based on either *rank position* or on (relevance or credibility) *scores*. For the desiderata pertaining to rank position, we need the following ancillary definition:

Let D_i be a document at rank i. We then define an *error* as any instance where

- either (a) the relevance of a document at rank i is greater than the relevance of a document at rank $i - 1$,
- or (b) the credibility of a document at rank i is greater than the credibility of a document at rank $i - 1$.

This assumes that documents are ranked decreasingly by relevance and credibility, i.e. that the "best" document occurs at the lowest (i.e. first) rank.

We define the following eight desiderata (referred to as **D1-D8** henceforth):

D1 Larger errors should be penalised more than smaller errors;

D2 Errors high in the ranking should be penalised more than errors low in ranking;

D3 Let δ^r be the difference in relevance score between D_i and D_{i-1} when D_{i-1} is more relevant than D_i. Similarly, let δ^c be the difference in credibility score between D_i and D_{i-1} when D_{i-1} is more credible than D_i. Then, larger δ^r and δ^c values should imply larger error;

D4 *Ceteris paribus*, a credibility error on documents of high relevance should be penalised more than a credibility error on documents of low relevance;

D5 The metric should be well-defined even if all documents have identical ranking/credibility scores;

D6 Scaling the document scores used to produce the ranking by some constant should not affect the metric;

D7 If all documents have the same relevance score, the metric should function as a credibility metric; and vice versa;

D8 We should be able to adjust (by some easily interpretable parameter) how much we wish to penalise low credibility with respect to low relevance, if at all.

Next, we present two types of evaluation measures of relevance and credibility that satisfy (wholly or partially) the above desiderata: Type I measures (Section 4) operate solely on the *rank positions* of documents; Type II measures (Section 5) operate solely on *document scores*.

4 TYPE I: RANK POSITION MEASURES

Given a ranking of documents that we want to evaluate (let us call this *input ranking*), we reason in terms of two additional *ideal rankings*: one by relevance only, and one by credibility only (the two ideal rankings are entirely independent of each other). So, for each document, we have:

(1) its rank position in the input ranking;
(2) its rank position in the ideal relevance ranking; and
(3) its rank position in the ideal credibility ranking.

The basic idea is then to take each adjacent pair of documents in the input ranking, check for errors in the input ranking compared to the ideal relevance and separately the ideal credibility ranking, and aggregate those errors. We explain next how we do this.

Let D_i be the rank position of document D in the input ranking. We then denote by $R^r_{D_i}$ the rank position of D_i in the ideal relevance ranking, and by $R^c_{D_i}$ the rank position of D_i in the ideal credibility ranking. Note that subscript $_i$ refers to the rank position of D in the input ranking *at all times*. That is, $R^r_{D_i}$ should be read as: the position in the ideal relevance ranking of the document that is at position i in the input ranking; similarly for $R^c_{D_i}$.

Let the *monus operator* $\dot{-}$ be defined on non-negative real numbers by:

$$a \dot{-} b = \begin{cases} 0 & \text{if } a \leqslant b \\ a - b & \text{if } a > b \end{cases} \quad (1)$$

That is, $a \dot{-} b$ is simply subtraction as long as $a > b$ and otherwise just returns 0. Then, using the monus operator and the notation introduced above, we define a "relevance error" (ϵ^r) and a "credibility error" (ϵ^c) as:

$$\epsilon^r = R^r_{D_i} \dot{-} R^r_{D_{i+1}} \qquad (2)$$

$$\epsilon^c = R^c_{D_i} \dot{-} R^c_{D_{i+1}} \qquad (3)$$

In the above, i and $i+1$ are the rank positions of two documents in the input ranking. Given two such documents, a "relevance error" occurs iff the document that is ranked lower (at rank i) in the input ranking is ranked after the other document in the ideal relevance ranking. Otherwise, the error is zero. Similarly for the "credibility error".

For example, if three documents A, B and C are ranked as C, A, B in the input ranking (i.e., $D_1 = C$, $D_2 = A$, $D_3 = B$), but ranked as $R^r = [A, B, C]$ in an ideal relevance ranking, there are two relevance errors, namely

(i) $R^r_{D_1} \dot{-} R^r_{D_2} = R^r_C \dot{-} R^r_A = 3 \dot{-} 1 = 2$, and
(ii) $R^r_{D_2} \dot{-} R^r_{D_3} = R^r_A \dot{-} R^r_B = 1 \dot{-} 2 = 0$.

We use the above "relevance error" and "credibility error" to define the two evaluation measures, presented next.

4.1 Normalised Local Rank Error (NLRE)

Let n be the total number of documents in the ranked list. We define the Local Rank Error (LRE) evaluation measure as $LRE = 0$ if $n = 1$, and otherwise:

$$LRE = \sum_{i=1}^{n-1} \frac{1}{\log_2(1+i)} \left((\mu + \epsilon^r)(\nu + \epsilon^c) - \mu\nu \right) \qquad (4)$$

where ϵ^r, ϵ^c are the relevance error and credibility error defined in Equations 2 – 3, and μ, ν are non-negative real numbers (with $\mu + \nu > 0$) controlling how much we wish to penalise low relevance with respect to low credibility. For instance, a high ν weighs credibility more, whereas a high μ weighs relevance more. The reason for the term $-\mu\nu$ inside the summation at the end is to ensure that the value of the LRE measure is zero if no error occurs.

Because Equation 4 is *large* for *bad* rankings and *small* for *good* rankings, we invert and normalise it (Normalised LRE or NLRE) as follows:

$$NLRE = 1 - \frac{LRE}{C_{LRE}} \qquad (5)$$

where C_{LRE} is the normalisation constant, defined as:

$$C_{LRE} = \sum_{j=0}^{\lfloor \frac{n}{2} - 1 \rfloor} \frac{(n - 2j - 1)^2 + (\mu + \nu)(n - 2j - 1)}{1 + \log_2(1 + j)} \qquad (6)$$

ensuring that $LRE/C_{LRE} \leqslant 1$. Note the "floor" function of the angular brackets above $\sum$ in Equation 6, which rounds the contents of the brackets down to the next (lowest) integer.

The somewhat involved definition of C_{LRE} is due to the fact that we wish the maximal possible error attainable (i.e., rankings that produce the largest possibly credibility *and* relevance errors) to correspond to a value of 1 for LRE/C_{LRE}. Observe that $NLRE$ is 1 if no errors of any kind occur (because, in that case, LRE is 0).

Our NLRE measure satisfies the desiderata presented in Section 3 as follows:

- **D1** holds if we interpret error size as the size of the rank differences;
- **D2** holds due to the discount factor of $1/\log_2(1+i)$;
- **D3** is satisfied in the sense that larger differences in *credibility* or *relevance* ranks mean larger error;
- **D4**: The credibility error is scaled by the relevance error, if there is any (i.e., they are multiplied). If there is no relevance error, the credibility error is still strictly greater than zero;
- **D5**: The measure is well-defined in all cases;
- **D6**: No scores occur explicitly, only rankings, so scaling makes no difference;
- **D7** is satisfied because if all documents have equal relevance, the relevance error will be zero. The resulting score will measure only credibility error. And vice versa;
- **D8** is satisfied through μ and ν.

We call NLRE a *local* measure because it is affected by differences in credibility and relevance between documents at each rank position in the input ranking. We present next a *global* evaluation metric that does not take such "local" effects at each rank into account (i.e., any differences in credibility and relevance between documents at rank i in the input ranking do not affect the global metric; only the total difference of credibility and relevance of the entire input ranking affects the global metric).

4.2 Normalised Global Rank Error (NGRE)

We define the Global Rank Error (GRE) evaluation measure as $GRE = 0$ if $n = 1$, and otherwise:

$$GRE = \left(1 + \mu \sum_{i=1}^{n-1} \frac{1}{\log_2(1+i)} \epsilon^r \right) \left(1 + \nu \sum_{i=1}^{n-1} \frac{1}{\log_2(1+i)} \epsilon^c \right) - 1 \qquad (7)$$

The notation is the same as for LRE. Similarly to LRE, we invert and normalise GRE, to produce its normalised version (NGRE) as follows:

$$NGRE = 1 - \frac{GRE}{C_{GRE}} \qquad (8)$$

where C_{GRE} is the normalisation constant, defined as:

$$C_{GRE} = \mu\nu \left(\sum_{j=0}^{\lfloor \frac{n}{2} - 1 \rfloor} \frac{n - 2j - 1}{1 + \log_2(1 + j)} \right)^2 + (\mu + \nu) \sum_{j=0}^{\lfloor \frac{n}{2} - 1 \rfloor} \frac{n - 2j - 1}{1 + \log_2(1 + j)} \qquad (9)$$

C_{GRE} is chosen to ensure that $GRE/C_{GRE} \leqslant 1$ and that $GRE/C_{GRE} = 1$ is possible iff the ranking has the maximal possible errors compared to both the ideal relevance and ideal credibility rankings. The square brackets above both $\sum$s in Equation 9 also use the floor function, exactly like in Equation 6.

As with NLRE, NGRE is 1 if no errors of any kind occur. In spite of the differences in computation, NGRE satisfies all eight desiderata for the same reasons given for NLRE.

The main intuitive difference between NLRE and NGRE is that in NGRE the credibility errors and relevance errors are cumulated separately, and then multiplied at the end. Thus, there is no immediate connection between credibility and relevance errors at the same rank (*locally*), hence we say that the metric is *global*.

The advantage of such a global versus local measure is that, in the global case, it is more straightforward to perform mathematical manipulations to achieve, e.g., normalisation, and easier to intuitively grasp what the measure means. The disadvantage is that local information is lost, and this may, in theory, lead to poorly performing measures. As the notion of "error" defined earlier is inherently a local phenomenon, the desiderata concerning errors are harder to satisfy formally for global measures.

5 TYPE II: DOCUMENT SCORE MEASURES

The two evaluation measures presented above (NLRE and NGRE) operate on the rank positions of documents. We now present three evaluation measures that operate, not on the rank positions of documents, but directly on document scores.

5.1 Normalised Weighted Cumulative Score (NWCS)

Given a ranking of documents that we wish to evaluate, let $Z^r(i)$ denote the relevance score with respect to some query of the document ranked at position i, and let $Z^c(i)$ denote the credibility score of the document ranked at position i. Then, we define the Weighted Cumulative Score (WCS) measure as:

$$WCS = \sum_{i=1}^{n} \frac{1}{\log_2(1+i)}(\lambda Z^r(i) + (1-\lambda)Z^c(i)) \quad (10)$$

where n is the total number of documents in the ranking list, and λ is a real number in $[0, 1]$ controlling the impact of relevance versus credibility in the computation. We normalise WCS by dividing it by the value obtained by an "ideal" ranking maximizing the value of WCS (this is inspired by the normalisation of the NDCG evaluation measure [12]):

$$NWCS = \frac{WCS}{IWCS} \quad (11)$$

where IWCS is the *ideal* WCS, i.e. the maximum WCS that can be obtained on an ideal ranking of the same documents.

NWCS uses a simple weighted combination of relevance or credibility *scores* in the same manner as the metric *NGRE*, but is applicable directly to relevance or credibility *scores* (instead of ranking positions).

Our NWCS measure satisfies the following of the desiderata presented in Section 3:

- **D1** is satisfied as both Z^r and Z^c occur linearly in WCS;
- **D2** is satisfied due to the logarithmic discounting for increasing rank positions;
- **D3** is satisfied by design as both Z^r and Z^c occur directly in the formula for WCS;
- **D5** is satisfied as the measure is well-defined in all cases;
- **D6** is satisfied due to normalization;
- **D7** is satisfied because the contribution of the credibility scores (if all are equal) is just a constant in each term (and vice versa if relevance scores are all equal);
- **D8** is satisfied due to the presence of λ.

Of all desiderata, only **D4** is not satisfied: there is no scaling of credibility errors based on relevance. Despite this, the advantage of NWCS is that it is interpretable in much the same way as NDCG.

The main idea of the next two measures is that any two separate measures of *either* relevance *or* credibility, but not both, can be combined into a single aggregating measure of relevance and credibility. We next present two such aggregating measures.

5.2 Convex aggregating measure (CAM)

We define the convex aggregating measure (CAM) of relevance and credibility as:

$$CAM = \lambda M^r + (1-\lambda)M^c \quad (12)$$

where M^r and M^c denote respectively any valid relevance and credibility evaluation measure, and λ is a real number in $[0, 1]$ controlling the impact of the individual relevance or credibility measure in the overall computation. CAM is normalized if both M_r and M^c are normalised.

Our CAM measure satisfies the following desiderata:

- **D1** is satisfied for the same reasons as NWCS;
- **D2** is not satisfied in general;
- **D3** is satisfied for the same reasons as NWCS;
- **D4** is not satisfied in general;
- **D5** is satisfied for the same reasons as NWCS;
- **D6** is not satisfied in general; it is satisfied if both M^r and M^c are scale-free;
- **D7** is satisfied because the contribution of the credibility scores (if all are equal) is just a constant in each term (and vice versa if relevance scores are all equal);
- **D8** is satisfied for the same reasons as NWCS.

With respect to **D2**, **D4**, and **D6** not being satisfied in general: The tradeoff in this case is that as CAM is just a convex combination of existing measures, the scores are readily interpretable by anyone able to interpret M^r and M^c scores.

5.3 Weighted harmonic mean aggregating measure ((WHAM) or "F-score for credibility and ranking")

We define the weighted harmonic mean aggregating measure (WHAM) as zero if either M^r or M^c is zero, and otherwise:

$$WHAM = \frac{1}{\lambda\frac{1}{M^r} + (1-\lambda)\frac{1}{M^c}} \quad (13)$$

where the notation is the same as for CAM in Equation 12 above. WHAM is the weighted harmonic mean of M^r and M^c. Observe that if $\lambda = 0.5$, WHAM is simply the F-1 scores of M^r and M^c. Note that WHAM is normalized if both M_r and M^c are normalised.

Similar definitions of metrics can be made that use other averages. For example, one can use the weighted arithmetic and geometric means instead of the harmonic mean.

Our WHAM measure satisfies the following desiderata:

- **D1** is satisfied for the same reasons as CAM;
- **D2** is not satisfied in general;
- **D3** is satisfied for the same reasons as CAM;
- **D4** is not satisfied in general;
- **D5** is satisfied for the same reasons as CAM;
- **D6** is not satisfied in general; it is satisfied if both M^r and M^c are scale-free;

Table 1: The 10 queries used in our experiments.

Query no.	Query
1	Smoking not bad for health
2	Princess Diana alive
3	Trump scientologist
4	UFO sightings
5	Loch Ness monster sightings
6	Vaccines bad for children
7	Time travel proof
8	Brexit illuminati
9	Climate change not dangerous
10	Digital tv surveillance

- **D7** is satisfied for the same reasons as CAM;
- **D8** is satisfied for the same reasons as CAM.

The primary advantage of CAM and WHAM is that their definitions appeal to simple concepts already known to larger audiences (convex combinations and averages), and hence the measures are simple to state and interpret. The consequent disadvantage is that this simplicity comes at the cost of not satisfying all desiderata.

We next present an empirical evaluation of all our measures.

6 EVALUATION

There are two main approaches for evaluating evaluation measures:

Axiomatic Define some general fundamental properties that a measure should adhere to, and then reflect on how many of these properties are satisfied by a new measure, and to what extent.

Empirical Present a drawback of existing standard and accepted measures, and illustrate how a new measure addresses this. Ideally, the new measure should generally correlate well with the existing measures, except for the problematic cases, where it should perform better [13].

We have already conducted the axiomatic evaluation of our measures, having presented 8 fundamental properties they should adhere to (Desiderata in Section 3), and having subsequently discussed each of our measures in relation to these fundamental properties in Sections 4 - 5. We now present the empirical evaluation. We first present our in-house dataset and experimental setup, and then our findings.

6.1 Empirical Evaluation

The goal is to determine how good our measures are at evaluating both relevance and credibility in ranked lists. We do this by comparing the scores of our measures to the scores of well-known relevance and separately credibility measures. This comparison is done on a small dataset that we create for the purposes of this work as follows[2]. We formulated 10 queries that we thought were likely to fetch results of various levels of credibility if submitted to a web search engine. These queries are shown in Table 1. We then recruited 10 assessors (1 MSc student, 5 PhD students, 3 postdocs, and 1 assistant professor, all within Computer Science, but none

---

[2]Our dataset is freely available here: https://github.com/diku-irlab/A66

Table 2: Conversion of graded assessments to binary. The same conversion is applied to both relevance and credibility assessments.

Graded	Binary
1 (not at all)	0 (not at all)
2 (marginally)	0 (not at all)
3 (medium)	1 (completely)
4 (completely)	1 (completely)

working on this project; 1 female, 9 males). Assessors were asked to submit each query to Google, and to assign separately a score of relevance and a score of credibility to each of the top 5 results. Assessors were instructed to use the same graded scale of relevance and credibility shown in the first column of Table 2.

Assessors were asked to use their own understanding of relevance and credibility, and not to let relevance affect their assessment of credibility, or vice versa (relevance and credibility were to be treated as unrelated aspects). Assessors were instructed that, if they did not understand a query, or if they were unsure about the credibility of a result, they should open a separate browser and try to gather more information on the topic. Assessors received a nominal reward for their effort.

Even though assessors used the same queries, the top 5 results retrieved from Google per query were not always identical. Consequently, we compute our measures separately on each assessed ranking, and we report the arithmetic average. For NLRE and NGRE, we set $\mu = \nu = 0.5$, meaning that relevance and credibility are weighted equally. Similarly, for NWCS, CAM, and WHAM, we set $\lambda = 0.5$.

As no measures of *both* relevance and credibility exist, we compare the score of our measures on the above dataset to the scores of:

- NDCG (for graded relevance), AP (for binary relevance);
- F-1, G-measure (for binary credibility).

F-1 was introduced in Section 2 for relevance. We use it here to assess credibility, by defining its constituent precision and recall in terms of true/false positives/negatives (as is standard in classification evaluation). The G-measure is the geometric mean of precision and recall, which are defined as for F-1.

To render our graded assessments binary (for AP, F-1, G-measure), we use the conversion shown in Table 2.

6.2 Findings

Table 3 displays the scores of all evaluation measures on our dataset. We see that relevance-only measures (NDCG, AP) give overall higher scores than credibility-only measures (F-1, G). It is not surprising to see such high NDCG and AP scores, considering that we assess only the top 5 ranks of Google. What is however interesting, is the comparatively lower scores of credibility (F-1 and G). This practically means that even the top ranks of a high-traffic web search engine like Google can be occupied by information that is not entirely credible (at least for this specially selected set of queries).

Table 3: Our evaluation measures compared to NDCG, AP, F-1 and G. For NDCG we see our graded assessments. For the rest, we convert our graded assessments to binary as follows: 1 or 2 = not relevant/credible; 3 or 4 = relevant or credible. All measures are computed on the top 5 results returned for each query shown in Table 1. We report the average across all assessors.

RELEVANCE	
NDCG	0.9329
AP	0.7842
CREDIBILITY	
F-1	0.4786
G	0.5475
RELEVANCE and CREDIBILITY	
NLRE	0.8262
NGRE	0.6919
NWCS	0.9413
$CAM_{NDCG,F-1}$	0.7058
$CAM_{NDCG,G}$	0.7402
$CAM_{AP,F-1}$	0.6311
$CAM_{AP,G}$	0.6659
$WHAM_{NDCG,F-1}$	0.6326
$WHAM_{NDCG,G}$	0.6900
$WHAM_{AP,F-1}$	0.6089
$WHAM_{AP,G}$	0.6448

Looking at our measures of evaluation and credibility, we see that they range from roughly 0.6 to 0.9. This coincides with the range between the score of credibility-only measures and relevance-only measures. All of our measures are strongly and positively correlated to NDCG, AP, F-1, and G (from Spearman's $\rho = 0.79$ for NDCG and F-1, up to $\rho = 0.97$ for NDCG and NLRE).

Table 4 shows examples of high divergence between the relevance and credibility of the retrieved documents, for three of our measures (the scores of our remaining metrics can be easily deduced from the respective relevance-only and credibility-only scores, as our omitted measures – CAM and WHAM – aggregate the existing relevance-only and credibility-only metrics shown in Table 4). Note that, whereas we found several examples of max relevance and min credibility in our data, there were (understandably) significantly fewer examples of max credibility and min relevance (this distribution is reflected in Table 4). We see that NWCS gives higher scores for queries 2 and 4-10 than NLRE and NGRE. For the first five examples (of max relevance and min credibility), this is likely because NWCS does not satisfy **D4**, namely that credibility errors should be penalised more on high relevance versus low relevance documents. We also see that NGRE gives consistently lower scores than NLRE and NWCS. This is due to its *global* aspect discussed earlier: NGRE accumulates credibility and relevance errors separately and then multiplies them at the end, meaning that local errors in each rank do not impact as much the final score (unlike NLRE and NWCS, which are both *local* in that sense, the first using document ranks, the second using document scores).

7 CONCLUSIONS

The credibility of search results is important in many retrieval tasks, and should be, we reason, integrated into IR evaluation measures that are, as of now, targetting mostly relevance. We have presented several measures and types of measures that can be used to gauge the effectiveness of a ranking, taking into account both credibility and relevance. The measures are both axiomatically and empirically sound, the latter illustrated in a small user study.

There are at least two natural extensions of our approach: First, the combination of rankings based on different criteria goes beyond the combination of relevance and credibility, and several such combinations are used in practice based on different criteria (e.g., combinations of relevance and upvotes on social media sites); we believe that much of our work can be encompassed in more general approaches, suitably axiomatised, that do not necessarily have to satisfy the same desiderata as those of this paper (e.g., do not have to scale credibility error by relevance errors as in our **D4**). Second, while we have chosen to devise measures that are both theoretically principled and conceptually simple using simple criteria (satisfaction of desiderata, local versus global, amenable to principled interpretation), there are many more measures that can be defined within the same limits. For example, our Type II measures are primarily built on simple combinations of scores or pre-existing measures that can easily be understood by the community, but at the price that some desiderata are hard or impossible to satisfy; however, there is no theoretical reason why one could not create Type II measures that incorporate some of the ideas from Type I metrics. We intend to investigate these two extensions in the future, and invite the community to do so as well.

Lastly, while the notion of credibility, in particular in news media, is subject to intense public discussion, very few empirical studies exist that contain user preferences, credibility rankings, or information needs related to credibility. The small study included in this paper, while informative, is a very small step in this direction. We believe that future substantial discussion of *practically relevant* research involving credibility in information retrieval would greatly benefit from having access to larger-scale empirical user studies.

REFERENCES

[1] Raju Balakrishnan and Subbarao Kambhampati. 2011. SourceRank: relevance and trust assessment for deep web sources based on inter-source agreement. In *Proceedings of the 20th International Conference on World Wide Web, WWW 2011, Hyderabad, India, March 28 - April 1, 2011*, Sadagopan Srinivasan, Krithi Ramamritham, Arun Kumar, M. P. Ravindra, Elisa Bertino, and Ravi Kumar (Eds.). ACM, 227–236. DOI:https://doi.org/10.1145/1963405.1963440
[2] Paul E. Black, Karen A. Scarfone, and Murugiah P. Souppaya (Eds.). 2008. *Cyber Security Metrics and Measures*. Wiley Handbook of Science and Technology for Homeland Security.
[3] Brian Brost, Ingemar J. Cox, Yevgeny Seldin, and Christina Lioma. 2016. An Improved Multileaving Algorithm for Online Ranker Evaluation. In *Proceedings of the 39th International ACM SIGIR conference on Research and Development in Information Retrieval, SIGIR 2016, Pisa, Italy, July 17-21, 2016*, Raffaele Perego, Fabrizio Sebastiani, Javed A. Aslam, Ian Ruthven, and Justin Zobel (Eds.). ACM, 745–748. DOI:https://doi.org/10.1145/2911451.2914706
[4] Brian Brost, Yevgeny Seldin, Ingemar J. Cox, and Christina Lioma. 2016. Multi-Dueling Bandits and Their Application to Online Ranker Evaluation. In *Proceedings of the 25th ACM International on Conference on Information and Knowledge Management, CIKM 2016, Indianapolis, IN, USA, October 24-28, 2016*, Snehasis Mukhopadhyay, ChengXiang Zhai, Elisa Bertino, Fabio Crestani, Javed Mostafa, Jie Tang, Luo Si, Xiaofang Zhou, Yi Chang, Yunyao Li, and Parikshit Sondhi (Eds.). ACM, 2161–2166.
[5] Chris Buckley and Ellen M. Voorhees. 2004. Retrieval evaluation with incomplete information. In *SIGIR 2004: Proceedings of the 27th Annual International ACM*

Table 4: Examples of max/min relevance and credibility, from our experiments. Only one out of the 5 retrieved documents is shown per query. The urls of the retrieved results are reduced to their most content-bearing parts, for brevity.

Query	Result (rank)	Relevance	Credibility	NDCG	AP	F-1	G	NLRE	NGRE	NWCS
	EXAMPLES OF HIGH RELEVANCE AND LOW CREDIBILITY									
2	www.surrealscoop.com. . . .princess-diana-found-alive (3)	4	1	.883	.679	.333	.387	.819	.585	.950
3	tonyortega.org. . . scientology. . . where-does-trump-stand (1)	4	1	.938	1.00	.571	.631	.949	.797	.913
4	www.ufosightingsdaily.com (1)	4	1	1.00	1.00	.333	.431	.808	.262	.941
6	articles.mercola.com. . .vaccines-adverse-reaction (4)	4	1	.938	.950	.571	.500	.872	.534	.927
8	www.henrymakow.com. . .brexit-what-is-the-globalist-game (1)	4	1	.884	.679	.000	.000	.889	.666	.985
10	educate-yourself.org. . .HDtvcovertsurveillanceagenda (3)	4	1	.979	1.00	.000	.000	.926	.885	.997
	EXAMPLES OF HIGH CREDIBILITY AND LOW RELEVANCE									
10	cctvcamerapros.com/Connect-CCTV-Camera-to-TV-s (2)	1	4	.780	.533	.571	.715	.863	.710	.931
10	ieeexplore.ieee.org/document/891879 (5)	1	4	.780	.533	.571	.715	.899	.605	.874

SIGIR Conference on Research and Development in Information Retrieval, Sheffield, UK, July 25-29, 2004, Mark Sanderson, Kalervo Järvelin, James Allan, and Peter Bruza (Eds.). ACM, 25–32. DOI : https://doi.org/10.1145/1008992.1009000

[6] Olivier Chapelle, Donald Metlzer, Ya Zhang, and Pierre Grinspan. 2009. Expected reciprocal rank for graded relevance. In Proceedings of the 18th ACM Conference on Information and Knowledge Management, CIKM 2009, Hong Kong, China, November 2-6, 2009, David Wai-Lok Cheung, Il-Yeol Song, Wesley W. Chu, Xiaohua Hu, and Jimmy J. Lin (Eds.). ACM, 621–630. DOI : https://doi.org/10.1145/1645953.1646033

[7] Aleksandr Chuklin, Pavel Serdyukov, and Maarten de Rijke. 2013. Click model-based information retrieval metrics. In The 36th International ACM SIGIR conference on research and development in Information Retrieval, SIGIR '13, Dublin, Ireland - July 28 - August 01, 2013, Gareth J. F. Jones, Paraic Sheridan, Diane Kelly, Maarten de Rijke, and Tetsuya Sakai (Eds.). ACM, 493–502. DOI : https://doi.org/10.1145/2484028.2484071

[8] Rob Ennals, Dan Byler, John Mark Agosta, and Barbara Rosario. 2010. What is disputed on the web?. In Proceedings of the 4th ACM Workshop on Information Credibility on the Web, WICOW 2010, Raleigh, North Carolina, USA, April 27, 2010, Katsumi Tanaka, Xiaofang Zhou, Min Zhang, and Adam Jatowt (Eds.). ACM, 67–74. DOI : https://doi.org/10.1145/1772938.1772952

[9] Katja Hofmann, Lihong Li, and Filip Radlinski. 2016. Online Evaluation for Information Retrieval. Foundations and Trends in Information Retrieval 10, 1 (2016), 1–117.

[10] Christopher Horn, Alisa Zhila, Alexander F. Gelbukh, Roman Kern, and Elisabeth Lex. 2013. Using Factual Density to Measure Informativeness of Web Documents. In Proceedings of the 19th Nordic Conference of Computational Linguistics, NODALIDA 2013, May 22-24, 2013, Oslo University, Norway (Linköping Electronic Conference Proceedings), Stephan Oepen, Kristin Hagen, and Janne Bondi Johannessen (Eds.), Vol. 85. Linköping University Electronic Press, 227–238. http://www.ep.liu.se/ecp_article/index.en.aspx?issue=085; article=021

[11] Zhicong Huang, Alexandra Olteanu, and Karl Aberer. 2013. CredibleWeb: a platform for web credibility evaluation. In 2013 ACM SIGCHI Conference on Human Factors in Computing Systems, CHI '13, Paris, France, April 27 - May 2, 2013, Extended Abstracts, Wendy E. Mackay, Stephen A. Brewster, and Susanne Bødker (Eds.). ACM, 1887–1892.

[12] Kalervo Järvelin and Jaana Kekäläinen. 2002. Cumulated gain-based evaluation of IR techniques. ACM Trans. Inf. Syst. 20, 4 (2002), 422–446. DOI : https://doi.org/10.1145/582415.582418

[13] Ravi Kumar and Sergei Vassilvitskii. 2010. Generalized distances between rankings. In Proceedings of the 19th International Conference on World Wide Web, WWW 2010, Raleigh, North Carolina, USA, April 26-30, 2010, Michael Rappa, Paul Jones, Juliana Freire, and Soumen Chakrabarti (Eds.). ACM, 571–580. DOI : https://doi.org/10.1145/1772690.1772749

[14] Elisabeth Lex, Inayat Khan, Horst Bischof, and Michael Granitzer. 2014. Assessing the Quality of Web Content. CoRR abs/1406.3188 (2014). http://arxiv.org/abs/1406.3188

[15] Christina Lioma, Birger Larsen, Wei Lu, and Yong Huang. 2016. A study of factuality, objectivity and relevance: three desiderata in large-scale information retrieval?. In Proceedings of the 3rd IEEE/ACM International Conference on Big Data Computing, Applications and Technologies, BDCAT 2016, Shanghai, China, December 6-9, 2016, Ashiq Anjum and Xinghui Zhao (Eds.). ACM, 107–117. DOI : https://doi.org/10.1145/3006299.3006315

[16] Stefano Mizzaro. 2008. The Good, the Bad, the Difficult, and the Easy: Something Wrong with Information Retrieval Evaluation?. In Advances in Information Retrieval , 30th European Conference on IR Research, ECIR 2008, Glasgow, UK, March 30-April 3, 2008. Proceedings (Lecture Notes in Computer Science), Iadh Ounis, Vassilis Plachouras, Ian Ruthven, and Ryen W. White (Eds.), Vol. 4956. Springer, 642–646. DOI : https://doi.org/10.1007/978-3-540-78646-7_71

[17] Meredith Ringel Morris, Scott Counts, Asta Roseway, Aaron Hoff, and Julia Schwarz. 2012. Tweeting is believing?: understanding microblog credibility perceptions. In CSCW '12 Computer Supported Cooperative Work, Seattle, WA, USA, February 11-15, 2012, Steven E. Poltrock, Carla Simone, Jonathan Grudin, Gloria Mark, and John Riedl (Eds.). ACM, 441–450. DOI : https://doi.org/10.1145/2145204.2145274

[18] Souneil Park, Seungwoo Kang, Sangyoung Chung, and Junehwa Song. 2009. NewsCube: delivering multiple aspects of news to mitigate media bias. In Proceedings of the 27th International Conference on Human Factors in Computing Systems, CHI 2009, Boston, MA, USA, April 4-9, 2009, Dan R. Olsen Jr., Richard B. Arthur, Ken Hinckley, Meredith Ringel Morris, Scott E. Hudson, and Saul Greenberg (Eds.). ACM, 443–452.

[19] Anne Schuth, Katja Hofmann, and Filip Radlinski. 2015. Predicting Search Satisfaction Metrics with Interleaved Comparisons. In Proceedings of the 38th International ACM SIGIR Conference on Research and Development in Information Retrieval, Santiago, Chile, August 9-13, 2015, Ricardo A. Baeza-Yates, Mounia Lalmas, Alistair Moffat, and Berthier A. Ribeiro-Neto (Eds.). ACM, 463–472.

[20] Anne Schuth, Harrie Oosterhuis, Shimon Whiteson, and Maarten de Rijke. 2016. Multileave Gradient Descent for Fast Online Learning to Rank. In Proceedings of the Ninth ACM International Conference on Web Search and Data Mining, San Francisco, CA, USA, February 22-25, 2016. 457–466.

[21] Julia Schwarz and Meredith Ringel Morris. 2011. Augmenting web pages and search results to support credibility assessment. In Proceedings of the International Conference on Human Factors in Computing Systems, CHI 2011, Vancouver, BC, Canada, May 7-12, 2011, Desney S. Tan, Saleema Amershi, Bo Begole, Wendy A. Kellogg, and Manas Tungare (Eds.). ACM, 1245–1254.

[22] C. J. Keith van Rijsbergen. 1974. Foundation of evaluation. Journal of Documentation 30, 4 (1974), 365–373.

[23] Janyce Wiebe and Ellen Riloff. 2011. Finding Mutual Benefit between Subjectivity Analysis and Information Extraction. IEEE Trans. Affective Computing 2, 4 (2011), 175–191. DOI : https://doi.org/10.1109/T-AFFC.2011.19

[24] Emine Yilmaz, Milad Shokouhi, Nick Craswell, and Stephen Robertson. 2010. Expected browsing utility for web search evaluation. In Proceedings of the 19th ACM Conference on Information and Knowledge Management, CIKM 2010, Toronto, Ontario, Canada, October 26-30, 2010, Jimmy Huang, Nick Koudas, Gareth J. F. Jones, Xindong Wu, Kevyn Collins-Thompson, and Aijun An (Eds.). ACM, 1561–1564. DOI : https://doi.org/10.1145/1871437.1871672

The Evolution of Computational Advertising

Suju Rajan
Criteo Research
s.rajan@criteo.com

ABSTRACT

Machine learning literature on computational advertising typically tends to focus on the simplistic CTR prediction problem which while being relevant is the tip of the iceberg in terms of the research challenges in the field. There have been several recent efforts, shaped by the realities of a complex ad ecosystem, to develop models that try to better encapsulate the journey of an ad from its impression to possibly leading to a purchase. In this talk, we will highlight the recent research challenges in the field of computational advertising & how it is evolving to incorporate ideas from areas such as reinforcement learning, econometrics, deep learning & large-scale recommender systems.

Author Keywords

Computational advertising; machine learning; recommender systems; deep learning

BIOGRAPHY

Suju Rajan is the VP, Head of Research at Criteo. At Criteo, her team works on all aspects of performance driven computational advertising, including, real-time bidding, large-scale recommendation systems, auction theory, reinforcement learning, online experimentation, metrics and scalable optimization methods. Prior to Criteo, she was the Director of the Personalization Sciences at Yahoo Research where her team worked on personalized recommendations for several Yahoo products. She received her PhD from the University of Texas at Austin.

Improved Query-Topic Models Using Pseudo-Relevant Pólya Document Models

Ronan Cummins
University of Cambridge
15 JJ Thomson Avenue
Cambridge, UK CB3 0FD
ronan.cummins@cl.cam.ac.uk

ABSTRACT

Query-expansion via pseudo-relevance feedback is a popular method of overcoming the problem of vocabulary mismatch and of increasing average retrieval effectiveness. In this paper, we develop a new method that estimates a *query-topic model* from a set of pseudo-relevant documents using a new language modelling framework.

We assume that documents are generated via a mixture of multivariate Pólya distributions, and we show that by identifying the topical terms in each document, we can appropriately select terms that are likely to belong to the *query-topic model*. The results of experiments on several TREC collections show that the new approach compares favourably to current state-of-the-art expansion methods.

CCS CONCEPTS

• **Information systems** → *Query representation*; *Query reformulation*; *Language models*;

1 INTRODUCTION

Query expansion is an effective technique for overcoming the problem of vocabulary mismatch. In pseudo-relevance feedback (PRF), expansion terms are selected from a set F of top ranked documents from an initial retrieval run using a term-selection algorithm and are added to the initial query in an attempt to improve retrieval. Query expansion via this method has been shown to improve average retrieval effectiveness [15]. The approach can also be used to suggest possible expansion terms to users, or to build topical models at run-time, where a few initial words provide a seed for the topic. In this paper we focus on the problem of estimating effective query-topic models via PRF in a new language modelling framework and provide a number of interesting theoretical insights.

The relevance modelling (RM) approach [14] has been shown to be an effective method for PRF. This approach builds a relevance model $\vec{\theta}_R$ from the top $|F|$ documents of an initial retrieval. Effectively the approach scores a term t as follows:

$$p(t|\vec{\theta}_R) = \frac{\sum_{d \in F} p(t|\vec{\theta}_d) \cdot p(q|\vec{\theta}_d)}{\sum_{d' \in F} p(q|\vec{\theta}_{d'})} \quad (1)$$

where $\vec{\theta}_d$ is the *smoothed* document model and $p(q|\vec{\theta}_d)$ is the query likelihood score (document score)[1]. The top-k terms are selected from this relevance model and are linearly interpolated with the original query. One weakness with this formulation is that each document model $\vec{\theta}_d$ includes a background model, and so noisy terms are generated by the relevance model $\vec{\theta}_R$. The general motivation for incorporating a background model is to explain non-topical aspects of documents (e.g. common words and noise), while topical aspects are explained by the unsmoothed document model. We argue that using a model which generates general background terms (noise) during feedback is theoretically anomalous and operationally non-optimal.

Consequently, in this paper we take a different approach to selecting expansion terms by firstly estimating the likelihood that a candidate term was drawn from the topical part of each of the feedback documents, and subsequently estimating a *query-topic model* (QTM) by estimating the probability that the term is topically related to the query. We show that this new approach outperforms the original relevance modelling approach to query expansion and also adheres to a number of recently proposed constraints [6] regarding the term-selection function for PRF. Furthermore, we adopt a recently developed document language model [8] that assumes that documents are generated from a mixture of multivariate Pólya distributions (aka. the Dirichlet-compound-multinomial). We show that this document model is more effective in the feedback step than using the multinomial language model with a Dirichlet prior. The contribution of this paper is three-fold:

- We develop a new *query-topic model* (QTM) useful for query expansion via PRF.
- We use the QTM with a recently developed document language model and show that it adheres to a number of recently developed PRF constraints.
- We show that the new method outperforms existing state-of-the-art PRF techniques on a number of TREC collections.

The remainder of the paper is as follows: Section 2 outlines related work in the area of PRF. Section 3 briefly introduces a recent document language modelling approach before developing a new method of estimating query-topic models for use with the aforementioned document model. Section 4 presents an analysis of the new feedback model. Section 5 describes the experimental setup and the results of those experiments. Finally, Section 6 concludes with a discussion.

ICTIR '17, October 01–04, 2017, Amsterdam, Netherlands
© 2017 ACM. 978-1-4503-4490-6/17/10...$15.00
DOI: https://doi.org/10.1145/3121050.3121053

---

[1]As it is often assumed that $p(\vec{\theta}_d|q) \propto p(q|\vec{\theta}_d)$ given a uniform prior over the documents.

2 RELATED WORK

Automatic query expansion via PRF has been proposed in information retrieval since the early 1970's and there exists extensive reviews [2, 4] and research [3, 7, 11–14, 18, 22, 23] in the area. In the language modelling framework, there has been a number of initial approaches to building query models. The idea of a query model was introduced by Zhai et al. [23] and the simple mixture model (SMM) approach to feedback was developed. The SMM approach aims to extract the topical aspects of the top $|F|$ documents assuming that the same multinomial mixture has generated each document in F. By fixing the initial mixture parameter (λ_{smm}), the topical aspects of the top $|F|$ documents can be estimated using Expectation-Maximisation (EM). Regularised mixture models [20] have been developed that aim to eliminate some of the free parameters in the SMM. However, this approach has been shown to be inferior to the SMM [15].

Lavrenko et al. [14] developed the idea of building generative relevance models (RM) and this idea was extended to pseudo-relevant documents. It was shown that when these relevance models were interpolated with the initial query model (an approach called RM3 [1, 15]), they were highly effective for query expansion. As per Eq. 1, the RM1 approach linearly combines the smoothed document models of the top $|F|$ documents. Essentially, the model assumes that short queries and long documents are generated by the same relevance model, and as a result the traditional relevance model also generates noisy non-topical background words. Consequently, empirical studies suggest [15] that different document representations are needed for the feedback step. They have shown that optimal performance with the RM3 method is achieved when the document model $\vec{\theta}_d$ in Eq. 1 remains unsmoothed during feedback. Essentially $p(t|\vec{\theta}_d)$ is estimated using the maximum likelihood of a term occurring in a feedback document.[2] Although using an unsmoothed document model in the feedback step is the optimal setting (as is confirmed by our experiments in Section 5), the theoretical anomaly remains (i.e. *why are different document representations needed for retrieval and feedback?*). The optimal RM3 approach is known to select common terms (possibly stopwords) and include them in the expanded query. We argue that this is because there is a modelling problem when using the RM approach with query-likelihood for short queries.

A pseudo-relevance based retrieval model using the Dirichlet compound multinomial (DCM) [21] (aka. multivariate Pólya distribution) was reported as outperforming the simple mixture model (SMM). However, in that work the initial document retrieval functions varied and the stronger RM3 baseline was not used. We implement and report a similar term-selection scheme using a single Dirichlet-compound-multinomial (PDCM) as a generative model for the top $|F|$ documents as a baseline.

As advances in document modelling are likely to yield improvements for principled PRF approaches, we also adopt a recently developed document language model based on the multivariate Pólya distribution [8]. A detailed comparative study [15] into PRF approaches reports that both RM3 and SMM achieve comparable performance but that RM3 has more stable parameter settings (i.e.

performing consistently well when the background mass is zero). More recently, positional pseudo-relevance (PRM) models [16] have also been developed which incorporate the proximity of candidate expansion terms to query terms in the feedback documents. We include a positional relevance model baseline (PRM2) in our experiments as a state-of-the-art relevance model that uses term proximity information in the set of feedback documents.

Others [5, 6, 10, 11] have studied desirable properties of effective term-selection scheme in PRF. Some of the useful *effects* outlined by Clinchant [6] are inherited from studies of constraints for document retrieval [9], while others [5] are explicitly developed for ranking terms for PRF. We perform an analysis of the pseudo-relevance approach developed in this work using the five constraints outlined in [6] (**TF**, **Concavity**, **IDF**, **DF**, and **Document length (DL)** effects) and the one non-redundant constraint [5] (the **document score (DS)** effect).

The **TF** effect captures the intuition that terms that occur more frequently in the documents in the feedback set are better candidate expansion terms and should receive a higher weight. While the **Concavity** effect ensures that this increase in weight should decay at higher term-frequencies in these documents. The **IDF** effect captures the intuition that rarer terms should be promoted if all else is equal. The **DF** effect states that a term that appears in a greater number of pseudo-relevant documents should receive a higher weight compared to terms occurring in less pseudo-relevant documents (given that the total occurrences of the term in the set of pseudo-relevant documents are equal and all else is equal). Interestingly, if the within document term-frequency aspect of the term-selection scheme is concave, the **DF** effect is usually present [5]. The **DL** effect penalises terms that appear in longer documents in the set F. Finally, the **DS** effect [5] captures the intuition that terms occurrences in high scoring pseudo-relevant documents should receive a higher selection weight than term occurrences in lower scoring pseudo-relevant documents.

3 DOCUMENT AND QUERY MODELLING

Before developing the new query-topic modelling approach, we briefly review a recently developed language model that we intend to use for modelling the documents in the feedback set F.

3.1 Smoothed Pólya Urn Document Model

Recently [8] it has been shown that modelling each document as a mixture of multivariate Pólya distributions improves the effectiveness of ad hoc retrieval. The model is known to capture word burstiness by modelling the dependencies between recurrences of the same word-type. Furthermore, the model ensures that each document adheres to both the *scope* and *verbosity* hypothesis [19]. Each document is modelled as follows:

$$\vec{\alpha}_d = (1 - \omega) \cdot \vec{\alpha}_{d\tau} + \omega \cdot \vec{\alpha}_c \tag{2}$$

where $\vec{\alpha}_d$, $\vec{\alpha}_{d\tau}$, and $\vec{\alpha}_c$ are the smoothed document model, unsmoothed document model[3], and background model respectively. The hyper-parameter ω controls the smoothing and is stable at

---

[2]The optimal RM3 uses $c(t, d)/|d|$ as $p(t|\vec{\theta}_d)$ in the feedback step where $c(t, d)$ is the count of term t in a document of $|d|$ tokens.

[3]For the purposes of this paper, we refer to the unsmoothed model as the *document-topicality model* as it explains words not explained by the general background model.

$\omega = 0.8$. Each of these models are multivariate Pólya distributions with parameters estimated as follows:

$$\vec{\alpha}_{d\tau} = \{m_d \cdot \frac{c(t,d)}{|d|} : t \in d\} \qquad \vec{\alpha}_c = \{m_c \cdot \frac{df_t}{\sum_{t'} df_{t'}} : t \in C\} \quad (3)$$

where m_d is the number of word-types (distinct terms) in d, $c(t,d)$ is the count of term t in document d, $|d|$ is the number of word tokens in d, df_t is the document frequency of term t in the collection C, and m_c is a background mass parameter that can be estimated via numerical methods (see [8] for details). The scale parameters m_d and m_c can be interpreted as beliefs in the parameters $c(t,d)/|d|$ and $df_t/\sum_{t'} df_{t'}$ respectively.

The query-likelihood approach to ranking documents can be used with these document models whereby one estimates the probability that the query is generated from the expected value drawn from each document model (i.e. $E[\vec{\alpha}_d]$ is a multinomial).[4] In this approach to retrieval, queries are generated by the expected multinomial as they are typically short and do not tend to exhibit word burstiness. In line with the original work [8], we refer to this document language model as the SPUD language model.

3.2 Query-Topic Models (QTM)

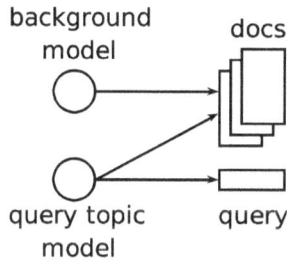

Figure 1: Query-Topic Model

In the original relevance model approach to expansion, candidate feedback terms are ranked according to the likelihood of the terms in the relevance model, where the relevance model is estimated as per Eq. 1. However, this model assumes that all the terms in the document are generated by the relevance model. We assume that documents are generated by both a topical model and a background model (Fig. 1), where we first need to estimate the probability that the term seen in a document is topical (i.e. $p(\vec{\alpha}_{d\tau}|t)$). Subsequently, given a set of feedback documents F, we rank terms as follows:

$$p(\vec{\theta}_Q|t) = \frac{\sum_{d \in F} p(\vec{\alpha}_{d\tau}|t) \cdot p(q|\vec{\alpha}_d)}{\sum_{d' \in F} p(q|\vec{\alpha}_{d'})} \quad (4)$$

which determines the probability that t was generated by the *query-topic model* (i.e. $\vec{\theta}_Q$) by using the probability that t is a topical term in d (i.e. $p(\vec{\alpha}_{d\tau}|t)$) and the probability that d is topically related to q (i.e. $p(q|\vec{\alpha}_d)$). While this looks somewhat similar to the relevance model approach (RM) [14] as it uses the query-likelihood document score $p(q|\vec{\alpha}_d)$, it differs in that it uses $p(\vec{\alpha}_{d\tau}|t)$ instead of $p(t|\vec{\alpha}_d)$. The

Bayesian inversion ranks terms by the likelihood of the term being generated by the topical part of the document, and then aggregates these probabilities over the top $|F|$ pseudo-relevant documents. Subsequently, the resulting probability $p(\vec{\theta}_Q|t)$ will be close to 1.0 when the term is likely be part of the query-topic model, and will be low when the term is unlikely to be part of the query-topic model. By assuming a uniform prior over the terms, the parameters of the query-topic model $\vec{\theta}_Q$ can be found by normalising over the number of feedback terms chosen as follows:

$$p(t|\vec{\theta}_Q) = \frac{p(\vec{\theta}_Q|t)}{\sum_{t'} p(\vec{\theta}_Q|t')} \quad (5)$$

As mentioned previously, one of the most prominent approaches to PRF (RM3) interpolates the pseudo-relevance model with the original query q. We follow this practise and smooth the query-topic model with the original query model ($\vec{\theta}_q$) as follows:

$$p(t|\vec{\theta}_{q'}) = (1 - \pi) \cdot p(t|\vec{\theta}_q) + \pi \cdot p(t|\vec{\theta}_Q) \quad (6)$$

where the parameter π determines how much mass to assign to the query-topic model as compared to the original query model. This interpolation is used in many language modelling approaches to feedback (e.g. RM3 [15] is recovered by substituting Eq. 1 for $p(t|\vec{\theta}_Q)$ above) and has been shown to be stable at $\pi \approx 0.5$.

Furthermore, the original query distribution is consistent with the model just presented. The terms in short queries are assumed to have been drawn directly from the *query-topic model* and are therefore deemed topical with a probability of 1.0 which are subsequently normalised to form $p(t|\vec{\theta}_q)$.[5] Thus far we have outlined a general method to estimate the QTM and therefore any plausible document language modelling approach can be used with it. While we have used the notation $\vec{\alpha}$ to denote the multivariate Pólya, the document models can be replaced with the original multinomial (denoted $\vec{\theta}$) with Dirichlet priors. In fact, we will show the results of doing so in Section 5.

3.3 QTM Using SPUD

We now outline a specific instantiation of the QTM using the SPUD document model outlined in Section 3.1. Given the SPUD language model (Eq. 2) and its parameters estimates (Eq. 3), the probability that the term t was generated from the *topical model* $\vec{\alpha}_{d\tau}$ of a document can be calculated via Bayes' theorem (assuming an equal prior on both models) as follows:

$$p(\vec{\alpha}_{d\tau}|t) = \frac{(1 - \omega) \cdot \alpha_{d\tau_t}}{(1 - \omega) \cdot \alpha_{d\tau_t} + \omega \cdot \alpha_{c_t}} \quad (7)$$

where $\alpha_{d\tau_t}$ and α_{c_t} are the parameters of t for the document-topicality model and background model respectively. A relatively simple intuition for this formula is that topical terms are those that are more likely generated from the topical part of a document than those that are generated by the background model. Interestingly, when plugging in the exact parameters for term t, the expression can be re-written in the following form:

---

[4]For the remainder of the paper when we write $p(q|\vec{\alpha}_d)$, we assume that a point estimate (the expectation) of the multivariate Pólya is taken.

[5]This assumption is likely valid for short queries. However, for longer queries it is likely that some words are generated by a background model and is worth investigating in future work.

$$p(\vec{\alpha}_{d\tau}|t) = \frac{c(t,d)}{c(t,d) + \frac{\omega \cdot m_c \cdot df_t}{(1-\omega) \cdot \sum_{t'} df_{t'}} \cdot \frac{|d|}{m_d}} \qquad (8)$$

where one can notice a concave term-frequency factor not dissimilar to the BM25 term-frequency factor (i.e. $\frac{c(t,d)}{c(t,d)+k_1}$). It should also be remarked that the formula promotes terms that are rarer in the collection and inherits verbosity normalisation from the SPUD model as $|d|/m_d$ is the average term-frequency in the document. We will analyse QTM$_{spud}$ more formally in the next section. For completeness, using the multinomial model with Dirichlet-priors in this feedback step leads to QTM$_{dir}$ as $p(\vec{\theta}_{d\tau}|t) = \frac{c(t,d)}{c(t,d)+\mu \cdot p(t|\theta_c)}$ where $p(t|\theta_c)$ is the maximum likelihood of seeing t in the collection c.

4 ANALYSIS

In this section, we conduct two analyses (a constraint analysis and a qualitative analysis) of the term selection method brought about by the QTM approach outlined in the previous section. For the constraint analysis, we limit ourselves to analysing five term-selection schemes; namely PDCM, SMM, RM3, QTM$_{dir}$, and QTM$_{spud}$. The PDCM approach assumes that the top $|F|$ documents returned for a query have been generated by a single DCM and estimates the parameters given the documents in F. Terms are then ranked according to their parameter value. SMM [23], RM3, and QTM have already been discussed and in fact, RM3 and SSM [6] have previously been analysed with regard to most of these constrains.

4.1 Constraint Analysis

Table 1: Adherence to Constraints

Method	DS	TF	Concavity	IDF	DL	DF
PDCM	no	yes	yes	no	yes	yes
SMM	no	yes	not sufficiently	yes	no	no
RM3	yes	yes	no	no	yes	no
QTM$_{dir}$	yes	yes	yes	yes	no	yes
QTM$_{spud}$	yes	yes	yes	yes	yes	yes

The RM3 and both QTM approaches adhere to the **DS** constraint as they use the query-likelihood score to promote terms that appear in documents that are more likely to be relevant (i.e. are highly scored). Neither SMM nor PDCM use the document score in their term selection scheme as they assume that all documents in F are equally relevant[6]. For the analysis of the remaining constraints, for simplicity we assume that documents in F have received the same document score (are all equally relevant).

All methods have a term-frequency aspect (**TF**) but this term-frequency aspect is not concave in the case of RM3 (i.e. the maximum likelihood $c(t,d)/|d|$ is a linear function).[7] Furthermore, previous research [6] points out that SSM does not sufficiently meet the **Concavity** constraint. However, Eq. 8 shows that both QTM approaches adhere to the **Concavity** constraint.

Only PDCM and RM3 do not adhere to the **IDF** constraint. This is because PDCM uses no background information, and in fact,

RM3 promotes terms that occur more frequently in the background collection when smoothing is employed in the feedback step (when smoothing is not used in the feedback step, then no background information is available and the **IDF** effect cannot exist). This has also been noted in recent research [11].

PDCM, RM3, and QTM$_{spud}$ penalise the weight contribution from terms in longer documents and so **DL** is satisfied. The only exceptions are SSM and QTM$_{dir}$. For QTM$_{dir}$ this is because the document length is absent in $p(\vec{\theta}_{d\tau}|t)$ (i.e. no verbosity normalisation is present).

Finally the **DF** constraint ensures that we should promote terms that appear in more pseudo-relevant documents when all else is equal (i.e. if the total occurrences of terms in F, the document lengths, and the document scores are all equal). Adherence to this constraint follows when the **Concavity** constraint is satisfied [5] and the aggregation function is a summation.[8]

4.2 Qualitative analysis

Table 2 shows the top 20 terms selected from four PRF approaches. QTM$_{dir}$ (not shown) returns term very similar to those returned by QTM$_{spud}$. The score for each of the terms is in its unnormalised form. We see that the two methods that do not adhere to the **IDF** constraint (PDCM and RM3) tend to select high frequency words (e.g. *said, from*) in the top $|F|$ documents without regard to their distribution in the entire collection. Although these frequent terms might not be highly detrimental when added to the initial query, it suggests that more expansion terms may be needed in order to achieve optimal performance. From a qualitative perspective, the QTM approach appears to promote expansion terms that are more semantically coherent when compared to PDCM and RM3. This would be of use in applications where one wished to generate topical models given a few initial terms. Furthermore, we can see that the score of the QTM$_{spud}$ approach has an intuitive interpretation as the probability that the term belongs to the query-topic model. All of the terms in red are those that are more likely to have been generated by the background model according to QTM$_{spud}$.[9]

5 EXPERIMENTAL EVALUATION

Our experiments have a number of aims. Firstly, we aim to determine the effectiveness of the new QTM model for query expansion when compared with a number of baseline approaches. Secondly, we wish to determine if QTM is empirically consistent with its theoretical derivation. To this end, we aim to show that during feedback the smoothed document models are effective and stable when using a similar parameter to that used during the initial retrieval step. We also aim to validate our choice of document model (multinomial vs multivariate Pólya) in the feedback step. Finally, we aim to perform a study of the performance of the approaches when varying the number of expansion terms used in two different settings.

We used a number of standard TREC[10] collections (robust-04, wt2g, wt10g, gov2, and ohsumed). Stemming and stopword removal

---

[6] This is a reasonable assumption for real relevance feedback.

[7] This stated violation is in contrast to the analysis in the original study [6]

[8] Space restricts the complete mathematical formalisms from being presented in this work.

[9] It would be interesting future work to investigate only selecting terms above a certain threshold (e.g. those terms that are more likely than not to be topical i.e. $p(\vec{\theta}_Q|t) > 0.5$).

[10] http://trec.nist.gov/

Table 2: Top 15 expansion words and their unnormalised term-selection value according to four PRF approaches. In all approaches the initial retrieval method is the SPUD language model with $\omega = 0.8$ and the set of pseudo relevant documents $|F| = 10$. Terms in red are those that receive a score of less than 0.5 according to the QTM_{spud} model, while terms in blue do not occur as top 15 expansion words for the other approaches.

		PRF methods for Topic 697 in **robust-04**						
Query	air traffic control							
Method	PDCM		$\text{SMM}_{\lambda=0.2}$		$\text{RM3}_{\omega=0}$		QTM_{spud}	
1	**air**	71.159	**air**	0.0793	**control**	0.0313	**traffic**	0.9835
2	**control**	68.542	**control**	0.0749	**air**	0.0310	**air**	0.9619
3	**traffic**	56.838	**traffic**	0.0655	**traffic**	0.0250	**control**	0.9227
4	system	33.123	system	0.0350	system	0.0125	aviat	0.8795
5	year	25.052	atc	0.0216	year	0.0109	airlin	0.8668
6	said	21.862	airport	0.0149	said	0.0105	airport	0.8389
7	from	16.890	safeti	0.0137	new	0.0072	transport	0.7684
8	problem	15.871	aviat	0.0135	from	0.0071	flight	0.7319
9	new	15.195	airlin	0.0134	european	0.0070	system	0.7141
10	ha	13.754	faa	0.0128	problem	0.0067	safeti	0.6251
11	airport	13.625	flight	0.0128	airlin	0.0059	problem	0.6243
12	which	13.521	problem	0.0126	ha	0.0056	radar	0.6196
13	have	13.409	european	0.0111	safeti	0.0055	inadequ	0.6132
14	safeti	12.724	facil	0.0103	airport	0.0054	rout	0.5859
15	airlin	12.695	europ	0.0100	europ	0.0053	delai	0.5552

(a small list of less than 30 words) was performed. The title fields of the associated topics are used as queries. As a first baseline, we use the language model with Dirichlet priors which was tuned for each collection ($\text{Dir}_{\hat{\mu}}$) and use the RM3 approach with $\mu = 0$ during the feedback step. This is currently a strong operational baseline. As a stronger set of baselines we use the $\text{SPUD}_{\omega=0.8}$ approach for retrieval with feedback approaches of PDCM, the simple mixture model (SMM), and the relevance model (RM3). Finally, we used a reportedly stronger positional relevance model baseline (PRM2) [17] that uses proximity information in the feedback documents where we set the proximity parameter to its suggested value $\sigma = 200$ [17]. In all experiments document retrieval is performed using the same function for both the original query and the expanded query.

To ensure a fair comparison, terms are ranked according to the selection function for each approach, are then normalised to sum to 1.0, and interpolated with the original query using π in Eq. 6. We tuned the three parameters $\pi \in \{0.0, 0.1, .., 0.9, 1.0\}$, $|F| \in \{5, 10, .., 45, 50\}$, and the number of feedback terms $|T| \in \{5, 10, ..., 45, 50\}$ using two-fold cross-validation[11] on each test collection. All approaches were implemented in Lucene and the code needed to replicate all of the results in this paper is available for download.[12]

5.1 Results

5.1.1 Smoothing Parameter During Feedback. Fig. 2 shows the effectiveness of three PRF approaches (SSM, RM3, and QTM_{spud}) as the background mass changes on three TREC collections (PDCM does not use a background model) during feedback. The same retrieval method (SPUD) was used in this experiment. The SMM

approach is relatively stable on these test collections at $\lambda_{smm} = 0.2$. We can see that the RM3 approach is most effective when using no smoothing ($\omega = 0.0$). This is consistent with previous research using the multinomial with Dirichlet priors [15] and confirms that different document representations are needed for initial retrieval and feedback when using RM3. The QTM_{spud} approach is most effective using the same background mass parameter that is used in the initial retrieval (i.e. $\omega = 0.8$). This result confirms that the background language model has useful information for term-selection. This also suggests that the QTM model is theoretically more consistent than RM3 as the same document representation is appropriate for initial retrieval and feedback. The remaining collections (ohsumed and gov2, not included in Fig. 2 due to space restrictions) show the same trend.

5.1.2 Effectiveness Comparison. Table 3 shows the effectiveness (MAP and NDCG@10) of the QTM model compared to the baselines on five test collections. The QTM_{spud} approach significantly outperforms the tuned RM3 approach on a number of collections. It is surprising that QTM_{spud} is competitive with the positional relevance model (PRM2) which uses proximity information. Furthermore, the QTM_{spud} approach outperforms the QTM_{dir} approach confirming that the Pólya document models are also better than the multinomial document models for feedback. This also suggests that the **DL** constraint is advantageous as it is the main difference between these methods. The improvements of QTM_{spud} over QTM_{dir} are consistent but small in magnitude. For the remainder of the paper, we focus on SSM, RM3 and the QTM PRF methods.

5.1.3 Number of Expansion Terms. Fig. 3 shows the performance of three approaches when the number of expansion terms vary. SMM is the worst approach and QTM_{spud} outperforms RM3. These differences tend to be less pronounced as more terms are added.

---

[11] using even and odd numbered topics as our two folds.
[12] https://github.com/anonymous/query-topic-model

Table 3: MAP (NDCG@10) of PRF approaches on 5 test collections (∗ means statistically significant compared to SPUD-RM3$_{\omega=0}$ at $p < 0.05$ using a paired t-test, while † means statistically significant when compared with QTM$_{dir}$ at $p < 0.05$. The best result per collection is in bold).

		ohsu	robust-04	wt2g	wt10g	gov2
	# docs	283k docs	528k	247k	1.69M	25.2M
	topics	1-63	301-450, 601-700	401-500	450-550	701-850
	# queries	63	249	50	100	149
Retrieval	Expansion					
Dir$_{\mu}$	None	0.321 (0.516)	0.256 (0.466)	0.311 (0.490)	0.194 (0.347)	0.303 (0.573)
Dir$_{\mu}$	RM3$_{\mu=0}$	0.374 (0.564)	0.288 (0.484)	0.346 (0.514)	0.213 (0.353)	0.332 (0.575)
SPUD	None	0.327 (0.520)	0.260 (0.480)	0.316 (0.495)	0.204 (0.366)	0.315 (0.596)
SPUD	SMM$_{\lambda=0.2}$	0.375 (0.568)	0.285 (0.471)	0.334 (0.510)	0.212 (0.363)	0.329 (0.568)
SPUD	PDCM	0.376 (0.565)	0.293 (0.489)	0.340 (0.511)	0.213 (0.368)	0.338 (0.598)
SPUD	PRM2	0.379 (0.567)	**0.305 (0.496)**	0.359 (**0.539**)	0.225 (**0.371**)	**0.350** (0.609)
SPUD	RM3$_{\omega=0}$	0.374 (0.572)	0.302 (0.494)	0.355 (0.535)	0.216 (0.362)	0.348 (0.604)
SPUD	QTM$_{dir}$	0.380 (0.558)	0.297 (0.491)	0.357 (0.517)	0.217 (0.357)	0.345 (0.628)
SPUD	QTM$_{spud}$	**0.384**∗ (**0.579**)	0.300† (0.493)	**0.364**† (0.529)	**0.220**∗ (0.374)	0.345 (**0.632**∗)

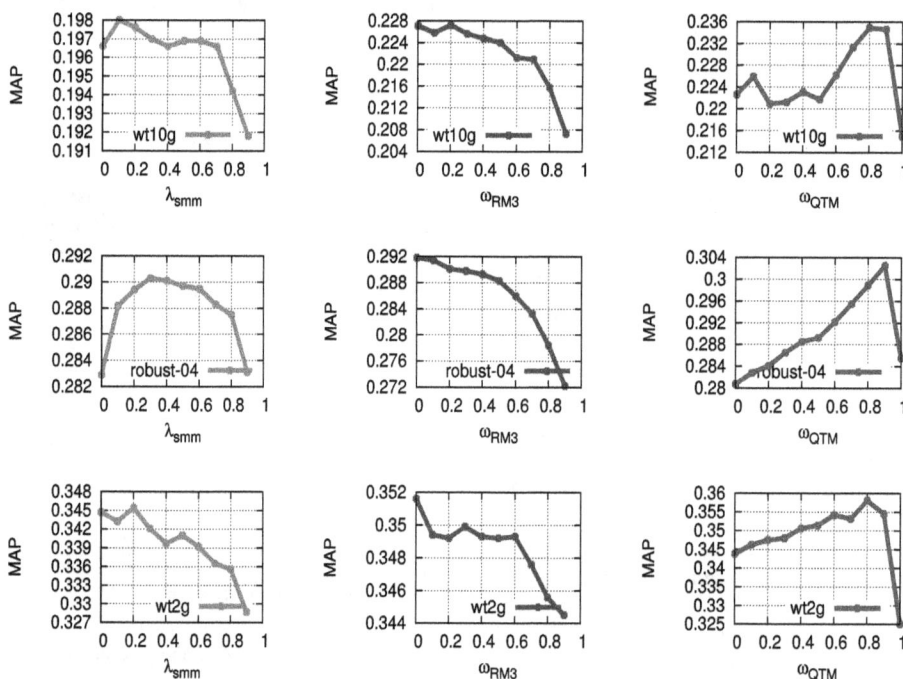

Figure 2: Retrieval effectiveness as background smoothing parameter in the feedback step changes in three PRF approach (SMM, RM3, and QTM from left to right).

We hypothesise that this is because as the number of expansion terms increase, the same terms tend to get added to the initial query. However, QTM$_{spud}$ retains its performance advantage when adding fewer expansion terms. In fact, during cross-validation we found that the optimal number of expansion terms for QTM is lower than for any of the other expansion methods studied here.

5.1.4 Removing Original Query Terms. Finally, we conducted an experiment of the PRF methods when varying the number of feedback terms while *removing terms* that occurred in the original query. For this experiment the original query terms were removed from the expanded query and the expanded query was renormalised. The results are outlined in Fig. 4 and show that the QTM$_{spud}$ approach creates queries that substantially outperform all other

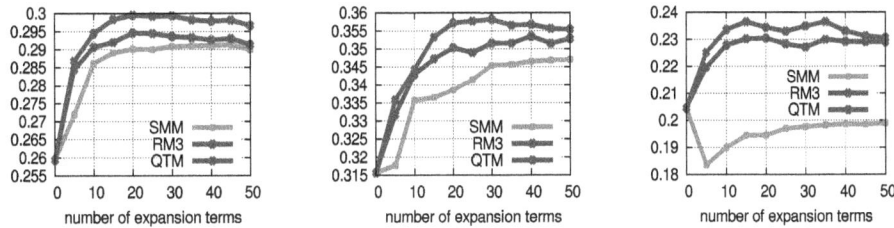

Figure 3: Retrieval effectiveness as number of expansion terms increase for three PRF approaches (SMM$_{\lambda=0.2}$, RM3$_{\omega=0}$, and QTM$_{spud}$) on three collections (robust-04, wt2g, and wt10g from left to right) for $|F| = 10$.

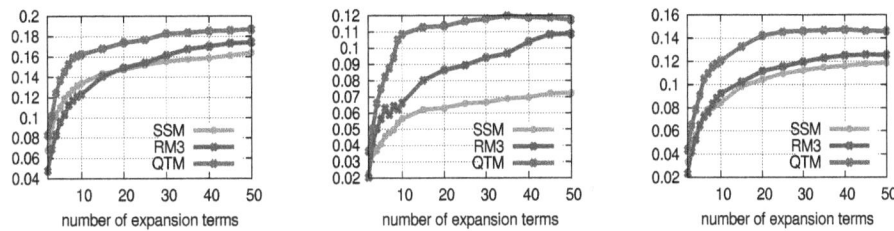

Figure 4: Retrieval effectiveness as number of expansion terms (removing original query terms) increase for three PRF approaches (SMM$_{\lambda=0.2}$, RM3$_{\omega=0}$, and QTM$_{spud}$) on three collections (robust-04, wt10g, and gov2 from left to right) for $|F| = 10$.

approaches for various lengths. This experiment yields valuable insights as it directly measures the retrieval effectiveness of only the feedback terms and their relative weightings.

6 DISCUSSION AND CONCLUSION

The QTM approach developed in this work is similar in spirit to the simple mixture model (SMM) outlined in the original work of Zhai and Lafferty [23]. However, there is no closed-form solution for the SMM approach and there is a free-parameter for which there is no obvious way of determining a suitable value (aside from tuning it empirically). While RM3 has stable performance, it is when different document representations are used for feedback (i.e. no background mass). Conversely for the QTM approach, we have shown that the same hyper-parameter values used to smooth documents for retrieval (i.e. $\omega = 0.8$ for SPUD), are close to optimal during the feedback process as shown in Fig. 2. This, unlike RM3, gives theoretical consistency to our approach. QTM achieves good performance at $|F| = 10$, $\pi = 0.5$, and with 20 or so expansion terms.

A brief analysis of the QTM$_{spud}$ approach has shown that it adheres to a number of previously proposed properties describing effective term-selection functions. It is interesting that these properties arise from modelling the PRF in a principled manner (without heuristically hand-crafting the function in any way). A qualitative analysis of the terms selected by the QTM$_{spud}$ indicates they are more topically coherent than those selected by RM3. This is because at its most optimal setting, RM3 selects the most frequent terms in the feedback documents without regard to their distribution in the collection. The QTM approach is competitive with several strong baselines, including a positional relevance model,

when using the same retrieval method. It is also worth pointing out that the absolute MAP values reported on a number of standard TREC collections are very competitive and actually outperform many previous studies. Future work will look at developing better expansion models for use with verbose queries.

REFERENCES

[1] Nasreen Abdul-jaleel, James Allan, W. Bruce Croft, O Diaz, Leah Larkey, Xiaoyan Li, Mark D. Smucker, and Courtney Wade. 2004. UMass at TREC 2004: Novelty and HARD. In *Proceedings of TREC-04*.

[2] Jagdev Bhogal, Andrew MacFarlane, and Peter Smith. 2007. A review of ontology based query expansion. *Information processing & management* 43, 4 (2007), 866–886.

[3] Guihong Cao, Jian-Yun Nie, Jianfeng Gao, and Stephen Robertson. 2008. Selecting Good Expansion Terms for Pseudo-relevance Feedback. In *Proceedings of the 31st Annual International ACM SIGIR Conference on Research and Development in Information Retrieval (SIGIR '08)*. ACM, New York, NY, USA, 243–250.

[4] Claudio Carpineto and Giovanni Romano. 2012. A Survey of Automatic Query Expansion in Information Retrieval. *ACM Comput. Surv.* 44, 1, Article 1 (Jan. 2012), 50 pages.

[5] Stéphane Clinchant and Éric Gaussier. 2011. A document frequency constraint for pseudo-relevance feedback models. In *CORIA 2011-COnférence en Recherche d'Information et Applications*. 73–88.

[6] Stéphane Clinchant and Eric Gaussier. 2013. A theoretical analysis of pseudo-relevance feedback models. In *Proceedings of the 2013 Conference on the Theory of Information Retrieval*. ACM, 6.

[7] Kevyn Collins-Thompson. 2009. Reducing the Risk of Query Expansion via Robust Constrained Optimization. In *Proceedings of the 18th ACM Conference on Information and Knowledge Management (CIKM '09)*. ACM, New York, NY, USA, 837–846.

[8] Ronan Cummins, Jiaul H. Paik, and Yuanhua Lv. 2015. A Pólya Urn Document Language Model for Improved Information Retrieval. *ACM Transactions of Informations Systems* 33, 4 (2015), 21.

[9] Hui Fang, Tao Tao, and ChengXiang Zhai. 2004. A Formal Study of Information Retrieval Heuristics. In *Proceedings of the 27th Annual International ACM SIGIR Conference on Research and Development in Information Retrieval (SIGIR '04)*. ACM, New York, NY, USA, 49–56.

[10] Hui Fang and ChengXiang Zhai. 2006. Semantic Term Matching in Axiomatic Approaches to Information Retrieval. In *Proceedings of the 29th Annual International ACM SIGIR Conference on Research and Development in Information Retrieval (SIGIR '06)*. ACM, New York, NY, USA, 115–122.

[11] Hussein Hazimeh and ChengXiang Zhai. 2015. Axiomatic Analysis of Smoothing Methods in Language Models for Pseudo-Relevance Feedback. In *Proceedings of the 2015 International Conference on The Theory of Information Retrieval (ICTIR '15)*. ACM, New York, NY, USA, 141–150.

[12] Saar Kuzi, Anna Shtok, and Oren Kurland. 2016. Query Anchoring Using Discriminative Query Models. In *Proceedings of the 2016 ACM International Conference on the Theory of Information Retrieval (ICTIR '16)*. ACM, New York, NY, USA, 219–228.

[13] Saar Kuzi, Anna Shtok, and Oren Kurland. 2016. Query Expansion Using Word Embeddings. In *Proceedings of the 25th ACM International on Conference on Information and Knowledge Management (CIKM '16)*. ACM, New York, NY, USA, 1929–1932.

[14] Victor Lavrenko and W Bruce Croft. 2001. Relevance based language models. In *Proceedings of the 24th annual international ACM SIGIR conference on Research and development in information retrieval*. ACM, 120–127.

[15] Yuanhua Lv and ChengXiang Zhai. 2009. A Comparative Study of Methods for Estimating Query Language Models with Pseudo Feedback. In *Proceedings of the 18th ACM Conference on Information and Knowledge Management (CIKM '09)*. ACM, New York, NY, USA, 1895–1898.

[16] Yuanhua Lv and ChengXiang Zhai. 2010. Positional Relevance Model for Pseudo-relevance Feedback. In *Proceedings of the 33rd International ACM SIGIR Conference on Research and Development in Information Retrieval (SIGIR '10)*. ACM, New York, NY, USA, 579–586.

[17] Yuanhua Lv and ChengXiang Zhai. 2011. Lower-bounding term frequency normalization. In *Proceedings of the 20th ACM international conference on Information and knowledge management (CIKM '11)*. ACM, 7–16.

[18] Javier Parapar, Manuel A Presedo-Quindimil, and Alvaro Barreiro. 2014. Score distributions for pseudo relevance feedback. *Information Sciences* 273 (2014), 171–181.

[19] S. E. Robertson and S. Walker. 1994. Some Simple Effective Approximations to the 2-Poisson Model for Probabilistic Weighted Retrieval. In *Proceedings of the 17th Annual International ACM SIGIR Conference on Research and Development in Information Retrieval (SIGIR '94)*. Springer-Verlag New York, Inc., New York, NY, USA, 232–241.

[20] Tao Tao and ChengXiang Zhai. 2006. Regularized Estimation of Mixture Models for Robust Pseudo-relevance Feedback. In *Proceedings of the 29th Annual International ACM SIGIR Conference on Research and Development in Information Retrieval (SIGIR '06)*. ACM, New York, NY, USA, 162–169.

[21] Zuobing Xu and Ram Akella. 2008. A New Probabilistic Retrieval Model Based on the Dirichlet Compound Multinomial Distribution. In *Proceedings of the 31st Annual International ACM SIGIR Conference on Research and Development in Information Retrieval (SIGIR '08)*. ACM, New York, NY, USA, 427–434.

[22] Hamed Zamani and W Bruce Croft. 2016. Embedding-based query language models. In *Proceedings of the 2016 ACM on International Conference on the Theory of Information Retrieval*. ACM, 147–156.

[23] Chengxiang Zhai and John Lafferty. 2001. Model-based Feedback in the Language Modeling Approach to Information Retrieval. In *Proceedings of the Tenth International Conference on Information and Knowledge Management (CIKM '01)*. ACM, New York, NY, USA, 403–410.

On the Additivity and Weak Baselines
for Search Result Diversification Research

Mehmet Akcay
Middle East Technical University & ASELSAN
Ankara, Turkey
meakcay@aselsan.com.tr

Ismail Sengor Altingovde
Middle East Technical University
Ankara, Turkey
altingovde@ceng.metu.edu.tr

Craig Macdonald
University of Glasgow
Glasgow, Scotland, UK
craig.macdonald@glasgow.ac.uk

Iadh Ounis
University of Glasgow
Glasgow, Scotland, UK
iadh.ounis@glasgow.ac.uk

ABSTRACT

A recent study on the topic of additivity addresses the task of search result diversification and concludes that while weaker baselines are almost always significantly improved by the evaluated diversification methods, for stronger baselines, just the opposite happens, i.e., no significant improvement can be observed. Due to the importance of the issue in shaping future research directions and evaluation strategies in search results diversification, in this work, we first aim to reproduce the findings reported in the previous study, and then investigate its possible limitations. Our extensive experiments first reveal that under the same experimental setting with that previous study, we can reach similar results. Next, we hypothesize that for stronger baselines, tuning the parameters of some methods (i.e., the trade-off parameter between the relevance and diversity of the results in this particular scenario) should be done in a more fine-grained manner. With trade-off parameters that are specifically determined for each baseline run, we show that the percentage of significant improvements even over the strong baselines can be doubled. As a further issue, we discuss the possible impact of using the same strong baseline retrieval function for the diversity computations of the methods. Our takeaway message is that in the case of a strong baseline, it is more crucial to tune the parameters of the diversification methods to be evaluated; but once this is done, additivity is achievable.

KEYWORDS

Additivity; result diversification; statistical significance

1 INTRODUCTION

Search result diversification in Information Retrieval (IR) is the process of (re-) ranking the retrieved documents for a query so that the top-ranked results would satisfy the users who all issue the same query but with diverse intents [22]. In the literature, search result diversification methods are broadly categorized as explicit and implicit [24]. In a nutshell, implicit methods only rely on the initially retrieved document list (the so-called candidate documents) to infer different subtopics (a.k.a., aspects or intents) of the query and re-rank the list. In contrast, explicit methods assume that query subtopics are made available (i.e., via using a topical taxonomy [1] or mining query logs [24]) and aim to use these subtopics to re-rank the candidate result list to surface results corresponding to different interpretations higher up the result list. In the last decade, several diversification methods have been investigated for and applied to adhoc text retrieval (e.g., web search [3, 14, 24], tweet search [12, 15]) but also in many other contexts, such as image search [16, 26], database and data stream querying [4, 10], and even recommender systems [25, 27, 28].

In a recent study, Kharazmi et al. [7] investigated the *additivity* of the findings with respect to different types of baselines for various IR tasks. First coined by Armstrong et al. [2], the additivity of a method refers to its capability to improve a strong baseline given an improvement over a weak one. Besides several other very useful and inspiring analyses and discussions, Kharazmi et al. also focussed on diversification, by employing three implicit and three explicit methods, and several baseline runs (i.e., adhoc runs submitted to TREC between 2009 and 2011 without any diversification effort) to investigate the additivity of the possible improvements made by these methods over weak and strong baselines. We emphasize that in this context, the term baseline refers to an adhoc retrieval method/system that returns a candidate result list (i.e., a run in TREC terminology) to be diversified, and a weak baseline run is such a list with a relatively low initial diversity performance (with respect to well-known evaluation metrics such as α-nDCG or ERR-IA). Their findings are quite striking: even when the diversification methods are found to consistently and significantly improve the weak baselines (and this only holds for the explicit diversification methods using the TREC official subtopics), these methods rarely improve the stronger ones; i.e., additivity does not occur.

The implications of the above conclusion are important. It says that in the future, researchers should use stronger baselines even for the initial retrieval stage to demonstrate the power of their diversification method, i.e., a simple adhoc run produced by a typical system (say, Lucene, Terrier or other research prototypes) or method (say, BM25) cannot be considered adequate. Given that at least some

ICTIR'17, October 1–4, 2017, Amsterdam, The Netherlands
© 2017 ACM. 978-1-4503-4490-6/17/10...$15.00
DOI: https://doi.org/10.1145/3121050.3121059

of these stronger baseline runs may involve several additional features that are extracted from external resources, such as proprietary datasets or even public ones that are no longer available (e.g., a modified web site or taxonomy), the necessity of such baselines may slow down the pace of experimentation in this subject area. Therefore, we believe that it is mandatory to repeat the procedure described by Kharazmi et al., and investigate their findings in a timely manner.

Our goal in this paper is to reproduce the major findings of the aforementioned previous work regarding the result diversification task, and question the validity of the resulting claims on additivity via additional experiments and analysis. In the previous works on explicit result diversification, it is widely reported that the official TREC subtopics yield much higher effectiveness than using subtopic definitions from other resources, such as web search engine suggestions (e.g., see [3, 14, 24]). It is also shown that explicit diversification, not surprisingly, outperforms the implicit approaches, especially when the official TREC subtopics are employed (e.g., see [11]). These observations are also verified by Kharazmi et al. in that significant improvements are either rare or even non-existent for the implicit methods and for the explicit methods with ODP-based subtopics even on the weaker baselines (see Fig. 3 in [7]). Thus, in this paper, we essentially focus on repeating the experiments employing explicit diversification methods and the official TREC subtopics, to investigate the new additivity claims of Kharazmi et al.

In doing so, our contributions are three-fold: (1) our experimental findings under exactly the same setup verify the results in [7]; (2) Moreover, our additional experiments where we set the λ trade-off parameter of some diversification methods (i.e. the parameter that balances the relevance to the main query and the diversity with respect to the query subtopics) for each baseline separately show that these methods can actually still significantly improve a non-trivial percentage of strong baselines, too; (3) We discuss the possible impact of using the same strong baseline retrieval function inside the diversification methods, i.e., to compute the relevance of a document to a subtopic, and provide some indirect evidence. Overall, our additional experiments and discussions show the potential of additivity of these diversification methods on strong baselines; and pinpoint the subtle issues (such as parameter tuning and relevance computation of documents to subtopics) that should be carefully handled while applying a diversification method to such baselines.

This paper is organized as follows. In Section 2, we briefly review the explicit diversification methods implemented for this work. In Section 3, we describe our experimental setup following the blueprint in [7]. Section 4 provides results of the repeated and additional experiments. In Section 5, we discuss the impact of modeling the document-subtopic relevance in this context. Finally, in Section 6, we conclude and summarize the main lessons learnt from this work.

2 EXPLICIT RESULT DIVERSIFICATION

In a typical result diversification scenario, for a query q, the adhoc retrieval results (i.e., a candidate ranking that typically includes from 50 up to 1000 documents) are given. The goal is to create a final ranking S of top-k documents (in practice, k is usually at most 20) that both maximizes the relevance to query q and its subtopics q_i, and minimizes the redundancy with respect to these subtopics [6]. As discussed above, both the earlier studies and Kharazmi et al. reported that the best diversification performance is obtained by

the methods that utilize an explicitly modeled set of the query's subtopics, T_q, provided beforehand. Therefore, in this work, we implement three explicit diversification approaches, namely, IA-Select [1] and xQuAD [19] as employed in [7], as well as CombSum, as a recently proposed method that is shown to be comparable to or better than both of the former methods [14] and PM2 [3], which is another state-of-the-art approach. Note that, in [7], another variant of xQuAD (referred to as xQuADRel [29]) has also been considered, but since their experiments revealed that it is always inferior to IA-Select and xQuAD in yielding significant improvements over the baseline runs, we use CombSum instead of xQuADRel. In the following, we briefly review these methods as implemented in our setup:

IA-Select This is a best-first greedy method [1] that scores the documents in each iteration and selects the one that is most likely to cover all query subtopics that are not yet covered by the documents that have already been selected for the final top-k results, S, in the previous iterations. While the original definition of the IA-Select's scoring function employs a slightly different notation, following the practice in [14, 19], we present it as follows:

$$S(q, d) = \sum_{q_i \in T_q} P(q_i|q)P(d|q_i) \prod_{d_j \in S} (1 - P(d_j, q_i)) \quad (1)$$

In IA-Select, $P(q_i|q)$ is the likelihood (or, importance) of subtopic q_i for the query q. The probability $P(d|q_i)$ represents the likelihood of observing document d for the subtopic q_i and is usually modeled based on the relevance score $rel(d, q_i)$ (normalized to the [0, 1] range) of the retrieval system that generates the candidate ranking (see Sections 3 and 5 for further discussions).

xQuAD Again operating in iterations, eXplicit Query Aspect Diversification (xQuAD) [19] is based on a probabilistic mixture framework that takes into account the relevance to the main query q as well as the relevance and diversity with respect to the query's subtopics. Its scoring function is as follows:

$$S(q, d) = (1-\lambda)P(d|q) + \lambda \sum_{q_i \in T_q} \left[P(q_i|q)P(d|q_i) \prod_{d_j \in S} (1 - P(d_j|q_i)) \right] \quad (2)$$

where $P(d|q)$ is typically modeled as $rel(d, q)$, i.e., the (normalized) relevance score of d for q as generated by a retrieval system, while the other probabilities are defined as in the case of IA-Select. Note that there is a trade-off parameter λ to balance the relevance and diversity of the results in the final ranking. For $\lambda = 0$, the final ranking is exactly the same as the candidate ranking, and for $\lambda = 1$, the $P(d|q)$ component is totally discarded, as in IA-Select.

CombSum This method is an adaptation of the score-based ranking aggregation technique CombSum [5, 9] to the diversification problem [14]. Instead of running in iterations, CombSum first ranks the documents for each subtopic by computing $P(d|q_i)$, and then combines these rankings and the ranking for the main query using the following function, where the probabilities are defined as above:

$$S(q, d) = (1 - \lambda)P(d|q) + \lambda \sum_{q_i \in T_q} P(q_i|q)P(d|q_i) \quad (3)$$

In summary, each of the diversification methods contains a notion of document-query relevance estimation (e.g. $P(d|q)$), which we denote as $rel(d, q)$, as well as a document-subtopic relevance (e.g. $P(d|q_i)$), which we denote as $rel(d, q_i)$. Furthermore, both xQuAD

Table 1: Score intervals for categorizing baseline runs.

Baseline level	ERR-IA@20	α-nDCG@20	P-IA@20
Weak	$\leqslant 0.18$	$\leqslant 0.23$	$\leqslant 0.10$
Medium	>0.18 & $\leqslant 0.33$	>0.23 & $\leqslant 0.41$	>0.10 & $\leqslant 0.19$
Strong	>0.33	>0.41	>0.19

Table 2: Number of baseline runs in each year and level w.r.t. each metric.

Dataset	Baseline level	ERR-IA	α-nDCG	P-IA	Total
TREC2009	Weak	31	16	25	
	Medium	0	15	6	31
	Strong	0	0	0	
TREC2010	Weak	11	3	7	
	Medium	15	22	18	26
	Strong	0	1	1	
TREC2011	Weak	0	0	0	
	Medium	6	5	3	14
	Strong	8	9	11	
Total	Weak	42	19	32	
	Medium	21	42	27	71
	Strong	8	10	12	

and CombSum have a parameter λ, which controls the trade-off between the importance between a document's relevance to the original query, and the coverage of subtopics. In the rest of this paper, we study the setting and instantiation of the methods with respect to $rel(d, q_i)$ and λ.

3 REPRODUCED EXPERIMENTAL SETUP FOR THE ANALYSIS OF ADDITIVITY IN DIVERSIFICATION

Baseline runs and categories. As in [7], we only use the TREC Web Track adhoc retrieval track submissions that are on the ClueWeb09 collection (Part-B) and employs no diversification methods. There were 34, 26 and 16 such runs submitted to TREC 2009, 2010 and 2011, respectively. Following [7], we remove the five lowest scoring (w.r.t. α-nDCG@20) of these 76 runs, to obtain a total of 71 runs.

Kharazmi et al. [7] categorized these runs into three levels, namely, weak, medium and strong baselines, based on the scores of certain evaluation metrics. In particular, for a given evaluation metric, the score range (i.e., the range between the minimum and maximum scores of the baseline runs) is partitioned into three equally sized regions to form these groups. We consider the ranges for α-nDCG and ERR-IA as proposed in [7], and further employ a third metric, P-IA, for additional insights. Table 1 provides the score boundaries, and Table 2 shows the number of runs that fall into each range with respect to each metric. Note that, the number of runs in each level with respect to α-nDCG and ERR-IA metrics (cf. Table 2) exactly match to those values reported in Table 3 of [7].

Diversification methods, query sets and subtopics. As discussed before, we focus on the most-effective diversification scenario, namely explicit diversification with the official TREC subtopics. We pre-process the subtopic descriptions so that they look like real

user queries, as has been performed in the literature [21]. In particular, we remove stopwords and generic terms like "find", "look for" and "information". We implement xQuAD, CombSum and IA-Select, as described in Section 2.

The query sets and their official subtopics from TREC 2009 to 2011 are used to diversify the top-100 candidate documents from the baseline runs of the corresponding year. As discussed in Section 2, all the aforementioned methods need to compute $rel(d, q)$ and $rel(d, q_i)$, i.e., the relevance score of the query and its subtopics to a candidate document, respectively. As all of the baseline runs provide the actual scores along with the candidate document ranking, we use the normalized version of these scores (by the sum of the scores of top-100 documents) for the former component, $rel(d, q)$ (Note that some runs involve negative scores that required further pre-processing before normalization).

For the latter component, $rel(d, q_i)$, the ideal case would be to obtain the document-subtopic scores using the exact retrieval system that yielded the candidate documents in each run. However, given the number and complexity of the methods in the baseline runs, this is practically unattainable. Thus, to compute document-subtopic scores, we employ a variant of the well-known Okapi BM25 weighting model [17], setting its parameters as follows $k_1 = 1.2$ and $b = 0.50$ (again, the actual BM25 scores are sum-normalized over the top-100 documents[1]). To do so, we use an index of ClueWeb09 Part-B collection using the open source Zettair retrieval system [30]. Although Kharazmi et al. [7] do not specify how exactly these computations are made, we verified through a personal communication [8] that they employed Indri with Okapi BM25 for computing $rel(d, q_i)$ in their work. Having said that, we further discuss the impact of this choice in Section 5.

In all our experiments, following [19], the subtopic probabilities $P(q_i|q)$ are computed uniformly as $1/|T_q|$, where T_q is the set of subtopics for a given query q. For xQuAD and CombSum, we set the trade-off parameter λ in three ways: First, we use the fixed value of $\lambda = 0.9$ reported in [7], which is said to be obtained via a 5-fold cross-validation process and by testing all values in the [0,1] range with a step size of 0.1 over the training sets. As confirmed by Kharazmi et al. [8], in their work the cross-validation has been applied over the runs, i.e., the best-performing λ parameter is determined over the training runs and then applied for the test runs in each fold. Second, we applied a similar procedure (i.e., a 5-fold cross-validation and scanning the [0,1] range) to determine the λ value that maximizes the α-nDCG@20 specifically for each run, i.e., in a *localized* fashion. In this case, for each run, we determine the best-performing λ over the training queries and then apply to the test queries—this mimics typical deployment of a run in a production environment, as well as in various research papers such as [19, 20]. Our λ parameter is more likely to be adjusted to the particular characteristics of a given run, rather than set for all runs in a training fold, as performed by [7]. Thirdly, we also report the performance using the *best* λ, which is again obtained per run but without using cross validation, as an upper-bound.

Evaluation metrics. To evaluate the diversification effectiveness, we compute three common metrics, namely, α-nDCG (with the default $\alpha = 0.5$), ERR-IA and Precision-IA, at the cut-off value of 20, using the ndeval software. We provide the evaluation results for our experiments at github.com/altingovde/ICTIR2017-DivAdditivity.

---

[1]This normalization is used in [14]; Santos [18] uses a slightly different normalization.

(a) IA-Select

(b) xQuAD

(c) CombSum

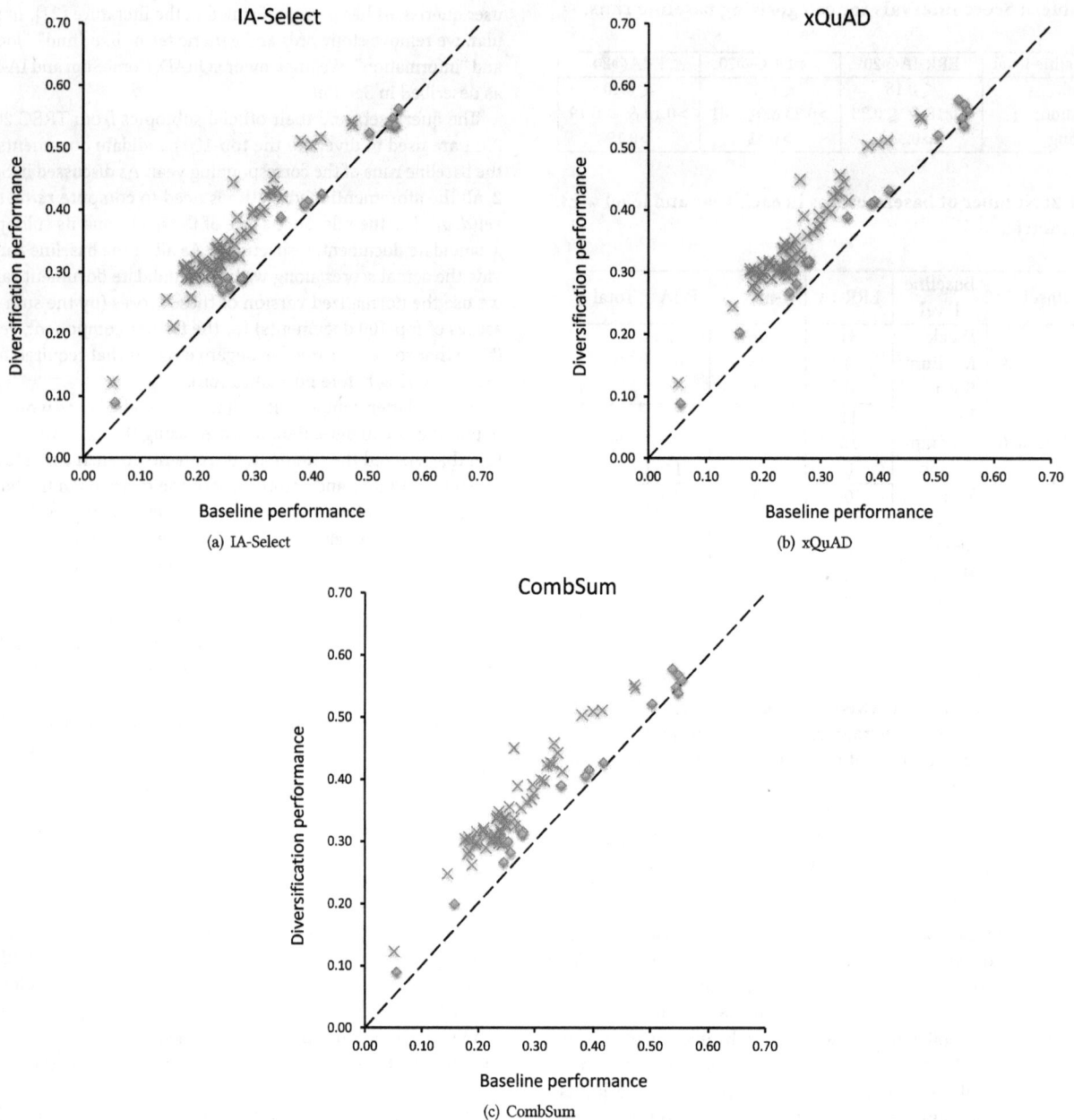

Figure 1: Scatter plots showing effectiveness of xQuAD and CombSum with trade-off parameter $\lambda = 0.9$. X- and y-axis show α-nDCG@20 scores for the baseline run and its diversified version, respectively. Points plotted as blue crosses are statistically significant improvements over the baseline, while red diamonds indicate no significant difference.

4 EXPERIMENTS AND EVALUATION

As our first goal is reproducing the findings of Kharazmi et al., Section 4.1 presents our experiments conducted in the same setup as theirs (to the greatest extent possible) and employing the reported Global λ value of 0.9 for xQuAD and CombSum methods. In the additional experiments given in Section 4.2, keeping all the other setup details the same, we demonstrate the impact of using the Local and Best λ values during diversification.

4.1 Reproduced Results using Global Trade-off Parameter

In this section, we report our findings for all three diversification methods using the global λ value of 0.9. Figure 1 presents the performances of the diversification methods applied over the baseline (non-diversified) runs in terms of the α-nDCG metric. From the figure, we observe that, as in [7], while weaker baselines (closer to y-axis in the plots) are almost always significantly improved

Table 3: Ratio of runs significantly improved for each baseline level using xQuAD and CombSum. Note that [7] did not report the CombSum method or P-IA metric.

Level	Method	Results from [7]			Our results (Global λ = 0.9)		
		ERR-IA	α-nDCG	P-IA	ERR-IA	α-nDCG	P-IA
Weak	xQuAD	34/42	18/19	N/A	30/42	17/19	21/32
	CombSum	N/A	N/A	N/A	30/42	17/19	22/32
Medium	xQuAD	3/21	25/42	N/A	13/21	33/42	14/27
	CombSum	N/A	N/A	N/A	13/21	33/42	12/27
Strong	xQuAD	0/8	1/10	N/A	1/8	3/10	7/12
	CombSum	N/A	N/A	N/A	1/8	3/10	7/12

Table 4: Ratio of runs significantly improved for each baseline level using IA-Select.

Level	Results from [7]			Our results		
	ERR-IA	α-nDCG	P-IA	ERR-IA	α-nDCG	P-IA
Weak	35/42	18/19	N/A	30/42	18/19	22/32
Medium	9/21	29/42	N/A	13/21	32/42	13/27
Strong	1/8	3/10	N/A	1/8	3/10	6/12

by the application of the diversification method (measured using a paired two-tailed t-test for $p < 0.05$), the improvements for the stronger baselines are not significant in most of the cases for all three methods. The trends across IA-Select, xQuAD and CombSum are similar, and for xQuAD and IA-Select they are consistent with the previously reported findings (see the top row of Fig. 3 in [7]).

As in [7], none of the diversification methods (with official subtopics) yields a significant degradation in the performance compared to their baseline runs; i.e, all the significant changes are improvements. We report the ratio of runs that are statistically significantly improved for each method per baseline category, i.e., weak, medium and strong, with respect to three evaluation metrics in Table 3 (for xQuAD and CombSum, with λ = 0.9) & Table 4 (for IA-Select[2]). Note that, the denominator of the ratios in the latter results denotes the number of baseline runs at each level for each metric, as provided in Table 2. Both Tables 3 & 4 report the respective results repeated from Table 5 in [7]. By comparing the columns across Tables 3 & 4, we note that our findings are generally consistent with the previous work: almost all weak baselines and the majority of the medium-level baselines are improved by the diversification methods, while the improvements for the strong baselines are rather moderate (i.e., no more than 30% for α-nDCG and ERR-IA). Having said that, for xQuAD, we find a considerably larger number of significant improvements over the medium and strong runs in terms of the ERR-IA metric. Yet another interesting finding is that, when the P-IA metric (which is not reported in [7]) is considered, the percentage of significantly improved strong baselines exceeds 50%, i.e., not really a moderate ratio as for the other two metrics. Overall, we conclude that we can successfully reproduce the main results of [7] for the result diversification task.

4.2 Additional Results using Local Trade-off Parameter

In this section, we investigate the impact of the trade-off parameter λ on the performance of the xQuAD and CombSum methods (recall that IA-Select has no λ parameter). To this end, for each run, we optimize λ (for the α-nDCG@20 metric) using a 5-fold cross validation and scanning the [0, 1] range with a step size of 0.01 . In Figure 2, we present the distribution of these Local λ values over the training folds (i.e., given 71 runs and 5-fold CV, we consider 355 folds in total). The plot clearly justifies our choice of setting the trade-off parameter separately for each run, as the values are quite scattered over the bins, e.g., even the largest bin (for the range [0.9, 1]) yields the best performance during the training for less than one fourth of the total number of folds.

In Table 5, we report the diversification performance using the Local λ values per run, as described above. In comparison to the Global λ column (repeated from Table 3 to facilitate comparison), there is a clear increase in the ratio of significantly improved runs for all baseline levels and methods in terms of all metrics. We concentrate on the strong baselines, as the majority of the other baselines are shown to improve even when the Global λ value is utilized. Table 5 reveals that xQuAD and CombSum yields statistically significant improvements for 70% and 60% (i.e., 7/10 and 6/10) of the strong baselines for the α-nDCG metric, respectively. In terms of the ERR-IA metric, both diversification methods now significantly improve 37.5% (i.e., 3/8) of the strong baselines. Even for P-IA, there is an improvement in the ratio of significantly improved strong runs (i.e., from 7/12 to 8/12). As before, we also plot the performance of diversification methods (with Local λ) applied over the baseline runs in Figure 3, which further reveals that none of the diversification methods yield any drop in the performance, as well as pictorially showing the larger number of significant increases for the two methods.

The Best λ column in Table 5 shows that when the optimal λ (for the α-nDCG@20 metric) for each baseline run is set, the ratio of significantly improved strong runs reaches 62.5% and 80% in terms of the ERR-IA and α-nDCG metrics (i.e., 5/8 and 8/10, respectively). While we essentially provide this setting as an upper-bound, given the small number of queries in the TREC campaigns, one could use a leave-one-out cross validation strategy per run, which would yield a similar performance to the Best λ. Finally note that all experiments in this paper use the same λ value applied uniformly over all the queries in the test fold. In the literature, it has been shown that different queries have different levels of ambiguity, and therefore benefit from different λ values [20] to further improve

Table 5: Ratio of runs that are significantly improved for each baseline level using XQuAD and CombSum with Global, Local and Best λ values.

Level	Diversity method	Global λ = 0.90			Local λ			Best λ		
		ERR-IA	α-nDCG	P-IA	ERR-IA	α-nDCG	P-IA	ERR-IA	α-nDCG	P-IA
Weak	xQuAD	30/42	17/19	21/32	33/42	19/19	24/32	37/42	19/19	28/32
	CombSum	30/42	17/19	22/32	32/42	19/19	24/32	37/42	19/19	29/32
Medium	xQuAD	13/21	33/42	14/27	18/21	36/42	18/27	20/21	40/42	19/27
	CombSum	13/21	33/42	12/27	17/21	36/42	18/27	20/21	40/42	20/27
Strong	xQuAD	1/8	3/10	7/12	3/8	7/10	8/12	5/8	8/10	8/12
	CombSum	1/8	3/10	7/12	3/8	6/10	8/12	5/8	7/10	8/12

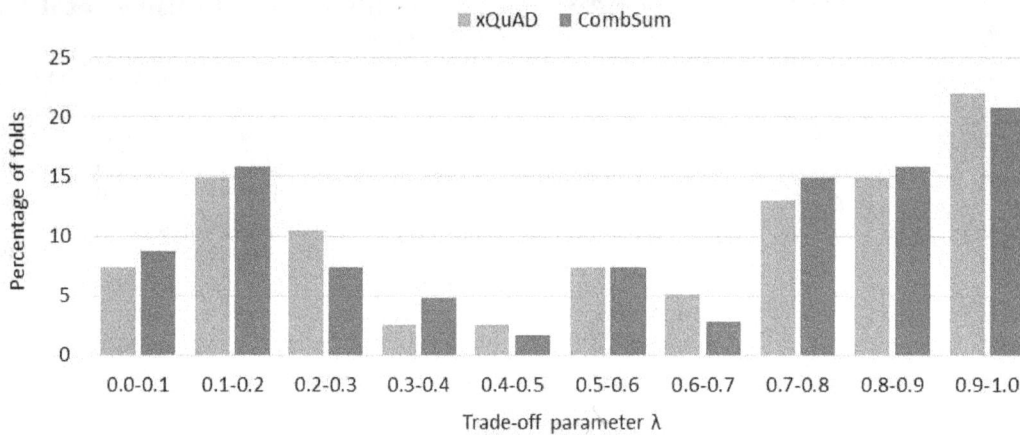

Figure 2: Distribution of trade-off λ parameter values over the 355 training folds.

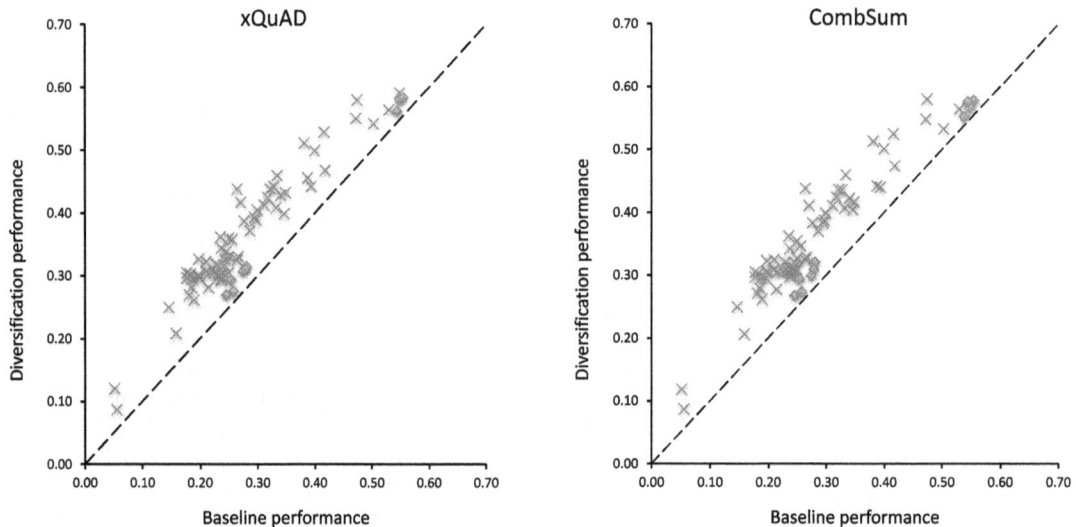

Figure 3: Scatter plots showing effectiveness of xQuAD and CombSum with the Local λ trade-off parameter. X- and y-axis show α-nDCG@20 scores for the baseline run and its diversified version, respectively. Points plotted as blue crosses are statistically significant improvements over the baseline, while red diamonds indicate no significant difference.

Table 6: α-nDCG@20 scores of the diversified results over ten strong baselines (wrt. α-nDCG) using xQuAD. We compute $rel(d, q)$ either based on the original scores in the run or using BM25, while the $rel(d, q_i)$ scores are always computed by BM25. The bold results are the ones that are higher within the same λ setup. The underlined scores are the highest in that row.

Run id	Original α-nDCG@20	Global $\lambda = 0.90$		Local λ	
		Original+BM25	BM25+BM25	Original+BM25	BM25 + BM25
2011SiftR1	0.5483	**0.5764**	0.5433	**0.5917**	0.5357
2011SiftR2	0.5372	**0.5793**	0.5442	**0.5615**	0.5362
DFalah11	0.5021	0.5240	**0.5266**	**0.5427**	0.5336
Otago2011cn	0.4160	**0.5170**	0.5141	**0.5286**	0.5178
liaQEWikiGoo	0.4725	**0.5548**	0.5440	**0.5490**	0.5430
srchvrs11b	0.5546	**0.5624**	0.5618	**0.5842**	0.5663
UAmsM705tiLS	0.5298	**0.5648**	0.5342	**0.5635**	0.5527
uogTrB47Vm	0.5691	0.5375	**0.5405**	**0.5795**	0.5376
uwBBadhoc	0.4731	**0.5397**	0.5327	**0.5788**	0.5418
uogTrB67	0.4178	**0.4310**	0.4265	**0.4674**	0.4330

the diversification performance – i.e. they can even outperform a uniform Best λ setting.

Indeed, there are other factors that may affect and potentially improve the diversification performance, such as the normalization of $rel(d, q)$ and $rel(d, q_i)$ scores, and setting the subtopic probabilities, $P(q_i|q)$. For the former component, Santos [18] employs a strategy that is again based on sum-normalization yet yields strict probability values for $P(d|q)$ and $P(d|q_i)$, while Ozdemiray and Altingovde [14] propose an alternative normalization strategy that improves the diversification effectiveness. It is also shown that exploiting the score distribution of candidate documents for each subtopic yields more accurate estimation of subtopic probabilities and subsequently, higher diversification performance [13]. With such optimizations, even more runs in Table 5 could have yielded statistically significant improvements; yet this direction is not explored here and left as a future work.

Our findings in this section imply that the diversification methods in question may still significantly improve the strong baselines as they do for the weaker ones. However, one might need to be more rigorous and careful tuning of the parameters in the case of strong baselines in comparison to applying them over the weaker baselines. This is contradictory to the claim by Kharazmi et al. in [7], that additivity "almost never" occurs for such diversification methods for strong baselines. Although it is preferable/recommendable to choose the stronger baselines whenever available, significant improvements over reasonable baselines may still be indicative, as well. Note that we still strongly encourage the use of a stronger baseline whenever available, as the actual improvements over the latter, albeit significant or not, would make more sense in real-world applications. We simply show that when such baselines are not available, using a medium level baseline is still viable.

5 DISCUSSION: IMPACT OF DOCUMENT-SUBTOPIC RELEVANCE

While we use BM25 to compute $rel(d, q_i)$ in the experiments of Section 4, this might be an important simplification, and the overall performance of the diversification methods (both metric scores and their statistical significance) could be increased by computing

such scores using the exact retrieval function used to compute the document-subtopic relevance score $rel(d, q)$.

Indeed, in a report on their TREC 2010 Web track participation using xQuAD, Santos et al. [23] showed that deploying a supervised learning-to-rank approach for both $rel(d, q)$ and $rel(d, q_i)$ could result in increased diversification effectiveness, as measured by α-nDCG, while outperforming the corresponding learned baseline run by 6%. On the other hand, using learning-to-rank only for $rel(d, q)$ within xQuAD only improved the baseline by 3.4%. As no significance tests were conducted in [23], this admittedly anecdotal evidence suggests that using strong baselines for both $rel(d, q)$ and $rel(d, q_i)$ are important for properly attaining the highest effectiveness, a point not considered by [7].

To further investigate the impact of the $rel(d, q_i)$ component would involve implementing all of the adhoc retrieval methods used in the baseline runs – unfortunately an unfeasible task. Instead, to illustrate the impact, we undertake the reverse, and for the top-100 documents of each run, we also compute the $rel(d, q)$ component using the typical BM25 function (i.e., in effect, once the top 100 candidate documents are obtained from the corresponding TREC adhoc run, we only use BM25 for diversification). Interestingly, Kharazmi et al. also applied this strategy [8] (i.e., computed both components $rel(d, q)$ and $rel(d, q_i)$ using BM25), and hence our analysis here may also help for shedding light on their findings in [7].

We experiment with the trade-off parameter computed as globally and locally, as in Section 4, and focus only on the strong baselines (wrt. α-nDCG), as the others are improved anyway. Table 6 shows that for both ways of setting λ, using the original scores of the run for the $rel(d, q)$ component almost always yields better α-nDCG scores (i.e., 18 out of 20 cases) and furthermore, for 7 (of 10) strong runs the highest scores are obtained by using their original scores together with the Local λ values, confirming the findings in the previous section. More interestingly, even with the Local or Best λ values, the percentage of statistically significant improvements over the non-diversified baseline is very low (i.e., 3/10) when BM25 is employed instead of the original scores (see Table 7). We believe that this latter observation further explains the low number of significant improvements for strong runs in [7]. Given the impact of the $rel(d, q)$ function in this setup, we argue

Table 7: Ratio of strong runs that are significantly improved (wrt. α-nDCG) using XQuAD (with Global, Local and Best λs) and $rel(d, q)$ computed using the original scores or BM25.

Diversity method	Global $\lambda = 0.90$		Local λ		Best λ	
	Original+BM25	BM25+BM25	Original+BM25	BM25+BM25	Original+BM25	BM25+BM25
xQuAD	3/10	2/10	7/10	3/10	8/10	3/10
CombSum	3/10	2/10	6/10	3/10	7/10	3/10

that this provides further evidence that using a $rel(d, q_i)$ score that matches the $rel(d, q)$ score used by the actual run may further improve the diversification performance, and therefore change the conclusions concerning the additivity of these methods.

6 CONCLUSIONS

In this work, we considered the additivity of search result diversification methods in general, and in particular we reproduced the recent study of Kharazmi et al. [7] which applied diversification methods to the TREC baselines runs. Going further than [7], we showed that the setting of the relevance/diversity trade-off parameter λ is key to the overall conclusions of the experiments. Indeed, we found that additivity is more likely to occur when λ is set appropriately for each baseline run, especially for the stronger runs. Furthermore, we showed evidence that the mismatch of the retrieval models used to calculate the relevance of a document to a query (denoted $rel(d, q)$) and to its subtopics (denoted $rel(d, q_i)$) has the effect of underestimating the additivity of the diversification methods. Overall, we have identified and shown two confounding aspects of the experiments reported in [7], which raise questions about the authors' conclusion that the diversification methods "almost never" improve over strong baselines. In fact our study shows that with the appropriate automatic tuning of the parameters of the diversification methods for each of the strong baselines (as might be performed in a deployment setting), additivity is achievable.

ACKNOWLEDGMENTS

We are grateful to the authors of [7] for their timely and detailed responses to our inquiries regarding their work. We also thank to Rodrygo L. T. Santos for fruitful discussions. This work is partially funded by the Royal Society (UK) under the Newton International Exchanges Scheme with grant no. NI140231. I. S. Altingovde is also supported by Turkish Academy of Sciences Distinguished Young Scientist Award (TÜBA-GEBİP 2016).

REFERENCES

[1] Rakesh Agrawal, Sreenivas Gollapudi, Alan Halverson, and Samuel Ieong. 2009. Diversifying Search Results. In *Proceedings of WSDM*. 5–14.
[2] Timothy Armstrong, Alistair Moffat, William Webber, and Justin Zobel. 2009. Improvements that don't add up: ad-hoc retrieval results since 1998. In *Proceedings of CIKM*. 601–610.
[3] Van Dang and W. Bruce Croft. 2012. Diversity by proportionality: an election-based approach to search result diversification. In *Proceedings of SIGIR*. 65–74.
[4] Elena Demidova, Peter Fankhauser, Xuan Zhou, and Wolfgang Nejdl. 2010. *DivQ: diversification for keyword search over structured databases*. In *Proceedings of SIGIR*. 331–338.
[5] Joseph A. Fox and Edward Shaw. 1994. Combination of multiple sources: The TREC-2 interactive track matrix experiment. In *Proceedings of SIGIR*.
[6] Sreenivas Gollapudi and Aneesh Sharma. 2009. An Axiomatic Approach for Result Diversification. In *Proceedings of WWW*. 381–390.

[7] Sadegh Kharazmi, Falk Scholer, David Vallet, and Mark Sanderson. 2016. Examining Additivity and Weak Baselines. *Transactions on Information Systems* 34, 4 (2016), 23.
[8] Sadegh Kharazmi, Falk Scholer, David Vallet, and Mark Sanderson. 2017. Personal communication. (May 2017).
[9] Joon Ho Lee. 1997. Analyses of multiple evidence combination. In *Proceedings of SIGIR*. 267–276.
[10] Enrico Minack, Wolf Siberski, and Wolfgang Nejdl. 2011. Incremental diversification for very large sets: a streaming-based approach. In *Proceedings of SIGIR*. 585–594.
[11] Kaweh Djafari Naini, Ismail Sengor Altingovde, and Wolf Siberski. 2016. Scalable and Efficient Web Search Result Diversification. *Transactions on the Web* 10, 3 (2016), 15:1–15:30.
[12] Kezban Dilek Onal, Ismail Sengor Altingovde, and Pinar Karagoz. 2015. Utilizing Word Embeddings for Result Diversification in Tweet Search. In *Proceedings of AIRS*. 366–378.
[13] Ahmet Murat Ozdemiray and Ismail Sengor Altingovde. 2014. Query Performance Prediction for Aspect Weighting in Search Result Diversification. In *Proceedings of CIKM*. 1871–1874.
[14] Ahmet Murat Ozdemiray and Ismail Sengor Altingovde. 2015. Explicit search result diversification using score and rank aggregation methods. *JASIST* 66, 6 (2015), 1212–1228.
[15] Makbule Gulcin Ozsoy, Kezban Dilek Onal, and Ismail Sengor Altingovde. 2014. Result Diversification for Tweet Search. In *Proceedings of WISE*. 78–89.
[16] Monica Lestari Paramita, Jiayu Tang, and Mark Sanderson. 2009. Generic and Spatial Approaches to Image Search Results Diversification. In *Proceedings of ECIR*. 603–610.
[17] Stephen Robertson and Hugo Zaragoza. 2009. The Probabilistic Relevance Framework: BM25 and Beyond. *Foundations and Trends in Information Retrieval* 3, 4 (2009), 333–389.
[18] Rodrygo L. T. Santos. 2013. *Explicit web search result diversification*. Ph.D. Dissertation. University of Glasgow.
[19] Rodrygo L. T. Santos, Craig Macdonald, and Iadh Ounis. 2010. Exploiting query reformulations for web search result diversification. In *Proceedings of WWW*. 881–890.
[20] Rodrygo L. T. Santos, Craig Macdonald, and Iadh Ounis. 2010. Selectively diversifying web search results. In *Proceedings of CIKM*. 1179–1188.
[21] Rodrygo L. T. Santos, Craig Macdonald, and Iadh Ounis. 2011. Intent-aware search result diversification. In *Proceedings of SIGIR*. 595–604.
[22] Rodrygo L. T. Santos, Craig Macdonald, and Iadh Ounis. 2015. Search Result Diversification. *Foundations and Trends in Information Retrieval* 9, 1 (2015), 1–90.
[23] Rodrygo L. T. Santos, Richard McCreadie, Craig Macdonald, and Iadh Ounis. 2010. University of Glasgow at TREC 2010: Experiments with Terrier in Blog and Web Tracks. In *Proceedings of TREC*.
[24] Rodrygo L. T. Santos, Jie Peng, Craig Macdonald, and Iadh Ounis. 2010. Explicit Search Result Diversification through Sub-queries. In *Proceedings of ECIR*. 87–99.
[25] David Vallet, Martin Halvey, Joemon M. Jose, and Pablo Castells. 2011. Applying soft links to diversify video recommendations. In *Proceedings of CBMI*. 73–78.
[26] Reinier H. van Leuken, Lluis Garcia Pueyo, Ximena Olivares, and Roelof van Zwol. 2009. Visual diversification of image search results. In *Proceedings of WWW*. 341–350.
[27] Saúl Vargas, Linas Baltrunas, Alexandros Karatzoglou, and Pablo Castells. 2014. Coverage, redundancy and size-awareness in genre diversity for recommender systems. In *Proceedings of RecSys*. 209–216.
[28] Saul Vargas and Pablo Castells. 2011. Rank and relevance in novelty and diversity metrics for recommender systems. In *Proceedings of RecSys*. 109–116.
[29] Saul Vargas, Pablo Castells, and David Vallet. 2012. Explicit relevance models in intent-oriented information retrieval diversification. In *Proceedings of SIGIR*. 75–84.
[30] Zettair. 2016. Zettair open-source search engine. http://www.seg.rmit.edu.au/zettair/. (2016).

Kullback-Leibler Divergence Revisited

Fiana Raiber
Yahoo Research, Israel
fiana@yahoo-inc.com

Oren Kurland
Technion, Israel
kurland@ie.technion.ac.il

ABSTRACT

The KL divergence is the most commonly used measure for comparing query and document language models in the language modeling framework to ad hoc retrieval. Since KL is rank equivalent to a specific weighted geometric mean, we examine alternative weighted means for language-model comparison, as well as alternative divergence measures. The study includes analysis of the inverse document frequency (IDF) effect of the language-model comparison methods. Empirical evaluation, performed with different types of queries (short and verbose) and query-model induction approaches, shows that there are methods that often outperform the KL divergence in some settings.

KEYWORDS

language models, weighted geometric mean

1 INTRODUCTION

Comparing a language model induced from the query with that induced from the document is a standard ranking approach in the language modeling framework to ad hoc document retrieval [20]. The Kullback-Leibler (KL) divergence has been the most commonly used measure for language-model comparison, as it is a natural choice for comparing probability distributions.

The KL divergence is rank equivalent to the cross entropy measure [20] which is in turn rank equivalent to a specific weighted geometric mean [19, 20]: that of the probabilities assigned to terms in the support of the query model[1] by the document language model; the probabilities assigned to these terms by the query language model serve as weights in the mean. Given the rank equivalence between the KL divergence and this weighted geometric mean, we study alternative weighted means for comparing the query and document language models; namely, the arithmetic and harmonic means, integrations of these with the geometric mean, and generalized versions of the means. In addition, we study alternative divergence measures.

Since using the KL divergence for ranking has an IDF (inverse document frequency) effect, we study this effect for the alternative language-model-comparison methods that we consider. The IDF effect holds if the impact of a term on the retrieval score becomes smaller when its corpus frequency increases.

---

[1]The support is the set of terms assigned a non-zero probability by the language model.

ICTIR '17, October 1–4, 2017, Amsterdam, The Netherlands
© 2017 ACM. ISBN 978-1-4503-4490-6/17/10...$15.00
DOI: http://dx.doi.org/10.1145/3121050.3121062

We perform extensive empirical evaluation of the various measures for comparing query and document language models using five TREC datasets. We vary the types of queries used (short titles vs. verbose descriptions+titles) and the query-model induction approach: unsmoothed maximum likelihood estimate (MLE) vs. pseudo-feedback-based query-model induction; specifically, we use the relevance model [21] and the mixture model [31].

We found that there are measures that can often outperform the KL divergence for certain types of queries and query-model induction methods. For example, the Power mean [6], which generalizes the harmonic and arithmetic means, and which under certain conditions converges to the geometric mean, outperforms the KL divergence when using MLEs induced from short title queries or pseudo-feedback-based query models. When using MLEs induced from verbose queries, KL is the best performing.

Our key contributions can be summarized as follows:

- We study various weighted means and divergence measures for comparing query and document language models; our study includes analysis of the IDF effect.
- We perform an extensive empirical evaluation and demonstrate that in some settings there are measures that often outperform the commonly used KL divergence.

2 RELATED WORK

Most work on using language models for ad hoc retrieval has focused on improving the language models induced from the query and a document rather than on the measure used to compare them [30]. There are studies of using various divergence measures to compare language models in natural-language-processing tasks; e.g. [23]. However, we are not aware of such in-depth studies for the ad hoc retrieval task. In contrast, document-query similarity estimates were compared in the vector space model [33].

The use of KL divergence for ad hoc retrieval was formally supported in [25]. KL was also shown to outperform a document likelihood approach for relevance-model-based ranking [21]. We show that there are measures more effective than KL for that end.

Axiomatic analysis of retrieval methods in the language modeling framework focused on the query likelihood model [14], translation models [18] and pseudo-feedback-based query models and their smoothing [9, 15]. For example, term frequency, document frequency and document length axioms have been devised and their empirical merits were demonstrated. In contrast, we evaluate different measures for comparing a query model with a document model and analyze whether they have an IDF effect.

3 COMPARING QUERY AND DOCUMENT LANGUAGE MODELS

We address the ad hoc retrieval task: ranking documents d in corpus $\mathcal{D}$ in response to query q. Let θ_q and θ_d denote the unigram language models induced from q and d, respectively. Henceforth, these are referred to as query and document (language) models, respectively. Various language-model induction methods have been used in work on ad hoc retrieval [30].

To rank documents in the corpus, the document and query language models can be compared [20]. Since the language models are probability distributions defined over the vocabulary, a natural similarity measure, which is the most commonly used in work on ad hoc retrieval, is the Kullback-Leibler (KL) divergence. As higher KL values correspond to decreased similarity, the negative KL divergence is used:

$$-KL(\theta_q, \theta_d) \overset{def}{=} -\sum_w p(w|\theta_q) \log \frac{p(w|\theta_q)}{p(w|\theta_d)} = H(\theta_q) - CE(\theta_q, \theta_d). \tag{1}$$

$H(\theta_q) \overset{def}{=} -\sum_w p(w|\theta_q) \log p(w|\theta_q)$ is the entropy of the query language model and $CE(\theta_q, \theta_d) \overset{def}{=} -\sum_w p(w|\theta_q) \log p(w|\theta_d)$ is the cross entropy between the query and document models. (As is the case for KL, higher values of CE correspond to decreased similarity.) Hereinafter, summations as that in Eq. 1 are applied only over terms w for which $p(w|\theta_q) > 0$ [21]; i.e., terms in the *support* of the query language model. Since the entropy of the query model does not affect ranking, KL and CE are rank equivalent: $KL(\theta_q, \theta_d) \overset{rank}{=} CE(\theta_q, \theta_d)$.

If an unsmoothed maximum likelihood estimate (MLE) is used for the query language model, then ranking produced using -CE (and therefore using -KL) is equivalent to that produced using the query likelihood method [20, 29]. Formally, $p(w|\theta_x^{MLE}) \overset{def}{=} \frac{\text{tf}(w \in x)}{|x|}$ is the MLE of term w with respect to the text (or text collection) x where $\text{tf}(w \in x)$ is the number of occurrences of w in x; $|x| \overset{def}{=} \sum_{w \in x} \text{tf}(w \in x)$ is x's length. Then, the following holds:

$$-CE(\theta_q^{MLE}, \theta_d) = \sum_w p(w|\theta_q^{MLE}) \log p(w|\theta_d) \tag{2}$$

$$= \frac{1}{|q|} \log \prod_w p(w|\theta_d)^{\text{tf}(w \in q)};$$

$\prod_w p(w|\theta_d)^{\text{tf}(w \in q)}$ is q's likelihood with respect to d.

3.1 The IDF Effect

An important implication of the rank equivalence between (negative) cross entropy used with a query MLE and the query likelihood method is the *IDF effect*. That is, Zhai and Lafferty [32] showed that for query likelihood, the effect of query terms on ranking is inversely related to their corpus frequency. Hence, this IDF (inverse document frequency) effect also governs ranking using cross entropy (and KL) with a query MLE.

An interesting question which was somewhat overlooked in past literature is whether using KL or CE with query models which are not maximum likelihood estimates results in an IDF effect.[2] Indeed, while MLE is the standard choice for inducing a query model using only the query terms, there are query models with a much broader support, e.g., pseudo-feedback-based query models [21, 31].

---

[2]In contrast, there has been work on the importance of selecting and increasing the probability in the query language model of terms with high IDF values (e.g., [9, 15]).

We now show that regardless of the query model utilized, using CE (and hence KL) for ranking results in an IDF effect. The formal argument is similar to that used to demonstrate the IDF effect for the query likelihood model [32]. We provide the details so as to later on contrast the IDF effect entailed by using KL and CE with that entailed by using alternative measures studied below.

We assume a standard smoothed unigram document language model θ_d. For the two most commonly used smoothing methods in work on ad hoc retrieval, Dirichlet and Jelinek-Mercer [32], the document language model is $\theta_d \overset{def}{=} (1 - \alpha_d)\theta_d^{MLE} + \alpha_d \theta_{\mathcal{D}}^{MLE}$; for Dirichlet, $\alpha_d = \frac{\mu}{|d|+\mu}$ where μ is a parameter; for Jelinek-Mercer, α_d is simply a constant. For $w \in d$ we define $p_s(w|\theta_d) \overset{def}{=} p(w|\theta_d) = (1-\alpha_d)p(w|\theta_d^{MLE}) + \alpha_d p(w|\theta_{\mathcal{D}}^{MLE})$. For $w \notin d$, we define $p_u(w|\theta_d) \overset{def}{=} p(w|\theta_d) = \alpha_d p(w|\theta_{\mathcal{D}}^{MLE})$; 's' and 'u' stand for "seen" and "unseen", respectively [32]. The negative CE is then:

$$-CE(\theta_q, \theta_d) = \sum_w p(w|\theta_q) \log p(w|\theta_d) \tag{3a}$$

$$= \sum_{w \in d} p(w|\theta_q) \log p_s(w|\theta_d) + \sum_{w \notin d} p(w|\theta_q) \log p_u(w|\theta_d) \tag{3b}$$

$$= \sum_{w \in d} p(w|\theta_q) \log \frac{p_s(w|\theta_d)}{p_u(w|\theta_d)} + \sum_w p(w|\theta_q) \log p_u(w|\theta_d) \tag{3c}$$

$$= \sum_{w \in d} p(w|\theta_q) \log \frac{p_s(w|\theta_d)}{\alpha_d p(w|\theta_{\mathcal{D}}^{MLE})} + \log \alpha_d - CE(\theta_q, \theta_{\mathcal{D}}^{MLE}) \tag{3d}$$

$$\overset{rank}{=} \sum_{w \in d} p(w|\theta_q) \log \left(1 + \frac{1 - \alpha_d}{\alpha_d} \frac{p(w|\theta_d^{MLE})}{p(w|\theta_{\mathcal{D}}^{MLE})}\right) + \log \alpha_d \tag{3e}$$

The transitions are based on separating groups of indices (Eq. 3b), ignoring document independent factors for ranking (Eq. 3e) and using definitions and arithmetic manipulations.

The summation in Eq. 3e is over terms in the query-model support that appear in d. It constitutes the "document-query match" which is based on the probability of query terms in the query ($p(w|\theta_q)$), document ($p(w|\theta_d^{MLE})$) and corpus ($p(w|\theta_{\mathcal{D}}^{MLE})$) models. The latter yields the "IDF effect" as it regularizes the impact of term occurrence in the document by occurrence in the corpus. Document length is used as a normalizer in $p(w|\theta_d^{MLE})$. If Dirichlet smoothing is applied, then α_d also (inversely) depends on document length.

3.2 Weighted Means

The negative cross entropy amounts to (cf. [19, 20]):

$$-CE(\theta_q, \theta_d) = \sum_w p(w|\theta_q) \log p(w|\theta_d) \overset{rank}{=} \prod_w p(w|\theta_d)^{p(w|\theta_q)}.$$

That is, negative CE is rank equivalent to a weighted geometric mean (henceforth **Geo**), $Geo(\theta_d; \theta_q)$, of the probabilities assigned to terms in θ_q's support by the document model θ_d; the probabilities assigned by θ_q serve as weights whose sum is 1.

The view of (negative) CE as a weighted geometric mean gives rise to the question, which to the best of our knowledge this paper is the first to explore, of whether using other means to compare the query and document language models can improve retrieval effectiveness. There are numerous weighted means (e.g., [4, 6]). In what follows we mainly focus on the three classical and most widely used means: arithmetic, geometric and harmonic, their integrations and generalizations. Table 1 presents the weighted means we study.

All these means, as well as the divergence measures we discuss in Section 3.3, include a "query-document match" component[3] which relies on occurrence of terms from the query model support in the document; document length normalizes this occurrence since MLE-based estimates are used. Hence, in addition to discussing general properties of the means and divergence measures, we study whether their query-document match component has an IDF effect. Analyzing more complicated connections between document length, IDF and term frequency (cf. [14]) is left for future work.

The weighted arithmetic mean (**Ari**) is less "conservative" than the weighted geometric mean applied by CE; i.e., it is less affected by outliers. Specifically, a low probability assigned by a document model to one of the terms in the query model support incurs higher penalty in Geo than in Ari. Using manipulations similar to those in Eq. 3, Ari amounts to:

$$Ari(\theta_d; \theta_q) \overset{rank}{=} (1 - \alpha_d) \sum_{w \in d} p(w|\theta_q) p(w|\theta_d^{MLE}) +$$
$$\alpha_d \sum_w p(w|\theta_q) p(w|\theta_D^{MLE}) .$$

The document-query match (the first summation) has no IDF effect.

The weighted harmonic mean (**Har**), which is more conservative than Geo, is the third classical mean. Using manipulations similar to those in Eq. 3, we arrive at:

$$Har(\theta_d; \theta_q) \overset{rank}{=} \Big(\sum_{w \in d} \frac{(\alpha_d - 1)p(w|\theta_q)p(w|\theta_d^{MLE})}{\alpha_d p_s(w|\theta_d)p(w|\theta_D^{MLE})}$$
$$+ \frac{1}{\alpha_d} \sum_w \frac{p(w|\theta_q)}{p(w|\theta_D^{MLE})} \Big)^{-1} .$$

The document-query match (first summation) has an IDF effect since $\alpha_d < 1$ and $p_s(w|\theta_d)$ increases with increasing values of corpus frequency. Note that the second summation has an "inverse" IDF effect (i.e., DF effect) which can be considered a drawback of Har: the more frequent a query term in the corpus, the higher the retrieval score.[4] However, if α_d is the same for all documents, then the second summation has no effect on ranking, and the entire retrieval score (used to rank documents) exhibits an IDF effect as was the case for the KL divergence in the transition from Eq. 3d to Eq. 3e . Indeed, using Jelinek-Mercer smoothing or assuming equal document lengths in analyzing the IDF effect yields a constant α_d. Using the equal document lengths assumption is in line with Fang and Zhai's methodology of analyzing the IDF effect [13]: assuming two documents of the same length, the document with more occurrences of query terms that are less frequent in the corpus should receive a higher retrieval score. Accordingly, hereinafter, and as mentioned above, our analysis of means and divergence measures will focus on whether the query-document match has an IDF effect.

The next two means integrate the geometric mean employed by negative CE with the arithmetic mean (**GeoAri**) and the harmonic mean (**GeoHar**). These means are computed in iterations that are guaranteed to converge. In the first iteration, $i = 1$, we initialize $g_1 = Geo(\theta_d; \theta_q)$, $a_1 = Ari(\theta_d; \theta_q)$ and $h_1 = Har(\theta_d; \theta_q)$. Then, for

Table 1: Weighted means. β and γ are free parameters.

M	$M(\theta_d; \theta_q)$	IDF Effect
Ari	$\sum_w p(w|\theta_q)p(w|\theta_d)$	✗
Har	$\left(\sum_w \frac{p(w|\theta_q)}{p(w|\theta_d)} \right)^{-1}$	✓
GeoAri	Integration of $Geo(\theta_d; \theta_q)$ and $Ari(\theta_d; \theta_q)$	✓
GeoHar	Integration of $Geo(\theta_d; \theta_q)$ and $Har(\theta_d; \theta_q)$	✓
Power	$\left(\sum_w p(w|\theta_q)p(w|\theta_d)^\beta \right)^{\frac{1}{\beta}}$	$\beta < 1$
Lehmer	$\frac{\sum_w p(w|\theta_q)p(w|\theta_d)^\gamma}{\sum_w p(w|\theta_q)p(w|\theta_d)^{\gamma-1}}$	$0 \leq \gamma < 1$

GeoAri, in iteration $i + 1$ we set $g_{i+1} = \sqrt{a_i g_i}$ and $a_{i+1} = \frac{1}{2}(a_i + g_i)$ until g_{i+1} and a_{i+1} converge to the same value.[5] Similarly, for GeoHar, we compute $g_{i+1} = \sqrt{h_i g_i}$ and $h_{i+1} = 2(h_i^{-1} + g_i^{-1})^{-1}$ until convergence.[6] Since Geo and Har have the IDF effect, and Ari does not, GeoHar has the effect while GeoAri has it to a somewhat limited extent. The following inequality holds for the means considered thus far:

$$Ari(\theta_d; \theta_q) \geq GeoAri(\theta_d; \theta_q) \geq Geo(\theta_d; \theta_q)$$
$$\geq GeoHar(\theta_d; \theta_q) \geq Har(\theta_d; \theta_q) .$$

The weighted **Power** mean is essentially a family of means that covers a wide range of aggregates bounded by the minimal and maximal values aggregated: $\lim_{\beta \to -\infty} Power(\theta_d; \theta_q) = \min_w p(w|\theta_d)$ and $\lim_{\beta \to \infty} Power(\theta_d; \theta_q) = \max_w p(w|\theta_d)$. For $\beta = 1$ and $\beta = -1$ Power amounts to the arithmetic and harmonic means, respectively. Furthermore, $\lim_{\beta \to 0} Power(\theta_d; \theta_q) = Geo(\theta_d; \theta_q)$. (Recall that Geo and negative CE are rank equivalent.) Using a similar transition to that from Eq. 3b to Eq. 3c it can be shown that the query-document match component in Power has an IDF effect for $\beta < 1$. In Section 4.2 we show that β close to 0 yields the best retrieval performance which also often transcends that of using Geo (CE).

As additional reference comparison we consider **Lehmer**, which is a special case of the Gini family of means [4]. For $\gamma = 1$ and $\gamma = 0$, Lehmer amounts to the arithmetic and harmonic means, respectively. It can be shown that the query-document match component in Lehmer has an IDF effect for $0 \leq \gamma < 1$, but not for $1 \leq \gamma \leq 2$. The analysis for $\gamma < 0$ and $\gamma > 2$ is quite involved and might require numerical simulation as the query-document match component and document-independent factor have mutual effects.

3.3 Divergence Measures

KL is a measure of the divergence between two probability distributions — query and document language models in our case. We therefore now turn to examine alternative divergence measures. These measures, presented in Table 2, were used in a variety of tasks, including term co-occurrence estimation [23], topic-based document segmentation [5], story link detection [7], query performance prediction [3] and static index pruning [8]. We rank documents by ascending values of the divergence measures.

---

[3]Other components are document-independent or α_d; sometimes, these two interact.
[4]This is also the case for the second summation in Ari.

[5]g_{i+1} is the geometric mean of g_i and a_i, while a_{i+1} is their arithmetic mean.
[6]g_{i+1} is the geometric mean of g_i and h_i, while h_{i+1} is their harmonic mean.

Table 2: Divergence measures. $p(w|\theta_{qd}^{[\eta]}) \stackrel{def}{=} \eta p(w|\theta_q) + (1 - \eta)p(w|\theta_d)$; η **is a free parameter.**

D	$D(\theta_q, \theta_d)$	IDF Effect
Hellinger	$\sqrt{\sum_w \left(\sqrt{p(w|\theta_q)} - \sqrt{p(w|\theta_d)}\right)^2}$	✓
TotalVariation	$\sum_w |p(w|\theta_q) - p(w|\theta_d)|$	✗
JensenShannon	$KL(\theta_q, \theta_{qd}^{[\eta]}) + KL(\theta_d, \theta_{qd}^{[\eta]})$; $\eta = \frac{1}{2}$	✓
J	$KL(\theta_q, \theta_d) + KL(\theta_d, \theta_q)$	✓
ResistorAverage	$\left(KL(\theta_q, \theta_d)^{-1} + KL(\theta_d, \theta_q)^{-1}\right)^{-1}$	✓
χ^2Neyman	$\sum_w \frac{(p(w|\theta_q)-p(w|\theta_d))^2}{p(w|\theta_d)}$	✓
χ^2Pearson	$\sum_w \frac{(p(w|\theta_q)-p(w|\theta_d))^2}{p(w|\theta_q)}$	✓
χ^2Symmetric	$\sum_w \frac{(p(w|\theta_q))-p(w|\theta_d))^2}{p(w|\theta_q)+p(w|\theta_d)}$	✓
Skew	$KL(\theta_q, \theta_{qd}^{[\eta]})$	✓

Most of the measures we consider are special cases of the f-divergence [11][7]. Given a convex function f defined over $(0, \infty)$ such that $f(1) = 0$, the f-divergence between θ_q and θ_d is:

$$\sum_w p(w|\theta_d) f\left(\frac{p(w|\theta_q)}{p(w|\theta_d)}\right).$$

Different choices of f result in different divergence measures. For example, setting $f(x) = x \log x$ results in the KL divergence, setting $f(x) = (1 - \sqrt{x})^2$ yields the **Hellinger** divergence, and setting $f(x) = |x - 1|$ results in the **TotalVariation** distance.

Some of the measures we consider are not metrics as they do not satisfy at least one of the following properties: non-negativity, identity of indiscernibles[8], symmetry and triangle inequality. KL divergence, for example, is not a metric since symmetry and triangle inequality do not hold. TotalVariation, on the other hand, is a metric satisfying all four properties.

Numerous symmetric versions of the KL divergence were proposed. These include **JensenShannon** [24] (defined using the mean language model of θ_q and θ_d), **J** [16] and **ResistorAverage** [17]. The J divergence is not a metric despite being symmetric since the triangle inequality does not hold. The square root of the Jensen-Shannon divergence is a metric.[9]

Three additional instances of the f-divergence are the asymmetric χ^2**Neyman** [26] and χ^2**Pearson** [27], where $\chi^2 Pearson(\theta_q, \theta_d) = \chi^2 Neyman(\theta_d, \theta_q)$, and their symmetric version χ^2**Symmetric**. The functions f in f-divergence that yield these three measures are $f(x) = \frac{(x-1)^2}{x}$, $f(x) = (1 - x)^2$ and $f(x) = \frac{(x-1)^2}{x+1}$, respectively.

The **Skew** divergence [22, 23] was proposed to address cases where $KL(\theta_x, \theta_y)$ is not defined because the support of θ_x is not a subset of the support of θ_y. In our case, $KL(\theta_q, \theta_d)$ is defined since smoothed document language models are used.

We next make a few observations about the IDF effect in the query-document match components of the divergence measures. It can be shown that Hellinger, χ^2Neyman, χ^2Pearson and χ^2Symmetric

exhibit the IDF effect. (More precisely, since we rank by ascending order of divergence values, the negative divergence measures exhibit, or not, the IDF effect.) In contrast, it is easy to verify that TotalVariation does not have an IDF effect.

For the negative J divergence, the negative $KL(\theta_q, \theta_d)$ employs an IDF effect since it is rank equivalent to $-CE(\theta_q, \theta_d)$ (see Eq. 1) and negative CE employs an IDF effect as shown in Eq. 3e. To estimate $-KL(\theta_d, \theta_q)$, we use an unsmoothed MLE for the document model and a query model smoothed via Jelinek-Mercer with the corpus (with parameter α_q), denoted θ_q^s. (See Section 4.1 for further details.) Using the fact that $KL(\theta_d^{MLE}, \theta_q^s) = -H(\theta_d^{MLE}) + CE(\theta_d^{MLE}, \theta_q^s)$, and applying manipulations as in Eq. 3, we get:

$$-KL(\theta_d^{MLE}, \theta_q^s) \stackrel{rank}{=} \sum_w p(w|\theta_d^{MLE}) \log\left(1 + \frac{1-\alpha_q}{\alpha_q} \frac{p(w|\theta_q)}{p(w|\theta_{\mathcal{D}}^{MLE})}\right)$$
$$+ \log \alpha_q - KL(\theta_d^{MLE}, \theta_{\mathcal{D}}^{MLE});$$

the summation is over w that are in both d and θ_q's support. High values of $p(w|\theta_{\mathcal{D}}^{MLE})$ reduce the value of the document-query match (the summation), and hence there is an IDF effect. This effect is somewhat counter balanced by the fact that documents with models similar to that of the corpus, i.e., with low $KL(\theta_d^{MLE}, \theta_{\mathcal{D}}^{MLE})$, are rewarded. Overall, since $-KL(\theta_q, \theta_d)$ and $-KL(\theta_d, \theta_q)$ have an IDF effect in their query-document match components, so does (negative) J divergence.

Using similar arguments to those used for the J divergence, we can show that ResistorAverage has an IDF effect. Along the same lines, the KL divergence factors that constitute JensenShannon and Skew have an IDF effect. However, in both measures, higher values of η make $\theta_{qd}^{[\eta]}$ more similar to θ_q. This causes loss of information about the original differences between θ_q and θ_d.

4 EMPIRICAL EXPLORATION

Our next goal is studying the retrieval effectiveness of using the different measures discussed above for comparing document and query language models.

4.1 Experimental Setup

The five datasets used for experiments are specified in Table 3. AP and ROBUST are small, mostly newswire, collections; GOV2 is a crawl of the .gov domain and CW09B is the Category B of the ClueWeb09 collection. An additional dataset, CW09BF, was created for ClueWeb09 Category B by filtering out from the initial document ranking documents assigned with a score below 50 by Waterloo's spam classifier [10]. Further details about the initial ranking are provided below. Unless stated otherwise, topic titles, which are short, served for queries. In Section 4.2.3 we also present evaluation when using verbose queries composed of both the title and description. We applied Krovetz stemming to documents and queries and removed stopwords on the INQUERY list only from queries. The Indri toolkit[10] was used for experiments.

We used a two-phase retrieval approach to compare the effectiveness of the different measures discussed in Section 3. In the first phase, an initial list of documents is retrieved using $KL(\theta_q, \theta_d)$,

---

[7]Also know as the Ali-Silvey distance [2].
[8]For metric D and a pair of models θ_x and θ_y, $D(\theta_x, \theta_y) = 0$ iff $\theta_x = \theta_y$.
[9]The f functions in f-divergence that yield the J and JensenShannon divergence are $f(x) = (x - 1) \log x$ and $f(x) = \frac{1}{2} \log \frac{2}{1+x} + \frac{1}{2} x \log \frac{2x}{1+x}$, respectively.

[10]www.lemurproject.org/indri

Table 3: TREC data used for experiments.

corpus	# documents	data	queries
AP	242,918	Disks 1 – 3	51 – 150
ROBUST	528,155	Disks 4 – 5 (–CR)	301 – 450, 600 – 700
GOV2	25,205,179	GOV2	701 – 850
CW09B CW09BF	50,220,423	ClueWeb09 Category B	1 – 200

where an unsmoothed unigram language model, specifically, a maximum likelihood estimate (**MLE**), is used to induce θ_q as is standard [20]. In the second phase, $M(\theta_d; \theta_q)$ or $D(\theta_q, \theta_d)$ is used to re-rank the 10000 most highly ranked documents in the initial ranking, where M and D are the weighted mean and divergence measures presented in Section 3, respectively. We take a re-ranking approach since applying numerous configurations of query expansion upon large-scale corpora is computationally expensive. For a uniform experimental setting, this approach is used in all cases even if query expansion is not employed. It is important to note that re-ranking an initial list of documents was shown to yield similar performance to ranking the entire corpus for pseudo-feedback query expansion which we use here, especially for precision-oriented evaluation metrics [12]. We further note that performance patterns similar to those reported here were also observed in experiments with re-ranking a shorter list of 1000 documents. (Actual numbers are omitted as they convey no additional insight.)

We use three query-model induction methods in the second phase. The first utilizes unsmoothed MLE induced from the original query as was the case in the first phase.[11] The additional two models are relevance model #3 (**RM3** [1, 21]) and the mixture model (**MM** [31]). For these two models, θ_q is induced from the top 50 ranked documents in the initial list. The resultant query language models are (much) richer than— i.e., their support is much larger than that of — the one induced using MLE from a short query; these query models represent expanded queries of the short title query.

The document model θ_d is in both phases a Dirichlet-smoothed unigram language model with the smoothing parameter μ=1000 [32]. Since the document model is smoothed, $KL(\theta_q, \theta_d)$ is always well defined (i.e., the support of θ_q is a subset of the support of θ_d). In contrast, $KL(\theta_d, \theta_q)$, which is used in J and ResistorAverage, might be undefined if the support of θ_d is not a subset of the support of θ_q. We took the following two approaches to address this issue: (i) applied Jelinek-Mercer smoothing [32] with $\lambda = 0.1$ to θ_q, or (ii) considered only terms that appear in the support of both θ_q and θ_d. The document model is unsmoothed in both cases, i.e., θ_d^{MLE} is used.[12] For the J divergence, the first approach was found in our experiments to be more effective for short title queries and is therefore used in Section 4.2.1, while the second was found to be more effective for longer queries with a larger support and is used in Sections 4.2.2 and 4.2.3. For ResistorAverage, the first approach resulted in better performance in all cases. We note that the first approach entails an IDF effect for $-KL(\theta_d^{MLE}, \theta_q)$ (see Section 3.3) while the second does not.

To estimate retrieval effectiveness, we use mean average precision (**MAP**), precision of the top 5 ranked documents (**p@5**), normalized discounted cumulative gain of the top 20 ranked documents (**NDCG20**) and reliability of improvement (**RI**) [28]. RI is the difference between the number of queries whose AP performance is improved and the number of queries whose AP performance is hurt compared to the initial ranking divided by the total number of queries. Ten-fold cross validation is used to set free-parameter values where MAP serves for optimization in the training phase. Folds are determined based on query IDs. The reported performance is the average over all queries in a dataset when these serve for testing. (Each query belongs to a single test fold.) Statistically significant differences of retrieval performance between two methods are computed over all the queries in a dataset when these serve for testing. The two-tailed paired t-test with $p \leq 0.05$ is used.

To construct RM3 and MM, the number of terms and the weight of the original query are set to values in $\{25, 50\}$ and $\{0.1, 0.2, \ldots, 0.9\}$, respectively. Unsmoothed document language models (MLE) are used to induce RM3. The mixture weight of the corpus in MM is in $\{0.1, 0.3, 0.5, 0.7, 0.9\}$. The values of η (in Skew), β (in Power) and γ (in Lehmer) are selected from $\{0.1, 0.2, \ldots, 0.9\}$, $\{\pm 0.05, \pm 0.15, \pm 0.25, \pm 0.5, \pm 1, \pm 2, \pm 3, \pm 10\}$, and $\{0, \pm 0.05, \pm 0.15, \pm 0.25, \pm 0.5, \pm 1, \pm 2, \pm 3, \pm 10\}$, respectively.

4.2 Experimental Results

4.2.1 Short Queries. Table 4 presents the results of using the unsmoothed MLE query language model θ_q^{MLE} — i.e., only the terms in the original short query are assigned with a non-zero probability. We see that in most cases Power is the best performing measure. Power outperforms KL in 12 out of the 15 relevant comparisons for the MAP, p@5 and NDCG20 evaluation metrics (5 datasets × 3 evaluation metrics) and in 5 of these the improvement is statistically significant; Power is outperformed (but not statistically significantly) by KL in a single case (NDCG20 for ROBUST). Power is the only measure among those considered that is never statistically significantly outperformed by KL. It is also the only measure with positive RI values across all five datasets, indicating that the number of queries for which average precision performance is improved compared to the initial ranking (KL) is higher than the number of queries for which performance is hurt.

Two additional measures outperforming KL in the majority of the relevant comparisons are GeoHar (in 8 relevant comparisons; 4 are statistically significant) and Lehmer (in 9 relevant comparisons; 5 are statistically significant). All other measures are outperformed by KL in most relevant comparisons and many of the differences are statistically significant.

The descending order of the seven weighted means according to a pairwise comparison of retrieval effectiveness[13] is Power, Lehmer, GeoHar, KL (Geo), Har, GeoAri and Ari. The poor performance of Ari could be explained by the fact that it has no IDF effect as shown in Section 3.2. Har is worse than Geo potentially due to being too conservative. GeoAri improves over Ari but not over Geo while GeoHar improves over both Geo and Har, which attests to the merits of integrating these two means. Power and Lehmer rely

---

[11]Note that the document ranking produced using $KL(\theta_q, \theta_d)$ in the second phase is in this case the same as the initial ranking.

[12]This is also the case for $KL(\theta_d, \theta_{qd}^{[\eta]})$ in JensenShannon. We note that JensenShannon is always well defined since θ_q is smoothed with θ_d in $\theta_{qd}^{[\eta]}$.

[13]The order is determined by counting the number of relevant comparisons (out of the 15) in which a method outperforms another method.

Table 4: Short title queries. Using unsmoothed MLE to induce query models. Because the KL divergence is used to produce the initial ranking, its RI is undefined. 'Init': initial ranking. 'k': statistically significant difference of retrieval effectiveness (MAP, p@5 and NDCG20) with the KL divergence. The best result in a column is highlighted.

	AP				ROBUST				GOV2				CW09B				CW09BF			
	MAP	p@5	NDCG20	RI	MAP	p@5	NDCG20	RI	MAP	p@5	NDCG20	RI	MAP	p@5	NDCG20	RI	MAP	p@5	NDCG20	RI
KL (=Init)	21.1	43.6	42.6	–	25.4	48.7	43.9	–	29.2	55.5	44.5	–	17.9	22.7	20.1	–	18.7	34.7	25.8	–
Ari	10.5_k	24.6_k	24.4_k	-69.7	6.4_k	14.5_k	12.7_k	-83.5	7.0_k	9.6_k	9.1_k	-93.2	6.6_k	5.8_k	6.0_k	-66.7	7.3_k	13.2_k	9.7_k	-67.2
Har	15.5_k	39.4_k	35.8_k	-55.6	22.7_k	47.1	41.3_k	-36.5	26.5_k	57.0	44.4	-24.3	19.5_k	28.6_k	23.8_k	27.3	19.1	35.5	26.7	8.6
GeoAri	18.0_k	41.4	39.1_k	-35.4	16.0_k	37.8_k	32.4_k	-70.7	17.1_k	34.5_k	27.4_k	-87.8	10.0_k	8.6_k	9.2_k	-66.7	12.4_k	23.9_k	16.9_k	-63.1
GeoHar	17.2_k	41.0	37.7_k	-47.5	24.0_k	47.7	42.1_k	-24.1	28.0_k	57.2	45.3	-8.1	19.6_k	27.6_k	23.3_k	35.4	19.4	35.9	26.8_k	19.7
Power	21.2	45.1	42.6	19.2	25.5	48.9	43.8	5.2	29.2	55.8	44.9_k	23.0	19.8_k	27.9_k	23.6_k	37.4	19.2	35.6	26.7_k	19.7
Lehmer	20.8	44.2	41.6_k	-9.1	25.0_k	48.8	43.7	-7.6	29.0	55.4	44.7	10.8	19.5_k	28.0_k	23.4_k	31.8	19.4	36.0	26.8_k	20.7
Hellinger	17.7_k	41.8	39.3_k	-30.3	14.2_k	34.1_k	28.9_k	-73.5	14.3_k	29.7_k	23.1_k	-89.2	9.9_k	10.8_k	10.0_k	-66.7	11.9_k	23.6_k	16.3_k	-65.2
TotalVariation	10.5_k	24.6_k	24.4_k	-70.7	6.4_k	14.5_k	12.7_k	-83.1	7.0_k	9.6_k	9.1_k	-92.6	6.6_k	5.8_k	6.0_k	-66.2	7.3_k	13.2_k	9.7_k	-67.2
JensenShannon	10.6_k	32.3_k	28.1_k	-74.7	8.3_k	22.9_k	18.9_k	-80.3	4.3_k	10.0_k	8.3_k	-94.6	4.4_k	10.1_k	7.3_k	-88.4	3.9_k	13.4_k	8.3_k	-85.9
J	19.0_k	41.0	40.7_k	-40.4	23.0_k	47.9	42.0_k	-30.9	28.5	60.4_k	46.3	-12.2	17.9	23.9	21.6	5.6	19.4	39.1_k	28.4_k	2.5
ResistorAverage	14.7_k	40.0	36.6_k	-66.7	15.5_k	40.2_k	33.7_k	-74.3	23.1_k	56.4	42.6	-51.4	16.8	21.5	19.6	4.0	18.2	37.2	26.7	-4.5
χ^2Neyman	15.5_k	39.4_k	35.8_k	-55.6	22.7_k	47.1	41.3_k	-36.5	26.5_k	56.9	44.4	-24.3	19.5_k	28.6_k	23.8_k	27.3	19.1	35.5	26.7	8.6
χ^2Pearson	10.6_k	25.3_k	24.6_k	-69.7	6.5_k	14.9_k	13.0_k	-83.9	7.1_k	10.1_k	9.4_k	-92.6	6.6_k	6.1_k	6.2_k	-66.2	7.4_k	13.5_k	9.8_k	-66.7
χ^2Symmetric	10.7_k	26.7_k	25.4_k	-67.7	6.6_k	15.3_k	13.3_k	-82.7	7.3_k	11.1_k	10.2_k	-92.6	6.8_k	6.5_k	6.4_k	-66.7	7.5_k	13.9_k	10.1_k	-67.2
Skew	9.1_k	22.4_k	21.3_k	-84.8	6.4_k	15.7_k	13.6_k	-87.6	3.1_k	6.2_k	4.5_k	-95.9	4.1_k	8.8_k	6.5_k	-86.4	3.8_k	10.7_k	7.6_k	-89.4
Cosine	7.5_k	21.8_k	19.4_k	-83.8	10.1_k	19.2_k	18.1_k	-89.6	4.1_k	13.4_k	8.7_k	-95.9	1.5_k	5.6_k	3.5_k	-88.9	1.4_k	5.8_k	3.1_k	-88.9

on a free parameter in contrast to the other means — some of which they generalize as noted in Section 3.2. We further study the effect of β on the retrieval performance of Power in Section 4.2.5.

The descending order of the ten divergence measures according to a pairwise performance comparison is KL, χ^2Neyman, J, ResistorAverage, Hellinger, χ^2Symmetric, JensenShannon, χ^2Pearson, TotalVariation and Skew. TotalVariation is low ranked potentially because it does not have an IDF effect. Skew is low ranked (and to some extent also JensenShannon) potentially due to smoothing the document model with the query model. KL, χ^2Neyman, J and ResistorAverage are presumably among the top 4 as they all have an IDF effect.

4.2.2 Pseudo-Feedback-Based Query Models.

Table 5 presents the results of using RM3 and MM as the query language models. (The initial ranking was attained, as described in Section 4.1, using an unsmoothed MLE induced from the title queries.) These query language models are much richer than the unsmoothed MLE query models explored in Section 4.2.1 ; i.e., their support is much larger. Two measures that stand out are the J divergence and Power. The former outperforms KL in 8 relevant comparisons for RM3 and in 13 for MM, while the latter outperforms KL in 12 relevant comparisons for RM3 and 10 for MM; some of these improvements are statistically significant. Both measures are statistically significantly outperformed by KL in at most two cases for RM3 and never for MM. The RI of both measures is always positive, whereas for the KL divergence it is positive in all but a single case: MM for CW09B.

Apart from Geo (KL), which is promoted to the second position after Power, the performance order of the weighted means remains the same as in Section 4.2.1. The top 4 divergence measures in descending order of pairwise comparisons for RM3 are J, KL, ResistorAverage and χ^2Neyman. For MM, χ^2Neyman and ResistorAverage switch places. These measures were also the top 4 in Section 4.2.1. The bottom 4 measures for both RM3 and MM are χ^2Pearson, JensenShannon, Skew and TotalVariation. These measures also appeared at the bottom of the list in Section 4.2.1.

4.2.3 Verbose Queries.

To further study the effect of the query-model support size on retrieval performance, we repeated the experiment from Section 4.2.1 but now using verbose queries composed of the topic's title and description. As a result, the support of the query model is (much) larger than that used in Section 4.2.1 where MLE of short title queries is used. The results are presented in Table 6. As was the case thus far, the two measures outperforming the KL divergence are the J divergence and Power. However, unlike the case in Sections 4.2.1 and 4.2.2, both measures are outperformed by KL in at least the same number of relevant comparisons in which they outperform it. Most performance differences between these measures and KL are not statistically significant. The performance-based ordering of the weighted means is as in Section 4.2.1, except that now Geo (KL) is promoted to the first rank. The top 4 divergence measures are KL, J, ResistorAverage and Hellinger, while the bottom 4 are JensenShannon, Skew, χ^2Pearson and TotalVariation as was the case in Sections 4.2.1 and 4.2.2.

4.2.4 Power vs. J divergence.

We saw that Power is the most effective weighted mean while J is the most effective divergence measure among the alternatives we considered. Table 7 contrasts their performance for: MLE query models induced from short (title) or verbose (title+description) queries, and pseudo-feedback-based query models (RM3 or MM). Evidently, Power is more effective than J for short title queries and for RM3, while the reverse holds for verbose queries and MM.

4.2.5 Further Analysis.

We showed that Power often outperforms KL for query models induced from short titles using unsmoothed MLE and those induced using pseudo feedback. In Figure 1 we study the effect of β on the MAP performance of Power. Short title queries and the MLE query model are used. We note that similar trends were also observed for RM3, MM and verbose queries. These results are omitted due to space considerations and as they convey no further insight. We see that the performance of Power is the highest for values of β close to 0. (Recall from Section 3.2 that Power converges to Geo as β approaches zero and that it has an IDF effect for $\beta < 1$.) A case in point, we found that

Table 5: Using RM3 and MM to induce query models. 'Init': initial ranking. 'i' and 'k' mark statistically significant differences of retrieval effectiveness (MAP, p@5 and NDCG20) with Init and KL divergence, respectively. The best result in a column per query model is highlighted.

		AP				ROBUST				GOV2				CW09B				CW09BF			
		MAP	p@5	NDCG20	RI	MAP	p@5	NDCG20	RI	MAP	p@5	NDCG20	RI	MAP	p@5	NDCG20	RI	MAP	p@5	NDCG20	RI
	Init	21.1	43.6	42.6	–	25.4	48.7	43.9	–	29.2	55.5	44.5	–	17.9	22.7	20.1	–	18.7	34.7	25.8	–
RM3	KL	27.1^i	48.7^i	46.5^i	43.4	28.8^i	48.8	44.6	23.7	32.8^i	58.0	47.3^i	43.9	19.0^i	26.1^i	22.5^i	11.6	19.9^i	37.2	27.1^i	13.6
	Ari	11.0^i_k	27.5^i_k	26.1^i_k	−64.6	6.4^i_k	14.6^i_k	13.1^i_k	−84.3	8.2^i_k	15.7^i_k	13.7^i_k	−91.9	6.6^i_k	5.7^i_k	6.1^i_k	−63.1	7.9^i_k	15.3^i_k	11.3^i_k	−63.1
	Har	17.8^i_k	40.8_k	40.0_k	−41.4	22.3^i_k	47.2	40.6^i_k	−37.3	23.8^i_k	53.5_k	42.3_k	−47.3	14.0^i_k	28.0^i	19.8_k	−28.8	14.9^i_k	32.2_k	22.3^i_k	−43.4
	GeoAri	24.1^i_k	45.1_k	45.0_k	20.2	24.0^i_k	45.1^i_k	41.1^i_k	−24.9	25.7^i_k	50.3^i_k	40.6^i_k	−35.1	12.3^i_k	14.4^i_k	13.6^i_k	−48.5	14.8^i_k	30.8^i_k	20.5^i_k	−42.4
	GeoHar	18.7^i_k	41.0_k	41.0_k	−26.3	23.9^i_k	47.6	42.3^i_k	−28.1	26.0^i_k	54.1_k	43.6_k	−32.4	15.7^i_k	29.0^i	20.9	−21.2	16.7^i_k	34.8	24.2_k	−25.3
	Power	26.8^i_k	48.9^i	46.5^i	42.4	28.9^i	49.3	44.7	24.1	33.2^i_k	58.8	47.5^i	39.9	19.4^i	28.3^i_k	23.3^i_k	21.2	19.9^i	37.4	27.2^i	6.6
	Lehmer	24.4^i_k	46.5	46.0^i	32.3	26.4^i_k	49.0	43.9	2.4	30.2_k	57.2	46.0	10.1	17.9_k	22.9_k	20.8_k	−5.1	19.0_k	35.8	26.1_k	−3.0
	Hellinger	25.1^i_k	47.1	46.0^i	22.2	22.8^i_k	46.1^i_k	40.8^i_k	−24.9	23.8^i_k	54.1_k	42.0_k	−39.2	15.5^i_k	27.0^i	20.1_k	−35.9	16.7^i_k	36.2	24.5_k	−28.8
	TotalVariation	13.8^i_k	43.2_k	36.6^i_k	−60.6	11.3^i_k	33.8^i_k	26.3^i_k	−82.7	11.7^i_k	41.1^i_k	30.3^i_k	−86.5	7.7^i_k	19.2_k	13.2^i_k	−78.8	8.8^i_k	26.3^i_k	16.7^i_k	−76.3
	JensenShannon	18.3^i_k	43.6	40.2_k	−34.3	13.9^i_k	36.5^i_k	30.6^i_k	−75.9	12.7^i_k	41.8^i_k	31.0^i_k	−85.1	9.8^i_k	23.5	16.1^i_k	−71.7	10.1^i_k	26.8^i_k	17.6^i_k	−69.7
	J	26.3^i_k	47.7	46.5^i	42.4	28.1^i_k	50.4_k	45.2^i	29.7	33.2^i_k	60.7^i_k	48.6^i_k	40.5	18.7	27.0^i	21.8^i	13.6	19.9^i	39.9^i_k	27.4^i	8.1
	ResistorAverage	23.5^i_k	47.5	45.1	10.1	22.0^i_k	44.8^i_k	40.0^i_k	−41.4	26.6^i_k	58.0	44.5_k	−29.7	18.5	28.3^i	21.9^i	9.1	19.1	40.0^i	26.7	6.1
	χ^2Neyman	19.3^i_k	41.8_k	40.9_k	−16.2	23.5^i_k	47.6	41.8^i_k	−30.5	26.0^i_k	56.1	44.1_k	−35.1	18.7	29.0^i	23.2^i	13.6	18.6_k	35.5	26.4	−7.6
	χ^2Pearson	19.4_k	44.4_k	42.1_k	−14.1	15.9^i_k	39.4^i_k	33.2^i_k	−64.3	15.5^i_k	46.2^i_k	34.3^i_k	−74.3	9.7^i_k	21.9_k	15.7^i_k	−72.7	11.1^i_k	30.6_k	19.6^i_k	−69.7
	χ^2Symmetric	21.2_k	45.5	43.5_k	0.0	16.8^i_k	40.6^i_k	33.9^i_k	−60.6	17.4^i_k	47.4^i_k	35.4^i_k	−67.6	11.7^i_k	23.6	17.5^i_k	−58.1	12.8^i_k	32.9_k	21.2^i_k	−60.6
	Skew	17.4^i_k	42.4_k	39.3_k	−42.4	14.1^i_k	35.3^i_k	30.0^i_k	−75.5	12.3^i_k	41.1^i_k	29.8^i_k	−87.8	9.1^i_k	21.4_k	14.3^i_k	−76.3	9.7^i_k	25.2^i_k	16.8^i_k	−72.2
MM	KL	27.8^i	50.1^i	46.9^i	22.2	27.1^i	47.5	43.2	24.1	32.1^i	58.0	45.4	31.1	18.9	24.8	21.8	−5.1	20.4^i	38.7^i	27.4	10.6
	Ari	18.7_k	38.0_k	36.6^i_k	−24.2	10.8^i_k	22.0^i_k	19.9^i_k	−68.7	10.7^i_k	21.1^i_k	16.5^i_k	−89.2	6.8^i_k	5.4^i_k	6.2^i_k	−65.7	8.0^i_k	14.7^i_k	11.9^i_k	−76.3
	Har	19.4_k	44.8_k	41.0_k	−23.2	22.5^i_k	46.4^i	40.5^i_k	−32.5	24.9^i_k	54.7	42.1_k	−44.6	13.5^i_k	26.0	18.1_k	−42.9	16.0^i_k	34.4_k	24.0_k	−33.3
	GeoAri	25.2^i_k	49.1^i	45.5	16.2	22.8^i_k	42.7^i_k	39.3^i_k	−28.5	24.8^i_k	47.4^i_k	39.0^i_k	−33.8	12.4^i_k	13.0^i_k	13.7^i_k	−53.5	15.4^i_k	31.7_k	21.9^i_k	−36.9
	GeoHar	22.1_k	43.8_k	41.4_k	−11.1	23.6^i_k	47.2	41.8^i	−30.1	26.9^i_k	56.6	43.7	−20.9	15.6^i_k	27.3^i	19.9	−27.3	17.6_k	36.6	25.4_k	−18.7
	Power	27.9^i	49.3^i	46.7^i	20.2	27.3^i	47.6	43.5	24.9	32.1^i	58.1	45.6	27.0	20.1^i_k	29.9^i_k	24.1^i_k	27.8	20.3^i	38.6^i	27.7^i	17.2
	Lehmer	27.6^i	49.9^i	46.9^i	22.2	26.0_k	45.8^i	42.5	8.8	30.1_k	57.3	46.4	21.6	17.8_k	23.3	20.3_k	−21.2	19.5_k	38.8^i	26.9	−6.6
	Hellinger	26.4^i_k	47.3	46.4	22.2	20.3^i_k	40.5^i_k	36.2^i_k	−24.1	23.2^i_k	50.7_k	37.8^i_k	−40.5	15.6^i_k	24.0	19.4_k	−40.9	17.0^i_k	37.4	24.2_k	−34.3
	TotalVariation	22.1_k	45.1_k	43.2_k	0.0	14.2^i_k	33.3^i_k	28.1^i_k	−54.2	15.2^i_k	38.4^i_k	28.0^i_k	−79.7	7.5^i_k	12.0^i_k	11.0^i_k	−78.8	10.0^i_k	24.5^i_k	17.3^i_k	−69.2
	JensenShannon	24.5^i_k	46.7	44.5	14.1	16.9^i_k	34.7^i_k	31.3^i_k	−47.8	13.2^i_k	32.4^i_k	25.0^i_k	−86.5	10.2^i_k	21.4	14.9^i_k	−74.7	10.7^i_k	25.6^i_k	16.8^i_k	−72.2
	J	28.2^i_k	49.7^i	47.3^i	21.2	27.3^i	48.5_k	43.8_k	24.9	32.2^i	58.2	46.5_k	39.2	19.2^i	26.1^i	21.8^i	12.6	20.8^i	41.8^i_k	29.0^i_k	27.8
	ResistorAverage	25.1^i_k	47.3	45.3	8.1	20.7^i_k	42.7^i_k	38.7^i_k	−32.5	26.9^i_k	54.7	42.5_k	−20.3	18.4	23.3	21.0	8.1	19.6	38.8	26.6	−1.0
	χ^2Neyman	21.6_k	46.5	43.4_k	−6.1	22.8^i_k	44.7^i_k	40.3^i_k	−31.3	26.3^i_k	56.2	44.3	−27.0	18.5	29.5^i_k	23.0^i	4.0	18.7_k	36.9	26.1	−8.1
	χ^2Pearson	22.9_k	46.3_k	43.5_k	4.0	14.6^i_k	33.7^i_k	28.5^i_k	−51.0	15.8^i_k	40.7^i_k	29.2^i_k	−71.6	10.5^i_k	22.9	16.7^i_k	−64.6	11.6^i_k	33.4_k	20.6^i_k	−58.1
	χ^2Symmetric	24.0_k	47.5	45.0	8.1	15.2^i_k	33.6^i_k	29.1^i_k	−45.4	16.6^i_k	43.0^i_k	31.1^i_k	−70.3	12.3^i_k	23.5	17.8_k	−55.6	13.1^i_k	34.4_k	21.7^i_k	−48.0
	Skew	23.8_k	46.7	43.7_k	14.1	16.8^i_k	32.6^i_k	29.1^i_k	−47.8	14.2^i_k	33.5^i_k	25.6^i_k	−86.5	9.5^i_k	18.2^i_k	13.3^i_k	−78.8	11.0^i_k	26.0^i_k	17.3^i_k	−73.7

Table 6: Verbose (title+description) queries. Using unsmoothed MLE to induce query models. Because the KL divergence is used to produce the initial ranking, its RI is undefined. 'Init': initial ranking. 'k': statistically significant difference of retrieval effectiveness (MAP, p@5 and NDCG20) with the KL divergence. The best result in a column is highlighted.

	AP				ROBUST				GOV2				CW09B				CW09BF			
	MAP	p@5	NDCG20	RI	MAP	p@5	NDCG20	RI	MAP	p@5	NDCG20	RI	MAP	p@5	NDCG20	RI	MAP	p@5	NDCG20	RI
KL (=Init)	23.8	49.1	46.0	–	28.4	54.8	47.3	–	30.0	61.4	47.1	–	18.1	29.2	24.2	–	18.1	36.1	26.6	–
Ari	9.8_k	29.3_k	26.6_k	−77.8	5.6_k	13.3_k	12.5_k	−93.6	7.2_k	10.9_k	9.8_k	−91.9	4.8_k	3.1_k	4.2_k	−63.1	6.2_k	12.0_k	8.7_k	−50.0
Har	10.2_k	25.5_k	24.2_k	−87.9	17.6_k	36.9_k	32.0_k	−82.7	15.5_k	45.5_k	31.9_k	−78.4	9.2_k	19.3_k	14.4_k	−66.7	8.8_k	20.4_k	14.1_k	−74.2
GeoAri	17.3_k	43.0_k	40.4_k	−57.6	14.8_k	35.9_k	29.7_k	−82.3	16.5_k	33.5_k	27.3_k	−83.8	8.6_k	7.3_k	8.6_k	−51.0	12.0_k	25.2_k	17.7_k	−30.8
GeoHar	15.3_k	33.5_k	32.2_k	−75.8	22.1_k	42.2_k	37.9_k	−69.9	20.0_k	51.1_k	36.7_k	−71.6	12.0_k	24.1_k	17.9_k	−59.6	11.4_k	25.1_k	17.9_k	−66.2
Power	23.8	48.7	46.7_k	9.1	28.0_k	53.9	47.2	−6.0	29.9	60.1	47.0	11.5	17.2_k	29.1	23.3_k	−35.4	17.8	37.0	26.5	20.7
Lehmer	23.2_k	48.1	45.4	−13.1	27.0_k	51.4_k	45.2_k	−34.1	27.3_k	57.8_k	44.6_k	−49.3	15.1_k	24.2_k	20.5_k	−51.0	15.8_k	32.5_k	24.0_k	−44.4
Hellinger	18.1_k	45.1	42.5_k	−43.4	16.6_k	39.4_k	32.7_k	−71.1	16.7_k	33.9_k	28.4_k	−85.1	11.5_k	18.7_k	15.0_k	−42.9	13.1_k	30.6_k	20.8_k	−30.8
TotalVariation	7.9_k	25.1_k	23.3_k	−73.7	5.0_k	12.9_k	11.5_k	−92.8	6.5_k	10.4_k	8.7_k	−95.9	3.6_k	3.0_k	3.3_k	−70.2	4.5_k	9.3_k	6.5_k	−67.2
JensenShannon	9.7_k	34.5_k	30.2_k	−83.8	9.0_k	26.9_k	22.0_k	−88.0	4.5_k	13.2_k	10.4_k	−97.3	4.3_k	12.1_k	8.5_k	−78.3	3.8_k	13.7_k	8.9_k	−75.8
J	23.8	49.7	46.0	−11.1	28.4	54.5	47.3	−3.2	29.8_k	59.6_k	47.0	−29.7	18.3_k	30.4	24.3	10.1	18.1	36.3	26.4	−3.5
ResistorAverage	12.7_k	42.0_k	36.2_k	−83.8	13.3_k	35.8_k	30.1_k	−86.7	19.9_k	53.5_k	39.6_k	−68.9	15.8_k	26.8	22.3	−10.1	16.3_k	36.1	25.5	−10.6
χ^2Neyman	12.1_k	30.9_k	28.0_k	−85.9	19.1_k	39.2_k	34.7_k	−78.7	17.8_k	49.3_k	35.2_k	−75.7	10.9_k	22.2_k	16.7_k	−60.6	10.4_k	23.4_k	16.9_k	−68.2
χ^2Pearson	8.2_k	26.9_k	24.7_k	−74.7	5.3_k	14.1_k	12.4_k	−92.0	6.8_k	10.8_k	9.9_k	−95.3	4.0_k	4.8_k	4.2_k	−67.2	5.1_k	10.8_k	8.1_k	−62.1
χ^2Symmetric	8.8_k	29.5_k	26.4_k	−75.8	5.8_k	16.1_k	13.6_k	−92.8	7.3_k	12.7_k	11.5_k	−94.6	4.7_k	6.8_k	5.5_k	−64.1	5.9_k	13.9_k	9.9_k	−58.1
Skew	8.3_k	29.3_k	24.6_k	−85.9	6.9_k	20.0_k	16.7_k	−88.8	3.4_k	8.9_k	6.4_k	−97.3	4.0_k	10.5_k	7.5_k	−77.3	3.6_k	11.6_k	8.0_k	−74.7

for $\beta = -0.05$ Power outperforms KL in terms of MAP for all five datasets. The performance for $\beta = -1$ (which amounts to Har), $\beta = 1$ (Ari) and especially for $\beta = 2$ (weighted quadratic mean) and $\beta = 3$ (weighted cubic mean) is often much lower than that attained for $\beta = -0.05$. The highest improvement over KL is attained for CW09B, the noisiest Web collection among those considered.

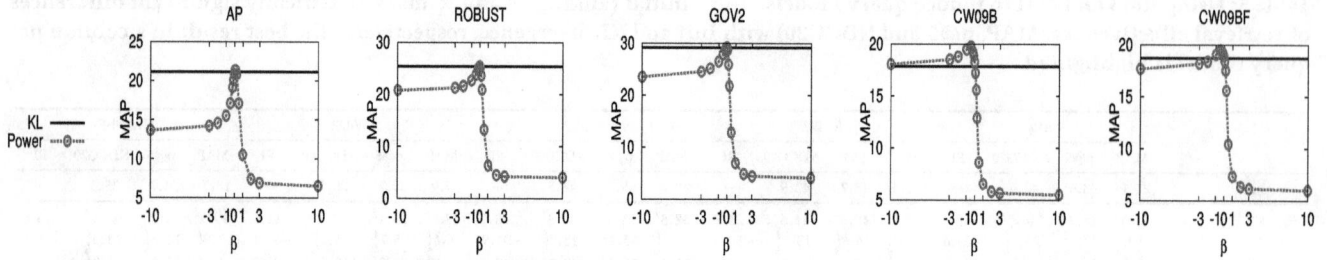

Figure 1: The effect of β on the MAP performance of Power. Short title queries and the MLE query model are used.

Table 7: Power vs. J divergence. The number of relevant comparisons out of 15 (5 datasets × 3 evaluation measures: MAP, p@5 and NDCG20) in which the method in the row (statistically significantly) outperforms the method in the column.

	Short Query MLE			RM3			MM			Verbose Query MLE		
	KL	Power	J	KL	Power	J	KL	Power	J	KL	Power	J
KL	0 (0)	1 (0)	7 (4)	0 (0)	1 (1)	5 (2)	0 (0)	4 (0)	1 (0)	0 (0)	12 (3)	5 (2)
Power	12 (5)	0 (0)	10 (6)	12 (3)	0 (0)	6 (4)	10 (3)	0 (0)	3 (3)	2 (1)	0 (0)	5 (1)
J	7 (3)	5 (1)	0 (0)	8 (5)	6 (2)	0 (0)	13 (6)	11 (4)	0 (0)	5 (1)	8 (3)	0 (0)

5 CONCLUSIONS

Motivated by the fact that comparing query and document language models using the KL divergence is rank equivalent to using a specific weighted geometric mean, we studied alternative weighted means as well as divergence measures; specifically, we analyzed the inverse document frequency (IDF) effect of the methods. Empirical evaluation showed that KL can be often outperformed in several settings by some alternatives.

Acknowledgments We thank the reviewers for their helpful comments. This paper is based upon work supported in part by the Israel Science Foundation under grant no. 433/12.

REFERENCES

[1] Nasreen Abdul-Jaleel, James Allan, W. Bruce Croft, Fernando Diaz, Leah Larkey, Xiaoyan Li, Marck D., and Courtney Wade. 2004. UMASS at TREC 2004 — Novelty and HARD. In *Proc. of TREC-13*.

[2] S. M. Ali and S. D. Silvey. 1966. A General Class of Coefficients of Divergence of One Distribution from Another. *Journal of the Royal Statistical Society. Series B (Methodological)* 28, 1 (1966), 131–142.

[3] Javed A. Aslam and Virgiliu Pavlu. 2007. Query Hardness Estimation Using Jensen-Shannon Divergence Among Multiple Scoring Functions. In *Proc. of ECIR*. 198–209.

[4] Gleb Beliakov, Humberto Bustince Sola, and Tomasa Calvo. 2016. *A Practical Guide to Averaging Functions*. Studies in Fuzziness and Soft Computing, Vol. 329. Springer.

[5] Thorsten Brants, Francine Chen, and Ioannis Tsochantaridis. 2002. Topic-based document segmentation with probabilistic latent semantic analysis. In *Proc. of CIKM*. 211–218.

[6] B.S. Bullen. 2003. *Handbook of means and their inequalities*. Springer-Science+Business Media, B.V.

[7] Francine Chen, Ayman Farahat, and Thorsten Brants. 2004. Multiple Similarity Measures and Source-Pair Information in Story Link Detection. In *Proc. of HLT-NAACL*. 313–320.

[8] Ruey-Cheng Chen, Chia-Jung Lee, and W. Bruce Croft. 2015. On Divergence Measures and Static Index Pruning. In *Proc. of ICTIR*. 151–160.

[9] Stéphane Clinchant and Éric Gaussier. 2013. A Theoretical Analysis of Pseudo-Relevance Feedback Models. In *Proc. of ICTIR*. 6.

[10] Gordon V. Cormack, Mark D. Smucker, and Charles L. A. Clarke. 2011. Efficient and effective spam filtering and re-ranking for large web datasets. *Information Retrieval* 14, 5 (2011), 441–465.

[11] Imre Csiszár. 1967. Information-type measures of difference of probability distributions and indirect observations. *Studia Sci. Math. Hungar.* 2 (1967), 299–318.

[12] Fernando Diaz. 2015. Condensed List Relevance Models. In *Proc. of ICTIR*. 313–316.

[13] Hui Fang, Tao Tao, and ChengXiang Zhai. 2004. A formal study of information retrieval heuristics. In *Proc. of SIGIR*. 49–56.

[14] Hui Fang and ChengXiang Zhai. 2005. An exploration of axiomatic approaches to information retrieval. In *Proc. of SIGIR*. 480–487.

[15] Hussein Hazimeh and ChengXiang Zhai. 2015. Axiomatic Analysis of Smoothing Methods in Language Models for Pseudo-Relevance Feedback. In *Proc. of ICTIR*. 141–150.

[16] Harold Jeffreys. 1939. *Theory of Probability*. Oxford University Press.

[17] Don Johnson and Sinan Sinanovic. 2001. Symmetrizing the Kullback-Leibler Distance. *IEEE Transactions on Information Theory* (2001).

[18] Maryam Karimzadehgan and ChengXiang Zhai. 2012. Axiomatic Analysis of Translation Language Model for Information Retrieval. In *Proc. of ECIR*. 268–280.

[19] Oren Kurland and Lillian Lee. 2010. PageRank without hyperlinks: Structural reranking using links induced by language models. *ACM Transactions on information systems* 28, 4 (2010), 18.

[20] John D. Lafferty and Chengxiang Zhai. 2001. Document language models, query models, and risk minimization for information retrieval. In *Proc. of SIGIR*. 111–119.

[21] Victor Lavrenko and W. Bruce Croft. Relevance Models in Information Retrieval. In *Language Modeling for Information Retrieval*. Number 13 in Information Retrieval Book Series. Kluwer, Chapter 2, 11–56.

[22] Lillian Lee. 1999. Measures of Distributional Similarity. In *Proc. of ACL*.

[23] Lillian Lee. 2001. On the effectiveness of the skew divergence for statistical language analysis. In *Proc. of AISTATS*. 65–72.

[24] Jianhua Lin. 1991. Divergence measures based on the Shannon entropy. *IEEE Trans. Information Theory* 37, 1 (1991), 145–151.

[25] Ramesh Nallapati. 2006. *The smoothed dirichlet distribution: Understanding cross-entropy ranking in information retrieval*. Ph.D. Dissertation. University of Massachusetts.

[26] Jerzy Neyman. 1949. Contribution to the theory of the χ^2 test. In *Proc. of the Berkeley symposium on mathematical statistics and probability*, Vol. 1. University of California Press Berkeley, 239–273.

[27] Karl Pearson. 1900. X. On the criterion that a given system of deviations from the probable in the case of a correlated system of variables is such that it can be reasonably supposed to have arisen from random sampling. *Philosophical Magazine Series 5* 50, 302 (1900), 157–175.

[28] Tetsuya Sakai, Toshihiko Manabe, and Makoto Koyama. 2005. Flexible pseudo-relevance feedback via selective sampling. *ACM Transactions on Asian Language Information Processing* 4, 2 (2005), 111–135.

[29] Fei Song and W. Bruce Croft. 1999. A general language model for information retrieval. In *Proc. of SIGIR*. 279–280.

[30] ChengXiang Zhai. 2008. Statistical Language Models for Information Retrieval: A Critical Review. *Foundations and Trends in Information Retrieval* 2, 3 (2008), 137–213.

[31] Chengxiang Zhai and John D. Lafferty. 2001. Model-based Feedback in the Language Modeling Approach to Information Retrieval. In *Proc. of CIKM*. 403–410.

[32] Chengxiang Zhai and John D. Lafferty. 2001. A Study of Smoothing Methods for Language Models Applied to Ad Hoc Information Retrieval. In *Proc. of SIGIR*. 334–342.

[33] Justin Zobel and Alistair Moffat. 1998. Exploring the similarity space. *ACM SIGIR forum* 18, 1 (1998), 18–34.

Text Retrieval based on Least Information Measurement

Weimao Ke
Drexel University
3141 Chestnut St
Philadelphia, Pennsylvania 19104
wk@drexel.edu

ABSTRACT

We developed a new information retrieval framework based on the Least Information (LI) metric. We derived multiple term weighting schemes and combined them with a vector space representation for ad hoc retrieval. Given probability distributions in a collection as prior knowledge, LI Binary (LIB) quantifies least information due to the binary occurrence of a term in a document whereas LI Frequency (LIF) measures least information based on the probability of drawing a term from a bag of words. Experiments on four benchmark TREC collections for ad hoc retrieval showed that LIT-based methods achieved superior performances compared to classic TF*IDF and BM25, especially for verbose queries and hard search topics. The least information theory is a method for entropy-based information measurement and offers a novel approach for IR modeling.

CCS CONCEPTS

•**Information systems** → **Probabilistic retrieval models**; *Similarity measures*; •**Mathematics of computing** → *Information theory*;

KEYWORDS

information measure, metric, information retrieval, probability distribution, entropy, term weighting, relevance, ranking, effectiveness

ACM Reference format:
Weimao Ke. 2017. Text Retrieval based on Least Information Measurement. In *Proceedings of ICTIR'17, October 1–4, 2017, Amsterdam, Netherlands.*, , 8 pages.
DOI: https://doi.org/10.1145/3121050.3121075

1 INTRODUCTION

Shannon's mathematical theory of communication, commonly known as the information theory, has been used in a wide spectrum of areas including digital coding, communication, and information technology applications [23, 24]. Modeling information as reduction of entropy (uncertainty) provides a valuable vehicle in the design and engineering of information systems. In information retrieval (IR), information and probability theories have provided

important guidance to the development of classic techniques such as TF*IDF, probabilistic retrieval, and language modeling [20].

Despite its broad use, there are assumptions that define the boundary of the classic information theory, beyond which its application requires careful examination of domain contexts [4, 21]. The original purpose of Shannon's theory, as noted in his master piece, was for engineering communication systems where the "meaning of information was considered irrelevant" [23, p. 379]. Information retrieval research is centered on the notion of relevance. To quantify the "relevant amount" of information requires extension of Shannon's theory, better clarification of the relationship between information and entropy, and justification of this relationship [24]. Although various measures such as mutual information and KL information (*relative entropy*) have been adopted, we observe that several important characteristics about an ideal information quantity in the IR context are yet to be met [14, 31].

In our research, we proposed the *Least Information Theory* (LIT) which quantifies the amount of information in probability distribution changes. The theory is built on the Shannon entropy but goes beyond the entropy-reduction notion of information. We have conducted experiments on related clustering and classification tasks and demonstrated strong performances of methods derived from LIT. Similar to *relative entropy*, LIT is a non-linear function of entropy. The theory demonstrates several characteristic that are desirable in applications such as information retrieval (IR). In this study, we apply the new theory in modeling ad hoc retrieval and show strong experimental results compared to classic TF*IDF and Okapi BM25 on multiple benchmark IR collections.

2 LIT AND BACKGROUND

Information and probability theories have provided important guidance on the development of classic techniques such as probabilistic and language modeling [20]. Information-theoretic measures such as mutual information and Kullback-Leibler (KL) divergence have also been used for various processes including feature selection and matching [2, 14, 31].

KL divergence measures information for discrimination between two probability distributions by quantifying the entropy change in an asymmetric manner [14]. KL divergence and its derived methods such as Jensen-Shannon divergence are broadly adopted in IR research [5, 16].

From an information-centric view, this research aims to develop a new model for ad hoc information retrieval. By quantifying the amount of information required to explain probability distribution changes, the *least information* theory (LIT) establishes an important information measurement and provides a new approach to evaluate relevance given term distributions in a document vs. in the collection. Here we present the Least Information Theory (LIT), which quantifies information via integration of Shannon entropy [13].

Let X be prior (initially specified) probabilities for a set of exhaustive and mutually exclusive inferences: $X = [x_1, x_2, .., x_n]$, where x_i is the prior probability of the ith inference on a given hypothesis. Let Y denote posterior (changed) probabilities after certain information is known: $Y = [y_1, y_2, .., y_n]$, where y_i is the *informed* probability of the ith inference. Uncertainties/entropies of the two distributions can be computed by Shannon entropy:

$$H(X) \quad = \quad -\sum_{i=1}^{n} x_i \ln x_i \tag{1}$$

$$H(Y) \quad = \quad -\sum_{i=1}^{n} y_i \ln y_i \tag{2}$$

The amount of information obtained from X to Y, in Shannon's treatment, can be measured via the reduction of entropy:

$$\Delta H \quad = \quad H(X) - H(Y) \tag{3}$$

We define dH_i as the amount of entropy change due to a tiny change dp_i of probability p_i:

$$dH_i \quad = \quad -\ln p_i \, dp_i \tag{4}$$

Every tiny change in the probabilities requires some explanation (information). Aggregating (integrating) the small changes of uncertainty leads to the amount of information required for a macro-level change. The least amount of information I_i required to explain the probability change of the ith inference as the integration (aggregation) of all tiny absolute (positive) changes of entropy dH_i:

$$I_i \quad = \quad \left| \int_{x_i}^{y_i} dH_i \right|$$
$$= \quad \left| y_i(1 - \ln y_i) - x_i(1 - \ln x_i) \right| \tag{5}$$

where x_i is the initial probability of the ith inference and y_i the posterior probability of the same inference. The total *Least Information* I is the sum of partial least information for every inference:

$$I \quad = \quad \sum_{i=1}^{n} I_i$$
$$= \quad \sum_{i=1}^{n} \left| y_i(1 - \ln y_i) - x_i(1 - \ln x_i) \right| \tag{6}$$

where n is the number of inferences, x_i is the initially specified probability of the ith inference, and y_i the revised probability of the ith inference.

2.1 Important Model Characteristics

Based on Equation 6, several important characteristics of *least information* can be observed. We summarize some of these characteristics below.

- Absolute information and symmetry: The amount of *least information* required for a probability change from X to Y is the same as that from Y to X, though their semantic meanings are different.
- Addition of continuous change: Amounts of *least information* for small, continuous probability changes in the same semantic directions add linearly to the amount of *least information* responsible for the overall change. In short, $I(X \rightarrow Z) = I(X \rightarrow Y) + I(Y \rightarrow Z)$, if and only if $X \rightarrow Y$ and $Y \rightarrow Z$ are in the same semantic direction.
- Unit Information: In the special case when there are two equally possible inferences, the amount of *least information* needed to explain an outcome (certainty) is one: $I(p_1 = p_2 = \frac{1}{2} \rightarrow p_1 = 1) = 1$, regardless of the log base in the equation.
- In the special case of reducing uncertain inferences to certainty (with the ultimate case):
  - With equally likely inferences, when there are more choices, the least information needed to explain an outcome is larger.
  - The less likely the outcome, the larger the amount of *least information* needed to explain it.
- Zero least information: The amount of *least information* is zero if and only if there is no change in the probability distribution (identical distributions).

2.2 Least Information Modeling for IR

In this work we apply the *least information theory* (LIT) to ad hoc information retrieval (IR), particularly for term weighting. In the bag-of-words approach to IR, a document can be viewed as a set of terms with probabilities (estimated by frequencies) of occurrence. While the entire collection represents the domain in which searches are conducted, each document contains various pieces of information which differentiate itself from other documents in the domain. By analyzing a term's probability (frequency) in a document vs. that in the collection, we can compute information presented by the document in the term to weight the term. In other words, taking domain distributions as prior knowledge, we can measure the amount of least information conveyed by a specific document when it is observed.

We conjecture that the larger amount *least information* is needed to explain a term's appearance in a document, the more heavily the term should be weighted to represent the document. Hence, we transform the question of document representation into weighting terms according to their amounts of *least information* in documents. In this study, we propose two specific weighting methods, one based on a binary representation of term occurrence (0 vs. 1) and the other based on term frequencies. These methods will be combined for vector representation.

2.2.1 LI Binary (LIB) Model. In the binary model, a term either occurs or does not occur in a document. If we randomly pick a document from the collection, the chance that a term t_i appears in the document can be estimated by the ratio between the number of documents containing the term n_i (i.e., document frequency) and the total number of documents N. Let $p(t_i|C) = n_i/N$ denotes the probability of term t_i occurring in a randomly picked document in collection C; $p(\bar{t}_i|C)$ is the probability that the term does not appear:

$$p(\bar{t}_i|C) = 1 - p(t_i|C) = 1 - n_i/N$$

When a specific document d is observed, it becomes certain whether a term occurs in the document or not. Hence the term probability given a specific document $p(t_i|d)$ is either 1 or 0. We define g_i as a function of probability p_i:

$$g_i \quad = \quad p_i(1 - \ln p_i) \tag{7}$$

The least amount of information from observing term t_i in document d can be computed by:

$$I(t_i, d) \quad = \quad \left| g(t_i|d) - g(t_i|C) \right|$$
$$+ \left| g(\bar{t}_i|d) + g(\bar{t}_i|C) \right| \tag{8}$$

The above equation gives the amount of information a term conveys in a document regardless of its semantic direction. When a query term t_i does not appear in document d, the least information associated with the term should be treated as *negative* because it makes the document less relevant to the term. Hence, the ranking function should not only consider the amount of information but also the *sign* (positive vs. negative) of the quantity. Hence, LI Binary (LIB) is computed by:

$$LIB_2(t_i, d) \quad = \quad g(t_i|d) - g(t_i|C)$$
$$- g(\bar{t}_i|d) - g(\bar{t}_i|C) \tag{9}$$

For term weighting, we are more interested in the likelihood of a term appearing in a document. Keeping only quantities related to t_i (and removing those associated with $\bar{t}_i$), we simplify the LIB equation to:

$$LIB(t_i, d) \quad = \quad g(t_i|d) - g(t_i|C) \tag{10}$$
$$= \quad g(t_i|d) - \frac{n_i}{N}\left(1 - \ln \frac{n_i}{N}\right) \tag{11}$$

The total least information of all query terms in the document d is computed by:

$$LIB(q, d) \quad = \quad \sum_{t_i \in q} LIB(t_i, d) \tag{12}$$

The quantity $LIB(t_i, d)$ depends on the observation of term t_i in the document: $g(t_i|d)$ is 1 when t_i appears in document d and 0 if otherwise, according to Equation 7. That is:

$$LIB(t_i, d) = \begin{cases} 1 - \frac{n_i}{N}\left(1 - \ln \frac{n_i}{N}\right) & t_i \in d \\ -\frac{n_i}{N}\left(1 - \ln \frac{n_i}{N}\right) & t_i \notin d \end{cases} \tag{13}$$

where n_i is the document frequency of term t_i and N is the total number of documents. The larger the LIB, the more information the term contributes to the document and should be weighted more heavily in the document representation. LIB is similar in spirit to IDF and its value represents the discriminative power of the term when it appears in a document.

2.2.2 LI Frequency (LIF) Model. In LI Frequency (LIF) model, we use term frequencies to model *least information*. Treating a document collection C as a meta-document, the probability of a randomly picked term from the collection being a specific term t_i can be estimated by: $p(t_i|C) = F_i/L$, where F_i is the total number of occurrences of term t_i in collection C and L the overall length of C (i.e., the sum of all document lengths).

When a specific document d is observed, the probability of picking term t_i from this document can be estimated by: $p(t_i|d) = tf_{i,d}/L_d$, where $tf_{i,d}$ is the number of times term t_i occurs in document d and L_d is the length of the document. Again, for each term t_i, there are two exclusive inferences, namely the randomly picked term being the specific term (t_i) or not ($\bar{t}_i$). To quantify a term's LIF weight, we measure *least information* that explains the change from the term's probability distribution in the collection to its distribution in the document in question:

$$LIF_2(t_i, d) \quad = \quad g(t_i|d) - g(t_i|C)$$
$$+ g(\bar{t}_i|C) - g(\bar{t}_i|d) \tag{14}$$

We focus on the quantities $g(t_i|d)$ and $g(t_i|C)$ to estimate *least information* of each term when a specific document is observed. Without quantities $g(\bar{t}_i|C)$ and $g(\bar{t}_i|d)$, LIF is computed by:

$$LIF(t_i, d) \quad = \quad g(t_i|d) - g(t_i|C) \tag{15}$$
$$= \quad \frac{tf_{i,d}}{L_d}\left(1 - \ln \frac{tf_{i,d}}{L_d}\right)$$
$$- \frac{F_i}{L}\left(1 - \ln \frac{F_i}{L}\right) \tag{16}$$

Hence, the LI Frequency (LIF) ranking score can be computed by the sum of *least information* in all query terms:

$$LIF(q, d) \quad = \quad \sum_{t_i \in q} g(t_i|d) - g(t_i|C) \tag{17}$$
$$= \quad \sum_{t_i \in q} \frac{tf_{i,d}}{L_d}\left(1 - \ln \frac{tf_{i,d}}{L_d}\right)$$
$$- \sum_{t_i \in q} \frac{F_i}{L}\left(1 - \ln \frac{F_i}{L}\right) \tag{18}$$

where $tf_{i,d}$ is term frequency of term t_i in document d and L_d is the document length. F_i is collection frequency of term t_i (sum of term frequencies in all documents) whereas L is the overall length of all documents. LIF can be compared to modeling term frequencies with document length and collection frequency normalization. For now, we use raw term frequencies with the Maximum Likelihood Estimator (MLE) to estimate probabilities and do not use any smoothing techniques to fine tune the estimates.

2.2.3 Fusion of LIB & LIF. While LIB uses binary term occurrence to estimate least information a document carries in the query terms, LIF measures the information based on term frequency. The two are related quantities with different focuses. As discussed, the LIB quantity is similar in spirit to IDF (inverse document frequency) whereas LIF can be seen as a means to normalize TF (term frequency). Given the classic fusion of TF and IDF, we reason that combining the two will potentiate each quantity's strength for term weighting, ultimately leading to improved document ranking. Hence we propose three fusion methods to combine the two quantities by addition and multiplication:

(1) LIB+LIF: To weight a term, we simply add LIB and LIF together by treating them as two separate pieces of information. The ranking score of a document is then the sum of all LIB+LIF quantities in the query terms.

(2) LIB*LIF: In this fusion method, we follow the idea of TF*IDF by multiplying LIB and LIF quantities for each term. Because individual *least information* values fall in the range of $[-1, 1]$ and can be negative, we normalize LIB and LIF values to $[0, 2]$ by adding 1 to each before multiplication. Again, document ranking is then based on the linear sum of LIB*LIF quantities in the query terms.

(3) LICos: This method combines LIB+LIF with cosine similarity in the vector space model (VSM). We use LIB+LIF for term weights to represent documents in VSM and rank documents based on their Cosine coefficients with the binary vector representation of a query.

These fusion methods allow us to examine potential strengths and weaknesses of *least information* modeling for IR. We study LIB and LIF individually as well as the above fusion methods in experiments. And given the effectiveness of TF*IDF and especially its BM25 variation in traditional ad hoc retrieval experiments, we use them as baselines in the experiments.

3 EXPERIMENTAL SETUP

3.1 Data Collections and Topics

We used the following data sets from the Linguistic Data Consortium and NIST for retrieval experiments: the TIPSTER corpus (Disks 2 and 3), TREC Disks 4 and 5, and the AQUAINT I corpus (roughly a million news documents from New York Times, AP, and Xinhua [29]). These data had been widely used in TREC for ad hoc retrieval experiments. We relied on the following TREC topics and relevance bases for IR evaluation:

- TREC 2 routing topics 51 - 100 with title, description, summary, narrative, and concepts (disk 3) [22];
- TREC 4 ad hoc topics 201 - 250 with natural language descriptions only (disks 2 and 3) [7];
- TREC 7 ad hoc topics 351 - 400 with title, description, and narrative (disks 4 and 5 minus the Congressional Record) [30];
- TREC 2005 HARD/Robust 50 topics with title, description, and narrative ranging from 303 - 689 (AQUAINT I data) [29].

These collections represent a diversity of text data and query tasks. In TREC 2, for example, the *concepts* field in 51 - 100 topics contains a verbose list of concepts to represent each search topic. Text queries automatically generated from the concept lists are likely to be more accurate than general descriptions in sentences. On the other hand, TREC 4 topics 201 - 250 only have natural language descriptions of queries. TREC 2005 HARD and Robust topics were developed as a list of *difficult* topics from previous years' ad hoc experiments. Using these diverse data and topics

enabled a relatively thorough examination of the proposed methods' effectiveness in various domain and task contexts.

3.2 Experimental System

We implemented the retrieval ranking methods using the Lucene core search engine library in Java [8]. We reused the Okapi BM25 implementation reported in [18] and validated by [20], which achieved highly competitive results in recent years' TREC competitions. We set parameter values $b = 0.75$ and $k_1 = 1.5$ for BM25, according to existing research on related data. In addition, we developed the following proposed methods for Lucene scoring (ranking): LIB, LIF, LIB+LIF, LIB*LIF, and LICos. Two classic TF*IDF methods, one with document length normalization (TF_N*IDF) and the other without (TF*IDF), were also implemented as baselines. We performed standard tokenization, casefolding, and stop-word removal for indexing. For each data collection, one set of experiments were conducted with stemming and the other without it.

3.3 Evaluation Metrics

We used human relevance judgment (QRELs) developed for TREC 2, TREC 4, TREC 7, and TREC 2005 HARD (Robust) tracks as the gold standard for each set of experiments. We compared the proposed methods with classic TF*IDF and Okapi BM25 methods. Evaluation metrics included mean average precision with arithmetic averaging (MAP) and geometric (gMAP), best precision at rank 10, normalized discounted cumulative gain at 10 ($nDCG_{10}$), and recall precision. While arithmetic average MAP provides a simple mean score across multiple queries, the geometric average (gMAP) is sensitive to poorly performed tasks and is a very useful metric developed for 2005 HARD track [29]. NDCG favors early retrieval of highly relevant documents in a ranked list and has become widely adopted for ranked retrieval evaluation [9].

4 EXPERIMENTAL RESULTS

Figure 1 provides an overview of major results. From the plots, the proposed LICos method appeared to have achieved best results and was better than BM25 in most experiments. All LIB related methods such as LIB, LIB+LIF, and LIB*LIF overwhelmingly outperformed TF*IDF methods, especially in TREC2, TREC7, and TREC'05 HARD (Robust) experiments. In many cases, the LIB-related methods were more than 100% better than TF*IDF baselines (i.e., relative scores > 2). LICos consistently outperformed BM25 in terms of *gMap* in all experiments, indicating that it did relatively well with *poorly* performed topics.

In sections 4.1 - 4.4, we discuss detailed experimental results on the four benchmark test collections. In each of Tables 1 - 6, one set of experiments were conducted with stemming and the other without. Best scores in each evaluation metric are highlighted in **bold** fonts. Section 4.5 presents our observation about the impact of query verbosity on proposed methods' effectiveness.

4.1 TREC 2 Topics on Disk 3

Table 1 shows results from experiments on disk 3. In TREC 2 topics, each query was described using a verbose list of concepts (good keywords). With these manually picked concept terms, which are

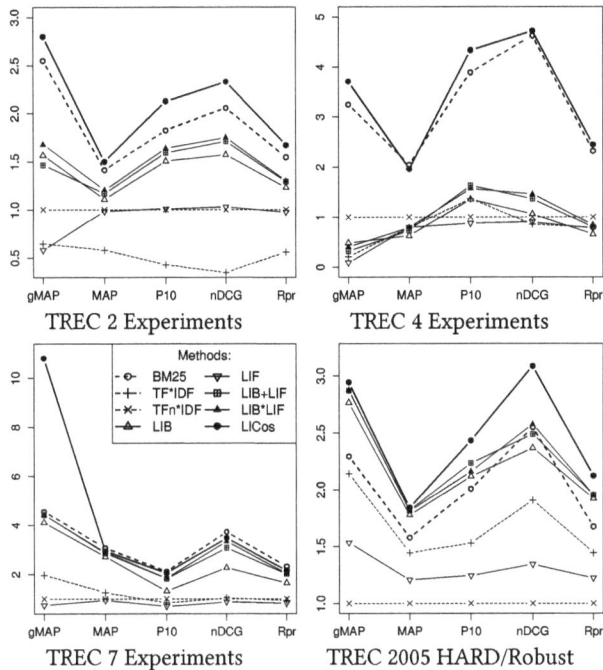

Figure 1: Overview of Experimental Results (with stemming). X has evaluation metrics. Y is relative performance score in each metric as a ratio to the TF_N*IDF baseline. TF_N*IDF scores are always 1 as the baseline. A score at 2, for example, indicates it is twice the baseline score.

Method	gMAP	MAP	P10	nDCG	R_{PR}
Concept-only Search Without Stemming					
BM25	0.288	0.407	0.597	0.504	0.451
TF*IDF	0.090	0.187	0.127	0.0911	0.182
TF_N*IDF	0.125	0.300	0.328	0.241	0.304
LIB	0.223	0.348	0.516	0.417	0.389
LIF	0.125	0.294	0.309	0.251	0.294
LIB+LIF	0.236	0.357	0.545	0.434	0.399
LIB*LIF	0.240	0.361	0.562	0.446	0.402
LICos	**0.301**	**0.413**	**0.635**	**0.523**	**0.464**
Concept-only Search With Stemming					
BM25	0.281	0.399	0.565	0.488	0.442
TF*IDF	0.0711	0.164	0.132	0.0822	0.160
TF_N*IDF	0.110	0.282	0.310	0.238	0.286
LIB	0.173	0.313	0.467	0.374	0.352
LIF	0.064	0.278	0.313	0.244	0.280
LIB+LIF	0.162	0.331	0.494	0.406	0.370
LIB*LIF	0.185	0.341	0.508	0.416	0.372
LICos	**0.309**	**0.423**	**0.659**	**0.554**	**0.477**

Table 1: TREC 2 Concept-only Retrieval (Disk 3)

overall quite precise in defining the topic, LICos (*least information* with cosine similarity) outperformed all the other methods in

every evaluation metric we used. Stemming appeared to further improve LICos's effectiveness. Overall, BM25 also performed very well and was second only to LICos in most cases, followed closely by LIB*LIF. Most proposed methods based on *least information*, especially LIB*LIF and LIB+LIF, outperformed ordinary TF*IDF and TF_N*IDF (with length normalization of TF) by a good margin.

4.2 TREC 4 Topics on Disks 2&3

Method	gMAP	MAP	P10	nDCG	R_{PR}
Desc-only Search Without Stemming					
BM25	0.155	**0.318**	0.515	**0.409**	**0.380**
TF*IDF	0.0178	0.108	0.141	0.0674	0.117
TF_N*IDF	0.0212	0.156	0.145	0.0914	0.163
LIB	0.0327	0.126	0.216	0.117	0.133
LIF	0.0052	0.135	0.139	0.086	0.141
LIB+LIF	0.0288	0.133	0.198	0.120	0.143
LIB*LIF	0.031	0.142	0.201	0.132	0.156
LICos	**0.191**	0.295	**0.536**	0.393	0.376
Desc-only Search With Stemming					
BM25	0.190	**0.316**	0.501	0.394	0.370
TF*IDF	0.0122	0.122	0.176	0.0728	0.126
TF_N*IDF	0.0584	0.155	0.129	0.0853	0.160
LIB	0.0282	0.0968	0.175	0.0905	0.105
LIF	0.00515	0.124	0.113	0.0768	0.125
LIB+LIF	0.0187	0.113	0.210	0.117	0.128
LIB*LIF	0.0235	0.123	0.202	0.125	0.135
LICos	**0.217**	0.304	**0.559**	**0.403**	**0.391**

Table 2: TREC 4 Desc-only Retrieval (Disks 2&3)

Table 2 shows results from TREC 4 experiments on disks 2 & 3. Again, LICos continued to dominate best scores, especially when stemming was used. TREC 4 topics only had descriptions written in natural language sentences. Stemming improved LICos effectiveness but slightly degraded BM25 performance.

While the two had very close scores in several metrics, LICos was consistently better than BM25 in terms of gMAP (geometric averaging MAP) and P_{10}. The evaluation metric gMap is biased toward poorly performed queries (*hard* tasks). LICos appeared to perform better on *difficult topics* than BM25 did to achieve a higher gMap. We shall see later most of the proposed methods performed well on TREC 2005 HARD/Robust's topics, which were considered *difficult* topics in TRECs.

4.3 TREC 7 Topics on Disks 4&5

In TREC 2 and TREC 4 experiments, we used two different fields/sources, namely *concepts* and *description*, to form long queries. In TREC 7 experiments, we used the *title* field to examine the effectiveness of the proposed methods with short queries. Table 3 shows results from these experiments, in which BM25 achieved slightly better scores in P_{10} and $nDCG_{10}$, which favor early retrieval of relevant documents. However, with short queries based on title, LICos performed much better than BM25 did in terms of gMAP, which biased toward poorly performed topics. This again indicates potential advantage of the

Method	gMAP	MAP	P10	nDCG	R_{PR}
Title-only Search Without Stemming					
BM25	0.0682	0.242	**0.482**	**0.337**	**0.360**
TF*IDF	0.0334	0.113	0.219	0.107	0.170
TF_N*IDF	0.0129	0.087	0.188	0.0844	0.172
LIB	0.0653	0.236	0.349	0.250	0.282
LIF	0.012	0.0813	0.150	0.0803	0.133
LIB+LIF	0.0665	0.248	0.411	0.305	0.331
LIB*LIF	0.0662	0.247	0.429	0.317	0.334
LICos	**0.173**	**0.251**	0.466	0.316	0.346
Title-only Search With Stemming					
BM25	0.0681	**0.242**	**0.479**	**0.346**	**0.374**
TF*IDF	0.0295	0.099	0.190	0.0963	0.151
TF_N*IDF	0.0150	0.079	0.228	0.0931	0.161
LIB	0.0615	0.215	0.299	0.211	0.265
LIF	0.0110	0.0744	0.159	0.0816	0.132
LIB+LIF	0.066	0.226	0.415	0.287	0.325
LIB*LIF	0.0662	0.229	0.420	0.311	0.327
LICos	**0.162**	0.232	0.466	0.323	0.347

Table 3: TREC 7 Title-only Retrieval (Disks 4&5)

Method	gMAP	MAP	P10	nDCG	R_{PR}
Title-only Search Without Stemming					
BM25	0.172	0.278	**0.416**	0.271	0.303
TF*IDF	0.174	0.282	0.410	**0.301**	0.301
TF_N*IDF	0.0823	0.194	0.231	0.147	0.210
LIB	0.192	**0.309**	0.409	0.280	0.322
LIF	0.0933	0.226	0.228	0.154	0.227
LIB+LIF	0.195	0.301	0.402	0.273	0.326
LIB*LIF	0.194	0.300	0.384	0.269	0.330
LICos	**0.225**	0.301	0.361	0.282	**0.340**
Title-only Search With Stemming					
BM25	0.166	0.263	0.381	0.273	0.296
TF*IDF	0.160	0.262	0.360	0.281	0.285
TF_N*IDF	0.056	0.175	0.197	0.118	0.191
LIB	0.194	**0.298**	0.388	0.246	0.316
LIF	0.0727	0.186	0.216	0.124	0.195
LIB+LIF	0.186	0.284	**0.410**	0.278	0.313
LIB*LIF	0.186	0.283	0.406	0.274	0.315
LICos	**0.214**	0.283	0.401	**0.295**	0.321

Table 4: TREC'05 Title-only Retrieval (AQUAINT)

proposed methods in search tasks that may have been challenging to traditional methods. The other proposed methods such as LIB, LIB+LIF and LIB*LIF came closely below BM25 but consistently outperformed TF*IDF methods by a large margin in each evaluation metric.

4.4 TREC 2005 HARD/Robust

Experiments on the earlier TREC collections above showed the proposed methods, especially the LICos method, performed very competitively and in many cases outperformed a well-tuned Okapi BM25. Now we discuss experiments on the more recent TREC 2005 HARD/Robust collection, in which 50 topics are considered difficult retrieval tasks. We used title, description, and title+description as queries in the experiments.

Table 4 shows retrieval performances using the topic *title* field for query representation. The proposed methods, especially LIB and LICos, achieved best results in terms of gMAP, MAP, and R_{PR}. BM25 and TF*IDF, without stemming, performed slightly better in P_{10} and $nDCG_{10}$. Overall the proposed methods dominated best results, especially when terms were stemmed.

When we used topic *descriptions* for query representation, as shown in Table 5, the proposed methods outperformed BM25 and TF*IDF methods across all metrics. In particular, LIB, LIB+LIF, and LICos produced very competitive results.

When both *title* and *description* fields were used (combined) for queries, the proposed methods demonstrated an even larger advantage over BM25 and TF*IDF, as shown in Table 5. Whereas LIB, LIB+LIF, and LIB*LIF all outperformed the classic methods, LICos (with stemming) achieved a score roughly 20% higher than that of BM25 in every metric.

TREC 2005 HARD/Robust topics represent *difficult* information needs, for which query specification is challenging. The proposed

Method	gMAP	MAP	P10	nDCG	R_{PR}
Desc-only Search Without Stemming					
BM25	0.204	0.275	0.336	0.239	0.290
TF*IDF	0.203	0.262	0.386	0.273	0.286
TF_N*IDF	0.0718	0.193	0.266	0.176	0.205
LIB	0.205	**0.308**	**0.404**	0.280	0.332
LIF	0.058	0.232	0.289	0.186	0.234
LIB+LIF	0.203	0.303	0.385	0.263	0.328
LIB*LIF	0.231	0.300	0.354	0.249	0.325
LICos	**0.243**	0.308	0.401	**0.292**	**0.338**
Desc-only Search With Stemming					
BM25	0.209	0.293	0.409	0.316	0.315
TF*IDF	0.202	0.266	0.350	0.270	0.283
TF_N*IDF	0.0663	0.197	0.243	0.159	0.209
LIB	0.232	**0.353**	0.460	0.318	0.377
LIF	0.0624	0.236	0.293	0.195	0.243
LIB+LIF	**0.275**	0.351	0.505	0.332	**0.387**
LIB*LIF	0.262	0.337	0.477	0.324	0.370
LICos	0.259	0.330	**0.518**	**0.377**	0.371

Table 5: TREC'05 Desc-only Retrieval (AQUAINT)

methods appeared to perform better with these *tougher* tasks, as was so suggested by the higher gMAP scores in earlier experiments. The methods also performed very competitively with long queries (concepts and descriptions). Overall, stemming improved the proposed methods' effectiveness.

Note that in all experiments, the proposed ranking methods based on *least information* were used without any tuning. Neither did we use additional data sources for query expansion. Although our results remain very competitive compared to reported results in

Method	gMAP	MAP	P10	nDCG	R_{PR}
Title+Desc Search Without Stemming					
BM25	0.226	0.297	0.458	0.329	0.338
TF*IDF	0.210	0.274	0.386	0.289	0.293
TF_N*IDF	0.0886	0.192	0.258	0.162	0.201
LIB	0.260	0.329	0.445	0.336	0.355
LIF	0.102	0.221	0.261	0.186	0.225
LIB+LIF	0.264	0.331	0.447	0.320	0.360
LIB*LIF	0.263	0.328	0.425	0.320	0.359
LICos	**0.264**	**0.331**	**0.490**	**0.394**	**0.397**
Title+Desc Search With Stemming					
BM25	0.217	0.291	0.458	0.362	0.332
TF*IDF	0.202	0.267	0.349	0.271	0.286
TF_N*IDF	0.0945	0.185	0.228	0.142	0.198
LIB	0.261	0.328	0.483	0.337	0.381
LIF	0.145	0.223	0.284	0.191	0.242
LIB+LIF	0.271	0.336	0.510	0.354	0.387
LIB*LIF	0.272	0.335	0.493	0.366	0.387
LICos	**0.278**	**0.340**	**0.555**	**0.439**	**0.421**

Table 6: TREC'05 Title+Desc Runs (AQUAINT)

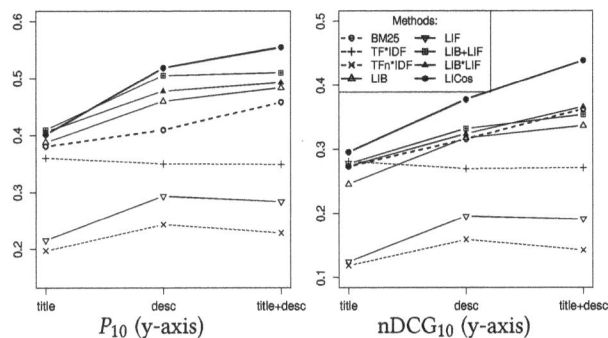

P_{10} (y-axis)   nDCG$_{10}$ (y-axis)

Figure 2: Retrieval effectiveness vs. query verbosity (TREC'05). X denotes query verbosity, ranging from *title-only*, *desc-only*, to *title+desc* query representations. Y is retrieval performance in terms of P_{10} and nDCG$_{10}$.

TREC, this is not a fair comparison because participating systems in TREC were often trained and tuned, sometimes with additional data. In TREC 2005 Robust track, for example, additional resources such as WordNet and Wikipedia were reportedly used to boost results [17].

4.5 Impact of Query Verbosity

We observed that query verbosity had an impact on the proposed methods' retrieval effectiveness. With (longer) verbose queries, methods such as LICos, LIB+LIF, and LIB*LIF appeared to outperform baseline methods by a greater margin. In TREC'05 experiments, for example, LICos with queries based on the *description* field produced P_{10} and nDCG$_{10}$ scores nearly 30% higher than those based on *title* queries (see Figure 2). The improvement was much larger than that of BM25. With verbose queries, having *good terms* (e.g., using the *concepts* field and adding *title* to *description*) for query representation also appeared to strengthen the proposed methods' advantage over BM25 and TF*IDF.

5 REFLECTIONS ON RELATED WORK

Term probability distribution analysis has been an important part of information retrieval modeling. Term frequency and document frequency are basic examples of these frequency (probability) distributions. While term frequency (TF) may indicate the degree of a document's association with a term, inverse document frequency (IDF) is a manifestation of a term's specificity, key to determine the term's value toward weighting and relevance ranking [27]. The two quantities we developed from the *least information* theory, namely LI Binary (LIB) and LI Frequency (LIB), can be related to IDF and TF, though their formulations are very different.

While a term's IDF is equivalent to the mutual information between the term and the collection [25], the probabilistic retrieval

framework provides an important theoretical ground to IDF weights [19]. Mutual information can be interpreted as *relative entropy* that quantifies the difference between the joint probabilities and product probabilities of two random variables [6]. Further development of notions around information-theoretic entropy led to theories such as *maximum entropy* and *minimum (mutual) information* principles, providing important guidance to inferential statistics for retrieval modeling [3, 10, 11, 26].

IDF can also be transformed into Kullback-Leibler (KL) information between term probability distributions in a document and in the collection [1], similar to the modeling of LIB in this work. KL divergence (relative entropy) measures information for discrimination between two probability distributions by quantifying the entropy change in a non-symmetric manner [14]. The non-symmetry of KL divergence is due to the assumption that one of the two distributions is considered *closer* to the ultimate case and the information quantity should be weighted by that distribution. This leads to the consequence that the (absolute) amount of information is different if simply the direction of change is different.

KL information has been used to support term-weighting models by measuring the divergence of the actual term distribution from that obtained under a random process [2]. Such models now serve as good baseline alternatives to the standard TF*IDF model. Research has also employed KL information in language modeling to measure the difference between document and query models for ranking and demonstrated strong empirical results [15, 28]. We believe that the *least information* can be integrated as an alternative to KL information with the aforementioned approaches.

The *least information theory* (LIT) quantifies information due to probability changes as a symmetric function of two distributions. Just as the probabilistic retrieval framework and KL information offer theoretical justification for IDF, *least information* provides the theory from which LIB is developed. While IDF can be obtained from the binary independent (probabilistic) model, LIB is derived from a binary model of *least information*. They both address a term's discriminative power or specificity. However, LIB falls in the range of $[0, 1]$ without normalization – it is close to 1 for extremely rare terms and 0 for stop-words.

6 CONCLUSION

Applying the *least information theory* (LIT) in information retrieval, we developed multiple quantities for document representation based on a term's probability distributions in a document vs. in the collection. Particularly, LI Binary (LIB) quantifies *least information* due to the binary occurrence of a term in a document, i.e., whether the term appears in the document or not. LI Frequency (LIF), on the other hand, measures the amount of *least information* based on the likelihood of drawing a term from a bag of words. While LIB and LIF are similar in spirit to classic IDF and TF respectively, the formulation is very different. Three additional quantities, namely LIB+LIF, LIB*LIF, and LICos, were developed for term weighting and document ranking.

Ad hoc retrieval experiments on four benchmark TREC collections showed that the proposed methods performed very competitively and in most cases outperformed classic TF*IDFs and a well-tuned BM25. LIT-based methods such as LICos and LIB+LIF were particularly effective with good query terms (e.g., using *concepts*), verbose queries (e.g., using *description + title*), and in *difficult* tasks (e.g., on TREC 2005 HARD/Robust collection). Note that none of the proposed methods based on *least information* involved training or tuning. For Okapi BM25, on the other hand, we adopted parameters that had demonstrated strong performances in existing experiments. Least information offers a means to quantify information and presents a new way of thinking for modeling information processes. We have used the theory in other important tasks such as clustering and classification, and obtained strong experimental results [12, 13]. While other IR models can be derived from LIT, the *least information theory* can also be used with existing frameworks. For example, it can be integrated with document and query language models, for which KL divergence has been used. With demonstrated experimental results in this work, broader research on *least information* modeling for IR is very promising.

ACKNOWLEDGMENTS

This work was supported in part by the National Science Foundation under grant no. 1646955.

REFERENCES

[1] Akiko Aizawa. 2000. The feature quantity: an information theoretic perspective of TFIDF-like measures. In *SIGIR'00*. 104–111.
[2] Gianni Amati and Cornelis Joost Van Rijsbergen. 2002. Probabilistic Models of Information Retrieval Based on Measuring the Divergence from Randomness. *ACM Trans. Inf. Syst.* 20, 4 (Oct. 2002), 357–389. https://doi.org/10.1145/582415.582416
[3] Javed A. Aslam, Emine Yilmaz, and Virgiliu Pavlu. 2005. The maximum entropy method for analyzing retrieval measures. In *SIGIR'05*. 27–34.
[4] Charles Cole. 1993. Shannon revisited: Information in terms of uncertainty. *Journal of the American Society for Information Science* 44, 4 (1993), 204–211.
[5] Inderjit S. Dhillon, Subramanyam Mallela, and Rahul Kumar. 2003. A divisive information theoretic feature clustering algorithm for text classification. *J. Mach.*

Learn. Res. 3 (March 2003), 1265–1287.
[6] Robert M. Fano. 1961. *Transmission of Information: A Statistical Theory of Communication.* MIT Press.
[7] D. Harman. 1995. Overview of the Fourth Text REtrieval Conference (TREC-4). In *The Fourth Text REtrieval Conference.* NIST, 1 – 24.
[8] Erik Hatcher, Otis Gospodnetić, , and Michael McCandless. 2010. *Lucene in Action* (second edition ed.). Manning Publications. 475 pages.
[9] Kalervo Jarvelin and Jaana Kekalainen. 2002. Cumulated gain-based evaluation of IR techniques. *ACM Transactions on Information Systems* 20, 4 (2002), 422–446.
[10] E. T. Jaynes. 1957. Information Theory and Statistical Mechanics. II. *Phys. Rev.* 108 (Oct 1957), 171–190. Issue 2.
[11] Paul B. Kantor and Jung Jin Lee. 1986. The maximum entropy principle in information retrieval. In *SIGIR'86.* 269–274.
[12] Weimao Ke. 2013. Information-theoretic Term Weighting Schemes for Document Clustering. In *Proceedings of the 13th ACM/IEEE-CS Joint Conference on Digital Libraries (JCDL '13).* ACM, New York, NY, USA, 143–152. https://doi.org/10.1145/2467696.2467698
[13] Weimao Ke. 2015. Information-theoretic term weighting schemes for document clustering and classification. *International Journal on Digital Libraries* 16, 2 (2015), 145–159.
[14] S. Kullback and R. A. Leibler. 1951. On information and sufficiency. *Annals of Mathematical Statistics* 22 (1951), 79–86.
[15] John Lafferty and Chengxiang Zhai. 2001. Document language models, query models, and risk minimization for information retrieval. In *Proceedings of the 24th annual international ACM SIGIR conference on Research and development in information retrieval (SIGIR '01).* 111–119.
[16] J. Lin. 2006. Divergence measures based on the Shannon entropy. *IEEE Trans. Inf. Theor.* 37, 1 (Sept. 2006), 145–151.
[17] Shuang Liu and Clement Yu. 2005. UIC at TREC2005: Robust Track. In *Text REtrieval Conference (TREC).*
[18] Joaquín Pérez-Iglesias, José R. Pérez-Agüera, Víctor Fresno, and Yuval Z. Feinstein. 2009. Integrating the Probabilistic Models BM25/BM25F into Lucene. *CoRR* abs/0911.5046 (2009).
[19] S. Robertson. 2004. Understanding inverse document frequency: on theoretical arguments for IDF. *Journal of Documentation* 60 (2004), 503–520.
[20] Stephen Robertson and Hugo Zaragoza. 2009. The Probabilistic Relevance Framework: BM25 and Beyond. *Foundations and Trends® in Information Retrieva* 3, 4 (2009), 333–389.
[21] J. S. Rowlinson. 1970. Probability, Information and Entropy. *Nature* 225, 5239 (28 03 1970), 1196–1198.
[22] S. Jones M. Hancock-Beaulieu M. Gatford S. Robertson, S. Walker. 1993. Okapi at TREC-2. In *The Second Text REtrieval Conference.* NIST, 21 – 34.
[23] Claude E. Shannon. 1948. A mathematical theory of communication. *Bell System Technical Journal* 27 (July and October 1948), 379–423 and 623–656.
[24] Debora Shaw and Charles H. Davis. 1983. Entropy and information: A multidisciplinary overview. *Journal of the American Society for Information Science* 34, 1 (1983), 67–74.
[25] M. Siegler and M. Witbrock. 1999. Improving the suitability of imperfect transcriptions for information retrieval from spoken documents. In *ICASSP'99.* IEEE Press, 505–508.
[26] Folke Snickars and Jrgen W. Weibull. 1977. A minimum information principle: Theory and practice. *Regional Science and Urban Economics* 7, 1 (1977), 137–168.
[27] Karen Spärck Jones. 2004. A statistical interpretation of term specificity and its application in retrieval. *Journal of Documentation* 60 (2004), 493–502.
[28] Tao Tao and ChengXiang Zhai. 2007. An exploration of proximity measures in information retrieval. In *Proceedings of the 30th annual international ACM SIGIR conference on Research and development in information retrieval (SIGIR '07).* 295–302.
[29] E.M. Voorhees. 2005. Overview of TREC 2005. In *Text Retrieval Conference (TREC).*
[30] Ellen M. Voorhees and Donna Harman. 1998. Overview of the Seventh Text REtrieval Conference (TREC-7). In *The Seventh Text REtrieval Conference.* NIST, 1 – 23.
[31] Yiming Yang and Jan O. Pedersen. 1997. A Comparative Study on Feature Selection in Text Categorization. In *ICML'97.* 412–420.

Mining the Temporal Statistics of Query Terms for Searching Social Media Posts

Jinfeng Rao,[1] Ferhan Ture,[2] Xing Niu,[1] and Jimmy Lin[3]

[1] Department of Computer Science, University of Maryland
[2] Comcast Applied AI Research Lab
[3] David R. Cheriton School of Computer Science, University of Waterloo
{jinfeng,xingniu}@cs.umd.edu,ferhan_ture@cable.comcast.com,jimmylin@uwaterloo.ca

ABSTRACT

There is an emerging consensus that time is an important indicator of relevance for searching streams of social media posts. In a process similar to pseudo-relevance feedback, the distribution of document timestamps from the results of an initial query can be leveraged to infer the distribution of relevant documents, for example, using kernel density estimation. In this paper, we explore an alternative approach to mining relevance signals directly from the temporal statistics of query terms in the collection, without the need to perform an initial retrieval. We propose two approaches: a linear ranking model that combines features derived from temporal collection statistics of query terms and a regression-based method that attempts to directly predict the distribution of relevant documents from query term statistics. Experiments on standard tweet test collections show that our proposed methods significantly outperform competitive baselines. Furthermore, studies of different feature combinations show the extent to which different types of temporal signals impact retrieval effectiveness.

1 INTRODUCTION

There is a large body of literature in information retrieval that has established the importance of understanding and modeling the temporal distribution of documents as well as queries for various information seeking tasks [5–9, 12, 16]. This is particularly important for searching rapidly-evolving, real-time social media streams such as Twitter, which is the focus of this work. Given an information need expressed as a query, we wish to develop ranking models that return relevant tweets. We refer to this problem as temporal ranking to emphasize the need to model temporal aspects of the information need as well as the document collection.

One successful approach to temporal ranking is to estimate the distribution of relevant documents using the distribution of document timestamps from the results of an initial query [8]. In the same way that pseudo-relevance feedback uses the results of an initial query to refine estimates of term distributions in relevant documents, this class of techniques can be viewed as performing inference on the distribution of document timestamps. The theoretical foundation of this approach lies in the temporal cluster hypothesis [8], which is the observation that relevant documents tend to cluster together in time. One effective implementation of this idea is to use kernel density estimation (KDE) to infer a "temporal prior" for a given information need.

In this work, we take a different approach to estimate the distribution of relevant documents: instead of relying on the results of an initial query, we attempt to exploit temporal signals embedded in the distribution of the query terms themselves. We call these *query trends*, which are generalizations of collection term statistics (of query unigrams and bigrams) in the temporal dimension. Specifically, we keep track of the number of occurrences of query terms across a moving window over the document collection.

Consider an example that illustrates our intuition: the distribution of relevant documents (i.e., from human judgments) for topic MB127 ("hagel nomination filibustered") from the TREC 2013 Microblog Track is shown on the top in Figure 1. The x axis denotes a timeline, with units in days anchored at the query time on the right edge. Of course, this distribution is not known at query time—it is the target of our prediction. The remaining rows in Figure 1 show *query trends*, the distribution of query terms in the collection across time, for the unigrams "filibustered", "hagel", "nomination", and the bigram "hagel nomination". Informally, our problem can be characterized as using query trends to predict the distribution of relevant documents (i.e., the top row in Figure 1).

From this example, it is apparent that there are correlations between query trends and the distribution of relevant documents. Furthermore, a key advantage of our approach over previous methods is that it eliminates the need for an initial retrieval, since temporal collection statistics can be compactly stored for efficient lookup [20] during query processing. From an efficiency perspective, this means that models based solely on query trends can be substantially faster than those that require an initial retrieval.

In this paper, we explore two different approaches to exploiting query trends:

- A linear ranking model that combines features based on the temporal collection statistics of query unigrams and bigrams, their entropies, other related signals.
- A regression-based method that attempts to directly predict the distribution of relevant documents from unigram and bigram query trends.

These two approaches are further combined in an ensemble model, which additionally includes features derived from previous work based on kernel density estimation.

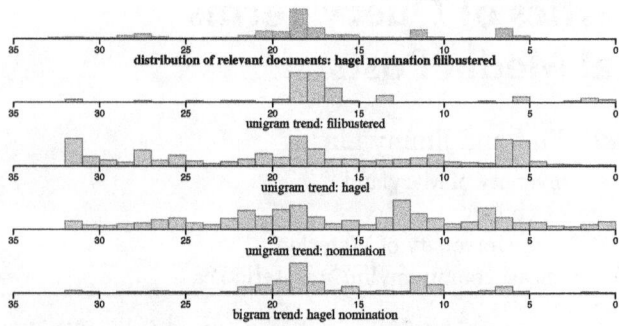

Figure 1: The temporal distribution of relevant documents (top row, in red) and unigram/bigram query trends (remaining rows, in blue) for MB127 ("hagel nomination filibustered") from the TREC 2013 Microblog Track. Informally, our problem can be characterized as using the blue distributions to predict the red distribution.

The main contribution of this work is the exploration of temporal collection statistics of query terms (what we call query trends) for temporal ranking. To our knowledge, our focus on such query term statistics is novel. Experimental evaluations on standard tweet test collections show that our proposed methods are significantly more effective than competitive baselines. Furthermore, detailed studies of different feature combinations show the extent to which different types of temporal signals impact retrieval effectiveness.

2 BACKGROUND AND RELATED WORK

We begin with an overview of related work on modeling temporal dynamics for document ranking and related tasks. Then we provide some technical details about recent work on temporal ranking to set up comparisons with our proposed methods.

2.1 Temporal Information Retrieval

There is a long thread of research exploring the role of temporal signals in search [5–9, 12, 17, 20], and it is well established that for certain tasks, better modeling of the temporal characteristics of queries and documents can lead to higher retrieval effectiveness.

For example, Jones and Diaz [10] studied the temporal profiles of queries, classifying queries as atemporal, temporally ambiguous, or temporally unambiguous. They showed that the temporal distribution of retrieved documents can provide an additional source of evidence to improve rankings. Building on this, Li and Croft [12] introduced recency priors that favor more-recent documents. Dakka et al. [5] proposed an approach to temporal modeling based on moving windows to integrate query-specific temporal evidence with lexical evidence. Efron et al. [7] presented several language modeling variants that incorporate query-specific temporal evidence. The most direct point of comparison to our work (as discussed in the introduction) is the use of non-parametric density estimation to infer the temporal distribution of relevant documents from an initial list of retrieved documents [8, 19]. Most recently, Rao et al. [17] proposed an end-to-end neural ranking model to integrate lexical and temporal signals, which has shown promising improvements over previous approaches.

There have been several other studies of time-based pseudo relevance feedback. Keikha et al. [11] represented queries and documents with their normalized term frequencies in the time dimension and used a time-based similarity metric to measure relevance. Craveiro et al. [4] exploited the temporal relationship between words for query expansion. Choi and Croft [3] presented a method to select time periods for expansion based on users' behaviors (i.e., retweets). Rao et al. [18] proposed a continuous hidden Markov model to identify temporal burst states in order to select better query expansion terms.

In addition to ranking, modeling temporal signals has also been shown to benefit related tasks such as behavior prediction [16], time-sensitive query auto-completion [21], and real-time event detection [1, 2]. For example, Radinsky et al. [16] built predictive models to learn query dynamics from historical user data.

One important difference between the above cited papers and our work lies in the source of the temporal signals. Temporal evidence in most previous studies comes either from behavior log data or from analyzing a candidate set of documents. We extend these approaches by incorporating the temporal distribution of collection term statistics as another source of temporal signal.

2.2 Temporal Modeling of Pseudo Trends

Consider the query-likelihood approach in the language modeling framework [15]: documents are ranked by $P(D|Q) \propto P(Q|D)P(D)$, where $P(Q|D)$ is the likelihood that the language model that generated document D would also generate query Q, and $P(D)$ is the prior distribution. Below, we discuss several ways to incorporate temporal signals within this general framework.

Recency Prior: One of the simplest way to let time influence ranking was proposed by Li and Croft [12], in the form of a document prior that favors recently published documents. If T_D is the timestamp associated with document D, $P(D)$ could take the form of an exponential distribution (with rate parameter $\lambda \geq 0$): $P(D) = \lambda e^{-\lambda T_D}$. Although previous studies have shown that recency priors increase overall effectiveness, they are by definition query-independent. This approach, however, is problematic because we know that dependencies between time and relevance vary from query to query [10].

Moving Window (WIN): Dakka et al. [5] proposed a query-specific way to combine lexical and temporal evidence in the language modeling framework by separating the two components: W_D, the document's content and T_D, the document's timestamp. This leads to the following derivation:

$$P(D|Q) = P(W_D, T_D|Q) \tag{1}$$
$$= P(T_D|W_D, Q)P(W_D|Q) \tag{2}$$
$$\sim P(T_D|Q)P(W_D|Q) \tag{3}$$

where the last step follows from Eq. (2) if we assume independence between content and temporal evidence. More generally, we take the view that there are two sources of evidence we need to integrate in document ranking: $P(R|W_D, Q)$, based on document content, and $P(R|T_D, Q)$, based on temporal evidence.

The content relevance term $P(R|W_D, Q)$ can be modeled through a standard query-likelihood model [15]. The temporal relevance term can be estimated through the temporal distribution of documents retrieved by query Q. Since this temporal distribution is estimated from the initial retrieved documents, we call this the *pseudo trend* approach, in contrast with our *query trend* methods. To estimate the pseudo trend, Dakka et al. [5] adopted a moving window technique to group retrieved document into discrete bins based on the publication time of the documents.

Kernel Density Estimation (KDE): Efron et al. [8] extended the pseudo trend approach by inferring a continuous density function using kernel density estimation. As discussed in the introduction, the theoretical motivation for modeling the distribution of initial retrieved documents is what Efron et al. [8] call the temporal cluster hypothesis: that relevant documents tend to cluster together in time, in the same way that van Rijsbergen's "classic" cluster hypothesis suggests that documents relevant to a query Q cluster in term space. An example of such cluster distributions can be found in the first row of Figure 1.

In the KDE approach, each document is modeled as a Gaussian kernel estimator and associated with a weight to denote its importance. Efron et al. proposed four weighting schemas: *uniform*, *score-based*, *rank-based*, and *oracle*. Uniform weights assume that each document contributes equally, score-based weights are derived from normalized retrieval scores, and rank-based weights are computed from an exponential decay function of the rank positions of the documents. Finally, oracle weights come from performing KDE directly on the relevant documents (i.e., from human judgments). Of course, we do not know the distribution of relevant documents at query time, but the oracle weights quantify the effectiveness upper bound of KDE-based techniques.

Once we obtain an estimate of the pseudo trend, we can then compute the temporal relevance term for each document given its publication timestamp. This feature is further integrated with the lexical relevance term in a simple log-linear model as follows:

$$
\begin{aligned}
\log P_\alpha(R|D, Q) = Z_\alpha + (1 - \alpha) \log P(R|W_D, Q) \\
+ \alpha \log P(R|T_D, Q)
\end{aligned}
\tag{4}
$$

where Z_α is a normalization constant. These scores are then used to rerank documents from the initial query.

3 APPROACH

3.1 Temporal Modeling of Query Trends

Instead of attempting to estimate the distribution of relevant documents from the results of an initial query—what we've called pseudo trend approaches in the previous section—we adopt the alternative approach of directly leveraging the temporal distribution of query term statistics, which we call query trends. This approach has the obvious advantage of not requiring an initial retrieval; temporal term statistics can be gathered and efficiently compressed for low-latency lookup [20] as part of the indexing process.

Intuitively, we would expect to find more relevant documents in temporal intervals where the query terms are bursty. We illustrate this in Figure 1 for topic MB127 ("hagel nomination filibustered") from the TREC 2013 Microblog Track, as described in the introduction. The top row shows the actual distribution of relevant documents, which is the target of our prediction and of course not known at query time. The remaining rows show the query

trends of the unigrams "filibustered", "hagel", "nomination", and the bigram "hagel nomination".[1] As we might expect, there are correspondences between peaks in the query trends and the actual distribution of relevant documents—for example, the few days when the unigram "filibustered" occurs most frequently are also when most of the relevant documents are clustered.

Of course, not all query trends are created equal. In the example in Figure 1, we see that the distribution of the unigram "nomination" is less predictive of the distribution of relevant documents. Overall, we find that less bursty terms are less useful, a notion we can formally capture by computing the entropy of the distribution. Given the counts of a particular unigram or bigram $t = \{c_1, c_2, ..., c_n\}$ across various time intervals (e.g., days), its entropy can be computed as follows:

$$
\text{Entropy}(t) = - \sum_i \frac{c_i}{C} \log \frac{c_i}{C}
\tag{5}
$$

where $C = \sum_i c_i$. Lower entropy indicates a less uniform distribution and thus more bursty behavior.

From the query trends we can derive a family of features for a learning-to-rank model. There is, however, one additional complication we need to address: queries vary in length, which means that different queries have different numbers of unigram and bigram query trends. This is problematic since the linear feature-based model we use assumes a fixed number of features. We address this issue in a more principled manner in the next section, but here we introduce features based on the unigram and bigram with the lowest entropy (thus, the largest burstiness). We call these the *representative* unigram and bigram query trend, respectively.

From the basic concepts introduced above, we propose the following features:

- The relative entropy of the representative unigram. The relative entropy reflects the burstiness of a unigram query trend, computed as the absolute difference between the unigram entropy and the maximum entropy. The maximum entropy is computed by assuming a uniform distribution over term counts. Note that queries can have different timespans (because each is associated with a different query time), and thus the maximum entropy is query-dependent; computing relative entropy normalizes for the effects of different query timespans.
- The relative entropy of the representative bigram. This feature is computed in exactly the same manner as described above, except on bigram query trends.
- Estimated density at the document's timestamp from the query trend of the representative unigram. This feature is document-dependent. First, we perform kernel density estimation over the representative query unigram. Then, for the particular document that we are scoring, we compute the estimated density at the document's timestamp.
- Estimated density at the document's timestamp from the query trend of the representative bigram. This is similar to above, except with bigrams.

In Section 3.3, we detail how these features are integrated into the final ranking model.

---

[1]The other query bigram "nomination filibustered" is ignored in this analysis because it does not occur with sufficient frequency (based on a simple threshold).

	Description
N_q	number of queries
N_p	number of sample points per query
N	$N_q \cdot N_p$, number of sample points across all queries
N_u	max. number of unigrams per query (default 10)
N_b	max. number of bigrams per query (default 10)
Y_i	$N_p \times 1$, densities computed from relevant docs for query i
Y	$N \times 1$, concatenation of densities $(Y_1, ..., Y_i, ..., Y_{N_q})$
U	$N \times N_u$, densities computed from unigram trends
B	$N \times N_b$, densities computed from bigram trends
E_u	$N_q \times N_u$, normalized relative unigram entropies
E_b	$N_q \times N_b$, normalized relative bigram entropies
R	$N_q \times 1$, ratio of max unigram to bigram entropy
w_i^u	$N_u \times 1$, weight vector for unigrams of query i
w_i^b	$N_b \times 1$, weight vector for bigrams of query i

Table 1: Notation Table.

3.2 Regression on Query Trends

The above feature engineering approach tries to predict the distribution of relevant documents via a single representative unigram or bigram query trend. An alternative is to integrate evidence from *all* unigram and bigram query trends. Such an approach, however, can be a double-edged sword. On the one hand, we observe that for many topics, the distribution of relevant documents has many peaks. In these cases, it is unlikely that a single unigram or bigram query trend is sufficient to reconstruct the reference distribution. Such cases would seemingly benefit from integrating multiple sources of evidence to overcome the limited signal from any individual query trend. On the other hand, we see that some query trends have low or even negative correlations with the actual distribution of relevant documents (e.g., query terms that aren't important to the information need). In these cases, the query trends merely introduce noise into the prediction. How to balance these two factors is a question we explore.

The basic idea behind our regression-based method is to predict the actual query distribution by integrating all unigram and bigram query trends. When a query arrives, we can apply the entropy computations and kernel density estimations on all query terms. Suppose we have computed an entropy of e_t and a kernel density function of f_t for each term t. We can then attempt to fit the actual density of relevant documents Y (which is obtained by KDE on the distribution of relevant documents) as follows:

$$Y \approx \sum_t w_t f_t \qquad (6)$$

where weight w_t is a function of entropy e_t and our goal is to learn this mapping function.

Note that approximating a continuous function from multiple kernel density functions is difficult, so instead we sample the distributions at fixed intervals. Now this model transforms into a non-linear regression problem. Given the unigram entropies E_u, bigram entropies E_b, unigram densities U at the sample points, and bigram densities B at the sample points, our task is to predict the densities Y at the same points. For more details about symbols used in this section, please refer to Table 1.

Two questions need to be answered in this non-linear regression problem. First, how to determine the importance of each term in contributing to the estimated density? Based on our observations, we find that terms with larger normalized entropies, i.e., a larger difference between its absolute entropy and the entropy of a uniform distribution, are more likely to reflect the true distribution of relevant documents. Therefore, we formulate the mapping from entropy to weights via an exponential increasing function, $w_t = \exp(\theta \cdot e_t) - 1$, where e_t is the normalized entropy of term t with its value ranging from zero to one. A term with zero normalized entropy would have zero weight, and thus can be ignored. The parameter θ controls the exponential rate. We use α for unigrams and β for bigrams as θ below.

The second question is how to differentiate contributions of unigrams from those of bigrams. For some queries, unigram query trends are more predictive, while for others, bigram trends are more predictive. How to evaluate their contributions for different queries is one key aspect of our model. To this end, for each query, we assign a weight $u_i \in [0, 1]$ to denote its unigram contribution; the corresponding bigram weight would be $1 - u_i$. We link the normalized unigram weight u_i to the entropy ratio R_i (which is the ratio of the maximum normalized unigram to bigram entropy for query i) by observing correlations between these two factors in training data. This mapping is normalized by a logistic function:

$$u_i = \text{logistic}(R_i, \gamma) = \frac{1}{1 + \exp(-\gamma R_i)} \qquad (7)$$

where

$$R_i = \frac{\max_u E_i^u}{\max_b E_i^b} - 1 \qquad (8)$$

and γ is a parameter to be estimated.

Intuitively, R_i greater than zero implies that the maximum normalized unigram entropy is larger than the maximum normalized bigram entropy. In this case, the logistic function would assign a unigram weight $u_i > 0.5$, and so unigrams would contribute more to the density estimate than bigrams. Finally, we desire that the integrated densities approximate the actual query density Y for each query i:

$$Y_i \approx u_i U_i w_i^u + (1 - u_i) B_i w_i^b \qquad (9)$$

where w_i^u and w_i^b are weight vectors of unigrams and bigrams of query i, respectively. Overall, we sum up the square loss between ground truth densities Y_i and the estimated densities $\hat{Y}_i$ over all queries, plus some regularization terms. The final loss function L is formulated as follows:

$$L = \sum_{i=1}^{N_q} \|Y_i - (u_i U_i (e^{\alpha E_i^u} - 1)^T + (1 - u_i) B_i (e^{\beta E_i^b} - 1)^T)\|^2 \\ + \lambda(\alpha^2 + \beta^2 + \gamma^2) \qquad (10)$$

where R_i and u_i are defined above.

Note that this model has three parameters (α, β, and γ) to be estimated, which are the weights of the entropy mapping function and the logistic function. Since the loss L is differentiable with respect to the three parameters, we can optimize the parameters using gradient-based methods. By constituting the logistic function into the overall loss function L, the gradients with respect to the parameters are computed as follows:

	Description
1	QL score
	Density estimate from:
2	KDE over initial retrieved docs (uniform)
3	KDE over initial retrieved docs (score-based)
4	KDE over initial retrieved docs (rank-based)
5	KDE over relevant docs (oracle)
	Section 3.1
6	Relative entropy of representative unigram
7	Relative entropy of representative bigram
	Density estimate from:
8	KDE of representative unigram distribution
9	KDE of representative bigram distribution
	Section 3.2
10	Density estimate from query trend regression model

Table 2: Summary of all features.

$$\text{term} = 2 \cdot \left(Y_i - (u_i U_i (e^{\alpha E_i^u} - 1)^T + (1 - u_i) B_i (e^{\beta E_i^b} - 1)^T) \right)$$

$$\frac{\partial L}{\partial \alpha} = - \sum_{i=1}^{N_q} \left(u_i \cdot \text{term}^T \cdot U_i \cdot (E_i^u \cdot e^{\alpha E_i^u})^T \right) + 2\lambda\alpha$$

$$\frac{\partial L}{\partial \beta} = - \sum_{i=1}^{N_q} \left((1 - u_i) \cdot \text{term}^T \cdot B_i \cdot (E_i^b \cdot e^{\beta E_i^b})^T \right) + 2\lambda\beta$$

$$\frac{\partial L}{\partial \gamma} = \sum_{i=1}^{N_q} \left(\text{term}^T \cdot \left(-U_i \cdot (e^{\alpha E_i^u} - 1)^T + B_i \cdot (e^{\beta E_i^b} - 1)^T \right) \right.$$
$$\left. \cdot R_i \text{logistic}(R_i, \gamma) \cdot (1 - \text{logistic}(R_i, \gamma)) \right) + 2\lambda\gamma$$

After solving the objective, we learn two mappings: an exponential mapping from entropy to term weight $w^t = \exp(\theta e) - 1$, and a logistic mapping from ratio to unigram weight $u = \text{logistic}(R, \gamma)$. We are then able to estimate densities for queries in the test data:

$$\hat{Y}_i = u_i U_i w_i^u + (1 - u_i) B_i w_i^b \qquad (11)$$

Finally, the estimated density $\hat{Y}_i$ serves as a feature in the final evidence combination approach (more details below).

3.3 Pulling Everything Together

To recap, we have introduced three families of features for modeling temporal evidence: KDE applied to initial retrieved documents [8] (Section 2.2), features derived from query trends (Section 3.1), and density estimates from a query trend regression model (Section 3.2). In total, we have ten features, including query-likelihood for capturing content relevance, which are summarized in Table 2.

As previously discussed, we integrate all these features in a linear feature-based ranking model [13]. The general form of such a model, extended from Eq. (4), is as follows:

$$S_d = \sum_i \alpha_i \cdot F_i(d, q) \quad \text{s.t.} \sum_i \alpha_i = 1. \qquad (12)$$

Naturally, we would like to understand the relative contributions of each type of feature, but it does not make sense to exhaustively

Method	Features
QL	1
IRD_u	1, 2
IRD_s	1, 3
IRD_r	1, 4
QT	1, 6–9
QT + IRD_r	1, 4, 6–9
Reg	1, 10
Reg + IRD_r	1, 4, 10
Oracle	1, 5

Table 3: Summary of different feature combinations.

explore all possible combinations. Thus, we took the middle road and explored a number of interesting feature set combinations, summarized in Table 3:

- Different weighting schemes for KDE applied to the initial retrieved documents. These are the same experimental conditions in Efron et al. [8] and Rao et al. [19]. For convenience, these models are referred to as IRD_u (uniform weights), IRD_s (score-based weights), and IRD_r (rank-based weights). Previous experiments [19] show that rank-based weights are the most effective overall, and thus for subsequent configurations we only use rank-based weights.
- Query trend features as a group (QT) and query trend features combined with KDE on the initial retrieved documents with rank-based weights (QT + IRD_r).
- Query trend regression (Reg) and query trend regression combined with KDE on the initial retrieved documents with rank-based weights (Reg + IRD_r).

Note that use of the IRD_r features requires an initial retrieval, and thus we lose the efficiency advantage of feature combinations that use only query trends.

4 EVALUATION

4.1 Experimental Setup

We evaluated our proposed methods on Twitter test collections from the TREC 2013 and 2014 Microblog Tracks (60 topics and 55 topics, respectively). Both use the Tweets2013 collection, which consists of approximately 243 million tweets crawled from Twitter's public sample stream between February 1 and March 31, 2013. NIST assessors provided relevance judgments on a three-point scale ("not relevant", "relevant", "highly relevant") but in this work we treated both higher grades as "relevant". We removed all retweets in our experiments since they are by definition not relevant according to the assessment guidelines.

To rule out the effects of different preprocessing strategies during collection preparation (i.e., stemming, stopword removal, etc.), we used the open-source implementations of tweet search provided by the TREC Microblog API[2] to retrieve up to 1000 tweets per topic using query likelihood (QL) for scoring. On this candidate set of documents we applied our various methods for reranking. Following the TREC Microblog Tracks, we used average precision (AP) and precision at 30 (P30) to measure effectiveness.

---

[2]https://github.com/lintool/twitter-tools

ID		Method	Odd-Even		Even-Odd		Cross	
			AP	P30	AP	P30	AP	P30
1		Query Likelihood (QL) [15]	0.271	0.475	0.357	0.564	0.315	0.520
2		Recency prior [12]	0.277	0.499[1]	0.359	0.574	0.313	0.534[1,4]
3		Moving Window (WIN) [5]	0.283[1]	0.487[1]	0.358	0.567	0.319	0.527
4	KDE [8]	IRD_u	0.273	0.481	0.350	0.566	0.308	0.515
5		IRD_s	0.274	0.487[1]	0.353	0.577[1]	0.314	0.530[1,4]
6		IRD_r	0.288[1,4,5]	0.517[1,3,4,5]	0.360	0.588[1,2,3,4]	0.327[1,2,4,5]	0.552[1,2,3,4,5]
7	This work	**QT**	0.278	0.492[1,4]	0.367[1,4,5]	0.587[1,2,3,4]	0.320	0.530[1,4]
8		**Reg**	0.276	0.488[1]	0.366[1,4,5]	0.576[1]	0.329[1,2,4,5]	0.535[1,4]
9		**QT-IRD_r**	0.290[1,2,4,5]	0.522[1,2,3,4,5]	**0.370**[1,2,3,4,5]	**0.598**[1,2,3,4,5]	0.328[1,2,4,5]	0.565[1,2,3,4,5]
10		**Reg-IRD_r**	**0.302**[1,2,3,4,5,6]	**0.535**[1,2,3,4,5]	0.368[1,2,3,4,5]	0.596[1,2,3,4,5]	**0.332**[1,2,3,4,5]	**0.566**[1,2,3,4,5]
11		Oracle	0.314[1,2,3,4,5,6]	0.536[1,2,3,4,5,6]	0.382[1,2,3,4,5,6]	0.636[1,2,3,4,5,6]	0.349[1,2,3,4,5,6]	0.586[1,2,3,4,5,6]

Table 4: Results from the TREC 2013/14 Microblog Track test collections: "Odd-Even" represents training on odd topics and testing on even topics; "Even-Odd" represents the opposite; "Cross" represents four-fold cross validation. Superscripts indicate the row indexes from which the metric differences are statistically significant ($p < 0.05$).

In our experiments, we examined four different ways of splitting the test collections into training and test sets:

- First, we trained on odd-numbered topics from the TREC 2013 and 2014 Microblog Tracks (57 topics) and evaluated on even-numbered topics (58 topics).
- Second, we swapped the training/test splits: training on even-numbered topics and testing on odd-numbered topics.
- Third, we performed four-fold cross validation across all topics.
- Finally, we performed a series of trials in which we randomly selected half the topics for training and used the remaining for testing. Results across multiple trials are aggregated.

We used coordinate ascent in RankLib[3] to learn the parameters in Eq. (12), optimizing and evaluating on the same metric.

Several baselines were used as points of comparison to our proposed methods. Query likelihood (QL) [15] was used as a lexical baseline. Temporal baselines included:

- Li and Croft's recency prior method [12].
- The moving window method of Dakka et al. [5].
- The kernel density estimation (KDE) methods of Efron et al. [8] with uniform weights (IRD_u), score-based weights (IRD_s), and rank-based weights (IRD_r).

In addition, we also include the KDE oracle as a reference upper bound. In this condition, we apply kernel density estimation over the distribution of the relevant documents based on human assessor judgments. This characterizes how much temporal signal can be extracted to improve relevance ranking, at least with this class of density estimation techniques.

To build the query trend features, we needed to precompute collection frequencies across time windows for the entire vocabulary. We aggregated term statistics and worked with query trends at the day granularity—that is, each term's trend is represented by an integer array of size 59, where each integer denotes the collection frequency for a single day. By discarding terms with a collection frequency lower than five, we extracted a total of 2.3 million unigrams and 23.1 million bigrams from the Tweets2013 collection. These term statistics are compressed with PForDelta [20], down to

a size of 0.26 GB for unigrams and 2.2 GB for bigrams. The average decoding time of the compressed term statistics is 5.1 μs per unigram and 5.8 μs per bigram on a commodity server. Due to the efficient compression, we are able to load the term statistics into memory to estimate query trend features very quickly.

4.2 Effectiveness of Temporal Models

Results of our experiments are summarized in Table 4. Each row denotes an experimental condition (numbered for convenience): the third column "Odd-Even" represents training on odd-numbered topics and testing on even-numbered topics; "Even-Odd" represents the opposite; "Cross" represents four-fold cross validation. The best result for each setting is in bold. We compared each method against all lexical and temporal baselines for statistical significance using Fisher's two-sided, paired randomization test [22]. Superscripts indicate the row indexes from which the metric differences are statistically significant ($p < 0.05$).

First, we observe that most temporal baselines (Recency, WIN, IRD_s, and IRD_r) outperform the lexical baseline in terms of P30, but generally not in terms of AP, suggesting that they are better suited to improving early precision. Among the temporal baselines, IRD_u performs consistently the worst and IRD_r outperforms the rest. Note that while IRD_s and IRD_r both place more weight on top-ranked documents, the gap in effectiveness comes from the fact that the retrieved scores of the top-ranked documents are generally quite similar. Thus, score normalization does not introduce sufficient bias to help us distinguish the high-ranking documents.

Second, we see that our query trend methods (QT and Reg) significantly outperform the lexical baselines in most conditions, suggesting that signals captured from temporal collection statistics are beneficial to relevance ranking. While these "vanilla" query trend methods alone do not significantly improve over the temporal baselines, combining them with the pseudo trend methods (as in QT+IRD_r and Reg+IRD_r) yields a boost in effectiveness. These ensemble methods are consistently more effective than the best-performing temporal baseline IRD_r. They also come close to the upper bound (oracle) in some conditions, especially for P30. For the Reg+IRD_r model, features 1, 4, and 10 (query likelihood, IRD_r, Reg

---

[3]https://sourceforge.net/p/lemur/wiki/RankLib/

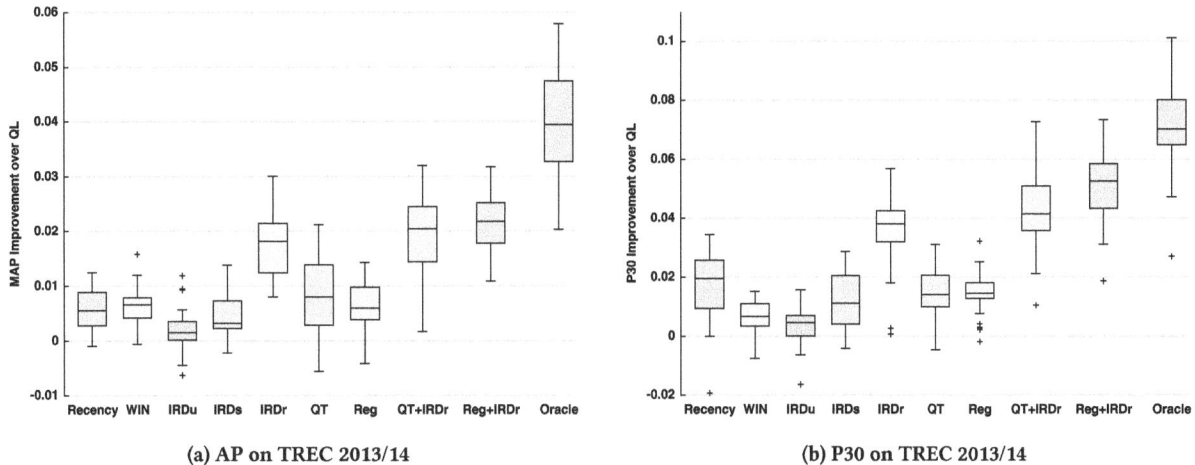

(a) AP on TREC 2013/14

(b) P30 on TREC 2013/14

Figure 2: Box-and-whiskers plots summarizing how much each temporal model outperforms the QL baseline across 30 random trials (half for training, half for testing) on the TREC 2013/14 Microblog Track test collections.

features) received weights 0.84, 0.10, and 0.06 in the Odd-Even split, respectively, which shows that the different sources of temporal evidence are complementary.

In the above experiments, we noticed variance in effectiveness under different conditions, depending on how the test collections are split into training/test sets. Our random split experiments were designed to factor out noise from this issue. In each trial, we trained on half of the topics (randomly selected) and evaluated on the other half. We then computed the effectiveness differences between each technique and the QL baseline. These differences, collected over 30 trials, are summarized in box-and-whiskers plots in Figure 2 for all temporal approaches. We show the distribution of effectiveness differences in terms of AP (left) and P30 (right). Each box represents the span between the first and third quartiles, with a horizontal line at the median value. Whiskers extend from the ends of each box to the most distant point whose value lies within 1.5 times the interquartile range. Points that lie outside these limits are drawn individually. These results capture the overall effectiveness of each method, better than metrics from any single arbitrary split.

From Figure 2, it is clear that IRD_r outperforms all baselines as well as the raw query trend approaches (QT and Reg). The ensemble approaches ($QT+IRD_r$ and $Reg+IRD_r$) yield further improvement over IRD_r, with $Reg+IRD_r$ coming out higher. Although we did not observe a statistically significant difference between our best ensemble method ($Reg+IRD_r$) and the best baseline (IRD_r) in our previous experiments, the box plots show that the effectiveness gains of $Reg+IRD_r$ are more consistent, This is especially true for P30 (right side of Figure 2): the median of $Reg+IRD_r$ is above 0.05 whereas IRD_r has a median below 0.04. Another observation is that the bottom of the $Reg+IRD_r$ box is still above the top of the IRD_r box, meaning that the top 75% of $Reg+IRD_r$ runs were better than the bottom 75% of IRD_r runs. Although it is difficult to definitively conclude statistical significance from these experiments, quantifying the variance associated with arbitrary training/test splits provides additional evidence supporting the effectiveness of our proposed methods.

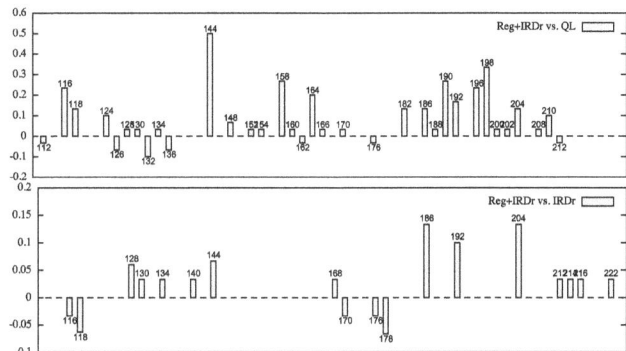

Figure 3: Per-topic improvements of the ensemble model $Reg+IRD_r$ compared to the QL baseline and IRD_r method.

4.3 Per-topic Analysis

In order to gain a better understanding of how different temporal features contribute to effectiveness in temporal ranking, we performed a topic-by-topic analysis along with an in-depth examination of the various component distributions. Due to a lack of space, here we present only results comparing the best-performing ensemble model ($Reg+IRD_r$) against the lexical baseline QL and the temporal baseline IRD_r. In Figure 3, we show per-topic differences as a bar chart, measured in terms of P30 on the even topics from the TREC 2013/14 Microblog Track test collections.

From the top bar chart in Figure 3, we can see that the ensemble model ($Reg+IRD_r$) improves over the QL baseline for most of the topics; there are only a few topics where effectiveness decreases (and not by much). From the bottom bar chart, we see that $Reg+IRD_r$ improves over IRD_r alone, which confirms that the regression model contributes additional signal over kernel density estimation alone.

In Figure 4 we take a closer look at the best-performing topic, MB144 "downtown abbey actor turnover". The top row shows the distribution of relevant documents (in red), the second row shows

139

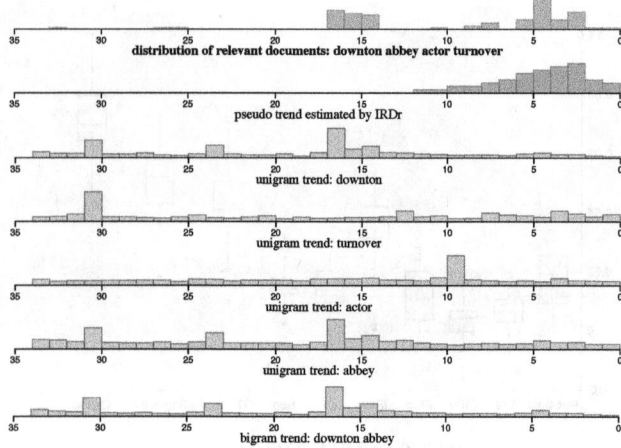

Figure 4: Analysis of MB144 ("downtown abbey actor turnover") from the TREC 2013 Microblog Track. Rows show: distribution of relevant documents (red), pseudo trend based on KDE (green), and query trends (blue).

the distribution inferred from the pseudo trend using IRD_r (in green), and the remaining rows show the query trends (in blue). Clearly, we can see that the distribution of relevant documents has two peaks, one around days 3–5 and the other around days 14–16. We can observe that the pseudo trend from IRD_r is able to capture the burst of relevant documents at days 3–5. We also see a strong correlation between the query trends (unigrams "downtown", "abbey", and the bigram "downtown abbey") and the ground truth relevance distribution at days 14–16. Thus, the combination of pseudo trend and query trend features allows us to nicely recover this multimodal distribution, which is affirmed by the large improvements for this topic compared to both QL and IRD_r. In addition, the regression model is able to smooth out noise from non-important terms "actor" and "turnover". This observation is confirmed in many other topics, like MB192 "whooping cough epidemic" and MB204 "sotomayor, prosecutor, racial comment", where we also observe strong correlations between query trends and the ground truth relevance distributions.

We also examined topics where effectiveness decreased with respect to IRD_r, such as MB116 "Chinese computer attacks" and MB118 "Israel and Turkey reconcile". We found that the representative query trends (the unigram "Chinese" for MB116 and the bigram "and Turkey" for MB118) are very different from the distribution of relevant documents, and thus our methods infer an inaccurate distribution. No approach is perfect, but overall our per-topic analysis affirms the effectiveness of our query trend methods.

5 CONCLUSION

Quite obviously, the temporal distribution of relevant documents provides an important signal for temporal ranking. As an alternative to previous pseudo trend methods that analyze the results of an initial query to infer this distribution, we propose query trend methods that attempt to make predictions directly from the temporal collection statistics of query terms. Experiments show that these sources of evidence are complementary, and the regression method

appears to be more effective than the feature-based approach. Although query trend methods alone, which do not require an initial retrieval, improve over a lexical baseline, combining query trends with pseudo trends yields the best results. This ensemble approach, however, *does* require an initial retrieval, which negates the performance advantages of query trend methods. Costly approaches that involve actually searching the collection appear to provide temporal signals that we currently cannot obtain from the temporal collection statistics of query terms alone.

6 ACKNOWLEDGMENTS

This work was supported by the Natural Sciences and Engineering Research Council (NSERC) of Canada, with additional contributions from the U.S. National Science Foundation under CNS-1405688. Any findings, conclusions, or recommendations expressed do not necessarily reflect the views of the sponsors.

REFERENCES

[1] Chao Zhang, Liyuan Liu, Dongming Lei, Quan Yuan, Honglei Zhuang, Tim Hanratty, and Jiawei Han. 2017. TrioVecEvent: Embedding-Based Online Local Event Detection in Geo-Tagged Tweet Streams. In *KDD*. 595–604.
[2] Chao Zhang, Guangyu Zhou, Quan Yuan, Honglei Zhuang, Yu Zheng, Lance Kaplan, Shaowen Wang, and Jiawei Han. 2016. GeoBurst: Real-Time Local Event Detection in Geo-Tagged Tweet Streams. In *SIGIR*. 513–522.
[3] Jaeho Choi and W. Bruce Croft. 2012. Temporal Models for Microblogs. In *CIKM*. 2491–2494.
[4] Olga Craveiro, Joaquim Macedo, and Henrique Madeira. 2014. Query Expansion with Temporal Segmented Texts. In *ECIR*. 612–617.
[5] Wisam Dakka, Luis Gravano, and Panagiotis G. Ipeirotis. 2012. Answering General Time-Sensitive Queries. *TKDE* 24, 2 (2012), 220–235.
[6] Anlei Dong, Ruiqiang Zhang, Pranam Kolari, Jing Bai, Fernando Diaz, Yi Chang, Zhaohui Zheng, and Hongyuan Zha. 2010. Time is of the Essence: Improving Recency Ranking Using Twitter Data. In *WWW*. 331–340.
[7] Miles Efron and Gene Golovchinsky. 2011. Estimation Methods for Ranking Recent Information. In *SIGIR*. 495–504.
[8] Miles Efron, Jimmy Lin, Jiyin He, and Arjen de Vries. 2014. Temporal Feedback for Tweet Search with Non-Parametric Density Estimation. In *SIGIR*. 33–42.
[9] Jonathan L. Elsas and Susan T. Dumais. 2010. Leveraging Temporal Dynamics of Document Content in Relevance Ranking. In *WSDM*. 1–10.
[10] Rosie Jones and Fernando Diaz. 2007. Temporal Profiles of Queries. *TOIS* 25, 3 (2007), Article 14.
[11] Mostafa Keikha, Shima Gerani, and Fabio Crestani. 2011. TEMPER: A Temporal Relevance Feedback Method. In *ECIR*. 436–447.
[12] Xiaoyan Li and W. Bruce Croft. 2003. Time-Based Language Models. In *CIKM*. 469–475.
[13] Donald Metzler and W. Bruce Croft. 2007. Linear Feature-Based Models for Information Retrieval. *Information Retrieval* 10, 3 (2007), 257–274.
[14] Gilad Mishne, Jeff Dalton, Zhenghua Li, Aneesh Sharma, and Jimmy Lin. 2012. Fast Data in the Era of Big Data: Twitter's Real-Time Related Query Suggestion Architecture. In *SIGMOD*. 1147–1157.
[15] Jay M. Ponte and W. Bruce Croft. 1998. A Language Modeling Approach to Information Retrieval. In *SIGIR*. 275–281.
[16] Kira Radinsky, Krysta Svore, Susan Dumais, Jaime Teevan, Alex Bocharov, and Eric Horvitz. 2012. Modeling and Predicting Behavioral Dynamics on the Web. In *WWW*. 599–608.
[17] Jinfeng Rao, Hua He, Haotian Zhang, Ferhan Ture, Royal Sequiera, Salman Mohammed, and Jimmy Lin. 2017. Integrating Lexical and Temporal Signals in Neural Ranking Models for Social Media Search. In *SIGIR Workshop on Neural Information Retrieval (Neu-IR)*.
[18] Jinfeng Rao and Jimmy Lin. 2016. Temporal Query Expansion Using a Continuous Hidden Markov Model. In *ICITR*. 295–298.
[19] Jinfeng Rao, Jimmy Lin, and Miles Efron. 2015. Reproducible Experiments on Lexical and Temporal Feedback for Tweet Search. In *ECIR*. 755–767.
[20] Jinfeng Rao, Xing Niu, and Jimmy Lin. 2016. Compressing and Decoding Term Statistics Time Series. In *ECIR*. 675–681.
[21] Milad Shokouhi and Kira Radinsky. 2012. Time-Sensitive Query Auto-Completion. In *SIGIR*. 601–610.
[22] Mark D. Smucker, James Allan, and Ben Carterette. 2007. A Comparison of Statistical Significance Tests for Information Retrieval Evaluation. In *CIKM*. 623–632.

Modeling Controversy within Populations

Myungha Jang, Shiri Dori-Hacohen and James Allan
Center for Intelligent Information Retrieval
College of Information and Computer Sciences
University of Massachusetts

ABSTRACT

A growing body of research focuses on computationally detecting controversial topics and understanding the stances people hold on them. Yet gaps remain in our theoretical and practical understanding of how to define controversy, how it manifests, and how to measure it. Since controversy is a complicated social phenomenon, it is difficult to understand what elements make up the controversy. Previous work has attempted to capture controversy algorithmically by studying cues for disagreement and polarity between different stance groups. However, we still lack a systematic understanding of how controversy should be defined and measured. In this paper, we propose a multi-dimensional model of controversy. Specifically, we introduce a model with two minimal dimensions: contention and importance. Our model departs from existing work by viewing controversy as a trait rooted in population. It suggests that controversy should be separately observed in a given population, rather than held as a fixed universal quantity. We model contention and importance within a population from a mathematical standpoint. To validate and evaluate the soundness of our theoretical model, we instantiate the model to algorithms for a diverse set of sources: polling, Twitter, and Wikipedia. We demonstrate that our controversy model holds an explanatory power for observed phenomena but also a predictive power for tasks, such as identifying controversial Wikipedia articles.

1 INTRODUCTION

Social networks, such as Twitter, Facebook, and discussion boards, have become one of the most popular places where controversial arguments are held. Accordingly, technological tools have also become critical in shaping these discussions by curating and filtering the content seen by each user. From a computational perspective, we currently do not understand controversy well enough. Algorithms based on an incomplete understanding of controversy are bound to fail in unexpected ways, which can replicate or even exacerbate the sources of human bias.

Recent work on controversy cuts across traditional disciplinary lines—including a wide variety of computational tasks along with the social sciences and the humanities—and has made significant strides in analyzing and detecting controversy (cf. [3, 12]). Nevertheless, there are serious gaps in our theoretical and practical

understanding of how to define controversy, how it manifests, and how it evolves. For example, polling organizations naturally select topics of broad interest and segment their results based on certain populations defined by demographics such as race and gender. These notions are surprisingly absent from algorithmic analyses of controversy. Instead, controversy has only been defined as an absolute, single value for an amorphous global population.

Meanwhile, there has been a growing disparity between scientific understanding and public opinion on certain controversial topics, such as climate change, evolution, and vaccination [19], with many scientists fighting these trends by arguing that "there is no controversy" [13] (referring to *scientific* controversy). Still, non-scientific claims and arguments have continued to proliferate, raising exposure to the supposedly non-existent controversies. As researchers studying controversies online, how can we reconcile the oft-repeated argument from the scientific community that "there is no controversy" with the practical appearance of wildly diverse opinions on many topics? In other words, is a topic like climate change controversial?[1]

We address these issues by proposing a theoretical model that defines controversy as a combination of at least "contention" and "importance" with respect to a given population. The model therefore captures the idea that not all controversies are of equal interest. It also suggests that the right question to be asked is not "is climate change controversial?" but instead "is climate change controversial to *a particular group?*"

Our framework departs from existing work on controversy in several important ways. First, we define controversy in terms of not only its topic but also a given population. Second, our model accounts for participants in the population who hold no stance on a specific topic and also allows for any number of stances rather than just a strict dichotomy. Third, our model allows that some items may be less controversial because they are contentious but not important (and vice versa). These elements give our model explanatory power that can be used to understand a large variety of observed phenomena, ranging from international conflict and community-specific controversies to high-stakes public controversies on well-understood phenomena such as climate change, evolution, and vaccination.

In order to ground our theoretical model, we examine a diverse collection of datasets from both online and offline sources. First, we examine several real-world polling datasets, including a poll that focuses on opinions about scientific topics, such as climate change and evolution, measured among the general US population and the scientific community [20]. Additionally, we look at Twitter coverage for three prominent controversies: the 2016 US Elections, the UK European Union membership referendum, commonly known

ICTIR'17, October 1–4, 2017, Amsterdam, The Netherlands.
© 2017 ACM. ISBN 978-1-4503-4490-6/17/10...$15.00
DOI: http://dx.doi.org/10.1145/3121050.3121067

---

[1] This differs from a value judgment, such as "Should climate change be controversial?".

as Brexit, and "The Dress," a photo that went viral when people disagreed on its colors. We cross-reference contention from Twitter with other data sources: a popular online poll for "The Dress," real voter data for Brexit, and the US Elections. Finally, we apply our model to Wikipedia and show that it can predict whether or not a Wikipedia article is controversial.

2 RELATED WORK

Most recent work on controversy has measured controversy as either a binary state or a single quantity, both of which are to be measured or estimated directly [2, 3, 15, 22]. With a few exceptions [1, 16], earlier work did not model controversy formally. Even when it did, the meaning of controversy was not modeled, but instead assumed to be a known quantity in the world. Most prior work in computer science does not define controversy and treats it as a global quantity (cf.[17, 28]). Past research shows that achieving inter-annotator agreement on the "controversy" label is challenging [10, 18].

Meanwhile, most of the work on controversy in the social sciences and the humanities is qualitative by nature and often focuses on one or two examples of controversy (c.f. [11, 24]). Otherwise, it works toward a more qualitative analysis of the overall patterns across controversies [9] with one notable exception [8]. Chen and Berger, while discussing whether controversy increases buzz and whether that is good for business, propose that "controversial issues tend to involve opposing viewpoints that are strongly held" [6]. However, these definitions leave a gap when people disagree on opinions that are strongly held on less important topics such as the color of a dress, the orientation of toilet paper. There may be "opposing viewpoints" in these topics, but there is no real controversy.

We depart from past research by modeling controversy as a multi-dimensional quantity within population. Similarly, Timmermans et al. also identified five aspects of controversy in news articles: time persistence, emotion, multitude of actors, polarity, and openness. While their approach is closest to our work, they have specifically targeted news articles and have not focused on actual modeling [26].

3 MODELING POPULATION-BASED CONTROVERSY

Controversy is a complicated social phenomenon. Since it is difficult to formally and systematically define what controversy is, there has been little effort to formulate a model that quantifies the level of controversy for a given topic.

As a motivating example, consider two controversies: "The Dress" and the Brexit referendum. First, "The Dress" refers to a photo that went viral over social media starting on Feb. 26, 2015 after people could not agree on its colors. The photo was posted to tumblr and made popular by a Buzzfeed article that asked "What color is this dress?" in a poll with two options: black and blue or gold and white. To date, over 37 million people viewed the article [14]. Second, the Brexit referendum, officially known as the UK European Union membership referendum, was a referendum that took place on June 23, 2016 in which 51.9% of UK voters voted to leave the European Union. The referendum had immediate political and

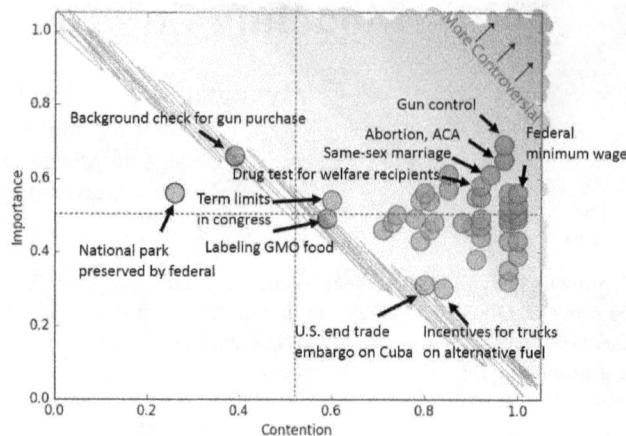

Figure 1: iSideWith topics plotted in the two-dimensional controversy plot of contention and importance. Contention scores are computed by our definition of contention and importance was given by users in the dataset. Sample topics are given in each quadrant of {low,high} importance and contention.

financial ramifications, including the worst one-day drop in the global stock market in history,

When observed by populations interested in each controversy, "The Dress" and Brexit were both extremely contentious. Nearly any group of people sampled from these populations was strongly divided in their opinion. However, it is clear that placing 'The Dress" and Brexit in the same bucket is problematic. Brexit affects the fate of entire nations, with far-reaching consequences on diplomatic relationships and the world economy. The other, a photo of the dress, caused a surprising divided reaction in color perception, went viral around the world, and was subsequently forgotten by nearly everyone. In other words, it had little impact on the world.

Therefore, we propose a new model in which controversy is composed of at least two orthogonal dimensions, which together play a role in determining how controversial a topic is for a given population, one of which is *contention*. However, this dimension alone cannot adequately explain less important controversies like "The Dress." An additional orthogonal metric is needed in order to distinguish between contention and controversy. Therefore, we hypothesize the existence of a notion of *importance* as a novel dimension of controversy. While more dimensions can be investigated, we hypothesize that these are the core features of controversy.

This framework is illustrated schematically in Figure 1, overlaying actual results including importance reported in the iSideWith dataset (see Table 2). The first dimension is contention, which we define as the proportion of people who are in disagreement. The other dimension is importance, which we loosely define as the level of impact of that issue to the world, and which was reported by users of iSideWith. In Figure 1, we hypothesize controversy to be a two-dimensional concept. An issue is more controversial when it has high contention and high importance (i.e., towards the right upper corner of Figure 5). Figure 1 shows a quadrant where an issue can have a {high, low} contention with a {high, low} importance.

Issues, such as gun control, abortion, and the Affordable Care Act, have high contention and high importance. Therefore, they are more controversial. Issues, such as whether the government should provide incentives for trucks to run on alternative fuels, is highly contentious but less important according to users.

Finally, we model the probability of controversy with a given topic T and a given population Ω. Let $Cont$ a binary random variable, which denotes the presence of controversy. Simiarly, let C and I be binary random variables, which denotes the presence of contention and importance of topic T.

We model $P(Cont|\theta)$, where $\theta = \{T, \Omega\}$ as the probability that topic T is controversial within the population Ω. Our model hypothesizes that the probability of controversy given T and Ω is the joint probability of two dimensions: contention (C) and importance (I), to be more rigorously defined later.

$$P(Cont|\theta) = P(C, I|\theta)$$

Here, $P(C, I|\theta)$ can be further decomposed as following:

$$P(C, I|\theta) = \frac{P(C, I, \theta)}{P(\theta)} = \frac{P(I|C, \theta) \cdot P(C|\theta) \cdot P(\theta)}{P(\theta)} = P(I|C, \theta) \cdot P(C|\theta)$$

To compute $P(I|C, \theta)$, the correlation between contention and importance of topic to a population has to be identified. While it is difficult to estimate the exact correlation in the real world, we assume that contention and importance are independent of each other, consisting of orthogonal dimensions of controversy. We therefore let $P(I|C, \theta) = P(I|\theta)$.

$$P(Cont|\theta) = P(C|\theta) \cdot P(I|\theta)$$

We now discuss the modeling of $P(C|\theta)$ and $P(I|\theta)$ and how to estimate them from the real data. Refer to Table 1 for the summary of the notations that are used in the model.

Table 1: Notation summary

Symbol	Definition
Ω	a population
$P(Cont|\theta)$	the probability that topic T is controversial in a given population Ω
$P(C|\theta)$	the probability that T is contentious in Ω
$P(I|\theta)$	the probability that T is important in Ω
C	a binary random variable for contention
c	a binary value to set C to be "contentious"
nc	a binary value to set C to be "non-contentious"
s	a stance with regard to topic T
$holds(p, s, T)$	a person p holds stance s with regard to topic T
$affected(T, p)$	a binary function that returns whether or not a person p is affected by topic T
$\hat{S}$	k stances with regard to topic T
s_0	a lack of stance
G_i	a group of people who hold stance s_i
O_i	an opposing group in the population that hold a stance that conflicts with s_i

3.1 Modeling Contention from Population

We define a measure we call *contention*, which quantifies the proportion of people in disagreement within a population. We begin with a general formulation of contention and then describe a special case in which stances are assumed to be mutually exclusive.

Let $\Omega = \{p_1..p_n\}$ be a population of n people. Let T be a topic of interest to at least one person in population Ω. We define C to be a binary variable to denote whether or not a given topic is contentious. Let us also define two binary values c and nc for C, each of which respectively means contentious and non-contentious. For example, $P(C = c|\Omega, T)$ denotes the probability that T is contentious in Ω, which we will simply denote it as $P(c|\Omega, T)$. Therefore, $P(c|\Omega, T) + P(nc|\Omega, T) = 1$ satisfies.

Let s denote a stance with regard to the topic T, and let the relationship $holds(p, s, T)$ denote that person p holds stance s with regard to topic T. Let $\hat{S} = \{s_1, s_2, ..s_k\}$ be the set of k stances with regard to topic T in the population Ω. We allow people to hold no stance at all with regard to the topic (either because they are not aware of the topic or because they are aware of it but do not take a stance on it). We use s_0 to represent this lack of stance. In that case, let

$$holds(p, s_0, T) \iff \nexists s_i \in \hat{S} \text{ s.t. } holds(p, s_i, T),$$

Let $S = \{s_0\} \cup \hat{S}$ be the set of $k + 1$ stances with regard to topic T in the population Ω. Therefore, $\forall p \in \Omega, \exists s \in S$ s.t. $holds(p, s, T)$. Now, let us define a measure $conflict$ to denote how much two stances are exclusive. $P(conflict|s_i, s_j) = 1$ indicates that s_i and s_j are in a complete conflict, meaning mutually-exclusive. In other words, $P(conflict|s_i, s_j) = 0$ indicates that two stances completely agree with each other. This probability measures the severity of conflict between two stances.

Not all stances are necessarily mutually exclusive or in a complete agreement. A stance of "abortion should be legalized only in certain circumstances" is not mutually exclusive to any of "pro-choice" or "pro-life" stances. In this case, the probability is somewhere in between 0 and 1. Note that a person can hold multiple stances simultaneously as long as none of the two stances are mutually exclusive. Also, not any stance can be jointly held with s_0. By definition, $P(conflict|s_i, s_i) = 0$ and $P(conflict|s_0, s_i) = 0$ satisfy.

Let a **stance group** in the population be a group of people that hold the same stance: for $i \in \{0..k\}$, let $G_i = \{p \in \Omega | holds(p, s_i, T)\}$. By construction, $\Omega = \bigcup_i G_i$. We let $P(conflict|G_i, G_j)$ be a probability that two groups of G_i and G_j are in a conflict, similarly as it was defined for two stances. As a reminder, our goal is to quantify the proportion of people who disagree. Intuitively, we would like to have that quantity grow when the groups in disagreement are larger. In other words, if we randomly select two people, how likely are they to hold conflicting stances?

We model contention directly to reflect this question. Let $P(c|\Omega, T)$ be the probability that if we randomly select two people in Ω, they will conflict on topic T. This is equal to:

$$P(c|\Omega, T) = P(p_1, p_2 \text{ selected randomly from } \Omega, \exists s_i, s_j \in S,$$
$$\text{s.t. } holds(p_1, s_i, T) \wedge holds(p_2, s_j, T)) \cdot P(conflict|s_i, s_j)$$

Alternatively:

$$P(c|\Omega, T) = P(p_1, p_2 \text{ selected randomly from } \Omega, \exists s_i, s_j \in S,$$
$$\text{s.t. } p_1 \in G_i \wedge p_2 \in G_j) \cdot P(conflict|G_i, G_j)).$$

Finally, we extend this definition to any sub-population of Ω. Let $\omega \subseteq \Omega, \omega \neq \emptyset$ be any non-empty sub-group of the population. Let $g_i = G_i \cap \omega$. Thus, by construction, $g_i \subseteq G_i$ and $\omega = \bigcup_i g_i$. The same model applies respectively to the sub-population. In other words, for any $\omega \subseteq \Omega$,

$$P(c|\omega, T) = P(p_1, p_2 \text{ selected randomly from } \omega$$
$$\wedge \exists i \text{ s.t. } p_1 \in g_i \wedge p_2 \in g_j) \cdot P(conflict|g_i, g_j).$$

Mutually exclusive stances. Most controversial topics have at least two exclusive mutually stances to bisect the community. In this section, we focus on the case of mutually exclusive stances and describe the model that can be defined. The model described here can be easily generalized by adjusting the value of $P(conflict|s_i, s_j)$.

Intuitively, a group is in the most contentious state when it is equally divided among the two stances. On the other hand, if a group is unequally divided among each stance, the stance of the smaller subgroup would be considered the minority, contributing to a smaller contention score. Our model captures this insight below.

Recall that stance group G_i is defined as the population of people who hold a stance s_i on T. We also define an **opposing group** in the population be a group of people that hold a stance that conflicts with s_i. For $i \in \{0..k\}$, let $O_i = \{p \in \Omega | \exists j \text{ s.t. } holds(p, s_j, T) \wedge conflict(s_i, s_j)\}$. The model with mutually exclusive stances can alternatively be expressed as:

$$P(c|\Omega, T) = P(p_1, p_2 \text{ selected randomly from } \Omega, \exists s_i, s_j \in S,$$
$$\text{s.t. } p_1 \in G_i \wedge p_2 \in O_i).$$

Note that we are selecting with replacement, and it is possible for $p_1 = p_2$. Strictly speaking, this model allows a person to hold two conflicting stances at once and thus be in both G_i and O_i, as in the case of intrapersonal conflict. This definition, while exhaustive to all possible combinations of stances, is very hard to estimate. We now consider a special case of this model with two additional constraints. Let every person have only one stance on a topic:

$$\nexists p \in \Omega, s_i, s_j \in S \text{ s.t. } i \neq j \wedge$$
$$holds(p, s_i, T) \wedge holds(p, s_j, T).$$

And, let every explicit stance conflict with every other explicit stance:

$$P(conflicts|(s_i, s_j)) = 1 \iff (i \neq j \wedge i \neq 0 \wedge j \neq 0)$$

This implies that $G_i \cap G_j = \emptyset$. Crucially, we set a lack of a stance to not be in conflict with any explicit stance. Thus, $O_i = \Omega \setminus G_i \setminus G_0$.

For simplicity, we estimate the probability of selecting p_1 and p_2 as selection with replacement[2]. Note that $|\Omega| = \Sigma_{i \in \{0..k\}} |G_i|$ and the probability of choosing any particular pair is $\frac{1}{|\Omega|^2}$. The denominator, $|\Omega|^2$, expands into the following expression:

$$|\Omega|^2 = (\Sigma_i |G_i|)^2 = \Sigma_{i \in \{0..k\}} |G_i|^2 + \Sigma_{i \in \{1..k\}} (2|G_0||G_i|)$$
$$+ \Sigma_{i \in \{2..k\}} \Sigma_{j \in \{1..i-1\}} (2|G_i||G_j|)$$

Depending on whether or not the pair of people selected hold conflicting stances, they contribute to the numerator in $P(c|\Omega, T)$ or $P(nc|\Omega, T)$, respectively. Therefore,

$$P(c|\Omega, T) = \frac{\Sigma_{i \in \{2..k\}} \Sigma_{j \in \{1..i-1\}} (2|G_i||G_j|)}{|\Omega|^2}$$

and $P(nc|\Omega, T) = 1 - P(c|\Omega, T)$.

As before, we can trivially extend this definition to any non-empty sub-population $\omega \subseteq \Omega$ using $g_i = G_i \cap \omega$.

Trivially, $P(C|\omega, T)$ is maximal when $|g_0| = 0$ and $|g_1| = ... = |g_k| = \frac{|\omega|}{k}$, and its value is $\frac{k-1}{k}$. This is subtly different from entropy due to the existence of s_0, as entropy would be maximal when $|g_0| = |g_1| = ... = |g_k| = \frac{|\omega|}{k-1}$.

Since the values of contention are $[0, \frac{k-1}{k}]$ rather than $[0, 1]$, we normalize by the maximal contention (divide the contention score by $\frac{k-1}{k}$) and take the non-contention score as 1 minus the new score. This normalization brings both contention and non-contention to a full range of $[0, 1]$, with a contention score of 1 signifying the highest possible contention regardless of the total number of stances.

3.2 Modeling Importance within Population

We now define a measure called *importance*. We loosely define importance as the level of impact that the issue brings to the world within a given population. In terms of importance of a topic T to population Ω, we interpret this as the number of people who think this topic is important to them. In other words, how many people are affected by T?

Let p be a person from some population and affected(T, p) be a binary function that returns whether p is affected by T. We let the probability that T is important to members of Ω be $P(I|\Omega, T)$. This is equivalent to the probability that T is important to the person p drawn from Ω.

$$P(I|\Omega, T) = P(p \text{ selected randomly from } \Omega \wedge affected(p, T))$$

Alternatively, we define Ω_T be the sub-population of Ω with those who are affected by T. $P(I|\Omega, T)$ can be computed by directly estimating $|\Omega_T|$.

$$P(I|\Omega, T) = \frac{|\Omega_T|}{|\Omega|}$$

Introducing importance into the controversy model allows us to penalize the controversy score for the contentious yet less important topics. For example, a sub-population ω_D that is affected by "The Dress" case is unarguably smaller than a sub-population ω_B that is affected by the Brexit Referendum. It follows that if we set Ω to the general population, we can now directly compare the importance of two topics in a general sense.

The *affected*(p) relationship is only defined conceptually here because its interpretation will vary with each dataset. In our experiments, we describe how to directly estimate the size of $|\Omega_T|$ from various datasets.

4 MODEL VALIDATION

We apply our model to the various data sources. To apply our theoretical model, we instantiate the model to algorithms that has been derived considering the characteristics of each dataset. We

---

[2]The calculation is very similar for selection without replacement, except for extremely small population sizes.

examine three different data sources: polling data, Twitter, and Wikipedia. We show that our model has both explanatory power and predictive power.

4.1 Contention in Polling

In the Pew and Gallup datasets, we used the topline survey results as reported by each organization. For a given poll topic T, ω is the set of respondents, s_i are the set of response possibilities, and "no answer" represents s_0. This determines g_i and thus allows us to calculate $P(c|\omega, T)$ as above.

4.1.1 US Scientists vs. General Population.
Using one dataset acquired from Pew Research Center, a non-partisan fact tank in the US, we are able to examine attitudes towards a number of issues among two populations: US adults and US scientists. The opinions for US adults was gathered among a representative sample of 2,002 adults nationwide, while the opinions for scientists were gathered among a representative sample from the US membership of the American Association for the Advancement of Science (AAAS) (Table 2)

As seen in Figure 2, for some topics, such as offshore drilling, hydraulic fracturing (fracking), and biofuel, contention was similar between US adults and scientists. On other topics, such as evolution, climate change, and the use of animals in research, contention varied widely depending on the population: the scientific community had low contention for these topics whereas they were highly contentious among US adults. This result precisely matches earlier work's intuitive notion of politically, but not scientifically, controversial topics [27]. The graph clearly demonstrates the notion that "there is no controversy" (among scientists) alongside the controversy in general population, with evolution as the most extreme case presented in this dataset (98% of AAAS members surveyed said that "humans and other living things have evolved over time", whereas 31% of the US adults said that they have "existed in their present form since beginning of time").

4.1.2 Per-state distribution of Contention in the U.S.
We obtained a dataset from the iSideWith.com website, a nonpartisan Voting Advice Application [5] which offers users the chance to report their opinions on a wide variety of controversial topics and outputs the information of which political candidate they most closely align with. We received the 2014 iSideWith dataset by request from the website owners, which includes nation-wide and per-state opinions over 52 topics. Each topic is posed as a question with two main options for answers, usually a simple "yes" or "no". Additionally, the dataset includes the average importance of the issue (both nation-wide and per-state) rated by the users.

Using the iSideWith dataset, we measure contention nation-wide and per-state on each of the 52 topics available. The two least contentious questions nation-wide were "Should National Parks continue to be preserved and protected by the federal government?" ($P(c|US, t) = 0.26$), and "Should every person purchasing a gun be required to pass a criminal and public safety background check?" ($P(c|US, t) = 0.39$). Several topics had over 0.99 contention nation-wide, such as "Should the US formally declare war on ISIS?" and "Would you support increasing taxes on the rich in order to reduce interest rates for student loans?" among others. We present the

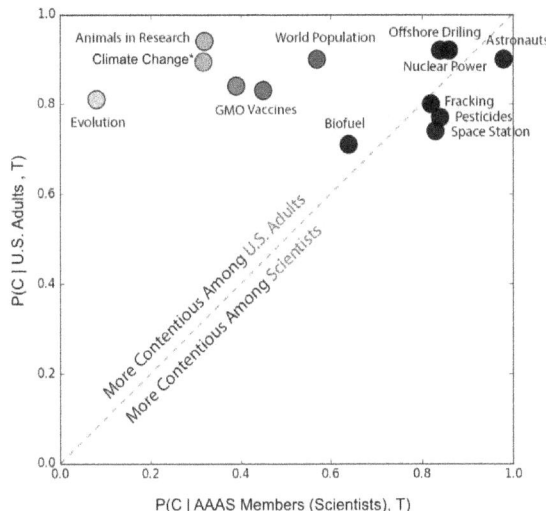

Figure 2: Contention in the scientific community vs. the general population for several controversial topics. The x=y line represents equal contention among both populations, with dots shaded according to their distance from the line. Note that the Climate Change question had 3 explicit stances and all other questions had 2.

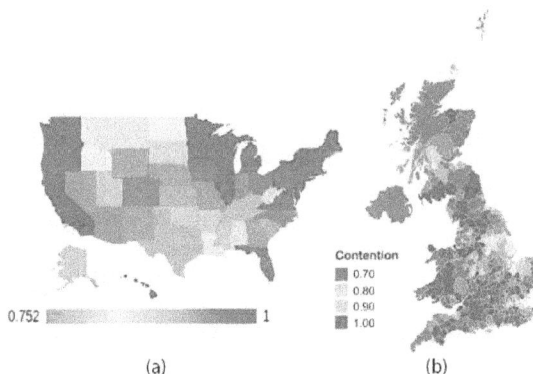

Figure 3: (a) Per-state contention for "Do you support increased gun control?". (b) Contention by voting district in the UK (The Electoral Comission 2016) Interactive maps for all iSideWith issues are available at http://ciir.cs.umass.edu/irdemo/contention

per-state contention for one such topic in Figure 3, which shows how contention varies geographically. An interactive demo with per-state contention on all 52 topics is available at http://ciir.cs.umass.edu/irdemo/contention.

4.2 Controversy in Twitter

Social media allows people to quickly respond to a topic, compared to surveys or other types of media. We turn to Twitter and observe how controversy changes over time on three well-known

Table 2: Datasets containing explicit stances

Dataset	Type	# Issues	Population(s)	Years	# People	Source
Pew Adults	Statistically Calibrated Phone Survey	13	US adults	2014	2.0K	[20, 21]
Pew AAAS	Statistically Calibrated Online Survey	13	US scientists	2014	3.7K	[20, 21]
iSideWith	Informal Online Polling	52	US people	2014	varies (M)	By request
Dress Buzzfeed	Informal Online Polling	1	Online readers	2015-2016	3.5M	[14]

contentious topics: "The Dress", the Brexit Referendum, and 2016 US Presidential Election.

To apply our model to Twitter, we create an instance of our model that automatically identifies a population for whom the topic is relevant, and identify stances of people on the topic to measure contention. Note that we need to identify the population of interest first to estimate $|g_0|$, the group that has an interest in the topic but that does not take any stance.

4.2.1 Measuring Contention in a Twitter Population.
We instantiate our model to compute the level of controversy for a given topic on Twitter. Instead of considering the entire Twitter population, we first automatically identify the sub-population interested in the topic T since the vast majority of people hold no stance even for the most controversial topics. Measuring contention within the relevant sub-population gives a more meaningful result on Twitter.

We start with a single hashtag "seeding" the topic, and the algorithm consists of three steps to identify the relevant sub-population and compute contention: (1) query hashtag expansion, (2) finding a population of interest, and (3) estimating the size of stance groups.

Query hashtag expansion: We start with the hashtag h of interest. Our goal here is to expand h to a set of k hashtags that are topically related to h, namely H_T

To do that, let $\mathcal{T}$ be a collection of tweets (e.g., the tweets collected for some day) and let $\mathcal{T}(h)$ be the subset of those tweets that contain the hashtag h. For any hashtag $h' \neq h$ that occurs in $\mathcal{T}(h)$, we calculate a TFIDF score as follows: TF is the number of times that h' occurs in $\mathcal{T}(h)$ and IDF is an inverse fraction of the frequency of h' in $\mathcal{T}$.

Note we aim to the topic T as the top k relevant hashtags H_T ranked by TFIDF in $\mathcal{T}$. However, one concern of that approach is that the hashtags in H_T is likely to vary greatly depending on which of them is chosen as a seed. To mitigate that risk, we create H_q for each hashtag $q \in H_T$. We then select the k hashtags that appear most often across all sets H_q. We call the resultant list T, and create a dataset $\mathcal{T}(T)$, which is a collection of tweets that contain any hashtag in T.

Identifying the population of interests to T: From $\mathcal{T}(T)$, we extract every user id who tweeted, is mentioned, or is retweeted. We consider this set of users as the population that shows interests in T. We call this sub-population ω_T as the people who are affected by T. ω_T is the population where the importance of T is maximized to 1 because by construction, it is the group of people who showed interests in T by explicitly discussing it on Twitter. Table 3 contains the size of $\mathcal{T}(T)$ and the identified population that shows interests.

Stance detection in the sub-population Automatic stance detection is an open problem [7, 12], so we use a simple and straightforward manual hashtag-based stance detection heuristic. We manually identified hashtags that explicitly indicate a stance. The full

Table 3: Twitter dataset with implicit stances

Topic	# Tweets	# Users	Dates
The Dress	359K	361K	Feb. 26-Mar. 3, 2015
Brexit Referendum	14.8M	12.4M	May. 1-Jul. 24, 2016
US Elections	9.3M	6.2M	Sep. 20- Nov. 30, 2016
Total	24.4M	18.9M	

list of hashtags used is available at http://ciir.cs.umass.edu/irdemo/contention.

This high-precision, low-recall process will omit some tweets that do not use precisely the hashtags selected, but those that are selected are likely to be on the expected stance. We leave analysis of the remaining tweets and other hashtags for future work in stance extraction.

Using the stance hashtags we created, we compute the size of the two stance groups per topic by counting the number of user ids in the tweets that contain any hashtag from each stance. As an estimate of G_0 (the group with no stance) on each topic, we used all other tweets collected via the Twitter Garden Hose API that day. Specifically, $|G_0| =$ count of all users collected $-|G_1| - |G_2|$.

4.2.2 Controversy Trends on Twitter.
We compute the final level of controversy by multiplying the contention computed on the identified population by the importance of that topic within the entire population that tweeted the same day. Figure 4 shows the controversy among all daily tweets by date for "The Dress," Brexit, and the 2016 US election. In all three plots, it shows marked peaks of contention around notable event times. For example, in the case of the US election, small peaks appear on the days of the presidential debates, and upon release of the extremely controversial Hollywood Access tape, with a much larger peak on election day. This showcases the strength of our model and its ability to track the difference between contention among the group for which the topic is relevant.

We compare $P(c|G_1 \cup G_2, T)$ from Twitter across a series of dates, along with the same probability calculated from external sources form comparison: the Buzzfeed poll on "The Dress" ($P(c|G_1 \cup G_2, T)$ = 0.88) [14], voting results on Brexit ($P(c|G_1 \cup G_2, T)$ = 1.00) [25], and the popular vote in the US Elections measured for the two main candidates ($P(c|G_1 \cup G_2, T)$ = 0.89). Additionally, Figure 3(b) shows the voting contention for each Unitary District of the UK (local Ireland results were not available), demonstrating the geographical variance of contention. Gibraltar, an extreme outlier both geographically and contention-wise, is omitted from the map ($P(c|Gibraltar, Brexit)$ = 0.16). The extremely low contention makes sense: Gibraltar is geographically located inside Europe, and 95.9% of its voters voted "remain".

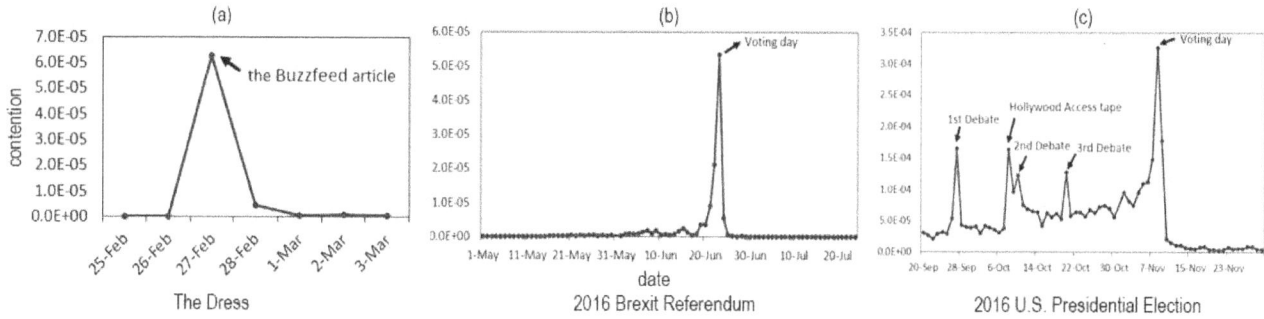

Figure 4: Controversy among all daily tweets by date for The Dress (left), Brexit (center) and 2016 US Elections (right), reported among all Gardenhose tweets that day (top) or only among those with an explicit stance (bottom). Notable peaks are annotated with associated events around that time. All dates are in UTC.

4.3 Controversy in Wikipedia

We now apply our model to the context of Wikipedia by measuring controversy among Wikipedia editor population.

4.3.1 Contention from Wikipedia Editor-population.
Rather than estimating stances, our challenge now becomes to provide an estimate for the *conflicts* function directly between pairs of editors. Several past researchers have noted the centrality of Wikipedia reverts to the study of controversies [4, 23, 29]. Yasseri et al. in particular established reverts as a central mechanism for detecting controversy-related disagreement in Wikipedia [29].

Let $\mathfrak{W} = \{D_1, D_2, D_3 ... D_n\}$ be the collection of articles in Wikipedia, and let p be the person (i.e., the editor) that instituted any change to a document (such as insertions, deletions, and substitutions).

Let $E_D = \{e_1, e_2, ... e_k\}$ be the set of k edits applied to the document D. Let $\omega_D = \{p \in \Omega | \exists \delta, (p, \delta) \in E_D\}$ be the set of people who created the edits in E_D (also called editors). Likewise, let

$$\Omega_{\mathfrak{W}} = \bigcup_{D \in \mathfrak{W}} \omega_D$$

be the set of all editors in Wikipedia.

One approach might be to simply consider any revert to represent a *conflicts* relationship. Let $conflicts_r(p_1, p_2) \equiv reverts(p_1, p_2) \lor reverts(p_2, p_1)$, in which case we get:

$$P(c|\Omega, D) = P(p_1, p_2 \text{ selected randomly from } \Omega \\ \land (reverts(p_1, p_2) \lor reverts(p_2, p_1)))$$

Unfortunately, this simple approach is likely to be too naive. We can conceptually distinguish between two types of reverts: those reverting vandalism and those reflecting opposing stances. To address this issue, Sumi et al., devised a reputation factor per editor, which grows proportionally with the number of edits the user contributes to this specific article [23].

The likelihood of an editor being a vandal is independent of all other editors. Adopting a probabilistic approach, we can reformulate the *conflicts* relationship, rather than being a binary value, into a probabilistic expression that captures the likelihood of a pair of editors reverting each other without vandalism. We can express this probability conditional on the existence of a mutual revert as

$$P(conflicts(p_1, p_2) | reverts(p_1, p_2) \land reverts(p_2, p_1)) \\ = P(p_1 \text{ is not a vandal}) * P(p_2 \text{ is not a vandal})$$

In order to progress further, we need to estimate the probability that a specific person p is (or is not) a vandal. Here, indirectly following Sumi et al.'s reputation factor, we choose to use the number of edits a user has contributed to E_D, divided by the largest reputation factor for any editor on the page. To state this formally, let

$$E_{p,D} = \{e \in E_D | \exists \delta, e = (p, \delta) \in E_D\}$$

be the set of edits contributed to document D by editor p. Let $N_p^D = |E_{p,D}|$ be the size of that set, i.e. the number of edits contributed to D by p. Let

$$N_{max}^D = \max_{p \in \omega_D} N_p^D.$$

Now, we estimate the probability of p's non-vandalism as

$$P(p \text{ is not a vandal}) = \frac{N_p^D}{N_{max}^D + 1}.$$

Note that this probability is independent for each editor and is in the range $[\frac{1}{N_{max}^D+1}, \frac{N_{max}^D}{N_{max}^D+1}]$.

We can marginalize over all pairs of editors for the document and incorporate this probability into our contention estimate. Let $MR_D = \{(p_i, p_j) | p_i, p_j \in \omega_D \text{ s.t. } i < j \land reverts(p_1, p_2) \land reverts(p_2, p_1)\}$ be the set of pairs that have mutually reverted each other. We can then calculate contention as follows:

$$P(c|\Omega, D) = \frac{\sum\limits_{p_1, p_2 \in \omega_D} P(conflicts(p_1, p_2))}{|\Omega|^2} = \\ \frac{1}{|\Omega|^2} * \sum_{(p_i, p_j) \in MR_D} \frac{N_{p_i, D}}{N_{max}^D + 1} * \frac{N_{p_j, D}}{N_{max}^D + 1}$$

Note that we select the editors from ω_D, yet we can measure contention over any superset of ω_D, for example $\Omega_{\mathfrak{W}}$. This allows us to compare contention across either local (article-specific) populations as well as larger ones, up to and including all of Wikipedia's editors.

Table 4: AUC measure reported on ranking controversial articles in Wikipedia by four scores.

	M [23]	C	MI	CI
AUC	0.649	0.649	0.630	**0.660**

4.3.2 Importance. We assume that an editor p who makes a change to the document is affected by the corresponding topic. Hence, we estimate $|\Omega_T|$ to be the size of the editors who have been involved with any change of the document.

$$P(I|T, \Omega_\mathfrak{W}) = \frac{|\omega_D|}{|\Omega_\mathfrak{W}|} \tag{1}$$

4.3.3 Ranking Controversial Articles in Wikipedia. We compare the contention derived from our model ("C") and controversy ("CI") scores, which is a version of C score multiplied by importance "I", against the state-of-the-art heuristic "M" score [23]. To verify the effectiveness of our new controversy score in predicting controversial Wikipedia articles, we rank all Wikipedia articles by four controversy-indicative scores: M, C, MI, and CI. To observe the effect of the importance score, we also devise an "MI" score, which is the M score weighted by its topic importance in Wikipedia. We used the truth data judgment for controversial Wikipedia articles from "the list of controversial issues" page [3] in Wikipedia as well as a previously collected annotated dataset [10]. Our judgment data contain 1,551 controversial articles. All articles that are not in the list are considered to be non-controversial. We then compute Area Under Curve (AUC) measure on the generated list.

Table 4 shows the AUC measure reported on ranking controversial articles by the four scores. While M and our C scores are comparable, CI score produced a better ranking than any of the measure. This result demonstrates that our model, when applied to Wikipedia, shows a competitive predictive power in classifying controversial articles in Wikipedia.

5 CONCLUSIONS

In this paper, we propose a theoretical model for controversy with respect to population. We argue that controversy is a multi-dimensional quantity that should only be understood in a given population and propose a model with two minimal dimensions: contention and importance. Contention mathematically quantifies the notion of "the proportion of people disagreeing on this topic" in a population-dependent fashion. On the other hand, importance measures how many people are affected by the given topic in the population. We validate our theoretical model on a wide variety of datasets from both offline and online sources, ranging from large informal online polls and Twitter data to statistically calibrated phone surveys and Wikipedia. Our experimental results show that our model has an explanatory power as well as a predictive power for the observed phenomenon.

6 ACKNOWLEDGEMENTS

The authors thank Marc-Allen Cartright, Jeff Dalton, Shay Hummel, Kiran Garimella, Seth Goldman, Justin Gross, Daniel Mishori, Brendan O'Connor, and Alena Vasilyeva for fruitful conversations. Special thanks to Taylor Peck and Nick Boutelier for providing us the iSideWith data set. This work was supported in part by the Center for Intelligent Information Retrieval and in part by NSF grant #IIS-1217281. Any opinions, findings and conclusions or recommendations expressed in this material are those of the authors and do not necessarily reflect those of the sponsor.

REFERENCES

[1] L. Amendola, V. Marra, and M. Quartin. 2015. The evolving perception of controversial movies. *Palgrave Communications* 1 (2015).

[2] R. Awadallah, M. Ramanath, and G. Weikum. 2012. Harmony and Dissonance : Organizing the People's Voices on Political Controversies. *New York* (feb 2012), 523–532.

[3] E. Borra, A. Kaltenbrunner, M. Mauri, U. Amsterdam, E. Weltevrede, D. Laniado, R. Rogers, P. Ciuccarelli, and G. Magni. 2015. Societal Controversies in Wikipedia Articles. *Proceedings CHI 2015* (2015), 3–6.

[4] U. Brandes, P. Kenis, J. Lerner, and D. Raaij. 2009. Network analysis of collaboration structure in Wikipedia. WWW.

[5] L. Cedroni. 2010. Voting Advice Applications in Europe: A Comparison. *Voting Advice Applications in Europe: The State of Art* (2010), 247–258.

[6] Z. Chen and J. Berger. 2013. When, Why, and How Controversy Causes Conversation. *Journal of Consumer Research* 40, 3 (2013), 580–593.

[7] M. Coletto, C. Lucchese, S. Orlando, and R. Perego. 2016. Polarized user and topic tracking in twitter. In *SIGIR*. ACM, 945–948.

[8] P.A. Cramer. 2011. *Controversy as News Discourse.* Springer Netherlands.

[9] Marcelo Dascal. 1995. Epistemology, Controversies, and Pragmatics. *Isegoría* 12, 8-43 (1995).

[10] S. Dori-Hacohen and J. Allan. 2013. Detecting controversy on the web. In *CIKM*.

[11] F.H.V. Eemeren and B. Garssen. 2008. *Controversy and confrontation: Relating controversy analysis with argumentation theory.* Vol. 6. John Benjamins Publishing.

[12] K. Garimella, Aristides Morales, G.D.F., and M. Mathioudakis. 2016. Quantifying controversy in social media. *WSDM* (2016).

[13] D. J. Helfand. 2016. *A Survival Guide to the Misinformation Age: Scientific Habits of Mind.* Columbia University Press.

[14] C. Holderness. 2015. What Colors Are This Dress? (2015). https://www.buzzfeed.com/catesish/help-am-i-going-insane -its-definitely-blue.

[15] M. Jang and J. Allan. 2016. Improving Automated Controversy Detection on the Web. In *SIGIR*.

[16] M. Jang, J. Foley, S. Dori-Hacohen, and J. Allan. 2016. Probabilistic Approaches to Controversy Detection. In *CIKM*.

[17] A. Kittur, B. Suh, B.A. Pendleton, and E. H h. Chi. 2007. He says, she says: conflict and coordination in Wikipedia. In *CHI*.

[18] M. Klenner, M. Amsler, and N. Hollenstein. 2014. Verb Polarity Frames: a New Resource and its Application in Target-specific Polarity Classification. In *KONVENS*.

[19] A.I. Leshner. 2015. Bridging the opinion gap. *Science* 347, 6221 (2015), 459.

[20] Pew Research Center. 2015. *An Elaboration of AAAS Scientists' Views.* Technical Report.

[21] Pew Research Center. 2015. *Public and Scientists' Views on Science and Society.* Technical Report.

[22] H. S. Rad and D. Barbosa. 2012. Identifying controversial articles in Wikipedia: A comparative study. In *WikiSym '12*. ACM.

[23] R. Sumi, T. Yasseri, A. Rung, A. Kornai, and J. Kertész. 2011. Edit Wars in Wikipedia. In *2011 IEEE Third Int'l Conference on Social Computing*.

[24] Mihály Szívós. 2005. Temporality, reification and subjectivity. *Controversies and Subjectivity* 1 (2005), 201.

[25] The Electoral Comission. 2016. EU referendum results. (2016).

[26] B. Timmermans, L. Aroyo, T. Kuhn, K. Beelen, E. Kanoulas, B. van de Velde, and G. van Eerten. 2017. ControCurator: Understanding Controversy Using Collective Intelligence. *Collective Intelligence* (2017).

[27] A. M Wilson and G. E Likens. 2015. Content volatility of scientific topics in Wikipedia: A cautionary tale. *PLoS ONE* 10, 8 (2015), 10–14.

[28] T. Yasseri, A. Spoerri, M. Graham, and J. Kertész. 2014. The most controversial topics in Wikipedia: A multilingual and geographical analysis. In *Global Wikipedia: International and cross-cultural issues in collaboration*. 178.

[29] T. Yasseri, R. Sumi, A. Rung, A. Kornai, and J. Kertész. 2012. Dynamics of conflicts in Wikipedia. *PloS one* 7, 6 (Jan. 2012), e38869.

---

[3] https://en.wikipedia.org/wiki/Wikipedia:List_of_controversial_issues

Recommendation with Social Relationships via Deep Learning

Dimitrios Rafailidis
Department of Computer Science
University of Mons
Mons, Belgium
dimitrios.rafailidis@umons.ac.be

Fabio Crestani
Faculty of Informatics
Università della Svizzera italiana (USI)
Lugano, Switzerland
fabio.crestani@usi.ch

ABSTRACT

While users trust the selections of their social friends in recommendation systems, the preferences of friends do not necessarily match. In this study, we introduce a deep learning approach to learn both about user preferences and the social influence of friends when generating recommendations. In our model we design a deep learning architecture by stacking multiple marginalized Denoising Autoencoders. We define a joint objective function to enforce the latent representation of social relationships in the Autoencoder's hidden layer to be as close as possible to the users' latent representation when factorizing the user-item matrix. We formulate a joint objective function as a minimization problem to learn both user preferences and friends' social influence and we present an optimization algorithm to solve the joint minimization problem. Our experiments on four benchmark datasets show that the proposed approach achieves high recommendation accuracy, compared to other state-of-the-art methods.

CCS CONCEPTS

•Information systems →Collaborative and social computing systems and tools;

KEYWORDS

Recommendation systems; deep learning; denoising autoencoders; social relationships; matrix factorization

1 INTRODUCTION

The collaborative filtering strategy has been widely adopted in recommendation systems, where users with similar preferences tend to get similar recommendations [14]. User preferences are expressed explicitly in the form of ratings or implicitly in the form of number of views, clicks, purchases, and so on. Matrix factorization techniques are representative collaborative filtering strategies, which factorize the data matrix with user preferences, to reveal the latent associations between users and items [16, 28]. However, in the real-world scenario the data sparsity of user preferences degrades the recommendation accuracy, as users select a few items and there are only a few preferences on which to base the recommendations. So, one of the motivations of this paper is concerned

with estimating how much data sparsity affects the performance of recommendation systems and with finding solutions to improve the performance of collaborative filtering in the presence of data sparsity. In the literature several methods have been proposed to overcome this problem. In [10, 12, 15, 18, 19, 38] are some examples of methods that have exploited users' social relationships in collaborative filtering, accounting for the fact that social friends have similar preferences. However, the preferences of social friends do not necessarily match, having different influence when generating recommendations [2, 9]. From the user feedback we have to learn both about her preferences and how much she is influenced by her friends. However, this is a challenging task, as it is difficult to determine how much her preferences are influenced by her friends when generating recommendations. In the context of social regularization in recommendation systems, recent studies try to capture the complex relationships between user preferences and those of her social friends [2, 9].

Various deep learning strategies have been proposed following the collaborative filtering strategy in recommendation systems e.g., Restricted Boltzmann Machines [7, 29, 39], Convolutional Neural Networks [21] and Deep Belief Networks [5, 35]. More recently, a few attempts have been made by following the deep learning strategy of Denoising Autoencoders [8, 31]. In [17, 30, 33, 34, 36], it has been shown that Denoising Autoencoders achieve high recommendation accuracy by learning the corrupted version of training data to learn the user preferences. This occurs because Denoising Autoencoders in collaborative filtering assume that the observed user-item interactions are a corrupted version of the user's preference set, thus learning a more robust mapping from the data [36]. In addition, the deep learning models in [17, 33, 34] exploit users' side information such as demographics and/or item features to further improve the recommendation accuracy. For instance, in [17] the user demographics are used to infer the user-user correlations when generating the recommendations. However the models in [17, 33, 34] do not exploit users' social relationships in their learning strategies. These models try to preserve the space of user/item attributes in each hidden layer with a projection matrix in their learning strategies. Instead, the goal of our study is to learn the users' similarities by considering users' sparse relationships. So, another motivation behind this paper is the investigation of how much user's preferences are influenced by her social friends when generating recommendations using a deep learning model.

The contributions of this paper are summarized as follows: (i) we define a joint objective function to enforce the latent representation of social relationships in the hidden layer of the Denoising Autoencoder, to be as close as possible to the latent representation of users when factorizing the user-item matrix. (ii) We formulate a joint objective function as a minimization problem to learn

ICTIR'17, October 1–4, 2017, Amsterdam, The Netherlands.
© 2017 ACM. 978-1-4503-4490-6/17/10...$15.00
DOI: https://doi.org/10.1145/3121050.3121057

both user preferences and the social influence of her friends and we present an optimization algorithm to solve the joint minimization problem. (iii) We design a deep learning architecture by stacking multiple marginalized Denoising Autoencoders, a scalable variant of Denoising Autoencoders, to generate the final recommendations. Our experiments on benchmark datasets show that the proposed approach outperforms competitive approaches that either follow other deep learning strategies or exploit in a different way users' relationships when generating recommendations.

The remainder of the paper is organized as follows. Section 2 reviews the related work, Section 3 provides some basic concepts of the deep learning strategy of Denoising Autoencoders and Section 4 details the proposed deep learning strategy. Section 5 evaluates the performance of the proposed approach and, finally, Section 6 concludes the study.

2 RELATED WORK

2.1 Social Recommendation

Many different strategies have been introduced to leverage the recommendation accuracy by exploiting the users' social relationships; for example, Ma et al. [19] present a social regularization method by sharing a common user-item matrix, factorized by ratings and social relationships. Jamali and Ester [12] extend [19] by weighting the user latent factors based on their social relationships. In [18], a social ensemble method is presented to combine matrix factorization with a social-based neighborhood model. Guo et al. [9] extend SVD++ [13] to learn both the user preferences and the social influence of her friends. The aforementioned methods exploit social relationships and use different squared loss functions to minimize the prediction/rating error. On the other hand, several methods focus on the ranking performance when generating the recommendations with social relationships. For example, Grimberghe et al. [15] combine Multi-Relational matrix factorization with the Bayesian personalized ranking framework of [27] to model users' feedback both on items and on social relationships. Zhao et al. [38] propose a social bayesian personalized ranking model that incorporates social relationships into a pair-wise ranking model, assuming that users tend to assign higher ranks to items that their friends prefer. In [11], Jamali and Ester combine Trust-Walker [10] with collaborative filtering to generate recommendations with social relationships. In [22], a collaborative ranking strategy is followed, considering how well the relevant items of users and their social friends have been ranked at the top of the list. In [23], authors extend the model presented in [22] by combing different collaborative ranking strategies into a joint model to leverage the recommendation accuracy. Chaney et al. [2] infer each user's preferences and the social influence of her friends by introducing a Bayesian model that performs Social Poisson factorization.

2.2 Recommendation via Deep Learning

One of the first attempts to generate recommendations via deep learning was made by Salakhutdinov et al. [29], where they use Restricted Boltzmann Machines instead of matrix factorization to perform collaborative filtering. Georgiev and Nakov[7] extend [29] by incorporating user-user and item-item correlations. Zheng et

al. [39] propose a a neural autoregressive architecture for collaborative filtering. Elkahky et al. [6] follow a deep learning strategy to map users and items to a latent space to maximize the similarity between users and their preferred items. They extend their model to jointly learn from features of items from different domains and user features, such as web browsing history and search queries, by introducing a multi-view Deep Neural Network learning model. In [21], Oord et al. use Convolutional Neural Networks to generate music recommendations. In this study, first they perform matrix factorization to compute the latent factors of songs and then they use Convolutional Neural Networks to map audio content to the latent factors. Dziugaite and Roy [5] combine a multi-layer feedforward Neural Network with matrix factorization to optimize the latent features. Wang et al. [35] propose a joint framework to learn the features of songs and generate recommendations using a Deep Belief Network.

Sedhain et al. [30] propose a user- and item-based collaborative filtering strategy with Autoencoders. Recently, Wu et al. [36] exploit the deep learning strategy of Stacked Denoising Autoencoders, assuming that the observed user-item interactions are a corrupted version of the user's preference set. In this study the model learns latent representations of corrupted user-item preferences that can best reconstruct the observed interactions. However, the side information of users or items are not exploited in this work. Instead, the studies in [17, 33, 34] couple matrix factorization with Stacked Denoising Autoencoders to generate recommendations with users' or items' side information. For example, Wang et al. [34] present a hierarchical Bayesian model which jointly performs deep learning via Stacked Denoising Autoencoders for learning the content information of articles and collaborative filtering for users' feedback. This work studies the particular problem of article recommendation, and improves the well-known model of Collaborative Topic Regression [32] by replacing its Topic Model component by a Bayesian Autoencoder, used for learning the latent feature representations for the articles. Similarly, Wang et al. [33] propose a probabilistic formulation for Stacked Denoising Autoencoders to generate tag recommendations. Li et al. [17] combine probabilistic matrix factorization [28] with marginalized Stacked Denoising Autoencoders [3] to exploit the side information of users' demographics and item features when generating the recommendations. Recently, a few deep learning strategies have been introduced to generate recommendations with social relationships, such as Denoising Autoencoders [4] and Restricted Boltzmann Machines [20]. Compared to marginalized Stacked Denoising Autoencoders, both deep learning strategies require a heavy computational cost to learn their models [3].

3 MARGINALIZED DENOISING AUTOENCODERS

According to [1] a basic block of an Autoencoder has two components, an encoder with an activation function $h(\cdot)$ that maps a d-dimensional input $\mathbf{a} \in \mathbb{R}^d$ to a hidden layer, resulting in a hidden representation $h(\mathbf{a})$. Then, a decoder uses a deactivation function $g(\cdot)$ to map the hidden representation back to the reconstructed version of $\mathbf{a}$, with $g(h(\mathbf{a})) \approx \mathbf{a}$. There are several choices for selecting the activation and deactivation functions, such as the identity and sigmoid functions. In this paper, we consider an identity activation function and a sigmoid deactivation function [30]. A Denoising Autoencoder is a variant of Autoencoder which corrupts the inputs before mapping them to the hidden representation, by randomly injecting artificial noise. This is achieved by adding zeros to inputs, usually based on Gaussian noise or binary masking noise with a probability p. The Stacked Denoising Autoencoders presented in [31] and [8] stack multiple Denoising Autoencoders to perform deep learning, by feeding the hidden representation of the l-th Denoising Autoencoder as input into to the $l + 1$ Denoising Autoencoder. In Stacked Denoising Autoencoders, the training is performed iteratively, layer by layer, thus having high computational cost because in each layer training with an optimization algorithm is required to learn the model parameters [3]. In this study we focus on the marginalized Denoising Autoencoders that lower the computational cost of conventional Denoising Autoencoders [3]. As opposed to the two level encoder and decoder in a block of a Denoising Autoencoder, the corrupted inputs are reconstructed with a single linear mapping (weight matrix) $W \in \mathbb{R}^{d \times d}$ that minimizes the following objective function:

$$\frac{1}{2n} \sum_{i=1}^{n} ||\mathbf{a}_i - W\tilde{\mathbf{a}}_i||^2 \tag{1}$$

where n is the number of samples in the input data, $\tilde{\mathbf{a}}_i$ is the corrupted version of $\mathbf{a}$ and the mapping W contains the reconstruction weights. As the features are randomly corrupted with probability p, c passes are performed over the input data, each time with different corruption to lower the variance. Let $A \in \mathbb{R}^{d \times n}$ be the data matrix and $\bar{A} = [A, A, \ldots, A] \in \mathbb{R}^{d \times cn}$ be its c-times repeated version. The corrupted version of $\bar{A}$ with different corruption at the c-th repeated version is denoted as $\tilde{A} \in \mathbb{R}^{d \times cn}$. Hence, Eq. (1) is reformulated as follows:

$$\min_{W} ||\bar{A} - W\tilde{A}||_F^2 \tag{2}$$

where $|| \cdot ||_F^2$ denotes the Frobenius norm. According to [3], in the case of $c \to \infty$, that is in the case of having infinitely many copies of noise data, the weight matrix W in Eq. (2) has the following closed-form solution $W = E[S]E[Q]^{-1}$, with $S = \tilde{A}\tilde{A}^T$, $Q = \tilde{A}\tilde{A}^T$, with $E[\cdot]$ being the expectation operator. Having a closed-form solution of the weight matrix W, we avoid to train the data via an optimization algorithm in each layer, thus reducing the computational cost of a Denoising Autoencoder block. To form a deep learning architecture, the basic blocks of marginalized Denoising Autoencoders are stacked in a similar way as in the case of conventional Denoising Autoencoders.

4 PROPOSED APPROACH

Problem definition. Given n users and m items, we assume that we have a user-item matrix $X \in \mathbb{R}^{n \times m}$, where X_{ij} denotes the number of times that user i has interacted with item j via implicit feedback e.g., number of views, clicks and so on, or via explicit feedback e.g., the rating that user i has assigned to item j. Let $A \in \mathbb{R}^{n \times n}$ be the adjacency matrix with the users' social relationships, then $A_{ij} = 1$ if users i and j are friends and 0 otherwise. Following the notation of matrix factorization techniques [16], the

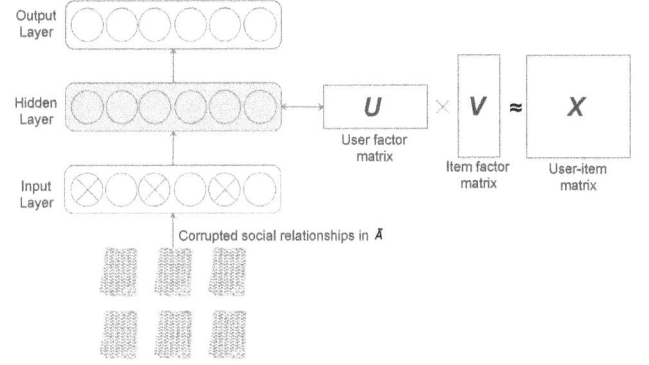

Figure 1: A basic block model of the proposed approach. The red line indicates the coupling of the latent representation of social relationships in the hidden layer with the user factor matrix U.

recommendations are generated by factorizing the matrix X. This is achieved by decomposing X as $X \approx UV^T$, which results in the following minimization problem:

$$\min_{U, V} ||X - UV^T||_F^2 \tag{3}$$

where $U \in \mathbb{R}^{n \times k}$ and $V \in \mathbb{R}^{m \times k}$ are the factor matrices of users and items, respectively, and k is the number of latent factors. The product UV^T results in a factorized matrix X', that is the low rank k approximation of X, with $X \approx X'$. Our problem is formally defined as follows:

DEFINITION 1 (PROBLEM). *"Given (i) a user-item matrix X and (ii) an adjacency matrix A with users' social relationships, the goal of the proposed approach is to compute the factorized matrix X' by learning both user preferences in X and the social influence of her friends in A."*

Overview. Figure 1 presents the framework of the proposed approach. A basic block model of our method consists of the input, hidden and output layers, and the matrix factorization of X. Let $\mathbf{a}_i \in \mathbb{R}^n$ be the representation of the social friends of user i, that is, a n-dimensional binary vector which corresponds to the i-th row of A. Following the deep learning strategy of Denoising Autoencoders [8, 31], first we apply the noise injection strategy by using binary masking noise with a probability p, to compute the corrupted social relationships in $\tilde{A} \in \mathbb{R}^{n \times cn}$. As A is sparse, we inject noise only to the non-zero values in $\tilde{A}$, that is, the social friends for each user. To learn both user preferences and the social influence of her friends we compute the latent representation in the hidden layer based on a weight matrix W, while at the same time we consider the factorization of X. This is achieved by enforcing the latent representation of the social relationships in the hidden layer to be as close as possible to the factor matrix $U \in \mathbb{R}^{n \times k}$. The red line in Figure 1 represents the coupling of the latent representation of social relationships in the hidden layer with the user factor matrix U.

The remainder of the Section is organized as follows. In Section 4.1 we detail how to couple the latent representation of the social relationships in the hidden layer with the user factor matrix U. In Section 4.2 we formulate the joint objective function as a minimization problem to learn both user preferences and the social influence of her friends in the factorized matrix and the marginalized Denoising Autoencoder, and then we present an optimization algorithm to solve the joint minimization problem. Finally, in Section 4.3 we design a deep learning architecture by stacking multiple block models of marginalized Denoising Autoencoders.

4.1 Latent Representation of Relationships in the Hidden Layer

For $\forall i = 1, \ldots, n$ we assume that a n-dimensional binary vector $\mathbf{a}_i \in \mathbb{R}^n$ can be mapped to a latent space representation $\mathbf{a}'_i = U^T \mathbf{a}_i \in \mathbb{R}^k$, based on the user factor matrix $U \in \mathbb{R}^{n \times k}$, with k being the number of latent factors. The similarity between two users in the latent space of the user factor matrix can be presented as the inner product in the users' latent space as follows:

$$sim(\mathbf{a}_i, \mathbf{a}_j) = \mathbf{a}'^T_i \mathbf{a}'_j = (U^T \mathbf{a}_i)^T U^T \mathbf{a}_i = \mathbf{a}_i^T U U^T \mathbf{a}_j^T \quad (4)$$

The matrix form of Eq. (4) can be formulated as the following minimization problem with respect to matrices U and W:

$$\min_{U, W} ||A^T U U^T A - WA||_F^2 \quad (5)$$

where $W \in \mathbb{R}^{n \times n}$ is the weight matrix in the hidden layer and the product WA corresponds to the latent representation of A in the hidden layer of the Autoencoder without denoising. According to Eq. (1) we consider the learning of W for the corrupted version of $\tilde{A}$, thus having the following objective function:

$$\min_{U, W} ||A^T U U^T A - WA||_F^2 + ||\tilde{A} - W\tilde{A}||_F^2 \quad (6)$$

where $\bar{A} \in \mathbb{R}^{n \times cn}$ is the c-times repeated versions of A, and $\tilde{A} \in \mathbb{R}^{n \times cn}$ is its corrupted version by randomly injecting noise based on the binary masking noise strategy.

4.2 Model Learning

By combining Eq. (6) with the objective function of matrix factorization in Eq. (3) we have the following *joint objective function*:

$$\min_{U, V, W} \mathcal{L} = ||X - UV^T||_F^2 + ||\bar{A} - W\tilde{A}||_F^2$$
$$+ ||A^T U U^T A - WA||_F^2 + \lambda(||U||_F^2 + ||V||_F^2) \quad (7)$$

where the last term is used to avoid model overfitting and λ is the regularization parameter. As mentioned in Section 4.1, the third term corresponds to the coupling of the latent representation of social relationships in the hidden layer with the user factor matrix U.

As the minimization problem of the joint objective function in Eq. (7) is non-convex with respect to the matrices (variables) U, V and W, we follow an alternative optimization strategy, that is, we update each variable by fixing the remaining two.

Considering only the related terms of $\mathcal{L}$ in Eq. (7) with respect to W, we have the following minimization problem when fixing U and V and updating W:

$$\min_{W} = ||\bar{A} - W\tilde{A}||_F^2 + ||A^T U U^T A - WA||_F^2 \quad (8)$$

According to the analysis in Section 3, we have the following closed-form solution of $W = E[S]E[Q]^{-1}$, where $S \in \mathbb{R}^{n \times n}$ and $Q \in \mathbb{R}^{n \times n}$ are calculated as follows:

$$S = \tilde{A}\tilde{A}^T + A^T U U^T A A^T$$
$$Q = \bar{A}\tilde{A}^T + AA^T \quad (9)$$

Next, by leaving out the unrelated terms of $\mathcal{L}$ with respect to U and V, the joint objective function in Eq. (7) can be rewritten as follows:

$$\mathcal{L}(U, V) = tr[(X - UV^T)(X - UV^T)^T]$$
$$+ tr[(A^T U U^T A - WA)(A^T U U^T A - WA)^T] \quad (10)$$
$$+ \lambda tr[UU^T + VV^T]$$

where $tr[\cdot]$ is the trace operator. By taking the partial derivatives of Eq. (10) with respect to matrices U and V we have:

$$\frac{\partial \mathcal{L}(U, V)}{\partial U} = 2(-XV + UV^T V)$$
$$+ 2AA^T U U^T (AA^T U + AA^T U U^T)$$
$$- 2A(A^T W^T A^T U + WAA^T U) + 2\lambda U \quad (11)$$

$$\frac{\partial \mathcal{L}(U, V)}{\partial V} = 2(-X^T U + VU^T U + \lambda V)$$

Then, we learn matrices U and V via gradient descent at the $t + 1$ iteration as follows:

$$U^{(t+1)} = U^{(t)} - \eta \frac{\partial \mathcal{L}(U^{(t)}, V^{(t)})}{\partial U^{(t)}}$$
$$V^{(t+1)} = V^{(t)} - \eta \frac{\partial \mathcal{L}(U^{(t)}, V^{(t)})}{\partial V^{(t)}} \quad (12)$$

where η is the learning parameter. In our implementation the maximum number of iterations is fixed to 1K. The algorithm terminates (converges) in less iterations if $(\mathcal{L}^{(t+1)} - \mathcal{L}^{(t)})/\mathcal{L}^{(t)} \leq 1e - 05$, where $\mathcal{L}^{(t)}$ is the value of the objective function $\mathcal{L}$ in Eq. (10) after the t-th iteration.

4.3 Deep Learning Architecture

Provided that stacking Denoising Autoencoders improves the performance of the models [8, 31], in our approach we form a deep learning strategy by stacking multiple block models of the proposed marginalized Denoising Autoencoders (Figure 1). This means that in our deep learning architecture the hidden representation of layer $l - 1$ is the input of the l-th (deeper) layer. Having in total l stacked layers, in layer $(l + 1)/2$ we have the deepest hidden representation of the social relationships. Since we have different social relationships' representations in the hidden layers, in our approach we assume that the factor matrix U should be close to the latent representation in the deepest hidden layer [17]. Consequently, in our approach we update the weight matrix W based on the closed-form solution $W = E[S]E[Q]^{-1}$ and we ignore the matrix factorization of X until we reach layer $(l + 1)/2$. As matrix S depends on U in Eq. (9), we initialize U by applying NMF [16] to X before the method starts. When we reach the deepest hidden layer $(l + 1)/2$, we minimize the joint objective function in Eq. (7) as presented in Section 4.2, where we update W and then calculate the factor matrices U and V based on Eq. (12). Having computed

U and V, the final recommendations are stored in the factorized matrix $X' = UV^T$.

5 EXPERIMENTS

5.1 Evaluation Setup

Datasets. In our experiments we use the following datasets, *Epinions*[1], *Flixster*[2], *Ciao*[3] and *FilmTrust*[4]. The statistics of the evaluation datasets are summarized in Table 1. We select these datasets as the number of social relationships varies and the users' feedback is at different levels of density.

Table 1: Dataset statistics.

	Epinions	Flixster	Ciao	FilmTrust
#users	71,002	147,612	7,375	1,508
#items	104,356	48,794	105,114	2,071
#ratings	571,235	8,196,077	284,086	35,497
#social rel.	508,960	7,058,819	111,781	1,853
density (%)	0.0077	0.1138	0.0366	1.1366

Training/test set split. Each dataset is divided into two subsets: the training and test sets. Following the evaluation protocol of similar studies [37, 38], for users with less than five ratings, one randomly selected rating is inserted into the test set. For users with five ratings or more, 10% of the randomly selected ratings are moved to the test set. The training set is further split into two subsets: the cross-validation training set and the cross-validation test set, which are used to determine the tuning parameters of each examined ranking model. We repeated our experiment ten times, and we report mean values and standard deviations on the (actual) test set over the runs.

Evaluation metrics. As relevant studies showed that rating error metrics, such as RMSE (Root Mean Squared Error) and MAE (Mean Absolute Error) do not necessarily reflect on the top-N recommendation performance, in our experiments we used the ranking-based metrics *recall (R@N)* and *Normalized Discounted Cumulative Gain (NDCG@N)* to evaluate the top-N recommendation performance of the examined models directly [15, 38]. *Recall (R@N)* is defined as the ratio of the relevant items in the top-N ranked list over all the relevant items for each user. The *Normalized Discounted Cumulative Gain (NDCG@N)* metric considers the ranking of the relevant items in the top-N list. For each user the Discounted Cumulative Gain is defined as: $DCG@N = \sum_{j=1}^{N} \frac{2^{rel_j}-1}{\log_2 j+1}$, where rel_j represents the relevance score of item j, that is binary relevance in our case. We consider an item as relevant if a user has rated it, and irrelevant otherwise. Alternatively, we could use a graded relevance in our evaluation, which is left for future work. The *Normalized Discounted Cumulative Gain NDCG@N* is the ratio of $DCG@N$ over the ideal $iDCG@N$ value for each user, that is, the $DCG@N$ value given the ratings in the test set. In our experiments we averaged $R@N$ and $NDCG@N$ over all users.

5.2 Compared Methods

We use as baselines the following social-based methods:

- `SocialMF`[5] [12]: a baseline model to exploit user's social relationships for recommendation systems. SocialMF weighs the user latent factors based on their social relationships when factorizing the user-item matrix.
- `TrustSVD`[5] [9]: a trust-based model which extends SVD++ to consider both explicit and implicit influence of ratings and social relationships.
- `SPF`[6] [2]: a probabilistic model that performs Social Poisson factorization. SPF incorporates user latent preferences for items with the latent influences of her friends, estimating how much each user is influenced by her social friends.

We also compare the following deep learning strategies:

- `CDAE`[7] [36]: a recently proposed model of Collaborative Denoising AutoEncoders, where the input is the user-item interactions, assuming that the input is a corrupted version of the user's full preference set. CDAE does not exploit the users' social relationships when generating recommendations.
- `mSDA-CF` [17]: a deep learning strategy that couples PMF [28] with marginalized Stacked Denoising Autoencoders for Collaborative Filtering. Instead of feeding mSDA-CF with users' demographics as in [17], in our setting we feed mSDA-CF with the binary matrix A that contains the users' social relationships.
- `SDAE`: the proposed deep learning model, which generates recommendation with Social relationships based on Denoising AutoEncoders. In our implementation we used the Deeplearning4j[8] library.

Parameter tuning. In the proposed SDAE method we varied the regularization parameter λ in Eq. (7) from 1e-04 to 1e-01, the learning rate η in Eq. (12) from 1e-05 to 1, the number of stacked layers from 1 to 20, the percentage of noise from 10% to 90%, and the number of latent factors from 10 to 100, by a step of 10. The parameter analysis of our deep learning architectures if further studied in Section 5.6. In CDAE we fixed the number of negative samples to 5, as suggested in [36] and we vary the learning rate η as in SDAE. Following [17], in mSDA-CF we tuned the parameters α and λ in 0-1 which control the approximation errors of PMF and the connection between the deepest hidden layer and the user latent factor matrix, respectively. We also varied the regularization parameter, the number of latent factors, the number of stacked layers and the percentage of noise as in SDAE. In SocialMF and TrustSVD we varied the regularization parameters as in [9] and we tuned the number of latent factors as in SDAE. In SPF we varied the number of latent factors as in the other methods and we fixed the hyperparameters to gamma priors on the latent variables, as suggested in [2]. In all the examined methods, we tuned the parameters based on the same cross validation strategy, and in our experiments we report the best results.

---

[1] https://alchemy.cs.washington.edu/data/epinions/
[2] http://www.cs.ubc.ca/~jamalim/datasets/
[3] http://www.jiliang.xyz/trust.html
[4] http://www.librec.net/datasets.html

[5] http://www.librec.net/
[6] https://github.com/ajbc/spf
[7] https://github.com/jasonyaw/CDAE
[8] http://deeplearning4j.org/stackeddenoisingautoencoder.html

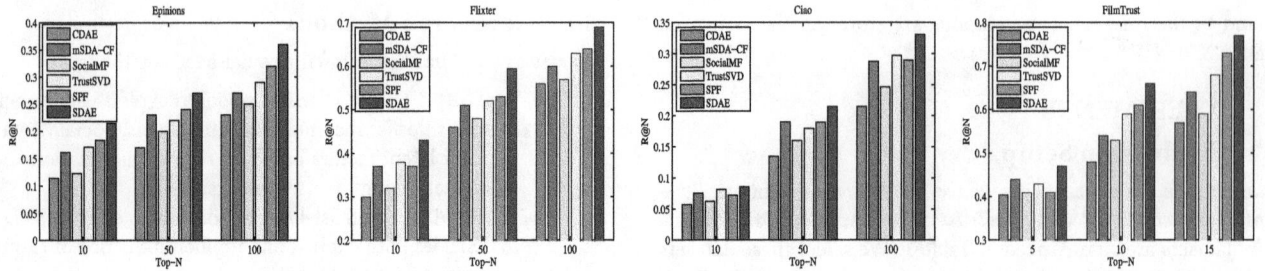

Figure 2: Effect on *recall (R@N)* when varying the number of the top-*N* recommendations.

Table 2: Effect on *NDCG@10* with 75% training set. Bold values denote the best scores for $^*p < 0.05$ in paired t-test, and the last row denotes the relative improvement (%), when comparing SDAE with the second best method.

75% training set	Epinions	Flixter	Ciao	FilmTrust
CDAE	.1396 ± .0015	.2673 ± .0040	.1271 ± .0032	.5463 ± .0148
mSDA-CF	.1867 ± .0061	.2986 ± .0099	.1834 ± .0031	.5910 ± .0098
SocialMF	.1572 ± .0047	.2724 ± .0051	.1374 ± .0077	.5734 ± .0171
TrustSVD	.1962 ± .0088	.3471 ± .0053	.1781 ± .0085	.5827 ± .0259
SPF	.2065 ± .0013	.3142 ± .0054	.1977 ± .0034	.6154 ± .0093
SDAE	**.2357 ± .0045***	**.3822 ± .0066***	**.2293 ± .0046***	**.6794 ± .0104***
Improvement (%)	14.15	12.42	15.94	10.40

5.3 Performance Evaluation

We evaluate the performance of the examined methods using 75% of the data as training set. Table 2 shows the effect on *NDCG@10* and Figure 2 shows the effect on *recall* by varying the number of the top-*N* recommended items. In Epinions, Flixter and Ciao we vary N in $\{10, 50, 100\}$, while in the smallest dataset of FilmTrust we vary N in $\{5, 10, 15\}$. We observe that CDAE has limited performance as it does not exploit the social relationships, thus being negatively affected by the sparsity in the evaluation datasets. mSDA-CF, TrustSVD, SPF and SDAE are superior to the baseline SocialMF method, because these models try to capture the user preferences and the friends' social influence in their learning strategies. Using the paired *t*-test ($p < 0.05$), we found out that SDAE is superior over all methods, achieving an average relative improvement of 13.22% and 12.72% in terms of *NDCG* and *recall*, respectively, when comparing it with the second best method (either TrustSVD or SPF). The advantage of our method is that our deep learning strategy can efficiently match the preferences of social friends, thus generating more accurate recommendations. Although mSDA-CF also follows a deep learning strategy, mSDA-CF is mainly designed to compute the user-user correlations based on the user attributes; this means that mSDA-CF tries to preserve the space of user attributes in each hidden layer, by using a projection matrix in its learning strategy. Instead, in the joint objective function of our model we try to learn the similarities between users based on their social relationships, while we consider the user preferences in the latent space of the user factor matrix at the same time, thus significantly outperforming mSDA-CF in all cases.

5.4 Effect of Sparsity

To evaluate the performance of the examined methods at different levels of sparsity, in this set of experiments we vary the size of the

Table 3: Effect on *NDCG@10* with 50% training set.

50% training set	Epinions	Flixter	Ciao	FilmTrust
CDAE	.1228 ± .0063	.2272 ± .0026	.1068 ± .0070	.4753 ± .0165
mSDA-CF	.1662 ± .0034	.2598 ± .0090	.1522 ± .0060	.5201 ± .0120
SocialMF	.1336 ± .0053	.2342 ± .0022	.1195 ± .0085	.4759 ± .0203
TrustSVD	.1727 ± .0047	.2856 ± .0074	.1567 ± .0053	.5186 ± .0092
SPF	.1837 ± .0026	.2765 ± .0045	.1720 ± .0023	.5354 ± .0139
SDAE	**.2145 ± .0022***	**.3401 ± .0095***	**.2086 ± .0083***	**.6251 ± .0103***
Improvement (%)	16.72	23.03	21.27	16.75

Table 4: Effect on *NDCG@10* with 25% training set.

25% training set	Epinions	Flixter	Ciao	FilmTrust
CDAE	.1117 ± .0076	.2090 ± .0046	.0971 ± .0042	.4325 ± .0088
mSDA-CF	.1529 ± .0080	.2442 ± .0055	.1400 ± .0056	.4785 ± .0136
SocialMF	.1242 ± .0098	.2178 ± .0044	.1100 ± .0094	.4426 ± .0111
TrustSVD	.1623 ± .0059	.2627 ± .0016	.1426 ± .0077	.4874 ± .0076
SPF	.1709 ± .0064	.2599 ± .0070	.1600 ± .0080	.49179 ± .0164
SDAE	**.2037 ± .0094***	**.3265 ± .0081***	**.1961 ± .0072***	**.5876 ± .0091***
Improvement (%)	19.23	25.64	22.58	19.48

training set. Tables 3 and 4 report *NDCG* in the reduced training sets and Figure 3 shows the effect on *recall (R@10)* by varying the size of the training set. Both *NDCG* and *recall* drop when reducing the size of the training set in all methods, as the users' selections are reduced, thus having a few selections on which to base the recommendations. We observe that SDAE constantly outperforms all methods. Compared to the second best method, SDAE on average achieves a relative improvement of 18.13% and 15.19% in terms of *NDCG* and *recall*, when varying the size of the training set in 25, 50 and 75%. An interesting observation is that when sparsity increases in the reduced training sets, SDAE achieves a relatively higher recommendation accuracy than the competitors, which confirms that SDAE can significantly handle the sparsity problem, by learning the preferences of each individual and exploiting her social relationships in its deep learning strategy.

5.5 Discussion

SDAE beats the competitors in all sets of experiments. Compared to the deep learning strategies CDAE and mSDA-CF, the proposed approach clearly achieves a significantly higher recommendation accuracy in all cases. This mainly happens because CDAE does not exploit the social relationships when generating the recommendations. mSDA-CF attempts to embed the space of user attributes in each hidden layer based on a projection matrix, which does not work well in the case of sparse social relationships. On the contrary, while considering the user preferences in the latent space of the user factor matrix, SDAE learns well similarities between users

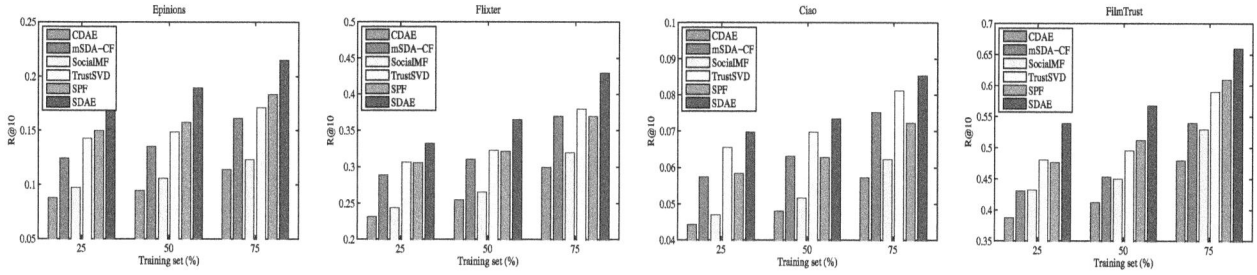

Figure 3: Effect on *recall (R@10)* when varying the size of the training set.

based on their social relationships (Section 4.1). The latent representation of relationships in the hidden layer enables it to take advantage of this, on top of the similar preferences. SDAE makes a very efficient use of the training data, as the limited loss in *NDCG* and *recall* passing from 75% to 25% of the training data shows. The method is also robust to data sparsity as it exploits the social relationships through the deep learning strategy. In fact, SDAE captures these better than mSDA-CF through the hidden layer.

SPF and TrustSVD have a relative good performance, compared to SocialMF, as SPF and TrustSVD follow different strategies to learn both about user preferences and the influence of her social friends, when factorizing the user-item matrix. However, both SPF and TrustSVD have limited recommendation accuracy, compared to SDAE. This occurs because the problem of recommendation becomes challenging when exploiting the user's social relationships, as recommendation strategies have to determine how much user preferences are influenced by her friends. In our architecture the proposed method follows a deep learning strategy by coupling the user latent factor matrix with the deepest hidden layer in the marginalized Denoising Autoencoder, thus leveraging the recommendation accuracy by correctly capturing the complex relationships between the selections made by social friends and those made by the user.

5.6 Parameter Analysis of Deep Learning Architecture

In Figure 4, we study the effect on *recall* of varying the percentage of injected noise in each input layer of SDAE. The proposed SDAE method has different performance due to the different characteristics of the evaluation datasets. We fix the percentage of injected noise to 70, 60, 50 and 30% for Epinions, Flixter, Ciao and FilmTrust, respectively. Based on the characteristics of the evaluation datasets in Table 1, we conclude that the number of social relationships and the number of users are the key factors to select the percentage of injected noise. For example, Filmtrust has the lowest number of social relationships and of users, thus requiring a lower percentage of injected noise. On the other hand, Epinions achieves the best performance when selecting a high percentage of injected noise. This happens because the input in the Denoising Autoencoder is the binary vector containing users with their social relationships. This means that when injecting too much noise the deep learning model becomes unstable for smaller datasets. Accordingly, SDAE has limited performance when the percentage of

injected noise is small, degrading the learning strategy of the Denoising Autoencoder [8].

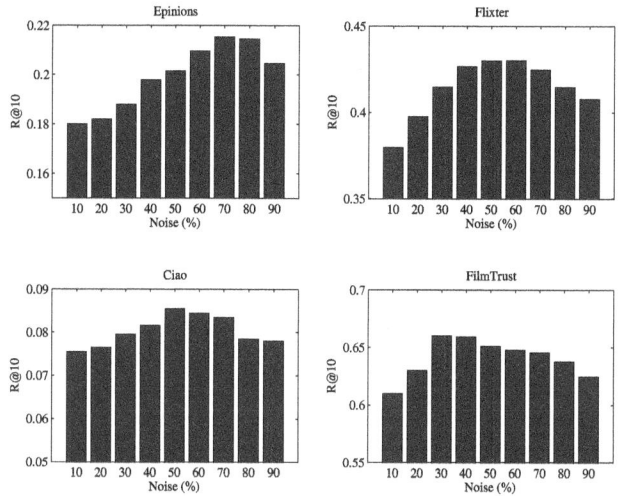

Figure 4: Effect on *recall (R@10)* when varying the percentage of injected noise.

Figure 5 shows the effect on *recall* of tuning the number of stacked layers to form the deep learning architecture in our model. The number of stacked layers is varied from 1 to 20 by a step of 1. In the case of selecting one layer we have a single-layer Denoising Autoencoder. We fix the number of stacked layers to 17, 13, 11 and 7 in Epinions, Flixter, Ciao and FilmTrust, accordingly. We observe that a larger number of stacked layers is required, depending on the dataset size. This occurs because SDAE has to follow a deeper learning strategy to efficiently capture both the user preferences and the social influence of her friends, when the dataset size is large. It is clear that the performance of SDAE slightly degrades, when a large number of stacked layers is selected for smaller datasets.

6 CONCLUSIONS

Our model generates recommendations with Social relationships based on marginalized stacked Denoising AutoEncoders, namely SDAE. This is achieved by formulating a joint objective function, which enforces the latent representation of the social relationships in the hidden layer of the marginalized Denoising Autoencoder to

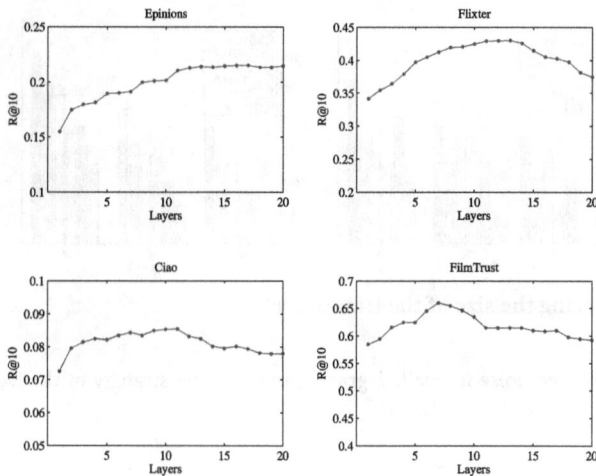

Figure 5: Effect on *recall (R@10)* when varying the number of stacked layers in our deep learning architecture.

be as close as possible to the latent representation of users, when factorizing the user-item matrix. The joint optimization problem is solved via an alternating optimization algorithm and gradient descent. Our experiments on benchmark datasets confirmed the superiority of the proposed approach over competitive strategies at different levels of sparsity. Compared to the second best method SDAE achieves a relative improvement of 16.65%, on average in all experiments. As future work we will consider the time dimension, to capture both user preferences and the social relationships' evolution over time in our deep learning strategy [24–26].

ACKNOWLEDGMENTS

Dimitrios Rafailidis was supported by the COMPLEXYS and IN-FORTECH Research Institutes of University of Mons.

REFERENCES

[1] Yoshua Bengio, Pascal Lamblin, Dan Popovici, and Hugo Larochelle. 2006. Greedy Layer-Wise Training of Deep Networks. In *NIPS*. 153–160.
[2] Allison June-Barlow Chaney, David M. Blei, and Tina Eliassi-Rad. 2015. A Probabilistic Model for Using Social Networks in Personalized Item Recommendation. In *RecSys*. 43–50.
[3] Minmin Chen, Zhixiang Eddie Xu, Kilian Q. Weinberger, and Fei Sha. 2012. Marginalized Denoising Autoencoders for Domain Adaptation. In *ICML*.
[4] ShuiGuang Deng, Longtao Huang, Guandong Xu, Xindong Wu, and Zhaohui Wu. 2017. On Deep Learning for Trust-Aware Recommendations in Social Networks. *IEEE Trans. Neural Netw. Learning Syst.* 28, 5 (2017), 1164–1177.
[5] Gintare Karolina Dziugaite and Daniel M. Roy. 2015. Neural Network Matrix Factorization. *CoRR* abs/1511.06443 (2015).
[6] Ali Mamdouh Elkahky, Yang Song, and Xiaodong He. 2015. A Multi-View Deep Learning Approach for Cross Domain User Modeling in Recommendation Systems. In *WWW*. 278–288.
[7] Kostadin Georgiev and Preslav Nakov. 2013. A non-IID Framework for Collaborative Filtering with Restricted Boltzmann Machines. In *ICML*. 1148–1156.
[8] Xavier Glorot, Antoine Bordes, and Yoshua Bengio. 2011. Domain Adaptation for Large-Scale Sentiment Classification: A Deep Learning Approach. In *ICML*. 513–520.
[9] Guibing Guo, Jie Zhang, and Neil Yorke-Smith. 2015. TrustSVD: Collaborative Filtering with Both the Explicit and Implicit Influence of User Trust and of Item Ratings. In *AAAI*.
[10] Mohsen Jamali and Martin Ester. 2009. *TrustWalker*: a random walk model for combining trust-based and item-based recommendation. In *KDD*. 397–406.
[11] Mohsen Jamali and Martin Ester. 2009. Using a trust network to improve top-N recommendation. In *RecSys*. 181–188.
[12] Mohsen Jamali and Martin Ester. 2010. A matrix factorization technique with trust propagation for recommendation in social networks. In *RecSys*. 135–142.
[13] Yehuda Koren. 2008. Factorization meets the neighborhood: a multifaceted collaborative filtering model. In *KDD*. 426–434.
[14] Yehuda Koren, Robert M. Bell, and Chris Volinsky. 2009. Matrix Factorization Techniques for Recommender Systems. *IEEE Computer* 42, 8 (2009), 30–37.
[15] Artus Krohn-Grimberghe, Lucas Drumond, Christoph Freudenthaler, and Lars Schmidt-Thieme. 2012. Multi-relational Matrix Factorization Using Bayesian Personalized Ranking for Social Network Data. In *WSDM*. 173–182.
[16] Daniel D. Lee and H. Sebastian Seung. 2000. Algorithms for Non-negative Matrix Factorization. In *NIPS*. 556–562.
[17] Sheng Li, Jaya Kawale, and Yun Fu. 2015. Deep Collaborative Filtering via Marginalized Denoising Auto-encoder. In *CIKM*. 811–820.
[18] Hao Ma, Irwin King, and Michael R. Lyu. 2009. Learning to recommend with social trust ensemble. In *SIGIR*. 203–210.
[19] Hao Ma, Haixuan Yang, Michael R. Lyu, and Irwin King. 2008. SoRec: social recommendation using probabilistic matrix factorization. In *CIKM*. 931–940.
[20] Trong T. Nguyen and Hady Wirawan Lauw. 2016. Representation Learning for Homophilic Preferences. In *RecSys*. 317–324.
[21] Aäron Van Den Oord, Sander Dieleman, and Benjamin Schrauwen. 2013. Deep content-based music recommendation. In *NIPS*. 2643–2651.
[22] Dimitrios Rafailidis and Fabio Crestani. 2016. Collaborative Ranking with Social Relationships for Top-N Recommendations. In *SIGIR*. 785–788.
[23] Dimitrios Rafailidis and Fabio Crestani. 2016. Joint Collaborative Ranking with Social Relationships in Top-N Recommendation. In *CIKM*. 1393–1402.
[24] Dimitrios Rafailidis and Alexandros Nanopoulos. 2014. Modeling the dynamics of user preferences in coupled tensor factorization. In *RecSys*. 321–324.
[25] Dimitrios Rafailidis and Alexandros Nanopoulos. 2015. Repeat Consumption Recommendation Based on Users Preference Dynamics and Side Information. In *WWW - Companion Volume*. 99–100.
[26] Dimitrios Rafailidis and Alexandros Nanopoulos. 2016. Modeling Users Preference Dynamics and Side Information in Recommender Systems. *IEEE Trans. Systems, Man, and Cybernetics: Systems* 46, 6 (2016), 782–792.
[27] Steffen Rendle, Christoph Freudenthaler, Zeno Gantner, and Lars Schmidt-Thieme. 2009. BPR: Bayesian Personalized Ranking from Implicit Feedback. In *UAI*. 452–461.
[28] Ruslan Salakhutdinov and Andriy Mnih. 2007. Probabilistic Matrix Factorization. In *NIPS*. 1257–1264.
[29] Ruslan Salakhutdinov, Andriy Mnih, and Geoffrey E. Hinton. 2007. Restricted Boltzmann machines for collaborative filtering. In *ICML*. 791–798.
[30] Suvash Sedhain, Aditya Krishna Menon, Scott Sanner, and Lexing Xie. 2015. AutoRec: Autoencoders Meet Collaborative Filtering. In *WWW - Companion Volume*. 111–112.
[31] Pascal Vincent, Hugo Larochelle, Yoshua Bengio, and Pierre-Antoine Manzagol. 2008. Extracting and composing robust features with denoising autoencoders. In *ICML*. 1096–1103.
[32] Chong Wang and David M. Blei. 2011. Collaborative topic modeling for recommending scientific articles. In *KDD*. 448–456.
[33] Hao Wang, Xingjian Shi, and Dit-Yan Yeung. 2015. Relational Stacked Denoising Autoencoder for Tag Recommendation. In *AAAI*. 3052–3058.
[34] Hao Wang, Naiyan Wang, and Dit-Yan Yeung. 2015. Collaborative Deep Learning for Recommender Systems. In *KDD*. 1235–1244.
[35] Xinxi Wang and Ye Wang. 2014. Improving Content-based and Hybrid Music Recommendation using Deep Learning. In *MM*. 627–636.
[36] Yao Wu, Christopher DuBois, Alice X. Zheng, and Martin Ester. 2016. Collaborative Denoising Auto-Encoders for Top-N Recommender Systems. In *WSDM*. 153–162.
[37] Xiwang Yang, Harald Steck, Yang Guo, and Yong Liu. 2012. On Top-k Recommendation Using Social Networks. In *RecSys*. 67–74.
[38] Tong Zhao, Julian McAuley, and Irwin King. 2014. Leveraging Social Connections to Improve Personalized Ranking for Collaborative Filtering. In *CIKM*. 261–270.
[39] Yin Zheng, Bangsheng Tang, Wenkui Ding, and Hanning Zhou. 2016. A Neural Autoregressive Approach to Collaborative Filtering. In *ICML*. 764–773.

Characterizing and Predicting Supply-side Engagement on Video Sharing Platforms Using a Hawkes Process Model

Rishabh Mehrotra
University College London
London, United Kingdom
r.mehrotra@cs.ucl.ac.uk

Prasanta Bhattacharya
National University of Singapore
Singapore, Singapore
prasanta@comp.nus.edu.sg

ABSTRACT

Video sharing platforms are one of the most popular and engaging platforms on the Internet today. Despite the increasing levels of user activity on these video platforms, current research on digital platforms have largely focused on social media and networking websites like Facebook and Twitter. We depart from previous work that have focused primarily on user demands (i.e. activity of viewers), and instead focus our attention to the supply-side activities on the platform (i.e. activity of video uploaders). We perform a large-scale empirical study by leveraging longitudinal video upload data from a major online video platform, demonstrating (i) heterogeneity of video types (e.g. presence of popular vs. niche genres), and (ii) inherent seasonality effects associated with video uploads. Through our analyses, we uncover a set of informative genre-clusters and estimate a self-exciting Hawkes point-process model on each of these clusters, to fully specify and estimate the video upload process. Additionally, we disentangle potential factors that govern user engagement and determine the video upload rates, which help supplement our analysis with additional explanatory power. Our results emphasize that using a parsimonious and relatively simple point-process model, we were able to obtain a high model fit, as well as perform prediction of video upload volumes with a higher accuracy than a number of competing models. The findings from this study can benefit platform owners in better understanding how their supply-side users engage with their site over time. We also offer a robust method for performing media upload prediction that is likely to be generalizable across media platforms which demonstrate similar temporal and genre-level heterogeneity.

1 INTRODUCTION

Video delivery and sharing platforms have witnessed exponential growth in recent times, with websites such as Youtube, Netflix and XVideos.com featuring among most frequently visited websites worldwide[1]. However, what sets these websites apart from other social media sites such as Facebook, Twitter and Reddit is the sheer

---

[1]http://www.alexa.com/topsites/countries;1/US

ICTIR'17, October 1–4, 2017, Amsterdam, The Netherlands
© 2017 ACM. ISBN 978-1-4503-4490-6/17/10...$15.00
DOI: http://dx.doi.org/10.1145/3121050.3121077

amount of data traffic that passes through their servers, as almost all content on these sites is available as streaming videos[2].

Despite the obvious importance of such video distribution and sharing platforms, academic research on such websites have been relatively lagging, with most choosing to focus on network-oriented sites instead [20] [19]. The extant research in the area of user-generated-content (UGC) too has been primarily focused on textual and pictorial content [18] [15] [4], and on issues related to UGC based predictions in the real world [1] [24] [21]. Most importantly, the few studies that have explicitly looked at video-based content, investigate demand-side research questions about video downloads, and consumption patterns [4, 9]. However, what lags in these previous investigations on the topic is an understanding of how the supply-side engagement develops on these platforms.

User engagement has been coined as the "emotional, cognitive and behavioral connection that exists between a user and a resource" [2]. While most users engage with these platforms as content-consumers, their engagement is sustained by a steady upload of videos from a relatively smaller sample of video uploaders who engage actively with the platform as content producers. As a result, it is imperative for such platforms to predict and understand user engagement so as to constantly attract content contributors by keeping them users engaged (for the purpose of this work, by "user" we imply users who contribute content, i.e., content producers).

In this current study, we depart from existing work by explicitly modeling the supply side engagement pattern of these video uploaders across different video genres. Specifically, we introduce a point process model to specify the content generation process and provide a mechanism for predicting future upload volumes and disentangling the contributing factors. For our empirical analysis, we use data from a large-scale adult entertainment website which is ranked among the top two most frequently visited adult entertainment sites on the Internet. Our dataset comprises information about the uploaded video (e.g. title, descriptions etc.) as well as user-generated tags associated with each upload. In order to uncover genre-level engagement patterns from the upload data, we first perform a clustering analysis, forming association clusters based on the co-occurrence of video tags which are selected by the users while uploading the video to the platform. Thus, videos which have a common set of associated tags are inducted into the same video cluster, implying that each video cluster qualitatively represents a specific genre or taste category.

Video uploads demonstrate a significant rate-heterogeneity depending on the specific video genre as is evident from the distinct upload patterns in each of the 4 illustrative clusters shown in Figure 1. Drawing on this insight, we perform predictive modeling on each

---

[2]http://www.cnet.com/news/netflix-youtube-gobble-up-half-of-internet-traffic/

of the clusters individually to generate insights about the upload process for the specific video genre. For our model estimations, we employ a parametric self-exciting process model, also termed as a Hawkes process model in literature [13]. Such models provide an elegant and parsimonious extension to the popular Poisson model, by incorporating the history of events into consideration. Self-exciting models are ideal candidates for fitting multi-spell events with bursty traffic where there are infrequent spikes in frequency followed by periods of mean-reveal when the frequency retreats to its mean value. In our current study, we apply the Hawkes model to each of the identified genres, also termed as clusters, and obtain parameter estimates that we later use to make predictions. We show that our model fits the data better than comparable variants of the Poisson model that have been used in recent research on Hawkes models. Moreover, our model provides lowest average prediction error spanning different splits of the training and test data, as compared to other baseline models.

In addition to predictive accuracy, we attempt to disentangle the effect of various factors contributing to the video upload process, and investigate which among them were the driving contributors to video uploads, spanning different clusters. Identifying the contributing factors helps in better understanding the psyche of users engaging with the platform as content contributors. We assert that the engagement driving factor derives from three major sources viz. self-reinforcement, popularity of other videos in the genre, and other exogenous events. We perform an explanatory analysis to estimate what fraction of the clustering in each genre can be attributed to each of these three sources. Thus, drawing on our self-excitation model, we are not only able to make accurate predictions of video uploads, but are also able to explain the source for these upload intensities across different video categories.

We contend that our study is among the first to go beyond consumer side view to analyze the supply side of videos generated in a real-world setting. While our empirical analysis leverages data from a large adult entertainment platform, the models and methods we use can easily be adapted to other video streaming platforms without any loss of generality. Specifically, we offer the following three contributions in the current paper: First, while several studies on UGC in general, and videos in particular have focused on modeling demand-side user engagement patterns (i.e. content consumption), this is among the first studies to analyze the user-generated supply side nature of these video distribution platforms. Second, we leverage a Hawkes point-process model to provide a robust predictive model which outperforms other comparable baselines that do not take into account the self-exciting nature of video uploads. Third, we go beyond prediction, to uncover potential factors that determine the video upload rate. This improves the analysis with additional explanatory power. We contend that these findings will increase our understanding of video-based UGC production on online entertainment platforms, and will aid platform owners in better understanding how their content producers engage with with the platform by producing content that has high genre-level and temporal heterogeneity.

2 RELATED WORK

We review some past work looking at user engagement on online

platforms along with a brief review of studies that look at video distributions.

User Engagement in Online Platforms:
Past work on user engagement on digital platforms have looked at metrics such as click-through rate, dwell time (i.e. time spent on the site), number of page views, site return rates etc. These metrics are often referred to as user engagement metrics, and have been widely used to quantify users' level of engagement on the site and hence relied upon as proxies for online engagement. Existing studies of user engagement with a web service can broadly be classified into three groups. First, some past studies have attempted to better characterize and explain different facets of online user behavior. For example, recent work has uncovered the relationship between goal success and system reuse [31], while some other studies have illustrated behavioral patterns of users (e.g. multitasking user behavior [16] or popularity, activity, and loyalty among online users [17]). Second, some prior work have focused on predicting future user engagement. For instance, [31] illustrated how users switch between different online systems over a period of 26 weeks. The authors uncovered switching strategies such as no switching, persistent switching, and oscillating behavior. The third group of user engagement studies have devoted attention to the development user engagement as an evaluation metric in controlled experiments [8, 14].

Video-based User Generated Content:
The massive growth of social media and social media powered digital plaforms has signficantly increased the volume of word-of-mouth (WOM) or user-generated content (UGC) generated on digital platforms. These user to user or site to user interactions, while mostly textual, have been succesffuly exploited to predict movie revenues, television success [1, 5, 29], election outcomes [23], product sales [12] and even firm equity values [21]. There have been related research on modeling the emergence and growth of such text-based user generated content as well [30, 32].

Self-exciting Point Processes:
Our approach in this work is based on the Hawkes Process which is a type of self-exciting point-process model. Such point-process models have been popularly used in recent studies to model natural phenomena like wildfire assessments [27], spiking in brain-waves [28], financial settings[10] and even online check-ins on a social media site[7].

3 DATASET DESCRIPTION

For our empirical analysis, we use data from a large-scale adult video sharing site[3] [22]. Such genre-based video sharing platforms like 9Gag.tv, XVideo.com etc. are unique in that they provide a fertile venue to study both genre-level heterogeneity (i.e. heterogeneity in uploader's video tastes), as well as temporal perturbations (i.e. periods of temporal clustering). Our dataset comprises an exhaustive collection of metadata from all videos published on the platform, since its creation in April 2007, up until February 2013, totalling over 800,000 videos from over 85000 uploaders. Table 1 describes the associated metadata which consists of an anonymized

---

[3] http://xhamster.com/

Metadata	Description	Example
upload_date	Day when the video was uploaded	4//30//2011
title	Title of the video	"Tea party at Dick's house"
channels	List of the video's tags	['Tea', 'Spoon', 'Sugar']
description	Description of the video	"What a spoon !"
nb_views	Number of times the video has been displayed	69
nb_votes	Number of users who voted for or against this video	42
nb_comments	Number of comments posted on this video	666
runtime	Length of the video in seconds	4815
uploader	Anonymized identifier of the uploader's username	6f60cbef5b891f80

Table 1: The metadata associated with each uploaded video on the website [22].

uploader identifier, video upload date and time, list of uploader contributed video-tags for the uploaded videos, and video popularity cues (e.g. number of views, comments etc).

The content on video sharing sites is often arranged in the form of diverse categories or tags for ease of access and use. While uploading any new video, the uploader is given the option of selecting tags from a set of existing tags. Often a video is tagged with multiple related tags. It is to be noted that the tags appear to form some clusters based on tag associativity, an insight we leverage later for better predictions.

4 MODELING VIDEO UPLOADS

Our aim in this research is to characterize the video upload process in such crowd-contributed video ecosystems so as to be able to uncover emerging genres in video uploads and predict future upload volumes for each of these themes, while at the same time explaining what factors might be generating the observed volumes. A multitude of factors influence the supply-side process of user contributions on such platforms. The inherent heterogeneity of content as reflected by the abundance of user-selected tags and categories poses interesting challenges in analyzing the content upload process. Additionally, the temporal variability introduced by seasonal trends and popularities form yet another aspect of the upload process.

We first explain the process of extracting different clusters of videos based on their tag associativity, following which, we present a Hawkes Process to model the upload process and predict future uploads.

4.1 Graph-based Tag Cluster Formation

Almost any web site that provides means for sharing user-generated multimedia content has tagging functionalities to let users annotate the material that they want to share. The tags are then used to retrieve the uploaded content, and to ease browsing and exploration of these collections, e.g. using tag clouds. These tags also provide additional contextual and semantic information by which users can organize and access shared media content. While uploading new media content, users typically associate their media with those tags which can potentially explain the content better to prospective viewers. Each media can thus be associated with different tags thereby forming a complex network of inter-tag relationships. When analyzing tag associations, it is often observed that some sets of tags co-occur together in a large proportions, suggesting that, together, they can be viewed as a high-level genre or category. While some of these genres or categories (e.g.funny cat videos) are

widely popular, others are very niche (e.g. black hole videos) with often a particular set of users responsible for most of the content generation and consumption in such categories. Often the content generation rate in niche videos are triggered by some external events (e.g. a recent movie related to Astronomy triggers an increased interest in black hole videos). This necessitates the need for segregating such categories of videos because the way a popular category gets flooded with user generated content varies drastically from the content generation process in such niche categories.

While videos do not have explicit category/cluster labels, we propose to make use of the associated tag information to uncover the various clusters underlying the videos. To this end, we formulate the tag associations in videos in a graph based setting. Given a set of videos along with their tag associations, we build a complete graph $G_V = (T, E, w)$, whose nodes T are the set of all tags associated with the set of videos V, and whose E edges are weighted by the tag-tag affinities. The weighting function w is a tag affinity function $w : E \to \mathbb{I}$ where $\mathbb{I}$ is the set of integers. For each pair of tags, the edge weight is defined as

$$w(t_1, t_2) = |\{v\}| \ s.t. \ t_1 \in tags(v) \ \& \ t_2 \in tags(v) \quad (1)$$

i.e., the total number of videos in which these two tags co-occur. Overall, the graph G_V describes the tag-affinity network for the set of videos V.

We define the video clusters as the set of vertex-partitions induced by the connected components of the graph G_V. The rationale is to drop weak edges, i.e., low tag-affinity and to build clusters on the basis of the strong edges, i.e. with high tag affinity, which identify the related tag pairs. The algorithm performs two steps:

1. **Graph Pruning:** given the graph G_V all the edges $e \in E$ whose weight is smaller than a given threshold, that is $w(t_1, t_2) < \eta$, are removed, thus obtaining a pruned graph G'_V.
2. **Connected Components:** in the second step, the connected components of the pruned graph G'_V are extracted.

Such connected components identify the genre-clusters of related tags which are returned by the algorithm.

4.2 Genre-Cluster Analysis

After constructing the tag-tag affinity graph for the contributed video tags and applying a vertex partitioning algorithm, we were able to uncover a total of 37 genre or category-based clusters from the entire dataset, such that videos within each cluster had similar tags. The average number of videos within each cluster was 19460,

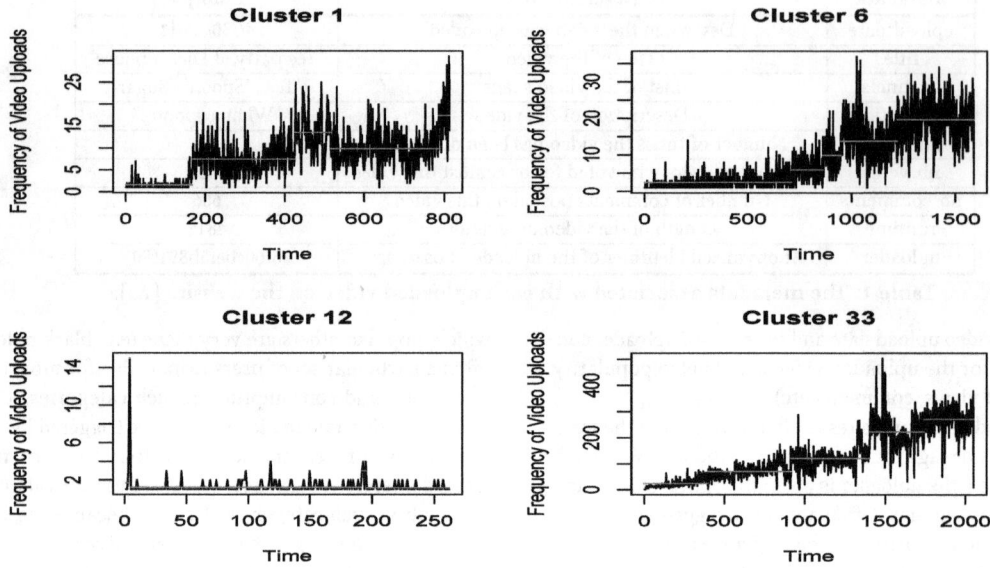

Figure 1: Variation in upload patterns across different clusters.

with the minimum and maximum number of videos in any cluster being 337 and 264509 respectively, for cluster numbers 12 and 33.

4.3 Modeling Video Uploads as a Hawkes Process

The *weighted connected components* of the tag affinity graph, as defined above, serve as the genre-clusters which represent the different types of video categories one usually observes on online video sharing sites. As is evident from the distinct upload patterns in each of the 4 illustrative clusters Fig. 1, video uploads demonstrate significant rate-heterogeneity depending on the specific video genre. Such cluster specific heterogeneity warrants the need to perform predictive modeling on each of the clusters individually to generate cluster-specific insights. We treat each such genre-clusters as a separate process and we adopt the parametric Hawkes process for each genre-cluster to model the cluster specific upload process.

4.3.1 Hawkes Process. A point process N is a random measure on a completely separable metric space S that takes values on $N \cup \{\infty\}$. In our case, a convenient way to view a realization of N is that of a list of times $t_1, t_2, ..., t_n$ at which events $1, 2, ...n$ occur. A point process is typically characterized by prescribing its conditional intensity $\lambda(t)$, which represents the infinitesimal rate at which events are expected to occur around a particular time t, given the history of the process up to t, $H_t = t_i : t_i < t$ [25] Thus, in a point process, $N(t)$ counts the number of points (i.e., occurrences of events) in $(-\infty, t]$, and the conditional intensity function $\lambda(t|H_t)$ denotes the expected instantaneous rate of future events at timestamp t depending on H_t, the history of events preceding t. An important example of a point process is the Poisson process, which always has a deterministic conditional intensity $\lambda(t)$. We say that a point process N is self-exciting if

$$Cov[N(t_1, t_2), N(t_2, t_3)] > 0 \tag{2}$$

for any $t_1 < t_2 < t_3$. This means that if an event occurs, a successive event becomes more likely to occur locally in time and space. This is, however, not true for a Poisson process which has independent increments, hence $Cov[N(t_1, t_2), N(t_2, t_3)] = 0$.

The Hawkes process is a specific class of self- or mutually-exciting point process models [13]. A univariate Hawkes process $\{N(t)\}$ is defined by its intensity function

$$\lambda(t) = \mu(t) + \int_{-\infty}^{t} \kappa(t - s)dN(s) \tag{3}$$

where $\mu : \Re \rightarrow \Re^+$ is a deterministic base intensity, $\kappa : \Re^+ \rightarrow R^+$ is a kernel function expressing the positive influence of past events on the current value of the intensity process. The process is well known for its self-exciting property, which refers to the phenomenon that the occurrence of one event in the past increases the probability of events happening in the future. Such a self-exciting property can either exist between every pair of events, as assumed in a normal univariate Hawkes process, or only exist between limited pairs of events.

4.3.2 Modeling Video Uploads. Each genre-cluster obtained via the connected components of the tag affinity graph is treated as a separate Hawkes Process. Each video upload in the genre-cluster is treated as an event in the given cluster specific point process. We model the intensity of video upload events involving a cluster c at time t as follows:

$$\lambda_c(t) = \mu_c + \sum_{p:t_p < t} g_c(t - t_p) \tag{4}$$

This intensity function can be interpreted as a rate at which video-uploads in a cluster occur. The summation in the second term is over all the events (i.e. uploads) that have happened up to time t. μ_c describes the background rate of event occurrence that is time-independent, whereas the second term describes the self-excitation part, so that a video upload in the past increases the probability of observing another upload in the (near) future. We will use a two-parameter family for the self-excitation term:

$$g_c(t - t_p) = \beta_c \, exp(-w_c(t - t_p)) \qquad (5)$$

where β_c describes the weight of the self-excitation term (compared to the background rate), while w_c describes the decay rate of the excitation. Intuitively, the decay term captures the notion that more recent upload events are more important.

Overall, each genre-cluster is defined by three sets of parameters of the Hawkes Process: $< \mu, \beta, w >$ representing the upload process characterized by the particular cluster. The estimates of these parameters were obtained by minimizing the negative of the log likelihood function [26].

5 DISENTANGLING THE CONTRIBUTING FACTORS

As can be seen in Fig 1, the average upload patterns across the different clusters are not static, but rather vary significantly with time and across clusters. Such a dynamic pattern can be attributed to the different factors which trigger users to contribute new media. In this section, we describe three primary mechanisms to describe the video upload process: (i) self-reinforcing behavior of users, (ii) trend-burst influence, also called here as the "popularity effect," and (iii) other exogenous factors. We are especially interested in disentangling the individual contributions of these three effects from the overall cumulative effect. The rich information in the data including the user information and the content popularity information allows us to construct a fine-grained model of the strength of the effect of one event on the other. We next describe the process of finding such relations, a technique which we use to uncover the relative contributions of these three different effects.

5.1 Inferring Correlations between Events

A Hawkes process model provides us with the flexibility to characterize the relationships between two events (e.g. between successive uploads, as in this study). We can infer the strength of the ties between two events by examining the intensity function for a given event which further allows us to infer the likelihood that the event was triggered by a specific historical event. A current event can potentially be triggered by any of the historical events. We use a probabilistic measure (introduced in [7]) described below, to model the strength of tie between i and j. For the given process (representing a specific genre-cluster c), the probability that the jth event is triggered by the $i - th$ event can be expressed as below:

$$p_{i \rightarrow j}^c = \frac{g_c(t_j - t_i)}{\mu_c + \sum_{p: t_p < t_j} g_c(t_j - t_p)} \qquad (6)$$

From the parameter values learnt in section 4.3 above, we can calculate the above probability based on the cluster specific $< \mu_c, \beta_c, w_c >$ values. Since we are interested in correlation of points for a given process (cluster) and not the correlation across different processes (clusters), we assume each process (cluster) has its own parameters which we estimate in isolation from each other.

5.2 Contributing Factors

Our goal here is disentangling and analyzing the different factors along with their individual contributions towards explaining the content creation volume in any particular genre-cluster. We consider three major factors that govern the content generation behavior observed in crowd-contributed websites. We describe each of the three in detail below. The user-views and comment information associated with each video serves as a proxy to estimate the relative popularity of the different videos, and along with the uploader's information, it provides us with the necessary equipment to tackle the disentanglement objective. Individual contributions from each of these factors allow us to construct a fine-grained model of the strength of the effect of one on another. While the ground truth cause for each video upload is unknown, we offer various ways to quantitatively test the validity of our factors.

5.2.1 Self-reinforcing Behavior. Often, users exhibit strong predictable behaviors in terms of their affinity towards a particular genre-cluster. Quite frequently, a particular user consistently uploads videos belonging to the same genre. Such a repetitive and self-reinforcing behavior observed on the platform is indeed a major factor governing the proportion of content in any particular cluster. A user who has already uploaded in a particular cluster is more likely to display behavioral consistency and upload again soon in this cluster and, conversely, a paucity of uploads strongly predicts fewer uploads in the future. This self-reinforcing tendency is measured using the event correlation equation described in subsection 5.1 by summing over upload events i and j that were initiated by a particular user. More specifically, we define the self-reinforcing score for a particular genre-cluster c as follows:

$$S_{self} = \frac{\sum_{t_i < t_j} p_{i \rightarrow j}^c \mathbb{I}_{u_i = u_j}}{\sum_{t_i < t_j} p_{i \rightarrow j}^c} \qquad (7)$$

where $\mathbb{I}$ is the indicator function which equals one if the uploader u_i is same as uploader u_j and i & j correspond to the upload event taking place in genre-cluster c.

5.2.2 Popularity Effect. The perceived *popularity* of an already uploaded content often lends a sense of validation to a prospective uploader who might use this information to decide whether or not to upload content of that genre [11]. Based on this intuition, we postulate that users are more likely to upload content if they perceive that the content they are uploading will be well-received by the content consumers. To incorporate this effect, we make use of a user specific *popularity effect* which is our second major factor governing the proportion of content in a particular cluster.

The average popularity of uploaded content would differ for different users - some users would have a relatively high popularity average while some would have a relatively low popularity average based on their past uploads. Indeed, different users have different notions of baseline popularity thresholds which are often impacted by how popular user's past uploads were. We quantify the popularity of any uploaded content in terms of the number of views and the number of comments it has received (popularity score for a video upload event i is notated as ψ_i). We model user specific popularity

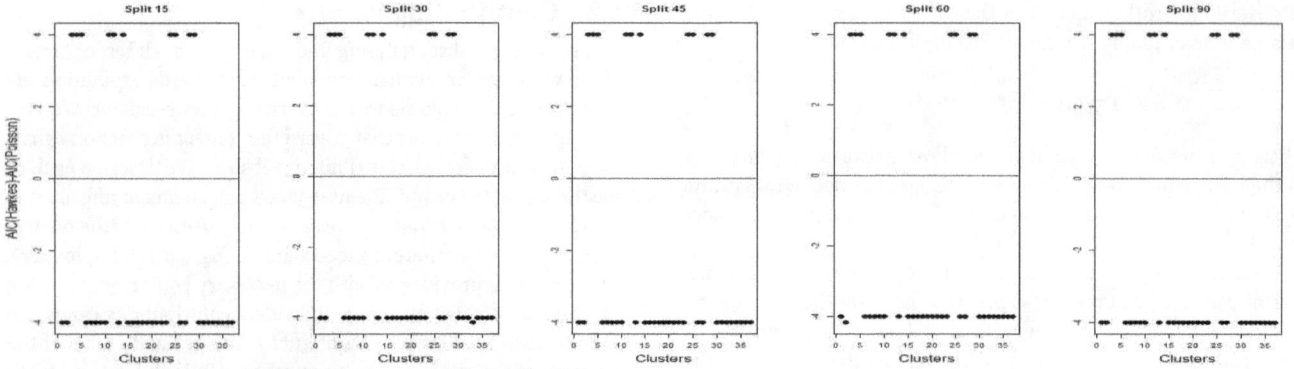

Figure 2: Comparison of model fit statistics: the difference in AIC scores among the proposed Hawkes process model and the Poisson model is plotted for each of the genre-clusters.

threshold by averaging over the user' past popularity score and postulate that past uploads by other users in a particular cluster which are, on average, more popular than the focal user's average popularity score, the *popularity effect*, will positively impact the uploader's decision to upload content to that cluster. We define the Popularity Effect score for any particular genre-cluster c as follows:

$$S_{pop} = \frac{\sum_{t_i < t_j} p_{i \to j}^c \mathbb{I}_{\psi_i > \psi_{avg_{u_j}}}}{\sum_{t_i < t_j} p_{i \to j}^c} \quad (8)$$

where ψ_i denotes the popularity of video event i, $\psi_{avg_{u_j}}$ denotes the average popularity score for user u_j and i, j correspond to the upload events taking place in the genre-cluster c. Thus, the term $\mathbb{I}_{\psi_i > \psi_{avg_{u_j}}}$ activates all past video upload events wherein the video i was more popular than user u_j's average popularity score. This effect models the increased likelihood of a upload event taking place in light of past popularity of content from the same cluster.

Exogenous Effect
If a upload event is not explained by either of the effects above, we consider it to be caused by some external (exogenous) factors. Indeed, other factors like website streaming quality, consumer demand, ease of content creation process, etc. might contribute towards explaining the observation that some genre-cluster have much more upload events than others. While modeling these effects individually provides stronger cues and insights about the overall upload process, for the current study, we accumulate them together as *Exogenous Effects*. The score for the exogenous effect is calculated based on the scores of the two main factors described earlier.

$$S_{exo} = 1 - S_{self} - S_{pop} \quad (9)$$

We make use of the above mentioned scores to evaluate the impact of these different factors towards guiding genre-cluster level upload behavior and present detailed results in Section 7.

6 EXPERIMENTAL EVALUATION

We next evaluate our performance in modeling and predicting video uploads via comparing goodness of fit and prediction errors of the proposed Hawkes process model with a number of baselines as described below.

6.1 Baselines

We compare the Hawkes process model to several other baselines based on nonhomogeneous Poisson processes(NHPP) as described below.

Baseline 1: piecewise-constant NHPP (PC-NHPP)
Content uploads rates for each cluster follow a cluster specific background rate: some popular genre-clusters generally notice much frequent uploads than other niche genre-clusters. We fit a piecewise-constant nonhomogeneous Poisson processes(NHPP) for each cluster and use the results as our first baseline.

Baseline 2: NHPP with drifting (NHPP-D)
We define the rate function as a linear function of time. On many genre-clusters, the video uploads become more frequent as time elapsed from the first upload. A sudden video upload suddenly sparks interest among consumers which excites uploaders to upload more content to this particular genre-cluster. To model this, we use a rate function defined as $\lambda(t) = \mu t + b$, where μ is the cluster specific the base rate.

Baseline 3: Hawkes process with no clusters
In this baseline, we consider all historic events ignoring the cluster assignments and model a single Hawkes process model on the entire data.

Baseline 4: ARIMA modeling
As a final baseline, we also estimate a time series model based on an autoregressive integrated moving average (ARIMA) specification. We implement a series of model specifications for each of the clusters by varying the autoregressive order, the moving average order and the degree of differencing. We finally select the model with the lowest AIC criterion and use it to make forecasts. The results are shown in Table 2.

6.2 Model Selection

For every genre-cluster, we fit the data to a Hawkes process using MLE and evaluate the goodness of fit compared against other baseline approaches (see Section 6.1 for the list of baselines). For evaluation we use the AIC score [3], which has been widely used for model selection. In addition to maximizing likelihood, AIC also

Splits	Hawkes	PC-NHPP	NHPP-D	No Cluster	Baseline 4
15	**31.99**	32.00	33.50	49.23	44.26
30	**27.76**	31.39	30.96	50.12	43.06
45	**35.25**	40.60	38.16	49.89	43.78
60	**37.43**	37.58	38.63256	51.22	44.02
90	**39.30**	41.90	42.89	51.45	44.79

Table 2: Predictive Analysis: the error in predicting total number of video uploads within a future window of 2 weeks. The splits highlight the number of training days used to construct the model.

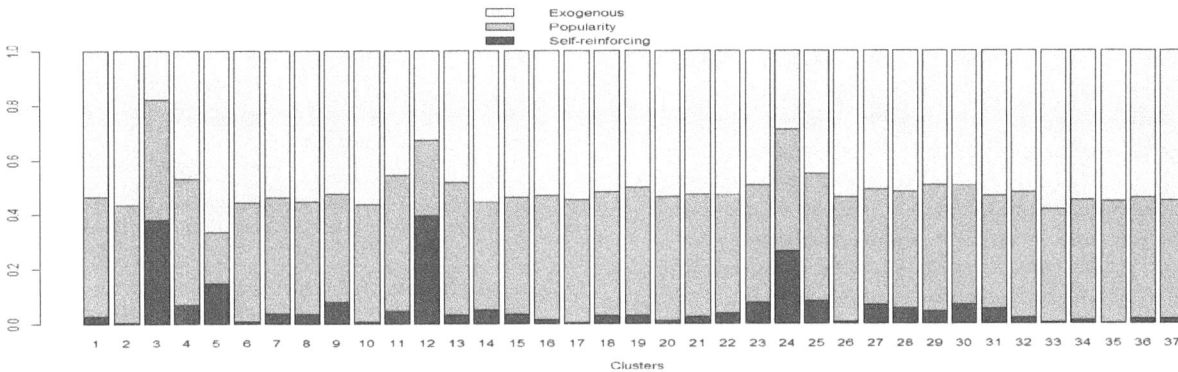

Figure 3: Relative impact of the three contributing factors across the different genre-clusters.

penalizes models with large number of parameters to discourage overfitting. The model with the smallest score is chosen from the candidates.

Figure 2 in the previous page shows a comparison of the model fit between our proposed Hawkes model and a homogeneous Poisson model, that is popularly employed to model count- or rate-related data. The difference in Akaike Information Criterion (AIC) between the Hawkes and Poisson model forms our key criteria for comparison. It is clear that across different sample sizes, denoted by the split values, our model shows superior model fit as compared to its Poisson counterpart. This is evidenced by a lower AIC value across most clusters for a given data size.

6.3 Predicting Video Uploads

To additionally evaluate the performance of the proposed Hawkes Process based model for modeling the video upload process, we evaluate our model on the task of video upload prediction. For all genre-clusters, we segregate the data into two components, training set and testing set and fit a separate Hawkes Process on the training data and perform MLE to obtain estimates of the model parameters. Using these parameters, we intend to predict the number of videos that would be uploaded in a given future time frame. With the estimated parameters, the rate function at time t can be computed based on the history up to time t and the parameters estimated from the training set. The number of events (video uploads) between time interval t and $t + \delta t$ can be computed using the counting process as below ($\delta t > 0$):

$$N(t + \delta t) - N(t) = \int_t^{t+\delta t} \lambda(\tau)d\tau \qquad (10)$$

In our experiments, we focus on predicting the number of videos uploaded in the time frame of two weeks. For this, we make use of a number of training-testing splits. The training splits consists

of data from the past 15 days, 30 days, 45 days, 60 days and 90 days. It is to be noted that the upload process at the web scale is highly susceptible to seasonal trends such that a holiday season experiences a surge in the number of videos uploaded as compared to a more monotone season. Hence, modeling dependencies in the upload process based on a longer historical past would add noise to the training phase.

We report results from our predictive analyses where the performance of the Hawkes model in predicting total number of video uploads to the site within a future window of 2 weeks is analyzed. As described in the previous section, we also run two comparable baseline models viz. a piecewise constant NHPP , and NHPP with drifting[6]. Our results as illustrated in Table 2 show that the Hawkes model outperforms both of the Poisson based baseline models across all sample sizes. The lower the prediction error, the better the model at predicting the upload volume. We find that our model is able to predict video uploads to the site with prediction error rates lowest among comparable models used in recent studies.

Impact of considering clusters:
As can be seen from the predictive results, cluster specific Hawkes process model performs better than the No Cluster Hawkes process model. Indeed this highlightsthe importance of modeling each cluster separately via a cluster specific model parameters.

Benefits over Time Series Model:
The performance of the ARIMA baseline is worse than that of the proposed model which highlights the fact that simple time series based models aren't generic enough to incorporate variations while Hawkes process is able to better model the temporal variations in the upload process.

7 IMPACT OF CONTRIBUTING FACTORS

One of the major goals of this study was to also disentangle the effect of various factors contributing to the video upload process, and investigate which among them were the driving contributors to video uploads, spanning different clusters. As mentioned in Section 5.2, we hypothesize that there are three major factors that contribute to temporal clustering viz. self-reinforcing behavior, popularity effect, and unobserved exogenous factors.

Figure 3 demonstrates the distribution of the self-reinforcing score, popularity effect score and exogenous effect score for each of our 37 clusters. We find evidence for both self-reinforcing behavior and popularity effect within each cluster. However, quite interestingly, we do find variation in the relative proportion of these two scores across the clusters. For instance, while most clusters report a higher popularity effect as compared to the self-reinforcing scores, clusters 3,12 and 24 report a higher than average self-reinforcing effect. Further, clusters 3 and 12 report even higher self-reinforcing scores than popularity effect. Taken together, these results hint of a strong genre-level dependency that exists on these video platforms, and while popularity of other videos in a genre is a leading driver for most genre of videos, this is not necessarily true for all genres. Our findings uncover this interesting interplay between video genres and the factors contributing to increased uploads.

8 CONCLUSION

The current study is among the first to fully characterize, explain and predict supply side engagement patterns on a large-scale online video sharing platform. We uncover significant user- and genre-level heterogeneities in online video uploads, and propose a parametric self-exciting point process model for modeling the same, after controlling for genre-level heterogeneity and temporal perturbations. We demonstrate a higher model fit as compared to a homogeneous-rate Poisson model, and also make more accurate predictions than comparable baseline models. Additionally, beyond predicting uploads, we also discuss possible reasons for the high-clustering behavior observed in our dataset. We posit that such clustering effects in uploader engagement could be the result of self-reinforcing behavior of the uploads, or due to popularity influence of other videos of the same genre, or even due to other exogenous factors that are not captured in our dataset. Based on our conditional intensity modeling, we are able to successfully disentangle the above three causes for the observed video clustering, thereby providing evidence that both self-reinforcement as well as the popularity effect have a strong role to play in producing the upload pattern displayed by our data. By providing a parsimonious model that combines the benefit of predictive modeling with strong explanatory power, and a unique dataset that allows us to investigate both genre-level and temporal heterogeneities, we offer researchers, policy makers, economists as well as platform owners with useful insights about the supply-side behavior of video-based entertainment sharing platforms.

REFERENCES

[1] Sitaram Asur and Bernardo A Huberman. Predicting the future with social media. In WI-IAT 2010.
[2] Simon Attfield, Gabriella Kazai, Mounia Lalmas, and Benjamin Piwowarski. 2011. Towards a science of user engagement (position paper). In WSDM workshop on user modelling for Web applications.
[3] Kenneth P Burnham and David R Anderson. 2002. Model selection and multimodel inference: a practical information-theoretic approach. Springer.
[4] Meeyoung Cha, Haewoon Kwak, Pablo Rodriguez, Yong-Yeol Ahn, and Sue Moon. 2007. I tube, you tube, everybody tubes: analyzing the world's largest user generated content video system. In Proceedings of the 7th ACM SIGCOMM conference on Internet measurement.
[5] Pradeep K Chintagunta, Shyam Gopinath, and Sriram Venkataraman. 2010. The effects of online user reviews on movie box office performance: Accounting for sequential rollout and aggregation across local markets. Marketing Science 29, 5 (2010), 944–957.
[6] Yoon-Sik Cho, Greg Ver Steeg, and Aram Galstyan. Where and Why Users "Check In". In AAAI 2014.
[7] Yoon-Sik Cho, Greg Ver Steeg, and Aram Galstyan. 2014. Where and Why Users fiCheck Infi. (2014).
[8] Alexey Drutsa, Anna Ufliand, and Gleb Gusev. 2015. Practical Aspects of Sensitivity in Online Experimentation with User Engagement Metrics. In Proceedings of the 24th ACM International on Conference on Information and Knowledge Management. ACM, 763–772.
[9] Flavio Figueiredo. On the prediction of popularity of trends and hits for user generated videos. In WSDM 2013.
[10] Vladimir Filimonov and Didier Sornette. 2013. Apparent criticality and calibration issues in the Hawkes self-excited point process model: application to high-frequency financial data. arXiv preprint arXiv:1308.6756 (2013).
[11] Paulo B Goes, Mingfeng Lin, and Ching-man Au Yeung. 2014. fiPopularity Effectfi in User-Generated Content: Evidence from Online Product Reviews. Information Systems Research (2014).
[12] Khim-Yong Goh, Cheng-Suang Heng, and Zhijie Lin. 2013. Social media brand community and consumer behavior: Quantifying the relative impact of user-and marketer-generated content. Information Systems Research 24, 1 (2013), 88–107.
[13] Alan G Hawkes. 1971. Spectra of some self-exciting and mutually exciting point processes. Biometrika (1971).
[14] Jin Young Kim and Emine Yilmaz. IR Evaluation: Designing an End-to-End Offline Evaluation Pipeline. In SIGIR 2015.
[15] Ravi Kumar, Jasmine Novak, and Andrew Tomkins. 2010. Structure and evolution of online social networks. In Link mining: models, algorithms, and applications.
[16] Janette Lehmann, Mounia Lalmas, Georges Dupret, and Ricardo Baeza-Yates. Online multitasking and user engagement. In CIKM 2013.
[17] Janette Lehmann, Mounia Lalmas, Elad Yom-Tov, and Georges Dupret. 2012. Models of user engagement. In User Modeling, Adaptation, and Personalization. Springer, 164–175.
[18] Jure Leskovec, Lars Backstrom, and Jon Kleinberg. 2009. Meme-tracking and the dynamics of the news cycle. In Proceedings of KDD 2009. ACM, 497–506.
[19] Jure Leskovec, Lars Backstrom, Ravi Kumar, and Andrew Tomkins. Microscopic evolution of social networks. In KDD 2008.
[20] Jure Leskovec and Eric Horvitz. Planetary-scale views on a large instant-messaging network. In WWW 2008.
[21] Xueming Luo, Jie Zhang, and Wenjing Duan. 2013. Social media and firm equity value. Information Systems Research (2013).
[22] Antoine Mazières, Mathieu Trachman, Jean-Philippe Cointet, Baptiste Coulmont, and Christophe Prieur. 2014. Deep tags: toward a quantitative analysis of online pornography. Porn Studies 1, 1-2 (2014), 80–95.
[23] Takis Metaxas and Eni Mustafaraj. 2012. Social media and the elections. (2012).
[24] Brendan O'Connor, Ramnath Balasubramanyan, Bryan R Routledge, and Noah A Smith. 2010. From tweets to polls: Linking text sentiment to public opinion time series. ICWSM (2010).
[25] Yosihiko Ogata. 1988. Statistical models for earthquake occurrences and residual analysis for point processes. J. Amer. Statist. Assoc. (1988).
[26] Roger D Peng. 2002. Multi-dimensional point process models in R. Department of Statistics, UCLA (2002).
[27] Roger Dean Peng. 2003. Applications of multi-dimensional point process methodology to wildfire hazard assessment. Ph.D. Dissertation. UCLA.
[28] Patricia Reynaud-Bouret, Christine Tuleau-Malot, Vincent Rivoirard, and Franck Grammont. 2013. Spike trains as (in) homogeneous Poisson processes or Hawkes processes: non-parametric adaptive estimation and goodness-of-fit tests. Journal of Mathematical Neuroscience (2013).
[29] Huaxia Rui and Andrew Whinston. 2011. Designing a social-broadcasting-based business intelligence system. ACM Transactions on Management Information Systems (TMIS) 2, 4 (2011), 22.
[30] Olivier Toubia and Andrew T Stephen. 2013. Intrinsic vs. image-related utility in social media: Why do people contribute content to twitter? Marketing Science (2013).
[31] Ryen W White, Ashish Kapoor, and Susan T Dumais. 2010. Modeling Long-Term Search Engine Usage.. In UMAP. Springer, 28–39.
[32] Zhiheng Xu, Yang Zhang, Yao Wu, and Qing Yang. 2012. Modeling user posting behavior on social media. In Proceedings of SIGIR. ACM, 545–554.

How to Exploit Relationships to Improve Predictions

Jennifer Neville
Purdue University
West Lafayette
neville@purdue.edu

ABSTRACT

The popularity of social networks and social media has increased the amount of information available about users' behavior online--including current activities, and interactions with followers, friends, and family. This rich relational information can be used to improve predictions even when individual data is sparse, since the characteristics of friends are often correlated. Although this type of network data offer several opportunities to improve predictions about users, the characteristics of online social network data also present a number of challenges to accurately incorporate the network information into machine learning systems. This talk will outline some of the algorithmic and statistical challenges that arise due to partially-observed, large-scale networks, and describe methods for semi-supervised learning, latent-variable modeling, and active sampling to address the challenges.

BIOGRAPHY

Jennifer Neville is the Miller Family Chair Associate Professor of Computer Science and Statistics at Purdue University. She received her PhD from the University of Massachusetts Amherst in 2006. She is currently an elected member of the AAAI Executive Council and she was recently PC chair of the 9th ACM International Conference on Web Search and Data. In 2012, she was awarded an NSF Career Award, in 2008 she was chosen by IEEE as one of "AI's 10 to watch", and in 2007 was selected as a member of the DARPA Computer Science Study Group. Her work, which includes more than 100 peer-reviewed publications with over 5000 citations, focuses on developing data mining and machine learning techniques for complex relational and network domains, including social, information, and physical networks.

ICTIR'17, October 1-4, 2017, Amsterdam, The Netherlands
© 2017 Copyright is held by the owner/author(s).
ACM ISBN 978-1-4503-4490-6/17/10.
DOI: https://doi.org/10.1145/3121050.3121081

Towards the Next Generation of Personal Assistants: Systems that Know When You Forget

Seyed Ali Bahrainian
University of Lugano, Faculty of Informatics
Lugano, Switzerland
bahres@usi.ch

Fabio Crestani
University of Lugano, Faculty of Informatics
Lugano, Switzerland
fabio.crestani@usi.ch

ABSTRACT

Recently a new class of personal assistants that are capable of addressing users' information needs proactively is emerging.

Users' information needs may include timely notifications about a certain context such as location, social interactions with other people, weather, other events, etc. Personal assistants can assist people by recommending the right information at just the right time and help them in accomplishing tasks. Because of the ubiquitous nature of mobile personal assistants, they have a broad range of potential capabilities. One of these potential capabilities is to carry out sophisticated tasks for supporting failing memories. Such support of human memory has been thus far limited, merely to setting reminders and calendar events.

In this paper, we present our work on developing a cutting-edge personal assistant for supporting failing memories in every day social interactions. Specifically, we envision a personal assistant that can anticipate the parts of a past conversation that you are likely to forget, hence remind you about them. Our experimental results on a real-world dataset of meetings reveals evidence that developing such systems is viable and can produce promising results.

KEYWORDS

Human Memory Augmentation; Meetings; Personal Assistants

ACM Reference format:
Seyed Ali Bahrainian and Fabio Crestani. 2017. Towards the Next Generation of Personal Assistants: Systems that Know When You Forget. In *Proceedings of ThematicWorkshops'17, October 1–4, 2017, Amsterdam, The Netherlands, , 9 pages.*
DOI: https://doi.org/10.1145/3121050.3121071

1 INTRODUCTION

Human memory is a critically important cognitive ability that we constantly rely on for carrying out various tasks in our daily lives. However, sometimes, due to the volume and intensity of information that we are exposed to on a typical day, or due to our lack of adequate attention, or yet due to aging, this critical cognitive ability fails to recall important events in our past. In a workplace environment, failing to recall important work related events can result

in frustration and disappointment. Discussions may be repeated and the work cycle may be prolonged. This can result in a waste of time, energy and resources, in addition to bringing tension and misunderstandings to the work place.

Aiding human memory [15] for later recall of workplace meetings has been tackled by summarizing, indexing [13], and generating memory cues [14] of digital records of meetings. An interesting research question in this domain is whether it is possible to build a system that can foresee which parts of a conversation you are likely to forget within a fixed time interval, hence setting proactive reminders to assist you with them. Such augmentation of human memory can effectively serve as a solution in preventing failure to recall past events. In this paper we present experiments that reveal an effective solution to this question.

In recent years, the different fields of lifelogging[9] and personal assistants have emerged in parallel which, if combined, may initiate an effort to build personal assistants that can analyze more data modalities and result in much more powerful personal assistants than exist today. The advent of various wearable data capture devices (e.g. wearable video/audio recorder or biophysical sensors) has also created new opportunities to utilize the collected data for various human-aid applications including the support of failing memories. The availability of smartwatches that are increasingly embedding biometrics sensors and are synchronized with smartphones is also creating the opportunity of developing personal assistants that can carry out augmentation of human memory.

The new paradigm of personal assistants such as Google Now, Microsoft Cortana or Apple's Siri seek to build on the notion of Just In Time Information Retrieval (JITIR) by 'offering proactive experiences that aim to recommend *the right information at just the right time* and help you get things done, even before you ask' [25]. These personal assistants are increasingly being built into other platforms. As an example, Google Now is built into Google home, and Microsoft Cortana is available on Windows desktop and thus we believe that they would play a significant role in the future.

In this paper, we focus on another aspect of JITIR for personal assistance by tracking one's conversations with the purpose of predicting the parts of a conversation that one may forget. To the best of our knowledge, this is the first work that aims at augmenting human memory by predicting the parts of a conversation that one is likely to forget. We use a real-world dataset of weekly meetings of six groups of people. In this dataset, we recorded real workplace conversations of each group (where a group consisted of two individuals) over the span of an entire month. In addition to recording the audio/video of a meeting, we record biophysical sensor data such as Electro-Dermal Activity (EDA) as well as first-person-view images captured automatically by each individual's wearable camera. By analyzing the recorded data, our proposed system extracts personalized insights for each user. Having access to such insights, a potential user of our system can be helped with remembering the things one is likely to forget, increasing self-awareness, being able to plan the future better, and more.

Thus, the main contributions of this paper are:

(1) We propose the idea of augmenting human memory by predicting the segments of a conversation that one is most likely to forget.

(2) We present a model capable of carrying out prediction of parts of a conversation that a person is likely to forget or remember.

The organization of this paper is as follows: Section 2 and 3 present the background and related work. Section 4, describes the dataset that we collected for this research. Section 5 presents our research goal. In Section 6, we present a preliminary analysis of the dataset. Sections 7 and 8 describe our methodology and evaluation. Finally, Section 9 concludes this paper and gives insight into future work.

2 BACKGROUND

Psychology of human memory has comprehensively studied how human memory recalls events or forgets them. One ground breaking work in this domain was the invention of the *forgetting curve* in 1885 by Ebbinghaus. The forgetting curve (which is an exponentially decreasing curve) shows that a human forgets on average about 77% of the details of what he has learned (for the first time) after six days. This motivated our goal in augmenting human memory to assist one in recalling details of his past events that one is likely to forget. Moreover, our study is motivated by a memory augmentation tool that we have already developed and deployed in the context of a project[1] for aiding people's memories in their workplace meetings [2]. This system takes as input transcriptions of audio recordings of one's conversations and images taken automatically by one's wearable camera at fixed time intervals. Both media types are time synchronized. The tool then processes the data by extracting topics of the transcribed conversations, detecting and recognizing faces in the images, and connecting the topics with their corresponding images. We refer to a topic connected with its corresponding image as an *event snippet*. Figure 1 shows an example of an event snippet. As shown in the figure, a topic is a set of words extracted from a fixed vocabulary that together represent a high-level concept. The rationale behind using topics is that they can effectively summarize long conversations and at the same time backtrack from a topic to its sentences of origin. This gives the user the opportunity to review the exact sentences from which a topic was extracted. Through pressing a button the system will display the next or previous topic. The system can also produce PDF document outputs of a set of event snippets representing a meeting, which could be easily reviewed to recall the context of the meeting in detail. We showed the efficacy of this system in improving users recall of past social interactions through a user study in [3].

[1] http://recall-fet.eu/

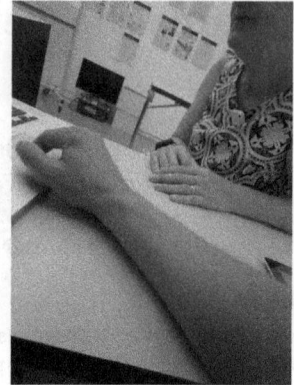

Buttons
Symbols
Readability
Understand
People
Meaning
Communicate
Difficulty
Visual
Practice

Figure 1: Sample output of our memory augmentation tool

Knowing which parts of a conversation are non-memorable /memorable can help further developing such system which can show event snippets as reminders, personalized for the memory of each user and customized for the specific parts of a conversation (i.e. content). This scenario motivates the work presented in this paper. Furthermore, the benefit of this research work is endorsed by other studies [16, 18, 24] which showed for people from different age groups (i.e. ranging from young to old) that replaying the recordings of their lives have significant effect in helping them better recall and remember past events.

3 RELATED WORK

In this section we briefly review some previous related work with a focus on three main areas as follows:

Aiding human memory: One of the first works on automatic augmentation of human memory was the Remembrance Agent [22] from MIT labs. The Remembrance Agent is a 'program which augments human memory by displaying a list of documents which might be relevant to the user's current context'. This information retrieval system ran continuously with no user intervention and acted as a human memory aid. The Forget-me-not system developed at the Rank Xerox Research Center [17] was another system that recorded where the user was, who he was with, who he phoned, and other such autobiographical information and stored and indexed them in a database for later retrieval. Rhodes et. al. [23] defined a class of software programs with the goal of JITIR. These programs were 'software agents that proactively present potentially valuable information based on a person's local context in an easily accessible yet non-intrusive manner'. One of the versions of these software agents visualized content using a wearable head-up display. Such systems could empower humans to live more independent and healthy lives by assisting them in recalling important events which could otherwise complicate their lives and cause them embarrassment and loss.

Memory augmentation in workplace meetings: Jaimes et.al. [14], proposed a video summarization tool that summaries and indexes a meeting's video recording. The system then allows users to use various types of queries and memory cues to find certain content in the meeting. Chen et.al. [6] also presents a memory augmentation tool and cites 'being reminded of information in a work situation (e.g. previous meetings with an individual' as an application of their system. A number of previous research proposed the use of summarization tools as opposed to indexing, by arguing that in many cases a user may not remember enough about a past meeting to even be able to formulate a query[2]. Thus, in such settings a summary of the meeting can reminisce the faint memories of that meeting.

Jaimes et.al. [14], ran a user study with 15 participants to research the common issues that people forget regarding a past meeting. They asked the participants using a questionnaire a week after a meeting and assessed the accuracy of answers. Their results show that on a scale, about 35% of the questions they asked about the content of a meeting were answered incorrectly. We note that these were only 35% of questions and not the actual meeting content. Motivated by the results of this work we aimed at predicting the parts of a meeting that one forgets.

Emotion, biometrics and memory: The work of [27] reveals that an emotion one experiences during an event does have an impact on recalling that memory later on. Furthermore, the level of attention during an experience is another important aspect that influences how much one can later recall that experience. To measure attention or emotional arousal researchers have used biophysical sensors such as Electro-Derlmal Activity (EDA). Braithwaite et.al. [5] states that 'the coupling between cognitive states, arousal, emotion and attention enables EDA to be used as an objective index of emotional states'. Additionally, the results of the research conducted by [29] confirm that EDA can be used as an attention index. Affective physiological signals such as EDA have been used by information retrieval researchers for understanding users' information needs as a form of implicit relevance feedback [1, 8, 19]. Moshfeghi et.al. [19] reports that affective signals were an effective complementary source of information for relevance judgment prediction across a number of search intentions. Edwards et.al. [8] also uses EDA to assess users search behaviors. In this study we use both EDA and sentiment as measures for predicting parts of a conversation that one may forget/remember.

4 RESEARCH GOAL

We hypothesize that the content of a conversation and the biophysical sensor recordings such as EDA have an impact on the degree that a person remembers each part of her conversations. If we would be able to show that there are correlations between such signals and memorability, this would mean that it would be possible to design models capable of anticipating the parts of a conversation that one is prone to forget. If so, the upshot would be an advancement in human memory health care. Therefore, by conducting a feasibility study, in this paper, we experimentally show the applicability of this new research direction. To achieve this goal in a ubiquitous setting, we only use easy-to-use wearable devices that one could practically use in every day life.

Research in the field of psychology of memory [27] shows that negative experiences are more memorable for people than positive ones. Can this finding be useful for our study? To answer this question we analyze the variations in sentiment expressed in different segments of a conversation. For processing the data, we examine

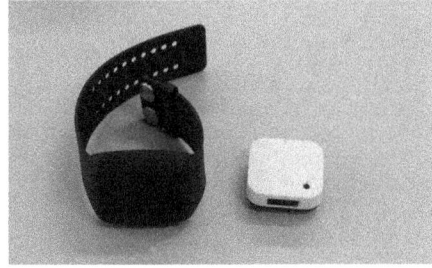

Figure 2: Empatica E4 biophysical sensor (left) and Narrative Clip Wearable Camera (right)

the effect of changes in the sentiments expressed in a recorded conversation via sentiment analysis of the transcribed conversations. Moreover, we utilize the EDA biometric signal which records the skin responses to any affective cause. We therefore test the effect of these two signals for the detection of forgettable/memorable segments of a conversation.

5 DATASET

Our dataset consists of recordings of workplace meetings of six groups of people. Each group consisted of two members. For each group, the audio of four consecutive meetings over four weeks in addition to their biophysical sensor readings were recorded. Our dataset is real-world and captured in the wild, meaning that the involved participants were asked to simply have their usual meetings with no regulations imposed from our side. The audio was recorded with an audio recorder and the biometrics were recorded using the Empatica E4 wristband sensor[2]. Figure 2 shows the Empatica E4 wristband next to a Narrative Clip wearable camera that is used to automatically capture images (e.g. the one shown in Figure 1).

Statistics of the Dataset Overall, there were 12 participants recruited for this study. For recruiting participants, we looked for groups of two people who usually had a weekly work-related meeting. No restrictions were imposed on the meetings from our side. Thus, we were able to collect a real-world dataset of workplace meetings. Due to the nature of this dataset (involving participants and being real-world) capturing it took a long time.

Converting audio to text: Subsequently, we transcribed all audio recordings of the meetings using an online transcription service[3] at a cost. The transcription error according to the service is 1%. The transcriptions of the conversations are time-stamped at fixed time intervals of one minute. Later in this section, we explain how we use the time stamps for synchronizing the transcribed text with other signals.

Basic statistics: Some important statistics of our transcribed audio recordings of meetings are reported in Figure 3. The report includes per-group statistics, such as total number of words in all four meetings, average number of words per meeting and the number of unique words in all four meetings. In general, Figure 3 shows the variability in the statistics of meetings and the behavior of the different groups.

---

[2]https://www.empatica.com/e4-wristband
[3]http://www.rev.com

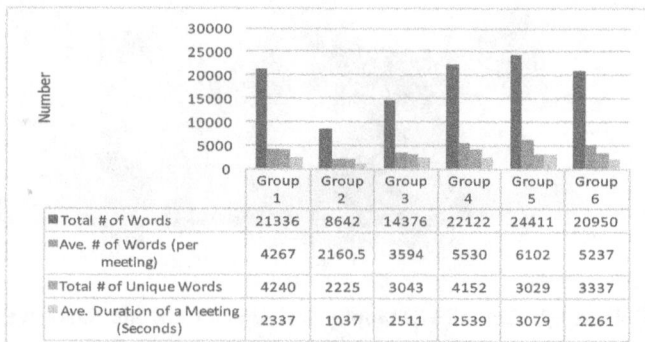

	Group 1	Group 2	Group 3	Group 4	Group 5	Group 6
Total # of Words	21336	8642	14376	22122	24411	20950
Ave. # of Words (per meeting)	4267	2160.5	3594	5530	6102	5237
Total # of Unique Words	4240	2225	3043	4152	3029	3337
Ave. Duration of a Meeting (Seconds)	2337	1037	2511	2539	3079	2261

Figure 3: Statistics of our Dataset

Overall, we recorded 917.6 minutes of audio, where the average duration of a meeting was 38.23 minutes. The average number of days in between every two consecutive meetings for all the 6 groups when rounded down to full days was 8.

Extracting Text Segments: we first extract text segments using the popular Texttiling [11] segmentation algorithm. This algorithm uses word co-occurrence patterns in sentences to detect changes in the topic of a segment.

Texttiling [11] is 'a technique for subdividing texts into multi-paragraph units that represent passages or subtopics'. It utilizes patterns of lexical co-occurrence and distribution as discourse cues for identifying major subtopic shifts. We note that the texttiling algorithm cuts segments in documents only at sentence endings. Therefore, one segment would contain one sentence at least. Our purpose behind using texttiling is to split a conversation into topically coherent segments, such that if one segment correlates with a change in biophysical responses of one of the people involved in a conversation, we would be able to infer that the topic discussed in that segment has triggered the change. This characteristic of the texttiling algorithm makes it useful for our goal.

Furthermore, in order to synchronize the biophysical sensor readings with the textual transcription of a conversation, we use the following steps:

(1) We use the per-minute time stamps of the transcribed audio and the number of words spoken within every one minute time lapse to determine the speed of the conversation.

(2) By using the ending points of each segment of the conversation (determined by the texttiling algorithm) along with the number of words within each segment, we compute a close estimation of the length of each segment in seconds.

To achieve this we locate the next per-minute time stamp directly after a segment end. Then since we know the time lapse until the per-minute time stamp, we only need to compute the time lapse until the end of the texttile segment and add it to the previously known duration of time. Additionally, we know the number of words spoken until the next per-minute time stamp and the number of words spoken until the end of the texttile segment. Therefore, we compute the duration in time for these words by:

$$DTime = \frac{\#w_{ts} \times 60}{\#w_n} \qquad (1)$$

where $DTime$ is the difference in time of the texttile segment with the next per-minute time stamp, $\#w_{ts}$ is the number of words in between the last per-minute time stamp and the next texttile segment ending, and $\#w_n$ is the number of words in between the previous per-minute time stamp and the following per-minute time stamp. The same method for synchronizing text and other signals holds if the beginning of a texttile segment is not at the start of a per-minute time stamp, but its somewhere in between.

The result of this step is multi-modal signals synchronized by time.

Labeling the Text Segments: we recorded four meetings per each group over four weeks. Immediately before the start of each meeting we held an interview with each participant, asking them to describe everything they remembered from their previous meeting. Thus one week after each meeting, we held what we call a recall session where each participant described everything one could recall while being audio recorded. Then, similarly to the meetings, the recordings of the recall sessions were transcribed.

Finally, by computing the Latent Semantic Indexing (LSI) [12] topic similarity (after preprocessing steps such as stop words removal, converting all words to lower case, etc.) on all segments of a meeting we created a topic model of that meeting. Subsequently, by querying the model with the two corresponding recall sessions, we automatically computed objective labels on how memorable each segment of a meeting was for an involved participant. This was done by comparing every segment of the meeting with the corresponding recall sessions based on the LSI topic model on the segments. Finally, the similarity between each segment and the corresponding recall sessions are computed based on cosine similarity. Therefore, by computing the semantic similarity between each segment and a segment we produce objective labels of how much a participant remembered or forgot.

Meetings differ from one another in terms of topics, depth, breadth, etc. Therefore, the range of similarity scores that are computed based on LSI differ from one meeting to another. Hence, for each meeting we normalize the scores by subtracting from the computed similarity score the average similarity score of all segments within that meeting. Finally, we determine a decision threshold for discriminating memorable from non-memorable. For this purpose, we examined the dataset of meetings to determine the decision threshold empirically. In order to determine this threshold, we manually looked into the dataset. We found out that a threshold value of 0.10 is optimal for distinguishing memorable segments from the others. The overall number of segments in our dataset is 1008, from which 616 segments are labeled as memorable and 392 labeled as forgotten. We note that the number of segments per meeting vary, because as explained earlier the segments were computed using the texttiling algorithm and each meeting may vary in the number of segments which are topically coherent.

6 PRELIMINARY ANALYSIS

In this section we present a preliminary analysis of our dataset through a case study to verify the applicability of our research goal. We will first, however, briefly describe the sentiment analysis algorithm that we implemented along with a brief explanation of EDA signals.

6.1 Sentiment Analysis Classifier

For analyzing sentiment, we implemented an unsupervised sentiment classifier similar to the one used in [4]. The reason that we used this classifier over the commonly used SentiStrength classifier [26] was that it significantly outperformed the SentiStrength classifier [26] on 3 different datasets. Therefore, by using this classifier we opted for a sentiment analyzer superior to the SentiStrength.

Here we briefly explain the sentiment classifier that we implemented. Each conversation segment is split into smaller text snippets based on the punctuation marks '.', '!' and '?'. We therefore define a text snippet as a number of words that occur in between two punctuation marks.

The algorithm first replaces slangs with their equivalences using a slang dictionary. To build this slang dictionary, we manually collected slang phrases to include in the dictionary by using as many online resources that we could find, and furthermore adding the slang dictionary of SentiStrength [26] to our collected dictionary.

Then in a second step, we used a modified sentiment lexicon to tag all sentiment-bearing words in each conversation with their corresponding sentiment scores. We further tagged all intensifier words (e.g. absolutely) and diminishers (e.g. might) with their corresponding scores. Additionally, we tagged negation words. Finally, if a word did not belong to any of the mentioned categories, it was tagged with the score '0'.

After having all the words in a document tagged either by their score or type, now we should handle occurrence of intensifiers, diminishers, and negations. First, the algorithm intensifies the strength of a sentiment-bearing word that appears after an intensifier word, by the score of that intensifier word. Analogously, in the case of diminishers, we weaken the strength of a sentiment-bearing word that appears after a diminisher word by the strength of that diminisher. Finally, for handling negations, we flip the polarity of the score of a sentiment-bearing word that appears after a negation. Furthermore, we weaken the flipped sentiment score by 1. That is, if the flipped score is positive, we subtract 1 from it and if it's negative we add 1 to it. Note that, while performing the above mentioned computations, in all cases we ignore the '0' tagged words that appear in between one of the above mentioned valence shifters and a sentiment-bearing words in a single text snippet.

In order to compute a sentiment score for a text snippet, we aggregate the words' scores. We define the decision threshold for classifying text snippets as '0'. That is, if the overall sentiment score of a document is less than or equal to '0' it is classified as negative, otherwise it is classified as positive.

As mentioned earlier, this classifier outperformed SentiStrength in terms of classification accuracy and F_1 measure and area under the curve of a receiver operating characteristic curve on three different datasets[4]. However, given the space limitations we will not present the details of the results of that experiment here.

Finally, for computing the overall sentiment score of each segment, we average the sentiment score of all text snippets present in that segment.

6.2 EDA Signal

EDA sensor reading is a measure of electrical skin response excreted by the eccrine glands, which is connected to the sympathetic nervous system [7]. It is most commonly associated with changes in sympathetic arousal. Anger, happiness, interest, excitement as well as disgust can all cause changes in EDA. It is important to note that EDA is not correlated with valence, so both positive and negative affect can alter sympathetic arousal [7]. Thus, changes in EDA are most commonly associated with changes in sympathetic arousal. However, factors that cause increased sweat production, such as humidity, room temperature, and physical exertion, can also cause increased EDA amplitude. However, in the case of our meetings dataset, since the participants stay in the same room throughout a meeting, such effects are controlled.

In the case of our meetings dataset, each meeting involving two persons who are both engaged in the conversation, it is reasonable to believe that most alteration in the EDA signal is caused by the content of the meeting. If there would have been more than two people in a meeting, there would have been the possibility that a person would have been left out of the conversation or would have not followed the conversation, hence our assumption in that case would not have been realistic. An EDA biophysical recording will contain an individual's response to the content of a meeting and the behavior of the other individual involved in the meeting.

6.3 Case Study

Now that we explained our sentiment analyzer and the basics of EDA, we can proceed with analyzing the data. We first start our analysis with a case study on the dataset. The goal of this case study is to examine whether there is any correlation between the sentiment expressed in the transcribed conversation and memorability, between EDA signal and memorability or even between EDA and the sentiment expressed in the text. The result of this analysis not only can help us in designing a model for predicting the memorable/ non-memorable moments of a conversation, but also can be used as a helpful finding for other researchers in the field.

Since we are dealing with time series data (a sequence of topically coherent segments extracted from a meeting along with their corresponding time-synchronized EDA signal) we use the Cross Correlation Function (CCF) which in essence is the convolution between two signals. The reason behind using CCF is that it analyzes the correlation between two signals at different lags (i.e. displacements of the signals). In our case each lag is a segment of a conversation. Such correlation analysis, for example, can reveal not only a possible correlation between sentiment of a segment and its corresponding memorability score, but also can show if there is a correlation between the sentiment of the previous or next segments and the memorability of the current segment. Thus, since CCF is a useful method for assessing the effects of different parts of two signals on one another we utilize it in this experiment.

The results of our case study on randomly selected participants and meetings are presented in Figures 4, 5, and 6. We randomly selected five participants from five different meetings of our dataset for this case study. Figure 4 shows that the there is a strong correlation between memorability and negative sentiment. Also, it shows that the segments that are preceded by segments with negative sentiment are more memorable. A segment of a meeting expressing negative sentiment, for example, could be regarding difficulties

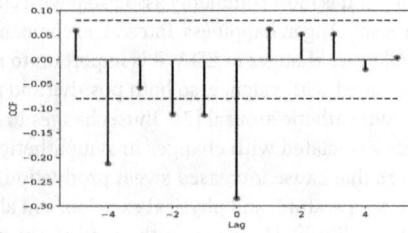

Figure 4: Cross Correlation between Sentiment and Memorability at different lags (each lag is a segment of a meeting)

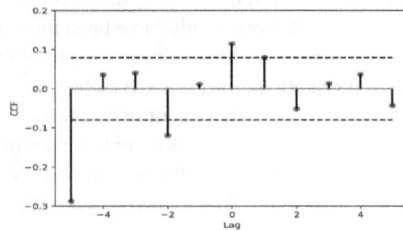

Figure 5: Cross Correlation between EDA and Memorability at different lags (each lag is a segment of a meeting)

and problems in a project, or in extreme cases arguing and strong disagreements between the involved participants. This finding also mirrors the results of psychology research such as [27] which show that negative experiences are more memorable for people than positive ones. The fact that we could support the findings of a psychology lab study with our study on a in-the-wild dataset using information retrieval techniques is an interesting finding.

We note that in Figures 4, 5, and 6 the height of the dashed lines (in both positive and negative directions) indicate the significance threshold and all bars that cross these lines being statistically significant.

Figure 5 reveals that memorability correlates with a rising EDA signal. However, we also observe that a memorable segment is preceded by a falling EDA signal. Thus, we conclude that shortly after a local minimum of an EDA signal we can find a significant reduction in forgetting, and thus an increase in memorability.

Furthermore, Figure 6 shows that an increase in sentiment intensity, regardless of the polarity, triggers the rise of the EDA signal. We note that since EDA is sensitive to both positive and negative emotions, we only computed the absolute sentiment score in Figure 6 and did not take into account the positiveness or negativeness of the sentiment scores. Hence, we can conclude that sentiment intensity correlates with an increase in the EDA signal.

7 METHODOLOGY FOR PREDICTING NON-MEMORABLE SEGMENTS

Now that we have a basic understanding of the problem of predicting non-mameorable/ memorable moments in a conversation, we strive for designing a model that can accurately foresee parts of a conversation that a person is likely to remember or forget.

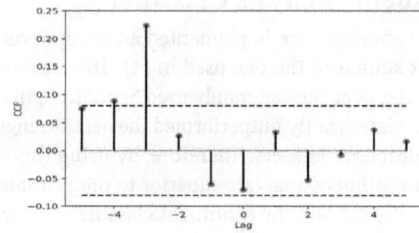

Figure 6: Cross correlation between sentiment and EDA at different lags (each lag is a segment of a meeting)

One of the best methods when dealing with time series data is Hidden Markov Models (HMM). In [20] we can find a number of time-series prediction tasks where HMMs hold the state-of-the-art performance, motivating our use of HMM for this task. We use an HMM in an unsupervised setting.

HMM is a generative probabilistic model in which a sequence of observable outputs is generated by a sequence of hidden states. In our work, we use HMM in a specific way to unpack the latent hidden structure in the meetings to predict the segments of a conversation that one forgets versus the ones that one remembers. In the following we explain the HMM architecture that we adopted based on the notation of (Rabiner, 1990) [21].

Among the various problems that HMM can solve, we aim at: *given the observation sequence of $O = O_1, O_2, \ldots O_T$, and a model $\lambda = (A, B, \Pi)$, how to select a corresponding state sequence $Q = q_1, q_2, \ldots q_T$ which is optimal in the sense that it best explains the observations*, where A is the state transition probability distribution, B is the observation symbol probability distribution and Π is the initial state distribution. To solve this problem the model λ is trained using the Baum-Welch algorithm given the input data. This algorithm implements an Expectation-Maximization algorithm to find the maximum likelihood estimate of the parameters of an HMM, given a set of observed feature vectors.

In the case of the problem we are addressing in this paper, our model architecture has seven states shown in Figure 7. We explain the observable outputs and the architecture in the next few paragraphs. Training the model starts by choosing an initial state q_1 according to the state distribution Π which assigns equal probability to all states. Furthermore, based on the state transition probability, the model moves to the next state and a new observation will be selected till all T observations in the sequence are generated. Given the observation sequence, the same explained process can be repeated to model an HMM. Subsequently, the Viterbi algorithm is used for decoding the most likely sequence of the transition states, hence predicting the forget/remember segments.

The architecture of the HMM that we deploy has seven states, and two output emission outputs. One of the two output emissions represents memorable segments while the other represents the forgotten segments. We use the Baum-Welch algorithm with 20 training cycles for learning the backward and forward probabilities. Additionally, the propagation of probability scores follows a Gaussian function. After the model is trained, we use the Viterbi algorithm to decode the best solution in the HMM network and

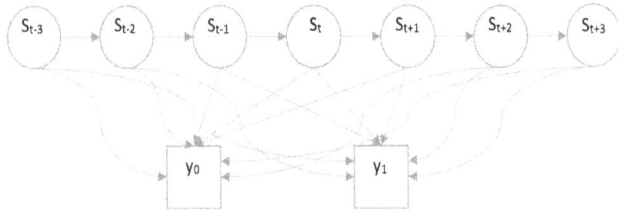

Figure 7: The architecture of the HMM proposed for memorability prediction. S stands for an HMM state.

Table 1: A comparison between our memorability prediction model against a random baseline

	F1 (%)	Prec. (%)	Recall (%)
Our Model	68.53	55.66	86.45
EDA Mean Slope (baseline)	59.81	50.45	73.43
Random (baseline)	55.08	59.97	50.97

find the best path. Viterbi is a back-tracking algorithm based on dynamic programming which defines $\delta_j(t)$, i.e. the single best path of length t which accounts for the observations and ends in state S_j, such that $\delta_j(t) = \max_{q_1 q_2 \ldots q_{t-1}} P(q_1 q_2 \ldots q_t = j, O_1 O_2 \ldots O_t | \lambda)$.

Figure 7 presents the architecture of our model. For determining the non-memorability/memorability of segment S_t, the model considers the features present in the sliding window of the three segments before it, the segment itself and the three segments after it. Each transition between states depicted in the figure, bears a probability score designating the strength of the transition. Furthermore, each of the states are connected to two output emission nodes, where one represents a non-memorable segment and the other represents a memorable segment. The result is an output prediction label for memorability of the segment S_t.

The features that we extract from the meeting contents and the corresponding biophysical signals are the moving average of the EDA signal per each meeting and participant as well as the corresponding sentiment signal expressed in the conversation. Furthermore, we compute the Canonical Correlation Analysis (CCA) of both signals. The use of CCA is motivated by the existing correlation between sentiment and EDA shown in a case study in Figure 5 as well as the correlation between each of these signals with memorability. CCA captures the co-variance between two signals and hence a suitable representation of the physical response of each participant in relation to an expressed sentiment within the conversation and vice versa.

Subsequently, for every segment of a conversation we keep a window of the CCA values corresponding to three segments before and after the target segment, and the CCA value corresponding to the target segment itself. For segments, such as the first segment of a meeting, that there is no CCA values for its previous segments, we use padding with identical values to the closest neighbor where such computation is viable. Therefore, for each segment of a conversation we feed the HMM a feature vector of length seven consisting of the described CCA values.

Finally, we compare the output of the HMM against the ground truth and evaluate the model.

The advantages of our approach are: first, it is unsupervised and there is no need for huge datasets to train it. Second, the use of CCA features, which capture co-variance between two signals is very critical to our approach due to the fact that CCA converts the data into a single signal which is normalized across different participants and meetings. This approach, generalizes our model to different participants and meetings.

8 EVALUATION

For evaluating our proposed model, we compute its precision, recall and F_1 measure by using our dataset. We compare the performance of our model against two baselines:

Random baseline: the random baseline is a model which predicts the labels of each conversation segment by assigning it a randomly generated label. For computing the random baseline, we find the average performance of 5 runs of a random predictor. Then we compare the results against the performance of our proposed prediction model. By including the random baseline in our experiments, we can show that the prediction of non-memorable segments of a conversation using our model is possible and the improvement over the random baseline is statistically significant.

Mean slope of EDA signal: as explained in Subsections 6.2 and 6.3, a rise in the EDA signal correlates with sympathetic arousal caused by an emotion such as anger, happiness, excitement, stress, interest, disgust, etc [10]. Thus, capturing rises and falls of an EDA signal can be a beneficial representative of the signal. In order to use an EDA signal we time-synchronize it with the corresponding transcription of a corresponding conversation, following the same procedure described in Section 5, and divide it in segments. Each segment of the EDA signal corresponds with its respective transcription segment. Then we compute the first derivative of each EDA segment between every two consecutive points in the signal (i.e. with a sampling rate of 5 seconds) and subsequently computing the average of all derivatives. This method was used in [10] to process an EDA signal for detecting emotions. For every two consecutive points in the EDA signal if the first point is less than the next point, the signal has a rising trend and the first derivative is positive. Thus, we consider a positive mean slope as a positive class and thus memorable. On the contrary, if the average slope would be negative or zero the segment is considered non-memorable.

Table 1 presents the results of performance comparison of our model against the two baselines. We observe that the performance of our model is significantly higher than both the Derivative of EDA and the random baseline. In order to confirm the statistical significance we used the two tailed paired t-test with the p-value of less than 0.05.

Thus, we experimentally demonstrated that this novel direction of research has the potential of turning into an important area of research that could truly help people throughout their everyday lives. People with good memories, or even people with mild memory deficiencies can benefit from such technology and live healthier lives with respect to their memory. Companies could use such technologies to improve the performance of their employees hence decreasing the work cycle. Such technology could be also used in the smart room scenario [28] to set personalized reminders for people to remind them about previous meetings.

Table 2: A detailed comparison between different features to train the HMM presented in Figure 7

	F_1 measure (%)
HMM + CCA	68.53
HMM + EDA	62.77
HMM + Sentiment	65.24

In a second experiment, we strive for testing the effect of sentiment and EDA signals independently in order to measure the contribution of each of these signals to the non-memorable/memorable segments prediction problem. To achieve this, we compare the performance of our HMM model trained with CCA features, against the same HMM once trained only with sentiment features and another time only with EDA features. We follow the same strategy of feeding the model with features of three segments before and after a target segment and the target segment itself. We compare the three models trained with three different features to examine the effectiveness of each signal. Table 2, presents the results of this experiment. The model trained using the CCA features outperforms both other models. Moreover, the sentiment features outperform the EDA features. This indicates that sentiment is a very strong feature in representing the content of a conversation. However, we observe that the EDA affective signal is still an important feature in combination with sentiment.

9   CONCLUSIONS

With the rapid proliferation of smartphones and wearable devices with powerful hardware, the possibility of developing various human aid applications that run on these devices is more than ever. One of the most important directions for human aid is assisting human memory by reminding one about the parts of a conversation that one is likely to forget. In this paper, we first presented a case study which revealed what are the significant patterns for detection of non-memorability/ memorability of conversations, in terms of sentiment and EDA signals. These new findings, can open a path to powerful memory augmentation and personal assistance tools of the future which may significantly improve the lives of many people by helping them reminisce their memories. Furthermore, based on our findings we introduced a novel method customized for each person for predicting the segments of a conversation that is likely to be forgotten. This could be helpful to focus the user's attention on those segments by showing her reminders. Our experimental results showed the efficacy of our proposed model.

This novel study can serve as a foundation for future work in the domain of memory augmentation. There are a number of directions for future work. Other signals such as heart rate or blood volume pressure can be investigated. Furthermore, an exploratory study of our dataset such as the effect of one attendee forgetting/ remembering a segment of meeting on the other attendee is another direction for future work.

REFERENCES

[1] Ioannis Arapakis, Joemon M. Jose, and Philip D. Gray. Affective Feedback: An Investigation into the Role of Emotions in the Information Seeking Process. In *Proceedings of the 31st Annual International ACM SIGIR Conference (SIGIR '08)*. 395–402.

[2] Seyed Ali Bahrainian and Fabio Crestani. 2016. Cued Retrieval of Personal Memories of Social Interactions. In *Proceedings of the First Workshop on Lifelogging Tools and Applications (LTA '16)*. 3–12.

[3] Seyed Ali Bahrainian and Fabio Crestani. 2017. Are conversation logs useful sources for generating memory cues for recalling past memories?. In *Proceedings of the Second Workshop on Lifelogging Tools and Applications (LTA '17)*.

[4] Seyed Ali Bahrainian and Andreas Dengel. 2015. Sentiment analysis of texts by capturing underlying sentiment patterns. In *Web Intelligence*, Vol. 13. 53–68.

[5] Jason J Braithwaite, Derrick G Watson, Robert Jones, and Mickey Rowe. A guide for analysing electrodermal activity (EDA) & skin conductance responses (SCRs) for psychological experiments. *Handbook of Psychophysiology* (????), 1017–1034.

[6] Yi Chen and Gareth JF Jones. 2010. Augmenting human memory using personal lifelogs. In *Proceedings of the 1st augmented human international conference*.

[7] Anne M.; Filion Diane L. Cacioppo John T. (Ed); Tassinary Louis G. (Ed); Berntson Gary G. Dawson, Michael E.; Schell. 2000. Sentiment in Short Strength Detection Informal Text. *Handbook of psychophysiology, 2nd ed.* (2000), 200–223.

[8] Ashlee Edwards, Diane Kelly, and Leif Azzopardi. The Impact of Query Interface Design on Stress, Workload and Performance. 691–702.

[9] Cathal Gurrin, Alan F. Smeaton, and Aiden R. Doherty. 2014. LifeLogging: Personal Big Data. *Foundations and Trends in Information Retrieval* (2014).

[10] Jennifer Healey and Rosalind Picard. 1998. Digital processing of affective signals. In *Proceedings of the IEEE International Conference on Acoustics, Speech and Signal Processing*, Vol. 6. 3749–3752.

[11] Marti A. Hearst. 1997. TextTiling: Segmenting Text into Multi-paragraph Subtopic Passages. *Comput. Linguist.* 23, 1 (1997), 33–64.

[12] Thomas Hofmann. 1999. Probabilistic Latent Semantic Indexing. In *Proc. of International ACM SIGIR Conference (SIGIR '99)*. 50–57.

[13] A. Jaimes, H. Bourlard, S. Renals, and J. Carletta. 2007. Recording, Indexing, Summarizing, and Accessing Meeting Videos: An Overview of the AMI Project. In *14th International Conference of Image Analysis and Processing - Workshops (ICIAPW 2007)*. 59–64.

[14] Ro Jaimes, Kengo Omura, Takeshi Nagamine, and Kazutaka Hirata. 2004. Memory cues for meeting video retrieval. In *In Proceedings CARPE 04*. 74–85.

[15] Vaiva Kalnikaité and Steve Whittaker. Software or Wetware?: Discovering when and Why People Use Digital Prosthetic Memory. In *Proceedings of the SIGCHI Conference on Human Factors in Computing Systems (CHI '07)*. 71–80.

[16] Basel Kikhia, Josef Hallberg, Kåre Synnes, and Zaheer Ul Hussain Sani. 2009. Context-aware life-logging for persons with mild dementia. In *Engineering in Medicine and Biology Society, 2009*.

[17] Mik Lamming and Mike Flynn. 1994. Forget-me-not: Intimate computing in support of human memory. 125–128.

[18] Matthew L. Lee and Anind K. Dey. 2008. Wearable experience capture for episodic memory support. In *12th IEEE International Symposium on Wearable Computers (ISWC 2008)*. Seoul, Korea, 107–108.

[19] Yashar Moshfeghi and Joemon M. Jose. 2013. An Effective Implicit Relevance Feedback Technique Using Affective, Physiological and Behavioural Features. In *Proceedings of the 36th International ACM SIGIR Conference (SIGIR '13)*. 133–142.

[20] Marcin Pietrzykowskiand and Wojciech Salabun. 2014. Applications of Hidden Markov Model: state-of-the-art. In *International Journal of Computer Technology and Applications*.

[21] Lawrence R. Rabiner. 1990. A Tutorial on Hidden Markov Models and Selected Applications in Speech Recognition. In *Readings in Speech Recognition*.

[22] Bradley Rhodes and Thad Starner. Remembrance Agent: A continuously running automated information retrieval system.

[23] B. J. Rhodes and P. Maes. 2000. Just-in-time Information Retrieval Agents. *IBM Syst. J.* 39 (2000), 685–704.

[24] Abigail Sellen, Andrew Fogg, Mike Aitken, Steve Hodges, Carsten Rother, and Kenneth R. Wood. 2007. Do life-logging technologies support memory for the past?: an experimental study using sensecam. In *In Proc. of the Conference on Human Factors in Computing Systems*. 81–90.

[25] Yu Sun, Nicholas Jing Yuan, Yingzi Wang, Xing Xie, Kieran McDonald, and Rui Zhang. 2016. Contextual Intent Tracking for Personal Assistants. In *Proceedings of the 22Nd ACM SIGKDD International Conference on Knowledge Discovery and Data Mining (KDD '16)*. 273–282.

[26] Mike Thelwall, Kevan Buckley, Georgios Paltoglou, Di Cai, and Arvid Kappas. 2010. Sentiment in Short Strength Detection Informal Text. *J. Am. Soc. Inf. Sci. Technol.* 61, 12 (Dec. 2010), 2544–2558.

[27] Tobias Grossmann Vaish, Amrisha and Amanda Woodward. 2008. Not All Emotions Are Created Equal: The Negativity Bias in Social-Emotional Development. *Psychological bulletin* 134.3 (2008), 383–403.

[28] A. Waibel, T. Schultz, M. Bett, M. Denecke, R. Malkin, I. Rogina, R. Stiefelhagen, and Jie Yang. 2003. SMaRT: the Smart Meeting Room Task at ISL. In *Acoustics, Speech, and Signal Processing, 2003. Proceedings. (ICASSP '03). 2003 IEEE International Conference on*, Vol. 4. IV-752–5 vol.4.

[29] Ryuichi et. al. Yoshida. Feasibility study on estimating visual attention using electrodermal activity. In *8th International Conference on Sensing Technology. 2014*.

On Effective Dynamic Search in Specialized Domains

Felipe Moraes
CS Dept, UFMG
Belo Horizonte, MG, Brazil
felipemoraes@dcc.ufmg.br

Rodrygo L. T. Santos
CS Dept, UFMG
Belo Horizonte, MG, Brazil
rodrygo@dcc.ufmg.br

Nivio Ziviani
CS Dept, UFMG & Kunumi
Belo Horizonte, MG, Brazil
nivio@dcc.ufmg.br

ABSTRACT

Dynamic search in specialized domains is a challenging task, in which systems must learn about the user's need from his or her interactive exploration. Despite recent initiatives to advance the state-of-the-art for this task, limited progress has been achieved, with the best performing dynamic search systems only marginally improving upon vanilla ad-hoc search systems. In this paper, we perform a comprehensive analysis of the impact of several components of a prototypical dynamic search system on the effectiveness of the entire system. Through a series of simulations, we discuss the impact of: producing an initial ranking of candidate documents, modeling the possible aspects underlying the user's query given his or her feedback, leveraging the modeled aspects to improve the initial ranking, and deciding when to stop the interactive process. Our results using data from the TREC 2015-2016 Dynamic Domain track shed light on these components and provide directions for the design of effective dynamic search systems for specialized domains.

CCS CONCEPTS

•Information systems →Retrieval effectiveness; *Users and interactive retrieval;*

KEYWORDS

Dynamic Search; Interactive Search; Search Effectiveness

1 INTRODUCTION

The need for exploration commonly arises in professional search settings such as in medical, legal, patent, military intelligence, and academic search, but also in personal searches such as in travel planning or personal health research [18, 29]. Exploratory searches often involve complex sessions, demanding multiple interactions between the user and a search system. Along the interactive process, the system must dynamically adapt to each feedback provided by the user in order to improve the understanding of the user's need and the usefulness of the subsequently retrieved documents [28].

Research on exploratory search has been supported by several initiatives. The Text REtrieval Conference (TREC) have hosted related research tracks on interactive search [1], search within sessions [6], search for task completion [31] and, more recently, dynamic search in specialized domains [9, 10]. The latter problem,

embodied by the TREC Dynamic Domain track,[1] is the focus of this paper.[2] Given an initial query, a dynamic search system must improve its understanding of the user's information need through a series of interactions. In each interaction, the user may provide the system with feedback on the relevance of specific passages of the retrieved documents with respect to one or more aspects underlying his or her information need. The system must then choose to either provide the user with further documents or end the interactive process. An effective system should be able to satisfy as many query aspects as possible (to maximize user satisfaction) with as few interactions as possible (to minimize user effort).

A dynamic search system must cope with four key problems: (i) produce an initial sample of candidate documents given the user's query and the domain of interest; (ii) decide whether the user's information need has been satisfied and eventually stop the interactive process; (iii) leverage the user's feedback to learn an improved aspect model; (iv) produce an enhanced ranking given the learned aspect model. As we will discuss in Section 2, several attempts have been made to produce dynamic search systems that could effectively tackle these problems. Nevertheless, as shown in Figures 1a-b for the two domains considered in the TREC 2016 Dynamic Domain track,[3] even the reportedly most effective system in each domain shows only marginal improvements compared to vanilla ad-hoc search baselines, which leverage no user feedback.

In this paper, we aim to better understand the challenges involved in building effective dynamic search systems. To this end, we isolate each of the aforementioned problems as a separate component of a dynamic search system. Through controlled simulations, we assess how the effectiveness of each component impacts the effectiveness of the whole system. In particular, we show that high-precision document samples are beneficial at early interactions, whereas high-recall samples help towards later interactions. Moreover, mishandled user feedback leads to inaccurate aspect models, which hinder the system effectiveness. Likewise, inaccurately estimating the coverage of the modeled aspects leads to poor reranking, which also hinders effectiveness. Lastly, despite the inherent trade-off, we show that stopping late typically incurs more effort than gain. To our knowledge, this is the first systematic attempt to shed light on the effectiveness of dynamic search in specialized domains.

2 RELATED WORK

In this section, we describe relevant related work on exploratory search in general and on dynamic search in particular.

ICTIR'17, October 1–4, 2017, Amsterdam, The Netherlands.
© 2017 ACM. 978-1-4503-4490-6/17/10...$15.00
DOI: http://dx.doi.org/10.1145/3121050.3121065

[1]http://trec-dd.org/

[2]A further related task on Dynamic Search for Complex Tasks has recently been proposed at CLEF: https://ekanou.github.io/dynamicsearch/

[3]Each plot shows average cube test (ACT) figures—the primary evaluation metric of the TREC 2016 Dynamic Domain track—along the interactive process. TREC 2015 results follow similar trends and are omitted for brevity.

(a) Ebola 2016

(b) Polar

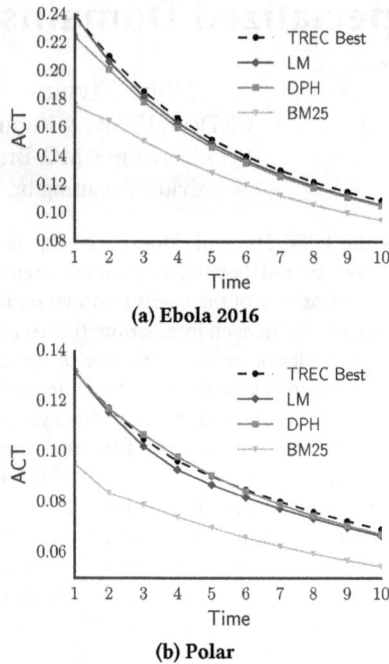

Figure 1: Per-domain ACT of the best dynamic search systems at the TREC 2016 Dynamic Domain track against ad-hoc search baselines (LM, DPH, and BM25). The best TREC systems were chosen as the most stable across iterations.

2.1 Exploratory Search

Several information retrieval researchers have investigated what makes a search process exploratory in nature [3, 18, 29]. For instance, Marchionini et al. [18] categorized information seeking tasks as lookup (or known-item) search tasks and exploratory search tasks, with the latter being further decomposed into learning and investigation tasks. Another example is the user study conducted by Wildemuth et al. [29], which provided an ample characterization of search tasks. Later, Athukorala et al. [3] described distinctive behaviors of search users during an exploratory search with respect to query length, scroll depth, and task completion time.

Many studies in exploratory search focused on developing user interfaces to support complex information needs [8, 22]. For instance, Ruotsalo et al. [22] proposed an interactive user interface that enhances a user's capacity to explore the results through a visualization of the possible aspects underlying his or her information need. Recently, Krishnamurthy et al. [12] presented an exploratory search system for domain discovery and used the TREC 2015 Dynamic Domain track data to perform user studies. While most research on exploratory search has focused on the user's perspective of the task, here we focus on the effectiveness of exploratory search from a system's perspective. In particular, we address a specific exploratory search task, namely, dynamic search.

2.2 Dynamic Search

Dynamic search is an exploratory search task [30]. Previous research in this area have focused on approaches for session search or multi-page search through reinforcement learning [11, 14, 15, 17,

26]. Sloan et al. [26] proposed a theoretical framework for multi-page dynamic search that learns the best policy based on implicit user feedback, such as clicks. Similarly, Luo et al. [14, 15, 17] proposed several approaches to leverage users' implicit feedback in the form of clicks and query reformulations within a session. These include reinforcement learning approaches such as Markov decision processes, direct policy learning, and dual-agent learning.

In contrast to the aforementioned approaches, we tackle dynamic search to aid user exploration in specialized domains, typically resulting from a focused crawl of the Web. In this setting, users provide explicit feedback on the relevance of each retrieved document with respect to multiple aspects underlying their information need. As part of the evaluation campaigns of the TREC 2015-2016 Dynamic Domain tracks [9, 10], several dynamic search approaches have been proposed that attempt to leverage such a structured feedback. In common, these approaches deploy a multi-step framework for dynamic search, as illustrated in Figure 2.

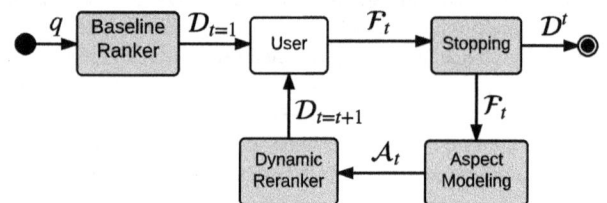

Figure 2: Flow diagram of a typical dynamic search system.

Given the user's query q, at the first step, a *baseline ranker* produces a sample of candidate documents $\mathcal{R}$. Standard ad-hoc retrieval models have been used for this step, including vector space, best matching, and language models [4]. At each time t, the user is presented with a batch of documents $\mathcal{D}_t$ selected from the list $\mathcal{R}$ of candidates and provides a set of feedback $\mathcal{F}_t$. In the second step, a *stopping* mechanism must choose to either continue the interactive process or to end the search session immediately. Stopping heuristics have been proposed that take into account the amount of irrelevant documents observed continuously or cumulatively up to the point of decision [19]. In the third step, the user feedback $\mathcal{F}_t$ on passages extracted from the presented ranking is used to update the system's knowledge about the multiple aspects $\mathcal{A}_t$ underlying his or her information need. Attempted solutions for *aspect modeling* include bag-of-passages modeling [20], clustering [13], and query expansion [21]. Lastly, in the fourth step, the updated aspect model $\mathcal{A}_t$ is used by a *dynamic reranker* to produce an improved result set $\mathcal{D}_{t+1}$, which is again presented to the user for feedback. Effective solutions here include mixture models [32], relevance feedback models [21], and result diversification models [25].

Table 1 organizes the official submissions to the TREC 2015-2016 Dynamic Domain tracks within the general framework described in Figure 2. As discussed in Section 1, not even the best among these approaches was able to consistently improve upon the baseline ranker component alone, which deploys feedback-ignorant ad-hoc search models. The primary goal of this paper is to investigate why this is the case. In the next section, we describe the experimental setup that supports our investigations in Section 4.

Table 1: Overview of dynamic search systems submitted to the TREC 2015-2016 Dynamic Domain tracks.

Group	Year	Baseline Ranker	Stopping	Aspect Modeling	Dynamic Reranker
georgetown_ir	2015	LM	none; cumul.	Passage Relevance	Mixture Models
LavalIVA	2015	Solr def.	none; cont.	Topic Modeling; K-means	Relevance Feedback
uogTr	2015	TF-IDF	none; cumul.	Topic Modeling	Explicit Diversification; Resource Allocation
georgetown	2016	LM; LM+Topic Modeling	none	Query Expansion	Relevance Model
IAPLab	2016	Indri def.+Topic Modeling	none		Markov Decision Processes
LavalLakehead	2016	TFIDF;BM25	none	Topic Modeling; K-Means; Entities	
RMIT	2016	LM	none		Relevance Feedback; Passage Retrieval
ufmg	2016	LM	cumul.; cont.	Passage Relevance	Explicit Diversification
UPD_IA	2016	BM25	none		Quantum Models

3 EXPERIMENTAL SETUP

In this section, we describe the setup that enables our controlled assessment of the effectiveness of dynamic search systems in Section 4. In particular, we detail the test collections and evaluation metrics used in our experiments. Additionally, we describe the reference models used to instantiate the baseline ranker, aspect modeling, and dynamic reranker components in Figure 2.

3.1 Test Collections

Our analysis follows the experimentation paradigm provided by the TREC 2015-2016 Dynamic Domain tracks [9, 10]. The TREC 2015-2016 Dynamic Domain tracks provide test collections targeting the following domains: (i) Ebola, related to the Ebola outbreak in Africa in 2014-2015; (ii) Illicit Goods, related to how illicit and counterfeit goods such as fake Viagra are made, advertised, and sold on the Internet; (iii) Local Politics, related to regional politics, the small-town politicians and personalities in the Pacific Northwest; (iv) Polar, related to the polar sciences. Each domain is indexed separately. In particular, we use Apache Lucene[4] for both indexing and retrieval, with Porter stemmer and standard stopwords removal. For parsing heterogeneous document formats (HTML, XML, RSS, etc.), we use the *AutoDetectParser* of Apache Tika.[5] Moreover, we remove duplicate documents based on their MD5 signature. Salient statistics of all domains are presented in Table 2.

Table 2: TREC 2015-2016 Dynamic Domain track collections. Q is the number of queries. A is the average number of aspects per query. RQ and RA are the average number of relevant documents per query and per aspect. D and U are the number of documents before and after duplicate removal.

Domain	TREC	Q	A	RQ	RA	D	U
Ebola	2015	40	5.7	603	136	6,831,397	5,409,275
Local Politics	2015	48	5.5	141	42	526,717	526,357
Illicit Goods	2015	30	5.3	39	9	497,362	319,538
Ebola	2016	27	4.4	414	121	194,481	193,310
Polar	2016	26	4.7	163	36	244,536	223,141

3.2 Evaluation Metrics

Given the interactive nature of the dynamic search task, we assess the effectiveness of a dynamic search system at different points in time, based upon the batch of documents $\mathcal{D}_t$ presented to the user at each time t. Following standard practice at the TREC 2015-2016 Dynamic Domain tracks [9, 10], we report the average cube test [16][6] at time t (ACT@t). ACT quantifies the ability of a system to fill an "information cube" representing the multiple aspects associated with the user's need. Accordingly, ACT measures the trade-off between the gain attained by satisfying different aspects and the effort incurred in doing so as time goes by. It is defined as:

$$ACT(q, \mathcal{D}) = \frac{1}{|\mathcal{D}|} \sum_t \frac{Gain(q, \mathcal{D}^t)}{Time(\mathcal{D}^t)}, \quad (1)$$

where $Time(\mathcal{D}^t)$ is the amount of time spent examining all documents $\mathcal{D}^t$ presented to the user from the beginning of the interactive process up to time t, and $Gain(q, \mathcal{D}^t)$ is defined as:

$$Gain(q, \mathcal{D}^t) = \sum_{j=1}^{|\mathcal{D}^t|} \sum_{i=1}^{|\mathcal{A}|} \Gamma_{ij}\, \theta_i\, \tilde{g}(a_i, d_j) \mathbb{1}\left(\sum_{k=1}^{j-1} \tilde{g}(a_i, d_k) < M \right), \quad (2)$$

where $\Gamma_{ij} = \gamma^{nrels(a_i, j-1)}$ is a discount factor for novelty, where $nrels(a_i, j-1)$ is the number of relevant documents for aspect a_i among the previously examined documents and $\gamma = 0.5$; θ_i is the a priori importance of aspect a_i, assumed uniformly distributed; $\tilde{g}(a, d)$ is the relevance grade assigned to document d with respect to aspect a, further normalized to lie in the range $[0, 1]$; $M = 1$ is a constant representing the maximum "height" to which the cube for any aspect can be filled; and $\mathbb{1}()$ is the indicator function.

3.3 Reference Components

The baseline ranker component in Figure 2 is responsible for returning a sample of candidate documents $\mathcal{R}$ for a query q. At time $t = 1$, the user is presented with a batch of documents $\mathcal{D}_1$, comprising the five highest scored documents in $\mathcal{R}$. At all other times $t > 1$, $\mathcal{D}_t$ is chosen by the dynamic reranker component from $\mathcal{R} \setminus \mathcal{D}^{t-1}$, where $\mathcal{D}^{t-1}$ denotes all documents returned before time t.

To study the impact of the baseline ranker component, we generate a variety of candidate samples $\mathcal{R}$ by perturbing a reference ranking produced by a field-based weighting model. In particular, we use a field-based extension of DPH [2] (henceforth "DPHF"), a hypergeometric model from the divergence from randomness framework, with field weights set to 0.15 and 0.85 for title and content. Besides being parameter-free, DPHF outperformed similar field-based extensions of best-matching and language models in

---

[4]https://lucene.apache.org/
[5]https://tika.apache.org/

[6]http://bit.ly/2pq0jq5

our preliminary investigations. Using DPHF, we retrieve the top 1,000 documents as a candidate set $\mathcal{R}$ for each query q.

At any time t, a feedback $f \in \mathcal{F}_t$ for a document $d \in \mathcal{D}_t$ is a tuple $f = \langle a, p, g \rangle$ comprising a passage p that the user deemed relevant to aspect a at a given relevance level $g \in \{1, 2, 3, 4\}$. The structured nature of the feedback associated with each aspect naturally lends itself amenable to some form of aggregate modeling. As illustrated in the magnified portion of Figure 3, as a reference aspect modeling component, we represent each aspect a as an aggregate of the relevant passages associated with it, with the content of each passage p weighted by its corresponding relevance grade g. As time progresses, new passages may be appended to a given aspect tree, and entirely new aspects may be discovered. Moreover, the relative importance of each aspect as perceived by the user can potentially change, as also illustrated in Figure 3 in different shades of gray. To restrict the number of confounding variables in our simulations, we assume a uniform and unchanged aspect importance at all times.

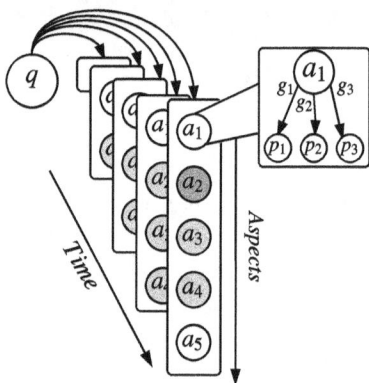

Figure 3: Query aspect modeling over time.

As reference models for dynamic reranking, we take two state-of-the-art diversification models: xQuAD [23] and PM2 [7]. In line with the goal of dynamic search, these models attempt to satisfy as many query aspects as possible (promoting diversity) and as early as possible (promoting novelty) [25].[7] Central to these models are estimates $P(d|q, a)$ of how well document d covers each aspect $a \in \mathcal{A}_t$ of query q. To assess the impact of the dynamic reranker component, we simulate coverage estimates of various performances. In our simulations, we gradually introduce noise into a perfect coverage matrix, which is defined as follows:

$$P(d|q, a) = \frac{g(a, d)}{\sum_{a_i \in \mathcal{A}_t} g(a_i, d)}, \quad (3)$$

where $g(a, d) = \max_{p \in d} g(a, p)$ is the highest relevance grade assigned to any passage p in document d that was judged relevant to aspect a. In other words, when estimating the aspect coverage of a document based on the user's passage-level feedback, we assume that the document is as relevant as its best passage.

4 EXPERIMENTAL EVALUATION

This section analyzes the impact of the four components illustrated in Figure 2 on the effectiveness of a dynamic search system. In particular, we aim to answer the following research questions:

Q1. How does the initial document sample impact the effectiveness of a dynamic search system?

Q2. What is the impact of feedback modeling on the system's knowledge of the aspects underlying the user's query?

Q3. How do improved coverage estimates impact the system's ability to dynamically adapt its ranking strategy?

Q4. What is the impact of early and late stopping strategies on the attained gain-effort trade-off?

The remainder of this section addresses each of these questions in turn. Our observations are based on ACT figures averaged across 171 queries from all five domains summarized in Table 2. Per-domain results follow similar trends and are omitted for brevity.

4.1 Baseline Ranker

The baseline ranker component may impact the effectiveness of a dynamic search system in different moments. In particular, to address Q1, we propose two complementary hypotheses:

H1. At earlier interactions, the effectiveness of the system is influenced by the precision attained by the baseline ranker.

H2. At later interactions, the effectiveness of the system is influenced by the recall attained by the baseline ranker.

Regarding H1, because little feedback is available at early interactions (with absolutely no feedback at $t = 1$), the overall system effectiveness depends on the relevance of the documents surfaced by the baseline ranker itself (i.e., precision). Regarding H2, the potential improvement brought by dynamically reranking the set of candidate documents at later interactions depends on the amount of relevant documents (i.e., recall) available in this set. To test these hypotheses, we simulate baseline rankers of various quality levels. Following Turpin and Scholer [27], for each query q, we generate a series of permutations of the reference ranking $\mathcal{R}$ produced by DPHF (as discussed in Section 3.3) by repeatedly swapping randomly chosen pairs involving one relevant document and one irrelevant document each, until a target average precision (AP) value is achieved. As target AP values for this simulation, we split the range $[0,1]$ of possible values into 20 equally sized bins (i.e., each bin has size 0.05) and randomly select 20 values from each bin, providing a total of 400 simulated permutations per query.

Figure 4 shows the effectiveness of three dynamic search systems (DPHF without reranking, DPHF+xQuAD, and DPHF+PM2) as we vary the quality of the baseline ranking produced by DPHF. Dynamic search effectiveness is given by ACT@t with $t \in \{1, 2, 10\}$,[8] whereas the effectiveness of the baseline ranker is given by either Precision@5 (Figures 4a-c) or Recall@500 (Figures 4d-f). To make sure documents below the 500 cutoff cannot contribute to the reported ACT figures, for this particular experiment, both xQuAD and PM2 are restricted to diversify the top 500 documents returned by the baseline ranker. In addition, to further isolate any impact from the dynamic reranker component itself, both xQuAD and PM2 leverage perfect coverage estimates, as given by Equation (3).

From Figure 4, we first note that dynamic search effectiveness (measured by ACT@t) is highly correlated with the effectiveness of the baseline ranker component (measured by either Precision@5

---

[7]Both xQuAD and PM2 are instantiated with their default setting of $\lambda = 0.5$.

[8]Note that, at $t = 1$, because no reranking is performed, the rankings produced by all three dynamic search systems (DPHF, DPHF+xQuAD, and DPHF+PM2) are identical.

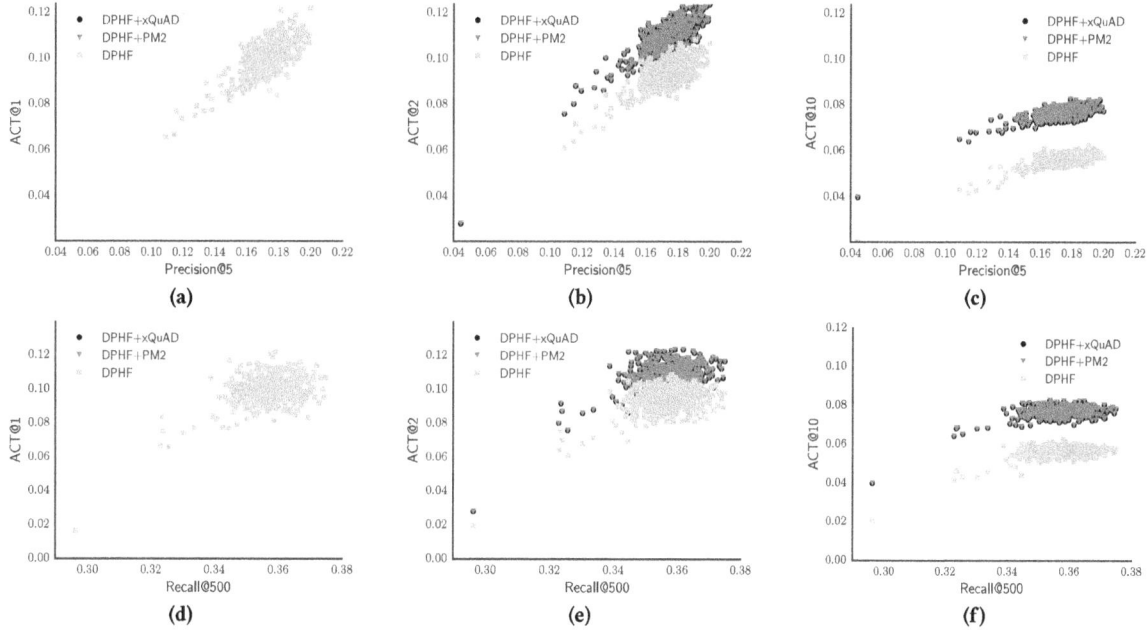

Figure 4: Impact of baseline rankers of various quality levels at times $t \in \{1, 2, 10\}$.

or Recall@500). From Figures 4a-c, we further observe that correlations with Precision@5 are stronger towards early interactions. In contrast, from Figures 4d-f, we note that correlations with Recall@500 are stronger at the last interaction. These observations are further corroborated by the quantitative figures reported in Table 3 in terms of the Pearson correlation between ACT@t and each of these metrics for all considered systems (i.e., DPHF, DPHF+xQuAD, and DPHF+PM2) and all times ($t \in \{1, 2, ..., 10\}$). In particular, correlations between ACT@t and Precision@5 peak at time $t = 3$ for DPHF and at $t = 2$ for both DPHF+xQuAD and DPHF+PM2 and then steadily decrease as time progresses. In turn, correlations between ACT@t and Recall@500 steadily increase as time goes by, peaking at $t = 10$ for all three systems. These observations hold regardless of whether the documents returned by the baseline ranker (DPHF) are dynamically reranked (by either xQuAD or PM2) and provide supporting evidence for both H1 and H2. Recalling Q1, the experiments in this section demonstrate that an effective baseline ranker impacts the effectiveness of a dynamic search system in different moments, with high-precision baseline rankers improving dynamic search effectiveness at early interactions, and high-recall baseline rankers bringing improvements towards later interactions.

4.2 Aspect Modeling

Section 4.1 showed how the precision and recall of the baseline ranker component may impact the effectiveness of the entire dynamic search system. In this section, we analyze the contribution of an accurate modeling of the multiple aspects $\mathcal{A}_t$ underlying the user's need based upon the feedback $\mathcal{F}_t$ provided by the user at each time t. To address Q2, we propose the following hypothesis:

H3. The effectiveness of a dynamic search system can be hindered by an inaccurate or incomplete aspect modeling.

Table 3: Correlation between ACT@t and Precision@5 or Recall@500 attained by the baseline ranker component.

	Precision@5			Recall@500		
t	DPHF	xQuAD	PM2	DPHF	xQuAD	PM2
1	0.8492	0.8492	0.8492	0.5218	0.5218	0.5218
2	0.8760	**0.8837**	**0.8838**	0.5673	0.5576	0.5586
3	**0.8769**	0.8784	0.8781	0.5905	0.5752	0.5764
4	0.8749	0.8686	0.8682	0.6051	0.5835	0.5844
5	0.8713	0.8584	0.8580	0.6143	0.5894	0.5900
6	0.8679	0.8496	0.8493	0.6211	0.5938	0.5943
7	0.8647	0.8421	0.8417	0.6260	0.5968	0.5972
8	0.8621	0.8360	0.8357	0.6300	0.5998	0.6003
9	0.8598	0.8311	0.8307	0.6332	0.6030	0.6035
10	0.8578	0.8274	0.8271	**0.6360**	**0.6061**	**0.6067**

To investigate this hypothesis, we perform two simulations that perturb the reference aspect model described in Section 3.3. First, we simulate the case where we may mishandle some of the user's feedback on different passages associated with a given query aspect a. Let $\kappa_a = \sum_{p \in \cup_t \mathcal{F}_t} \tilde{g}(a, p)$ denote the accuracy of the aspect model built for a, where $\tilde{g}(a, p)$ denotes the relevance grade assigned to a passage p with respect to aspect a, normalized by the total grade of all passages relevant to a (i.e., the "relevance mass" of passage p).[9] In our simulation, a mishandled feedback on passage p for aspect a incurs a probability $(1 - \kappa_a)$ of zeroing out coverage estimates $P(d|q, a)$ of any document d given this aspect, hence introducing noise in the subsequent dynamic reranking. Conversely, with probability κ_a, perfect estimates are used, as defined

---

[9]In practice, because the summation encompasses only passages to which the user provided feedback at some time t (as opposed to all relevant passages in the ground-truth), the maximum accuracy an aspect can attain is typically under 1.

in Equation (3). In our second simulation, we consider all aspects as perfectly accurate (i.e., $\kappa_a = 1, \forall a \in \mathcal{A}_t$) and evaluate the impact of incomplete aspect models, by mishandling entire aspects as opposed to individual passages. For this simulation, we zero out coverage estimates $P(d|q, a)$ of all documents that are relevant to a mishandled aspect a.

Figure 5 shows the impact on dynamic search effectiveness in terms of ACT@10 for DPHF, DPHF+xQuAD, and DPHF+PM2 as we perturb the underlying aspect model. To this end, in Figure 5a, we vary the *probability* of mishandling individual passages within the range [0,1] with steps of 0.05. In Figure 5b, we vary the *fraction* of mishandled aspects, also within the range [0,1] with steps of 0.05. In both figures, for a given step, the whole process is repeated 100 times, with error bars denoting standard deviations. Recall that DPHF alone is not affected by perturbations, as it does not leverage any user feedback for reranking. As a result, it provides a natural lower bound for both DPHF+xQuAD and DPHF+PM2.

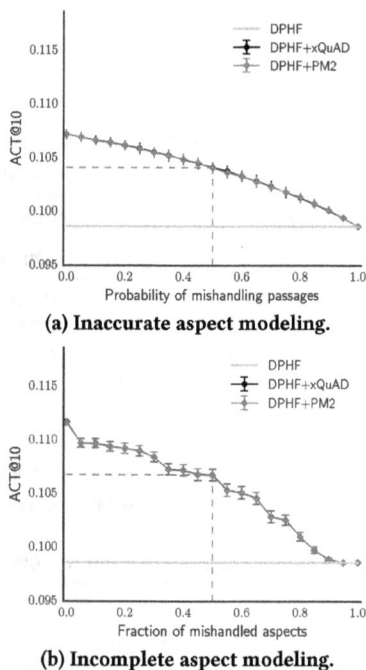

(a) Inaccurate aspect modeling.

(b) Incomplete aspect modeling.

Figure 5: Impact of inaccurate or incomplete aspect models.

From Figures 5a-b, we note that, as we increase either the probability of mishandling feedback on individual passages or the fraction of mishandled aspects, dynamic search effectiveness is hindered, which answers Q2 by providing supporting evidence for H3. On the other hand, these results demonstrate a reasonable resilience of both xQuAD and PM2 to inaccurate or incomplete aspect models. In particular, as highlighted in Figure 5a, mishandling feedback on individual passages with 50% probability accounts for 35.8% of the total drop in ACT@10. In turn, mishandling 50% of all aspects underlying a query accounts for 37.8% of the total drop in Figure 5b.

4.3 Dynamic Reranker

In Section 4.2, we investigated how perturbed aspect models could impact the effectiveness of a dynamic search system. In that investigation, we isolated the impact of the dynamic reranker component, by leveraging perfect estimates of the coverage of each document with respect to each modeled aspect. In this section, we address Q3, by investigating the impact of the dynamic reranker component itself. To this end, we propose the following hypothesis:

H4. The effectiveness of a dynamic search system can be enhanced by improved document coverage estimates for a given aspect model, more so for narrower queries.

Accurate coverage estimates have been shown to contribute to the effectiveness of explicit diversification approaches, such as xQuAD and PM2 [24], which are used here as reference models for dynamic reranking. Our hypothesis is that such estimates will also be key in a dynamic search scenario, particularly for narrower queries, which have a smaller number of relevant aspects and hence are arguably harder to diversify. To test this hypothesis, we simulate increasingly inaccurate coverage estimates, by gradually adding noise to the perfect estimates given by Equation (3). Inspired by related research on differentially private recommender systems [5], we perturb the relevance grade $g(a, d)$ assigned to document d with respect to aspect a by adding a Laplacian noise $Y \sim \text{Laplace}(0, b)$ to it. In this paper, we parameterize b as Δ_a/ϵ. The sensitivity parameter Δ_a captures the dispersion of relevance grades associated with aspect a, as the difference between the maximum and minimum values returned by $g(a, d)$ for all documents $d \in \mathcal{R}$ sampled for the query q. In turn, the leakage parameter ϵ determines how much of the perfect coverage estimates is allowed to "leak" to the dynamic reranker. In other words, lower ϵ values denote noisier coverage estimates, whereas higher ϵ values denote cleaner estimates.

Figure 6 shows the ACT@10 attained by DPHF, DHF+xQuAD, and DPHF+PM2 as we vary the leakage parameter ϵ in the range [0.1,20] with steps of 0.1. For a given step, the entire process is repeated 100 times. On the x-axis, instead of reporting actual leakage values, which cannot be easily interpreted, we indicate how much the resulting (perturbed) coverage estimates differ from perfect coverage estimates. To this end, for each aspect a, we compute the ordering over all documents $d \in \mathcal{R}$ induced by the perturbed coverage estimates $P(d|q, a)$ and compute its nDCG using the expected ordering (induced by the perfect coverage estimates) as ground-truth. The aspect nDCG for a query q is then computed by averaging over the nDCG obtained for its aspects $a \in \mathcal{A}_t$.

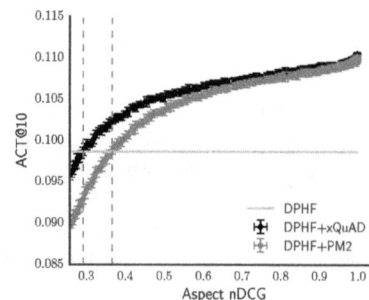

Figure 6: Impact of perturbed coverage estimates.

From Figure 6, we first note that DHF+xQuAD and DPHF+PM2 increasingly outperform the DPHF baseline ranker as their underlying coverage estimates improve, in support of *H4*. In particular, xQuAD begins to outperform DPHF at a critical leakage (CL) point of 0.3, measured in terms of aspect nDCG. On the other hand, PM2 requires slightly improved coverage estimates at a CL point of 0.4. To better understand the impact of improved coverage estimates, Figure 7 provides a breakdown analysis of the results in Figure 6 for queries organized in different bins in the range {1, 2, ..., 10} according to the number of relevant aspects underlying each query.[10]

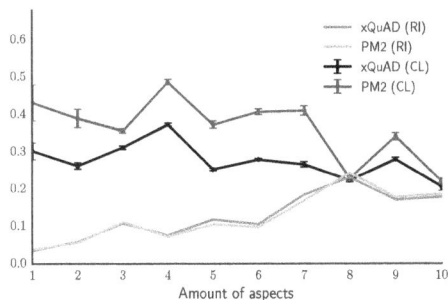

Figure 7: Critical leakage (CL) and room for improvement (RI) for queries with different numbers of relevant aspects.

From Figure 7, we observe a slight decrease in CL as the number of aspects per query increases, particularly for PM2. In addition to CL points, Figure 7 also shows the room for improvement (RI) in each bin, measured as the difference between the ACT@10 attained by the dynamic reranker (xQuAD or PM2) with perfect coverage estimates and the ACT@10 attained by the baseline ranker (DPHF). As shown in the figure, RI increases with the number of aspects per query. These results suggest that narrower queries (i.e., those with fewer aspects) are indeed harder to improve and demand better coverage estimates, which provides further support for *H4*. Recalling *Q3*, the results in this section demonstrate the positive impact of improved coverage estimates—and hence, of an improved dynamic reranker—on the effectiveness of a dynamic search system.

4.4 Stopping Strategies

In the previous sections, we evaluated the impact of the baseline ranker, aspect modeling, and dynamic reranking components under the assumption that the user would interact with a dynamic search system indefinitely. In this section, we address question *Q4*, by investigating the impact of alternative strategies for stopping the interactive process. To this end, we define an oracle stopping strategy, which stops immediately after the last relevant document has been returned, hence providing an optimal gain to the user. At the same time, this strategy may naturally incur additional user effort by extending the interactive process. To better understand this gain-effort trade-off, we simulate suboptimal stopping strategies by increasingly perturbing the stopping decision made by the oracle. Precisely, after receiving the user feedback $\mathcal{F}_t$ at time t, the oracle decides whether or not to stop. With probability τ, this decision is kept; conversely, with probability $(1 - \tau)$, it is flipped.

Figure 8 shows the dynamic search effectiveness attained by DPHF[11] in terms of ACT@10 as we vary the probability τ of keeping the oracle's stopping decision in the range [0,1] with steps of 0.05. For a given step, the entire process is repeated 100 times, with error bars denoting standard deviations. In addition to the simulated strategies, we consider three heuristic strategies: (i) *none*, which always decides not to stop; (ii) *cumul.*, which decides to stop after observing n_1 irrelevant documents cumulatively; and (iii) *cont.*, which decides to stop after observing n_2 irrelevant documents contiguously. The latter two heuristics were investigated by Maxwell et al. [19] and are tested here with parameters $n_1, n_2 \in \{10, 20\}$.

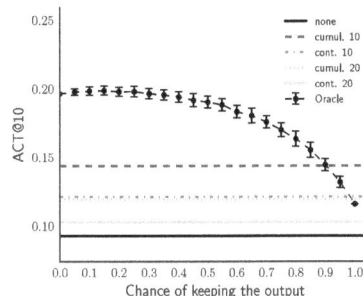

Figure 8: Impact of different stopping strategies for DPHF.

From Figure 8, we first note that the unperturbed oracle strategy (i.e., $\tau = 1$) attains a suboptimal gain-effectiveness trade-off, as measured by ACT@10. While it performs better than the *none* and *cont.* 20 strategies, it is outperformed by all other heuristics, with *cumul.* 10 achieving the highest ACT@10 among them. The underperformance of the oracle is further exacerbated when contrasting it to the increasingly perturbed simulated strategies, which attain the highest ACT@10 by completely flipping all decisions made by the oracle at full perturbation (i.e., $\tau = 0$). This apparent contradiction can be explained by the fact that the oracle strategy optimizes solely for gain, regardless of the incurred effort. In practice, such a gain-oriented strategy tends to stop much later than other effort-oriented strategies. For instance, intuitively, *cumul.* tends to stop earlier than *cont.* since, by definition, $n_1 \leq n_2$ (i.e., it is easier to observe a certain number of irrelevant results cumulatively than contiguously). On the other hand, it is not as apparent why early stopping strategies attain a better gain-effort trade-off. To further analyze this point, we propose the following hypothesis:

H5. Stopping late tends to incur more effort than gain.

To test this hypothesis, we further contrast the five heuristic strategies in Figure 8 in terms of their gain-effort trade-off. Figure 9 breaks down the impact of these heuristics by deconstructing the ACT metric (see Equation (1)) in terms of its two core components: *Gain* and *Time*, with the latter providing a simple proxy for user effort. We observe that strategies that cause no stopping (*none*) or a late stopping (e.g., *cont.* 20) naturally attain more gain compared to early stopping strategies (e.g., *cumul.* 10). Conversely, late stopping strategies naturally incur more effort. We can also observe that, because the amount of relevant documents is finite and typically small, gain rapidly tails off, while effort increases

---

[10]Queries with more than 10 relevant aspects are discarded from this analysis, as they are substantially fewer, amounting to only 9% of all queries.

[11]The same conclusions apply to DPHF+xQuAD and DPHF+PM2.

linearly as time progresses. As a result, although ACT measures the speed of fulfilling the user's information need with multiple aspects, our analysis suggests that it is biased in favor of systems that stop as early as possible, which supports *H5*. Recalling *Q4*, the results in this section demonstrate the trade-off between the gain attained and the effort incurred by continuing the interaction process. While the ACT metric aims at quantifying this trade-off, in practice, the harsh penalty incurred by its effort model discourages late stopping. While alternative effort models could be deployed (e.g., log-based), we leave this investigation to future work.

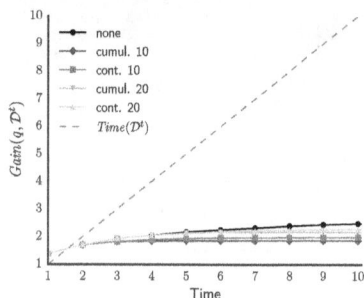

Figure 9: Gain-effort trade-off of stopping strategies.

5   CONCLUSIONS

In this paper, we investigated the role of different components on the effectiveness of a dynamic search system for specialized domains. Through a comprehensive analysis, we found that a high-precision baseline ranker may improve dynamic search at early interactions, whereas a high-recall baseline ranker tends to favor later interactions. Moreover, mishandling the user's feedback on individual passages associated with an aspect or on entire aspects may lead to decreased effectiveness. Likewise, we demonstrated the need for accurately estimating the coverage of each retrieved document with respect to each query aspect, particularly for queries with fewer aspects, which seem inherently harder to improve. Finally, we found that early stopping strategies achieve a better gain-effort trade-off compared to late stopping strategies, which highlights the challenge of promoting effective exploration in this task.

In the future, we plan to extend our analysis to encompass other elements of user interaction, including query reformulations and other forms of implicit feedback, as well as temporal characteristics of the feedback provided within a session. We also plan to further invest in concrete instantiations of each of the four components simulated in this study, so as to harness the potential they demonstrated. In addition to interactive diversification models, a promising direction here includes online learning models. Lastly, another interesting direction for future work involves improved models of the gain-effort trade-off for dynamic search evaluation.

ACKNOWLEDGMENTS

This work was partially funded by projects InWeb (MCT/CNPq 573871/2008-6) and MASWeb (FAPEMIG/PRONEX APQ-01400-14), and by the authors' individual grants from CNPq and FAPEMIG.

REFERENCES

[1] James Allan. 2006. HARD Track Overview in TREC 2005: High Accuracy Retrieval from Documents. In *Proceedings of TREC*.
[2] Giambattista Amati, Edgardo Ambrosi, Marco Bianchi, Carlo Gaibisso, and Giorgio Gambosi. 2016. FUB, IASI-CNR and University of Tor Vergata at TREC 2007 Blog Track. In *Proc. of TREC*.
[3] Kumaripaba Athukorala, Dorota Głowacka, Giulio Jacucci, Antti Oulasvirta, and Jilles Vreeken. 2016. Is exploratory search different? A comparison of information search behavior for exploratory and lookup tasks. *JASIST* (2016).
[4] Ricardo A. Baeza-Yates and Berthier A. Ribeiro-Neto. 2011. *Modern Information Retrieval - the concepts and technology behind search, Second edition*. Pearson Education Ltd., Harlow, England.
[5] Arnaud Berlioz, Arik Friedman, Mohamed Ali Kaafar, Roksana Boreli, and Shlomo Berkovsky. 2015. Applying Differential Privacy to Matrix Factorization. In *Proc. of RecSys*.
[6] Ben Carterette, Paul Clough, Mark Hall, Evangelos Kanoulas, and Mark Sanderson. 2016. Evaluating Retrieval over Sessions: The TREC Session Track 2011-2014. In *Proc. of SIGIR*.
[7] Van Dang and W. Bruce Croft. 2012. Diversity by Proportionality: An Election-based Approach to Search Result Diversification. In *Proc. of SIGIR*.
[8] Gene Golovchinsky, Abdigani Diriye, and Tony Dunnigan. 2012. The Future is in the Past: Designing for Exploratory Search. In *Proc. of IIIX*.
[9] Grace Hui Yang, John Frank, and Ian Soboroff. 2015. TREC 2015 Dynamic Domain Track Overview. In *Proc. of TREC*.
[10] Grace Hui Yang and Ian Soboroff. 2016. TREC 2016 Dynamic Domain Track Overview. In *Proc. of TREC*.
[11] Xiaoran Jin, Marc Sloan, and Jun Wang. 2013. Interactive Exploratory Search for Multi Page Search Results. In *Proc. of WWW*.
[12] Yamuna Krishnamurthy, Kien Pham, Aécio Santos, and Juliana Freire. 2016. Interactive Exploration for Domain Discovery on the Web. In *Proc. of KDD IDEA*.
[13] S. Lloyd. 2006. Least Squares Quantization in PCM. *IEEE Trans. Inf. Theor.* (2006).
[14] Jiyun Luo, Xuchu Dong, and Hui Yang. 2015. Learning to Reinforce Search Effectiveness. In *Proc. of ICTIR*.
[15] Jiyun Luo, Xuchu Dong, and Hui Yang. 2015. Session Search by Direct Policy Learning. In *Proc. of ICTIR*.
[16] Jiyun Luo, Christopher Wing, Hui Yang, and Marti Hearst. 2013. The Water Filling Model and the Cube Test: Multi-dimensional Evaluation for Professional Search. In *Proc. of CIKM*.
[17] Jiyun Luo, Sicong Zhang, and Hui Yang. 2014. Win-win Search: Dual-agent Stochastic Game in Session Search. In *Proc. of SIGIR*.
[18] Gary Marchionini. 2006. Exploratory Search: From Finding to Understanding. *Commun. ACM* (2006).
[19] David Maxwell, Leif Azzopardi, Kalervo Järvelin, and Heikki Keskustalo. 2015. Searching and Stopping: An Analysis of Stopping Rules and Strategies. In *Proc. of CIKM*.
[20] Felipe Moraes, Rodrygo L. T. Santos, and Nivio Ziviani. 2016. UFMG at the TREC 2016 Dynamic Domain track. In *Proc. of TREC*.
[21] J. J. Rocchio. 1971. Relevance feedback in information retrieval. In *The Smart retrieval system - experiments in automatic document processing*, G. Salton (Ed.). Englewood Cliffs, NJ: Prentice-Hall, 313–323.
[22] Tuukka Ruotsalo, Jaakko Peltonen, Manuel J. A. Eugster, Dorota Glowacka, Aki Reijonen, Giulio Jacucci, Petri Myllymäki, and Samuel Kaski. 2015. SciNet: Interactive Intent Modeling for Information Discovery. In *Proc. of SIGIR*.
[23] Rodrygo L.T. Santos, Craig Macdonald, and Iadh Ounis. 2010. Exploiting Query Reformulations for Web Search Result Diversification. In *Proc. of WWW*.
[24] Rodrygo L. T. Santos, Craig Macdonald, and Iadh Ounis. 2012. On the role of novelty for search result diversification. *Information Retrieval* (2012).
[25] Rodrygo L. T. Santos, Craig Macdonald, and Iadh Ounis. 2015. Search result diversification. *Found. Trends Inf. Retr.* 9, 1 (2015), 1–90.
[26] Marc Sloan and Jun Wang. 2015. Dynamic Information Retrieval: Theoretical Framework and Application. In *Proc. of ICTIR*.
[27] Andrew Turpin and Falk Scholer. 2006. User Performance Versus Precision Measures for Simple Search Tasks. In *Proc. of SIGIR*.
[28] Ryen W. White. 2016. *Interactions with Search Systems*. Cambridge University Press.
[29] Barbara M. Wildemuth and Luanne Freund. 2012. Assigning Search Tasks Designed to Elicit Exploratory Search Behaviors. In *Proc. of HCIR*.
[30] Hui Yang, Marc Sloan, and Jun Wang. 2015. Dynamic Information Retrieval Modeling. In *Proc. of WSDM*.
[31] Emine Yilmaz, Manisha Verma, Rishabh Mehrotra, Evangelos Kanoulas, Ben Carterette, and Nick Craswell. 2015. Overview of the TREC 2015 Tasks Track. In *Proc. of TREC*.
[32] Chengxiang Zhai and John Lafferty. 2001. Model-based Feedback in the Language Modeling Approach to Information Retrieval. In *Proc. of CIKM*.

Investigating per Topic Upper Bound for Session Search Evaluation

Zhiwen Tang
Department of Computer Science
Georgetown University
zt79@georgetown.edu

Grace Hui Yang
Department of Computer Science
Georgetown University
huiyang@cs.georgetown.edu

ABSTRACT

Session search is a complex Information Retrieval (IR) task. As a result, its evaluation is also complex. A great number of factors need to be considered in the evaluation of session search. They include document relevance, document novelty, aspect-related novelty discounting, and user's efforts in examining the documents. Due to increased complexity, most existing session search evaluation metrics are NP-hard. Consequently, the optimal value, i.e. the upper bound, of a metric highly varies with the actual search topics. In Cranfield-like settings such as the Text REtrieval Conference (TREC), scores for systems are usually averaged across all search topics. With undetermined upper bound values, however, it could be unfair to compare IR systems across different topics. This paper addresses the problem by investigating the actual per topic upper bounds of existing session search metrics. Through decomposing the metrics, we derive the upper bounds via mathematical optimization. We show that after being normalized by the bounds, the NP-hard session search metrics are then able to provide robust comparison across various search topics. The new normalized metrics are experimented on official runs submitted to the TREC 2016 Dynamic Domain (DD) Track.

KEYWORDS

Session Search; Evaluation; Normalization

1 INTRODUCTION

Session search is a complex search task which involves multiple iterations of searches in order to accomplish a complex information need. In the process, multiple queries are issued or reformulated and multiple runs of search results are returned by the search engine and examined by the user. Session search systems learn the users' search intents from the interactions to satisfy the complex information need of the entire session. The complexity of session search results comes from many factors, including the relevance of documents, the cost of reviewing documents, how to discount the relevance score of a document that is ranked lower in a list or is returned later at a later iteration. The challenge of evaluating session search lies in how to evaluate the search engine effectiveness throughout the entire course of the search.

Most metrics measure the amount of information a user gains during a search session. The gain is usually represented as the sum of relevance of the documents that have been returned so far. The relevance scores are usually assigned by third party annotators as ground truth scores. They can be graded or binary scores. Generally, as shown in previous research, it is believed that there is a positive correlation between a third party annotated relevance score and a user's satisfaction level [1, 6]. In this paper, instead of a user study, we will mainly focus on discussing evaluation in the Cranfield-like settings which rely on third party annotations.

Discounting document relevance is a common technique used in IR evaluation. There are two main types of discounting methods. First, discounting is done based on ranking orders. The idea is that the relevance scores of the lower ranked documents are discounted (as in DCG [7]) because it is assumed that users are less likely to read those documents hence less gains come from them. Second, discounting is done based on content redundancy. The relevance scores of documents that repeat on topics that have appeared in earlier documents are discounted (as in α-nDCG [4]), too.

Some IR evaluation metrics also take into account users' efforts (sometimes also known as *cost*). The cost can be regarded as a user's effort, both mentally and/or physically, spent in the session. It is usually simplified as the time spent in completing the entire task/session [12, 16], or the aggregated lengths of documents a user has read [19]. As more user efforts are put into search activities, the user's satisfaction level is expected to decrease. Kokubu et al. has found a positive correlation between user satisfaction and the reciprocal rank of relevant results in QA systems [10], which implies that a user is more satisfied if less documents are needed to examine in order to find the answers. The cost of a document may be discounted as well (as in Expected Utility [19]).

Most session search metrics handle all of the above factors and usually combine them into a single formula. The complexity of these metrics is quite high and most of them are NP-Hard. Consequently, the optimal value, i.e. the upper bound, of a metric highly varies with the actual search topics. That is to say, the bounds are not only decided by the mathematical definition of each metric, but also affected by the ground truth data of each topic. For instance, some search topics might be easy (with high optimal value for those topics) because many relevant documents are available and many search systems can achieve pretty high evaluation metric scores on those topics; while other topics might just be difficult for all search systems (with low optimal values for those topics). In Cranfield-like settings such as the Text REtrieval Conference (TREC), however, evaluation metric scores for systems are usually averaged across

ICTIR'17, October 1–4, 2017, Amsterdam, The Netherlands
© 2017 ACM. ISBN 978-1-4503-4490-6/17/10...$15.00
DOI: http://dx.doi.org/10.1145/3121050.3121069

Table 1: Document Relevance Scores in Ground Truth

topic	document
1 (2 subtopics)	d1(1.1, 1) d2(1.2, 3)
2 (4 subtopics)	d1(2.1, 4) d2(2.2, 4) d3(2.2, 2) d4(2.3, 4) d5(2.4, 4)

Table 2: The Importance of Normalization

systems	CT-topic 1	CT-topic 2	CT avg	normalized-CT avg
optimal	4	17	/	/
system 1	1	16	8.5	0.596
system 2	3	14	8.5	0.787

all search topics without considering the per topic upper bound a metric could achieve. Neglecting the differences in those bounds could be unfair when evaluating the systems across different topics.

A toy example is shown in Tables 1 and 2. Suppose two systems are evaluated on two topics with two and four subtopics respectively. In Table 1, $d1(1.1, 1)$ means document $d1$ is relevant to subtopic 1.1 with a relevance score of 1 (scaled from 1 to 5). Assume that each system returns five documents. *System 1 found $d1$ for topic1* and $d1, d3, d4, d5$ for *topic 2; System 2 found $d2$ for topic 1* and $d1, d2, d4, d5$ for *topic 2.* Other documents returned are irrelevant. Suppose that Cube Test [12] is used to evaluate session search effectiveness. We also assume that equal amount of time is needed to read each document and the discounting factor is 0.5. The optimal scores and the actual scores are shown in Table 2. As we can see here, the two systems' averaged CT scores are the same (8.5) thus it is hard to tell which system is better. However, the raw CT scores do not reflect the actual performance of the two systems. *Topic 2* has a high upper bound (17), which suggests an easy search topic. Therefore, the higher CT score from *system 1* (16) does not support that it is a better system than *system 2* which does an impressive job on the more difficult topic (*topic 1* with an upper bound of 4). The issue can be resolved by proper normalizing the raw scores by the per topic upper bounds, as shown in the last column in Table 2. The example demonstrates that knowing the per topic metric bounds is very important in fairly evaluating IR systems.

In this paper, we investigate existing session search evaluation metrics and focus on the following Research Question (**RQ**): *What is the best possible optimal metric value that a system could achieve?* To answer this question, we first take apart existing session search metrics into components. We then analyze the rationale behind each component and the ways used to combine them. Based on the component-based analysis, we compute the optimal score or the bounds of these metrics, which are then used for score normalization later. The new normalized metrics are experimented on the official runs submitted to the TREC 2016 Dynamic Domain (DD) Track. Our results show that these NP-hard session search metrics are then able to provide robust comparison across different topics.

This paper is organized as follows. Literature review is in section 2. Existing session search metrics are analyzed in sections 3 and section 4. The optimization method is detailed in section 5 and the experiments are shown in section 6. Section 7 concludes the paper.

2 RELATED WORK

2.1 Session Search Evaluation

Different from ad-hoc retrieval where a single query is asked and a single ranked list of documents is returned for that query, session search involves multiple ranked lists of documents generated from multiple runs of queries. To the best of our knowledge, the following metrics have been proposed to evaluate the effectiveness of session search results. They are Session-based DCG (sDCG) [8], Cube Test (CT) [12] and Expected Utility (EU) [19].

Relevance is a critical element in IR evaluation. sDCG [8] is a session search evaluation metric mainly about relevance. It extends the Discounted Cumulative Gain (DCG) [7]. Besides being discounted based on ranking position in the same list, documents ranked at a later iteration also get discounted because they are assumed less likely to be read. In this metric, discounted relevance is the main factor being considered.

Novelty of documents is another important factor in IR evaluation. IR systems that return more novel results should be rewarded more. Metrics use nuggets (in EU [19]), subtopics (in CT [12]), or intents to refer to the similar idea of "aspects" that compose into a complete search topic for a session. If a document is related to a nugget/subtopic that is previously found, then its relevance score should be discounted.

Recent research has shown that another dimension, the effort spent by the user, should also be incorporated into IR evaluation[21]. Metrics measure the user effort include CT [12], EU [19] and Time-bias gain [16]. The first two are session search evaluation metrics. CT represents the effort as the time spent reviewing the documents. EU represents it as the total lengths of documents having been read. Time-bias gain calculates the expected time spent reading the documents.

Many session search metrics assumes that the user will read all the document returned in every iteration from the beginning to the end. However, it is probably not true. Users may choose to stop early or read the documents in a different order. Kanoulas et al. addressed this problem by incorporating the user's reviewing paths into IR evaluation [9]. EU [19] also takes the reviewing path into consideration. Since users may not read all the documents, the utility of the search session may differ for different users. EU uses a uniformly distributed user model to calculate the final scores.

2.2 Score Normalization and Optimization

Table 2 demonstrates that topic difficulty level could affect fairness in IR evaluation. It has been a while since this issue was recognized. As an early attempt, Robertson proposed to use Geometric Mean of Average Precision (GMAP) [13], which can be seen as the arithmetic mean of the logarithms of Average Precisions (AP). GMAP reduces the variance among high AP scores and enlarges the variance among low AP scores. However, the physical meaning of the logarithm function remains unclear.

Another approach was proposed by Webber et al. to first standardize the raw scores, then map the standardized scores into the range of [0, 1] by applying the cumulative density function of a standard normal distribution [17]. Their method provides the opportunity of comparing the scores across different topics and collections. Sakai used a similar method [15], where a linear transformation is applied to the standardized scores. Lee et al. proposed to use Generalized Adaptive-Weight Mean (GAWM) to aggregate the scores from different topics [11]. Based on the Fixed Point Theorem, GAWM assigns more weights to topics on which the search systems' effectiveness has higher variance.

In various ways, these existing methods are able to average scores across different topics. However, what is missing is that they all provide little information about how to make use of the averaged scores to guide an IR system to do better. Here we propose to inform the search systems not only the averaged scores, but also how far away they are from the best they can do via providing the knowledge of per topic upper bounds of the metrics.

The work most relevant to our paper is [3]. It computes the optimal values of a few IR metrics, including S-recall, S-precision [22] and α-DCG [4], which are not used for session search though. In [3], Carterette found that optimizing metrics considering document novelty is usually NP-Complete [3]. Given different search topics, the performance of search systems varies and there is no general guideline for optimizing novelty and relevance at the same time. Our paper is along the same line of research of [3], with an emphasis on session search metrics.

3 EXISTING SESSION EVALUATION METRICS

The complexity of the session search task poses challenges to its evaluation. This section presents existing session search metrics, sDCG [8], Cube Test [12] and Expected Utility [19]. The following notations are used in the rest of the paper.

For a search session:

- i: the index of a search iteration in a session with total L iterations, $i = 1, ..., L$.
- $list_i$: the returned document list at the ith iteration.
- j: the position of a document within an iteration, $j = 1, ..., |list_i|$.
- k: the id of a document in the entire corpus, $k = 1, ..., n$.
- c: a subtopic/nugget of the search topic.
- θ_c: the importance/relevance of a subtopic or nugget.

For document $d_{i,j}$, which is at the jth position in the ith iteration:

- $rel_c(i, j)$ is the relevance score of $d_{i,j}$ regarding c if we consider subtopic/nugget level relevance. Otherwise if we only consider document level relevance, $rel(i, j)$ is the relevance score of $d_{i,j}$.
- $cost(i, j)$: the cost or user effort of examining $d_{i,j}$.

Dynamic parameters during the session:

- $n(c, i, j - 1)$: the number of documents that are relevant to c returned before the jth document in the ith iteration.
- γ, bq, b : novelty, iteration, and within-iteration position discounting factors.

The definitions of sDCG, Cube Test and Expected Utility are shown in formulas 1, 2 and 3, respectively.

$$sDCG = \sum_{i=1}^{L} \sum_{j=1}^{|list_i|} \frac{rel(i, j)}{(1 + \log_b j) * (1 + \log_{bq} i)} \tag{1}$$

$$CT = \frac{\sum_{i=1}^{L} \sum_{j=1}^{|list_i|} \sum_c \theta_c * rel_c(i, j) * \gamma^{n(c, i, j-1)}}{\sum_{i=1}^{L} \sum_{j=1}^{|list_i|} cost(i, j)} \tag{2}$$

For simplification, without loss of generality, the cap for maximum relevant scores of CT is neglected here. We also assume that the amount of time needed for reviewing each document in CT is equal.

$$EU = \sum_{\omega} P(\omega) \left(\sum_{(i,j) \in \omega} \left(\sum_{c \in d_{i,j}} \theta_c * \gamma^{n(c, i, j-1)} \right) - a * cost(i, j) \right) \tag{3}$$

Expected Utility assumes that a user only reviews a subset of documents being returned, which is denoted as ω. $P(\omega)$ is the probability that ω are reviewed. a is a coefficient to adjust the relationship between the gain and cost. The cost of reviewing each document is measured by their document lengths.

As we can see, all these metrics attempt to handle multiple aspects of session search, such as relevance and novelty of documents and time spent reviewing them. Mixing various factors into a single metric has two consequences. First, it is difficult to understand them. Second, most metrics here are NP-hard thus they would be unreliable to be directly used as optimization goals in supervised ranking algorithms such as in learning to rank. In the following sections, we decompose these metrics into a few simple components and further analyze them.

4 DECONSTRUCTING THE METRICS

We observe that there are common components shared by almost all the session search metrics. They are *gain, cost, ranking discount* and *novelty discount*.

Gain: the gain of each document is its raw relevance score. *Gain* represents the amount of useful information a user can learn from the document.

Cost: the cost of each document is its length or time spent examining it. *Cost* represents the effort the user needs to spend on that document.

Both *Gain* and *Cost* are inherent attributes of a document. It means they are irrelevant to the environment or context in which the document is present. Such context includes being at a specific position among a list and the content of other documents being examined before.

When considering the context, the raw *Gain* or *Cost* of a document may be adjusted to reflect the influences of the context. For instance, they are usually being discounted when a document appears at a lower ranking position, or the document contains redundant information compared to an early document. We thus have two types of discounts.

Ranking discount: Discounting that is based on the original ranking position of a document. It is irrelevant to the document's own content. The rationale behind the ranking discount is that the lower a document ranks, the less likely the user will read it, the less the expected gain or expected cost comes out of this document. Decaying functions like logarithmic reduction factor $\frac{1}{1+\log_b x}$ are commonly used in ranking discount.

Novelty discount: Nuggets and subtopics both measure a user's knowledge coverage. If a document is related to a subtopic/nugget that the user read before, then it contributes less novel information about this subtopic/nugget, for which its value will be discounted. Decaying functions like exponential discounting function γ^x are commonly used in novelty discount. Novelty discount can be seen as a general form of ranking discount, where the ranking order is one within each subtopic or nugget.

Let us denote *Gain, Cost, Ranking discount* and *Novelty discount* by A, B, C, and D:

A = raw gain of each document B = ranking discount

C = novelty discount D = raw cost of each document

We propose to view metrics shown in formula 1, 2 and 3 as combinations of A, B, C, and D and apply a component-based analysis.

Specifically, sDCG does not take novelty into account, thus it only has components $A+B$. The definition of sDCG can be rewritten as

$$sDCG = Discounted\ Gain = \sum_d rank\_discount_d * gain_d$$

Ranking discount is not considered in CT, thus CT can be seen as $A + C + D$. Its definition can be rewritten as

$$CT = \frac{Discounted\ Gain}{Cost} = \frac{\sum_d \sum_c novelty\_discount_{d,c} * gain_{d,c}}{\sum_d cost_d}$$

EU takes all the components into consideration. It can be regarded as $A + B + C + D$:

$$EU = Discounted\ Gain - Discounted\ Cost$$

$$= \sum_d \sum_c novelty\_discount_{d,c} * rank\_discount_d * gain_{d,c}$$

$$- \sum_d rank\_discount_d * cost_d$$

An interesting question arose out of our abstraction is how to combine the *(Discounted) Gain* and *(Discounted) Cost* when both are present. CT divides *Gain* by *Cost* while EU subtracts *Cost* from *Gain*. Which one is more appropriate, subtraction or division?

Subtracting *Cost* from *Gain* is like calculating a "net gain". The assumption here is that *Gain* and *Cost* are of the same nature and can be directly added or subtracted. Is this true? In session search, *Cost* is the amount of time needed to review the documents or the aggregated length of reviewed documents, for which its unit can be seconds or words. *Gain* is the information obtained from the reviewed documents and its unit is still unknown. Based on dimensional analysis [2], if two things do not belong to the same dimension, it is probably incorrect to add or subtract them with each other (eg. adding area into length). Even if both measure the same thing, it may still not be ideal to sum them up unless the exchange rate is fixed (eg. 1 foot = 0.3048 meters).

When combining measurements from two different dimensions, in this case gain and cost, we think using division is more appropriate. No matter whether *Gain* and *Cost* measure in the same dimension or not, the result of division can still be seen as a measurement of the rate to achieve that gain. An effective IR system should return more *Gain* with the same *Cost* or provide the same *Gain* with less *Cost*. CT can be regarded as a speed function measuring how fast an IR system can satisfy an information need.

5 FINDING THE UPPER BOUND VALUES

This section focuses on computing the bound of the metrics after decomposing them into components. For a given topic, the bound of a metric is one of the topic's inherent propertites and is very useful

in identifying where to make improvement to a search system. For example, if a system receives a very low score on a topic, it might be because of the poor retrieval model, or be because of a very difficult search topic. Without knowing the optimal score on the topic, it is difficult to separate the two cases. Moreover, without knowing the bound of every topic, it might also be unfair to average the scores across topics.

As an evaluation scheme, suppose we know the ground truth of a given search topic, which consists of the relevance scores and reviewing cost of each document, the importance of every subtopic and the number of documents returned at each iteration. The research problem here is to calculate the optimal scores (bounds) for these NP-hard metrics for a given topic.

After knowing the bounds, **normalizing the scores** would be straightforward. Normalization requires not only the upper bound, but also the lower bound. In this paper, for a given metric, the normalized score of a search system is

$$score_A = \sum_t \frac{raw\_score(t,A) - lower\_bound(t)}{upper\_bound(t) - lower\_bound(t)} \quad (4)$$

where A is the system, t is the topic and $raw\_score(t,A)$ is the raw metric value of system A on topic t. Note that for sDCG and CT, the lower bound is always zero, we thus will only focus on calculating their upper bounds. However, the lower bound of EU could be negative so both upper and lower bounds will be studied.

5.1 Optimization Methods

Components A (gain) and D (cost) become constants once ground truth data is provided. The challenge of computing the optimal scores/upper bounds lies in components B (ranking discount) and C (novelty discount). As discussed before, novelty discount could be seen as a more general form of ranking discount. Both components share the property that the lower (later) a document ranks, the more discount it receives. It implies that we can use the same optimization framework for both types of discounts.

For a single document ranked list, its discounted gain can be expressed as $\sum_j rel(j) * discount(j)$, where $rel(j)$ is the relevance score of the jth document in this list. Since $discount(j)$ is only related to the ranking position j and not relevant to the document's relevance or reviewing cost, computing the optimal score or the bound of the ranked list is equivalent to finding the best permutation of documents that optimizes the metric score. The ranked list can be optimized based on the *rearrangement inequality* [5].

The *rearrangement inequality* states that

$$x_1 y_n + ... + x_n y_1 \le x_{\sigma(1)} y_1 + ... + x_{\sigma(n)} y_n \le x_1 y_1 + ... + x_n y_n$$

for all the real numbers $x_1 \le ... \le x_n$ and $y_1 \le ... \le y_n$. Moreover, $x_{\sigma(1)}, ... x_{\sigma(n)}$ is a permutation of $x_1, ..., x_n$. In our case, $rel(j)$ can be seen as x_i and $discount(j)$ can be regarded as y_i. The position that has the larger $discount(j)$ should be reserved for a document that has higher rel_j, if we would like to calculate the max value.

This method is also referred as *Probability Ranking Principle* in IR [14], which states that the overall effectiveness of an IR system can be achieved the best by ranking the documents by their usefulness in descending order. The method can give a feasible optimal score if only one ranking order needs to be optimized. However, when multiple ranked lists are required to be optimized simultaneously,

---

ALGORITHM 1: optimal score on a single ranking list

Input:

$|list_i|$ where $i = 1, 2...L$,

raw (relevance/cost) scores: r_k of document d_k, $k = 1, 2, ..., n$,

discount function: $discount(i, j)$

optimization direction: $IsMaximize = true$ or $false$

Output: optimal score on a single ranked list

$POS = \{(1, 1), ..., (1, |list_1|), (2, 1), ..., (L, |list_L|)\}$

// Set of all possible document ranking positions

$SP = Queue(sort(POS)$ by $discount(i, j)$ in ascending order$)$

if $IsMaximize$ **then**

    $D = Queue(sort(d_k)$ by r_k in ascending order$)$

end

else

    $D = Queue(sort(d_k)$ by r_k in descending order$)$

end

$opt = 0$

while SP is not empty and D is not empty **do**

    $(i, j) = SP.deQueue()$

    $d_k = D.deQueue()$

    $opt+ = r_k * discount(i, j)$

end

return opt

---

e.g. the optimization of CT requires the optimization of the ranked list within each subtopic, there may not exist a ranking order that can optimize all lists. Nonetheless, optimizing each required ranking list independently can approximate an overall bound.

Greedy algorithms have been proposed to approximate the optimal score in novelty-related metrics [3, 4], where multiple ranked lists are required to be optimized simultaneously. However, the focus of a greedy algorithm is to produce an ideal document list, which is not required for score normalization. It is also shown that the results yielded by a greedy algorithm can be far below the optimal score on certain topics [3]. From this point of view, optimization based on *rearrangement inequality* is more proper because it is able to lead to a tighter bound and is very efficient especially when the number of relevant documents is large.

Our optimization algorithm is shown in Algorithm 1. It handles both minimization and maximization based on different settings. In the algorithm, all the possible slots are first ranked based on the discount value it will receive. When maximization is needed, a document with higher raw score will be put at a position with higher $discount(i, j)$ value. When minimization is needed, the document with higher raw score will be assigned to a position with lower $discount(i, j)$ value. The algorithm forms the basis for optimizing of the session search metrics in the rest of this section.

5.2 sDCG

sDCG is essentially discounted cumulated gain for a search session. Computing the optimal sDCG score can be expressed as

$$maximize \sum_{i=1}^{L} \sum_{j=1}^{|list_i|} \frac{rel(i, j)}{(1 + \log_b j) * (1 + \log_{bq} i)} \quad (5)$$

Since subtopics are not considered in sDCG, only one document ranking list needs to be optimized. Algorithm 1 can be directly used by setting $IsMaximize = true$ and $discount(i, j) = \frac{1}{(1 + \log_b j) * (1 + \log_{bq} i)}$.

Different from the normalization method proposed in [8], there is no duplicated result in our ideal ranked lists. Our optimal sDCG score represents the optimal performance a system can achieve in the session. The range of sDCG score of any system on a topic is $[0, opt]$ when the session length L is fixed.

5.3 Cube Test

Computing the optimal score of CT is not as intuitive as that of sDCG. In fact, computing the optimal score of Cube Test is NP-Hard even for a special case of CT, which is defined as

$$maximize \ CT = \frac{\sum_c \sum_d novelty\_discount_{d,c} * gain_{d,c}}{\sum_d cost_d} \quad (6)$$

where $cost_d = 1$, $novelty\_discount_{d,c}$ is boolean and is set to 1 iff. document d is the first relevant document found on subtopic c.

In the special case, the discounted cumulated gain can be considered as the number of subtopics found by the IR system and the aggregated cost is the number of documents returned. The optimal CT score in this special case should have the highest number of subtopics found with the minimum number of documents returned.

The optimization problem can be transformed into the *Minimum Edge Dominating Set* problem in graph theory, which is NP-Hard [20]. An *edge dominating set* is a subset of edges satisfying the property that every edge that is not in this subset is adjacent to at least one edge in this subset. The *minimum edge dominating set* is one such subset of edges that has the smallest size.

Here each document is considered as an edge and each subtopic is considered as a vertex. Then, documents (edges) in the *minimum edge dominating set* are the ones that need to be returned so as to achieve the optimal performance in the special form of CT. Because the special CT is NP-Hard, computing the optimal value of general CT is also NP-Hard. Nonetheless, CT's upper bound can still be computed based on *rearrangement inequality*. The optimal CT can be achieved by

$$maximize \sum_{i=1}^{L} \sum_{j=1}^{|list_i|} rel_c(i, j) * \gamma^{\sum_{l=1}^{i-1} |list_l| + (j-1)} \ \forall c$$

$$minimize \sum_{i=1}^{L} \sum_{j=1}^{|list_i|} cost(i, j) \quad (7)$$

Formula 7 requires to maximize a number of objective functions and minimize one objective function. The number of objective functions need to be maximized equals to the number of subtopics, i.e., $\#(c)$. The upper bound of CT can be derived by optimizing each of these target functions independently using Algorithm 1 and then combine them according to formula 2. For the maximization target functions, the input contains the raw relevance scores of all the documents regarding a given subtopic, and $discount(i, j) = \gamma^{\sum_{l=1}^{i-1} |list_l| + (j-1)}$. For the minimization target function, the input contains the raw cost scores of all the documents, and

$discount(i, j) = 1$. The approximated upper bound may not be feasible in real situations. However, it provides good approximations of the real bound.

5.4 Expected Utility

EU assumes that the user will scan the returned document in a top-down fashion with a probability p of stopping at some document in the current iteration. Once the user stops reviewing, (s)he will start the next search iteration. In order to make the computation tractable, Yang et al. [19] approximated the computation of EU by formula 8.

$$EU = \frac{1}{1-\gamma}\left(\sum_c \theta_c \left(1 - \gamma^{\sum_\omega P(\omega)n(c,\omega)}\right)\right) - a\sum_\omega P(\omega)len(\omega)$$
(8)

where $n(c, \omega)$ is the number of appearances of nugget c in the reviewed document subset ω and $len(\omega)$ is the total length of documents in ω.

The computation of $\sum_\omega P(\omega)n(c,\omega)$ and $\sum_\omega P(\omega)len(\omega)$ can be further expanded. $\sum_\omega P(\omega)n(c,\omega) = \sum_{i=1}^{L}\sum_{h_i=1}^{|list_i|} P(h_i)\sum_{j=1}^{h_l} rel_c(i,j)$
$= \sum_{i=1}^{L}\sum_{j=1}^{|list_i|} rel_c(i,j)\sum_{h_i=j}^{|list_i|} P(h_i) \sum_{i=1}^{L}\sum_{j=1}^{|list_i|} rel_c(i,j)(1-p)^{j-1}$,
where h_i is the position where the user stops in the ith iteration of the session. Similar transformation can also be applied to $\sum_\omega P(\omega)len(\omega) = \sum_{i=1}^{L}\sum_{j=1}^{|list_i|} cost(i,j)(1-p)^{j-1}$.

In EU, each nugget c has its own graded importance score θ_c. The relevance between a document and a nugget $rel_c(i, j)$ is binary (a document does or does not contain a nugget). The cost of a document, $cost(i, j)$, is its length.

The maximization of formula 8 is also NP-Hard. It is achieved by

$$maximize \sum_{i=1}^{L}\sum_{j=1}^{|list_i|} rel_c(i,j) * (1-p)^{j-1} \; \forall c$$
$$minimize \sum_{i=1}^{L}\sum_{j=1}^{|list_i|} cost(i,j) * (1-p)^{j-1}$$
(9)

Using similar methods as in CT, the upper bound of EU can be obtained by maximizing #(c) target functions and minimizing 1 target function independently with Algorithm 1. Note that the lower bound of EU is negative. It is because an IR system may return documents that are all irrelevant but still requires user's effort to read them, which leads to a negative EU score. The lower bound of EU can be derived by

$$maximize \sum_{i=1}^{L}\sum_{j=1}^{|list_i|} cost(i,j)(1-p)^{j-1}$$
(10)

which can also be approximated using Algorithm 1.

6 EXPERIMENTS

In this section, we experiment on the dataset and the official runs submitted to the TREC 2016 Dynamic Domain (DD) Track [18]. The dataset contains documents in various formats, including html pages and tweets. Each search topic contains several subtopics addressing different aspects of the topic. Every document may be relevant to multiple subtopics with different relevant grades. Subtopics within a topic are assigned identical weights. In total, there are

Table 3: Topic sample in TREC-DD 2016

Topic/Subtopic id	Topic/Subtopic name
DD16-1	US Military Crisis Response
– DD16-1.1	West African mission
– DD16-1.2	Key Personnel
– DD16-1.3	Personnel safety protocols

53 topics and 242 subtopics, with an average of 4.57 subtopics per topic. The ground truth data was created by NIST assessors. It contains 14,597 relevant documents, with an average of 291.47 relevant documents per topic[1]. Table 3 shows an example topic from TREC 2016 DD Track.

We have conducted two sets of experiments. The first mainly studies the upper bounds (or the bound size, if the lower bound of the metric is negative) of the session search metrics. The second studies the influence of score normalization.

6.1 Plotting the Bounds

Figures 1(a), 1(b) and 1(c) plot the upper bounds/ bound sizes on different topics for sDCG, Cube Test and Expected Utility respectively at different session lengths. Within each figure, we also show the statistics for the corresponding metric in a table. The statistics include the min, max, average, median and standard deviation of the bounds. The bounds are computed as in Section 5. The runs we studied are the 21 official runs submitted to TREC 2016 DD Track.

We observe that differences among the bounds of a metric across different topics are huge and non-negligible for all three session search metrics. This conclusion is true regardless of how many search iterations having been conducted. It suggests that without proper score normalization, it would be unfair to compare across different topics. A metric score averaged for all topics would be biased towards topics that have higher bounds.

For a particular search topic, as more search iterations are conducted, we observe that the metrics' upper bound/bound size changes. They change differently for the three metrics. The optimal sDCG score increases as the search goes on with more iterations. It is because sDCG is essentially a gain function and it ignores the cost of search. Therefore, more search iterations would always increase chances of getting more relevant documents. On the other hand, the upper bound of CT decreases as the search keeps going. It suggests that the rate of gaining relevant information is decreasing as more iterations are used. It makes sense since once a user has learned relevant information in the initial runs, (s)he will not be too surprised for more relevant information at the later iterations thus the gains from those later iterations decrease. However, this observation might also only be related to the TREC 2016 DD dataset and tasks, where the search topics are mostly factual and informational. For navigational or learning-intensive search topics, we might be able to observe a different learning rate. Lastly, we observe that the bound size of EU enlarges as the session length increases. It comes from the fact that EU is a "net gain" function, more iterations mean more possible gain as well as more possible cost.

---

[1]Some documents are relevant to multiple topics

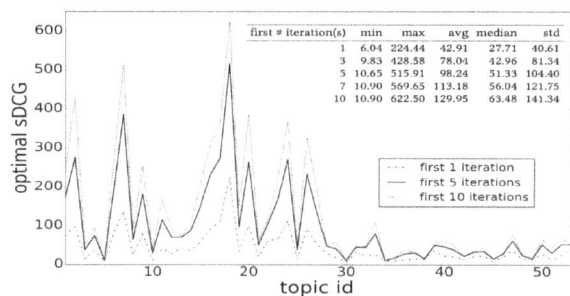

(a) optimal sDCG on TREC16-DD topics

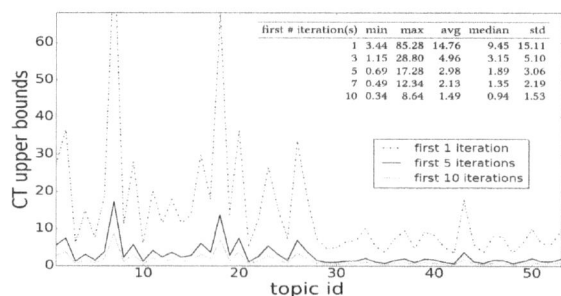

(b) CT upper bounds on TREC16-DD topics

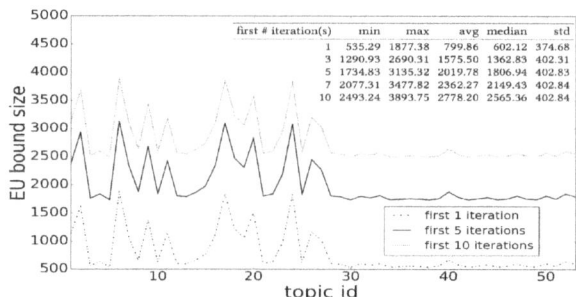

(c) EU bound size on TREC16-DD topics

Figure 1: Upper bounds/ bound sizes on TREC16-DD topics

Moreover, as more iterations conducted in a session, the differences of the metric bounds across topics also change in various ways. For sDCG, the differences among topics become bigger. As a result, the optimal sDCG on different topics become more polarized as the number of iterations increases. For CT, this difference reduces a bit which indicates the system performance gets similar among the topics when more iterations are used. But the differences are still huge and cannot be neglected. For EU, the differences among topics remain relatively the same as the session develops.

Regardless of the changes on the upper bounds/bound sizes as more iterations are conducted, the difference of the optimal value a metric would produce for different topics is large and should not be ignored. We recommend taking per topic bounds into account for fairer evaluation.

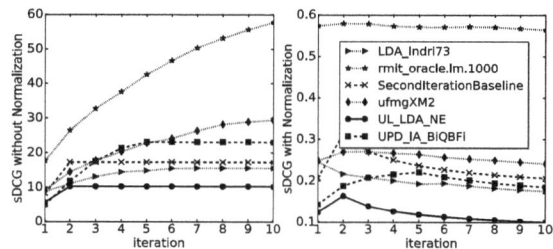

Figure 2: sDCG on TREC16-DD

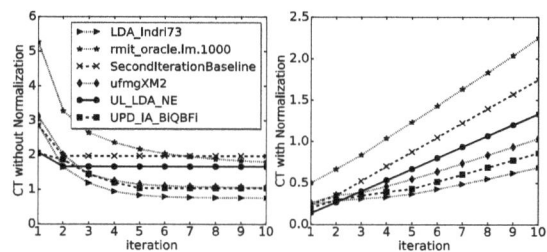

Figure 3: CT on TREC16-DD

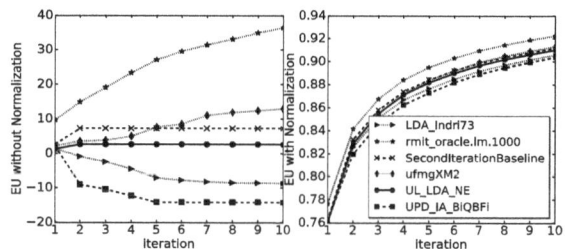

(a) $a = 0.001$

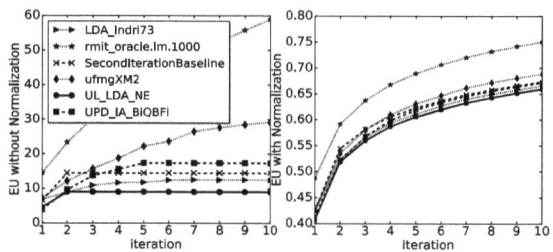

(b) $a = 0.0001$

Figure 4: EU on TREC16-DD

6.2 Normalizing Effect

Twenty-one runs from six groups are submitted to TREC 2016 DD Track. We select six representative runs, one from each team, to examine the effects of score normalization. Figures 2, 3 and 4 plot the raw scores without and with normalization. The scores are averaged across all topics for selected runs.

Figure 2 compares the raw (left) and the normalized (right) sDCG scores. The raw sDCG scores are non-decreasing as the number of iterations increases. It is because sDCG is essentially cumulated gains. However, the normalized sDCG scores could increase, decrease or remain as a constant as the number of iterations increases. It suggests that some systems actually have been close to the optimal sDCG score at certain points whereas others do not perform that well. We notice that systems such as *LDA_Indri*73 and *UL_LDA_NE*, whose raw sDCG values increase (non-decrease) in Figure 2 (left) but decreases after being normalized (Figure 2 (right)). It suggests that even though the raw gains keep increasing, they increase at a much slower rate than that of the optimal sDCG increases.

Figure 3 compares the raw (left) and the normalized (right) CT scores. Most raw CT scores are decreasing, suggesting that as more iterations are involved, the rate of getting relevant information by those systems reduces. Some raw CT scores remain the same because their systems stop the search after a certain number of iterations. Based on the definition of CT in formula 2, after a system stops, its gain and cost in the following iterations are all zero therefore its CT score won't be affected. On the other hand, all the normalized CT scores increase as the session develops. It is yielded from the sharply declining upper bounds of CT. We even see some normalized CT scores increase so much that they become greater than 1. The normalized CT scores actually imply that, in session search, choosing the right time to stop the search can help an IR systems maintain its efficiency so as to improve users' satisfaction.

Figure 4 compares the raw (left) and the normalized (right) EU scores. As the number of iterations increases, the raw EU scores may increase (Figure 4(a)) or decrease (Figure 4(b)) while the normalized EU scores always increase. We realize that whether the raw EU score would increase or decrease is highly influenced by the choice of the parameter a in formula 3. With different parameter settings, the raw EU curves for the same run could be completely different. It confirms our conclusion that it is not appropriate to directly add or subtract gain by cost. On the other hand, the shape of the normalized EU score is not sensitive with different parameter settings. As a result, the normalization based on the metric bounds yields a more robust metric. Meanwhile, the increase of normalized EU score suggests an enlarged gap between the raw score and the metric's lower bound while the change on the difference between the raw score and upper bound may vary. Nonetheless, the enlarged gap suggests that all the systems have at least moved away from the worst case (the lower bounds).

7 CONCLUSIONS AND DISCUSSION

Session search brings rich interactions between the user and the search system. The evaluation of session search encompasses many factors in search, such as relevance, novelty, and user's effort. As more factors are included into the evaluation, many metrics for session search evaluation become NP-Hard. In this paper, we deconstruct those metrics, compute the optimal scores and use them for score normalization. Through experimenting on the TREC 2016 DD Track, we observe that (i) the variation of bounds of session search metrics on different topics is big and cannot be ignored; (ii) Using the bounds for normalization of those complex session metrics can

bring in more fairness into evaluating across topics and yield more reliable evaluation. In addition, the upper bounds of the metrics could potentially be used as optimizing criteria for search systems to decide when to stop the search. Suppose a system has completed k iterations, by giving the upper bound of the first $k + 1$ iterations and computing its actual score in the first k iterations, the system could potentially make a better judgment on whether to continue or stop searching.

8 ACKNOWLEDGEMENTS

This research was supported by NSF grant IIS-145374 and DARPA FA8750-14-2-0226. Any opinions, findings, conclusions, or recommendations expressed in this paper are of the authors, and do not necessarily reflect those of the sponsor.

REFERENCES
[1] Azzah Al-Maskari and Mark Sanderson. 2010. A review of factors influencing user satisfaction in information retrieval. *Journal of the American Society for Information Science and Technology* 61, 5 (2010), 859–868.
[2] Jean Baptiste Joseph Baron Fourier. 1878. *The analytical theory of heat.* The University Press.
[3] Ben Carterette. 2009. An analysis of NP-completeness in novelty and diversity ranking. In *ICTIR'2009.* Springer, 200–211.
[4] Charles LA Clarke, Maheedhar Kolla, Gordon V Cormack, Olga Vechtomova, Azin Ashkan, Stefan Büttcher, and Ian MacKinnon. 2008. Novelty and diversity in information retrieval evaluation. In *SIGIR'2008.* ACM, 659–666.
[5] Godfrey Harold Hardy, John Edensor Littlewood, and George Pólya. 1952. *Inequalities.* Cambridge university press.
[6] Scott B Huffman and Michael Hochster. 2007. How well does result relevance predict session satisfaction?. In *SIGIR'2007.* ACM, 567–574.
[7] Kalervo Järvelin and Jaana Kekäläinen. 2002. Cumulated gain-based evaluation of IR techniques. *ACM Transactions on Information Systems (TOIS)* 20, 4 (2002), 422–446.
[8] Kalervo Järvelin, Susan L Price, Lois ML Delcambre, and Marianne Lykke Nielsen. 2008. Discounted cumulated gain based evaluation of multiple-query IR sessions. In *ECIR'2008.* Springer, 4–15.
[9] Evangelos Kanoulas, Ben Carterette, Paul D Clough, and Mark Sanderson. 2011. Evaluating multi-query sessions. In *SIGIR'2011.* ACM, 1053–1062.
[10] Tomoharu Kokubu, Tetsuya Sakai, Yoshimi Saito, Hideki Tsutsui, Toshihiko Manabe, Makoto Koyama, and Hiroko Fujii. 2005. The Relationship between Answer Ranking and User Satisfaction in a Question Answering System.. In *NTCIR'2005.*
[11] Chung Tong Lee, Vishwa Vinay, Eduarda Mendes Rodrigues, Gabriella Kazai, Nataša Milic-Frayling, and Aleksandar Ignjatovic. 2009. Measuring system performance and topic discernment using generalized adaptive-weight mean. In *CIKM'2009.* ACM, 2033–2036.
[12] Jiyun Luo, Christopher Wing, Hui Yang, and Marti Hearst. 2013. The water filling model and the cube test: multi-dimensional evaluation for professional search. In *CIKM'2013.* ACM, 709–714.
[13] Stephen Robertson. 2006. On GMAP: and other transformations. In *CIKM'2006.* ACM, 78–83.
[14] Stephen E Robertson. 1977. The probability ranking principle in IR. *Journal of documentation* 33, 4 (1977), 294–304.
[15] Tetsuya Sakai. 2016. Simple and Effective Approach to Score Standardisation. In *ICTIR'2016.* ACM, 95–104.
[16] Mark D Smucker and Charles LA Clarke. 2012. Time-based calibration of effectiveness measures. In *SIGIR'2012.* ACM, 95–104.
[17] William Webber, Alistair Moffat, and Justin Zobel. 2008. Score standardization for inter-collection comparison of retrieval systems. In *SIGIR'2008.* ACM, 51–58.
[18] Grace Hui Yang and Ian Soboroff. 2016. TREC 2016 Dynamic Domain Track Overview. (2016).
[19] Yiming Yang and Abhimanyu Lad. 2009. Modeling expected utility of multi-session information distillation. In *ICTIR'2009.* Springer, 164–175.
[20] Mihalis Yannakakis and Fanica Gavril. 1980. Edge dominating sets in graphs. *SIAM J. Appl. Math.* 38, 3 (1980), 364–372.
[21] Emine Yilmaz, Manisha Verma, Nick Craswell, Filip Radlinski, and Peter Bailey. 2014. Relevance and effort: an analysis of document utility. In *CIKM'2014.* ACM.
[22] Cheng Xiang Zhai, William W Cohen, and John Lafferty. 2003. Beyond independent relevance: methods and evaluation metrics for subtopic retrieval. In *SIGIR'2003.* ACM, 10–17.

Information Retrieval Evaluation as Search Simulation: A General Formal Framework for IR Evaluation

Yinan Zhang
Department of Computer Science
University of Illinois at
Urbana-Champaign
Urbana, IL 61801
yzhng103@illinois.edu

Xueqing Liu
Department of Computer Science
University of Illinois at
Urbana-Champaign
Urbana, IL 61801
xliu93@illinois.edu

ChengXiang Zhai
Department of Computer Science
University of Illinois at
Urbana-Champaign
Urbana, IL 61801
czhai@illinois.edu

ABSTRACT

While the Cranfield evaluation methodology based on test collections has been very useful for evaluating simple IR systems that return a ranked list of documents, it has significant limitations when applied to search systems with interface features going beyond a ranked list, and sophisticated interactive IR systems in general. In this paper, we propose a general formal framework for evaluating IR systems based on search session simulation that can be used to perform reproducible experiments for evaluating any IR system, including interactive systems and systems with sophisticated interfaces. We show that the traditional Cranfield evaluation method can be regarded as a special instantiation of the proposed framework where the simulated search session is a user sequentially browsing the presented search results. By examining a number of existing evaluation metrics in the proposed framework, we reveal the exact assumptions they have made implicitly about the simulated users and discuss possible ways to improve these metrics. We further show that the proposed framework enables us to evaluate a set of tag-based search interfaces, a generalization of faceted browsing interfaces, producing results consistent with real user experiments and revealing interesting findings about effectiveness of the interfaces for different types of users.

CCS CONCEPTS

• **Information systems** → **Evaluation of retrieval results**;

KEYWORDS

IR evaluation; User simulation; Interface card

ACM Reference format:
Yinan Zhang, Xueqing Liu, and ChengXiang Zhai. 2017. Information Retrieval Evaluation as Search Simulation: A General Formal Framework for IR Evaluation. In *Proceedings of ICTIR '17, Amsterdam, Netherlands, October 01-04, 2017,* 8 pages.
https://doi.org/.1145/3121050.3121070

1 INTRODUCTION

Information Retrieval (IR) is an empirically defined task in the sense that there is no way to mathematically prove one IR system is better than another, and the question of which IR system is the best can only be answered based on how well the system can help users finish a task. Thus, how to appropriately evaluate an information retrieval (IR) system has always been one of the most important research questions in IR [10, 14, 22]. So far, the dominant methodology for evaluating an IR system has been the Cranfield evaluation methodology proposed in 1960s [24]. The basic idea is to build a test collection that consists of a sample of queries, a sample of documents, and a set of relevance judgments (indicating which documents are relevant/non-relevant to which queries). An IR system can then be evaluated using such a test collection as follows. First, we run the system on the test collection to generate retrieval results for each of the test queries. We then quantitatively evaluate the system results for each query with various measures (such as precision and recall) based on the relevance judgments. Measures on all the queries can be aggregated to quantify the performance of a system on the whole set of queries. Such a methodology has also been widely used for evaluating many other empirical tasks, including particularly machine learning tasks.

A key benefit of using the Cranfield evaluation methodology is that the test collection, once built, would be reusable as many times as we want to, which enables repeatedly using the *same* test collection to compare different systems or examine the effectiveness of each component in a complicated system. Such reusability is key to ensure reproducibility of IR experiments. The Cranfield evaluation methodology has played a crucial role in advancing IR technologies, and the reusability of the created test collections has enabled the development of many effective retrieval algorithms that are used in many modern search engine applications today.

Unfortunately, the Cranfield evaluation methodology, in its current form, can only be used for evaluating simple IR systems that return a ranked list of documents, and would encounter significant difficulty when applied to more sophisticated IR systems which have become increasingly popular due to the advancement in technologies for human-computer interaction. In particular, it is hard to use it to evaluate an interactive IR system where we need to assess the overall performance of a system over an entire interactive search session and compare two different search interfaces that may go beyond a ranked list of documents (e.g., an interface with features such as query suggestion or faceted browsing); such sophisticated IR systems have so far been evaluated primarily through controlled user studies [14] or a proxy of such a user study experiment by performing search log analysis [9]. However, the experiment results obtained in such a way would be hard to reproduce due to the difficulty in completely controlling the users.

In this paper, we propose a general formal framework for evaluating IR systems based on search session simulation that can be used to evaluate *any* IR system with *reproducible experiments*, including systems with sophisticated retrieval interfaces. The key idea is to build "user simulators," which are software programs that can simulate how a user would interact with a search engine (interface) when trying to finish a task. With a set of such user-task simulators, we can then test each IR system by having the system interact with the simulators. The interaction sequence of system responses and user actions can then be used to compute various quantitative measures of the system based on how effective the system has helped the (simulated) user finish a task.

We show that such a simulation-based evaluation framework is, in fact, a generalization of the traditional Cranfield evaluation method to enable reproducible experiments to evaluate or compare sophisticated IR systems. The current ranked list evaluation method can be derived quite naturally as a specific instantiation of the framework, where the simulated search session is a user sequentially browsing the presented search results.

One immediate benefit of the proposed framework is that it enables us to examine any existing evaluation metric *formally* from the perspective of user simulation, which further helps reveal the exact assumptions a metric has made (often implicitly) about the simulated users. The analysis also helps provide an interpretation of any metric from a user's perspective. We formally study several widely used measures, Precision, Recall, and Average Precision (AP), and reveal the assumptions made by these measures.

A more important benefit of the framework is that it would enable us to evaluate more complicated IR systems that are hard to evaluate with existing evaluation methods. As a case study to pursue this benefit, we build search session simulators to evaluate a set of tag-based search interfaces, a generalization of faceted browsing interfaces, with validation of our proposed framework from real user experiments and interesting findings about effectiveness of the interfaces for different types of users.

2 RELATED WORK

Evaluation has always been a central research topic in IR; the three surveys by Sanderson [22], Kelly [14], and Harman [10] have covered most progress in IR evaluation research, though many newer papers on the topic have been published since those three surveys were written, notably the axiomatic approaches to IR evaluation [4], and applications of statistical analysis techniques. Cranfield test-collection evaluation methodology proposed a long time ago [24] remains the dominant evaluation method in IR for comparing different retrieval algorithms today, and the ranking performance is often assessed using measures such as Precision, Recall, MAP and/or NDCG. It was demonstrated in [20] that MAP could be derived under certain user behavior assumptions, which was one of the initial attempts to interpret IR evaluation metrics from the perspective of user behavior models. Additional evaluation measures have been proposed and used for evaluating various IR tasks, such as α-NDCG[8], Rank-based Precision [18], Expected Reciprocal

Rank [6], and time-based measures [23]. A very recent study [27] proposed a novel Bejeweled Player Model for evaluating IR systems, which could not only cover many existing metrics as special case but also provide a more principled and refined model for users' stopping behaviors when scanning along a ranked list. However, while these approaches work well for evaluating retrieval results in the form of a ranked list, it is unclear how it can be applied to evaluate an interactive retrieval system associated with more diversified interface elements and user behaviors. The proposed simulation-based evaluation framework breaks this limitation and generalizes the previous evaluation method to provide a principled way to evaluate any interactive system.

User studies are also often conducted to evaluate an IR system, including both small-scale controlled studies and larger-scale user studies using A/B test. While such an evaluation method involves real users and accurately reflects the utility of a retrieval system in application settings, it has a serious drawback (as compared with Cranfield evaluation method) in not being reproducible. A main point of our paper is that the only way to enable reproducible experiments with interactive IR systems is through user simulation. The framework can be regarded as both a generalization of the test collection approach to enable evaluation of interactive IR systems, and an "artificial" way to perform interactive user studies.

A previous work [5] has already made an attempt to evaluate session search by doing simulation; our work is a step forward to propose a more general framework. Indeed, it appears that we have no choice but to use such a simulation framework if we want to perform reproducible experiments to evaluate an interactive retrieval system with sophisticated interfaces since this appears to be the only way to control the user. Our work is also related to the recent work by the Glasgow group on user simulation (see, e.g., the simulation toolkit [16]), but our goal of doing simulation is different, i.e., it is to evaluate an arbitrary IR system.

There have been extensive studies on evaluating ranking systems' performance using simulated user [5, 15, 26]. Traditional IR studies have long been focusing on modeling users' click behaviors [7] and relevance feedback [13, 15]. Recent studies have gone beyond click models to simulate other aspects of user behavior, including simulating user queries [26] (often based on language models [2, 12, 26]), simulating a user's stopping behavior [17, 25] based on gain/cost ratio [19], and query reformulation [5]. A common weakness of these studies is that they are mostly based on random sampling instead of learning from real user behavior [5]. As a result, it remains a challenge how to fairly compare different algorithms using results generated by these simulators. However, they can be leveraged to build an accurate simulator for use in the proposed evaluation framework.

The line of work on economic models for IR [1, 3] studied user interactions with an interactive IR system from the perspective of economic factors, e.g. reward/cost. Our proposed framework also models user reward/cost factors but focuses on evaluating the IR system.

3 SEARCH SIMULATION FRAMEWORK

In this section, We formally characterize our proposed search simulation framework for interactive IR evaluation. We first explicitly define the basic components in the framework at the level of the whole interaction.

Definition 3.1 (System, User, Task and Interaction Sequence). In any interaction involving two parties issuing actions to each other in turn, we define the *(interactive) system S* to be the party to be evaluated, the *user U* to be the other party, the *task T* to be the user's information need, and the *interaction sequence I* to be the whole process of the interaction.

A user may have different information need, or task, when using a system, and the user with a specific task may result in different interaction sequences due to the randomness of the user actions and the system responses.

Definition 3.2 (Simulator). A *simulator* is a (synthetic) user with a task, created for the purpose of evaluating a system.

In general, a system's performance over an interaction sequence can be measured in two dimensions from a user's perspective: reward and cost:

Definition 3.3 (Interaction / Simulator Reward and Cost). For an interaction sequence I between a user U with task T and an interactive system S, the *interaction reward $R(I, T, U, S)$* and the *interaction cost $C(I, T, U, S)$* respectively represent the overall amount of reward and cost the user gets from the whole interaction. For a simulator simulating a user U with task T and an interactive system S, the *simulator reward $R(T, U, S)$* and the *simulator cost $C(T, U, S)$* respectively represent the expected interaction reward and cost over all possible interaction sequences: $R(T, U, S) = E(R(I, T, U, S))$ and $C(T, U, S) = E(C(I, T, U, S))$, where the expectation is taken with respect to the distribution of all possible interaction sequences, $p(I|T, U, S)$.

Note that $p(I|T, U, S)$ would be entirely concentrated on a single interaction sequence if the interaction is deterministic.

The simulator reward $R(T, U, S)$ and cost $C(T, U, S)$ provide a complete and interpretable characterization of the utility of system S to user U with task T: $C(T, U, S)$ measures the effort made by a user, while $R(T, U, S)$ gives the reward that a user would receive for the effort. We chose to maintain reward and cost as two separate measures because the desired trade-off between them is inevitably application-specific, thus it should be treated as an external application of our framework. Moreover, we can easily further define the average utility and cost of a system over a group of simulators to obtain an overall reward and cost, or first combine reward and cost for each individual simulator and then compute the average over a group of simulators; these again would be better treated as applications of the framework. We will see some interesting examples in Section 4.

The formalism established above serves as a high-level framework for assessing interactive retrieval systems in general on the whole interaction level, in particular by evaluating the reward and cost of a task oriented user when interacting with the system through an interaction sequence. To assess the reward and cost at a finer level, we must define the interaction sequence in more detail. To this end, we follow the Interface Card Model [28] and partition the interaction between a user and an interactive IR system into a series of interaction laps:

Definition 3.4 (Lap, Action and Interface Card). The *lap* $t = 1, 2, \ldots$ is the time unit of the interaction between a user and a system in which the user and the system each acts once in turn. In each lap t, the user first issues an *action a^t*, and the system then reacts by generating an *interface card q^t*. The *stopping action a_B^t* is a special action the user could issue in each lap which ends the interaction.

It is often the case that there is certain level of intrinsic randomness in the user action and the system's interface cards. In this work, we focus more on the user side, and we will later adopt a user action model describing the probabilistic distribution of the user actions at each lap.

When different users interact with the same system, or even when the same user interacts with the same system at different times, the user might tend to issue different actions, depending on e.g. the user's habits, information need (task), and any past interactions between the user and the system. We characterize such user side information by user state (which we adopt from [29]):

Definition 3.5 (User State). At each lap t, the *user state z^t* denotes the collection of all the information that as a whole is sufficient to determine how likely the user issues each possible action given any interface card the system issues. The user state starts from the initial user state z^1, which depends on the user U and the task T and follows an *initial user state distribution $p_I(z^1)$*. The user state then transitions across laps probabilistically via the *user state transition function $p_T(z^{t+1}|z^t, a^t, q^t)$*.

Intuitively, the user state in many cases could be in the form of a multi-dimensional vector where each element denotes some aspect of the status of the interaction process, e.g. the stage of the interaction process, the remaining information need, etc. Based on the user state, we formalize the action model of the user:

Definition 3.6 (User Action Model). The *user action model* specifies the probability distribution of the user issuing each possible user action in a given lap, where the probabilities are conditioned on the user state and the interface card: $p(a^{t+1}|z^t, q^t)$.

We can now define the interaction sequence on a finer level:

Definition 3.7 (Interface Card Interaction Sequence). For an interaction process between a system S and a user U with task T, the interaction sequence I is composed of the sequence of user states, the user actions and the interface cards in the whole interaction: $I = ((z^1, a^1, q^1), (z^2, a^2, q^2), \ldots, (z^n, a^n, q^n))$, where n denotes the total number of laps in the interaction. We define I^t to be the partial interaction sequence from lap 1 to lap t, $1 \le t \le n$. ($I = I^n$.)

The interaction reward and cost can now be refined as follows:

Definition 3.8 (Cumulative / Lap Reward and Cost). For user U with task T, system S and interaction sequence I, the *cumulative reward* and *cumulative cost* at lap t are respectively the total reward and cost the user obtains by the end of lap t: $R^t(I, T, U, S) = R(I^t, T, U, S)$, and $C^t(I, T, U, S) = C(I^t, T, U, S)$. The *lap reward* and *lap cost* are respectively the difference of cumulative reward and cost between consecutive laps: $r^t(I, T, U, S) = R^t(I, T, U, S) - R^{t-1}(I, T, U, S)$, and $c^t(I, T, U, S) = C^t(I, T, U, S) - C^{t-1}(I, T, U, S)$. (We define $R^0(I, T, U, S) = C^0(I, T, U, S) = 0$.)

The notion of cumulative reward and cost provides the basis for the simulator to track the reward and cost measures progressively along the interaction process. The lap reward and cost may depend on many factors related to the user's current status and past interactions. To simplify the discussion, we assume that the user state contains the information sufficient to determine the lap reward and cost (in addition to the user action model) given any interface card:

Definition 3.9 (Action Reward and Cost). The lap reward and cost are determined by the user's action, the user state, and the system's previous interface card (if any), and are also called the *action reward and* action cost: $r^t(I, T, U, S) = r(a^t|z^t, q^{t-1})$, $c^t(I, T, U, S) = c(a^t|z^t, q^{t-1})$. (There will not be the term q^{t-1} when $t = 1$.)

We expand out the cumulative interaction reward and cost as a summation over action reward and cost, forming the computational basis for our proposed search simulation evaluation framework:

$$R^t(I, T, U, S) = \sum_{i=1}^{t} r(a^i|z^i, q^{i-1}) \tag{1}$$

$$C^t(I, T, U, S) = \sum_{i=1}^{t} c(a^i|z^i, q^{i-1}) \tag{2}$$

4 ANALYSIS OF EXISTING METRICS

In this section, we formally analyze some commonly used existing evaluation metrics using the proposed framework to reveal the (implicit) assumptions made underlying each measure and understand how we should interpret them based on the reward and cost defined on the user simulation.

We first instantiate the framework to obtain a general simulator for classical IR metrics:

Definition 4.1 (Classical IR simulator). The simulator's task is to find relevant documents by going through a ranked list of documents. At each lap t, the interface card is the document ranked at position t. The user is assumed to sequentially browse the list and choose from three actions: click, skip or stop at each lap t. We assume the simulator will always click a relevant document, and when seeing a non-relevant document, the user may skip or stop depending on the specific setting. The lap reward is 1 for a relevant document and 0 otherwise, and the cumulative reward is thus the number of relevant documents the simulator scanned through. The lap cost is 1 for each document scanned by the simulator, and the cumulative cost is the total number of documents the simulator scanned through. The cumulative reward and cost are recorded in the user state.

The classical IR simulator serves as a common basis for further instantiations into specific simulators corresponding to each classical IR evaluation metric. In the following sections, we assume we have a test collection consisting of a number of queries and the relevance judgment labels of a set of documents with respect to each query, and our goal is to evaluate a ranked list of results generated by a system in response to a query. We will show that Precision, Recall, and Average Precision can all be interpreted from the perspective of our proposed reward and cost measures when specific simulators are used. These simulators can help reveal the assumptions made

by these measures and also provide interpretations of them from a user's perspective.

We first examine precision and recall, two of the most fundamental metrics in IR:

Definition 4.2 (Precision). Given a list of retrieval results, the traditional measure Precision can be defined as the ratio of interaction reward and cost, i.e., $R(I, T, U, S)/C(I, T, U, S)$, of a classical IR simulator that would never stop until having scanned through the whole result list.

The Precision Simulator shows clearly that Precision is focused on measuring the reward per unit of cost, but does not take into consideration of task completion; the task is not well specified, but the implied task can be assumed to be to find as many relevant documents as possible.

Definition 4.3 (Recall). Suppose there are N relevant documents in the collection. Given a list of retrieval results, the traditional measure Recall can be defined as the task completion percentage $R(I, T, U, S)/N$, i.e. the interaction reward relative to the best possible interaction reward for perfectly completed task, for a classical IR simulator that never stops until having scanned through the whole list.

It is easy to see that the assumed task in the Recall Simulator is to find *all* relevant documents. Meanwhile, Recall is only focused on the collected reward, but does not measure the cost at all. Even if we combine Precision and Recall, there is still no direct measure of the cost, and the cost is only indirectly reflected in the Precision (relative to the reward). Interestingly, we can interpret the reciprocal of Precision as the average cost per relevant document (more generally, cost/reward ratio).

Definition 4.4 (Precision@K / Recall@K). Precision@K and Recall@K are defined similarly as how Precision and Recall are defined except that such a simulator would stop when the accumulated cost (which is equal to the number of documents examined by the simulator) reaches K.

This definition shows that Precision@K and Recall@K can be interpreted as Precision and Recall with a "cost budget," i.e., the simulated user wants to control the amount of effort. We can thus easily generalize both measures by allowing variable cost in examining each document/snippet (e.g., examining a longer document/snippet would have a higher cost) and using a cost threshold τ_c, leading to Precision@τ_c and Recall@τ_c, respectively.

We now examine one of the most important measures, Average Precision (AP). We first define the variable-recall simulator:

Definition 4.5 (Variable-Recall Simulator). A variable-recall simulator is a classical IR simulator whose task is to collect N' relevant documents, where $1 \leq N' \leq N$ (N is the total number of relevant documents). The simulated user never stops scanning through the list until either the task is completed or the list is exhausted.

Definition 4.6 (Average Precision). In the simulation framework, Average Precision can be defined as the average ratio of the interaction reward and cost: $R(I, T, U, S)/C(I, T, U, S)$ for a set of N variable-recall simulators, each with the task of collecting $1, 2, \ldots, N$ relevant documents, respectively.

By examining AP in the simulation framework, we see that AP should be interpreted as the average performance of a system on a set of *different* retrieval tasks or *different* simulated users. While the Precision and Recall simulators only simulate a single user/task, the AP simulator simulates a set of users with variable recall demand; this explains why AP is more discriminative than Precision/Recall, and is thus also more suitable for comparing two ranked lists. This analysis result further suggests that in general, we can systematically vary the parameter of any simulator (recall in the case of AP) to obtain more discriminative measures that can better detect even the smallest differences between two ranking methods; AP is only one of the many such possibilities and may not necessarily be the best one.

The variant of AP@K can be easily derived by setting a cost budget for all the simulated users as in the case of Precision/Recall@K.

Many other evaluation metrics such as Mean Reciprocal Rank (MRR) [6], Ranked-Based Precision (RBP) [18], Normalized Discounted Cumulative Gain (NDCG), time-based measures [23], can also be studied rigorously in the framework to reveal their assumptions about users and tasks. For example, MRR is obtained when a precision simulator has a task of only finding one relevant document (and then stop). RBP assumes, on top of the precision simulator, a constant stopping rate at each position of the ranked list. In NDCG, the discounting factors for each ranked position also correspond to the simulator's stopping rate at each position, and the overall gain calculated is the simulator's expected reward over all stopping positions. The time-based evaluation is closely related, only except that the probability of stopping depends on the time spent into the search session (i.e., time cost) instead of on the lap count. Due to the space, we cannot include details of these derivations.

We could also easily extend our instantiations to generalizations of evaluation metrics on session search. For example, Session NDCG [11] could be derived similarly as classic NDCG, only with the additional simulator action model for continuing / abandoning the search after scanning through the document list of each query in the session. The U-measure based on trail-text proposed in [21], as another example, could be derived from our proposed framework by dividing the simulator's interaction with the system into word-level laps, and the simulator may abandon the search after reading till each word (e.g. in snippet, document, etc.).

The great generality of our framework is not a coincidence; it is a natural consequence of the basis of our framework - the simulator and the reward / cost measures - which are the minimal basis that maps to real world users and what they care about in an IR system; all existing metrics tried to achieve the same goal but with additional simplification assumptions for the sake of computational convenience. In particular, for example, our analysis based on the simulator models suggest that one major class of assumption underlying the existing evaluation metrics is on when and how likely the user stops throughout the interaction, and every assumption has its own advantages as well as drawbacks when compared with real user behaviors. A very important future direction is thus to study users' stopping tendencies more rigorously and propose more realistic user stopping action models, which can then be used in the proposed framework to derive more meaningful metrics than the existing ones.

5 SIMULATED EVALUATION ON TAG-BASED SEARCH INTERFACE

In this section, we apply our proposed general framework on interactive retrieval systems that do not follow a simple ranking interface, and show that an instantiation of our proposed general framework could lead to novel evaluation method for interactive systems where no traditional evaluation methodology could be applied in a principled way.

We focus on a set of interactive retrieval interfaces where, in addition to lists of documents, tags related to the document contents are used to facilitate user navigation. A common example of such tag-based search interfaces is the faceted browsing interface, where facet filters serve as tags to help users zoom into specific subsets of the documents. The Interface Card Model (ICM) proposed in [28] led to a novel method for optimizing tag-based search interfaces via automatically adjusting the interface layout based on the screen size and the estimated user interest. To evaluate and compare these relatively more sophisticated interactive retrieval interfaces, traditional evaluation methodologies focusing mainly on assessing ranked lists of documents could not be easily applied, because the user-system interactions do not adopt a sequential scanning manner. This is also the reason why the authors in [28] could only rely on real user experiments for the comparison experiments. In this work, as an example of demonstrating the effectiveness of our proposed search simulation framework, we show that an instantiation of the framework could lead to reasonable evaluation practices of the search interfaces on different types of users (or simulators), and we also validate the simulation by comparing the simulator behaviors with real user behaviors.

To instantiate the search simulation framework into a simulator model for the tag-based search interfaces, we assume that each screen the simulator sees is an interface card; the simulator could either select a document or a tag (if shown) on the screen, or click some other control buttons (e.g. scroll down / next page) to look for new content, and then the system displays a new interface card to the user and the interaction goes on. In the traditional faceted-browsing interfaces, the interface layout is *static*: on a moderate sized screen, there is typically a tag list on the left and a document list on the right, where the user could either scan through the documents, or scan through the tags to narrow down the set of documents shown on the right; on a very small screen (e.g. of a smart phone), only one of the two lists (i.e. the tag list or the document list) could be displayed at a time, and there usually is an extra button for the user to switch between the two lists. On the contrary, the interfaces proposed in [28], which we designate by "ICM interfaces," automatically adjust their layouts (e.g. between only showing tags, only showing documents, showing half-screen tags and half-screen documents, etc.), and the user either clicks a shown document / tag or click "next page" in each interaction lap.

We define the instantiation of our proposed search simulation framework for the case of tag-based search interfaces as follows:

Definition 5.1 (Tag-based search interface simulator). A *tag-based search interface simulator* U is assumed to be interested in one or a few documents in the collection, which are designated by the simulator's *target* document(s). The simulator's task T is to find all target document(s). The simulator's action model on the interface cards in a tag-based search interface is defined as follows (assuming τ, τ_1 and τ_2 are constants between 0 and 1):

(1) If the simulator sees a target document, they always click it, and in cases of multiple target documents, they click one of them uniformly randomly.

(2) Otherwise, if the simulator sees a tag related to a target document, they always click it, and in cases of multiple related tags, they click one of them uniformly randomly.

(3) Otherwise, they seek for the next card in a way depending on the type of the interface:

　a. On an ICM interface, they always click next card;

　b. On a moderately sized traditional static interface displaying both a tag list and a document list, the simulator scrolls down the document list with probability τ (designated as the *document tendency value*) and scrolls down the tag list with probability $(1-\tau)$;

　c. On a very small traditional static interface displaying only a tag list *or* a document list, if the simulator faces a document list (which is usually the case for the initial interface card), they scroll it down with probability τ_1 (designated as the *document inertia value*) and switch to the tag list with probability $(1-\tau_1)$; if the simulator faces a tag list, they scroll it down with probability τ_2 (designated as the *tag inertia value*) and switch to the document list with probability $(1-\tau_2)$.

(4) The simulator only and always stops when all target documents are found.

The lap cost is 1 for each lap the simulator undergoes, and the overall evaluation metrics is the simulator's interaction cost $C(I, T, U, S)$ for completing the task.

The implicit user state of the simulator is the task, i.e. the set of target documents, plus, for interacting with the very small static interface, the additional binary status of whether the user is browsing the document list or the tag list. The parameters τ, τ_1 and τ_2 could be very different for different types of users, and could be learned from user search logs.

Such an instantiation is apparently an overly simplified model for users in the real world, and it could be easily extended in a lot of aspects to reflect more realistic settings (e.g. with consideration of information scent when the simulator decides on what link to follow). As the very first example of instantiating our proposed search simulation framework, we stick with this simplified simulator model and demonstrate that it could lead to fairly reasonable and interesting evaluation results, leaving further extensions of the simulator to future research work.

5.1 Simulated Evaluation

We implemented the tag-based search interface simulators and use them to evaluate and compare the static interfaces and the ICM interfaces on a medium screen as well as on a small screen, where we used the New York Times API[1] to obtain news articles and keywords respectively as our documents and tags. The medium screen could hold up to 2 documents or 8 tags; on the static interface, 1 document alongside 4 tags on the left are displayed at a time. The small screen could hold up to 1 document or 4 tags; on the static interface, the (simulated) user needs to switch between the document list and the tag list. We vary the number of documents in

[1] https://developer.nytimes.com/

the collection as well as the parameters τ, τ_1 and τ_2. We assume the simulator is interested in only one (uniformly randomly selected) document in the collection in each search session, and we record down the average number of laps for the simulator to find the target document across multiple simulated sessions, which is an unbiased estimate of the simulator's interaction cost.

5.1.1 Medium screen. Figure 1 shows the interaction cost against different document tendency values τ on a medium screen with the static interface, and we set the number of documents in the collection to be either 30 or 100. It is firstly not surprising to find that the interaction cost is always lower on a collection of 30 documents than on a collection of 100 documents across all τ values, as it naturally takes less laps for the simulator to navigate in a smaller collection. It could also be observed that the cost tends to grow higher when τ is either too low or too high, suggesting that it is not a good idea for the simulator to stick too much to the document list (high τ), or too much to the tag list (low τ). Such an implication makes sense: sticking too much to the document list is essentially giving up the "zoom-in" functionality provided by the tags, whereas sticking too much to the tag list makes the simulator pay too little attention to the documents, which are after all what the simulator is really looking for. It is also interesting to observe that the negative effect of sticking too much to the document list (high τ) is weaker on the smaller collection, which is reasonable as keeping scrolling through a small collection is not a problem as serious as keeping scrolling through a large collection.

Note that the curves are observed to fluctuate a lot around their overall trends, since the effectiveness of the tags (news keywords) in helping the simulator narrow down to specific documents (news articles) could vary significantly depending on the specificity of the tags. Such fluctuations will also be seen in the other experiments we report.

Figure 1: Cost for different document tendency values (τ) on medium screen with static interface

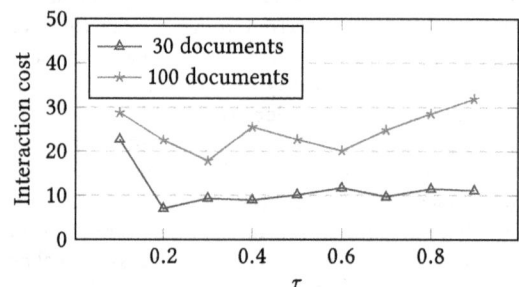

To use our simulators to compare the static interface with the ICM interface, we set $\tau = 0.3$ for the static interface, and Figure 2 shows the simulation result on both interfaces with various number of documents in the collection. Despite the expected fluctuations, we clearly observe that the ICM interface achieves more efficient navigation across all #documents than the static interface, and the interaction cost grows at a slower pace in the ICM interface than in the static interface as the collection size grows. We also tried setting τ to other values and obtained similar results. Such comparison outcomes coincide with the findings from real user studies in [28].

Figure 2: Cost comparison for medium screen

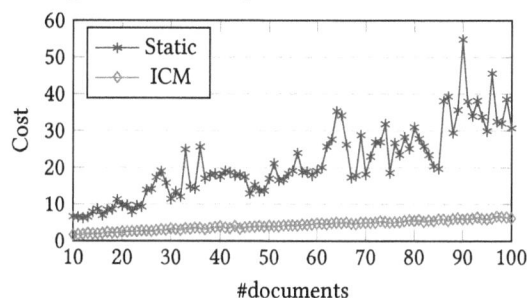

Figure 4: Cost comparison for small screen

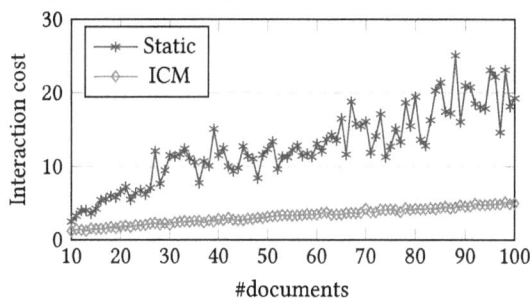

5.1.2 Small screen. On a small screen with static interface, there are two parameters, the document inertia τ_1 and the tag inertia τ_2, underlying the simulator's action model. Figure 3 shows the interaction cost for different combinations of τ_1 and τ_2 on top of a collection of 30 and 100 documents, with brighter color for lower cost and darker color for higher cost. In addition to what we observed on the medium screen - the cost in navigating through a smaller collection is lower than that in navigating in a larger collection - there are a couple of interesting findings unique to the small screen. Firstly, for both collection sizes, the cost is generally lower when the tag inertia is high ($\tau_2 \geq 0.7$), i.e. when the simulator tends to scan more tags before switching back to the document list. It is a reasonable strategy for the simulator to keep scanning through more tags, since discovering a good tag would eventually shrink the number of documents to look through even though it takes a few more scrolls on the tag list in the short run. Secondly, given a relatively high tag inertia τ_2, it is a good idea to keep the document inertia low in the smaller collection ($\tau_1 \leq 0.6$), while it is better to raise it higher in the larger collection (($\tau_1 \geq 0.5$). Such a finding also makes intuitive sense: when the document collection grows larger, the simulator should be more patient in scrolling through the document list rather than quickly jumping back to the tag list.

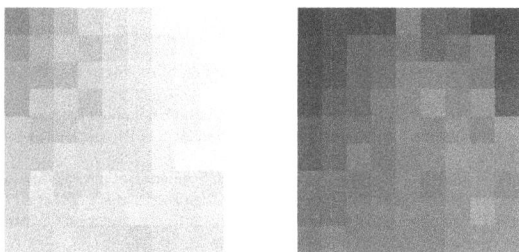

Figure 3: Heat maps of interaction cost (in log scale) for different document inertia (τ_1) and tag inertia (τ_2) values on small screen with static interface. Left: #documents = 30; right: #documents = 100. Top to bottom: τ_1 = 0.1 to 0.9; left to right (in each heat map): τ_2 = 0.1 to 0.9.

To compare the static interface with the ICM interface on the small screen, we set $\tau_1 = 0.5$ and $\tau_2 = 0.8$ for the simulator, and Figure 4 shows the interaction cost for the simulator on the two interfaces across different collection sizes. The comparison result is analogous to the one for the medium screen: the ICM interface achieves lower cost than the static interface, and the cost also grows slower on the ICM interface as the collection grows. The finding again coincides with those found in the real user studies in [28].

5.2 Validation from real user experiment

We conducted real user experiments on Amazon Mechanical Turk[2] following the scheme described in [28], and compare real user behaviors with the behaviors of our simulators. We gave users the task of finding a target news article of their choice and asked them to navigate through the static interface and the ICM interface, on both medium screens and small screens, and we record down the users' clicks throughout the interaction. On the medium sized static interface, we compute the users' average rate of choosing to scroll the document list across all laps as $\hat{\tau}$; on the small static interface, we compute the users' average rate of choosing to scroll the list across all document screens and all tag screens as $\hat{\tau}_1$ and $\hat{\tau}_2$, respectively. Table 1 displays the result.

Screen size	Sample size	Workers' average
Small	42	$\hat{\tau}_1 = 0.845, \hat{\tau}_2 = 0.370$
Medium	38	$\hat{\tau} = 0.211$

Table 1: Real user action averages

It could be observed that on the medium static screen, the users have a relatively low tendency ($\hat{\tau} = 0.211$) on average to stick to scrolling the document list, and such a $\hat{\tau}$ value also led to a fairly good interaction cost measure in our simulation experiments as observed in Figure 1. In other words, the real users are generally able to utilize the tags nearly optimally in facilitating their navigation on the medium static screen. On the small static screen, on the other hand, the users have a high inertia ($\hat{\tau}_1 = 0.845$) of keeping scrolling through the document list, but a relatively low inertia ($\hat{\tau}_2 = 0.370$) of scrolling through the tag list. Such a combination of $\hat{\tau}_1$ and $\hat{\tau}_2$ values resides in the lower-left portion in the two heat maps in Figure 3, which led in sub-optimal interaction cost measures in our simulation experiments. The users navigating on the small static interface do not tend to switch to the tag list when they are scrolling through the documents, and even when they switch to the tag list, they quickly switch back to the document list without exploring more tags when they could not find a relevant tag. The reason is most likely that the small screen only has space for either the document list or the tag list, and is initially showing the document list, so a lot of users merely follow the document list, and might only consider the switch as a glimpse of what tags might be there and do not recognize the power of exploring more tags; on the contrary, the medium screen always displays both the documents and the tags, so the users are free to explore both lists without taking any extra effort in switching between the lists.

[2]https://www.mturk.com/

The authors in [28] conducted real user experiments to compare the ICM and static interfaces on small and medium screens, and concluded that the ICM interface is more efficient in helping users navigate, and also that the benefit of ICM over the static interface is more striking on the small screen than on the medium screen. In our experiment and analysis, with the tag-based search interface simulator as an extension of our proposed search simulation framework, we reached the same conclusion that the ICM interface is better as shown in Figure 2 and 4, which validates that our proposed search simulation framework could reliably assess the effectiveness of search interfaces. More interestingly, by comparing the real users' actions with the spectrum of our simulators' action model, we observe that the real users adopt a nearly optimal strategy on the medium screen yet a sub-optimal strategy on the small screen, which are novel insights into the reason why the difference between ICM and static interfaces in user navigation efficiency is more significant on the small screen as concluded in [28]. Such novel insights would be hardly possible to draw without establishing the proposed search simulation framework. These results also highlight another important benefit of the proposed simulation framework for understanding user behavior in detail by fitting simulators to real user interaction log data.

6   CONCLUSIONS AND FUTURE WORK

We presented a new general framework for evaluating arbitrary information retrieval (IR) systems based on search session simulation. The motivation for this framework is to enable reproducible experimental evaluation of sophisticated IR systems, particularly interactive IR systems, in the same spirit as the Cranfield evaluation methodology. The main idea is to generalize the current Cranfield evaluation method based on a test collection to one based on a set of user-task simulators and measures defined on a whole interaction session. We examine multiple commonly used measures in IR evaluation in this framework and show that they can all be derived as special cases of the framework under various assumptions about the user that they (implicitly) intend to simulate. Analysis of these assumptions reveals insights about how to improve these measures, which not only are practically useful, but also point out interesting new research directions. We also propose a way to construct user simulators for evaluating a set of tag-based search interfaces, and conduct simulation experiments to assess the effectiveness of different interface layout strategies. We show that such systems, which cannot be evaluated using any existing method in a principled way, can now be evaluated using the constructed simulators with interesting observations.

The proposed framework lays a theoretical foundation for experimental studies of sophisticated IR systems and opens up many new research directions. For example, we can use the framework to derive potentially better metrics than the existing ones that we analyzed, and to further analyze many more evaluation metrics of various tasks. The framework also opens up many interesting opportunities to leverage search log data to build various realistic user simulators for evaluating potentially very complicated search systems.

REFERENCES

[1] Leif Azzopardi. 2014. Modelling Interaction with Economic Models of Search. In *SIGIR '14*. 3–12.
[2] Leif Azzopardi, Maarten de Rijke, and Krisztian Balog. 2007. Building simulated queries for known-item topics: an analysis using six european languages.. In *SIGIR '07*. 455–462.
[3] Leif Azzopardi and Guido Zuccon. 2016. An Analysis of the Cost and Benefit of Search Interactions. In *ICTIR '16*. 59–68.
[4] Luca Busin and Stefano Mizzaro. 2013. Axiometrics: An Axiomatic Approach to Information Retrieval Effectiveness Metrics.. In *ICTIR '13*. 8.
[5] Ben Carterette, Ashraf Bah, and Mustafa Zengin. 2015. Dynamic Test Collections for Retrieval Evaluation.. In *ICTIR '15*. 91–100.
[6] Olivier Chapelle, Donald Metlzer, Ya Zhang, and Pierre Grinspan. 2009. Expected reciprocal rank for graded relevance. In *CIKM '09*. 621–630.
[7] Aleksandr Chuklin, Ilya Markov, and Maarten de Rijke. 2015. *Click Models for Web Search*. Morgan & Claypool Publishers.
[8] Charles L.A. Clarke, Maheedhar Kolla, Gordon V. Cormack, Olga Vechtomova, Azin Ashkan, Stefan Büttcher, and Ian MacKinnon. 2008. Novelty and Diversity in Information Retrieval Evaluation. In *SIGIR '08*. 659–666.
[9] Susan Dumais, Edward Cutrell, JJ Cadiz, Gavin Jancke, Raman Sarin, and Daniel C. Robbins. 2003. Stuff I've Seen: A System for Personal Information Retrieval and Re-use. In *SIGIR '03*. 72–79.
[10] Donna Harman. 2011. *Information Retrieval Evaluation*. Morgan & Claypool Publishers.
[11] Kalervo Järvelin, Susan L Price, Lois ML Delcambre, and Marianne Lykke Nielsen. 2008. Discounted cumulated gain based evaluation of multiple-query IR sessions. In *ECIR*. Springer, 4–15.
[12] Chris Jordan, Carolyn R. Watters, and Qigang Gao. 2006. Using controlled query generation to evaluate blind relevance feedback algorithms.. In *JCDL*. ACM, 286–295.
[13] Kalervo JÄrvelin. 2009. Interactive relevance feedback with graded relevance and sentence extraction: simulated user experiments.. In *CIKM* (2009-11-17). ACM, 2053–2056.
[14] Diane Kelly. 2009. Methods for Evaluating Interactive Information Retrieval Systems with Users. *Foundations and Trends in Information Retrieval* 3, 1-2 (2009), 1–224.
[15] Heikki Keskustalo, Kalervo JÄrvelin, and Ari Pirkola. 2008. Evaluating the effectiveness of relevance feedback based on a user simulation model: effects of a user scenario on cumulated gain value. *Inf. Retr.* 11, 3 (2008), 209–228.
[16] David Maxwell and Leif Azzopardi. 2016. Simulating Interactive Information Retrieval: SimIIR: A Framework for the Simulation of Interaction. In *SIGIR '16*. 1141–1144.
[17] David Maxwell, Leif Azzopardi, Kalervo JÄrvelin, and Heikki Keskustalo. 2015. An Initial Investigation into Fixed and Adaptive Stopping Strategies.. In *SIGIR*. ACM, 903–906.
[18] Alistair Moffat and Justin Zobel. 2008. Rank-biased Precision for Measurement of Retrieval Effectiveness. *ACM Trans. Inf. Syst.* 27, 1, Article 2 (Dec. 2008), 27 pages.
[19] Peter Pirolli and Stuart Card. 1999. Information Foraging. *Psychological Review* 106 (1999), 643–675.
[20] Stephen Robertson. 2008. A New Interpretation of Average Precision. In *SIGIR '08*. 689–690.
[21] Tetsuya Sakai and Zhicheng Dou. 2013. Summaries, Ranked Retrieval and Sessions: A Unified Framework for Information Access Evaluation. In *SIGIR '13*. 473–482.
[22] Mark Sanderson. 2010. Test Collection Based Evaluation of Information Retrieval Systems. *Foundations and Trends in Information Retrieval* 4, 4 (2010), 247–375.
[23] Mark D. Smucker and Charles L.A. Clarke. 2012. Time-based Calibration of Effectiveness Measures. In *SIGIR '12*. 95–104.
[24] Karen Sparck Jones and Peter Willett (Eds.). 1997. *Readings in Information Retrieval*. Morgan Kaufmann Publishers Inc., San Francisco, CA, USA.
[25] Paul Thomas, Alistair Moffat, Peter Bailey, and Falk Scholer. 2014. Modeling decision points in user search behavior.. In *IIiX*. ACM, 239–242.
[26] Suzan Verberne, Maya Sappelli, Kalervo JÄrvelin, and Wessel Kraaij. 2015. User Simulations for Interactive Search: Evaluating Personalized Query Suggestion.. In *ECIR*, Vol. 9022. 678–690.
[27] Fan Zhang, Yiqun Liu, Xin Li, Min Zhang, Yinghui Xu, and Shaoping Ma. 2017. Evaluating Web Search with a Bejeweled Player Model. In *SIGIR '17*. 425–434.
[28] Yinan Zhang and Chengxiang Zhai. 2015. Information Retrieval As Card Playing: A Formal Model for Optimizing Interactive Retrieval Interface. In *SIGIR '15*. 685–694.
[29] Yinan Zhang and Chengxiang Zhai. 2016. A Sequential Decision Formulation of the Interface Card Model for Interactive IR. In *SIGIR '16*. 85–94.

A User Re-Modeling Approach to Item Recommendation using Complex Usage Data

Oren Sar Shalom*
IBM Research - Haifa, Israel
& Bar Ilan University
orensr@il.ibm.com

Haggai Roitman
IBM Research - Haifa, Israel
haggai@il.ibm.com

Yishay Mansour
Tel Aviv University, Israel
mansour@tau.ac.il

Amir Amihood†
Bar Ilan University, Israel
& Johns Hopkins University
amir@esc.biu.ac.il

ABSTRACT

We study the problem of item recommendation using complex usage data. We assume that users may interact with items in various ways, each such interaction generates a usage point which may be accompanied with multiple feedback types. In addition, each user may interact with each item multiple times. We propose a generic framework that re-models the user vectors as a post-processing step that can be applied to any Matrix Factorization (MF) method. Using an evaluation on several heterogeneous real-world datasets, we demonstrate the effectiveness of the approach and demonstrate its superiority over two alternative methods.

1 INTRODUCTION

In most real life scenarios, user-item interactions may be quite complex. Each such interaction may record multiple and diverse feedback types that could potentially be utilized for better learning of the user preferences for item recommendation. Additionally, a user may have multiple interactions with each item, implying repetitive preference patterns, which could be further utilized for enhancing the learning.

As an illustrative example, let us consider an online digital store use case. A user may view an item page, purchase it, write a review, etc. All in all, the user has several interactions with an item, each one defines a single *usage point*. A usage point may be associated with multiple *feedback types*, which can be diverse such as categorical, ordinal or numerical; discrete or continuous; explicit or implicit. For example, an item view event records a usage point that provides two feedback types: the type of the event itself ("view") and the event's time. While the first feedback type is categorical, the second one is continuous. Both feedback types are implicit. A usage point recorded for an item "review" event may provide the additional feedback of the rating, which is explicit and discrete.

Considering several feedback sources may help a Recommender System (RS) to better model its users' tastes. For example, augmenting a RS with additional implicit feedback sources may help to elevate its accuracy in situations where explicit feedback is insufficient [8, 11, 29].

Matrix Factorization (MF) is nowadays the leading method for implementing Recommender Systems (RS) [15]. MF methods are usually learned from user-item interaction data. However, handling rich user-item interactions data, such as in the use case above, using existing MF methods is hard, as there is no natural way to incorporate all possible properties of this data into these methods. Moreover, existing MF methods cannot trivially model users who interacted with the same item on different occasions, having each usage point recorded with various feedback types. Utilizing such data in a generic (domain-independent) way still remains a great challenge for RS designers.

1.1 A User Re-modeling Approach

We propose a novel generic framework for utilizing complex usage data for item recommendation. The approach is domain independent, capable of utilizing diverse feedback sources, independently of their types, including an unbounded number of interactions with the same user-item pair.

The proposed approach is applied as a post-processing step on the output of any underlying MF method, "upgrading" it to support complex usage data. By applying a retrospective analysis of the usage points, the approach learns for any given user the personalized weight (importance) of each item in her interactions history. Then, the method incorporates both the personalized weights and the latent item vectors originally inferred by the underlying MF method and derives a refined user-model (hence "user re-modeling").

Since a user may have an unbounded number of usage points with the same item, we make the observation that each *usage point* may differ in its contribution to the *item* importance. Such relative contribution is assumed to depend on the various feedback types accompanying each usage point. As an example, a usage point that records an item purchase may be more important than a usage point of the same item that records an item page view. As another example, by using the time of the usage points, our algorithm may reveal that recent usage points provide more up-to-date feedbacks

* This paper is part of the author's PhD thesis.
† Partially supported by ISF grant number 571/14.

on the user's tastes. Additionally, the very existence of multiple interactions with an item implies its personalized importance. Finally, a novel data-driven pooling (aggregation) scheme is proposed which estimates the personalized importance of an item by aggregating over the importance estimates of the various usage points of that item in the user's interaction history.

1.2 Contributions of the Approach

The key contribution of this paper is a framework that learns complex usage data. Specifically, we handle three different data phenomena, which are:

(1) Usage points may be associated with a varied number of feedback types. For instance, a "click" event may be accompanied with time only while a "purchase" event with time and amount.

(2) The feedback types are diverse and may be of any kind such as categorical, ordinal or numerical; discrete or continuous; explicit or implicit.

(3) Users may interact with the same item multiple times.

Each one of these data phenomena is very common in real life scenarios. Yet, so far, there exists no single generic algorithm that can handle any of these phenomena. Our approach is the first that considers *all* of these data phenomena and learns how to optimally incorporate them for item recommendation.

Another advantage is its deployment. As in any real-life production system, after a recommendation system is deployed, it is extremely hard, even sometimes impossible to modify its behavior. Our method allows utilizing the aforementioned data phenomena in an existing (possibly domain tailored) system without requiring actual change to the underlying MF method. This is accomplished by applying our approach as a *post-processing* step to *any* MF method.
in Section 5.

Finally, better modeling user interactions may mitigate the user cold start problem [2], a prominent problem in most real-life scenarios [24].

2 RELATED WORK

The majority of state-of-the-art recommender system implementations have been designed to consume only a single type of user feedback for user tastes learning [11, 23]. Some previous studies have suggested that combining several feedback sources together may improve recommendation quality (e.g., [12, 13, 17, 18, 29]), and some actual (domain-specific) recommender system implementations have been proposed [5, 6, 9, 14, 19, 26, 29, 31, 32].

Among these works, Tang et al. [29] have presented an empirical study over LinkedIn data with three prototype methods for incorporating multiple feedback types. However, the relative importance of various feedback types in [29] was manually determined and no attempt was done to automatically learn such weights.

Rendle [20] has developed *Factorization Machines* (FM), that can process rich user-item interaction vectors and mimic most factorization models using feature engineering. Previously, FM has obtained state-of-the-art results in context-aware recommendations [22]. For example, second order FM can learn to what extent a given user may prefer to watch movies on weekends and a given movie may

be preferred to be watched on weekends. However, this interpretation does not trivially hold in the multiple feedback types setting (i.e., it is less informative to know to what extent a user prefers to purchase items or just add them to her cart; yet we would like to know what is the importance of an item due to such interactions).

The authors of [27] coped with the problem of multiple relation types between entities (users and items in our case). They have considered binary relationships, which can be extended to categorical relations as well. In [19], they have trained a linear regression model using several feedback types (e.g., user ratings, track playcounts and recency) to predict user ratings for music recommendation. In [25], they considered recency, popularity etc. to optimize recommended lists. Yin et al. [31] recommended jokes to the JokeBox application users by augmenting explicit user votes with (implicit) pseudo-votes estimated from user application dwell times. Some other previous works have modeled multi-feedback data settings as *Heterogenous Information Networks* (HIN) [32]. Yu et. al [32] predicted item ratings by applying a Non-Negative MF method on several similarity matrices; each matrix was induced by PathSim – a graph path based entity similarity measure. Shi et. al [26] have provided further improvement by considering explicit user ratings. Guo et. al [9] proposed an alternative recommendation approach based on a random-walk on the HIN hyper-graph.

Finally, a couple of previous works [5, 6] have employed ensemble methods [1] as a post-processing step, used to combine the recommendations of several underlying recommenders; each trained over a single feedback type. Domingues et al. [6] have simply averaged the item scores obtained from several independent recommenders, each trained on a (single) different feedback type. Da Costa and Manzato [5] proposed an ensemble approach that predicted item rating as the linear combination of several item ratings, each initially predicted by a given underlying recommender trained using a single feedback type. The relative importance of each feedback type was then learned using Rendle et al. [21] LearnBPR algorithm.

2.1 Main Differences

We distinguish our work from prior methods on several aspects. First, most previous works have focused on the implementation of *customized* recommender systems that were employed only in a single domain (e.g., music, movies, etc.). In addition, such works rely on *specific feedback types* and their blends. As an example, common to HIN recommendation approaches is a preliminary *manual* path types ("MetaPaths") selection step, which *requires deep domain expertise* and should be applied before any recommendation could be done [9, 26, 32]. For these two reasons, re-utilizing most previous works within new domains or using them with new feedback types is quite complicated. On the other end, our method only requires some underlying MF method, with no restrictions on it.

Continuous feedback types encode valuable data. For example, the time of the usage point was shown in our experiments to be beneficial. Other continuous feedback types can be the watching duration in a movie recommender system and the dwell-time in an e-commerce system. Although some previous works have incorporate multiple feedback types, most of these works cannot handle continuous feedback types (e.g., [27, 29]).

Similarly to [5, 6, 29], in this work we propose a post-processing approach. Yet, compared to them, whose methods heavily rely on inputs generated by *several base recommenders*, our approach only requires *a single base* MF method as an input. Additionally, compared to [5], which requires to design its "blend" of underlying (single feedback type) methods based on available feedback types (e.g., explicit feedback is handled by a SVD++ recommender, implicit feedback by a BPR recommender, etc.), our approach is oblivious to feedback type, and therefore, may consume the result of any underlying MF method applied to the problem.

One of the corner stones of our method is the ability to learn how to handle multiple occurrences of the same user-item pair. Previous works apply naïve aggregations (e.g., summation) of feedback obtained from multiple usage points [9, 26]. As we will motivate later, a more sophisticated aggregation function should be applied, where this work is the first to consider and solve this issue.

3 APPROACH

We now describe our approach. We start by introducing several basic notations that will be used throughout the rest of this paper. Next, we shortly discuss how a user may be re-modeled, assuming that the personalized weight of each item is given. We then show how such weights can be obtained, based on the feedback types accompanying the usage points. We conclude this section with a discussion on parameter learning within our approach.

3.1 Preliminaries

Let u denote a single user and let i denote a single item. Every user u may interact with any item i and let R_u denote the set of items in user u's interaction history. To capture the mutli-feedback aspect of user interactions, we assume that each interaction may provide up to l different feedback types. We further assume that a user may interact multiple times with any given item; each such interaction defines a single *usage point*. Such repetitive preferential behavior is actually quite common in real-life. For example, in the music domain, a user may listen to the same song again and again. Accordingly, let R_{ui} denote the sequence of usage points in user u's interaction history with a given item i; and let $R_{ui}^{(j)}$ denote the jth usage point in R_{ui}. Each usage point $R_{ui}^{(j)}$ is defined as a real vector of size l, with entry $R_{ui}^{(j)}[m]$ ($1 \leq m \leq l$) capturing the feedback obtained for the mth feedback type; If no such feedback exists, then we simply assign $R_{ui}^{(j)}[m] = 0$. For instance, an entry may hold the time of the usage point. We can further have type-dependent time entries (e.g., purchase-time or click-time when only one of them has a nonzero value).

In this work, we assume a latent factor model of users and items [15]. Hence, we associate each user u with a user-factors vector $p_u \in \mathbb{R}^f$, and each item i with an item-factors vector $q_i \in \mathbb{R}^f$. Using such a model, the predicted score of user u to item i is given by [1] $\hat{r}_{ui} = p_u^T q_i$, where this score is correlated with the likelihood that the user will interact with the item.

---

[1] We omit the bias terms for clarity of presentation.

3.2 User re-modeling

Let $\mathcal{M}$ be an underlying MF method. Similarly to any MF method, it cannot learn how to consider the various feedback types nor how to aggregate repetitive interactions with the same item. We now describe a novel user re-modeling approach that improves $\mathcal{M}$ to support these data phenomena using a post-processing step.

To this end, a set of latent item vectors $\{q_i\}$ derived by $\mathcal{M}$ is provided as an input to our approach. Since users choose to interact with items, and not the other way around, we concentrate only in understanding the importance of the items to the users. We therefore fix the item vectors, and for a given user u, we wish to estimate a new user-factors vector $\hat{p}_u$ (hence "re-modeling") that captures the *personalized importance* of each item $i \in R_u$ to user u; further denoted hereinafter as w_{ui} and termed "*item weight*".

Given the history of a user R_u, most existing approaches assume that every missing item $i' \notin R_u$ is inferior to any item $i \in R_u$ [11, 21]; an assumption that may not always hold. We take a novel approach, which does not require this assumption, where we choose $\hat{p}_u$ that maximizes the weighted average of the predicted scores of items in R_u. Formally, let us assume for a moment that the personalized item weights $\{w_{ui}\}$ are given. We now "re-create" user u's vector $\hat{p}_u$ as follows:

$$\underset{\hat{p}_u}{\text{argmax}} \; \frac{1}{\|\hat{p}_u\|} \sum_{i \in R_u} w_{ui}(\hat{p}_u^T q_i) \quad (1)$$

It can be easily shown that the objective defined by Eq. 1 has an infinite number of optimal solutions (i.e., user vectors $\hat{p}_u$). Each such optimal user vector $\hat{p}_u$ further takes the following form[2]:

$$\hat{p}_u \overset{\cdot}{=} Z_u^{-1} \cdot \sum_{i \in R_u} w_{ui} q_i, \quad (2)$$

where $Z_u > 0$ and is independent of $\hat{p}_u$. We shall later on suggest a particular instantiation of Z_u, used for practical reasons as the user vector of interest in this work (see Section 3.4).

We now describe the main part of the algorithm, that learns the item weights $\{w_{ui}\}$.

3.3 Item Weights Estimation

We first assume that each item weight w_{ui} depends on the relative importance of the different usage points in R_{ui}. Therefore, each usage point $R_{ui}^{(j)} \in R_{ui}$ may contribute differently to the overall weight w_{ui}, according to the different feedback types associated with that usage point. Next, using a pooling approach, the weight w_{ui} is obtained by aggregating over all item i's usage point importance estimates.

3.3.1 Usage Point Weights Estimation. We now define $\theta \in \mathbb{R}^l$, a real parameter vector, having entry $\theta^{(m)}$ models the relative importance (weight) of the mth feedback type. Using such weights allows to capture situations in which different feedback types provide a variable level of "useful" evidence on user tastes (e.g., time of event). In this work, we consider θ to be a global parameter. We note that, such a parameter can be individually derived for each user u (i.e., θ_u). Due to space considerations, we refrain from using this extension and leave this for future work.

---

[2] The proof is rather straight forward and is based on the fact that we use a cosine-like measure.

Given θ, let z_{ui}^j denote the relative importance of usage point $R_{ui}^{(j)}$ and is simply calculated as $z_{ui}^j = \theta^T R_{ui}^{(j)}$. We note that, while we choose a simple linear correlation for this purpose, any other function could be incorporated. For example, introducing a squared kernel could allow the algorithm to learn that in the case of purchases, usage points in the recent or in the distant past are less important then ones in the intermediate term. Such kernel would boost the performance of the method as it better reflects user behavior patterns.

Mathematically, usage point weights can be negative. However, according to our experiments, negative weights did not seem to affect behavior, thus we would like to consider only non-negative weights. This would mean that we take the maximum of the learned weight and 0. In our implementation 0 values cause infinite gradients, thus we take the maximum between the weight and some small constant real number τ (in our case, we fixed $\tau = 0.01$). That is, we define: $h_\tau(x) = max\{x, \tau\}$. Note that, the rectified linear unit (ReLU), a commonly used activation functionin Neural Networks, is a special case of this definition, with $\tau = 0$.

Another domain-specific phenomenon that needs to be addressed is the following. There are some domains where a small sample of usage points is sufficient to determine the user taste (e.g., in deciding movie tastes). In this case, we may want to adjust the relative weight of the items in a non-linear way that will differentiate in a more drastic manner between weights and make the larger weighed items dominate the user tastes. On the other hand, there are domains with a vast number of items and tastes (e.g., food retail), where we do not want to exaggerate the weight difference. We achieve this by raising the weights to a power γ, which is a learned (real number) parameter in our approach, i.e.:

$$w_{ui}^{(j)} = \left[h_\tau(z_{ui}^j) \right]^\gamma . \tag{3}$$

3.3.2 Usage Point Weights Aggregation. The overall weight w_{ui} is now obtained by aggregating over the usage point weights $\{w_{ui}^{(j)}\}$. We adopt a pooling approach for this purpose. Using such an approach allows to reduce an arbitrary number of features to a fixed size, as we may have a variable number of usage point weights $\{w_{ui}^{(j)}\}$ based on the number of such points recorded in R_{ui} for each item i. The most popular pooling function in Neural Networks is *max-pooling* [16] while in the field of recommender systems, the common approach is sum-pooling [11].

We next make an observation that, the actual choice of a pooling operation may be domain-dependent. While in many recommendation scenarios, a reasonable assumption would be to emphasize more the highly weighted usage points, in some cases, the opposite may be true. For example, in the services domain, some user may use some service several times, but a single bad experience may determine the personalized weight of this service to that user. In this case, we may actually want to consider the minimum weight.

We now make another observation that, considering the length of item usage histories (i.e., $|R_{ui}|$) may be also important. On the one hand, interacting with the same item over and over again can imply a special importance of that item. As an example, considering the movies domain; the fact that a user has repeatedly seen a movie may be very significant. On the other hand, in the food retail domain, repeated purchases of the same item (e.g., bread, milk, etc.) have much less importance.

Motivated by these two observations, we now introduce a more general pooling approach. Let α and β be two learnable parameters, the final item weight w_{ui} is calculated as follows:

$$w_{ui} = \left\| \{w_{ui}^{(j)}\} \right\|_\alpha \cdot |R_{ui}|^\beta . \tag{4}$$

This weight function is composed of two main parts. The first is a L_α-norm[3], given by:

$$\left\| \{w_{ui}^{(j)}\} \right\|_\alpha \overset{def}{=} \left(\sum_{j=1}^{|R_{ui}|} w_{ui}^{(j)\alpha} \right)^{\frac{1}{\alpha}} .$$

This part aggregates over the weights of the different usage points. When $\alpha = 1$ we obtain the sum of usage point weights; as α increases, more emphasis is given to usage points with a higher weight $w_{ui}^{(j)}$; and as α approach infinity, this is equivalent to taking the maximum weight. We acknowledge that when $0 < \alpha < 1$ this is a definition of a distance, which is not a norm. Since $\|x\|_\alpha = 1/\|1/x\|_{-\alpha}$, then in case $\alpha < 0$, as α decreases, more emphasis is given to usage points with a lower weight. This part may be considered as a soft and learnable version of max- and min-pooling.

The second part of w_{ui} allows to weigh each item i in proportion to the number of user u's interactions with item i (i.e., $|R_{ui}|$). For $\beta > 0$, a higher importance is given to longer item interaction histories; for $\beta = 0$ we ignore this property; and for $\beta < 0$ shorter histories are preferred. This part increases the expressiveness of the pooling method, and allows, for example, to model average-pooling. Note that, the commonly used sum-pooling is a private case of this pooling method, having $\alpha = 1$ and $\beta = 0$.

3.4 Learning the Parameters

We conclude this section with a description of how the various parameters introduced in the preceding sections (i.e., $\theta, \gamma, \alpha, \beta$) are learned. The common evaluation metrics in recommender systems domain are based on the same basic idea: *hide the last usage point of the user, and reward in case it was ranked high by the recommender* [3]. Motivated by that, in order to learn the various parameters, for each given user u, we first sort the usage points of *all* her item interactions histories R_{ui} chronologically. We then hide the last usage point; let i' denote the item whose usage point was hidden. We want to learn a parameter set that would rank the hidden item as high as possible. Since ranking is not a differentiable function, we simply try to maximize the predicted score of the hidden item i'. We acknowledge that, other differentiable functions may be applicable for this purpose (e.g., [28]). However, once again we prefer to focus on the novelty of our approach, and therefore, choose a simple differentiable function.

Formally, let $\hat{r}_{ui'} = \hat{p}_u^T q_{i'}$ be the score of the hidden item based only on the revealed items in the corresponding user u's item interactions history. The objective is, therefore, to maximize $\hat{r}_{ui'}$. Since a few number of parameters are learned (i.e., γ, α, β and one parameter per each feedback type), the whole training process can be done in a manner of minutes on a small sample of users, regardless

---

[3]By definition, $w_{ui}^{(j)}$ are all positive. Hence, we do not write their absolute value as required by the L_α-norm definition.

to the actual size of the usage data. Overall our goal is to maximize the hidden items' scores :

$$\max_{\theta, \gamma, \alpha, \beta} \sum_{(u, i') \in TrainingSet} \hat{r}_{ui'} \qquad (5)$$

We note that if the item vectors were not fixed, then an optimal solution would set the same vector to all users and items. In this case we could potentially learn the item vectors by using negative sampling. Yet, we defer such an extension to future work as it will result in a runtime linear in the number of items in the usage data.

We now note that, according to $\hat{r}_{ui'}$ definition, it follows that it directly depends on the weights $\{w_{ui}\}$. Since the maximization of the linear objective defined in Eq. 5 has no constraints on these weight values, it is possible that some or even all of them will not be finite after parameter learning. To avoid such undesired outcome, we now restrict $\hat{p}_u$ to be a linear combination that lies in the convex hull of the item vectors $\{q_i\}_{i \in R_u}$. Therefore, we further normalize the objective by setting $Z_u = \sum_{i \in R_u} w_{ui}$ for every user u. This in turn, re-creates an optimal user vector $\hat{p}_u$ that is defined as the *weighted centroid* of the underlying MF method $\mathcal{M}$'s latent item vectors $\{q_i\}_{i \in R_u}$, as follows:

$$\hat{p}_u = \frac{\sum_{i \in R_u} w_{ui} q_i}{\sum_{i \in R_u} w_{ui}} \qquad (6)$$

Since the scores $\hat{r}_{ui'}$ are computed in a feed-forward fashion, our learning is done using back-propagation with parameter tying [10], further implemented using AdaGrad. For a given parameter $x \in \{\alpha, \beta, \gamma, \theta\}$ to be optimized and a learning rate η, its general update formula is given by: $x \leftarrow x + \eta \frac{\partial \hat{r}_{ui'}}{\partial x}$. Using the facts that: $\frac{\partial \hat{r}_{ui'}}{\partial \hat{p}_u} = q_{i'}$ and $\frac{\partial \hat{p}_u}{\partial w_{ui}} = \frac{Z_u q_{i'} - \sum_{i \in R_u} w_{ui} q_i}{Z_u^2} = \frac{q_i - \hat{p}_u}{Z_u}$, the general form of the partial derivation $\frac{\partial \hat{r}_{ui'}}{\partial x}$ is calculated as follows:

$$\frac{\partial \hat{r}_{ui'}}{\partial x} = \frac{\partial \hat{r}_{ui'}}{\partial \hat{p}_u} \cdot \sum_{i \in R_u} \frac{\partial \hat{p}_u}{\partial w_{ui}} \cdot \frac{\partial w_{ui}}{\partial x} = q_{i'} \cdot \sum_{i \in R_u} \left(\frac{q_i - \hat{p}_u}{Z_u} \right) \cdot \frac{\partial w_{ui}}{\partial x}. \quad (7)$$

The exact $\frac{\partial w_{ui}}{\partial x}$ derivative calculation for each parameter is given by the following final set of equations:

$$\frac{\partial w_{ui}}{\partial \alpha} = \frac{w_{ui}}{\alpha} \cdot \left[\frac{\sum_{j=1}^{|R_{ui}|} w_{ui}^{(j)\alpha} \ln w_{ui}^{(j)}}{\sum_{j=1}^{|R_{ui}|} w_{ui}^{(j)\alpha}} - \frac{\ln \sum_{j=1}^{|R_{ui}|} w_{ui}^{(j)\alpha}}{\alpha} \right], \quad (8)$$

$$\frac{\partial w_{ui}}{\partial \beta} = w_{ui} \ln |R_{ui}|, \qquad (9)$$

$$\frac{\partial w_{ui}}{\partial \gamma} = \frac{w_{ui}}{\sum_{j=1}^{|R_{ui}|} w_{ui}^{(j)\alpha}} \cdot \sum_{j=1}^{|R_{ui}|} w_{ui}^{(j)\alpha} \ln h_\tau(z_{ui}^j), \qquad (10)$$

$$\frac{\partial w_{ui}}{\partial \theta^{(m)}} = \sum_{j=1}^{|R_{ui}|} \mathbb{1}_{[z_{ui}^j > \tau]} \cdot \gamma \cdot z_{ui}^{j \, \gamma - 1} \cdot R_{ui}^{(j)}[m] \qquad (11)$$

4 EVALUATION

We now describe the evaluation of our proposed approach, dubbed "*User Re-Modeling*" and denoted $URM_{[\mathcal{M}]}$ (for a given underlying MF method $\mathcal{M}$). We first describe our datasets and experimental setup and then we report the results.

4.1 Datasets

Our evaluation is based on three real-world datasets that belong to heterogenous domains. These datasets vary in their recommendable item and feedback types that can be utilized within our proposed approach. Therefore, using these different datasets allows to evaluate the *robustness* of our approach given different item recommendation tasks and available feedback types.

MovieLens[4]: This dataset contains about 20 million ratings and 465,000 tag applications that were applied to more than 27,000 movies by about 138,000 users. Each user interaction has a recorded timestamp. Tags that were assigned by the same user to an item within a 24-hour window were accounted as been applied within a single usage point. Therefore, usage points in this dataset are associated with four feedback types: *type* (either rating or tag), *time*, explicit *rating* (5-star scale) in the case of rating events, and *tag count* in the case of tagging events (i.e., the number of tags applied to the item by the user in a given usage point). Since we are only interested in studying users with several feedback types, following previous recommendation [5], we kept only those users whose interaction history includes at least one rating usage point and at least one tagging usage point, regardless of item identity. This has left us with 3,136,408 usage points recorded for 7,801 users that interacted with 25,649 movies. Having similar considerations, we applied the same filtering step on the two other datasets, which details are described next.

Last.fm:[5] This dataset contains social networking and usage history from a set of about 2,000 users from Last.fm (http://www.last.fm) online music system [4]. The data is composed of tags assigned to artists by users. Each tagging has a timestamp. Once again, tags that were assigned by the same user to an item (artist) within a 24-hour window were aggregated. A symmetric user friendship list is also supplied, and used to increase the number of usage points in this dataset to 1,296,274 as follows: every tag used by a given user was assumed to be implicitly used by that user's friends. The basic assumption made here is that, users that are friends also tend to share the same artist tastes. Overall, this dataset has three feedback types: *type* (either tag or friend tag), *timestamp* and *tag count*.

Yelp:[6] This dataset contains about 1.5M *reviews* and 495,000 *tips* on more than 60,000 businesses made by about 367,000 users. The number of usage points in this dataset are 2,064,372. The basic feedback type in this dataset is again the event's *type* (either review or tip). Reviews are further associated with *date* and explicit *rating*. Each tip includes a *timestamp* and the *number of users who liked it*. This in all, translates to five different feedback types available within usage points of this dataset.

4.2 Setup

4.2.1 Underlying MF methods. Recall that, our approach may be applied as a post-processing step on the outputs of any given underlying MF method. For that purpose, we chose two state-of-the-art MF methods to serve as the underlying MF method $\mathcal{M}$ for

---

[4]http://grouplens.org/datasets/movielens/20m/
[5]http://grouplens.org/datasets/hetrec-2011/
[6]http://www.yelp.com/dataset_challenge

our approach, namely WRMF [11] and BPR [21]. Both methods' implementations are based on the MyMediaLite[7] recommender systems library [7], and their corresponding user re-modeling versions using our approach are denoted URM[WRMF] and URM[BPR].

On each dataset, the two underlying methods were trained over uniform feedback usage points (i.e., all feedback events were considered with no type distinction[8]). The optimal latent dimension in all domains for both methods was between 40 to 60. Following previous recommendations [11, 21], *any* implicit feedback obtained in different usage points of a given (u, i) user-item pair (denoted hereinafter r_{ui}) was aggregated. Using the latent item vectors $\{q_i\}$ inferred by each method $\mathcal{M}$, we re-created the user models $\hat{p}_u$ for recommendation as was described in Section 3. The details of both methods are now shortly described.

The *Weighted Regularizd Matrix Factorization* method [11] (WRMF) is based on the assumption that any implicit feedback r_{ui} encodes some signal about user u's taste towards item i. Such signal is first binarized as follows: $b_{ui} = 1$ if $r_{ui} > 0$, else $b_{ui} = 0$. Next, a set of parameters $c_{ui} = 1 + a \cdot r_{ui}$ further model the confidence of each observation b_{ui} (with $a = 40$, following previous recommendations [11]). WRMF learns latent user and item vectors by minimizing the following regularized cost function:

$$\min_{p_*, q_*} \sum_{u, i} c_{ui} (b_{ui} - p_u^T q_i)^2 + \lambda \left(\sum_u \|p_u\|^2 + \sum_i \|q_i\|^2 \right). \quad (12)$$

The *Bayesian Personalized Ranking* method [21] (BPR) learns a personalized ranking of items to a given user using implicit feedback. Such feedback is assumed to represent positive observations about the user's taste. Hence, non-observed user-item interactions are assumed to represent negative feedback on the user's tastes. Accordingly, BPR tries to fit a ranking model that assigns positive scores only to observed interactions (and negative to the rest). For that, for each user u, a relative order is defined over all items, with $i <_u i'$ whenever $i \in R_u$ and $i' \notin R_u$. BPR's objective is then to maximize the following optimization criterion:

$$\max_{p_*, q_*} \sum_{i <_u i'} \ln \sigma(\Delta \hat{r}_{u(ii')}) - \lambda \left(\sum_u \|p_u\|^2 + \sum_i \|q_i\|^2 \right), \quad (13)$$

where $\Delta \hat{r}_{u(ii')} = \hat{r}_{ui} - \hat{r}_{ui'} \overset{def}{=} p_u^T q_i - p_u^T q_{i'}$.

4.2.2 Multi-feedback baselines. Our choice of baseline multi-feedback types methods had two main considerations. First, the baselines should be strong enough to outperform other alternatives. Second, the baseline should be also applied as a post-processing step on the outputs of an underlying MF method.

The first baseline is the Ensemble method, proposed by da Costa and Manzato [5] and its implementation is openly available[9]. This method was previously shown to provide a significant improvement over several state-of-the-art uni-feedback recommender systems. In addition, this method has been shown to outperform other multi-feedback alternatives, including an implementation based on

libFM's *Factorization Machines [20]* and several alternative ensemble methods. Therefore, the Ensemble method serves as a *strong* baseline for comparison.

Per each feedback type, this method first applies a uni-feedback MF algorithm, trained using that feedback source only. To this end, let $\hat{r}_{ui}^m$ denote the predicted score of user u to item i by a given uni-feedback recommender method, when using only the mth feedback type. For a given user u, the method predicts a given item i's score to be the linear combination of uni-feedback item scores: $\hat{r}_{ui} = \sum_{m=1}^l \phi^{(m)} \hat{r}_{ui}^m$. Here, $\phi^{(m)}$ encodes the relative importance (weight) of the mth feedback type. By replacing $\Delta \hat{r}_{u(ii')} = \sum_{m=1}^l \phi^{(m)} \left(\hat{r}_{ui}^m - \hat{r}_{ui'}^m \right)$ in Eq. 13 and further regularizing ϕ, the Ensemble method learns the parameter vector ϕ using Rendle et al.'s LearnBPR algorithm [21].

The second baseline, the CombMNZ method is a generic unsupervised fusion approach for combining the results of several base rankers, commonly serving as a competitive baseline[10] in many similar data settings [30]. Let $R_{u,m}^{[k]}$ further denote the list of top-k items recommended by a given underlying uni-feedback method $\mathcal{M}$ using the mth feedback type ($1 \leq m \leq l$); CombMNZ returns the top-k items with the highest fused score, where the item combined score is calculated as follows:

$$\text{CombMNZ}(i|u) = \text{NZ}(i) \cdot \sum_{m=1}^l \hat{r}_{ui}^m, \quad (14)$$

and $\text{NZ}(i) = \#\{i \in R_{u,m}^{[k]}\}$ is the number of top-k lists that include item i, and each $\hat{r}_{ui}^m$ is further 0-1 (i.e., max-min) normalized when $i \in R_{u,m}^{[k]}$; otherwise: $\hat{r}_{ui}^m = 0$ [30].

Following [5], we used the SVD++ [14] method for explicit feedback sources (i.e., ratings and reviews in the MovieLens and Yelp datasets, respectively). For implicit feedback types we have tried both WRMF and BPR. Due to space considerations, we only report on the best "blends" that we found for each dataset. For example, in the MovieLens dataset, we found that using BPR worked better than WRMF. On the other end, the opposite was true for the Yelp dataset, etc. Since none of the two underlying MF methods can handle continuous feedback types, compared to our method, we cannot evaluate these multi-feedback alternative approaches using time feedback. Hence, to have a fair comparison with these two multi-feedback baseline methods, we further ignored the time feedback within our approach in the first part of the evaluation.

4.2.3 Evaluation Protocol & Measures. Multi-feedback methods (ours and the two baselines) were further applied on the outputs of the underlying uni-feedback recommenders (i.e., WRMF, BPR, and SVD++). Specifically to our approach, for each underlying MF method $\mathcal{M} \in \{$WRMF, BPR$\}$, we used all training users in order to learn the latent item vectors $\{q_i\}$. We then applied our method on a sample of the same training users in order to learn the various parameters (see Section 3.4)[11]. Each test user u was then re-modeled

---

[7]http://mymedialite.net/

[8]We note that, each such underlying method instantiation provided a much better performance compared to the alternative of training the same method using only a single feedback source.

[9]http://www.github.com/ArthurFortes/AF_Recommender_tool/

[10]We also tried the simple CombAVG approach used in [6], but we found CombMNZ to provide a much better baseline to compare with.

[11]We also tried to train the MF models with a portion of the training users, and then to learn the parameters of our method using the rest of the users. However, across all datasets, this approach led to inferior results.

	MovieLens			Last.fm			Yelp		
	MRR@1	MRR@3	MRR@10	MRR@1	MRR@3	MRR@10	MRR@1	MRR@3	MRR@10
WRMF	.007	.011	.018	.096	.107	.117	.120	.185	.240
BPR	.012	.019	.025	.049	.064	.073	.011	.019	.030
Ensemble	.014	.018	.022	.143	.166	.190	.022	.038	.050
CombMNZ	.004	.017	.027	.111	.141	.169	.004	.076	.126
URM$^{-T}_{[\text{WRMF}]}$	$.012^*_c$	$.019^*$	$.024^*$	$.180^*_{ec}$	$.201^*_{ec}$	$.209^*_{ec}$	$.116_{ec}$	$.179_{ec}$	$.235_{ec}$
URM$^{+T}_{[\text{WRMF}]}$	$\mathbf{.019}^*_{ec}$	$\mathbf{.027}^*_{ec}$	$\mathbf{.033}^*_{ec}$	$\mathbf{.205}^*_{ec}$	$\mathbf{.219}^*_{ec}$	$\mathbf{.230}^*_{ec}$	$\mathbf{.128}^*_{ec}$	$\mathbf{.193}^*_{ec}$	$\mathbf{.248}^*_{ec}$
URM$^{-T}_{[\text{BPR}]}$	$.016^*_{ec}$	$.023^*_{ec}$	$.030^*_{ec}$	$.156^*_{ec}$	$.172^*_{ec}$	$.182^*_c$	$.036^*_{ec}$	$.056^*_e$	$.075^*_e$
URM$^{+T}_{[\text{BPR}]}$	$.017^*_{ec}$	$\mathbf{.027}^*_{ec}$	$\mathbf{.033}^*_{ec}$	$.161^*_{ec}$	$.175^*_{ec}$	$.189^*_c$	$.038^*_{ec}$	$.064^*_e$	$.075^*_e$

Table 1: Comparison of our approach with the two underlying MF methods and the two multi-feedback type baselines. Yelp results are reported in a 10^{-1} scale. The superscript $*$ and subscripts e and c next to each URM$_{[\mathcal{M}]}$ result further denote a statistical significant difference with the underlying uni-feedback MF method $\mathcal{M}$, Ensemble and CombMNZ, respectively ($p < 0.05$).

(i.e., $\hat{p}_u$) and the top-k items i with the highest predicted score (i.e., $\hat{r}_{ui} = \hat{p}_u^T q_i$) were recommended.

On each dataset, we ran two versions of our approach based on whether we considered the time feedback or not. The first version, denoted URM$^{+T}_{[\mathcal{M}]}$ includes the time feedback. To this end, for each usage point, its time is considered as any other feedback type, represented by usage recency[12]. Noting that for different users we might have different time scales, for each user, we further *Z-normalized* the times. The second version, denoted URM$^{-T}_{[\mathcal{M}]}$, excludes the time feedback and was used for proper comparison with the two other multi-feedback alternatives.

Using each dataset, we evaluated our approach and the various baseline methods using an *"All But (Last) One"* protocol [3] (i.e., the hidden item belongs to the last usage point). Since a RS should recommend on valuable items, usage points with a low explicit rating (2 or less stars) or of type "friend tag" were not considered as hidden items. Recommender systems usually present a few items at once, where the exact amount is system dependent. Hence the item a user may pick would be among the first few items on the list. Therefore, we chose several representative values for the size of the list k, namely $k \in \{1, 3, 10\}$. Our evaluation metric is **MRR@k** (Mean Reciprocal Rank), which returns the inverse of the rank of the hidden item. It returns the zero value if the rank is above k. We used 5-fold cross validation and report the average results. Statistical significant differences were measured using the paired two-tailed Student's t-test ($p < 0.05$).

4.3 Results

Table 1 summarizes the overall results of our evaluation.

4.3.1 Comparison with the underlying MF methods. We first compare our approach (URM$^{+T}_{[\mathcal{M}]}$) to the two underlying MF methods (i.e., WRMF and BPR). First, we observe that, none of the two underlying methods was better than the other for all datasets. While the BPR method was better for the MovieLens dataset, the WRMF had better performance for the two other datasets. We next observe that, overall, the URM$^{+T}_{[\mathcal{M}]}$ approach has provided a notable boost in performance (sometimes two or even three times better) to that of

the corresponding underlying method $\mathcal{M}$ on which it was applied as a post-processing step.

4.3.2 Comparison with multi-feedback baselines. We next compare our approach (URM$^{-T}_{[\mathcal{M}]}$) to the two baseline multi-feedback methods (i.e., Ensemble and CombMNZ). First we observe that, none of the two baseline multi-feedback methods was better than the other for all the datasets. For example, while Ensemble was better than CombMNZ in the Last.fm dataset, this is not the same for the two other datasets. For the MovieLens and Yelp datasets, the Ensemble method had a better accuracy (i.e., MRR@1) than CombMNZ; yet, for $k \in \{3, 10\}$ the opposite was true.

Next, comparing the two instantiations of our approach side by side with the two alternative multi-feedback methods, we can observe that, overall, our approach provided a better accuracy. First, for the MovieLens and Yelp datasets, URM$^{-T}_{[\text{BPR}]}$ and URM$^{-T}_{[\text{WRMF}]}$ respectively had the overall best performance than any other method. For the Last.fm dataset, on the other hand, URM$^{-T}_{[\text{WRMF}]}$ was the overall best choice.

Finally, comparing the two versions of our approach implementations, URM$^{+T}_{[\mathcal{M}]}$ (with the time feedback) and URM$^{-T}_{[\mathcal{M}]}$ (without the time feedback), we can observe that, an additional boost is further achieved by considering the time feedback (between +3.5% and +58% more, depending on the dataset and the underlying uni-feedback method). Among all methods, URM$^{+T}_{[\text{WRMF}]}$ was the dominant one.

4.3.3 Post-learning domain analysis. Analyzing the various parameter values that were learned by our approach (i.e., α, β, γ and θ) further reveals interesting domain-dependent user behavioral patterns. For example, recall that, while the α parameter determines the type of pooling operation that we perform on each item's usage history R_{ui}, the β parameter determines the importance of the history's length $|R_{ui}|$. The average (α, β) values learned (using the two underlying methods) for the MovieLens, Last.fm and Yelp datasets were approximately $(1.94, 2.43)$, $(1.01, 4.16)$ and $(-1.21, 0.41)$, respectively. Using these numbers, we can first observe that since $\beta > 0$ in all datasets, repeated interactions with the same item increase its weight. Moreover, since $\alpha > 0$ in both the MovieLens and Last.fm datasets, when aggregating repeated interactions with the same item, highly weighted usage points are emphasized more.

---

[12]Such recency is simply given by time that elapsed between a given usage point time and the recommendation time.

In contrast, since $\alpha < 0$ in the Yelp dataset, the personalized weight of an item is dictated by usage points with a lower weight.

We next make another interesting observation by analyzing the domain-variability of the γ parameter, with an average value of 3.28, 0.8, 1.1 for the MovieLens, Last.fm and Yelp datasets, respectively. For the MovieLens and Yelp datasets, γ amplifies the value of each usage point weight $w_{ui}^{(j)}$, while for the Last.fm dataset it attenuates the weight values. This in turn, implies that, for example, in the MovieLens dataset, the importance of a movie to a user will be effected by (probably fewer) usage points that have significantly higher "confidence" than the others (as given by z_{ui}^{j}). On the other end, an artist's importance in the Last.fm datase should be determined by more usage points whose "confidence" is predicted to be less reliable (hence the attenuation is applied). In all datasets, the average value of γ is higher when we include time comparing to the case when we omit it. This can be explained by the fact that a model that considers also the time has more confidence in the most valuable usage points. Therefore less usage points are needed in order to model the users, and the value of γ is increased.

We conclude with some "anecdotal" insights that came from analyzing the values of the feedback type importance weights $\theta^{(m)}$. In the MovieLens dataset, a review has more weight than a single tag only if it is rated 4 stars or above. In the Yelp dataset, a review has more weight than a tip only if it is rated 3 stars or above. We also discovered a weak positive correlation between the weight and the number of likes a tip got. We argue that, in general, more effort is invested in writing tips that would gain more likes; and this in turn, implies on their importance. As a last example insight, in the Last.fm dataset, a tag is more important than a friend-tag, but the recency of the event influences more (e.g., a recent friend-tag has more weight than an old tag).

5 SUMMARY

In this work we faced a problem that is relevant to any recommendation setting. Our approach can be used to incrementally incorporate new feedback types into any existing baseline MF methods . Since our approach is applied as a post-processing step, no actual change is required to the underlying MF method that is employed.

REFERENCES
[1] Ariel Bar, Lior Rokach, Guy Shani, Bracha Shapira, and Alon Schclar. Improving simple collaborative filtering models using ensemble methods. In Multiple Classifier Systems, pages 1–12. Springer, 2013.
[2] J. Bobadilla, F. Ortega, A. Hernando, and A. GutiéRrez. Recommender systems survey. Know.-Based Syst., 46:109–132, July 2013.
[3] John S. Breese, David Heckerman, and Carl Kadie. Empirical analysis of predictive algorithms for collaborative filtering. In Proceedings of the Fourteenth Conference on Uncertainty in Artificial Intelligence, UAI'98, pages 43–52, San Francisco, CA, USA, 1998. Morgan Kaufmann Publishers Inc.
[4] Iván Cantador, Peter Brusilovsky, and Tsvi Kuflik. 2nd workshop on information heterogeneity and fusion in recommender systems (hetrec 2011). In Proceedings of the 5th ACM conference on Recommender systems, RecSys 2011. ACM.
[5] Arthur F. da Costa and Marcelo G. Manzato. Exploiting multimodal interactions in recommender systems with ensemble algorithms. Inf. Syst., 56(C):120–132, March 2016.
[6] Marcos Aurélio Domingues, Fabien Gouyon, Alípio Mário Jorge, José Paulo Leal, João Vinagre, Luís Lemos, and Mohamed Sordo. Combining usage and content in an online music recommendation system for music in the long-tail. In Proceedings of the 21st International Conference on World Wide Web, WWW '12 Companion, pages 925–930, New York, NY, USA, 2012. ACM.
[7] Zeno Gantner, Steffen Rendle, Christoph Freudenthaler, and Lars Schmidt-Thieme. Mymedialite: A free recommender system library. In Proceedings of the fifth ACM conference on Recommender systems, pages 305–308. ACM, 2011.
[8] David Goldberg, David Nichols, Brian M. Oki, and Douglas Terry. Using collaborative filtering to weave an information tapestry. Commun. ACM, 35:61–70, December 1992.
[9] Chun Guo and Xiaozhong Liu. Automatic feature generation on heterogeneous graph for music recommendation. In Proceedings of the 38th International ACM SIGIR Conference on Research and Development in Information Retrieval, SIGIR '15, pages 807–810, New York, NY, USA, 2015. ACM.
[10] John J Hopfield. Neural networks and physical systems with emergent collective computational abilities. Proceedings of the national academy of sciences, 79(8):2554–2558, 1982.
[11] Yifan Hu, Yehuda Koren, and Chris Volinsky. Collaborative filtering for implicit feedback datasets. In Proceedings of the 2008 Eighth IEEE International Conference on Data Mining, ICDM '08, pages 263–272. IEEE Computer Society, 2008.
[12] Gawesh Jawaheer, Martin Szomszor, and Patty Kostkova. Comparison of implicit and explicit feedback from an online music recommendation service. In Proceedings of the 1st International Workshop on Information Heterogeneity and Fusion in Recommender Systems, HetRec '10, pages 47–51, NY, USA. ACM.
[13] Joseph A. Konstan, Bradley N. Miller, David Maltz, Jonathan L. Herlocker, Lee R. Gordon, and John Riedl. Grouplens: Applying collaborative filtering to usenet news. Commun. ACM, 40(3):77–87, March 1997.
[14] Yehuda Koren. Factorization meets the neighborhood: A multifaceted collaborative filtering model. In Proceedings of the 14th ACM SIGKDD International Conference on Knowledge Discovery and Data Mining, KDD '08, pages 426–434, New York, NY, USA, 2008. ACM.
[15] Yehuda Koren, Robert Bell, and Chris Volinsky. Matrix factorization techniques for recommender systems. Computer, 42(8):30–37, August 2009.
[16] Alex Krizhevsky, Ilya Sutskever, and Geoffrey E Hinton. Imagenet classification with deep convolutional neural networks. In Advances in neural information processing systems, pages 1097–1105, 2012.
[17] David M. Nichols. Implicit rating and filtering. In In proceedings of the Fifth DELOS Workshop on Filtering and Collaborative Filtering, pages 31–36, 1997.
[18] Douglas W Oard and Jinmook Kim. Modeling information content using observable behavior. ASIST Annual Meeting, pages 481–488, 2001.
[19] Denis Parra and Xavier Amatriain. Walk the talk: Analyzing the relation between implicit and explicit feedback for preference elicitation. In Proceedings of UMAP'11.
[20] Steffen Rendle. Factorization machines with libfm. ACM Trans. Intell. Syst. Technol., 3(3):57:1–57:22, May 2012.
[21] Steffen Rendle, Christoph Freudenthaler, Zeno Gantner, and Lars Schmidt-Thieme. Bpr: Bayesian personalized ranking from implicit feedback. In the Twenty-Fifth Conference on Uncertainty in Artificial Intelligence, UAI '09.
[22] Steffen Rendle, Zeno Gantner, Christoph Freudenthaler, and Lars Schmidt-Thieme. Fast context-aware recommendations with factorization machines. In Proceedings of the 34th international ACM SIGIR conference on Research and development in Information Retrieval, pages 635–644. ACM, 2011.
[23] Francesco Ricci, Lior Rokach, Bracha Shapira, and Paul B. Kantor. Recommender Systems Handbook. Springer-Verlag, Inc., New York, NY, USA, 2010.
[24] Oren Sar Shalom, Shlomo Berkovsky, Royi Ronen, Elad Ziklik, and Amir Amihood. Data quality matters in recommender systems. In Proceedings of the 9th ACM Conference on Recommender Systems, pages 257–260. ACM, 2015.
[25] Oren Sar Shalom, Noam Koenigstein, Ulrich Paquet, and Hastagiri P Vanchinathan. Beyond collaborative filtering: The list recommendation problem. In Proceedings of the 25th International Conference on World Wide Web, pages 63–72. International World Wide Web Conferences Steering Committee, 2016.
[26] Chuan Shi, Zhiqiang Zhang, Ping Luo, Philip S. Yu, Yading Yue, and Bin Wu. Semantic path based personalized recommendation on weighted heterogeneous information networks. In Proceedings of the 24th ACM International on Conference on Information and Knowledge Management, CIKM '15, pages 453–462, New York, NY, USA, 2015. ACM.
[27] Ajit P Singh and Geoffrey J Gordon. Relational learning via collective matrix factorization. In Proceedings of the 14th ACM SIGKDD international conference on Knowledge discovery and data mining, pages 650–658. ACM, 2008.
[28] Harald Steck. Gaussian ranking by matrix factorization. In Proceedings of the 9th ACM Conference on Recommender Systems, pages 115–122. ACM, 2015.
[29] Liang Tang, Bee-Chung Chen, Deepak Agarwal, and Bo Long. An empirical study on recommendation with multiple types of feedback.
[30] Shengli Wu. Data fusion in information retrieval, volume 13. Springer Science & Business Media, 2012.
[31] Peifeng Yin, Ping Luo, Wang-Chien Lee, and Min Wang. Silence is also evidence: Interpreting dwell time for recommendation from psychological perspective. In Proceedings of the 19th ACM SIGKDD International Conference on Knowledge Discovery and Data Mining, KDD '13, pages 989–997, New York, NY, USA. ACM.
[32] Xiao Yu, Xiang Ren, Yizhou Sun, Quanquan Gu, Bradley Sturt, Urvashi Khandelwal, Brandon Norick, and Jiawei Han. Personalized entity recommendation: A heterogeneous information network approach. In Proceedings of the 7th ACM International Conference on Web Search and Data Mining, WSDM '14, pages 283–292. ACM, 2014.

The Positive and Negative Influence of Search Results on People's Decisions about the Efficacy of Medical Treatments

Frances A. Pogacar[1], Amira Ghenai[1], Mark D. Smucker[2], and Charles L. A. Clarke[1]

[1] David R. Cheriton School of Computer Science, University of Waterloo, Canada
[2] Department of Management Sciences, University of Waterloo, Canada
{fapogacar,aghenai,mark.smucker,charles.clarke}@uwaterloo.ca

ABSTRACT

People regularly use web search engines to investigate the efficacy of medical treatments. Search results can contain documents that present incorrect information that contradicts current established medical understanding on whether a treatment is helpful or not for a health issue. If people are influenced by the incorrect information found in search results, they can make harmful decisions about the appropriate treatment. To determine the extent to which people can be influenced by search engine results, we conducted a controlled laboratory study that biased search results towards correct or incorrect information for 10 different medical treatments. We found that search engine results can significantly influence people both positively and negatively. Importantly, study participants made more incorrect decisions when they interacted with search results biased towards incorrect information than when they had no interaction with search results at all. For search domains such as health information, search engine designers and researchers must recognize that not all non-relevant information is the same. Some non-relevant information is incorrect and potentially harmful when people use it to make decisions that may negatively impact their lives.

KEYWORDS

Health Search; User Study; Misinformation; Harmful Effects

1 INTRODUCTION

Wei Zexi, a 21 year old Chinese student, died on April 12, 2016, of synovial sarcoma, a form of cancer [10]. In the early stages of his illness, doctors treated him with conventional treatments. But when these treatments were not successful, his family reportedly spent 200,000 yuan (US$30,650) on an experimental treatment not approved for use in China. Wei Zexi's story is notable because he found the hospital offering the treatment via the Baidu search engine. The treatment did not help, and he later learned, via a friend using the Google search engine outside of China, that there was no scientific evidence that this treatment would help him. Shortly before his death, he wrote a web posting denouncing Baidu for

violating his trust. Following the web post and his death, public outrage resulted in the Chinese government passing new regulations regarding search engines [1]. Apparently, Wei Zexi had found the treatment via an advertisement on Baidu's search results page, and among these new regulations was the requirement that search engines clearly identify advertisements as different from natural or organic search results [1].

When people search for health information online, as 72% of U.S. internet users do, the majority are seeking information about a health issue or medical treatment [7]. While the majority of U.S. internet users are confident searchers, and believe they are finding accurate information [12], it is likely that there are many like Wei Zexi who have used a search engine for health information and have ended up making incorrect decisions that either wasted their money or negatively impacted their health. Indeed, White and Hassan [16] have shown that search engines can be biased towards incorrectly indicating that medical treatments help when they do not, and that these errors may be amplified by people's bias towards positive information [14]. If people find and believe incorrect information regarding medical treatments, there is the potential for these people to be harmed.

To measure the actual effect of search bias on people's ability to correctly determine the efficacy of medical treatments, we conducted a controlled laboratory study with 60 participants. In our study, we biased search results towards being correct or towards being incorrect. We also controlled the topmost rank of a correct result to investigate the effect of rank.

Our study's participants had to determine the efficacy of ten different medical treatments. We asked participants to pretend that they had a question about the effectiveness of a medical treatment and that they had decided to use a search engine to help them answer the question. For each of the ten treatments, we either presented the participants with a search results page or a control condition where they had to directly answer the question without any search results at all.

We found that:

- Search results have a statistically significant, strong effect on people's ability to make correct decisions. Results biased towards incorrect information reduced people's accuracy from 43% to 23%. Results biased towards correct information increased accuracy from 43% to 65%.
- The topmost rank of a correct result appears to have some effect on people's accuracy. While not statistically significant, when shown results biased towards correct information, participants' accuracy was only 59% if the top two results were incorrect compared to 70% accuracy when the rank 1 item was correct.

ICTIR '17, October 1–4, 2017, Amsterdam, Netherlands.
© 2017 Copyright held by the owner/author(s). Publication rights licensed to ACM.
ISBN 978-1-4503-4490-6/17/10...$15.00
DOI: https://doi.org/10.1145/3121050.3121074

- Knowledge of the medical treatment can perhaps inoculate people against incorrect information. We found more self-reported knowledge to reduce the effect of incorrect information on accuracy (p = 0.04).
- Like White and Hassan [16], we found that participants were biased towards saying treatments were helpful.

In addition, we collected information about search behaviour via a questionnaire and report on participant's confidence in their answers and their click behaviour.

Our results demonstrate that search engines have a great potential to both help and harm people. Indeed, when searchers decide that ineffective treatments will help them, they open themselves up to at best being swindled out of money and at worst being harmed by these ineffective treatments either directly or from lack of proper treatment.

We next review related work, and then cover the details of the study and present the study's results. Following the results, we discuss implications and conclude the paper.

2 RELATED WORK

Our work builds directly on the results of White and his co-authors [14–17]. White has established that web search engines have a bias towards search results that report that medical treatments help health issues even when the evidence is either inconclusive or actually says that the treatment is unhelpful. White's work has looked at both medical queries with yes and no answers [14, 15] and queries about the efficacy of medical treatments [16, 17]. An example of a yes/no question from [15] is "Does mono in children cause bruising?" An example of an efficacy query from [17] is "Does melatonin work for jet lag".

A key finding of this body of work is that people are both biased towards answers of "yes" and "helps" and that people's beliefs are difficult to change if they are already decided on an answer. White [15] did find that when search results are biased towards one answer (yes or no) and these answers are all ranked above the contradictory answers (all yes above all no, and vice versa), that people could be influenced to select the dominant answer in search results. When the correct answer to a question was *yes*, White was able to get participants to correctly answer 74.9% of the time. When the correct answer was *no*, users' accuracy could reach 63.1% when the results were biased to *no* and all *no* results were ranked above *yes* answers.

Our work specifically looks at searcher accuracy for determining the efficacy of medical treatments rather than yes/no questions. While White and Horvitz [17] looked at search accuracy for efficacy queries, they did not measure the impact of bias and rank on accuracy. White and Horvitz [17] examined organic search results, which have an uncontrolled bias, as well as controlled search results with a 50/50 mix of answers, i.e. unbiased search results. In this paper, we look at biasing results both towards correct and towards incorrect results. We also look specifically at the rank of the topmost correct document, which is a more subtle notion of rank than White [15] examined where he ranked all yes/no answers above all no/yes answers.

Both White [15] and White and Horvitz [17] focus their study on the process by which search engine results can change searcher beliefs. To study the dynamics of search beliefs, White and his co-authors first asked study participants about their beliefs before searching. In this paper, we purposely avoided asking study participants about their beliefs prior to searching for fear of biasing participants towards their pre-existing beliefs. If we were to ask participants for their prior beliefs, this would mean that to change their belief, a participant would need to admit to the experimenter that their prior belief was wrong. Instead, our control condition is to measure participant's accuracy without any exposure to search results. While we cannot measure how a single participant changes their belief, we can measure how a population's accuracy can be influenced. White [15] and White and Horvitz [17] both found that it is difficult to change beliefs, while we show that with a significant bias in results, large shifts in a population's accuracy can be achieved. As an additional aspect of our work, we examine the impact of participants' self-reported knowledge of the medical treatments and health issues.

Other than the work of White and co-authors, the work most relevant to our paper is that of Epstein and Robertson [6], who studied the impact of search results in the political domain. Epstein and Robertson designed large scale, controlled experiments to understand the influence of search engine results on political elections. Results showed that preferences of undecided voters can be significantly influenced and that the extent of the influence was associated with certain demographic characteristics. Epstein and Robertson's work is similar to ours as we both study the influence of search results on people's decisions, but while Epstein and Robertson focus heavily on the effect of rank on preferences in the political domain, we explore how search results, biased with correct and incorrect information, as well as rank, can lead participants towards or away from correct decisions in the health domain.

In other related work, Kammerer et al. [8] designed a controlled user study to understand the behaviour of people when evaluating web search sources regarding medical issues. Kammerer et al. [8] chose two medical treatments for a health issue, crafted search results using different types of sources (medical institutions, journals, forums, etc.), and then asked participants to evaluate which treatment was better. Using eye tracking, participant logs and verbal protocols, results showed that people spend less time and effort evaluating search results when information sources seem accurate and reliable. Even though their study design is similar to ours, their main focus was to evaluate the validation of sources. In this paper, we evaluate the influence of search bias and rank when searching the efficacy of medical treatments.

Kulshrestha et al. [9] studied search bias in Twitter, a social media website. More specifically, Kulshrestha et al. [9] introduced three different aspects of bias for search systems: query bias, output bias, and ranking bias. Results showed that query bias (such as query topic or how the query is phrased) and ranking bias play an important role in producing bias in search results.

3 METHODS AND MATERIALS

To measure the effect of search results bias on people's ability to correctly determine the efficacy of medical treatments, we created a controlled, within-subjects, laboratory study. We first provide an overview of the experiment and then detail each of the parts.

3.1 Overview

Our experiment had two independent variables each with two levels. The first independent variable was the search results bias with the levels: *correct* and *incorrect*. The second independent variable was the rank of the topmost correct search result with levels of 1 and 3, indicating the position of the first correct result. The experiment also had a control condition, in which no search results are presented to the user. The two independent variables with two levels each, plus a control, produces five experimental conditions. Participants had to determine the efficacy of medical treatments and a treatment could be either *helpful* or *unhelpful*. So that each of the five experimental conditions would be measured on both *helpful* and *unhelpful* treatments, we selected five of each for a total of ten treatments. The experiment had two dependent variables: 1) the fraction of *correct* decisions and 2) the fraction of *harmful* decisions made by the participant. In addition, we collected data from a questionnaire and feedback on each decision made. We also logged computer interactions for the entire study.

3.2 Medical Treatments

To select our medical treatments, we first received from White and Hassan [16] a list of 249 treatments that they had judged for their study. White and Hassan together determined the effectiveness of each treatment by reading the corresponding Cochrane Review [4, 5] and then reaching a consensus to determine the treatment's efficacy. A Cochrane Review is a systematic review that synthesizes the clinical evidence and informs clinical decision making. White and Hassan settled on three categories of efficacy: *helps*, *inconclusive*, and *does not help*.

For each medical treatment in our study, our participants needed to decide on its efficacy by selecting one of these three categories. We described the categories to our study participants as follows:

- **Helps**: The medical treatment **helps** if the treatment is effective and has a direct positive influence on the specified illness.
- **Inconclusive**: The effectiveness of a medical treatment is **inconclusive** if medical professionals are still unsure if the treatment will have a positive, negative or no influence on the specified illness.
- **Does not help**: The medical treatment **does not help** if the treatment is ineffective and either has no effect or has a direct negative influence on the specified illness.

To help our study participants better understand each category, these definitions modify and expand upon the definitions that White and Hassan [16] used in their paper. To save space in this paper, we report results using the labels: *helpful*, *inconclusive*, and *unhelpful*.

Table 3 shows the ten treatments we selected for our study. Each medical treatment is associated with a stated health issue. We selected five *helpful* and five *unhelpful* treatments, and we tried to select treatments and health issues that might be of interest to university students, who would form the majority of our study participants.

3.3 Control Condition

The control condition required participants to decide on the efficacy of a medical treatment without any assistance, i.e., they were not shown a search engine results page (SERP). This control condition allows us to determine the fraction of correct and harmful decisions that participants would make if they did not interact with a search engine. Participants experienced the control condition for two of the ten medical treatments that they judged.

3.4 Search Results - Independent Variables

For eight of the ten medical treatments, we instructed participants to pretend that they had a question about the effectiveness of a medical treatment and had decided to use a search engine to help them answer the question. In these cases, we showed participants a web page that looked like a search engine results page (SERP) with ten search results displayed with snippets.

All ten of the search results were about the medical treatment, but they were biased towards either *correct* or *incorrect* information regarding the efficacy of the medical treatment.

To bias our search results towards correct information, we selected eight of the results to be correct and two to be incorrect. A correct result is a document that contains information about the efficacy of the medical treatment that supports the truth, and an incorrect result contains information that contradicts the true efficacy of the medical treatment. To bias the search results towards incorrect information, we selected eight to be incorrect and two to be correct.

Our amount of bias is similar to that which can be found in actual search engines. White and Hassan [16] found that, for a major web search engine, at rank 10, on average, 80.69% of the results for a query about a medical treatment reported that the treatment was *helpful*. The remainder of the top 10 results consisted of 12.29% being *inconclusive* and 7.01% being *unhelpful*.

In addition to controlling the result bias to be correct or incorrect, we also controlled the rank of the topmost correct document to be either at rank 1 or at rank 3. We selected these ranks because eye tracking studies show that the first two results are viewed at very high rates, but that attention from rank 1 to rank 3 drops by about 50% [11].

For each participant and each display of search results, we used randomization to generate the search results. For each medical treatment, we had pools of 8-10 correct and 8-10 incorrect documents. To generate search results biased towards *correct* information, we randomly selected two incorrect documents and eight correct documents from their respective pools. Conversely, for results biased towards *incorrect* information, we randomly selected two correct and eight incorrect documents from their respective pools. The topmost correct document was randomly assigned into rank 1 or rank 3, corresponding to the experimental condition. If the experimental condition had the topmost correct document in rank 3, then rank 1 and rank 2 were assigned two random incorrect documents. The rest of the incorrect and correct documents were then randomly distributed across the remaining ranks. After generating search results pages, we verified that the correct and incorrect documents were randomly distributed among the ranks and across the participants.

3.5 Documents and Snippets

In order to build search engine result pages for every medical treatment, we collected documents containing information about the treatment's efficacy. We used Bing, Yahoo, and Google to collect a total of 158 documents relevant to determining the efficacy of the ten medical treatments. As described in the previous section, for each medical treatment we created pools of 8-10 correct and 8-10 incorrect documents. A correct document contains information about the efficacy of the medical treatment that supports the truth (see Table 3). An incorrect document contains information that contradicts the true efficacy of the medical treatment.

We divided the task of collecting and labeling documents as either correct or incorrect between two of the paper's authors. For some of the medical treatments, it was difficult to find eight documents stating that the medical treatment was unhelpful. In these cases, we selected documents that did not directly support or oppose the truth, but rather listed negative side effects or possible harm of the treatment.

For the search results pages, we showed the document's title, its url, and a snippet. We manually constructed the snippets. For topics T1-T8 (Table 3), one of the authors selected the first two sentences of the document as the snippet. For topics T9 and T10, a different author selected what appeared to be the most important and descriptive sentences. We did not realize that different techniques were employed until after the experiment was concluded. Given that we did not see significantly different click behavior across the different medical treatments, we do not believe that the different selection of snippets affects the results. As part of publication, we intend to release copies of these documents and the snippets for others to be able to replicate the experiment.

3.6 Dependent Variables

We study two dependent variables. The first is the fraction of decisions that are correct. A participant's decision about the efficacy of a medical treatment is correct if their decision matches the truth (Table 3). Note that if a participant decides that the efficacy of a medical treatment is inconclusive, that decision will always be wrong because our ten medical treatments are either helpful or unhelpful.

Our second dependent variable is the fraction of decisions that are harmful. We consider a harmful decision to be one where the participant decides that the efficacy is the opposite of the truth, i.e., the participant decides a medical treatment is helpful when in fact it is unhelpful, or unhelpful when it is helpful. If a participant decides that a medical treatment's efficacy is inconclusive, we do not count that as a harmful decision because our reasoning is that the participant will still need to find more information before making a final decision.

3.7 Study Design

After consenting to participate, participants filled out a questionnaire to capture demographic information as well as information about their usage of search engines for health related purposes. Following the questionnaire, the participants read instructions and had to answer correctly a set of questions regarding the study before they could proceed with the study. Next the participants had a chance to practice with the system by determining the efficacy of two medical treatments not used in the main study. For one medical treatment, they could use search results and for the other

they experienced the control condition, with no search results. The participants then began the main study where they had to decide on the efficacy of the ten medical treatments while experiencing the experimental conditions. For each medical treatment decision task, we asked pre-task and post-task questions. Before the task, we asked participants about their knowledge of the health issue and treatment. After the task we asked the participants about their confidence in their answer. At the end of the study, participants were debriefed and provided with the truth about each of the medical treatments.

3.7.1 User Interface. We built the study as a web application. For 8 of the 10 medical treatments, participants interacted with a search engine results page. For the other two medical treatments, the participants received the control condition, with no search results. We modelled the search results page after the traditional style of web search engines. At the top of the page, we displayed the medical treatment question that the user is asked to answer followed by a short boxed paragraph showing definitions of the health issue and treatment. We obtained the definitions from either Merriam-Webster's[1] or the Mayo Clinic's[2] medical dictionaries. We showed the definitions to avoid confusion and to make sure participants had a basic understanding of what was meant by the health issue and medical treatment. The medical treatment question and definitions remained visible throughout the entire task.

The search results page allowed participants to click on the search results, but they could not issue additional queries or obtain additional results. On the right side of the search results page, we displayed a reminder of the definitions of the different categories of medical treatment efficacies: *helps*, *does not help* and *inconclusive*.

For every document summary, we first showed the document title followed by a snippet and a link to the actual page. When a participant clicked on a search result, we took them to a screenshot of the web page rather than to the actual web page. We did this because we wanted to make sure that the participant was not able to click on any links and view any pages outside the scope of the study. In addition, this approach allowed us to be certain that each participant was exposed to the same version of the web page, and we did not have to fear the loss of pages during the study. We placed a button at the bottom of the search results page that, when pressed, took the user to a page to submit their decision regarding the efficacy of the medical treatment.

3.7.2 Balanced Design. We used a 10x10 Graeco-Latin square to create a fully balanced design and randomize medical treatments and experimental conditions. We create each 10x10 block by first creating four smaller 5x5 squares as follows. To balance the *helpful* medical treatments with the *unhelpful* ones, we generated three Latin Squares: one for the five experimental conditions, one for the five helpful medical treatments and one for the five unhelpful medical treatments. Overlaying the Latin square of experimental conditions over the helpful treatments and over the unhelpful treatments individually, we create two separate Graeco-Latin squares ensuring that both the *helpful* treatments and *unhelpful* treatments

---

[1]https://www.merriam-webster.com/
[2]http://www.mayoclinic.org/

have an equal and systematic balance of the experimental conditions. Finally by randomizing the columns and rows, this process creates two separate 5x5 Graeco-Latin Squares - one for the *helpful* treatments and one for the *unhelpful* treatments. Repeating the above process generates two new Graeco-Latin squares for *helpful* and *unhelpful* treatments and gives us four separate Graeco-Latin Squares (two *helpful* and two *unhelpful*). Combining the four squares we generate a 10x10 Graeco Latin square, and randomize the columns and rows and then randomly assign participants to each row.

3.8   Participants

We obtained ethics approval from our university and then recruited participants via posters and email announcements to different graduate student email lists at the university. All participants gave their informed consent. Following their participation, we debriefed all participants and provided them with the correct answers regarding the efficacy of the medical treatments. We paid participants $15. Participants were 60 students (27 male, 33 female) from different majors (36 from engineering and mathematics, 20 from arts and sciences and 4 from other majors) with an age between 18 and 36 years old (22% less than 20, 50% between 20 and 25 and 28% greater than 25, with an average age of 23).

3.9   Data Cleaning

During the course of the study, four participants had to be replaced because of failure to successfully complete the study due to technical or other issues. After a careful examination of the study data from the 60 participants, we did not find any irregularities and thus did not clean or modify the data before analysis.

3.10   Statistical Significance and Modelling

To determine the statistical significance of our results, we used generalized linear (logistic) mixed effect models as implemented in R [13] and the lme4[2] package. We used logistic regression because our dependent variables of correct and harmful decisions are binary outcomes. We modeled participants and medical treatments as random effects. Our independent and explanatory variables were fixed effects. We test the effect of each independent and explanatory variable on our dependent variables individually. To analyze the significance of these variables, for each variable we build and compare two models using a likelihood ratio test that reports a Chi-Square test statistic and p-value. The first model is the complete model. The complete model includes the dependent variable, the applicable independent variables, and the random effects. The second model is the null model, which includes everything in first model minus the variable of interest. With the two models, the null model, without the variable of interest, and the complete model, with the variable of interest, we perform the likelihood ratio test. The p-values are then determined by chi-square tests on the log-likelihood values.

When analyzing our entire dataset, which includes all five experimental conditions (a 2x2 factorial design plus one control), we do not include the Topmost Correct Rank as a fixed effect in the model. This is because the control condition has no search results, and therefore rank is not applicable. The majority of our other analyses

are done on the four search results experimental conditions without the control. For these analyses, we include both independent variables of Search Results Bias and Topmost Correct Rank in our models.

4   RESULTS AND DISCUSSION

The main results of our study focus on the effect of our independent variables on the participants' ability to correctly determine the efficacy of the ten medical treatments. The participants either interact with controlled search results to help them answer the question, or they are asked to directly answer the question without any search results (control condition). The search results are either biased towards correct or incorrect information regarding the medical treatment, with the topmost correct document at rank 1 or rank 3.

Table 1 reports the fraction of correct and harmful decisions of the 60 participants corresponding to the independent variables of Search Results Bias and Topmost Correct Rank. Refer to Section 3.6 for the definitions of correct and harmful decisions. We see that results with the rank 1 document correct and biased towards correct information can lead to increased accuracy up to 70%, while lowering harmful decisions from 20% to 6%. Conversely, results biased towards incorrect information significantly reduces accuracy from 43% to 23%, while doubling the incidence of harmful decisions.

Table 2 reports the statistical significance of the independent variables on the dependent variables from Table 1. Measuring significance using the techniques described in Section 3.10, we found the effect of the search result bias is statistically significant on the fraction of correct decisions and harmful decisions. We found that the topmost correct rank had less of an effect on the dependent variables, yet it did demonstrate some explanatory significance for our model with a nearly statistically significant effect (p = 0.06) on the fraction of harmful decisions made by the participant.

These results demonstrate the strong effect that search results can have on people's ability to use search results to correctly determine the efficacy of medical treatments. We have shown that with exposure to correct information, searchers perform better. On the other hand, we see that there is harm that can be done by incorrect information. For our experimental conditions where the search bias is towards incorrect information, the results show that participants actually perform worse than if they had no search results at all. Although the bias is towards incorrect information, the search results still contain two correct documents, with one always located in the top three ranks of the result list. The possibility to find the correct information is there, yet participants perform worse than if they were given no extra information.

Table 3 shows the fraction of correct decisions made by the participants for each of the ten medical treatments. For nine of the ten treatments, we see that search results biased towards incorrect information, decreases the accuracy with respect to the control. The treatment that does not behave as expected is T6 *Does caffeine help asthma?* (truth = helpful). For this specific treatment, the search results biased towards incorrect information improves performance over the control. The control shows that most participants generally begin with an incorrect belief. We may speculate that when exposed to the search results, participants may find the correct documents

Independent Variables		Dependent Variables	
Results Bias	Topmost Correct Rank	Fraction of Decisions	
		Correct	Harmful
Incorrect	3	0.23 ± 0.04	0.41 ± 0.05
Incorrect	1	0.23 ± 0.04	0.35 ± 0.04
Control (No search results)		0.43 ± 0.05	0.20 ± 0.04
Correct	3	0.59 ± 0.05	0.13 ± 0.03
Correct	1	0.70 ± 0.04	0.06 ± 0.02

Table 1: Main results. Users either interact with a page of search results or had to determine the efficacy of the medical treatment with no search results (control condition). We biased the search results towards incorrect or correct answers. We also controlled the topmost correct result to be at either rank 1 or 3. Based on the decisions the 60 participants made, we compute the fraction of correct and harmful decisions. Fractions are shown along with their standard errors. Table 2 reports the statistical significance of the independent variables.

Independent Variable	Dependent Variable	Pr(>Chisq)
Search Results Bias	Correct Decision	$\ll 0.001$
Search Results Bias	Harmful Decision	$\ll 0.001$
Topmost Correct Rank	Correct Decision	0.16
Topmost Correct Rank	Harmful Decision	0.06

Table 2: Statistical significance of independent variables. When the dependent variable is either the participant making a correct or a harmful decision, the search bias is statistically significant for the outcomes in Table 1. The rank of the topmost correct result shows significance near the 0.05 level with a p-value of 0.06 when the dependent variable is whether or not the participant makes a harmful decision.

and this slightly improves their performance. For eight of the ten treatments, we see that search results biased towards correct information, increases the accuracy with respect to the control. The two cases which do not behave as expected are T7 *Does cinnamon help diabetes?* (truth = unhelpful) and T9 *Does surgery help obesity?* (truth = helpful). For T9, the accuracy decreases slightly under the *correct* search results and may be due to random noise. On the other hand, T7 creates some speculation for what is actually going on for that specific treatment. A follow up study, including observations and debriefing participants would help better analyze these trends.

As White and Hassan [16] have demonstrated, participants and search engines have strong biases towards positive information. We split our data by the medical treatment type of *helpful, inconclusive, unhelpful* to investigate the trends and behaviours of our participants. Table 4 shows this data separately for the control condition and the other experimental conditions. Both tables show that there is an overall bias towards deciding that a health treatment is *helpful*. For the control condition, where the medical treatment is truly unhelpful, results show that participants correctly answer *unhelpful* about as often as they answer *inconclusive*. For the controlled experimental conditions, where the medical treatment is

truly unhelpful, results show that participants are actually more likely to answer *inconclusive* than to decide that the treatment is *unhelpful*. This suggests that users are looking for information that is positive, and would rather respond *inconclusive* than believe that a treatment is *unhelpful*. This is a dangerous bias. When a treatment is truly unhelpful, searchers want to find positive information, and therefore can be heavily influenced by search results with incorrect information, claiming that the treatment is *helpful*.

4.1 Knowledge and Confidence

Before participants saw any search results for a given medical treatment, we asked them separately about their knowledge of the health issue and the medical treatment. Participants answered the questions on a rating scale, which we coded from 1 to 5 to mean "nothing", "heard of it", "know generally about it", "quite familiar", and "know extensive details". Knowledge of the health issue and medical treatment were positively correlated as determined by the Pearson correlation coefficient of $r = 0.40$ ($p \ll 0.001$). After submitting their decision about the medical treatment, we asked participants to report their confidence in their answer on a 5 point scale from 1="very uncertain" to 5="very certain".

We did not find that knowledge had a statistically significant effect on our dependent variables, but we did see a general trend for more knowledge to result in a greater fraction of correct decisions when the search results were biased towards incorrect information. Looking closer, we decided to group decisions made with the two highest levels of knowledge into one group, *high* and the lowest three levels of knowledge into another group, *low*.

Considering only the experimental conditions when the search results are biased towards incorrect information, we can examine the fraction of correct decisions made plus and minus its standard error for both low and high knowledge levels of both health issue and medical treatment. The fraction of correct decisions and its standard error for *low health issue* knowledge was 0.19 ± 0.03. When the knowledge of the health issue is *high*, the fraction increases to 0.28 ± 0.04. Applying a Chi-squared test, the difference between these two rates is not statistically significant (p=0.14).

When the knowledge of the *medical treatment* is low, the fraction correct is 0.20 ± 0.03 and it increases to 0.34 ± 0.06 when knowledge is *high*. The difference between these rates is statistically significant (p=0.04). Knowledge of medical treatment can result in a significantly higher fraction of decisions made correctly when exposed to search results biased towards incorrect information. Table 3 shows that under the control condition, the fraction of decisions made correctly was 0.43 ± 0.05. Applying a two-sided t-test to compare the control condition to the decision made with high knowledge of the medical treatment, we fail to reject the null that they are the same rates (p=0.21). Even so, having knowledge of the health issue and medical treatment are not enough to raise performance above no exposure to search results. In other words, it is not as though the knowledgeable participants could fully ignore the incorrect information and only focus on the correct information and exceed the control condition's performance.

If we perform these same analyses for the fraction of decisions that are harmful, we find that more knowledge is associated with

T	Medical Treatment (Cochrane ID Suffix)	Efficacy	Fraction of Decisions Correct		
			Control (no search results)	Search Results Bias	
				Incorrect	Correct
T1	Do antioxidants help female subfertility? (7807.pub2)	Unhelpful	0.58 ± 0.15	0.08 ± 0.06	0.71 ± 0.09
T2	Do benzodiazepines help alcohol withdrawal? (5063.pub3)	Helpful	0.33 ± 0.14	0.29 ± 0.09	0.63 ± 0.10
T3	Do insoles help back pain? (5275.pub2)	Unhelpful	0.33 ± 0.14	0.17 ± 0.08	0.50 ± 0.10
T4	Do probiotics help treat eczema? (6135.pub2)	Unhelpful	0.33 ± 0.14	0.17 ± 0.08	0.75 ± 0.09
T5	Do sealants prevent dental decay in the permanent teeth? (1830.pub4)	Helpful	0.67 ± 0.14	0.46 ± 0.10	0.83 ± 0.08
T6	Does caffeine help asthma? (1112.pub2)	Helpful	0.08 ± 0.08	0.25 ± 0.09	0.79 ± 0.08
T7	Does cinnamon help diabetes? (7170.pub2)	Unhelpful	0.50 ± 0.15	0.00 ± 0.00	0.38 ± 0.10
T8	Does melatonin help treat and prevent jet lag? (1520)	Helpful	0.67 ± 0.14	0.38 ± 0.10	0.79 ± 0.08
T9	Does surgery help obesity? (3641.pub3)	Helpful	0.67 ± 0.14	0.46 ± 0.10	0.63 ± 0.10
T10	Does traction help low back pain? (3010.pub5)	Unhelpful	0.17 ± 0.11	0.08 ± 0.06	0.46 ± 0.10
	Overall		0.43 ± 0.05	0.23 ± 0.03	0.65 ± 0.03

Table 3: This table shows the medical treatments with their corresponding efficacy and suffix to their Cochrane [5] source ID. The Cochrane ID has been condensed from the full ID. The prefix for each suffix listed in the table is 14651858.CD00*. Each treatment is also assigned a label T1 - T10 that we use throughout the paper to refer to specific medical treatments. The table also shows the fraction of decisions correctly made by participants for each of the 10 medical treatments under the control condition, and the experimental conditions of search results biased toward incorrect and correct information. Fractions are shown along with their standard errors.

Control Condition (No Search Results)

Truth	Participant Decision			Total
	Unhelpful	Helpful	Inconclusive	
Unhelpful	23	16	21	60
Helpful	8	29	23	60
Total	31	45	44	120

Experimental Conditions (Interact with Search Results)

Truth	Participant Decision			Total
	Unhelpful	Helpful	Inconclusive	
Unhelpful	79	64	97	240
Helpful	50	132	58	240
Total	129	196	155	480

Table 4: Confusion matrices. These tables show the decisions made by the study participants regarding the efficacy of the 5 helpful and 5 unhelpful medical treatments. The upper table shows the decisions under the control condition when participants decide without any assistance at all. The lower table shows the decisions made under the experimental conditions that allow the participants to interact with controlled search results.

more harmful decisions. On investigation, we found that this is because people who are less knowledgeable are more likely to decide a medical treatment is *inconclusive*, which highlights a limitation of analyzing results in terms of the fraction of harmful decisions.

For the confidence of the decision, we found that participants who decide that a medical treatment's efficacy is *inconclusive*, are less confident in their answer than those deciding a treatment is *unhelpful* or *helpful*.

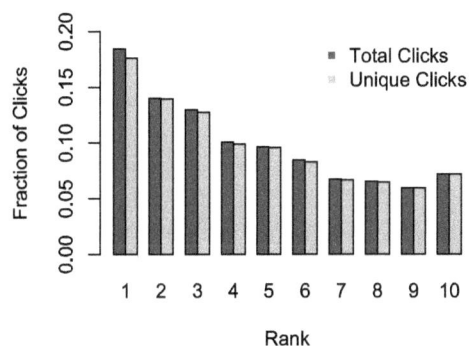

Figure 1: This graph shows the fraction of total clicks and unique clicks for each of the 10 search result ranks.

4.2 Clicks

Figure 1 shows the distribution of clicks over the search result ranks. We see that the total number of clicks and unique number of clicks per question and overall are very similar. The biggest difference between the total clicks and unique clicks occurs at rank 1, which shows that rank 1 is so important that some participants click on it multiple times in the same session. The overall distribution of clicks over search rank shows a similar result to what is seen with real search engines and provides some evidence that our participants interacted with our search results in a realistic fashion.

Over the four SERP experimental conditions, the average number of total clicks per question was 3.50 ± 0.1. For all correct decisions of SERP experimental conditions, the average number of total clicks was 3.73 ± 0.2. For all incorrect decisions of SERP experimental conditions, the average number of total clicks was 3.32 ± 0.2. For all harmful decisions of SERP experimental conditions (response was opposite to the correct answer), the average number of clicks was

Dependent Variables	Average Number of Clicks
Harmed Decisions	3.02 ± 0.3
Unharmed Decisions	3.65 ± 0.3
Correct Decisions	3.73 ± 0.2
Incorrect Decisions	3.32 ± 0.2

Table 5: Average Number of Clicks for each dependent variable: Correct Decisions, Harmful Decisions. This analysis only applies to the 4 SERP experimental conditions. Control data (No SERP) is not relevant.

3.02 ± 0.3. Conversely, all unharmful decisions of SERP experimental conditions (their response was correct), the average number of clicks was 3.65 ± 0.3. The difference between the mean number of clicks for correct and harmful decisions is statistically significant. Participants that interact more with the search results are more likely to make a correct decision and may be working harder to determine the correct answer.

5 CONCLUSION

When people use search engines to answer health questions, their interaction with the system has the potential for both positive and negative outcomes. When people find medical treatments or information that will prolong or improve their life, or that of a loved-one, search engines demonstrate an ability to make people's lives better. When search engines intermix correct and incorrect information, we have shown that there is the potential for harm.

In this paper, we showed that search results can significantly affect people's decisions about the efficacy of medical treatments. Compared to not using a search engine, when people interacted with search results biased toward incorrect information, their accuracy dropped from 43% to 23%. Thankfully, when people interact with search results biased towards correct information, their accuracy climbed to 65% (Table 3).

There has long been people who prey on the hopes of others for cures to terrible diseases, and now their webpages can become intermingled with those of reputable medical organizations. For example, a search for Hoxsey Therapy, an ineffective cancer treatment [3], on today's popular web search engines, returns a mix of results that either explain it is ineffective or explain how it can help a patient with cancer. We found that people are biased towards wanting treatments to be helpful, and this bias combined with incorrect information has the potential to cause people harm.

The implications of these results extend beyond health search. Information retrieval researchers typically use curated collections. These curated collections contain high quality and trustworthy documents. On the open web, we already know that there is spam, and we actively filter it out of web results. We now can see that web search needs more than spam filtering. Web search also needs a form of automated curation to be available to searchers so that they can have confidence in the quality of the information being provided to them. It is not enough to rely on searchers' own media literacy to protect them from incorrect information.

Likewise, information retrieval evaluation needs to expand its understanding of the effects of documents beyond graded relevance.

Non-relevant does not always mean innocuous. A document that leads a searcher to form a harmful belief about a medical treatment is damaging. A non-relevant document in today's effectiveness measures only causes a loss of time or effort and is represented as having zero gain. An incorrect document can increase the likelihood of a searcher forming a harmful belief and undoing the value of relevant documents, i.e. an incorrect document could be perceived to have some notion of a *negative gain*, which to our knowledge, is a new concept in information retrieval.

ACKNOWLEDGMENTS

We thank Ryen White for his assistance, feedback, and sharing of resources. Nimesh Ghelani and Gaurav Baruah both assisted with the running of the study. We thank the University of Waterloo Survey Research Centre for their advice. This work was supported in part by the Natural Sciences and Engineering Research Council of Canada (Grants CRDPJ 468812-14 and RGPIN-2014-03642), in part by Google, in part by the Qatar Foundation for Education, Science and Community Development, and in part by the University of Waterloo.

REFERENCES

[1] Alyssa Abkowitz. 2016. China Issues New Internet Search Rules Following Baidu Probe; Regulator mandates 'objective, fair and authoritative results'. *Wall Street Journal (Online)* (Jun 26 2016).

[2] Douglas Bates, Martin Mächler, Ben Bolker, and Steve Walker. 2015. Fitting Linear Mixed-Effects Models Using lme4. *Journal of Statistical Software* 67, 1 (2015), 1–48. DOI:http://dx.doi.org/10.18637/jss.v067.i01

[3] Barrie R. Cassileth and Helene Brown. 1988. Unorthodox cancer medicine. *CA: A Cancer Journal for Clinicians* 38, 3 (1988), 176–186.

[4] A Cipriani, TA Furukawa, and C Barbui. 2011. What is a Cochrane review? *Epidemiology and psychiatric sciences* 20, 03 (2011), 231–233.

[5] J. P. T. Higgins (Ed.). 2008. *Cochrane Handbook for Systematic Reviews of Interventions*. Vol. 5. The Cochrane Collaboration. www.cochrane-handbook.org.

[6] Robert Epstein and Ronald E Robertson. 2015. The search engine manipulation effect (SEME) and its possible impact on the outcomes of elections. *Proceedings of the National Academy of Sciences* 112, 33 (2015), E4512–E4521.

[7] Susannah Fox and Maeve Duggan. 2013. Health Online 2013. Pew Research Center. (2013).

[8] Yvonne Kammerer, Ivar Bråten, Peter Gerjets, and Helge I Strømsø. 2013. The role of Internet-specific epistemic beliefs in laypersons' source evaluations and decisions during Web search on a medical issue. *Computers in Human Behavior* 29, 3 (2013), 1193–1203.

[9] Juhi Kulshrestha, Motahhare Eslami, Johnnatan Messias, Muhammad Bilal Zafar, Saptarshi Ghosh, IIEST Shibpur, India Krishna P Gummadi, and Karrie Karahalios. 2017. Quantifying Search Bias: Investigating Sources of Bias for Political Searches in Social Media. In *Proc. of CSCW*.

[10] Yadan Ouyang. 2016. Student's death highlights gaps in China's health regulations. *Lancet Oncology* 17, 6 (2016), 709.

[11] Bing Pan, Helene Hembrooke, Thorsten Joachims, Lori Lorigo, Geri Gay, and Laura Granka. 2007. In Google We Trust: Users' Decisions on Rank, Position, and Relevance. *Journal of Computer-Mediated Communication* 12, 3 (2007), 801–823.

[12] Kristen Purcell, Joanna Brenner, and Lee Rainie. 2012. Search Engine Use 2012. Pew Research Center. (2012).

[13] R Core Team. 2014. *R: A Language and Environment for Statistical Computing*. R Foundation for Statistical Computing, Vienna, Austria. http://www.R-project.org/

[14] Ryen White. 2013. Beliefs and biases in web search. In *SIGIR*. ACM, 3–12.

[15] Ryen W White. 2014. Belief dynamics in Web search. *Journal of the Association for Information Science and Technology* 65, 11 (2014), 2165–2178.

[16] Ryen W White and Ahmed Hassan. 2014. Content bias in online health search. *ACM Transactions on the Web (TWEB)* 8, 4 (2014), 25.

[17] Ryen W White and Eric Horvitz. 2015. Belief dynamics and biases in web search. *ACM Transactions on Information Systems (TOIS)* 33, 4 (2015), 18:1–18:46.

Personalized Navigation and Random Walk on a Complex Heterogeneous Graph

Xiaozhong Liu*
School of Informatics and Computing
Indiana University Bloomington
Bloomington,IN, USA 47405
liu237@indiana.edu

Yingying Yu[†]
School of Software
Dalian University of Foreign
Languages
Dalian, China 116044
uee870927@126.com

Zhuoren Jiang
Institute of Computer Science and
Technology
Peking University
Beijing, China 100871
jiangzr@pku.edu.cn

Chun Guo
School of Informatics and Computing
Indiana University Bloomington
Bloomington,IN, USA 47405
chunguo@indiana.edu

Scott Jensen
Lucas College and Graduate School of
Business
San Jose State University
San Jose, CA, USA 95192
scott.jensen@sjsu.edu

ABSTRACT

As data in many disciplines continues to grow at a frantic pace, a more heterogeneous set of information sources both can and need to be connected in innovative ways to improve information search and recommendation systems. Using information retrieval (IR) as an example, classical search techniques are based on limited information, including query terms, the content of documents, and basic user characteristics. However, recent studies have started to investigate additional information resources, including semantic web data, knowledge graphs, linguistic features, user email account content, social networks, user behavior, the search context, and other sources. Intuitively, a heterogeneous graph integrating all these information sources could enhance search performance. However, the complexity of such graphs challenge most existing graph mining algorithms. In this study, we propose a novel approach for a personalized random walk over a complex heterogeneous graph; which we refer to as Personalized Graph Navigation (PGN). Unlike earlier expert-guided random walk approaches, by using an EM framework, PGN estimates the personalized usefulness probability distribution for each edge type (the latent variable), which can be used as a random walk navigation profile for a user on a heterogeneous graph. While PGN can cope with information retrieval/recommendation problems at a low cost, this method also transforms a complex heterogeneous graph into a homogeneous graph, allowing existing homogeneous graph mining algorithms to be applied to a heterogeneous graph.

*Xiaozhong Liu is the corresponding author

[†]Yingying Yu is the co-corresponding author

ICTIR'17, October 1–4, 2017, Amsterdam, The Netherlands
© 2017 ACM. ISBN 978-1-4503-4490-6/17/10...$15.00
DOI: http://dx.doi.org/10.1145/3121050.3121061

KEYWORDS

Personalization; Complex Heterogeneous Graph Mining; Random Walk; Information Retrieval; Information Recommendation

1 INTRODUCTION AND MOTIVATION

Over the past decade, information search has evolved beyond considering only a user's query and a corpus of documents. Similarly, recommendation systems have evolved beyond the limitations of just a user-item rating matrix. Additional data, especially user data generated from multiple sources, has been successfully used to enhance the performance of information retrieval/recommendation systems. For example, early works in music recommendation used classical item-based or user-based methods that employed a user-music rating matrix as input [8]. However, recent studies have found that additional, often novel data sources both specific to a song (e.g., the artist, album, genre, user-generated tags, or playlists including the song), as well as specific to a user (the user's social network, favorite music/artist/album, comments, and bookmarks), can potentially be useful for both music search and recommendation. In this study, we incorporate various types of information into complex heterogeneous graphs[1].

Integrating additional data can potentially enhance both search and recommendation results, but there are two major challenges. **The first challenge is that most existing text or graph based algorithms cannot efficiently cope with very complex heterogeneous data;** including multi-graph integration [34], hyperedge [4], sequential relation path [16] and meta-path [30] approaches. For instance, [16] proposed an approach to ranking that used a number of (expert generated) relation paths or meta-paths over a relatively simple heterogeneous graph based on expert generated hypotheses as to which nodes (objects) and edges (relationships) were more important for ranking. However, in a complex heterogeneous graph it can be difficult to exhaustively examine all of the potentially useful path

---

[1]There is no official definition of "complex heterogeneous graphs". In this study, the complex heterogeneous graph means the graph with at least 10 different types of edges.

types. Furthermore, if a large number of random walk-based ranking functions are used, the computational cost can be prohibitive.

The second challenge is that the usefulness of each data type varies depending on the user. Using music recommendation as an example, some users can be characterized as idolaters who prefer to listen to music from particular artists (e.g., they prefer an artist or album-related path), while other users prefer to listen to specific types of music (e.g., they prefer genre, playlist or tag-related paths). A single ranking model cannot tailor its recommendation results to satisfy both types of users. Expressed as paths over a graph, Figure 1 shows that $user_1$ has two preferred paths from a song they know (M_1) to a new song (M_2): $music \rightarrow artist \rightarrow genre \rightarrow music$ and $music \rightarrow playlist \rightarrow music$. On the other hand, $user_2$ is a simple idolater, so $music \rightarrow artist \rightarrow music$ works best for her. When complex heterogeneous data are brought together in a graph, being able to personalize the navigation path is critical.

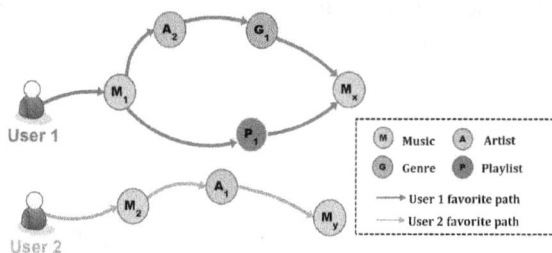

Figure 1: Personalized ranking over a heterogeneous graph.

In this study, we propose a novel method, Personalized Graph Navigation (PGN), for personalized random walk, search and recommendation over a complex heterogeneous graph. Given a user and a specific search or recommendation task, we simplify the problem by introducing a new latent variable, the **personalized edge type usefulness probability distribution**, which enables an innovative approach to estimating a user profile. More importantly, this latent variable allows a complex heterogeneous graph to be simplified to a homogeneous graph where the random walk probability is navigated using a classical *edge transitioning probability* combined with a novel *personalized edge type usefulness probability*. In order to estimate the user profile, we employ an iterative EM (expectation-maximization), where the E-step ranks objects in the graph using the existing user profile and then in the M-step the user profile is maximized for the specific search or recommendation task. We repeat this process until the user profile and object ranking stabilize.

The contributions of this paper are fourfold. First, we propose a new method, personalized graph navigation (PGN), for personalized information search and recommendation. Second, we show that the proposed method can efficiently cope with complex heterogeneous data without human intervention. Third, by using the new latent variable (personalized edge type usefulness probability distribution), a complex heterogeneous graph can be converted to a homogeneous graph for random walk and ranking. Then, we could apply homogeneous graph mining algorithms to heterogeneous graphs. Lastly, we validate the proposed method using two relatively complex datasets: music graph (with 6 types of nodes and 18 types of edges) and scholarly graph (with 5 types of nodes and 26 types of edges) to perform a music/scholarly recommendation tasks.

2 RELATED WORK

Personalized search and recommendation have been investigated and a number of personalization algorithms are well documented. For example, memory-based collaborative filtering (CF) algorithms, (e.g., item/user-based CF [26], and matrix factorization [15]) have been used successfully in information recommendation to generate high quality results. However, all of these algorithms are based mainly on a user-item rating matrix and studies have found that item content can be used to enhance performance [26].

In contrast to the CF algorithms used in personalized recommendation, personalized search tends to use additional data sources, including query logs [25], query session [9], user browsing behavior [11], and knowledge-bases [5]. Personalization algorithms allow different users to receive results tailored to them for the same search query. Hannak et al. [13] found that on average, 11.7% of the Google search results show differences due to personalization. However, most prior personalization studies have only included a small number of different data sources when generating a user profile, and as data become more complex and heterogeneous, these existing methods may no longer be appropriate.

Graph mining has proven to be one of the most efficient means for information search and recommendation and a number of algorithms are well documented. Web pages and scholarly publications are examples of interconnected graphs based on hyperlinks or citations, and PageRank has been used to identify important nodes in a graph. Random walk based search and ranking algorithms over such graphs have been extensively investigated (e.g., query expansion [6], term weighting [3], and query log mining [7]), and graph analysis has been used to enhance recommendation results [24]. For instance, [17] proved that user trust and information cascades exist in social networks and recommendation datasets. Meanwhile, previous studies [10, 32] have also employed graph mining to address personalization. Meng et al. [22], applied the personalized random walk to a multi-layer graph for citation recommendation, where different kinds information are treated equally in the graph. However, most existing work on ranking is based on a homogeneous graph containing a single type of object or link. Intuitively, with multiple kinds of data available, a heterogeneous graph may be a better data structure for search and recommendation tasks.

In recent years the mining of heterogeneous graphs has attracted increased research interest. Taking bibliographic databases as an example, authors, venues, and publications can be represented as different types of nodes that are related through different types of edges such as citation, authorship, and co-author for academic search and recommendation [18, 19]. The heterogeneous objects and relationships in such a graph provide flexibility in defining possible paths for a 'random walk' over the graph. For instance, PathSim [30] proposed extending the measure of similarity in a graph by measuring the number of connecting paths with the same semantics based on meta-paths between nodes and [1, 27] utilized heterogeneous graphs for link prediction. Using scholarly search as an example, two publications can be connected via the meta-path *Author-Paper-Author* or *Author-Venue-Author* [18, 31], where each meta-path can be used as a ranking function for the results presented to the user. Meta-path-based graph mining has been applied to a number of graph-related tasks, including similarity search [30], relationship prediction [29], user-guided clustering [31], and recommendation [18]. These meta-path approaches employ a supervised random walk over the heterogeneous graph, and prior studies have shown that a supervised random walk can significantly enhance classical unsupervised graph mining methods. The approach presented in this paper also employs a supervised random walk method as investigated in [16, 18]. Graph techniques similar to meta-paths include hyperedges as applied to music recommendation in [4], sequential relation path as used in [16] for scholarly recommendation, and multi-graph integration as applied to scholarly recommendation [34]. All of these methods require somehow expert assistance.

Although existing heterogeneous graph mining solutions have shown great promise, there are three reasons such solutions may be challenged by complex heterogeneous graphs. First, when the network is relatively simple, human generated meta-paths can be quite effective. For instance, Baluja et al., [2] provided personalized video suggestions based on a graph consisting of two types of objects. When a heterogeneous graph is relative simple, users can easily propose a small number of meta-paths as hypotheses for ranking. However, as graphs become more complex, it is not feasible for humans to consider all of the meta-paths for ranking. Second, even if all of the meta-paths on a complex graph could be considered [12] or a large number of homogeneous graphs could be integrated through a learning to rank approach [34], the high computational cost is likely to be prohibitive for a large complex dataset. Third, existing meta-path based methods cannot address the personalized information needs of different users. Intuitively, different users may prioritize different paths when identifying the resources most useful to them.

3 RESEARCH METHODS
3.1 Definitions

An information network represents an abstraction of the real world; focusing on the objects and interactions (links) between those objects. A heterogeneous graph can be defined as $G = (\mathcal{V}, \mathcal{E})$ where $\mathcal{V}$ is a set of nodes (objects) and $\mathcal{E}$ is a set of edges (links). Since there are multiple types of objects in the graph, an object type mapping function $\tau : \mathcal{V} \rightarrow \mathcal{A}$ maps each object $v \in \mathcal{V}$ to a particular object type $\tau(v) \in \mathcal{A}$, where $\mathcal{A}$ is the set of object types in the graph's schema. Similarly, a link type mapping function $\phi : \mathcal{E} \rightarrow \mathcal{R}$ maps each link $e \in \mathcal{E}$ to a particular relation type $\phi(e) \in \mathcal{R}$, where $\mathcal{R}$ represents the set of relation types in the graph's schema. If two links belong to the same relation type, the two links share the same starting object type and ending object type. The complexity of the graph increases as the number of object and relation types in the graph's schema increases.

A general recommendation task on a heterogeneous graph is denoted as $T = (Q \rightsquigarrow C)$, which means, given specific query object(s) $Q \in \mathcal{V}$ and $\tau(Q) = \dot{A}_Q \in \mathcal{A}$, the recommendation algorithm returns a list of candidate objects $C \in \mathcal{V}$ where $\tau(C) = \dot{A}_C \in \mathcal{A}$. For instance, for most e-commerce services, Q can be a user, and C can be target items or digital products recommended to the user. An information retrieval task can be converted to a similar form from a relevance feedback viewpoint [18], where a text query can be converted to a number of relevant document nodes (Q) on the graph (if user node doesn't exist on the graph), and a random walk function can search for additional relevant documents (C).

Actually, the boundary between homogeneous and heterogeneous graphs can start to blur. By ignoring the object and relation types for a graph, it can be converted from a heterogeneous graph to a homogeneous one. For either type of graph, a random walk function (from Q to C) can be used to rank results. However, in most cases, while the random walk on a homogeneous graph can be unsupervised, it is necessary to provide a hypothesis-driven tour definition (e.g, a meta-path) for a random walk on a heterogeneous graph.

3.2 Personalized Navigation on Graph

As mentioned above, most existing heterogeneous graph mining algorithms first require a domain expert to generate random walk (ranking) hypotheses, which can be problematic for complex heterogeneous graphs. Existing methods also cannot address personalization, allowing different users to apply different kinds of random walk functions (e.g., meta-paths), over the target graph. In this study, we propose PGN as a novel method to personalize tour navigation and random walk over a complex heterogeneous graph. Unlike traditional approaches, the PGN algorithm does not require a meta-path based hypothesis for ranking. Instead, for user u and task T, a new latent variable, the personalized edge type usefulness probability distribution $P_T(\theta_\phi|u)$ is used for random walk navigation over the graph, where ϕ represents the edge type. By using this variable we can tailor the random walk probability from one node (V_j) to another connected node (V_k) on the graph:

$$P(V_j \xrightarrow{e_l} V_k|u) = P(V_j \xrightarrow{e_l} V_k) \cdot P_T(\tau(V_j) \xrightarrow{\phi(e_l)} \tau(V_k)|u)$$

where $P(V_j \xrightarrow{e_l} V_k)$ is the edge transition probability between two connected nodes V_j and V_k via edge e_l, and $P_T(\tau(V_j) \xrightarrow{\phi(e_l)} \tau(V_k)|u)$ is the edge type usefulness probability for user u extracted from the latent variable $P_T(\theta_\phi|u)$. When an edge type is less useful for a given target user and task, the edge type usefulness probability will be low, reducing the likelihood that a random walk would transition from the starting node to the end node; even if the edge transition probability between those two nodes is high.

3.3 Heterogeneous Graph Random Walk and $P_T(\theta_\phi|u)$ Inference

While the new latent variable can be applied to a number of homogeneous graph mining algorithms, in this section we investigate its application to the random walk algorithm as a specific case. The key issue is to infer $P_T(\theta_\phi|u)$ for each target user. To reduce the computational cost, the inference of $P_T(\theta_\phi|u)$ (using the EM framework) is integrated into the recursive PageRank-based random walk process. We call this PGNRank (see Algorithm 1):

Initially the edge type usefulness probability is set to $\frac{1}{|\phi|}$ for every edge, where $|\phi|$ is the total number of edge types in the graph's schema. The Expectation step (t iteration), calculates the PGNRank score as follows for each node in the graph based on the edge type usefulness probability of the prior iteration $P_T^{(t)}(\theta_\phi|u)$:

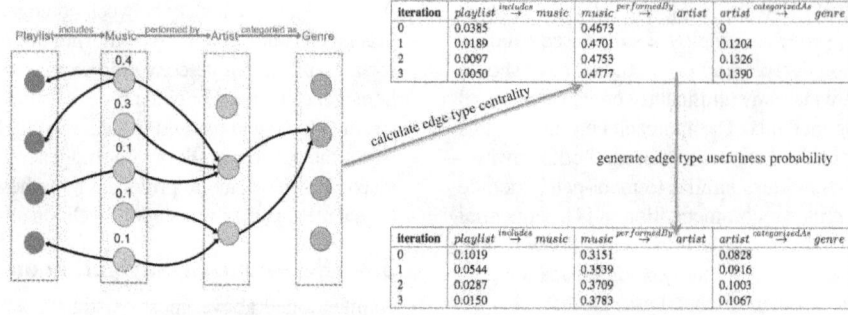

iteration	playlist $\xrightarrow{includes}$ music	music $\xrightarrow{performedBy}$ artist	artist $\xrightarrow{categorized\ as}$ genre
0	0.0385	0.4673	0
1	0.0189	0.4701	0.1204
2	0.0097	0.4753	0.1326
3	0.0050	0.4777	0.1390

calculate edge type centrality

generate edge type usefulness probability

iteration	playlist $\xrightarrow{includes}$ music	music $\xrightarrow{performedBy}$ artist	artist $\xrightarrow{categorised\ as}$ genre
0	0.1019	0.3151	0.0828
1	0.0544	0.3539	0.0916
2	0.0287	0.3709	0.1003
3	0.0150	0.3783	0.1067

Figure 2: Edge Type Usefulness Probability Optimization Toy Example.

Algorithm 1 Heterogeneous Graph based PGNRank and $P_T(\theta_\phi|u)$ Inference via EM approach

1: Initially (0): all $\phi \in \mathcal{R}$ get the same probability score for $P_T^{(0)}(\theta_\phi|u)$
2: **procedure** E-STEP: RANKING
3:    Calculate the PGNRank score $PGNRank^{(t+1)}(\mathcal{V}|u)$ using $P_T^{(t)}(\theta_\phi|u)$ and PageRank
4:    Call M-Step
5: **end procedure**
6: **procedure** M-STEP (T): UPDATE $P_T^{(t+1)}(\theta_\phi|u)$
7:    $P_T^{(t+1)}(\theta_\phi|u) = \underset{P_T(\theta_\phi|u)}{argmax}PGNRank(\mathcal{V}|P_T^{(t)}(\theta_\phi|user_x))$
8:    **if** object ranking and $P_T(\theta_\phi|u)$ stabilize **then**
9:       Algorithm End
10:    **else**
11:       Call E-Step
12:    **end if**
13: **end procedure**

$$PR^{(t+1)}(V_k) = d \sum_{V_j \in In(V_k)} PR^{(t)}(V_j) \cdot P^{(t)}(V_j \xrightarrow{e_l} V_k|user_x)$$
$$+ (1-d)Prior(V_k)$$

where $PR^{(t+1)}(V_k)$ is the PGNRank score for node V_k for the $t+1$ iteration, and $P^{(t)}(V_j \xrightarrow{e_l} V_k|user_x)$ is the new random walk function proposed in the last section. Note that the new random walk function requires both the edge transition probability and the edge type usefulness probability from the prior iteration (i.e., $P_T^{(t)}(\tau(V_j) \xrightarrow{\phi(e_l)} \tau(V_k)|user_x)$).The node prior probability, $Prior(V_k)$, follows the definition in PageRank with priors [32], which can be the preferred objects for the user as extracted from the training data. Using music recommendation as an example, the node prior can be calculated based on the user's historical listening history.

In the Maximization step, we need to update the $P_T^{(t+1)}(\theta_\phi|u)$ distribution by $\underset{P_T(\theta_\phi|u)}{argmax}PGNRank(\mathcal{V}|P_T^{(t)}(\theta_\phi|u))$. In this paper, we use the edge type convergence probability to update the usefulness probability of each edge type $P_T^{(t+1)}(\tau_i \xrightarrow{\phi_l} \tau_j|u)$. If a number of edges of type ϕ_l start at nodes of type τ_i, and those nodes are important in iteration t (the nodes have high PGNRank scores), and those edges converge on a small set of nodes of type τ_j, that will increase the ranking of those nodes of type τ_j in iteration $t+1$. The

reverse edges (with type ϕ_l^{-1} and start nodes of type τ_j and end nodes of type τ_i) will be maximized in subsequent iterations.

Using music recommendation again as an example, for a given user, if a number of music nodes have high PGNRank scores in iteration t, and those songs are performed by a small number of artists, the edge type convergence probability is high and the importance of the edge type $Music \xrightarrow{performedBy} Artist$ can be high. In the $t+1$ iteration, the $Music \xleftarrow{performedBy^{-1}} Artist$ type edges from artists to music (songs) will not only enhance the rankings of the music already identified as important in the prior iteration t, but will also find additional music that is important because it is performed by artists important to that user.

For edge type $\tau_i \xrightarrow{\phi_l} \tau_j$, the convergence probability of edge type ϕ_l can be estimated by the probability that node instances of τ_i meet each other via paths containing edges of type ϕ_l. The more important the edge type ϕ_l is, the more likely we are able to find other important nodes of either type τ_i or τ_j.

The edge type convergence $C^{t+1}(\tau_i \xrightarrow{\phi_l} \tau_j|u)$ is defined in formula (1). The proposed algorithm incorporates two different kinds of indicators: the importance probability of the starting node type τ_i (by using the accumulated PGNRank scores of the τ_i typed nodes from E-step), and the probability that two starting type nodes meet via an ϕ_l type edge. For the latter, the numerator is the chance that one important node instance ($\in \tau_i$) reaches another one by random walk via an edge of type ϕ_l, (i.e., all the instances of $V_{\tau_{i_1}} \xrightarrow{e_{\phi_{l_1}}} V_{\tau_j} \xleftarrow{e_{\phi_{l_2}}} V_{\tau_{i_2}}$). The denominator is all possible combination of two randomly selected path instances ($\in \phi_l$). The edge type usefulness probability can be updated by incorporating the convergence scores:

$$P_T^{t+1}(\phi_l|u) = \frac{P_T^t(\phi_l|u) + C^{t+1}(\phi_l|u)}{\sum_{\phi_a}^{|\phi|}[P_T^t(\phi_a|u) + C^{t+1}(\phi_a|u)]}$$

Figure 2 shows a (toy) example in which the top ranked music nodes (based on initial PGNRank scores for a given user) are more likely to be connected to the same artists (via $Music \xrightarrow{performedBy} Artist$ type edges) than to the same playlists (via $Music \xrightarrow{includes^{(-1)}} Playlist$ type edges). In this example, since the $Artist$ nodes are more likely to be connected to multiple highly ranked music nodes

$$C^{t+1}(\tau_i \overset{\phi_l}{\to} \tau_j | u) = \frac{\sum_{V_{\tau_i}} PR^t(V_{\tau_i}|u)}{\sum_V PR^t(V|u)} \cdot \frac{\sum_{V_{\tau_{i1}}} \overset{e_{\phi_{l1}}}{\to} V_{\tau_j} \overset{e_{\phi_{l2}}}{\leftarrow} V_{\tau_{i2}} [PR^t(V_{\tau_{i1}}|u) \cdot P(e_{\phi_{l1}}) \cdot PR^t(V_{\tau_{i2}}|u) \cdot P(e_{\phi_{l2}})]}{\sum_{e_{\phi_{lm}}}^{|\phi_l|} \sum_{e_{\phi_{ln}}}^{|\phi_l|} [PR^t(V_{\tau_i}^{\phi_{lm}}|u) \cdot P(e_{\phi_{lm}}) \cdot PR^t(V_{\tau_i}^{\phi_{ln}}|u) \cdot P(e_{\phi_{ln}})]} \tag{1}$$

than are *Playlist* nodes, the *Music* $\overset{performedBy}{\to}$ *Artist* edge type will have a higher convergence and usefulness probability in the t M-step. In the $t+1$ E-step, the updated edge type usefulness will help the random walk function locate other important music nodes that can be reached by traversing edges originating at important artists. Similarly, in the $t+1$ M-step, convergence and usefulness probability of the *Artist* $\overset{categorizedAs}{\to}$ *Genre* type edges will be influenced by multiple edges from important artists merging at the same genre type node. Values for the first four iterations of calculating the recursive edge type convergence and usefulness probability are depicted in Figure 2, and the results for the $P_T(Music \overset{performedBy}{\to} Artist|u)$ is higher than the other edge types.

This EM process is repeated until both the PGNRank score distribution and edge type usefulness distribution stabilize (i.e., $P_T^t(\phi|u) \approx P_T^{t+1}(\phi|u)$ and $PGNRank^{(t)}(\mathcal{V}|u) \approx PGNRank^{(t+1)}(\mathcal{V}|u)$).

The proposed algorithm provides two benefits. First, by leveraging the personalized navigation method, the revised PageRank method generates a general ranking list of all the nodes $\mathcal{V}$ in the heterogeneous graph. Because each node is associate with a node type, the general node ranking can be converted into $|\phi|$ ranking lists, and each list ranks all of the nodes of a specific node type. Second, the algorithm generates an edge type usefulness probability distribution, $P_T(\theta_\phi|u)$, which is a novel user profile (for random walk navigation). We propose that this user profile is more stable than the graph content. Using citation recommendation as an example, the user profile as calculated represents the generalized behavior that a specific user exhibits when traversing the graph and selecting papers, authors, or venues to expand on the graph.

When the graph is dynamically expanding, i.e., for a time Δt, a number of new nodes $\Delta \mathcal{V}$ and new edges $\Delta \mathcal{V}$ will have been added to the graph. We can rank the importance of the new nodes by using the user profile, i.e., based on the random walk probability given $P_T(\theta_\phi|u)$. For information recommendation or retrieval problems, in order to enhance the algorithm performance, we can keep the user profile training offline, and random walk based ranking online. The assumption is that the user profile is more stable than the ranking results (e.g., user online music listening behavior is relatively stable).

More importantly, $P_T(\theta_\phi|u)$ and the new random walk method enable us to apply existing homogeneous graph mining methods to a complex heterogeneous graph.

4 EXPERIMENT

4.1 Dataset

The proposed PGN method is validated using complex heterogeneous graphs based on data collected in two different domains. To the best of our knowledge, the schemas for these graphs are more complex than those used in most prior studies on heterogeneous graph mining. The first graph is for a music sharing network and is based on a dataset containing metadata and user generated data from

Xiami.com, a popular music social network/music streaming service in China. Xiami captures user-contributed and editor-curated metadata about different music entities [12]. It also allows users to build a personal profile, record their listening history, create customized playlists, and socialize with other users within the community. As shown in Figure 3, the schema for the graph based on the Xiami data consists of 6 types of nodes and 18 types of edges (including the inverse edges for the reverse relationships). For this study, the experiment dataset contains 56,055 artists, 43,086 albums, 1,233,651 songs, 633 genres, 677,275 users, 305,916 playlists, and a total of 8,388,014 relationships between these entities. The proposed task for the experiment is music recommendation (recommending songs to the user), i.e., $T = (U \rightsquigarrow S)$ on the graph.

The second graph is a scholarly network based on a dataset we collected from the ACM Digital Library. As shown in Figure 3, the schema for this graph consists of 5 types of nodes and 26 types of edges (including the inverse edges). The dataset contains information on 171,025 papers, 270,576 authors, 586 venues, 3,910 keywords (topics), 2,679 (ACM) categories and a total of 4,824,349 relationships between these entities. The proposed task for this experiment is scholarly recommendation (recommending papers to an author), i.e., $T = (A \rightsquigarrow P)$ on the graph. Citation recommendation without personalization has previously been explored in [16, 18].

Performance on the music recommendation task is evaluated by randomly selecting 342 users from the dataset whose listening history contains more than 50 songs. For the scholarly recommendation task, we select 300 authors from the ACM data who have a publishing record containing citations to over 50 papers. We set these thresholds to make sure there were enough training/test instances for each user. For both tasks, after identifying the users or authors for the evaluation, 40% of their listening/citation history was removed from both the graph and the user-item matrix to work as ground truth. We also removed the "playlists" that created by the 342 testing users to avoid any leak of the ground truth.

Given space limitations, we provide detailed results for the music graph and general results for the scholarly graph. More detailed results can be found on the project website.

4.2 Recommendation Baselines

Music Graph: For music recommendation we compare the proposed PGN approach to three collaborative filtering (CF) algorithms [8] and a meta-path based approach [28–31] using five different expert-generated meta-path ranking functions. The three CF algorithms used are popularity-based CF (**POP**), item-based CF (**CF_IS**), and implicit matrix factorization (**CF_IMF**) [14].

Unlike the KDD-Cup 2011 Yahoo! Music Recommendation challenge [8] which included explicit user ratings for songs, we use play counts in our dataset. Play counts are considered to be implicit feedback from a collaborative filtering perspective [21]. Having listened to a song only once doesn't necessarily mean a user dislikes the

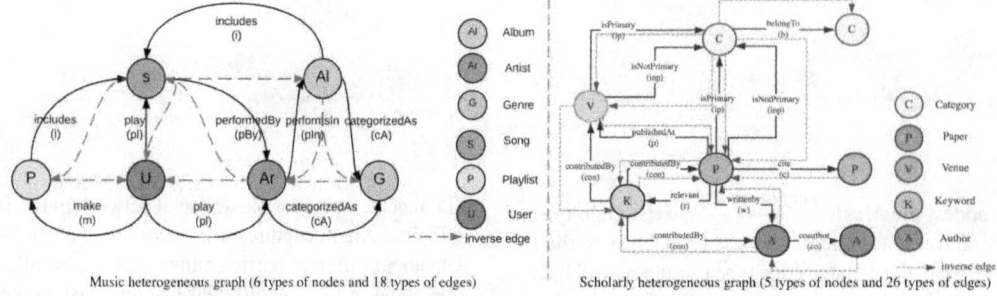

Figure 3: Music and Scholarly (Complex) Heterogeneous Graph Schema.

song; the user simply may not have had a second chance to listen to it yet. But an explicit rating of 1 (on a 1-to-5 scale) generally means the user is not quite into that song. Researchers have developed separate CF approaches for implicit datasets. In the implicit matrix factorization model[14], play count is used to represent confidence in the preference rather than the preference itself. The performance of matrix factorization (**CF_IMF**) improves as the number of factors considered goes up. We experimented with different numbers of factors and report recommendation performance results using 50 factors, which we found to be the best-performing parameter setting for this baseline method.

For the meta-path based baseline approach we use the following five expert-generated meta-path ranking functions:

- **[MP1]:** $U \xrightarrow{pl} S \xleftarrow{i} P \xrightarrow{i} S$ [*Hypothesis: the playlist containing a song the user has played can be useful in finding other important songs*]

- **[MP2]:** $U \xrightarrow{pl} S \xrightarrow{pBy} Ar \xleftarrow{pBy} S$ [*Hypothesis: The artist performing a song the user has played can be useful in finding other important songs*]

- **[MP3]:** $U \xrightarrow{pl} S \xrightarrow{pBy} Ar \xrightarrow{pIn} Al \xrightarrow{i} S$ [*Hypothesis: Album(s) from the artist performing a song the user has played can be useful in finding other important songs*]

- **[MP4]:** $U \xrightarrow{pl} S \xleftarrow{i} Al \xleftarrow{pIn} Ar \xleftarrow{pBy} S$ [*Hypothesis: The artist(s) performing on an album containing a song the user has played can be useful in finding other important music*]

- **[MP5]:** $U \xrightarrow{pl} S \xleftarrow{i} P \xleftarrow{m} U \xrightarrow{m} P \xrightarrow{i} S$ [*Hypothesis: The playlists created by a user who created a playlist containing a song the user played can be useful in finding other important music*]

For each meta-path, the query node is the target user U, and we retrieve a number of candidate music nodes S by following the target meta-path [18]. A meta-path can be represented as: $\dot{A}_Q \xrightarrow{R_1} \dot{A}_1 \xrightarrow{R_2} \dot{A}_2 \dots \xrightarrow{R_{l-1}} \dot{A}_{l-1} \xrightarrow{R_l} \dot{A}_R$, where $\dot{A}_Q$ is the query node type, and $\dot{A}_R$ is the recommended node type. Then, the meta-path-based ranking function can be used to calculate the ranking score for each candidate recommendation node. The random walk based relevance measure between v_i and v_j is defined as:

$$s(v_i, v_j | \mathcal{P}) = \sum_{t = v_i \rightsquigarrow v_j | \mathcal{P}} RW(t)$$

where t is a tour from v_i to v_j following a specific meta-path $\mathcal{P}$, and $RW(t)$ is the random walk probability of the tour t. Suppose $t = (v_i, v_{i+1}, \dots, v_{i+k}, \dots, v_j)$, the random walk probability is then $RW(t) = \prod_{k=0}^{k=j-i-1} w(v_{i+k}, v_{i+k+1})$, where $w(v_{i+k}, v_{i+k+1})$ is the weight of edge $v_{i+k} \rightarrow v_{i+k+1}$. More detailed ranking functions can be found in [18, 28].

From a ranking viewpoint, a stronger method is learning to rank, and each meta-path can be used as a ranking feature, (i.e., use learning to rank to train a ranking model $\Phi(\mathcal{P}_1, \mathcal{P}_2 \dots, \mathcal{P}_t)$, where $\mathcal{P}_i$ ($1 \leq i \leq t$) is a meta-path based ranking feature). As this study is not focused on learning to rank, we used a relatively simple algorithm, Coordinate Ascent [23], which iteratively optimizes a multivariate objective ranking function. Previous studies [16, 18] have shown that learning to rank + meta-path solutions perform well for a number of search and recommendation tasks.

For the music recommendation task, the primary evaluation metric is MAP@500, and we also explore precision and NDCG at different cut off values k as evaluation metrics. For scholarly recommendation, P@10 and NDCG@10 can be more important [18].

Scholarly Graph: For the scholarly recommendation task we compared PGN with a heterogeneous graph random walk method [16, 18]. Given space limitations, we provide evaluation details on the project website. The five baseline meta-paths used are described below. We also use Coordinate Ascent [23] to generate learning to rank models for evaluation.

- **[MP1]:** $A \xleftarrow{w} P \xrightarrow{c} P \xrightarrow{ip} C \xleftarrow{ip} V \xleftarrow{p} P$ [*Hypothesis: author cited paper is primary to the same category that venue is primary to can be useful to find other important papers*]

- **[MP2]:** $A \xleftarrow{w} P \xrightarrow{c} P \xrightarrow{r} K \xrightarrow{con} P$ [*Hypothesis: author cited paper is relevant to the topic can be useful to find other important papers*]

- **[MP3]:** $A \xleftarrow{w} P \xrightarrow{c} P \xrightarrow{ip} C \xrightarrow{b} C \xleftarrow{ip} P$ [*Hypothesis: author cited paper is primary to the category that belongs to other category can be useful to find other important papers*]

- **[MP4]:** $A \xleftarrow{w} P \xrightarrow{c} P \xrightarrow{w} A \xrightarrow{co} A \xleftarrow{w} P$ [*Hypothesis: author cited paper's author's coauthors can be useful to find other important papers*]

- **[MP5]:** $A \xleftarrow{w} P \xrightarrow{c} P \xrightarrow{w} A \xrightarrow{con} K \xrightarrow{con} P$ [*Hypothesis: author cited paper's author contribute to the topic can be useful to find other papers*]

4.3 Experiment Results

We tune the parameter α (in the PGN random walk function) to optimize the recommendation performance. For the music recommendation task we find the optimal value of $\alpha = 0.65$ using MAP@500 [8]. Using the same procedure, we find an optimal value of $\alpha = 0.85$ for scholarly recommendation via NDCG10 [18]. In order to save space, we only present the MAP@500 result for the music graph (primary metric) in Figure 4.

Personalized Navigation vs. Meta-path: In this experiment, we compare the proposed method with different meta-path solutions. Each of the individual meta-paths and the learning to rank baselines are compared to PGN in Table 1. It is clear that different meta-path

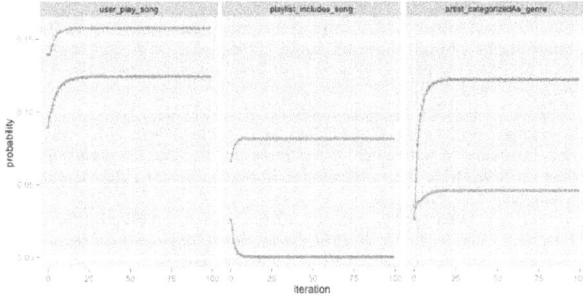

Figure 4: Edge Type Usefulness Probability Comparison (of 2 Randomly Selected Users).

Table 1: Meta-path vs. Personalized Graph Navigation

-	PGN	MP-L2R	MP1	MP2	MP3	MP4	MP5
Music Recommendation Task, $T = (U \rightsquigarrow S)$							
MAP100	0.0451†	0.0153	0.0118	0.0023	0.0041	0.0102	0.0065
MAP300	0.0701†	0.0284	0.0193	0.0043	0.0092	0.0142	0.0143
MAP500	0.0802†	0.0359	0.0237	0.0056	0.0128	0.0164	0.0190
NDCG100	0.2279†	0.1361	0.1172	0.0427	0.0532	0.0736	0.0683
NDCG300	0.2133†	0.1447	0.1130	0.0456	0.0700	0.0705	0.0872
NDCG500	0.2447†	0.1804	0.1373	0.0594	0.0949	0.0858	0.1133
Scholarly Recommendation Task, $T = (A \rightsquigarrow P)$							
NDCG5	0.0764†	0.0441	0.0008	0.0361	0.0005	0.0251	0.0268
NDCG10	0.0752†	0.0496	0.001	0.0371	0.0006	0.0289	0.0292
NDCG15	0.0781†	0.0561	0.0013	0.0407	0.0006	0.0337	0.0325
NDCG20	0.0790†	0.0611	0.0021	0.0456	0.0007	0.0366	0.0373
P5	0.1488†	0.0805	0.0061	0.0717	0.0014	0.0669	0.0608
P10	0.1195†	0.0785	0.0044	0.0608	0.001	0.0604	0.0539
P15	0.1067†	0.0783	0.0041	0.0587	0.0014	0.0578	0.0503
P20	0.0942†	0.0773	0.0051	0.0585	0.0014	0.0543	0.0515

† significance $p < 0.0001$

Table 2: CF, Meta-Path and PGN for music recommendation

	POP	CF_IMF	CF_IS	PGN	PGN + CF	MP L2R
MAP20	0.0036	**0.0175**	0.0149	0.0171	**0.0227†**	0.0053
MAP50	0.0051	0.0275	0.0243	**0.0312†**	**0.0407†**	0.0095
MAP100	0.0067	0.0369	0.0333	**0.0451†**	**0.0583†**	0.0153
MAP300	0.0101	0.0532	0.0504	**0.0701†**	**0.0915†**	0.0284
MAP500	0.0121	0.0605	0.0584	**0.0802†**	**0.1061†**	0.0359
MAP	0.0203	0.0828	0.0752	**0.1073†**	**0.1405†**	0.0610
NDCG20	0.1094	**0.3387**	0.2776	0.2944	**0.3803†**	0.1524
NDCG50	0.0873	**0.2665**	0.2257	0.2590	**0.3257†**	0.1429
NDCG100	0.0741	0.2198	0.1887	**0.2279†**	**0.2797†**	0.1361
NDCG300	0.0650	0.1799	0.1583	**0.2133†**	**0.2532†**	0.1447
NDCG500	0.0780	0.2047	0.1839	**0.2447†**	**0.2906†**	0.1804
NDCG	0.1812	0.3614	0.3001	**0.4060†**	**0.4607†**	0.3628
P20	0.1268	**0.3732**	0.3218	0.3184	**0.4165†**	0.1783
P50	0.0995	**0.2845**	0.2541	0.2798	**0.3551†**	0.1690
P100	0.0823	0.2278	0.2066	**0.2367†**	**0.2948†**	0.1586
P300	0.0598	0.1479	0.1415	**0.1612†**	**0.2026†**	0.1232
P500	0.0506	0.1168	0.1133	**0.1279†**	**0.1614†**	0.1053

† significance $p < 0.0001$

ranking functions perform differently for the music and scholarly recommendation tasks, and the learning to rank based function significantly outperforms each meta-path ranking feature individually. For music recommendation, PGN significantly ($p < 0.0001$) outperforms all the meta-path based ranking methods, including learning to rank (MP-L2R). For scholarly recommendation, PGN (NDCG and precision) scores outperform all other methods for top 5,10, 15, 20 results. When $k > 500$, MP-L2R performs better than PGN. When we add PGN to the L2R model, the new result (PGN + Meta-Path) performs better than all other methods for all the metrics.

In the second experiment, we compare the PGN method with the baseline methods for music recommendation. The result is presented in Table 2. For the collaborative filtering baseline calculations, the matrix factorization algorithm outperforms both item-based and popularity approaches. This is consistent with previous studies. For $MAP@k$, $NDCG@k$ and $P@k$ evaluation, when k equals 20 or 50, the matrix factorization algorithm performance surpasses the PGN algorithm alone. When $k > 100$, PGN significantly ($p < 0.0001$) outperforms all the CF baselines. In order to enhance the recommendation performance, we trained another learning to rank model (PGN+CF), which integrates three personalized recommendation algorithms: item-based, matrix factorization, and PGN. It is clear that PGN+CF is the best performing algorithm ($p < 0.0001$).

Unlike traditional meta-path approaches, the PGN algorithm generates a computational profile for each user, and each profile is represented by an edge type usefulness probability distribution. Based

on this analysis, we find that PGN can efficiently distinguish a user's personal music listening or scholarly citation behavior. For instance, Figure 4 compares three different types of edges in the music recommendation graph for two different users: $U \xrightarrow{pl} S$ (user-plays-song), $P \xrightarrow{i} S$ (playlist-includes-song) and $Ar \xrightarrow{cat} G$ (artist-categorizedAs-genre). It is clear that the proposed method can optimize the edge type usefulness for different users. For instance, playlist can be quite important for $user_2$ compared to $user_1$. For most users in this experiment, the $user - plays - song$ type edge was found to be the most important one (the edge type usefulness probability is higher than for other types of edges). This makes sense because the $user - plays - song$ relation, representing (other) users' tastes in music listening, can be an alternate for item-based collaborative filtering, which has proven to be one of the most efficient means for music recommendation to date. In most cases, $P_T^{(t+1)}(\theta_\phi | u)$ stabilizes in about 25 to 50 iterations (the same pattern holds for scholarly recommendation), which is faster than the PageRank based object ranking convergence rate. Note that this profile is created for the music recommendation task. If we were to switch to a different search or recommendation task (e.g., artist or playlist recommendation), the user profile could change.

5 ANALYSIS AND CONCLUSION

In this study, we propose a novel method for personalized random walk navigation on the complex heterogeneous graph. In the experiment, we employ two relatively complex graphs to music/scholarly recommendation problems to validate the proposed method. However, this approach can be generalized to solve other novel search or recommendation problems when faced with complex data; two such examples are web search and job recommendations:

- **Information Retrieval Scenario:** using *Web page + User information + Social network + Query log + Domain information + Name Entities...* to address web search problem.
- **Information Recommendation Scenario:** using *User working experience + User background + Social network + User family + Company information + Business category + Job requirement...* to address job recommendation problem.

Intuitively, the more data or the more types of data we use, the better the performance we could achieve. However, novel types of data may not necessarily be useful or equally useful for all user(s). For instance, social network information may not help some users in searching for relevant web pages (even though [20] proved the potential usefulness of social network for information retrieval). The proposed PGN algorithm addresses this problem by leveraging the personalized navigation user profile. Unlike previous studies [32, 33] in personalized graph mining, PGN can cope with very complex heterogeneous graphical data, and the latent variable $P_T(\theta_\phi|u)$ is shown to be efficient for personalized music recommendation.

Compared to meta-path solutions, PGN has three advantages. First, it can efficiently cope with complex heterogeneous graph data without human intervention. Second, PGN provides a personalized random walk on the graph, i.e., between two nodes on the graph, different users may prefer different optimized paths. Last but not least, the latent variable $P_T(\theta_\phi|u)$ and the new navigation algorithm can transform the heterogeneous graph into a (personalized) homogeneous graph, making **it feasible to apply any homogeneous graph mining algorithms to complex heterogeneous data.**

However, there are two major limitations of this study. First, although the proposed method may work well when training data is available, when training data is not available or sparse, the proposed method may not perform as well. Second, even though we can theoretically apply any homogeneous graph mining algorithm by using the latent variable, existing graph indexation algorithms and graph databases cannot handle this new data structure. In the future, we will investigate new method to address these problems.

REFERENCES

[1] Lars Backstrom and Jure Leskovec. 2011. Supervised random walks: predicting and recommending links in social networks. In *Proceedings of the fourth ACM international conference on Web search and data mining*. ACM, 635–644.

[2] Shumeet Baluja, Rohan Seth, D Sivakumar, Yushi Jing, Jay Yagnik, Shankar Kumar, Deepak Ravichandran, and Mohamed Aly. 2008. Video suggestion and discovery for youtube: taking random walks through the view graph. In *Proceedings of the 17th international conference on World Wide Web*. ACM, 895–904.

[3] Roi Blanco and Christina Lioma. 2012. Graph-based term weighting for information retrieval. *Information retrieval* 15, 1 (2012), 54–92.

[4] Jiajun Bu, Shulong Tan, Chun Chen, Can Wang, Hao Wu, Lijun Zhang, and Xiaofei He. 2010. Music recommendation by unified hypergraph: combining social media information and music content. In *Proceedings of the international conference on Multimedia*. ACM, 391–400.

[5] Pablo Castells, Miriam Fernández, David Vallet, Phivos Mylonas, and Yannis Avrithis. 2005. Self-tuning personalized information retrieval in an ontology-based framework. In *On the Move to Meaningful Internet Systems 2005: OTM 2005 Workshops*. Springer, 977–986.

[6] Kevyn Collins-Thompson and Jamie Callan. 2005. Query expansion using random walk models. In *Proceedings of the 14th ACM international conference on Information and knowledge management*. ACM, 704–711.

[7] Nick Craswell and Martin Szummer. 2007. Random walks on the click graph. In *Proceedings of the 30th annual international ACM SIGIR conference on Research and development in information retrieval*. ACM, 239–246.

[8] Gideon Dror, Yahoo Labs, Noam Koenigstein, Yehuda Koren, and Markus Weimer. 2012. The Yahoo! music dataset and KDDCup'11. In *JMLR Workshop and Conference Proceedings: Proceedings of KDD Cup 2011 Competition*. 3–18.

[9] Carsten Eickhoff, Jaime Teevan, Ryen White, and Susan Dumais. 2014. Lessons from the journey: A query log analysis of within-session learning. In *Proceedings of the 7th ACM international conference on Web search and data mining*. ACM, 223–232.

[10] Yasuhiro Fujiwara, Makoto Nakatsuji, Hiroaki Shiokawa, Takeshi Mishima, and Makoto Onizuka. 2013. Efficient ad-hoc search for personalized pagerank. In *Proceedings of the 2013 ACM SIGMOD International Conference on Management of Data*. ACM, 445–456.

[11] Susan Gauch, Jason Chaffee, and Alexander Pretschner. 2003. Ontology-based personalized search and browsing. *Web Intelligence and Agent Systems* 1, 3-4

(2003), 219–234.

[12] Chun Guo and Xiaozhong Liu. 2015. Automatic Feature Generation on Heterogeneous Graph for Music Recommendation. In *Proceedings of the 38th International ACM SIGIR Conference on Research and Development in Information Retrieval*. ACM, 807–810.

[13] Aniko Hannak, Piotr Sapiezynski, Arash Molavi Kakhki, Balachander Krishnamurthy, David Lazer, Alan Mislove, and Christo Wilson. 2013. Measuring personalization of web search. In *Proceedings of the 22nd international conference on World Wide Web*. International World Wide Web Conferences Steering Committee, 527–538.

[14] Yifan Hu, Y. Koren, and C. Volinsky. 2008. Collaborative Filtering for Implicit Feedback Datasets. In *Eighth IEEE International Conference on Data Mining*. 263–272. DOI: http://dx.doi.org/10.1109/ICDM.2008.22

[15] Yehuda Koren. 2008. Factorization meets the neighborhood: a multifaceted collaborative filtering model. In *Proceedings of the 14th ACM SIGKDD international conference on Knowledge discovery and data mining*. ACM, 426–434.

[16] Ni Lao and William W Cohen. 2010. Relational retrieval using a combination of path-constrained random walks. *Machine learning* 81, 1 (2010), 53–67.

[17] Jure Leskovec, Ajit Singh, and Jon Kleinberg. 2006. Patterns of influence in a recommendation network. In *Advances in Knowledge Discovery and Data Mining*. Springer, 380–389.

[18] Xiaozhong Liu, Yingying Yu, Chun Guo, and Yizhou Sun. 2014. Meta-Path-Based Ranking with Pseudo Relevance Feedback on Heterogeneous Graph for Citation Recommendation. In *Proceedings of the 23rd ACM International Conference on Conference on Information and Knowledge Management*. ACM, 121–130.

[19] Xiaozhong Liu, Yingying Yu, Chun Guo, Yizhou Sun, and Liangcai Gao. 2014. Full-text based context-rich heterogeneous network mining approach for citation recommendation. In *Proceedings of the 14th ACM/IEEE-CS Joint Conference on Digital Libraries*. IEEE Press, 361–370.

[20] Ariel Maislos, Ruben Maislos, and Eran Arbel. 2007. Apparatus and computer code for providing social-network dependent information retrieval services. (Oct. 25 2007). US Patent App. 11/923,762.

[21] Brian McFee, Thierry Bertin-Mahieux, Daniel PW Ellis, and Gert RG Lanckriet. 2012. The million song dataset challenge. In *Proceedings of the 21st international conference companion on World Wide Web*. ACM, 909–916.

[22] Fanqi Meng, Dehong Gao, Wenjie Li, Xu Sun, and Yuexian Hou. 2013. A unified graph model for personalized query-oriented reference paper recommendation. In *Proceedings of the 22nd ACM international conference on Conference on information & knowledge management*. ACM, 1509–1512.

[23] Donald Metzler and W Bruce Croft. 2007. Linear feature-based models for information retrieval. *Information Retrieval* 10, 3 (2007), 257–274.

[24] Da-Cheng Nie, Zi-Ke Zhang, Qiang Dong, Chongjing Sun, and Yan Fu. 2014. Information Filtering via Biased Random Walk on Coupled Social Network. *The Scientific World Journal* 2014 (2014).

[25] Fabrizio Silvestri. 2010. Mining query logs: Turning search usage data into knowledge. *Foundations and Trends in Information Retrieval* 4, 1—2 (2010), 1–174.

[26] Xiaoyuan Su and Taghi M Khoshgoftaar. 2009. A survey of collaborative filtering techniques. *Advances in artificial intelligence* 2009 (2009), 4.

[27] Karthik Subbian, Arindam Banerjee, and Sugato Basu. 2015. PLUMS: predicting links using multiple sources. In *Proceedings of the 2015 SIAM International Conference on Data Mining*. SIAM, 370–378.

[28] Y. Sun, R. Barber, M. Gupta, C. Aggarwal, and J. Han. 2011. Co-author relationship prediction in heterogeneous bibliographic networks.. In *Proc. 2011 Int. Conf. Advances in Social Network Analysis and Mining (ASONAM'11)*. Kaohsiung, Taiwan.

[29] Y. Sun, J. Han, C. C. Aggarwal, and N. Chawla. 2012. When will it happen? relationship prediction in heterogeneous information networks. In *Proc. 2012 ACM Int. Conf. on Web Search and Data Mining (WSDM'12)*. Seattle, WA.

[30] Y. Sun, J. Han, X. Yan, P. S. Yu, and T. Wu. 2011. PathSim: Meta path-based top-k similarity search in heterogeneous information networks. In *Proc. 2011 Int. Conf. Very Large Data Bases (VLDB'11)*. Seattle, WA.

[31] Y. Sun, B. Norick, J. Han, X. Yan, P. S. Yu, and X. Yu. 2012. Integrating metapath selection with user guided object clustering in heterogeneous information networks. In *Proc. of 2012 ACM SIGKDD Int. Conf. on Knowledge Discovery and Data Mining (KDD'12)*. Beijing, China.

[32] Scott White and Padhraic Smyth. 2003. Algorithms for estimating relative importance in networks. In *Proceedings of the ninth ACM SIGKDD international conference on Knowledge discovery and data mining*. ACM, 266–275.

[33] Shinjae Yoo, Yiming Yang, Frank Lin, and Il-Chul Moon. 2009. Mining social networks for personalized email prioritization. In *Proceedings of the 15th ACM SIGKDD international conference on Knowledge discovery and data mining*. ACM, 967–976.

[34] Ding Zhou, Shenghuo Zhu, Kai Yu, Xiaodan Song, Belle L Tseng, Hongyuan Zha, and C Lee Giles. 2008. Learning multiple graphs for document recommendations. In *Proceedings of the 17th international conference on World Wide Web*. ACM, 141–150.

Mobile Vertical Ranking based on Preference Graphs

Yuta Kadotami
Waseda University, Tokyo, Japan
kdtm-783640@ruri.waseda.jp

Yasuaki Yoshida
Yahoo Japan Corporation, Tokyo, Japan
yayoshid@yahoo-corp.jp

Sumio Fujita
Yahoo Japan Corporation, Tokyo, Japan
sufujita@yahoo-corp.jp

Tetsuya Sakai
Waseda University, Tokyo, Japan
tetsuyasakai@acm.org

ABSTRACT

We consider the problem of ranking relevant verticals for a given mobile search query so as to satisfy the average user. To this end, we utilise real mobile search click logs, and apply a graph contruction algorithm proposed by Agrawal *et al.* who tackled the problem of automatically assigning relevance labels to URLs for general web search. While Agrawal *et al.* ordered URLs based on pairwise preferences and then partitioned the ordered URL list to determine absolute relevance grades, our objective is to *rank* a given set of *verticals* for a given query, to help search engine companies select which verticals to include in a search engine result page for a small smartphone screen. We show that "Click > Skip Other" preference rules consistently outperform more conservative rules such as "Click > Skip Previous," and that our best graph-based vertical ranking methods substantially and statistically significantly outperform a competitive baseline that ranks verticals based on click counts.

CCS CONCEPTS

•**Information systems → Query log analysis; Combination, fusion and federated search; Retrieval on mobile devices;**

KEYWORDS

click logs; mobile search; pairwise preferences; vertical ranking

1 INTRODUCTION

Search engines are returning increasingly rich *Search Engine Result Pages* (SERPs) in response to user queries, and moving away from the classical "10-blue-link" paradigm, especially in mobile search where information presented on a small smartphone screen is expected to satisfy the user's information need quickly. More specifically, for some queries, modern search engines return *verticals* [3] such as images, video, maps, recipes, online shopping items, community question answering contents, etc.

We consider the problem of ranking relevant verticals for a given mobile search query so as to satisfy the average user. To this end,

we utilise real mobile vertical search click logs, and apply a graph contruction algorithm proposed by Agrawal *et al.* [1] who tackled the problem of automatically assigning relevance labels to URLs for general web search. While Agrawal *et al.* ordered URLs based on pairwise preferences and then partitioned the ordered URL list to determine absolute relevance grades, our objective is to *rank* a given set of *verticals* for a given query, to help search engine companies select which verticals to include in a SERP for a small smartphone screen. We show that "Click > Skip Other" preference rules, which generalise the *probabilistic click log rule* of Agrawal *et al.*, consistently outperform more conservative rules such as "Click > Skip Previous" [7], and that our best graph-based vertical ranking methods substantially and statistically significantly outperform a competitive baseline that ranks verticals based on click counts.

2 PRIOR ART

2.1 Tasks Related to Vertical Ranking

Our problem is related but different from *vertical results presentation* or *block ranking* [2, 10], which places a block of vertical instances above, below, or between blocks of "organic" web search results. Given our focus on mobile search, we simply rank vertical instances, transform the list into a list of vertical *types*, and assume that our top-ranked vertical type will be used for selecting one or more vertical instances that will be placed at the top of the mobile SERP to try to satisfy the user immediately.

The TREC Federated Web Search Track organised a *Vertical Selection Task* [5]. In this task, participating systems were required to select relevant ones from a set of 24 verticals for each query. Each vertical corresponds to several *resources*: for example, the image vertical contained resources such as Flickr and Picasa. For the evaluation, relevant verticals for a given query were determined based on the top performing resource (in terms of graded precision) for each vertical, and *set* retrieval measures such as F-measure were used. According to a study by the Federated Web Search track coordinators [15], the gold standard verticals thus constructed in a bottom-up manner align fairly well with verticals selected subjectively through a user study.

The NTCIR-12 iMine Task organised a *Vertical Incorporating Subtask* [14]. This is a diversified search task; its novelty compared to traditional diversified search is that participating systems were allowed to insert "virtual documents" (i.e., verticals) within the diversified SERP containing organic web documents. There were five possible virtual documents allowed, including "Vertical-Image," "Vertical-Encyclopedia," "Vertical-Shopping" etc.

2.2 Labelling URLs based on Preference Graphs

The present study aims at achieving effective vertical ranking for a given mobile query by leveraging the algorithm of Agrawal *et al.* [1] whose aim was to automatically assign graded relevance labels to URLs for general web search. Their algorithm comprises three steps: *constructing a preference graph*, *ranking graph nodes*, and *partitioning graph nodes*. The third step involves mapping a sorted list of URLs to graded relevance levels; since the present study aims at *ranking* verticals for a given query rather than identifying a *set of* relevant verticals as in the TREC Vertical Selection task, we briefly describe only the first two steps of the algorithm below.

2.2.1 Constructing a Preference Graph.
For a given query with click data, the algorithm first constructs a graph where each node represents a URL and an edge (u, v) from node u to node v means "u is preferred over v." Moreover, (u, v) has a weight $w_{u,v}$, which reflects how often u was preferred over v in the click data. Whether a URL was preferred over another is estimated using one specific *preference rule* such as "Click > Skip Previous" [7]. For example, let $URL(i)$ denote the URL at Rank i, and suppose that in a SERP in a particular user session, $URL(2)$ was clicked but $URL(1)$ was not. From this fact, the "Click > Skip Previous" rule increments $w_{URL(2), URL(1)}$ by one.

Agrawal *et al.* [1] extended the deterministic preference rules of Joachims *et al.* [7] and introduced the *probabilistic click log rule*, which generates multiple pairwise preferences probabilistically given a single click. They leverage a user model (based on a user study from prior art [4]) which says that "Given a click at Rank j, the user has read all snippets from Ranks 1 through j with 100% probability, and the snippet at Rank $i(> j)$ with some probability $P(i, j)$ which decreases as i gets large. Agrawal *et al.* remark that the decreasing probability curve is not very steep: for example, given a click at Rank 1, their model assumes that 10% of the user population will still read the snippet at Rank 10. Given a click at Rank j, Agrawal *et al.*'s rule increments $w_{URL(j), URL(i)}$ with 100% probability for $i = 1, \ldots, j - 1$ (which generalises "Click > Skip Above"), and with $100P(i, j)\%$ probability for $i > j$ (which generalises "Click > Skip Below").

2.2.2 Ranking Graph Nodes.
This second part of the algorithm obtains a partially ordered list of URLs from a given preference graph. While Agrawal *et al.* [1] considered three ordering methods, namely, Δ-*order*, *PageRank* [9], and *Pivot* (i.e., the Bucket Pivot Algorithm [6]), we discuss the first two only, as Pivot was less effective than these two in their experiments.

Δ-order simply ranks the nodes (i.e., URLs) by the difference between the sum of weights of outgoing edges and the sum of weights of incoming edges. Formally, given a preference graph $G = (V, E)$, the score of node $u \in V$ is computed as follows for ranking the nodes in V:

$$\Delta(u) = \sum_{v \in V, (u,v) \in E} w_{u,v} - \sum_{v \in V, (v,u) \in E} w_{v,u} . \quad (1)$$

The well-known PageRank algorithm can also be applied to the preference graph to compute a score for each node and to rank them. The only departure from the original PageRank for web page ranking is that the edges are reversed; in our context, an edge going from u to v means that u is preferred over v. While Agrawal *et al.* [1] chose an outgoing link (u, v) proportionally to its weight $w_{u,v}$ instead of choosing one uniformly at random, we consider both options, and call these node ranking methods *WRageRank* (Weighted PageRank) and *UPageRank* (UniformPageRank), respectively.

3 DATA AND METHOD

We now describe how we applied the algorithm of Agrawal *et al.* to the problem of vertical ranking for a given mobile search query.

3.1 Data

We obtained a Japanese mobile query log and click data from a major Japanese search engine company, Yahoo! Japan. From head queries obtained in March 2016, we randomly sampled 1,200 queries for our experiments: the query set size was determined based on a budget constraint for obtaining gold standard vertical data by hiring assessors. Each query is associated with one or more *SERP records*, and each SERP record contains information such as which verticals were shown at which positions, clicked URLs, click timestamps, and so on. In our experiments, we consider the following 12 major vertical types, which the Japanese search engine offers: *image, recipe, Q&A, video, news, map, dictionary, shopping, auction, realtime, celebrity info,* and *local info*.

Our raw SERPs are somewhat more complex than flat lists of URLs: between organic web results, sometimes blocks of verticals are inserted, and each block generally contains its own ranked list of a few vertical instances. Moreover, in our SERP *records*, organic web URLs and the URLs of verticals that were *not* clicked are missing. Hence, for a given query, we need to (a) create nodes from combinations of ranks and verticals instead of actual URLs; and (b) obtain a flat list of verticals, in which the ranks do not necessarily reflect the absolute positions within the original SERP. To achieve (b), we consider the following two simple strategies:

Flattening Simply collapse the original SERP into a flat ranked list of verticals, e.g., "$recipe_1, recipe_2, image_3, video_4, recipe_5, \ldots$," where each subscript represents the relative position in the resultant list.

Flattening+Merging Further collapse the above list by merging consecutive verticals that are of the same type. For example, the above flat ranked list is converted into "$recipe_1, image_2, video_3, recipe_4, \ldots$." Note that this new $recipe_1$ corresponds to "$recipe_1, recipe_2$" in the Flattening example.

3.2 Adapting the Algorithm for Vertical Ranking

Given a query, we first apply either **Flattening** or **Flattening+Merging** to define the graph nodes, and then adopt the algorithm of Agrawal *et al.* to establish the weighted edges across the nodes. For the latter step, we consider the rules shown in Table 1: one graph is created using exactly one of these rules. R6 generalises the probabilistic click log rule of Agrawal *et al.* [1]: while they assumed a decreasing probability curve over ranks (See Section 2.2.1), we were not sure if this was the right assumption in our particular setting, because absolute rank information is not available in our data. We therefore considered the following three user behaviour models to determine

Table 1: Preference Rules

Rule ID	Rule
R1	Click > Skip Next
R2	Click > Skip Above
R3	Click > Skip Previous
R4	Last Click > Skip Above
R5	Click > Click Above
R6 (Models 1-3)	Click > Skip Other

Table 2: Assessors' ratings and final relevance levels.

assessors' ratings	#instances (percentage)		final relevance levels	#instances (percentage)	
2-2-2	418	(10.62%)	2	1,262	(32.06%)
2-2-1	488	(12.40%)			
2-2-0	356	(9.04%)			
1-1-2	327	(8.31%)	1	1,264	(32.11)
1-1-1	120	(3.05%)			
0-1-2	456	(11.58%)			
1-1-0	361	(9.17%)			
0-0-2	322	(8.18%)	0	1,411	(35.84%)
0-0-1	596	(15.14%)			
0-0-0	493	(12.52%)			
total	3,937	(100%)	total	3,937	(100%)

$P(i, j)$, i.e., the probability of having read the snippet at i given a click at rank j:

Model 1 A uniform model, which lets $P(i, j) = 1$ for all i;

Model 2 An exponential decay model, which lets $P(i, j) = 1$ for $i \leq j + 1$, and $P(i, j) = 2^{-(i-j-1)}$ for $i > j + 1$;

Model 3 A linear decay model, which lets $P(i, j) = 1$ for $i \leq j + 1$, $P(i, j) = 1 - (i - j - 1)/10$ for $j + 1 < i \leq j + 11$, and $P(i, j) = 0$ for $i > j + 11$.

While Agrawal *et al.* incremented $w_{URL(j), URL(i)}$ by one with $100P(i, j)\%$ probability, our implementation increments it by $P(i, j)$ with 100% probability (for $i \neq j$), so that every pairwise preference instance contributes to the edge weights.

After contructing a preference graph for each of the *eight* different rules indicated in Table 1, the nodes in each graph were ranked using one of the three methods described in Section 2.2.2. Finally, since our task is to obtain a ranked list of vertical *types* for a given query, the sorted list of vertical instances were transformed into a list of vertical types, by using the "take one best" approach. For example, if the sorted list of instances implied "*recipe > recipe > image > video > recipe*" when viewed at the vertical type level, we obtain "*recipe > image > video*."

4 EVALUATION

4.1 Ground Truth and Evaluation Measure

The methods described in Section 3 generate, for each query given, a ranked list of vertical types. Although we consider 12 vertical types, only those that were present in our click data are included in the ranking for a particular query. Such a list can be evaluated using ranked retrieval measures such as nDCG (normalised Discounted Cumulative Gain) if we can define an *ideal* ranked list. To this end, we hired nine assessors who belong to the Computer Science department of Waseda University: to each of the aforementioned 1,200 queries, three assessors were assigned to independently provide an absolute relevance rating to each vertical type. No vertical *instances* were provided to the assessors: for example, they were asked to rate the vertical type "*image*" for a given query, rather than an actual image retrieved for that query. The levels of relevance ratings were described to the assessors as follows:

2 The user who entered this query will probably access this vertical type;

1 The user who entered this query may or may not access this vertical type depending on the context;

0 The user who entered this query will probably not access this vertical type.

Subsequently, the ratings of the three assessors were consolidated by a majority vote, so that the final relevance levels reflect the view

of at least two assessors. Exceptions are when there were complete disagreements (0-1-2): for these cases, we let the final relevance level be one.

Table 2 shows the statistics of the assessors' individual ratings and the final relevance levels. For example, the number of query-vertical pairs that received completely unanimous ratings ("2-2-2," "1-1-1," or "0-0-0") is given by $418 + 120 + 493 = 1, 031$ (26.19% of the total query-vertical pairs); the number of "semi-unanimous" pairs (i.e., those that are not completely unanimous but do not contain a 2-versus-0 conflict) is $488 + 327 + 361 + 596 = 1, 772$ (45.01%). This level of inter-assessor agreement seems reasonable.

Clearly, the above method is not the only possible way to construct the ground truth data for vertical ranking. As was mentioned above, we made assessors rate vertical *types* rather than vertical *instances*, because vertical instances retrieved for a particular query are highly dependent on the search engine, and we wanted to avoid the vertical *type* preferences getting affected by the quality of those particular vertical instances. However, we are open to considering alternative approaches to ground truth construction in future work. For example, it may be worthwhile to explore the bottom-up labelling approach used in the TREC 2014 Federated Web Track Vertical Selection task, where the top performing resource (i.e., a specialised search engine) was used to automatically define which vertical types are relevant to a given query (See Section 2.1).

We used the "Microsoft version" of nDCG with an exponential gain value setting [12] to compare the system's vertical list with the ground truth for each query. The comparison depth differs across queries, as different queries have ranked lists that contain different numbers of vertical types.

4.2 Results and Discussions

Table 3 shows the results of our vertical ranking experiments in terms of mean nDCG over 1,200 queries. Two baseline results are also provided: a system that ranks the given set of vertical types at random, and one that simply ranks the vertical types according to the click counts for each query. It can be observed that the latter is a strong baseline. Parts (a) and (b) show the results for **Flattening** and **Flattening+Merging**, respectively. Recall that these two strategies define what constitute the nodes in a preference graph. On the other hand, recall that the three ordering methods,

Table 3: Effectiveness of vertical ranking in terms of mean nDCG over 1,200 queries.

random	0.7550		
click counts	0.8430		
(a) Flattening			
rule	Δ-order	UPageRank	WPageRank
R1	0.8307	0.8208	0.8215
R2	0.8536	0.8355	0.8434
R3	0.7868	0.7949	0.7951
R4	0.8233	0.8149	0.8193
R5	0.8511	0.8349	0.8446
R6 (Model 1)	0.8630	**0.8713**	0.8671
R6 (Model 2)	0.8623	0.8707	0.8590
R6 (Model 3)	0.8617	0.8707	0.8662
(b) Flattening+Merging			
rule	Δ-order	UPageRank	WPageRank
R1	0.8143	0.8129	0.8158
R2	0.7900	0.7680	0.7792
R3	0.5944	0.5858	0.5852
R4	0.6877	0.6750	0.6878
R5	0.7980	0.7818	0.7831
R6 (Model 1)	0.8482	0.8657	0.8631
R6 (Model 2)	0.8570	0.8640	**0.8703**
R6 (Model 3)	0.8576	0.8640	0.8699

Δ-order, UPageRank and WPageRank, define how the nodes of a given preference graph are finally transformed into a partially ordered list of verticals.

The following main observations can be made from the Table 3:

- On average, the best method based with **Flattening** is the combination of R6 (Model 1: uniform probability distribution) with UPageRank; we call this method **Best-F**. Similarly, the best method based with **Flattening+Merging** is the combination of R6 (Model2: exponential decay) with WPageRank; we call this method **Best-FM**.
- On average, each **Flattening+Merging** method underperforms the corresponding **Flattening** method, except when R6 (Model 2) or R6 (Model 3: linear decay) is combined with WPageRank; hence, merging consecutive verticals of the same type prior to graph construction is generally not a good idea.
- On average, the results with R6 outperform those with R1-R5, which is in line with the results of Agrawal *et al.* on automatic relevance labelling for web pages. On the other hand, the differences due to the three user models appear to be inconsequential; it is not clear if a decaying probability curve is necessary for this particular task.
- The least effective rule, for both **Flattening** and **Flattening+Merging**, is clearly R3 ("Click > Skip Previous").

We conducted a randomised Tukey HSD test using the Discpower tool [13][1] with 5,000 trials to compare the Click Counts baseline, **Best-F**, and **Best-FM**. These two graph-based methods statistically significantly outperform the Click Count baseline ($p \approx 0.000$; with substantial *effect sizes* [13] over Click Counts, $ES_{HSD} = 0.2504$

for **Best-F** and $ES_{HSD} = 0.2416$ for **Best-FM**); whereas, the difference between the two methods is not statistically significant ($p = 0.979$; $ES_{HSD} = 0.0089$).

5 CONCLUSIONS AND FUTURE WORK

We considered the problem of ranking verticals by relevance for a given mobile search query for the purpose of satisfying an average user. We showed that "Click > Skip Other" preference rules consistently outperform more conservative rules such as "Click > Skip Previous," and that our best graph-based vertical ranking methods substantially and statistically significantly outperform the Click Count baseline. On the other hand, the effect of user models on "Click > Skip Other" seems negligible, which probably reflects the fact that our data lack information on the absolute ranks within the SERPs. Our future work includes: (a) exploring alternative ways to obtain the ground truth vertical data; (b) clustering queries prior to graph construction based on co-clicks and session data [8, 11], so that vertical preferences can be obtained for a given *search intent* rather than a query; and (c) handling tail queries with few clicks, for which it is difficult to obtain reliable preference graphs.

REFERENCES

[1] Rakesh Agrawal, Alan Halverson, Krishnaram Kenthapadi, Nina Mishra, and Panayiotis Tsaparas. 2009. Generating labels from clicks. In *Proceedings of ACM WSDM 2009*. 172–181.
[2] Jaime Arguello, Fernando Diaz, and Jamie Callan. 2011. Learning to Aggregate Vertical Results into Web Search Results. In *Proceedings of ACM CIKM 2011*. 201–210.
[3] Jaime Arguello, Fernando Díaz, Jamie Callan, and Jean-François Crespo. 2009. Sources of evidence for vertical selection. In *Proceedings of ACM SIGIR 2009*. 315–322.
[4] Edward Cutrell and Zhiwei Guan. 2007. What are you looking for?: an eye-tracking study of information usage in web search. In *Proceedings of the ACM CHI 2007*. 407–416.
[5] Thomas Demeester, Dolf Trieschnigg, Dong Nguyen, Ke Zhou, and Djoerd Hiemstra. 2015. Overview of the TREC 2014 federated Web search track. In *Proceedings of TREC 2014*.
[6] Aristides Gionis, Heikki Mannila, Kai Puolamäki, and Antti Ukkonen. 2006. Algorithms for Discovering Bucket Orders from Data. In *Proceedings of ACM KDD 2006*. 561–566.
[7] Thorsten Joachims, Laura Granka, Bing Pan, Helene Hembrooke, Filip Radlinski, and Geri Gay. 2007. Evaluating the accuracy of implicit feedback from clicks and query reformulations in web search. *ACM TOIS* 25, 2 (2007).
[8] Makoto P. Kato, Tetsuya Sakai, and Katsumi Tanaka. 2012. Structured query suggestion for specialization and parallel movement: effect on search behaviors. In *Proceedings of WWW 2012*. 389–398.
[9] Lawrence Page, Sergey Brin, Rajeev Motwani, and Terry Winograd. 1999. The PageRank Citation Ranking: Bringing Order to the Web. Technical Report. Stanford InfoLab.
[10] Ashok Kumar Ponnuswami, Kumaresh Pattabiraman, Qiang Wu, Ran Gilad-Bachrach, and Tapas Kanungo. 2011. On Composition of Federated Web Search Result Page: Using Online Users to Provide Pairwise Preference for Heterogeneous Verticals. In *Proceedings of ACM WSDM 2011*. 715–724.
[11] Eldar Sadikov, Jayant Madhavan, Lu Wang, and Alon Halevy. 2010. Clustering Query Refinements by User Intent. In *Proceedings of WWW 2010*. 841–850.
[12] Tetsuya Sakai. 2014. Metrics, Statistics, Tests. In *PROMISE Winter School 2013: Bridging between Information Retrieval and Databases (LNCS 8173)*. 116–163.
[13] Tetsuya Sakai. 2014. Statistical Reform in Information Retrieval? *SIGIR Forum* 48, 1 (2014), 3–12.
[14] Takehiro Yamamoto, Yiqun Liu, Min Zhang, Zhicheng Dou, Ke Zhou, Ilya Markov, Makoto P Kato, Hiroaki Ohshima, and Sumio Fujita. 2016. Overview of the NTCIR-12 IMine-2 task. In *Proceedings of NTCIR-12*. 94–123.
[15] Ke Zhou, Thomas Demeester, Dong Nguyen, Djoerd Hiemstra, and Dolf Trieschnigg. 2014. Aligning Vertical Collection Relevance with User Intent. In *Proceedings of ACM CIKM 2014*. 1915–1918.

[1] http://research.nii.ac.jp/ntcir/tools/discpower-en.html

Enhanced Probabilistic Classify and Count Methods for Multi-Label Text Quantification

Roy Levin[*]
Microsoft
Herzliya, Israel
rolevin@microsoft.com

Haggai Roitman
IBM Research - Haifa
Haifa, Israel 31905
haggai,doronc,shaie@il.ibm.com

ABSTRACT

In this work we address the problem of Multi-Label Text Quantification. To this end, for a given collection of documents, each was pre-classified with one or more labels by some multi-label classifier, our goal is to find an estimate of the cardinality of each actual label set, as accurate as possible. We present two enhanced Probabilistic Classify and Count (PCC) methods that focus on improving the quantification accuracy by employing another supervised learning phase. Using a real-world multi-label documents dataset, we report on an experimental evaluation that compares the estimated label counts produced by our solution (and several alternatives) to the actual label counts derived from labels assigned by human experts. Our results confirm that, using our solution, the quantification accuracy can be significantly improved.

1 INTRODUCTION

Multi-label classification is the problem of annotating data instances with multiple predefined labels. Single-label classification is a special case in which there is only one correct label for each instance. Classification of text documents [1] is a common example in which a single item may be assigned with multiple labels, e.g., a newspaper article that is related to both finance and technology.

Multi-label classification problems have been extensively studied and many methods have been proposed (Tsoumakas and Katakis [11] present a thorough overview for many of the common methods). Modern applications include examples such as multi-document summarization, protein function classification, music categorization, semantic scene classification and many others [11].

The **Text Quantification** problem [10], which we deal with in this paper, further requires to provide an estimate of the number of documents on each class[1], as accurate as possible. At a first glance, the solution to the problem seems straight forward: *use the best existing text categorization method to solve this multi-label text classification problem and then merely count the number of instances annotated with each of the labels.* However, due potential

---
[*]Work was done while the author was in IBM Research - Haifa
[1]We use the terms "label", "category" and "class" interchangeably throughout the paper.

ICTIR '17, October 01–04, 2017, Amsterdam, Netherlands.
© 2017 ACM. ISBN 978-1-4503-4490-6/17/10...$15.00
DOI: https://doi.org/10.1145/3121050.3121083

distribution drift effects and the fact that even state-of-the-art text classifiers are far from perfect, producing a quantification in such a way may actually be highly inaccurate [10].

Rather than counting the output classes of the classifier for each document, it has been shown that, summing the posterior probabilities assigned to each class by the classifier (if the classifier provides such) can significantly improve the quantification accuracy [3]. This technique is termed *Probabilistic Classify and Count* or **PCC** for short. In this paper, we further extend this approach by calibrating a given classifier's posterior probability for the specific task of text quantification. This is in comparison to merely using the posterior of the classifier which was adjusted for the task of classification. Using a real world manually labeled dataset obtained from a large enterprise corpus, we compare the accuracy of the quantification produced by our extended technique to some baseline approaches including PCC [3]. Our results confirm that the accuracy can be further improved.

2 PROBLEM DEFINITION

Let d denote a single document and let $C = \{c_1, c_2, \ldots, c_m\}$ denote a set of m possible labels, also termed document categories or classes. In a multi-labeling setting, each document d may be associated with multiple labels $C(d) \subseteq C$. A classifier φ trained over a given labeled dataset $\mathcal{D} = \{d, C(d)\}$ maps each possible input document d' into a set of labels $C_\varphi(d') \subseteq C$.

For a given dataset $D = \{d_1, \ldots, d_n\}$ and label $c \in C$, let $n(c|D) \in \{0, \ldots, n\}$ denote the **actual** number of documents in D that include that label. The objective of the multi-label quantification task is to find, for **any** input dataset D and label $c \in C$, a count estimate $\mu(c|D)$ which is as close as possible to the actual count $n(c|D)$. As in any estimation settings, the estimator $\mu(c|D)$ may be biased, producing estimates of $n(c|D)$ that deviate from the actual counts.

For a given document dataset D to be quantified according to labels in C, the amount of deviation between the actual counts and the estimated counts is captured by the *Concordance Ratio* (CR), defined as follows:

$$CR_\mu(C|D) = \frac{1}{|C|} \sum_{c \in C} \frac{\min(\mu(c|D), n(c|D))}{\max(\mu(c|D), n(c|D))}, \quad (1)$$

For simplicity, we assume here that for every $c \in C$, it follows that $\mu(c|D) \geq 1$ or $n(c|D) \geq 1$. (If this is not the case, the formula can be easily fixed, e.g., by adding 1 to $\mu(c|D)$ and to $n(c|D)$). Note that, if for every label $c \in C$, $\mu(c|D)$ correctly estimates $n(c|D)$, then

$CR_\mu(C|D) = 1$. On the other hand, if $\mu(c|D)$ completely underestimates $n(c|D)$ (i.e., $\mu(c|D)=0$ and $n(c|D) > 0$) or completely overestimates $n(c|D)$ (i.e., $\mu(c|D) > 0$ and $n(c|D) = 0$), then $CR_\mu(C|D) = 0$. In any other case: $CR_\mu(C|D) \in (0, 1)$.

Our goal in this work is, therefore, to **maximize** $CR_\mu(C|D)$ by estimating the label counts $n(c|D)$ as accurately as possible.

3 ENHANCED PCC METHODS

3.1 Baseline Methods

We start with a description of our baseline methods. The first, is a straight forward approach which simply counts documents according to a given classifier's labeling decisions [10]. We call this approach **Simple Classify and Count** (SCC for short). The second method, **Probabilistic Classify and Count** (PCC for short) [3], is based on the posterior probabilities of a given classifier [3]. Note that, many existing classifiers directly provide scores that are in the form of posteriors [4] (e.g., Naive Bayes, MaxEnt, etc.), while the scores of others (e.g., SVM) may be transformed into posteriors (e.g., using the softmax function) [4]. Therefore, for a given dataset D with label posteriors $p_\varphi(c|d)$ of classifier φ for every $d \in D$, the expected label counts are estimated by PCC as follow:

$$\mu(c|D) \stackrel{def}{=} \sum_{d \in D} p_\varphi(c|d) \qquad (2)$$

3.2 PCC-PAV Method

One direction towards a better estimate of the label counts is to try to improve the label posteriors' estimation. Various methods have been studied for increasing the accuracy of the posterior probabilities estimation of a given classifier [8, 13]. These methods employ another supervised learning step and produce a **calibrated** posterior probability $p_\varphi^*(c|d)$ based on the score the classifier assigns to each label-document pair $s_\varphi(c, d)$ and its actual precision. In our case, replacing $p_\varphi(c|d)$ with $p_\varphi^*(c|d)$ has the potential to improve the basic PCC method and provide a more accurate estimate of the expected count of each label.

A highly effective method for learning the calibrated posterior probability is by using the *Pair Adjacent Violators* algorithm or **PAV** for short [13]. For multi-label problems, scores are calibrated for each binary classifier using PAV and combined to obtain multi-label probabilities [13]. The PAV algorithm is commonly used for implementing **isotonic regression** [2], aiming at correct ranking by the classifier and is defined as follows.

Let $d_1, \ldots, d_n$ be a sequence (order) of documents of a given dataset D (of size n), such that for every $k > j \in \{1, \ldots, n\}$ the the following holds: $s_\varphi(c, d_k) \geq s_\varphi(c, d_j)$. Let $p_k^c \in \{0, 1\}$ denote an indicator recieving the value 1 if $c \in C(d_k)$ and 0 otherwise. Therefore, we wish to find a sequence of **non-decreasing** real values $(y_1^c, \ldots, y_n^c)$ which **minimizes** the following quadratic error:

$$E_c(y, p) = \sum_{i=1}^{n} \left(y_i^c - p_i^c \right)^2. \qquad (3)$$

We refer to this method as the **PCC – PAV** method. The PAV[2] algorithm solves this constraint programming problem in $O(n)$ operations.

---

[2] A MathLab implementation is available in [6].

3.3 PCC-EPAV Method

A notable weakness of the PAV algorithm for the quantification task (rather than the classification task which is what it was designed for) is that it does not enforce any constraints on the expected total counts of a given label in the dataset. Adding a constraint that the expected count of the calibrated posterior probabilities for a category will be equal to the actual counts observed in the training data $\mathcal{D}$, makes sense for the quantification task, i.e.:

$$\sum_{d \in D} p_\varphi^*(c|d) = n(c|\mathcal{D}). \qquad (4)$$

Therefore, we now introduce a more refined version of the PCC-PAV method, termed **PCC Enhanced PAV** (**PCC-EPAV** for short). This method further adds a new constraint additionally to the existing PAV constraint (i.e., $y_1^c \leq y_2^c \leq \ldots \leq y_n^c$) and constructs a quadratic programming problem whose objective is again to minimize $E_c(y, p)$. Such problems can be generally solved by using a Quadratic Programming Solver. Existing quadratic programming solvers use heuristics to reach good approximations in reasonable time depending on the size of the problem (i.e., the number of variables and constraints). Even so, when the number of variables and constraints is high such problems become unpractical.

In our experiments we use an open source math programming framework written in Java called *oj! Algorithms* [9]. However, using this approach the number of variables and constraints are very large (above 170,000 in our experiments) causing the solver to run for a very long time and consume very large amounts of memory (in our experiments 8GB of RAM did not suffice).

3.3.1 Data Unification Approach. We next introduce a novel technique, termed **Document Unification**, which effectively reduces the complexity of solving the Quadratic Program problem and works as follows. We define a *Delta-Score Threshold* δ such that for every $k < j \in \{1, \ldots, n\}$ the variables y_k^c and y_j^c are unified if $|s_\varphi(c, d_k) - s_\varphi(c, d_j)| \leq \delta$. In addition, y_k^c and y_j^c are also unified if $p_k^c = p_{k+1}^c = \ldots = p_j^c$ regardless of their scores. We denote by y'^c a single unified variable. Such step, therefore, introduces new constraints to the problem, which we now further term the *Unification Constraints*.

When probabilities are unified a few things need to be rewritten in the quadratic program formulation. First, each probability p'^c now needs to be some function of all the probabilities of the unified documents. Second, as p'^c is now a combination of multiple original probabilities p_k^c, the distance measure between y'^c and p'^c now needs to be weighted according to the number of documents it represents. Third, the score of the "unified document" d', $s'_\varphi(c, d')$, needs to represent the scores of all the corresponding unified documents.

The algorithm for generating the unified probabilities and their corresponding weights is depicted in Algorithm 1. The algorithm iterates over the documents in D in ascending order according to the original scores assigned by the classifier $s_\varphi(c, d)$ and it constantly maintains an active "chunk" of documents whose probabilities and scores match the Unification Constraints.

Once the unified scores $\left(s'_\varphi(c, d'_1), \ldots, s'_\varphi(c, d'_q)\right)$, probabilities $\left(p'^c_1, \ldots, p'^c_q\right)$ and weights $\left(w^c_1, \ldots, w^c_q\right)$ are calculated we formulate the following Quadratic Program whose objective is to minimize the weighted squared distance between the (unified) calibrated posterior probabilities and the (unified) probabilities generated by Algorithm 1, that is: **minimize** $\sum_{k=1}^{q} w^c_k \cdot \left(y'^c_k - p'^c_k\right)^2$

subject to:

(1) $\forall k \in \{1, \ldots, q\}, \quad y'^c_k \in [0, 1]$ (**proper probabilities**).

(2) $\forall k \in \{1, \ldots, q-1\}, \quad y'^c_k \leq y'^c_{k+1}$ (**isotonic**).

(3) $\sum_{k=1}^{q} y'^c_k = n(c|\mathcal{D})$ (**actual count match**).

3.3.2 Posterior derivation. After solving the Quadratic Program and finding the calibrated posterior probabilities $y'^c_1, \ldots, y'^c_q$ we can calculate the posterior probability for a given label c of an unseen new document d whose classifier score is $s_\varphi(c, d) = s$ as follows. If there exists $k \in \{1, 2, \ldots, q\}$ such that $s'_\varphi(c, d_k) = s$, then we return y'^c_k. Otherwise, we need to find the two closest scores $s'_\varphi(c, d'_k)$ and $s'_\varphi(c, d'_{k+1})$ (s.t. $s \in [s'_\varphi(c, d'_k), s'_\varphi(c, d'_{k+1})]$) and use linear interpolation to estimate the calibrated posterior probability. That is, we return:

$$p^*_\varphi(c|d) = y'^c_k + \frac{y'_{k+1} - y'_k}{s'_\varphi(c, d_{k+1}) - s'_\varphi(c, d_k)} \cdot \left(s - s'_\varphi(c, d_k)\right) \quad (5)$$

4 EVALUATION

4.1 Dataset

Our dataset is comprised of more than $170,000$ real short text comments (around 20 words per comment on average) written as answers by employees to human resources (HR) questionnaires that have been conducted in $M = 14$ different companies during a period of several years. We refer to the comments written by employees of a particular company as the comments belonging to that company. The comments have been manually categorized by experts to $m = 16$ predefined HR categories such as "*Work-Life Balance*", "*Growth and Development*", "*Compensation and Benefits*", etc. Each comment has been annotated with up to 5 matching labels.

4.2 Setup

4.2.1 Environment. Our algorithms were implemented in Java and open source tools as described in Section 3. The experiments were conducted on a computer with a 64 bit ICore 7 Dual-Core Intel processor and with 8GB of RAM.

4.2.2 Classifiers. Recall that, our quantification methods require a classifier as an input. We ran our experiments with the following three different classifiers:

(1) Naive Bayes (NB) with Absolute Discount Smoothing [12].
(2) SVMLight's Support Vector Machine (SVM) [7].
(3) Stanford's Maximum Entropy (MaxEnt) [5].

We do not provide further details about these classifiers as the classification task itself is not the focus of this paper. Since our basic problem is a multi-label classification problem, in order to use the

above classifiers without modification, we transformed the problem by creating m binary classifiers $\varphi_c : D \to \{c, \neg c\}$, one for each label $c \in C$. This is an effective technique which is commonly used for multi-label classification (further dubbed PT4 [11]).

To assess the quality of the classifiers, we ran $M = 14$ total tests. In each test, we isolated the comments belonging to one company from the training set and used it as a test set for evaluating the classifiers (i.e., in all our tests the training set and test set were disjoint). For each classifier we measured four standard quality measures, namely: Precision, Recall, F-Measure and Accuracy. The quality measures of the three classifiers are reported in Table 1. We can observe that, the classifiers do a decent job on the dataset achieving, on average, around $70\% - 80\%$ precision and around 55% recall with well above 90% accuracy.

Measure	NB	SVM	MaxEnt
Precision	0.698	0.795	0.690
Recall	0.579	0.544	0.568
F-Measure	0.631	0.644	0.622
Accuracy	0.923	0.934	0.922

Table 1: Average quality measures of the three classifiers used for the evaluation

---

Algorithm 1 Document Unification

Input: $\left(s_\varphi(c, d_1), \ldots, s_\varphi(c, d_n)\right)$ - sorted in ascending order - - document scores assigned by the classifier -

Input: $\left(p^c_1, \ldots, p^c_n\right)$ - sorted by ascending $s_\varphi(c, d_i)$ - - $p^c_i = 1$ if document d_i is correctly classified - - $p^c_i = 0$ otherwise -

Input: δ - the delta score threshold -

Output: $\left(\left(s'_\varphi(c, d'_1), \ldots, s'_\varphi(c, d'_q)\right), \left(p'^c_1, \ldots, p'^c_q\right), \left(w^c_1, \ldots, w^c_q\right)\right)$ - Unified scores, probabilities and weights -

1: $\bar{t} \leftarrow 0$ (* Comment: active chunk document count *)
2: $\bar{s} \leftarrow 0$ (* Comment: active chunk score sum *)
3: $\bar{p} \leftarrow 0$ (* Comment: active chunk probability sum *)
4: $q \leftarrow 0$
5: **for** $i = 1$ to n **do**
6:   **if** $i > 1$ and $\left(p^c_i = \bar{p}/\bar{t} \text{ or } |s_\varphi(c, d_i) - s_\varphi(c, d_{i-1})| \leq \delta\right)$ **then**
7:     $\bar{t} \leftarrow \bar{t} + 1$
8:     $\bar{s} \leftarrow \bar{s} + s_\varphi(c, d_i)$
9:     $\bar{p} \leftarrow \bar{p} + p^c_i$
10:   **else**
11:     $q \leftarrow q + 1$
12:   **end if**
13:   $s'(c, d_q) \leftarrow \bar{s}/\bar{t}$
14:   $p'^c_q \leftarrow \bar{p}/\bar{t}$
15:   $w^c_q \leftarrow \bar{t}$
16: **end for**
17: **return** $\left(\left(s'_\varphi(c, d'_1), \ldots, s'_\varphi(c, d'_q)\right), \left(p'^c_1, \ldots, p'^c_q\right), \left(w^c_1, \ldots, w^c_q\right)\right)$

4.2.3 Quantifiers. Our experimental results were obtained by applying the three classifiers (NB, SVN and MaxEnt) with the various quantification methods described in Section 3 over our dataset. Again, each of the experiments reported here is based on $M = 14$ different runs. In each such run, we isolated the comments belonging to one company from the training set and used it as a test set for evaluating each method. Therefore, as before, the training and test sets are always disjoint. Statistical significant differences in quality between each pair of methods was further measured using the paired two-side Student's t-test for 95% of confidence.

As the simplest baseline approach we start by learning the *expected* label counts based on the training data $\mathcal{D}$. Hence, for a given label c's prior probability $p(c|\mathcal{D})$, this method simply estimates its expected label count as $\mu(c|D) = |D| \cdot p(c|\mathcal{D})$. That is, the method does not even examine the unseen (test) dataset for producing the quantification — they are based solely on the training dataset. We refer to this naive approach as **Simple Expected Counts** (**SEC** for short). The SEC (maximum) Concordance Ratio of 0.721, therefore, sets a lower bound on the performance of the evaluated algorithms.

Next, we tested the Simple Classify and Count (SCC) and Probabilistic Classify and Count (PCC) methods and our two quantification posterior probability adjusting methods PCC-PAV and PCC-EPAV, applied every time over each different classifier's posterior probabilities.

4.3 Results

Table 2 reports on the average Concordance Ratios for our dataset. We note that, we did not manage to obtain a posterior probability for each possible label from the SVMLight's basic SVM classifier implementation. Therefore, the result for the PCC baseline is missing in Table 2 and there is no similar comparison with the other two methods.

	NB	SVM	MaxEnt
SCC	0.761	0.690	0.812_p
PCC	0.798_s	-	0.756
PCC-PAV	0.801_s	0.825_s	0.840_{sp}
PCC-EPAV	0.825_{sp}^{v}	0.841_{sp}^{v}	0.852_{sp}^{v}

Table 2: Average Concordance Ratios of the various text quantification methods (using various classifiers). The letters s, p and v denote a statistical significant difference with the SCC, PCC and PCC-PAV methods, respectively.

We further note that, due to potential distribution drift effects [10], the Concordance Ratios (especially those of SCC) clearly do not correspond with the quality of the classifiers in Table 1.

4.3.1 Quantification results analysis. Analyzing the results in Table 2 we first observe that, there was no single dominant quantification approach among the SCC and PCC methods. We can further observe that, calibrating the posteriors by the PCC-PAV method significantly improved the quantification quality applied on the outputs of the SVM and MaxEnt classifiers (with only a slightly better, yet insignificant, result for the NB classifier). Finally, overall, the extended PCC-EPAV approach, which further

applies the Document Unification step, has provided the best quantification quality, with a further +3%, +2% and +1.4% (significant) performance improvement to that of PCC-PAV for the NB, SVM and MaxEnt classifiers, respectively.

4.3.2 PCC-EPAV Parameters and Runtime. Using cross-validation, we ran the unification step of the PCC-EPAV Method (see Algorithm 1) with a Delta-Score Threshold value $\delta = 0.005$ for the NB and MaxEnt classifiers and with $\delta = 0.025$ for the SVM classifier. With this setting, the number of variables and constraints was around 200 and the running time of the QP-solver we used ranged between 2 and 16 seconds.

Recall that, by decreasing the Delta-Score Threshold towards zero, PCC-EPAV will produce more accurate posterior probabilities (and hence, more accurate summaries). Yet, this comes at the expense of increasing the number of variables and constraints, and therefore, increasing running time and memory complexity.

5 SUMMARY

In this paper we addressed the task of multi-label text quantification. We presented two new methods PCC-PAV and PCC-EPAV that improved the quantification accuracy by summing the **adjusted** posterior probabilities of a given classifier. We showed how these posteriors can be adjusted specifically to the task of quantification (rather than classification). We further proposed a novel Document Unification step, applied within the PCC-EPAV method that significantly boosted the quantification quality. Finally, using a real-world multi-labeled documents dataset, we showed that these two methods outperformed existing methods which simply relay on the original posterior probabilities as provided by the classifier.

REFERENCES

[1] Charu C Aggarwal and ChengXiang Zhai. A survey of text classification algorithms. In *Mining text data*, pages 163–222. Springer, 2012.

[2] RE Barlow and HD Brunk. The isotonic regression problem and its dual. *Journal of the American Statistical Association*, 67(337):140–147, 1972.

[3] Antonio Bella, Cesar Ferri, José Hernández-Orallo, and Maria Jose Ramirez-Quintana. Quantification via probability estimators. In *Data Mining (ICDM), 2010 IEEE 10th International Conference on*, pages 737–742. IEEE, 2010.

[4] Christopher M Bishop et al. *Pattern recognition and machine learning*, volume 1. springer New York, 2006.

[5] Chih-Chung Chang and Chih-Jen Lin. Web site. http://nlp.stanford.edu/downloads/classifier.shtml, 2013.

[6] L. Dumbgen. Statistical software (matlab). http://www.math.mu-luebeck.de/workers/duembgen/software/software.html, 2000.

[7] Thorsten Joachims. Web site. http://svmlight.joachims.org/, 2008.

[8] Alexandru Niculescu-Mizil and Rich Caruana. Predicting good probabilities with supervised learning. In *Proceedings of the 22Nd International Conference on Machine Learning*, ICML '05, pages 625–632, New York, NY, USA, 2005. ACM.

[9] ojAlgo github:. https://github.com/optimatika/ojAlgo.

[10] Fabrizio Sebastiani. *Advances in Information Retrieval: 36th European Conference on IR Research, ECIR 2014, Amsterdam, The Netherlands, April 13-16, 2014. Proceedings*, chapter Text Quantification, pages 819–822. Springer International Publishing, Cham, 2014.

[11] Grigorios Tsoumakas and Ioannis Katakis. Multi-label classification: An overview. *International Journal of Data Warehousing and Mining (IJDWM)*, 3(3):1–13, 2007.

[12] Quan Yuan, Gao Cong, and Nadia Magnenat Thalmann. Enhancing naive bayes with various smoothing methods for short text classification. In *Proceedings of the 21st International Conference Companion on World Wide Web*, WWW '12 Companion, pages 645–646, New York, NY, USA, 2012. ACM.

[13] Bianca Zadrozny and Charles Elkan. Transforming classifier scores into accurate multiclass probability estimates. In *Proceedings of the eighth ACM SIGKDD international conference on Knowledge discovery and data mining*, pages 694–699. ACM, 2002.

Retrieving Compositional Documents Using Position-Sensitive Word Mover's Distance

Martin Trapp[1,2], Marcin Skowron[1,3], Dietmar Schabus[1]

[1]Austrian Research Institute for Artificial Intelligence (OFAI), Vienna, Austria
[2]Signal Processing and Speech Communication Lab., Graz University of Technology, Graz, Austria
[3]Dept. of Computational Perception, Johannes Kepler University Linz, Linz, Austria
firstname.lastname@ofai.at

ABSTRACT

Retrieving similar compositional documents which consist of ranked sub-documents, such as threads of healthcare web fora containing community voted comments, has become increasingly important. However, approaches for this task have not exploited the semantic relationships between words so far and therefore do not use the effective generalization property present in semantic word embeddings. In this work, we propose an extension of the Word Mover's Distance for compositional documents consisting of ranked sub-documents. In particular, we derive a Position-sensitive Word Mover's Distance, which allows to retrieve compositional documents based on the semantic properties of their sub-documents. Additionally, we introduce a novel benchmark dataset for this task, to facilitate other researchers to work on this relevant problem. The results obtained on the novel dataset and on the well-known MovieLense dataset indicate that our approach is well suited for retrieving compositional documents. We conclude that incorporating semantic relations between words and sensitivity to the position and presentation bias is crucial for effective retrieval of such documents.

1 INTRODUCTION

Recent work in machine learning and Natural Language Processing (NLP) has collectively developed effective methods for semantic analysis of words [13, 15] and textual documents [3, 8], e.g. books. In particular, leveraging the semantic relationships between words, using word embeddings [13, 15], has led to the Word Mover's Distance (WMD) [7, 9] which has shown to be an effective approach for semantic-aware document similarity. Using the WMD, Kusner et al. [9] were able to show impressive results on various document retrieval tasks. On the other hand, comparing compositional documents which consist of ranked sub-documents, e.g. rank based on the number of community votes, has gained increasing imporance in the field of information retrieval, e.g. [4, 19]. However, despite the recent advances in semantic analysis of documents, to the best of our knowledge, there has not been a transition of such methods to the task of comparing compositional documents as of yet. Moreover, even though comparing compositional documents is a

relevant problem with multiple applications, only a very limited amount of benchmark data is available.

In this paper, we tackle the problem of *finding similar compositional documents based on the similarities of their ranked sub-documents*. We consider ranked sub-documents to be textual documents, e.g. comments in a forum thread, with the order of sub-documents given by a rank which reflects the amount of community votes. Specifically, we show how to leverage recent advances in machine learning and NLP to formulate a Position-sensitive Word Mover's Distance (P-WMD) which allows to compare compositional documents based on the semantic properties of their ranked sub-documents. In addition, we introduce the twin films dataset[1], a new openly accessible benchmark dataset for this task. The twin films dataset contains community-voted short descriptions in the form of plot keywords for each film, and it is well suited as a benchmark dataset for further research in this direction.

2 BACKGROUND

In the following we briefly review relevant background material and introduce the mathematical notation used in this paper.

2.1 Word Embeddings

Word embeddings aim to represent semantic relationships of words in vector spaces which consist of fewer dimensions than the dictionary size. Recent advances in this field [13, 15] allow for efficient computation and have also gained increasing importance in the field of information retrieval, e.g. [5]. Specifically, Mikolov et al. [13] proposed an efficient architecture in which each word vector is trained by maximising the conditional log probability of neighbouring words given the current word.

2.2 Word Mover's Distance

Based on the work on semantic word embeddings, Kusner et al. [9] recently proposed the Word Mover's Distance (WMD) as an effective approach for document similarity computation. By leveraging the semantic relationships of words, captured in word embeddings, the WMD measures similarity between documents on a semantic level. At a high level explanation, the WMD computes the minimal cost required to "transport" words from one document to another, where the cost is influenced by the distance of the words in the semantic space. Therefore, the WMD can be seen as a special case of the Earth Mover's Distance (EMD) [16], which is also known as the Wasserstein distance [12], for document similarity tasks. More formally, let us assume a D-dimensional word embedding $X \in \mathcal{R}^{D \times N}$

ICTIR '17, October 01–04, 2017, Amsterdam, Netherlands.
© 2017 Copyright held by the owner/author(s). 978-1-4503-4490-6/17/10.
DOI: https://doi.org/10.1145/3121050.3121084

[1]The twin films data set and the code are available on https://github.com/trappmartin/PWMD_ICTIR2017.

for a set of N words and let $x_i \in \mathcal{R}^D$ be the embedding vector of the ith word in the vocabulary. Let $c_i \geq 0$ define the frequency count of the ith word and let $z = \sum_{i=1}^{N} c_i$ be a normalisation constant. We define $d = \{d_i\}_{i=1}^{N}$ and $d' = \{d'_i\}_{i=1}^{N}$ to be the normalised Bag Of Words (BOW) representations of two documents. Each column $d_i = \frac{1}{z} c_i$ represents the relative frequency count of a word in the respective document. As for the EMD, the WMD uses a transportation matrix $T \in \mathbb{R}_{\geq 0}^{N \times N}$, where T_{ij} describes how much of word i in document d travels to word j in d'. Formally, the WMD solves the following linear program:

$$\underset{T \in \mathbb{R}_{\geq 0}^{N \times N}}{\text{minimize}} \sum_{i=1}^{N} \sum_{j=1}^{N} T_{ij} ||x_i - x_j||_2$$

$$\text{subject to} \sum_{j=1}^{N} T_{ij} = d_i, \ \sum_{i=1}^{N} T_{ij} = d'_j \ \forall i, j \quad (1)$$

Informally, the WMD assigns a smaller distance to documents that share many semantically similar words than to documents with many semantically different words. Intuitively, the WMD is therefore well suited for various retrieval tasks in the natural language domain. In the following, we will show how to utilize the WMD when the aim is to compute the distance between compositional documents consisting of ranked sub-documents.

3 POSITION-SENSITIVE WORD MOVER'S DISTANCE

As discussed in prior work [4], compositional documents with ranked sub-documents are susceptible to a position bias [17]. In particular, displaying sub-documents in an order affects the perception, resulting in top-ranked items being more popular than low-ranked items. In addition, presenting summary information of the ranked sub-documents to the user can lead to a presentation bias [21]. Recent work by Lee et al. [11] proposed to include the position and presentation bias into the modelling process, using a Bayesian nonparametric model and allowing the model to be sensitive to the bias. We refer to [14, 20] for more details on Bayesian nonparametric models. Lee at al. [11] also showed that the sensitivity to the position and presentation bias depends on the community. In particular, the community *stackoverflow* turned out to have a higher sensitivity than the related community *mathoverflow*. Therefore, it is crucial for effective retrieval of such compositional documents to integrate the bias, but also to control the sensitivity. In the case of compositional documents, the linear program described in Equation 1 can be extended as follows:

$$\underset{T \in \mathbb{R}_{\geq 0}^{N \times N}}{\text{minimize}} \sum_{i=1}^{N} \sum_{j=1}^{N} T_{ij} ||x_i - x_j||_2$$

$$\text{subject to} \sum_{j=1}^{N} T_{ij} = \frac{1}{z} \sum_{p=1}^{P} c_{pi} \ \forall i \quad (2)$$

$$\sum_{i=1}^{N} T_{ij} = \frac{1}{z'} \sum_{p=1}^{P} c'_{pj} \ \forall j$$

where c_{pi} and c'_{pi} are frequency counts of the ith and jth word in the pth sub-document of a document. Note that we are using P to

Table 1: Examples from twin films dataset.

First Film	Second Film
Oscar Wilde (1960)	The Trials of Oscar Wilde (1960)
Prefontaine (1997)	Without Limits (1998)
Kundun (1997)	Seven Years in Tibet (1997)
A Hijacking (2012)	Captain Phillips (2013)

indicate the number of ranked sub-documents for both documents. Without loss of correctness, the number of ranked sub-documents can vary for the two documents. By integrating the bias directly into the normalised BOW representation, we can allow the WMD to be sensitive to the position and presentation bias. Formally, we define r_p to be the rank of the pth sub-document. Further, we borrow the bias term by Lee at al. [11] and define the position and presentation bias as:

$$b_p = \left(\frac{1}{1 + r_p} \right)^{\gamma} \quad (3)$$

where $\gamma \geq 0$ is a sensitivity parameter which allows us to control the effect of the position and presentation bias. We refer to Lee at al. [11] for more details on the choice of the bias term. We can now define the normalised rank-weighted BOW representation $\hat{d} = \{\hat{d}_i\}_{i=1}^{N}$ as follows:

$$\hat{d}_i = \frac{1}{z} \sum_{p=1}^{P} b_p c_{pi} \quad (4)$$

The Position-sensitive Word Mover's Distance (P-WMD) is therefore defined by solving the following linear program:

$$\underset{T \in \mathbb{R}_{\geq 0}^{N \times N}}{\text{minimize}} \sum_{i=1}^{N} \sum_{j=1}^{N} T_{ij} ||x_i - x_j||_2 \quad (5)$$

$$\text{subject to} \sum_{j=1}^{N} T_{ij} = \hat{d}_i, \ \sum_{i=1}^{N} T_{ij} = \hat{d}'_j \ \forall i, j \quad (6)$$

Note that this formulation allows us to use the word centroid distance [9], providing efficient computation of the transportation problem. As described in previous work [1, 10], word embeddings tend to suffer from the hubness problem which is critical for retrieval tasks. We propose to reduce the hubness of the P-WMD using mutual proximity [18], which transforms the P-WMD to a statistical distance.

4 TWIN FILMS DATASET

Twin films can be characterized as films which have the same or very similar plot but were produced by two different studios around the same time. Explanations for the phenomenon are diverse, ranging from industrial espionage to topical issues [2], e.g. the refugee crisis. We acquired a dataset based on an list of twin film examples listed on Wikipedia[2] to tackle the problem of finding the twin film. The dataset consists of 111 twin film pairs (first film, second film) and is composed of 221 unique films which have been carefully

---

[2]https://en.wikipedia.org/wiki/Twin_films, last accessed: 16.02.2016

Table 3: *R*-precision scores on twin films dataset. The best result is highlighted in bold.

Method	Random	BOW	TFIDF	WMD	P-WMD
R-precision	0.005	0.171	0.072	0.459	**0.523**

revised. The films present in the dataset range over several genres and sub-genres and cover a wide range of production dates (1938–2016). Table 1 lists a few samples from our twin films dataset, where we treat the first film to be considered as the query object. To summarize the synopsis of the films, we additionally extracted the plot keywords listed at IMDB[3] for each of the 221 films. The position of each plot keyword on IMDB depends on the number of up-votes given by the community members resulting in a position bias of the keywords. Additionally, the plot keywords listed on IMDB are biased by the presentation used on the film description page, as only the five highest ranked keywords are shown.

Table 2 lists the top five plot keywords for a few samples of our twin films dataset. Note that the IMDB plot keywords do not necessarily contain only a single token but rather describe properties of the plot using concatenated tokens, e.g. *long-distance-runner* in Prefontaine (1997). We have therefore pre-processed all plot keywords as follows: (1) each keyword has been split into its individual words using hyphen as the delimiter, (2) all occurrences of stop words have been removed and (3) all tokens have been transformed to lowercase. Note that it was not possible to retrieve plot keywords for all 221 films, resulting in a sub-set of 108 twin film pairs which contain plot keywords for both films.

5 EXPERIMENTAL RESULTS

To asses the effectiveness of our approach, we performed a set of evaluations on the introduced twin films dataset and on the MovieLense dataset [6]. We used a sensitivity of $\gamma = 0.75$ for all experiments, as this value roughly represents the sensitivity of the majority of online communities discussed in [11]. Note that an optimal sensitivity value can be found using grid search if a validation set is available.

5.1 Twin Films Benchmark

We compared the performance of our P-WMD against three other methods: Bag Of Words (BOW), Term Frequency–Inverse Document Frequency (TFIDF) and the original Word's Mover Distance (WMD). As for each query object (first twin film) exactly one film has to be retrieved, we used the *R*-precision metric. In particular we define the *R*-precision as the average precision with the number of relevant documents equal to one ($R = 1$). The *R*-precision of random guessing can therefore be computed by $\frac{R}{\#Films}$, where *#Films* is the number of films in the dataset. All *R*-precision scores on the twin films dataset, including random guessing, are shown in Table 3. As indicated in the results table, our P-WMD approach outperforms all other approaches by a clear margin. In addition to the evaluation using *R*-precision scores, we assessed the recall@*k* for the range of $k = \{1, \dots, 10\}$. The resulting recall@*k* scores are

---

[3]http://www.imdb.com, last accessed: 16.02.2016

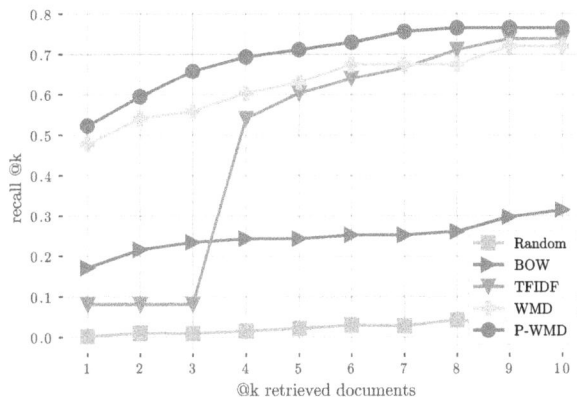

Figure 1: Comparison of recall at different values of k on the twin films dataset.

shown in Figure 1. The recall@*k* scores indicate that our P-WMD achieves an improvement upon the WMD for all values of *k* considered in the evaluation. Recall@*k* of the random guessing has been estimated using 200 random trials. The stable recall@*k* results indicated that the P-WMD is a robust approach for retrieving compositional documents based on the semantic properties of their ranked sub-documents. These results and the *R*-precision results indicate that the P-WMD is well suited for such retrieval tasks.

5.2 MovieLense Benchmark

In addition to the evaluation on the twin films dataset, we assessed the performance of our proposed P-WMD on the MovieLense dataset [6] by measuring the relative improvement over a baseline. The MovieLense dataset consists of 100k film ratings from 1000 users on 1700 films. The data was collected through the MovieLense web site and is an established dataset for research on recommender systems. In order to allow for an evaluation consistent to those on the twin films dataset, we considered the problem of retrieving the genre of a film based on a similarity space constructed from plot keywords. Note that the plot keywords do not necessarily reflect information about the genres, resulting in weak performance (*F1* score) of all approaches.

We automatically retrieved IMDB IDs and IMDB plot keywords for all 1700 films. As the MovieLense dataset provides information on the film genre, we used the provided data as ground truth. We assessed the performance of this multi-label task using the macro-averaged F_1 score and used leave-one-out to estimate the generalization error. To obtain predictions for the film genres given the plot keywords of a film, we computed the majority vote using the k-Nearest Neighbour classifier. We used Bag Of Words (BOW) as the baseline approach and measured the relative improvements of the leave-one-out macro-averaged F_1 scores over the baseline score. The relative improvement of a method is computed using $\frac{F1_{method}}{F1_{baseline}} - 1$. Figure 2 shows the improvements obtained by all approaches when $k = 2$ neighbours or $k = 5$ neighbours are considered in the estimation of the genres for a movie. Considering the large margin to TFIDF and WMD with $k = 2$, our P-WMD seems to

Table 2: Top five plot keywords of examples from twin films dataset.

Film	Plot Keywords (Top 5)
Oscar Wilde (1960)	homosexual-history, grapes, playwright, grape, london-fog
The Trials of Oscar Wilde (1960)	gay-husband, gay-interest, homosexuality, homosexual, gay
Prefontaine (1997)	oregon, long-distance-runner, runner, olympics, watching-television
Without Limits (1998)	oregon, car-crash, death, university-of-oregon, coach
Kundun (1997)	tibet, chinese, dalai-lama, lama, tibetan
Seven Years in Tibet (1997)	dalai-lama, tibet, austria, mountain, himalaya
A Hijacking (2012)	somali-pirate, pirate, cargo-ship, ransom, ceo
Captain Phillips (2013)	ship, hostage, lifeboat, somalian-pirate, leader

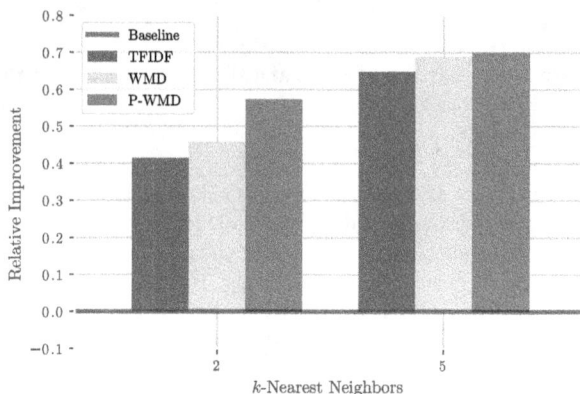

Figure 2: Relative improvements, estimated using leave-one-out, of the macro-averaged F_1-score over BOW using k-Nearest Neighbour classification.

be more robust for compositional documents resulting in less noise in the distance space and therefore resulting in a higher relative improvement than the other methods. As expected, with increased k the relative improvement over the baseline of the P-WMD is approximately the same as for the original Word Mover's Distance.

6 CONCLUSION

We presented an effective approach for retrieving compositional documents consisting of ranked sub-documents by incorporating the position and the presentation bias into the Word Mover's Distance. As datasets for such retrieval tasks are rare and difficult to obtain, we additionally introduced a new benchmark dataset on twin films. While the formulation of our Position-sensitive Word Mover's Distance allows for efficient computation, integrating the position and the presentation bias has shown to lead to an improvement over state-of-the-art approaches on both the twin films and the established MovieLense dataset. We could further identify a larger improvement if a small number of neighbours is used in the k-Nearest Neighbour classification task, indicating that our approach produces less noise and is suitable for retrieving compositional documents based on their ranked sub-documents. We further conclude that exploiting semantic properties of words and integrating the position and presentation bias is important to achieve convincing

results. In further work, we will investigate the integration of the position and presentation bias into the supervised Word Mover's Distance.

ACKNOWLEDGMENTS

This research is partially funded by the Austrian Science Fund (FWF): P 27530.

REFERENCES

[1] M. Artetxe, G. Labaka, and E. Agirre. 2016. Learning principled bilingual mappings of word embeddings while preserving monolingual invariance. In *Proceedings of EMNLP*.
[2] Henrik Arvidsson. 2016. Först till kvarn i Drömfabriken. (16 02 2016). http://www.dn.se/kultur-noje/film-tv/forst-till-kvarn-i-dromfabriken
[3] J. A Aslam and M. Frost. 2003. An Information-theoretic Measure for Document Similarity. In *Proceedings of ACM SIGIR*. 449–450.
[4] J. HD Cho, P. Sondhi, C. Zhai, and B. R Schatz. 2014. Resolving healthcare forum posts via similar thread retrieval. In *Proceedings of ACM BCB*. 33–42.
[5] D. Ganguly, D. Roy, M. Mitra, and G. JF Jones. 2015. Word embedding based generalized language model for information retrieval. In *Proceedings of ACM SIGIR*. 795–798.
[6] F Maxwell Harper and Joseph A Konstan. 2016. The movielens datasets: History and context. *ACM TiiS* 5, 4 (2016), 19.
[7] G. Huang, C. Guo, M. J Kusner, Y. Sun, F. Sha, and K. Q Weinberger. 2016. Supervised Word Mover's Distance. In *Proceedings of NIPS*. 4862–4870.
[8] R. Kiros, Y. Zhu, R. R Salakhutdinov, R. Zemel, R. Urtasun, A. Torralba, and S. Fidler. 2015. Skip-Thought Vectors. In *Proceedings of NIPS*. 3294–3302.
[9] M. J Kusner, Y. Sun, N. I Kolkin, and K. Q Weinberger. 2015. From Word Embeddings To Document Distances.. In *Proceedings of ICML*, Vol. 15. 957–966.
[10] A. Lazaridou, G. Dinu, and M. Baroni. 2015. Hubness and Pollution: Delving into Cross-Space Mapping for Zero-Shot Learning. In *Proceedings of ACL*.
[11] M. Lee, S. H Jin, and D. Mimno. 2016. Beyond Exchangeability: The Chinese Voting Process. In *Proceedings of NIPS*. 4934–4942.
[12] E. Levina and P. Bickel. 2001. The earth mover's distance is the mallows distance: Some insights from statistics. In *Proceedings of ICCV*, Vol. 2. 251–256.
[13] T. Mikolov, I. Sutskever, K. Chen, G. S Corrado, and J. Dean. 2013. Distributed representations of words and phrases and their compositionality. In *Proceedings of NIPS*. 3111–3119.
[14] P. Orbanz and Y. W Teh. 2011. Bayesian nonparametric models. In *Encyclopedia of Machine Learning*. Springer, 81–89.
[15] J. Pennington, R. Socher, and C. D Manning. 2014. GloVe: Global Vectors for Word Representation. In *Proceedings of EMNLP*. 1532–1543.
[16] Y. Rubner, C. Tomasi, and L. J Guibas. 2000. The earth mover's distance as a metric for image retrieval. *IJCV* 40, 2 (2000), 99–121.
[17] M. J Salganik, P. S Dodds, and D. J. Watts. 2006. Experimental study of inequality and unpredictability in an artificial cultural market. *Science* 311, 5762 (2006), 854–856.
[18] D. Schnitzer, A. Flexer, M. Schedl, and G. Widmer. 2012. Local and global scaling reduce hubs in space. *JMLR* 13 (2012), 2871–2902.
[19] A. Singh, P. Deepak, and D. Raghu. 2012. Retrieving Similar Discussion Forum Threads: A Structure Based Approach. In *Proceedings of ACM SIGIR*. 135–144.
[20] M. Trapp. 2015. BNP.jl: Bayesian nonparametrics in Julia. In *Bayesian Nonparametrics: The Next Generation Workshop at NIPS*.
[21] Y. Yue, R. Patel, and H. Roehrig. 2010. Beyond position bias: Examining result attractiveness as a source of presentation bias in clickthrough data. In *Proceedings of WWW*. 1011–1018.

Personalised Search Time Prediction using Markov Chains

Vu Tran
University of Duisburg-Essen
vtran@is.inf.uni-due.de

David Maxwell
University of Glasgow
d.maxwell.1@research.gla.ac.uk

Norbert Fuhr
University of Duisburg-Essen
norbert.fuhr@uni-due.de

Leif Azzopardi
University of Strathclyde
leif.azzopardi@strath.ac.uk

ABSTRACT

For improving the effectiveness of *Interactive Information Retrieval (IIR)*, a system should minimise the search time by guiding the user appropriately. As a prerequisite, in any search situation, the system must be able to estimate the time the user will need for finding the next relevant document. In this paper, we show how Markov models derived from search logs can be used for predicting search times, and describe a method for evaluating these predictions. For personalising the predictions based upon a few user events observed, we devise appropriate parameter estimation methods. Our experimental results show that by observing users for only 100 seconds, the personalised predictions are already significantly better than global predictions.

1 INTRODUCTION

Interactive Information Retrieval (IIR) is a complex, non-trivial process where searchers undertake a variety of different actions over the course of a search session [7]. With a large number of variables that can impact upon how an individual searches, modelling the IIR process is extremely complex and has attracted a large amount of attention from the community (e.g. [1–4, 6, 10, 11, 14, 17]). For quantitative modelling of IIR, the *Interactive Probability Ranking Principle (IPRP)* [6] formulates a general principle for structuring the interaction between a user and a system. It assumes that the user performs a sequence of decisions about choices offered to him or her by said system. Each choice involves a certain degree of *effort* (or *cost*) for evaluating it, and when it is accepted (with some probability), it results in a certain *benefit*. The IPRP then derives a criterion for the optimum ordering of the choices such that the expected benefit of the decision list is maximised. As the IPRP is a rather general framework, it does not specify the type of costs and benefits to be considered.

A natural choice for measuring costs and benefits is to use time. The economic approach for modelling IIR [2] uses the same *'currency'*. It is straightforward to measure the cost of specific actions (e.g. the average time it takes a user to formulate a query, to look at

a result snippet, or scan through a potentially relevant document). However, estimating benefit is a much more complex issue, as there is no simple method for doing this for the various actions possible in a specific situation (e.g. how much does it help reformulating the query or inspecting a results list item?). Tran and Fuhr [15] proposed regarding the (saved) *Time To the next Relevant document (TTR)* as benefit. However, they were only able to estimate TTR values retrospectively, and did not try to make any predictions.

We address in this paper the issue of TTR estimation as an important step towards estimating the benefit of potential user actions. This will allow us to apply the IPRP for *user guidance*. However, retrieval time depends heavily upon the specific user due to individual factors, such as typing and reading speed. Thus, general TTR estimates are of little help. Instead, we require a *personalisation* of these estimates. Moreover, time estimates are closely related to time-based *evaluation* [12] of IIR as shorter times yield improved quality in terms of time-based measures.

To the best of our knowledge, this is the first paper aiming at estimating search times. As a preliminary study, we will only regard a simplified version of the general problem: instead of estimating times for all possible actions and situations, we only look at the time from the first/next snippet (after the first query or a relevant document) to the next relevant document. While these estimates themselves may be of little practical value, the methods described here can be used as a baseline for further research focusing on situation- and action-specific estimates. To this end, we focus on the following two research questions.

RQ1 Is it possible to attain reasonable TTR estimates, or do actual search times vary too much to make such predictions feasible?

RQ2 Can we personalise these estimates so that the average prediction error is smaller for these individual estimates?

2 RELATED WORK

Several different approaches have been proposed for modelling complex IIR processes. Zhang and Zhai [17] presented the *card model* as a theoretical framework for optimising the contents of the screen presented in a specific situation. As optimising criterion, they used information gain, which in terms of the IPRP can be regarded as a heuristic approach for estimating the difference between cost and benefit. However, it is unclear if and how information gain is related to evaluation criteria for entire search sessions.

In terms of general user modelling, Azzopardi [2] presented *Search Economic Theory (SET)*, based upon the approach of the IPRP framework [6]. With SET, user effort was measured via use of a

ICTIR '17, October 1–4, 2017, Amsterdam, Netherlands
© 2017 Association for Computing Machinery.
ACM ISBN 978-1-4503-4490-6/17/10...$15.00
https://doi.org/10.1145/3121050.3121085

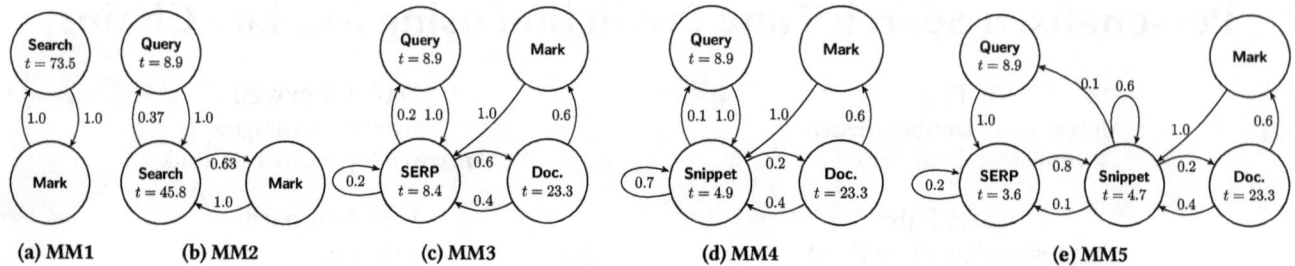

Figure 1: Five state diagrams – from *MM1* at subfigure *(a)* to *MM5* at subfigure *(e)* – representing the five Markov chains used for this study. Each of the diagrams highlights the states and transitions between them. Also included are the times and transition probabilities when each of the models were trained over *33 searchers, over two topics, yielding 66 sessions* (refer to Section 4 - *Predicting Interactions*), using the complete interaction data from each of their search sessions.

cost function. Using simulated interactions with cognitive load as the cost, Azzopardi [2] compared a variety of search strategies, examining the cost of interaction for a given level of expected output, or gain. Kashyap et al. [8] define a cost model for browsing facets to minimise the cost of interaction, and thereby increasing the usefulness of the interface.

These models commonly use cost (effort) and gain (benefit) measures to maximise the expected gain, although there are only few studies that actually estimated them. Tran and Fuhr [15] combined eyetracking data with system logs to model the search process as a Markov chain, where a searcher would transition between a variety of different states, including (re)formulating a query, examining the attractiveness of snippets, the examination of documents, and selecting relevant documents. With this Markov chain, they were able to estimate values for the IPRP with effort as the time spent on each state, and benefit saved as the TTR. The authors then extended the Markov chain to a more detailed one [16], where each result rank has its own state. By estimating the expected benefit for each state, they were able to tell the user at which rank it is better to formulate a query (instead of going further down the result list). Similar to this, Smucker and Clarke [13] modelled the *switching behaviour* of users engaging with ranked lists which provide different levels of gain and show at what point it is optimal to *'switch'*.

3 USER DATA AND MARKOV MODELS

For this study, we were provided with interaction logs from 48 subjects who participated in a user study, each using the same search system to undertake ad-hoc topic retrieval over the TREC AQUAINT collection [9]. Subjects undertook two time-limited search tasks, with each task limited to a total of 20 minutes (1200 seconds), and were assigned to one of four experimental conditions[1]. Over the two search tasks, subjects *on average* submitted 11.7 queries and examined 38.5 documents. In this preliminary analysis, we use a subset of the interaction data from 36 subjects which were assigned to the first three conditions. This is due to the fact that there were no significant differences between the first three conditions; the remaining 12 subjects differ significantly in terms of interaction times from the first three conditions.

Considering the interaction log data we acquired, we propose five different models based upon discrete time, discrete state Markov chains with costs as times spent on each state (refer to Figure 1). We start with a very simple model (*MM1*) and increase the complexity with each model (up to *MM5*). The aim of this approach is to cover log files with different levels of granularity. As a baseline, we predict the average search time, which is represented here as Markov model *MM1* comprising the two states *(i) search* and *(ii) marking a document as relevant*. In the second model *MM2*, we added state, *(iii) query*, for formulating a query. We added more details in the search process by replacing the search with *SERP*, examining the *Search Engine Results Page (SERP)* and *document*, assessing a document for relevance, naming this model *MM3*. For *MM4*, we changed SERP interactions to *snippet* interactions. Instead of simply modelling all the time spent on a SERP as a single state, we split it into one state per snippet examined. These simplistic representations of SERP/snippet interactions were then replaced by a fifth, amalgamated Markov chain, *MM5*, where we consider both the SERP interaction time and snippet time. Here, SERP time is assumed as the time spent after submitting the query or asking for the next 10 results, until the requested SERP time is displayed (due to the underlying search engine, this took several seconds). The snippet time then refers to the actual time spent per snippet (subject to the approximations described below).

4 EXPERIMENTAL METHOD

Interpreting Log Data The user study log file contains a series of events: *query box focus, query submitted, view SERP page x, snippet hovers* (both in and out, with the mouse cursor), and *view* and *mark* documents. Each event has a timestamp, with document-centric events also containing the original rank. We considered the query state as the point from which a searcher focused on the query box to submitting their query. Examining a document was interpreted as the duration from which a document was displayed to a subject to the time that they either marked the document as relevant, or left the document altogether (i.e. returning back to the corresponding SERP). SERP time was considered as the duration from which SERP *x* was displayed to the subject, to the point that they left the SERP by either: focusing on the query box (to reformulate); viewing a document; or viewing the next/previous SERP *y*. For *MM5*, the SERP time was considered as the duration from viewing SERP *x* to

---

[1]Space restrictions limit a more thorough explanation of the user study; refer to [9] for further details.

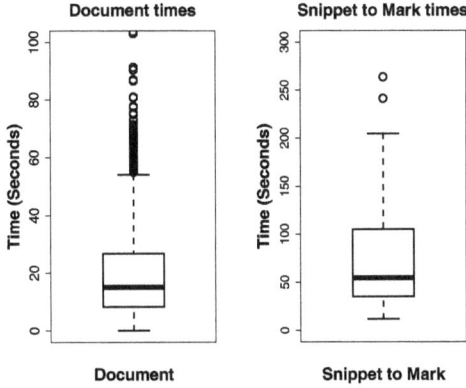

Figure 2: Time distribution on documents and snippet-to-mark from the actual user study log data (refer to Maxwell and Azzopardi [9]).

Figure 3: The mean absolute error of the predictions for each Markov chain model over the cutoff times (refer to Section 4). Note that the absolute error is compared over the various interaction data cutoff times.

the time the first result item was examined (via the first recorded hover in event), and from the previous action (e.g. marking a document) to the viewing of SERP y. Snippet time was considered as the duration the subject spent examining a snippet. Since hovering events proved to be unreliable, we had no direct information on these events. Instead, we assumed that the subject looked sequentially through the snippets, and when he or she clicks on a document, we divided the time since the SERP examination began by the rank of the viewed document. Based upon this assumption, we created the corresponding number of snippet events. In the case where no snippet on the SERP was clicked, we created artificial snippet events with the average duration per snippet derived from the observed clicks.

As can be seen from Figure 2, document times varied substantially, with a fairly large number of outliers (those that are more than 3.5 standard deviations away from the mean, i.e. above 58 seconds). As it is impossible to predict such outliers, one reasonable solution would be to discard these sessions. However, since we have only a limited amount of empirical data, we decided to keep these sessions, but to 'cap' the outlier document times, by assuming that the user did not spend more than 58 seconds per document.

Measures Examined The most obvious time to predict was the span from query formulation until finding the first relevant document. However, since users were asked to find as many relevant documents as possible – and with our limited number of observed search sessions – it was more sensible to be able to make predictions for each relevant document found. After finding a relevant document, users typically go back to a SERP and look at the next snippet. For this reason, the most appropriate time to be considered is the one from the first/next snippet viewed (or SERP in case of **MM3**) to marking a document relevant.

Estimating Times and Probabilities The transition probability between any two states s_i and s_j is estimated using a maximum likelihood estimation: $P_{r(s_i,s_j)} = N_{ij}/N_i$, where N_{ij} is the number of times we observed a transition from state s_i to state s_j, and N_i is the total number of transitions from state s_i to any other state in the training data. In a similar way, the expected time spent for each

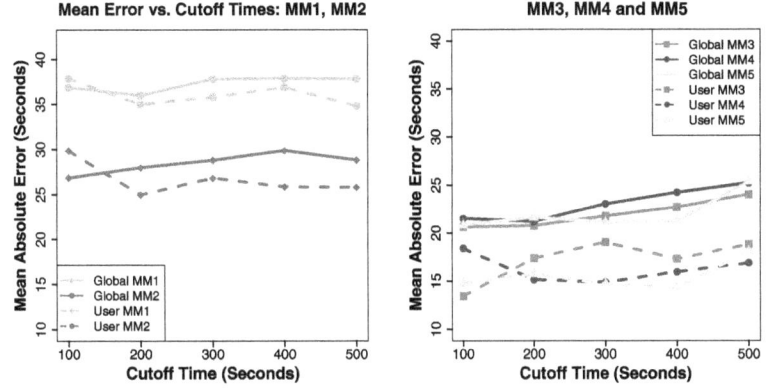

state (*Query, SERP, Snippet, Document*) is computed as the average of the observed times in these states respectively.

With our Markov chains, we estimate the so-called *mean first passage time*, which is the expected time from one state to another. We explain this method for the case of **MM4** here. Let us denote the four Markov states q, s, d and m, the time in these states t_q, t_s, t_d and t_m, and the transition probability from state x to state y as p_{xy}. The expected times T_q, T_s and T_d for reaching the mark state from the query, snippet/SERP or document states respectively can then be computed via the following linear equation system.

$$T_q = t_q + p_{qs}T_s$$
$$T_s = t_s + p_{sq}T_q + p_{ss}T_s + p_{sd}T_d$$
$$T_d = t_d + p_{ds}T_s$$

We derived the actual observed behaviours from the user study log data. The actual time $\hat{T}_s$ (snippet or SERP to mark) was calculated as $\hat{T}_s = (\hat{T}_{lM} - \hat{T}_{fS})/|M|$. Here, $\hat{T}_{lM}$ is the timestamp of the last mark in the session. Since we are making predictions for the remainder of a session at specific cutoff times, $\hat{T}_{fS}$ is the timestamp of the first snippet seen for which we have not yet reached a marked document. Finally, $|M|$ denotes the number of documents marked in the remainder of the session.

Predicting Interactions We worked with 72 sessions (36 subjects with 2 topics each) in total. A pilot study showed no major differences between the two topics; as such, we consider both topics together. We used 12 fold cross-validation for all tests, meaning our training group and our test group contained 66 and 6 sessions respectively. When selecting subjects for training and testing, we created stratified samples by selecting the first three experimental conditions. This helped us to factor out the effects across the different experimental conditions. We evaluate our predictions with the actual observed data and present the mean absolute errors.

Global models are trained over 66 entire subsamples of session data as our baselines and tested on the remaining subsample. Sessions were cutoff into time slices, from 0 seconds (at the initial query focus) to periods ranging from 100 up to 500 seconds in steps of 100 seconds. These cutoffs provided us with five variations of the same log data, with each increase in time providing more interaction data. We then used the remainder of the sessions to evaluate our predictions by comparing the predictions from our generated models against the observed behaviours.

Personalised models are built from cutoff data of each individual subject. For building these models after some short observation time, we face the problem of parameter estimation: some transitions or states even may not yet have been observed for a specific subject. For the states, we use the following Bayesian formula to estimate the time: $T_x = \overline{T}_x v + Cm/v + m$, where $\overline{T}$ is the time of the global model at the given point of time, and v is the total number of observations until that point. C is the mean time of that state across the entire session, and m is the weight given to the prior estimate that is based on the distribution of average times derived from the entire session.

As for the probabilities for our personalised models, even a few observed events will not lead to good estimates using the standard maximum likelihood technique. Thus, we instead use Bayes' estimates with beta priors where the parameters of the beta distribution are derived from the overall distribution of probabilities in the training sample via the *method of moments* [5].

5 RESULTS

Figure 2 shows the overall distribution of the actual snippet times. Even after capping the document viewing times as described above, there is still a large variance in these times, making the task of predicting these times extremely difficult.

The mean absolute error of the various models investigated are depicted in Figure 3, where we show these errors for various cutoff times. All approaches consider the snippet-to-mark times for marks occurring after the cutoff time. For the user models, user-specific parameters are derived from the observations occurring before the cutoff time (i.e. these models are trained for some time, allowing them to make predictions for session's remainder). Significance tests are achieved using 2-tailed paired t-tests, with $p < 0.05$.

Given that the average snippet-to-mark time is 73.5 seconds, the relative errors are not very satisfactory for most of the approaches – which is at least partially due to the high variance of the values to be predicted. Comparing the performance of the five models *MM1-5*, it is obvious that the first two models are outperformed by the three latter ones. Specifically, *MM1* produces very high errors due to the fact that it does not distinguish between querying and result examinations. With this distinction, both global and user-specific models of *MM2* perform significantly better than those of *MM1*, showing that the complexity of a user's interaction requires a model with a certain level of detail. With even more details, *MM3-5* show much better performance than *MM1-2*, although the improvement seems to stagnate when comparing *MM3*, *MM4* and *MM5* to each other. This shows that increasing detail boosts the results only to a certain point, and after this point, results increase moderately.

Comparing the global models with the user-specific ones, we can see that the latter models are much better, even with very little training time. Only for the simple, poor-performing models *MM1* and *MM2*, personalisation is of limited value. For *MM3-5*, after only 100 seconds of training, all user-specific models are significantly better than their corresponding global ones, and this holds true also

for the rest of the session. Earlier results without Bayes' estimators showed a different picture: the personalised models were worse than the global ones until 400 seconds.

6 CONCLUSIONS AND FUTURE WORK

User guidance for maximising the expected benefit of a search session is a major goal of quantitative models of IIR. In this paper, we devised a method for estimating these benefits in terms of search time, which is directly related to time-based evaluation measures. Moreover, we have shown that we can significantly improve global estimates by generating user-specific predictions after having observed the user for a short time.

Although the models regarded here are still fairly simple, these results are rather promising. Future work will focus on more complex models, considering (for example) rank positions of snippets, or the number of query reformulations. Only with these extensions will it be possible to guide the user (e.g. *go to the next rank*, or *reformulate your query* [16]). Moreover, we have considered only one type of search task here. Models for other types of tasks will also have to be developed (as well as classification methods for recognising the current user's task type). Nevertheless, the work presented in this paper is an important first step along this path.

Acknowledgements This work was supported by *ESF ELIAS* grant nos. 7109 (Tran) and 7271 (Maxwell), *GSF* grant no. FU 205/26-1 (Tran), and *EPSRC* grant no. 1367507 (Maxwell). Our thanks to the three anonymous reviewers for their feedback.

REFERENCES

[1] M. Ageev, Q. Guo, D. Lagun, and E. Agichtein. 2011. Find it if you can: a game for modeling different types of web search success using interaction data. In *Proc. 34th ACM SIGIR*. 345–354.
[2] L. Azzopardi. 2011. The Economics in Interactive Information Retrieval. In *Proc. 34th ACM SIGIR*. 15–24.
[3] F. Baskaya, H. Keskustalo, and K. Järvelin. 2013. Modeling behavioral factors in interactive information retrieval. In *Proc. 22nd ACM CIKM*. 2297–2302.
[4] A. Borisov, I. Markov, M. de Rijke, and P. Serdyukov. 2016. A Context-aware Time Model for Web Search. In *Proc. 39th ACM SIGIR*. 205–214.
[5] K.O. Bowman and L.R. Shenton. 2007. The beta distribution, moment method, Karl Pearson and RA Fisher. *Far East J. of Theoretical Statistics* 23, 2 (2007), 133.
[6] N. Fuhr. 2008. A Probability Ranking Principle for Interactive Information Retrieval. *Information Retrieval* 11, 3 (2008), 251–265.
[7] P. Ingwersen and K. Järvelin. 2005. *The Turn: Integration of Information Seeking and Retrieval in Context*.
[8] A. Kashyap, V. Hristidis, and M. Petropoulos. 2010. FACeTOR: Cost-driven Exploration of Faceted Query Results. In *Proc. 19th ACM CIKM*. 719–728.
[9] D. Maxwell and L. Azzopardi. 2014. Stuck in Traffic: How Temporal Delays Affect Search Behaviour. In *Proc. 5th ACM IIiX*. 155–164.
[10] D. Maxwell, L. Azzopardi, K. Järvelin, and H. Keskustalo. 2015. Searching and Stopping: An Analysis of Stopping Rules and Strategies. In *Proc. 24th ACM CIKM*. 313–322.
[11] P. Pirolli and S.K. Card. 1999. Information foraging. *Psychological Review* 106 (1999), 643–675. Issue 4.
[12] M.D. Smucker and C.L.A. Clarke. 2012. Time-based Calibration of Effectiveness Measures. In *Proc. 35th ACM SIGIR*. 95–104.
[13] M.D. Smucker and C.L.A. Clarke. 2016. Modeling Optimal Switching Behavior. In *Proc. 1st ACM CHIIR*. 317–320.
[14] P. Thomas, A. Moffat, P. Bailey, and F. Scholer. 2014. Modeling Decision Points in User Search Behavior. In *Proc. 5th ACM IIiX*. 239–242.
[15] V. Tran and N. Fuhr. 2012. Using Eye-Tracking with Dynamic Areas of Interest for Analyzing Interactive Information Retrieval. In *Proc. 35th ACM SIGIR*. 1165–1166.
[16] V. Tran and N. Fuhr. 2013. Markov Modeling for User Interaction in Retrieval. In *MUBE SIGIR Workshop*.
[17] Y. Zhang and C. Zhai. 2015. IR As Card Playing: A Formal Model for Optimizing Interactive Retrieval Interface. In *Proc. 38th ACM SIGIR*. 685–694.

An Exploration of Serverless Architectures
for Information Retrieval

Matt Crane and Jimmy Lin

David R. Cheriton School of Computer Science
University of Waterloo, Ontario, Canada
{matt.crane,jimmylin}@uwaterloo.ca

ABSTRACT

Serverless architectures represent a new approach to designing applications in the cloud without having to explicitly provision or manage servers. The developer specifies functions with well-defined entry and exit points, and the cloud provider handles all other aspects of execution. In this paper, we explore a novel application of serverless architectures to information retrieval and describe a search engine built in this manner with Amazon Web Services: postings lists are stored in the DynamoDB NoSQL store and the postings traversal algorithm for query evaluation is implemented in the Lambda service. The result is a search engine that scales elastically with a pay-per-request model, in contrast to a server-based model that requires paying for running instances even if there are no requests. We empirically assess the performance and economics of our serverless architecture. While our implementation is currently too slow for interactive searching, analysis shows that the pay-per-request model is economically compelling, and future infrastructure improvements will increase the attractiveness of serverless designs over time.

1 INTRODUCTION

Servers, referring to both software stacks and the machines they run on, are central to the architecture of information retrieval systems. In the standard design, a search service waits for requests from a client based on some well-known protocol (e.g., HTTP or an RPC framework such as Thrift), executes the query, and returns the result. In a distributed search architecture, each server may only be responsible for a small partition of the entire document collection, and there may be many replicas of the same service, but servers remain the basic building block.

The advent of cloud computing means that physical machines are nowadays increasingly replaced by on-demand virtualized instances under a pay-as-you-go model. However, running a search engine still requires managing servers in some form. Even if there are no requests, one still needs to pay for some basic level of provisioning, in anticipation of incoming queries. As the query load increases, one then needs to provision more servers and load balance across them. Although there are tools to assist with scaling

up (and down) elastically, our goal is to explore alternative architectures that simplify management.

A new trend in cloud computing under the banner of serverless architecture or serverless computing aims to divorce the execution of stateless services from the server machines they run on (whether physical or virtualized). For example, Amazon's Lambda service lets a developer run code without provisioning or managing servers. The developer specifies a block of code that needs to be executed with well-defined entry and exit points, and Amazon handles the actual execution of the code—from a few times per day to thousands of requests per second.

This paper explores applications of serverless architectures for information retrieval and describes a search application built entirely using this approach with Amazon Web Services. Our key insight is that search breaks down into two components: postings lists that comprise the index and postings traversal algorithms that manipulate the postings to compute query results. The postings lists represent the "state" of the application, which we store in Amazon's DynamoDB NoSQL store. The "stateless" query evaluation algorithm is encapsulated in Lambda code that fetches postings of query terms stored in DynamoDB to compute query results.

The contribution of this work is the first application of serverless computing to information retrieval that we are aware of. We show that it is indeed possible to build a fully-functional search engine that does not require the explicit provisioning or management of servers. Experimental results show that our design yields end-to-end query latencies of around three seconds on a standard web test collection of approximately 25 million documents. While this latency is not acceptable for interactive retrieval today, the economics of the pay-per-request model is compelling. We believe that our design is interesting, and as serverless architectures gain popularity, infrastructure improvements will increase the attractiveness of our approach over time.

2 BACKGROUND

Serverless computing represents the logical extension of the "as a service" cloud computing trend that began in earnest a decade ago (even though precedents date back many decades to the advent of timesharing machines). Infrastructure as a service (IaaS) provides elastic, on-demand computing resources, usually in the form of virtual machines—Amazon's EC2 was the first and remains the most prominent example of this model, although Microsoft, Google, and many others have similar offerings. These cloud providers also offer storage and other infrastructure components (e.g., network virtualization) in a pay-as-you-go manner. Platform as a service (PaaS) raises the level of abstraction, where the cloud provider manages a complete computing platform—a typical example is Google App

Engine, which supports hosted web applications. Database as as service (DBaaS), such as Amazon's Relational Database Service (RDS), Microsoft's Azure SQL, and Google's Cloud SQL, provides managed database services that simplify provisioning, administering, and scaling relational databases in the cloud.

Database and storage as a service can be viewed as providing developers the ability to offload the management of "state" to a cloud provider. Many modern web applications centralize state in a database or some backend data store to simplify design and to support horizontal scalability. Therefore, most, if not all, application logic becomes stateless, in the sense that state is not preserved across multiple invocations of a particular functionality. Thus, the application just becomes a bunch of functions that access a common data store. If the responsibility of managing state is then pushed to a hosted cloud solution, then all that is left is a bunch of functions. In such an architecture, the developer does not really care how these functions are executed—hence, serverless.

Serverless computing does not actually mean that code can run without servers—but rather that from the developer's perspective, the execution of self-contained functions becomes someone else's problem, namely, that of the cloud provider. The developer does not need to worry about spinning up servers (or VM images), aggregating multiple execution instances to increase utilization, load balancing across multiple server instances, scaling up and down elastically, etc. The advent of lightweight containers with additional namespace virtualization and tooling, exemplified by Docker [11], makes serverless computing practical.

To date, most discussions of serverless computing take place in the context of redesigning user-facing applications in this paradigm. Such a decomposition is consonant with the "mircoservices" architecture that is in vogue today. For example, Hendrickson et al. [7] speculate about what it would take to rebuild Gmail in a completely serverless design, and the breakthroughs necessary to make it a reality. In this paper, we focus on the backend and explore what serverless information retrieval might look like.

3 SERVERLESS DESIGN

This section describes the design of our serverless search architecture, shown in Figure 1. We explain how index structures are mapped to DynamoDB and how the query evaluation algorithm is implemented using Lambda functions. At present, we have designed our system entirely around Amazon Web Services and thus vendor lock-in is a concern. Other cloud providers offer similar capabilities, although they are not as mature as Amazon's services. Cloud interoperability is an important issue in its own right, but beyond the scope of our work.

In this paper, we consider the JASS score-at-a-time query evaluation algorithm on impact-ordered indexes [9]. This approach has been shown to be both effective and efficient compared to state-of-the-art document-at-a-time approaches [4]. Query evaluation in JASS begins with lookup of postings corresponding to query terms. Each postings list comprises a sequence of decreasing impact scores, each of which is associated with a run of sorted docids (which we call a segment). To simplify our implementation, we currently do not compress docids [10]. Segments from postings lists of all query terms are sorted in decreasing impact score and processed in that

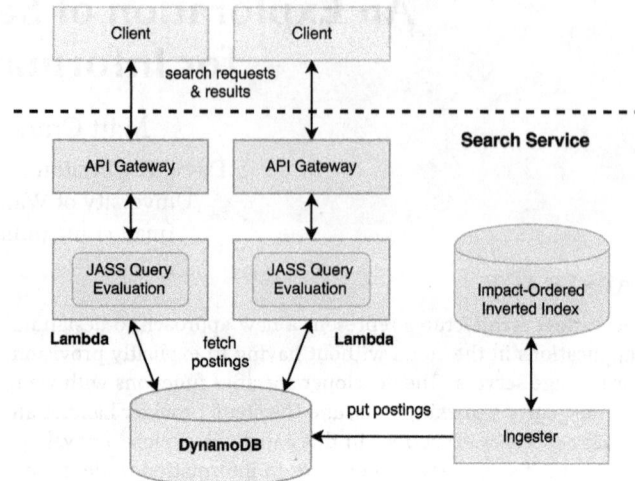

Figure 1: Our serverless search architecture. AWS infrastructure is shown in blue (Lambda and DynamoDB) and our custom components are shown in green.

order. For each segment, its impact score is loaded, and for each docid in the segment, the impact score is added to its accumulator. In JASS, the accumulators are implemented as an array of 16-bit integers, one per document, indexed by the docid. To avoid sorting the accumulators once all postings segments have been processed, a heap of the top k can be maintained during processing. That is, after adding the current impact score to the accumulator, we check if the document score is greater than the smallest score in the heap; if so, the pointer to the accumulator is added to the heap. After all postings segments have been processed, the top k elements are extracted from the heap and returned as results.

3.1 DynamoDB Index Storage

DynamoDB [5] is Amazon's fully-managed NoSQL store that supports a basic key–value model. One of its key features is that the user pays only for data storage and read/write operations. This pricing model is truly pay-per-request, in contrast to Amazon's Relational Database Service (RDS), which requires payment for server instances, regardless of query load.

DynamoDB has three core components: tables, items, and attributes. Tables store collections of related data. An item is an individual record within a table, and an attribute is a property of an item. In DynamoDB, items in the same table can have attributes that are not shared across all items. DynamoDB supports two types of primary keys: One attribute is selected as the partition key and is used internally by the service itself for data placement. Optionally, a second attribute can be selected as the sort key. No two items within a table can share a primary key, but DynamoDB supports additional indexes.

At construction time, each DynamoDB table needs to have a name and an associated primary key defined. Otherwise, the tables are schemaless, which means that neither the attributes, nor their types, have to be defined prior to data insertion. DynamoDB items have a size limit of 400KB, which is an important limitation we need to overcome (details below).

A naïve mapping from an inverted index to a NoSQL store would be to use the term as the partition key, and to store the postings for that term as the value. The issue with this design is that even for small collections, the size of the postings lists will exceed the 400KB size limit of DynamoDB items. Fortunately, the organization of impact-ordered indexes presents a natural way of breaking up the postings—by their impact scores. However, with sufficiently large collections, a postings segment (particularly for small impact scores) can still exceed the 400KB limit. To accommodate this we introduce the notion of "groups", an ordering of different runs of docids that share the same impact score. In DynamoDB, we use a hybrid sort key comprised of the impact score and the group number within that impact score.

Recall that for JASS score-at-a-time traversal we must retrieve postings for a term and a given impact score. Unfortunately, our hybrid sort key design does not make this easy to do. As a workaround, we created a secondary index on the postings table with the term as the hash key and the impact score as the sort key to support querying directly by impact score. Because there is no uniqueness constraint for primary keys in a secondary index, this approach works regardless of whether or not the postings for an impact score are split across DynamoDB items (i.e., different groups). In addition to the postings table, we created a separate metadata table, which stores the number of documents in the collection (necessary for the initialization of query evaluation) as well as a list of impact values that have postings for each term. This design allows us to avoid fetching non-existent impact scores.

Finally, we built an ingester program that takes impact-ordered indexes from an external source and inserts the postings into DynamoDB according to our design. Our current implementation is rather naïve and does not manage "hotspots" in the underlying DynamoDB table that develop when inserting many items with the same partition key, and hence does not achieve high throughput.

3.2 Lambda Query Evaluation

Amazon's Lambda lets developers run code without provisioning or managing servers, although creating a Lambda requires specifying the amount of memory that is available to each code invocation (up to a maximum of 1.5GB) and a timeout period (not exceeding 300 seconds). Code invocations are charged according to the duration of the execution, rounded up to the nearest 100ms in a very fine-grained manner. While there are no specifications of computational resources provided to execute the Lambda, both the network bandwidth [6] and the amount of processing power [2] have been observed to scale linearly with the memory requested.

Lambda code must be written in a supported language: JavaScript, Python, Java, or C#. However, there is no restriction against invoking code written in other languages. It is trivial, and indeed common usage, to bundle resources such as native binaries and libraries along with the function code itself. Our Lambda function is implemented in Python, which then invokes a program written in C++ that performs the actual query evaluation.

When an invocation request arrives at the API Gateway (a trigger that invokes a Lambda on HTTP events), Amazon is responsible for provisioning the necessary resources to execute the Lambda and managing its lifecycle. All of this happens without our intervention.

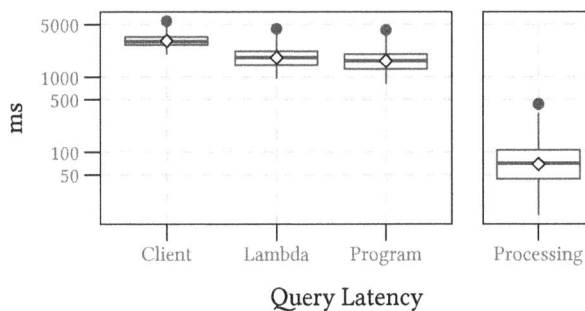

Figure 2: Performance of our serverless architecture.

Within the Lambda itself, our code first requests information about the number of documents and the impact scores for the query terms from the metadata table. After fetching this information, the accumulators and the heap are initialized, followed by the actual processing of the impact segments of the query terms in descending order. For each impact score, the DynamoDB requests are issued asynchronously, and the results are processed when available. While it would be possible to perform all requests asynchronously, this was not done since it would not yield a correct score-at-a-time traversal order. After processing has completed, the top k results are returned ($k = 1000$ in our experiments). Our implementation currently returns internal numeric docids instead of external (string) docids that are collection-specific.

4 EXPERIMENTS

To validate our design, we implemented the serverless retrieval architecture described in the previous section on the Gov2 collection, comprised of around 25 million web pages. For evaluation, we used topics 701–850 (with stopwords removed) used in the Terabyte Tracks from TREC 2004 to 2006 [3]. For expediency, we only ingested into DynamoDB the postings lists of the query terms.

4.1 Performance Analysis

We report experimental results in Figure 2, showing standard box-and-whiskers plots for query latency, with the mean shown as a white diamond. Latency figures are broken down as follows: "Client" is measured from the search client using the Unix command time (mean: 3087ms), "Lambda" is the billable duration as measured by Amazon (mean: 1887ms), "Program" is the internal timing by our query evaluation algorithm (mean: 1722ms), and "Processing" captures the amount of time spent performing query evaluation outside of waiting for DynamoDB requests (mean: 87ms). The difference between the "Program" and "Lambda" measurements captures the overhead of the Python Lambda invoking the native C++ binaries for query evaluation. The difference between "Lambda" and "Client" represents the additional overhead of invoking the Lambda itself and retrieving the results. Overall, everything other than the "Processing" measurement reflects overheads of the serverless architecture in various forms.

Even with all the "obvious" optimizations that we have implemented, end-to-end client query latency is longer than is typically considered usable for an interactive search application. To better contextualize these results, a recent open-source reproducibility challenge organized by Lin et al. [8] reported a query latency of JASS under similar experimental conditions as 51ms (same collection, same queries, on an EC2 instance). This compares favorably with our "Processing" time, and the performance gap can be likely attributed to CPU differences in the underlying instances.

Overall, our experiments identified many sources of latencies in the current design, the biggest of which involves fetching postings from DynamoDB. There is substantial room for improvement, and we would expect that as serverless designs become more popular, Amazon would address these bottlenecks over time. Beyond DynamoDB latencies, there are a few obvious inefficiencies: for example, the invocation overhead of the C++ program can be eliminated if AWS supported C++ Lambdas. Furthermore, there is time wasted in needless data conversion—all Lambda requests and responses must be in JSON format and binary attributes in DynamoDB are encoded in base64, which is slow to decode. It would not be very difficult for Amazon to provide the developer more fine-grained control over serverless execution in these regards.

Beyond these experiments, there are several additional questions regarding our setup. In performance evaluations, it is customary to distinguish "cold" runs and "warm" runs, where the latter benefit from caching effects. Since both DynamoDB and Lambda are fully-managed services, this is difficult for us to accomplish as many aspects of execution are not as transparent as we would like. However, since our work is primarily a feasibility study, we defer these more detailed explorations to future work.

4.2 Cost Analysis

A key feature of our serverless design is the pay-per-request model and the automatic horizontal scalability of Lambda and DynamoDB in response to demand. In this section, we provide a cost analysis comparison of serverless and server-based architectures.

For a fair comparison, we once again turn to results from the reproducibility study of Lin et al. [8], which also examined JASS on the same collection and queries. On an EC2 r3.4xlarge instance, Lin et al. reported a query latency of 51ms on a single thread. Since the instance has 16 vCPUs, if we assume linear scaling, we arrive at a throughput of around 313 queries per second on a fully-loaded server. This instance costs USD$1.33 per hour regardless of load, which means that the cost is the same whether the server executes zero, one, or one million queries in any given hour. On the other hand, Lambda is charged on a per-request basis in increments of 100ms. The average billable time for our system was 1887ms per query, which translates to USD$0.000047951. DynamoDB storage is charged at USD$0.25 per GB per month plus additional costs for read and write operations. However, our usage levels remain in the DynamoDB "free tier" for these experiments, although a heavier query load would not substantially affect our analysis.

In Figure 3, we model the per-query cost in cents for the server-based and serverless architectures assuming the configurations above, as a function of query load in queries per second (qps). The Lambda design has a constant cost per query, while the EC2 instance becomes more cost-effective at higher loads, with the breakeven point around 7.7 queries per second. In addition, with Lambda we achieve (potentially unlimited) scalability without manual intervention. While a load of 7.7 qps seems low, consider that

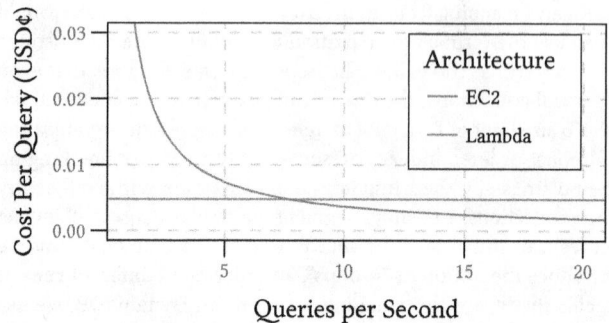

Figure 3: Cost of serverless vs. server-based architectures.

in the overview of the TREC 2016 Open Search Track [1], it was revealed that CiteSeerX receives nearly 100,000 queries per day, which translates into 1.2 qps on average. We venture that in all but the most demanding applications (e.g., commercial search engines), a serverless design would be compelling from a cost perspective.

5 CONCLUSIONS

Trends point to an inevitable move of computing to the cloud, and serverless architectures reflect this evolution. This work represents, to our knowledge, the first design of a serverless architecture for information retrieval. We readily concede that this initial iteration suffers from performance issues, although our cost analysis justifies the pay-per-request model for most search needs. We expect that future improvements in cloud infrastructure, along with additional optimizations in our design, will render serverless information retrieval increasingly attractive.

REFERENCES

[1] Krisztian Balog, Anne Schuth, Peter Dekker, Narges Tavakolpoursaleh, Philipp Schaer, and Po-Yu Chuang. 2016. Overview of the TREC 2016 Open Search Track.
[2] cecilia@aws. 2014. Re: Lambda CPU relative to which instance type? (9 Dec. 2014). Retrieved February 2, 2017 from https://forums.aws.amazon.com/message.jspa?messageID=588722
[3] Charles Clarke, Nick Craswell, and Ian Soboroff. 2004. Overview of the TREC 2004 Terabyte Track. In TREC.
[4] Matt Crane, J. Shane Culpepper, Jimmy Lin, Joel Mackenzie, and Andrew Trotman. 2017. A Comparison of Document-at-a-Time and Score-at-a-Time Query Evaluation. In WSDM. 201–210.
[5] Giuseppe DeCandia, Deniz Hastorun, Madan Jampani, Gunavardhan Kakulapati, Avinash Lakshman, Alex Pilchin, Swaminathan Sivasubramanian, Peter Vosshall, and Werner Vogels. 2007. Dynamo: Amazon's Highly Available Key-value Store. In SOSP. 205–220.
[6] Vineet Gopal. 2015. Powering CRISPR With AWS Lambda. (25 Sept. 2015). Retrieved February 6, 2017 from http://benchling.engineering/crispr-aws-lambda/
[7] Scott Hendrickson, Stephen Sturdevant, Tyler Harter, Venkateshwaran Venkataramani, Andrea C. Arpaci-Dusseau, and Remzi H. Arpaci-Dusseau. 2016. Serverless Computation with OpenLambda. In HotCloud.
[8] Jimmy Lin, Matt Crane, Andrew Trotman, Jaime Callan, Ishan Chattopadhyaya, John Foley, Grant Ingersoll, Craig Macdonald, and Sebastiano Vigna. 2016. Toward Reproducible Baselines: The Open-Source IR Reproducibility Challenge. In ECIR. 408–420.
[9] Jimmy Lin and Andrew Trotman. 2015. Anytime Ranking for Impact-Ordered Indexes. In ICTIR. 301–304.
[10] Jimmy Lin and Andrew Trotman. 2017. The Role of Index Compression in Score-at-a-Time Query Evaluation. Information Retrieval 20, 3 (2017), 199–220.
[11] Dirk Merkel. 2014. Docker: Lightweight Linux Containers for Consistent Development and Deployment. Linux Journal 2014, 239 (2014), Article No. 2.

Acknowledgments. This work was supported by the Natural Sciences and Engineering Research Council (NSERC) of Canada, with additional contributions from the U.S. National Science Foundation under CNS-1405688.

Robust Standard Deviation Estimation for Query Performance Prediction

Haggai Roitman, Shai Erera, Bar Weiner

IBM Research - Haifa

Haifa, Israel 31905

haggai,shaie,barw@il.ibm.com

ABSTRACT

We derive a robust standard deviation estimator for post-retrieval query performance prediction. To this end, we propose a novel bootstrap sampling approach which is inspired by user search behavior. Using an evaluation with several TREC benchmarks and a comparison with several different types of baselines, we demonstrate that, overall, our estimator results in an enhanced query performance prediction.

1 BACKGROUND

We address the problem of post-retrieval query performance prediction [2] (QPP). A post-retrieval QPP method predicts the query's performance based on the quality of its retrieved result list [2].

A common approach utilized by many state-of-the art post-retrieval QPP methods is the analysis of retrieval scores [6, 8, 10, 13, 15, 18]. Specifically, the **standard deviation** of retrieval scores has been employed as a strong indicator of query performance [6, 8, 13, 15]. Higher standard deviation usually attests to lower chance of query-drift [13] or higher content diversity [3], which in turn, is assumed to result in a better query performance. Various alternative methods have been proposed for estimating the standard deviation for QPP [6, 8, 13, 15]. Each of these methods mostly differs in the way documents from the query's corresponding result list are selected for the estimation.

Inspired by [9, 12], we propose a new standard deviation estimator that utilizes several document result lists as reference lists for enhanced QPP. Each such list is sampled from the original retrieved result list. This in comparison to most previous works which directly estimate the standard deviation using only the original retrieved result list [6, 8, 13, 15]. To this end, various document samples are obtained using a novel bootstrap sampling approach. The proposed sampling approach simulates a random user that "browses" the retrieved result list and "clicks" on the documents that should be included in a given sample. Various samples are further weighted based on their presumed quality [9, 12]. Noting that score divergence may be query-dependent [6, 13, 15], we further normalize the bootstrap estimate to ensure inter-query compatibility. We show that, the *Normalized Query Commitment* (NQC) method [13] can be derived as a private instance of our estimator.

ICTIR '17, October 01–04, 2017, Amsterdam, Netherlands.

© 2017 ACM. ISBN 978-1-4503-4490-6/17/10...$15.00

DOI: https://doi.org/10.1145/3121050.3121087

Using an evaluation with several TREC benchmarks and a comparison with several different types of baselines (including two variants of the Bagging method [1]), we demonstrate that, overall, our estimator results in an enhanced query performance prediction.

2 ESTIMATION APPROACH

For a given query q and corpus C, let D denote the result list of the top-k documents $d \in C$ with the highest retrieval scores $s(d|q)$.

We focus on post-retrieval QPP [2]. Therefore, our goal is to estimate *the likelihood of finding relevant information for q in D* [2]. Similar to many previous works [6, 8, 10, 13, 15, 18], we estimate such likelihood by analyzing the retrieval scores $s(d|q)$ of the documents in D. Specifically, we focus on the (retrieval scores) standard deviation, hereinafter denoted $\sigma_{s|q}$, as the indicator of query performance. Higher standard deviation usually attests to lower chance of query-drift [13] or higher content diversity [3], which in turn, is assumed to result in a better query performance.

2.1 Robust Standard Deviation estimator

Our goal is to estimate $\sigma_{s|q}$ as accurately as possible. To this end, we propose a novel bootstrap sampling approach that estimates $\sigma_{s|q}$ using $N \geq 1$ samples $D_1, D_2, \ldots, D_N$; each sample satisfies $D_j \subseteq D$ and contains $|D_j| = l \leq k$ documents.

Our proposed bootstrap estimator, hereinafter named **RSD**[1], is calculated as follows:

$$\hat{\sigma}_{s|q} \overset{def}{=} \sqrt{\sum_{j=1}^{N} \omega(D_j) \cdot \widehat{var}(s|q, D_j)} \qquad (1)$$

$\widehat{var}(s|q, D_j) \overset{def}{=} \frac{1}{l-1} \sum_{d \in D_j} \left(s(d|q) - \hat{\mu}_{D_j} \right)^2$ denotes the (unbiased)

variance estimate of sample D_j's document scores, where $\hat{\mu}_{D_j} \overset{def}{=} \frac{1}{l} \sum_{d \in D_j} s(d|q)$ denotes D_j's mean score. $\omega(D_j)$ is a non-negative real weight, which denotes the relative importance of sample D_j.

2.2 Bootstrap sampling approach

Each $\widehat{var}(s|q, D_j)$ is estimated based on a random sample of documents $D_j \subseteq D$ obtained by a new proposed **ranked-biased**, **WOR** (without replacement) and **round-robin** bootstrap sampling approach. Using this approach, each new sample D_j is obtained by simulating the behavior of a "random user" who "browses" the documents in D, retrieved in response to the user's query q.

---

[1]RSD stands for "Robust Standard Deviation".

The random user is assumed to scan the result list D from top to bottom. On each document, its likelihood of being included in D_j is assumed to be relative to its likelihood of being "clicked" by the random user. Similar to real-world search settings, such random clicks are assumed to be rank-biased [4]. Therefore, the higher document d's ($\in D$) rank is, the higher its chance of being clicked by the random user (hence **ranked-biased** sampling). Let r_d denote document d's ($\in D$) rank ($1 \leq r_d \leq k$) and let $u \sim U[0, 1]$. Using an acceptance-rejection approach, d is included ("clicked") in sample D_j, if the following condition[2] is satisfied: $\sum_{r=r_d}^{k} p(r) \geq u$, where $p(r) \stackrel{def}{=} \frac{2(k+1-r)}{k(k+1)}$ ($1 \leq r \leq k$) denotes the rank distribution.

We also assume that, the random user may click each document only once (hence a **WOR** sampling). Finally, for a given required sample size $|D_j| = l \leq k$, the random user is assumed to click exactly l documents in D. Therefore, whenever the random user has reached the bottom of the list and there are still documents to click, the random user continues her scan again from the top of the list (hence a **round-robin** sampling).

2.3 Sample weighting

We next suggest three variants of the RSD estimator, which was defined in Eq. 1, based on the sample weighting scheme $\omega(D_j)$ that is being employed. The first weighting scheme (denoted "uni") assumes that all samples have the same importance and assigns $\omega_{\text{uni}}(D_j) \stackrel{def}{=} \frac{1}{N}$. Using the uni scheme we estimate the standard deviation according to the average of the samples' variances.

Inspired by [9, 12], we note that, each sample D_j can be treated as a *reference list* for prediction [12]. Hence, different samples can be weighted according to their own predicted query performance. Further following [12], as a second weighting scheme (denoted "sim"), we measure $\omega_{\text{sim}}(D_j) \stackrel{def}{=} sim_{RBO(p)}(D_j, D)$ using the rank-biased overlap [16] (RBO) similarity measure. p is a free parameter set to 0.95, following [12]. Here, each sample D_j is assumed to be a pseudo effective (PE) reference list [12]; therefore, the higher the similarity between D and D_j, the more important D_j is [12].

We also propose a third weighting scheme inspired by the WIG [18] method[3] (denoted "wig"), which is calculated as: $\omega_{\text{wig}}(D_j) \stackrel{def}{=} \frac{1}{l} \sum_{d \in D_j} (s(d|q) - s(C|q))$, where $s(C|q)$ denotes the corpus query likelihood. $s(C|q)$ can be estimated by treating the corpus as a single document. According to $\omega_{\text{wig}}(D_j)$, a sample D_j whose document scores' deviate more from the corpus score (which acts as an ineffective reference document [18]), is assumed to contain better documents, and therefore, receives a higher weight[4].

Overall, using the three sample weighting schemes, we obtain three variants of our proposed RSD estimator, hereinafter denoted RSD[uni], RSD[sim] and RSD[wig], respectively.

2.4 Query-sensitive normalization

We note that, score divergence may be query-dependent [6, 13, 15]. Hence, following [6, 13, 15], to ensure inter-query compatibility, we further normalize our estimate of $\hat{\sigma}_{s|q}$ as follows:

$$\hat{\sigma}_{s|q}^{norm} \stackrel{def}{=} \frac{\hat{\sigma}_{s|q} \cdot nperp(q|R)}{|s(C)|}. \qquad (2)$$

Here, similar to [13, 15], $|s(C)|$ denotes the (absolute) corpus query likelihood. Similar to WIG, such normalization utilizes the corpus as an ineffective reference document; the higher $|s(C)|$ is, the more difficult query q is assumed to be [13, 15].

We further introduce a second (and new) normalization term $nperp(q|R)$, which models to what extent q provides a correct representation of the (hidden) information need I_q [14]. Thus, the higher $nperp(q|R)$ is, the better q's performance is assumed to be. To this end, assuming that the relevance model [7] R induced from D approximates I_q, the representativeness of q (having n_q unique terms) given R is calculated according to the *normalized perplexity*: $nperp(q|R) \stackrel{def}{=} \frac{2^{H(q|R)}}{2^{\log n_q}}$. $H(q|R) \stackrel{def}{=} -\sum_{w \in q} p(w|R) \log p(w|R)$ is the weighted entropy of query q given R, where for each term $w \in q$ we assign the weight of 1 and 0 to the rest of the vocabulary [14]. Therefore, a query q that is more "anticipated" by the relevance model R, is assumed to provide a better representation of I_q.

3 EVALUATION

3.1 Datasets

Corpus	#documents	Queries	Disks
AP	242,918	51–150	1–3
TREC4	567,529	201–250	2–3
TREC5	524,929	251–300	2&4
ROBUST	528,155	301–450, 601–700	4&5-{CR}
WT10g	1,692,096	451–550	WT10g
GOV2	25,205,179	701–850	GOV2

Table 1: TREC benchmarks used for the evaluation.

Table 1 summarizes the TREC corpora and queries used for the evaluation. These benchmarks were used by many previous QPP works [2]. Titles of TREC topics were used as queries, except for the TREC4 benchmark, where no titles are available and topic descriptions were used instead. The Apache Lucene[5] open source search library was used for indexing and searching documents. Documents and queries were processed using Lucene's English text analysis (i.e., tokenization, Porter stemming, stopwords, etc.). As the underlying retrieval method, we used Lucene's Dirichlet-smoothed query-likelihood implementation with $\mu = 1000$ [17].

3.2 Baselines

We compared the three (normalized) variants of our proposed RSD estimator (i.e., RSD[uni], RSD[sim] and RSD[wig]) with several different types of baseline QPP methods.

---

[2]Note that, the first document in D is always "clicked" by the random user.

[3]WIG's original prediction is given by $\frac{\omega_{\text{wig}}(D_j)}{\sqrt{|q|}}$. Yet, we do not divide in $\sqrt{|q|}$ since query q is fixed across all samples.

[4]To avoid negative weights we further take $\omega'_{\text{wig}}(D_j) = \max\{0, \omega_{\text{wig}}(D_j)\}$.

[5]http://lucene.apache.org

As a first line of baselines, we compared with the Clarity [5], WIG [18] and QF methods [18], which are commonly used as competitive post-retrieval QPP methods [2]. The Clarity [5] method estimates query performance proportionally to the divergence between the relevance language model [7] induced from D and that induced from C. The WIG method [18] estimates query performance according to the difference between the average retrieval score in D and that of C. The QF method predicts query performance according to the overlap between D and another list $D' \subseteq C$ (measured as $|D \cap D'|$), obtained by evaluating a new (weighted) query q' over C. q' is formulated from the top-n terms with the highest contribution to the KL-divergence between the relevance model induced from D and the background (corpus) model.

The next line of baselines we compared with were QPP methods that estimate the standard deviation in several alternative ways. This includes among others: σ_m which calculates the standard deviation using the top-m documents in D, hereinafter denoted $D^{[m]}$; using $m = 100$ following [8]; $\sigma_{\max}$ which takes the maximum standard deviation over all rank cutoffs [8]; $\sigma_{50\%}$ which considers only the document scores in D that are above the median score [6]; its extension $n(\sigma_{50\%}) \overset{def}{=} \frac{\sigma_{50\%}}{\sqrt{|q|}}$ [6]; and σ_k which adaptively decides on the rank cutoff for standard deviation calculation, with its tuning parameter set to $\lambda = 5$, following [6, 8].

We also compared with the NQC [13] method which can be derived as a private instance of RSD using D as a single "sample" and further setting $\omega(D) = 1$ and $nperp(q|R) = 1$. We also compared with the UEF[NQC] method [11], a more robust version of NQC, which multiplies the NQC value in the similarity $sim(D, \pi_D)$ (measured using Pearson's correlation on document scores [11]). π_D denotes the permutation of D obtained by re-ranking its documents using the relevance model induced from $D^{[m]}$. Finally, as another alternative that considers score "variance", we implemented the SMV method [15], whose prediction is calculated as follows: $\frac{1}{k|s(C)|} \sum_{d \in D} s(d) \left| \ln \frac{s(d)}{\mu_D} \right|$.

In order to evaluate the effect of our proposed bootstrap sampling approach, we further implemented two alternative standard deviation estimators based on the bootstrap-aggregation (Bagging) method [1]. Similar to RSD, Bagging uses a bootstrap sampling approach to obtain several estimates of the variance, which are then averaged to obtain an aggregated estimate of the standard deviation[6]. Differently from RSD, the original Bagging's bootstrap sampling scheme, now denoted Bagging[org], is rank-oblivious and randomly selects documents with replacements (WR). We further implemented an extended approach, denoted Bagging[rank] which utilizes a rank-biased sampling approach similar to RSD (yet it still allows replacements). Similar to RSD, both Bagging variants were further normalized[7].

3.3 Setup

We predicted the performance of each query based on its top-1000 retrieved documents [2]. Following the common practice [2], we

assessed prediction over queries quality according to the correlation between the predictor's values and the actual average precision (AP@1000) values calculated using TREC's relevance judgments. To this end, we report the Pearson's-ρ (P-ρ) and Kendall's-τ (K-τ) correlations which are the most common measures [2].

Most of the methods that we evaluated (including the RSD variants) required tuning some free parameters. Common to all methods is the free parameter $k \overset{def}{=} |D|$, which is the number of top scored documents (out of a total of 1000 retrieved documents) **to be used for the prediction**. To this end, for each method we selected $k \in \{5, 10, 20, 50, 100, 150, 200, 500, 1000\}$.

Next, some of the methods we evaluated required to tune additional parameters. For example, Clarity, QF, UEF[NQC] and $nperp(q|R)$, all utilize a relevance model [7] (RM1) that is induced from $D^{[m]}$, with $m \in \{1, 3, 5, \ldots, |D|\}$. Following [5, 11, 18], in all these methods, we further clipped the induced relevance model at the top-n terms cutoff, with $n \in \{5, 10, 20, 50, 100, 150, 200, 250\}$.

Finally, the number of bootstrap samples utilized by the RSD and Bagging variants was fixed to $N = 100$. Each documents sample size (**for all samples**) was further tuned as follows: $l \in \{30, 50, 100, 150, 200\}$.

Following [12, 13], training and testing of all methods was performed using a holdout (2-fold cross validation) approach. Accordingly, on each benchmark, we generated 30 random splits of the query set; each split had two folds. The first fold was used as the (query) train set, where parameters were tuned to maximize P-ρ. The second fold was kept untouched for testing. We recorded the average prediction quality (i.e., P-ρ and K-τ) over the 30 splits. Finally, we measured statistical significant differences of prediction quality using a two-tailed paired t-test with (Bonferroni corrected) $p < 0.05$ computed over all 30 splits.

3.4 Results

The results of our evaluation are summarized in Table 2. We first compare RSD to those baseline methods that predict query performance using only the (single) original retrieved result list D (either based on standard deviation or not). We then evaluate the impact of RSD's bootstrap sampling approach. Finally, we compare the three RSD variants to each other.

3.4.1 Original result list based prediction vs. RSD. Comparing RSD side by side with the various single result list baselines (i.e., Clarity, WIG, QF and the various standard deviation estimation alternatives), we observe that, RSD provides a much better query performance prediction quality. Overall, compared to the **best alternative among these methods**, the best RSD variant (which was in all cases RSD[wig]) has provided an average improvement in prediction quality of 9.1%(±2.4%) and 8.5%(±3.9%) in P-ρ and K-τ, respectively. Such improvement was further statistically significant in most cases. This empirical result attests to the merits of using several reference lists for the standard deviation estimation based on our bootstrap sampling approach. Further notable is the improvement over NQC (including UEF[NQC]), which, as we have shown, can be derived as a private instance of our estimator.

---

[6] An alternative is to average over standard deviation estimates, each obtained by a different bootstrap sample. Yet this version was found to be inferior in our evaluation.

[7] The unnormalized variants were significantly inferior to the normalized ones.

Method	AP		TREC4		TREC5		Robust		WT10g		GOV2	
	P–ρ	K–τ	P–ρ	K–τ	P–ρ	K–τ	P–ρ	K–τ	P–ρ	K–τ	P–ρ	K–τ
Clarity	.596	.428	.456	.380	.490	.258	.477	.328	.380	.240	.407	.305
QF	.575	.385	.632	.570	.413	.310	.483	.371	.436	.343	.515	.383
WIG	.526	.380	.533	.502	.347	.252	.411	.358	.434	.364	.535	.387
σ_{100}	.381	.306	.335	.302	.270	.261	.468	.378	.475	.334	.421	.305
σ_{max}	.381	.309	.411	.331	.333	.227	.344	.347	.405	.296	.402	.301
$\sigma_{50\%}$	.341	.308	.278	.254	.202	.191	.395	.331	.376	.333	.383	.289
$n(\sigma_{50\%})$	.510	.396	.301	.281	.231	.240	.461	.367	.436	.350	.411	.302
σ_k	.475	.370	.487	.402	.450	.329	.501	.386	.352	.301	.402	.286
NQC	.554	.361	.624	.562	.483	.318	.575	.406	.486	.354	.432	.304
UEF[NQC]	.613	.394	.639	.569	.520	.332	.615	.418	.518	.361	.455	.327
SMV	.631	.398	.524	.499	.459	.268	.586	.432	.292	.206	.418	.304
Bagging[org]	.678	.462	.629	.567	.557	.369	.593	.412	.519	.330	.530	.365
Bagging[rank]	.682	.457	.632	.571	.564	.375	.606	.430	.529	.348	.537	.369
RSD[uni]	$.703^{ob}$	$.469^{ob}$	.633	.574	$.590^{ob}_s$	$.405^{ob}$	$.622^{ob}_s$	$.438^{ob}_s$	$.553^{ob}_s$	$.366^b$	$.568^{ob}_s$	$.371_s$
RSD[sim]	$.694^{ob}$	$.466^o$	.634	.571	$.570^{ob}$	$.395^{ob}$	.606	.421	$.524^o$	$.362^o$	.553	.363
RSD[wig]	$.710^{ob}_{us}$	$.473^{ob}_{us}$	$.651^b$	$.581^b$	$.618^{ob}_{us}$	$.421^{ob}_{us}$	$.649^{ob}_{us}$	$.441^{ob}_{us}$	$.561^{ob}_{us}$	$.387^{ob}_{us}$	$.576^{ob}_{us}$	$.403^{ob}_{us}$

Table 2: Comparison between the RSD variants and the alternative baseline methods. Bold values mark the best performing method per usecase. The superscripts o and b denote a statistically significant better performance of a given RSD variant compared to all other alternative baselines that use only the original (single) result list for prediction and the two Bagging variants, respectively. The subscripts u and s further denote statistically significant better performance of either the RSD[uni] or RSD[wig] variants compared to the RSD[uni] and RSD[sim] variants, respectively. All significance notations are further reported using a Bonferroni correction for $p < 0.05$.

3.4.2 Impact of RSD's bootstrap sampling approach. We next evaluate the impact of RSD's bootstrap sampling approach by comparing its RSD[uni] variant with the two Bagging variants. We first note that, these two Bagging variants, in most cases, also outperform the prediction quality of the other alternative baseline methods which only make use of the original result list. Among the two Bagging variants, Bagging[rank] was (slightly) better.

Similar to Bagging, the RSD[uni] variant treats every sample evenly. Hence, we can evaluate the impact of our proposed bootstrap sampling approach that is employed in RSD[uni] by directly comparing it with that employed by the Bagging[rank] variant. To recall, compared to Bagging, RSD does not allow document repetitions and further utilizes a round-robin sampling scheme. Overall, RSD[uni] outperformed the prediction quality of Bagging (an average improvement of 3.6%($\pm$0.8%) and 2.6%($\pm$1.5%) in P-ρ and K-τ, respectively). This is yet another empirical testimony that, our new proposed bootstrap sampling approach, which is inspired by user search behavior, is better tailored for QPP.

3.4.3 Comparison of RSD variants. Among the three RSD variants that we evaluated, RSD[wig] had the best prediction quality, with an average improvement of 2.6%($\pm$0.6%) and 2.9%($\pm$1.4%) in P-ρ and K-τ, respectively, over the next best RSD variant (which was RSD[uni] in most cases). Notable is the significant difference between RSD[sim] and RSD[wig]. This empirical result implies that, a better reference lists prediction combination strategy would probably be to use another QPP method (in our case a variant of WIG was utilized) rather than to use inter-list similarity as was originally proposed in [12].

REFERENCES

[1] Leo Breiman. Bagging predictors. *Mach. Learn.*, 24(2):123–140, August 1996.
[2] David Carmel and Oren Kurland. Query performance prediction for ir. In *Proceedings of SIGIR '12*.
[3] David Carmel, Elad Yom-Tov, Adam Darlow, and Dan Pelleg. What makes a query difficult? In *Proceedings of SIGIR '06*.
[4] Nick Craswell, Onno Zoeter, Michael Taylor, and Bill Ramsey. An experimental comparison of click position-bias models. In *Proceedings of WSDM '08*.
[5] Steve Cronen-Townsend, Yun Zhou, and W. Bruce Croft. Predicting query performance. In *Proceedings of SIGIR '02*.
[6] Ronan Cummins, Joemon Jose, and Colm O'Riordan. Improved query performance prediction using standard deviation. In *Proceedings of SIGIR '11*.
[7] Victor Lavrenko and W. Bruce Croft. Relevance based language models. In *Proceedings of SIGIR '01*.
[8] Joaquín Pérez-Iglesias and Lourdes Araujo. Standard deviation as a query hardness estimator. In *Proceedings of SPIRE'10*.
[9] Haggai Roitman. An enhanced approach to query performance prediction using reference lists. In *Proceedings of SIGIR '17*.
[10] Haggai Roitman, Oren Sar-Shalom, Shai Erera, and Bar Weiner. Enhanced mean retrieval score estimation for query performance prediction. In *Proceedings of ICTIR '17*.
[11] Anna Shtok, Oren Kurland, and David Carmel. Using statistical decision theory and relevance models for query-performance prediction. In *Proceedings of SIGIR '10*.
[12] Anna Shtok, Oren Kurland, and David Carmel. Query performance prediction using reference lists. *ACM Trans. Inf. Syst.*, 34(4):19:1–19:34, June 2016.
[13] Anna Shtok, Oren Kurland, David Carmel, Fiana Raiber, and Gad Markovits. Predicting query performance by query-drift estimation. *ACM Trans. Inf. Syst.*, 30(2):11:1–11:35, May 2012.
[14] Mor Sondak, Anna Shtok, and Oren Kurland. Estimating query representativeness for query-performance prediction. In *Proceedings of SIGIR '13*.
[15] Yongquan Tao and Shengli Wu. Query performance prediction by considering score magnitude and variance together. In *Proceedings of CIKM '14*.
[16] William Webber, Alistair Moffat, and Justin Zobel. A similarity measure for indefinite rankings. *ACM Trans. Inf. Syst.*, 28(4):20:1–20:38, November 2010.
[17] C. X. Zhai and J. Lafferty. A study of smoothing methods for language models applied to ad hoc information retrieval. In *Proceedings of SIGIR '01*.
[18] Yun Zhou and W. Bruce Croft. Query performance prediction in web search environments. In *Proceedings of SIGIR '07*.

Term-Mouse-Fixations as an Additional Indicator for Topical User Interests in Domain-Specific Search

Daniel Hienert and Dagmar Kern

GESIS – Leibniz Institute for the Social Sciences

Cologne, Germany

firstname.lastname@gesis.org

ABSTRACT

Models in Interactive Information Retrieval (IIR) are grounded very much on the user's task in order to give system support based on different task types and topics. However, the automatic recognition of user interests from log data in search systems is not trivial. Search queries entered by users a surely one such source. However, queries may be short, or users are only browsing. In this paper, we propose a method of term-mouse-fixations which takes the fixations on terms users are hovering over with the mouse into consideration to estimate topical user interests. We analyzed 22,259 search sessions of a domain-specific digital library over a period of about four months. We compared these mouse fixations to user-entered search terms and to titles and keywords from documents the user showed an interest in. These terms were found in 87.12% of all analyzed sessions; in this subset of sessions, per session on average 11.46 term-mouse-fixations from queries and viewed documents were found. These terms were fixated significantly longer with about 7 seconds than other terms with about 4.4 seconds. This means, term-mouse-fixations provide indicators for topical user interests and it is possible to extract them based on fixation time.

KEYWORDS

Mouse Movements, Search Terms, Search Process, Session, Task

1 INTRODUCTION & RELATED WORK

Knowing the user's search task and the current interest would be very valuable for supporting the actual information need. However, this is still a challenging issue in real-world and live situations. There are various research attempts to model and predict user needs and interests, for example, based on user queries [e.g. 7], context [e.g. 11] and search histories [e.g. 9, 10]. As eye-tracking data is still not practical in long-term real-life user studies, we logged the position of the mouse on a term as well as its dwell time and used this as indicators for user's interest in this term.

Mouse-movement has been shown to be a promising candidate for gathering further information about user behavior. Mouse

trajectories, for example, are utilized to infer and disambiguate navigation and informational search intents [3]. Huang et al. [6] found that cursor hovering and scrolling on landing pages are good indicators to decide if a user has examined a search result. Mouse movement and scrolling are used in addition to click-through-rate and dwell time to better estimate document relevance [2]. The approaches above focus thereby on areas of interests on result lists and landing pages. The approach by Ageev et al. [1] goes one step further and considered single fixated terms on the landing pages and used them among other things for generating result summaries of the corresponding document. Liu et al. [8] combine existing click models with mouse movement information to enhance the prediction of result examination. Therefore, they collected a large-scale data set with a commercial search engine. Other studies in this context base their findings predominantly on task-based evaluations in laboratory settings.

In our research, we also refer to real-world interaction data collected in a digital library for social science information and focus on mouse-fixated terms in whole user sessions. We address the following research questions:

R1: Can we find indicators of topical user interests such as user search terms and topics from document clicks in mouse-fixated terms?

R2: Is it possible to distinguish between terms in a list of mouse-fixated terms the user showed an interest in and terms the user had fixated more or less unconsciously?

With our work, we contribute to this research field by analyzing a log file of about 22,000 search sessions of a domain-specific digital library.

2 EXPERIMENT

2.1 Environment

Sowiport[1] is a digital library for social science information such as bibliographic records, full texts, and research projects. It contains more than nine million records from 22 German- and English-language databases; the main audience is German-speaking. Users are supported in their search process with a number of services [cp. 4]. Figure 1 shows the search result page of Sowiport. By clicking on the title of a result entry the user is forwarded to the corresponding detailed view page (see Figure 2). This page contains further information about the selected bibliographic record. Amongst typical literature metadata like

ICTIR '17, October 01-04, 2017, Amsterdam, Netherlands

© 2017 Copyright is held by the owner/author(s). Publication rights licensed to ACM.

ACM ISBN 978-1-4503-4490-6/17/10...$15.00

https://doi.org/10.1145/3121050.3121088

---

[1] http://sowiport.gesis.org

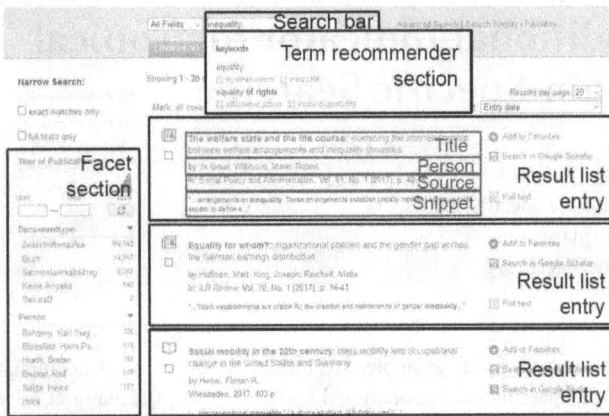

Figure 1: Overview of the different AOIs on the search result page (black frame) with metadata fields (blue frame).

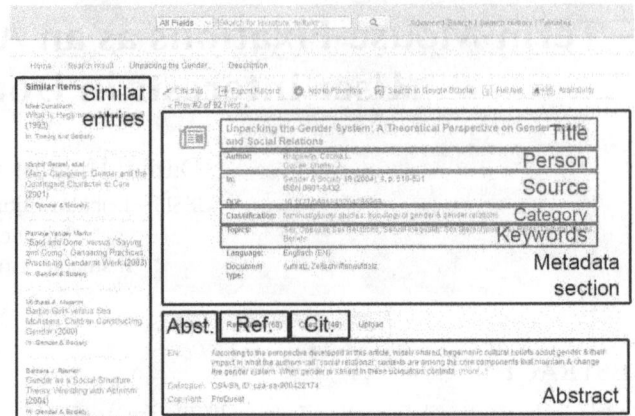

Figure 2: AOIs on the detailed view page with metadata fields.

author and source, it usually provides keywords and sometimes even categories. These keywords and categories are manually assigned from information professionals using the thesaurus for the social sciences[2] (TheSoz), the classification for the social sciences[3] and similar classification systems.

2.2 Mouse Tracker

We have implemented our own JavaScript mouse tracker and integrated it in Sowiport to capture aggregated mouse fixations over terms. The framework can be customized to capture only mouse fixations in certain areas of interest (AOI). In our case, we limited the recording of the search result page to the term recommender section, the result list entries (with the metadata fields: title, person, journal/proceedings source, and snippet), and the facet section. The recording of the detailed view page is limited to the metadata section (with the metadata fields: title, person, journal/proceedings source, category, and keywords), abstract, references, citations and similar entries section. Figure 1 gives an overview of different AOIs and metadata fields on the search result page and Figure 2 on the detailed view page.

When the user hovers with the mouse over a word in these areas the algorithm creates a new entry for this term in the term-mouse-fixation data file[4]. To achieve a good aggregation level already in this stage words are cleaned from English and German stop words and stemmed with a Porter stemmer. Fixation times for each stemmed term are summed up for every time the user hovers over an instance on the whole website. This means, the fixation time describes how long a user has fixated a unique term with the mouse over the whole session. For each term, the aggregated fixation time, the first-time-fixation, last-time-fixation, the AOI and metadata field are recorded. Each time the user submits a search query with the search form the term-mouse-fixation data is stored in the logging database together with the session-id, timestamp and user search terms.

2.3 Methodology for User Queries

In a first step, we check for the correspondence of term-mouse-fixations to *user search terms*. The overall goal is to check whether user search term(s) from user queries have been fixated with the mouse in the search session at all. For each user session and its user queries a list of distinct user search terms is built. User search terms with more than two characters are cleaned from English/German stop words and stemmed by a Porter stemmer. The list of term-mouse-fixations is additionally cleaned with a blacklist of terms which are part of the user interface and have no substantive topical meaning (e.g. "Authors:"). Then, the algorithm compares each user search term to the list of term-mouse-fixations. The comparison checks for in-word-inclusion, this means user search terms in the middle of term-mouse-fixations are also recognized. This is especially important for the German language where a lot of compounds are used. Found user search terms in term-mouse-fixations are collected throughout the user session. Based on this we compute the average fixation time of all found user search terms and compare it to the average fixation time of terms in term-mouse-fixations which are no user search terms. Additionally, we analyze the source AOIs and metadata fields for found search terms in term-mouse-fixations.

2.4 Methodology for Document Clicks

Similarly, we check for the correspondence of term-mouse-fixations to topics from *documents clicks*. We define a *document click* as a click in a result list entry that leads to further information about the document or to the document itself. These are mainly clicks on the title to see the detailed view (Figure 2) of a document within Sowiport and clicks on elements in the sidebar of a result item which lead to the full text outside Sowiport. We assume that these clicks indicate a certain user interest in this document. For each *document click* we collect the metadata of the corresponding document. As documents in our collection are well described by title and keywords we focus in the following on these fields. Titles are tokenized, stop word cleaned and like the keywords stemmed. The algorithm then compares if either document keywords or title terms can be found within the term-mouse-fixations. Found title terms and

---

[2] http://www.gesis.org/en/services/research/tools/social-science-thesaurus/

[3] http://www.gesis.org/angebot/recherchieren/tools-zur-recherche/klassifikation-sozialwissenschaften/

[4] The term-mouse fixation data file is stored on the client-side and is deleted after 12 hours of inactivity.

keywords are collected for the whole user session. Again, for each session, we compute the average fixation times for found title terms and keywords and compare them to the average fixation time of those mouse-term-fixations which are no title terms or keywords.

3 RESULTS

3.1 Evaluation Data Set

The final data set has been recorded from 18th October 2016 to 13th February 2017. User sessions are limit to those with at least one submitted search query which results in 22,259 sessions with 80,796 searches and 105,286 document clicks. On average a session lasts 64 minutes, and about 57 distinct terms have been fixated within the session with the mouse. Figure 3 shows the distribution of first-time mouse-fixation by AOIs and metadata fields. More than half of the fixated terms are first hovered in the result list entries (58.46%), followed by the metadata section in the detailed view (21.11%), the facets (9.21%) and by other AOIs. The metadata fields title (25.79%), person (24.19%) and snippet (21.99%) are relatively evenly distributed.

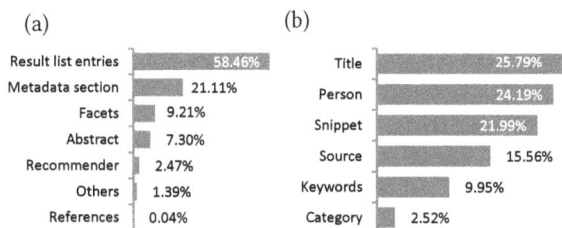

Figure 3: Proportion of first-time mouse-fixation in (a) AOI and (b) metadata field.

3.2 User search terms in term-mouse-fixations

Now we can check how many of the search terms the user has explicitly entered into the search bar can be found in term-mouse-fixations.

About half of the user search terms (47.41%) have been fixated with the mouse within the session. We call this proportion "*found terms*" in term-mouse-fixations. Inversely, "*other terms*" are the proportion in term-mouse-fixations which have no correspondence to user search terms. *Found terms* have been fixated significantly longer with the mouse (9.11 seconds) than *other terms* (4.41 seconds). These are statistically significant different groups found with a single factor ANOVA test with $\alpha=0.01$ and $F=1,736.13$.

Figure (4a) shows the AOI where the *found search terms* come from based on first fixation. Most terms have been fixated in the result list entries (49.45%), followed by the metadata section (23.68%), the term recommender section (15.46%), the facets (4.85%), and in the abstract (4.63%). Figure (4b) shows the distribution of metadata fields in which terms have been fixated. 26.93% came from the title, 8.84% from the snippet, 8.84% from the keywords, 6.16% from the persons, 5.20% from the source and 1.81% from the category. The rest to 100% has no metadata field information.

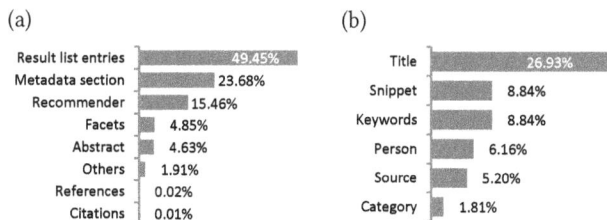

Figure 4: Source of found search terms in term-mouse-fixations: (a) AOI and (b) metadata field.

3.3 Document topics in term-mouse-fixations

Next, we check for correspondence of term-mouse-fixations with topics from *document clicks* in the result list.

First, we compare term-mouse-fixations with title terms from clicked documents and found that for 72.13% of the clicked documents at least one title term is found in the term-mouse-fixation of the appropriate session. Regarding the number of found title terms on average 2.48 of 4.05 terms (61.23%) of a single document are found. Fixation times are significantly longer with 8.79 seconds for *found title terms* vs. 4.32 seconds for the rest of term-mouse-fixations (significantly different with ANOVA, $\alpha=0.01$ and $F=1786.68$).

For the *keywords* of the clicked documents, we found a similar result. For 75.06% of all document clicks at least one keyword can be found in the term-mouse-fixations of the appropriate session. Regarding the number of found keywords on average 3.51 of 11.4 keywords (30.79%) of a single document can be found in term-mouse-fixations of the appropriate session. Found keywords have been fixated significantly longer with 6.42 seconds than other term-mouse-fixations with 4.33 seconds (significantly different with ANOVA, $\alpha=0.01$ and $F=563.84$).

3.4 Combined results

Finally, we can combine the check for inclusion of user search terms, title terms and keywords from document clicks in term-mouse-fixations within the same user session. We then find on average 11.45 terms in 87.12% of the sessions. Found terms have an average fixation time of 7.06 seconds, other terms 4.43 seconds (significantly different with ANOVA, $\alpha=0.01$ and $F=1,296.30$).

4 DISCUSSION

So far, mouse movements, clicks, and scrolling data have been used as an articulation of user behavior to understand the user's interest for e.g. certain areas or documents. In this paper, we go one step deeper and consider the term under the mouse cursor as a point of interest. In a prior eye tracking study, we found that for a specific exploratory task users are scanning the user interface with their eyes for new search terms and later use them in their search queries [5]. These terms have been fixated several times before they were used as search terms. As eye tracking is still not available in real world settings, we want to know if users' mouse pointer behavior can provide enough information to assume topical user interest. Therefore, we formulated the following research question: *(R1) Can we find indicators of topical user interests such as user search terms and topics from document clicks in mouse-fixated terms?*

User search terms are a very concrete and condensed articulation of user interests, and we found that in almost half of the user sessions (47.41%) the user search terms can be found in the term-mouse-fixations. If we compare Figure 3 and Figure 4 we can see that the metadata fields person, snippet, and source are often first-time hovered with the mouse, but the most user search terms originated from title and keywords. This is analog to our results in the eye tracking experiment [5] where user search terms have been most times fixated in these fields. Document clicks are a second indicator for analyzing user interest. Here, we focus on the two most preferred sources for user search terms – title and keywords. We found that for 72.13% of the documents, the user showed an interest in, at least one title term and in 75.06% of all clicked documents at least one keyword is found in term-mouse-fixations. On average 2.48 title terms and 3.51 keywords per single document are represented. We assume this as a reasonable representation of the document's topic itself and therefore for the user's topical interest. If we combine these findings, we can find in 87.12% of the sessions 11.45 terms from user queries and topics of clicked documents.

For a practical use of our previous findings, it is essential that we can determine mouse-fixated terms the user shows an interest in. On average 57 terms have been fixated in a search session, but only a share of them can be used to represent topical user interests. We address this issue in our second research question: *(R2) Is it possible to distinguish between terms in a list of mouse-fixated terms the user showed an interest in and terms the user had fixated more or less unconsciously?* We found a strong proof that accumulated fixation times can be used to extract these terms. Fixation times are significantly longer for found search terms (9.11s), keywords (6.42s) and title terms (8.79) from document clicks. The fixation times for the rest of term-mouse-fixations are very stable at around 4.4s. With this knowledge, we have one indicator to distinguish between important and unimportant terms in the sense of user interests. To make the prediction for user topical interest more precise, we consider using term overlaps between documents. The general assumption here is that keywords which occur simultaneously in several clicked document of a user's search session express even more strongly her interest. Based on the evaluation data set we computed the fixation times of keywords which occur in two to five different clicked documents of a search session. For keywords in x documents of a session, we found fixation times from 6-10s for keywords (2 docs: 6.69s, 3 docs: 7.79s, 4 docs: 8.84s, 5 docs: 9.74s). Again, the fixation times for other terms in term-mouse fixation remain stable at around 4.4 to 4.8 seconds. This means, even terms representing indicators of stronger user interest (contained in several different documents of a session) show linear higher fixation times. This is a further indication that term-mouse-fixation times can be used for the extraction of interesting terms.

Nevertheless, the approach of term-mouse-fixations also has some limitations. Mouse moving behavior can be very individual for a single user. For example, while one user extensively moves the mouse for reading assistance, the other user does not. This can result, e.g., in large deviations of fixation times and may influence the quality of extracted topical user interest on single session level.

5 CONCLUSION & FUTURE WORK

In this work we analyzed logfiles of a domain-specific digital library and we found that in 87% of the sessions we can find 11.45 terms per session from user queries, title, and keywords from clicked documents in term-mouse-fixations. These terms have significantly longer term-mouse-fixation times (7.06s) than the rest of the term-mouse fixations (around 4.43s). With the difference in fixation time, we can extract these terms from the whole list of term-mouse-fixations. These terms are indicators for user interests articulated through search queries and document clicks. One current line of research in IIR is to find the user's task(s) within a search session. The type of the task and the topic can help to better support the user in different search situations and for different search topics. Different sources of background knowledge can be used to understand these topics such as user queries, actions, the context or history. In our research, we found with term-mouse-fixations an additional source of information to understand the user's topics. Combining different sources may lead to a better estimation of topical user interests. In the end, we could rank search results according to the extracted user interest or more personalized recommendations could be given. In future work, we want to determine the quality of the assumed user interest based on keywords and title terms by performing a long-term field study with Sowiport in which we offer the extracted topics from term-mouse-fixations as suggested search terms.

ACKNOWLEDGMENTS This work was partly funded by the DFG, grant no. MA 3964/5-1; the AMUR project at GESIS.

REFERENCES

[1] Ageev, M. et al. 2013. Improving Search Result Summaries by Using Searcher Behavior Data. *Proceedings of the 36th International ACM SIGIR Conference on Research and Development in Information Retrieval* (New York, NY, USA, 2013), 13–22.

[2] Guo, Q. and Agichtein, E. 2012. Beyond Dwell Time: Estimating Document Relevance from Cursor Movements and Other Post-click Searcher Behavior. *Proceedings of the 21st International Conference on World Wide Web* (New York, NY, USA, 2012), 569–578.

[3] Guo, Q. and Agichtein, E. 2008. Exploring Mouse Movements for Inferring Query Intent. *Proceedings of the 31st Annual International ACM SIGIR Conference on Research and Development in Information Retrieval* (New York, NY, USA, 2008), 707–708.

[4] Hienert, D. et al. 2015. Digital Library Research in Action - Supporting Information Retrieval in Sowiport. *D-Lib Magazine*. 21, 3/4 (2015).

[5] Hienert, D. and Lusky, M. 2017. Where Do All These Search Terms Come From? – Two Experiments in Domain-Specific Search. *Advances in Information Retrieval: 39th European Conference on IR Research, ECIR 2017, Aberdeen, UK, April 8-13, 2017, Proceedings*. J.M. Jose et al., eds. Springer International Publishing. 15–26.

[6] Huang, J. et al. 2012. Improving Searcher Models Using Mouse Cursor Activity. *Proceedings of the 35th International ACM SIGIR Conference on Research and Development in Information Retrieval* (New York, NY, USA, 2012), 195–204.

[7] Liu, F. et al. 2002. Personalized Web Search by Mapping User Queries to Categories. *Proceedings of the Eleventh International Conference on Information and Knowledge Management* (New York, NY, USA, 2002), 558–565.

[8] Liu, Z. et al. 2017. Enhancing Click Models with Mouse Movement Information. *Inf. Retr.* 20, 1 (Feb. 2017), 53–80.

[9] Qiu, F. and Cho, J. 2006. Automatic Identification of User Interest for Personalized Search. *Proceedings of the 15th International Conference on World Wide Web* (New York, NY, USA, 2006), 727–736.

[10] White, R.W. et al. 2013. Enhancing Personalized Search by Mining and Modeling Task Behavior. *Proceedings of the 22Nd International Conference on World Wide Web* (New York, NY, USA, 2013), 1411–1420.

[11] White, R.W. et al. 2009. Predicting User Interests from Contextual Information. *Proceedings of the 32Nd International ACM SIGIR Conference on Research and Development in Information Retrieval* (New York, NY, USA, 2009), 363–370.

The Pareto Frontier of Utility Models as a Framework for Evaluating Push Notification Systems

Gaurav Baruah and Jimmy Lin

David R. Cheriton School of Computer Science
University of Waterloo, Ontario, Canada
{gbaruah,jimmylin}@uwaterloo.ca

ABSTRACT

We propose a utility-based framework for the evaluation of push notification systems that monitor document streams for users' topics of interest. Our starting point is that users derive either positive utility (i.e., "gain") or negative utility (i.e., "pain") from consuming system updates. By separately keeping track of these quantities, we can measure system effectiveness in a gain vs. pain tradeoff space. The Pareto Frontier of evaluated systems represents the state of the art: for each system on the frontier, no other system can offer more gain without more pain. Our framework has several advantages: it unifies three previous TREC evaluations, subsumes existing metrics, and provides more insightful analyses. Furthermore, our approach can easily accommodate more refined user models and is extensible to different information-seeking modalities.

1 INTRODUCTION

There is growing interest in push notification systems that prospectively monitor continuous document streams to identify relevant, novel, and timely content, delivered to users as push notifications. The Temporal Summarization [2, 8], Microblog [11], and Real-Time Summarization [12] Tracks at recent Text Retrieval Conferences (TRECs) all explore this basic idea.

We propose a novel framework for evaluating push notification systems that focuses on the Pareto Frontier of a utility model in which users derive positive utility (i.e., gain) from consuming relevant content and negative utility (which we refer to as "pain") from consuming non-relevant content. A system occupies a point in this pain vs. gain tradeoff space, and instead of trying to collapse both quantities into a single-point metric (as previous evaluations attempt to do), we examine the Pareto Frontier of systems in this utility space. Systems that lie on the frontier are all "optimal" in the sense that for a particular level of gain, no other system offers a user experience with less pain.

Our framework makes the following contributions to the evaluation of push notification systems:

- It provides a unified evaluation methodology that encompasses multiple recent TREC evaluations.

- It subsumes previous metrics used in those evaluations.
- It provides more insightful comparisons of system effectiveness that capture different operating points.
- It is extensible to different information-seeking modalities and more refined user models.

This paper details our evaluation framework, applies it to previous TREC evaluations, and elaborates on each of the points above.

2 BACKGROUND AND RELATED WORK

Work on prospective information needs against document streams dates back at least a few decades. Early examples include the TREC Filtering Tracks from 1995 [10] to 2002 [15] and research under the umbrella of topic detection and tracking (TDT) [1]. Over the past few years, we have seen renewed interest in this area, due to the growing popularity of social media and the tighter response cycles demanded by various end users (e.g., journalists, politicians, traders, etc.) to act on high-velocity information.

The TREC Temporal Summarization (TS) Tracks [3, 8], which took place from 2013 to 2015, imagined a stream of newswire articles that a system processed in real time to incrementally select relevant non-redundant sentences pertinent to events of interest such as the 2012 Pakistan garment factory fires or the 2012 Buenos Aires train crash. The putative user of such a system might be a disaster relief coordinator or a journalist, and although somewhat under-specified in the evaluation itself, system output (i.e., "updates") might be proactively delivered to the user via push notifications. Alternatively, based on the model of Baruah et al. [6], users may periodically poll the system for updates.

The Temporal Summarization Tracks evaluated system output in terms of two metrics, expected gain, $(1/|S|) \sum_{s \in S} G(s)$, and comprehensiveness, $(1/|Z|) \sum_{s \in S} G(s)$, where S is the set of updates returned by the system, Z is the number of relevant updates, and G computes the gain for an update. Typically, G factors in redundancy (i.e., systems are not rewarded for returning two updates that "say the same thing"), verbosity (i.e., shorter updates are preferred over longer updates), and also timeliness (i.e., incorporating some type of latency penalty). The exact details varied across track iterations, but the overall form remained constant. Expected gain is analogous to precision and comprehensiveness is analogous to recall, so these two metrics are quite familiar to any IR researcher.

At around the same time as the TS evaluations, the TREC Microblog (MB) Tracks were exploring information needs against social media streams (specifically Twitter). For the evaluation in 2015, systems were given "interest profiles" and the task was to monitor the live Twitter stream to identify relevant and novel tweets in a timely fashion, which were putatively delivered to users as push notifications. For example, a user might be interested in anecdotes of people injured while playing Pokémon Go and wished to be notified whenever there are such reports. The convergence of the TS and MB Tracks led to their merger in TREC 2016 to form the Real-Time Summarization (RTS) Track, following the basic setup of content filtering on tweets. The novel aspect of the evaluation in 2016 was live user participation, in which system updates were actually delivered as push notifications to users' mobile devices, who provided judgments *in situ* [12, 16].

The MB and RTS evaluations used metrics that were heavily borrowed from the TS evaluations, although the exact formulation differed. Nevertheless, both evaluations measured expected gain as well as cumulative gain (what TS called comprehensiveness). Once again, these are basically variants of precision and recall. The MB and RTS evaluations additionally re-introduced a linear utility metric that dates back to the TREC Filtering Track in 1990s [10, 15]: gain minus pain (GMP), which is a linear interpolation between positive and negative utility based on an arbitrary weight. Our utility-based framework is derived from this formulation, but with a critical difference: instead of interpolating gain and pain to produce a single-point metric, we separately present the two quantities in an effectiveness tradeoff space.

3 EVALUATION MODEL

We assume a task model in which users specify prospective information needs against a stream of discrete text units (sentences, tweets, etc.). The system monitors this stream, and whenever it identifies a relevant piece of text, the user is proactively notified—in operational terms, this might be a push notification to the user's mobile device, a notification pop-up on the user's desktop, or some other mechanism of grabbing the user's attention. Generically, we call these updates. This task setup broadly encompasses the TREC evaluations described in Section 2.

To evaluate such systems, we assume a simple user model: that the user will read each update with some probability p, which we call the persistence parameter. A high persistence value models an "eager" user, and a low persistence value models a user who is likely to ignore the updates. In addition, we assume that unread updates are accumulated in a "holding area" somewhere on the user's device, e.g., a mobile app, a desktop notification tray, etc. Whenever the user examines an update, we assume that the user will also read each subsequent item in the holding area with probability p. The decision is made independently with respect to each item and does not take into account the item's relevance (similar to RBP [14]).

Given this user model, we can construct a utility model for evaluating systems. Whenever the user reads an update, she derives some utility: we refer to positive utility as "gain" and negative utility as "pain". For a particular topic, over a specified evaluation period, a particular system or algorithm delivers to the user a certain amount of pain and gain. We average across multiple topics to arrive at a system's overall effectiveness. To enable meaningful averaging, gain is normalized to the maximum gain based on the evaluation ground truth (e.g., all nuggets in the evaluation pools).[1] Thus,

each system can be represented as a point in the gain vs. pain tradeoff space. Below, we explain precisely how gain and pain are operationalized in the three evaluations we examined.

Temporal Summarization. We applied our evaluation framework to data from the TS Track at TREC 2014 (TS14). All the TS evaluations employed a nugget-based evaluation methodology [3], and thus expected gain (i.e., the precision-like metric) and comprehensiveness (i.e., the recall-like metric) were both measured in terms of nuggets. For a given run, TS14 evaluated updates using normalized Expected Gain (nEG) and Comprehensiveness (C).

In our analysis, positive utility (i.e., gain) is accumulated when the user encounters a nugget in an update and negative utility (i.e., pain) is accumulated when the user encounters a non-relevant update. Reading behavior is dictated by the user persistence model described above. We do not penalize gain for latency or verbosity [3, 6] in order to keep our implementation straightforward and intuitive, and pain in this case is simply the number of non-relevant updates consumed. As will be described later, our basic framework can be enriched with more refined user models.

There is one additional detail to note: A few systems in TS14 returned an enormous number of updates (on the order of 10^4 updates per topic). It is inconceivable that so many updates would actually be delivered to a user, and therefore we preprocessed these runs prior to analysis. Fortunately, systems returned a confidence score with each update, and therefore in our experiments only updates above a normalized confidence score of 0.7 are pushed to the simulated user. We set this threshold to balance the volume of system output with the number of unjudged updates; because of the pooled evaluation procedure, most of the updates from the high volume systems were unjudged. This preprocessing was necessary to bring the TS14 runs closer in line to a "reasonable" push notification scenario, although changing the threshold does not impact our findings (since it has the effect of throwing away mostly unjudged updates and affects only the high-volume runs). Updates with a normalized score below 0.7 are assumed to still be available in the "holding area", but in practice since the user consumes these updates in score order, they are rarely read based on our user model.

Microblog and Real-Time Summarization. We analyzed data from the TREC 2015 Microblog Track (MB15) and the TREC 2016 Real-Time Summarization Track (RTS16). For both, positive utility accumulates when the user reads a relevant tweet (defined in the same way as in the official evaluation), and negative utility accumulates when the user reads a non-relevant tweet (as in the official evaluation, just the count of non-relevant tweets).

Since in both MB15 and RTS16, each system was limited to pushing ten tweets per topic per day, we assumed that all system updates were delivered to users. Unread notifications are assumed to be stored in a time-ordered queue on the user's mobile app, to be consumed or ignored based on our persistence model.

4 RESULTS AND ANALYSIS

Evaluation results for TS14, MB15, and RTS16 are shown in Figure 1 based on the pain and gain definitions described in the previous section, modeled with a persistence of $p = 0.5$, i.e., half the push notifications are ignored. Each point represents an individual system in the evaluation.

---

[1]Note that this maximum gain may or may not be achievable based on a particular user model. For example, a low persistence user may never have the opportunity to accumulate much gain, even if every update contains relevant information. This design represents one of many possible choices, each with advantages and disadvantages.

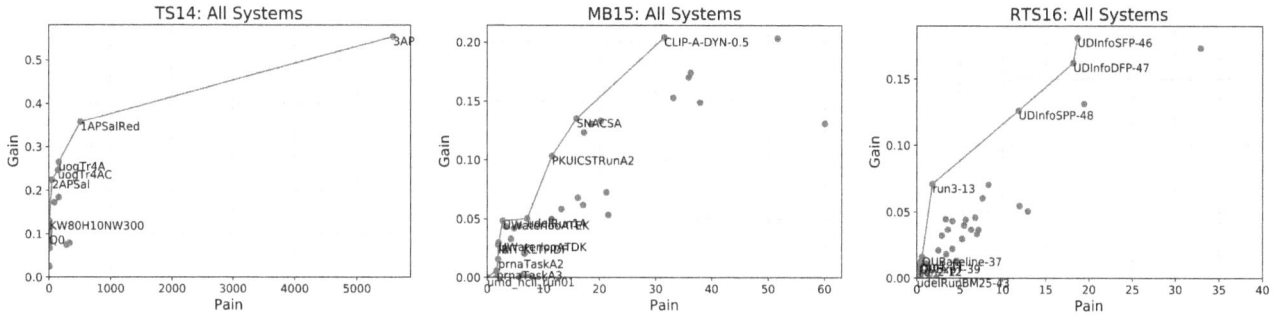

Figure 1: Application of our evaluation framework to the TS14, MB15, and RTS16 evaluations, with persistence $p = 0.5$. The Pareto Frontier represents the best achievable gain for a given level of pain.

The Pareto Frontier (outlined in each figure) contains the set of systems such that, for each system, it is not possible to achieve greater gain without incurring greater pain. Each system along the frontier can claim to be "optimal", in the sense that for the particular level of gain achieved, the system has the minimum pain. Put differently, all systems in the interior are dominated by systems along the frontier, in that for a particular level of gain, there is an alternate system (on the frontier) which provides at least that level of gain with smaller pain—and therefore a rational user would always prefer the system on the frontier. Systems on the frontier, however, are not comparable since they represent different gain vs. pain tradeoffs—deciding between them would require knowing actual user preferences (more below). Naturally, the frontier is not continuous, and hence we interpolate between systems.

In what follows, we elaborate on the four key advantages of our evaluation framework that were outlined in the introduction:

Unified evaluation framework. We provide a unified view across three different TREC evaluations that share underlying similarities, but which up until now have employed different evaluation methodologies. Across these evaluations, we see the broad contours of system design and the tradeoffs in building push notifications: in all cases, the Pareto Frontier rises steeply in the beginning and then falls off. This suggests that there are a number of "obviously good" updates that are fairly easy to identify, but the marginal cost of discovering additional useful updates increases, such that the highest levels of recall can't be achieved (with present systems) without an inordinate amount of pain. This is most apparent in the TS14 evaluation, where the frontier really levels off at higher gain.

Subsumption of previous metrics. In our framework, each system is represented by a point in the gain vs. pain tradeoff space. This position encodes representations that are comparable to all existing metrics for TS, MB, and RTS. Expected gain relates to the slope of the line connecting each point to the origin. Recall metrics (e.g., comprehensiveness) can be visualized as the position on the y axis of each system. Linear utility corresponds to a weighted linear combination of the x and y positions. Furthermore, it is easy to construct iso-metric lines (i.e., lines along which systems have the same metric value): radial lines of different slopes emanating from the origin, parallel horizontal lines, and parallel diagonal lines for the three metrics above, respectively. Thus, our evaluation framework not only unifies but also subsumes previous evaluations—no information about previous metrics is lost.

More insightful analyses. Beyond unifying previous evaluations and subsuming existing metrics, our framework addresses specific issues with previous metrics and supports more insightful analyses. In previous evaluations, precision and linear utility are hard to interpret because they don't factor in update volume: for example, a system that returns 100 "good" and 100 "bad" updates receives the same score as a system that returns 1000 "good" and 1000 "bad" updates. In both cases, the precision is 0.5 and the linear utility is zero (assume equal weight on gain and pain). However, it is obvious that these two systems provide a completely different user experience. If we sort systems in terms of effectiveness by either metric, we are hiding important differences in how systems actually appear to real users.

In fact, any single-point metric necessarily encodes a particular user model representing a specific operating point, which is not ideal because we currently have little evidence of what users actually want in a push notification system (e.g., guidance from user studies). Specifically, the Pareto Frontier recognizes that there are different operating points for push notification systems in the space of pain vs. gain. Some operating points are more plausible than others (for example, in TS14 it is unlikely that users would be willing to endure over 5000 units of pain), but ultimately we need guidance from real-world users. Until then, we argue that it is dangerous to optimize on any single-point metric.

With guidance from our user model, we can explore different usage scenarios in our evaluation framework to conduct more insightful analyses. For example, the current user model contains a persistence parameter, which characterizes the extent to which a user will pay attention to or ignore a notification: we can vary the persistence parameter to model different types of users and note how the Pareto Frontier changes in each case. Figure 2 shows some of these results: we plot the Pareto Frontiers for three different values of persistence $p = \{0.1, 0.5, 0.9\}$. In all three evaluations, we only focus on low-pain systems (note the range of the x axis compared to Figure 1). From the plots, we see that although the Pareto Frontier changes, its overall shape and the systems that lie on the frontier remain similar. Put differently, "good" systems seem to be invariant with respect to different user models, which suggests that our evaluation framework is robust with respect to different parameter settings.

Extensibility. Beyond merely exploring parameters in the existing model, our framework can be extended with richer user and utility

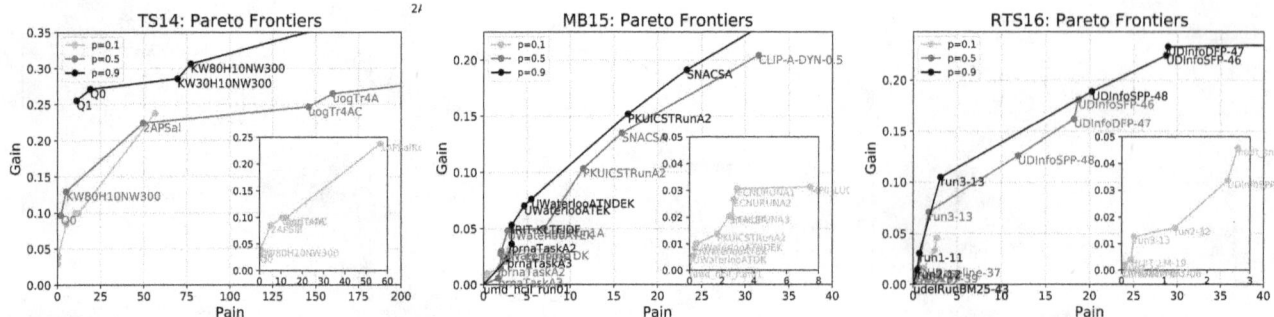

Figure 2: Pareto frontiers for the TS14, MB15, and RTS16 evaluations, modeling users with different persistence, $p = 0.1, 0.5, 0.9$

models based on advances in our understanding of user behavior, operationalized in user simulations [4, 5]. Concrete examples include accurate models of user reading speed [7] in the calculation of pain and gain, time-based calibration of effectiveness measures for more accurately capturing utility [17], incorporating negative higher-order relevance [9], and modeling users' propensity to browse deep down a ranked list of items [13]. These improvements could all be applied to replace our simple persistence model.

In fact, our framework can even accommodate completely different modalities of information seeking with respect to prospective information needs. In this work we assume that system updates are delivered as push notifications, potentially interrupting the user. Alternatively, Baruah et al. [6] considered the scenario where updates accumulate without explicit notification, and a simulated user periodically returns to examine system output (unprompted by the system itself). Pull-based and push-based consumption of updates are merely the ends of a spectrum, and real-world users are likely to employ a combination of both strategies. It is certainly possible to capture these different modalities in our framework using a more refined user model, which would translate into different gain and pain measurements. However, our notion of a gain vs. pain tradeoff space remains relevant, and the Pareto Frontier can still serve as an important construct for understanding the state of the art.

5 FUTURE WORK AND CONCLUSION

Our evaluation framework immediately suggests a gap in our understanding of push notifications systems: What is the pain tolerance of users in operational systems, and how does that tolerance vary with the volume of updates? Based on the latest evaluation results from the TREC 2016 Real-Time Summarization Track, the best systems can achieve a gain vs. pain ratio of roughly one for low volume pushes [12], which corresponds to a precision of 0.5. In other words, roughly half of the content pushed is not relevant. Furthermore, beyond a certain volume, current systems are not able to maintain even a one-to-one gain vs. pain ratio. Is this "good enough"? It seems unlikely to us, but empirically, what is the threshold for a system to be usable in practice?

An important related question concerns update volume [16]: What is the right number of notifications to push within some time interval? One imagines that even for a fast moving topic, users will get annoyed if they are constantly bombarded by notifications, even if all the updates are relevant. On the other hand, a user might also express annoyance at a system for failing to deliver an important

update. All of the questions above point to the need for user studies to enrich our understanding of the push notification problem. Our framework can help to contextualize these studies.

Extensions to the user and utility models mentioned in the previous section represent another promising area of future work, as well as modeling hybrid push/pull interactions. We believe that our framework can provide a unified view to evaluate systems that address prospective information needs. Specifically, there is great potential in mixed-initiative interfaces that are both reactive and proactive as appropriate.

REFERENCES
[1] James Allan. 2002. *Topic Detection and Tracking: Event-Based Information Organization*. Kluwer Academic Publishers, Dordrecht, The Netherlands.
[2] Javed Aslam, Matthew Ekstrand-Abueg, Virgil Pavlu, Richard McCreadie, Fernando Diaz, and Tetsuya Sakai. 2014. TREC 2014 Temporal Summarization Track Overview. In *TREC*.
[3] Javed Aslam, Matthew Ekstrand-Abueg, Virgil Pavlu, Fernando Diaz, and Tetsuya Sakai. 2013. TREC 2013 Temporal Summarization. In *TREC*.
[4] Leif Azzopardi. 2016. Simulation of Interaction: A Tutorial on Modelling and Simulating User Interaction and Search Behaviour. In *SIGIR*. 1227–1230.
[5] Leif Azzopardi, Kalervo Järvelin, Jaap Kamps, and Mark D. Smucker. 2011. Report on the SIGIR 2010 Workshop on the Simulation of Interaction. *SIGIR Forum* 44, 2 (2011), 35–47.
[6] Gaurav Baruah, Mark D. Smucker, and Charles L. A. Clarke. 2015. Evaluating Streams of Evolving News Events. In *SIGIR*. 675–684.
[7] Charles L. A. Clarke and Mark D. Smucker. 2014. Time Well Spent. In *IIiX '14*. 205–214.
[8] Qi Guo, Fernando Diaz, and Elad Yom-Tov. 2013. Updating Users about Time Critical Events. In *ECIR*. 483–494.
[9] Heikki Keskustalo, Kalervo Järvelin, Ari Pirkola, and Jaana Kekäläinen. 2008. Intuition-Supporting Visualization of Userfs Performance Based on Explicit Negative Higher-Order Relevance. In *SIGIR*. 675–682.
[10] David D. Lewis. 1995. The TREC-4 Filtering Track. In *TREC*. 165–180.
[11] Jimmy Lin, Miles Efron, Yulu Wang, and Garrick Sherman. 2015. Overview of the TREC-2015 Microblog Track. In *TREC*.
[12] Jimmy Lin, Adam Roegiest, Luchen Tan, Richard McCreadie, Ellen Voorhees, and Fernando Diaz. 2016. Overview of the TREC 2016 Real-Time Summarization Track. In *TREC*.
[13] David Maxwell, Leif Azzopardi, Kalervo Järvelin, and Heikki Keskustalo. 2015. Searching and Stopping: An Analysis of Stopping Rules and Strategies. In *CIKM*. 313–322.
[14] Alistair Moffat and Justin Zobel. 2008. Rank-Biased Precision for Measurement of Retrieval Effectiveness. *ACM TOIS* 27, 1, Article 2 (Dec. 2008), 27 pages.
[15] Stephen Robertson and Ian Soboroff. 2002. The TREC 2002 Filtering Track Report. In *TREC*.
[16] Adam Roegiest, Luchen Tan, and Jimmy Lin. 2017. Online In-Situ Interleaved Evaluation of Real-Time Push Notification Systems. In *SIGIR*.
[17] Mark D. Smucker and Charles L. A. Clarke. 2012. Time-based Calibration of Effectiveness Measures. In *SIGIR*. 95–104.

Acknowledgments. This work was supported by the Natural Sciences and Engineering Research Council (NSERC) of Canada, with additional contributions from the U.S. National Science Foundation under CNS-1405688.

Advanced Hidden Markov Models for Recognizing Search Phases

Sebastian Dungs
University of Duisburg-Essen
Duisburg, Germany
sebastian.dungs@uni-due.de

Norbert Fuhr
University of Duisburg-Essen
Duisburg, Germany
norbert.fuhr@uni-due.de

ABSTRACT

Although cognitive IR approaches usually distinguish between different search phases, there are no automatic methods for recognizing these phases. In this paper, we use constrained Hidden Markov Models (HMM), for addressing this issue. Especially, we develop a hybrid form of HMM combining both discrete and continuous signal values, which improves the recognition process. Furthermore, we show how the new model can be used for predicting the time to the next relevant document, which is a prerequisite for the application of the interactive probability ranking principle.

CCS CONCEPTS

• **Information systems** → **Users and interactive retrieval**; *Personalization*; *Task models*;

KEYWORDS

Interactive Retrieval, User Modelling, Hidden Markov Model

1 INTRODUCTION

Users' behaviour in complex search tasks has been studied extensively, both in real world and in online scenarios. The degree of detail varies, starting from high level models like Wilson's information behaviour research[14] to more specific approaches like Kuhlthau's information search process model[5] or Ellis' behavioural model[1]. While these models all have a different focus, the claim of the existence of search *phases* is a recurring thought.

A search phase is a combination of users' mental state, current work task and search engine state, which is categorized into a set of prototypical states. In a typical complex search tasks users undergo an unknown number of phase changes which are stimulated by the search engine output or by users' reasoning efforts. Longitudinal empirical research has tried to shed light on qualitative aspects of these search phases[7, 12], while some researchers additionally imply a temporal order of phases[5].

In this work we follow the temporal ordered search phase approach and try a novel quantitative approach in detecting these phases by using Hidden Markov Models (HMM). Using HMM to learn search phase parameters allows for an automatic probabilistic categorization of observed user actions.

The realization of such automated search phase detection would be beneficial to the Interactive Information Retrieval (IIR) research community in at least two scenarios:

Developers of cognitive models have pointed out that different functions and types of system support are needed in the various phases, e. g., query suggestions or result ranking could be phase-dependent. Huurdeman & Kamps[4] propose an adaptive interface, which offers certain elements only when needed by the user.

As a theoretic framework, Fuhr[2] proposed the Probability Ranking Principle for interactive IR (iPRP), which allows for calculation of optimal ordering of a set of choices (e.g. a result list). The iPRP assumes a set of parameters that characterize the interaction between user and search engine. Following this idea Tran and Fuhr[10, 11] use Markov models for describing the search process, but do not consider search progress in terms of search phases. With the work presented in this paper we take a first step in this direction.

Since search phases are not directly observable, we have to use HMMs. However, the most common type of HMMs deal with discrete signals, in order to estimate transition probabilities. For the iPRP, we also need to consider times for the different user actions carried out during a search. For this purpose, we introduce a hybrid form of HMM, utilizing both discrete and continuous signal values in a single model. All categorical user actions are associated with a distribution function describing their expected durations. Based on search phases, different distribution functions are learnt for each type of user action. This way, we can derive both average times and transition probabilities from log data; then we can apply well-established methods like Viterbi-Algorithm as well as the new hybrid approach for calculating the expected time the user needs for finding the next relevant document. This parameter is crucial for the application of the iPRP, as the different possible actions in a situation are compared wrt. their potential benefit, which can be measured in the time to the next relevant document—which, in turn, forms the basis for time-based evaluation measures.

While the full implementation of the iPRP in a productive search engine is still a great challenge, we believe that search phase dependent system adaptation even of isolated features like ranking function or selection of search suggestions has a large potential for improving search efficiency and success. The presented work in this paper can be seen as a first step in this direction and an outline of its evident extension.

First, we take a look at existing literature on search phases and briefly examine how HMM and related techniques have been used in IIR research. In Section 3 we introduce our HMM framework and the data set used. Section 4 describes our two modelling approaches.

ICTIR '17, October 1–4, 2017, Amsterdam, Netherlands
© 2017 Copyright held by the owner/author(s). Publication rights licensed to ACM.
ACM ISBN 978-1-4503-4490-6/17/10…$15.00
https://doi.org/10.1145/3121050.3121090

2 RELATED WORK

Carol C. Kuhlthau's Information Search Process model[5] is a qualitative information seeking model that categorizes user behaviour in six phases. It gives a very broad view on the topic by also including users' feelings.

Vakkari[12] extended the work of Kuhlthau by studying the effects of task stages (phases) on users' interaction with information systems. He found that the information sought for, the relevance judgements and the search tactics are differing in dependence on the users' current search phase.

Huurdeman & Kamps[4] looked at search phase dependent interface component usage patterns. Although their initial results are promising, they still lack a method of phase detection. Instead the authors use a fixed time interval.

Hidden Markov Models and their related concepts have been used extensively in many domains, including bioinformatics and speech recognition. Yue et al.[15] applied HMM to model and analyse collaborative web search sessions. Based on a lab study they demonstrated that HMM can be used to identify interaction patterns.

He et al.[3] and Wang et al.[13] used Partially Observable Markov Models and click trough data to estimate searchers' viewing behaviour. Partially Observable Markov Decision Processes were proposed by Luo et al.[6] amongst others to model search sessions including a reward function. However, the derivation of such a reward function remains an open issue.

Tran and Fuhr[11] employed Markov Models for analysing users' performance in search tasks based on eye tracking data. They showed the appropriateness of their method, but did not try to make predictions based on their models.

3 METHOD

Now we introduce a simple definition of two search phases and give details on the modelling framework and the data set used.

The various cognitive IR models differ in the number of search phases they distinguish. As this paper is a first step towards automatic detection of these phases, we start with a simple approach of considering only two phases. We assume an explorative search task were users have to first familiarize themselves with a topic to later enter a phase of document 'inspection'. Consequently, the first search phase *Searching* is a rough adaptation of Kuhlthau's Exploration and Formulation stages, while the second search phase *Finding* maps to Kuhlthau's Collection stage.

While a two phase approach is most likely an oversimplification, all proposed methods can be easily extended to a higher number of phases, in order to mirror established longitudinal models. The addition of a single search phase would for instance allow for an implementation of Vakkari's[12] pre-focus, focus formulation, post-focus model.

3.1 Data Set

For our experiments, we received an anonymized log of the productive *Sowiport*[1] search engine developed at the *GESIS – Leibniz-Institute for the Social Sciences*. The data was gathered in an 18 month period and consists of more than 3 million log entries.

Based on anonymous user ID hashes and timestamps all log entries were grouped in a set of sequences S where each $\sigma_i \in S$ comprises all log entries of a single session in chronological order.

Short σ_i with less than 4 implicit relevance judgements as well as σ_i containing implausible log entries (i.e. negative times) were removed from the log. After cleaning S had a size of 1642 elements which were included in the analysis described below.

3.2 Modelling Framework

Implementation of the modelling framework is based on the publicly available library Jahmm[2] which was used with minor modifications. Given appropriate initial models and the set of sequences S the libraries' implementation of the Baum-Welch-Algorithm for HMM parameter optimization can be used. Two distinct modalities of operation were explored based on how the emission alphabet E is extracted from S:

3.2.1 Discrete Emission HMM. In this most straightforward version of HMM, E is generally considered to be a finite set of discrete nominal values. While in theory the size of E is not constraint, for reasons of easier comprehension and computation the alphabet is usually kept small. Here we use an alphabet of size four $E = \{$Query, Snippet, Abstract, Mark$\}$, were *Query* categorizes all search queries, *Snippet* and *Abstract* categorize all actions related to viewing a document's snippet and abstract respectively and *Mark* sums up all user actions that implicitly indicate a document's relevance.

Since the Sowiport search engine produced a total of 54 distinct types of log entries (E') a mapping had to be introduced. Each $\epsilon_i \in E$ is represented by various $\epsilon_i' \in E'$ whereas some ϵ_i' were not considered for further analysis (meta log entries, e.g. user login).

The discrete model was built by defining four hidden states in total, where one state is associated with the user actions Query, Snippet and Abstract and one with implicit relevance signals (Mark) for each search phase respectively. For convenience the former is referred to as $Work_S$ ($Work_F$) while the latter is called $Mark_S$ ($Mark_F$) in searching (finding) phase. Transition from phase *Searching* to *Finding* is set to occur only from $Mark_S$, while the *Finding* phase is not left for the remainder of a session once entered. All other transition as well as emission probabilities were learnt using Baum-Welch algorithm.

3.2.2 Hybrid HMM with mixed signal values. The major limitation of the model described above is the neglect of user action durations. As we will see later, the average times for certain action types differ substantially between the two search phases. Thus, for recognizing search phases, this information should also be considered.

Therefore, a hybrid hidden Markov user model was built where the definition of the emission alphabet E is extended. In this hybrid model each $\epsilon_i \in E$ is a tuple of nominal user action and its respective duration. The nominal user actions remain unchanged Query, Snippet, Abstract and Mark. Since there exists no straight forward way to instantiate a HMM with tuple emissions, hidden states were used to code nominal user actions. Given the four possible user actions multiplied by the two phases searching and finding the final model has 8 hidden states. Thus, nominal actions are mapped to

---

[1]http://sowiport.gesis.org/

[2]https://github.com/KommuSoft/jahmm

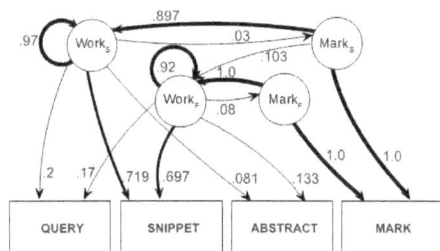

Figure 1: Discrete emission Hidden Markov Model

states as Q_S: Query action in phase *Searching*, Q_F: Query action in phase *Finding*, S_S: Snippet action in phase *Searching* and so on.

Additionally, probability distribution functions (PDF) of action duration were extracted from the log data for all four nominal user actions. The HMM was then initialized by assigning each user action's PDF to their respective hidden states for both phases. Using Baum-Welch parameter optimization, each PDF was tuned with respect to being either associated with phase *Searching* or *Finding*. Additionally, all hidden state transition probabilities were learnt with the exception, that a transition from phase *Searching* to phase *Finding* is only possible from state $Mark_S$. This constraint has been introduced to make the transition point more explicit. Once the *Finding* phase has been entered, the user stays in that phase for the remainder of that session.

The next section presents the results of both modelling approaches described above.

4 RESULTS

The discrete observation HMM categorizes users' actions in search phases, with each phase consisting of a work and a mark state. Figure 1 gives an overview of the model's state transition probabilities (circle to circle edge) and the states' emission probabilities (circle to rectangle edge). Here we only have two states in each phase: Work and Mark. The major difference in the two phases lies in the fact that the transition from Work to Mark has a probability of 3% in *Searching*, but 8% in the *Finding* phase. Thus, on average users need fewer actions for locating the next relevant document once they have reached the second phase. This observation is in line with related research findings[8, 9]. We see that already a very simple model is able to recognize the major difference between the two phases.

Now we turn to the hybrid HMM, which also considers action durations (Figure 2). Here each state corresponds to one specific discrete emission, so we have omitted these signals from the figure and encoded it in the state name[3]. Comparing the probabilities for the transitions to Q_S vs. Q_F, we see that users are more likely to reformulate their queries in the *Finding* phase, while they look at more snippets in the *Searching* phase (transition $S \rightarrow S$, 85.8% vs. 70.6%). In the *Finding* phase, they identify more snippets which are potentially relevant (transition $S \rightarrow A$, 7.8% vs. 3.8% in the Searching phase). The dominant user action after encountering a

---

[3]Please note that the hybrid model is not just a refinement of the discrete model. Due to the additional consideration of the times spent for the various actions, the transition probabilities in the hybrid model differ to a certain extent (e.g. the transition probabilities from Searching to Finding are 10.3% vs. 12.3%).

Table 1: Mean user action duration

	Query	Snippet	Abstract
Searching	7.5 sec.	2.5 sec.	36 sec.
Finding	2.2 sec.	1.6 sec.	23 sec.

relevant document is issuing a query (66.9%) in *Finding* as opposed to 41.3% in *Searching*. This behaviour could be an indication of what Vakkari calls a post-focus phase[12], where rechecking of information occurs. Overall, Figure 2 shows that users search more effectively in the *Finding* phase, by formulating better queries.

As the hybrid model also considers the duration of states, the average values can be extracted directly from the learnt HMM (Table 1). It can be seen that all average durations are lower in the *Finding* phase. While the comparison of the probabilities shows that users make better decisions in the *Finding* phase, the time values indicate that they also work more efficiently by needing less time for the different types of actions.

As mentioned already in the introduction, a potential applications of search phase detection (besides phase-dependent system behaviour) is the prediction of search times for the iPRP. Since we want to regard the time needed for each relevant document, it makes sense to consider the time from the first snippet after a query (or a mark!) until the next relevant document is identified (mark). For evaluating the quality of the model's predictions, we applied 10-fold cross validation. After having trained a HMM on the training folds, for each session in the test fold we compared actual times taken from the log to predicted times generated by using four different methods:

Baseline: We use the Viterbi algorithm to determine the most likely hidden state path given a sequence of observations. For each hidden state we generate an observation based on the states' probability distribution function. The expected time to next mark is calculated by summing up the generated emissions. This acts as our baseline.

Searching: For detecting potential bias in our model we also calculate expected times assuming that the user stays in the *Searching* phase, again using Viterbi algorithm. This method uses only the left side of the model shown in Figure 2—with a slight adjustment of M_S's transition probabilities.

Finding: As before, but now with phase *Finding* transition probabilities and times only. This is equivalent to using only the right side of the model depicted in Figure 2.

Hybrid: Here we use the full expressive power of the hybrid model. Instead of using Viterbi for a binary assumption on user's current search phase, a probabilistic phase assignment is achieved by comparing states' emission probability functions to emissions observed previously in the search session. Expected time to next mark is then calculated as a weighted mean of both conditions' predictions.

Figure 3 depicts a box plot of the distribution of the relative errors for all methods. The Viterbi and the Searching only methods show about the same performance, both having a positive bias (i.e., on average the estimates are too high), while the Finding only method shows negative bias. Solely the Hybrid method gives unbiased

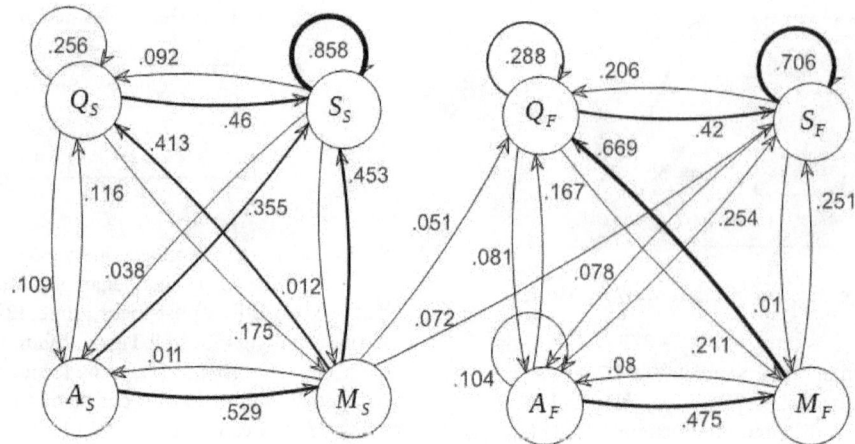

Figure 2: Hybrid model's state transition probabilities (emissions omitted)

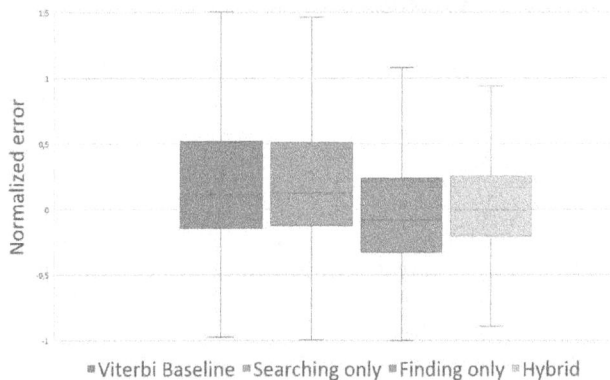

Figure 3: Quality of snippet to mark time prediction

estimates (compare solid line in bars), indicating its superiority over the simpler methods. Additionally, the Hybrid method significantly outperforms the baseline method given its mean absolute relative error in the test runs (385 vs. 561, t-test $p < 0.01$).

5 CONCLUSION AND OUTLOOK

Extensive research on user behaviour in complex search scenarios has shown that users' search sessions can be divided in different search phases. In this paper, we describe approaches for automatic detection of search phases. We use two variants of constrained hidden Markov models, besides one based on discrete signals only also a hybrid one combining both discrete and continuous signal values. The parameter of these models are in line with earlier research focusing on cognitive models.

Besides allowing a system to adapt its behaviour to the current search phase the user is in, our approach can also be used for predicting the search time, which is a prerequisite of the iPRP. The experimental results show that the full-fledged hybrid model is best suited for this task.

In future work, we will vary the number of search phases, and also investigate the effect of adaptive system behaviour.

ACKNOWLEDGMENTS

This work was supported by the Deutsche Forschungsgemeinschaft (DFG) under grant No. GRK 2167, Research Training Group "User-Centred Social Media".

REFERENCES

[1] D. Ellis. 1989. A Behavioral Approach to Information Retrieval System Design. *J. Doc.* 45, 3 (Oct. 1989), 171–212. https://doi.org/10.1108/eb026843
[2] Norbert Fuhr. 2008. A probability ranking principle for interactive information retrieval. *Information Retrieval* 11, 3 (2008), 251–265.
[3] Y. He and K. Wang. 2011. Inferring search behaviors using partially observable markov model with duration (pomd). In *Proc. 4th ACM WSDM*. 415–424.
[4] Hugo C. Huurdeman and Jaap Kamps. 2014. From Multistage Information-seeking Models to Multistage Search Systems. In *Proceedings of the 5th Information Interaction in Context Symposium (IIiX '14)*. ACM, New York, NY, USA, 145–154. https://doi.org/10.1145/2637002.2637020
[5] Carol C Kuhlthau. 1991. Inside the search process: Information seeking from the user's perspective. *JASIST* 42, 5 (1991), 361.
[6] Jiyun Luo, Sicong Zhang, Xuchu Dong, and Hui Yang. 2015. *Designing States, Actions, and Rewards for Using POMDP in Session Search*. Springer International Publishing, Cham, 526–537. http://dx.doi.org/10.1007/978-3-319-16354-3_58
[7] Lokman I. Meho and Helen R. Tibbo. 2003. Modeling the Information-seeking Behavior of Social Scientists: Ellis's Study Revisited. *J. Am. Soc. Inf. Sci. Technol.* 54, 6 (April 2003), 570–587. https://doi.org/10.1002/asi.10244
[8] Nils Pharo and Ragnar Nordlie. 2012. Examining the Effect of Task Stage and Topic Knowledge on Searcher Interaction with a "Digital Bookstore". In *Proceedings of the 4th Information Interaction in Context Symposium (IIiX '12)*. ACM, New York, NY, USA, 4–11. https://doi.org/10.1145/2362724.2362730
[9] Amanda Spink, Howard Greisdorf, and Judy Bateman. 1998. From highly relevant to not relevant: examining different regions of relevance. *Information Processing & Management* 34, 5 (1998), 599–621.
[10] Vu T. Tran and Norbert Fuhr. 2012. Using Eye-Tracking with Dynamic Areas of Interest for Analyzing Interactive Information Retrieval. In *Proc. 35th ACM SIGIR*. 1165–1166.
[11] Vu T. Tran and Norbert Fuhr. 2013. Markov Modeling for User Interaction in Retrieval. In *SIGIR 2013 Workshop on Modeling User Behavior for Information Retrieval Evaluation (MUBE 2013)*.
[12] Pertti Vakkari. 2001. A theory of the task-based information retrieval process: a summary and generalisation of a longitudinal study. *Journal of documentation* 57, 1 (2001), 44–60.
[13] K. Wang, N. Gloy, and X. Li. 2010. Inferring Search Behaviors Using Partially Observable Markov (POM) Model. In *Proc. 3rd ACM WSDM*. 211–220.
[14] T.D. Wilson. 1999. Models in information behaviour research. *Journal of Documentation* 55, 3 (1999), 249–270. https://doi.org/10.1108/EUM0000000007145 arXiv:http://dx.doi.org/10.1108/EUM0000000007145
[15] Z. Yue, S. Han, and D. He. 2014. Modeling Search Processes Using Hidden States in Collaborative Exploratory Web Search. In *Proc. 17th CSCW*. 820–830.

Uncovering Like-minded Political Communities on Twitter

Ophélie Fraisier
CEA-Tech en Occitanie
IRIT, Université de Toulouse, CNRS
31400, Toulouse, France
ophelie.fraisier@cea.fr

Guillaume Cabanac
IRIT, Université de Toulouse, CNRS
31062, Toulouse, France
guillaume.cabanac@irit.fr

Yoann Pitarch
IRIT, Université de Toulouse, CNRS
31062, Toulouse, France
yoann.pitarch@irit.fr

Romaric Besançon
CEA, LIST
91191, Gif-sur-Yvette, France
romaric.besancon@cea.fr

Mohand Boughanem
IRIT, Université de Toulouse, CNRS
31062, Toulouse, France
mohand.boughanem@irit.fr

ABSTRACT

Stance detection systems often integrate social clues in their algorithms. While the influence of social groups on stance is known, there is no evaluation of how well state-of-the-art community detection algorithms perform in terms of detecting *like-minded communities*, i.e. communities that share the same stance on a given subject. We used Twitter's social interactions to compare the results of community detection algorithms on datasets on the Scottish Independence Referendum and US Midterm Elections. Our results show that algorithms relying on information diffusion perform better for this task and confirm previous observations about retweets being better vectors of stance than mentions.

CCS CONCEPTS

• **Applied computing → Sociology;** • **Information systems →** *Web mining*;

KEYWORDS

Stance detection, Social media, Benchmarking

1 INTRODUCTION

The impact of communities and homophily[1] on the construction of people's opinions have been studied by sociologists for decades. Bourdieu [3] noted that choosing between opinions usually meant choosing between groups supporting underlying opinions. Subsequent studies showed that these observations still held true on virtual social media, where users tended to interact with people sharing their opinions rather than debating with opponents, a phenomenon known as *"echo chambers"* [11, 13].

---

[1]Homophily is the principle that a contact between similar people occurs at a higher rate than among dissimilar people.

This project is co-financed by the European Union – Europe is committed to Midi-Pyrénées with the European fund for regional development.

With the rapid growth of user-generated content, many researchers decided to built opinion mining systems, to automatically detect the subjective information users shared in their writings on the web [12]. These systems led to stance detection, which can be used in online social media to automatically determine the stance of specific users in favor or against a particular topic. Successful detection of stance can be very useful in various downstream tasks, such as information retrieval, text summarization or irony detection.

But an important question remains unanswered: can social interactions and communities alone be used to determine users' stances? We decided to use the phenomenon of *echo chambers* and community detection to try to answer this question. This paper makes the following contributions: (a) a comparison of state-of-the-art community detection algorithms, testing their ability to uncover underlying groups who share a common stance and (b) a comparison between the potential of retweet, mention, and their combination graphs, as a means to uncover like-minded communities.

2 RELATED WORK

The relationship between opinions and social relations has been exploited in opinion mining for many years, with researchers trying to deepen their analysis by using social theories [20]. Some researchers, while not formally using community detection, integrated some aspects of it to improve their opinion classification systems. Speriosu et al. [19] used for example label propagation along the follower graph to assign polarity labels to tweets. On the other hand, opinion was sometimes used as a feature to detect like-minded community in conjonction with classical algorithms. Dinsoreanu and Potolea [9] exploited opinions extracted from documents and the infomap community detection algorithm to detect consistent communities of users.

Several benchmarks compared performances on ground-truth communities and some systems are explicitly made for detecting like-minded communities — like Deepak et al. [8] who used a bottom-up hierarchical clustering approach — but we did not find a benchmark focusing on how classical algorithms performed when detecting like-minded communities.

3 EXPERIMENTAL SETUP

3.1 Definitions

In this paper, we define a *community* as a group of users interacting for enough time and with enough commitment for connections to appear in the cyberspace [17].

The *stance* of a user is its publicly stated viewpoint on a particular subject. In our experiments, we focused on datasets with political viewpoints. Each dataset contains N stances, with $N \geq 2$. A stance may be shared by users belonging to different communities, and a community may contain several stances. Our aim is to detect if some algorithms obtain better performances in finding communities as homogeneous as possible in terms of stances, that is communities where a large majority of users share the same stance. We will call them *like-minded communities*.

3.2 Algorithms

We chose to compare in this study some popular and easily-accessible graph-based community detection algorithms[2], implemented in the *igraph* library [6]. Table 1 lists some characteristics of the algorithms presented below.

Table 1: Characteristics of community detection algorithms, including complexity on typical sparse data – W stands for edges weights and D for edges direction.

Family	Algorithm	W	D	Complexity
Modularity maximisation	Fast-greedy [22]	✓	✗	$O(mn \log n)$
	Leading eigenvectors [14]	✗	✗	$O(n^2)$
	Multi-level [1]	✓	✗	$O(n)$
Information diffusion	Infomap [18]	✓	✓	$O(n(n+m))$
	Label propagation [16]	✓	✗	$O(n+m)$
Random walk	Walktrap [15]	✓	✗	$O(n^2 \log n)$

Modularity maximisation. The modularity measures the number of intra-community links versus links joining communities. Fast-greedy attempts to maximize modularity of the community structure by merging pairs of communities with a bottom-up approach. Leading eigenvectors uses a matrix-based approach analogous to a spectral partitioning method. Multi-level iteratively merges partitions representing local maxima of modularity at different scales.

Information diffusion. Infomap attempts to create communities according to the flow of information present in the network. Label propagation is a simple iterative process where, at each step, each node adopts the label most present in its neighbors.

Random walk. Walktrap detects communities based on a distance that quantify the structural similarity between vertices using random walks.

3.3 Interactions

In this work we consider only the two main tweet-level interactions[3]: retweets (RT) and mentions (@). Retweeting means sharing another user's tweet with one's followers while mentioning is citing another user's username. Three graphs are built per dataset: one per interaction plus one taking into account both interactions indifferently. In these graphs, vertices are users and edges are interactions. The weight of the edges are the number of times the

users interacted. A vertex can represent an annotated or a non-annotated user: annotated users are those for which we know the stance, whereas non-annotated users appear in annotated users' tweets because of mentions or retweets, but we do not know their stance. When a directed graph is required by the algorithm, we follow the information path: from retweeted users to users sharing tweets, and from mentioning users to users being cited.

3.4 Scoring functions

To compare the performance of algorithms on like-minded communities we used the *purity* [10] and the *normalized mutual information* [7], defined as follows:

$$\text{Purity}(\Omega, \mathbb{C}) = \sum_k \frac{\max_j |\omega_k \cap c_j|}{N} \qquad \text{NMI}(\Omega, \mathbb{C}) = \frac{2 \times I(\Omega, \mathbb{C})}{H(\Omega) + H(\mathbb{C})}$$

with Ω the partition of detected communities, $\mathbb{C}$ the set of stances, ω_k the set of annotated users in community k, c_j the set of annotated users in class j, N the total number of annotated users in P, I the mutual information, and H the entropy.

Purity is known to be biased in favor of small communities but in our case, since we want communities as homogeneous as possible, it is still a valid indicator. To examine the consistency of the community detection, we also used the *standard deviation* (SD) of the intra-communities purity scores.

4 EXPERIMENTS

4.1 Datasets

The use of community detection algorithms as a mean to detect like-minded communities forces us to have a non-negligible amount of interactions between the users. For this reason we cannot use datasets built around keywords, like the ones featured in the task 6 of SemEval2016[4] because users in this kind of datasets seldom interact with one another. We used two datasets published by Brigadir et al. [4], both constructed by gathering all available tweets for a fixed subset of users (see Table 2). DMI-TCAT [2] collected the tweets from Twitter API, based on the released users accounts and tweets ids.

Scottish Independence Referendum (SR). This dataset was originally collected from Aug 11th to Oct 19th 2014. It reflects the debate around the Scottish Independence referendum of the 18th of September 2014. The official "Yes" and "No" campaigns were very active on social media. To be included as a "Yes" or "No" supporter, users had to be part of the Scottish Independence Referendum Electoral Commission or unambiguously self-identify as such on their profile.

Table 2: Dataset sizes[5]

Dataset	Stance	Original		Retrieved	
		Users	Tweets	Users	Tweets
SR	Yes	618	799,096	535	344,563
	No	610	570,024	508	263,569
ME	Democrat	942	89,296	701	56,671
	Republican	997	80,840	756	56,506

---

[2]We used non-parametric algorithms with respect to the number of communities to detect since, as expressed in Section 3.1, the ideal situation for us is not having one unique community per stance, but simply having homogeneous communities.

[3]We did not consider the *Follow* interaction because it is a user-level interaction, so hardly comparable with retweets and mentions, and it shows a more passive way of participating on Twitter.

[4]http://alt.qcri.org/semeval2016/task6/

[5]The differences between the original sizes and the retrieved ones are due to users having deleted their tweets and their accounts since the initial crawl.

US Midterm Elections (ME). This dataset concerns the US Midterm elections held on the 4th of November 2014 and was originally collected from Oct 10th to Nov 20th 2014. Third parties were ignored so users are either "Democrat" or "Republican". They were selected thanks to several sources listing official Twitter accounts of campaigners in these elections.

4.2 Scores on all users

Table 3 presents some characteristics of the resulting graphs. Given the construction method for the graphs, we do not have annotated users in all communities. In order to measure consistent scores, we exclusively consider communities having at least 3 annotated users (see Table 4). We will discard from the observations below the scarce cases where we only have one community to analyse, since standard deviation and NMI cannot be calculated on a unique community.

Table 5 presents the scores by interaction and algorithm. The first observation we can make is that retweets appear to be more important in terms of stance diffusion. For retweets, while almost all algorithms obtain a purity score of more than 90%, LABEL PROPAGATION and INFOMAP obtain smaller standard deviation values. LABEL PROPAGATION also obtain the best NMI scores for both dataset. For mentions, results are more variable. INFOMAP, FAST-GREEDY and

WALKTRAP obtain good performances. Taking into account both interactions does not seem to offer an advantage, since purity and NMI scores for these graphs are inferior to those of the retweet graphs. All in all, algorithms based on information diffusion seem to have a slight advantage. They consistently detect communities with a high purity, and despite the fact that they detect more communities, they still obtain better NMI scores than the other algorithms most of the time. For all graphs, MULTI-LEVEL and LABEL PROPAGATION are the quickest algorithms with a runtime under 2 seconds. The slowest ones are FASTGREEDY and WALKTRAP, with a runtime up to 25 minutes for the Scottish Independence Referendum dataset, and up to 75 minutes for the US Midterm Elections dataset. These observations are not really surprising given the respective complexities of the algorithms (see Table 1).

4.3 Scores on annotated users only

One important caveat of this analysis is of course the communities without annotated users. Indeed, since all interactions are used to

Table 3: Characteristics of the constructed graphs – D is the density measure and C the clustering coefficient.

		# Vertices	# Edges	Degrees			D	C
				Mean	Med	Max		
Using interactions between all users								
SR	RT	78,854	266,146	7	1	7,391	10^{-5}	0.019
	@	59,122	200,631	7	1	1,721	10^{-4}	0.044
	Both	120,165	443,322	7	1	7,785	10^{-5}	0.031
ME	RT	149,137	291,137	4	1	10,125	10^{-5}	0.001
	@	23,148	35,141	3	1	2,278	10^{-4}	0.004
	Both	163,646	320,007	4	1	10,288	10^{-5}	0.001
Using interactions between annotated users only								
SR	RT	898	16,938	38	21	302	0.042	0.298
	@	258	278	2	1	237	0.008	0.002
	Both	902	16,938	38	21	302	0.041	0.298
ME	RT	973	2,056	4	2	69	0.004	0.134
	@	126	125	2	1	122	0.015	0.000
	Both	989	2,180	4	2	123	0.004	0.106

Table 4: Number of communities containing at least 3 annotated users – the algorithms are represented by their initials.

Algorithm		Scottish Referendum			Midterms Elections		
		RT	@	Both	RT	@	Both
Using interactions between all users							
Modularity maximisation	F	15	34	27	39	45	39
	LE	19	1	1	3	19	1
	M	17	36	29	43	47	43
Information diffusion	I	102	85	38	112	159	103
	LP	4	2	3	74	135	98
Random walk	W	15	34	27	39	45	37
Using interactions between annotated users only							
Modularity maximisation	F	4	2	4	49	2	49
	LE	4	2	2	33	2	n/a
	M	4	2	5	46	2	40
Information diffusion	I	138	2	137	111	2	122
	LP	4	2	4	94	2	94
Random walk	W	4	2	4	49	2	45

Table 5: Scores for the SR and ME datasets – best scores are presented in bold and cases for which we have one community only to analyse in gray and in italic (see table 4).

	Algorithm		Scottish Referendum			Midterms Elections		
			RT	@	Both	RT	@	Both
	Using interactions between all users							
Purity	*Modularity maximisation*	F	0.97	0.78	0.86	0.93	0.63	0.77
		LE	0.87	*0.51*	*0.51*	0.62	0.58	*0.51*
		M	0.97	0.72	0.84	0.87	0.66	0.78
	Information diffusion	I	0.96	**0.80**	**0.88**	**0.97**	0.79	**0.91**
		LP	**0.98**	0.53	0.54	0.93	0.78	0.90
	Random walk	W	0.97	0.78	0.86	0.93	0.63	0.77
SD	*Modularity maximisation*	F	0.16	**0.13**	**0.15**	0.14	**0.12**	**0.15**
		LE	0.15	*n/a*	*n/a*	0.24	0.15	*n/a*
		M	0.17	0.15	0.16	0.17	**0.12**	0.17
	Information diffusion	I	0.10	0.19	0.17	0.10	0.18	**0.15**
		LP	**0.02**	0.33	0.24	**0.09**	0.17	**0.15**
	Random walk	W	0.16	**0.13**	**0.15**	0.14	**0.12**	**0.15**
NMI	*Modularity maximisation*	F	0.55	0.12	**0.25**	**0.28**	0.02	0.12
		LE	0.33	*n/a*	*n/a*	0.14	0.023	*n/a*
		M	0.52	0.08	0.21	0.22	0.04	0.13
	Information diffusion	I	0.22	**0.13**	0.21	0.24	**0.11**	**0.20**
		LP	**0.85**	0.01	0.01	0.25	**0.11**	**0.20**
	Random walk	W	0.55	0.12	**0.25**	**0.28**	0.02	0.12
	Using interactions between annotated users only							
Purity	*Modularity maximisation*	F	**0.99**	**0.76**	**0.99**	**0.98**	0.58	0.94
		LE	0.98	**0.76**	0.86	0.86	0.58	*n/a*
		M	**0.99**	**0.76**	0.98	**0.98**	0.58	0.94
	Information diffusion	I	0.96	0.75	0.97	0.97	0.58	**0.96**
		LP	**0.99**	0.74	0.98	**0.98**	0.58	0.94
	Random walk	W	**0.99**	**0.76**	**0.99**	**0.98**	0.58	0.94
SD	*Modularity maximisation*	F	0.01	0.06	0.01	0.06	0.06	0.10
		LE	0.02	0.06	0.16	0.07	0.06	*n/a*
		M	0.01	0.06	0.01	0.06	0.06	0.10
	Information diffusion	I	0.09	0.09	0.09	0.08	0.06	**0.09**
		LP	0.01	0.09	0.01	0.08	0.06	**0.09**
	Random walk	W	0.01	0.06	0.01	0.06	0.06	0.10
NMI	*Modularity maximisation*	F	**0.88**	**0.18**	**0.86**	**0.32**	0.001	**0.29**
		LE	0.69	**0.18**	0.50	0.26	0.001	*n/a*
		M	0.84	**0.18**	0.81	**0.32**	0.001	**0.29**
	Information diffusion	I	0.22	0.15	0.23	0.24	0.001	0.23
		LP	0.86	0.15	0.85	0.27	0.001	0.24
	Random walk	W	**0.88**	**0.18**	**0.86**	**0.32**	0.001	**0.29**

construct the retweets and mentions graphs, we have a majority of users for whom we do not know the stance, and therefore a lot of communities for which we cannot evaluate stance homogeneity since they do not contain enough annotated users. To overcome this issue, we opted for detecting communities on the sub-graphs representing the interactions between annotated users only (see Table 3 for sub-graphs characteristics).

The results (see Table 5) show again that, even when using only the interactions between the subset of users used to build the datasets, stance can be determined by community. [6] By focusing on annotated users only, we obtain for almost all graphs better scores. Interestingly, for retweets, algorithms based on information diffusion do not seem to have an advantage over the others, contrary to the previous section. This may be due to the fact that focusing on interactions between annotated users does not allow to properly model the diffusion of information.

5 DISCUSSION

Retweet graphs generally seem to be a better way to detect homogeneous like-minded communities than mention graphs. This is consistent with the previous observations made in the literature so far [5].

When considering retweet interactions, the leading algorithms are LABEL PROPAGATION and INFOMAP, two algorithms relying on information diffusion. This is a valuable observation, suggesting that, in a certain way, stance "follows" information on Twitter. These observations suggest that to efficiently detect like-minded communities on Twitter, it is a better idea to look at the information circulating between users rather than considering purely structural criteria. However the direction of diffusion does not seem to be important, since the implementation of label propagation we used in this work considers undirected edges. For mentions however, we can see that these algorithms do not really have an advantage compared to others, suggesting that mention graphs do not have the same underlying principles that retweet graphs, stressing a difference in use between these interactions.

This work featured only two interactions taken separately and focuses mainly on atypical users, limiting the generalization capability of this study. The formation and diffusion of stances is a much more complex process, still hard to grasp by computing methods. We may assume that every interactions on social media has its own role in this process. It would be interesting to expand this comparison to more algorithms, datasets (including some with more than 2 stances), and interactions, and to see how well the systems taking into account several interactions [21] perform on like-minded communities.

6 CONCLUSION

In this article, we compare the performances of three classes of community detection algorithms for the detection of like-minded communities on Twitter. Despite the growing integration of social features in opinion mining systems, there is no existing comparison of state-of-the-art community detection methods on this particular task.

We found out that algorithms based on information diffusion seem to perform better when using retweet interactions and upheld the fact that retweets are a better vector of opinion than mentions. Overall, label propagation seems to be a good choice for detecting like-minded communities, it achieves excellent results and is one of the fastest among the algorithms we benchmarked.

Our results confirms that popular community detection algorithm can indeed be used as-is to reliably detect users' stance under certain conditions.

REFERENCES

[1] Vincent D Blondel, Jean-Loup Guillaume, Renaud Lambiotte, and Etienne Lefebvre. 2008. Fast Unfolding of Communities in Large Networks. *JSTAT* 10 (2008), P10008. DOI:http://dx.doi.org/10.1088/1742-5468/2008/10/P10008

[2] Erik Borra and Bernhard Rieder. 2014. Programmed Method: Developing a Toolset for Capturing and Analyzing Tweets. *AJIM* 66, 3 (2014), 262–278. DOI:http://dx.doi.org/10.1108/AJIM-09-2013-0094

[3] Pierre Bourdieu. 1973. L'opinion Publique n'existe pas. *Les temps modernes* 318 (1973), 1292–1309.

[4] Igor Brigadir, Derek Greene, and Pádraig Cunningham. 2015. Analyzing Discourse Communities with Distributional Semantic Models. In *WebSci*. 1–10. DOI:http://dx.doi.org/10.1145/2786451.2786470

[5] M. D. Conover, J. Ratkiewicz, M. Francisco, B. Gonçalves, A. Flammini, and F. Menczer. 2011. Political Polarization on Twitter. In *ICWSM*. 89–96.

[6] Gabor Csardi and Tamas Nepusz. 2006. The Igraph Software Package for Complex Network Research. *InterJournal* Complex Systems (2006), 1695.

[7] Leon Danon, Albert Díaz-Guilera, Jordi Duch, and Alex Arenas. 2005. Comparing Community Structure Identification. *JSTAT* 09 (2005), P09008. DOI:http://dx.doi.org/10.1088/1742-5468/2005/09/P09008

[8] Talasila Sai Deepak, Hindol Adhya, Shyamal Kejriwal, Bhanuteja Gullapalli, and Saswata Shannigrahi. 2016. A New Hierarchical Clustering Algorithm to Identify Non-Overlapping Like-Minded Communities. In *HT*. 319–321. DOI:http://dx.doi.org/10.1145/2914586.2914613

[9] Mihaela Dinsoreanu and Rodica Potolea. 2015. Opinion-Driven Communities' Detection. *IJWIS* 10, 4 (2015), 324–342. DOI:http://dx.doi.org/10.1108/IJWIS-04-2014-0016

[10] M. Girvan and M. E. J. Newman. 2002. Community Structure in Social and Biological Networks. *NAS* 99, 12 (2002), 7821–7826. DOI:http://dx.doi.org/10.1073/pnas.122653799

[11] Shanto Iyengar and Sean J. Westwood. 2015. Fear and Loathing across Party Lines: New Evidence on Group Polarization. *AJPS* 59, 3 (2015), 690–707. DOI:http://dx.doi.org/10.1111/ajps.12152

[12] Bing Liu. 2012. Sentiment Analysis and Opinion Mining. *Synthesis Lectures on HLT* 5, 1 (2012), 1–167. DOI:http://dx.doi.org/10.2200/S00416ED1V01Y201204HLT016

[13] Miller McPherson, Lynn Smith-Lovin, and James M Cook. 2001. Birds of a Feather: Homophily in Social Networks. *Annual Review of Sociology* 27, 1 (2001), 415–444. DOI:http://dx.doi.org/10.1146/annurev.soc.27.1.415

[14] M. E. J. Newman. 2006. Finding Community Structure in Networks Using the Eigenvectors of Matrices. *PRE* 74, 3 (2006). DOI:http://dx.doi.org/10.1103/PhysRevE.74.036104

[15] Pascal Pons and Matthieu Latapy. 2005. Computing Communities in Large Networks Using Random Walks. In *ISCIS*. Vol. 3733. 284–293. DOI:http://dx.doi.org/10.1007/11569596_31

[16] Usha Nandini Raghavan, Réka Albert, and Soundar Kumara. 2007. Near Linear Time Algorithm to Detect Community Structures in Large-Scale Networks. *PRE* 76, 3 (2007). DOI:http://dx.doi.org/10.1103/PhysRevE.76.036106

[17] Howard Rheingold. 1993. *The virtual community: Finding commection in a computerized world*. http://www.rheingold.com/vc/book/

[18] M. Rosvall, D. Axelsson, and C. T. Bergstrom. 2009. The Map Equation. *EPJ ST* 178, 1 (2009), 13–23. DOI:http://dx.doi.org/10.1140/epjst/e2010-01179-1

[19] Michael Speriosu, Nikita Sudan, Sid Upadhyay, and Jason Baldridge. 2011. Twitter Polarity Classification with Label Propagation over Lexical Links and the Follower Graph. In *EMNLP*. 53–63.

[20] Jiliang Tang, Yi Chang, and Huan Liu. 2014. Mining Social Media with Social Theories: A Survey. *ACM SIGKDD Explorations Newsletter* 15, 2 (2014), 20–29. DOI:http://dx.doi.org/10.1145/2641190.2641195

[21] Lei Tang, Xufei Wang, and Huan Liu. 2012. Community Detection via Heterogeneous Interaction Analysis. *DMKD* 25, 1 (2012), 1–33. DOI:http://dx.doi.org/10.1007/s10618-011-0231-0

[22] Ken Wakita and Toshiyuki Tsurumi. 2007. Finding Community Structure in Mega-Scale Social Networks. In *WWW*. 1275. DOI:http://dx.doi.org/10.1145/1242572.1242805

---

[6]We must note that LEADING EIGENVECTOR does not succeed in extracting communities on the graph taking into account both interactions (see Table 4).

Quantization in Append-Only Collections

Salman Mohammed, Matt Crane, and Jimmy Lin

David R. Cheriton School of Computer Science
University of Waterloo, Ontario, Canada
{salman.mohammed,matt.crane,jimmylin}@uwaterloo.ca

ABSTRACT

Quantization, the pre-calculation and conversion to integers of term/document weights in an inverted index, is a well studied aspect of search engines that substantially improves retrieval efficiency. Previous work has considered the impact of quantization on effectiveness–efficiency tradeoffs in retrieval, for example, exploring the relationship between collection size and quantization range in static web collections. We extend previous work to append-only collections and examine whether quantization settings derived from prior time periods can be applied to future time periods. Experiments confirm that previous results generalize to a collection with different characteristics and with a different ranking function, and that in an append-only collection, we can use previous quantization settings in future time periods without substantial losses in either effectiveness or efficiency.

1 INTRODUCTION

The query latency of search engines is dominated by the time taken to traverse postings in the inverted index to compute the relevance score of documents with respect to queries. This can be reduced in several ways, for example, by using a postings traversal algorithm that skips documents that cannot enter the final ranked list (such as WAND [2]) or using an anytime algorithm to enforce an upper bound on the number of postings processed (such as JASS [9]); see Crane et al. [4] for a recent comparison of these approaches.

Quantization describes another class of techniques for improving the efficiency of query evaluation. This approach has a long history: Persin et al. [12] proposed ordering postings by decreasing term frequency. This not only allows documents with the highest term frequencies to be processed first, but also amortizes the cost of computing the term frequency component of the ranking function across documents sharing the same term frequency.

Moffat et al. [10] observed that approximations to components of the ranking function (in particular, the document length) are as effective as exact values. Anh et al. [1] further observed that term/document weights can be pre-computed. However, such values are floating point and do not compress well, which is addressed by quantizing scores into q-bit integers. The result is a so-called *impact-ordered* index. Several approximations were explored by

Anh et al. [1], who showed that either a linear mapping, or alternatively skewing to provide extra granularity to lower scores, works well. With quantization, query evaluation reduces to integer additions. Subsequently, Crane et al. [5] showed that there is a relationship between the size of the document collection, query efficiency, and the number of quantization bits needed to maintain the power of the search engine to discriminate between documents (by reducing the number of scoring ties).

To our knowledge, prior work in quantization has focused on static collections. That is, the entire collection has been indexed and quantization can occur with the benefit of knowing that no more documents are to be added, which would change the quantization range. In this paper, we extend previous work to handle append-only collections, which we define as collections that can be split into temporal blocks that accumulate over time, each of which can be considered static.

We frame our research around the question of whether we can calculate quantization parameters using an earlier temporal block and apply the parameters to future blocks without negatively impacting effectiveness. For simplicity, we use uniform linear scaling of the term/document weights across the collection proposed by Anh et al. [1]. As our question is primarily framed in terms of effectiveness, we conducted our experiments, without loss of generality, using the ATIRE search engine [13]. This approach also allows for direct comparisons to the results of Crane et al. [5].

2 APPEND-ONLY COLLECTIONS

Problematically for collections that grow over time, such as in a typical web search engine (where a crawler continuously adds new pages) or Twitter (where new tweets are constantly being posted), quantization will degrade search effectiveness over time. Based on Crane et al. [5], while eight bits are sufficient for a collection of 25M documents, nine bits are needed for 50M documents. A naïve solution would be to re-quantize the entire collection when such bit thresholds are crossed. However, in the process of quantization, the information that is needed to re-quantize the index is discarded. It is possible to re-quantize to a smaller number of bits, but this is the opposite of what we desire.

However, if we consider append-only collections where past documents are considered static and there is a method by which the collection can be partitioned into blocks, then it may be possible to learn quantization settings on one block and apply those settings to future blocks. This would allow quantization during indexing, rather than as a separate post-indexing process, meaning that the benefits of quantization can apply to non-static collections.

To study whether this approach is feasible, we experimented on the Tweets2013 collection used for the TREC 2013 and 2014 Microblog Tracks [7, 8]. The collection contains approximately

Documents	254,456,742
Size	11.4GB
Unique Terms	89,759,296
Total Terms	3,221,307,052
Date Range	February, 1 2013 to March, 28 2013
TREC Queries	MB 111–225

Table 1: Tweets2013 collection statistics.

254 million tweets gathered over February and March 2013, and provides an obvious temporal partitioning—this is exactly the implementation used by Twitter's Earlybird search engine [3]. Although Twitter recently switched to relevance ranking of search results (from reverse chronological order), it appears that the implementation still depends on retrieving candidate tweets and then reranking them [6]. Although the Tweets2013 collection includes information about tweets that were subsequently deleted by users, we ignore this information and include all tweets. This is justified because deletes are typically handled via so-called tombstones: they are kept in the index but filtered from query results.

For queries, we used topics from the TREC 2013 and 2014 Microblog Tracks, each of which includes a query time. In the track setup, results exploited term statistics of tweets posted after the query time,[1] but the track guidelines required that results only contain tweets posted before the query time [7, 8]. This requirement was relaxed in our experiments, as we are not directly interested in absolute effectiveness, but rather only in relative comparisons to a non-quantized index. To measure effectiveness, the relevance judgments were also split to contain judgments for only those tweets that occur within the period being assessed. This means that our results are not directly comparable to other results reported in the literature that conformed to the official track guidelines.

Table 1 shows collection statistics for the Tweets2013 collection.[2] We see that this collection is quite different from web collections that have been previously used to study quantization—two obvious differences are the number and length of documents, which affects the vocabulary size as well. Crane et al. [5] used BM25 as the ranking function, but it is widely known that BM25 does not work well for tweet collections since tweets are relatively uniform in length, which negates the effects of the length normalization factor in BM25. Instead, for our experiments we used the LMJM ranking function [16], with $\lambda = 3000$ (the ATIRE default). Ranking functions based on language modeling have been shown to perform better for tweets [11].

We additionally examined the ClueWeb09 Category B (CW09B) collection, which contains 50 million documents crawled from the web in early 2009. For queries we used TREC queries 51–150. The collection was distributed in crawl order, which provides an approximate temporal ordering. One can imagine a web search engine performing quantization as crawling and indexing proceeds. We tested only on folders in the collection that start with the en00 prefix, as the enwp files are injected outside of crawling.[3]

---

[1] Although it was shown that use of this "future information" had no significant impact on retrieval effectiveness [14].
[2] Note that we discarded the last few days of the complete collection as to work with complete weeks in our partitioning scheme.
[3] http://www.lemurproject.org/clueweb09/datasetInformation.php

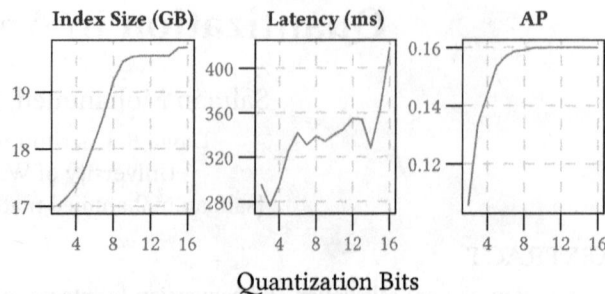

Figure 1: Effects of the number of quantization bits using LMJM on the Tweets2013 collection with respect to index size (measured in GB), mean query latency ($k = 1000$, measured in ms), and effectiveness (measured using AP).

3 EXPERIMENTS

Our experiments were conducted on an otherwise idle server with two Intel E5-2670 2.60GHz CPUs (8 cores) with 256GB of memory, running Linux kernel 3.13.0. All implementations were single threaded. Source code for our experiments is available online for reproducibility purposes.[4]

3.1 Analysis of the Complete Collection

In light of the different collection characteristics and the ranking function, our first experiment aimed to verify that the effects of quantization observed by Crane et al. [5] generalize. Figure 1 shows the effects that the number of quantization bits has on the index size (measured in GB), query latency for $k = 1000$, and search effectiveness (measured using AP) over the entire collection. The query latency is represented as the average time for queries in the test collections, and for an individual query we selected the minimum time from five runs. The minimum was selected because noise introduced in timing can only be additive, and thus the minimum is closer to the ground truth than either the mean or median. While recent work by Crane et al. [4] have suggested that only showing the mean latency has a number of drawbacks, we are merely attempting to replicate results from prior work. Indeed, what we see is entirely consistent with what has been reported in the literature.

3.2 Prediction of Quantization Settings

Having confirmed that the trends observed in prior work apply to this tweet collection and ranking function, we now turn our attention to the dynamic nature of the collection. To test this we split the collection into weeks (recall that we only examined the eight full weeks in the collection). In addition, we also performed experiments on the CW09B collection, split using the folder layout described in the previous section.

When documents from the current period are being indexed, we can use the quantization settings learned from the previous period to quantize term/document weights on the fly, rather than as a post-processing step. The quantization settings are the number of bits and the range of the observed weights. The concerns with this are two-fold: First, the range of the values may be substantially different across time periods, affecting the uniformity of the quantization.

---

[4] https://github.com/snapbug/quant-time

Subset	Documents	Terms		LMJM Score		Required Bits		Crane et al. [5]	
		Unique	Total	min	max	$p < 0.05$	$p < 0.01$	AP	P@20
Complete	254,456,742	89,759,296	3,221,307,052	0.092340	21.275933	6	6	15	10
Week 1	30,010,597	18,247,199	379,188,879	0.092185	19.136566	13	3	9	6
Week 2	26,213,500	16,449,208	329,256,187	0.091704	18.995803	5	4	9	6
Week 3	30,050,788	18,431,524	380,556,865	0.092369	19.140002	3	3	9	6
Week 4	30,531,252	19,089,511	387,982,579	0.092652	19.159073	3	3	9	6
Week 5	30,241,679	18,949,096	384,368,344	0.092664	19.149702	4	4	9	6
Week 6	31,054,512	19,333,063	394,602,513	0.092643	19.175997	3	3	9	6
Week 7	31,053,073	19,455,396	394,973,784	0.092724	19.176866	3	3	9	6
Week 8	31,581,904	19,615,690	398,909,012	0.092153	19.187290	5	4	9	6

Table 2: Collection statistics and quantization range for the entire collection and weekly subsets of Tweets2013. Final columns show the required number of bits for different significance levels with respect to AP (experimentally determined), and values predicted by Crane et al. [5] for $p < 0.01$.

Second, the number of bits devoted to quantization may be either too low—resulting in a significant loss in effectiveness—or too high—resulting in a loss in efficiency.

Table 2 shows collection statistics for the different weekly temporal subsets of Tweets2013 as well as the quantization settings. For example, there are 30 million tweets from the first week of February, which contain 380 million occurrences of 18 million unique terms. The range of LMJM term/document weights for this week was 0.092185–19.136566. As shown in the table, the range of the weights is remarkably consistent, within the same granularity, across different temporal subsets.

The table also shows the minimum number of bits required to maintain effectiveness with respect to average precision. Following Crane et al. [5], we selected the smallest number of bits needed to maintain effectiveness that is not significantly different at both $p < 0.05$ and $p < 0.01$ from a non-quantized index (calculated using a two-tailed paired t-test). We also require that no higher bit setting has a statistically significant difference: since quantized ranking converges to results from a non-quantized index as the number of bits increases, if there is a higher bit setting that is significantly different, then the non-difference at the lower setting is likely due to noise, rather than any "real" difference.[5]

The final two columns in Table 2 show the estimated numbers of bits that are needed in terms of AP and P@20 using the relationship and parameters described by Crane et al. [5]. Clearly, this vastly overestimates the required number of bits compared to the $p < 0.01$ setting (the setting used to derive the relationship) when targeting either metric. There is an obvious need to consider collection characteristics and the ranking function, which Crane et al. [5] did not do. The predicted values more closely match the results we derive for subsets of the CW09B collection, which is unsurprising given the collections the formula was derived from.

Figure 2 shows the effects of quantization on mean latency and AP per week. For example, the minimum number of bits required, at the $p < 0.05$ level, for Week 7 is three, while for Week 8 it is five. Applying the value learned from the week 7 subset to the week 8 subset would result in a loss in AP, compared to the oracle

minimum bits, of 0.0272, bringing it to a level that is significantly different from a non-quantized index. Accompanying this is a mean query latency decrease of 5% (2ms).

Figure 3 shows the changes in AP and mean latency when using the learned settings from the previous period, with $p < 0.05$, compared to the oracle setting. Whether the setting was over, equal to, or under the oracle value for the current period is identified by both shape and color. The figure clearly shows that in general whenever the bit setting was greater than needed, the mean latency suffered. While the AP values are higher, these are not significantly different from a non-quantized index. When the prediction was lower than the oracle, the mean efficiency improved at the cost of statistically significant differences in AP.

4 CONCLUSIONS AND FUTURE WORK

We have shown that the overall results of Crane et al. [5] extend to another collection (with very different characteristics) as well as a different ranking function. We were then able to divide collections into temporal subsets and show that by using settings obtained for one period, we can effectively quantize the next time period without substantial loss in effectiveness or efficiency.

There are a number of open questions worth exploring: The formula provided by Crane et al. [5] vastly overpredicts the number of bits required for the Tweets2013 collection, since it does not account for collection characteristics and the ranking function. The number of bits required for this collection is surprisingly low, especially given the gains observed by resolving tie-breaks [15]. Finally, we only explore the scenario where judgments are applied to a future time period, as opposed to the entire collection cumulatively. While this is not unrealistic for tweets since users generally care about the most recent posts, such a setup may be questionable in the web scenario. We save these issues for future work.

REFERENCES

[1] Vo Ngoc Anh, Owen de Kretser, and Alistair Moffat. 2001. Vector-Space Ranking with Effective Early Termination. In *SIGIR*. 35–42.
[2] Andrei Z. Broder, David Carmel, Michael Herscovici, Aya Soffer, and Jason Zien. 2003. Efficient Query Evaluation using a Two-Level Retrieval Process. In *CIKM*. 426–434.
[3] Michael Busch, Krishna Gade, Brian Larson, Patrick Lok, Samuel Luckenbill, and Jimmy Lin. 2012. Earlybird: Real-time Search at Twitter. In *ICDE*. 1360–1369.

---

[5]This requirement was also used by Crane et al. [5], although the description is missing from that paper.

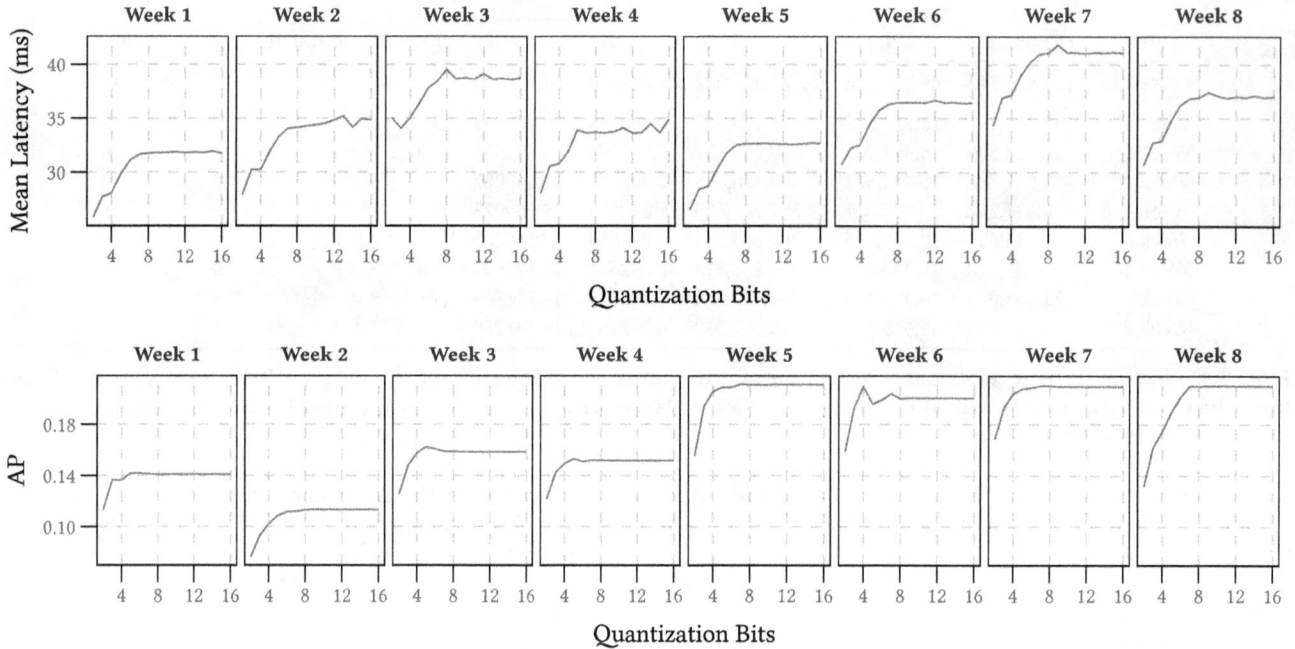

Figure 2: Effects of quantization bits on mean latency (top) and AP (bottom) for weekly subsets of the Tweets2013 collection.

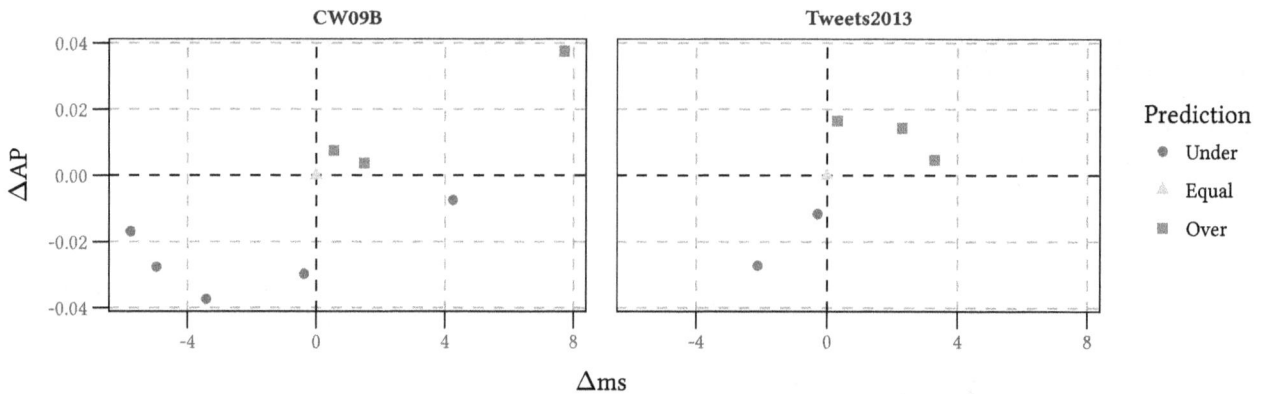

Figure 3: Changes in AP and mean latency using settings from the previous block (CW09B) or week (Tweets2013) compared to the oracle setting (when requiring *n.s.* at $p < 0.05$ compared to a non-quantized index).

[4] Matt Crane, J. Shane Culpepper, Jimmy Lin, Joel Mackenzie, and Andrew Trotman. 2017. A Comparison of Document-at-a-Time and Score-at-a-Time Query Evaluation. In *WSDM*. 201–210.

[5] Matt Crane, Andrew Trotman, and Richard O'Keefe. 2013. Maintaining Discriminatory Power in Quantized Indexes. In *CIKM*. 1221–1224.

[6] Lisa Huang. 2016. Moving Top Tweet Search Results from Reverse Chronological Order to Relevance Order. (19 Dec. 2016). Retrieved July 31, 2017 from https://blog.twitter.com/2016/moving-top-tweet-search-results-from-reverse-chronological-order-to-relevance-order

[7] Jimmy Lin and Miles Efron. 2013. Overview of the TREC-2013 Microblog Track. In *TREC*.

[8] Jimmy Lin, Miles Efron, Yulu Wang, and Garrick Sherman. 2014. Overview of the TREC-2014 Microblog Track. In *TREC*.

[9] Jimmy Lin and Andrew Trotman. 2015. Anytime Ranking for Impact-Ordered Indexes. In *ICTIR*. 301–304.

[10] Alistair Moffat, Justin Zobel, and Ron Sacks-Davis. 1994. Memory Efficient Ranking. *IP&M* 30, 6 (1994), 733–744.

[11] Jesus A. Rodriguez Perez, Andrew J. McMinn, and Joemon M. Jose. 2013. University of Glasgow (UoG_TwTeam) at TREC Microblog 2013. In *TREC*.

[12] Michael Persin, Justin Zobel, and Ron Sacks-Davis. 1996. Filtered Document Retrieval With Frequency-sorted Indexes. *JASIS* 47, 10 (1996), 749–764.

[13] Andrew Trotman, Xiang-Fei Jia, and Matt Crane. 2012. Towards an Efficient and Effective Search Engine. In *OSIR Workshop*.

[14] Yulu Wang and Jimmy Lin. 2014. The Impact of Future Term Statistics in Real-time Tweet Search. In *ECIR*. 567–572.

[15] Yue Wang, Hao Wu, and Hui Fang. 2014. An Exploration of Tie-breaking for Microblog Retrieval. In *ECIR*. 713–719.

[16] Chengxiang Zhai and John Lafferty. 2001. A Study of Smoothing Methods for Language Models Applied to Ad Hoc Information Retrieval. In *CIKM*. 334–342.

Acknowledgments. This work was supported by the Natural Sciences and Engineering Research Council (NSERC) of Canada, with additional contributions from the U.S. National Science Foundation under CNS-1405688.

Emotion Detection from Text via Ensemble Classification Using Word Embeddings

Jonathan Herzig
IBM Research - Haifa
Haifa 31905, Israel
hjon@il.ibm.com

Michal Shmueli-Scheuer
IBM Research - Haifa
Haifa 31905, Israel
shmueli@il.ibm.com

David Konopnicki
IBM Research - Haifa
Haifa 31905, Israel
davidko@il.ibm.com

ABSTRACT

Emotion detection from text has become a popular task due to the key role of emotions in human-machine interaction. Current approaches represent text as a sparse bag-of-words vector. In this work, we propose a new approach that utilizes pre-trained, dense word embedding representations. We introduce an ensemble approach combining both sparse and dense representations. Our experiments include five datasets for emotion detection from different domains and show an average improvement of 11.6% in macro average F1-score.

1 INTRODUCTION

Emotions are an important element of human nature and detecting them in the textual messages written by users has many applications in information retrieval [17] and human-computer interaction [6]. A common approach to emotion analysis and modeling is categorization, e.g., according to Ekman's basic emotions; namely, anger, disgust, fear, happiness, sadness, and surprise [9]. Approaches to categorical emotion classification based on text often employ supervised machine learning classifiers, which require labeled training data.

Currently, two types of datasets labeled with emotions are publicly available: manually labeled, and pseudo-labeled. Manual annotation requires high cognitive capabilities of multiple human annotators per sample. As a result, the quality of these datasets is usually high. However, the task is tedious, time-consuming, and expensive [4], and thus, these datasets are usually small (in the order of thousands of annotated samples). Manual annotations are usually applied to domain specific datasets (e.g., news headlines). To overcome these limitations, pseudo-labeled datasets are gathered from social media platforms where social media posts are explicitly tagged by the author by using the hashtag symbol (#) or by adding emoticons [1]. This tagged data can be used to create large-scale training data labeled with emotions in a non-specific domain as in [20].

Given such a dataset (manually or pseudo labeled), it is then common to train a linear classifier based on bag-of-words (BOW)

[1] http://techcrunch.com/2013/04/09/facebook-mood/

representation: representing text samples as sparse vectors, where each vector entry corresponds to the presence of a specific feature (such as n-grams, punctuation and other) [21].

As reported recently by [11], deep learning is a promising approach for solving NLP tasks including text classification. While the aforementioned approach utilizes BOW representation and linear classifiers, neural network methods are based on dense vector representations of text samples (word embedding) and are non-linear. Such word embedding representation captures syntactic and semantic knowledge, which can improve the emotion detection task. For example, in such a representation the words "awful" and "terrible" are expected to have similar vector representations.

Generating high quality word vectors requires large-scale data and computing power. When generation is not an option, one can utilize pre-trained representations; the most popular pre-trained representations are based on word2vec [18] and GloVe [23] algorithms, and were trained on large corpora.

Inspired by the good results of the deep learning approach, we aim at using these techniques for emotion detection. Pseudo-labeled large-scale data is suitable for deep learning techniques, however, it exhibits low accuracy when classifying domain specific data, even after domain adaptation [20] (using linear models). On the other hand, the manually annotated data is highly accurate, but it is not large enough to form an appropriate base for deep learning techniques, as these models tend to overfit small size datasets. In order to utilize the high quality but small size datasets, we propose an *ensemble* approach that combines both a linear model based on BOW, and a non-linear model based on the pre-trained word vectors. In addition, we propose a new method for realizing a sentence level representation from the single words vectors.

To our knowledge, this is the first research that shows how to utilize pre-trained word vectors to improve emotion detection from text in domain-specific datasets.

2 RELATED WORK

Approaches to categorical emotion classification often employ one-vs-rest machine learning classifiers (a binary classifier for each emotion), typically SVM [19, 25] or logistic regression [32], using textual features such as n-grams, lexicon based, and POS features.

In the domain of sentiment analysis, which is closely related to emotion detection, Tang et al. [30] showed that encoding sentiment information into the word embeddings using Twitter data, as a part of a neural network based system, outperformed previous approaches. [16, 29] focused on generating document level embeddings in sentiment classification. These works all require the availability of large-scale data. In our setting, we only have small datasets, thus, we used pre-trained vectors.

Pre-trained word vectors were used as an input to neural networks to improve sentiment analysis classification [14, 27]. This approach also requires large-scale data for the neural network training. Forgues [10] used pre-trained word vectors and a linear classifier to classify user intents in dialog systems, however their task and methodology is different than ours.

3 EMOTION CLASSIFIERS

In this section we describe the two different classifiers we created and an ensemble method that combines their output. The two classifiers are based on different document representations. Depending on the dataset being used, the classification task can be represented as a multi-class or a multi-label problem. For both types of problems we used a one-vs-rest SVM classifier. Thus, given some test sample, a classifier outputs the decision function value for each emotion that appears in the training data. The classes associated with the test sample are then taken to be the emotion with the highest decision function value (for multi-class) or the set of emotions with a positive decision function value (for multi-label).

3.1 BOW Classifier

In our first approach we used an SVM classifier with a linear kernel, and represented every document as a BOW. We extracted various n-grams (after lemmatization), punctuation and social media features. Namely, unigrams, bigrams, NRC lexicon features (number of terms in a post associated with each affect label in NRC lexicon [22]), and presence of exclamation marks, question marks, usernames, links, happy emoticons, and sad emoticons.

We used TFIDF weights for the values of n-gram features (this was experimentally superior to using binary weights), and removed n-grams that appeared in less than two documents. We further removed 10% of the remaining features that got the lowest scores in a χ^2 statistical test. We handled negation similarly to [24].

3.2 Word Embedding-Based Classifier

Word embedding based vectors can be combined to represent a document into a fixed size vector. We have experimented with several document representations, combining the word vectors, following the notation:

$$d_{we}(t_1, ..., t_k) = \frac{1}{\sum_{i=1}^{k} a_i} \sum_{i=1}^{k} a_i \cdot v(t_i), \qquad (1)$$

where d_{we} is the word embedding based vector representation for document d with k terms, v is some pre-trained word-to-vector mapping (described in Section 5), and a_i is some weight indicating the relative importance of term t_i. The document representations we experimented with include:

CBOW (continuous bag of words) [18]: in this case, $\forall i, a_i = 1$, which means uniform weights for all terms.

TFIDF weights: a_i is the TFIDF weight for term t_i. In case t_i was not present in the training data, we smoothed its IDF weight as if it appeared in one document (this yielded better performance than discarding the term).

Classifier weights (CLASS): in this approach we calculated a weight function, $w(t, e)$ for each term t in the training data which indicates its importance in classifying a document as expressing

emotion e. We did this by first representing the documents in a BOW binary vector representation where we only extracted unigram features. Then, for each e we trained an SVM model with a linear kernel and took $m(e, t)$ to be the weight associated by the model with each term t in the training data. Motivated by Guyon [12] who showed that $|m(e, t)|$ is an indicative feature selection criterion, we define:

$$w(t, e) = \frac{|m(e, t)| - \mu_e}{\sigma_e}, \qquad (2)$$

where μ_e and σ_e are the corresponding average and standard deviation of model weights in absolute value. We now define:

$$a_i = \begin{cases} 1 & t_i \notin V \text{ or } w(t_i, e) < 1 \\ w(t_i, e) & \text{else} \end{cases} \qquad (3)$$

, where V is the vocabulary generated from the training data. In words, a low constant weight is assigned to terms which did not appear in the training data, or were found to be less discriminative. For other terms, the weight is proportional to the words discriminative power. This method captures the notion that some terms in a document are more important in its embedded representation since they are more informative given the classification task. Note that, in this method, a different document representation is used for every emotion e since the discriminative power of every word (and hence its weight a_i) is different for each emotion. This is a novel embedded document representation method, and as detailed in Section 5, it is superior in comparison to the other representation methods we experimented with.

Similarly to our BOW classifier, we used an SVM classifier in this approach as well, but since we represented a document as a low-dimensional vector, we allowed non-linearity by using an RBF kernel. This yielded better results than using a linear kernel.

3.3 Ensemble Methods

Ensembles tend to achieve better results when there is a significant diversity among the classifiers [15]. Thus, we utilized the above classifiers that are based on different document representations, to form an ensemble model. As a preliminary step, we transformed the above classifiers' decision function value output to represent probabilities, using softmax transformation for multi-class problems [8], and sigmoid transformation for multi-label problems. The ensemble methods we experimented with, follow the notation:

$$m_{en}(d) = \alpha \cdot (m_{bow}(d)) + (1 - \alpha) \cdot (m_{we}(d)), \qquad (4)$$

where $m_{en}(d)$ is the output probability vector for the ensemble classifier given a test document d, $m_{bow}(d)$ and $m_{we}(d)$ are the output probability vectors of the BOW and the word embedding based classifiers respectively, and α is a parameter which corresponds to the specific ensemble method used. We have experimented with the following weighed average probabilities methods: equal weights ($\alpha = 0.5$), stacking (α is learned by an additional classifier) and precision-based weighting [3] (α reflects the ratio between the macro precision scores for the two classifiers over the training data). We have found in our setting that precision-based weighting achieved the best performance, thus we report results using this method only.

Dataset	Size	Emotion Classes	Problem	# Annotators
ISEAR	7666	anger, disgust, fear, guilt, joy, sadness, and shame	multi-class	1
SemEval	1250	anger, disgust, fear, happiness, sadness, and surprise	multi-class	6
Fairy Tales	1207	angry-disgusted , fear, happiness, sadness, and surprise	multi-class	6
Blog Posts	4090	anger, disgust, fear, happiness, sadness, surprise, and neutral	multi-class	4
Twitter Dialogs	1056	confusion, frustration, anger, sadness, happiness, hopefulness, disappointment, gratitude, politeness, and neutral	multi-label	5

Table 1: Datasets characteristics.

Dataset	Previous Work	Performance	BOW	Metric
ISEAR	[7]	0.702	**0.712**	accuracy
SemEval	[19]	**0.516**	0.464	macro F1
Fairy Tales	[5]	0.619	**0.691**	accuracy
Blog Posts	[2]	0.739	**0.779**	accuracy
Twitter Dialogs	[13]	0.440	**0.472**	macro F1
Average	-	0.603	**0.624**	-

Table 2: BOW baseline performance comparison with published results using the published metric.

Dataset	Word2Vec			GloVe		
	CBOW	TFIDF	CLASS	CBOW	TFIDF	CLASS
ISEAR	.566	.543	.610	.577	.562	**.620**
SemEval	.477	.486	.482	.495	**.502**	.499
Fairy Tales	.617	.630	.688	.661	.680	**.710**
Blog Posts	.506	.528	.634	.505	.533	**.635**
Twitter Dialogs	.441	.450	.447	.469	**.480**	.479
Average	.521	.528	.572	.541	.551	**.589**

Table 3: Macro F1-scores for each pre-trained word vector source and embedded representation method.

4 DATASETS

We experimented with the following five emotion detection datasets from different domains (summarized in Table 1):

- **ISEAR** [26] contains labeled sentences where participants who have different cultural backgrounds reported experiences and reactions for seven emotions.
- **SemEval** [28] contains newspaper headlines labeled with the six Ekman emotions by six annotators. For our experiments, we considered the most dominant emotion as the headline label as in [19].
- **Fairy Tales** [1] includes sentences from fairy tales, labeled with five emotions by six annotators. For our experiments, we used only sentences with high annotation agreement of four identical emotion labels, as in [5].
- **Blog Posts** [2] consists of emotion-rich sentences collected from blogs labeled with emotions by four annotators. We considered only sentences for which the annotators agreed on the emotion category, as in [2].
- **Customer Support Dialogs in Twitter** [13] consists of customer turns from customer support dialogs in Twitter, labeled by five annotators with nine emotions relevant to customer care.

5 EXPERIMENTS

5.1 Experimental Setup

We tuned the hyper-parameters for our classifiers using a grid search over a validation dataset collected from Twitter, presented in [33]. This process yielded the following hyper-parameter values that we used in all of our experiments below. Penalty parameter for BOW classifier: $C = 0.5$; Penalty and kernel parameters for the word embedding based classifier: $C = 4, \gamma = 0.1$.

We evaluated our methods for each dataset by using 10-fold cross-validation. Our baseline is the BOW classifier described above. This

was used as a state-of-the-art approach for emotion detection in short texts in many cases, e.g., [19, 31] and more.

Emotion detection datasets are labeled with multiple emotions and are imbalanced. Thus, we evaluated the classification performance for all emotion classes by using macro average F1-score. We used scikit-learn [2] for an SVM implementation and spaCy [3] for n-grams extraction.

5.2 BOW Classifier Comparison

We compared our BOW classifier baseline with previous work which presented cross-validation results on the datasets we experimented with. Table 2 shows results presented in the original work that introduced the dataset, or in an advanced work. The table shows that our BOW classifier results correspond to previous work, which validates our baseline's implementation.

5.3 Word Embedding Methods Comparison

We compared the quality of two publicly available pre-trained word vector sources, based on GloVe[4] and Word2Vec (GoogleNews)[5], in terms of emotion detection performance. Vectors from both sources are 300 dimensional.

Table 3 depicts the macro F1-scores for each dataset and each document representation method that is based on word vectors, as detailed in Section 3.2. Results show that for all datasets and representation methods, word vectors trained by GloVe achieved higher performance than using Word2Vec based vectors. For example, on average, CBOW representation for GloVe source showed a 4% improvement in F1-score relative to Word2Vec. Thus, we used GloVe based pre-trained word vectors below. Also, the CLASS method we

---

[2] http://scikit-learn.org/stable/
[3] https://spacy.io/
[4] http://nlp.stanford.edu/data/glove.840B.300d.zip
[5] https://code.google.com/archive/p/word2vec/

Dataset	BOW	EN-CBOW	EN-TFIDF	EN-CLASS
ISEAR	0.617	0.626	0.625	**0.641***
SemEval	0.464	0.516	**0.525***	0.517*
Fairy Tales	0.638	0.700	0.729*	**0.733***
Blog Posts	0.560	0.590	0.612*	**0.663***
Twitter Dialogs	0.472	0.512	**0.522***	0.516*
Average	0.550	0.589	0.603	**0.614**

Table 4: Macro F1-scores for all datasets using ensembles. "*" marks a significantly better model ($p < 0.001$) than the baseline model, using McNemar's test.

proposed outperformed the other embedded document representation methods.

5.4 Ensemble Results

Table 4 depicts the macro F1-scores for each dataset, and for the different models: BOW is our baseline, presented in Section 3.1. EN-CBOW, EN-TFIDF and EN-CLASS are the ensemble models of BOW and the corresponding embedded representations presented in Section 3.2.

Our ensemble methods outperformed the baseline for each document representation method. The best result, which is also significantly better for each dataset, is of EN-CLASS model that achieved an average relative improvement of 11.6% in F1-score over all datasets. These results indicate the advantage in combining both BOW and embedded document representations for emotion detection from text.

6 CONCLUSIONS

This work studied the use of pre-trained word vectors for emotion detection. We presented CLASS, a novel method for representing a document as a dense vector based on the importance of the document's terms in respect to emotion classification. Our results show that an ensemble that combines BOW and embedded representations using our CLASS method, outperforms previous approaches for domain-specific datasets. In comparison to other deep-learning methods, our approach fits a small number of model parameters and requires little computing power.

For Future work we plan to investigate the use of deep learning models trained on domain adapted pseudo-labeled large-scale datasets. We also plan to investigate transfer learning for multi-domain emotion detection.

REFERENCES

[1] Ebba Cecilia Ovesdotter Alm. 2008. *Affect in text and speech*. ProQuest.
[2] Saima Aman and Stan Szpakowicz. 2007. Identifying expressions of emotion in text. In *Text, Speech and Dialogue*. Springer, 196–205.
[3] Alina Andreevskaia and Sabine Bergler. 2008. When Specialists and Generalists Work Together: Overcoming Domain Dependence in Sentiment Tagging.. In *ACL*. 290–298.
[4] Lea Canales and Patricio Martinez-Barco. 2014. Emotion Detection from text: A Survey. *Processing in the 5th Information Systems Research Working Days (JISIC 2014)* (2014), 37.
[5] Soumaya Chaffar and Diana Inkpen. 2011. Using a heterogeneous dataset for emotion analysis in text. In *Advances in Artificial Intelligence*. Springer, 62–67.
[6] Roddy Cowie, Ellen Douglas-Cowie, Nicolas Tsapatsoulis, George Votsis, Stefanos Kollias, Winfried Fellenz, and John G Taylor. 2001. Emotion recognition in human-computer interaction. *Signal Processing Magazine, IEEE* 18, 1 (2001), 32–80.
[7] Taner Danisman and Adil Alpkocak. 2008. Feeler: Emotion classification of text using vector space model. In *AISB 2008 Convention Communication, Interaction and Social Intelligence*, Vol. 1. 53.
[8] Kaibo Duan, S Sathiya Keerthi, Wei Chu, Shirish Krishnaj Shevade, and Aun Neow Poo. 2003. Multi-category classification by soft-max combination of binary classifiers. In *Multiple classifier systems*. Springer, 125–134.
[9] Paul Ekman. 1992. An argument for basic emotions. *Cognition & Emotion* 6, 3-4 (1992), 169–200.
[10] Gabriel Forgues, Joelle Pineau, Jean-Marie Larchevêque, and Réal Tremblay. 2014. Bootstrapping Dialog Systems with Word Embeddings. (2014).
[11] Yoav Goldberg. 2017. Neural Network Methods for Natural Language Processing. *Synthesis Lectures on Human Language Technologies* 10, 1 (2017), 1–309.
[12] Isabelle Guyon and André Elisseeff. 2003. An introduction to variable and feature selection. *The Journal of Machine Learning Research* 3 (2003), 1157–1182.
[13] Jonathan Herzig, Guy Feigenblat, Michal Shmueli-Scheuer, David Konopnicki, Anat Rafaeli, Daniel Altman, and David Spivak. 2016. Classifying Emotions in Customer Support Dialogues in Social Media. In *17th Annual Meeting of the Special Interest Group on Discourse and Dialogue*. 64.
[14] Yoon Kim. 2014. Convolutional Neural Networks for Sentence Classification. *CoRR* abs/1408.5882 (2014).
[15] Ludmila I Kuncheva and Christopher J Whitaker. 2003. Measures of diversity in classifier ensembles and their relationship with the ensemble accuracy. *Machine learning* 51, 2 (2003), 181–207.
[16] Quoc V Le and Tomas Mikolov. 2014. Distributed representations of sentences and documents. *arXiv preprint arXiv:1405.4053* (2014).
[17] Irene Lopatovska and Ioannis Arapakis. 2011. Theories, methods and current research on emotions in library and information science, information retrieval and human–computer interaction. *Information Processing & Management* 47, 4 (2011), 575–592.
[18] Tomas Mikolov, Kai Chen, Greg Corrado, and Jeffrey Dean. 2013. Efficient estimation of word representations in vector space. *arXiv preprint arXiv:1301.3781* (2013).
[19] Saif Mohammad. 2012. Portable features for classifying emotional text. In *Proceedings of NAACL HLT*. 587–591.
[20] Saif M. Mohammad. 2012. #Emotional Tweets. In *Proceedings of the First Joint Conference on Lexical and Computational Semantics - Volume 1: Proceedings of the Main Conference and the Shared Task, and Volume 2: Proceedings of the Sixth International Workshop on Semantic Evaluation (SemEval '12)*.
[21] Saif M Mohammad. 2015. Sentiment analysis: Detecting valence, emotions, and other affectual states from text. *Emotion Measurement* (2015).
[22] Saif M Mohammad and Peter D Turney. 2013. Crowdsourcing a word–emotion association lexicon. *Computational Intelligence* 29, 3 (2013), 436–465.
[23] Jeffrey Pennington, Richard Socher, and Christopher D. Manning. 2014. GloVe: Global Vectors for Word Representation. In *EMNLP*. 1532–1543.
[24] Nataliia Plotnikova, Micha Kohl, Kevin Volkert, Andreas Lerner, Natalie Dykes, Heiko Ermer, and Stefan Evert. 2015. KLUEless: Polarity classification and association. In *Proceedings of the 9th International Workshop on Semantic Evaluation*. 619–625.
[25] Ashequl Qadir and Ellen Riloff. 2014. Learning Emotion Indicators from Tweets: Hashtags, Hashtag Patterns, and Phrases. In *Proceedings of EMNLP*. 1203–1209.
[26] Klaus R Scherer and Harald G Wallbott. 1994. Evidence for universality and cultural variation of differential emotion response patterning. *Journal of personality and social psychology* 66, 2 (1994), 310.
[27] Aliaksei Severyn and Alessandro Moschitti. 2015. UNITN: Training Deep Convolutional Neural Network for Twitter Sentiment Classification. In *Proceedings of the 9th International Workshop on Semantic Evaluation (SemEval 2015)*. 464–469.
[28] Carlo Strapparava and Rada Mihalcea. 2007. Semeval-2007 task 14: Affective text. In *Proceedings of the 4th International Workshop on Semantic Evaluations*. Association for Computational Linguistics, 70–74.
[29] Duyu Tang, Bing Qin, and Ting Liu. 2015. Document Modeling with Gated Recurrent Neural Network for Sentiment Classification. In *Proceedings of the 2015 Conference on Empirical Methods in Natural Language Processing*. 1422–1432.
[30] Duyu Tang, Furu Wei, Nan Yang, Ming Zhou, Ting Liu, and Bing Qin. 2014. Learning Sentiment-Specific Word Embedding for Twitter Sentiment Classification.. In *ACL (1)*. 1555–1565.
[31] Bincy Thomas, KA Dhanya, and P Vinod. 2014. Synthesized feature space for multiclass emotion classification. In *Networks & Soft Computing (ICNSC), 2014 First International Conference on*. IEEE, 188–192.
[32] W. Wang, L. Chen, K. Thirunarayan, and A. P. Sheth. 2012. Harnessing Twitter Big Data for Automatic Emotion Identification. In *Privacy, Security, Risk and Trust (PASSAT), 2012 International Conference on and 2012 International Confernece on Social Computing (SocialCom)*. 587–592.
[33] Yichen Wang and Aditya Pal. 2015. Detecting emotions in social media: a constrained optimization approach. In *Proceedings of the 24th International Conference on Artificial Intelligence*. AAAI Press, 996–1002.

Upper Bound Approximations for BlockMaxWand

Craig Macdonald
University of Glasgow
Glasgow, Scotland, UK
craig.macdonald@glasgow.ac.uk

Nicola Tonellotto
ISTI-CNR
Pisa, Italy
nicola.tonellotto@isti.cnr.it

ABSTRACT

BlockMaxWand is a recent advance on the Wand dynamic pruning technique, which allows efficient retrieval without any effectiveness degradation to rank K. However, while BMW uses docid-sorted indices, it relies on recording the upper bound of the term weighting model scores for each *block* of postings in the inverted index. Such a requirement can be disadvantageous in situations such as when an index must be updated. In this work, we examine the appropriateness of upper-bound approximation – which have previously been shown suitable for Wand– in providing efficient retrieval for BMW. Experiments on the ClueWeb12 category B13 corpus using 5000 queries from a real search engine's query log demonstrate that BMW still provides benefits w.r.t. Wand when approximate upper bounds are used, and that, if approximations on upper bounds are tight, BMW with approximate upper bounds can provide efficiency gains w.r.t. Wand with exact upper bounds, in particular for queries of short to medium length.

KEYWORDS

Wand, BlockMaxWand, upper-bounds approximations

1 INTRODUCTION

The efficiency of a search engine is important, for example to ensure user satisfaction (users will not wait a long time for results), and also to minimise the resources that must be deployed by the search engine (number of servers needed to ensure low response times). A key factor in ensuring such low response time is the layout and traversal strategies of the inverted index underlying the search engine. In this paper, we are concerned with the efficient traversal of docid-sorted inverted index posting lists, as these are more commonly deployed in industry [4], rather than impact sorted postings lists.

Among techniques, the Wand technique [1], and the more recent variant BlockMaxWand (BMW) [6] are advantageous to deploy, as they enable effecient retrieval of K documents without degrading effectiveness to rank K (also known as safe-to-rank K). In particular, Wand and BMW determine the query terms that must be matched for the next document to be retrieved, based on upper bounds of the scores of the query terms, and the score of the current K-th ranked document. Efficiency is therefore enhanced as the decompression

of postings and the scoring of documents that cannot make the current K ranked documents are *skipped*. The advance offered by BMW is that upper bounds are calculated for blocks of postings, offering tighter upper bounds than a single upper bound for the entire posting list, and hence more skipping is achieved.

Upper bounds for a given weighting model are typically calculated by pre-scoring all postings for each query term in the inverted index. However, such pre-calculated upper bounds have disadvantages [8], for instance that they are sensitive to changes in weighting model scores, as might be caused by additions/deletions to the index, or by changes to the weighting model parameters. In [8], the authors proposed *approximations* for upper bounds for Wand, applicable to various weighting models. Such approximations are "less tight" than the exact (empirically-derived) calculated upper bounds, but only require more basic statistics such as the maximum within-document term frequency in each posting list.

However, no previous work has addressed the application of upper bounds for BMW. Hence, in this work, our central contribution is to experiment to address a central research question: are approximations of UBs good enough for efficient retrieval using BMW? The remainder of this paper is as follows: Section 2 provides an overview of the Wand and BMW techniques; Section 3 describes the calculation of exact and approximate upper bounds on term weighting score contributions. In Section 4 we demonstrate and analyse the applicability of approximate upper bounds for BMW. Section 5 provides concluding remarks.

2 QUERY PROCESSING

In document-at-a-time (DAAT) query processing, the query term postings lists are processed in parallel keeping them aligned by docid. The score of each document is computed fully by considering the contributions of all query terms $t \in Q$ before moving to the next document. However, processing queries exhaustively with DAAT can be very inefficient, and therefore various techniques to enhance retrieval efficiency have been proposed, by dynamically pruning docids that are unlikely to be retrieved. Among them, the most popular today is Wand [1]. This processing strategy uses additional information for each term in the form of its maximum score contribution, or *upper bound* $\sigma(t)$, thus allowing to skip large segments of posting lists if they only contain terms whose sum of maximum scores is smaller than the scores of the top K documents found up to that point. Wand relies on upper-bounding the contribution that each term can give to the overall document score, allowing to skip whole ranges of docids [8].

Wand employs a *global* per-term upper bound, that is, the maximum score among *all* documents in a given term's posting list. Such maximum score could be significantly larger than the typical score contribution of that term, in fact limiting the opportunities to skip large amounts of documents. To tackle this problem, Ding and

Suel [6] proposed to augment the inverted index data structures with additional information to store more accurate upper bounds: at indexing time each posting list is split into consecutive blocks of constant size, e.g. 128 postings per block. For each block B the score upper bound $\sigma^B(t)$ is stored, together with largest docid of each block. These *block* term upper bounds can then be exploited by adapting existing algorithms such as Wand to make use of the additional information. The resulting algorithm is BlockMaxWand (BMW) [6]. The authors reported an average query response time reduction of BMW compared to Wand of 64% – 67%. Experiments in [5] reported a reduction of 66% by BMW with respect to Wand. A more recent work [2] explored the performance of BMW compared to Wand on different document collection and different query logs. They reported average reductions up to only 26%. However, for long queries and large collections, Wand outperforms BMW, because of its complex logic for skipping blocks using block upper bounds.

In the following, we discuss how recent advances in determine *approximate* upper bounds can be applied for both Wand and BMW.

3 DEFINING UPPER BOUNDS

As shown in the previous section, both Wand and BMW rely on upper bounds for the maximum contribution of the weighting model for each query term, i.e. $\sigma(t)$ for an entire posting list, or $\sigma^B(t)$ for a block of postings B. In the following, we discuss both the classical empirical evaluation of *exact* upper bounds – by pre-scoring of the index – as well as recent advances in *approximate* upper bounds.

3.1 Exact Upper Bounds

Classically, such upper bounds can be calculated exactly by pre-scoring of each term's postings list $p(t)$:

$$\sigma_{\text{EXACT}}(t) = \max_{d \in p(t)} w(tf_d, l_d) \qquad (1)$$

for some weighting model $w(\cdot, \cdot)$ calculated using the within-document term frequency tf_d and length of document d. These upper bounds are then stored within an augmented inverted index data structure.

However, as highlighted in Section 1, the exact pre-calculation of $\sigma_{\text{EXACT}}(t)$ has some disadvantages:

(1) Adaptation of the weighting model, or its hyper-parameters;
(2) Adaptation of the index, e.g. adding or removing documents, thereby changing global statistics of the index (number of documents, average document length);
(3) Adaptation of a given term's posting list, e.g. adding or removing documents, thereby changing the statistics of the term (e.g. IDF).

Given these disadvantages, the use of pre-calculated exact upper bounds that are stored within an augmented inverted index may not be suitable for some retrieval environments. For this reason, Macdonald et al. [8] investigated the use of approximate upper bounds for Wand. Below, we discuss approximate upper bounds, and their application to Wand and BMW.

3.2 Approximate Upper Bounds

Approximate upper bounds [8] are upper bounds $\sigma_{\text{APPROX}}(t)$ that can be calculated based on raw index statistics. They are designed

to be *safe*, i.e. $\sigma_{\text{APPROX}}(t) \geq \sigma_{\text{EXACT}}(t)$, which means that given in retrieving K documents, effectiveness to rank K will not be negatively impacted (also known as safe-to-rank K). Moreover, the *accuracy* of the approximate upper bounds – the extent that they over-estimate the actual exact upper bound is important: widely inaccurate upper bounds will lead to the unnecessary scoring of documents that could never make the top K retrieved set as their approximate scoring was over-estimated. Hence, the absolute error $\sigma_{\text{APPROX}}(t) - \sigma_{\text{EXACT}}(t)$ should be minimised.

To derive approximate upper bounds for weighting models such as BM25, Dirichlet Language Modelling (LM), and DLH13 from the Divergence from Randomness framework, Macdonald et al. [8] proposed a methodology based on partial differentiation of the weighting models w.r.t. term frequency tf_d and document length l_d.

Indeed, as weighting models are typically monotonically increasing in tf_d (this was characterised as TFC1 in the formalised heuristics identified by Fang et al. [7]), an upper bound is typically found at (or just before) $tf_{\max}$, where $tf_{\max} = \max_{d \in p(t)} tf_d$. Moreover, as longer documents have lower scores (due to document length normalisation, denoted as LNC1 in [7]), for all documents in a posting list, l_d cannot be less than tf_d. Thus an approximate upper bound that is appropriate for a number of weighting models is:

$$\sigma_{\text{APPROX}}(t) = w(tf_{\max}, tf_{\max} + \epsilon) \qquad (2)$$

where ϵ is a small number, required for some weighting models that are not defined when $l_d = tf_d$; $\epsilon = 0$ for BM25 and Dirichlet LM, and $\epsilon = 1$ for DLH13.

As is clear from Equation (2), approximate upper bounds can be easily obtained for models such as BM25 based on storing $tf_{\max}$ alone, a statistic for each term that can be easily calculated and stored within the lexicon structure of the inverted index. It does not require knowledge of the collection's statistics, nor the weighting model hyper-parameter settings that will be applied at retrieval time, and can be easily updated when new documents are added to a term's posting list.

Within the empirical studies reported in [8], approximate upper bounds were found to be suitable for Wand and the simpler MaxScore dynamic pruning technique, but no work has investigated their applicability to the more complex BMW technique, which relies on upper bounds calculated for each block B of postings. Indeed, the central aim of this work is to investigate the usability of approximate upper bounds for blocks in the context of BMW, i.e. $\sigma_{\text{APPROX}}^B(t)$ calculated as per Equation (2), but using the maximum frequency observed in the block of postings, $tf_{\max}^B$. Like those reported in [8] for Wand, our experiments show that the approximations can be used for BMW, but cannot match the efficiency of exact upper bounds. Approximate upper bounds, being greater than exact upper bounds, limit the skipping abilities of BMW, forcing more blocks to processed because their approximate contributions would beat the current top K documents threshold. Nevertheless, we will show that they allow to improve over the efficiency of Wand when using exact upper bounds.

4 EXPERIMENTS

Motivated by the unknown applicability of approximate upper bounds for BMW, in the following, we experiment to address two research questions:

Table 1: Mean query times (in ms) for different weighting models with both exact and approximate upper bounds (denoted ✗ and ✓, resp.). Percentage reductions are shown for BMW w.r.t. Wand, (denoted Δs), and of BMW with approximate upper bounds w.r.t. Wand with exact upper bounds (Γs).

Model	Approx.	$K = 20$				$K = 1000$			
		Wand	BMW	Δ(%)	Γ(%)	Wand	BMW	Δ(%)	Γ(%)
BM25	✗	58.67	38.71	34.02	16.02	113.06	88.46	21.76	8.55
	✓	59.18	49.27	16.75		113.91	103.39	9.24	
LM	✗	172.52	68.72	60.17	44.66	285.00	130.10	54.35	44.10
	✓	217.41	95.47	56.09		359.42	159.31	55.68	
DLH13	✗	139.67	74.42	46.72	-17.40	235.42	137.68	41.52	-4.34
	✓	167.62	163.97	2.18		272.23	245.63	9.77	

RQ1: What is the impact of upper bound approximations on BMW in terms of efficiency?

RQ2: Can we obtain efficiency benefits when using upper bound approximations with BMW w.r.t. Wand when using exact upper bounds?

In the remainder of this section, we define the experimental setup under which our experiments are conducted and we report the results and analysis addressing our two research questions.

All of our experiments are conducted on the TREC ClueWeb12 category B13 corpus[1], which consists of 50M Web documents. We index all 50M documents of the ClueWeb12 corpus using the Terrier IR platform [9], removing stopwords and applying Porter stemming. Our index is compressed using Elias-Fano encoding provided in [11], widely considered to be the state-of-the-art in terms of fast decompression. For the block upper bounds, we assume the standard block size of 128 postings.

For retrieval, we follow best practices in sampling a significant number of queries from a real search engine, namely 5,000 random queries from the MSN 2006 query log [3]. We conduct efficiency timings using a machine equipped with 32 GB RAM and an 8-core Intel i7-4770K processor. The entire index is loaded in memory. All experiments are performed on a single core. While the resulting response times using a single machine for retrieval are marginally higher than would be expected for interactive retrieval in a deployed Web search engine, following previous work [12], this does not detract from the generality of the findings, and avoids the complexities of performing experiments in a distributed retrieval environment.

Table 1 reports the mean response times, in milliseconds for Wand and BMW for $K = 20$ and $K = 1000$, for BM25, Dirichlet LM and DLH13 weighting models, when exact or approximate upper bounds are used. We also note the percentage reduction in mean response times of BMW vs. Wand, denoted Δ(%), and of BMW with approximate upper bounds w.r.t. Wand with exact upper bounds, denoted with Γ(%).

We firstly compare BMW with Wand when using exact upper bounds. Indeed, on analysing Table 1, observe that BMW with exact upper bounds provides clear improvements in mean query times for all weighting models, with greater benefits when K is smaller. In particular, LM obtains reductions in mean response

time, which are > 50%. This is confirmed by the reduction on the total number of postings processed by BMW. These results confirm the findings in [10], where the authors analysed the performance of BMW and Wand in terms of number of processed documents. Indeed, in line with our results, they reported that BMW only marginally improved the performance over Wand for BM25, while BMW markedly boosted the performance when using LM for scoring.

Next, we consider the approximate upper bounds, and observe that using the approximate upper bounds increases the response times of both Wand (as expected from [8]) and also BMW. Moreover, the benefits of BMW over Wand are reduced when approximate upper bounds are used in place of exact upper bounds, both in terms of mean query response times and number of processed postings (e.g. for BM25, $K = 20$, BMW reduces response times by 34% compared to Wand for exact upper bounds, and only 17% for approximate upper bounds). Nevertheless, clear benefits w.r.t. the corresponding Wand processing with approximate upper bounds are still present when documents are evaluated with LM (e.g. for $K = 20$, BMW reduces response times by 60% compared to Wand for exact upper bounds, and 56% for approximate upper bounds). However, when documents are evaluated with DLH13, BMW with approximate upper bounds is marginally worse than Wand with exact upper bounds, with higher losses when K value is small. This loss can be explained by Figure 1, which reports the distribution of the absolute difference between approximate and exact upper bounds for all the blocks associated with query terms, for the different weighting models. BM25 exhibits the best error distribution due to the saturating effect of the Robertson's TF component in BM25 (TFC2 in [7]), the IDF component is dominant for large values of tf_{max}^B. Hence its benefits are limited since the block upper bounds are similar in magnitude to the corresponding term upper bound. For LM, the block upper bounds are not concentrated towards the corresponding term upper bound [10], and the error distribution is skewed towards a small percentage of normalised absolute error. The absolute errors reported for DLH13 are relatively larger than the corresponding errors for other weighting models, i.e. the approximate upper bounds for DLH13 are significantly larger than the corresponding exact upper bounds, causing a large number of blocks to be accessed during query processing that do not contain documents that are retrieved in the final top K set.

Hence, regarding RQ1, we conclude that the use of approximate upper bounds with BMW provides a relatively small performance loss with BM25 and LM, while for DLH13 the upper bound approximations cause a reasonable loss in efficiency w.r.t. exact upper bounds. Nevertheless, BMW still provides benefits w.r.t. Wand when approximate upper bounds are used.

Next, we address RQ2, by comparing the efficiency of BMW with approximate upper bounds versus the efficiency of Wand with exact upper bounds. In doing so, we also make use of Figure 2, which reports the mean, median and errors bars of query times for Wand (with exact upper bounds) and BMW (with exact and approximate upper bounds) for multi-term queries ($K = 20$), broken down by number of terms, for different weighting models. For BM25, BMW with approximate upper bounds provides clear benefits for 2 and 3 terms queries w.r.t. Wand with exact upper bounds, and for LM clear benefits are present also for queries with more terms. As

[1]http://lemurproject.org/clueweb12/

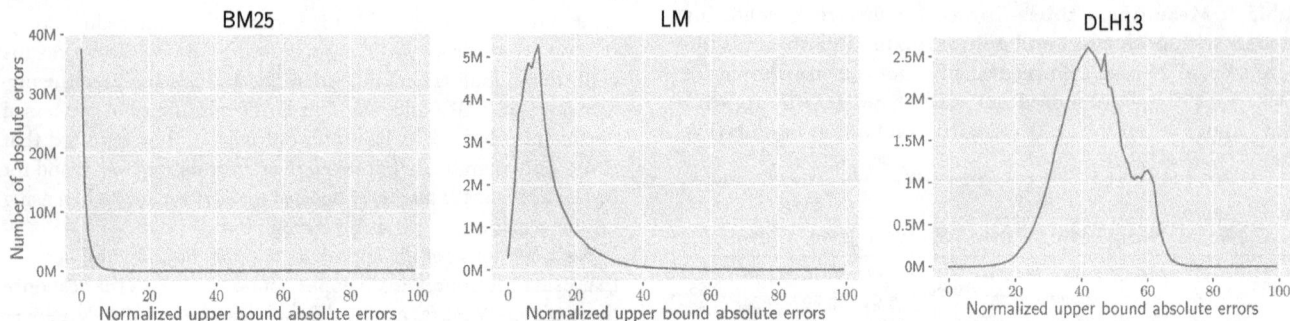

Figure 1: Distribution of block upper bound absolute errors for all the blocks associated with query terms, for different weighting models.

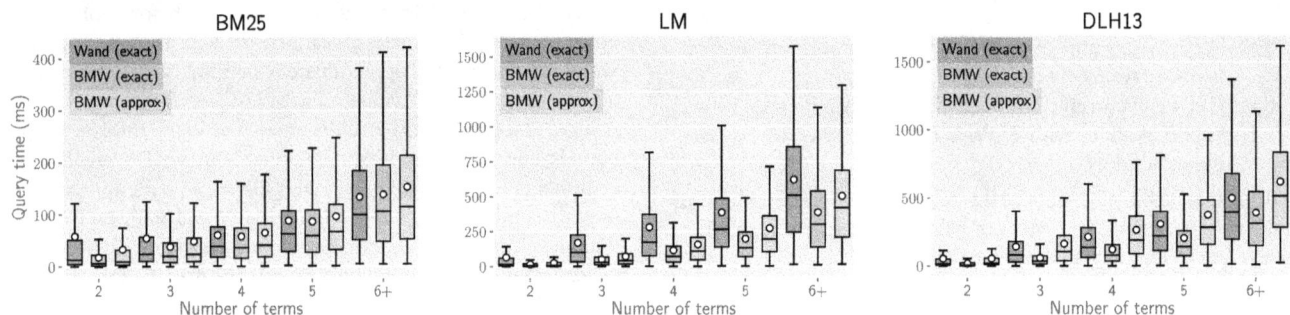

Figure 2: Mean, median and error bars (in ms) for Wand **(with exact upper bounds) and** BMW **(with exact and approximate upper bounds) for multi-term queries ($K = 20$), broken down by number of terms, for different weighting models.**

reported in Table 1 (Γ column), the overall percentage reduction of BMW with approximate upper bounds w.r.t. Wand with exact upper bounds is 8% – 16% for BM25, with larger improvements for the smaller K value, and above 40% for LM, regardless of the value of K. However, DLH13 suffers from the aforementioned approximation looseness, hence it cannot compete with BMW using exact upper bounds. Overall, for RQ2, we conclude that, if approximations of the upper bounds are sufficiently tight, BMW with approximate upper bounds can provide efficiency benefits w.r.t. Wand with exact upper bounds, in particular for queries of short or medium lengths. This is also apparent from Table 1, where we observe BMW is more sensitive to the accuracy of the upper bounds than Wand– indeed, for DLH13, $K = 20$, using approximate upper bounds only slightly degrade the efficiency of Wand (139 $\rightarrow$ 167 ms), it more than doubles the response time of BMW (74 $\rightarrow$ 163 ms). This highlights the importance of tight upper bounds approximations on the resulting efficiency of BMW.

5   CONCLUSIONS

In this paper, we demonstrated the applicability of approximate upper bounds to the BMW, which can result in marked benefits to efficiency compared to Wand using exact upper bounds (up to 44% in the case of LM). This ensures that efficient but safe retrieval can

be attained in scenarios where exact upper bounds cannot be maintained. However, our results also provide insight into the importance of the tightness of the approximate upper bounds for efficient BMW, and how this varies across different weighting models.

REFERENCES

[1] Andrei Z. Broder, David Carmel, Michael Herscovici, Aya Soffer, and Jason Y. Zien. 2003. Efficient query evaluation using a two-level retrieval process. In *CIKM.* 426–434.
[2] Matt Crane, J. Shane Culpepper, Jimmy Lin, Joel Mackenzie, and Andrew Trotman. 2017. A Comparison of Document-at-a-Time and Score-at-a-Time Query Evaluation. In *WSDM.* 201–210.
[3] Nick Craswell, Rosie Jones, Georges Dupret, and Evelyne Viegas (Eds.). 2009. *Proceedings of the Web Search Click Data Workshop at WSDM 2009.*
[4] Jeffrey Dean. 2009. Challenges in building large-scale information retrieval systems: invited talk. In *WSDM.*
[5] Constantinos Dimopoulos, Sergey Nepomnyachiy, and Torsten Suel. 2013. Optimizing Top-k Document Retrieval Strategies for Block-max Indexes. In *WSDM.* 113–122.
[6] Shuai Ding and Torsten Suel. 2011. Faster top-k document retrieval using block-max indexes. In *SIGIR.* 993–1002.
[7] Hui Fang, Tao Tao, and ChengXiang Zhai. 2004. A Formal Study of Information Retrieval Heuristics. In *SIGIR.* 49–56.
[8] Craig Macdonald, Iadh Ounis, and Nicola Tonellotto. 2011. Upper-bound Approximations for Dynamic Pruning. *ACM Trans. Inf. Syst.* 29, 4 (2011), 17:1–17:28.
[9] Iadh Ounis, Gianni Amati, Vassilis Plachouras, Ben He, Craig Macdonald, and Christina Lioma. 2006. Terrier: A High Performance and Scalable IR Platform. In *OSIR.*
[10] Matthias Petri, J. Shane Culpepper, and Alistair Moffat. 2013. Exploring the Magic of WAND. In *ADCS.* 58–65.
[11] Sebastiano Vigna. 2013. Quasi-succinct indices. In *WSDM.* 83–92.
[12] Lidan Wang, Jimmy Lin, and Donald Metzler. 2010. Learning to Efficiently Rank. In *SIGIR.* 138–145.

Merge-Tie-Judge: Low-Cost Preference Judgments with Ties

Kai Hui

Max Planck Institute for Informatics

Saarbrücken Graduate School of Computer Science

Saarbrücken, Germany

khui@mpi-inf.mpg.de

Klaus Berberich

htw saar

Max Planck Institute for Informatics

Saarbrücken, Germany

kberberi@mpi-inf.mpg.de

ABSTRACT

Preference judgments have been demonstrated to yield more accurate labels than graded judgments and also forego the need to define grades upfront. These benefits, however, come at the cost of a larger number of judgments that is required. Prior research, by exploiting the transitivity of preferences, successfully reduced the overall number of preference judgments required to $O(N_d \log N_d)$ for N_d documents, which is still prohibitive in practice. In this work, we reduce the overall number of preference judgments required by allowing for ties and exploiting that ties naturally cluster documents. Our novel judgment mechanism *Merge-Tie-Judge* exploits this "clustering effect" by automatically inferring preferences between documents from different clusters. Experiments on relevance judgments from the TREC Web Track show that the proposed mechanism requires fewer judgments.

ACM Reference format:

Kai Hui and Klaus Berberich. 2017. *Merge-Tie-Judge*: Low-Cost Preference Judgments with Ties. In *Proceedings of ICTIR '17, October 1–4, 2017, Amsterdam, The Netherlands, , 4 pages.*

DOI: http://dx.doi.org/10.1145/3121050.3121095

1 INTRODUCTION

Offline evaluation in information retrieval aims at evaluating rankings of documents from rivaling systems based on a set of test queries. There exist two approaches to collect judgments, namely, graded judgments, where documents are labeled independently with a predefined grade, and preference judgments, where judges provide a relative ranking for a pair of documents. Preference judgments have been demonstrated to be a more robust mechanism than graded judgments [3, 6, 8]. Despite their advantages, they have seen little adoption in practice, and graded judgments remain prevalent. One reason for this is the inherently larger number of judgments required, given that preference judgments need to consider all pairs of documents. By assuming transitivity, this number is reduced to $O(N_d \log N_d)$ [1, 3, 9] for N_d documents, which is still impractical [7] for large N_d. More recently, we [4] demonstrated that the introduction of ties can dramatically reduce the number of judgments, when assuming transitivity. That is, when ties are included, different orders of judgments can lead to different

numbers of judgments. Intuitively, ties cluster documents into a smaller number of tie partitions, where a single tie partition contains documents that are mutually tied. Ideally, one would desire to simultaneously merge the tied documents into several tie partitions, and to judge the preferences among these tie partitions instead of among documents. In this way, the number of judgments can be reduced from $O(N_d \log N_d)$ to $O(N_t \log N_t + N_d)$, where N_t is the number of tie partitions [4].

Inspired by this, we propose a novel labeling mechanism, coined *Merge-Tie-Judge*, to take advantage of the "clustering effect" of ties by dynamically merging documents into tie partitions in the judgment procedure. Akin to Song et al. [10], we assume that transitivity strictly holds, so that preferences can be inferred based on transitivity without incurring conflicts.

Contribution. A novel judgment mechanism is proposed to specifically consume preference judgments with ties, which is more robust than the existing method, and can further reduce the number of judgments required.

2 RELATED WORK

In early work, Rorvig [9] proposed that preference judgments could be used beyond the scaling-based judgments due to the applicability of simple scalability on documents. Since then, the advantages of preference judgments over graded judgments have been empirically tested and confirmed [3, 5, 8, 10]. However, the quadratic nature of the number of judgments required is overwhelming in practice [2]. Therefore, one important topic regarding preference judgments is to reduce the number of judgments. Assuming transitivity among preference judgments, the complexity is reduced from $O(N_d^2)$ to $O(N_d \log N_d)$ [1, 3, 10], by avoiding a full comparison among all document pairs. More recently, we [4] demonstrated that the introduction of ties can further dramatically reduce the number of judgments, when assuming transitivity. They analytically derived and empirically simulated the number of judgments required in preference judgments. They also argued that it is possible to further reduce the number of judgments by merging documents that are judged as ties simultaneously. Ideally, the number of judgments can be reduced from $O(N_d \log N_d)$ to $O(N_t \log N_t + N_d)$, where N_t is the number of tie partitions. Inspired by the theoretical analyses [4], we further propose *Merge-Tie-Judge* which implements this "cluster effects" in this work.

3 METHOD

3.1 Mechanism Framework

In the *Merge-Tie-Judge* mechanism, the "cluster effect" is leveraged explicitly. Intuitively, a cluster of documents grows via incoming tie judgments, by either adding a tied document to it or by merging it with other clusters. The follow-up judgments are made based on these merged clusters, the number of which keeps decreasing as more and more tie judgments are made.

Input *All documents $\mathcal{D}$, document pairs $\mathcal{E}$, initialization of tie probabilities $\mathcal{P}^t$, hyper parameter JudNumber4SVM.*

Output *Sorted clusters of tied documents: $\mathcal{J}ud = \{jud_{ij} = c_i > c_j \text{ or } c_i \prec c_j | c_i, c_j \in C\}$, where $c_. = \{d_i | d_i \in \mathcal{D} \text{ that are tied}\}$.*

/* $C_{>c}$ and $C_{<c}$: sets of clusters that are better or worse than c, initialized as empty.   */

Initialization *Clusters $C = \{c_i = \{d_i\} | d_i \in \mathcal{D}\}$, TranTracker $= \{(c_i, C_{<c}, C_{>c}) | c_i \in C\}$;*

StopCondition $\forall\, c_i, c_j \in C, c_i \prec c_j \text{ or } c_i > c_j \in \mathcal{J}ud$

while *not StopCondition* **do**

  /* Select two clusters for judgment.   */

  if $|\mathcal{J}ud| < $ *JudNumber4SVM* **then**

  | $c_i, c_j, \mathcal{P}^t = ActiveSVM(C, \mathcal{J}ud)$;

  else

  | $c_i, c_j = SelectClusterPair4Judgment(C, \mathcal{P}^t)$;

  end

  $jud_{ij} = ManualJudgment(c_i, c_j)$;

  if jud_{ij} *is* $c_i \sim c_j$ **then**

    /* Merge c_i, c_j into new cluster c_n, and update C.   */

    $C, c_n = MergeClusters(c_i, c_j, C)$

  end

  /* Update $\mathcal{J}ud$, adding incoming and inferred judgments.   */

  $\mathcal{J}ud = UpdateTranTracker(TranTracker, \mathcal{J}ud, jud_{ij})$

  /* Update $\mathcal{P}^t$ for document pairs that are judged, 0 for non-tie and 1 for tie.   */

  $\mathcal{P}^t = UpdateTieProbability(\mathcal{P}^t, \mathcal{J}ud)$

end

Algorithm 1: *Merge-Tie-Judge*

The basic data structure here is the cluster of tied documents, which is initialized with a single document. When collecting judgments, two clusters are merged when at least one document pair from either side is judged as a tie; meanwhile the transitivity relationship for an individual cluster c is tracked with *TranTracker*, recording clusters that are judged better than ($C_{>c}$) or worse than it ($C_{<c}$). When a document pair is judged as a non-tie ($\prec$ or $>$), the transitivity property is applied over all clusters involved, and the *TranTracker* is updated accordingly. For example, if a new judgment indicates $c_i > c_j$, then we need to update *TranTracker* for c_i and c_j, as well as for clusters that are better than c_i, i.e., $c \in C_{>c_i}$, and that are worse than c_j, i.e., $c \in C_{<c_j}$, adding $jud_{ij} = c_i > c_j$ as well as the inferred pairwise judgments to $\mathcal{J}ud$, namely, $\{jud_{kl} = c_k > c_l | c_k \in C_{>c_i}, c_l \in C_{<c_j}\}$.

Another important data structure is $\mathcal{P}^t$, which tracks an estimate of the probability of being tied for every pair of clusters, and

$\mathcal{P}^t_{ij} = P(c_i \sim c_j)$. During iterations, the next cluster pair to judge is selected according to $\mathcal{P}^t$: the cluster pair with the largest tie probability is chosen for judgment. It could be initialized randomly or based on prior knowledge, which is introduced in next section. After initialization, we keep updating $\mathcal{P}^t$ to reflect new judgments, and to compute tie probabilities among emerging clusters. In *UpdateTieProbability*, the tie probability between two emerging clusters is computed as the sum of the tie probability between old cluster pairs residing in either side. This aggregation represents the union of the involved document pairs are tied. Thus, the larger the clusters, the more likely they are picked out for judgment.

3.2 ActiveSVM for Tie Inference

As mentioned, the tie probability $\mathcal{P}^t$ introduced above can be initialized randomly. We argue that manual judgment procedure is special in the sense that it is too expensive to repeat dozens of times in practice. Thereby, the average number of judgments could be misleading, especially when the variance is large. In other words, though the average number of judgments is acceptable, the judgment mechanism may still result in an extreme large number of judgments in practice. Therefore, we propose to reduce the variance by introducing a predictor, i.e., $ActiveSVM(C, \mathcal{J}ud)$ in Algorithm 1. The prediction function will be triggered when positive *JudNumber4SVM* is set. The prediction can be cast as a supervised binary classification problem, where an ActiveSVM method is employed to initialize $\mathcal{P}^t$ to encode the prior knowledge.

Active Support Vector Machine. The support vector machine (SVM) is employed to make predictions. A document pair d_i, d_j is denoted as p_{ij}, meanwhile its corresponding label is $y_{ij} = 0$ or 1, corresponding to non-tie and tie. The classification problem aims at learning the function between the feature vector of each pair, i.e., $\Phi(p_{ij})$, and the binary label. Given that the ultimate target is to collect labels over document pairs with fewer manual judgments, the number of judgments for making prediction is desired to be small. Henceforth, the *ActiveSVM* with **Ratio Margin** strategy proposed by Tong and Koller [11] is used, which is designed to approach the optimized hyperplane with a small number of labeled data points. In each iteration, for each unlabeled document pair, two new classifiers w_+ and w_- are trained by hypothetically assigning the document pair a positive (tie) or a negative judgment (non-tie) respectively. The next pair to label is selected according to ratio between m_+ and m_-, by picking out $min(\frac{m_+}{m_-}, \frac{m_-}{m_+})$, where $m_.$ is the sum of margins of the classifier defined as follows.

$$m_+ = \sum_{p_{ij} \in \text{Support Vectors}} w_+ \Phi(p_{ij})$$

$$m_- = \sum_{p_{ij} \in \text{Support Vectors}} w_- \Phi(p_{ij})$$

4 EVALUATION

We now describe the experiments to examine the proposed *Merge-Tie-Judge* mechanism by comparing it with *Quick-Sort-Judge* [10]. To empirically compare the number of judgments from graded judgments and from preference judgments, we equivalently answer a question: "to approach the same ground truth generated with the graded judgments from TREC, how many judgments are required with preference judgments". We denote this number as *equivalent judgment number* (EquJn). As discussed in Section 3.2, we further examine the robustness of the proposed mechanism.

4.1 Evaluation Setting

Our experiments are based on 2011–2014 Trec Web Track's[1] queries and the corresponding labeled documents (qrel) for adhoc tasks, including 200 queries and 64k graded judgments. Only the judged documents are considered in this work. The judgments from Trec contain at most six relevance levels: junk pages (*Junk*), non-relevance (*NRel*), relevance (*Rel*), high relevance (*HRel*), key pages (*Key*) and navigational pages (*Nav*), corresponding to six graded levels, i.e., -2, 0, 1, 2, 3, 4. The concrete assignments varied from year to year, where *Junk* and *NRel* are always merged as *NRel* in this work, given the limited occurrences of *Junk* judgments (less than 5%). To employ the system rankings from rivaling systems as features in *ActiveSVM*, we also obtained the runs submitted by participants of the Trec Web Track. There are 62 runs from 2011, 48 runs from 2012, 61 runs from 2013, and 42 runs from 2014.

Collecting preference judgments. Ideally, we should rejudge the documents with preference judgments and compare them with the original graded judgments from Trec. Given the unaffordable number of document pairs to judge, instead, we employ the existing graded judgments from the Trec Web Track to create preference judgments in a straightforward manner. In particular, the preference judgments are created for two documents according to the comparison of their graded judgments, namely, if the label for d_1 is l_1 and the label for d_2 is l_2, the preference between these two documents is $d_1 > d_2$ when $l_1 > l_2$; $d_1 \sim d_2$ when $l_1 = l_2$ and $d_1 < d_2$ otherwise. In this way, after collecting judgments for all document pairs, we can simulate the same ground truth from graded judgments. Note that, in practice, it is unlikely to create exactly the same ground truth from judgments collected with different methods. This setting is mainly for allowing comparisons between preference and graded judgments under the same conditions, and also for guaranteeing the same amount of ranking information is collected by different competing mechanisms.

Competing mechanisms. The number of judgments with graded judgments is simply the total number of documents to judge, denoted as #Document. As a comparisons, we implement *Quick-Sort-Judge* (QSJ) from Song et al. [10]. The *Quick-Sort-Judge* is similar to a randomized *QuickSort* method, where, during each iteration, a document is randomly chosen as a pivot document. Thereafter, all remaining documents are grouped into worse than (<), better than (>) or tied with (~) per manual judgments. The mechanism terminates when all documents have been recursively sorted, and the results are based on 300 repetitions.

We examine the proposed *Merge-Tie-Judge* (MTJ), where ActiveSVM is used to initialize $\mathcal{P}^t$ as described in Section 3.2. We employ rankings from different systems in Trec as features to train ActiveSVM. In our preliminary experiments, the optimal setting of *JudNumber4SVM* varies a lot over different queries, as results of the difference of the quality of system rankings (features) and of the instinct difficulty to make prediction etc.. Therefore, we further demonstrate that the number of judgments over one year

[1]http://trec.nist.gov/tracks.html

is robust within a range of settings for *JudNumber4SVM* $\in [5, 35]$. In addition, we also include the variants of *Merge-Tie-Judge* when initialized $\mathcal{P}^t$ randomly, namely, employing random probability in place of ActiveSVM, and denote it as *Merge-Tie-Judge-Random* (*MTJR*), whose results are also based on 300 repeats.

4.2 Equivalent Number of Judgments

In this section, we examine the *equivalent judgment number* from different competing mechanisms. The results for *Merge-Tie-Judge* and its comparison relative to *Quick-Sort-Judge* are summarized in Table 1. For *Merge-Tie-Judge*, we report the results under the average, best, and worst situations with different *JudNumber4SVM* in Table 1. We can see that the number of judgments is reduced significantly by 5.9%, 6.8% and 4.7% under average, best, and worst situations respectively, in comparison with *Quick-Sort-Judge*. Beyond that, the results from Merge-Tie-Judge, together with Merge-Tie-Judge-Random and *Quick-Sort-Judge* are visualized in Figure 1, where different mechanisms are reported in terms of mean, minimum, maximum, and the 95% confidence interval. We can see that there is no overlap of the 95% confidence interval from two variants of *Merge-Tie-Judge* and the one from *Quick-Sort-Judge*. Therefore, we can conclude that in terms of the number of judgments, both *Merge-Tie-Judge* and *Merge-Tie-Judge-Random* are significantly better than *Quick-Sort-Judge*.

4.3 Robustness

As mentioned, the robustness of the judgment mechanism is also important. Especially, one may desire, even in the worst case, the number of judgments from a mechanism still to be close to the number of judgments on average. From Figure 1, *Quick-Sort-Judge* fails to meet this expectation since the largest number of judgments could be multiple times larger. We report the coefficient of variation (Cv) to quantify the robustness in Table 1, which equals the ratio of the standard deviation to the mean. We can see that *Merge-Tie-Judge* is much more robust among a wide range of *JudNumber4SVM*, and the coefficient of variance is only 3.2% of the one from *Quick-Sort-Judge*. In addition, in Figure 1, from the distance between minimum and maximum number of judgments, as well as from the length of their confidence interval, it is obvious that both *Merge-Tie-Judge* are much more robust. Finally, compared with *Merge-Tie-Judge-Random*, *Merge-Tie-Judge* enjoy a better robustness with *ActiveSVM*, reducing the possible number of judgments into a small range.

5 DISCUSSION

The transitivity has been examined among weak preference judgments via crowdsourcing [5]. It has been demonstrated that transitivity holds for only 75% document triples. However, from Table 2 therein, it can be also seen that it is among tie judgments the transitivity does not hold, namely, only 32% of document triples are transitive. Whereas, for the remaining situations, the transitivity still holds for more than 90% of document triples. In other words, given $d_1 > d_2, d_2 > d_3$, no matter whether ties are allowed or not, one can always infer that $d_1 > d_3$ with transitivity. Similarly, given $d_1 > d_2, d_2 \sim d_3$, in more than 90% situations, one can infer that $d_1 > d_3$. However, given three document $d_1 \sim d_2$ and $d_2 \sim d_3$, one can not infer that $d_1 \sim d_3$, because they are not transitive anymore.

Table 1: *Equivalent judgment number* when using *Quick-Sort-Judge (QSJ)* and *Merge-Tie-Judge* with *ActiveSVM*. The statistics reported are based on *JudNumber4SVM* ∈ [5, 35]. Both absolute number of judgment (EquJn) and the relative comparison with document number (% more) are reported for average, best (minimum number of judgments) and worst (maximum number of judgments) situations. The number in the bracket is the relative reduction w.r.t. mean value in *QSJ*. The coefficient of variation (Cv) is reported in the rightmost column.

Year	Average EquJn	% more	Best EquJn	% more	Worst EquJn	% more	Cv	QSJ	% more	Cv	#Document
Wt11	23,818 (5.2%)	22.9%	23,680 (5.7%)	22.2%	23,977 (4.6%)	23.7%	0.0027	25,122	29.6%	0.159	19,381
Wt12	21,087 (6.7%)	31.3%	20,845 (7.7%)	29.8%	21,289 (5.8%)	32.6%	0.0046	22,587	40.7%	0.176	16,055
Wt13	19,557 (6.4%)	35.1%	19,365 (7.3%)	33.8%	19,887 (4.8%)	37.4%	0.0055	20,897	44.4%	0.167	14,474
Wt14	21,106 (5.5%)	46.3%	20,887 (6.5%)	44.8%	21,546 (3.5%)	49.3%	0.0083	22,331	54.8%	0.154	14,429
Summary	85,568 (5.9%)	33.0%	84,777 (6.8%)	31.8%	86,699 (4.7%)	34.8%	-	90,937	41.3%	-	64,339

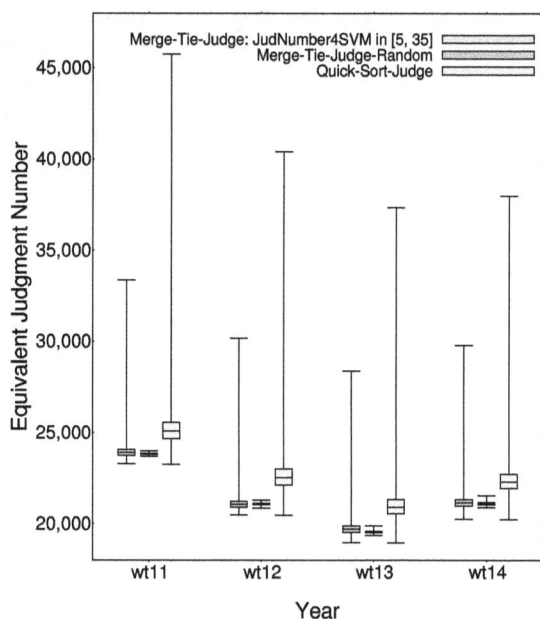

Figure 1: Comparison of number of judgments from different mechanisms. The x-axis is different years and y-axis represents the *equivalent judgment number*. The fewer *equivalent judgment number* the better. *Quick-Sort-Judge* is reported as a baseline; *Merge-Tie-Judge*, which implements *ActiveSVM*, and *Merge-Tie-Judge-Random* are both reported. For random mechanism, the mean, minimum, maximum as well as the 95% confidence interval are plotted.

As mentioned, this is due to the effects that it is hard to tell whether two documents should be judged as tied or non-tied, when their relevance are very close [5].

On the other hand, in *Merge-Tie-Judge*, non-ties are used to determine the relative order of tie partitions or of documents, meanwhile ties are used to grow the tie partitions. Given the degraded transitivity brought by ties, one can regard such tie partitions as documents, among which the mutual preferences are not of interest, and only the strict preferences among tie partitions are employed for evaluation. Recall that we [5] demonstrated the quality from weak preferences is significantly better than the one from graded

judgments. Thus judgment mechanisms employing ties, like *Merge-Tie-Judge* and Quick-Sort-Judge [10], actually exchange 33% more judgments relative to graded judgments (Table 1) for a better judgment quality. Should one desire to collect strict preferences among all documents, which has the best judgment quality, at least 800% more judgments have to be made [4].

6 CONCLUSION

In this work, a robust judgment mechanism, named *Merge-Tie-Judge*, is proposed, utilizing the "cluster effect" of tie judgments, bringing down the number of judgments. For future work, in awareness of the importance of ties, they are worth being carefully defined and exploited to make them more applicable. Moreover, novel judgment mechanisms are desired, addressing the conflicts among preference judgments by tolerating intransitive judgments.

REFERENCES

[1] N. Ailon and M. Mohri. An efficient reduction of ranking to classification. *arXiv preprint arXiv:0710.2889*, 2007.

[2] M. Bashir, J. Anderton, J. Wu, P. B. Golbus, V. Pavlu, and J. A. Aslam. A document rating system for preference judgements. In *Proceedings of the 36th international ACM SIGIR conference on Research and development in information retrieval*, pages 909–912. ACM, 2013.

[3] B. Carterette, P. N. Bennett, D. M. Chickering, and S. T. Dumais. Here or there: Preference Judgments for Relevance. In *Advances in Information Retrieval*, ECIR '08, pages 16–27. Springer, 2008.

[4] K. Hui and K. Berberich. Low-cost preference judgment via ties. In *Advances in Information Retrieval*, ECIR '17, pages 626–632. Springer, 2017.

[5] K. Hui and K. Berberich. Transitivity, time consumption, and quality of preference judgments in crowdsourcing. In *Advances in Information Retrieval*, ECIR '17, pages 239–251. Springer, 2017.

[6] G. Kazai, N. Craswell, E. Yilmaz, and S. Tahaghoghi. An analysis of systematic judging errors in information retrieval. In *Proceedings of the 21st ACM International Conference on Information and Knowledge Management*, CIKM '12, pages 105–114, New York, NY, USA, 2012. ACM.

[7] S. Niu, J. Guo, Y. Lan, and X. Cheng. Top-k learning to rank: labeling, ranking and evaluation. In *Proceedings of the 35th international ACM SIGIR conference on Research and development in information retrieval*, pages 751–760. ACM, 2012.

[8] K. Radinsky and N. Ailon. Ranking from pairs and triplets: Information quality, evaluation methods and query complexity. In *Proceedings of the Fourth ACM International Conference on Web Search and Data Mining*, WSDM '11, pages 105–114, New York, NY, USA, 2011. ACM.

[9] M. E. Rorvig. The simple scalability of documents. *Journal of the American Society for Information Science*, 41(8):590, 1990.

[10] R. Song, Q. Guo, R. Zhang, G. Xin, J.-R. Wen, Y. Yu, and H.-W. Hon. Select-the-best-ones: A new way to judge relative relevance. *Information processing & management*, 47(1):37–52, 2011.

[11] S. Tong and D. Koller. Support vector machine active learning with applications to text classification. *The Journal of Machine Learning Research*, 2:45–66, 2002.

Evaluating and Analyzing Click Simulation in Web Search

Stepan Malkevich
St. Petersburg State University
St. Petersburg, Russia
stepamalkevich@yandex.ru

Ilya Markov
University of Amsterdam
Amsterdam, The Netherlands
i.markov@uva.nl

Elena Michailova
St. Petersburg State University
St. Petersburg, Russia
e.mikhaylova@spbu.ru

Maarten de Rijke
University of Amsterdam
Amsterdam, The Netherlands
derijke@uva.nl

ABSTRACT

We evaluate and analyze the quality of click models with respect to their ability to simulate users' click behavior. To this end, we propose distribution-based metrics for measuring the quality of click simulation in addition to metrics that directly compare simulated and real clicks. We perform a comparison of widely-used click models in terms of the quality of click simulation and analyze this quality for queries with different frequencies. We find that click models fail to accurately simulate user clicks, especially when simulating sessions with no clicks and sessions with a click on the first position. We also find that click models with higher click prediction performance simulate clicks better than other models.

CCS CONCEPTS

•**Information systems** →**Web search engines**; **Information retrieval**; **Retrieval models and ranking**;

1 INTRODUCTION

Simulation has long played a role in information retrieval (IR). Queries have been simulated [2] and so have labeled test collection [3]. Several recent workshops and tutorials have focused on simulating user interactions and search behavior; see, e.g., [1]. Simulating user search behavior in information retrieval and web search is crucial not only for academic researchers, who may not have access to large-scale search logs, but also for commercial systems, where online experiments with real users cannot scale infinitely. Clicks are a particularly important aspect of online user behavior; clicks are widely used both to evaluate the quality of search [13], as a predictive signal [8], and to improve the quality of search [15].

To simulate clicks, researchers and practitioners use clicks models [6, 16]. For example, such simulated clicks have been recently used in interleaving experiments [7, 14]. Little attention has been given to the problem of click simulation on its own and to measuring the quality of this simulation [16]. It is not clear, for instance,

which click models simulate clicks better and why, i.e., what theoretical properties of click models affect the quality of click simulation. In this paper we fill this gap by evaluating and analyzing the simulation quality of the most widely-used and well-performing click models, namely, DBN [5], CCM [12] and UBM [10].

Our contributions are the following. First, we propose to consider distribution-based metrics to measure the quality of click simulation in addition to metrics that directly compare simulated and real clicks. Second, we perform a thorough comparison of the above-mentioned click models in terms of the quality of click simulation.

2 RELATED WORK

Click simulation is used to either evaluate the quality of click models [16, 17] or to simulate online experiments in cases where real users are not available [7, 14]. Zhu et al. [17] simulated clicks to estimate the query-document CTR and then compared this estimated CTR to the real CTR value. Xing et al. [16] directly evaluated click simulation by calculating the mean average error (MAE) between the ranks of the first/last simulated clicks and the ranks of the real clicks. In this work we take a close look at click simulation and follow the latter approach to evaluate the simulation quality. In addition, we propose distribution-based measures for evaluation of click simulation.

Hofmann et al. [14] proposed probabilistic interleaving and used simulated clicks to evaluate the proposed method. Similarly, Chuklin et al. [7] simulated clicks to evaluate vertical-aware interleaving. However, the quality of click simulation itself was not taken into account. In this work, we aim to directly evaluate this quality, which will further inform and support various applications of click simulation.

3 BACKGROUND

Click models. We consider click models that have been shown to have the best performance in terms of modeling and predicting clicks [6]: the user browsing model (UBM) [10], the dynamic Bayesian network model (DBN) [5], and the click chain model (CCM) [12].

The UBM model includes two types of parameters: (i) the probability $\gamma_{rr'}$ of examining a snippet of a search result, which depends on the rank r of the result and on the rank r' of the previously clicked result, and (ii) the probability α_{qd} of snippet d being attractive to a user given query q. According to UBM, a snippet is clicked if, and only if, it is both examined and attractive, i.e., with

ICTIR'17, October 1–4, 2017, Amsterdam, Netherlands.
© 2017 ACM. ISBN 978-1-4503-4490-6/17/10...$15.00
DOI: https://doi.org/10.1145/3121050.3121096

probability $\gamma_{rr'}\alpha_{qd}$. UBM was reported to outperform DBN and CCM in terms of log-likelihood and perplexity [6, 11].

DBN considers not only the attractiveness probability of a snippet α_{qd}, but also the satisfactoriness probability σ_{qd} of the actual search result d after it is clicked. DBN follows the cascade assumption [9] and assumes that a user examines a snippet at rank r with probability γ if, and only if, she examined a snippet at rank $r-1$ and was not satisfied with it (this happens with probability $1 - \alpha_{qd}\sigma_{qd}$). Similarly, according to UBM, a snippet is clicked if, and only if, it is both examined and attractive, where the examination probability is calculated recursively.

The CCM model also contains the set of attractiveness parameters α_{qd} and, similarly to DBN, follows the cascade assumption. CCM introduces three examination parameters $\tau_1-\tau_3$ that determine the examination probability for a snippet at rank r based on the examination and attractiveness of the snippet at rank $r-1$. Just as before, a snippet is clicked if, and only if, it is both examined and attractive.

Click simulation. We simulate clicks using Algorithm 1, as described in [6]. For each rank r (line 1) the algorithm calculates

---

Algorithm 1 Simulating user clicks for a query session.

Input: click model M, query session s
Output: vector of simulated clicks $(c_1, \ldots, c_n)$
1: **for** $r \leftarrow 1$ *to* $|s|$ **do**
2:     Compute $p = P(C_r = 1 \mid C_1 = c_1, \ldots, C_{r-1} = c_{r-1})$ using previous clicks $c_1, \ldots, c_{r-1}$ and the parameters of model M
3:     Generate random value c_r from $Bernoulli(p)$

---

the probability p of clicking on that rank, given all previous clicks $c_1, \ldots, c_{r-1}$ (line 2). This probability is calculated using a click model M; all click models are able to calculate the conditional probability of a click on a result using previously observed clicks in the same query session. Based on the obtained conditional click probability p the algorithm generates a random value from a Bernoulli distribution with parameter p (line 3). This random value indicates the presence of a click. If it equals 1, then model M simulates a click, otherwise model M simulates the absence of a click.

4 EVALUATION METRICS

The quality of click simulation is usually measured by comparing real clicks and simulated clicks. In particular, Xing et al. [16] measure the mean absolute error (MAE) in predicting the first clicked rank and the last clicked rank. We consider these metrics in our work. Note that for sessions without clicks we assume that the rank of the first/last click is zero.

At the same time, we argue that directly comparing real and simulated clicks is too strict and a good click simulator does not necessarily have to have (and even should not have) low MAE of the first/last clicked rank. Consider that we observe two sessions for the same query. In the first session we observe a click at some rank, while in the second session we do not observe any click. Assume that a click simulator simulates an opposite situation: no clicks in the first session and a click at the same rank in the second session. In this case, MAE will be large, because, strictly speaking, the clicks

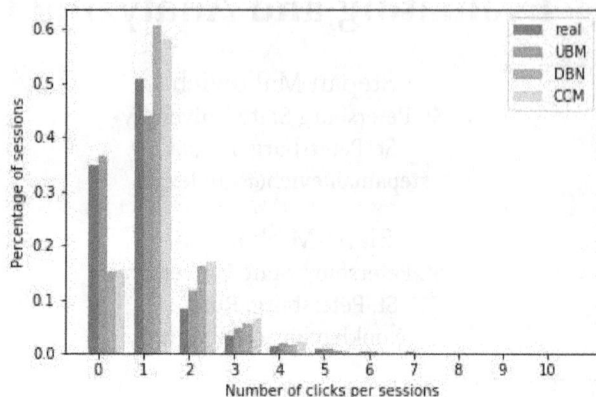

(a) Distributions of clicks over sessions.

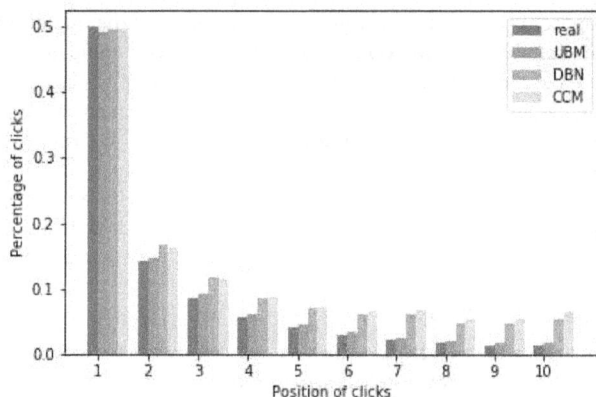

(b) Distribution of clicks over ranks.

Figure 1: Click distributions considered in this paper.

are not simulated correctly. On the other hand, the distribution of clicks among sessions and over ranks is preserved. Moreover, we argue that a realistic click simulator must preserve the distribution of clicks and should not necessarily simulate exactly same clicks in exactly same sessions. Therefore, we propose to measure the Kullback-Leibler divergence between the distribution of real clicks and the distribution of simulated clicks in addition to measuring MAE of the first/last clicked ranks.

There are two natural click distributions to look at. First, the distribution of clicks over sessions (see Figure 1(a)), which shows the percentage of sessions with a certain number of clicks. Second, the distribution of clicks over ranks (see Figure 1(b)), which shows how many times a certain rank was clicked.

Note that directly measuring the KL-divergence between the real and simulated distribution of clicks does not give any meaningful information. Consider the following example. The actual clicks for a query q_1 are $[1, 0, 1, 0, 0, 0, 0, 0, 0, 0]$, while a simulator predicts $[0, 1, 0, 1, 0, 0, 0, 0, 0, 0]$. For a query q_2 the situation is reversed: the actual clicks are $[0, 1, 0, 1, 0, 0, 0, 0, 0, 0]$, while the predicted clicks are $[1, 0, 1, 0, 0, 0, 0, 0, 0, 0]$. In this case, the global KL-divergence between the distribution of real clicks and the distribution of simulated clicks is 0.0, while the simulation is actually wrong. For this reason, we measure a local KL-divergence for every query and then calculate a weighted average of local divergences as follows:

$$KL\text{-}div = \frac{\sum_{q \in Q} KL\text{-}div(q) \cdot s_q}{\sum_{q \in Q} s_q} \qquad (1)$$

where Q is the number of unique queries and s_q is the number of sessions observed for a particular query q. We calculate this metric for both click distributions: distribution over sessions and distribution over ranks. Lower values of the metrics denote better click simulation performance.

5 EXPERIMENTAL SETUP

Dataset. In our experiments, we use a publicly available click log published by Yandex[1] within the personalized web search challenge.[2] This click log consists of 27 days of search activity, where each day contains more than 2 million query sessions (2,413,800 on average). We split the data in two parts: first 14 days for training and last 13 days for testing. We train click models on all query sessions of the first 14 days (33,310,079 sessions). Due to limited computational resources we measure the quality of click simulation on the first 100K query sessions of each test day, which results in 1,300,000 sessions for testing. Since query sessions are independent and their order within a day is not specified, using the first 100K sessions of a day is equivalent to considering random sessions.

Baselines. We compare the simulation performance of the DBN, CCM and UBM models to the following naïve baselines: (i) always simulate no clicks (**baseline 1**), and (ii) always simulate a click on the first position (**baseline 2**). We considered these simple simulators as baselines due to specific properties of the data: 35% of the test sessions have no clicks and 51% of the test sessions have a click on the first position.

6 EXPERIMENTAL RESULTS AND ANALYSIS

In this section we first compare the click simulation performance of the UBM, DBN and CCM click models to that of the baselines presented above. Then we discuss the relative performance of click models compared to each other.

Baselines vs. click models. Table 1 summarizes the simulation performance of the click models and baselines in terms of the MAE of the first/last clicked rank and the KL-divergence of the click distribution over sessions (session-based KL) and over ranks (rank-based KL).

Table 1 shows that Baseline 2, which always simulates a click on the first position, achieves the best performance in terms of all metrics. This is not surprising as 51% of the sessions in the test set contain a click on the first position. An interesting result here is that advanced click models, such as UBM, DBN and CCM, cannot simulate sessions with a click on the first position as accurate as Baseline 2.

Baseline 1, which simulates no clicks, performs worse than Baseline 2, because there are fewer sessions without clicks (35%) than with a click on the first position (51%). Baseline 1 also outperforms the click models in terms of all but one metric, which means that the considered click models cannot accurately simulate sessions

Table 1: Simulation performance of click models.

Model	MAE		KL-divergence	
	First rank	Last rank	Session-based	Rank-based
Baseline 1	0.97	1.36	1.79	1.63
Baseline 2	0.69	1.18	1.61	0.85
UBM	0.96	1.69	1.84	1.26
DBN	1.55	2.34	1.94	1.44
CCM	1.54	2.42	1.99	1.43

without clicks either. (The rank-based KL-divergence of Baseline 1 is worse than that of the click models, because this baseline does not simulate any click at any rank).

In Tables 2 and 3 we take a closer look at the click simulation quality for queries with different frequencies: frequent queries with more than 100 sessions, torso queries with 10–100 sessions and rare queries with 1–10 sessions. Here the situation is slightly different. Baseline 2 is still the best in almost all cases, apart from the session-based KL-divergence for frequent queries (Table 3). Baseline 1 is better than click models in terms of MAE, but not in terms of KL-divergence for frequent and torso queries.

Overall, naïve baselines almost always outperform advanced click models in terms of both MAE and KL-divergence apart from some cases for frequent and torso queries. These results suggest the following. First, click models cannot accurately simulate sessions with no clicks and with a click on the first position, which is crucial in a web search scenario, where such sessions comprise the majority of cases. Ways of improving the simulation accuracy of click models in these cases should be considered. Second, the metrics used in this study do not take into account the "usefulness" of simulated clicks. Naïve baselines that always simulate the same click pattern are not useful in practical applications, such as training a ranker using clicks.

Table 2: MAE of the first/last clicked rank for queries with different frequencies.

Model	Frequent (100+)		Torso (10–100)		Rare (1–10)	
	First	Last	First	Last	First	Last
Baseline 1	0.93	1.12	0.97	1.28	0.99	1.51
Baseline 2	0.52	0.76	0.68	1.07	0.78	1.45
UBM	0.72	1.12	0.92	1.53	1.12	2.06
DBN	1.07	1.55	1.44	2.10	1.85	2.89
CCM	1.07	1.58	1.44	2.16	1.84	3.00

Table 3: Session- and rank-based KL-divergence for queries with different frequencies.

Model	Frequent (100+)		Torso (10–100)		Rare (1–10)	
	Session	Rank	Session	Rank	Session	Rank
Baseline 1	0.0046	0.0211	0.08	0.35	3.67	3.18
Baseline 2	0.0021	0.0017	0.05	0.05	3.33	1.74
CCM	0.0008	0.0048	0.07	0.15	4.12	2.88
DBN	0.0007	0.0046	0.06	0.15	4.02	2.91
UBM	0.0007	0.0019	0.06	0.11	3.80	2.55

Relative performance of click models. First, it has to be noted that the mean absolute errors for the UBM model, presented in Table 1, are higher than those reported in [16]. We believe this is because we use a different dataset compared to [16].

Second, it is clear that UBM simulates clicks better than DBN and CCM in terms of both MAE and KL-divergence. This also holds for all query frequencies (see Tables 2 and 3). UBM was reported to outperform DBN and CCM in terms of click prediction performance, measured by log-likelihood and perplexity [6, 11]. Although there is an intuitive relation between the quality of click prediction and the quality of click simulation, this intuition has not been confirmed so far. Our results show that indeed the best-performing click model in terms of log-likelihood and perplexity is also the best-performing click simulator in terms of MAE and KL-divergence.

Third, Tables 1–3 show that DBN and CCM perform similarly to each other in terms of click simulation. They were also shown to have similar log-likelihood and perplexity when predicting clicks [6, 11]. This further confirms the above discussion.

Finally, Tables 2 and 3 show that click models simulate clicks best for frequent queries and worst for rare queries. This is a known limitation of click models: they do not perform well for rare queries [11]. Our results confirm that this also holds for click simulation.

Overall, our results confirm the intuition that a click model with better log-likelihood and perplexity in a click prediction task should also simulate clicks better.

7 CONCLUSION

We considered the problem of click simulation in web search and studied the ability of click models to simulate clicks. To measure the quality of click simulation, we used metrics that directly compare real and simulated clicks and proposed to use distribution-based metrics that compare the distributions of real and simulated clicks. We compared the simulation quality of the best-performing and widely-used click models, namely UBM, DBN and CCM, and analyzed this performance for queries with different frequencies.

Our main findings are the following. First, click models do not simulate accurately sessions without clicks and sessions with a click on the first position. In a web search scenario, considered in this work, such sessions comprise the majority of oberved sessions. Thus, in this scenario, naïve baselines that simulate no clicks and a click on the first position outperform advanced click models in terms of click simulation. This finding suggests that click models should consider ways of dealing with sessions with no clicks and sessions with a click on the first position. Second, we confirmed the intuition that click models that have high click prediction performance (usually measured with log-likelihood and perplexity) also have the best click simulation performance. Particularly, the UBM model was shown to be the best in predicting clicks and it appears to be the best in simulating clicks compared to DBN and CCM. This finding suggests that building click models with high log-likelihood will result in better click simulators.

There are a few directions for future work. First, we plan to study click simulation in scenarios other than web search, e.g., exploratory search, academic search, search in digital libraries and archives. We expect that user click behavior in these scenarios will differ significantly from that in web search. In particular, there may be much fewer sessions with no clicks or only one click. Second, in addition to directly evaluating the performance of click simulators we plan to consider and evaluate various applications of click simulation, e.g., building rankers using simulated clicks. This way we will evaluate the "usefulness" of simulated clicks. Finally, we plan to consider recently proposed neural click models [4] for the task of click simulation and evaluate their simulation performance. We expect that these neural models will capture more complex patterns in user click behavior and, therefore, simulate clicks better. In particular, we expect them to better deal with sessions with no clicks or only one click.

Acknowledgments. This research was supported by Ahold Delhaize, Amsterdam Data Science, the Bloomberg Research Grant program, the Criteo Faculty Research Award program, the Dutch national program COMMIT, Elsevier, the European Community's Seventh Framework Programme (FP7/2007-2013) under grant agreement nr 312827 (VOX-Pol), the Microsoft Research Ph.D. program, the Netherlands Institute for Sound and Vision, the Netherlands Organisation for Scientific Research (NWO) under project nrs 612.-001.116, HOR-11-10, CI-14-25, 652.002.001, 612.001.551, 652.001.003, and Yandex. All content represents the opinion of the authors, which is not necessarily shared or endorsed by their respective employers and/or sponsors.

REFERENCES

[1] Leif Azzopardi. 2016. Simulation of Interaction: A Tutorial on Modelling and Simulating User Interaction and Search Behaviour. In *SIGIR*. ACM, 1227–1230.

[2] Leif Azzopardi, Maarten de Rijke, and Krisztian Balog. 2007. Building simulated queries for known-item topics: An analysis using six European languages. In *SIGIR*. ACM.

[3] Richard Berendsen, Manos Tsagkias, Wouter Weerkamp, and Maarten de Rijke. 2013. Pseudo test collections for training and tuning microblog rankers. In *SIGIR*. ACM, 53–62.

[4] Alexey Borisov, Ilya Markov, Maarten de Rijke, and Pavel Serdyukov. 2016. A Neural Click Model for Web Search. In *WWW*. 531–541.

[5] Olivier Chapelle and Ya Zhang. 2009. A dynamic bayesian network click model for web search ranking. In *WWW*. 1–10.

[6] Aleksandr Chuklin, Ilya Markov, and Maarten de Rijke. 2015. *Click Models for Web Search*. Morgan & Claypool.

[7] Aleksandr Chuklin, Anne Schuth, Katja Hofmann, Pavel Serdyukov, and Maarten de Rijke. 2013. Evaluating Aggregated Search Using Interleaving. In *CIKM*. ACM Press, New York, NY, USA.

[8] Aleksandr Chuklin, Pavel Serdyukov, and Maarten de Rijke. 2013. Click model-based information retrieval metrics. In *SIGIR*. 493–502.

[9] Nick Craswell, Onno Zoeter, Michael Taylor, and Bill Ramsey. 2008. An experimental comparison of click position-bias models. In *WSDM*. 87–94.

[10] Georges E. Dupret and Benjamin Piwowarski. 2008. A user browsing model to predict search engine click data from past observations. In *SIGIR*. 331–338.

[11] Artem Grotov, Aleksandr Chuklin, Ilya Markov, Luka Stout, Finde Xumara, and Maarten de Rijke. 2015. A Comparative Study of Click Models for Web Search. In *CLEF*. 78–90.

[12] Fan Guo, Chao Liu, Anitha Kannan, Tom Minka, Michael Taylor, Yi-Min Wang, and Christos Faloutsos. 2009. Click chain model in web search. In *WWW*. 11–20.

[13] Katja Hofmann, Lihong Li, and Filip Radlinski. 2016. Online Evaluation for Information Retrieval. *Foundations and Trends in Information Retrieval* 10, 1 (2016), 1–117.

[14] Katja Hofmann, Shimon Whiteson, and Maarten de Rijke. 2011. A probabilistic method for inferring preferences from clicks. In *CIKM*. ACM Press, New York, NY, USA.

[15] Thorsten Joachims. 2002. Optimizing Search Engines Using Clickthrough Data. In *KDD*. 133–142.

[16] Qianli Xing, Yiqun Liu, Jian-Yun Nie, Min Zhang, Shaoping Ma, and Kuo Zhang. 2013. Incorporating User Preferences into Click Models. In *CIKM*. 1301–1310.

[17] Zeyuan Allen Zhu, Weizhu Chen, Tom Minka, Chenguang Zhu, and Zheng Chen. 2010. A Novel Click Model and Its Applications to Online Advertising. In *WSDM*. 321–330.

An Initial Investigation of Query Expansion Bias

Colin Wilkie
School of Computing Science
University of Glasgow
Glasgow, Scotland
c.wilkie.3@research.gla.ac.uk

Leif Azzopardi
Computer & Information Sciences
University of Strathclyde
Glasgow, Scotland
leif.azzopardi@acm.org

ABSTRACT

Query expansion is a useful retrieval mechanism for creating more verbose queries from the users initial key word search. Query expansion generally have multiple parameters that allow the user to define how many terms and where those terms come from are introduced to the expanded query. However, the idea that query expansion may be introducing biases into the system by selecting terms from overly retrievable documents has never been formally evaluated. In this work, the relationship between performance and retrievability bias is explored when various query expansion methods are employed to aide retrieval. Several parameters are altered, independently, to identify those that have an impact on bias. Parameters altered include; Rocchio's beta, length normalisation parameters, the number of terms added and the number of documents those terms are extracted from. The evaluation performed here identifies a strong correlation between performance and retrievability bias, suggesting that performance is increased by making the system more biased thus more likely to pick terms from a set of overly retrievable documents.

1 INTRODUCTION

Information Retrieval's (IR) primary objective is to return all of the most relevant information ordered in an useful way to a user, given their information need. One function of an IR system is to infer a users information need when provided with a few key words that a user believes reflects their search goal. However, these key words often form a very vague query that could cover a massive range of documents, thus methods have been developed to bolster the users key words with additional content in the hopes that this new query will identify the most relevant documents. A Query Expansion (QE) mechanism must identify documents that are relevant to the original query and extract new terms from these documents to expand the user query with meaningful content. This new query should then identify more relevant documents that satisfy the users information need. Obviously, the documents selected are of vital importance to the success of the method as terms extracted from non-relevant documents may cause the query to drift from the users intended information need. Ideally, the user would deem

which documents are relevant to them and allow the QE mechanism to select the terms from them, however this is often not possible and instead the QE must rely on some pseudo relevance feedback (PRF) [8]. Pseudo relevance feedback assumes that the top n documents are relevant and as such, important terms from these documents will improve the users query. This technique can lead to improved performance but it is pivotal that the terms are extracted from the appropriate documents. To this end, QE can be adjusted in various ways to alter the weightings terms receive as well as how many terms are extracted and which documents are taken into consideration.

This method of query improvement clearly opens doors for biases to creep into the system, for example, overly retrievable documents may be given the opportunity to contribute terms which then increases their relevance when the document may not be relevant to the original query at all. Ideally, QE would select a relevant document and extract important terms that steer the query towards a specialised set of relevant documents that may not be easy to retrieve with particular terms.

This work investigates the impact of QE on the relationship between retrievability bias and performance [10]. The main question is whether the gain in performance that is often found is the result of an increase in bias. Identifying the effect of QE on retrievability bias, we can then correlate the bias with the performance metrics. By doing so, we can infer whether the introduction (or reduction) of bias in the system increases (or decreases) the performance of the system and whether or not this is beneficial to the user.

2 BACKGROUND

Retrievability, a document centric evaluation method, has become a popular method of evaluation in domains where system bias influences retrieval. Retrievability, proposed by Azzopardi and Vinay [2], provides an alternative view on how an IR system interacts with a collection by evaluating how *likely* a document is to be retrieved by a particular configuration of an IR system. The retrievability $\mathbf{r}$ of a document $\mathbf{d}$ with respect to the configuration of an IR system is defines as:

$$\mathbf{r(d)} \propto \sum_{q \in Q} f(\mathbf{k_{dq}}, \mathbf{c})$$

where q is a query from the large query set Q. $\mathbf{k_{dq}}$ is the rank at which d is retrieved given q, therefore the utility function $f(\mathbf{k_{dq}}, \mathbf{c})$ determines the score that document d attains for query q given the rank cutoff c. $\mathbf{r(d)}$ is calculated by summing over all queries q in query set Q. Theoretically, Q represents the universe of all possible queries, but in practice Q is very large set of queries [1, 2, 4, 5, 10]. The standard measure of retrievability used employs the utility function $f(\mathbf{k_{dq}}, \mathbf{c})$, such that if a document, d, is retrieved in the top

c documents given q, then $f(k_{dq}, c) = 1$, otherwise $f(k_{dq}, c) = 0$. This measure provides an intuitive value for each document as it is simply the number of times that the document is retrieved in the top c documents. Documents falling outside the the the top c attain no scores.

To convert the $r(d)$ for each document into a single value describing bias, inequality metrics that assess the distribution of wealth in a population are used. However, the retrievability fits this paradigm as the documents retrievability can be considered its wealth wealth and the collection is the population that the retrievability is distributed amongst. The Gini Coefficient [6] is one inequality metric that can be used to to calculate the level of inequality in a population by comparing the distribution to the Lorenz Curve.

An interesting line of research emerging from the theory of retrievability is how performance metrics relate to retrievability bias. Wilkie and Azzopardi have conducted several studies investigating this relationship [9–11]. The first of these works investigated how retrievability bias related to both performance and document lengths [9]. In this study, Wilkie and Azzopardi investigated how altering the length normalisation parameters of the BM25 and PL2 retrieval models impacted both the performance and the bias that the systems exerted upon the collection. Their findings indicated that the relationship between bias and performance was non-linear and that TREC performance metrics had a poor match up with bias (i.e. the parameter where performance was at its highest was not the parameter where the least amount of bias was found). In a follow up study by Wilkie and Azzopardi, system ranking based on performance and retrievability bias was performed [10]. The results demonstrated a much stronger correlation between bias and performance when a range of retrieval models were utilised. They found that choosing a less biased retrieval system would often improve performance while also reducing bias. From these two studies it could be concluded that when choosing a retrieval model, models which exert less bias are generally better performers. However, when tuning the length normalisation parameter of a retrieval model selecting the least bias setting for that parameter will often not lead to optimal performance. In many cases, the difference in the best performance and performance at the least biased setting was not significant however and so it was stated that the least biased point of length normalisation is a good starting point when tuning a system. A final study by Wilkie and Azzopardi on the relationship between bias and performance employed the use of a large number of evaluation metrics including some recently proposed metrics that were more user centric than TREC metrics. Again, they investigated how altering the length normalisation parameter of retrieval models impacted the relationship between bias and performance. They found that when employing metrics like Time Biased Gain and U-Measure in almost all cases, the parameter setting that minimised bias also maximised performance. Again suspecting that the poor match up for TREC metrics occurred due to length biases in the relevancy pools, the authors investigated these pools and found that there was a strong length bias towards longer documents in the relevancy pools of the TREC collections.

While the studies performed by Wilkie and Azzopardi were conducted in the domain of ad hoc web and news search, Bashir and Rauber have performed studies investigating retrievability bias

in the patent retrieval domain [3, 5]. In these studies, the authors find a stronger link between recall and retrievability bias than what was observed by Wilkie and Azzopardi in ad-hoc search. These results lead Bashir and Rauber to investigate methods of QE which account for retrievability bias [4]. In this study, Bashir and Rauber compare the bias of a number of competing retrieval models and QE methods in a study to demonstrate how their new cluster based QE method provides results that are less biased than all other approaches compared. The authors work was motivated by the finding that current QE methods would often increase retrievability bias by extracting terms from the highly retrievable documents, thus making them more retrievable. However, in their study the QE methods investigated were only investigated on their default settings and the performance of the methods was never evaluated. Therefore, the relationship between bias and performance when QE is performed remains completely unknown.

Converse to Bashir and Rauber, Pickens *et al* evaluated the performance of the traditional QE methods against their new QE method, the reverted index [7]. In this work, Pickens *et al* explored the parameter space of multiple QE methods and evaluated performance at each setting to find what the impact of altering each parameter was.

Between the work of Bashir and Rauber, and the work of Pickens *et al* there is an interesting gap in the literature about the relationship between bias and performance when QE is employed to improve performance. No previous work has explored the parameter space available in QE and quantified both bias and performance to determine whether QE improves performance by employing a more biased retrieval model or if its success is due to a reduction in bias.

3 EXPERIMENTAL METHOD

3.1 Research Questions

The hypothesis of this study states that performing QE during retrieval leads to increases in retrievability bias. This work seeks to answer several research questions in the following experiments. The first question investigates how altering length normalisation in retrieval model impacts both bias and performance. Previous work by Wilkie and Azzopardi [11] has shown that employing the length normalisation setting that minimises bias does not maximise performance. As such, in QE we expect that due to there being two rounds of retrieval under the one system that the bias may be compounded and biased systems will introduce larger biases. The next question concerns how much weight should be applied to the new expansion terms compared with the original query terms. Does weighting the original query terms lower than the expansion terms introduces more bias to the system as the expansion terms are being extracted from documents which may be highly retrievable, thus bolstering the retrievability of these already retrievable documents? The next research question investigates the length of the queries that are issues to the retrieval system. As QE adds new terms to the original query, we investigate whether generating longer queries using QE actually increases biases as longer documents have more chance to match more terms. Finally, the work explores the impact that the number of documents the QE terms are extracted from has on the performance and bias relationship. It is posited that

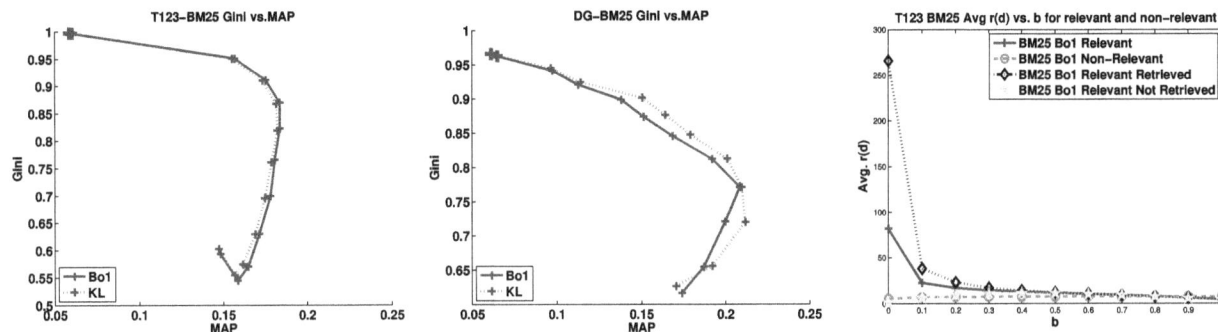

Figure 1: Plots of Gini vs. MAP Altering the b parameter of BM25 (Left & Middle). The larger points indicate $b = 0.0$. **And plots of Average r(d) vs. b for BM25 using Bo1 expansion on T123 (Right).**

using more documents from the rankings should help lower bias by utilising a larger sample of documents which would allow for more diverse terms to be generated for the expanded query. Following is the experimental methodology employed to achieve the results required for this investigation.

3.2 Data and Materials

Collections The experiments were performed on three TREC test collections: two news collections, TREC123 (T123) and Associated Press (AP), and one web collection; .Gov (DG). Each collection was indexed on Terrier[1] with stop words removed and Porter Stemming.

Retrieval Models Experiments were performed using 3 common retrieval models implemented in Terrier: BM25, DPH and TF.IDF. For the parameterised BM25 model, only the **b** parameter was altered as it influences length normalisation, leaving the remaining parameters of BM25 to their default values ($k_1 = 1.2$ and $k_3 = 8$). These models were selected to fit a range of profiles of performance and bias.

Query Expansion Models Experiments were performed using two common query expansion models, KullbackâĂŞLeibler divergence (KL) and Bose-Einstein (Bo1). These models both feature a suite of tuneable parameters. The first of these parameters is the Rocchio's beta, a parameter that is used to alter the weighting applied to the original query terms and the new expanded terms. Parameters specifying how many terms should be extracted and from how many documents these terms are to be selected from were also altered for the corresponding research questions.

Performance and Retrievability Bias To measure the performance in each of the experiments Mean Average Precision (MAP) was used. The retrievability bias was quantified using the Gini Coefficient similar to previous studies [2, 4, 11]. To quantify the bias of the system these steps are followed: first, generate a very large set of bigrams for each collection using automatic extraction where bigrams which occur at least 20 times were selected. Next, launch this query set for the corresponding collection and compute the document retrievability scores. Following this, Gini is used to compute the bias of the system using the **r(d)** scores. This outputs a

decimal between 0 and 1 that represents the level of bias the system exerts on the collection, this can then be used to compare systems.

3.3 Experiments

Experiment 1: Altering the Parameters of the Retrieval Model The first experiment altered the b parameter between the bounds of 0 and 1, traversing the space in steps of 0.1 (i.e 0, 0.1, 0.2, ..., 0.9, 1). Additionally, in these experiments Bo1 and KL were used with their parameters at default values of: $Rocchio's \beta = 0.4$, extracting 10 terms for expansion from the top 3 documents.

Experiment 2: Altering Rocchio's Beta in the QE Method The second experiment consisted of altering the Rocchio's Beta for the employed QE method on each of the retrieval models. As BM25 has the adjustable b parameter, for the remaining experiments it was fixed to $b = 0.7$. For QE, 10 terms were extracted from the top 3 documents.

Experiment 3: Altering the Number of Terms for Expansion The third experiment again utilised both QE methods on the 3 retrieval models similar to the previous experiment. In this experiment, Rocchio's Beta was set to 0.4 while the number of terms extracted was explored. In each run, a different number of expansion terms were selected from the top 3 documents. The number of terms extracted were: 1, 2, 3, 4, 5, 6, 7, 8, 9, 10, 12, 15, 20, 25 and 50. This approach replicated some of the experiments performed by Pickens (et al) [7] where performance was evaluated. We will also evaluate retrievability bias, an evaluation that has not previously been performed.

Experiment 4: Altering the Number of Documents for Expansion The final experiment follows the same method as Experiment 3 however, the number of documents that terms are extracted from are altered. 10 terms are extracted from a varying number from the top x documents (1, 2, 3, 4, 5, 6, 7, 8, 9, 10, 12, 15, 20, 25, 50).

4 RESULTS AND ANALYSIS

The results of the experiments are presented in this section, however for brevity, focus is placed on the results of T123 as similar patterns are observed on the other collections. When increasing the b parameter for length normalisation in BM25 using the Bo1 and KL QE methods, results similar to those observed by Wilkie

---

[1]http://terrier.org/

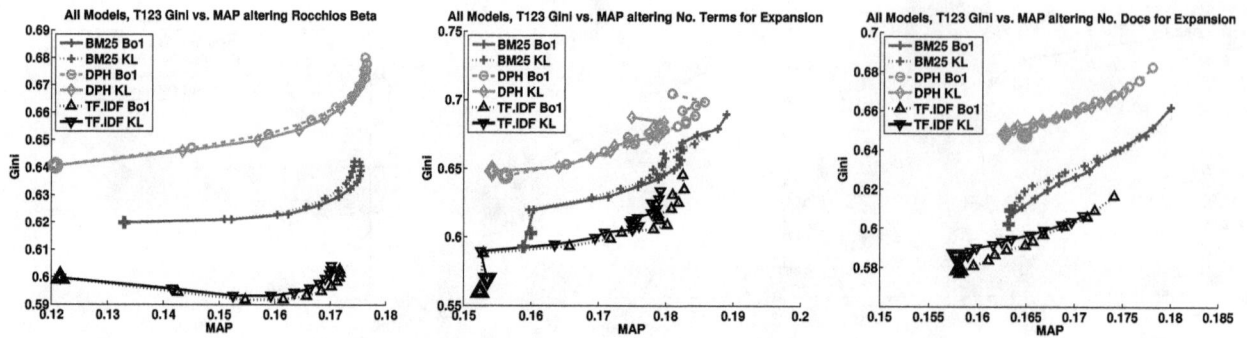

Figure 2: Plots of Gini vs. MAP for BM25, DPH and TF.IDF when varying Rocchio's Beta (Left), the number of documents for expansion (Middle) or the number of terms for expansion (Right). The larger points towards the left of each graph indicate the smallest settings.

and Azzopardi when no QE was performed [9] were evident in the left and middle plots of Figure 1. In terms of MAP, from $b = 0.0$ (the poorest performing point on the graph) there is a steady increase in MAP until the maximum MAP is found at $b = 0.3$ for T123 and $b = 0.7$ for DG for both Bo1 and KL. The difference here can be attributed to the variance in length between the collections and that DG has an average document length of 1108 compared with T123 of 439 meaning more length normalisation must be applied to DG to improve performance (thus a higher value of b). In terms of bias there is a steady decrease from $b = 0.0$, the most biased point, until the minimum point of bias of $b = 0.9$ for T123 and $b = 1.0$ on DG for both QE methods. Obviously, the point of minimum bias does not coincide with the point of maximum performance, also observed by Wilkie and Azzopardi. The rightmost plot of Figure 1 demonstrates how at low settings of b, the models apply very high retrievability to relevant documents making the rest of the collection unretrievable. As these low b settings do not correspond with high performance scores, it is evident that a small set of the relevant documents are receiving huge $r(d)$ scores, dragging the average up (supported by the standard deviation at $b = 0.0$ of 2600 compared to 8 at $b = 1.0$) as this is a small set of the whole collection.

For the second experiment where the Rocchio's Beta was altered, results are shown in the left plot of Figure 2. In all cases, an increase in Rocchio's β leads to improvements in performance however, gains are diminishing. In terms of bias for this experiment, for BM25 and DPH a direct correlation between performance and retrievability bias is observed, signifying that as performance improves, bias also increases.

The central plot of Figure 2 shows how the findings agree with Pickens *et al* [7] in that there is a constant increase in MAP as we add more terms for expansion. Similar to the finding in the previous experiment, there is a corresponding rise in bias as performance increases. Again, suggesting that the terms extracted are relevant but are causing the retrieval system to focus on a smaller set of documents than when done without QE. The Rocchio's Beta appears to have most impact on performance while the number of terms has the biggest impact on bias.

The final experiment yields very similar findings to the previous two experiments where a steady rise in MAP and a corresponding

rise in bias is observed as more documents become available to select terms from.

5 CONCLUSION

Given the results presented, the following conclusions about QE's effect on retrievability bias and performance can be drawn. Increases in the number of terms and number of top documents used to extract the terms leads to increases in MAP as well as in bias, meaning the system is selecting useful terms for expansion but in doing so, is narrowing the set of documents that can be retrieved to a subset of the collection. Altering Rocchio's beta on each model, it was again evident that applying higher weight to the expansion terms lead to improvements in MAP and increases in bias. Finally, altering the b parameter for BM25 provided results that reflect previous findings when no QE is performed where no match up between maximum performance and minimum bias appears. These findings suggest that the effectiveness of QE is in part, linked with an increase in bias associated with the system.

REFERENCES

[1] L. Azzopardi and R. Bache. On the relationship between effectiveness and accessibility. In *Proc. of the 33rd ACM SIGIR*, pages 889–890, 2010.
[2] L. Azzopardi and V. Vinay. Retrievability: An evaluation measure for higher order information access tasks. In *Proc. of the 17th ACM CIKM*, pages 561–570, 2008.
[3] S. Bashir and A. Rauber. Analyzing document retrievability in patent retrieval settings. In *Database and Expert Systems Applications*, pages 753–760. 2009.
[4] S. Bashir and A. Rauber. Improving retrievability of patents with cluster-based pseudo-relevance feedback documents selection. In *Proc. of the 18th ACM CIKM*, pages 1863–1866, 2009.
[5] S. Bashir and A. Rauber. Improving retrievability of patents in prior-art search. In *Proc. of the 32nd ECIR*, pages 457–470, 2010.
[6] J. Gastwirth. The estimation of the lorenz curve and gini index. *The Review of Economics and Statistics*, 54:306–316, 1972.
[7] J. Pickens, M. Cooper, and G. Golovchinsky. Reverted indexing for feedback and expansion. In *Proc. of the 19th ACM CIKM*, pages 1049–1058, 2010.
[8] J. J. Rocchio. Relevance feedback in information retrieval. 1971.
[9] C. Wilkie and L. Azzopardi. Relating retrievability, performance and length. In *Proc. of the 36th ACM SIGIR conference*, pages 937–940, 2013.
[10] C. Wilkie and L. Azzopardi. Best and fairest: An empirical analysis of retrieval system bias. *Advances in Information Retrieval*, pages 13–25, 2014.
[11] C. Wilkie and L. Azzopardi. A retrievability analysis: Exploring the relationship between retrieval bias and retrieval performance. In *Proc. of the 23rd ACM CIKM*, pages 81–90, 2014.

Towards Learning Reward Functions from User Interactions

Ziming Li
University of Amsterdam
Amsterdam, The Netherlands
z.li@uva.nl

Julia Kiseleva
UserSat.com & University of Amsterdam
Amsterdam, The Netherlands
j.kiseleva@uva.nl

Maarten de Rijke
University of Amsterdam
Amsterdam, The Netherlands
derijke@uva.nl

Artem Grotov
University of Amsterdam
Amsterdam, The Netherlands
a.grotov@uva.nl

ABSTRACT

In the physical world, people have dynamic preferences, e.g., the same situation can lead to satisfaction for some humans and to frustration for others. Personalization is called for. The same observation holds for online behavior with interactive systems. It is natural to represent the behavior of users who are engaging with interactive systems such as a search engine or a recommender system, as a sequence of actions where each next action depends on the current situation and the *user reward* of taking a particular action. By and large, current online evaluation metrics for interactive systems such as search engines or recommender systems, are static and do not reflect differences in user behavior. They rarely capture or model the *reward* experienced by a user while interacting with an interactive system. We argue that knowing a user's reward function is essential for an interactive system as both for learning and evaluation. We propose to learn users' reward functions directly from observed interaction traces. In particular, we present how users' reward functions can be uncovered directly using *inverse reinforcement learning* techniques. We also show how to incorporate user features into the learning process. Our main contribution is a novel and dynamic approach to restore a user's reward function. We present an analytic approach to this problem and complement it with initial experiments using the interaction logs of a cultural heritage institution that demonstrate the feasibility of the approach by uncovering different reward functions for different user groups.

CCS CONCEPTS

• **Information systems** → *Users and interactive retrieval*; • **Computing methodologies** → *Inverse reinforcement learning*;

KEYWORDS

Inverse reinforcement learning, online evaluation, interactive systems

1 INTRODUCTION

Understanding and modeling user behavior is a fundamental problem for any interactive system as insight into user behavior will lead towards "proper" evaluation: what satisfies user needs and what frustrates users. We know that users have different preferences and can display different behavior [20, 32]. Despite this key lesson, the evaluation metrics in use today do not take differences in user behavior into account. Existing methods are directed towards generalization [12] rather than personalization [35]. This stops us from deciphering fine-grained user feedback. The idea of designing an interactive system that dynamically reacts to user actions by employing the reinforcement learning (RL) paradigm as proposed in Figure 1 is appealing. A key problem preventing this is that we do not know the users' *true* reward functions.

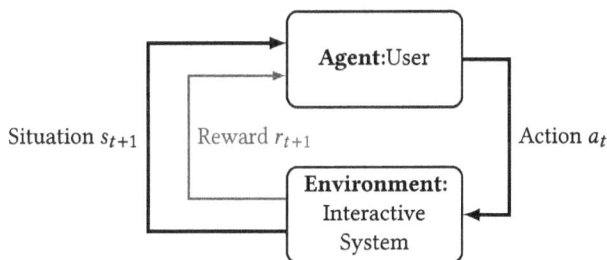

Figure 1: The user-system interface.

Let's consider an example of interactive system—a web search engine. Assume a user issues the query "panda" and the search engine returns a diverse search engine result page (SERP) that contains answers from various verticals: text, images, videos. If our user is a child, he will most likely click on an image result, and adults may prefer to read a Wikipedia page. According to existing evaluation paradigms, based, e.g., on the number of satisfied clicks [23], both outputs are successful because the user clicks on the SERP [5]. To increase user satisfaction, search engines are currently showing diverse SERPs, but this is no silver bullet. With the popularity of mobile phones, we are moving to an era of personal assistants on mobile devices [17, 18] and direct answers [34], where the screen size is small or a system is expected to give the best result that directly answers user needs. In such scenarios it is not an option for an interactive system to offer a broad selection of alternatives. Instead, the interactive system has to discover, during successive interactions, a user's preferences.

Our long-term goal is to dynamically process user feedback for evaluating user reward during an interactive session and to respond accordingly as presented in Figure 1. For example, if a user clicks on images after issuing the query "panda," an interactive system can infer a user's reward to provide a *better* experience for the next step in the interaction.

The main aim of this paper is *to study how user reward functions can be learned from their interactions,* which we break down into the following concrete research questions.

RQ1: How to define user reward? We model the interactive user-system interface in Figure 1 using Reinforcement Learning (RL) [30]. More specifically, a user is an agent who interacts with an environment, which is an interactive system, in a sequential manner with discrete time steps, $t = 0, 1, 2, 3, \ldots$. At each time step t, the user receives some representation of the system, which we call *situation,* $s_t \in S$, where S is the set of possible system situations, and on that the user performs an action, $a_t \in A$, where A is the set of actions possible in the situation s_t. We propose the following way of modeling the user reward function: one time step later, the user receives a numerical reward, $R_{t+1} \in R$, and finds himself in a new situation, s_{t+1}. While examining interactive user behavior, we should consider the reward function unknown and to be restored though empirical detection. This is specifically important for multi-attribute reward functions as in our case. A unit of user interactions with the system within some time period $[t_i, t_{i+j}]$, called a *user session.*

RQ2: How to recover a user reward function? Our problem fits the setting of Inverse Reinforcement Learning (IRL) [25], which is defined as follows: **given:** (1) sequential users' interactions with a system over time in a variety of circumstances, and (2) a system model; **determine:** the reward function of the users.

RQ3: How to incorporate user features into the learning process? IRL techniques have successfully been applied for the apprenticeship (or imitation) learning problem [25], to discover the reward function whose optimization would produce *desirable behavior.* One of the prominent examples is self-driving cars, where one recovers the reward function based only on expert driving behavior. In contrast, we attempt to restore reward function(s) covering various types of user behavior (similar to driving styles in [1]). Similar to [4] we incorporate into our learning process user features that can be organized in two groups: (1) *static user features* remain unchanged during the user session, e.g., age, gender; (2) *dynamic user features* describe user behavior in the particular situation s_t, e.g., time spent.

To confirm our hypothesis that different types of users have different reward functions, we perform a preliminary reward learning experiment for which we choose onsite logs of physical interactions in a museum because user features are explicitly given.

2 BACKGROUND AND RELATED WORK

Evaluation. Information Retrieval (IR) is about getting the right information to the right people in the right way. Evaluation has historically been one of IR's key concerns. Offline, system-oriented evaluation, with a strong focus on assessing the degree to which a system is able to successfully identify documents that are relevant to a query, has received considerable attention [27]. In parallel, user-oriented evaluation methods for interactive information retrieval received considerable attention [16]. Increasingly, though, there is a

realization that system aspects and user aspects should be assessed in tandem. In online experimentation the two aspects naturally come together [15].

Online controlled experiments, such as A/B testing or inter-leaving, have become widely used techniques for controlling and improving search quality based on data-driven decisions [19]. This methodology has been adopted widely [3, 7, 9, 31]. An A/B test is a between-subject test designed to compare two variants of a method (e.g., ranking on the SERP, ad ranking, colors and fonts of the web result title) at the same time by exposing them to two user groups and by measuring the difference between them in terms of a *key metric* (e.g., revenue, number of visits, etc.).

There are many existing studies towards better online evaluation that are devoted to improving the sensitivity of our measurement methods [28], inventing new metrics [8, 10] or improving existing ones [9]. An important goal of recent studies is to make metrics more consistent with long-term goals [19]. User engagement metrics show different aspects of user experience. For instance, they can reflect (1) *user loyalty* – the number of sessions per user [29]; (2) *user activity* – the number of visited web pages [21] or the absence time [10]. Periodicity engagement metrics of user behavior, which result from the discrete Fourier transform of state-of-the-art engagement measures, have also been proposed [8]. Few studies have looked at evaluating intelligent assistants in online settings [17, 18, 33, 34], where user satisfaction [16] is defined and predicted at the session level.

Most existing studies are directed towards generalization from user interaction rather than understanding the behavior of individuals. Very few works [2] have explored why users behave in particular ways by applying economic models.

Reinforcement learning in interactive systems. Several authors have adopted a Reinforcement Learning (RL) perspective on IR problems. Hofmann et al. [12, 14] seem to have been the first; they use RL for online evaluation and online learning to rank and define reward functions directly in terms of NDCG [13]. Later work on RL in IR predefined reward functions as the number of satisfied clicks in session search [22, 23]. Odijk et al. [26] use RL for query modeling and define reward in terms of retrieval performance (NDCG). Applications of IRL in interactive systems are relatively rare. Ziebart et al. [36] use IRL for predicting the desired target of a partial pointing motion in graphical user interfaces. Monfort et al. [24] use IRL to predict human motion when interacting with environment. It is not straightforward to apply IRL for interactive systems as it is often unclear how one should deal with user features [4].

To summarize, the key distinctions of our work compared to previous work are that we introduce a new problem (recovering user reward functions from interaction data) and propose a method to address the problem.

3 LEARNING USER REWARD FUNCTIONS

We start by investigating *RQ1: How to define user reward?* To model the user reward function, presented in Figure 1, we use a finite Markov Decision Process (MDP). An MDP is a tuple (S, A, T, d_0, γ, R), where S is a set of N states (possible system situations); A is a set of K actions; T is a set of state transition probabilities $P_{sa}(\cdot)$ is a state transition probability upon taking action a in state s; the initial distribution of states is d_0 and $\gamma \in [0, 1)$ is a discount factor; R is a user reward function, where $R(s, a)$ is a reward given for action a in situation s. Given a current state s and action a together with any next state s', the expected value of the next reward is: $r(s, a, s') = \mathbb{E}(R_{t+1} \mid S_t = s, A_t = a, S_{t+1} = s')$.

An MDP without reward function is denoted as MDP/R, i.e., a tuple (S, A, T, d_0, γ). Let $\mathbf{f} : S \to [0, 1]^k$ be a vector of features over states. There is a "true" reward function R that is given by a linear combination of k features f_i with weights θ_i where $\theta^T \in \mathbb{R}^k$. We assume that the reward function is defined as $R(s) = \theta^T \cdot \mathbf{f}(s)$. In our setting, $\mathbf{f}$ is a vector of features describing user behavior, e.g., time a user spent interacting with the system state. The desired vector θ^T specifies the relative weighting between these features.

A *policy* is a map π from situations, $s_t \in S$, and actions, $a_t \in A$, to the probability $\pi(a_t \mid s_t)$ of taking action a_t when in state s_t. The value function V for policy π is:

$$\mathbb{E}_{s_0 \sim d_0}[V^\pi(s_0)] = \mathbb{E}\left[\sum_{t=0}^\infty \gamma^t R(s_t) | \pi\right] = \theta^T \cdot \mathbb{E}[\sum_{t=0}^\infty \gamma^t \mathbf{f}(s_t) \mid \pi]. \quad (1)$$

The expectation is taken with respect to random sequences of situations $s_0, s_1, \ldots$ drawn from the starting situation $s_0 \sim d_0$. The goal of RL is to find π such that $V^\pi(s)$ is maximized. There exists at least one optimal policy π^* such that $V^\pi(s)$ is simultaneously maximized for all $s_t \in S$ by $\pi^* = \pi$ [25].

We need to estimate a user's features expectations μ_E. Given a set of m user sessions $\{s_0^i, s_1^i, s_2^i, \ldots\}_{i=0}^m$, generated by users, we empirically estimate $\mu_E \approx \hat{\mu}_E = 1/m \cdot \sum_{i=0}^m \sum_{t=0}^\infty \gamma^t \mathbf{f}(s^i)$.

Next, we consider **RQ2: How to recover a user reward function?** The problem of IRL is to find a reward function that can explain the observed user behavior. We formulate the problem as follows: **given** (1) an MDP/R, (2) $\mathbf{f}$, (3) user feature expectations μ_E; **determine** a policy whose performance is close to the observed user group behavior based on the unknown user reward function $R = \theta^T \cdot \mathbf{f}$. There are a number of available IRL methods [1, 6, 25, 37, 38]. For our preliminary experiments we adopt Maximum Entropy IRL (MaxEnt) [37] to recover the user reward functions.

4 INCORPORATING USER FEATURES

We report on a preliminary experiment aimed at assessing the feasibility of uncovering the reward function from interaction data.

Data. The dataset we use [11] is extracted from the physical interaction logs of an archaeological museum. Besides common exhibitions, this museum also provides additional information that can be obtained from different POIs. The contents at each POI are based on one specific topic and there are 8 topics in total. According to the corresponding topic, each POI shows 3 related objects and the objects at different POIs can be accessed in any order. Users can enter their personal information and preference at the beginning to personalize the contents being shown. The original dataset consists of 5 months of onsite logs with about 21,000 sessions. Each record contains one user's personal information (e.g., age and language) and the interaction order with different objects at POIs. The starting time and how long the interaction lasts for each object are also recorded. After filtering the sessions which did not have any interactions or necessary user information (such as age), 4,694 out of 21,000 interaction sessions remain and constitute our final data.

Experimental design. To address **RQ3: How to incorporate user features into the learning process?** we propose the following experiment. We focus on exploring the difference between the reward functions of different groups. According to the user's age, we divide the data into two groups, child and adult, with 1,135 and 3,559 sessions, respectively. To indicate each interaction situation, we consider three kinds of features: "*topic*" (8 different types, including: *appearance, death, religion, architecture, entertainment, food, trade, army*), "*object order*" (3 objects for each topic) and "*duration time*" (discretized in 3 bins denoting 0–30s, 30–90s and more than 90s). One-hot encoding is used in our experiment as some features are categorical. In this manner, 14 features are selected and 72 situations are defined. With respect to the action feature, we use the object's topic number to denote an action; taking a specific action means the user will transition to the situations that has the same topic number. We identified 8 actions in this dataset. In terms of transition probability, we simply count the occurrence frequency in the behavior history to estimate the probability for possible situations when the current situation and action are determined.

Experiments and results. Table 1 shows part of the learned weights of the reward function. The feature "*architecture*" negatively contributes to the user reward function for the Adult group. With respect to the feature "*death*," the Child group has a higher weight, which makes intuitive sense as children are more curious about scary contents. For the Adult group, objects of "*food*" contribute most to the reward while it is also the most popular topic for children. For the Adult group, "*religion*" has a higher weight compared to "*appearance*" while it is same for the Child group. But for "*trade*" and "*army*", these two groups have different preference. Another interesting phenomena is that most weights of object order of the Adult group are in a small scope compared to Child group, which can be explained as that adults will interact with all the three objects with the same topic while most children will only view objects in the front of the object order. As we can see, there really does exist a difference between different groups' reward functions and this kind of difference was also reported in the setting of self-driving cars [1].

5 CONCLUSIONS AND FUTURE WORK

In this conceptual paper we investigated *how reward functions can be directly learned from users' interplays with an interactive system.*

First, we explored **RQ1: How to define user reward?** We used a container of different features (such as system features and user features) to represent all possible situations. The user reward function, then, is a linear combination of situation features that we used to explain demonstrated user behavior.

Second, to answer **RQ2: How to recover a user reward function?** we proposed to use IRL techniques. We adopted maximum entropy *IRL* to recover the users reward functions. Our experimentation with a physical interaction dataset showed that the reward functions of different user groups have different priorities about features. Some features have a bigger impact on one user group's reward than on another group's.

Third, we studied **RQ3: How to incorporate user features into the learning process?** In the dataset used, explicit user features are given. We see two ways of incorporating user features into the learning process: (1) Grouping based on static user features; explicit user

Table 1: The recovered weights of reward function.

Group	Appearance	death	religion	architecture	entertainment	food	trade	army	object1	object2	object3
Adult	0.3378	0.1340	1.0539	-0.7106	0.9119	1.3577	0.4174	0.6783	0.6161	0.6556	0.6171
Child	0.9436	0.6479	1.2215	0.2658	1.2394	1.5001	0.7700	0.4649	0.9405	0.7115	0.7368

features are needed and we recover the reward functions for all the groups separately; the drawback is that groups need to be predefined and the number of user features should be relatively small. (2) Using user features to describe the situation. In many scenarios, such as web search, explicit user features may be unavailable and the first method is not applicable. How to adjust the reward for different users without predefined groups?

In conclusion, recovering user reward functions is (1) feasible, (2) a promising direction, and (3) applicable in many scenarios, including personal assistants, web search, recommender system.

As we are only at the beginning of our investigations into user reward functions, many questions remain open. (1) How can we make the reward function more complex, e.g., non-linear, rather than assuming that the function is a linear combination of situation features? (2) How can we make the system learn the rewards for different users automatically and return personalized rewards? To achieve this goal, user features should be taken into account during the learning process which can balance the reward for different users. Besides static user features, dynamic user features could also influence the decisions of users and need to be considered if possible. (3) How can we solve the computational problem of very large state spaces? The presence of very many features implies that many states will be defined, which in turn may reduce learning efficiency. Automatic feature construction and feature selection can be considered. (4) With more diverse and complicated features being considered, how can we adopt emerging techniques (such as deep inverse reinforcement learning) to mine user interaction scenarios effectively and efficiently?

Acknowledgments. This research was supported by Ahold Delhaize, Amsterdam Data Science, the Bloomberg Research Grant program, the Criteo Faculty Research Award program, the Dutch national program COMMIT, Elsevier, the European Community's Seventh Framework Programme (FP7/2007-2013) under grant agreement nr 312827 (VOX-Pol), the Microsoft Research Ph.D. program, the Netherlands Institute for Sound and Vision, the Netherlands Organisation for Scientific Research (NWO) under project nrs 612.001.-116, HOR-11-10, CI-14-25, 652.002.001, 612.001.551, 652.001.003, and Yandex. All content represents the opinion of the authors, which is not necessarily shared or endorsed by their respective employers and/or sponsors.

REFERENCES

[1] P. Abbeel and A. Y. Ng. Apprenticeship learning via inverse reinforcement learning. In *ICML*, page 1. ACM, 2004.
[2] L. Azzopardi. Modelling interaction with economic models of search. In *SIGIR*, pages 3–12. ACM, 2014.
[3] E. Bakshy and D. Eckles. Uncertainty in online experiments with dependent data: an evaluation of bootstrap methods. In *KDD*, pages 1303–1311, 2013.
[4] N. Banovic, T. Buzali, F. Chevalier, J. Mankoff, and A. K. Dey. Modeling and understanding human routine behavior. In *CHI*, pages 248–260. ACM, 2016.
[5] A. Borisov, I. Markov, M. de Rijke, and P. Serdyukov. A neural click model for web search. In *WWW*, pages 531–541, 2016.
[6] A. Boularias, J. Kober, and J. Peters. Relative entropy inverse reinforcement learning. In *AISTATS*, pages 182–189, 2011.
[7] A. Deng, T. Li, and Y. Guo. Statistical inference in two-stage online controlled experiments with treatment selection and validation. In *WWW*, pages 609–618, 2014.
[8] A. Drutsa, G. Gusev, and P. Serdyukov. Engagement periodicity in search engine usage: Analysis and its application to search quality evaluation. In *WSDM*, pages

27–36, 2015.
[9] A. Drutsa, G. Gusev, and P. Serdyukov. Future user engagement prediction and its application to improve the sensitivity of online experiments. In *WWW*, pages 256–266, 2015.
[10] G. Dupret and M. Lalmas. Absence time and user engagement: evaluating ranking functions. In *WSDM*, pages 173–182, 2013.
[11] S. H. Hashemi and J. Kamps. Skip or stay: Users' behavior in dealing with onsite information interaction crowd-bias. In *CHIIR*, pages 389–392, 2017.
[12] K. Hofmann, S. Whiteson, and M. de Rijke. Balancing exploration and exploitation in learning to rank online. In *ECIR*, pages 251–263. Springer, 2011.
[13] K. Hofmann, A. Schuth, S. Whiteson, and M. de Rijke. Reusing historical interaction data for faster online learning to rank for IR. In *WSDM*, pages 183–192. ACM, 2013.
[14] K. Hofmann, S. Whiteson, and M. de Rijke. Balancing exploration and exploitation in listwise and pairwise online learning to rank for information retrieval. *Information Retrieval Journal*, 2013, February.
[15] K. Hofmann, L. Li, and F. Radlinski. Online evaluation for information retrieval. *Foundations and Trends in Information Retrieval*, 10(1):1–117, 2016.
[16] D. Kelly. Methods for evaluating interactive information retrieval systems with users. *Foundations and Trends in Information Retrieval*, 3(1–2):1–224, 2009.
[17] J. Kiseleva, K. Williams, A. H. Awadallah, I. Zitouni, A. Crook, and T. Anastasakos. Predicting user satisfaction with intelligent assistants. In *SIGIR*, 2016.
[18] J. Kiseleva, K. Williams, J. Jiang, A. H. Awadallah, I. Zitouni, A. Crook, and T. Anastasakos. Understanding user satisfaction with intelligent assistants. In *CHIIR*, pages 121–130, 2016.
[19] R. Kohavi, A. Deng, R. Longbotham, and Y. Xu. Seven rules of thumb for web site experimenters. In *KDD*, pages 1857–1866, 2014.
[20] M. Kosinski, D. Stillwell, and T. Graepe. Private traits and attributes are predictable from digital records of human behavior. *Proceedings of the National Academy of Sciences*, 110:5802–5805, 2013.
[21] J. Lehmann, M. Lalmas, G. Dupret, and R. A. Baeza-Yates. Online multitasking and user engagement. In *CIKM*, pages 519–528, 2013.
[22] J. Luo, X. Dong, and H. Yang. Learning to reinforce search effectiveness. In *ICTIR*, pages 271–280. ACM, 2015.
[23] J. Luo, X. Dong, and H. Yang. Session search by direct policy learning. In *ICTIR*, pages 261–270. ACM, 2015.
[24] M. Monfort, A. Liu, and B. Ziebart. Intent prediction and trajectory forecasting via predictive inverse linear-quadratic regulation. In *AAAI*, 2015.
[25] A. Y. Ng, S. J. Russell, et al. Algorithms for inverse reinforcement learning. In *ICML*, pages 663–670, 2000.
[26] D. Odijk, E. Meij, I. Sijaranamual, and M. de Rijke. Dynamic query modeling for related content finding. In *SIGIR*, pages 33–42. 2015, August.
[27] M. Sanderson. Test collection based evaluation of information retrieval systems. *Foundations and Trends in Information Retrieval*, 4(4):247–375, 2010.
[28] A. Schuth, F. Sietsma, S. Whiteson, D. Lefortier, and M. de Rijke. Multileaved comparisons for fast online evaluation. In *CIKM*. 2014, November.
[29] Y. Song, X. Shi, and X. Fu. Evaluating and predicting user engagement change with degraded search relevance. In *WWW*, 2013.
[30] R. S. Sutton and A. G. Barto. *Introduction to reinforcement learning*, volume 135. MIT Press Cambridge, 2012.
[31] D. Tang, A. Agarwal, D. O'Brien, and M. Meyer. Overlapping experiment infrastructure: More, better, faster experimentation. In *KDD*, pages 17–26, 2010.
[32] H. Wei, F. Zhang, N. J. Yuan, C. Cao, H. Fu, X. Xie, Y. Rui, and W.-Y. Ma. Beyond the words: Predicting user personality from heterogeneous information. In *WSDM*, pages 305–314, 2017.
[33] K. Williams, J. Kiseleva, A. Crook, I. Zitouni, A. H. Awadallah, and M. Khabsa. Is this your final answer? evaluating the effect of answers on good abandonment in mobile search. In *SIGIR*, 2016.
[34] K. Williams, J. Kiseleva, A. C. Crook, I. Zitouni, A. H. Awadallah, and M. Khabsa. Detecting good abandonment in mobile search. In *WWW*, pages 495–505, 2016.
[35] W. Zhang, U. Paquet, and K. Hofmann. Collective noise contrastive estimation for policy transfer learning. In *AAAI*, pages 1408–1414, 2016.
[36] B. Ziebart, A. Dey, and J. A. Bagnell. Probabilistic pointing target prediction via inverse optimal control. In *IUI*, pages 1–10. ACM, 2012.
[37] B. D. Ziebart, A. L. Maas, J. A. Bagnell, and A. K. Dey. Maximum entropy inverse reinforcement learning. In *AAAI*, volume 8, pages 1433–1438, 2008.
[38] B. D. Ziebart, J. A. Bagnell, and A. K. Dey. The principle of maximum causal entropy for estimating interacting processes. *IEEE Transactions on Information Theory*, 59(4):1966–1980, 2013.

Benchmark for Complex Answer Retrieval

Federico Nanni
University of Mannheim
federico@informatik.uni-mannheim.de

Bhaskar Mitra
Microsoft and University College London
bmitra@microsoft.com

Matt Magnusson
University of New Hampshire
magnusson3@gmail.com

Laura Dietz
University of New Hampshire
dietz@cs.unh.edu

ABSTRACT

Providing answers to complex information needs is a challenging task. The new TREC Complex Answer Retrieval (TREC CAR) track introduces a large-scale dataset where paragraphs are to be retrieved in response to outlines of Wikipedia articles representing complex information needs. We present early results from a variety of approaches – from standard information retrieval methods (e.g., TF-IDF) to complex systems that adopt query expansion, knowledge bases and deep neural networks. The goal is to offer an overview of some promising approaches to tackle this problem.

1 INTRODUCTION

Over the last two decades, research in information retrieval (IR) has developed a variety of approaches for answering queries regarding precise facts – such as "Population New York City", "Who is Bill de Blasio?" or "Neighborhoods in Manhattan" – via the identification, extraction, and synthesis of pieces of information from textual sources. However, for more complex queries, such as "Benefits of immigration for NYC culture" current systems still rely on presenting the traditional ten blue links to the user as an answer.

To solicit works in this direction, and following the output of the recent SWIRL 2012 workshop on frontiers, challenges, and opportunities for information retrieval report [2], a new TREC track on Complex Answer Retrieval[1] (TREC CAR) for open-domain queries has been recently introduced [10].

The task and related dataset are based on the assumption that each Wikipedia page represents a complex topic, with further details under each sections. Accordingly, paragraphs contained in a section such as "Cultural diversity – Demographic" of the page "Culture of New York City", offer one aspect of the open-domain query "Culture of New York City". The goal of the task is presented as such: given an outline of a page (in the form of the page title and hierarchical section headings), retrieve a ranking of passages for each section. While assessed manually in the future, in this work, a passage is relevant for a section if and only if it is contained in the original article in the corresponding section.

[1] http://trec-car.cs.unh.edu/

Contribution. Many different approaches can be applied to this problem. This can address the ways a query can be expanded (using textual or structural information from knowledge bases), the way query and passages can be represented as vectors (e.g., word embedding vectors), and applications of deep neural networks and learning to rank. Given the recent release of the dataset, with this work we intend to support the future participants of the TREC CAR task by studying the performance of a variety of methods—to highlight which of them may be the most promising directions.

Additionally with the publication of this paper, we make our code and data available online.[2]

Outline. We give an overview of related work in Section 2, describe the data set and our experimentation environment in Section 3 and 4. Section 5 provides details of the approaches. We evaluate empirically in Section 6 before concluding the paper.

2 RELATED WORK

A wide variety of approaches are applicable to the TREC CAR problem. In the following, we cover three central ones, namely passage retrieval, query expansion using knowledge bases and the recent advancement in the use of deep neural network models for information retrieval.

Passage Retrieval. Passage retrieval is often cast as a variation on document retrieval, where the document retrieval model is applied only to a fragment of the text. The applications include search snippet detection, which aims to summarize the query-relevant parts of a document. Scores under the passage model can be combined with those from the containing document to improve performance [6] or to include quality indicators [5]. These approaches have been adapted to retrieve answers for questions [1]. Passage retrieval models can be extended to combine terms and entity-centric knowledge [8, 11]. For certain Wikipedia categories, template of articles can be extracted and automatically populated [24]. Furthermore, Banerjee and Mitra [4] found that training a lexical classifier per section heading obtains good results for article construction.

Neural-IR. With the comeback of neural networks, the IR community is exploring pre-trained word-vector approaches as well as dedicated neural networks for ranking. Pre-trained word- and entity-embeddings are publicly available in the form of word2vec,[3] GloVe,[4] DESM,[5] NTLM,[6] wiki2vec,[7] and RDF2Vec[8] vectors. Much

[2] https://federiconanni.com/trec-car-benchmark/
[3] https://code.google.com/archive/p/word2vec/
[4] http://nlp.stanford.edu/projects/glove/
[5] https://www.microsoft.com/en-us/download/details.aspx?id=52597
[6] http://www.zuccon.net/ntlm.html
[7] https://github.com/idio/wiki2vec
[8] http://data.dws.informatik.uni-mannheim.de/rdf2vec/

of the work in this area focuses on the applications of these shallow distributional models to IR tasks, although recently deeper architectures have also been investigated [18, 26].

Query Expansion with KB. Pseudo relevance feedback [15] is one of the most popular query expansion methods in which frequent words in top documents of a first retrieval run are extracted. This idea is generalized to expansion with multiple sources [7] based on terms and phrases. Recent developments in entity linking algorithms and object retrieval make it feasible to tap into the rich information provided by KBs [9, 14, 17], and exploit disambiguation and confidences for query and document representation [13, 21]. Further work on entity aspects [22] and effective learning-to-rank approaches for latent entities [25] are a promising avenue.

3 DATA SET

To study complex answer retrieval, the TREC CAR organizers extract a large and comprehensive benchmark from Wikipedia articles [10].[9] English Wikipedia is processed to separate articles into outlines of hierarchical section headings and contained paragraphs (discarding info boxes, images and wrappers - v1.4). The hierarchical outlines are provided as complex information needs, where for each heading a ranking of paragraphs is to be retrieved. Automatic relevance data (qrels files) are provided based on whether a paragraph was listed in a given section.

Train data. For 50% of all articles, both outlines and articles are made available as training data for supervised machine learning as well as a resource for the Rocchio method discussed below.

Test200. As the track focuses on knowledge-centric topics (in contrast to biographies), 200 manually selected outlines are provided as a representative test collection. Together, these 200 outlines include approximately 2300 headings, each resulting in a query.

4 EXPERIMENTATION ENVIRONMENT

We focus on the task of retrieving and ranking paragraphs for each heading of the outline. We consider the 2300 sections in Test200 corpus: First we experiment in a "safe" experimentation environment before applying approaches to the entire collection of seven million paragraphs. The goal is to simulate a noisy candidate generation method, which is guaranteed to include all relevant paragraphs for the heading with a set of nearly-relevant negatives.

For each heading, we construct a **train set** by selecting, for every true paragraph under the heading, five paragraphs from different sections of the article, and five paragraphs from a different article.

Similarly we construct a **test set** that includes all paragraphs from the article, as well as the same amount of paragraphs drawn from other articles. All articles are provided in random order. On average this process yields a mean of 35 paragraphs per section.

5 EXAMINED APPROACHES

The setup of TREC CAR is a bit unusual as all headings of an article are given at once, with the goal of producing a separate ranking for each heading. In this early work, we are breaking each outline into several independent queries, one per heading h as follows: We identify the path from the heading to the root, and concatenate all all headings together with the page title to obtain the query.

For example, if h corresponds to heading H2.3.4 the query is the concatenation of H2.3.4, H2.3, H2 and the page title.

Based on these queries, we experiment with different query expansion approaches and vector space representations of queries and paragraphs (TF-IDF, GloVe embeddings and RDF2Vec embeddings). We examine BM25, cosine similarity, learning to rank [16] and a state-of-the-art neural network model [19].

5.1 Query Expansion Techniques

We experiment three different query expansion approaches. We combine them with other scores, to, for instance, obtain RM3.

Expansion terms (RM1). Feedback terms are derived using pseudo relevance feedback and the relevance model [15]. Here we use Galago's implementation[10] which is based on a Dirichlet smoothed language model for the feedback run. In the experimental setting, we achieve the best performance expanding the queries with top 10 terms extracted from the top 10 feedback paragraphs.

Expansion entities (ent-RM1). Another way of expanding queries is by retrieving relevant entities. As for retrieving supporting terms, we derive a set of feedback entities by a search of the index using the heading-query and deriving several entities. In the experimental setting, best performance are achieved using 10 entities.

Paragraph Rocchio. Inspired by the work of Banerjee and Mitra [4], we retrieve other paragraphs, which have an identical heading to our heading-query, from folds 1 to 4 of the collection (omitting the fold where test200 originates from). For example, given a query such as "Demographic", regarding the entity United States, we collect supporting paragraphs from the pages of other entities (e.g., United Kingdom), which have as well a a section titled "Demographic". Headings are pre-processed with tokenisation, stopword/digit removal and stemming. This way, we can retrieve at least one supporting paragraph for 1/3 of our heading-queries. In the experimental setting, we test expansion using from 1 to 100 supporting passages and we obtain best performance expanding the query with 5 passages.

5.2 Vector Space Representations

We study three variations for representing the content in the vector space model.

TF-IDF. Representing each word in the vocabulary as its own dimension in the vector space, queries and paragraphs are represented as their TF-IDF vector. We are using the logarithmic L2-normalised variant. We perform stemming as a pre-processing step.

Word Embeddings. Using the pre-trained word embedding GloVE [20] of 300 dimensions, every word w in query or paragraph is represented as a K-dimensional vector $\vec{w}$. A vector representation for the whole paragraph $\vec{d}$ (complete query $\vec{q}$) is obtained by a weighted element-wise average of word vectors $\vec{w}$ in the paragraph (query). To give more attention to infrequent word, we use the TF-IDF of each word w to weights.

$$\vec{d} = \frac{1}{|d|} \sum_{w \in d} \text{TF-IDF}(w) \cdot \vec{w}$$

Entity Embeddings. Queries and paragraphs are represented as their mentioned DBpedia entities, using the entity linker TagMe

---

[9]Dataset available at: http://trec-car.cs.unh.edu/datareleases/v1.4-release.html

[10]lemurproject.org/galago.php

[12] (with default parameters). Next, we obtain latent vector representations $\vec{e}$ of each linked entity e using pre-computed **RDF2Vec** 300d entity embeddings [23]. Vector representations of paragraphs $\vec{d}$ (queries $\vec{q}$) are computed by a weighted element-wise average of entity vectors $\vec{e}$. By casting a paragraph as a bag-of-links we adapt TF-IDF to entity links (link statistics from DBpedia 2015-04 [3]):

$$\vec{d} = \frac{1}{|\{e \in d\}|} \sum_{e \in d} \text{TF-IDF}(e) \cdot \vec{e}$$

5.3 Ranking Approaches

We include four different ranking approaches.

Okapi BM25. Results are ranked using Okapi BM25 with k_1=1.2 and b=0.75, using the implementation of Lucene 6.4.1. Porter stemming and stopword removal was applied to paragraphs and queries.

Cosine Similarity. Paragraphs are ranked by cosine similarity (**cs**) between vector representations of the query and the paragraph.

Learning to Rank. We combine the ranking scores of different baselines with supervised machine learning in a learning-to-rank setting, for producing a final ranking of relevant paragraphs. We use RankLib [11] with 5-fold cross validation using a linear model optimized for MAP, trained with coordinate ascent.

Deep Neural Network. The Duet model is a state-of-the-art deep neural network (DNN) recently proposed by Mitra et al. [19] for ad-hoc retrieval. The Duet architecture learns to model query-paragraph relevance by jointly learning good representations of the query and the paragraph text for matching, as well as by learning to identify good patterns of exact matches of the query terms in the paragraph text. We use the Duet implementation available publicly[12] under the MIT license for our experiments. Training on folds 1 to 4 of the collection, we only consider the first ten words for the query and the first 100 words for the passage as inputs. We use 64 hidden units in the different layers of the network, as opposed to 300 in the original paper, to reduce the total number of learnable parameters of the model. We trained the model for 32 epochs with a learning rate of 0.001 which was picked based on a subset of the training data. Each epoch was trained over 1024 minibatches, and each minibatch contained 1024 samples. Each training sample was a triplet consisting of a query, a positive passage, and a negative passage. The training time was limited to 60 hours.

6 EVALUATION

We present experiments both on a small set and on the full data set.

6.1 Experimentation Environment

The experimentation environment (Section 4) provides a "safe environment" by simulating a noisy candidate method for each section. Results are presented in Table 1. The approach *bm25 query only* sets the baseline of our work.

Not all query expansion approaches and vector space representation methods improve over this baseline. This is particularly true for query expansion with terms or entities (through RM3 = query + RM1) as well as RDF2Vec embeddings. On the contrary, the most promising results among the methods which employ cosine similarity as a ranking function, are obtained when the query is expanded

---

[11]lemurproject.org/ranklib.php
[12]https://github.com/bmitra-msft/NDRM/blob/master/notebooks/Duet.ipynb

Table 1: Results on experimentation environment.

	MAP	R-Prec	MRR
BM25			
query only	0.304	0.225	0.388
TF-IDF (cs)			
query only	0.328	0.212	0.385
query + RM1	0.325	0.206	0.385
query + Rocchio	0.401	0.286	0.467
GloVe (cs)			
query only	0.329	0.210	0.387
query + RM1	0.255	0.148	0.305
query + Rocchio	0.350	0.236	0.410
RDF2Vec (cs)			
entity-query only	0.313	0.200	0.369
ent-query + ent-RM1	0.322	0.209	0.379
ent-query + ent-Rocchio	0.316	0.205	0.376
Learning to Rank			
all (cs) scores	0.412	0.295	0.478
Duet model			
query only	**0.465**	**0.359**	**0.552**

Table 2: Results of the initial candidate selection.

	MAP	R-Prec	MRR
BM25			
query only	**0.140**	**0.110**	**0.202**
TF-IDF (cs)			
query only	0.035	0.025	0.053
query + Rocchio	0.029	0.020	0.041

with Rocchio vectors trained on paragraphs from sections with the same heading. This finding reconfirms the results of previous work on the automatic generation of Wikipedia articles based its structural information [4]. The results show that common traits between Wikipedia sections with the same heading are better captured using the TF-IDF word vector than through word- and entity-embedding vectors suggest that a possible improvement over these baselines could by obtained by training embeddings for this task.

In comparison to these unsupervised retrieval models, both supervised Learning to Rank and the Neural Duet model out-perform all previously described baselines. In particular, the Duet model yields a substantial improvement over all presented approaches, showing the potential of neural-IR for the task. It is important to remark that neural deep models take days to train even on a GPU. In addition they are data-hungry, with performances improving significantly with more training data as shown in Figure 1.

6.2 Experiments on Full TREC collection

Moreover, we conduct experiments on the entire paragraph collection.

Candidate Selection. Many of the previously presented methods, such as the Duet model, require a candidate generating method. We test three candidate methods: BM25, TF-IDF, and TF-IDF with Rocchio expansion. For each query, the methods produce a candidate

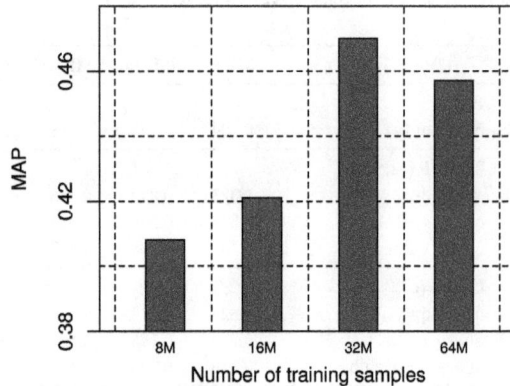

Figure 1: Effect of training data size on the performance of the Duet model. Training on four folds, reporting MAP on holdout fold.

Table 3: Results on the Paragraph Collection after candidate method. ▼ Worse according to paired-t-test with $\alpha = 5\%$.

	MAP	R-Prec	MRR	w/o BM25 MAP
BM25 candidate	0.140▼	0.110	0.202	-
theoretical upper-bound	0.382	0.382	0.537	0.382
TF-IDF (cs)				
BM25 + query + Rocchio	0.143▼	0.112	0.206	0.085
GloVe (cs)				
BM25 + query + Rocchio	0.150▼	0.119	0.217	0.082
Duet model				
BM25 + query only	**0.160**	**0.130**	**0.229**	0.094

set of 100 paragraphs. The results are presented in Table 2. While this is a challenging task, encouraging performance are obtained by *BM25 query only*, which we use in the following. Since not all relevant paragraphs are contained in the candidate set, the theoretically achievable performance of following methods is upper-bound by MRR is 0.537 and MAP/R-Prec is 0.382.

We evaluate the three best systems from Table 1 on the candidate set, combining candidate method BM25 and other components with learning to rank (5-fold cross validation) in Table 3. The combination of BM25 score and duet model is significantly outperforming all other methods, demonstrating the strength of neural method (although the Duet is by far the most expensive method to train). However, if the combination with the BM25 score is left out, all methods are significantly loosing in performance (see last column in Table 3).

7 CONCLUSIONS

In this paper, we present the performance of a variety of approaches, from established baselines to more advanced systems, in the context of the new TREC-CAR track on Complex Answer Retrieval.

Our results show that Neural retrieval methods provides best results only (!) when combined with the score of the candidate method. Among fast to train methods, we find that BM25 is a strong baseline, and that a Rocchio classifier based on headings is better than query expansion with pseudo-relevance feedback (RM3). We offer this empirical analysis as a complement to the publicly available TREC CAR dataset, to support future participants of the track and the IR community.

Acknowledgements

The publication is funded in part through the scholarship of the Eliteprogramm for Postdocs of the Baden-Württemberg Stiftung (project "Knowledge Consolidation and Organization for Query-specific Wikipedia Construction").

REFERENCES

[1] Elif Aktolga, James Allan, and David A. Smith. 2011. Passage reranking for question answering using syntactic structures and answer types. In *Advances in Information Retrieval*. Springer.
[2] James Allan, Bruce Croft, Alistair Moffat, and Mark Sanderson. 2012. Frontiers, challenges, and opportunities for information retrieval: Report from SWIRL 2012 the second strategic workshop on information retrieval in Lorne. In *ACM SIGIR Forum*, Vol. 46. ACM, 2–32.
[3] Sören Auer, Christian Bizer, Georgi Kobilarov, Jens Lehmann, Richard Cyganiak, and Zachary Ives. 2007. *Dbpedia: A nucleus for a web of open data*. Springer.
[4] Siddhartha Banerjee and Prasenjit Mitra. 2015. WikiKreator: Improving Wikipedia Stubs Automatically.. In *ACL (1)*. 867–877.
[5] Michael Bendersky, W Bruce Croft, and Yanlei Diao. 2011. Quality-biased ranking of web documents. In *WSDM*.
[6] Michael Bendersky and Oren Kurland. 2008. Utilizing passage-based language models for document retrieval. In *Advances in Information Retrieval*. Springer.
[7] Michael Bendersky, Donald Metzler, and W Bruce Croft. 2012. Effective query formulation with multiple information sources. In *WSDM*.
[8] Roi Blanco and Hugo Zaragoza. 2010. Finding support sentences for entities. In *SIGIR*.
[9] Jeffrey Dalton, Laura Dietz, and James Allan. 2014. Entity Query Feature Expansion Using Knowledge Base Links. In *SIGIR*.
[10] Laura Dietz and Ben Gamari. 2017. TREC CAR: A Data Set for Complex Answer Retrieval. Version 1.4. (2017). http://trec-car.cs.unh.edu
[11] Laura Dietz and Michael Schuhmacher. 2015. An interface sketch for queripidia: Query-driven knowledge portfolios from the web. In *Proc. Workshop on Exploiting Semantic Annotations in IR*. ACM, 43–46.
[12] Paolo Ferragina and Ugo Scaiella. 2010. Tagme: on-the-fly annotation of short text fragments (by wikipedia entities). In *CIKM*. ACM.
[13] Faegheh Hasibi, Krisztian Balog, and Svein Erik Bratsberg. 2016. Exploiting Entity Linking in Queries for Entity Retrieval. In *ICTIR*. 209–218.
[14] Alexander Kotov and ChengXiang Zhai. 2012. Tapping into knowledge base for concept feedback: leveraging conceptnet to improve search results for difficult queries. In *WSDM*.
[15] Victor Lavrenko and W Bruce Croft. 2001. Relevance based language models. In *SIGIR*.
[16] Hang Li. 2014. Learning to rank for information retrieval and natural language processing. *Synthesis Lectures on Human Language Technologies* 7, 3 (2014).
[17] Xitong Liu and Hui Fang. 2015. Latent entity space: a novel retrieval approach for entity-bearing queries. *Information Retrieval Journal* 18, 6 (2015).
[18] Bhaskar Mitra and Nick Craswell. 2017. Neural Models for Information Retrieval. *arXiv preprint arXiv:1705.01509* (2017).
[19] Bhaskar Mitra, Fernando Diaz, and Nick Craswell. 2017. Learning to Match Using Local and Distributed Representations of Text for Web Search. In *www*.
[20] Jeffrey Pennington, Richard Socher, and Christopher D Manning. 2014. Glove: Global Vectors for Word Representation.. In *EMNLP*, Vol. 14.
[21] Hadas Raviv, Oren Kurland, and David Carmel. 2016. Document Retrieval Using Entity-Based Language Models. In *SIGIR*.
[22] Ridho Reinanda, Edgar Meij, and Maarten de Rijke. 2015. Mining, ranking and recommending entity aspects. In *SIGIR*.
[23] Petar Ristoski and Heiko Paulheim. 2016. Rdf2vec: Rdf graph embeddings for data mining. In *ISWC*. Springer.
[24] Christina Sauper and Regina Barzilay. 2009. Automatically generating Wikipedia articles: A structure-aware approach. In *IJCNLP*.
[25] Chenyan Xiong and Jamie Callan. 2015. Esdrank: Connecting query and documents through external semi-structured data. In *CIKM*.
[26] Ye Zhang, Md Mustafizur Rahman, Alex Braylan, Brandon Dang, Heng-Lu Chang, Henna Kim, Quinten McNamara, Aaron Angert, Edward Banner, Vivek Khetan, and others. 2016. Neural Information Retrieval: A Literature Review. *arXiv preprint arXiv:1611.06792* (2016).

Detecting Seasonal Queries Using Time Series and Content Features

Behrooz Mansouri
School of Electrical and Computer
Engineering, University of Tehran
Iran
b.mansouri@ut.ac.ir

Mohammad Sadegh Zahedi
School of Electrical and Computer
Engineering, University of Tehran
Iran
s.zahedi@ut.ac.ir

Maseud Rahgozar
Database Research Group, Control and
Intelligent Processing Center of Excellence,
School of Electrical and Computer
Engineering, University of Tehran
Iran
rahgozar@ut.ac.ir

Ricardo Campos
Polytechnic Institute of Tomar
LIAAD INESC TEC
Portugal
ricardo.campos@ipt.pt

ABSTRACT

Many user information needs are strongly influenced by time. Some of these intents are expressed by users in queries issued indistinctively over time. Others follow a seasonal pattern. Examples of the latter are the queries "*Golden Globe Award*", "*September 11th*" or "*Halloween*", which refer to seasonal events that occur or have occurred at a specific occasion and for which, people often search in a planned and cyclic manner. Understanding this seasonal behavior, may help search engines to provide better ranking approaches and to respond with temporally relevant results leading into user's satisfaction. Detecting the diverse types of seasonal queries is therefore a key step for any search engine looking to present accurate results. In this paper, we categorize web search queries by their seasonality into 4 different categories: Non-Seasonal (NS, e.g., "*Secure passwords*"), Seasonal-related to ongoing events (SOE, "*Golden Globe Award*"), Seasonal-related to historical events (SHE, e.g., "*September 11th*") and Seasonal-related to special days and traditions (SSD, e.g., "*Halloween*"). To classify a given query we extract both time series (using the document publish date) and content features from its relevant documents. A Random Forest classifier is then used to classify web queries by their seasonality. Our experimental results show that they can be categorized with high accuracy.

KEYWORDS

Temporal IR; Temporal Query Classification; Seasonal Queries;

1 INTRODUCTION

The importance of time cannot be neglected on web search. The temporal intent of the searcher adds an important dimension to the relevance judgments of web queries. However, lack of understanding their temporal requirements, increases the difficulty in clearly understand the real intention behind the

ICTIR '17, October 1–4, 2017, Amsterdam, Netherlands
© 2017 Association for Computing Machinery.
ACM ISBN 978-1-4503-4490-6/17/10...$15.00
https://doi.org/10.1145/3121050.3121100

user's query. Identifying the query temporal nature offers search engines the chance to provide better ranking approaches leading into user's satisfaction. For example, a search engine retrieving results for the query "*Halloween*" will mostly return recent pages related to this event during peak times (a likely indication of the approaching of the event), while Wikipedia-like pages during non-peak times. In this work, we are particularly concerned in identifying seasonal queries, a sub-type of temporal queries. Seasonal queries are issued periodically usually triggered by expected events occurring at specific planned and repeated occasions. During the occurrence of the event or on the days before or after it, an increase in the number of published documents and queries that concern the event can be observed. Figure 1 shows an example of this user behavior for the queries "*Golden Globe Award*" (Seasonal-related to ongoing event), "*September 11th*" (Seasonal-related to historical events) and "*Halloween*" (Seasonal-related to special days and traditions) from January 2004 (which marks the beginning of the Google Trends feature) to April 2017. The figure portraits a time series built by query frequency volume. A large number of spikes - mostly corresponding to the occurrence or celebration of the event - can be observed for each query, thus proving its seasonality.

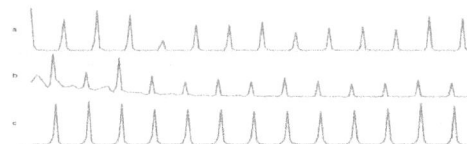

Figure 1: Query frequency pattern examples from Google Trends from January 2004 to April 2017. (a: "Golden Globe Award", b: "September 11th", c: "Halloween").

The genesis of detecting seasonality, dates back to 2010, when Zhang et al. [14] proposed to detect recurrent queries of related-events occurring at predictable time intervals, by using a machine learning classifier which is built on top of query logs, search sessions, clicks and time series features. A similar work was proposed by Shokouhi [13] who used seasonality of query volume time series to detect seasonal queries. In their work, they used time series decomposition techniques to measure seasonality of queries. In addition to the methods above,

Kulkarni et al. [16] analyzed a query log over the course of 10 weeks to explore how query's intent change over time. There has also been substantial work involving the dynamics and the classification of time-sensitive queries. The temporal dynamics of web queries have been commonly studied by building time series for queries based on their past frequency at uniform intervals and extracting time series features [5,8,13]. An interesting tutorial on this topic has been given by Radinsky et al. [12]. Other than frequency volume, previous researches used click log, query reformulation and relevant documents to better understand user temporal intent [1, 3, 11, 14]. In particular, Jones and Diaz [8], introduce a model to measure the distribution of documents retrieved in response to a query over the time domain in order to create a temporal profile for a query. They introduced three temporal classes of queries: atemporal, temporally ambiguous and temporally unambiguous. Campos et al. [1] also propose to classify queries into one of these three categories using information extracted from web snippets. Metzler et al. [11] in turn, used query logs to investigate implicitly year qualified queries. The work by Gupta and Berberich [5] describes a taxonomy of temporal classes at different granularities. Ghoreishi and Aixin [3] and Kanhabua et al. [9] studied event-related queries within Temporalia task of NTCIR [7] which considers 4 classes: atemporal, past, present, and future. A fully detailed description on Temporal IR applications can be found in the survey of Campos et al. [2]. In the next section, we present our classification taxonomy. The remainder of this paper is organized as follows. Section 3 describes the features used for classification. Section 4 outlines our experiment results. Finally, Section 5 provides some conclusions.

2 SEASONAL QUERIES CLASSIFICATION

Despite previous attempts to tackle the problem of identifying seasonal queries, no one so far, has considered to use content features as a means to understand the reasons for seasonality. Different approaches have been presented for this purpose [13 - 14], however mostly focused on identifying seasonal queries based on time series and query reformulation data. In this work, we plan to use relevant published documents as a way to capture seasonality. In particular, we use time series and content features to capture valuable information. This may be understood as an important contribution to the community. As an additional contribution, we present a new taxonomy which distinguishes between the different types of seasonal queries: Non-Seasonal (NS), Seasonal-related to ongoing event (SOE), Seasonal-related to historical events (SHE) and Seasonal-related to special days and traditions (SSD). In particular, NS refer to those types of queries that do not show any seasonal spike in their related time-series (e.g., "passwords"); SOE concern events that in each episode a new story - which is different from previous ones - happens (e.g. "US Presidential Elections", "Olympics"); SHE shows periodic spikes because of an old, usually historical event, for which users are tempted to search whenever the celebration date approaches (e.g. "September attacks", "Adolf Hitler Death",

"Iranian Revolution"). Finally, SSD concern special days and traditions (e.g. "Halloween", "Thanksgiving Day").

Detecting the different types of seasonal queries can be very useful for search engines aiming to adapt their results depending on the type of seasonal query detected. Our assumption, which we will confirm by query log analysis, is that different queries, despite having the same time series shape (recall Figure 1), may present different requirements in terms of the results to be returned to the user. For example, seasonal queries such as "Halloween" may require more recent pages during peak times, whereas an historical seasonal query such as "September 11th", which is often issued by users each year, demands, instead, more Wikipedia-like pages. To validate our assumption, we conduct a user survey on two-year query log of a Persian commercial search engine. We studied user's behavior towards seasonal queries under peak and non-peak times, where peak time is defined as the time that goes from a week before and a week after the occurrence of the seasonal event, and non-peak time is defined as the rest of the time that do not fit within the previous interval. For this purpose, we selected 150 seasonal queries with a two-year query log frequency higher than 100. These queries concern well-known seasonal events that took place on repeated occasions (e.g., "Halloween") during this two-year time period. All the queries were then manually classified into each one the three seasonal classes by 4 professional editors. An inter-rater reliability analysis using the Fleiss Kappa statistics was performed to determine consistency among the editors. Overall, the annotators obtained about 0.88 of agreement level, which represents a high agreement between editors. 41 queries were labeled SHE (Seasonal-related to historical events), 50 SOE (Seasonal-related to ongoing event) and 59 SSD (Seasonal-related to special days and traditions). For each query, we considered the top-200 clicked pages (100 pages from peak time and 100 from non-peak time) totalizing 30.000 web pages. We then asked one student to look at the content of each web page and to manually classify them with regards to recency, oldness and Wikipedia-like page (a type of page that is usually retrieved for seasonal events). In particular, each web page is classified into: (1) Recent Pages; which provide information about the most recent episode of the event, (2) Wikipedia-Like Pages; which gives general information about the event and (3) Old Pages; which concerns the old episodes of the event. Table 1 summarizes the result of our study, by showing the percentage of clicked pages per page categories during peak and non-peak times for each seasonal query class.

Table 1: **Percentage of clicked pages per seasonal queries during peak and non-peak times**.

Seasonal Query Class	Recent Pages		Wikipedia-Like Pages		Old Pages	
	Peak	Non-Peak	Peak	Non-Peak	Peak	Non-Peak
SOE	**92.1%**	51.4%	2.5%	7.1%	5.4%	41.5%
SHE	54.7%	7.3%	44.9%	**90.6%**	0.4%	2.1%
SSD	**94.3%**	4.9%	4.1%	91.3%	1.6%	3.8%

Based on our experiment, we were able to confirm that, despite having the same time series shape, different seasonal queries may require a different type of results. Thus, detecting the different type of seasonal queries may reveal an important feature for any search engine looking to provide better ranking approaches. Our experiments on query logs show that the results to be retrieved should differ during peak and non-peak times for each seasonal category class. Observing the results for SOE queries one can conclude that during peak times, users prefer most recent web pages thus retrieving more fresh documents seems to be the best choice. This contrasts with non-peak periods, for which temporal diversity is suggested. Likewise, considering peak times on SHE queries, users are mostly interested in getting to know about recent commemorative and memorial gatherings. However, in contrast to SOE queries, a notable amount of users were also interested in Wikipedia-like pages. On non-peak times, Wikipedia-like pages were also dominantly clicked compared to other type of web pages. Finally, SSD queries were mostly favored with recent pages during peak times, while Wikipedia-like pages were preferred on non-peak times.

3 OUR APPROACH

To detect the different types of seasonal queries, we expand the queries with two types of features: (i) time-series; (ii) content features.

3.1 Time Series Features

A time series is a sequence of values of a particular measure taken at regularly spaced intervals over time. In the context of web search, a time series can be constructed for a query based on the queries past frequency or generated on top of the retrieved documents published time. In this work, we chose the latter. Thus, instead of resting on query log features, we follow a metadata-based approach which rests on top the documents published time. Here we introduce our 7-time series features: (1) **Autocorrelation** indicates how well a time series is similar to a time-shifted copy of itself. We used lag-1 autocorrelation of a time series which is the correlation of each value with the immediately preceding observation. Time series of queries with strong inter-day dependency have higher autocorrelation value [10]. Autocorrelation of time series T with lag=1 can be calculated as follows ($\bar{t}$ is the mean value of time series):

$$Autocorrelation(T) = \frac{\sum_{i=1}^{N-1}(t_i - \bar{t})(t_{i+1} - \bar{t})}{\sum_{i=1}^{N}(t_i - \bar{t})} \qquad (1)$$

(2) **Seasonality** represents the cosine similarity between time series and its seasonal component. Different decomposition approaches can be applied to time series in order to analyze its seasonal components. In this work, we use Holt-Winters decomposition technique [4]. After decomposing the time series, we remove its trend component from the time series as it just shows the overall trend of a query and then calculate the cosine similarity between the seasonal component and the remaining components. Considering S as seasonal component of time series and $\hat{T}$ as time series with removed trend component seasonality of time series T is:

$$Seasonality(T) = \frac{S.\hat{T}}{\|S\|.\|\hat{T}\|} \qquad (2)$$

(3) **Kurtosis** calculates how much of the probability distribution is contained in the peaks and how much in the low-probability regions [8] and is calculated as the ratio of the fourth moment and variance squared. (4) **Randomness Test** is used to analyze the distribution of a set of data to see if it is random. We calculate p-value of Mann-Kendall rank test [11] and use it as a feature of randomness. (5) **SSE** (Sum of Squared Errors) of a prediction model can show how the time series is unplanned at a given point. We estimate predicted values using Holt-Winters [4] approach. (6) **Modality** in time series show number of detected modes. Seasonal queries should have multi-modal time series. In our work, we used Dip test [6] to calculate number of modes. (7) **Mean** value of time series.

3.2 Content Features

In addition to time series features (over a metadata-based approach), we also consider six content features: (1) **Content clarity:** shows how specific a query is, and it is measured by calculating the KL-divergence between the collection language model and the relevant documents language model. A higher KL-divergence value indicates that the query is clear and that its related documents concern a more specific topic. (In this work, we used unigram language model). (2) **Year expressions:** The number of year expressions mentioned in relevant documents is an important feature which help us to differentiate between seasonal queries. For SOE queries, multiple year expressions with high frequency are expected. SSD queries in turn, are mostly characterized by one high frequency year expression. Finally, SHE queries have no year expression with high frequency. Based on this, we also consider: (3) **number of total year expressions**; (4) **number of distinct year expressions**; (5) **difference between the first and second frequent year expressions** (different between their frequency); and (6) **number of distinct year expressions** with frequency higher than 20.

4 EXPRIMENTS

4.1 Dataset and Experimental Setting

Our experiments were conducted on 300 Persian web queries (150 selected from Section 2, divided as follows: 41 SHE (Seasonal-related to historical events), 50 SOE (Seasonal-related to ongoing event) and 59 SSD (Seasonal-related to special days and traditions); plus 150 non-seasonal queries randomly selected from the query logs). Our dataset is publicly available[1]. To conduct our experiments, we make use of Hamshahri news dataset [15], which covers a wide range of news in Persian language, including politics, entertainment and sports, and resort to the set of queries introduced in Section 2. For each query, top-200 relevant documents were retrieved using Okapi BM25 retrieval model. As each document has a publication date this dataset suits our experiment. Time series were then generated

---

[1] http://dbrg.ut.ac.ir/SeasonalQueryDataset/

using documents publish date. To extract year expressions, we consider any number between 1990 and 2030 (Gregorian calendar), and 1300 to 1400 (Jalali calendar) a year expression. We used 10-fold stratified cross validation, and averaged the results over 10 runs. We used Random Forest for the classification and compared it with LibSVM, AdaBoost, and Naïve Bayes.

4.2 Feature Evaluation

In order to study the importance of our features we used information gain ratio (IGR) on training data. Auto correlation (0.371 of IGR) and seasonality (0.337) were the most important time series feature in terms of measuring the periodicity of time series. The distinct (0.337), seasonality (0.325) and also the total number of year expressions (0.319) are also important features to discriminate between the different seasonal categories. In contrast, some time series features like modality (0.124) randomness (0.048) were less discriminative.

4.3 Experimental Results

In order to classify queries into seasonal categories we use Random Forest (RF) classifier due to its properties like bagging and boosting. We compared its effectiveness against three baseline models: LibSVM, Naïve Bayes and AdaBoost. The results of our experiments are shown in Table 2. All the results are statistically significant when comparing RF classifier with each one of the baselines, with p-value < 0.05 using the matched paired one-sided t-test. A careful observation of the results led us to conclude that RF Classifier achieved the highest effectiveness with 0.887 F-measure which outperforms the 3 other classifiers.

Table 2: **Performance of different classifiers**

Model	Precision	Recall	F-measure
Random Forest	0.887	0.887	0.887
LibSVM	0.799	0.797	0.790
Naïve Bayes	0.820	0.757	0.757
AdaBoost	0.794	0.847	0.820

To better analyze the outcomes of our approach, we present in Table 3 the confusion matrix for the Random Forest classifier. As this table shows, instances of SSD queries (Seasonal-related to special days and traditions) were wrongly labeled as NS (non-seasonal queries). The main reason for that is the stable and non-periodic shape of time series for some of its queries. This can be observed in Figure 2 for the query "*Father's Day*", which despite being an SSD query, portraits a steady non-periodical shape.

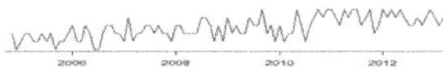

Figure 2: **Time series built over top-200 relevant documents publish time retrieved for the query "Father's day".**

Also, some queries from SOE (Seasonal-related to ongoing event) were wrongly categorized as SHE (Seasonal-related to historical events). Our exploration of the results, shows that, while SOE queries are characterized by multiple occurrences, top-200 retrieved documents are formed, mostly, by texts referring to a very specific episode of the event. For example, for the query "*Oscar*", most of the documents retrieved in the top-200 relate to

2012 when a Persian movie ("Separation") won the Oscar for the best movie. Yet this query is related to several all Oscar events. On the other hand, NS queries behaved well and 96% of its queries were correctly classified.

Table 3: **Confusion matrix for the Random Forest classifier**

Real \ Classified	NS	SOE	SHE	SSD
NS	144	2	2	2
SOE	1	40	5	4
SHE	2	2	34	3
SSD	7	1	3	48

5 CONCLUSIONS

Seasonal queries are a sub-type of temporal queries, characterized by a change of search intents over time. Understanding this seasonal behavior, may help search engines to provide better ranking approaches and to respond with temporally relevant results leading eventually into user's satisfaction. Ideally, search engines would have different retrieval strategies for any of the different categories, using this additional information to provide better responses for their users. In this paper, we proposed an approach for identifying different seasonal queries by using time series and content features. We show how users' behavior toward these queries are different. Random Forest classifier is used for classification and achieved 88.7% F-Measure. As part of future work, we plan to propose a ranking approach that use the proposed taxonomy to better rank the retrieved results. Although our approach is totally independent of any language, we plan to do the same study on an English dataset.

6 ACKNOWLEDGMENTS

This research was funded by Project "TEC4Growth - Pervasive Intelligence, Enhancers and Proofs of Concept with Industrial Impact/NORTE-01-0145-FEDER-000020" which is financed by the North Portugal Regional Operational Programme (NORTE 2020), under the PORTUGAL 2020 Partnership Agreement, and through the European Regional Development Fund (ERDF).

REFERENCES

[1] Campos, R., Dias, G., and Jorge, A. (2011). What is the Temporal Value of Web Snippets. In WWW-TWAW'11, pp. 9-16.
[2] Campos, R., Dias, G., Jorge, A., and Jatowt, A. (2014). Survey of Temporal Information Retrieval and Related Applications. In CSUR, 47(2). Article No.: 15.
[3] Ghoreishi, S., and Aixin, S. (2013). Predicting Event-Relatedness of Popular Queries. In CIKM'13, pp. 1193-1196.
[4] Goodwin, P. (2010). The Holt-Winters Approach to Exponential Smoothing: 50 Years Old and Going Strong. In The Int. Journal of Applied Forecasting, 19, pp. 30-33.
[5] Gupta D. and Berberich, K (2015). Temporal Query Classification at Different Granularities. In SPIRE'15, pp. 156-164.
[6] Hartigan, J. A., and Hartigan, P.M. (1985). The Dip Test of Unimodality. In The Annals of Statistics, 13(1), pp 70-84.
[7] Joho, H., Jatowt, A., Blanco, R., Naka, H., and Yamamoto, S. (2011). In NTCIR'11.
[8] Jones R. and Diaz, F (2007). Temporal Profiles of Queries. In TOIS, 25(3).
[9] Kanhabua, N., Nguyen, T., and Wolfgang, N. (2015). Learning to Detect Event-Related Queries for Web Search. In WWW'15, pp. 1139-1344.
[10] Kendall, M. G. (1948). Rank Correlation Methods.
[11] Metzler, D., Jones, R., Peng, F., and Zhang, R. (2009). Improving Search Relevance for Implicitly Temporal Queries. In SIGIR'09, pp. 700-701.
[12] Radinsky, K., Diaz, F., Dumais, S., Shokouhi, M., Dong, A., and Chang, Y. (2013). Temporal Web Dynamics and its Application to Information Retrieval". In WSDM'13
[13] Shokouhi M (2011). Detecting Seasonal Queries by Time-Series Analysis. In SIGIR'11, pp. 1171-1172.
[14] Zhang, R., Konda, Y., Dong, A.; Kolari, P.; Chang, Y., and Zheng, Z. (2010). Learning Recurrent Event Queries for Web Search. In EMNLP'10, pp. 1129-1139.
[15] AleAhmad, A., Amiri, H., Darrudi, E., Rahgozar, M. and Oroumchian, F., 2009. Hamshahri: A standard Persian text collection. Knowledge-Based Systems, 22(5)
[16] Kulkarni, A., Teevan, J., Svore, K. M., and Dumais, S.T. (2011). Understanding Temporal Query Dynamics. In WSDM'11, pp. 167-176.

A Contextual Bandit Approach to Dynamic Search

Angela Yang
Department of Computer Science
Georgetown University
Washington, D.C. 20057
asy24@georgetown.edu

Grace Hui Yang
Department of Computer Science
Georgetown University
Washington, D.C. 20057
huiyang@cs.georgetown.edu

ABSTRACT

When users engage in complex search tasks, they encounter two main questions at each point in the search: how to re-formulate the query and whether to continue the search or stop. In this paper, we propose a contextual bandit algorithm to model the dynamic search process. The proposed algorithm uses the context surrounding the current state of the search to select how the search will continue through different query re-formulation tactics. Furthermore, the algorithm automatically decides stopping condition for a search process. Using data from the Text REtrieval Conference (TREC) 2016 Dynamic Domain Track, we evaluate our system's search effectiveness over time and compare to the official runs. Our results show that the use of context as well as an automated stopping condition is effective in a dynamic search system.

1 INTRODUCTION

Dynamic search is a complex search process which involves multiple iterations of searches to accomplish an overall goal. A search topic can be broken down into subtopics that the user navigates through and discovers through their search. For example, a user looking for places to eat in New York City might choose to search the topic "NYC restaurants." In her initial search, she might find a wide variety of relevant information. Thus, she will choose one subtopic, such as "New York style pizza," and continue the search with that subtopic. Afterwards, she may choose another subtopic that she discovered, such as "Michelin star restaurants," and search on this new subtopic. Her complex search task would not be finished until she has searched through the different subtopics in her search task and her information need is fulfilled.

As we can see, in the current setting of a complex search task, a user with a broad information need goes through multiple iterations of query re-formulation to find relevant documents. This process is repeated until their information need has been satisfied. However, this current search process leaves a lot of responsibility with the user, especially placing the burden of query formulation and decisions of navigation on their shoulders. A few efforts [1, 4, 6] have thought about an alternative setting that instead shifts the responsibility to the systems.

ICTIR '17, October 1–4, 2017, Amsterdam, The Netherlands
© 2017 ACM. ISBN 978-1-4503-4490-6/17/10...$15.00
DOI: http://dx.doi.org/10.1145/3121050.3121101

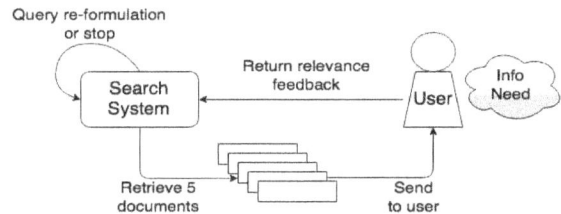

Figure 1: The TREC Dynamic Domain search process

The Text REtrieval Conference (TREC) Dynamic Domain (DD) Track [6], introduced in 2015, researches dynamic search using a simulated user called the "jig," that provides feedback for the documents returned by a search system. The task can be visualized in figure 1. In the TREC-DD task, the system uses a seed query to begin the search, providing 5 documents to the simulated user for feedback at each iteration. This feedback, instead of being click data, comes in the form of whether or not that document was relevant, and if it was, which passages within it were relevant and how relevant they were. Using that feedback, the system should then make a decision of whether to stop the search or continue it by retrieving 5 more documents in the next iteration.

Previous submissions to the Dynamic Domain Track use methods such as MDP [6] and passage language models [1]. While most algorithms focus on the document retrieval portion of the search process and manually specify the search's stopping condition, this paper proposes the addition of search completion automation.

In this paper, we propose using the context surrounding the current search to aid the system through the use of a contextual bandit algorithm. We ran our system on the TREC-DD 2016 Ebola dataset, and compared our system's runs with baselines extracted from the TREC-DD 2016 submitted runs. We also analyzed the search policy created by our system to better understand how the system navigated through the dynamic search. Our proposed system shifts more of the search responsibility from the user to the system, leading to a smarter and more agile search system.

2 PRELIMINARIES: CONTEXTUAL BANDITS

Contextual bandit algorithms [7] are a type of reinforcement learning algorithm that uses the context given at each iteration to select an action that will maximize some sort of reward. Contextual bandits are similar to the multi-armed bandit with the augmentation of a historical context that is utilized alongside the reward from previous iterations to select an action. The context can be historical data that was collected since the start of the process, such as in Shivaswamy and Joachims [5], or use the contextual features of the current action to influence the bandit selection policy, such as in LinUCB by Lihong et al. [2].

The LinUCB algorithm was originally designed for personal news recommendation. LinUCB uses contextual information gathered from the user and news articles to estimate a reward for each action. At each iteration, they pick the action that maximizes their estimated reward, using

$$a_t \overset{\text{def}}{=} \underset{a \in A_t}{\operatorname{argmax}} \left(\mathbf{x}_{t,a}^\top \hat{\theta}_a + \alpha \sqrt{\mathbf{x}_{t,a}^\top \mathbf{A}_a^{-1} \mathbf{x}_{t,a}} \right) \tag{1}$$

where a_t signifies the selected action, $\mathbf{x}_{t,a}$ is the feature vector with an unknown but estimated coefficient vector $\hat{\theta}_a$ and α is a constant. $\sqrt{\mathbf{x}_{t,a}^\top \mathbf{A}_a^{-1} \mathbf{x}_{t,a}}$ is the standard deviation of the expected reward, where $\mathbf{A}_a^{-1}$ is the inverse of a matrix made by adding a design matrix corresponding to the previous contexts to an identity matrix the size of the context. In [2], they use click data as reward.

We adapt the LinUCB algorithm as its use of context at each iteration to select an action fits well with the multi-iterative approach of a dynamic search process. Our adaptation of LinUCB emphasizes the use of the context surrounding the search iteration, such as what the user found relevant and where previous actions have explored in the information space, to select what the appropriate next action should be. Furthermore, while [2] defines its action as the actual news article that is selected, we define actions as the tactics used to edit the query to retrieve documents, with the feedback information returned from the simulated user as the reward.

3 IMPLEMENTATION

Our framework uses a LinUCB contextual bandit algorithm[1] built on top of a search engine[2] to interact with the simulated user in order to navigate through the dynamic search process. At each iteration t, the bandit is provided with contextual information about the current state of the search. This feature vector is used by the bandit along with the reward information about each action to select one of four actions to play for that iteration. The relevance feedback provided in response to the documents retrieved by that action is then used to calculate a reward for the action selected. This process is repeated until the search is finished.

3.1 Bandit Actions

We design four actions in the bandit: add, remove, weight and stop. These actions use query re-formulation tactics in order to explore the search topic through its different subtopics. The actions "add," "remove," and "weight," explore the topic through a widening or narrowing focus of the search, while the action "stop" is akin to ending the search in that topic, and (if applicable) starting a new search in a different topic. The next topic can be randomly chosen.

3.1.1 Add. The action "add" provides more detail to the search by adding another word to the query in order to explore a new, more specific subtopic in the search. We use a form of tf-idf to

---

[1]We used the open source python package Striatum bandit at https://github.com/ntucllab/striatum.
[2]We used the Indri 5.8 search enginehttps://www.lemurproject.org/indri/.

Table 1: Actions and Their Associated Directions

Action	Search Direction
Add	Explore a more detailed subtopic "Kaci Hickox"→"Kaci Hickox actions"
Remove	Broaden search from subtopic "existing robots"→"robots"
Weight	Search for more documents within the same subtopic "1.0 US 1.0 Military 1.0 crisis 1.0 response" →"0.8 US 0.85 Military 1.0 crisis 0.9 response"
Stop	End search for one topic "alleged alternative Ebola treatments"

select the word:

$$s_w = \underset{w \in D_{rel}}{\operatorname{argmax}} \left(\frac{freq_{w,d}}{len(d)} * \ln(\frac{size(D_{rel})}{docfreq_w}) \right) \tag{2}$$

The score s_w of any given word is the maximum tf-idf score received for that word w in any document d in the set of relevant documents D_{rel} retrieved that iteration. In equation 2, the term frequency is calculated using $freq_{w,d}$, the frequency of a word in a document, divided by the document length, and inverse document frequency is calculated using the natural log of the total number of relevant documents that iteration divided by $docfreq_w$, the number of documents containing that word. The word with the highest score is considered to be the most representative word found in the documents with positive feedback, and is therefore selected to be added to the query.

In table 1, the example for "add" shows how the search is narrowed from a general search on the woman Kaci Hickox to a more specific search on her actions in particular.

3.1.2 Remove. The action "remove" also applies tf-idf like "add" to select which word to remove. This action widens the search from the previous subtopic. Notably, while the "add" action uses the set of relevant documents, "remove" uses the set of irrelevant documents in the feedback, or D_{nonrel} instead of D_{rel}. This generates a set of least relevant words retrieved in the last iteration. We then select the word in the current query that has the highest score in the set to be removed.

The example for "remove" shown in table 1 demonstrates this as the removal of the term "existing," which widens the search from searching about the currently existing robots being used to aid health care workers to all robots both existing and merely proposed to aid in the Ebola outbreak.

3.1.3 Weight. The action "weight" modifies the weights to each query term. This can be considered a continued search on the current subtopic with a shift in its focus. We calculate the adjustment as $weight_{t-1} \pm \alpha(rel(w))$, such that it is addition if the term is relevant and subtraction if irrelevant, and where $\alpha < 1$ is a constant and $rel(w)$ is the degree to which the term w is relevant or irrelevant. We decide the degree of a term's relevance or irrelevance by creating two lists—the top 20 most frequent words in the relevant documents and that in the irrelevant documents. A term's relevance or irrelevance is proportional to its rank on either list. Using mathematical representation, a term's weight is adjusted according

Table 2: The features of the search

#	context feature	explanation
1	# of documents seen	how far search is
2	# of relevant documents last iteration	current effectiveness
3	# of relevant documents seen	depth of search
4	# of times action weight called	search path direction
5	# of times action add called	search path direction
6	# of times action remove called	search path direction

to eq. 3, with α set as 0.2, meaning a maximum of 0.2 is added (if relevant) or subtracted (if irrelevant) from the weight at any one time.

$$w_t = \begin{cases} w_{t-1} + .2(\frac{20-rel(w)}{20}) & \text{if word } w \text{ is relevant} \\ w_{t-1} - .2(\frac{20-rel(w)}{20}) & \text{if word } w \text{ is irrelevant} \end{cases} \quad (3)$$

3.1.4 Stop. While most dynamic search systems being proposed set a stopping condition for the search manually, either through the number of iterations or number of relevant documents seen, we propose giving the bandit an action "stop" to decide the search's stopping condition automatically.

The action "stop" ends the search of one topic and, if applicable, starts the next one. For example, once the bandit has searched the topic "alleged alternative Ebola treatments" adequately and found enough information, the bandit will select the action "stop" and end the search on that topic. The bandit will then start the search on the next topic in the list provided by TREC, "urbanization/urbanisation."

3.2 Bandit Reward and Context Features

3.2.1 Reward. A reward is given to denote the effectiveness of an action. In a search process, the reward for an iteration can be considered the amount of information gained at that iteration. Therefore, we define the reward r_t for a selected action at iteration t as the sum of the relevance score RS for each relevant passage p in the set of all documents D retrieved at that iteration.

$$r_t = \sum_{p \in D} RS_p \quad (4)$$

The relevance score for a relevant passage is a score from 1 to 5, with 5 meaning extremely relevant and 1 being only marginally relevant. Note that the reward is never negative but it can be 0 if there were no relevant passages, which would show that the action was not effective in retrieving relevant documents for that iteration. The reward for "stop" is calculated using the set of documents retrieved by the next topic's initial search.

3.2.2 Context. The context given to the LinUCB model consists of six features, listed in table 2. These features span different aspects of the previous iteration(s) in order to provide the bandit with more information about the current state of the search and search path. Using the reward and the context, the bandit selects the action to play at each round that will maximize the reward.

4 RESULTS

Experiments were run on the Ebola dataset from TREC 2016 DD Track dataset, using the ground truth and topics provided by TREC

Table 3: Search effectiveness from Iteration 1 to Iteration 10 on TREC DD 2016 Ebola Dataset (* indicates stat. significant improvement over rmit-lm-psg-max, (p<0.05, t-test, one-sided))

Algorithm	CT@1	ACT@1	CT@10	ACT@10
LinUCB	0.278	0.208	0.098*	0.135*
rmit-lm-psg-max	0.246	0.268	0.049	0.089
LDA_Indri73	0.260	0.187	0.069	0.115
TREC Median	0.260	0.187	0.076	0.119
TREC Best	0.319	0.236	0.176	0.150

Table 4: A comparison of the scores of system with manual search completion and automated search completion (* indicates stat. significant improvement of automated system over manual system, (p<0.05, t-test, one-sided)).

Algorithm	1	3	5	7	10
Manual CT	0.277	0.139	0.090	0.068	0.049
Automated CT	0.277	0.149	0.116	0.104*	0.098*
Manual ACT	0.208	0.170	0.141	0.122	0.101
Automated ACT	0.208	0.172	0.153*	0.143*	0.135*

to retrieve results and generate relevance feedback. Since a relevant document is no longer relevant the second time it is seen, we prevent duplicate documents being retrieved for any one topic by assigning a prior value of $-1e-24$ to a document that was retrieved once to reduce the chance that it is retrieved again.

Results were evaluated using the official TREC-DD metrics, the Cube Test (CT) and Average Cube Test (ACT) [3]. CT and ACT metrics show gain over time, with gain calculated using

$$\text{Gain}(q, d_j) = \sum_i \Gamma \theta_i rel(d_j, c_i) \mathbb{1}(\sum_{k=1}^{j-1} rel(d_k, c_i < \text{MaxHeight}) \quad (5)$$

where $rel()$ is the relevance of document d_j to subtopic c_i, θ_i denotes the importance of the subtopic, Γ is the discount factor for previous gains to that subtopic, and $\mathbb{1}$ is the indicator function. MaxHeight constrains the gain such that once an information need has been fulfilled (has reached 1), no further gain can be added. CT at each iteration representing the change in information gain that occurred through that iteration.

4.1 Search Effectiveness

We compare our results to other TREC-DD 2016 submitted runs. The TREC median and best scores are aggregated from the median and best score of all the runs at each iteration. We also compare our system with a submitted run called rmit-lm-psg-max[1] that uses a passage language model for document ranking, which represents a vastly different approach to the one presented in this paper, and a submitted run, LDA_Indri73 [6] that uses MDP, a more similar approach to our system. The results in table 3 show that our bandit achieves significantly better CT and ACT scores compared to rmit-lm-psg-max by the tenth iteration. Our system also shows scores similar to the TREC median scores and LDA_Indri73 from iteration one to iteration ten.

Table 5: Example policy created by the bandit algorithm.

Action	Results
Add "Kaci Hickox actions"→"Kaci Hickox actions CDC"	3 relevant
Add "Kaci Hickox actions CDC"→"Kaci Hickox actions CDC obtain"	5 relevant
Weight "1.0 Kaci 1.0 Hickox 1.0 actions 1.0 CDC 1.0 obtain"→"1.0 Kaci 1.0 Hickox 1.0 actions 0.91 CDC 1.0 obtain"	4 relevant
Weight "1.0 Kaci 1.0 Hickox 1.0 actions 0.91 CDC 1.0 obtain"→"0.93 Kaci 0.96 Hickox 1.0 actions 0.91 CDC 1.0 obtain"	2 relevant
Stop	
Weight "1.0 natural 1.0 immunity"→".87 natural .9 immunity"	1 relevant
Weight ".87 natural .9 immunity"→".7 natural 1.0 immunity"	no relevant
Stop	

Our comparison with TREC best, however, shows that there is still much potential for our system to improve. The basic algorithms used for our actions and our use of the contextual bandit algorithm overall provides an effective method for retrieving relevant documents and selecting when to stop but leave room for continued improvement.

As most of our actions use quite straightforward tactics for query re-formulation, it is clear there is large room to improve the search effectiveness if we employ more sophisticated query re-formulation tactics. Nonetheless, these comparisons show that using the context of the current iteration to select the next action in the search provides a good method for navigating through the search and finding relevant documents. These results also indicate that our approach is effective with even a simple set of actions.

4.2 Automated Search Completion

To analyze the effects of automating the search completion, we ran our system with a manually set stopping condition instead of the "stop" action. Table 4 shows a comparison of that run with our automated system. Both systems begin with the same effectiveness, but the faster rate of decrease in the manual system demonstrates that our system is capable of detecting a good end to the search and provides a statistically significant improvement for our system's search effectiveness.

4.3 Bandit Search Policy

The policy created by the bandit to make decisions on how to navigate through the search focused on retrieving as many relevant documents as possible.

For example, table 5 shows an example from a search on Kaci Hickox, who resisted a quarantine as she insisted she was not infected. First, the bandit selected "add", and found that had good results. Specifically, the bandit system found that exploring a subtopic on her actions against the CDC led to many relevant documents.

Then, when the bandit discovered a subtopic that seemed to be very relevant (with 5 relevant documents), it chose to continue the search that subtopic with a shift in focus through the action "weight," also to good results. It finally ended the search when the effectiveness started to decrease.

During another search task, the bandit system tried using action weight to good results, turning "1.0 natural 1.0 immunity" to ".87 natural .9 immunity," with 1 relevant document. It therefore continued to choose action weight again. However, the new query ".7 natural 1.0 immunity" retrieved no relevant documents. At this point, the bandit system chose to stop the search, deciding that there had been enough relevant documents retrieved and that the search was becoming ineffective.

These examples demonstrate that the bandit understands the search path being explored and the search's current effectiveness. It is able to discover the strategies that lead to relevant results, and chooses "stop" at points when the effectiveness of the search begins to drop off.

5 CONCLUSIONS

In this paper, we proposed a solution to the dynamic search task that uses the context of the current search state in order to determine the next action in the search. We designed actions, add, remove, weight and stop, to explore the information space in order to find relevant documents quickly and exhaustively before deciding to end the search. Based on our system's interaction with the TREC-DD Ebola domain, we found that taking into account the context of the current search is relevant towards improving the search's effectiveness over time. In the future, we can continue to improve these results by applying more advanced query expansion and weight adjustment techniques to increase the bandit's search effectiveness over time. Further research can also be done on the search completion and next topic selection portion of the search, in order to build an even more advanced search system.

6 ACKNOWLEDGEMENTS

This research was supported by NSF grant IIS-145374 and DARPA FA8750-14-2-0226 and the SIGIR student travel grant. Any opinions, findings, conclusions, or recommendations expressed in this paper are of the authors, and do not necessarily reflect those of the sponsor.

REFERENCES

[1] Ameer Albahem, Lawrence Cavedon, Damiano Spina, and Falk Scholer. 2016. RMIT @ TREC 2016 Dynamic Domain Track: Exploiting Passage Representation for Retrieval and Relevance Feedback. In *TREC '16*.
[2] Lihong Li, Wei Chu, John Langford, and Robert E. Schapire. 2010. A Contextual-bandit Approach to Personalized News Article Recommendation *(WWW '10)*. 10.
[3] Jiyun Luo, Christopher Wing, Hui Yang, and Marti Hearst. 2013. The Water Filling Model and the Cube Test: Multi-dimensional Evaluation for Professional Search *(CIKM '13)*. 6.
[4] Felipe Moraes, Rodrygo L. T. Santos, and Nivio Ziviani. UFMG at the TREC 2016 Dynamic Domain track.
[5] Pannagadatta K. Shivaswamy and Thorsten Joachims. 2012. Multi-armed Bandit Problems with History. In *AISTATS '12*.
[6] Hui Yang and Ian Soboroff. 2016. TREC 2016 Dynamic Domain Overview. In *TREC '16*.
[7] Li Zhou. 2015. A Survey on Contextual Multi-armed Bandits. *CoRR* (2015).

Modeling Information Flow in Dynamic Information Retrieval

Felipe Moraes
Department of Computer Science
Universidade Federal de Minas Gerais
Belo Horizonte, MG, Brazil
felipemoraes@dcc.ufmg.br

Mário S. Alvim
Department of Computer Science
Universidade Federal de Minas Gerais
Belo Horizonte, MG, Brazil
msalvim@dcc.ufmg.br

Rodrygo L. T. Santos
Department of Computer Science
Universidade Federal de Minas Gerais
Belo Horizonte, MG, Brazil
rodrygo@dcc.ufmg.br

ABSTRACT

User interaction with a dynamic information retrieval (DIR) system can be seen as a cooperative effort towards finding relevant information. In this cooperation, the user provides the system with evidence of his or her information need (e.g., in the form of queries, query reformulations, relevance judgments, or clicks). In turn, the system provides the user with evidence of the available information (e.g., in the form of a set of candidate results). Throughout this conversational process, both user and system may reduce their uncertainty with respect to each other, which may ultimately help in finding the desired information. In this paper, we present an information-theoretic model to quantify the flow of information from users to DIR systems and vice versa. By employing channels with memory and feedback, we decouple the mutual information among the behavior of the user and that of the system into directed components. As a result, we are able to measure: (i) by how much the DIR system is capable of adapting to the user; and (ii) by how much the user is influenced by the results returned by the DIR system. We discuss implications of the proposed framework for the evaluation and optimization of DIR systems.

CCS CONCEPTS

•**Information systems** →**Users and interactive retrieval;**
•**Mathematics of computing** →*Information theory;*

KEYWORDS

Directed Information Flow; Search Effectiveness; Formal Methods

1 INTRODUCTION

Nowadays people spend a considerable part of their daily lives interacting with information retrieval systems across multiple devices, from web search engines to personal assistants running on a variety of smart devices. To better support information seeking, modern information retrieval systems must dynamically adapt their retrieval strategy as they interact with the user. In particular, given a user's query, a *dynamic information retrieval* (DIR) system [17, 18] may respond with an initial result set that best matches its understanding of the user's information need. This set may provide the user with an improved understanding of the information available

ICTIR'17, October 1–4, 2017, Amsterdam, The Netherlands
© 2017 ACM. 978-1-4503-4490-6/17/10...$15.00
DOI: 10.1145/3121050.3121102

to the system, prompting him or her to respond back (e.g., by performing a query reformulation, a relevance judgment, or a click). The system may then adapt to the user's response and retrieve a further (ideally improved) result set. This conversational process may continue until the desired information is retrieved to the user or until the user decides to abandon the interaction.

The effectiveness of a DIR system is a function of the gain it provides (in terms of the relevance of the retrieved results) and the effort it incurs (in terms of the total interaction time) to the user [13]. Quantifying such effectiveness is challenging, primarily because the behavior of both the user and the system is inherently uncertain. On the one hand, user actions cannot be fully determined by the system outputs alone, as they also depend on non-observable variables, including the user's cultural background and state of mind. On the other hand, system outputs may not be fully determined by the user actions alone, as the system may benefit from further exploration of the output space to improve its knowledge about the user's need [9]. User modeling under uncertainty has been recently investigated in the context of click models for web search [5], which are probabilistic graphical models aimed at describing and predicting user behavior when interacting with a search engine. In turn, probabilistic retrieval systems have been mostly investigated in the context of the *multi-armed bandit problem* in reinforcement learning [15], in which the system faces a trade-off between exploring new knowledge and exploiting existing knowledge [8].

To provide a unified analysis of the mutual interaction between a user and a DIR system, we propose an information-theoretic model to quantify the amount of information flowing between both agents. Building upon recent advances in information theory [16], we quantify not only the correlation between user and system behavior, but also how much they influence each other. In particular, a high flow from user to system may indicate a highly *sensitive* system, i.e., one that could effectively learn about the user's information need and adapt accordingly. In turn, a high flow from system to user may indicate a highly *influential* system, i.e., one that could effectively teach the user about the available information. While system influence may be interpreted as a measure of retrieval effectiveness—as the user behavior is highly influenced by the system's responses—, system sensitivity could measure lack of privacy—since the more tailored the system is to a particular user, the more information about this user is revealed to an observer of the system's behavior.

In the remainder of this paper, after a brief review of crucial concepts from information theory, we formalize the proposed theoretical model and discuss the challenges involved in instantiating it in a practical scenario as well as implications for evaluating and optimizing DIR systems.

2 PRELIMINARIES

In this section we briefly review key concepts from information theory; for more details we refer to [6]. Let $\mathcal{A} = \{a_1, \ldots, a_n\}$ and $\mathcal{B} = \{b_1, \ldots, b_m\}$ be two finite sets with associated random variables A and B, and following probability distributions p_A and p_B, respectively. (We shall omit the subscripts from distributions when they are clear from the context.)

The *entropy* of A is defined as $H(A) = -\sum_{a \in \mathcal{A}} p(a) \log p(a)$, and it measures the uncertainty of A: the higher its value, the less information one has about the value of A. It takes its minimum value $H(A) = 0$ when p_A is a point-mass distribution, and maximum value $H(A) = \log |\mathcal{A}|$ when p_A is the uniform distribution. Usually the base of the logarithm is set to be 2 and the entropy is measured in *bits*. The *conditional entropy* of A given B is defined as $H(A|B) = -\sum_{a \in \mathcal{A}, b \in \mathcal{B}} p(a, b) \log p(a \mid b)$, and it measures the uncertainty of A when B is known. It takes minimum value $H(A|B) = 0$ when A is completely determined by B, and maximum value $H(A|B) = H(A)$ when A and B are independent. The *mutual information* between A and B is defined as $I(A; B) = H(A) - H(A|B)$, and it measures the amount of information about A that one gains by observing B. It can be shown that mutual information is symmetric, $I(A; B) = I(B; A)$, and that $0 \leq I(A; B) \leq H(A)$.

A (*discrete memoryless*) *channel* C is a tuple $(\mathcal{A}, \mathcal{B}, p_{A|B})$, where $\mathcal{A}$ and $\mathcal{B}$ are sets of *input* and *output* symbols, respectively, and $p_{B|A}(b_j \mid a_i)$ is the probability of the channel producing output symbol b_j when the input symbol is a_i. An input distribution p_A over $\mathcal{A}$ determines, together with the channel C, the joint distribution $p_{AB}(a_i, b_j) = p_A(a_i) p_{B|A}(b_j \mid a_i)$, and consequently $I(A; B)$. The maximum $I(A; B)$ over all possible input distributions is the channel's *capacity*, and it represents the maximum rate by which information can be transmitted using the channel.

3 INFORMATION-THEORETIC MODEL OF DIR SYSTEMS

In this section we present an information-theoretic model for reasoning about the flow of information between a user and a DIR system, when both agents can behave probabilistically. We start by introducing some notation. When we have a *sequence* of symbols (ordered in time) from a set $\mathcal{A}$, we use a Greek letter α_t to denote the symbol at time t, and α^t to denote the sub-sequence $\alpha_1 \alpha_2 \ldots \alpha_t$. We use A^t to denote the sequence of t consecutive occurrences $A_1, \ldots, A_t$ of the random variable A. Moreover, we use $\mathcal{A}^*$ to denote the Cartesian product of set $\mathcal{A}$ with itself a non-negative number of times (so the elements of $\mathcal{A}^*$ are all finite strings whose symbols are elements of $\mathcal{A}$), and $\mathbb{D}\mathcal{A}$ to denote the set of all probability distributions on the set $\mathcal{A}$.

3.1 Formalization of probabilistic DIR systems

Let $\mathcal{A} = \{a_1, \ldots, a_n\}$ be the set of all possible *user's actions*, where each $a_i \in \mathcal{A}$ represents a possible input the user can provide to the DIR system (e.g., the posing of a query, or the relevance judgment of some retrieved result). Let $\mathcal{D} = \{d_1, \ldots, d_m\}$ be the set of all possible *result sets* the DIR system can return to the user (e.g., a list of documents). The user and the DIR system can interact, and a *session* of length $T \geq 1$ of the interactive process is an alternating sequence $\alpha_1 \, \delta_1 \, \alpha_2 \, \delta_2 \, \ldots \, \alpha_T \, \delta_T$ in which each α_t and δ_t represent

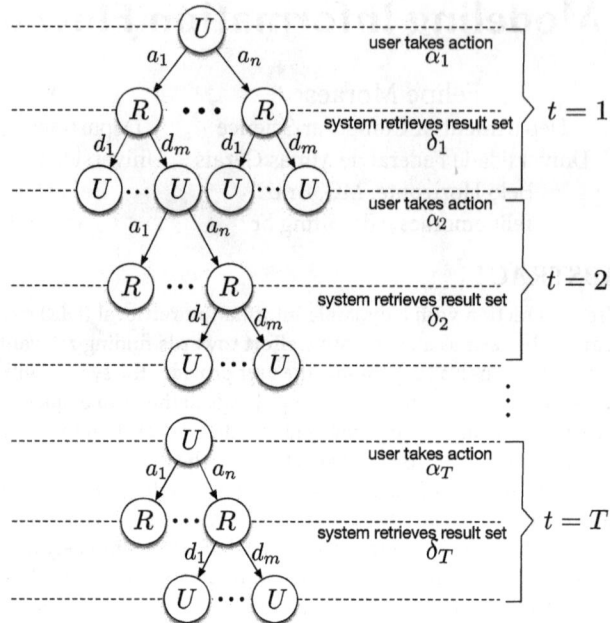

Figure 1: A tree depicting all possible sessions between user U and DIR system R. Each edge would also be labeled with a probability, which is omitted from the figure for simplicity.

the action taken by the user and the result set returned by the system, respectively, at time step $1 \leq t \leq T$. A (*session*) *history* up to time t is the sub-sequence $\alpha_1 \delta_1 \ldots \alpha_t \delta_t$ of a session, and we may denote it simply by α^t, δ^t, where α^t is the *action history* (i.e., the projection of h onto $\mathcal{A}^*$), and δ^t is the corresponding *result-set history* (i.e., the projection of h onto $\mathcal{D}^*$).

A *DIR system* is modeled as a probabilistic function $R : \mathcal{A}^* \times \mathcal{D}^* \rightarrow \mathbb{D}\mathcal{D}$ mapping each session history to a distribution on result sets. The function R can be represented as a family $\{p(\delta_t \mid \alpha^t, \delta^{t-1})\}_{t=1}^T$ of conditional probability distributions, where, for each $1 \leq t \leq T$, $p(\delta_t \mid \alpha^t, \delta^{t-1})$ is the probability of R retrieving result-set δ_t, at time t, given that the session history so far is α^t, δ^{t-1}.

A *user* is modeled as a probabilistic function $U : \mathcal{A}^* \times \mathcal{D}^* \rightarrow \mathbb{D}\mathcal{A}$ mapping each history to a distribution on user actions. The function U can be represented as a family $\{p(\alpha_t \mid \alpha^{t-1}, \delta^{t-1})\}_{t=1}^T$ of conditional probability distributions, where each $p(\alpha_t \mid \alpha^{t-1}, \delta^{t-1})$ represents the probability of the user taking action α_t, given the history $\alpha^{t-1}, \delta^{t-1}$ so far.

All possible sessions of an interactive process between DIR system R and user U can be represented as a probabilistic automaton like the one in Figure 1. In such an automaton: (i) there is a node for each point in time an agent (user or DIR system) can make a move; (ii) from each node there is an emanating edge labeled with a possible move available for the agent, together with the probability of the agent choosing that move; (iii) every session (resp., history) is represented by a path from the root to a leaf (resp., some node), and the probability of the session (resp., history) can be computed by multiplying the probabilities of the edges in a path from the root to the corresponding node.

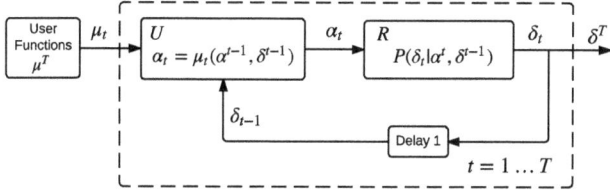

Figure 2: Model of interaction process between user U and DIR system R, using a channel with memory and feedback.

3.2 DIR systems as channels w/ memory and feedback

In order to quantify the information flow from U to R, and vice versa, in a session of the interactive process, we map the probabilistic automaton representing an interactive process to the model of discrete channels with memory and feedback proposed by Tatikonda and Mitter [16], and adapted to interactive systems by Alvim et al. [1].

The model, represented in Figure 2, can be decomposed into components as follows. The behavior $p(\delta_t \mid \alpha^t, \delta^{t-1})$ of the DIR system is modeled as the internal channel R taking user actions as inputs and producing result sets as outputs. The result set produced is then fed back to the user with delay one (i.e., a result set δ_t produced at time t will only become available to the user at time $t + 1$). Since R can be used repeatedly, its behavior after T uses can be fully described by the joint probability distribution relating the sequences α^T of inputs and δ^T of outputs as follows:

$$p(\alpha^T, \delta^T) = \prod_{t=1}^{T} p(\alpha_t \mid \alpha^{t-1}, \delta^{t-1})p(\delta_t \mid \alpha^t, \delta^{t-1}). \quad (1)$$

The first term $p(\alpha_t \mid \alpha^{t-1}, \delta^{t-1})$ indicates that the channel supports *feedback*, i.e., the occurrence of a current input α_t may depend on past outputs δ^{t-1} from the channel.[1] The second term $p(\delta_t \mid \alpha^t, \delta^{t-1})$ indicates that the channel may present *memory*, in the sense that the production of an output δ_t may not depend only on the current input α_t, but on the whole previous history α^t, δ^{t-1}.

Computing the capacity of channels with memory and feedback is a significantly more complex task than it is for simple information-theoretic channels (i.e., memoryless, and without feedback). Tatikonda and Mitter's method does it by representing the channel with memory and feedback from A^T to D^T (the inner channel R in Figure 2) as an equivalent channel without memory or feedback from user-behavior functions U^T to D^T (represented as everything inside the dotted-line in Figure 2). Because this outer channel is a simple channel, its capacity can be computed using usual methods. However, to do so, their model limits the production of inputs to the channel to deterministic functions. This limitation means that the term $p(\alpha_t \mid \alpha^{t-1}, \delta^{t-1})$ in Equation (1), which corresponds to the user's behavior in the interactive process, cannot be directly captured in the model. To circumvent this problem, here we follow Alvim et al.'s approach [1] and externalize the probabilistic

behavior of the user to a distribution on deterministic *user-behavior functions* μ_t.[2]

3.3 Information flow in DIR systems

To quantify the flow of information in a DIR system, we employ the concepts of directed information flow and capacity in channels with memory and feedback.

3.3.1 A brief review of directed information. In the presence of feedback, mutual information $I(A^T; D^T)$ does not represent the information flow from A^T to D^T. Intuitively, this is due to the fact that mutual information expresses correlation, and therefore it is increased by feedback. The appropriate measure of transmission of information in such a channel is *directed information* [14].

Definition 3.1. In a channel with feedback, the *directed information from input A^T to output D^T* is defined as

$$I(A^T \rightarrow D^T) = \sum_{t=1}^{T} I(A^t; D_t \mid D^{t-1});$$

and the *directed information from D^T to A^T* is defined as

$$I(D^T \rightarrow A^T) = \sum_{t=1}^{T} I(A_t; D^{t-1} \mid A^{t-1}).$$

Note that directed information is not symmetric: the flow from A^T to D^T considers the correlation between A^t and D_t, whereas the flow from D^T to A^T considers the correlation between D^{t-1} and A_t. Intuitively, this is because α^t influences δ_t, but, in the other direction, it is δ^{t-1} that influences α_t. It can be proven [16] that

$$I(A^T; D^T) = I(A^T \rightarrow D^T) + I(D^T \rightarrow A^T),$$

i.e., the traditional concept of mutual information is the sum of the directed information in both directions in a channel with memory and feedback. In particular, if a channel does not have feedback, then $I(D^T \rightarrow A^T) = 0$ and $I(A^T; D^T) = I(A^T \rightarrow D^T)$, which recovers the traditional definition of information flow in such channels. In a channel with feedback, however, the correct measure of information transmitted is directed information $I(A^T \rightarrow D^T)$, and not mutual information.

The concept of capacity is generalized for channels with feedback as follows. Let $\mathbb{D}U^T = \{\{p(\alpha_t \mid \alpha^{t-1}, \delta^{t-1})\}_{t=1}^{T}\}$ be the set of all input distributions. For finite T, the *capacity* of a channel $\{p(\delta_t \mid \alpha^t, \delta^{t-1})\}_{t=1}^{T}$ is

$$C_T = \sup_{\mathbb{D}U^T} \frac{1}{T} I(A^T \rightarrow D^T).$$

---

[1]In this paper we use the term "feedback" only to denote its usual meaning in information theory, as opposed to its usual meaning in retrieval systems.

[2] To formalize the transformation, let us call $\mathcal{U}_t$ the set of all measurable maps $\mu_t : \mathcal{D}^{t-1} \rightarrow \mathcal{A}$ endowed with a probability distribution, and let U_t be the corresponding random variable. Let $\mathcal{U}^T$, U^T denote the Cartesian product on the domain and the random variable, respectively. A *user-behavior function* is an element $\mu^T = (\mu_1, \ldots, \mu_T) \in \mathcal{U}^T$. Note that, by probability laws, $p(\mu^T) = \prod_{t=1}^{T} p(\mu_t \mid \mu^{t-1})$. Hence the distribution on $\mathcal{U}^T$ is uniquely determined by a sequence $\{p(\mu_t \mid \mu^{t-1})\}_{t=1}^{T}$. We will use the notation $\mu_t(\delta^{t-1})$ to represent the $\mathcal{A}$-valued t-tuple $(\mu_1, \mu_2(\delta^1), \ldots, \mu_t(\delta^{t-1}))$. We, then, formally capture a user in our model as a family $\{\mu_t \mid \mu^{t-1}\}_{t=1}^{T}$ of distributions on user-behavior functions defined as $p(\mu_1) = p(\alpha_1 \mid \alpha^0, \delta^0) = p(\alpha_1)$, and $p(\mu_t \mid \mu^{t-1}) = \prod_{\delta^{t-1}} p(\mu_t \mid \mu^{t-1}(\delta^{t-2}), \delta^{t-1})$ for $2 \leq t \leq T$.

3.3.2 Interpretation in terms of DIR systems. Taking advantage of the disentanglement of the information flow from user to DIR system from the information flow in the opposite direction, we can provide a refined analysis of an interactive process as follows.

$I(A^T \to D^T)$ can be used as a measure of how *sensitive* to the user the DIR system is, as it quantifies how much the DIR system's outputs are tailored to the user's actions. The higher the value of $I(A^T \to D^T)$, the more the result sets retrieved by the DIR system will differ from user to user. This has an interesting application at enforcing privacy in the user interaction. For instance, the DIR system could be parameterized to restrict itself to a certain (perhaps user-defined) level of sensitivity, so that no user information beyond the target level can flow to the system. Moreover, since $I(A^T \to D^T) = \sum_{t=1}^{T} H(A_t|A^{t-1}, D^{t-1}) - H(A^T|D^T)$, the term $\sum_{t=1}^{T} H(A_t|A^{t-1}, D^{t-1})$ can be interpreted as the *entropy of the user* and used to measure how unpredictable the user's behavior is.

On the other hand, $I(D^T \to A^T)$ is a measure of how *influential* the retrieval system is on the user. The higher its value, the more the user's actions differ from what they would be in case the result sets were just being randomly produced. This can be interpreted as a measure of the retrieval effectiveness of the system as interaction progresses, providing an alternative to current DIR evaluation efforts. Moreover, it could serve as a criterion for optimizing DIR systems, perhaps constrained to a particular sensitivity level, as previously discussed.

Finally, since the capacity C_T is the maximum information flow over all possible distributions on user-behavior functions, it is an accurate theoretical limit for the retrieval system's ability to produce results tailored to users.

4   CONCLUSIONS

A dynamic information retrieval (DIR) system aims to identify relevant information through a series of interactions with the user. An effective DIR system should be able to satisfy the user's information need with as few interactions as possible, by dynamically adapting itself in response to user actions. In this paper, we proposed an information-theoretic model for quantifying the flow of information between a user and a DIR system throughout the interactive process. Our proposed model allows for decoupling the mutual information between the user and the system into separate flows of information from the user to the system and from the system to the user. We discussed a possible interpretation for the information flow in each direction and pointed out potential applications for the evaluation and optimization of DIR systems.

An exact computation of information flows is intractable, as it would require computing the probability of observing a system input or output given all possible interaction histories.[3] Hence, an important direction for future investigation involves methods for approximate estimation of information flows. Promising candidates here include several techniques developed for the analysis of quantitative information flow in the context of security, which involve a mixture of model-checking techniques and/or statistical analysis, such as [4, 7, 11]. Another practical limitation of the proposed

model is the unsigned nature of the computed information flows. In fact, directed information (as Shannon's mutual information) is agnostic to the meaning of the information flowing: it can measure by how much one agent's state is affected about the other agent's state (e.g., user and DIR system), but it cannot reflect whether the information flowing is helpful or unhelpful. This limitation restricts the interpretability of system sensitivity and influence. Future extensions should consider advanced information-theoretic metrics, which can take into consideration the meaning of information, such as the *g*-leakage framework [3] and its generalized capacities [2]. Lastly, in addition to the potential applications discussed in Section 3.3, we plan to investigate the applicability of the proposed model in scenarios such as statistical translation models [10] as well as conversational machines using neural networks [12]. In particular, the latter achieved state-of-the-art performance by using a mutual information-based optimization criterion. As future work, we plan to extend our measure of influence in this scenario, where a dual optimization criterion could improve the precision of the quality of messages produced by a dialogue system.

ACKNOWLEDGMENTS

This work was partially funded by projects InWeb (MCT/ CNPq 573871/2008-6) and MASWeb (FAPEMIG/PRONEX APQ-01400-14), and by the authors' grants from CNPq, CAPES and FAPEMIG.

REFERENCES

[1] Mário S. Alvim, Miguel E. Andres, and Catuscia Palamidessi. 2012. Quantitative Information Flow in Interactive Systems. *JCS* (2012).

[2] Mário S. Alvim, Konstantinos Chatzikokolakis, Annabelle McIver, Carroll Morgan, Catuscia Palamidessi, and Geoffrey Smith. 2014. Additive and Multiplicative Notions of Leakage, and Their Capacities. In *Proc. of CSF*.

[3] Mário S. Alvim, Konstantinos Chatzikokolakis, Catuscia Palamidessi, and Geoffrey Smith. 2012. Measuring Information Leakage Using Generalized Gain Functions. In *Proc. of CSF*.

[4] Rohit Chadha, Umang Mathur, and Stefan Schwoon. 2014. Computing Information Flow Using Symbolic Model-Checking. In *Proc. of FSTTCS*.

[5] Aleksandr Chuklin, Ilya Markov, and Maarten de Rijke. 2015. *Click Models for Web Search*. Morgan & Claypool.

[6] Thomas M. Cover and Joy A. Thomas. 1991. *Elements of Information Theory*. J. Wiley & Sons, Inc.

[7] Deniz Gencaga, Kevin H. Knuth, and William B. Rossow. 2015. A Recipe for the Estimation of Information Flow in a Dynamical System. *Entropy* (2015).

[8] Artem Grotov and Maarten de Rijke. 2016. Online learning to rank for information retrieval: SIGIR 2016 Tutorial. In *Proc. of SIGIR*. 1215–1218.

[9] Leslie Pack Kaelbling, Michael L. Littman, and Andrew W. Moore. 1996. Reinforcement Learning: A Survey. *JAIR* (1996).

[10] Maryam Karimzadehgan and ChengXiang Zhai. 2010. Estimation of Statistical Translation Models Based on Mutual Information for Ad Hoc Information Retrieval. In *Proc. of SIGIR*.

[11] Yusuke Kawamoto, Fabrizio Biondi, and Axel Legay. 2016. *Hybrid Statistical Estimation of Mutual Information for Quantifying Information Flow*.

[12] Jiwei Li, Michel Galley, Chris Brockett, Jianfeng Gao, and Bill Dolan. 2016. A Diversity-Promoting Objective Function for Neural Conversation Models. In *NAACL*.

[13] Jiyun Luo, Christopher Wing, Hui Yang, and Marti Hearst. 2013. The Water Filling Model and the Cube Test: Multi-dimensional Evaluation for Professional Search. In *Proc. of CIKM*.

[14] James L. Massey. 1990. Causality, Feedback and Directed Information. In *Proc. of SITA*.

[15] Richard S Sutton and Andrew G Barto. 1998. *Reinforcement learning: An introduction*. MIT press Cambridge.

[16] Sekhar Tatikonda and Sanjoy K. Mitter. 2009. The Capacity of Channels With Feedback. *IEEE Trans.Inf.Theory* (2009).

[17] Ryen W. White. 2016. *Interactions with Search Systems*. Cambridge University Press.

[18] Grace Hui Yang, Marc Sloan, and Jun Wang. 2016. *Dynamic Information Retrieval Modeling*. Morgan & Claypool Publishers.

---

[3]It can be shown that the computational complexity is $O(|\mathcal{A}|^T |\mathcal{D}|^T \times k)$, where $|\mathcal{A}|$ is the number of user actions, $|\mathcal{D}|$ is the number of documents, k is a constant to produce $|\mathcal{D}|$, and T is the number of interactions.

On the Effectiveness of Bayesian Network-based Models for Document Ranking

Xing Tan, Fanghong Jian and Jimmy Xiangji Huang
Information Retrieval and Knowledge Management Research Lab
School of Computer Science, Central China Normal University, Wuhan, China
School of Information Technology, York University, Toronto, Canada
xtan@yorku.ca,jfhrecoba@mails.ccnu.edu.cn,jhuang@yorku.ca

ABSTRACT

Theoretical soundness and technical feasibility of treating the problem of document ranking in IR as an inference problem in Bayesian Networks, was studied recently. A pilot framework was also proposed there. In this paper, we provide two implementations of the framework: BNBM25, the one based on BM25, and BNMATF, which is based on MATF, a recently proposed innovative ranking function. We empirically verify the effectiveness of these two implementations on several standard test collections. Positive, significant results are obtained. Potentials of this BN-based framework in addition to its verified effectiveness are also discussed. As a result of the study, we believe that the technique is promising, worthy of further analysis and application.

KEYWORDS

Info. Retrieval; Bayesian Networks; Stochastic Sampling

1 INTRODUCTION

A specific probabilistic graphical model [3] for document ranking is recently proposed in [10]. In the paper, a simple and straightforward two-layer (one for documents and the other for words) Bayesian Network (BN) is constructed, where posterior probabilities for the network are estimated through statistical sampling, since exact specification of them are not computationally feasible. Some initial experiments on the effectiveness of the model are performed on computer-generated documents in [10], and it is conjectured that in practise, this new model performs comparably to the baseline BM25, on real-world document collections, such as the standard ones WT10G or AP90.

In this paper, we demonstrate empirically that this conjectured comparability holds. We show that when posteriors of the model are estimated with reference to BM25, performance of the accordingly built BN-based model (name it BNBM25) is comparable to that of BM25. In a similar manner, we tried MATF (proposed recently in [6], standing for Multi-Aspect TF), an innovative term weighting function that almost always outperforms with good margin all baselines. We found that the performance of BNMATF is comparable to the one of MATF too. We believe that this comparability can be

generally observed for any existing term weighting function other than BM25 or MATF.

As being done in [10], we use the so-called *rejection sampling* to estimate the posteriors. A few additional aspects actually need to be considered when working on real-world document collections with rejection sampling: We need to address in particular two questions. One, how would we numerically characterize a sample, i.e., a collection of documents? Two, how would we decide an appropriate threshold value, so much so it is never the case where too many samples are accepted, or rejected? In responding to the first question, we simply calculate the average over all documents in a given sample. For the second question, it turns out that, a better threshold value is case-by-case on query, and on the actual collection that is being queried.

The impact and significance of this new framework and its models in our opinion goes beyond simply another term-weighting function with effectiveness. It transforms the problem of document ranking into probabilistic inference in probabilistic graphical models, and potentially into probabilistic and logic inference in a model that is mixed with probability theory and first-order logic theory. Feasibility of a future model obtained from this combination is also discussed in loose sense.

The remainder of this paper is organized as follows. Section 2 presents the background and preliminaries. In Section 3, we explain how we would implement the model BNBM25 and BNMATF using BM25 and MATF, respectively. Experimental results are reported and analyzed in Section 4. Conclusive remarks are presented in Section 5.

2 PRELIMINARIES

In this section, term weighting ranking functions BM25 [5, 9] and MATF [6], and the idea of BN for document ranking [10], are briefly reviewed.

2.1 Concepts for Probabilistic Models in IR

Given a set of documents $\mathcal{D} = \{d_1, \ldots, d_M\}$ where $|\mathcal{D}| = M$, a set of terms $\mathcal{T} = \{t_1, \ldots, t_N\}$ where $|\mathcal{T}| = N$, and a collection of query terms $\vec{q}$ such that $\vec{q} \subset \mathcal{T}$, documents in $\mathcal{D}$ can be completely ranked in order by $score(\vec{q}, d_i)$, a function which returns a numeric score for each document $d_i \in \mathcal{D}$ with respect to $\vec{q}$. Top S elements will be put in set $\mathcal{S}$, where $|\mathcal{S}| = S$.

Let $tf_{t,d}$ denote *term frequency*, number of occurrences of term t in document d; df_t denotes *document frequency*, number of documents in $\mathcal{D}$ containing the term t; and $idf_t = \log(M/df_t)$ denotes *inverse document frequency*. Summing up on $tf_{t,d} \times idf_t$ for each term $t \in \vec{q}$ with respect to d defines a baseline: $score_{base}(\vec{q}, d) = \sum_{t \in \vec{q}} (tf_{t,d} \times idf_t)$.

2.2 Ranking Formulas: BM25 & MATF

Several variants and extensions to $tf\text{-}idf$ baseline $score_{base}$ have been proposed over the years. Among them, BM25 is probably the most influential one; MATF, meanwhile, is recently proposed and quite effective.

t in $\mathcal{D}$ and in $\mathcal{S}$, and denoted by cf_t and sf_t, respectively. Specifically, BM25 score function $score_{bm25}(\vec{q}, d)$ is defined as

$$\sum_{t \in \vec{q}} idf_t^{bm25} \cdot \frac{(k_1 + 1)tf_{t,d}}{k_1\big((1-b) + b \cdot (\frac{|d|}{avdl})\big) + tf_{t,d}} \cdot \frac{(k_3+1)tf_{t,\vec{q}}}{k_3 + tf_{t,\vec{q}}},$$

where $|d|$ denotes the length of the document d, and $avdl$ denotes the average length of documents in $\mathcal{D}$; constant $k_1 > 0$ controls the scaling of document term frequency $tf_{t,d}$; constant $k_3 > 0$ controls the scaling of query term frequency $tf_{t,\vec{q}}$; constant $b \in [0,1]$ controls the level of document normalization; When $b = 0$, normalization is not in effect, and when $b = 1$, full level of normalization proportional to the ratio of $\frac{|d|}{avdl}$ is applied. Finally, $idf_t^{bm25} = \log \frac{M - df_t + 0.5}{df_t + 0.5}$ is a variant to idf_t.

Defining MATF calls for several additional notations (All copied from [6]): *Relative Intra-document TF (RITF)* is defined as $ritf_{t,d} = \log_2(1 + tf_{t,d})/\log_2(1 + tf_d^{ave})$, where tf_d^{ave} denotes average term frequency of d. *Length Regularized TF (LRTF)* is defined as $lrtf_{t,d} = tf_{t,d} \cdot \log_2(1 + avdl/|d|)$. Let $britf_{t,d}$ be defined as $ritf_{t,d}/(1 + ritf_{t,d})$, and $blrtf_{t,d}$ be defined as $lrtf_{t,d}/(1 + lrtf_{t,d})$, we have

$$tff_{t,d} = w \cdot britf_{t,d} + (1-w) \cdot blrtf_{t,d},$$

where $w = 2/(1 + log_2(1 + |\vec{q}|))$.

Let cf_t denote total number of occurrences of t in $\mathcal{D}$; $aef_t = cf_t/df_t$ denotes the average elite set term frequency (AEF). Term discrimination frequency is defined as

$$tdf_t = idf_t \cdot (aef_t/(1 + aef_t))$$

MATF $score_{matf}(\vec{q}, d)$ finally is defined as $\sum_{t \in \vec{q}}(tff_{t,d} \cdot tdf_t)$. (Formula 13 in [6]). In general better than BM25 performance of MATF is observed, according to [6].

2.3 BN for Document Ranking

Demonstrated in [10], a document ranking problem in probabilistic IR models can be converted into probabilistic inference in Bayesian Networks. Given again $\mathcal{D}$, $\mathcal{T}$, and $\vec{q}$, a BN model (shown in Figure 1) is constructed with two sets of random variables $\mathcal{D}$ and $\mathcal{T}$. Each $D_i \in \mathcal{D}$ takes two values: d_i^1, d_i^0, representing "D_i selected with respect to a query" (d_i^1) or not (d_i^0); Similarly, each $T_j \in \mathcal{T}$ takes two values: t_j^1, t_j^0, representing "T_j is a query term" (t_j^1) or not (t_j^0). The BN is a two-layer directed graph containing a node in the top layer for each document variable D_i and a node in the bottom layer for each term variable T_j. In the graph, an edge from D_i to T_j represents that term T_j appears in the document D_i. It is assumed no edges between document variables in $\mathcal{D}$, and no edges between term variables in $\mathcal{T}$.

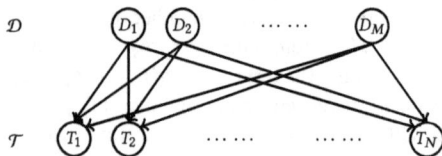

Figure 1: A BN Graph for Document Ranking (Source: Figure 2 in [10]).

Additional remarks for this BN model: 1) $P(D_i)$ represents the distribution that D_i is selected in $\mathcal{S}$ or not and $P(d_i^1) = S/M$; 2) there are too many conditional distributions $P(T_j|D1, \ldots, D_M)$, to be specified individually; 3) the value of posterior probability of $P(d_i^1|\mathbf{q})$, however, can be estimated through stochastic sampling; and 4) with respect to $\vec{q}$, all documents in $\mathcal{D}$ can be ranked according to the values of $P(d_i^1|\mathbf{q})$, for $1 \le i \le M$.

$P(D_i)$, the prior distribution over D_i, and $P(T_j|D1, \ldots, D_M)$, the conditional probability distribution of T_j given $D_1, D_2, \ldots$, and D_M. Since $P(D_i)$ represents the distribution that D_i is selected in $\mathcal{S}$ or not, for any document D_i in $\mathcal{D}$, the probability that D_i is eventually selected into S equals the ratio of the size of $\mathcal{S}$ to the size of $\mathcal{D}$, i.e., $P(d_i^1) = S/M$.

actual content of $\mathcal{S}$, the set of documents selected. That is to say, specifically, for each subset of $\mathcal{D}$ (totally 2^M of them), we need to specify a distribution for t_j^1, the event that t_j is actually a query term. Since the number of parents of a term in the network is not bounded by a constant, we know that exact inference here has exponential time complexity in worst cases. Nevertheless what we really need is to calculate, for any document variable D_i where $1 \le i \le M$, the relevance of D_i to evidence q, i.e., the posterior probability of $P(d_i^1|\mathbf{q})$, the value of which can be estimated through stochastic sampling. For simplicity in explanation, we assume that q contains only one term t, without loss of generality.

3 BNBM25 & BNMATF

In this section, we explain the key ingredients regarding implementation of BNBM25 & BNMATF. Test collections used to test these two models, and settings for evaluating these models are also introduced.

3.1 Implementations

Implementation of this BN-based framework for document ranking requires a workable solution to the important question: Given a sample, should it be accepted or rejected?

More formally, suppose we have a set of samples $\mathcal{P}$ where $|\mathcal{P}| = P$, for any sample (say the jth one P^j, where $1 \le j \le P$), the expected number of documents in P^j is S. These documents are put in the set $\mathcal{S}^j$, hence $|\mathcal{S}^j| = S$. Given P^j, we need to figure out a way to assign a numerical score $score_{bn}(\vec{q}, \mathcal{S}^j)$ and a threshold value $thld$ such that P^j is accepted iff

$$score_{bn}(\vec{q}, \mathcal{S}^j) \ge thld. \tag{1}$$

If P^j is accepted, it is added to the set $\mathcal{P}^{accepted}$.

Eventually, when sampling finishes, the number of samples in $\mathcal{P}^{accepted}$ containing d can be counted out. This number is used to rank d.

Assuming $score(\vec{q}, d)$ is known for all $d \in \mathcal{D}$, given again P^j, we can straightforwardly instantiate the above inequality by respectively taking averages on scores over the set $\mathcal{S}^j$ and the set $\mathcal{D}$, and then comparing the two averages:

$$\frac{\sum_{d \in \mathcal{S}^j} score(\vec{q}, d)}{S} \ge \frac{\sum_{d \in \mathcal{D}} score(\vec{q}, d)}{M} \tag{2}$$

In this paper we consider $score(\vec{q}, d)$ that is based on BM25 and MATF, respectively. That is,

$$\frac{\sum_{d \in \mathcal{S}^j} score_{bm25}(\vec{q}, d)}{S} \ge \frac{\sum_{d \in \mathcal{D}} score_{bm25}(\vec{q}, d)}{M} \tag{3}$$

$$\frac{\sum_{d \in \mathcal{S}^j} score_{matf}(\vec{q}, d)}{S} \ge \frac{\sum_{d \in \mathcal{D}} score_{matf}(\vec{q}, d)}{M} \tag{4}$$

For a total of $\mathcal{P}$ samples, it is hard to tell beforehand with a given *thld*, how many samples in $\mathcal{P}$ would eventually be accepted. At one extreme, the value of *thld* is too high, such that no sample in $\mathcal{P}$ is accepted and consequently the method does not demonstrate any ranking functionality at all; At the other extreme where *thld* is too low in value, all samples would be accepted. As a consequence, each $d \in \mathcal{D}$ would be expected to receive same score, the method would have no capability in ranking documents either. Hence we introduce a heuristic parameter α which determines how many samples would be accepted

$$score_{bn}(\vec{q}, \mathcal{S}^j) \geq \alpha \cdot thld. \qquad (5)$$

It is probably useful that given a query $\vec{q}$, we run a few thousand samples first simply for deciding the actual value of α. We want two-thirds of the samples to be accepted, for example.

3.2 Experimental Settings

We conduct experiments on eight standard test collections including AP90, AP88-89, AP88-90, SJMN, and etc. Sizes and genres of them are different in general (Table 1).

Table 1: Test Collections Used

Collection	#of Docs	Size	Single Term Queries
AP90	78,321	0.23Gb	57, 75, 77, 78
AP88-89	164,597	0.50Gb	57, 75, 77, 78
AP88-90	242,918	0.73Gb	57, 75, 77, 78
SJMN	90,257	0.29Gb	57, 75, 77, 78
FT	210,158	0.56Gb	349, 364, 367, 392, 395
LA	131,896	0.48Gb	349, 364, 367, 392, 395
TREC8	528,155	1.85Gb	403, 417, 424
WT2G	247,491	2.14Gb	403, 417, 424

In the effort to simplify explanations, and without loss of generality, twelve single-term queries are reported in the paper[1]: Among them, Query 57, 75, 77 and 78 are drawn from collections AP/SJMN; Query 349, 364, 367, 392 and 395 are from SJMN/FT; Query 403, 417 and 424 are from TREC8/WT2G. Judgments for these queries are available. Each term is stemmed by using Porter's English stemmer and standard stop-words in English are removed. Mean Average Precision (MAP), the standard metric for relevance assessment is employed to measure and compare performance of models.

Values of BM25 parameters k_1, k_3, and b, respectively, are set to 1.2, 8, and 0.35. As reported in [11, 12], this setting can achieve best BM25 MAP for most datasets used. The sampling ratio $\gamma = S/M$ is set to 0.05. Other combinations of values for k_1, k_3, b, and γ are also tested, with results quite similar to the ones reported in Section 4 obtained. Sample size varies from 1K up to 5M.

4 RESULTS & ANALYSIS

BNBM25 and BM25 are compared on MAP in Figure 2. Each subfigure corresponds to one of the eight test collections currently used in our research. Taking the top-left subfigure as an example: it depicts results obtained on the collection AP90; In this subfigure, the green bar, which is at a level slightly over 0.5, is the MAP of BM25 on AP90. The other five color-lines refer to different BNBM25 models in stepwise variation of the value of α (from 30% up to 70%). MAP values are averaged over the four queries for AP90 (the first row of Table 1).

---

[1]Nevertheless the models demonstrate quite similar behavior and performance on multiple-term queries on all these test collections.

In all these eight cases, we observe that as the sample size increases, BNBM25 models tend to climb up to reach the green bars (MAPs of BM25), lending us quick support in claiming that, BNBM25 and BM25 are comparable in performance, should the sample size be large enough.

Interestingly, there are cases (AP88-89 and SJMN for examples) where MAP of BNBM25 surpasses that of BM25 with sample sizes fairly small. Difference on MAP values at maximum can be greater than 10% (observed in subfigure for SJMN, the redline at sample size equaling 10K). We believe this is an indication that statistical randomness in BN models by itself potentially can bring in additional ranking power. By all means at its base level, BNBM25 exerts its function solely on BM25. Hence it appears to be reasonable to conjecture that occurrences of better than BM25 performance of BNBM25 are only due to the introduction of statistical sampling in BNBM25. When sample size further increases, performance of BNBM25 converges to the one of BM25, in the sense that BNBM25 approaches BM25 from both below and above, and the favorable effect of randomness gradually fades out. That is, as correctly conjectured in [10], BM25 asymptotically dominates.

Figure 3 compares BNMATF and MATF. A similar argument can be used to conclude that, performance of BNMATF converges to MATF as sample size increases. In Figure 3, MAP of BN25 remains to be represented by the green bars. The black, dotted bars correspond to MAP values of MATF. It is observed that, for everyone of the seven out of the 8 subfigures in Figure 3, the black bar is on top of the green bar, a positive reflection of significance of MATF over the baseline BM25, claimed in [6]. Since BNMATF in Figure 3 is driven to catch up MATF on MAP, BNMATF has a tendency to asymptotically surpasses BM25, for all cases where MATF surpasses BM25.

5 SUMMARY & FUTURE WORK

Research reported in this paper verifies effectiveness and contributes to a better understanding of a BN-based framework for document ranking proposed initially in [10]. More precisely, through working on a variety of different data collections, we demonstrate that performance of BNBM25 is comparable to the one of baseline BM25, and performance of BNMATF is comparable to the one of MATF. Not surprisingly, BM25 is outperformed by BNMATF in general.

Although only BM25 and MATF are considered in this paper, we believe it is the case that for most term-weighting models (probably language-models too), a corresponding BN model can be derived within the framework. In fact, any ranking function on input query $\vec{q}$ and document d (e.g., BM25, MATF, and etc.), can be used to decide whether or not a given sample $\mathcal{S}$ should be accepted in terms of its relevance to $\vec{q}$ the query – we currently take simple average on individual ranking scores over all documents in $\mathcal{S}$.

Further refinements on methods calculating the numerical score of a sample can, we believe, lead directly to improved performance of BN-based models. With evidences reported in this paper, BN-based models offer new opportunities for getting deeper understanding of existing term weighting models, and for building up better future term weighting models. For example, the bag-of-words assumption can be extended to be applied to samples instead of documents, as such, a score function for individual samples (not individual documents) can be developed consequently. This idea provides an interesting direction for future research.

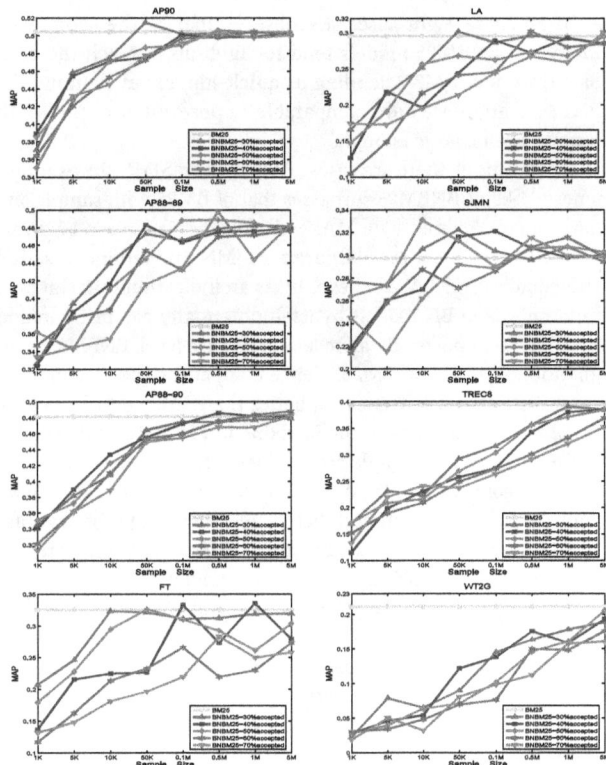

Figure 2: Comparisons on MAP Between BNBM25 and BM25 with Varying Ratios of Accepted Samples.

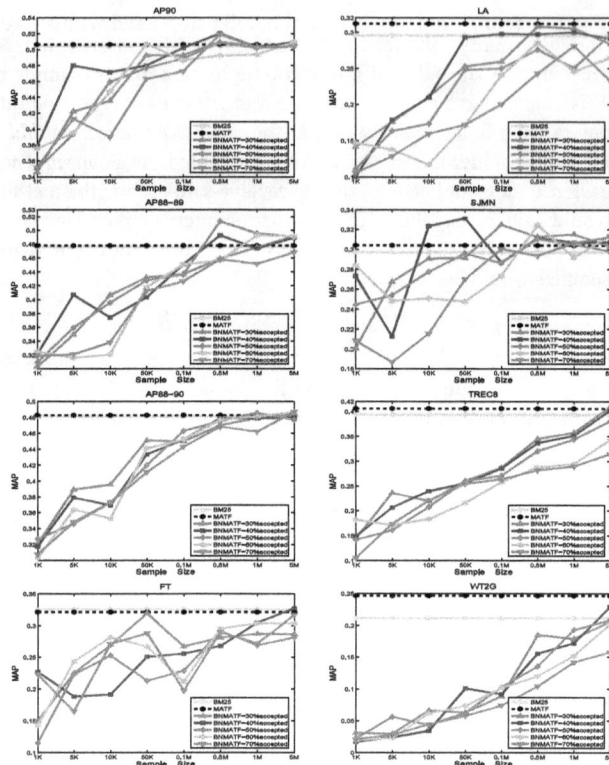

Figure 3: Comparisons on MAP Among BM25, MATF and BN-MATF.

Some engineering efforts are required on tuning up the parameter α introduced in Formula 5, so a great portion of samples can actually be accepted, leading to faster convergence of the model. It takes time taking samples, thus it is challenging for the proposed BN-models to win on time-efficiency easily, when competing with existing term weighting models. That being the case, efficiency should be improved with significance when more advanced sampling strategies, such as the many ones listed in [3], are further incorporated into the model.

More interestingly and perhaps more important, the framework in our opinion establishes a cross-bridge connection between probabilistic ranking in traditional information retrieval models and probabilistic inference in Bayesian Networks. Although exact inference in this new framework is not computationally feasible (it is NP-hard [1]), most approximate inference methods (such as, of course, statistical sampling methods) should be applicable here.

From these BN-based models, document ranking can be further conveyed into a world more expressive in representational power, that is, a world of 1) first-order objects in terms of documents and words, 2) relationships between these objects in view of relevancy, novelty, and diversity; and 3) uncertainties of knowledge about these relationships. As a matter of fact, a variety of different foundational work and formalisms on relational probabilistic models are covered in [2]. Future retrieval models, built in a way where probability theory and logic theory are combined (for examples, consider using Markov Logic Networks [8], Probabilistic Soft Logic [7], or Multi-Entity Bayesian Networks [4]), are expected to achieve further improved performance on effectiveness, efficiency, and possibly other metrics.

6 ACKNOWLEDGEMENTS

This research is supported by a Discovery grant from the Natural Sciences and Engineering Research Council of Canada (NSERC), an NSERC CREATE award in ADERSIM and an ORF-RE (Ontario Research Fund - Research Excellence) award in BRAIN Alliance.

REFERENCES

[1] Gregory F. Cooper. 1990. The computational complexity of probabilistic inference using Bayesian belief networks. *Artificial Intelligence* 42, 2 (1990), 393 – 405.
[2] Lise Getoor and Ben Taskar. 2007. *Introduction to Statistical Relational Learning.* The MIT Press.
[3] Daphne Koller and Nir Friedman. 2009. *Probabilistic Graphical Models: Principles and Techniques - Adaptive Computation and Machine Learning.* The MIT Press.
[4] Kathryn Blackmond Laskey. 2008. MEBN: A Language for First-order Bayesian Knowledge Bases. *Artificial Intelligence* 172, 2-3 (Feb. 2008), 140–178.
[5] Christopher D. Manning, Prabhakar Raghavan, and Hinrich Schütze. 2008. *Introduction to Information Retrieval.* Cambridge Univ. Press, New York, NY, USA.
[6] Jiaul H. Paik. 2013. A Novel TF-IDF Weighting Scheme for Effective Ranking. In *Proc. of the 36th ACM SIGIR.* 343–352.
[7] Jay Pujara, Hui Miao, Lise Getoor, and William W. Cohen. 2015. Using Semantics and Statistics to Turn Data into Knowledge. *AI Magazine* 36, 1 (2015), 65–74.
[8] Matthew Richardson and Pedro Domingos. 2006. Markov Logic Networks. *Mach. Learn.* 62, 1-2 (Feb. 2006), 107–136.
[9] S. E. Robertson and S. Walker. 1994. Some Simple Effective Approximations to the 2-Poisson Model for Probabilistic Weighted Retrieval. In *Proc. of the 17th ACM SIGIR.* 232–241.
[10] Xing Tan, Jimmy Xiangji Huang, and Aijun An. 2016. Ranking Documents Through Stochastic Sampling on Bayesian Network-based Models: A Pilot Study. In *Proc. of the 39th ACM SIGIR.* 961–964.
[11] Jiashu Zhao, Jimmy Xiangji Huang, and Ben He. 2011. CRTER: Using Cross Terms to Enhance Probabilistic IR.. In *Proc. of the 34th ACM SIGIR.* 155–164.
[12] Jiashu Zhao, Jimmy Xiangji Huang, and Zheng Ye. 2014. Modeling Term Associations for Probabilistic Information Retrieval. *ACM Trans. Inf. Syst.* 32, 2 (2014), 1–47.

On Fine-Grained Geolocalisation of Tweets

Jorge David Gonzalez Paule[1], Yashar Moshfeghi[2],
Joemon M. Jose[3] and Piyushimita (Vonu) Thakuriah[4]
[1,3]School of Computing Science, [4]Urban Big Data Centre, University of Glasgow, Glasgow, UK
[2]Department of Computer & Information Sciences, University of Strathclyde, Glasgow, UK
j.gonzalez-paule.1@research.gla.ac.uk,yashar.moshfeghi@strath.ac.uk,
Joemon.Jose@glasgow.ac.uk,Piyushimita.Thakuriah@glasgow.ac.uk

ABSTRACT

Recently, the geolocalisation of tweets has become an important feature for a wide range of tasks in Information Retrieval and other domains, such as real-time event detection, topic detection or disaster and emergency analysis. However, the number of relevant geo-tagged tweets available remains insufficient to reliably perform such tasks. Thus, predicting the location of non-geotagged tweets is an important yet challenging task, which can increase the sample of geo-tagged data and help to a wide range of tasks. In this paper, we propose a location inference method that utilises a ranking approach combined with a majority voting of tweets weighted based on the credibility of its source (Twitter user). Using geo-tagged tweets from two cities, Chicago and New York (USA), our experimental results demonstrate that our method (statistically) significantly outperforms our baselines in terms of accuracy, and error distance, in both cities, with the cost of decrease in recall.

CCS CONCEPTS

•Information systems → Social networking sites; Location based services; Information retrieval;

KEYWORDS

Information Retrieval; Geolocalisation; Fine-Grained; Twitter; User Credibility; Weighted Majority Voting

ACM Reference format:
Jorge David Gonzalez Paule[1], Yashar Moshfeghi[2],
Joemon M. Jose[3] and Piyushimita (Vonu) Thakuriah[4]. 2017. On Fine-Grained Geolocalisation of Tweets. In *Proceedings of ICTIR '17, October 1–4, 2017,Amsterdam, Netherlands*, , 4 pages.
DOI: https://doi.org/10.1145/3121050.3121104

1 INTRODUCTION

In recent years, social media services such as Twitter have gained increasing popularity within the research community since their data is spatially fine-grained (i.e. at street or neighborhood level). Such a characteristic has provided new opportunities for a broad range of applications in Information Retrieval (IR) including real-time event detection [2], sentiment analysis [3], topic detection

[7], and disaster and emergency analysis [1, 8, 11]. However, since only a very small sample of messages in the Twitter stream contain geographical information [5], geo-locating (or geolocalising) individual tweets has become an important yet challenge task. In this paper, we focus on geolocalisation of tweets at a fine-grained level. To tackle this problem, we propose a novel approach to combine evidence gathered from geo-tagged tweets that are similar based on their contents to a given non-geo-tagged tweet.

Several approaches have been proposed in the past to provide fine-grained geolocalisation of tweets, e.g. [9, 13]. These works first create a document for each predefined geographical area by concatenating the texts of the tweets belonging to that area. They then create a vector representation of that area from the generated document using a bag-of-word approach. To geolocate a given tweet, they then find the most similar area to that tweet based on its content-similarity, using the generated vectors [9]. Paraskevopoulos and Palpanas [13], in addition to above, have also considered time-evolution characteristics in their matching algorithm. Although these approaches have provided important insights on how to tackle fine-grained geolocalisation of tweets, due to the noisy nature of Twitter data [19], such an aggregation method could affect the accuracy of matching algorithms and in turn, decrease the accuracy of the geolocalisation.

In this work, we adopted a weighted majority voting algorithm to the problem of fine-grained geolocalisation of tweets. In particular, we estimated the geographical location of a given non-geo-tagged tweet by collecting the geo-location votes of the geo-tagged tweets that are most similar regarding their contents to that tweet. The weights of the votes were calculated based on the credibility of its source, (i.e. Twitter user). We then performed an exhaustive study of different models across two test collections generated based on tweets gathered from two different cities to validate our models. Our experimental results showed significant improvements regarding accuracy and reduction of geographical distance error compared to our baselines.

The rest of the paper is organised as follows. First, we discuss previous research and motivate our work. Second, we introduce our approach for fine-grained geolocalisation of a non-geo-tagged tweet. Finally, we present our experimental setup and discuss our results.

2 BACKGROUND

Several research efforts have identified the problem of geolocalising individual non-geo-tagged tweets. For example, Schulz et al. [18] tackled this problem by exploiting different spatial indicators of a tweet – i.e. tweet text or user profile – and mapping them to different geo-spatial datasets such as DBpedia Spotlight or Geonames.

More recently, other works tackled this problem by dividing the geographical space into areas of a given size and then modelled the language for each area [9, 13, 17, 20]. Then, a ranking approach is used to retrieve the most likely area based on the probability that a non-geo-tagged tweet was issued in that area. However, these studies used a coarse-grained level of granularity – i.e. zip codes to city or country level. In contrast, the problem we aim to tackle is the geolocalisation of Twitter posts at a fine-grained level – i.e. street or neighbourhood level.

An example of previous work on fine-grained geolocalisation is the work by Kinsella et. al. [9]. They attempted to predict location from country level to postal code level. As a result, the accuracy of their model decreases significantly when trying to predict at such fine-grained level. Another example of fine-grained geolocalisation is the work by Paraskevopoulos et. al. [13]. The authors refined the approach proposed by Kinsella et. al. [9] by dividing the geographical space into fine-grained squares of size $1km$. Also, the authors reduced the granularity of time by considering time slots of 4 hours, and computing the number of tweets by time for each candidate location compared with the global activity of the city. In this way, the model promotes short-term events in detriment of long-term events.

Inspired by Paraskevopoulos et. al. [13], we follow the strategy of dividing the city into squares of size $1km$. However, the time dimension is out of the scope of this paper. Thus we consider short-term and long-term events alike. Moreover, the works above perform a concatenation of texts of tweets belonging to a predefined area to represent that area as a single bag-of-word vector. We believe that by concatenating the content of the tweets, relevant information can be missed when predicting a location. In contrast to these works, we consider each tweet individually, representing each area as multiple bag-of-word vectors during the prediction process.

Also, our approach take into account the credibility of tweets. Other works have also considered the credibility of tweets. For example, McCreadie et. al. [11] has considered the idea of assigning a credibility score to tweets but for the disaster and emergency detection task. They have computed the credibility score using regression models with text features and user information. They have used this score to inform the user about the veracity/credibility of events derived from social media. We also incorporate the credibility of tweets in our fine-grained geolocalisation approach. But in contrast to McCreadie et. al. work, we incorporate this score as a weight of each vote in our adopted majority voting approach. The majority voting algorithm is a well known, fast and effective strategy widely adopted for prediction and re-ranking tasks [4, 12, 16]. However, to the best of our knowledge, this is the first time the majority voting is considered to tackle the geo-location of tweets. Next section describes our approach in detail.

3 FINE-GRAINED GEOLOCALISATION

Our proposed approach consists of three steps. First, we create a grid to divide the geographical area into squares of size $1km$ and associate each geo-tagged tweet to an area based on its location. As discussed in Section 2, the grid approach has been widely used in the literature to represent geographical areas at different

levels of granularity [9, 13]. Second, we obtained the Top-N content-based similar geo-tagged tweets to a non-geo-tagged using different retrieval models (see Section 4.1). Finally, we combine evidence gathered from the Top-N tweets by adopting a weighted majority voting algorithm where the weight is calculated based on the credibility information of tweets source.

3.1 Combining Evidence using Weighted Majority Voting

In order to combine evidences gathered from the Top-N content-based similar geo-tagged tweets to a non-geo-tagged tweet t_{ng}, we adopted a weighted majority voting algorithm [4, 12, 16] as follows. We represent each element of the Top-N tweets as a tuple (t_i, l_i, s_i) where l_i is the location associated to a geo-tagged tweet t_i posted by the source s_i. We then select the most frequent location within the Top-N set and associate that as the geo-location of a given tweet. In formal definition:

$$Location(t_{ng}) = \underset{l_j \in L}{\mathrm{argmax}} \left(\sum_{i=1}^{N} W_{t_i} * Vote(t_i^{l_i}, l_j) \right) \qquad (1)$$

where L is the set of locations (l_j) in the Top-N tweets and $t_i^{l_i}$ is the location of the i-th tweet in the rank. Then, a vote is given to the location l_j by the tweet t_i as follows:

$$Vote(t_i^{l_i}, l_j) = \begin{cases} 1 & t_i^{l_i} = l_j \\ 0 & t_i^{l_i} \neq l_j \end{cases} \qquad (2)$$

The vote of the tweet t_i is weighted by:

$$W_{t_i} = \frac{|\{t_{si} \in TN_i \mid distance(t_{s_i}, t_{v_i}) \leq 1km\}|}{|TN_i|} \qquad (3)$$

where W_{t_i} is based on the credibility of tweet's source s_i. The credibility of tweet's source is calculated as follows. First, we obtain the Top-N content-based most similar tweets for every tweet in a validation set (see Section 4). Second, we calculate the geographical distance (see Section 4) between the tweet in the validation set and each element in its Top-N. Next, for each source s_i we define a set TN_i that contains all the tweets appearing in any of the Top-N rankings (t_{si}) produced for each tweet in the validation set (t_{vi}). Finally, the credibility of source s_i is given by the ratio of all tweets in TN_i placed within less than $1km$ distance from the tweets in the validation set (t_{vi}).

Finally, the location l_j that obtains the highest number of tweet votes is returned as the final predicted geo-location of a given non-geo-tagged tweet.

4 EXPERIMENTAL SETUP

In this section, we describe the experimental setup that supports the evaluation of our proposed approach for fine-grained geolocalisation of non-geo-tagged tweets.

Data: Previous studies have shown that geo-tagged and non-geo-tagged data have the same characteristics [6]. Thus, models built from geo-tagged data can be generalised to non-geo-tagged data. We, therefore, experimented over a ground truth sample of

English geo-tagged tweets located in two different cities: Chicago and New York City (USA) with 131,273 and 155,114 tweets respectively. Tweets were collected from the Twitter Public stream during March 2016.

To evaluate our approach, we divided our dataset into three subsets. We used the first three weeks of tweets in our collection (i.e. the first three weeks of March) as a training set. We then randomly divided the last week data into validation and test sets to ensure that they have similar characteristics. Therefore, for Chicago dataset, our training, validation and test sets contained 111,627, 9,823 and 9,823 geo-tagged tweets respectively. For New York dataset, our training, validation and test sets contained 128,746, 13,184 and 13,184 geo-tagged tweets respectively.

4.1 Models

4.1.1 Baseline Models. We implemented our baseline (denoted by "Baseline") inspired by Paraskevopoulos et al. [13] work. To do so, for each of our cities, we first created a grid structure of squared areas with a side length of 1 km. For each of these defined squared areas, we created a document by concatenating the text of the tweets associated with each area. We then indexed these documents. As a preprocessing step, usernames and hashtags were preserved as tokens, all hyperlinks were removed from tweets, and re-tweets were preserved in the dataset. Then, we retrieved the most content-based similar document (Top-1) for each non-geo-tagged tweet. As the model returns the Top-1 tweet, the longitude and latitude coordinates of the tweet are returned as the predicted location instead of the squared area associated to the post. We investigated several retrieval models to maximise the performance of our baseline. Five different retrieval models were evaluated: Divergence From Randomness (dfr), Language Model with Dirichlet Smoothing (lmd), IDF (idf), TF-IDF (tf_idf) and BM25 (bm25) using the Apache Lucene[1] implementation. The difference between our baseline and the work by [13] are two-fold. First, we removed stop-words [10] and applied Porter stemming.[2] Second, we also did not consider the time dimension, as described in Section 2.

4.1.2 WMV Models. We also implemented our proposed approach explained in Section 3, denoted by "WMV". We used the same squared areas defined for our baseline models. However, in WMV model, each of these defined squared areas was represented as multiple bag-of-word vectors where each vector represents a single tweet associated with that area. By doing this, we treated each tweet as a single document for the retrieval task. We performed the same preprocessing step applied in our baseline models.

Similarly to our baselines, we investigated the same five retrieval models to maximise the performance of our approach. The results indicated that using IDF gave us the best performance. This is consistent with previous research findings [15].

We apply our weighted majority voting algorithm on top of the retrieval task. We considered the Top-3, -5, -7 and -9 content-based most similar tweets obtained from the retrieval task. The final

---

[1]http://lucene.apache.org/
[2]We also tried our baseline without removing stop-words and applying Porter stemming, but resulted in the lower performance and hence we did not report them due to lack of space.

predicted location is the predefined area that obtain the highest number of votes.

Metrics: To evaluate the effectiveness of our approach, the following metrics are reported. **Average Error distance (km):** we compute the distance on Earth (Haversine formula [14]) between the predicted location and the real coordinates of the tweet in our ground truth. **Accuracy@1km:** the accuracy of the model is measured by determining whether a predicted location lies within a radius of $1km$ from the real location. **Recall:** we consider Recall as the fraction of tweets in the test set that was geolocalised by our approach regardless of the distance error.

5 RESULTS

Table 1 and 2 shows the average error distance, accuracy, and recall for our approach evaluated on the Chicago and New York datasets respectively. A paired t-test was conducted to assess if the difference in effectiveness between the models is statistically significant. As shown in Table 1 and 2, our approach ("WMV") (statistically) significantly outperforms the best performed baseline (i.e. "Baseline_lmd") in terms of accuracy and error distance, in both cities, across all the investigated values of N for the Top-N tweets, with the cost of decrease in recall.

Table 1: Results for Chicago city dataset. The table presents the Average Error Distance in kilometres (A_Err_km), Accuracy at 1 kilometre (Acc@1km) and Recall for our proposed approach ("WMV") against our Baseline using the Top-N (@TopN) elements in the rank. Significant differences with respect to our best Baseline ("Baseline_lmd") are denoted by * and ** where p<0.05 and p<0.01 respectively.

Chicago			
Model	A_Err_km	Acc@1km	Recall
Baseline_tf_idf	8.100	42.40%	99.97%
Baseline_idf	14.056	13.18%	99.97%
Baseline_dfr	8.586	37.40%	99.97%
Baseline_lmd	6.185	47.79%	99.97%
Baseline_bm25	7.637	41.76%	99.97%
WMV@Top3	3.849**	61.17%**	83.28%**
WMV@Top5	3.669**	62.78%**	79.08%**
WMV@Top7	3.170**	66.82%**	70.41%**
WMV@Top9	2.576**	71.29%**	62.28%**

Table 2: Results for New York city dataset. The table presents the Average Error Distance in kilometres (A_Err_km), Accuracy at 1 kilometre (Acc@1km) and Recall for our proposed approach ("WMV") against our Baseline using the Top-N (@TopN) elements in the rank. Significant differences with respect to our best Baseline ("Baseline_lmd") are denoted by * and ** where p<0.05 and p<0.01 respectively.

New York			
Model	A_Err_km	Acc@1km	Recall
Baseline_tf_idf	7.505	38.39%	99.98%
Baseline_idf	12.755	12.78%	99.98%
Baseline_dfr	7.609	36.28%	99.98%
Baseline_lmd	7.169	37.29%	99.98%
Baseline_bm25	7.460	38.25%	99.98%
WMV@Top3	4.234**	52.33%**	75.84%**
WMV@Top5	4.362**	51.98%**	75.09%**
WMV@Top7	4.008**	54.81%**	67.83%**
WMV@Top9	3.476**	59.23%**	59.94%**

Additionally, our findings show that as the number of voting candidates (i.e. Top-N) increases, our approach achieves lower error distance, higher accuracy but lower recall. Therefore, considering the Top-3 tweets resulted in the best trade-off regarding error distance, accuracy and recall. Also, we observed that our approach performed similarly across both cities despite their geographical and cultural differences. Such similarity in performance suggests that our approach can be generalised and adapted to different cities. Our promising results show the potential of our approach for fine-grained geolocalisation of tweets.

6 CONCLUSIONS

In this work, we proposed an approach for fine-grained geolocalisation of tweets by adopting a weighted majority voting algorithm. The weight of each tweet vote is obtained by calculating the credibility of its source (i.e. Twitter user). Our baseline model is inspired by Paraskevopoulos [13] work, where a grid approach were applied to divide a city into a set of predefined geographical areas of size $1\ km$. However, in contrast to this work, we did not concatenate the text of tweets into a document to create a single bag-of-word vector to represent a predefined area. Our approach, instead, treats each tweet individually as a single document and represent each area as multiple bag-of-word vectors.

We then indexed these documents and then retrieved the most content-based similar document for each non-geo-tagged tweet. Also, we investigated several retrieval models to find the best performance for our baseline and our proposed approach. For our baseline approach, the geographic location associated with the Top-1 retrieved document is then assigned to the tweet, since each predefined area is only represented by a single document. In our approach, we assign the most voted area of the Top-N content-based similar tweets where N is set to 3, 5, 7 and 9.

To demonstrate the effectiveness of our approach, we conducted an experiment on two datasets of geo-tagged tweets collected from two different cities, Chicago and New York, with 131,273 and 155,114 tweets respectively. The data was collected during March 2016. Our experimental results show that our weighted majority voting approach (statistically) significantly outperforms the best-performed baseline (i.e. "Baseline_lmd") in terms of accuracy and error distance, in both cities, across all the investigated values of N for the Top-N tweets, with the cost of decrease in recall in the two cities of study. Also, we observed that as the number of voting candidates (i.e. Top-N) increases, our approach achieves lower error distance, higher accuracy but lower recall. This behaviour is observed across both datasets which suggest that our approach can be generalised and adapted to different cities.

This shows the power of our proposed approach in predicting geolocation of tweets, and can substantially expand the sample of geo-tagged data at a fine-grained level (i.e. street level or neighbourhood level), helping to a wide range of tasks in information retrieval, including real-time event detection, topic detection and disaster and emergency analysis. In future work, we will investigate whether we can improve recall while maintaining the high accuracy of our approach.

Acknowledgements: The research leading to these results has received funding from the European Research Council under the European Union's Seventh Framework Programme (FP7/2007-2013)/ ERC grant agreement n° 632075.

REFERENCES

[1] Ji Ao, Peng Zhang, and Yanan Cao. 2014. Estimating the Locations of Emergency Events from Twitter Streams. *Procedia Computer Science* 31 (2014), 731 – 739. DOI:http://dx.doi.org/10.1016/j.procs.2014.05.321 2nd International Conference on Information Technology and Quantitative Management, ITQM 2014.

[2] Farzindar Atefeh and Wael Khreich. 2015. A Survey of Techniques for Event Detection in Twitter. *Comput. Intell.* 31, 1 (Feb. 2015), 132–164. DOI:http://dx.doi.org/10.1111/coin.12017

[3] Eric Baucom, Azade Sanjari, Xiaozhong Liu, and Miao Chen. 2013. Mirroring the Real World in Social Media: Twitter, Geolocation, and Sentiment Analysis. In *Proceedings of the 2013 International Workshop on Mining Unstructured Big Data Using Natural Language Processing (UnstructureNLP '13).* ACM, New York, NY, USA, 61–68. DOI:http://dx.doi.org/10.1145/2513549.2513559

[4] T.-H. Chiang, H.-Y. Lo, and S.-D. Lin. 2012. A Ranking-based KNN Approach for Multi-Label Classification. In *Proceedings of the Asian Conference on Machine Learning (Proceedings of Machine Learning Research)*, Steven C. H. Hoi and Wray Buntine (Eds.), Vol. 25. PMLR, Singapore Management University, Singapore, 81–96. http://proceedings.mlr.press/v25/chiang12.html

[5] Mark Graham, Scott A. Hale, and Devin Gaffney. 2013. Where in the World are You? Geolocation and Language Identification in Twitter. *CoRR* abs/1308.0683 (2013). http://arxiv.org/abs/1308.0683

[6] Bo Han, Paul Cook, and Timothy Baldwin. 2014. Text-based Twitter User Geolocation Prediction. *J. Artif. Int. Res.* 49, 1 (Jan. 2014), 451–500. http://dl.acm.org/citation.cfm?id=2655713.2655726

[7] Liangjie Hong, Amr Ahmed, Siva Gurumurthy, Alexander J. Smola, and Kostas Tsioutsiouliklis. 2012. Discovering Geographical Topics in the Twitter Stream. In *Proceedings of the 21st International Conference on World Wide Web (WWW '12).* ACM, New York, NY, USA, 769–778. DOI:http://dx.doi.org/10.1145/2187836.2187940

[8] Muhammad Imran, Carlos Castillo, Fernando Diaz, and Sarah Vieweg. 2015. Processing Social Media Messages in Mass Emergency: A Survey. *ACM Comput. Surv.* 47, 4, Article 67 (June 2015), 38 pages. DOI:http://dx.doi.org/10.1145/2771588

[9] Sheila Kinsella, Vanessa Murdock, and Neil O'Hare. 2011. "I'M Eating a Sandwich in Glasgow": Modeling Locations with Tweets. In *Proceedings of the 3rd International Workshop on Search and Mining User-generated Contents (SMUC '11).* ACM, New York, NY, USA, 61–68. DOI:http://dx.doi.org/10.1145/2065023.2065039

[10] Christopher D. Manning, Prabhakar Raghavan, and Hinrich Schütze. 2008. *Introduction to Information Retrieval.* Cambridge University Press, New York, NY, USA.

[11] Richard McCreadie, Craig Macdonald, and Iadh Ounis. 2016. EAIMS: Emergency Analysis Identification and Management System. In *Proceedings of the 39th International ACM SIGIR Conference on Research and Development in Information Retrieval (SIGIR '16).* ACM, New York, NY, USA, 1101–1104. DOI:http://dx.doi.org/10.1145/2911451.2911460

[12] Mawloud Mosbah and Bachir Boucheham. 2015. *Majority Voting Re-ranking Algorithm for Content Based-Image Retrieval.* Springer International Publishing, Cham, 121–131. DOI:http://dx.doi.org/10.1007/978-3-319-24129-6_11

[13] Pavlos Paraskevopoulos and Themis Palpanas. 2015. Fine-Grained Geolocalisation of Non-Geotagged Tweets. In *Proceedings of the 2015 IEEE/ACM International Conference on Advances in Social Networks Analysis and Mining 2015 (ASONAM '15).* ACM, New York, NY, USA, 105–112. DOI:http://dx.doi.org/10.1145/2808797.2808869

[14] C. C. Robusto. 1957. The Cosine-Haversine Formula. *The American Mathematical Monthly* 64, 1 (1957), 38–40. http://www.jstor.org/stable/2309088

[15] Jesus Alberto Rodriguez Perez and Joemon M. Jose. 2015. On Microblog Dimensionality and Informativeness: Exploiting Microblogs' Structure and Dimensions for Ad-Hoc Retrieval. In *Proceedings of the 2015 International Conference on The Theory of Information Retrieval (ICTIR '15).* ACM, New York, NY, USA, 211–220. DOI:http://dx.doi.org/10.1145/2808194.2809466

[16] Lior Rokach. 2010. *Pattern Classification Using Ensemble Methods.* World Scientific Publishing Co., Inc., River Edge, NJ, USA.

[17] Stephen Roller, Michael Speriosu, Sarat Rallapalli, Benjamin Wing, and Jason Baldridge. 2012. Supervised Text-based Geolocation Using Language Models on an Adaptive Grid. In *Proceedings of the 2012 Joint Conference on Empirical Methods in Natural Language Processing and Computational Natural Language Learning (EMNLP-CoNLL '12).* Association for Computational Linguistics, Stroudsburg, PA, USA, 1500–1510. http://dl.acm.org/citation.cfm?id=2390948.2391120

[18] Axel Schulz, Aristotelis Hadjakos, Heiko Paulheim, Johannes Nachtwey, and Max Mühlhäuser. 2013. A Multi-Indicator Approach for Geolocalization of Tweets. https://www.aaai.org/ocs/index.php/ICWSM/ICWSM13/paper/view/6063

[19] Jaime Teevan, Daniel Ramage, and Meredith Ringel Morris. 2011. #TwitterSearch: A Comparison of Microblog Search and Web Search. ACM.

[20] Benjamin P. Wing and Jason Baldridge. 2011. Simple Supervised Document Geolocation with Geodesic Grids. In *Proceedings of the 49th Annual Meeting of the Association for Computational Linguistics: Human Language Technologies - Volume 1 (HLT '11).* Association for Computational Linguistics, Stroudsburg, PA, USA, 955–964. http://dl.acm.org/citation.cfm?id=2002472.2002593

On Search Powered Navigation

Mostafa Dehghani
University of Amsterdam
dehghani@uva.nl

Glorianna Jagfeld
University of Stuttgart
jagfelga@ims.uni-stuttgart.de

Hosein Azarbonyad
University of Amsterdam
h.azarbonyad@uva.nl

Alex Olieman
University of Amsterdam
olieman@uva.nl

Jaap Kamps
University of Amsterdam
kamps@uva.nl

Maarten Marx
University of Amsterdam
maartenmarx@uva.nl

ABSTRACT

Query-based searching and browsing-based navigation are the two main components of exploratory search. Search lets users dig in deep by controlling their actions to focus on and find just the information they need, whereas navigation helps them to get an overview to decide which content is most important. In this paper, we introduce the concept of *search powered navigation* and investigate the effect of empowering navigation with search functionality on information seeking behavior of users and their experience by conducting a user study on exploratory search tasks, differentiated by different types of information needs. Our main findings are as follows: First, we observe radically different search tactics. Using search, users are able to control and augment their search focus, hence they explore the data in a depth-first, bottom-up manner. Conversely, using pure navigation they tend to check different options to be able to decide on their path into the data, which corresponds to a breadth-first, top-down exploration. Second, we observe a general natural tendency to combine aspects of search and navigation, however, our experiments show that the search functionality is essential to solve exploratory search tasks that require finding documents related to a narrow domain. Third, we observe a natural need for search powered navigation: users using a system without search functionality find creative ways to mimic searching using navigation.

1 INTRODUCTION

Knowledge graphs and other hierarchical domain ontologies hold great promise for complex information seeking tasks, yet their massive size defies the standard and effective way smaller hierarchies are used as a static navigation structure in faceted search or standard website navigation. As a result, we see only limited use of knowledge bases in entity surfacing for navigational queries, and fail to realize their full potential to empower search. Seeking information in structured environments consists of two main activities: *exploratory browsing* and *focused searching* [4, 11, 12]. Exploratory browsing refers to activities aimed at better defining the information need and increasing the level of understanding of the information space, while focused searching includes activities such as query refining and comparison of results, which are performed after the information need has been made more concrete. Based on the interplay of these two actions, a search system is supposed to provide a connected space of information for the users to *navigate*, as well as *search* to adjust the focus of their browsing towards useful content.

In this paper, we introduce the concept of *Search Powered Navigation (SPN)*, which enables users to combine navigation with query based searching in a structured information space, and offers a way to find a balance between exploration and exploitation. We hypothesize that SPN enables users to exploit the semantic structure of a large knowledge base in an effective way. We test this hypothesis by conducting a user study in which users are engaged in exploratory search activities and investigate the effect of SPN on the variability in users' behaviour and experience. We employed an exploratory search system on parliamentary data in two modes, *pure navigation* and *search powered navigation*, and tested two types of tasks, broad-and focused-topic tasks.

In our study, the primary goal is *to investigate information seeking behavior and user experience when navigation is empowered by a search functionality*. We break it down into the following two research questions:

RQ1 What is the effect of search powered navigation on user behavior in different types of exploratory search tasks?

RQ2 Does empowering navigation with search improve user experience in different types of exploratory search tasks?

There is a large body of research focusing on user behavior in exploratory search from different angles. Athukorala et al. [1] investigated user behavior in terms of narrowing or broadening queries in exploratory search. Diriye et al. [5] discussed different factors that generally influence exploratory search like objective, search activities, conceptual complexity, procedural complexity, and domain knowledge. In terms of investigating user behavior during search, there are also relevant studies conducted in the context of general web search [6] and website browsing [2]. White and Drucker [10] also studied the interaction flow in web search and investigated user behavioural variability based on users' queries, interactions, time, and the types of visited webpages.

2 CASE STUDY SYSTEM OVERVIEW

For our study, we have used an exploratory search system, the WikiCat Browser, which maps parliamentary data into a conceptually structured space to facilitate exploring the data.

WikiCat Browser. The WikiCat Browser is a search system developed for exploratory search to browse and investigate parliamentary debates from a particular point of view. It projects the parliamentary speeches to the Wikipedia categorical structure, based on Wikipedia

ICTIR'17, October 1–4, 2017, Amsterdam, The Netherlands
© 2017 Copyright held by the owner/author(s). Publication rights licensed to ACM.
ISBN 978-1-4503-4490-6/17/10...$15.00
DOI: https://doi.org/10.1145/3121050.3121105

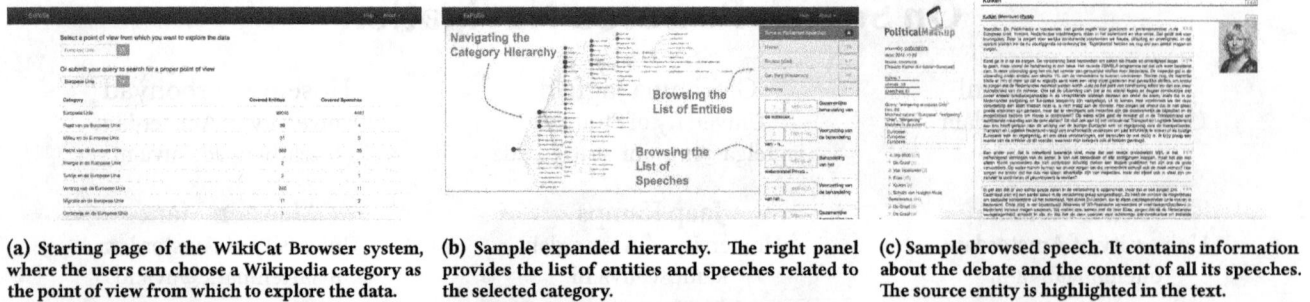

(a) Starting page of the WikiCat Browser system, where the users can choose a Wikipedia category as the point of view from which to explore the data.

(b) Sample expanded hierarchy. The right panel provides the list of entities and speeches related to the selected category.

(c) Sample browsed speech. It contains information about the debate and the content of all its speeches. The source entity is highlighted in the text.

Figure 1: WikiCat Browser system

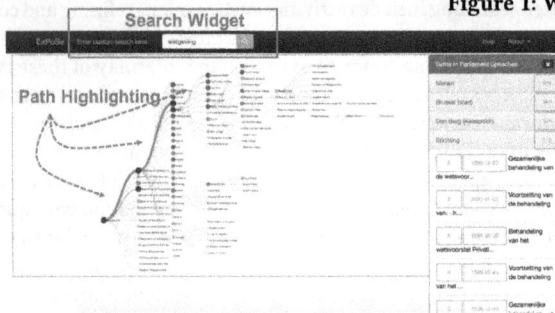

Figure 2: The WikiCat Browser system with SPN. The users can submit a textual query which highlights the paths in the hierarchy based on their likelihood of leading to speeches relevant to the query.

named entities mentioned in the parliamentary speeches. A customized entity linker for parliamentary conversation [4, 9] is employed to recognize and disambiguate both the general and domain specific entities from all the speeches.

In this system, first, the user has to chose the point of view from the set of Wikipedia categories. To assist users in choosing a good staring point of view, the WikiCat Browser provides a search tool, which was first introduced to the system for the experiments presented in this paper. Given a free text query, the search tool retrieves a ranked list of categories according to the BM25 similarity of the query to the content of the debates grouped under each category (Figure 1a). In the selected hierarchy, each node is a Wikipedia category representing one topic. The users can explore the category hierarchy by clicking on a node which expands its descendants, i.e. sub-categories (Figure 1b). Importance and recency of the categories are visualized by the size and color of the nodes, respectively. The importance of each node denotes how much the topic of that category is addressed in the parliamentary debates, based on the frequency of entities under this category. The recency of each node shows how recently the topic of the category was discussed, calculated from the dates of the debates in this category.

Besides expanding each category, the users can browse the list of entities under the category by clicking on the category name. For each entity, the users can browse the list of all speeches in which this entity occurs. The list of speeches is ordered by the number of occurrences of the corresponding entity. For each speech the title of the debate and its date is shown. By clicking on the speech title, the full content of the speeches with the related entities highlighted in the text is displayed (Figure 1c).

As example of the type of search questions that can be addressed with the WikiCat Browser constitutes analysing the relation between national laws of the European country and the European union legislation. As a reasonable approach, we would like to investigate

when EU legislation was discussed in the Dutch parliament and in the context of which (proposed) Dutch laws, i.e. we want to project debates in the Dutch parliament to topics related to the European Parliament in terms of both the subject matter and time.

Search-Powered Navigation. In order to investigate the effect of search on the browsing behaviour of the users, we designed search-powered navigation (SPN) for the WikiCat Browser. SPN provides the ability to *search* during the data navigation. It allows the users to submit a textual query at any step in the navigation. The system ranks different navigation paths based on their likelihood to leading to data relevant for the query (Figure 2).

SPN is integrated as a search bar in the navigation window of the WikiCat Browser. Every time the user submits a query, the system calculates the similarity of the full content of all speeches in the collection with the given query. The scores at the speech level are used to calculate the scores at the entity level based on their occurrences in different speeches and their corresponding scores. Finally, the normalized scores of all entities under each category are summed to obtain the likelihood score of the category. This score determines the weight of the edge from the previous level of the hierarchy to the category.

In the user interface, the weights of different edges are represented by their thickness. At each level in the navigation hierarchy, SPN provides a ranking of paths that are likely to lead to speeches relevant for the query. In line with the general purpose of the WikiCat Browser system, which is exploratory search, SPN does not provide a direct ranking of speeches but hints the user to more promising paths. In that way, the users still can explore the full search space but obtain some guidance in their decision making process. In our experiments we show that the imposed bias by SPN for steering users to relevant information does not keep them from exploring the space.

3 EXPERIMENTAL SETUP

We have conducted a descriptive user study [7] by asking the users to do exploratory search tasks on Dutch parliamentary debates from 1994 to 2014, once by means of the pure navigational system and once using the system with SPN.

With regard to the requirements of simulated work task situations [3], we selected 14 search tasks, comprising seven broad-topic and seven focused-topic tasks and defined task scenarios for the users. Broad-topic tasks, on the one hand, are supposed to be addressed by a diverse set of debates and there is no concrete answer to them. Focused-tasks, on the other hand, are supposed to be addressed by a small fraction of debates. In the broad-topic tasks, the users had to find out the general attitude or opinion of the Dutch parliament on the following seven topics: *Immigration, Islam, World War II, Taxes, Holocaust, Dutch Golden Age, European Union*. In the focused-topic

Table 1: Per-session statistics from search sessions for both systems in both types of tasks averaged over all search sessions. Numbers marked by ᵃ or ᵛ differ significantly from all other numbers in the same column (two-tailed t-test, p-value < 0.05).

Task	System	avg. num. of root selection	avg. depth of selected root in Wikipedia hierarchy	avg. num. of node expansions	avg. num. of entity list loading	avg. num. of speech list loading	avg. num. of speech content browsing	avg. session duration (min)	avg. rating summaries/speeches (10 point scale)
Broad Topic	WikiCat	3.1	5.1	15.1	29.5	16.7	18.2	22.2	5.12
	WikiCat + SPN	2.2	4.7	11.8	20.8	12.4	13.1	18.2	7.78
Focused Topic	WikiCat	8.7ᵃ	9.3ᵃ	9.5ᵛ	31.6ᵃ	9.2	4.9	33.4	3.44
	WikiCat + SPN	3.3	6.3	13.9	16.4	7.6	4.1	27.1	4.62

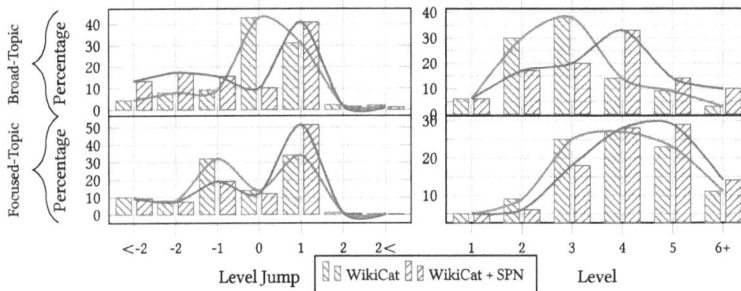

(a) Distribution of level jumps.   (b) Distribution of level visits.

Figure 3: Distribution of level jumps and visits for focused and broad topics.

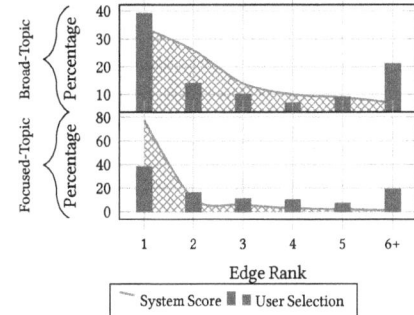

Figure 4: Percentage of selected edges on different ranks versus distribution of scores assigned to edges.

tasks, the users should find Dutch parliamentary debates related to the following seven particular cases: *Unsuccessful operation of "baby Jelmer" in Groningen University Hospital; The trial and death of Slobo-dan Milosevic in the Hague; Role of Dutchbat soldiers in the Srebrenica massacre; New year's fire in a cafe in Volendam; The fireworks disaster in Enschede; H5N1 (a variant of the bird flu virus);* and *Fitna (an anti-Islam film by the Dutch parliamentarian Geert Wilders).*

In our study, 14 participants (5 undergraduate and 9 graduate students) were enrolled, six male and eight female, who had an average age of 26 (SD = 2.01). All participants had more than 10 years of computer experience, a fairly high ability of online search, but inexperienced in the political domain and Dutch parliament. The participants were each given two broad-topic and two focused-topic tasks. They had to complete one broad-topic task and one focused-topic task using the original WikiCat Browser system, and the two remaining tasks using the system with SPN. To control the order bias, we randomly divided the users into two equally sized groups. The first group started off with the baseline system, while the second group used the system with SPN first. In all experiments, the participants were asked to provide a set of relevant speeches along with a short summary of the obtained information.

Based on our setup, each task was performed twice with the original WikiCat Browser system and twice with the system with SPN, each time by a different participant. In total, we had 56 search sessions. Additionally, the users were asked to fill out a basic pre-search questionnaire with their general information, including age, education, gender, and a self-assessment of their domain knowledge and their ability to use search systems. After each task, they filled out a post-search questionnaire to rate the difficulty of the task and their satisfaction [8]. During the experiments, we logged all interactions of the users with systems.

4 RESULTS AND DISCUSSION

In this section, we analyze the effect of our different conditions, search vs. no search, broad vs. focused topic tasks on the naviga-tional behavior of the users and their experience during search. We describe the navigational model in terms of *level visits* and *level jumps*. A *level visit* is counted if the user expands the children of a node on a certain level or loads the list of entities of the node. The *level jump* denotes the difference of the node levels of a pair of consecutively visited nodes. Additionally, we recorded statistics on the different actions the users can take during browsing which implicitly indicate how user experience changes in terms of time and effort. The results are shown in Table 1.

4.1 Effect of SPN on user behaviour

We analyze in what ways adding search functionality influences the navigational behavior. According to the plots in the upper part of Figure 3a, for broad-topic tasks the users of the WikiCat Browser system tend to visit nodes from the same layer when exploring the space (high percentage of zero level jumps), which corresponds to a **breadth-first** navigation. However, as the lower part of Figure 3a shows, when their navigation is empowered by a search utility, they tend to have more forward moves and visit nodes in the next levels (high percentage of level jumps = 1), which corresponds to a **depth-first** exploration of the hierarchy. For the focused-topic tasks, the traversal approach is **depth-first** for both systems. This pattern can be explained by the information need. Since the users are not able to evaluate the quality of a taken path until they are deep enough to access a narrow part of the search space. The main difference in the browsing behaviour of the users is that they backtrack a lot using the baseline system (high percentage of negative level jumps). The reason for this is that the users need to try more different paths when they have no strong clue of the content of the documents in the deeper levels. Figure 4 demonstrates the percentage of the selected edges on different ranks versus the distribution of their scores. In the broad-topic tasks, the system assigns rather high scores to the edges in the second and third ranks, while in the focused-topic tasks, the score distribution is pretty skewed, where the top-ranked edge receives a considerable share of the score distribution. Regardless of the task, the users choose the top-ranked edge at each point to deepen their exploration in about 40% of the cases. Interestingly, the users were still motivated to explore lower ranked edges irrespective of the score distribution of the edges. Moreover, contrary to the concern that search may limit the extent of exploration, the users are more confident to go deeper in the hierarchy with the system with SPN (cf. Figure 3b).

4.2 Does SPN improve user experience?

First we investigate the general user behavior with regards to the task type, then we study how empowering navigation with search improves user experience in each type of task.

We look at the effect of different tasks on the navigational model. As expected the users explore more of the search space in the broad-topic tasks because they require more browsing. In average the rate of node expansions and data loading including entities, speeches, and content of speeches displayed in Table 1 are higher in both systems compared to the focused-topic tasks. As can be seen from Figure 3b, in general the users tend to visit deeper levels in focused-topic tasks. It is noteworthy that in both systems, all the data of the deeper levels is also accessible from higher levels. However, with regard to the sorting strategy of displayed information, the more popular the data is (i.e. more frequent entities in each category), the higher it is ranked in the browsing panel. Hence, for the broad-topic tasks, which are mostly addressable with popular entities and speeches, the users find their needed information on top of the lists already at higher levels and they see no need to go deeper. In contrast, for the focused-topic tasks, which are mostly related to particular entities that are not necessarily popular overall, in the higher levels the users need to scroll down a long list to find a related data among lots of unrelated data. Thus, according to our observations, they prefer to descend in the hierarchy to narrow down the search space.

We further investigated whether the search functionality is a useful addition to an exploratory search system. As can be seen in Table 1, the average number of loaded entities, speeches or their content is generally lower for the system with SPN compared to the original WikiCat Browser system in both types of tasks. This can be attributed to the fact that users skip loading the intermediary data when their navigation is facilitated by search. They quickly get to the target content, which leads to shorter search sessions. We assessed the quality of the search results by asking two experts in the Dutch political domain to rate set of relevant speeches and summaries retrieved by the users. The assessors were not informed about the participants and the system used to compile the summaries and speeches. As can be seen from the last column in Table 1, the users were more successful in the broad-topic tasks compared to the focused-topic tasks, regardless of the search system. However, the search functionality improved the quality of the results in both tasks significantly. In summary, we conclude that the search lays the ground for a better navigation of the users, enabling them to explore better content.

In our study, in the focused-topic tasks, the users are supposed to find a needle in a haystack of data. Using the original WikiCat Browser system, if they fail to express the information need using a set of proper entities, it is less likely that they find paths leading to the relevant content. The statistics in Table 1 reveal an interesting behavior of the users' faced with the original WikiCat Browser system to perform focused-topic tasks. In this setting, the average number of node expansions is significantly lower compared performing the same type of tasks with the system with SPN. This runs contrary to

our expectations, since in the system with no navigation aid, users are supposed to try different paths by expanding a lot of nodes, as it is the case in the broad-topic tasks. However, considering the high average number of root selections and their high average depths in the focused-topic tasks using the original WikiCat Browser system, we noticed that the users seemed to creatively simulate the search in their navigation when they needed it. They went back to the starting page of the system, where they can choose the root of the hierarchy they want to navigate through, using the search functionality provided for choosing the root node. Then, instead of navigating from there to deep levels, they shallowly evaluate the selected hierarchy and again go back to the starting page to choose a better root node by reformulating their query. They repeat this procedure until they get access to a proper root node which is fairly deep in the hierarchy. Thus, the users try different nodes as the starting node using the search instead of trying to locate them via navigation.

5 CONCLUSIONS

We introduced the concept of "search powered navigation" as a way to empower users with the semantic structure of large knowledge bases, and build a proof-of-concept system to investigate the viability of this approach to support exploratory search tasks. In a user study, we showed that a search functionality can be a viable and effective addition to a navigational exploratory search system. This was reflected in faster task completion and better search results using the system with the additional search feature. While users tended to search the data in a breadth-first manner in the pure navigational baseline exploratory search system, an additional search functionality lead to a depth-first investigation of the data. Furthermore, we found that a search functionality is essential to be able to efficiently address focused-topic tasks.

Acknowledgments This research is funded in part by the Netherlands Organization for Scientific Research (NWO; ExPoSe project, NWO CI # 314.99.108).

REFERENCES

[1] K. Athukorala, A. Oulasvirta, D. Glowacka, J. Vreeken, and G. Jacucci. Narrow or broad?: Estimating subjective specificity in exploratory search. In *CIKM '14*, pages 819–828, 2014.
[2] M. H. Blackmon, M. Kitajima, and P. G. Polson. Tool for accurately predicting website navigation problems, non-problems, problem severity, and effectiveness of repairs. In *CHI '5*, pages 31–40, 2005. ISBN 1-58113-998-5.
[3] P. Borlund. The IIR evaluation model: a framework for evaluation of interactive information retrieval systems. *Information research*, 8(3), 2003.
[4] M. Dehghani, G. Jagfeld, H. Azarbonyad, A. Olieman, J. Kamps, and M. Marx. Telling how to narrow it down: Browsing path recommendation for exploratory search. In *Proceedings of the CHIIR '17*, 2017.
[5] A. Diriye, M. L. Wilson, A. Blandford, and A. Tombros. Revisiting exploratory search from the HCI perspective. In *HCIR 2010*, pages 99–102, 2010.
[6] I. Hsieh-Yee. Research on web search behavior. *Library & Information Science Research*, 23(2):167–185, 2001.
[7] D. Kelly. Methods for evaluating interactive information retrieval systems with users. *Found. Trends Inf. Retr*, 3(1–2):1–224, 2009. ISSN 1554-0669.
[8] D. Kelly, J. Arguello, A. Edwards, and W.-c. Wu. Development and evaluation of search tasks for IIR experiments using a cognitive complexity framework. In *ICTIR '15*, pages 101–110, 2015.
[9] A. Olieman, H. Azarbonyad, M. Dehghani, J. Kamps, and M. Marx. Entity linking by focusing on dbpedia candidate entities. In *ERD '14*, pages 13–24, 2014.
[10] R. W. White and S. M. Drucker. Investigating behavioral variability in web search. In *WWW '07*, pages 21–30, 2007.
[11] R. W. White and R. A. Roth. Exploratory search: beyond the query-response paradigm. *Morgan and Claypool Publishers*, 3, 2009.
[12] M. L. Wilson, B. Kules, B. Shneiderman, et al. From keyword search to exploration: Designing future search interfaces for the web. *Foundations and Trends in Web Science*, 2(1):1–97, 2010.

The Treatment of Ties in AP Correlation

Julián Urbano
Delft University of Technology
Delft, The Netherlands
urbano.julian@gmail.com

Mónica Marrero
Delft University of Technology
Delft, The Netherlands
m.marrerollinares@tudelft.nl

ABSTRACT

The Kendall tau and AP correlation coefficients are very commonly use to compare two rankings over the same set of items. Even though Kendall tau was originally defined assuming that there are no ties in the rankings, two alternative versions were soon developed to account for ties in two different scenarios: measure the accuracy of an observer with respect to a true and objective ranking, and measure the agreement between two observers in the absence of a true ranking. These two variants prove useful in cases where ties are possible in either ranking, and may indeed result in very different scores. AP correlation was devised to incorporate a top-heaviness component into Kendall tau, penalizing more heavily if differences occur between items at the top of the rankings, making it a very compelling coefficient in Information Retrieval settings. However, the treatment of ties in AP correlation remains an open problem. In this paper we fill this gap, providing closed analytical formulations of AP correlation under the two scenarios of ties contemplated in Kendall tau. In addition, we developed an R package that implements these coefficients.

KEYWORDS

Evaluation; Correlation; Kendall; Average Precision; Ties

1 INTRODUCTION

The Kendall τ [5] and Yilmaz τ_{ap} [17] rank correlation coefficients are frequently employed in Information Retrieval to compare two rankings X and Y given to a set of n items. For instance, Baeza-Yates et al. [1] compared the ranking of webpages produced by crawling algorithms with the ranking produced by PageRank, and White et al. [15] compared different rankings of terms in a study of implicit feedback. These correlation coefficients are particularly common in evaluation studies to compare the rankings of retrieval systems produced by different evaluation conditions, such as different evaluation measures [9], topic sets [3], assessors [14], experts vs. non-experts [2], or even to compare it to the ranking produced by user ratings [10] or the ranking over populations of topics [13].

Both τ and τ_{ap} were originally defined under the assumption that no ties are present in either ranking, so that every item is assigned one integer rank from 1 to n. However, in practical applications

there are cases in which several items are considered equal and no preference is given to any of them. As Kendall [6] put it himself:

> *this effect may arise either because the objects really are indistinguishable, [...] or because the observer is unable to discern such differences as exist.*

According to Student [12], Pearson was first in contemplating the issue of ties in ranking problems, for which he suggested several ways to assign ranks to tied items [8]. Following Pearson, Student investigated the effect of ties in the calculation of the Spearman ρ correlation coefficient through its analogy to the product-moment correlation between the rankings. Woodbury [16] also studied the treatment of ties in Spearman ρ, but suggested a different alternative. Following a general definition of correlation by Daniels [4], Kendall [6] applied the principles of Student and Woodbury to his τ correlation coefficient, and identified the two versions as pertaining to two different scenarios:

a) The variant by Woodbury [16] assumes that one of the rankings, say X, is in fact a true and objective ranking in which no ties are present, and Y is the ranking given by an observer which may sometimes fail to distinguish some items and therefore assigns them the same rank. The correlation in this scenario is hence used as a measure of the *accuracy* of the observer. He coined this coefficient τ_a.

b) The variant by Student [12] assumes that both X and Y are rankings given by two observers, both of which may decide to tie some items. In this case, there is no objective ranking to compare with, so the correlation is used as a measure of *agreement* between the two observers. He coined this coefficient[1] τ_b.

As will be evident in the following sections, these two scenarios are fundamentally different and may lead to significantly different scores, so it is important to choose the most appropriate in each case. To the best of our knowledge though, the τ_{ap} correlation coefficient of Yilmaz et al. [17] has not been defined in the presence of ties as τ has. Smucker et al. [11] briefly confronted this problem in scenario a), but approached it numerically. In this paper we fill this gap and provide closed analytical formulations of τ_{ap} under both scenarios of ties. Of course, we coin them $\tau_{ap,a}$ and $\tau_{ap,b}$.

In addition, and to promote its use, we provide implementations of these correlation coefficients in a fully-fledged R package called `ircor`, available from http://github.com/julian-urbano/ircor/.

2 CORRELATION WITHOUT TIES

Let $X = \langle x_1, \ldots, x_n \rangle$ be the true ranking of a set of n items, and let $Y = \langle y_1, \ldots, y_n \rangle$ be an alternative ranking given to the same items.

---

[1]Initially, Kendall [6] used the terms τ_W and τ_S after Woodbury and Student, but he recoined them as τ_a and τ_b when enumerated both scenarios a) and b)) in his later book [7], similar to what we did here.

For illustration purposes, let us consider the following ranks given to a set of $n = 6$ items: $X = \langle 1, 2, 3, 4, 5, 6 \rangle$ and $Y = \langle 2, 3, 1, 4, 6, 5 \rangle$. If our items were identified by letters we would have rankings $X = \langle A, B, C, D, E, F \rangle$ and $Y = \langle C, A, B, D, F, E \rangle$. If we consider all items in pairs, a distance between the two rankings can be computed by counting how many pairs are concordant or discordant between the two rankings: a pair is concordant if their relative order is the same in both rankings, and discordant otherwise. Kendall [5] followed this idea to define his τ correlation coefficient

$$\tau = \frac{\#concordants - \#discordants}{\#total} = \frac{4}{n(n-1)} \sum_{i<j} c_{ij} - 1, \quad (1)$$

where c_{ij} equals 1 if items i and j are concordant (recall that no ties are permitted yet):

$$c_{ij} = \begin{cases} 1 & sign(x_j - x_i) = sign(y_j - y_i) \\ 0 & \text{otherwise} \end{cases}. \quad (2)$$

In our example, the pair (B, C) is discordant because it has ranks $(2, 3)$ in X and ranks $(3, 1)$ in Y. Counting all pairs as in (1), the correlation is $\tau = 0.6$. The fraction of concordant pairs can be interpreted as the expected value of a random experiment: pick two arbitrary items and return 1 if they are concordant, or 0 if they are discordant. The Kendall τ coefficient can thus be interpreted in terms of the probability of concordance.

Yilmaz et al. [17] followed this idea to define a correlation coefficient with the same rationale as Average Precision, thus penalizing more heavily if swaps occur between items at the top of the ranking, much like AP penalizes more if the non-relevant documents appear at the top of the search results. The random experiment is now as follows: pick one item at random from Y and another one ranked above it, and return 1 if they are concordant, or 0 if they are discordant. Their AP correlation coefficient is similarly calculated by traversing the ranking Y from top to bottom[2]:

$$\tau_{ap} = \frac{2}{n-1} \sum_{i=2}^{n} \left(\frac{\#concordants\ above\ i}{i-1} \right) - 1 =$$

$$= \frac{2}{n-1} \sum_{i=2}^{n} \sum_{j<i} \frac{c_{ij}}{i-1} - 1. \quad (3)$$

In our example, we find $\tau_{ap} = 0.32$.

3 CORRELATION WITH TIES

Under the considerations of Woodbury [16] and Student [12], a tie reflects the *inability* of the observer to decide which of two items should be ranked first. Therefore, in the presence of a tie a pair of items can be considered neither concordant nor discordant; it is simply ignored. In the following subsections, we discuss how ties affect τ_a and τ_b, and provide the corresponding definitions for τ_{ap}.

3.1 Correlation as Measure of Accuracy

For illustration purposes, let us consider the true objective ranking $X = \langle 1, 2, 3, 4, 5, 6 \rangle$ and the ranking $Y = \langle 2, 4, 1, 4, 6, 4 \rangle$ estimated by an observer, in which items B, D and F are tied. The observer was unable to distinguish these three items, but she should have because

there really is an objective order. When counting the number of concordant pairs in (1), we can not really penalize or reward pairs (B, D), (B, F) and (D, F) because the observer did not really decide in either direction. However, these pairs are still counted in the denominator because she was *expected* to distinguish them. The correlation is thus defined as

$$\tau_a = \sum_{i<j} \frac{sign(x_j - x_i) \cdot sign(y_j - y_i)}{n(n-1)/2}, \quad (4)$$

Note that a concordant pair contributes +1 in the numerator, and a discordant pair contributes −1. A tied pair, on the other hand, contributes 0 in spite of it being expected in the denominator. In our example, the correlation is $\tau_a = 0.4$.

Woodbury [16] noted an interesting way of looking at the problem of ties in this scenario: what is the *average* correlation over all the possible permutations of the tied items in Y? As it turns out, if we replace any tied set t by integer ranks and average for all $t!$ possible orders we obtain the same formula as in (4). In our example there are six permutations: $\langle 2, 3, 1, 4, 6, 5 \rangle$, $\langle 2, 3, 1, 5, 6, 4 \rangle$, $\langle 2, 4, 1, 3, 6, 5 \rangle$, $\langle 2, 4, 1, 5, 6, 3 \rangle$, $\langle 2, 5, 1, 3, 6, 4 \rangle$ and $\langle 2, 5, 1, 4, 6, 3 \rangle$, with τ scores of $0.6, 0.467, 0.467, 0.333, 0.333$ and 0.2, respectively; their average is indeed $\tau_a = 0.4$. This result is precisely what we use next to define the corresponding version of τ_{ap} correlation: $\tau_{ap, a}$.

Back in (3), we can see that all untied items will contribute the same in all permutations when acting as the pivot item i. If there are groups of ties above it, each of their items will be concordant or discordant with respect to the pivot i, *regardless* of their position within the tie. For instance, when the pivot is E ($i = 6$), items B and D are both concordant and F is discordant, regardless of the position they have within their tied group. On the other hand, when the pivot i is a tied item we have to consider two terms separately:

I) The contribution of all items ranked above its tied group.
II) The contribution of the items within the group in all permutations in which they are ranked above the pivot.

Let t_i be the number of items tied with the pivot i, inclusive, and let p_i be the position of the first item in the group (the typical ranks used in sports). In our example, the estimated ranking is $Y = \langle C, A, (B, D, F), E \rangle$, so there are $t_3 = t_4 = t_5 = 3$ items in the tie, the first of which appears in position $p_3 = p_4 = p_5 = 3$. Note that if i is not tied, then $t_i = 1$ and $p_i = i$.

For the first term I, we can see that the items above the tied group which are concordant with the pivot remains the same in all permutations. In our example, A is always concordant with the pivot B regardless of the permutation, and C is always discordant. In general, the number of concordants above the pivot i is

$$\sum_{j<p_i} c_{ij}. \quad (5)$$

However, these items will have a different contribution depending on the specific position within the tie that the pivot has in each permutation. Across all $t_i!$ permutations, a tied item will have position p_i a total of $(t_i - 1)!$ times, position $p_i + 1$ another $(t_i - 1)!$ times, etc. Therefore, just like the factor $i-1$ normalizes the number of concordants in (3), these positions normalize the number of

---

[2]Throughout the paper, indexes refer to items sorted by the order given in Y (eg. in $Y = \langle 2, 3, 1 \rangle$, the sorted items are $\langle C, A, B \rangle$, so $i = 2$ refers to item A).

concordants in (5), so the average contribution of term I is:

$$\sum_{j<p_i} c_{ij} \cdot \sum_{k=1}^{t_i} \frac{1}{t_i\,(p_i + k - 2)}. \tag{6}$$

For the second term II, we shall calculate the average contribution of all pairs within the tied group and over all permutations. There are $\binom{t_i}{2}$ such pairs to consider across $t_i!$ permutations. Note that two arbitrary items R and S will appear in order (R, S) in half the permutations and in the order (S, R) in the other half; on average, every pair will thus be concordant in half the cases. Without loss of generality, let us assume that the correct order is in fact (R, S).

Again, the individual contribution of this pair needs to be normalized according to the position of the pivot S. When it is in position p_i (ie. the first of the group), the pair (R, S) is not possible because R can never appear before S. When the pivot is in position $p_i + 1$ (ie. the second of the group), there are $(t_i - 2)!$ permutations in which R is arranged before it. When the pivot is in position $p_i + 2$, there are $2(t_i - 2)!$ permutations with R arranged before it: $\langle R, *, S, \dots \rangle$ and $\langle *, R, S, \dots \rangle$. In general, when the pivot S is in position $p_i + k$, there are $k \cdot (t_i - 2)!$ permutations where R appears before it.

As before, these positions are used to normalize the contribution of each pair, and the number of permutations is used to average these contributions across permutations. All in all, there are thus $\binom{t_i}{2}$ pairs of items in the tied group, each of which can appear in positions $k = 1, \dots, t_i-1$ within the group a total of $k \cdot (t_i-2)!$ times, in each of which it contributes one concordant pair normalized by $p_i + k - 1$. Averaging over all $t_i!$ permutations, term II becomes

$$\frac{1}{2} \sum_{k=1}^{t_i-1} \frac{k}{p_i + k - 1}. \tag{7}$$

Putting together terms I and II, the $\tau_{ap,a}$ correlation is therefore

$$\tau_{ap,a} = \frac{2}{n-1} \Bigg(\sum_{i=t_1+1}^{n} \sum_{j<p_i} c_{ij} \cdot \sum_{k=1}^{t_i} \frac{1}{t_i\,(p_i + k - 2)} + \\ \sum_{i=1}^{n} \frac{1}{2t_i} \sum_{k=1}^{t_i-1} \frac{k}{p_i + k - 1} \Bigg) - 1, \tag{8}$$

where the second term II is further divided by t_i because it will be added t_i times when traversing the tied elements in the outer summation. There are three final remarks worth mentioning. First, note that the summation is taken over all items in the estimated ranking Y, but the order in which the tied items are arranged does not alter the final score. Second, in the absence of ties the third summation equals $1/(i - 1)$ and the last summation equals 0, so $\tau_{ap,a}$ reduces to τ_{ap}. Third, because tied groups are disjoint and the summation considers separately the contribution of items outside and within groups, this formulation generalizes to several tied groups. Also note that in the extreme case that the observer ties all elements, $\tau_{ap,a}$ equals 0, as does τ_a. In our example, the correlations with each of the permutations are $0.32, 0.22, 0.253, 0.153, 0.22$ and 0.087, for an average of $\tau_{ap,a} = 0.209$.

3.2 Correlation as Measure of Agreement

When both X and Y are produced by observers, there is no notion of true and objective ranking. Similar to the scenario of τ_a, if either

observer produced a tie for a pair of items, we can not really reward or penalize his indecision, regardless of how the other observer ranked them. However, in this scenario all these tied pairs are not really expected to be untied from one observer to another: whether the other observer is right or wrong with respect to some unknown truth, the fact remains that his agreement with the current observer can not be measured. In the extreme case of an observer tying all items, τ_a is 0 to reflect that he is no better than chance at ranking the items, but τ_b would be undefined because there is no pair of systems to calculate his agreement with the other observer. The correlation is thus defined as

$$\tau_b = \sum_{i<j} \frac{sign(x_i - x_j) \cdot sign(y_i - y_j)}{\sqrt{n(n-1)/2 - t_X}\,\sqrt{n(n-1)/2 - t_Y}}, \tag{9}$$

where t_X and t_Y are the number of tied pairs in X and Y, respectively. Note that (4) and (9) differ only in the denominator, reflecting out intuition as to how the former expects all possible pairs to be concordant, while the latter only expects this of the untied pairs. Indeed, the fact that the denominator includes one term for each ranking nicely shows that both observers may expect a different number of concordant pairs, according to their own ranking and regardless of the other. Note that in this case it does not make sense to average over all permutations, because not all pairs are expected.

To illustrate, let us include a tie between the third and fourth elements (C and D) of the first ranking in the previous example, so that one observer produced ranking $X = \langle 1, 2, 3.5, 3.5, 5, 6 \rangle$ and the other one produced the same $Y = \langle 2, 4, 1, 4, 6, 4 \rangle$ as before. In this case there are $t_X = 1$ and $t_Y = 3$ tied pairs, so the denominator is 12.961. In the numerator there are 8 concordant pairs and 3 discordants, so the final correlation is $\tau_b = 0.386$.

It is not immediate how to adapt AP correlation in this scenario, because (3) is computed by traversing the estimated ranking from top to bottom, computing concordants with an objective truth. However, here there is no notion of true and estimated ranking, so in principle we can not decide which of the two rankings we traverse. In situations like this, Yilmaz et al. [17] suggested to compute a symmetrized version of τ_{ap} by computing the mean of the correlation of X with respect to Y and the correlation of Y with respect to X, that is, assuming that one ranking is the truth and the other one the estimate, and vice-versa.

Approaching $\tau_{ap,b}$ as a symmetrized version still requires two changes in the original formulation of (3) in order to mimic the behavior of τ_b. First, if the pivot i is part of a tied group we need only count its concordants among all items ranked above the group (term I in $\tau_{ap,a}$), because the items within the group will not contribute anything (term II in $\tau_{ap,a}$). The number of concordants is thus as in (5), but normalized by $p_i - 1$ rather than by $i - 1$. In our example, if the pivot is D ($i = 4$) in Y, only items C and A are ranked above its group, of which only A is concordant in X. By ignoring B and F from Y we mimic the second term in the denominator of τ_b as well as the second term in the numerator (ie. do not expect those pairs), and by ignoring C from X we mimic the first term in the numerator (ie. neither reward nor penalize a pair that is expected).

Second, the outer normalization by $n - 1$ that averages across all pivots now needs to normalize only across the number of pivots that are not tied with the top item. To clarify, consider the toy example in which the top m items are tied: by (5) there are no pairs

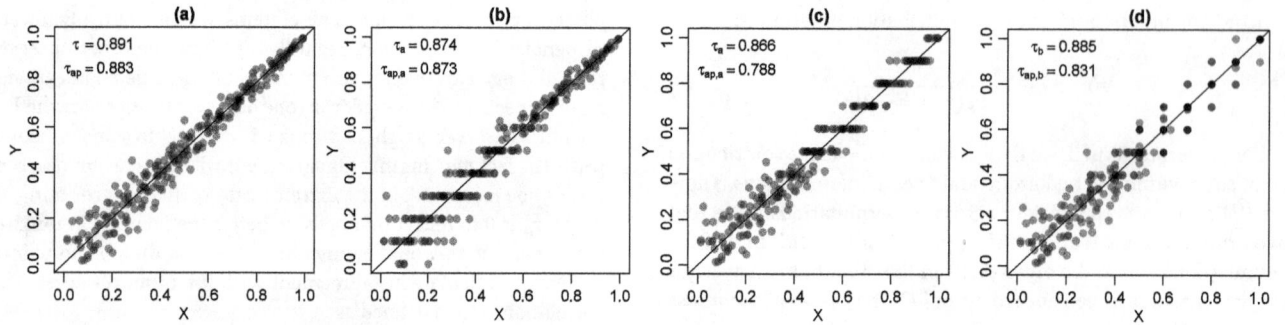

Figure 1: (a) No ties. (b) Small effect of ties at the bottom. (c) Large effect of ties at the top. (d) Ties in both rankings.

to consider concordance above those pivots because $p_i = 1$, so there is no point in counting them for the outer summation and normalization. This (still asymmetric) $\tau_{ap,ties}$ would therefore be

$$\tau_{ap,ties} = \frac{2}{n - t_1} \sum_{i=t_1+1}^{n} \sum_{j < p_i} \frac{c_{ij}}{p_i - 1} - 1. \qquad (10)$$

In our example, we find that $\tau_{ap,ties}$ of Y with respect to X is 0.12, while it is 0.16 when correlating X with respect to Y. The final $\tau_{ap,b}$ is defined as the average

$$\tau_{ap,b} = \frac{\tau_{ap,ties}(X,Y) + \tau_{ap,ties}(Y,X)}{2}, \qquad (11)$$

which in our case is $\tau_{ap,b} = 0.14$. There are three final remarks worth mentioning. First, note that the summation in (10) is taken over the items in the "estimated" ranking, but the order in which tied elements are arranged does not affect the final score because it only considers pairs above the group. Second, in the absence of ties $\tau_{ap,ties}$ in reduces to the original τ_{ap} because $t_i = 1$ and thus $p_i = i$. Third, because tied groups are disjoint, this formulation generalizes to several tied groups. Also note that in the extreme case that one observer ties all elements, $\tau_{ap,b}$ is not defined because there are no pairs to compare with, as happens with τ_b.

4 CONCLUSIONS AND FUTURE WORK

In this paper we tackled the problem of ties in the calculation of the τ_{ap} correlation coefficient. Following the principles by which Kendall [6] adapted his τ correlation to cope with ties under two different scenarios, we provided closed analytical formulations of τ_{ap} to accept ties in either ranking. Thanks to the accompanying software implementation, researchers can easily substitute τ_{ap} for τ to incorporate its top-heaviness component in problems where ties are possible.

For future work we will consider a third scenario that Kendall [6] mentioned implicitly but did not consider explicitly (see the quote in the introduction). In both τ_a and τ_b he assumed that a tie was given when the observer was unable to discern a difference, but it may be the case that the tied elements are in fact equal in the true ranking. In principle, this is an scenario for the measurement of the accuracy of an observer, so in τ_a this would mean that a tie in the true ranking is what we expect the observer to tell. If the observer orders the pair of items in either way, it should be discordant because he should have tied it. Similarly, if a pair is not

tied in the true ranking but the observer did tie it, it should be considered discordant as well.

Yet another scenario to consider is that in which a tie means that the two items are very close together, within some threshold. For instance, two systems may be tied if their $nDCG$ difference is smaller than 0.05. While this scenario surely is appealing because it allows us to compute correlations under customizable thresholds, it appears to be problematic because the ties are no longer transitive.

ACKNOWLEDGMENTS

Zizou entrenador. Casemiro titular.

REFERENCES

[1] Ricardo Baeza-Yates, Carlos Castillo, Mauricio Marin, and Andrea Rodriguez. 2005. Crawling a country: better strategies than breadth-first for web page ordering. In *ACM WWW*. 864–872.
[2] Peter Bailey, Nick Craswell, Ian Soboroff, Paul Thomas, Arjen P. de Vries, and Emine Yilmaz. 2008. Relevance Assessment: Are Judges Exchangeable and Does it Matter?. In *ACM SIGIR*. 667–674.
[3] Ben Carterette, Virgil Pavlu, Hui Fang, and Evangelos Kanoulas. 2009. Million Query Track 2009 Overview. In *TREC*.
[4] H. E. Daniels. 1944. The Relation between Measures of Correlation in the Universe of Sample Permutations. *Biometrika* 33, 2 (1944), 129–135.
[5] Maurice G. Kendall. 1938. A New Measure of Rank Correlation. *Biometrika* 30, 1 (1938), 81–93.
[6] Maurice G. Kendall. 1945. The Treatment of Ties in Ranking Problems. *Biometrika* 33, 3 (1945), 239–251.
[7] Maurice G. Kendall. 1948. *Rank Correlation Methods* (4th ed.). Charles Griffin & Company Limited.
[8] Karl Pearson. 1907. *On Further Methods of Determining Correlation*. Technical Report.
[9] Tetsuya Sakai. 2007. On the Reliability of Information Retrieval Metrics Based on Graded Relevance. *Information Processing and Management* 43, 2 (2007), 531–548.
[10] Mark Sanderson, Monica Lestari Paramita, Paul Clough, and Evangelos Kanoulas. 2010. Do User Preferences and Evaluation Measures Line Up?. In *ACM SIGIR*. 555–562.
[11] Mark D. Smucker, Gabriella Kazai, and Matthew Lease. 2013. Overview of the TREC 2013 Crowdsourcing Track. In *TREC*.
[12] Student. 1921. An Experimental Determination of the Probable Error of Dr. Spearman's Correlation Coefficients. *Biometrika* 13, 2/3 (1921), 263–282.
[13] Julián Urbano and Mónica Marrero. 2016. Toward Estimating the Rank Correlation between the Test Collection Results and the True System Performance. In *ACM SIGIR*. 1033–1036.
[14] Ellen M. Voorhees. 1998. Variations in Relevance Judgments and the Measurement of Retrieval Effectiveness. In *ACM SIGIR*. 315–323.
[15] Ryen W White, Ian Ruthven, Joemon M Jose, and CJ Van Rijsbergen. 2005. Evaluating implicit feedback models using searcher simulations. *ACM TOIS* 23, 3 (2005), 325–361.
[16] Max A. Woodbury. 1940. Rank Correlation When There are Equal Variates. *Annals of Mathematical Statistics* 11, 3 (1940), 358–362.
[17] Emine Yilmaz, Javed A. Aslam, and Stephen Robertson. 2008. A New Rank Correlation Coefficient for Information Retrieval. In *ACM SIGIR*. 587–594.

Differential Privacy for Information Retrieval

ICTIR 2017 Tutorial

Grace Hui Yang
Georgetown University
Washington, D. C.
huiyang@cs.georgetown.edu

Sicong Zhang
Georgetown University
Washington, D. C.
sz303@georgetown.edu

ABSTRACT

Information Retrieval (IR) research has extensively utilized personalization to advance its state-of-the-art. In this process, many IR algorithms and applications require the use of users' personal information, contextual information and other sensitive and private information. However, while IR researchers are making progress, there is always a concern over violations to the users' privacy. Sometimes, the concern becomes so overwhelming that IR research has to stop to avoid leaking users' privacy. The good news is that there have been increasing attentions paid on the joint field of privacy and IR – privacy-preserving IR. As part of the effort, this tutorial offers an introduction to differential privacy (DP), one of the most advanced techniques in privacy research, and provides necessary set of theoretical knowledge for applying privacy techniques in IR. Differential privacy is a technique that provides strong privacy guarantees for data protection. Theoretically, it aims to maximize the data utility in statistical datasets while minimizing the risk of exposing individual data entries to any adversary. Differential privacy has been applied across a wide range of applications in database, data mining, and IR. This tutorial aims to lay a theoretical foundation of DP and how it can be applied to IR. We hope the attendees of this tutorial will have a good understanding of DP and the necessary knowledge to work on this newly minted joint research field of privacy and IR.

KEYWORDS

Differential Privacy; Privacy-Preserving Information Retrieval

1 MOTIVATION

The rapid development of big data, social networks, mobile services and the growing popularity of digital communications have profoundly changed Information Retrieval (IR). Many recent advances in IR research rely on sensitive and private data such as large-scale query logs, users' search history, and location information. It is understandable that the sensitive and private data is kept within commercial companies without being shared with the research community. However, the concern of privacy sometimes is so overwhelming that it has hurt IR research in the past. For instance, the TREC Medical Record Retrieval Tracks [21] are halted because of the privacy issue and the TREC Microblog Tracks [10] could not provide participants with a standard testbed of tweets to ensure a fair comparison. The proper use of privacy techniques to empower privacy-preserving IR [25] should be studied at a timely manner.

The major concerns about privacy in IR include how to properly use personalized data for IR research and how to preserve privacy when releasing them. For instance, web query logs and medical records could not be shared with the public or the researchers without proper treatment. However, without having enough education in privacy research, it is very challenging to study how to make sure data used in IR research can be shared with a certain degree of privacy guarantee and at the same time its IR utility is preserved. This tutorial focuses on the latest technology of differential privacy in particular and how it can be used in IR.

Differential privacy (DP) is the state-of-the-art approach which provides a strong privacy notion and has been widely used in the database and data mining communities. Differential privacy provides guarantees which can be theoretically proved that no individual user in the datasets could be identified. Recent research has shown that differential privacy provides the strongest privacy guarantees among all other privacy techniques and has been shown to be effective in supporting multiple IR tasks [4, 6, 7, 19, 26].

Since privacy-preserving IR is a joint field in both privacy and IR, the success of this field requires researchers from both sides to understand techniques from each other. Therefore, it is necessary to introduce promising privacy techniques such as DP to IR researchers and practitioners. In this tutorial, we focus on introducing the theory of differential privacy as well as how it can be applied to IR research. We cover successful examples of using DP to support IR tasks such as web search, query suggestion, and geological information retrieval. We hope that this tutorial could be a milestone in the development of privacy-preserving IR and enable more valuable research in this promising new joint field.

2 LEARNING OBJECTIVES

The objective of this tutorial is to provide a comprehensive and up-to-date introduction to differential privacy for IR research. We also present a handful of recent IR and mining applications utilizing DP. By the end of this tutorial, the attendees are able to:

- Master DP's mathematical foundation.
- Have a sound understanding of how DP connects to IR.
- Have knowledge of how DP is used in the state-of-the-art research in IR and data mining.
- Be able to generalize the use of DP in other privacy-preserving IR scenarios.

ICTIR '17, October 1–4, 2017, Amsterdam, Netherlands
© 2017 Copyright held by the owner/author(s).
ACM ISBN 978-1-4503-4490-6/17/10.
https://doi.org/10.1145/3121050.3121107

3 TUTORIAL ORGANIZATION

Tutorial Length: A half-day (3 hours plus breaks).
Prerequisite: Basic knowledge of IR and a good understanding of probability and statistics.

Theme 1 Privacy-Preserving IR and Early Attempts - 50 mins

(1) Background: Privacy concerns in IR. [27]
(2) Privacy-Preserving Information Retrieval (PPIR): General Methodologies.
(3) Naive privacy techniques [3].
(4) K-Anonymity [16], T-Closeness [9], L-Diversity [11].
(5) Recent research topics in Privacy-Preserving IR [14, 24, 25].

Theme 2 Theory of Differential Privacy - 50 mins

(1) Background knowledge in probability.
(2) Mathematical definition of DP [4].
(3) Characteristics of DP.
(4) Analysis about DP.

Theme 3 IR applications using Differential Privacy - 50 mins

(1) Why differential privacy is applicable to IR.
(2) Query Log Anonymization [6, 7, 26, 28].
(3) Geographic IR [18–20].
(4) Other applications that use DP.

Theme 4 Other applications using Differential Privacy - 30 mins

(1) Differential Privacy in Social Network Analysis [17].
(2) Histogram Publication for Dynamic Datasets [8].
(3) Text Mining [5, 22], Frequent Graph Pattern Mining [13] and Data Sequence Mining [1, 2, 15, 23].
(4) Inference from Geo-location Data [12].
(5) Wrapping up the tutorial.

4 CONCLUSIONS

Privacy in IR is an emerging field of research. This tutorial introduces a state-of-the-art privacy technique – differential privacy – to the IR community. The purpose of this tutorial is to provide necessary background knowledge for IR researchers to solve the privacy issues in their related research. Differential privacy is a theoretical framework that requires good mathematical skills and deep understanding to master it. It is not trivial to learn this subject however due to the serious concerns over privacy issues and the strong privacy guarantee provided by this latest technique, we think it is necessary for anyone who would like to pursue research in privacy-preserving IR to master this subject. We hope the tutorial to help lay a solid theoretical foundation for IR researchers and practitioners to use DP to solve many privacy problems in IR.

5 ACKNOWLEDGMENTS

This research was supported by NSF grant IIS-145374 and DARPA grant FA8750-14-2-0226. Any opinions, findings, conclusions, or recommendations expressed in this paper are of the authors, and do not necessarily reflect those of the sponsor.

REFERENCES

[1] Raghav Bhaskar, Srivatsan Laxman, Adam Smith, and Abhradeep Thakurta. 2010. Discovering Frequent Patterns in Sensitive Data. In *KDD '10*.
[2] Rui Chen, Gergely Acs, and Claude Castelluccia. 2012. Differentially Private Sequential Data Publication via Variable-length N-grams. In *Proceedings of the 2012 ACM Conference on Computer and Communications Security (CCS '12)*.
[3] Alissa Cooper. 2008. A Survey of Query Log Privacy-enhancing Techniques from a Policy Perspective. *ACM Trans. Web* 2, 4, Article 19 (Oct. 2008), 27 pages.
[4] Cynthia Dwork, Frank McSherry, Kobbi Nissim, and Adam Smith. Calibrating Noise to Sensitivity in Private Data Analysis. In *Proceedings of the Third Conference on Theory of Cryptography (TCC'06)*.
[5] Arik Friedman and Assaf Schuster. 2010. Data mining with differential privacy. In *KDDâĂŹ10*. ACM, 493–502.
[6] Michaela Gotz, Ashwin Machanavajjhala, Guozhang Wang, Xiaokui Xiao, and Johannes Gehrke. 2012. Publishing Search Logs – A Comparative Study of Privacy Guarantees. *IEEE Trans. on Knowl. and Data Eng.* 24, 3 (March 2012).
[7] Aleksandra Korolova, Krishnaram Kenthapadi, Nina Mishra, and Alexandros Ntoulas. Releasing Search Queries and Clicks Privately. In *WWW '09*.
[8] Haoran Li, Li Xiong, Xiaoqian Jiang, and Jinfei Liu. 2015. Differentially Private Histogram Publication for Dynamic Datasets: an Adaptive Sampling Approach. In *CIKM '15*.
[9] N. Li, T. Li, and S. Venkatasubramanian. t-Closeness: Privacy Beyond k-Anonymity and l-Diversity. In *ICDE 2007*.
[10] Jimmy Lin, Miles Efron, Yulu Wang, and Garrick Sherman. 2014. *Overview of the TREC-2014 Microblog track*. Technical Report. DTIC Document.
[11] Ashwin Machanavajjhala, Daniel Kifer, Johannes Gehrke, and Muthuramakrishnan Venkitasubramaniam. 2007. L-diversity: Privacy Beyond K-anonymity. *ACM Trans. Knowl. Discov. Data* 1, 1, Article 3 (March 2007).
[12] Cyrus Shahabi, Liyue Fan, Luciano Nocera, Li Xiong, and Ming Li. Privacy-preserving Inference of Social Relationships from Location Data: A Vision Paper. In *SIGSPATIAL '15*. Article 9, 4 pages.
[13] Entong Shen and Ting Yu. 2013. Mining Frequent Graph Patterns with Differential Privacy. In *KDD '13*.
[14] Luo Si, Grace Hui Yang, Sicong Zhang, and Lei Cen. 2014. Proceeding of the 1 st International Workshop on Privacy-Preserving IR: When Information Retrieval Meets Privacy and Security. *PIR* (2014).
[15] S. Su, S. Xu, X. Cheng, Z. Li, and F. Yang. 2015. Differentially Private Frequent Itemset Mining via Transaction Splitting. *IEEE Transactions on Knowledge and Data Engineering* 27, 7 (July 2015).
[16] Latanya Sweeney. 2002. k-anonymity: A model for protecting privacy. *International Journal of Uncertainty, Fuzziness and Knowledge-Based Systems* 10, 05 (2002).
[17] Christine Task and Chris Clifton. 2012. A Guide to Differential Privacy Theory in Social Network Analysis. In *ASONAM '12*.
[18] Hien To, Liyue Fan, and Cyrus Shahabi. 2015. Differentially Private H-Tree. In *GeoPrivacy'15*. Article 3, 8 pages.
[19] H. To, G. Ghinita, L. Fan, and C. Shahabi. 2017. Differentially Private Location Protection for Worker Datasets in Spatial Crowdsourcing. *IEEE Transactions on Mobile Computing* 16, 4 (April 2017), 934–949.
[20] Hien To, Kien Nguyen, and Cyrus Shahabi. 2016. Differentially Private Publication of Location Entropy. In *GIS '16*. Article 35, 10 pages.
[21] Ellen M Voorhees and William R Hersh. 2012. Overview of the TREC 2012 Medical Records Track.. In *TREC*.
[22] L. Xu, C. Jiang, J. Wang, J. Yuan, and Y. Ren. 2014. Information Security in Big Data: Privacy and Data Mining. *IEEE Access* 2 (2014), 1149–1176. DOI: http://dx.doi.org/10.1109/ACCESS.2014.2362522
[23] S. Xu, S. Su, X. Cheng, Z. Li, and L. Xiong. 2015. Differentially private frequent sequence mining via sampling-based candidate pruning. In *ICDE 2015*.
[24] Grace Hui Yang and Ian Soboroff. 2015. Privacy Preserving IR 2015: A SIGIR 2015 Workshop.. In *SIGIR Forum*, Vol. 49. 98–101.
[25] Hui Yang, Ian Soboroff, Li Xiong, Charles L.A. Clarke, and Simson L. Garfinkel. 2016. Privacy-Preserving IR 2016: Differential Privacy, Search, and Social Media. In *SIGIR '16*.
[26] Sicong Zhang, Grace Hui Yang, Lisa Singh, and Li Xiong. 2016. Safelog: Supporting Web Search and Mining by Differentially-Private Query Logs. In *2016 AAAI Fall Symposium Series*.
[27] Sicong Zhang, Hui Yang, and Lisa Singh. 2014. Increased Information Leakage from Text.. In *PIR 2014@ SIGIR*. 41–42.
[28] Sicong Zhang, Hui Yang, and Lisa Singh. 2016. Anonymizing Query Logs by Differential Privacy. In *SIGIR '16*.

Bandit Algorithms in Interactive Information Retrieval

Dorota Glowacka
Department of Computer Science
University of Helsinki
glowacka@cs.helsinki.fi

ABSTRACT

The multi-armed bandit problem models an agent that simultaneously attempts to acquire new knowledge (exploration) and optimize his decisions based on existing knowledge (exploitation). The agent attempts to balance these competing tasks in order to maximize his total value over the period of time considered. There are many practical applications of the bandit model, such as clinical trials, adaptive routing or portfolio design. Over the last decade there has been an increased interest in developing bandit algorithms for specific problems in information, such as diverse document ranking, news recommendation or ranker evaluation. The aim of this tutorial is to provide an overview of the various applications of bandit algorithms in information retrieval as well as issues related to their practical deployment and performance in real-life systems/applications.

CCS CONCEPTS

•**Information systems** →**Personalization;** *Information retrieval diversity;* •**Computing methodologies** →*Online learning settings;*

KEYWORDS

bandit algorithms, information retrieval, recommender systems, exploration-exploitation trade-off, interactive search, personalization, system optimization

1 MOTIVATION

With ever increasing amount and type of data available on the web, search engines have gradually developed into complex systems that combine many ranking criteria with the aim of producing the optimal result list in response to usersfi queries. Traditional approaches, where a ranking algorithm are trained off-line with manually annotated data can be very expensive due to the involvement of human experts. Creation of new algorithms in this way can also be to slow to respond to rapid growth of new data or changes of documents' relevance to a given query over time. Additionally, it may not always be possible for experts to annotate data as might be the case in personalised search, where the perceived relevance of a given document is usually very subjective.

A response to these issues has been emergence of new branches of information retrieval, such as online learning to rank, interactive information retrieval or dynamic information retrieval. These

approaches often employ various reinforcement learning methods, of which bandit algorithms are the most popular. The bandit problem models an agent that simultaneously attempts to acquire new knowledge (exploration) and optimize his decisions based on existing knowledge (exploitation). The agent attempts to balance these competing tasks in order to maximize his total value over the period of time considered. This aspect of bandit algorithms allow the search engine to gradually build the user model without getting stuck in a local search space, while engaging the user in the search loop. The simplicity and ease of implementation of bandit algorithms also adds to their popularity in the information retrieval community. Over the past decade there has been an increase in the number of new bandit algorithms as well as new applications for these algorithms. However, not all of these algorithms are equality suitable to all information retrieval settings or all types of data.

Bandit algorithms have been studied extensively by the statistics and machine learning communities since 1950-ies. However, only recently has there been a growing interest in the application of bandits in information retrieval and related areas. We now have a handful of bandit algorithms aimed specifically at solving IR problems, such as online learning to rank, ranker evaluation or click models. The goal of this tutorial is to bring together current efforts in the area, summarize the research performed so far and give a holistic view on the challenges of applying bandit algorithms in the information retrieval domain.

2 FORMAT AND DETAILED SCHEDULE

The tutorial will consist of three parts: 1) overview of bandit algorithms; 2) application of bandits in information retrieval; 3) Optimization of information retrieval systems based on bandit algorithms. In the first part will provide an overview of bandit algorithms and how they develop overtime starting from Gittins indices and then gradually follow the algorithmic development of bandits: Upper Confidence Bound (UCB) algorithms, multi-armed bandits, dependent arm bandits, contextual bandits, dueling bandits, collaborative bandits, etc. The basic aspects of bandit algorithms, such as the reward function and the exploration-exploitation trade-off will be introduced as well. The first part of the tutorial aims to not only familiarize the audience with the mathematical and statistical foundations of of bandits but also provide them with an intuition how they can be applied to real-life problems through examples from various areas, such as clinical trials, economics or information retrieval.

Topics covered in the first part of the tutorial:
- Gittins indices [9], UCB [4]
- multi-armed bandits [5, 15]
- dependent arm bandits [22, 23]
- contextual bandits [18]
- dueling bandits [30]

ICTIR'17, October 1–4, 2017, Amsterdam, The Netherlands.
© 2017 Copyright held by the owner/author(s). 978-1-4503-4490-6/17/10.
DOI: http://dx.doi.org/10.1145/3121050.3121108

- collaborative bandits [19]
- exploration-exploitation trade-off [4]

The second part of the tutorial, which will constitute the majority of the tutorial, will focus on the application of bandit algorithms in various areas of information retrieval with an emphasis on the limitations of different types of bandits in various applications as well as issues related to implementation, scalability, training and dealing with specific types of data (ads, newspaper articles, multimedia, etc.). This part of the tutorial will be divided into four sub-parts: 1) click models and online learning to rank using bandit algorithms; 2) online advertising and news recommendation; 3) multimedia retrieval approaches supported by bandit algorithms; 4) bandit algorithms in recommender systems.

Topics covered in the second part of the tutorial:

- click models and bandit algorithms [24]
- online learning to rank and the exploration/exploitation problem [11]
- dynamic information retrieval in the context of bandit algorithms [27]
- ranker evaluation [31]
- news item recommendation [18]
- online advertising [17]
- recommender systems [17, 19]
- multimedia retrieval: images, music, video [12, 16, 29]

In the third part of the tutorial I will present example information retrieval systems based on bandits and discuss how such systems can be optimized and personalized through user involvement. This part will be largely based on our recent research into this area. I will discuss user study methods that we specifically developed to optimize and test document retrieval systems based on bandit algorithms.

Topics covered in the third part of the tutorial:

- examples of information retrieval and recommender systems based on bandits [2, 6, 8, 10, 20, 25, 26]
- issues related to deploying bandits in online systems [7, 28]
- personalization [1, 21]
- system optimization [3, 13, 14, 30]

REFERENCES

[1] K. Ahukorala, A. Medlar, K. Ilves, and D. Glowacka. 2015. Balancing exploration and exploitation: Empirical parameterization of exploratory search systems. In *Proceedings of the 24th ACM International on Conference on Information and Knowledge Management.* 1703–1706.
[2] S. Andolina, K. Klouche, J. Peltonen, M. Hoque, T. Ruotsalo, D. Cabral, A. Klami, D. Glowacka, P. Floreen, and G. Jacucci. 2015. IntentStreams: Smart Parallel Search Streams for Branching Exploratory Search. In *Proceedings of the 20th International Conference on Intelligent User Interfaces.*
[3] K. Athukorala, A. Medlar, A. Oulasvirta, G. Jacucci, and D. Glowacka. 2016. Beyond Relevance: Adapting Exploration/Exploitation in Information Retrieval. In *Proceedings of the 21st International Conference on Intelligent User Interfaces.*
[4] P. Auer. 2002. Using confidence bounds for exploitation-exploration trade-offs. *Journal of Machine Learning Research* 3, Nov (2002), 397–422.
[5] P. Auer, N. Cesa-Bianchi, and P. Fischer. 2002. Finite-time analysis of the multi-armed bandit problem. *Machine learning* 47, 2-3 (2002), 235–256.
[6] P. Auer, Z. Hussain, S. Kaski, A. Klami, J. Kujala, J. Laaksonen, A. P. Leung, K. Pasupa, and J. Shawe-Taylor. 2010. Pinview: Implicit Feedback in Content-Based Image Retrieval.. In *WAPA.* 51–57.
[7] P. Daee, J. Pyykkö, D. Glowacka, and S. Kaski. 2016. Interactive Intent Modeling from Multiple Feedback Domains. In *Proceedings of the 21st International*

[8] Y. Gao, K. Ilves, and D. Glowacka. 2015. OfficeHours: A System for Student Supervisor Matching Through Reinforcement Learning. In *Proceedings of the 20th International Conference on Intelligent User Interfaces Companion.*
[9] John C Gittins. 1979. Bandit processes and dynamic allocation indices. *Journal of the Royal Statistical Society. Series B (Methodological)* (1979), 148–177.
[10] D. Glowacka, T. Ruotsalo, K. Konuyshkova, K. Athukorala, S. Kaski, and G. Jacucci. 2013. Directing Exploratory Search: Reinforcement Learning from User Interactions with Keywords. In *Proceedings of the 2013 International Conference on Intelligent User Interfaces.*
[11] K. Hofmann, S. Whiteson, and M. de Rijke. 2013. Balancing exploration and exploitation in listwise and pairwise online learning to rank for information retrieval. *Information Retrieval* 16, 1 (2013), 63–90.
[12] S. Hore, L. Tyrvainen, J. Pyykko, and D. Glowacka. 2014. A reinforcement learning approach to query-less image retrieval. In *International Workshop on Symbiotic Interaction.* 121–126.
[13] A. Kangasrääsiö, Y. Chen, D. Glowacka, and S. Kaski. 2016. Interactive Modeling of Concept Drift and Errors in Relevance Feedback. In *Proceedings of the 2016 Conference on User Modeling Adaptation and Personalization.*
[14] A. Kangasrääsiö, D. Glowacka, and S. Kaski. 2015. Improving Controllability and Predictability of Interactive Recommendation Interfaces for Exploratory Search. In *Proceedings of the 20th International Conference on Intelligent User Interfaces.*
[15] R. Kleinberg, A. Slivkins, and E. Upfal. 2008. Multi-armed bandits in metric spaces. In *Proceedings of the fortieth annual ACM symposium on Theory of computing.* 681–690.
[16] K. Konyushkova and D. Glowacka. 2013. Content-based image retrieval with hierarchical Gaussian Process bandits with self-organizing maps. In *ESANN.*
[17] A. Lacerda. 2017. Multi-Objective Ranked Bandits for Recommender Systems. *Neurocomputing* (2017).
[18] L. Li, W. Chu, J. Langford, and R. E. Schapire. 2010. A contextual-bandit approach to personalized news article recommendation. In *Proceedings of the 19th international conference on World wide web.* 661–670.
[19] S. Li, A. Karatzoglou, and C. Gentile. 2016. Collaborative filtering bandits. In *Proceedings of the 39th International ACM SIGIR conference on Research and Development in Information Retrieval.*
[20] A. Medlar, K. Ilves, P. Wang, W. Buntine, and D. Glowacka. 2016. PULP: A System for Exploratory Search of Scientific Literature. In *Proceedings of the 39th International ACM SIGIR Conference on Research and Development in Information Retrieval.*
[21] A. Medlar, J. Pyykkö, and D. Glowacka. 2017. Towards Fine-Grained Adaptation of Exploration/Exploitation in Information Retrieval. In *Proceedings of the 22Nd International Conference on Intelligent User Interfaces.*
[22] S. Pandey, D. Agarwal, D. Chakrabarti, and V. Josifovski. 2007. Bandits for taxonomies: A model-based approach. In *Proceedings of the 2007 SIAM International Conference on Data Mining.* 216–227.
[23] S. Pandey, D. Chakrabarti, and D. Agarwal. 2007. Multi-armed bandit problems with dependent arms. In *Proceedings of the 24th international conference on Machine learning.* 721–728.
[24] F. Radlinski, R. Kleinberg, and T. Joachims. 2008. Learning diverse rankings with multi-armed bandits. In *Proceedings of the 25th international conference on Machine learning.*
[25] T. Ruotsalo, J. Peltonen, M. Eugster, D. Glowacka, K. Konyushkova, K. Athukorala, I. Kosunen, A. Reijonen, P. Myllymäki, G. Jacucci, and S. Kaski. 2013. Directing Exploratory Search with Interactive Intent Modeling. In *Proceedings of the 22Nd ACM International Conference on Information & Knowledge Management.*
[26] T. Ruotsalo, J. Peltonen, M. J.A. Eugster, D. Glowacka, A. Reijonen, G. Jacucci, P. Myllymaki, and S. Kaski. 2015. SciNet: Interactive Intent Modeling for Information Discovery. In *Proceedings of the 38th International ACM SIGIR Conference on Research and Development in Information Retrieval.*
[27] M. Sloan and J. Wang. 2012. Dynamical information retrieval modelling: a portfolio-armed bandit machine approach. In *Proceedings of the 21st International Conference on World Wide Web.*
[28] A. Vorobev, D. Lefortier, G. Gusev, and P. Serdyukov. 2015. Gathering additional feedback on search results by multi-armed bandits with respect to production ranking. In *Proceedings of the 24th international conference on World wide web.*
[29] X. Wang, Y. Wang, D. Hsu, and Y. Wang. 2014. Exploration in interactive personalized music recommendation: a reinforcement learning approach. *ACM Transactions on Multimedia Computing, Communications, and Applications (TOMM)* 11, 1 (2014), 7.
[30] Y. Yue and T. Joachims. 2009. Interactively optimizing information retrieval systems as a dueling bandits problem. In *Proceedings of the 26th Annual International Conference on Machine Learning.*
[31] M. Zoghi, S. Whiteson, and M. de Rijke. 2015. MergeRUCB: A method for large-scale online ranker evaluation. In *Proceedings of the Eighth ACM International Conference on Web Search and Data Mining.*

Efficiency/Effectiveness Trade-offs in Learning to Rank

Claudio Lucchese
ISTI-CNR, Pisa, Italy
Ca' Foscari University of Venice, Italy
c.lucchese@isti.cnr.it

Franco Maria Nardini
ISTI-CNR
Pisa, Italy
f.nardini@isti.cnr.it

ABSTRACT

In the last years, Learning to Rank (LtR) had a significant influence on several tasks in the Information Retrieval field, with large research efforts coming both from the academia and the industry. Indeed, efficiency requirements must be fulfilled in order to make an effective research product deployable within an industrial environment. The evaluation of a model can be too expensive due to its size, the features used and several other factors. This tutorial discusses the recent solutions that allow to build an effective ranking model that satisfies temporal budget constrains at evaluation time.

KEYWORDS

Learning To Rank; Efficiency/Effectiveness trade-offs.

ACM Reference format:
Claudio Lucchese and Franco Maria Nardini. 2017. Efficiency/Effectiveness Trade-offs in Learning to Rank. In *Proceedings of ICTIR'17, October 1–4, 2017, Amsterdam, Netherlands.*, 2 pages.
DOI: https://doi.org/10.1145/3121050.3121109

1 ORGANIZERS

Claudio Lucchese (http://hpc.isti.cnr.it/~claudio) is associate professor with the Ca' Foscari University of Venice and adjunct researcher at the ISTI–CNR. He received his MS.c. and Ph.D. from the Ca' Foscari di Venezia University in 2003 and 2008, respectively. His main research activities are in the areas of data mining techniques for information retrieval, large-scale data processing and cloud computing. He has published more than 90 papers on these topics in peer-reviewed international journals and conferences.

Franco Maria Nardini (http://hpc.isti.cnr.it/~nardini) is a researcher with the Italian National Research Council. He received the Ph.D. in Information Engineering from the University of Pisa in 2011. His research interests focus on Web Information Retrieval (IR), Data Mining (DM), and Machine Learning. He served as program committee member of several top-level conferences of IR and DM. He authored more than 50 papers in peer-reviewed international journal, conferences and other venues.

Claudio Lucchese and Franco Maria Nardini received the Best Paper Award at SIGIR 2015 for their work on efficient traversal of LtR models [22].

2 MOTIVATION AND OBJECTIVES

Learning to Rank (LtR) has recently received increasing attention both from the academia and the industry. In a production environment, the quality of a LtR solution is indeed bounded by the time budget available for evaluating it. State-of-the-art solutions that aim at building models with high effectiveness, may produce models that cannot be used in practice. Such solutions must therefore be re-designed and optimized in order to take efficiency into account.

Note that efficiency constraints are relevant beyond the real-time IR engine scenario and they become an issue in every other application where an accurate LtR model must be applied to a large collection of instances (e.g., a collection of Web pages) even in batch mode. Therefore, in addition to being able to build an accurate LtR model, it is becoming more and more valuable the capability of building and tuning models in order to improve their efficiency at evaluation time.

The aim of the tutorial is two-fold. First, we aim at providing an overview of Learning to Rank for Web information retrieval along with how Learning-to-Rank solutions have been adopted and employed in real-world search engines. The analysis is provided both from a efficiency and an effectiveness point of view. Secondly, we aim at providing attendees with a set of tools/techniques allowing them to analyze and tune the efficiency of LtR models. To do so, we plan two "hands-on" sessions where attendees will have the opportunity to run and profile several state-of-the-art solutions in the field. Slides of the tutorial and code/datasets used during the hands-on session will be made available at http://learningtorank.isti.cnr.it/.

At the end of the tutorial, the attendees will be able to master open source solutions for the efficient evaluation of LtR models and to fine tune and optimize such models to reduce their evaluation cost by a factor larger than 10x without reducing its quality.

3 DESCRIPTION OF THE TUTORIAL

The tutorial consists of two sessions of 90 minutes each mixing theory and experiments, with formal analyses of LtR methods, technical details on query processing enhanced by LtR, interleaved with illustration examples, source code and discussion of experimental outcomes. Session I is aimed at introducing the key concepts and algorithms while Session II is more practical as it is aimed at analyzing and experiment live some of selected technical contributions.

Session I

Introduction to LtR and aims of the tutorial. (10 min.)
The tutorial starts with an introduction on LtR [17], its historical evolution and main results [29] and the illustration of the goals of the tutorial.

LtR in Web Information Retrieval (20 min.)
The role of LtR in modern Web search engines. We review the main approaches of LtR. Focus on tree-based LtR models [4, 13].

Discussion of the quality vs. efficiency trade-off in the use of LtR models [7].

Web Search Architectures (20 min.)
Detailed description of a query processor employing LtR: multi-stage ranking and challenges in each stage [11].

Efficiency in Learning to Rank (40 min.)
Detailed analysis of state-of-the-art solutions for improving the efficiency of LtR models along different dimensions.

- *Feature analysis*: i) removing features to speed up both training and model evaluation [15]; ii) introducing meta-features for list-aware query-document representation [21]; iii) reducing feature evaluation cost [30].
- *Pruning forests of regression trees*: i) borrowing drop-out from artificial Neural Networks [25]; ii) removing trees at learning time [20]; iii) post-learning tree removal [19].
- *Optimizing efficiency within the model learning process*: i) jointly optimizing quality and discarding features in linear models [26]; ii) learning compact and fast trees [2]; iii) oblivious trees for boosting efficiency and generalization power [24]; iv) a novel cascade ranking model that simultaneously improve ranking effectiveness and retrieval efficiency [27]; v) methods for learning *temporally constrained* ranking functions [28].
- *Approximate score computation and dynamic trade-off prediction*: i) optimization strategies to allow short-circuiting score computations in additive LtR models [5]; ii) dynamically predicting the size of the result set to optimize the performance of the entire retrieval system [10].
- *Efficient traversal of tree-based LtR models*: i) standard approaches: Conditional Operators, If-Then-Else [12, 22]; ii) vectorized traversal of trees [3]; iii) novel parallel traversal strategies: QuickScorer [12, 22, 23]; iv) cache-conscious optimization strategies for tree-based models [16].

Session II

Publicly Available Resources for Efficiency in LtR (15 min.)
Review of public datasets for LtR and their limitations [8, 12]; ii) review of LtR software libraries: QuickRank [6], RankEval [18], XGBoost [9], LightGBM[1], jForests [14].

Hands-on 1: Analysis of different scoring solutions (20 min.)
In-deep analysis of several state-of-the-art strategies for scoring documents with forests of regression trees. We share the source code of state-of-the-art solutions, including QuickScorer [22] (under NDA), and discuss CPU and cache profiling.

Hands-on 2: Efficiency/Effectiveness trade-offs (45 min.)
We show how to apply several of the orthogonal strategies discussed in the first session to gain a more efficient ranking model without losing effectiveness. Given a model learnt with a state-of-the-art algorithm such as LambdaMART, we will show how to reduce its runtime cost by a factor larger than 10x.

Final Discussion and Conclusion (10 min.)
Final questions, discussion and concluding remarks.

Acknowledgments. This work was supported by EC H2020 INFRAIA-1-2014-2015 SoBigData: Social Mining & Big Data Ecosystem (654024).

REFERENCES

[1] Microsoft LightGBM. https://github.com/Microsoft/LightGBM.

[2] Nima Asadi and Jimmy Lin. 2013. *Training Efficient Tree-Based Models for Document Ranking*. Springer, 146–157.

[3] Nima Asadi, Jimmy Lin, and Arjen P. de Vries. 2014. Runtime Optimizations for Tree-Based Machine Learning Models. *IEEE TKDE* 26, 9 (2014), 2281–2292.

[4] Christopher JC Burges. 2010. From ranknet to lambdarank to lambdamart: An overview. *Learning* 11, 23-581 (2010), 81.

[5] B. Barla Cambazoglu, Hugo Zaragoza, Olivier Chapelle, Jiang Chen, Ciya Liao, Zhaohui Zheng, and Jon Degenhardt. 2010. Early Exit Optimizations for Additive Machine Learned Ranking Systems. In *Proc. WSDM*. ACM, 411–420.

[6] G. Capannini, D. Dato, C. Lucchese, M. Mori, F. M. Nardini, S. Orlando, R. Perego, and N. Tonelotto. 2015. QuickRank: a C++ Suite of Learning to Rank Algorithms. In *Proc. IIR*.

[7] G. Capannini, C. Lucchese, F. M. Nardini, S. Orlando, R. Perego, and N. Tonelotto. 2016. Quality versus efficiency in document scoring with learning-to-rank models. *IP&M* 52, 6 (2016), 1161 – 1177.

[8] Olivier Chapelle and Yi Chang. 2011. Yahoo! learning to rank challenge overview.. In *Yahoo! Learning to Rank Challenge*. 1–24.

[9] Tianqi Chen and Carlos Guestrin. 2016. Xgboost: A scalable tree boosting system. In *Proc. SIGKDD*. ACM, 785–794.

[10] J. Shane Culpepper, Charles L. A. Clarke, and Jimmy J. Lin. 2016. Dynamic Trade-Off Prediction in Multi-Stage Retrieval Systems. *CoRR* abs/1610.02502 (2016). http://arxiv.org/abs/1610.02502

[11] Van Dang, Michael Bendersky, and W Bruce Croft. 2013. Two-Stage learning to rank for information retrieval. In *Proc. ECIR*. Springer, 423–434.

[12] D. Dato, C. Lucchese, F. M. Nardini, S. Orlando, R. Perego, N. Tonelotto, and R. Venturini. 2016. Fast Ranking with Additive Ensembles of Oblivious and Non-Oblivious Regression Trees. *ACM TOIS* 35, 2, Article 15 (Dec. 2016), 31 pages.

[13] Jerome H Friedman. 2001. Greedy function approximation: a gradient boosting machine. *Annals of statistics* (2001), 1189–1232.

[14] Yasser Ganjisaffar, Rich Caruana, and Cristina Lopes. 2011. Bagging Gradient-Boosted Trees for High Precision, Low Variance Ranking Models. In *Proc. SIGIR*. ACM, 85–94.

[15] A. Gigli, C. Lucchese, F. M. Nardini, and R. Perego. 2016. Fast Feature Selection for Learning to Rank. In *Proc. ICTIR*. ACM, 167–170.

[16] Xin Jin, Tao Yang, and Xun Tang. 2016. A Comparison of Cache Blocking Methods for Fast Execution of Ensemble-based Score Computation. In *Proc. SIGIR*. ACM, 629–638.

[17] Tie-Yan Liu and others. 2009. Learning to rank for information retrieval. *Foundations and Trends® in Information Retrieval* 3, 3 (2009), 225–331.

[18] C. Lucchese, C. I. Muntean, F. M. Nardini, R. Perego, and S. Trani. 2017. RankEval: An Evaluation and Analysis Framework for Learning-to-Rank Solutions. In *Proc. SIGIR*. ACM, 1281–1284.

[19] C. Lucchese, F.M. Nardini, S. Orlando, R. Perego, F. Silvestri, and S. Trani. 2016. Post-Learning Optimization of Tree Ensembles for Efficient Ranking. In *Proc. SIGIR*. ACM, 949–952.

[20] C. Lucchese, F.M. Nardini, S. Orlando, R. Perego, F. Silvestri, and S. Trani. 2017. X-DART: Blending Dropouts and Pruning for Efficient Learning To Rank. In *Proc. SIGIR*. ACM.

[21] C. Lucchese, F.M. Nardini, S. Orlando, R. Perego, and N. Tonelotto. 2015. Speeding Up Document Ranking with Rank-based Features. In *Proc. SIGIR*. ACM, 895–898.

[22] C. Lucchese, F.M. Nardini, S. Orlando, R. Perego, N. Tonelotto, and R. Venturini. 2015. QuickScorer: A Fast Algorithm to Rank Documents with Additive Ensembles of Regression Trees. In *Proc. SIGIR*. ACM, 73–82.

[23] C. Lucchese, F.M. Nardini, S. Orlando, R. Perego, N. Tonelotto, and R. Venturini. 2016. Exploiting CPU SIMD Extensions to Speed-up Document Scoring with Tree Ensembles. In *Proc. SIGIR*. ACM, 833–836.

[24] Ilya Segalovich. 2010. Machine learning in search quality at Yandex. *Invited Talk, Proc. SIGIR* (2010).

[25] Rashmi Korlakai Vinayak and Ran Gilad-Bachrach. 2015. DART: Dropouts meet Multiple Additive Regression Trees. In *Proc. AISTATS*, Vol. 38. 489–497.

[26] Lidan Wang, Jimmy J. Lin, and Donald Metzler. 2010. Learning to efficiently rank. In *Proc. SIGIR*. ACM, 138–145.

[27] Lidan Wang, Jimmy J. Lin, and Donald Metzler. 2011. A cascade ranking model for efficient ranked retrieval. In *Proc. SIGIR*. 105–114.

[28] Lidan Wang, Donald Metzler, and Jimmy J. Lin. 2010. Ranking under temporal constraints. In *Proc. CIKM*. ACM, 79–88.

[29] Qiang Wu, Christopher JC Burges, Krysta M Svore, and Jianfeng Gao. 2010. Adapting boosting for information retrieval measures. *Information Retrieval* 13, 3 (2010), 254–270.

[30] Zhixiang Eddie Xu, Matt J Kusner, Kilian Q Weinberger, Minmin Chen, and Olivier Chapelle. 2014. Classifier cascades and trees for minimizing feature evaluation cost. *Journal of Machine Learning Research* 15, 1 (2014), 2113–2144.

LEARning Next gEneration Rankers (LEARNER 2017)

Nicola Ferro
University of Padua, Padua, Italy
ferro@dei.unipd.it

Claudio Lucchese
Ca' Foscari University of Venice and ISTI-CNR, Pisa, Italy
c.lucchese@isti.cnr.it

Maria Maistro
University of Padua, Padua, Italy
maistro@dei.unipd.it

Raffaele Perego
ISTI-CNR, Pisa, Italy
r.perego@isti.cnr.it

ABSTRACT

The aim of LEARNER@ICTIR2017 is to investigate new solutions for LtR. In details, we identify some research areas related to LtR which are of actual interest and which have not been fully explored yet. We solicit the submission of position papers on novel LtR algorithms, on evaluation of LtR algorithms, on dataset creation and curation, and on domain specific applications of LtR.

LEARNER@ICTIR2017 will be a gathering of academic people interested in IR, ML and related application areas. We believe that the proposed workshop is relevant to ICTIR since we look for novel contributions to LtR focused on foundational and conceptual aspects, which need to be properly framed and modeled.

KEYWORDS

learning to rank; user behaviour; datasets; evaluation

1 WORKSHOP DESCRIPTION AND MOTIVATIONS

Ranking is forever at the core of *Information Retrieval (IR)* since it allows to sift out non relevant information and to select a list of items ordered by their estimated relevance to a given query. Documents, information needs, search tasks and interaction mechanisms between users and information systems are getting more and more complex and diversified, and this calls for more and more sophisticated techniques able to cope with this emerging complexity and the high expectations of users.

Learning to Rank (LtR), and *Machine Learning (ML)* in general, have proven to be very effective methodologies to address these issues, significantly improving over state-of-the-art traditional algorithms. Popular areas of investigation in LtR are related to efficiency, feature selection, supervised learning, but many new angles are still overlooked. The goal of this workshop is to investigate how to improve ranking, in particular LtR, by bringing in new perspectives which have not explored or fully addressed yet by our community after the 2011 Yahoo Learning to Rank Challenge [3].

ICTIR '17, October 01-04, 2017, Amsterdam, Netherlands
© 2017 Copyright held by the owner/author(s).
ACM ISBN 978-1-4503-4490-6/17/10.
https://doi.org/10.1145/3121050.3121110

For example, user behaviour in interacting with search results is a prominent research area in IR, but traditional offline LtR approaches limit themselves to consider, e.g., the number of clicks on a document or the dwell time, as features without embedding or exploiting user dynamics in the LtR algorithm itself. The user dynamic changes with queries of different types, with the length of the user session, with the difficulty and complexity of the search task, and this calls for novel evaluation measures and LtR algorithms [8]. On the other hand, online ranking algorithms iteratively exploit user interaction in A/B testing-like settings to choose among rankers and interleave their outputs, but they do not modify the ranking algorithms according to such user interaction. We would like to explore how to bridge the gap between these two approaches to LtR and create new solutions that leverage the best of the two worlds.

As another example, efficiency is a core theme in LtR and it is traditionally approached by studying how to optimize such algorithms from a time and/or space perspective [2, 12]. Nevertheless, the cost of applying the models generated by those algorithms in a real production environment has received limited attention. Ranking is typically organized in pipelined stages, where increasingly accurate and expensive models are used to rank documents coming from the previous stage and prune the ones that are not likely to appear in the top-K results. How to optimally design and train such a complex pipeline is still an open problem.

On the other side, learning with effectiveness centric techniques is getting more and more costly, especially when large amounts of data need to be processed. Indeed, to sustain a reasonable ranking speed, additional hardware and energy costs are required [17]. Therefore, a tradeoff between the effectiveness and quality of the ranking and the ranking speed represents a challenging and compelling area of research. This is of particular importance when academic research and knowledge need to be transferred to business applications [16].

A possible approach to reduce annotation costs consists in limiting the size of the training dataset. LtR algorithms tend to perform the training phase on the whole datasets to leverage the benefit of using a large amount of annotated data. However, when the whole dataset is used, even low quality data are included and this affects the global effectiveness [13]. New research directions deal with the proposal of novel techniques to select training data by preserving and/or increasing the effectiveness and efficiency of rankers. For instance, a compression-based selection process can be used to create small and yet highly informative and effective initial sets that can later be labeled and used to bootstrap a LtR system [14].

Another key area of investigation to bridge between offline and online approaches is personalized LtR algorithms able to account for user profile, interests, current user context, preferences in diversity of results, relevance feedback and more. When rankers are trained on batch data they can not adapt to user preferences and satisfy changing user needs [4]. On the other side, utilizing interaction data to improve search algorithms is challenging. Recently [9] analyzed the problem of bias in click data that affects LtR algorithms when used as training signal. For example, using clicks and no clicks as relevant or non relevant judgements leads to biased rankers, since the presentation position has a strong influence on where users click. Moreover, when it comes to personal content search, there are no multiple observations across different users for the same query-document pair [1]. Indeed, user queries are personal, therefore they might not generalize well across different users, and documents (e.g. emails or private files) are not shared between different users.

We also solicit the submission of papers which deal with hybrid approaches between LtR and deep learning. Recently, deep learning applied to IR has received an increasing attention from the research community, as witnessed by the tutorial on deep learning for IR [11] and the neu-IR workshop [5] proposed at SIGIR 2016. Neural networks were proposed to improve multiple aspects of IR, for instance to learn user interests and preferences [15], to model the novelty of a document for diversification [18], and in combination with traditional models as BM25 to define new ranking functions [6].

Finally, reproducibility of the experimental results is an increasing concern in IR and in computer science, in general [7]. In particular, we think that the lack of large real-world information-rich datasets and the difficulty of generating them is hindering further developments of LtR in the academic community. We welcome the contribution of novel datasets to the community and the proposal of methodologies for evaluating the quality of the datasets currently available. Moreover, we encourage the submission of papers related to new approaches to evaluate bias and variance of LtR as well as to explain and interpret the outputs of LtR algorithms, also using visual analytics techniques [10].

2 SCOPE

A (not exhaustive) list of relevant topics for the LEARNER@ICTIR2017 workshop is reported below:

- Next Generation LtR Algorithms:
  - Unsupervised approaches to LtR, active learning for LtR, transfer learning for LtR;
  - Incremental LtR, online, or personalized LtR;
  - Embedding user behaviour and dynamic in LtR;
  - Cost-Aware LtR;
  - List-based approaches for result list diversification and/or clustering;
  - Bias/Variance and other theoretical characterizations or ranking models;
  - Feature engineering for ranking;
  - Deep neural networks for ranking;
  - Understanding and explaining complex LtR models, also via visual analytics solutions.
- Evaluation of LtR Algorithms:
  - Quality measures accounting for user behaviour and perceived quality;

- Quality measures accounting for models failures, redundancy, robustness, sensitivity, etc.;
  - Evaluation of ranking efficiency vs. quality trade-off;
  - Visual analytics solutions for exploring and interpreting experimental data;
  - Reproducibility of LtR experiments.
- Datasets:
  - Measuring quality of training datasets: noise, contradictory examples, redundancy, difficulty of building a good model, features quality, coverage of application domain use cases;
  - Creation and curation of datasets: compression, negative sampling, aging, dimensionality reduction;
  - Contributing novel datasets to the community.
- Applications:
  - Application of LtR to verticals or to other domains (e.g., recommendation, news, product search, social media, job search, ...);
  - LtR beyond documents: keyword-based access to structured data, multimedia, graphs, etc.

Acknowledgments. This work was partially supported by the EC H2020 Program INFRAIA-1-2014-2015 SoBigData: Social Mining & Big Data Ecosystem (654024), and SID16 Ferro, PRAT 2016: Improving Information Retrieval Effectiveness via Markovian User Models.

REFERENCES

[1] M. Bendersky, X. Wang, D. Metzler, and M. Najork. Learning from User Interactions in Personal Search via Attribute Parameterization. In WSDM, pages 791–799, ACM, 2017.
[2] B. B. Cambazoglu, and R. Baeza-Yates. Scalability and Efficiency Challenges in Large-Scale Web Search Engines. In SIGIR, pages 1223–1226, ACM, 2016.
[3] O. Chapelle, Y. Chang, and T. Liu. Future Directions in Learning to Rank. Yahoo! Learning to Rank Challenge, pages 91–100, PMLR, 2011.
[4] S. Chaudhuri, and A. T. Tewari. Online Learning to Rank with Feedback at the Top. In AISTAT, pages 277–285, PMLR, 2016.
[5] N. Craswell, W. B. Croft, J. Guo, B. Mitra, and M. de Rijke. Neu-IR: The SIGIR 2016 Workshop on Neural Information Retrieval. In SIGIR, pages 1245–1246, ACM, 2016.
[6] M. Dehghani, H. Zamani, A. Severyn, J. Kamps, and W. B. Croft. Neural Ranking Models with Weak Supervision. In SIGIR, ACM, 2017.
[7] N. Ferro. Reproducibility Challenges in Information Retrieval Evaluation. In Data and Information Quality, 2(8):1–4, ACM, 2017.
[8] N. Ferro, C. Luchesse, M. Maistro, and R. Perego. On Including the User Dynamic in Learning to Rank. In SIGIR, ACM, 2017.
[9] T. Joachims, A. Swaminathan, and T. Schnabel. Unbiased Learning-to-Rank with Biased Feedback. In WSDM, pages 781–789, ACM, 2017.
[10] J. Krause, A. Perer, and K. Ng. Interacting with Predictions: Visual Inspection of Black-box Machine Learning Models. In CHI, pages 5686–5697, ACM, 2016.
[11] H. Li, and Z. Lu. Deep Learning for Information Retrieval. In SIGIR, pages 1203–1206, ACM, 2016.
[12] C. Lucchese, F. M. Nardini, S. Orlando, R. Perego, F. Silvestri, and S. Trani. Post-Learning Optimization of Tree Ensembles for Efficient Ranking. In SIGIR, pages 949–952, ACM, 2016.
[13] Q. Ma, B. He, Ben and J. Xu. Direct Measurement of Training Query Quality for Learning to Rank. In SAC, pages 1035–1040, ACM, 2016.
[14] R. M. Silva, G. C. M. Gomes, M. S. Alvim, and M. A. Gonçalves. Compression-Based Selective Sampling for Learning to Rank. In CIKM, pages 247–256, ACM, 2016.
[15] Y. Song, A. M. Elkahky, and X. He. Multi-Rate Deep Learning for Temporal Recommendation. In SIGIR, pages 909–912, ACM, 2016.
[16] M. Tsagkias, and W. Weerkamp. Building a Self-Learning Search Engine: From Research to Business. In SIGIR, pages 523–524, ACM, 2016.
[17] L. Wang, J. Lin, D. Metzler, and J. Han. Learning to Efficiently Rank on Big Data. In WWW, pages 209–210, ACM, 2014.
[18] L. Xia, J. Xu, Y. Lan, J. Guo, and X. Cheng. Modeling Document Novelty with Neural Tensor Network for Search Result Diversification. In SIGIR, pages 395–404, ACM, 2016.

Search-Oriented Conversational AI (SCAI)

Mikhail Burtsev
MIPT
Moscow, Russia
burtcev.ms@mipt.ru

Aleksandr Chuklin
Google Research Europe
Zürich, Switzerland
chuklin@google.com

Julia Kiseleva
UserSat.com & University of Amsterdam
Amsterdam, the Netherlands
j.kiseleva@uva.nl

Alexey Borisov
Yandex & University of Amsterdam
Moscow, Russia
alborisov@yandex-team.ru

ABSTRACT

The aim of SCAI@ICTIR2017 is to bring together IR and AI communities to instigate future direction of search-oriented conversational systems. We identified the number of research areas related to conversational AI which is of actual interest to both communities and which have not been fully explored yet. We think it's beneficial to exchange our visions. We solicit the paper submissions and more importantly proposals for panel discussions where researchers can exchange opinions and experiences. We believe that the proposed workshop is relevant to ICTIR since we look for novel contributions to search-oriented conversational systems which are a new and promising area.

CCS CONCEPTS

• **Information systems** → *Users and interactive retrieval*; *Evaluation of retrieval results*; **Search interfaces**; • **Human-centered computing** → *HCI design and evaluation methods*;

KEYWORDS

Personal assistants, evaluation, conversational search, deep learning, dialogues systems

1 OBJECTIVES, GOALS, RELEVANCE TO ICTIR

There is a gradual shift towards searching and presenting the information in a conversational form. Chatbots, personal assistants in our phones and eyes-free devices are being used increasingly more for different purposes, including information retrieval and exploration. On the other side, information retrieval empowers dialogue systems to answer questions and to get context for assisting user in her tasks. With the recent success of deep learning in different areas of natural language processing, this appears to be the right foundation to power search conversationalization. While there is a significant progress in building goal-oriented dialogue systems [1, 3] and open-domain chit-chat bots [2], more remains to

be done for theory and practice of conversation-based search and search-based dialogues.

This workshop aims to bring together AI/Deep Learning specialists on one hand and search/IR specialists on the other hand to lay the ground for search-oriented conversational AI and establish future directions and collaborations.

1.1 Format

Half day workshop.

1.2 Submissions

4–6 pages in ACM format:

- conceptual papers
- experimental papers
- preliminary results of http://convai.io competition
- panel discussion proposals

2 EXPECTED OUTCOMES

We expect participants to get together and discuss current problems of the area and compile a list of relevant algorithms and methods to address them.

Target audience: intersection of web search, dialogues systems and deep learning communities

Estimated number of participants: 40

3 TOPICS OF INTERESTS

- Surfacing search results in form of a dialogue (how to present information that search gives us in a form of a dialogue? Which model to use for dialogue-state tracking?)
- Evaluation of search-oriented conversational AI: despite early attempts at computing dialogue system's quality in a scalable way [4], this is still a relevant issue
- From conversational AI to personal assistants (how to maintain a stable and consistent assistant behaviour)
- The role of personalization for conversational AI and for its evaluation (users are different, can we personalize their experience?)
- Deep Learning for conversational AI
- (Deep) Reinforcement Learning for conversational AI
- Voice as input (voice interactions with a personal assistant: how it will affect existing models?)

ICTIR '17, October 01-04, 2017, Amsterdam, Netherlands
© 2017 Copyright held by the owner/author(s).
ACM ISBN 978-1-4503-4490-6/17/10...$15.00
https://doi.org/.1145/3121050.3121111

4 BIO OF ORGANIZERS

Mikhail Burtsev (MIPT). Mikhail is a head of Neural Nets and Deep Learning lab at the Moscow Institute of Physics and Technology. Research and development in the lab are focused on the problem of conversational intelligence. This challenge is addressed in the lab by a spectrum of modern DL methods such as hierarchical recurrent neural architectures, attention, memory and reinforcement learning. The lab is a lead co-organizer of ongoing NIPS Conversational Intelligence Challenge (convai.io) . The competition aims at measuring the quality of state-of-the-art dialogue systems, and collecting an open-source dataset of human evaluated dialogues.

Aleksandr Chuklin (Google Research Europe). Aleksandr is currently based in Zürich, Switzerland working at Google Research Europe. The focus of his research is digital eyes-free assistants, such as Google Home or Amazon Echo, where dialogue plays major role. In particular, Aleksandr aims at rethinking information retrieval and exploration for this new surface and finding new ways of evaluating user experience. He has experience in modeling and evaluating user experience of traditional search and aims to transfer this expertise over to the world of eyes-free assistants. Aleksandr received his PhD from the University of Amsterdam. He has a number of publications and tutorials at WSDM, SIGIR, CIKM, ECIR and served as a PC member of WSDM and CIKM.

Julia Kiseleva (UserSat.com & UvA). Julia is currently running spin-off UseSat.com and a postdoctoral researcher at University of Amsterdam. She received her PhD from University of Eindhoven University of Technology in 2016. The focus of Julia's research is understanding and predicting user satisfaction with variety of search systems. Currently Julia is mostly focused on understanding user interaction patterns with personal assistants such as Siri, Google Now and Cortanta. Julia is chair of Russian Summer School in Information Retrieval this year and publicity chair at ICTIR.

Alexey Borisov (Yandex). Alexey is an applied researcher at Yandex. He is pursuing a (part-time) doctorate in Computer Science at the University of Amsterdam under the supervision of Maarten de Rijke. His research interests lie at the intersection of deep learning and several IR/NLP fields: modeling user behavior, semantic matching and conversational systems. He received the best student paper award from SIGIR 2016 for his work on (neural) modeling times between user actions.

REFERENCES

[1] Antoine Bordes and Jason Weston. 2016. Learning end-to-end goal-oriented dialog. *arXiv preprint arXiv:1605.07683* (2016).

[2] Jiwei Li, Will Monroe, Tianlin Shi, Alan Ritter, and Dan Jurafsky. 2017. Adversarial learning for neural dialogue generation. *arXiv preprint arXiv:1701.06547* (2017).

[3] Pararth Shah, Dilek Hakkani-Tür, and Larry Heck. 2016. Interactive reinforcement learning for task-oriented dialogue management. In *NIPS 2016 Deep Learning for Action and Interaction Workshop.*

[4] Marilyn A Walker, Diane J Litman, Candace A Kamm, and Alicia Abella. 1997. PARADISE: A framework for evaluating spoken dialogue agents. In *Proceedings of the eighth conference on European chapter of the Association for Computational Linguistics.* Association for Computational Linguistics, 271–280.

Author Index

www.ingramcontent.com/pod-product-compliance
Lightning Source LLC
Chambersburg PA
CBHW080914220326

41598CB00034B/5570